"*Majority World Theology* provides a survey of the development of Christian thought in the whole world. It explores the basic Christian doctrines in the context of a crosscultural dialogue and gives us vivid ethnographic descriptions and indigenized understandings of Christian faith. Its publication will surely enrich academic studies and cultural exchanges of world religions today."

Zhuo Xinping, Institute of World Religions of the Chinese Academy of Social Sciences, and chairperson of the Chinese Association of Religious Studies

"A well-written and much-needed book. Through these essays [in *Jesus Without Borders*] the reader travels around the world and gets a flavor of the rich theological ferment underway in world Christianity."

Emmanuel Katongole, University of Notre Dame

"Different societies vary in exactly how they understand Christ's gospel message in terms of their own culture. The rewarding essays in *Jesus Without Borders* offer an impressively wide-ranging survey of those diverse responses and understandings of Christology. Provocative and interesting."

Philip Jenkins, Baylor University

"The authors make a remarkable connection between the theology process and the real-life experience of God's people. . . . [*The Church from Every Tribe and Tongue*] succeeds in being both biblically truthful and culturally applicable, emphasizing that the Word of God is for the whole of humanity throughout its entire history and various cultures. Each author represents contemporary rationale among an extensive selection of traditional academics. The book will inspire and challenge local and global church leaders and theologians."

Julie Ma, associate professor of missions and intercultural studies, Oral Roberts University

"If *The Church from Every Tribe and Tongue* teaches us anything, it is that the question, 'What does it mean to be the church?' cannot be divorced from other fundamental matters. *Where* is the church located? How are the people of God to define their identity and mission in *that place*? These creative Majority World voices open up new vistas that can only arise from and in commitment to their contexts. But these essays are not simply reflections from diverse parts of the globe that can be held at arm's length as an interesting exercise in ecclesiology. They are profound explorations of the inexhaustible riches of the Word that reveal fresh insights into the church as a situated community."

M. Daniel Carroll R., Blanchard Professor of Old Testament, Wheaton College and Graduate School

"This volume [*The Church from Every Tribe and Tongue*], like its predecessors, aptly captures a plethora of perspectives on what it means to be the church. It evokes different emotions as we encounter the familiar and the unfamiliar. . . . These contributions should help Christians everywhere not only to broaden their vision of the church but also to feel a kindred spirit with each other."

Simon Chan, former Earnest Lau Professor of Systematic Theology, Trinity Theological College, Singapore

"[*The Spirit over the Earth*] discusses a foundational subject—the role of the Holy Spirit in the work and witness of the global church. It is appropriate that the coming of world Christianity should move discussion of the Holy Spirit to front and center for communities of faith across the world. The authors are to be congratulated for bringing to our attention the diverse and lively ways in which we see the Spirit's manifestation in our midst today."

Lamin Sanneh, Yale Divinity School

"[*Jesus Without Borders*] provides all of us with a kind of stereophonic listening to one another across the cultures that shape us but should not define us as Christians. The whole Majority World Theology series promises to be a refreshingly reciprocal contribution to global theology."

Christopher J. H. Wright, Langham Partnership

MAJORITY
WORLD
THEOLOGY

CHRISTIAN DOCTRINE
IN GLOBAL CONTEXT

Edited by Gene L. Green,
Stephen T. Pardue, *and* K. K. Yeo

IVP
Academic

An imprint of InterVarsity Press
Downers Grove, Illinois

InterVarsity Press
P.O. Box 1400, Downers Grove, IL 60515-1426
ivpress.com
email@ivpress.com

InterVarsity Press® is the book-publishing division of InterVarsity Christian Fellowship/USA®, a movement of students and faculty active on campus at hundreds of universities, colleges, and schools of nursing in the United States of America, and a member movement of the International Fellowship of Evangelical Students. For information about local and regional activities, visit intervarsity.org.

Cover design and image composite: David Fassett
Interior design: Daniel van Loon
Images: abstract painting: © beastfromeast / DigitalVision Vectors / Getty Images
   watercolor background: © Sergey Ryumin / Moment Collection / Getty Images
   night sky: © Khaneeros / iStock / Getty Images Plus
   rough textured paper: © tomograf / E+ / Getty Images
   3D earth illustration: © Svetlana Borovkova / iStock / Getty Images Plus

ISBN 978-0-8308-3180-7 (print)
ISBN 978-0-8308-3181-4 (digital)

Printed in the United States of America ♾

InterVarsity Press is committed to ecological stewardship and to the conservation of natural resources in all our operations. This book was printed using sustainably sourced paper.

Library of Congress Cataloging-in-Publication Data
Names: Green, Gene L., editor. | Pardue, Stephen T., editor. | Yeo, Khiok-Khng, editor.
Title: Majority world theology / edited by Gene L. Green, Stephen T. Pardue, K. K. Yeo.
Description: Downers Grove, IL : InterVarsity Press, [2020] | Includes bibliographical references and index.
Identifiers: LCCN 2020043827 (print) | LCCN 2020043828 (ebook) | ISBN 9780830831807 (print) | ISBN 9780830831814 (digital)
Subjects: LCSH: Theology. | Globalization—Religious aspects—Christianity.
Classification: LCC BR118 .M355 2020 (print) | LCC BR118 (ebook) | DDC 230—dc23
LC record available at https://lccn.loc.gov/2020043827
LC ebook record available at https://lccn.loc.gov/2020043828

P	25	24	23	22	21	20	19	18	17	16	15	14	13	12	11	10	9	8	7	6	5	4	3	2
Y	43	42	41	40	39	38	37	36	35	34	33	32	31	30	29	28	27	26	25	24	23	22

To our brothers and sisters in the Majority World

who offer us renewed visions of the faith

CONTENTS

PART THREE: THE SPIRIT OVER THE EARTH

PNEUMATOLOGY IN THE MAJORITY WORLD

PART FOUR: SO GREAT A SALVATION

SOTERIOLOGY IN THE MAJORITY WORLD

PART FIVE: THE CHURCH FROM EVERY TRIBE AND TONGUE

ECCLESIOLOGY IN THE MAJORITY WORLD

PART SIX: ALL THINGS NEW

ESCHATOLOGY IN THE MAJORITY WORLD

PREFACE

Gene L. Green, Stephen T. Pardue, and K. K. Yeo

YOU HAVE NO DOUBT HEARD that Christianity has undergone a massive shift in its center of gravity. While in 1910 over 80 percent of the Christian population lived in the Global North, just one hundred years later residents of the Global South—also called the Majority World since it is home to the majority of the world's population—had become Christianity's largest stakeholders, with over 60 percent of the world Christian population living in Africa, Asia, and Latin America.[1] In the last decade those trends have continued, with churches in the Majority World enjoying steady (and in some cases dramatic) growth, while those in North America and Europe largely remain steady or shrink as a percentage of the population.

Because of the continuing growth of Christianity in Asia, Africa, and Latin America, these regions have increasingly become new centers of Christian vitality. As Andrew Walls and others have noted, whenever the Christian faith takes root in new cultures, the church's understanding of the faith inevitably grows as it sees Scripture with new eyes and recognizes aspects of Christ and his kingdom that it had overlooked and under-

appreciated.[2] Currently this is not just a hypothesis about what *might* happen in an era of world Christianity; it is what *has actually occurred* while the faith has taken root around the globe. As the churches in these dynamic regions have been cultivating the Christian faith in new soil, the Spirit has blessed their work and allowed it to bear good fruit that the rest of the church should be eager to enjoy. This volume represents a landmark attempt to harvest much of that fruit and make it accessible to as many contemporary readers as possible.

When we first conceived this project, it was precisely because we had each spent years getting acquainted with the striking vitality of Majority World Christianity and wanted to give our students and colleagues the chance to "taste and see" what God was doing. By then, it had already become common for missiologists and church historians to observe the shifts in world Christianity and to see how this was necessarily reshaping their various disciplines.[3] But in spite of the reality that most Christians had been living outside of North America and Europe for some time already, theology and biblical studies

---

[1]Pew Research Center, "Global Christianity: A Report on the Size and Distribution of the World's Christian Population," December 19, 2011, www.pewforum.org/2011/12/19/global-christianity-exec.

[2]Andrew F. Walls, *The Cross-Cultural Process in Christian History: Studies in the Transmission and Appropriation of Faith* (Maryknoll, NY: Orbis, 2002).

[3]See Philip Jenkins, *The Next Christendom* (Oxford: Oxford University Press, 2002).

had remained largely unchanged, with textbooks and other resources often failing to reckon with this development at all. A number of notable exceptions had charted some progress, but given the scale and diversity of Majority World Christianity, we recognized the need for far more resources to offer readers direct access to the voices of dynamic Majority World scholars who were bringing new perspectives to the theological calling.[4]

In charting the way forward, we developed a vision for global conversations that would allow readers to hear the diverse and rich contributions of Christians from all over the globe. With the help of key partners, we were able to develop an annual gathering of eight global scholars who would offer essays from their own perspectives and regions on a particular theological topic. Following the presentations, we discussed, argued, and ate together. After we dispersed, we agreed to put the papers into a form that would let readers be a part of the emerging conversation, seeing a snapshot of contemporary catholic theology in the making.

Our primary goal in these meetings and in the essays they produced was to bring readers into acquaintance with a catholic vision of the Christian faith and theology, one in which the whole church shared in the task of discerning and proclaiming the gospel using the resources available in, and across, their cultures and traditions. As much as possible, we also sought to avoid the siloing so common in Western academia by bringing together a mixture of theologians and biblical studies specialists. This en-riched the conversations further, making them not only crosscultural but cross-disciplinary, and it also helped ensure that the conversations were constantly engaged with Scripture as the ultimate source of authority and vitality for Christian theology.

Through our annual gatherings we sought to curate a theological resource that would be catholic in its composition and dynamics, cross-disciplinary in its method, and evangelical in its orientation toward Scripture as the ultimate source of divine revelation. Yet too often contemporary contextual theologies seem to live untethered from the reality of the church in ages past, participating in a dictatorship of the present rather than the democracy of the dead. We recognized this as a threat to genuine catholicity, since the universal church includes not just the contemporary church in all its diversity but also the church in ages past.

Moreover, beyond simply following a demand to "honor our parents," we saw that engaging the early church in general, and the ecumenical creeds in particular, had the salutary effect of broadening our horizons as contemporary global Christians. It served as a reminder of how Christianity has flourished in the past not by trying to escape from its cultural context but by using available cultural tools to protect, proclaim, and reinvigorate the good news of Christian faith. Thus, by ensuring that essays engaged in some way with relevant sections of the early church's creeds, we put our contemporary contextual theologies into conversation with the contextual theologies of the church

---

[4]See, e.g., Walter Dietrich and Ulrich Luz, eds., *The Bible in a World Context: An Experiment in Contextual Hermeneutics* (Grand Rapids: Eerdmans, 2002); Timothy C. Tennent, *Theology in the Context of World Christianity: How the Global Church Is Influencing the Way We Think About and Discuss Theology* (Grand Rapids: Zondervan, 2007); K. K. Yeo, *Musing with Confucius and Paul: Toward a Chinese Christian Theology* (Eugene, OR: Cascade, 2008); William A. Dyrness et al., eds., *Global Dictionary of Theology: A Resource for the Worldwide Church* (Downers Grove, IL: IVP Academic, 2008); Jeffrey P. Greenman and Gene L. Green, eds., *Global Theology in Evangelical Perspective: Exploring the Contextual Nature of Theology and Mission* (Downers Grove, IL: IVP Academic, 2012).

through the centuries. We sought biblically grounded, historically informed, and contextually engaged theological discourse.

Though we could have organized the conversations in any number of ways, we wanted to connect them as much as possible with theological topics that were often studied in seminaries around the globe. So over the course of six years, we focused on six theological loci: the doctrine of the triune God, Christology, pneumatology, soteriology, ecclesiology, and eschatology. After our first year of meeting and curating essays, we were hooked. The authors brought an amazing dynamism to the conversation, and we discovered insights that were genuinely new and enduringly good as we argued with each other and engaged Scripture and the early church.

We are delighted that it is now possible for readers to have the fruit of all these lively, rich exchanges in one volume. In this global conversation, you will meet forty-six scholars and pastors from every part of the globe, and you will see them sort out how Scripture, tradition, and culture fit together to guide the church's theological reflection today. We trust you will find this a useful and transforming experience, and we hope that it will inspire further conversation in your community, whether you are in an Indigenous community, Los Angeles, Madrid, Beijing, Buenos Aires, or Bethlehem.

THE TRINITY AMONG THE NATIONS

THE DOCTRINE OF GOD IN THE MAJORITY WORLD

Part One

INTRODUCTION TO PART ONE

TRINITY 101: KALEIDOSCOPIC VIEWS OF GOD IN THE MAJORITY WORLD

K. K. Yeo

CHRISTIANITY HAS MADE a unique claim among world religions: God is one, and there are three persons (Father, Son, and Spirit) who are God. In the Christology section of this volume (part two), scholars from the global church present a thesis that God is Christlike. Yet much more can be said about God. In this section, the thesis advanced is: God is one and trinitarian—but this is more easily asserted than proved. Indeed, "One is in danger of losing [one's] soul by denying the Trinity and of losing [one's] wits by trying to understand it"—but believe and understand we must.[1] Our understanding of this doctrine has great consequences for how we apprehend who God is and how God works in history; it also has rich implications for how we understand who we are as God's creatures, who we are as a church, and what Christian ministry, mission, and spiritual life entail.

This introductory chapter serves as a guide to help readers study this doctrine, and to avoid studying it in isolation or from an exclusively Western perspective.[2] We invite you to sit at a roundtable with nine biblical and theological scholars from the Majority World church. The gifts they bring are more than their academic qualifications and areas of expertise. They offer perspectives as Christian believers who breathe the air and drink the water of their homelands, live in the sociopolitical and cultural contexts of their countries, and serve their local churches and communities. These scholars, who hold diverse perspectives on scriptural reading, creedal understanding, and who God is and how God relates to their life-worlds, are committed to honest discourse. Their works are invaluable to us as we seek a clearer and fuller understanding of the basic issues of this foundational confession of our faith. While it should be clear that there are diverse understandings of the Trinity even within evangelical Western scholarship and in the Majority World, the editors of this

---

[1]Bruce M. Stephens, *God's Last Metaphor: The Doctrine of the Trinity in New England Theology* (Ann Arbor, MI: Scholars Press, 1981), 75. Or Augustine: "If you can understand it, it is not God."

[2]Basic texts from the Western perspectives abound; I recommend a few: Alister McGrath, *Christian Theology: An Introduction*, 3rd ed. (Malden, MA: Blackwell, 2001); Colin E. Gunton, *Father, Son and Holy Spirit: Essays Toward a Fully Trinitarian Theology* (London: T&T Clark, 2001); R. Kendall Soulen, *The Divine Name(s) and the Holy Trinity*, vol. 1, *Distinguishing the Voices* (Louisville: Westminster John Knox, 2011).

collection are not theological policemen. Rather, our task is to bring the global church to theological dialogue regarding kaleidoscopic understandings of the Trinity, but a dialogue that is bound and strengthened by our evangelical faithfulness to Scripture and tradition as well as our dynamic contexts.

WHY STUDY THE TRINITY?

The liturgical contexts and doxological purposes in the formation of the Holy Scriptures, Christian creeds, and theological endeavors speak volumes about the significance of this study. Surely, the study of the Trinity is not simply an academic exercise; admittedly, it is a complex doctrine. The human quest to know how things look in light of the triune God is noble. Since "faith seeks understanding" (*fides quaerens intellectum*, according to Anselm), Christian life is most fruitful when it is informed and renewed by our knowledge of God.

The Latin phrase *lex orandi, lex credendi, lex vivendi* ("the law of prayer/worship, the law of belief, the law of living") summarizes well the way our worship life informs how we believe and live.[3] Since we become what we worship—"for ruin or for restoration"—it is important to pursue the knowledge of God in order to know God more certainly (in creed) and fully (in worship), thus grounding the ethical and ecclesial bearing of believers to live in the trinitarian life of God for God's glory and for the good of the world.[4] The end of Christian theology is the beginning of doxology—a worship of the triune God that carries the following life currency:

1. to restore who we are as the *imago Dei* in Christ by the Spirit;

2. to transform who we are as the body of Christ in the world for the reign of truth (authenticity), love (justice), and beauty (power);[5] and

3. to envision all of creation as children of God as they live in the divine economy/community of ecological diversity in unity, mutual hospitality, and interdependence.

All nine essays in part one are written out of such passion for the topic and out of a shared commitment to the evangelical cause (the gospel of Christ) and to interpreting all life events through this theology (the triune God). This allegedly abstract, seemingly useless, but truly transcendent doctrine may in fact be "a practical doctrine with radical consequences for Christian life."[6]

WHITHER TRINITY?

Our nine scholars are part of a revival of the study of the doctrine of the Trinity in the twentieth and twenty-first centuries. A sketch of the current landscape of various trinitarian views below will help us locate the terrain of the eight main chapters in this part.[7]

---

[3]See also the discussion of Miroslav Volf and Michael Welker regarding the significance of trinitarian life in their *God's Life in Trinity* (Minneapolis: Fortress, 2006).

[4]G. K. Beale, *We Become What We Worship: A Biblical Theology of Idolatry* (Downers Grove, IL: IVP Academic, 2008): "What people revere, they resemble, either for ruin or for restoration." See Rom 1:20-28; 1 Cor 10:14-22.

[5]See Stephen M. Garrett, *God's Beauty-in-Act: Participating in God's Suffering Glory* (Eugene, OR: Pickwick, 2013).

[6]Catherine Mowry LaCugna, *God for Us: The Trinity and Christian Life* (San Francisco: HarperSanFrancisco, 1991), ix. See, however, Thomas H. McCall's caution that "Trinitarian theology should not conflate Trinitarian doctrine with sociopolitical theological agendas" (*Which Trinity? Whose Monotheism? Philosophical and Systematic Theologians on the Metaphysics of Trinitarian Theology* [Grand Rapids, MI: Eerdmans, 2010], 224-27). Even so, his conclusion on 246-53 regarding the understanding of the God-world relation is insightful.

[7]The list has not included those views in the Old and New Testaments, the creedal formulations of this doctrine by the Latin and Greek fathers, and those before the twentieth century. For more, see Stanley Grenz, *Rediscovering the Triune God: The Trinity in Contemporary Theology* (Minneapolis: Fortress, 2004); McCall, *Which Trinity? Whose Monotheism?*; and Stephen R. Holmes, *The Quest for the Trinity: The Doctrine of God in Scripture, History and Modernity* (Downers Grove, IL: IVP Academic, 2012).

The debate about immanent and transcendent understanding of the Trinity seems to occupy the mind of the European scholars. Related issues are the relationship between Trinity and Christology (Karl Barth, N. T. Wright), person and nature (T. F. Torrance), history and revelation (Wolfhart Pannenberg), person and community (Jürgen Moltmann, John Zizioulas), and immutability and change (Richard Bauckham). Taking a step further than the European scholarship, North American scholars wrestle with the social and relative models of the Trinity. Major themes that have surfaced in their deliberation are identity and narrative (Robert Jenson, Michael Rea), God for us (Catherine M. LaCugna, Gerald Bray), God in relationship to Wisdom/Sophia (Elizabeth Johnson), Friend (Sallie McFague), or the Holy Spirit (Steven M. Studebaker).

Latin American scholars, however, take their lived experience as a necessary lens for focusing on the communal understanding of Trinity. While their concerns regarding the Trinity are not antagonistic to that of the North Atlantic region, their formulations give rich nuances to our understanding of the Trinity in the context of justice. Leonardo Boff uses the language of a perichoretic community of equals; Justo L. González speaks of a Trinity of minority; and José Míguez Bonino mentions the Trinity at work in community. Antonio González, a writer in this part, writes of act of love as God's essence, whereas Rosalee Velloso Ewell, another writer in this part, celebrates the reign of the Trinity in community through the Spirit.

A highly contextual theology of the Trinity is seen in the works of African scholars as well. Common themes in the African Trinity have to do with God in light of African traditional reli-gions (John Mbiti) and parent ancestor (Charles Nyamiti). Our African writer in this part, Samuel Waje Kunhiyop, recounts an African Trinity in the African Orthodox and Islamic contexts.

Asian scholars have considered the signifi-cance of their indigenous worldviews and the multireligious contexts. Natee Tanchanpongs's essay reviews and assesses, for example, Jung Young Lee's yin-yang philosophical under-standing of Trinity, Brahmabandhab Upadhyay's Hindu religious categories (*sat*, *cit*, *ananda*), and Nozomu Miyahira's relational and communal language (Trinity as three betweenness and one concord). The other two essays in this part are more constructive: Atsuhiro Asano discusses the motherly relatedness and care of God in the Pauline Epistles and in the experience of Jap-anese Christians; Zi Wang revisits the challenge of translating the name of God as *Shang-ti* and *Shin*, and she then uses Paul's crosscultural her-meneutic to suggest a way forward.

There are exciting voices emerging from the margins. The Kairos Palestine Document claims the promise of the gracious God in the land and its suffering people, and the Rainbow Spirit Elders and Aborigines in Australia call God to be their Creator Spirit. Randy Woodley's essay in this part represents the struggle of many Native American Christians in embracing God and all creations, and asks what it means to name God as *Uhahetaqua, Atanati, Usquahula*.

Theologians in the West keep revising, and at times departing from, their own classical formu-lations of this doctrine.[8] Scholars from the Ma-jority World who seek fidelity to the doctrine find that their new linguistic and cultural con-texts compel them to think anew. At times, their stance seems critical and reactionary, and at

---

[8]See Holmes, *Quest for the Trinity*, 24.

other times their constructive theologies show originality coupled with continuity. Among themselves they also find nuances and disagreements; thus the need for dialogue and debate with each other.

The answer to the question "Whither Trinity?" has over the centuries been contingent on the threeness-oneness problem and on defining more precisely key terms such as *one*, *three*, *person/prosōpon/persona*, and *essence/nature/substance/ousia*. Most of the essays in this part discuss these issues. Part of the challenge is using a limited linguistic tool to depict God, who is incomparable. How can a line, being a one-dimensional tool, depict a cube, which is a three-dimensional reality? Although languages are metaphorical and creative, analogy still falls short of allowing us to conceptualize precisely who God is and what God does. Yet the recognition that language is inadequate does not mean that we are limited to silence or to a *via negativa* (see Asano's essay). Rather, the scriptural narrative suggests that we need to deliberate more, speak more, and consult more languages for a fuller understanding (see the essays by Woodley, Wang, and Velloso Ewell).

For example, what does it mean to say that "God is one," or to refer to "the oneness of God" (Deut 6:4-9)? The term *one* is used not in a quantitative (numerical) sense but in a qualitative sense to indicate the sovereignty of God in his nature, will, and action. Whether one accepts the existence of other gods (thus the difference between monotheism and monolatrism), the oneness of God calls for exclusive devotion to

God *alone*, who is *most sovereign* above all (Is 45:23; 1 Cor 8:1-6).[9] I propose that the biblical faith is one of *soteriological* monotheism (thus monolatrism), not primarily metaphysical or numerical monotheism. Even in Old Testament usage, the word *one* is used to express a nuanced meaning: "The Hebrew *'echad* means 'one' (Gen. 1:9; Exod. 12:49; Josh. 23:10); but also 'one and the same' (Gen. 40:5; Job 31:15); or 'only' or 'alone' (1 Kings 4:19; Josh. 6:11); or *first* (Gen. 1:5; Exod. 39:10)," Anthony Thiselton writes. In other words, God is unique, one and only; "there is no other [God]" (Deut 4:39-40) or no other like him; he is incomparable (Ex 15:11; Ps 35:10; Is 40:12-17; 44:7; 45:21-22). No class, genus, or category will fit God precisely; no language can fully describe God; there is no equal (Is 40:25) to God; God is the real "I AM WHO I AM" (Ex 3:14). Anthony Thiselton correctly privileges the meaning of *one* to God's *doing*: "If 'one' carries with it an application in terms of the *one living God in action*, this is no different from the *unity of focus* in which God as Father, Son, and Holy Spirit are *one in action and self-giving* in 1 Cor. 12:4-7, where distinctive actions of Father, Son, and Spirit are also identified."[10] Thus the oneness of God entails also the *unity* of the triune God; in other words, biblical monotheism and trinitarian faith are inseparable.

As we explicate unity as oneness, we come to another difficult term, *person*. There is one God (Mt 28:19; Deut 6:4; Is 45:5; 1 Tim 2:5), not three Gods, although the Athanasian Creed states, "The Father is God, the Son is God, and the Holy Spirit is God" (*Ita deus Pater, deus Filius, deus*

---

[9]Monotheism professes belief in (and worships) only one God, and states that other gods are forceless idols (and therefore do not exist); monolatrism acknowledges the existence of *many* gods but allows *worship* of only one God. See the following scriptural witnesses: "the gods of the peoples are idols" (Ps 96:5); "all gods bow down before him" (Ps 97:7); and 1 Cor 8; 10 regarding whether idols have forces or not. The phrase "God is one" in Romans speaks of God's impartiality to save all through Christ and thus is in line with soteriological/christological monotheism.

[10]Anthony Thiselton, *The Hermeneutics of Doctrine* (Grand Rapids, MI: Eerdmans, 2007), 461n55, 462, emphasis original.

Spiritus sanctus; Jn 6:27; Heb 1:8). Why is the sum of three "is-es" still one? During the patristic period, the Latin/Western and Greek/Eastern churches used *substantia/ousia* ("essence/nature") to speak of the oneness of God, and *persona/prosōpon/hypostasis* ("person") to speak of the threeness of God. In our modern English usage, *person* means an individualized being with their own personality (thus Karl Barth refused to speak of God as three persons).[11] In antiquity, however (e.g., Tertullian), the Latin word *persona* (Greek: *prosōpon*) means a mask worn by an actor in performing a drama (yet the New Testament usage of *prosōpon* and *hypostasis* is nuanced beyond the concept of masking to unmasking, i.e., the understanding of role-playing of God's being and unmasking of God's mystery; "face to face" in 1 Cor 13:12; see Bray's essay in this part). Simply put, in trinitarian theology the threeness of God means that the three-foldness, or three persons of the Godhead, plays three roles in history for working out the drama of redemption.

The threeness of God can sound like tritheism (a belief in three equal, closely related Gods). To avoid the error of tritheism, theologians also speak of the unity/oneness of the Trinity, which means that the Father, Son, and the Holy Spirit share the same essence/nature/*ousia* (Jn 10:30), honor (Jn 5:23), and glory (Jn 17:5), to the extent that they have perfect communion in will,

knowledge, and love (Mt 11:27; 1 Cor 2:10). Yet the oneness of God is not modalism (a belief in one God who reveals himself in three forms) either. So, at the same time that it acknowledges the oneness of God, the creed holds to three persons in the Godhead, each having their own uniqueness. For example, in matters of personal relations, the Father is viewed (if not strictly, at least partly) from the perspective of begetting (Eph 1:3; 3:14), the Son is viewed from the perspective of filiation, or being begotten (Mt 3:17; Jn 19:7; Heb 1:2-3), and the Spirit is viewed from the perspective of spiration (Ezek 37:9; Jn 20:22). The three persons of God have individual differences in some responsibilities and functions (Jn 16:14; Phil 2:6-11; 1 Cor 11:3), which are undertaken with voluntary dependence and subordination (an order of priority in work rather than subordination in essence).[12] While threeness in oneness will always be a mystery (a positive, dynamic, and revelational one rather than a kept-in-the-dark mystery), the term *triune* (or "three-in-one") seems to speak best of God's distinctiveness and relatedness.[13]

I applaud the minds of the Greek and Latin fathers, whose analytical and abstract categories have helped us know God more certainly. Their gift to the church is seen in their language, which is highly philosophical and scientific, although many of the linguistic expressions they used are

---

[11]This is a difficult topic. Karl Barth refused to use the term *person* in relation to the Father, Son, and Holy Spirit because his contemporary understanding associated *person* with personality or the I-center axis of consciousness. Instead, he uses "mode of being" (*Seinsweise*). Barth said that there is "only one Willer and Doer that the Bible calls God," not "three divine 'I's but thrice of the one divine 'I'" (Karl Barth, *Church Dogmatics* [Edinburgh: T&T Clark, 1956–1975], I/1, 348, 351). But the New Testament witness is that Jesus has his own will and action (only the Son is born of the Virgin Mary, baptized at the Jordan River, suffered under Pontius Pilate, is fully divine and fully human), which is quite different from the action and will of the Father. See the following footnote.

[12]The relationship among the three persons of the Trinity is much more complex than this would indicate; see Wolfhart Pannenberg, *Systematic Theology*, trans. Geoffrey W. Bromiley (Edinburgh: T&T Clark, 1991), 1:320: "Relations among the three persons that are defined as mutual self-distinction cannot be reduced to relations of origin in the traditional sense. The Father does not merely beget the Son. He also hands over his kingdom to him and receives it back from him. . . . The Spirit is not just breathed. He also fills the Son and glorifies him in his obedience to the Father, thereby glorifying the Father himself."

[13]God is both unknowable and distinct from the world; and yet, at the same time, God is knowable in his relations with the world through Jesus (the incarnated, crucified, and resurrected one) and the Holy Spirit (the indwelling and transforming one).

not found in the Bible explicitly. The church fathers were doing first-rate crosscultural biblical interpretation as they employed the languages and related concepts (e.g., "unnamable and ineffable" God) of Neo-Platonism and Aristotle in reading the Bible. Those cultures that do not have a language system similar to that of the West, before dismissing what the classical traditions in the West have done, need to listen to their voices, since monolinguistic interpretations tend to espouse limited views and can lead to idolatrous readings. More importantly today, however, we need a similar crosscultural interpretation that is true to our own contexts and vernacular categories (see Wang's and Woodley's essays). I believe that this kind of Christian hermeneutics has "saved" or fulfilled the Platonic and Aristotelian philosophies in Western civilization. Similarly, Christian theology, if done well today, will indeed have a positive effect on our cultures when Christians are true to the triune God as they find contextual material to incarnate the biblical faith (see Velloso Ewell and Asano's essays).

Whither Trinity? Whatever language (which is the soul of a culture) we use, it is important to hold to monotheistic (oneness) and trinitarian (threeness) affirmations in close, healthy tension. As Thomas McCall advocates:

1. Trinitarian theology should be committed to monotheism.

2. Trinitarian theology should insist on the full divinity of the distinct persons, and it should avoid whatever might compromise the full equality and divinity of the persons.

3. Trinitarian theology should insist on an understanding of persons . . . who exist together in loving relationships of mutual dependence.[14]

Without such commitment, "God without Christ and the Spirit is remote and unavailing, Christ without God and the Spirit is a martyred saint, the Spirit without God and Christ is power bereft of form and direction. Faith lives from the interconnection of the three."[15]

A good example of this is found in Gregory of Nyssa's *On the Trinity*, where he defends the idea of unity within the Godhead over the "subordinated-and-created-Son" idea of Arianism and the "imperfect-humanity-but-divine-Logos-as-Christ-soul" idea of Apollinarianism.[16] Gregory argues that the word *Godhead* refers not to God's nature, for God's nature is unknowable and therefore cannot be expressed positively. He says that *Godhead* must refer to an operation (*energeia*) of God, which "has its origin in the Father, proceeds through the Son, and reaches its completion by the Holy Spirit. . . . Operation is not divided among the persons involved."[17] Gregory does not speak of the Godhead as three substances. Gregory accepts the threeness of God in that the three persons of the Godhead are distinct only as *hypostases*: the unbegotten Father, the begotten Logos, and the proceeding Spirit. Gregory puts much emphasis on the oneness (or unity) of God in the sense that the three persons are undistinguished in essence or substance (*ousia*).

Jürgen Moltmann, revising somewhat the Western trinitarian formulation, offers another example when he speaks of the "togetherness" of

---

[14]McCall, *Which Trinity? Whose Monotheism?*, 229-46.
[15]Soulen, *Distinguishing the Voices*, 4.
[16]In Peter C. Hodgson and Robert H. King, eds., *Readings in Christian Theology* (Philadelphia: Fortress, 1985), 60-64.
[17]Hodgson and King, *Readings in Christian Theology*, 62-63. See Ps 84:9; Mt 9:4; Acts 5:3, which refer to the Father and the Son and the Holy Spirit as God respectively.

a family rather than oneness/unity of persons.[18] Likewise, Leonardo Boff, a Majority World scholar from Brazil (see also González and Velloso Ewell's chapters), underlines the trinitarian communion: "The Trinitarian vision produces a vision of a church that is more communion than hierarchy, more service than power, more circular than pyramidal, more loving embrace than bending the knee before authority."[19]

Naming the Unnamable Triune God

In naming God, we name who we are.[20] In Genesis 1, God named the world into existence, and soon Adam was gifted with the speech-act of naming other creatures and Eve, by which Adam entered into an intersubjective relationship with them. Thus theology is to speak well of God, with clarity, eloquence, and power; and theological prolegomena always involve language, especially naming God, enabling us to relate to our source and destiny. Naming is not simply a substitution of words for things they represent; it is neither a magical charm nor an arbitrary, useless label.[21] For when language is used aptly, it can lead the user to participate in the mystery of the event (i.e., the event re-presents the mystery), in this case the trinitarian life. The divine invitation for humans to contemplate and declare God's name, and thus express divine uniqueness and action, renders people receptive to God's presence and his promised blessings.[22]

How do we name God? This is Moses' question to God: "Who shall I say sent me?" (Ex 3:13). Exodus 3:14-15 reveals three divine names in response to Moses' query: "I AM WHO I AM," "I AM [has sent me to you]," and "YHWH" (these four Hebrew letters, referred to as the Tetragrammaton, are without vowels and therefore cannot be pronounced; thus pious Jews often use the surrogates "the Name" [*ha-Shem*] or "the LORD" [*Adonai*] instead). The locus classicus for God's transcendence *and* immanence, being *and* doing, monotheism *and* trinitarianism (or singularity and triunity), is found in these three names of God (Ex 3:12-15) as we do a *synergic/confluencing reading* of both the Hebrew and the Greek texts within the canonical wholeness.[23]

Two points should be kept in mind at this point. First, the trinitarian monotheism ("I AM WHO I AM," "I AM," and YHWH)[24] of Exodus 3 is used repeatedly, with some variations, in regard to Jesus' claims about himself in the New Testament (see the Gospel of John, the Pauline Epistles, and Revelation especially).[25] Although the Old Testament narrates a rigorously monotheistic Israelite faith, and the idea of the threeness of God is vague,[26] it is possible to think of the "divine plurals" of Genesis (Gen 1:26; 3:22; 11:7)

---

[18]Jürgen Moltmann, *The Trinity and the Kingdom of God: The Doctrine of God*, trans. Margaret Kohl (London: SCM Press, 1981), 160. See McCall, *Which Trinity? Whose Monotheism?*, 164-66.

[19]Leonardo Boff, *Trinity and Society*, vol. 2, *Liberation and Theology* (London: Burns & Oates, 1988), 154.

[20]For more, see Paul Ricoeur, "Naming God," in *Figuring the Sacred: Religion, Narrative and the Imagination*, trans. David Pellauer, ed. Mark I. Wallace (Minneapolis: Fortress, 1995), 227-28.

[21]The word *name* is not simply a noun; it can be verb, adjective, parable, or even narrative.

[22]Soulen, *Distinguishing the Voices*, 133-73.

[23]For more, see K. K. Yeo, "The 'Yin and Yang' of God (Exod. 3:14) and Humanity (Gen. 1:27)," *Zeitschrift für Religions- und Geistesgeschichte* 46, no. 4 (1994): 319-32.

[24]See John I. Durham, *Exodus*, Word Biblical Commentary (Waco, TX: Word, 1987), 34-41, for various interpretations and literature.

[25]The following New Testament texts have explicit references to Christ's preexistence: Jn 1:1; 8:58; 17:5; 1 Cor 8:6; 10:4; 2 Cor 8:9; Phil 2:6; Col 1:15; Heb 1:2; 11:26; Rev 22:13. The Gospel of John presents Christ as the Logos of God, thus implying that Jesus the Word is God. *Logos* bespeaks a divine being who is with God before time, and that Logos is God. Note how the Greek fathers' use of *Logos* resonates with the Platonic idea that sees Logos as an agent in creation and an intelligible structure immanent in nature. See Soulen's masterful treatment of this subject in *Distinguishing the Voices*, 127-256.

[26]E.g., the plural "divine messengers" (or angels of God; Gen 18:2-8), or the tendency to read the trinitarian view or the idea of "majesty plural" into the word *elohim* (plural of "God" in Hebrew).

and Isaiah (Is 6:8) as a rich resource for the New Testament's trinitarian overtones.[27] These are then further developed by the church fathers in clearer formulations of the Trinity.[28] Note, for example, the Jewish experience of Yahweh or Elohim as God the Father who *saves* through his Word (*dabar*) and the Breath/Spirit (*ruach*).[29] Francis Watson's thick reading of Genesis 1 regarding the three distinct modes of divine creative action interprets Genesis 1: the first divine creativity is the transcendent divine command ("God said, 'Let there be light' . . . and there was light"); the second is the material involvement ("God said, 'Let there be a firmament' . . . and God made the firmament"); the third is mediation by indwelling ("God said, 'Let the earth put forth vegetation.' . . . The earth brought forth vegetation").[30] Holmes comments that "he [Watson] reads this as an account of *triune divine action,* indivisibly united, but representing the particular modes of relation of the three persons."[31]

Second, the understanding of God as both the immanent and the transcendent one is expressed in the Hebrew "I am who I am" (*'ehyeh 'asher 'ehyeh*) and its abbreviated form, "I am" (*'ehyeh*); both phrases are closely related to the Tetragrammaton (YHWH), the most holy and personal name of God. All three names seem to have derived from *hyh* ("be" or "being"), which can be translated as "to be," "to become," or even "isness." The verb *hyh* is the first-person *qal* imperfect, connoting continuing action or reality. According to A. T. van Leeuwen, "The name Yahweh, which is in origin Kenite or Ugaritic, takes us back to an indefinable power encountered in the lightning and thunder."[32] The verb *hayah*, when it refers to God, "expresses his personal, dynamic, active being vis-à-vis his people and his creation."[33] In other words, when "is" or "am" is used in Hebrew, its *verbal* significance is stressed. When "is" is used to refer to God, most English translations correctly render it as "came to" or "happened."[34] Thus "Yahweh" means "I make to be, whatever comes to be" in a causative sense, marking God as the Wholly Other *and* Wholly Immanent, a God in relationship with the world and history.[35] The context of the Exodus 3 passage also suggests God's doings. Exodus 3:6, 15-16 emphatically declares God to be the God of the past, of Abraham, Isaac, and Jacob, who acted for them. God relates to the world in creation, preservation, direction, redemption.

Yet the Bible of the early church, the Septuagint (Greek Old Testament), translates the

---

[27]The God of the Old Testament reveals himself not as a singular "I" but as a personal being whose plenitude surpasses in richness all human understanding. G. A. F. Knight calls this the "qualitative plural," meaning the diversity in unity of God. See his *A Biblical Approach to the Doctrine of the Trinity* (Edinburgh: Oliver & Boyd, 1953), 20.

[28]C. Kavin Rowe, "Luke and the Trinity: An Essay in Ecclesial Biblical Theology," *Scottish Journal of Theology* 56 (2003): 4: "The creeds can serve as hermeneutical guidelines to reading the Bible because it is in fact the biblical text itself that necessitated the creedal formulations."

[29]See the excellent chapter on the Holy Spirit and the Trinity by Steven M. Studebaker, *From Pentecost to the Triune God* (Grand Rapids, MI: Eerdmans, 2012), 53-100.

[30]Francis Watson, *Text, Church, and World: Biblical Interpretation in Theological Perspective* (Edinburgh: T&T Clark, 1994), 140-45.

[31]Holmes, *Quest for the Trinity*, 48 (emphasis added).

[32]A. T. van Leeuwen, *Christianity in World History*, trans. H. H. Hoskins (New York: Charles Scribner's Sons, 1964), 48. Just like another name of God, El or Elohim expresses "life in its power" or means "to be strong," "to be mighty" (Alan Richardson, *A Theological Word Book of the Bible* [New York: Macmillan, 1950], 91).

[33]Van Leeuwen, *Christianity in World History*, 47; Durham, *Exodus*, 39; Thorleif Boman, *Hebrew Thought Compared with Greek*, trans. Jules L. Moreau (Philadelphia: Westminster, 1960), 47: "The *hayah* of God is to act as God, to deal as God, and to carry into effect as God. . . . Continuously he shows himself in manifestation of grace and mighty acts as the God of Israel."

[34]See Is 55:11, "So shall my word be," which goes on to state what it will do.

[35]"With reference to the Lord the verb is used when he *does* something, when he *acts*" (Andrio König, *Here Am I* [Grand Rapids, MI: Eerdmans, 1982], 67 [emphasis added]).

Hebrew verb "I am [who I am]" into a Greek participle functioning as a noun, "I am the being" (*egō eimi ho ōn*), thus providing the basis for Philo, as well as Origen and other church fathers, to perceive God essentially as Being. Is the Septuagint a mistranslation? Is the Hebrew Bible more authoritative than the Greek Bible? My answer is that it takes at least two languages to understand God, whose doing *and* being are in unity, and thus to perceive God more fully as the immanent-transcendent one. A Hebrew understanding must cross over its linguistic presuppositions and learn from the Greek the name of God, which embraces his "is-ness" or "being" as a nonsymbolic, ineffable, primordial concept or "pure being/substance."[36] Likewise, the Greek understanding must go beyond its philosophical assumption and learn from the Hebrew "I AM" and YHWH as a dynamic, active, living God who continuously acts in and interacts with his people and creation. This to me is the beginning of ecumenical theology. One should not bow to the god of logic (speculation), for one should only bow to the relational God of logic.

The essays that follow in this section raise a series of questions: How should non-Western Christians name God? Why are Allah, Shang-ti, and Shin appropriate, but Zeus and Buddha are not? Is Moltmann's understanding of a crucified God a modern form of patripassianism, that is, God the Father suffered on the cross and therefore changes in his divine nature? As the conversation in this section will show, taking Scriptures, Christian traditions, and the contexts of the Christians seriously will provide a generative hermeneutics regarding how we name and understand God. This project works hard to invite Majority World readers to construct a theology, such as naming God, via a creative dialogue—using criteria such as that of Natee Tanchanpongs (biblical authenticity and his notion of moving toward Scriptures and context of readers), as well as the three patterns of naming the persons of the Trinity advocated by Kendall Soulen:[37]

1. A theological pattern that identifies the three persons in terms of the giving, receiving, and glorification of the divine name, the unspoken and untranslatable Tetragrammaton (YHWH)—referred to obliquely (the name, the LORD) or as a divine passive ("Blessed are . . . be comforted" in the beatitudes in Mt 5, or "I am raised up" in Mt 26:32).

2. A christological pattern that identifies the three persons as the Father, the Son, and the Holy Spirit. This pattern is relatively fixed in that it revolves chiefly around a limited set of male kinship terms (Father, Son, Spirit).

3. A pneumatological pattern that identifies the three persons by using an open-ended variety of ternaries (variables of three), such as "Love, Lover, Beloved" (1 Jn 4:8, 16) or "God, Word, Breath." And here we can add more contextual ternaries: "Root-Tree-Fruit, Sun-Ray-Apex, Fountain-River-Stream" (Tertullian); "Archetype, Image, Purifying Sun" (Basil the Great); "Revealer, Revelation, and Revealed-ness" (Barth, influenced by German idealism of absolute subject); "Primordial Being, Expressive Being, and Unitive Being" (John Macquarrie), "*Dao, De,*

---

[36]Similarly, the "Wholly Other" terminology used by Karl Barth, Søren Kierkegaard, and Rudolf Otto; see Otto's *The Idea of the Holy: An Inquiry into the Nonrational Factor in the Idea of the Divine and Its Relation to the Rational*, trans. J. W. Harvey (Oxford: Oxford University Press, 1950).

[37]Soulen, *Distinguishing the Voices*, 22. See also Sallie McFague, *Models of God: Theology for an Ecological, Nuclear Age* (Philadelphia: Fortress, 1987).

Qi" (Paul S. Chung, influenced by Daoist cosmology); "Mother Sophia, Jesus Sophia, Spirit Sophia" (Elizabeth Johnson, influenced by biblical feminism).

It is our theological task to look for contextual and appropriate imagery to portray the mysterious, paradoxical nature of the Trinity, who is always in relation to and in interaction with the world. The content of the New Testament gospel message, expressed in narrative with multiple and spontaneous symbolic expressions of the mysterious God, can be translated into an ontological metaphysics. But one would want to avoid using highly abstract ontological terms to refer to the Trinity, making God into a static, aloof, and uncaring God. Most Majority World scholars in part one lean toward the immanent and social aspects of the Trinity (following perhaps Moltmann's social trinitarian understanding based on the ancient doctrine of *perichoresis*, although classically the doctrine refers to the depth of the ontological identity of Father, Son, and Spirit!). They raise a critical question: Is ontology about the nature of a pure/essential substance? (Bray says no.) Or is it about a personal existence that is relational at its base? The answer will determine for us whether freedom is a property of the person (*hypostasis*) or of the substance (*ousia*).[38] I find Karl Barth's dialectic understanding of the totally other God who makes himself known in Jesus Christ to be persuasive, and his strong thesis that "the One who loves in freedom" is necessarily triune.[39]

Conclusion

We are always at risk of projecting our minds and images onto God, even though we profess that God creates us in his image. This is what the third commandment (Ex 20:7) warns against—not to take the name of God in vain—even as we are mandated and gifted to name him. Despite the risk of erring, devotion to God requires that we be faithful, for "the doctrine of the Trinity is basically an attempt to bring together the *incredible richness of the Christian understanding of God*. It is the distillation of the kaleidoscopic Christian experience of God in the light of its scriptural foundations."[40] The hope and courage of our faith comes from the reality of the triune God himself. We witness from the gospel narrative the moment when "the innermost life of the Trinity is at stake." That is when "the Father suffers the death of the Son . . . and when in his descent into hell the Son loses the Father . . . the Father loses the Son."[41] It is significant that the quest for the fuller reality of the Trinity is read in light of the Easter event. Thiselton writes of the power of the post-Easter triune God: "The Easter witnesses saw 'the glory of God in the face of Jesus Christ' (2 Cor. 4:6), as Jesus appeared in the likeness of God (2 Cor. 4:4), and as 'the reflection of God's glory and the exact imprint of God's very being' (Heb. 1:3). This raising takes place through the agency and activity of the Holy Spirit (Rom. 1:4; 8:11; 1 Pet. 3:18)."[42] In other words, the eternal love of the triune God has touched our historical process, so that although we often oscillate between tritheism and modalism, we can trust that God-in-Christ through

---

[38]See John D. Zizioulas (Greek Orthodox) following the Cappadocian fathers (e.g., St. Basil) on connecting being with personhood and relationality in his *Being as Communion: Studies in Personhood and the Church* (London: Darton, Longman & Todd, 1985).

[39]Barth, *Church Dogmatics*, 1/1, 322.

[40]Alister McGrath, *Understanding the Trinity* (Grand Rapids, MI: Zondervan, 1988), 116, emphasis added.

[41]Moltmann, *Trinity and the Kingdom of God*, 81.

[42]Thiselton, *Hermeneutics of Doctrine*, 458-59.

the power of the Spirit will enable our myriad namings of God to embrace the fuller reality of the triune God—even as we are known by him (1 Cor 8:3; see Gal 4:9).

We often contemplate, as Job queries, "Can we know the deep [and beautiful/glorious] things of God?" (Job 11:7). No (*via negativa*) *and* yes (through Christ)—"No one knows the Father except the Son" (Mt 11:27). Through the person and event of Christ with the agency of the Holy Spirit, "God's being [and doing] is thinkable again," so that we can view ourselves and the world through God's eyes.[43] Sitting at a roundtable with our brothers and sisters from "every tribe and language and people and nation" (Rev 5:9; 7:9; 13:7; 14:6) in a mansion with many windows will grant us a kaleidoscopic lens of the Easter reality—over and over again—as the biblical matrix patterns for us, the creedal affirma-tions guide us, and our contexts/horizons ground us in a more comprehensive view of the Trinity. Just as Paul's theology leads him to doxology, our knees will bend toward the earth and our songs rise to the heaven: "O the depth of the riches and wisdom and knowledge of [the triune] God!" (Rom 11:33-34).

POSTSCRIPT

The editors wish to express our heartfelt gratitude to the following partners in ministry for generously encouraging and sacrificially supporting this project: Michael Thomson at Wm. B. Eerdmans Publishing Company, Shen Li and Moses Cui in Beijing, the SEED Research Institute, the Earle M. and Virginia M. Combs Foundation, ScholarLeaders International, and the Rivendell Steward's Trust.

---

[43]Eberhard Jüngel, *God as the Mystery of the World* (Grand Rapids, MI: Eerdmans, 1983), 111, taken from Thiselton, *Hermeneutics of Doctrine*, 474.

ONE GOD IN TRINITY
AND TRINITY IN UNITY

Gerald Bray

THE DOCTRINE OF THE TRINITY is fundamental to Christian faith. It has frequently been challenged, both inside and outside the church, but it has never been dislodged from its central position. The language used to explain it was developed in the early centuries of the church against the backdrop of Greek philosophy and Roman law, but it was not decisively shaped by them. On the contrary, Christians forged a new perception out of existing terminology and used it to impose their doctrine of God on what was to become the Western world. Since the sixteenth century that synthesis has been challenged, and more recently it has been dismissed altogether by Enlightenment and post-Enlightenment thinkers, but it continues to be defended by able Christian thinkers and remains a productive source of new thought. Today the church has to absorb that heritage and apply it in Majority World contexts, where the intellectual history of the doctrine may be unfamiliar. New expressions of it may have to be found, but the substance of the traditional teaching must not be lost or diminished in the process.

THE CHRISTIAN DOCTRINE OF GOD

Few people would dispute that the doctrine of the Trinity is fundamental to the Christian faith. Even those who think it ought to be reformulated recognize that it lies at the heart of our prayers, hymns, and blessings. Jesus himself, just before he ascended into heaven, gave his disciples the Great Commission, to go into the whole world preaching the gospel and baptizing the nations in the name of the Father, the Son, and the Holy Spirit (Mt 28:19). The Great Commission is a reminder to us that from the very beginning the three persons of the Godhead have been part of the church's message to the whole world.[1] The word *Trinity* may not have been used to describe it in New Testament times, but the idea was there, and it has always been characteristic of Christianity. It was unknown to Judaism and as yet untested among (non-Jewish) Gentiles—a unique understanding of the one God that continues to challenge the church today as we seek to express it in our ongoing mission to new generations and cultures.

It may be true that the early church separated from Judaism more because it was prepared to

---

[1]See A. W. Wainwright, *The Trinity in the New Testament* (London: SPCK, 1962); J. N. D. Kelly, *Early Christian Doctrines*, 5th ed. (London: Black, 1977), 83-137, 252-79, for a comprehensive presentation of the evidence.

admit Gentile believers without expecting them to become Jews first than because of its trinitarian beliefs about God. As far as we can tell, the Jewish opponents of Paul and the other apostles did not accuse them of preaching that there were three gods instead of one, though their claim that Jesus was the Messiah who had come down from heaven was clearly unacceptable to them.[2] The divinity of Christ was a doctrine that Jews could not accept, but Christians seem to have escaped the charge of tritheism because they always insisted that he was a revelation of the one God of the Bible, not a second deity that had appeared on earth. Much the same must be said for Christian teaching about the Holy Spirit. He was divine, but he was not a third god, a belief that might have been easier for Jews to accept because they did not distinguish him as a person. The Old Testament is full of references to "the Spirit of God," which are usually understood to be no more than a particular way of speaking about him, and as long as there was no formulated doctrine of the Trinity, Christian references to him could probably have been interpreted in that light.

Christians have always claimed to be monotheists—believers in one God—and for the most part Jews and Muslims have allowed that claim, even though they have both rejected the doctrine of the Trinity on the ground that it is incompatible with true monotheism.[3] From their point of view, Christianity is inconsistent or mistaken in the way it honors Jesus Christ as God and regards the divine Spirit as a third divine person. To their minds, Jesus was no more than an extraordinarily gifted prophet and teacher, and the Holy Spirit can only be a particular characteristic of God that is frequently used to describe him. In response to this, Christians have traditionally replied that it is their experience of God that has forced them to develop a trinitarian understanding of him and that to abandon that understanding is to abandon the message of Christ himself. This is not to say that the church has never felt a need to seek theological reconciliation with the other great monotheistic religions. In our modern and increasingly globalized world there is considerable pressure on the three religions of Abraham, as they are often called, to patch up their differences and live in harmony.

According to one way of thinking that has been popular since the eighteenth-century Enlightenment in Europe, Jews, Christians, and Muslims all have their own understanding of God, but they all worship the same God, and so they ought to be able to accept one another as brothers and sisters in a common religious enterprise. That view did not get very far at the time, but it has come into its own in recent years, partly because of the horrors of the Holocaust and partly because of the rise of militant fundamentalism and continuing conflicts in the Middle East. These things have added a sense of urgency to the appeal that the great faiths should stand together, if not actually unite. Christians are now in danger of appearing to be the odd ones out because they cling to a doctrine of God that adherents of the other two faiths find unacceptable. Given that Christians claim to be monotheists, is the Trinity not an unnecessary complication that can and should be sidelined in the interests of peace and harmony?

It must be said that there are some within the Christian fold who are more than a little

---

[2]This is an obscure and highly contested subject. For a recent treatment, see Leo Duprée Sandgren, *Vines Intertwined: A History of Jews and Christians from the Babylonian Exile to the Advent of Islam* (Peabody, MA: Hendrickson, 2010).

[3]For a full discussion of the issues involved, see G. Emery and P. Gisel, *Le christianisme est-il un monothéisme?* (Geneva: Labor et Fides, 2001).

sympathetic to this plea. Such people may incline to the view that the Trinity developed
against a backdrop of ancient Greek philosophy
that has fundamentally distorted the faith and
ought to be abandoned as a matter of principle,
and not just as a diplomatic gesture in the direction of other monotheists. Surely it must be
possible, they would argue, to honor Christ and
speak of the Holy Spirit without having to say
that they are divine in the same way that God the
Father is. They point out that there were many in
the early church who regarded the Father of
Jesus Christ as God in the Old Testament sense
and who sought to interpret Jesus and the Holy
Spirit as manifestations of him that were not
separate persons in their own right. Can we not
go back to that time and recover a supposedly
"lost" Christianity that might bring us closer to
our Jewish and Muslim colleagues?[4]

This theme, or variations of it, is common
among liberal Christians, who often find it relatively easier to make common cause with similarly liberal Jews and Muslims than any of these
do with more conservative followers of their
own religion. Yet at the same time, there has
been a remarkable revival of interest in the doctrine of the Trinity in Western theology, so much
so, in fact, that it is now almost impossible to
write a book on any theological subject without
exploring its trinitarian dimension in the process.[5] Much of that is a fad and is overdone, but
that does not matter. What is important is that
the Trinity has become a benchmark for modern

Christian theology so that whatever is said about
other doctrines must take it into account and
show how it relates to our understanding of
every aspect of the Christian message.[6]

These two tendencies—the pressure for
movement toward a generic monotheism and
the revival of trinitarian teaching—coexist in
the modern church, and so far nobody seems to
have noticed that they are mutually incompatible, perhaps because their proponents move
in different circles. Those who emphasize the
commonality of the religions of Abraham often
prioritize interfaith dialogue and are likely to
include a significant number of lay Christians
who have little knowledge of, or time for, what
they regard as theological subtleties such as the
Trinity. In contrast, those who find the Trinity
everywhere in Christian teaching are more likely
to be theologians with an investment in system-
atizing their own subdisciplines around a
common theme. Dialogue with other faiths is
unlikely to be very high on their agenda, if it
figures at all. But in a global world, this inconsis-
tency cannot continue forever. Sooner or later
there will be conflict, and it is not unreasonable
to suppose that it will erupt with particular force
in the Majority World, where young Christians
are confronted with a need to deepen their own
faith and at the same time deal with the ever-
present challenge of militant Islam. People in
that situation cannot afford the luxury of academic religious dialogue. They have to give a
reason for the hope that is within them and be

---

[4]On this subject, see Stephen Holmes, *The Quest for the Trinity: The Doctrine of God in Scripture, History and Modernity* (Downers Grove,
IL: IVP Academic, 2012). For the challenge to traditional theism presented by process theology, see Bruce G. Epperly, *Process Theology:
A Guide for the Perplexed* (London: T&T Clark, 2011); John B. Cobb Jr. and Clark H. Pinnock, *Searching for an Adequate God: A Dialogue
Between Process and Free Will Theists* (Grand Rapids, MI: Eerdmans, 2000).

[5]Much of this recent revival has been influenced by such works as Colin E. Gunton, *The Promise of Trinitarian Theology* (Edinburgh:
T&T Clark, 1991), and T. F. Torrance, *The Trinitarian Faith* (Edinburgh: T&T Clark, 1988).

[6]See Paul M. Collins, *The Trinity: A Guide for the Perplexed* (London: T&T Clark, 2008). For a wide-ranging exposition of the different
views held on the subject at the present time, see Robert J. Wozniak and Giulio Maspero, *Rethinking Trinitarian Theology: Disputed
Questions and Contemporary Issues in Trinitarian Theology* (London: T&T Clark, 2012).

prepared to suffer for it at the hands of people who are determined to stamp out their witness. It is not enough to say that Muslim fundamentalists are a tiny minority even in their own cultures. That is true, but as Christians in many Islamic countries can testify, they are a hyperactive minority that is capable of doing great harm, not least to them. They certainly cannot be dismissed as an eccentric irrelevance in the way that similar Christian groups can be.

Christians in the Majority World are thus faced with a series of questions about the doctrine of the Trinity that they must answer if they are to survive and prosper. The first and most basic of these is straightforward—Do we need the Trinity at all? Can we not express our belief in God, Christ, and the Spirit in some simpler way that will avoid giving offense to other monotheists? How important is the traditional doctrine of the Trinity for expressing our Christian convictions? Can we safely leave it to one side as a complicated problem that the ordinary person does not need to bother with? Can it be reconstructed in a way that would help to indigenize it in recently Christianized cultures, making it seem less of a Western import and more attuned to the thoughts and needs of new believers? Or is the doctrine of the Trinity so totally bound up with ancient Greek thought that if the latter is discarded it would collapse of its own accord? In other words, can it be expressed in other thought forms, or is it just the product of a tradition that was once dominant but that is now being challenged and may soon lose its remaining influence in the Christian world?

At this point we should perhaps stand back from particular contexts and consider how far the challenge of trinitarian doctrine is common to the entire Christian world. In the West it takes particular forms that on the surface may appear to be alien in many parts of the Majority World, but we should not be misled by this. The problems we face go right back to the beginnings of the Christian faith, before there was a West or a Majority World in the modern sense. Christians have always had to explain a belief that on the surface makes no sense and appears to be unnecessarily complicated. Had it been to their advantage not to construct such a doctrine, it is hard to believe that they would have done it in defiance of their own best interests. It flies in the face not only of Judaism but of the Greek philosophical tradition as well.[7] If the Jews could not conceive of any plurality in God, the Greeks could not think of the supreme being in personal terms. To them, ultimate reality was an idea, not a person with whom they could have an interactive relationship. It is true that their gods were personal, rather in the way that Hindu gods are, but that merely emphasized that they were not absolute, and therefore not what the Jews meant by God at all. To be personal was to be relational, but in the Greek mind to be relational was to be relative—none of their personal gods could claim to be the one true Being in himself.

For the Christian church faced with these challenges, the basic questions were the same then as they are now. What lies at the heart of the universe? How can we relate to that reality, if indeed we can? The gospel message was that God, the ultimate Being, had revealed himself to the world in Jesus Christ and continues to do so in and through his Holy Spirit. This was the context in which Christians sought to answer these questions, and the result was the doctrine of the Trinity. Whatever we do with that doctrine today, the

---

[7]For this development, see R. P. C. Hanson, *The Search for the Christian Doctrine of God* (Edinburgh: T&T Clark, 1988).

same questions confront us as Christians in the modern world, whether we accept the Western tradition as normative for the whole church or seek to replace it with something we think is more attuned to our own needs and circumstances.

THE TRADITIONAL DOCTRINE

Before we examine what possibilities there might be for revising the traditional doctrine of the Trinity, we have to understand what that is and how it came into being. The detailed history has often been recounted elsewhere, and there is neither the time nor the need for us to cover the ground again. But if we are thinking of building anew, we have to understand what building blocks were felt to be necessary for the construction of the traditional doctrine and why they were pieced together in the way they were. We must also appreciate that there were a number of other possible constructs, some of which were very appealing to large numbers of early Christians, but that in the end they were all found to be inadequate for one reason or another. What we have inherited has stood the test of time and surpassed the claims of its rivals, and so it must be taken seriously, even if we think there may be reasons for thinking it can (or must) be reformulated in the modern theological and missional context.

The first principle of traditional Western trinitarianism is that God is one. Whatever else we say about him, we cannot allow the fundamental unity of his divine being to be compromised. The second principle is that the Father, the Son, and the Holy Spirit coexist within that divine being.[8] They are not different names for the same objective being, because they interact with one another and there are some things that only one of them has done, such as become a man in Jesus Christ. We are therefore forced to insist on their distinctiveness, however we choose to describe it. Whether they are equal to one another is more difficult to determine. As part of God's being they must be the same, since God's being is one, but in their relationships to each other they reveal a pattern in which the Father appears to be somehow greater than either the Son or the Spirit. How the Son and the Holy Spirit are related to each other is much less clear and has been the subject of an ongoing and still-unresolved controversy, but they are not interchangeable. Furthermore, there is an order among them that allows the Father to send the Son into the world, but not the other way around, and that also allows the Holy Spirit to take the Son's place in the life of the church without repeating his atoning sacrifice on the cross. To what extent their different functions reflect a fundamental difference that is inherent in their identities is one of the most enduring questions of trinitarian theology. Have the persons acted as they have by their own free choice, or is there something in who they are that predetermined how they would act?

The early Christians tackled this question by starting with the assumption that the one God could be equated with the Father. When Jesus told his disciples to pray to God as their Father, they could hardly have imagined that the Father could have been anyone other than the God of Abraham, Isaac, and Jacob, in whom they already believed. What Jesus was teaching them was to look at him in a new way.[9] Just as his God was their God, so his Father would be their Father too. That basic assumption led the first generations of the church to think of the Son and

[8]See G. L. Prestige, *God in Patristic Thought*, 2nd ed. (London: SPCK, 1952).
[9]This is fully explained in Gerald L. Bray, *God Has Spoken* (Wheaton, IL: Crossway, 2014).

the Spirit as extensions of the Father, but they soon found themselves in trouble with that analysis. For example, they could say that the Son was the mind of the Father, but not that the Father lost his mind when the Son became a man. They could also imagine that Father, Son, and Holy Spirit were distinguished by their functions, so that the Father was the Creator, the Son was the Redeemer, and the Holy Spirit was the Sanctifier. That sounded better, but in the end it did not work very well because the New Testament tells us that the Son was also the Creator (Jn 1:3; Col 1:15-16), the Father was the Redeemer (Jn 3:16), and both the Father and the Son are sanctifiers. Separation according to function did not work, nor could it, since it is hard to see how redemption can be distinguished from sanctification in the new creation. What the members of the Godhead do, they do together.

The end result of these attempts to account for the threeness in God was to reinforce the supremacy of the Father and downgrade the divinity of the Son. The Holy Spirit was seldom mentioned at this early stage, but we can probably assume that if the Son was regarded as being less than fully God, the same would also have been true of the Spirit. By the time the church emerged from the shadows of persecution into the daylight of legality, the various options that had been canvassed for the previous 250 years were fading into the background. In their place, however, came the greatest challenge of all—the heresy we now know as Arianism. How much Arianism had to do with Arius, the Alexandrian presbyter after whom it is named, and whether it can really be seen as a single

belief system are questions we can leave to the historians.[10] For our present purposes, the problem was that the Arians denied the divinity of the Son and insisted that he was no more than the greatest of the creatures. It is true that they thought he had been created in heaven before the foundation of the world and that he was closer to God the Father than any angel was, but despite his lofty status, he was still not God.

Arianism owed its popularity to its simplicity. There is only one God, and that God is the Father, so the Son is by definition not God, even if he is as close to divinity as it is possible for a creature to be. Its opponents argued that between the Creator and the creation there is a great gulf fixed—if the Son was a creature, then not only was he not God but he could not be our Savior or Mediator either. As a creature he had no special standing with the Creator, and if he became sin for us, as the New Testament says he did, then he became a sinner and had no authority to save us from our transgressions. The crisis that Arianism produced led to the First Council of Nicaea, in 325, where a serious attempt was made to sort out the terminology used to describe the Son.

The fathers of Nicaea recognized that the Son has his own identity, quite distinct from that of the Father, but they insisted that he was fully and properly God at the same time. To describe him, they said that he was "consubstantial" with the Father, meaning by this that his being was the same as that of the Father. The main problem they faced was that the Greek word for "consubstantial" (*homoousios*) was not in the New Testament but had apparently been used by

---

[10]See, e.g., Rowan Williams, *Arius: Heresy and Tradition* (London: Darton, Longman & Todd, 1987); Michele René Barnes and D. H. Williams, eds., *Arianism After Arius: Essays on the Development of the Fourth-Century Trinitarian Conflicts* (Edinburgh: T&T Clark, 1993). There is also a lengthy exposition in Aloys Grillmeier, *Christ in Christian Tradition*, trans. John Bowden, 2nd ed. (London: Mowbray, 1975), 1:219-328.

third-century heretics who wanted to say that the Son was the Father in another form, or "mode" of being. That would have destroyed his distinct identity because he would have been no more than a façade behind which the Father was to be found hiding, a heresy we now know as modalism or Sabellianism, after the man who is supposed to have advocated it. It was true, of course, that Jesus had told his disciples that he and the Father were one, but whatever that meant, it did not mean that he was merely the Father in disguise. The New Testament evidence presents us with two subjects who are in conscious dialogue with each other, and that had to be accounted for. The modalist approach would have meant that when Jesus prayed to his Father he was either talking to himself or he was a man talking to God in the Arian sense of a creature speaking to the Creator.

Neither of these options was adequate. By adopting the word *consubstantial*, the First Council of Nicaea sought to establish parameters within which the debate must proceed, but it could not produce a definitive solution to the problem raised by confessing the divinity of the Son. Their failure in this respect became obvious in the following generation. Granted that we must say the Son is consubstantial with the Father, in what sense is this true? Human beings are consubstantial with one another—we share the same kind of being and nature, we can copulate and reproduce, we can even share blood and body parts to a limited degree. This is possible because we are like one another without being exactly the same, and it was natural for some people to want to interpret the Father, Son, and Holy Spirit in an analogous way. The snag was that while human beings exist in plurality,

there is only one God. Father, Son, and Holy Spirit are not related to each other like Tom, Dick, and Harry—three separate beings sharing the same analogous nature. Rather, they are three distinct identities sharing the same being, and for this a new terminology had to be found.

In searching for the right words to use, the early church found it relatively easy to agree about how to describe the oneness of God. This was his being or substance and his nature, which were one and the same.[11] For example, God was good, but he was fully and absolutely good, and so Father, Son, and Holy Spirit were each fully and absolutely good too. Here the logic of monotheism is plain to see, and at this level the early Christian understanding of God is scarcely different from either the Jewish or the Muslim one.

It was much harder for the church to find a word to describe the threeness in that one divine being. The two most successful terms were the Greek *hypostasis* and the Latin *persona*. *Hypostasis* can be found in the New Testament, in Hebrews 1:3, where the Son is described as the "*character* of the Father's *hypostasis*," whatever that is supposed to mean. There has been considerable debate about this over the years, but the context suggests that the best translation is something like "the exact replica of the Father's identity." A *character* was a copy or a stamp, hence the idea of replica, while a *hypostasis* was an underlying reality. The snag was that the word was often used as a synonym for "being," and in its Latin form, *substantia*, that is what it came to mean more or less exclusively. Thus while Greeks could and did say that there were three *hypostases* in the one being of God, the Latins could not translate this as "three substances in the one substance."

---

[11]On this concept and its relationship to Greek philosophy in particular, see Christopher Stead, *Divine Substance* (Oxford: Clarendon, 1977).

To get around this problem Tertullian came up with the word *persona*, which had originally meant a mask in the theater but had come to signify an agent in a lawsuit as well. A *persona* was someone who could act in a court of law, a dimension that was missing from the word *hypostasis*.[12] The difference can be seen in that whereas *hypostasis* was not confined to human beings, since animals and inanimate objects can also have an identity, *persona* more or less was. I say "more or less" because in Roman law not every human being was a legal *persona*—women, children, and slaves were all excluded—and it was possible for a business entity to acquire legal personality, or as we would say today, to be "incorporated," which simply means "to be given a body."

Whether the word *persona* occurs in the Bible or not is hard to say. Its Greek equivalent, *prosōpon*, certainly does, especially in the phrase *prosōpon pros prosōpon*, which is the standard translation of the Hebrew for "face to face." Its most famous occurrence in the New Testament is in 1 Corinthians 13:12, where Paul says that though we now see through a glass darkly, we shall then see "face to face." The mystery will be unveiled, and we shall know God just as he knows us. What is particularly interesting is that in this passage, *prosōpon* cannot possibly mean mask because it is explicitly used to describe the exact opposite. For Paul, to see God "face to face" is to be unmasked; it is, in effect, what we could now quite happily refer to as "person-to-person" contact. In other words, Paul's use of the word *prosōpon* is closer to what we now understand as *person* than it is to the original meaning of *mask*,

and it is on that basis that the early Christians took it over for theological purposes.

In finding this word Tertullian struck it rich, as we might say today. It enabled him to say that in God there were three persons in one substance—the same formula we continue to use now. He may not have understood it in precisely the way that we do, but his terminology was sufficiently flexible that it could adapt to later theological developments and survive without change. The Greek world hesitated over this for a long time, preferring the formula "three *hypostases* in one being" but occasionally flirting with *prosōpon* as an alternative. The question was finally resolved at the Council of Chalcedon in 451, where it was decreed that *hypostasis* and *prosōpon* were synonymous and could be used interchangeably. In practice, what that meant was that the word *hypostasis* was redefined so as to accord with the Latin *persona*, which also became the model for understanding *prosōpon*.

The details are complex, but the underlying principles are clear enough. What the Chalcedonian Definition achieved was a balance between two different levels of perception that can be traced back to a number of Greek thinkers of the late fourth century but that was not formally canonized until the council.[13] Chalcedon got to that point by making a clear distinction between the level of particular identities in God, where there were three persons, and the level of his being, which was only one. Previously it had usually been imagined that the one somehow expanded into three or that the three coalesced into the one, but by positing two different levels of analysis, Chalcedon was able to avoid this. In

---

[12]The fullest discussion of this is in R. Braun, *Deus Christianorum: Recherches sur le vocabulaire doctrinal de Tertullien*, 2nd ed. (Paris: Etudes Augustiniennes, 1977), 207-42. For a more recent and wide-ranging treatment of the word *person*, see B. Meunier, *La personne et le christianisme ancien* (Paris: Cerf, 2006).

[13]On Chalcedon, see R. V. Sellers, *The Council of Chalcedon* (London: SPCK, 1961).

its understanding, which in many ways reflects that of the great Cappadocian fathers of the late fourth century, the one did not become three or the three one. Instead, the three were simultaneously present in the one and the one in the three, and there was no crossover from one level to the other. In other words, the Father could no longer be seen as God in the true or absolute sense in a way that did not apply equally to the Son and the Holy Spirit, because although the last two depended on the Father with respect to their personal identities, they did not do so in regard to their common being, in which they all shared equally. The Father might personify the mysterious being of God to a degree that the Son and the Holy Spirit did not, but if so, that was because he remained eternally transcendent in heaven and not because he was innately superior to the other two persons.

Just as importantly, though this is not always properly recognized, the Chalcedonian Definition of faith gave priority to the three persons of the Godhead over their one being or nature. It envisaged a God whose three persons possess their one nature and are free to use it to shape their common divine will. This conclusion was imposed on them by the incarnation of the Son, because in that act he took on a second, human nature while remaining the divine person, with his divine nature, that he was in eternity. That he could do this, without involving the Father and the Holy Spirit in the same process, showed that as a divine person the Son was not bound by his divine nature but was able to transcend it and become a man, not by diminishing his divinity but by adding to it. It took several more centuries to work out the finer points of this doctrine, but

the essential framework was laid at Chalcedon, and that has remained the standard formulation of trinitarian doctrine ever since. There were dissenters at Chalcedon who refused to sign on to its Christology, but even they accepted the trinitarian aspect of the decisions taken there, so that all Christians now confess that God is three persons in one being or substance and interpret these terms in basically the same way.

RECONSTRUCTING THE DOCTRINE

What was decided at Chalcedon and the councils that later clarified its definition has remained the official orthodoxy of most of the Eastern and all of the Western churches from then until now. It was questioned from time to time, especially after the rise of Islam, and during the Middle Ages it was elaborated by a number of philosophical theologians who sought to integrate the doctrine of the Trinity into their systematization of truth. To a man such as Richard of St. Victor in the twelfth century, the Trinity was not only a revealed doctrine but also an essential part of created reality, reflected in any number of analogies that were readily available to those who used their minds to think about them and could be used to explain the underlying structure of the universe.[14] It was not until the sixteenth century, when Renaissance humanists uncovered vast tracts of ancient philosophy and science that had either been lost or forgotten, and when the Protestant Reformers called into question the biblical foundations of the church's teaching, that serious attempts were made to overturn it on the ground that it was a philosophical construct and not part of God's revelation at all.

The most important of these attempts to undo the Trinity was something close to what we now

---

[14]Richard has been rediscovered recently in the English-speaking world. See, e.g., Ruben Angelici, *Richard of Saint Victor: On the Trinity* (Eugene, OR: Cascade, 2011); Boyd Taylor Coolman and Dale M. Coulter, *Trinity and Creation* (Hyde Park, NY: New City, 2011), 195-352.

call Unitarianism, though that doctrine emerged independently in the early eighteenth century. We meet it in the pages of Calvin's *Institutes of the Christian Religion* (1.13), where the great Reformer had to deal with unnamed men who were attacking the legitimacy of the traditional theological terminology. In the early seventeenth century this way of thinking was generally associated with Socinianism, a doctrine derived from the teaching of Lelio Sozzini and his nephew Fausto, two Italian lawyers who propagated it.[15] Socinianism was regarded as a great danger in the early seventeenth century, but although it was largely snuffed out, at least in Western Europe, it left an abiding legacy. Its principle that theological doctrine should always be susceptible to rational analysis was attractive to many and became a commonplace even among some theologians, such as the famous Hugo Grotius, who dissented from the Sozzini and argued against them. Three persons in one divine being did not make logical sense, and so the doctrine of the Trinity was living on borrowed time in a world that was increasingly governed by the power of reason.

Eighteenth-century Unitarianism was a kind of upgraded Socinianism in which the antitrinitarian element, as its name indicates, was unmistakable. It was never accepted as orthodox teaching by any Christian church, and to this day Unitarians are not officially recognized as Christians, but their impact has been far greater than such rejection and denial might suggest. For although no church has ever adopted Unitarian beliefs outright, many leading theologians have shared the mindset that produced it and have taught a theoretically "orthodox" form of Christianity that for all intents and purposes is indistinguishable from Unitarianism. The doctrine of the Trinity has been progressively sidelined in Western seminaries to the point where few pastors and even fewer laypeople know what to say about it. Worse still, they do not think that the Trinity is very important. They believe that they can preach and teach the gospel on the basis of the Bible without indulging in such theological abstractions and find it hard to see why anyone should challenge them in this belief. They do not ignore Jesus Christ, who remains central to their perception of God's revelation to the world, and many of them pay great attention to the Holy Spirit. What they find difficult is linking them together as three equal persons in one God, but that, of course, is what the doctrine of the Trinity is all about.

It is essential to understand that the antitrinitarianism of the past five centuries has been the outward and visible sign of a progressive but often covert secularization in Western society. Belief in miracles, superstitions of various kinds, and reliance on divine revelation as opposed to human reason have all been dismissed as relics of a medieval past. The concept of God has occasionally survived in the form of a "supreme being," "intelligent designer," or "first principle" that holds the universe together, but whether there really is such a thing is debated, and if there is, whether it ought to be equated with the Christian God is regarded as a matter of personal opinion.[16] Christians will tend to do that,

---

[15] On Socinianism, see Philip Dixon, *Nice and Hot Disputes: The Doctrine of the Trinity in the Seventeenth Century* (London: T&T Clark, 2003); Sarah Mortimer, *Reason and Religion in the English Revolution: The Challenge of Socinianism* (Cambridge: Cambridge University Press, 2010).

[16] It is significant that the defenders of "intelligent design" in the United States have insisted that theirs is not a religiously based theory but one that can be justified on scientific principles alone. Equally significant is the fact that the courts have generally disagreed with them when the matter has been put to adjudication. For a discussion of modern theism that does not involve trinitarian belief, see David J. Bartholomew, *God, Chance and Purpose: Can God Have It Both Ways?* (Cambridge: Cambridge University Press, 2008).

either from conviction or tradition, and others will not, but to the liberal mind that does not matter very much. As long as people recognize that there is something out there that is bigger than themselves, we can get along by calling it different things and relating to it in different ways. However we approach it, though, the Trinity is an irrelevance, either because it is a mistaken formulation held over from a bygone era by the weight and inertia of traditional orthodoxy, or because it is an irretrievably Western picture of God. This, by and large, is where the West and its theologians are coming from today, though by no means all of them have succumbed to this logic. On the contrary, there has been a major trinitarian revival in the late twentieth century, which started against that background and must be seen in that light, but has headed off in quite a different direction.

When we turn to the Majority World, the theological picture is more complex. The influence of Western secularism is certainly widespread, especially in those countries that have come under communist rule at some stage, but not only there. The governing elites have almost all been educated in Western universities and have absorbed their philosophy to a greater or lesser degree. As a result, in most cases local universities and other centers of learning act as secularist embassies in what is intellectually a foreign country to them. The grassroots church, however, appears very different. In Western countries, secularization has taken hold of a large proportion of the population. Some people remain religious, and a great many are privately superstitious, but for the most part such things are kept out of the public domain. Religion has become a private matter left to the individual conscience, which in practice means that God cannot be mentioned in public discourse in any

serious way. This is true even in theological faculties, where the methods of debate and research parallel those used in every other academic discipline. Belief in God can be studied as a social phenomenon, but it cannot be used as the basis for constructing policy. Here we have gone well beyond any form of Unitarianism into outright atheism, where the Christian doctrine of the Trinity has no logical place.

In the Majority World, by contrast, spirituality is the stuff of everyday life. Whether people believe in spirits, pagan gods, or some higher form of religion, the whole of life is permeated with a sense of the presence of the divine. What Christianity has done, especially in Africa, has been to structure that instinctive awareness in a systematic way that appeals to history, philosophy, and personal experience. What was previously mysterious, disordered, or threatening has become clear, orderly, and positive. At this level, it must be recognized that Islam has performed a similar function in the places where it has gone, and it is here that the potential for conflict between the two great religions arises. Christian systematization of the spiritual world includes a doctrine of the Trinity, but its Islamic equivalent does not. More importantly, Islam does not simply ignore the Trinity—it excludes it. Where the prevailing culture is still animist or polytheist, a different problem arises. People there may have little trouble understanding that there are three divine persons, but why should there be only three? And how does that affect our understanding and experience of God, who can surely be called by many names without detracting from his supreme sovereignty? In these contexts, the church faces a different battle, though in a curious way, the two worlds can overlap at the academic level. Liberal theologians who call for a restructuring of the Christian doctrine of God to take account of modern perceptions of reality may sound very much like, and even make common cause with, representatives of the conservative Majority World who want to explain God in terms that are meaningful to their own people. For different reasons, both types of people find traditional orthodoxy hard to swallow, and there is a very real possibility that the Western liberals will deconstruct Christian doctrine in a way that will appeal to Majority World thinkers who want to appear to be sophisticated and who will be attracted by the apparent simplicity and practicality of what amounts to Unitarianism. Why learn a complex theological formula when a simple "love God and your neighbor" will apparently do instead?

How can we deal with these challenges, and in what way can the West and the Majority World work together? First of all, Western theologians need to recognize that most of the criticisms leveled against traditional trinitarian doctrine, which have to do with the supposedly inappropriate use of the terms *person* and *substance* in the way we define it, are misguided. The charge made against *substance* is that it is an outdated scientific concept. It has been abandoned in physics, the argument goes, so it should be abandoned in metaphysics as well. The root of the problem here is philosophical, not theological. There has always been a complex and difficult relationship between these two disciplines, but theologians must point out that the biblical revelation has never been captive to any secular philosophy. It does not need the word *substance* to describe God, who is there whatever term we use. In fact, there is a long tradition of Christian thought that has rejected the use of words such as *substance* and *being* to describe God precisely because he cannot be pinned down in this way. To define him in terms derived from natural science is to make an intellectual idol of him. That may be more sophisticated than statues of gold and silver, but it is just as inaccurate and unacceptable. Whatever we say about God in human language, it is only an approximate and therefore inadequate description of him.

At the same time, we must insist that God is really there, that he has a presence that cannot be denied, and that he is fundamental to our existence. In much Western thought, the abandonment of terms such as *substance* has led not to a deeper theological understanding, but to atheism, and it is this that we must do all in our power to avoid. For this reason, we probably cannot abandon the vocabulary of *substance* as long as there is no alternative readily available, but we can certainly reassure our critics that we are not wedded to it as a matter of principle. Come up with something better and we shall be only too willing to adopt it.

Where *person* is concerned, the main objection is that in modern secular usage the term refers to a "center of consciousness" that is supposed to be the unique possession of each individual. But there cannot be three centers of consciousness in God, because if there were, there would be three different gods and not one. This argument is appealing at first sight, but it is flawed. First of all, to assert that a person is a center of consciousness raises doubts about the status of human beings who, for one reason or another, are not conscious. We cannot explore this theme in detail here, but suffice it to say that Christian opposition to abortion and euthanasia is rooted in the belief that a person cannot be defined in that way. The Christian hope in life after death is also bound up with this—an inert corpse is not the end of our life but the sign that we have moved on to a higher reality. For Christians, to be a human person is to be created in the image and likeness of God, because God is personal. Even if we are not conscious, this is still true.

But equally important, and it is here that the West and the Majority World can perhaps most easily converge, to be a person is to exist in relationships—with God primarily, but also with other human beings. It is often said nowadays that the West is too individualistic, whereas the Majority World places a much higher value on the importance of community. How true this really is is hard to say. It seems probable that the Majority World is moving in the direction of greater individualism, and there are signs that the West is rediscovering the importance of community.[17] Be that as it may, there is no doubt that both worlds are built on a structure of relationships, however they are defined. The persons of the Trinity are the ultimate example of this—the absolute relationships into which believers are integrated by being united with Christ in the power of the Holy Spirit. This is true whoever we are, wherever we come from, and whatever intellectual or cultural formation we have had. The rediscovery of this principle in Western theology has given new life to the doctrine of the Trinity, which is now interpreted much more in the context of interpersonal relationships than it ever used to be. This is perhaps the most encouraging sign that theological renewal in the West is possible and that it can connect with the concerns and experience of the Majority World at the deepest level.

The Christian doctrine of the Trinity is that God is love and that he manifests himself to us as a community in which his love is perfected. Love is not a substance, not a thing that can be objectified and defined, but it is a reality and constitutes the being of God. Those who live in love are the persons of the Trinity, and it is as persons created in God's image that we are invited to share in their eternal fellowship. We cannot exclude the possibility that this reality might be expressed in other ways, and perhaps one day new doctrinal definitions will be found that can describe it as well or better than what has been achieved in the past. But whatever the future holds in this respect, it is certain that nothing that does not contain and enhance this reality will ever take the place of traditional trinitarian doctrine, nor is it likely that this truth will be expressed in one cultural context to the exclusion of others. Jesus commissioned his followers to make disciples of all the nations, baptizing them in the name of the Father, the Son, and the Holy Spirit. Over the centuries the church has proclaimed this message not so much by adapting to the prevailing cultural norms as by transforming them into something higher, which only divine revelation is capable of expressing adequately. Let us pray that as our mission enters a new phase this conviction and this awareness will continue to guide us and that we may be led into all truth as we believe our forefathers in the faith were.

FURTHER READING

Collins, Philip M. *The Trinity: A Guide for the Perplexed*. London: T&T Clark, 2008.

Gunton, Colin E. *The Promise of Trinitarian Theology*. Edinburgh: T&T Clark, 1991.

Holmes, Stephen. *The Quest for the Trinity*. Downers Grove, IL: IVP Academic, 2012.

Torrance, T. F. *The Trinitarian Faith*. Edinburgh: T&T Clark, 1988.

Wozniak, Robert J., and Giulio Maspero. *Rethinking Trinitarian Theology*. London: T&T Clark, 2012.

---

[17]See, e.g., Alan J. Torrance, *Persons in Communion: Trinitarian Description and Human Participation* (Edinburgh: T&T Clark, 1996).

BEYOND *HOMOIOUSIOS* AND *HOMOOUSIOS*

EXPLORING NORTH AMERICAN INDIGENOUS CONCEPTS OF THE SHALOM COMMUNITY OF GOD

Randy S. Woodley

THE FOURTH-CENTURY BATTLE over the interpretation of a single developed trinitarian theology laid the groundwork for numerous binary trajectories, with some resulting in Christian imperialism. Western Christianity's early preoccupation with divine ontology, coupled with the military might of the Christian empire and the West's inability to hold the mystery of God in tension, has beleaguered Christians and other monotheists for centuries. An Indigenous understanding of the divine shalom community may offer different choices that are perhaps closer to the constructed understandings of Trinity held by early followers of the Christ. In their various perceptions, early Jewish Christians recognized and acknowledged a place in their worldview for a trinitarian construct without the trappings of extrinsic categorization

or the burden of ontological fixation. If we must talk of God in ontological terms, which again is beyond any of our comprehension, then perhaps the image of the community of the Creator, existing eternally in shalom relationality, can lead us beyond much of the former dialogue that has centered itself on ontological substance, and toward a better understanding of our own communal ontology.[1]

INTRODUCTION

There is no way for us today to gauge the perceptual difficulties early Jewish followers of Jesus went through when moving from a monotheistic construct of God to a trinitarian construct. From what we can garner from the writings of the New Testament, it is apparent that the divinity of Jesus struck them with such

---

[1]Shalom, as used in Scripture, is a very broad theological construct. I am using it according to Walter Brueggemann's model, which he describes as follows: "That persistent vision of joy, well-being, harmony and prosperity is not captured in any single word or idea in the Bible; a cluster of words is required to express its many dimensions and subtle nuances: love, loyalty, truth, grace, salvation, justice, blessings, righteousness. But the term that in recent discussions has been used to summarize that controlling vision is *shalom*. Both in such discussion and in the Bible itself, it bears tremendous freight—the freight of a dream of God that resists all our tendencies to division, hostility, fear, drivenness, and misery. *Shalom* is the substance of the biblical vision of one community embracing all creation. It refers to all those resources and factors that make communal harmony joyous and effective." Walter Brueggemann, *Peace: Living Toward a Vision* (St. Louis: Chalice, 2001), 14.

intensity that an alternative view of the divine was impending and necessary.[2] Therefore, it is paramount in discussing Jesus' divinity to acknowledge that according to several writers in the New Testament, Jesus is recognized as the divine Creator. The literary structure of New Testament references to Christ as Creator are predominately in formulaic style, meaning they may have been mnemonic devices memorized as poems or sung as hymns. These formulaic patterns suggest that the early Jewish understanding of Christ as Creator somehow equated Jesus with YHWH and that it was a popular theme in the early church. Here is the account found in the Gospel of John.

> In the beginning was the Word, and the Word was with God, and the Word was God.
>
> He was in the beginning with God.
>
> All things came into being through him, and without him not one thing came into being. What has come into being in him was life, and the life was the light of all people. (Jn 1:1-4)[3]

In the writer's mind, Jesus is preexistent, is divine, was God's instrument in creation, and gave life to all creation. In the same chapter, John 1:10-14, the writer speaks of God's redemptive value in Christ. The writer seems to have a fluid understanding of Jesus the man and Jesus the preexistent Christ who is Creator. The writer of John also appears to understand the very same Jesus as the redeemer of all things. In a similar formulaic pattern to the one found in John, Paul writes,

> He is the image of the invisible God, the firstborn of all creation;
>
> for in him all things in heaven and on earth were created, things visible and invisible, whether thrones or dominions or rulers or powers—all things have been created through him and for him.
>
> He himself is before all things, and in him all things hold together.
>
> He is the head of the body, the church; he is the beginning, the firstborn from the dead, so that he might come to have first place in everything.
>
> For in him all the fullness of God was pleased to dwell, and through him God was pleased to reconcile to himself all things, whether on earth or in heaven, by making peace through the blood of his cross. (Col 1:15-20)

In this text Paul understands:

- Christ as preexistent

- Christ as having supremacy over all creation

- Christ as God's instrument in creation

- All creation as being created by Christ

- All creation made for Christ

- Christ making shalom with all creation by his redemptive atonement

Paul's explanation parallels John's understanding of Christ the human, Christ the Creator, and Christ the Redeemer. Paul references another formulaic description of Christ as Creator in 1 Corinthians 8:6: "Yet for us there is one God, the Father, from whom are all things and for whom we exist, and one Lord, Jesus Christ, through whom are all things and through whom we exist." Once again, Paul states that through Jesus Christ, God made all creation, and through Christ we all have life.

A fourth reference, possibly constructed in a similar kind of formula, is found in the letter to

---

[2]The Gospels and much of Paul's writings are largely a defense of Christ's divinity without the direct assertion that Christ himself understood his purpose to be more than that of the expected Jewish Messiah.

[3]Unless otherwise noted, Scripture quotations in this chapter follow the NRSV.

the Hebrews: "Long ago God spoke to our ancestors in many and various ways by the prophets, but in these last days he has spoken to us by a Son, whom he appointed heir of all things, through whom he also created the worlds" (Heb 1:1-2). As with the other passages, the writer of Hebrews begins by reasoning that, through Christ, God created all of creation and that all creation belongs to him. Later, the same writer ties the creation act to Christ's redemptive actions by saying, "It was fitting that God, for whom and through whom all things exist, in bringing many children to glory, should make the pioneer of their salvation perfect through sufferings" (Heb 2:10).

In this great mystery of incarnation and reconciliation, those who walked with or near the incarnated Christ came to an understanding that he was the orchestrator of creation. Without a better understanding of God's plan through Jesus Christ as both Creator and as Savior/Reconciler (shalom bringer), we in the modern church may have overzealously developed an imbalanced salvation theology that favors the otherworldly over our physical realities. Among traditional Indigenous peoples, God inhabits all creation. God is in every tree, every rock, and every stream.[4]

The Creator of all things is also the reconciler of all things, and all things (i.e., all creation) are being created for Christ. Paul, in the Colossians passage, even says Christ "holds all things together." It may be said that since all things are redeemable in Christ, then restoring the world to God's intentions of shalom is the point of Christ's redemption. The basic issue in our day is perhaps the breadth of healing God has made available in Christ. If Jesus died for all creation, and not just the human "soul," and not even just for humans (all things), then the concept of redemption is much broader than many Christians have traditionally thought. Redemption (our salvation) is reconciliation of and for the whole earth.

Part of the problem contributing to a limited view of salvation is Western Christianity's insistence on binary choices (i.e., divine/human, created/not created, Creator/Redeemer, Father/Son), which may be compounded in both the English language and Western logic. For example, in the Cherokee language we are able to use a phrase that points to Jesus as the *Creator-Son*. This linguistic construction references Jesus' sonship in relation to the Father while at the same time referencing his role in creation. The word *son* in Cherokee is related to the word for egg. An egg is both chicken and egg at the same

---

[4]The idea of physical *place* should not be overlooked when referencing the Trinity. As a settler-colonial society, the West has placed an emphasis on *time* to the deprecation of serious thinking concerning *place*. The emphasis of time over place naturally bends Christianity toward an abstract trajectory to the point where systematic theology and practical theology become two distinct realities. The author understands that it is difficult to form a righteous theology of place when the historical reality begins from a place of stolen land, but as a result, in a Western worldview Trinity is a very abstract or even ethereal ideal. Among Indigenous peoples, when thinking about the trinitarian community, *place* can take on relational aspects that are neglected by an emphasis on time.

Many traditional Native Americans would understand the nature of God in regard to creation to be panentheistic. Pantheism, on the one hand, is the belief that the created order *is* God and God *is* the created order. Panentheism, on the other hand, is a constructed word from the Greek meaning "all-in-God," with the distinction that, while the world and universe are contained within God, God is greater than the whole of the universe and creation. From this position there can be significant variation on how the relationship between God and creation plays out. Also, as stated, the fingerprint of God or DNA is on all creation, allowing trinitarian concepts to become tangible and accessible. For a detailed philosophical article on panentheism, see John Culp, "Panentheism," in *Stanford Encyclopedia of Philosophy*, ed. Edward N. Zalta, spring 2013 ed., http://plato.stanford.edu/entries/panentheism/. For a more complete historical theology, see Sean M. McDonough, *Christ as Creator: Origins of a New Testament Doctrine* (Oxford: Oxford University Press, 2009).

time.[5] Respected Keetoowah Cherokee tradition keeper Thomas Belt, in an essay coauthored with Margaret Bender, says concerning the Cherokee word for egg,

> In Cherokee, one's child is *agwe'tsi,* "my egg." The child is inseparable from the speaker in two ways: first, a possessive pronoun is built into the word as a prefix (in this case in the form *agw-,* "my") so that no child is an abstraction but is always the child of a specific person in a conversation; second, a child's biological origin as a part of the parent is reinforced throughout life since the word for child also means "egg."[6]

When used with the word for Creator, the Son becomes connected to the Creator through relationship and becomes indistinguishable from that relationship. In this simple linguistic formula Jesus is acknowledged as both divine Creator and divine Son. The implications of embracing broader understandings of Christ as the one who creates all things and as the one who restores all things has tremendous significance for the *missio Dei* as well as theological import.[7] The God who creates all creation also sends, is sent to, and will restore all creation. Jesus, the Creator-Son, is one in indistinguishable relationship with God, sent by God, to redeem all things to God. This brings us back to the problem of the modern West and the dilemma the title of this essay alludes to: Is Jesus the same as or similar to God?

GIVING ONE IOTA

The early church, in defending Christ's divinity against various heresies, primarily Arianism (the Son is the first and highest creation of the Father), Ebionism (the Son is only apparently divine), and docetism (the Son is only apparently human), created a quandary for trinitarians and nontrinitarians alike. How can Christians, after investing in centuries of persecuting one another for various trinitarian positions surrounding Christ, move beyond the ontology of trinitarian *personae*?

One of the earliest controversies in Christianity focused on Jesus Christ, the Son, in the trinitarian construct. The two Greek words representing one significant dispute were *homoiousios,* "of a similar substance," and *homoousios,* "of the same substance." It has been pointed out many times that these two words differ by a single letter, *iota,* the smallest in the Greek alphabet.

I would like to suggest in this essay (even while attempting to convey my own ontological understanding) that we can move beyond traditional arguments concerning the ontology of God. The ontological question of the Trinity is one we may *ask* but not one over which we should *divide* ourselves. Ontological notions of God require proof beyond what any human can produce, so ultimately our understanding of God's ontological essence may be simply a matter

---

[5]I first heard the term *Creator-Son* used in 2001 by fellow Cherokee theologian Robert Francis, who later told me he had earlier heard me use it in a song. I use the term *Creator-Son* to designate "Creator" as Jesus' relationship to the Trinity and the efficacy of his role in the whole creation process. The use of the term *Son* refers to Jesus' *kenosis* as the member of the Trinity who became the "Son of Man" on earth. As I will explain, this idea is inherent in the Cherokee language.

[6]Thomas Belt and Margaret Bender, "Speaking Difference to Power: The Importance of Linguistic Sovereignty," in *Foundations of First Peoples' Sovereignty: History, Education and Culture,* ed. Ulrike Wiethaus (New York: Peter Lang, 2008), 189.

[7]Given that *shalom* has never been used as a model for mission among Native Americans, the relationality of the Trinity could serve as a vital missional model in this process. Since the widespread understanding of *shalom* is found among almost all North American Indians, there is an immediate common point of reference between Native American symbols, stories, and ceremonies that promote harmony and what the Bible presents as God's vision of *shalom.*

of our best understandings and faith.[8] We Christians accept the construct of a monotheistic faith. As evangelicals we accept the inclusion of Jesus and Spirit as in eternal relationship with God. In terms of how we pray (and avoiding modalism), we believe in faith that God hears us, yet the full answer to who God is remains a great mystery. Without certainty of proof, we must admit that the great mystery is just that—a mystery to us.

A Different Way of Thinking

There may be room in the "Native American Old Testament" for renewed trinitarian constructs, especially given the similarities between Native American views and those of shalom as developed in Judaism.[9] Similar to the early Jewish Christian monotheistic community, Native Americans are able to look back from the vantage point of history to understand God as a great mystery or even a divine trinitarian mystery. Although rare, some pre–European invasion Indigenous Native North American sects even held a trinitarian view of the Creator. Aboriginal North Americans are not dependent on Western church history, church councils, and doctrinal development in order to validate their views of trinitarian plausibility. Reexamining Native American views of God in light of past trini-

tarian revelation may provide new light from an alternative worldview, which could lead to a deeper understanding of the divine mystery and the earthly shalom community.

Indigenous peoples do not think about theology in the same categories as Westerners.[10] Only within the last several decades have Native American Christians begun to do significant work on compiling, writing, and sharing their understanding of Christian theology. Many factors help explain why this is the case, but primarily, Native Americans have not been encouraged to share their perspectives in Western-dominated Christian theological circles. Particular to the subject at hand is not that Indigenous peoples are not thinking about concepts such as Trinity, but rather they are struggling to find ways to communicate their insights in ways that are true to their culture and worldviews.

Indigenous North American cultural understandings, worldviews, and ways of disseminating knowledge are drastically different from Western paradigms and are often diametrically opposed to them. Further complicating things is the problem that not only are the categories incompatible with Indigenous thinking, but there is also currently no existing model or construct for translating traditional Native beliefs into

---

[8]I often use a phrase in my courses, "There is no such thing as theology, there are only theologies." When humans attempt to articulate their understandings and experiences of the divine, those descriptions become inseparably bound to ourselves and to our own experiences, which give formation to the language we have available to comprehend. All our explanations inevitably assume a sense of anthropomorphism.

[9]See Steve Charleston's essay, "The Old Testament of Native America," in *Native and Christian: Indigenous Voices on Religious Identity in the United States and Canada*, ed. James Treat (New York: Routledge, 1996), which helps deepen our understanding of these two ancient covenants. Charleston avers, "God spoke to generations of Native People over centuries of our spiritual development. We need to pay attention to that voice, to be respectful of the covenant" (69). The sources confirming the commonly held principles of harmony among Native Americans are many and varied in nuance, but it can be stated without great disputation that most North American Indigenous tribes held to a lifeway of harmony. In general, the list of tribes whose overriding lifeway/philosophy promotes harmony could include almost every North American Native tribal group. The similarities between God's vision of shalom and what Native Americans view as the harmony way are incontrovertible. There are many innate aspects in Native American cultures that promote biblical shalom, or what we as First Nations call shalom by other names. For a more thorough understanding of the intersection of the Native American harmony way and Walter Brueggemann's construct of shalom, see my "The Harmony Way: Integrating Indigenous Values Within Native North American Theology and Mission" (PhD diss., Asbury Theological Seminary, 2010).

[10]For example, consider the North American Institute for Indigenous Theological Studies (NAIITS), which is one example of how Indigenous theological dialogue is changing. For information on NAIITS see www.naiits.com/.

Western Christian theology. Indigenous theologians who wish to discuss such topics are at a disadvantage with few choices available.

The choice most often taken by the Indigenous theologian is assimilative, learning all the histories and categories of the West, even though to many Indigenous theologians they seem anemic and separate from the whole of reality. Another alternative (and these are not mutually exclusive choices) is to simply begin by sitting down and asking other Indigenous thinkers the question, "What do our elders, spiritual leaders, and other traditional people say about this theological concept?" Since the answer to that question will typically be, "Nothing directly," Indigenous scholars can begin exploring what aspects of their traditional beliefs carry the same concepts or fit within the same paradigms as the Christian beliefs they are seeking to understand.[11]

While Native North Americans do have room in their worldview for Trinity, and sometimes even with direct historic evidence of a trinitarian understanding of God, this understanding has been overlooked because of categorical differences. These categorical differences, the result of a Western paradigm for approaching theological study, are directly traced back to Greek systems of thought, having influenced Western thinkers how to extrinsically categorize and dissect concepts, and define objects by their attributes and separate them accordingly. This type of thinking has been the dominating influence in Western doctrinal development. Aboriginal Americans have no such major influence. Because of this, America's First Nations have their own way of understanding the relational independence, interdependence, and connectivity of the trinitarian mystery.

Native American views of God are defined almost completely by relationality rather than by function.[12] In other words, the different aspects of the Trinity are not determined by their function so much as by how they relate in community.[13] Recent theological discussions are focusing more on sacred community/*perichoresis* in developing an understanding that the ontology of the Trinity is not to be found in the persons but rather in the relationship (Zizioulas, Barth, Moltmann, Boff, Grenz, Olson).[14] In

---

[11]It should not be surprising that there are few direct parallels between Native American theological beliefs and modern theological Christian constructs. This does not mean that there are no opportunities for crossover between them or that traditional Native beliefs are incompatible with Christian theological concepts. In fact, many Indigenous Christian thinkers would argue that there is a great amount of support for Christian beliefs in traditional Native religious understandings. For example, there have been strong parallels drawn between traditional Native beliefs and the Jewish concept of shalom theology (Woodley, "Harmony Way"). This is not an unfounded opinion. It has been pointed out that much of the Jewish Old Testament theology omits significant aspects of the Christian faith—the Trinity, for example—and yet still is seen as supportive of the Christian faith. In regard to the Old Testament, the more "ancient" religious traditions are reinterpreted and filtered through the lens of our later understandings and given new meaning. This is what many Indigenous followers of Jesus are attempting to do with their traditional Native beliefs.

[12]The relationality of the Christian Trinity as community becomes all-important for Indigenous peoples. The pre-Enlightenment worldviews of the writers of the New Testament have a great affinity with non-Western/communal Indigenous-oriented thinking, such as is found among Native North Americans. Since we see little writing about the Trinity (proper) in Scripture, one interpretation may be that the church of the New Testament was able to hold the tension of the three-in-one with less difficulty than the later, Greek-influenced theologians who followed them.

[13]A word should be said about parallels concerning First Nations constructs of the Sacred Spirit and the Holy Spirit (*holy* is a synonym for *sacred*). The Spirit is recognized as a continual working of God on the earth and is the source of life as well as our connection to God. It is God's Spirit working on earth that is the all-encompassing manifestation of God's presence here. In this sense, and because of the length of this essay, suffice it to say that the way Western thinkers frame the Spirit is similar to the way Native people do. The Spirit functions in everything and in everyday life as God's presence. The primary difference would be the Indigenous thought concerning God's active presence in all creation. In other words, nothing is inanimate to the Indigenous mind.

[14]Early Christian uses of the *perichoresis* have been ascribed to church leaders such as Gregory of Nazianzus, Hilary of Poitiers, Athanasius, Maximus the Confessor, Gregory of Nyssa, and John of Damascus. Regardless of their different understandings and usages, the point I am making is that the concept of *perichoresis* was marginalized by the Western church until recently.

terms of common dialogue potential with First Nations theologians, this is a positive change from the usual Western form. Non-Western thinkers tend to be able to hold two seemingly opposite views in tension with little problem. The theological difficulty for Native Americans may come when discussing the independent aspects of the Trinity rather than relational inter-connectivity.[15] Recent postmodern theological discussions also promise meaningful dialogue with Indigenous peoples.[16]

INDIGENOUS NORTH AMERICAN TRINITARIAN CONCEPTS

Because early European settler-colonial literature is so sparse concerning the subject at hand, we only have the records of a few eyewitnesses to rely on concerning early Indigenous American constructs of the divine Trinity. Among Cherokee scholars there is general acknowledgment of an ancient trinitarianism, but it is based on little written record or deep traditional knowledge. A trinity of creator beings is found in the oral traditions among the Cherokee and several other tribes. One of these references is an account by a writer in the 1930s describing an ancient Cherokee concept of a Supreme Trinity. The writer records, "Much like our Trinity, they were called *Uhahetaqua,* the Supreme Power, and *Atanati* and *Usquahula.* Although they were three distinct beings they were always unanimous in thought and action."[17]

A second reference hints at the ontological unity of purpose of the Cherokee Trinity:

The other "sect," with far fewer followers, believed that there were only three beings above, "always together and of the same mind," who sit in three white seats and receive all prayers and determine when each person must die. Such interpretations were strengthened by the recognition that those who held to the three primordial beings were apparently well versed in traditional Cherokee religion.[18]

A fascinating trinitarian account in colonial Native American encounters comes from the journals of John Wesley. The following excerpt, from Wesley's 1736 journal, reflects his experience among another southeastern Indian tribe, the Chickasaw Indians:

Tues. 20 [July]—Five of the Chicasaw Indians (twenty of whom had been in Savannah several days) came to see us, with Mr. Andrews, their interpreter. They were all warriors, four of them head men. The two chief were Paustoobee and Mingo Mattaw. Our conference was as follows:

Q. Do you believe there is One above who is over all things? Paustoobee answered,

A. We believe there are four beloved things above; the clouds, the sun, the clear sky, and He that lives in the clear sky.

Q. Do you believe that there is but One that lives in the clear sky?

A. We believe there are two with him, three in all.[19]

---

[15]Ironically, this would seem to be the opposite of the issue that Western theologians have. An example of this kind of categorization would be the church split between the Western and Eastern churches in the eleventh century. At its heart, the issue revolved around the *filioque* controversy, which was a debate about the categories of the trinitarian figures and their roles in regard to each other independently.

[16]Olson, Grenz, Boff, and even Moltmann might be considered viable candidates, but in particular I am referring to Austin J. Roberts, *Perichoresis and Process: The Eco-theologies of Jürgen Moltmann and John Cobb* (Claremont, CA: Imago Futura, 2012).

[17]Hugh T. Cunningham, "A History of the Cherokee Indians," *Chronicles of Oklahoma* 8, no. 3 (September 1930): 291.

[18]Lee Irwin, "Museum of the Cherokee Indian in Cooperation with the Cherokee Historical Association and Western Carolina University Different Voices Together: Preservation and Acculturation in Early 19th Century Cherokee Religion," *Journal of Cherokee Studies* 18 (1997): 12.

[19]*The Works of John Wesley*, vol. 1, *Journals from October 14, 1735 to November 29, 1745*, 3rd ed. (Peabody, MA: Hendrickson, 1984), 37.

Further in his journal, after clarifying that this Native traditional belief is in reference to the one God and not angels or spirit beings, Wesley simply moves on without further questions. It is unclear whether Wesley found it surprising that the Chickasaws had a trinitarian theology, or whether he completely missed what they were saying, or perhaps he simply had no way of processing what they were describing.[20] However, it is obvious from his journal that such trinitarian beliefs were in fact held and espoused by traditional Natives.[21]

Some have argued that all Native American thinking concerning the Trinity was later adaptations of reports of the Christian Trinity. This position does not explain the fact that a trinity of creator beings is found in early Native American literature and in the oral traditions, particularly among the Cherokee. Early reports of Cherokee trinitarianism are recognized and confirmed by a variety of scholars, of whom perhaps the most prolific and respected in Cherokee literature is William G. McLoughlin. Says McLoughlin, "Myths, now lost, may have told of three superior beings that later myths call the 'Creators' or the 'Masters of Life' or 'Givers of Breath' who were responsible for giving life to human beings, but these myths have not survived except as we find them in the later 'fractured myths' of the early nineteenth century."[22] Again, McLoughlin leaves room for the authentic possibility of divine triune Cherokee creators by stating, "Creation and genesis myths in this period [circa 1821] took many forms, indicating their popularity and the unsettled nature of Indian speculation about this question. They differed as to whether there was one, two or three creators at work."[23]

Another report from a southeastern Indian tribe from an earlier time period (circa 1728) concerns the Saponi, a Siouan tribe in Virginia, which confirms the plausibility of a Creator within a communal theistic structure. William Byrd explains what was reported to him by his Saponi guide, Bearskin:

> He told us he believed that there was one Supreme God, who had several Subaltern Deities under Him. And that this Master-God made the World a long time ago. That he told the Sun, the Moon, and Stars, their business in the Beginning, which they, with good looking after, have faithfully performed ever since. That the same Power that made all these things at first, has taken care to keep them in the same Method and Motion ever since.[24]

There are also nonsoutheastern Native American tribes who have theological constructs that appear to be trinitarian in some fashion. For example, Cree theologian Ray Aldred has suggested the possibility that the Cree worship a Supreme Being, yet with three manifestations of power, including Manitou, Thunderbird, and Bear.[25] The point here is that there is little angst

---

[20]My opinion is that Wesley was unable to grasp the possibility of a Trinity construct among a people he considered to be pagan. Wesley's inability to compare trinitarian views was based on the typical bias of the era.

[21]It should be mentioned here that though there are no particular distinctions made in these trinitarian traditions that represent a specific concept of the Holy Spirit in the Trinity, this should not be surprising. As we have discussed, such categorization would be completely foreign to a Native way of thinking. The essential aspect of these stories, however, is that they represent the concept of a three-in-one view of the Great Spirit that, though not generally held by all Native traditions, was at least an accepted construct among some.

[22]William G. McLoughlin, *The Cherokees and Christianity, 1794–1870: Essays on Acculturation and Cultural Persistence*, ed. Walter H. Conser Jr. (Athens: University of Georgia Press, 1994), 160.

[23]McGloughlin, *Cherokees and Christianity*, 163.

[24]John R. Swanton, *The Indians of the Southeastern United States* (1946; Washington, DC: Smithsonian Institution Press, 1977), 749-50.

[25]From a conversation with Ray Aldred (Cree) on April 25, 2005. I have chosen to focus this study on Trinity beliefs in the southeast because of my familiarity with the literature. By doing this, I have resisted the temptation to interpolate, and I have left room for others to explore their own tribal beliefs without undue influence as a result of my naiveté. I mention my conversation with Ray because he is familiar with both the culture and literature that put forth a Cree Trinity construct.

and tension regarding such matters among American Indians.

THE GREAT MYSTERY AS THREE IN ONE

I think neither Jesus nor the early church ever imagined a religion where orthodoxy was enforced by anyone, much less the state during and after the Constantinian era. In the Nicene Creed we find the first universal document representing orthodox Christianity influenced by the utopian legacies of the Greeks, in propositional form and in adherence to truthful knowledge rather than truthful moral character, along with Roman imperialism. Numerous examples in the Gospel writings lead readers to believe that Jesus would condemn rather than embrace the offspring of such a marriage (Mt 21:28-32; Lk 4; 10:29-37). Heterodoxy may or may not have been the norm in the Gospels, but the Christ who is presented in the Gospel accounts would certainly not pardon most forms of an enforced orthodoxy. Says respected elder and Seneca scholar John Mohawk,

> Once established, the institutions that represented the utopian vision of the Kingdom of God—the Roman and Greek churches—took steps to strengthen and fortify their control, particularly any deviation in matters of doctrine and belief. The survival strategies of institutions that inherit utopian legacies can become intensely repressive in nature, policing behavior and even thought in order to maintain their control. In the Christian establishment these strategies produced repression, excommunications, the search for heretics, the Inquisition, witchcraft trials, and the ruthless use of torture, executions, and even mass slaughter—all in the cause of advancing a religion that once claimed itself committed to the principles of peace.[26]

References to American Indian historic trinitarian constructs of the deity are few and far between. Even I, a Cherokee scholar, feel somewhat apprehensive in discussing the mystery of the great mystery in such detail. Yet bridges need to be built in order to promote mutual understanding and respect between settler-colonial theologies and American Indigenous theologies. Osage scholar George Tinker, relying on the work of Seneca scholar Barbara Mann, effectively argues both for an American Indian reciprocal dualism and that God cannot be one.[27] Says Tinker,

> So first of all, the notion of a single creator immediately participates in the dysfunctionality of the number one, signaling a hierarchical order of creation. The dualistic opposite, rather than a feminine co-participant, is then abject evil, or the Devil, something entirely lacking in Indian cultures until it was read back into our traditions by missionaries who needed to find (and still do) an equivalent evil to fit their own theologies. For Indian folk, the notion of a single, male sky god is decisively unbalanced and leads to chaos, competition, male supremacy, racial hierarchy, and competing notions of a single (doctrinal?) truth over against falsehood, hearsay, and evil. It immediately allows for an anthropology that is decidedly anthropocentric and elevates the human (superior) over all other life-forms (the inferior), and equally allows for the elevation of male over female—since it is the male/man/*adam* who is particularly made in the image of the christian, male sky god.[28]

---

[26]John Mohawk, *Utopian Legacies: A History of Conquest and Oppression in the Western World* (San Francisco: Clear Light, 2000), 262-63.
[27]This argument is made by Seneca scholar Barbara Mann, *Iroquoian Women: The Gantowisais* (New York: Peter Lang, 2000), 63, and Osage scholar George Tinker in his essay, "Why I Do Not Believe in a Creator," in *Buffalo Shout, Salmon Cry: Conversations on Creation, Land Justice, and Life Together*, ed. Steve Heinrichs (Waterloo, ON: Herald, 2013), 171-72. While Tinker is attempting to make the point that the understanding of one Creator is a missionary construct perpetuated for convenience by colonized Native Americans, the same rationale for his argument can be used to explain that God is not one but three in one.
[28]Tinker, "Why I Do Not Believe," 172.

I believe (and my guess is that Tinker does as well) that American Indian theological divine premises are probably more varied, complex, and left to mystery than a complementary dualism, or as he calls it, "collateral-egalitarian image schema as community," would suggest.[29] The brilliance of his argument is that a single, noncomplex divine ontology cannot exist in harmony with what we all see plainly in creation. However, it is easy to understand how any religion viewed through the imperial cultural lens of kings and kingdoms, especially those in which that religion is married to the state, will produce a hierarchical, single, high god-king.

Also, I would argue that the DNA of the Creator is primarily found in the witness of that which has been created, and nature is more complex than a theory based on dualities would suggest. I would like to propose that when we focus on the divine ontology our focus should primarily be on the communal aspects of God, nature, and human organizing.

When considering the dynamics of Trinity, if God does exist as *one in one* (an A alone model), then the lens of imperialism would be at least partially correct in believing God is something akin to a benevolent dictator. In such a model it would make sense that God orders all creation to act within certain reasonable parameters and human organization should reasonably follow in step with a hierarchical model of organization. In the God-as-one-in-one model, God's love is given to creation because of God's inherent wisdom as the Creator, and we become wise through giving the Creator our patronage and our worship. American settler-colonial organizing appears to reflect this understanding. The difficulty is that grasping how much this understanding forms and reflects our theology is likely impossible, though there does seem to be a relationship between the two. The problem with God as one in one is the incongruence with both nature and social relationships. Nothing of creation reflects such a simplistically individualistic model.

If the divine ontology is *two in one*, then perhaps the imagery of a perfect marriage is appropriate for the divine being. The divine couple, if you will, respond to each other in love and as an example, expecting all creation to do likewise. In a sense, God as *two in one* simply mirrors a double benevolent dictatorship of two who rule instead of one. In the A to B model, there are only three possibilities of relational dynamics, that is, A to B, B to A, and A together with B.

God as *three in one* presents the first possibility of matching the relational and ontological DNA found in all creation and human community. The basic building block of human life, all the way down to subatomic particles, is both simple and complex, containing a harmonious existence of unity and diversity.[30] Imagining the divine being as three in one is also the first opportunity to reveal God as community operating in deference and preference to one another as one intersocial being. Rather than the limited relationship of only three possible permutations of the two-in-one model, the relational possibilities of God's ontology as three in one (A-B-C) become much more complex, presenting an extraordinary number of relational permutations. An A-B-C ontology is much closer to the makeup of all creation, as well as reflecting how we relate

---

[29]Tinker, "Why I Do Not Believe," 172.

[30]For the implications of unity and diversity in all creation and the Scriptures, see Randy Woodley, *Shalom and the Community of Creation: An Indigenous Vision* (Grand Rapids, MI: Eerdmans, 2012), 80-91; and my earlier book, *Living in Color: Embracing God's Plan for Ethnic Diversity* (Downers Grove, IL: InterVarsity Press, 2004).

to one another in human community. In the trinitarian model, God is community, which may also reflect the divine sense of community in all creation; in other words, community is innate to, and created by, the community of the Creator.

An A-B-C imagery of the divine may include aspects or characteristics of the other two models, but it is infinitely more beautiful in its simplicity, and yet more complex than the alternatives. I understand the community-of-the-Creator model expressed in the Gospels concerning Jesus, whose actions and teachings surrounding human community were a direct result of a shalom community ethic, based primarily through a harmonious, communal lens. Jesus' understanding of God's kingdom is a shalom community of egalitarianism, where peace reigns and the most marginalized in society are cared for.

Jesus spent his life forming community. He included the outcast and disenfranchised. Women, shepherds, lepers, tax gatherers, Gentiles, the infirm, and others who made up the marginalized of society formed his community. Jesus' teachings, exemplified by parables such as those found in Luke 15, point directly to God's deepest desires being for community.[31] Other New Testament writings expound on the value of unity and diversity and egalitarian community as the norm of the church (1 Cor 11–12; 1 Pet 4:8-11). The image of God as community and as a model of community, I would argue, goes far deeper in our souls than that of the image of a God who is expecting community. If we must talk of God in ontological terms, which, again, is beyond any of our comprehension, then perhaps the image of the community of the Creator, existing eternally in shalom relationality, can lead us beyond much of the former dialogue that has centered itself on ontological substance and toward a better understanding of our own communal ontology.

FURTHER READING

Boff, Leonardo. *Trinity and Society*. Reprint, Eugene, OR: Wipf & Stock, 2005.

Deloria, Vine, Jr. *God Is Red: A Native View of Religion*. Golden, CO: Fulcrum, 2003.

Grenz, Stanley. *The Social God and the Relational Self*. Louisville: Westminster John Knox, 2001.

Kärkkäinen, Veli-Matti. *The Trinity: Global Perspectives*. Louisville: Westminster John Knox, 2007.

Kidwell, Clara Sue, Homer Noley, and George E. Tinker. *A Native American Theology*. Maryknoll, NY: Orbis, 2003.

LaCugna, Catherine Mowry. *God for Us: The Trinity and Christian Life*. San Francisco: HarperSanFrancisco, 1993.

Moltmann, Jürgen. *The Trinity and the Kingdom*. Minneapolis: Fortress, 1993.

Rahner, Karl. *The Trinity*. New York: Crossroad, 1997.

Twiss, Richard. *Rescuing Theology from the Cowboys: An Emerging Indigenous Expression of the Jesus Way in North America*. Downers Grove, IL: InterVarsity Press, 2015.

Volf, Miroslav. *After Our Likeness: The Church as the Image of the Trinity*. Grand Rapids, MI: Eerdmans, 1997.

Woodley, Randy. *Shalom and the Community of Creation: An Indigenous Vision*. Grand Rapids, MI: Eerdmans, 2012.

Zizioulas, John. *Communion and Otherness: Further Studies in Personhood and the Church*. London: T&T Clark, 2007.

Also see all volumes of the *Journal of North American Institute for Indigenous Theological Studies* (Winnipeg).

---

[31]See my exposition of Lk 15 in *Shalom and the Community of Creation*, 80-91.

THE TRINITY IN AFRICA

TRENDS AND TRAJECTORIES

Samuel Waje Kunhiyop

GOD AND THE IDEA OF the Trinity are no strange beliefs in Africa. The Supreme Being (God) is a commonly held belief among all African peoples, predating Christianity and Islam. Africa also played a formative role in the development of the concept of the Trinity. Tertullian, an African theologian, is credited with being the first theologian to coin the word *Trinity*. The Ethiopian Orthodox Church is the only church in Africa that traces its trinitarian beliefs and practice to the fourth century. The thesis of this chapter is that though classical trinitarian belief is historically and biblically and theologically true, its presence in the contemporary African church is practically disregarded and absent. The church is recommended to go back and emphasize trinitarian theology in its theology and practice.

INTRODUCTION

Christians do not just believe in God; they affirm the real existence of three persons in the Godhead, namely, God the Father, God the Son, and God the Holy Spirit. Obviously, this is not a simple and straightforward belief. This highly thought-out and very complex concept has been in existence from the rise of Christianity to its present articulated position. The belief in the triune God is not just an abstract theological postulation by sophisticated theologians but has serious meaning and implications for Christian spirituality and practice. Why is a study on the Trinity important? Harold O. J. Brown struck it well. "Without a coherent doctrine of the Trinity, the New Testament witness to the activity of God in Christ and in the work of the Holy Spirit will tend to force one either into modalism or a kind of tritheism."[1] In other words, one cannot ignore it and not fall into serious heresy of some sort.

Though, as I will argue, biblical Christianity cannot exist without trinitarian theology, sadly we find that Christianity as practiced in most of contemporary African Christianity either ignores, disregards, or simply does not appreciate its meaning and significance. This development is especially worrisome as the Pentecostal movement is attracting millions of members who are untaught and ignorant of key cardinal doctrines of the Christian church.

In some Christian circles, preachers make pronouncements such as "Don't expect to

---

[1]Harold O. J. Brown, *Heresies: The Image of Christ in the Mirror of Heresy and Orthodoxy from the Apostles to the Present* (Grand Rapids, MI: Baker, 1988), 154.

understand it, just believe or accept." The problem is that the statement is half true and half false. Yes, it is true that we cannot understand the Trinity fully, but this does not mean that we are unable to understand anything. Yes, it is a mystery, but it does not mean that God has not revealed anything about this concept and that we cannot say anything intellectually rational about it. This is a sad commentary on the church and should not be the case.

In this chapter, I will examine this doctrine not only from a historical and biblical perspective but even more so from an African historical, cultural, and religious context. I will look critically at the Ethiopian Orthodox Church, the oldest form of Christianity in Africa, and how it has been able to continue emphasizing the Trinity as a cardinal aspect of its life and practice. This chapter will also survey both contemporary distortions of the Trinity in the African church and Islamic rejection of the Trinity. I will also provide a biblical summary of trinitarian theology, and note how it should influence spiritual life and practice.

AFRICAN CONCEPT OF GOD

There is no gainsaying that Africans who come to the Christian faith already have a belief in the existence of God and the spirit world. Evidence for the African belief in God can be seen in the variety of names for God among all African peoples, as well as in religious beliefs and practices, rituals and sacrifices. God is viewed as supreme, all-powerful, all-knowing, loving, and caring. The most important and critical question is: Is the Supreme Being whom Africans acknowledge the same as the God of the Bible? John Mbiti, probably the most prominent and

influential African theologian on this subject, considers this to be the case. So does Bolaji Idowu, who argues on the basis of general revelation that God has revealed himself to Africans and is worshiped by them.[2]

At most, the beliefs and practices of African traditional religion convey only a faint and incomplete understanding of who God is. For example, even if we grant the concept of the supreme God who is the same as the God of the Bible, we must ask, What about the concept of the triune God in African conceptions of God? Some African theologians have argued that the concept of the Trinity is present and well-articulated in the African understanding of God. A. Okechukwu Ogbonnaya, who opposes monotheism (Idowu) and polytheism as depictions of the African understanding of God, postulates:

> The Concept of the One is present in African religions, but so also is the concept of the Many. . . . The concept of the Divine as community actually does more justice to African conceptions of God. For this, we need another term, a word like communotheism; a community of gods. Community, in the African sense, will reflect better the affirmation of both the One and the Many than the categories of monotheism and polytheism. The noun communotheism communicates the idea that Divinity is communal.[3]

Ogbonnaya uses community theism from an African perspective to explore the Christian concept of the Trinity. What is unclear is the identity of the community gods. It is not explained who these community gods are. To his credit, there are great lessons to be learned about the relational aspect of the Godhead in terms of relationships between the persons. However, it

---

[2]Bolaji Idowu, *Towards an Indigenous Church* (London: Oxford University Press, 1965), 24-26.
[3]A. Okechukwu Ogbonnaya, *On Communitarian Divinity: An African Interpretation of the Trinity* (St. Paul, MN: Paragon, 1998), 27-28.

must be pointed out that the image of the community of relationships between (among?) the gods in the African sense at best underscores the importance of relationships but fails to deal with the equality in the Godhead that biblical Christianity affirms. The point is, relational and communal aspects of the Trinity are not the same as the metaphysical issues involved in the Trinity. This is a category mistake. For Ogbonnaya, the Trinity must be true because Africans so perceive it in their world. As I argue in *African Christian Theology*, seeking to justify and authenticate our theology from our own experience or from below has inherent weaknesses.[4] If the concept is true, it must be derived first from above or as revealed in his Word. Otherwise we end up with a doctrine that is our cultural conception. The Bible is the textbook for evaluating our doctrine, not our worldview or context, although we acknowledge that our worldview and context do influence our use and application of the Bible. Clearly, though there is a community of gods, the supreme God is ontologically not equal to the other gods. We also affirm the pervasive nature of the idea of community in Africa; without it one cannot fully understand the African worldview. The most severe criticism of communotheism or social theory is that of polytheism—a plurality of gods. A plurality of gods is closer to polytheism and tritheism, which both biblical revelation and historic, biblical Christianity see as heretical. Community among these many gods cannot be postulated as the best tool for understanding and stating trinitarian theology.

TRINITY IN AFRICAN CHRISTIANITY

The earliest contact between Africans and the idea of the Trinity goes back as early as the fourth century, when the Ethiopians were introduced to Christianity. History has it that "paganism and Judaism were practised side by side in Ethiopia before the introduction of Christianity."[5] In their pre-Jewish and pre-Christian religion, the Ethiopians were polytheistic, with temples, altars, and statues of gods all over the land.

There is also biblical and historical evidence that Judaism was introduced into Ethiopia. The Bible tells of the story of the queen of Sheba of Ethiopia visiting King Solomon during his peak period as king of Israel (1 Kings 10:1-13; 2 Chron 9:1-9). The Kebre Negest (The Glory of the Kings), which was composed around AD 1320 with both pre-Christian and Christian materials, recounts the visit of the queen of Sheba to King Solomon in Jerusalem. It is believed that her relationship with King Solomon resulted in the birth of a son. According to tradition, this son, who was named Manilek, visited his father Solomon when he grew up, and King Solomon sent him back to Ethiopia accompanied by some Israelites to serve him, with Levites as priests, who brought back the ark of the covenant. From then onward, Judaism was practiced in Ethiopia.[6]

In the New Testament, Acts 8:26-40 tells us that a certain eunuch, the treasurer of Queen Candace of Ethiopia, went to Jerusalem to worship the God of Israel. There he met Philip, who baptized him. According to tradition, he returned home and evangelized his people.

---

[4]Samuel Waje Kunhiyop, *African Christian Theology* (Grand Rapids, MI: Zondervan, 2012), 78-80.

[5]Sergew Hable Selassie, "The Establishment of the Ethiopian Church," in *The Church of Ethiopia: A Panorama of History and Spiritual Life* (Addis Ababa: Ethiopian Orthodox Church, 1997), 1.

[6]D. A. Hubbard, "Queen Sheba," in the *International Standard Bible Encyclopedia*, ed. Geoffrey W. Bromiley (Grand Rapids, MI: Eerdmans, 1988), 4:8-10; D. Harvey, "Sheba, Queen of," in *Interpreter's Dictionary of the Bible*, ed. George A. Buttrick (Nashville: Abingdon, 1962), 4:311-12.

St. Frumentius played a key role in the conversion of Emperor Ezana around AD 330. A
Greek inscription belonging to Ezana states: "In
the faith of God and the power of the Father, the
Son and the Holy Ghost." From henceforth and
even to the present, Christianity has played a
prominent role in the national life of Ethiopians.
Unlike other lands, Christianity came through
the royal families and then to the ordinary people.
The kings, and especially the late emperor Haile
Selassie, were not only seen as the political heads
but also the spiritual leaders. It is for this reason
that Haile Selassie was buried in the Ethiopian
Orthodox Church in Addis Ababa. For our particular interest, Ethiopian Christianity emerged
in the context of the Arian controversy, when the
divinity of Christ was hotly debated. The Ethiopian church stood by the side of Athanasius and
the Nicene Creed, which affirmed the full deity of
Christ and also affirmed the threeness of the
Godhead, Father, Son, and Holy Spirit. The Ethiopian Orthodox Church proudly stands in the
tradition of the Nicene Creed and publicly displays its belief in the Trinity—in fact, the most
prominent church in Addis Ababa, where the late
emperor Haile Selassie is buried, is called "The
Trinity Orthodox Ethiopian Church."[7]

The theology of the Trinity, as we have seen, is
a very pronounced aspect of the Ethiopian
church. The Trinity is not only stated in their
books but also expressed in church paintings.
These images and paintings are meant to be kept
before the eyes of the worshiper's prayerful gaze,
to inspire prayer, meditation, and devotion. They
are intended for the worshiper for two ways of
seeing, "to see and to be seen." It is believed that
when praying in front of the paintings, not only
are worshipers looking at pictures but the spirit
of the subject of the pictures is also looking at
worshipers at the same time.

ISLAMIC CONCEPT OF GOD

The African Christian cannot discuss the Trinity
without interacting with Islam, whose understanding of God sharply contrasts with the
Christian view of God. Often, these two major
religions collide head-on over their contrasting
views of God. Islam was founded in the seventh
century and borrowed some of its beliefs from
Judaism and Christianity. From Judaism, it
stresses absolute monotheism to the exclusion of
any plurality within the Godhead. Many heresies
such as Arianism and other heretical views were
already prevalent in the seventh and eighth centuries. The major thrust of Islam is its teaching
on God, and this has become the major sour
point with Christianity. Robert Letham writes,
"Its doctrine of God is the major weakness of
Islam. It is the root of all other problems. It is
here that the Christian apologete and evangelist
can probe, with sensitivity and wisdom. While
the Trinity is one of the major stumbling blocks
to Muslims turning to Christ, it must be presented with intelligence and skill."[8] In Islam,
therefore, the idea of a Trinity is repugnant and
unacceptable (see Qur'an 4:471; 5:76). Allah is
one, Islam teaches, and cannot have a son, for it
is not befitting for God to have a son. Despite
Islam's rejection of the Trinity, the Trinity is a
critical element of Christian faith and nonnego-
tiable in reaching out to Muslims. Without
going into too much discussion, what is most

---

[7]Selassie, "Establishment of the Ethiopian Church"; Lule Melaku, *History of the Ethiopian Orthodox Tewahedo Church: From the Reign
of Emperor Caleb to the End of the Zagwe Dynasty and from the Classical (Golden) Age to the Present* (Addis Ababa: Elleni, 2010), parts
2-3; Bantalem Tadesse, *A Guide to the Intangible Treasures of Ethiopian Orthodox Tewahido Church: Historic Perspectives and Symbolic
Interpretations of Festivals* (Addis Ababa: Kalu, 2010).

[8]Robert Letham, *The Holy Trinity in Scripture, History, Theology and Worship* (Phillipsburg, NJ: P&R, 2004), 446.

productive in dialogue with Muslims is to discuss the divine attributes of Christ, which are also found in God. These include, among others, creation (see Qur'an 4:171; 3:49; 5:11; 19:34; 22:34; 22:73; compare Jn 1:1-5), sovereignty (Qur'an 3:45-50; compare Mk 4:37-41), holiness (Qur'an 3:45; 19:16-19; compare Lk 7:48; Jn 1:29), omniscience (Qur'an 4:171; compare Mic 5:2; Jn 8:58); Judge (Qur'an 4:158; 43:61; 4:78-80; compare Mt 24–25; Rev 21–22).

One attribute of God that is lacking in Islam is the concept of God as love. Islam emphasizes the justice and power of God and that God or "Allah cannot love."[9] Love cannot be found in a monad god but can only be properly expressed among persons. This is readily available within the Godhead and has also been exhibited toward his created world: "God so loved the world that he gave his only begotten son" (Jn 3:16).

DISTORTIONS OF THE TRINITY IN CONTEMPORARY AFRICAN CHRISTIANITY

The heresies of the Trinity were not only found in the early church and the West; they are duplicated today, and some new variations have arisen. We need only mention a few. Theism holds to belief in God and nothing more. African Christians are susceptible to this error due to their cultural worldview, which does not have a clear understanding of the triune God. The triune God easily loses its uniqueness in a general and ambiguous belief in God. In many instances, believers feel comfortable just referring to God as the supernatural or the supreme God. This vague theism is found in interreligious discussions with other faiths such as African traditional religions, Jehovah's Wit-

nesses, and Islam. This is done in order to remove offense to those who are nontrinitarian. While it is true that Christians need not be unnecessarily provocative, Christians cannot afford to downplay the triune confession of God; otherwise they will have reduced Christianity to just another theistic religion.

Modalism is the belief that God is one but has manifested himself in three modes at various historical moments, for example, that God revealed himself as the Father in the Old Testament period, as Jesus in the New Testament, and as the Holy Spirit in the church age. This modalistic view of God has been quite common, especially among the older version of African Initiated Churches that did not have the benefit of formal training in theology. In its early stages, the Cherubim and Seraphim Church held to this version of modalism. Apostle Abana allocates the three ages to the three persons, stating, "As the names are three, so also is the Bible divided into three parts: the name of the Father means God the Father and refers to Genesis through Malachi; the name of the Son means Jesus Christ and refers to Matthew through Jude; and the name of the Holy Ghost refers to Revelation, which is the last book of the Bible."[10] Captain Christianah Abiodun Emanuel, one of the pioneers of the Cherubim and Seraphim movements, holds the same view. This is the heresy of modalism, which the early church condemned.

Unitarianism of the Spirit is a reductionistic posture that emphasizes the third person of the Trinity, the Holy Spirit. Modern African Christianity, particularly Pentecostal and charismatic movements, revolves around the experience of the Holy Spirit. Prayers by ministers and evangelists of certain Christian groups and individuals

---

[9]Letham, *Holy Trinity*, 444.

[10]J. Akinyele Omoyajowo, *Cherubim and Seraphim: The History of an African Independent Church* (New York: Nok, 1982), 101.

are a clear indication that there is a move toward a unitarianism of the Spirit. While the church certainly needs to experience the Holy Spirit's gifts, it is equally dangerous to overemphasize this aspect to the detriment of God the Father and God the Son. The Spirit who empowers reconciliation and liberation is the Spirit of Christ and of the one Christ called "Abba, Father."

Jesusology is another distortion of the use and name of Jesus in Christian worship. Just as in the case of the Holy Spirit, there has been a development in recent years in the use of the name of Jesus as a magical means of getting answers to prayer. Apart from the baptismal formula, dedications, consecrations, and benedictions—which generally remain trinitarian—the church and believers use the name of Jesus in total disregard of the triune God in worship and prayer.

In a functional Trinity view, the triune God is used in some instances as a means of achieving personal needs. In prayers and worship, one often has the feeling that the names of God, especially the Son and the Holy Spirit, are used as a magical means to acquire personal needs such as guidance, protection, and judgment against perceived or even real enemies. The phrase "in the name of Jesus" is invoked by the believer in prayer over and over to emphasize the power in Jesus' name. The blood of Jesus is used to protect children from spiritual attack, for protection against accidents, and so on. The Holy Spirit is invoked to punish enemies or opposition. The selection of verses of Scripture to justify such use is rampant in churches. Selective and wrong use of the triune God in prayers and worship is a distortion.

THE KNOWLEDGE OF GOD

For the Christian faith, divine revelation is a fundamental belief without which Christianity has no basis for existence. Without the self-disclosure of God to his creation, creation would not be able to know anything about God. Revelation in the strictest sense means God's initiative, disclosure, and unveiling. Divine revelation is therefore cardinal to the Christian religion. Its understanding of revelation is set forth in the Bible, the Word of God. Our understanding of revelation as Christians ultimately must be drawn from an understanding of Scripture, the primary vehicle of divine revelation. However, since revelation has also been experienced by human beings in every culture, it is critical that we understand revelation from an African perspective and how this Christian experience relates to divine revelation. The only true source of knowledge about God is his personal revelation of himself in Jesus Christ and the recording of that revelation in the inspired, inerrant, and infallible Holy Scriptures. Indeed, Scripture insists that knowledge of a personal and sovereign God combined with worship of him through other divinities boils down to idolatry: "For although they knew God, they neither glorified him as God nor gave thanks to him, but their thinking became futile and their foolish hearts were darkened. . . . They exchanged the truth about God for a lie, and worshiped and served created things rather than the Creator" (Rom 1:21, 25 NIV).

THE GOD OF THE SCRIPTURES AND TRINITY IN HISTORY

The Bible teaches that God is self-existent. When Moses asks God who he is, God simply replies, "I AM WHO I AM" (Ex 3:13-14). The psalmist regards any questioning of the fact of God's existence as foolishness (Ps 14:1), and most Africans would agree. There is thus no need to explore the proofs of the existence of God in this work. What is important is to seek to understand more about God, and the only way to achieve such understanding is to examine his self-revelation in his written Word. When we do this, we discover that God exists in Trinity, is transcendent and immanent, sovereign, omnipotent, holy, just, and loving.

If there is one thing that our brief history brings to mind immediately, especially from the Ethiopian Orthodox Church, it is that the contemporary church in Africa does not lose touch or interest in the history or tradition of her past. There are several advantages in looking back at the history and the traditions of the church.

First of all, it reminds the church of her roots and traditions and helps us to tread in its paths. It is unfortunate that the history of missions often stops with the pioneers who brought the gospel to Africans from the United States, Canada, England, Australia, and so on but never traces its faith to, or builds it on, its traditions. The consequence, of course, is that the contemporary African church neither cares nor knows the beliefs, traditions, and roots of its forebears. Very few church members know anything beyond the early Christian missionaries and converts, and clearly almost nothing about the history of the early church.

Second, as a consequence of the above point, contemporary African churches do not know the difference between right and wrong belief, orthodox and heretical teachings. The Ethiopian Orthodox Church, which emphasizes right belief going back to the early history of the church, always ensures through its recitation of them that these beliefs are neither abandoned nor discontinued in church life and practice.

Third, reminding ourselves of the past ensures continuity with the past traditions that the

church must adhere to. The church in Africa lacks continuity with the past traditions. Every church comes and goes with its own inventions of what it considers right or wrong belief. We must remind ourselves that the church of Jesus Christ did not begin today, and we must appreciate and carry on the traditions of the past and pass it on to future generations.

All these historic creeds affirm trinitarian theology, which should be the universal teaching of the Christian church. The church in Africa must also be seen as affirming, teaching, and upholding these creeds.

The triune God in spirituality. The very essence of Christianity is trinitarian. Every aspect of the Christian life and experience is and must be rooted in the Father, the Son, and the Holy Spirit. One would have a very truncated view of the Christian life without the Trinity. Our salvation cannot be understood without it. The Father loved us, Jesus died for us, and the Holy Spirit lives and enables us to understand the Word and live life in accordance with the will of God. "A living relationship with God requires that each of the persons be honored and adored in the context of their revealed relations with each other. The nature of our response in worship is to be shaped by the reality of the one we worship."[11] The clear teaching of Scripture is that we pray to the Father, in the name of Jesus Christ, and by the enablement of the Holy Spirit. However, one finds that in these days, this order is not observed, as believers often confuse it or ignore it in prayer. For example, it is quite common to hear worshipers pray to the Holy Spirit to take vengeance on their enemies. In the New Testament, the Father is addressed through the Son, by the power of the Holy Spirit.

[11]Letham, *Holy Trinity*, 419.

The triune God in worship. True worship is the acknowledgment and adoration of the Father, Son, and Holy Spirit—very trinitarian (Eph 2:18). "Prayer, worship, and communion with God are by definition Trinitarian. As the Father has made himself known through the Son 'for us and our salvation' in or by the Spirit, so we are all caught up in this reverse movement. We live, move, and have our being in a pervasively Trinitarian atmosphere."[12] One essential aspect of worship is prayers to the triune God (Jn 4:24; Rev 5:11).[13] Another is hymns. Our songs in worship should reflect our trinitarian understanding of God. Charles Wesley (1707–1788) composed a hymn in 1746 that does just this, something Christians would do well to emulate in their song-making and worship.

> Father of Mankind, Be ever ador'd:
> Thy Mercy we find, In sending our Lord,
> To ransom and bless us; Thy Goodness we praise,
> For sending in Jesus, Salvation by Grace.
> O Son of His Love, Who deignest to die,
> Our Curse to remove, Our Pardon to buy;
> Accept our Thanksgiving, Almighty to save,
> Who openest Heaven, To all that believe.
> O Spirit of Love, Of Health, and Power,
> Thy working we prove; Thy Grace we adore,
> Whose inward Revealing applies our Lord's Blood,
> Attesting and sealing us Children of God.

This hymn clearly articulates the drama of salvation. Without a clear understanding of the Father, Son, and Holy Spirit, our understanding of salvation will be incomplete. Songs should play a key role in clarifying our redemption. Choruses and short songs that are commonplace in African churches should reflect this trinitarian belief among believers.

CONCLUSION

First, the African church must recover its past, its history, and its traditions. The church in Africa does not stand in isolation from the church Christ has been building over the centuries. Though the primary and fundamental source of the Christian life is Holy Scripture, we must not forget that from the Old Testament to the New Testament to the early church and succeeding generations, Christ has been at work in his church. The church has grappled with many issues and drawn some universal conclusions. These universal conclusions, which include among others the Trinity and the hypostatic union, are important beliefs and considered orthodox (right doctrine) not only for past generations of believers but even for today. The Ethiopian Orthodox Church is a model of such a church that has held on to this orthodox belief and practice.

Second, the church in Africa must consciously and deliberately evolve ways of reintroducing and retrenching the belief in and practice of the Trinity as an essential part of the church. Some of these methods may include recitation of the Apostles' and the Nicene Creeds every Sunday. The Ethiopian Orthodox Church makes pictures of the Trinity, and this helps believers and worshipers to keep trinitarian theology in view. In spite of its shortcomings, it is true that a picture is worth more than a thousand words. In a nonliterate society, the idea of pictures sends the message across very distinctly. This is more so when biblical exposition and recitation of church creeds go hand in hand, and this ought to provide safeguards against misconstruing such images. Of course rote memory can be counterproductive,

---

[12]Letham, *Holy Trinity*, 7-8.
[13]Letham, *Holy Trinity*, 412, 419.

but when included in songs, praise, or story-telling about the early church, one can have a balanced position.

Third, the pulpit should take the lead on the exposition of the theology of the Trinity. Many believers are not able to remember when their pastor preached on the Trinity except when saying the benediction, wedding blessings, or launching or dedicating a church building, musical instrument, or home. The pulpit must take center stage in helping the congregation to know what the church has believed over the years and what the Bible clearly teaches. Letham does not underemphasize the importance of preaching.

> Chief of all, the Trinity must be preached and must shape preaching. Preaching is the highest point of worship. Not only must the Trinity be preached, but all preaching must be shaped by the active recognition that the God whose word is so proclaimed is triune. A Trinitarian mindset must become as integral to the preacher as the air we breathe. The most practical preaching is that which enables us to advance in our knowledge of the God who is three persons.[14]

Fourth, materials and manuals about the Trinity should be made available to all the believers. Those who become full members should be conversant with the essentials of the church, which must include teaching on the Trinity. Believers need to be conversant with the Apostles' Creed, the Nicene Creed, and the Athanasian Creed.

Fifth, and finally, Christians in Africa must reinstate and develop a trinitarian theology that is relevant to the rise of an aggressive and violent Islam. Militant Islam falls short of a loving and caring God as provided in a trinitarian theology that depicts God as loving and caring, who loves to save and not to kill his enemies.

Ultimately, grasping God's triunity is about God, not about believers or even ourselves. The doxology says it very well.

> Praise God from whom all blessings flow,
> Praise Him all his creatures here below,
> Praise him above you heavenly hosts,
> Praise Father, Son and Holy Ghost,
> Amen.

FURTHER READING

Bray, Gerald. *Creeds, Councils and Christ: The Continuity Between Scripture and Orthodoxy in the First Five Centuries.* Leicester, UK: Inter-Varsity Press, 1984.

Ela, Jean Marc. *My Faith as an African.* Translated by John P. Brown and Susan Perry. Maryknoll, NY: Orbis, 1981.

Idowu, Bolaji. *Towards an Indigenous Church.* London: Oxford University Press, 1965.

Kombo, James Owino. *The Doctrine of God in African Christian Thought: The Holy Trinity, Theological Hermeneutics and the African Intellectual Culture.* The Netherlands: Hotei, 2007.

———. "The Trinity in Africa." *Journal of Reformed Theology* 3 (2009): 125-43.

Kunhiyop, Samuel Waje. *African Christian Ethics.* Grand Rapids, MI: Zondervan, 2008.

———. *African Christian Theology.* Grand Rapids, MI: Zondervan, 2012.

Letham, Robert. *The Holy Trinity in Scripture, History, Theology, and Worship.* Phillipsburg, NJ: P&R, 2004.

Mangayi, J. S., and J. Buitendag. "A Critical Analysis of African Traditional Religion and the Trinity." *Teologiese Studies/Theological Studies* 69 (2013), www.hts.org.za/index.php/HTS/article/view/1934/3679.

Ogbonnaya, A. Okechukwu. *On Communitarian Divinity: An African Interpretation of the Trinity.* St. Paul, MN: Paragon, 1998.

---

[14]Letham, *Holy Trinity*, 423.

Omojajowo, J. Akinyele. *Cherubim and Seraphim: The History of an African Independent Church*. New York: Nok, 1982.

Parrinder, Edward Geoffrey. *African Traditional Religion*. Westport, CT: Greenwood, 1970.

Sellassie, Sergew Hable. *The Church of Ethiopia: A Panorama of History and Spiritual Life*. Addis Ababa: Ethiopian Orthodox Church, 1997.

Thurmer, John. *A Detection of the Trinity*. Exeter, UK: Paternoster, 1984.

THE TRINITY AS GOSPEL

Antonio González

THE DIVINITY OF JESUS is not a contradiction to Jewish monotheism, but rather a way of its messianic fulfillment. Jewish monotheism was not a simple metaphysical affirmation of the uniqueness of God, but originated as an affirmation of the exclusive rule of God. Therefore, all other sources of power were radically called into question in the context of Jewish monotheism, including the power of the king. This is the root of the historical and theological difficulties that the Hebrew Bible shows when it comes to understand and justify the existence of Israel as a state. Jesus' message about the kingdom of God should be understood against the background of this affirmation of the exclusive rule of God. This is also the reason why the resurrected and exalted Jesus could not be understood as an intermediate being between humanity and God. In this context, it is comprehensible why the inclusion of Jesus in the divinity of the only God took place so early, and in a Jewish context.

The doctrine of the Trinity belongs to the core of Christian beliefs. Nevertheless, for some Christians and many non-Christians, the Trinity is a strange entity in the history of monotheism. Many would suspect that the doctrine of the Trinity is the result of the introduction of Chris-

tianity in the Hellenistic world of the first centuries of our era. In this context, the first Gentile Christians, principally Paul, would have been the main culprits in the beginning of the exaltation of Jesus as a heavenly figure, thereby opening in this way the possibility of the subsequent proclamation of Jesus as God. This proclamation, supposedly done for the first time by the early church councils, also included the idea of the deity of the Holy Spirit and therefore became the ground for the doctrine of the Trinity.[1]

LATIN AMERICAN CONTEXT

We can observe various responses to these difficulties within the Latin American context. All of them seek to underscore the relevance of the Trinity for the present moment in Latin America, especially for the millions who live under oppressive situations. In this sense we could say that all the different ways we think about the Trinity respond to what we may call the "perspective of the poor." This is a characteristic of liberation theology, although it is found in various other theological forms.

In the first place, in some quarters the doctrine of the Trinity has been accepted as a late development that now has practically become

---

[1]Especially the Councils of Nicaea (325) and Constantinople (381).

insignificant for the church. Clearly there is an appreciation of the fact that in the past speculative theology used trinitarian categories. These became a way to think about the implications of the fact that God had manifested himself in Jesus Christ. However, in the present time the important consideration is not the speculation about the character of God himself but rather to center our attention on Jesus Christ. This means we cannot start from a previous concept of God, including the doctrine of the Trinity, but we must begin with Jesus Christ. The proclamation of Jesus' divinity would not, in this sense, mean that Jesus is God but rather affirms that God is Jesus, that is to say, only in Jesus can we know who God is. This sense, in spite of being important, leaves opaque the very idea of the Trinity, and some have consequently considered it to be radically obsolete. Rather, what is important is to underline the humanity of Jesus and his importance as a model for discipleship.

In liberation theology we also encounter a second perspective regarding the Trinity, which, instead of considering it obsolete, values it as essential to Christian thought. From this perspective, pure monotheism holds within it a tendency toward legitimizing oppression. The image of one unique God in the heavens tends to favor totalitarian or dictatorial government in the land: only one can govern. In this point we can clearly see the influence of Erik Peterson's thesis, which wrestled with monotheism's import in the context of national socialism.[2] In the case of liberation theology, some extended this analysis to the structures of their own church. The image of an exclusive government in

heaven favored authoritarian models in the church, with exclusive power centered on one person, the same as what occurs when the church concedes all the government's power to one person. In the face of these celestial images that legitimate political or ecclesiastical power, this stream of liberation theology emphasizes the image of the Trinity as community. And if God is a community, this favors the establishment of egalitarian relations on earth that reflect the reality of God. On the other hand, every authoritarian structure on earth comes under critique in the light of the communitarian and egalitarian God of the Trinity.[3]

In my view, these two lines of thinking need to be revised for various reasons. In the first place, both lines of reflection presuppose that divine revelation is structured like a mirror, such that what we see on earth is in some way a reflection of the model, which is in heaven. Therefore some assert that what we know about God is only that which is reflected in Christ, or they affirm the idea that a celestial model is paradigmatic for earthly governmental structures. Second, we have to ask whether this idea of a celestial model or paradigm does greater justice to the "perspective of the poor," as emphasized repeatedly in Latin American theology. How does a celestial model help those who are oppressed in their earthly life? And, in the third place, we should question the idea, commonly held in Latin American theology, that the Trinity comes from a later speculation in the history of theology, given that its biblical foundations are weak.

At this point something needs to be said about those biblical foundations. As we know,

---

[2]See Erik Peterson, *Der Monotheismus als politisches Problem: Ein Beitrag zur Geschichte der politischen Theologie im Imperium Romanum* (Leipzig: Hegner, 1935).

[3]See Leonardo Boff, "Trinidad," in *Mysterium liberationis: Conceptos fundamentales de la teología de la liberación*, ed. Jon Sobrino and Ignacio Ellacuría (Madrid: Trotta, 1990), 513-30, esp. 514-16.

the Pauline letters represent the most complete ancient collection of New Testament writings. However, perceptions about Paul are changing significantly in two fundamental ways. On one hand, current Pauline scholarship stresses the so-called new perspective on Paul.[4] According to this perspective, in its many variants, Paul belonged completely to the Jewish world and was by no means trying to build some kind of synthesis between the Hebraic faith and the Hellenistic world with its plurality of gods. On the other hand, many New Testament scholars are now ready to admit that the proclamation of Jesus' deity was by no means a slow process, which would have only taken place when Christianity was adapted to Hellenistic culture. Many scholars think that the first Christians, even those before Paul, did in fact believe Jesus belonged to the deity of God.[5]

How is this possible? How could a group of Jewish believers come so early to proclaim the deity of the Messiah? These results are even stranger when we recognize that these early Christians were by no means thinking that they were giving up the story of strict Old Testament monotheism.[6]

Some have tried to solve these difficulties by affirming that the Jewish monotheism of the first century was not as strict as it became later, this development being partly due to the discussions in rabbinic Judaism against the Christian movement. In this sense, some have thought that some figures such as the divine Wisdom could be

understood as precedents and conditions that made the "high" Christology of the New Testament possible.[7] The problem is that such figures as Wisdom, although present, are relatively scarce in the New Testament writings. For a growing number of scholars, these intermediate figures played no role in the rapid development of New Testament Christology and are not especially relevant for the doctrine of the Trinity.[8]

Following and radicalizing the path opened by authors such as Richard Bauckham, Gordon Fee, and N. T. Wright, I will try to show that the reasons for the early development of Christology in a mainly Jewish monotheistic milieu are directly related not to the possible Jewish ideas of intermediate beings but to the central New Testament ideas about the kingdom of God and the messianic position of Jesus. As a result of this, early Christian belief in the deity of Jesus would need to be thought in complete continuity with Old Testament monotheism. If such is the case, the doctrine of the Trinity would not be a strange addition to the history of monotheism but rather the culmination of this history. Let us think about this in more detail.

MONOTHEISTIC EXCLUSIVITY

To properly understand the development of the Christian doctrine of God, it is essential to understand the meaning of God's exclusivity in the Hebrew Scriptures. The monotheism of Israel is not a result of philosophical speculation about the unity of God. On the contrary, it is God's

[4]Beginning with E. P. Sanders's book *Paul and Palestinian Judaism: A Comparison of Patterns of Religion* (Philadelphia: Fortress, 1977). The term *new perspective* was later coined by James D. G. Dunn.
[5]See N. T. Wright, *Paul in Fresh Perspective* (Minneapolis: Fortress, 2005). See also Larry Hurtado, *Lord Jesus Christ: Devotion to Jesus in Earliest Christianity* (Grand Rapids, MI: Eerdmans, 2003).
[6]See Gordon D. Fee, *Pauline Christology: An Exegetical-Theological Study* (Peabody, MA: Hendrickson, 2007).
[7]See Martin Hengel, *Der Sohn Gottes: Die Entstehung der Christologie und die jüdisch-hellenistische Religionsgeschichte*, 2nd ed. (Tübingen: Mohr Siebeck, 1977).
[8]See Richard Bauckham, *Jesus and the God of Israel: God Crucified and Other Studies on the New Testament's Christology of Divine Identity* (Grand Rapids, MI: Eerdmans, 2008). See also the already quoted book of Fee, *Pauline Christology*, 595-630.

saving action in the history of Israel that brings about the idea of the uniqueness of God. Here the idea of God's kingdom, God's rule over Israel, plays a decisive role.

To see this, we can look at the actual canon of the Torah and examine the place where the idea of God's kingdom appears for the first time. It is in the book of Exodus just at the moment when the people of God arrive safely at the other side of the sea. Moses then sings, and at the end of his song he proclaims: "The LORD will reign forever and ever" (Ex 15:18). The place of this affirmation is extremely significant. It is when the rule of Pharaoh is broken, when his sovereignty does not reach God's people, that the people can truly proclaim that God is now their king and that he will be forever. The rule of God, the kingdom of God, reveals itself as an exclusive rule, which is incompatible with the rule of Pharaoh.

It is important to observe that we have a structure here that is opposite from the structure of myths. According to Mircea Eliade, the myths of religions usually regard the images of the gods in heaven as some kind of model or paradigm of the realities on earth.[9] For example, the pantheon of the gods in heaven is the paradigm of the royal court of the "real" kings of Mesopotamia.[10] A female goddess in heaven is the model of a priestess, or a queen, and so on. This is of course also a structure of ideological justification. The king god explains and blesses the rule and power of his human image on earth.

What we see in the Hebrew Scriptures is a wholly different structure. The God of Israel is able to have a direct relationship with his people, without intermediate figures. If God is king, the people of God do not need another king. God can rule his people directly, as long as his people desire to be ruled by God. This is the reason why, in the first book of Samuel, the introduction of state and monarchy is a big problem. As God says to the prophet, the people who ask for a king are not just rejecting Samuel; they are rejecting God himself as their king (1 Sam 8:7).[11]

We can see this same structure in other areas. The idea of God being a warrior, a "Lord of the hosts," is the basis for the affirmation that the people do not need to prepare for war. God will fight the battles of his people (Ex 14:14). That is why the people should reduce their army and trust God, who will take care of their defense. Again, the God in heaven does not work as a heavenly paradigm, designed to justify the warriors on earth. On the contrary: because God is a warrior, the people do not need to worry about war.[12] The same can be said about the image of God as master. God became a master of all the Israelites when he redeemed them from slavery in Egypt, and this is the very reason to limit slavery in Israel (Lev 25:54-55).

In short, the direct rule of God means that God assumes the roles of domination. By doing this, these roles are limited or excluded from his people. The people of God are designed in the Torah like brothers and sisters, and among them there should not be significant social differences. This is the reason for the many social measures we find in the Torah (Ex 21:1-11; 23:12; Lev 25:8-55; Deut 15:1-18; 23:15).[13] We can also say that the connection between monotheism and

---

[9]See Mircea Eliade, *Aspects du Mythe* (Paris: Gallimard, 1963).

[10]Jean Bottéro, *La plus vieille religion: En Mésopotamie* (Paris: Gallimard, 1998).

[11]See Norbert Lohfink, *Das Jüdische am Christentum: Die verlorene Dimension* (Freiburg im Breisgau: Herder, 1987), 71-102.

[12]John Howard Yoder, *The Original Revolution: Essays on Christian Pacifism* (Scottdale, PA: Herald, 2003).

[13]In Deut 26:12-15 we have "the first known tax for a social program," according to Frank Crüsemann, *The Torah: Theology and Social History of Old Testament Law* (Edinburgh: T&T Clark, 1996), 218.

social justice is a direct one. Social justice is not a secondary consequence of monotheism but the very expression of God's direct and exclusive rule over his people. This is precisely what the true prophets of Israel said.

Here we can see a decisive difference with Greek philosophical theism. For the Greek philosophers, the affirmation of some sort of Supreme Being was always compatible with the idea that many other realities could be considered divine, somehow participating in the same divine character. Instead, biblical monotheism is exclusive, and this exclusivity is directly related to the idea of an exclusive rule of God.

In due time, this exclusive rule of God came to embrace all peoples and all realities. God was perceived as the king not only over Israel, but also as the king who rules the entire history of humankind. At the same time, this universal rule is the rule of a Creator God, who does not need any other kind of eternal realities beside him. He creates all things, and all things are created realities. No reality, no star, no moon, no sun, no person, no animal can therefore aspire to be some kind of companion or alternative to God (Gen 1:14-19).

Here we encounter something different from what has been thought in European theology, from Peterson to Moltmann, and also something different from what Latin American theology assumed when it wanted to situate itself with the perspective of the poor. In the history of Israel, the idea of one exclusive God, instead of signifying the legitimation of authoritarian forms of power on earth, was the means by which those powers were critiqued. A good part of Latin

American theology seems to have continued thinking in this way of a celestial image that functions as a paradigm for its earthly reflection, a thought common in the history of religions. But for Israel, if God is the king over his people, there is no place for the other kings. For this precise reason it is not strange that Jesus assumes the category of the "kingdom of God" as the central theme of his proclamation.

JESUS AND THE EXCLUSIVITY OF GOD

These Hebrew ideas about God are essential if we are to understand the early and quick development of Christian Christology and the basis of the doctrine of the Trinity. Although usually forgotten, the Old Testament is essential for the doctrine of the Trinity. Without the Hebrew Scriptures, it is impossible to understand the Christian doctrine of God.

When we read the Hebrew Scriptures as a whole, we cannot avoid a sense of failure. The people of God were not able to exist among the nations as a living testimony of the exclusivity of God. The Deuteronomistic writers and the prophets blame the people as a whole, and specifically the kings, for this disaster. The people, again and again, forsake the exclusivity of God and the fulfilling of the Torah. For many Jews of the first centuries, there had been no real restoration after exile.[14]

In this context, Jesus preaches the gospel of the kingdom of God (Mk 1:15). The gospel is the good news of God coming to rule over his people.[15] This rule is again a direct one. The kingdom of God is close. Saying this, Jesus is connecting with the hopes expressed by the prophets concerning a direct rule of God over

---

[14]See N. T. Wright, *The New Testament and the People of God* (Minneapolis: Fortress, 1992), 268-71.
[15]See N. T. Wright, "Paul and Caesar: A New Reading of Romans," in *A Royal Priesthood: The Use of the Bible Ethically and Politically*, ed. Craig Bartholomew (Carlisle, UK: Paternoster, 2002), 173-93.

his people (Jer 23:1-8; Ezek 34:1-22).[16] To put it briefly, we can see this direct rule of God in four aspects of Jesus' teaching and activity.

1. Jesus teaches about God as Father, an image already present but not very developed in the Hebrew Bible. God's rule is like the benevolent rule of a paterfamilias, who takes care of his people. As a matter of fact, Jesus' followers probably organized themselves in houses. In those houses it was possible to share goods, help each other, forgive debts, and so on. But these houses had no other father than God. Again, the rule of God is exclusive. Against what feminist theology used to think, if God is Father, patriarchalism has no place. And against what was thought in the first currents of liberation theology, the image of God as Father, far from favoring the patriarchalism of traditional agrarian societies or ecclesial patriarchalism, instead justly critiques them.[17] Jesus' disciples should not call anybody "father," because they have only one Father in heaven (Mt 23:9). A person entering the kingdom of God may leave father, mother, brothers, and sisters, but they will recover all of them, hundreds of times, except the fathers (Mk 10:29-30).

2. Jesus depicts God as a landowner. As a matter of fact, this is the subject of many of his parables (Mt 20:1-16; Mk 12:1-10; 13:33-37; Lk 12:35-38, 42-46; 15:11-32; 16:1-9; 17:7-10). In them, Jesus connects with the Old Testament image of God as the real owner of the land and the farmers just being tenants of their fields (Lev 25:23-24). This meant that all the people would come back to the lands of their ancestors after a period of forty-nine years, putting an end to extreme social differences (Lev 25:8-22). In Jesus' parables, the coming of the kingdom is compared to the coming of the real owner of the land. This is again an exclusive process. God, as the real owner, will take back his own land, which is now in the hands of tenants who have usurped a land that does not belong to them. In other words: if God is landowner, the time for other landowners is limited.

If we situate ourselves in the perspective of the poor, as liberation theology suggests, now we truly have good news for the poor. The good news for the poor does not consist in proposing a celestial model that should be imitated. The good news is such when we hear the announcement of what God has done in our favor. The proclamation that God is the King who has returned to reign, and that he is the landowner who returns to claim his land, announces precisely the beginning of the end of oppression.

3. In this context we can also understand Jesus' nonviolence. If God is king, he will protect his people. The people only have to trust God. If you take this Old Testament teaching to its ultimate fulfillment, you will not reduce the army, as Gideon did (Judg 7:1-25) or as Deuteronomy teaches (Deut 17:14-20). Radical faith in God's protection means that Jesus' followers will not have any army. They will trust God, looking for new and creative ways to act in front of their enemies (Mt 5:38-48). The exclusive kingdom of the mighty God makes warriors unnecessary.

Here we also encounter the necessity of radicalizing some of the common ideas found in Latin American theology. Like the majority of Christian theologians from the sixth century onward, liberation theology understood that, in certain circumstances, it was legitimate to resort

---

[16]Note that Ezekiel, after affirming the future direct sovereignty of God over his people, does not call the future David "king," but only "prince," in Ezek 34:24.

[17]As Boff suggested in "Trinidad," 515.

to violence against the oppressor. With that, liberation theology did nothing more than apply the traditional doctrine of "just war" to revolutionary situations, something Augustine of Hippo, who took it from Cicero, utilized to legitimate the new "Christian" emperors' recourse to violence. The similar revolutionary experience in Latin America belies the wisdom of this option. In reality, the radical discipleship of Jesus, which liberation theology insistently proposes, and the very idea of the kingdom of God must rather be carried out in postures that are consequently pacifist.

4. This context of the direct and exclusive kingdom of God makes us understand what has usually been called the messianic secret. The reason for this secret is not the assumption that Jesus did not understand himself as Messiah, and the disciples did only after the resurrection. Rather, the reason for this secret is that Jesus did not like the "political" or the "violent" ideas about a Messiah. The problem is more deeply theological. Jesus was proclaiming the coming of the kingdom, and this was an exclusive kingdom. But the main meaning of Messiah for first-century Jews was none other than the anointed king, wherein lies the problem. If this kingdom of God is a direct and exclusive one, there is little room for another king in it.

As a matter of fact, many symbolic actions of Jesus, such as his own baptism and the election and sending of the Twelve, are clear allusions to the "young" Israel, the Israel that existed without state or king for almost two hundred years.

Here we have great insight into the messianic consciousness of Jesus. At the decisive moments, Jesus did not deny that he was the expected Messiah. But, at the same time, he corrected this title with the image of the Son of Man (Mk 8:27-33; 14:61-62). The Son of Man, as is well known, is not only an image of humility. On the contrary, the strange figure of the Son of Man from Daniel 7 prompts interesting associations:

1. The Son of Man is a human image, in contrast to the history of empires in the human story, which represent themselves as beasts (lions, leopards, tigers, eagles, dragons, etc.), because they are beasts. The kingdom of God is a human kingdom, a kingdom with a human face.

2. The Son of Man shares his kingdom. The dominion is given to the Son of Man but also to the people of the saints of the Most High (Dan 7:18). This shared kingdom is an important motif in Jesus' preaching and also for early Christians (Mt 17:25-27; 18:28; 2 Tim 2:12; Rev 5:10).[18]

3. The Son of Man is depicted as moving toward the throne of God. Here we also approach the question of the deity of Jesus.

RESURRECTION AS MESSIANIC EXALTATION

The resurrection of Jesus was interpreted very early as messianic exaltation. By his resurrection, Jesus was declared Messiah (Rom 1:4), solving this issue once and for all. This declaration as Messiah obviously means that Jesus is now in a ruling position. Jesus has been declared king. Not a king in the palaces of Jerusalem but a king who now rules from heaven. As Paul puts it, Jesus is "at the right hand of God" (Rom 8:34). It seems from this text that Paul is presupposing that the Christians of Rome, whom he has not yet met, already share this knowledge.

---

[18]See Gerd Theissen and Annette Merz, *Der historische Jesus: Ein Lehrbuch* (Göttingen: Vandenhoeck & Ruprecht, 1996).

Along this line, many other texts suppose that Jesus, now resurrected, shares the very ruling position of God. Some texts speak about only one throne in heaven, shared by God and the Messiah (Rev 22:1). Other texts speak about a single kingdom that belongs to God and to the Messiah (Eph 5:5). Note that in Greek, as in Hebrew, the word usually translated as "kingdom" means, in the first place, the very act of ruling as king. God the Father and his Messiah share only one throne; together they are but one act of royal ruling over his people.

And here is the main point. This ruling act of the Messiah could not be correctly understood if the first Christians had placed Jesus as an intermediate being between God and his people, or between God and his creation. Here all speculation about first-century intermediate figures is useless. Jesus could not have been understood as an intermediate figure. Why? We already know: putting Jesus as an intermediate figure between God and his creation stood in contradiction with the exclusive character of God's rule, as it was understood in the past both by the Hebrew Bible and by Jesus. If the first Christians wanted to be loyal to the central core of Jesus' message about the kingdom of God, they could not introduce an intermediate creature in a ruling position between God and the rest of his creation.

They could not. Obviously the temptation was there. The books of Chronicles sometimes say that the kings of Israel were seated on God's throne over Israel (1 Chron 29:23; 2 Chron 9:8). However, this throne is no longer in Jerusalem but in heaven. Of course, one could then think that Jesus is now some kind of angel, who reigns sitting on the throne of God. Probably some tendencies of the so-called Jewish Christianity thought like this.[19] But in doing so, they became paradoxically less "Jewish" than the "orthodox" Christians because they dared to put an angel, a being different from God, in a ruling position that only suits God himself. As a matter of fact, some of these groups ended up with a very Hellenistic worldview, introducing not just one but a long cascade of intermediate entities between God and the creation.[20]

The letter to the Hebrews begins with the affirmation that Jesus cannot be an angel. Then the letter quotes Psalm 45:6-7, applying it to the Messiah. As it is a psalm, it is God's Word, and this means that God himself addresses his Messiah as "God." The context is again the kingdom of God, which now Jesus himself shares with the Father.

Although the letter to the Hebrews resumes this development, the process had begun before. Being loyal to Jesus, and being loyal to the history of monotheism, the first Christians could not understand Jesus as an intermediate figure between God and creation. The kingdom is only one. The act of reigning is only one. But God and the Messiah share this sole rule. And this means that the Messiah belongs in the monotheism of God. Jesus is Lord (*kyrios*), the same Lord of the Septuagint translation of the Old Testament. Paul expresses it very early, inserting Jesus in the Shema of Israel (1 Cor 8:6; see Deut 6:4 LXX).[21]

Now we can better understand the reasons why some great Pauline exegetes have commented on the speed of the process wherein Jesus was identified with God, and why this

---

[19]Hans-Joachim Schoeps, *Theologie und Geschichte des Judenchristentums* (Tübingen: Mohr, 1949), 71-116.

[20]Jean Daniélou, *Théologie du judéo-christianisme* (Tournai, Belgium: Desclée, 1958).

[21]N. T. Wright, *What Saint Paul Really Said: Was Paul of Tarsus the Real Founder of Christianity?* (Grand Rapids, MI: Eerdmans, 1997), 65-67.

process took place not in a Hellenistic context but in a Jewish context. This also explains why the first Christians, while proclaiming Jesus as Lord, never thought they were leaving their traditional monotheism. On the contrary, they were in some sense being faithful to the most exclusive character of Hebrew monotheism, which does not tolerate other ruling figures besides God. The ruling act of Jesus is the same as the ruling act of God, and therefore Jesus belongs in the midst of the royal deity of God.

THE CROSS AND REDEMPTION

When we look back from the exaltation of resurrection and we look back to the cross, we have to think again. If Jesus belongs to the monotheism of God, his whole life is now the story of God. We can say, with Tom Wright, that the story of Jesus is the story of God becoming king.[22] But the cross is part of this story. God was in the place most opposite from any idea of power and glory. God was with Jesus on the cross.

The event at the cross, then, has a radically unexpected meaning. Jesus has experienced the abandonment of God, which means that God himself has experienced the abandonment of God. God has taken on himself the destiny of the cursed and the sinners, the destiny of all supposedly abandoned by God. There is no place nor situation that is too far away from God. This is the core of redemption: Jesus was made sin for us (2 Cor 5:21).

In the Old Testament, God had assumed the roles of king, of master, and of warrior. This already had important consequences, because in assuming these roles God was revealing his will of enabling a people without domination. Now, on the cross, we come to the full revelation of

what it really means to be king, master, or warrior. The king, master, and warrior reveals himself as a servant and a slave. There is no more radical expression of God's love for humankind (Rom 5:8).

At the same time, the unity of God is not broken. Even to the point of extreme humiliation and death, God continues to be the only God of monotheism. In the midst of extreme abandonment, Father and Son are still the one and only God. This unity is the fellowship of the Spirit. In the difference of Father and Son, the Spirit is not only the eternal essence of God but also a personal relation between Father and Son.

This difference and unity can be seen through Jesus' earthly life. In his ministry, Jesus reveals himself as the true Son, representing as such the original mission of all of Israel. As Son, he has an intimate relation with his Father. In Jesus' earthly life, Father and Son are revealed as such because they have a relationship. In his relation with the Father, the Son is Son because he has a Father, and the Father is Father because he has a Son. Relation means difference and unity. Because of this unity, the life and ministry of Jesus are led by the Spirit in complete unity with the Father.

From this point of view it becomes important to emphasize, as occurs in some streams of Latin American theology, that we only know who God is through Jesus Christ. He is the same as the prologue of John tells us (Jn 1:18). However, Jesus not only reveals himself but also reveals himself as the Son. Upon revealing himself as the Son, he reveals to us that God is also Father. The manifestation of who God is, for this reason, does not stop in Jesus. The revelation has a relational structure, although this relational structure is not a celestial model but rather that of the incarnation.

[22]N. T. Wright, *How God Became King: Getting to the Heart of the Gospels* (San Francisco: HarperOne, 2012).

This same structure is found in our redemption. Our separation from God as sinners is bridged by the grace of Jesus, who approaches the lost and experiences our deserved destination. Reached by Jesus, we are introduced into the very fellowship of God with God, who is the Spirit. The Spirit brings us into the relationship of the Son with the Father, which means that we are inserted into the core of God's life. As we are introduced into this relationship of the Son with the Father, we are able to cry out, "Abba, Father" (Rom 8:15; Gal 4:6). The Spirit adopts us as children of God, brothers and sisters of Jesus, and thus we belong to God's family.

The early "trinitarian" expressions in the New Testament (Mt 28:19; Lk 3:22; Jn 3:34-35; 14:16, 26; 15:26; 16:7, 13-15; 2 Cor 13:14; 2 Thess 2:13-14; 1 Pet 1:2) have their roots not only in the experiences of the churches with the Spirit but also in the certainty that Christ's abandonment by God was never a division in God. Here again the resurrection is the proof of the unity of the Spirit. It was the Holy Spirit, in unity with Father and Son, who raised Jesus from the dead, keeping the eternal unity of the monotheistic God.[23]

The "perspective of the poor," as expressed in liberation theology, could never do justice to the essential importance of the theology of the Holy Spirit. From the point of view of the first liberation theology, the Pentecostal movements that were outside the usual clerical controls appeared as substantially alien developments, and consequently their proponents were painted as conservatives who were linked with North American imperialism. From that perspective, the first liberation theologians found it incomprehensible that the movements were actually composed of the poor whose perspective they themselves had tried to assume. These were those who were incorporated into the charismatic and Pentecostal movements. However, an adequate trinitarian theology culminates precisely in the thought of the active presence of God in his people, especially among the poorest of his people. It is precisely this presence of God in the midst of his people, and not the communitarian images in the heavens, that implies a constituent demand for equality and fraternity.[24]

BEYOND SUBJECTS

Upon reaching this point, it becomes clear that we cannot understand the three divine persons as "subjects," as modern philosophy and theology tend to do. The idea of God as subject does not appear to leave room for trinitarian thought: or it affirms one unique subject in heaven, or affirms three subjects, something that approaches tritheism instead of the Trinity.[25]

When the ancient councils of the church introduced the word *person* (*hypostasis* or *prosōpon*), they never thought of it in a modern sense. For example, in the Third Council of Constantinople (681), the monotheletists defended the idea that in Jesus there was only one will because they tended to think that in Jesus there was only one nature. The orthodox party, on the contrary, defended the view that in Jesus there were two wills because of his two natures. In both cases, they were clear that the will was not an attribute of the one person of Jesus but an

---

[23]As a matter of fact, the New Testament ascribes the resurrection to the Son himself (Jn 10:17-18), to the Father (mostly; see Acts 5:30), and also to the Spirit (Rom 1:4; 8:11).

[24]A fresh perspective on Latin American Pentecostalism can be found in C. Álvarez, ed., *Pentecostalismo y liberación: Una experiencia latinoamericana* (San José: Departamento Ecuménico de Investigaciones, 1992).

[25]An extreme example of this is Jürgen Moltmann, *Trinität und Reich Gottes: Zur Gotteslehre* (Munich: Kaiser, 1980), 187-94. Some Latin American theologians, such as Leonardo Boff, are close to Moltmann's position.

attribute of his nature. On the contrary, the modern idea of person as subject has no doubt that the will is an attribute of the person.

If Christianity would have come to the triune image of God by means of "intermediate figures," it would be easy to think of the Trinity as a unity of three different subjects. But this idea of person as subject is not in the New Testament, and it is also not what the ancient church tried to say.

What we have in the Scriptures is the image of a God who has revealed himself in his act of liberating and ruling his people. This ruling is so radical that God is also proclaimed the Creator of the whole reality. In the New Testament, the rule of God shows itself as an act of extreme and radical love, even to the point of death. After the definitive revelation of God in Jesus we can say that God is love (1 Jn 4:8). The act of love is the very essence of God, according to the Scriptures. God is not primarily a thing but an act, the pure act of love.

By revealing himself as love, God has revealed personal relations in himself. Love means relationships, and these are eternal relationships. God did not begin to be love in the moment of time when we experienced loving relationships with him. God is eternal love, and this means that God is love beyond the realm of creation. The loving relations in God are eternal relations. God has revealed himself as love, and this means that God has revealed himself as that which he eternally is. Trinity is not an appearance toward creatures but the essence of God as love.

The words used by the ancient church (*prosōpon*, *hypostasis*) do not mean an isolated subject but relations. The word *hypostasis* primarily refers to an act, the act of supporting something or somebody. The word *prosōpon* means primarily the act of looking at, and

therefore the act of facing, and then a face, or the front of something. To say that in God there are persons means that in God there are three eternal relations.

God as Father has revealed himself as the eternal Source of himself, including all relations included in his pure act of love. God has revealed himself as the eternal Gift of himself to the Father. And God has revealed himself as eternal fellowship between Father and Son. As eternal Source, God is creator. As eternal Gift, God is the only redeemer of believers. As eternal Fellowship, God is the sanctifying Spirit in us (2 Cor 13:14).

We can conclude, then, that the doctrine of Trinity essentially belongs to the Christian image of God, having its roots in the exclusivity of God, in the way this exclusivity is understood in the Hebrew Scriptures. However, the Trinity is not principally a celestial model but rather the very structure of the solidarity of the unique God with his people. It is a solidarity that is inseparable from the biblical idea of an exclusive monotheism of God. Precisely because it points to solidarity, and precisely because monotheism is exclusive, trinitarian language is situated precisely in the "perspective of the poor," that which liberation theology longs for. From this perspective, God is not only the eternal Father, Creator, and Almighty who makes the sun to shine on the just and the sinners. God is also God the Son, committed unto death to the oppressed, the sinners, and all those who appear to be rejected by God. And God is also the Spirit, who raised Jesus from the dead, and who lives filling his people with life and giving gifts to his people. Precisely because God is like this, so also his Holy Scriptures speak to us of him.

FURTHER READING

Boff, Leonardo. *Trinity and Society*. Maryknoll, NY: Orbis, 1988.

Díaz, Miguel H. "The Life-Giving Reality of God from Black, Latin American, and US Hispanic Theological Perspectives." Pages 259-73 in *The Cambridge Companion to the Trinity*, edited by Peter C. Phan. Cambridge: Cambridge University Press, 2011.

González, Antonio *God's Reign and the End of Empires*. Miami: Convivium, 2012.

———. *The Gospel of Faith and Justice*. Maryknoll, NY: Orbis, 2005.

Kärkkäinen, Veli-Matti. *The Trinity: Global Perspectives*. Louisville: Westminster John Knox, 2007.

LEARNING TO SEE JESUS
WITH THE EYES OF THE SPIRIT

THE UNLIKELY PROPHETS OF GOD'S REIGN

C. Rosalee Velloso Ewell

THIS CHAPTER JOURNEYS through a couple of Old Testament prophets (Jeremiah and Jonah) and Paul's correspondence with the Corinthians in order to examine the implications of the doctrine of the Trinity for how we understand the prophetic role of the church today. It offers a brief overview of how the Bible has been read in Latin America and the place of the Trinity within such readings. Then it sketches the lives of two biblical prophets in order to focus on how Christians are enabled to see Jesus through the work of the Holy Spirit in the gathered community. This trinitarian work has implications not only for scriptural reading and the formulation of doctrine but also for what can be called holistic evangelism: the witness of the church in today's society in all areas of life.

> *Credo in Deum Patrem omnipotentem;*
> *Creatorem coeli et terrae.*
> *Et in Jesum Christum, Filium ejus unicum,*
> *Dominum nostrum;*
> *qui conceptus est de Spiritu Sancto, natus ex*
> *Maria virgine . . .*
> I believe in God the Father Almighty, Maker of
> heaven and earth.

> And in Jesus Christ his only Son our Lord;
> who was conceived by the Holy Ghost, born of
> the Virgin Mary . . .

Jürgen Moltmann once asked, "Why are most Christians in the West, whether they be Catholics or Protestants, really only 'monotheists' where the experience and practice of their faith is concerned? Whether God is one or triune evidently makes as little difference to the doctrine of faith as it does to ethics."[1] I would argue that is this the case not only in the West but, with some exceptions, describes an aspect of Christian faith and practice in Latin America as well.

All theologies, all scriptural interpretations, are contextual. Whether one's theology challenges consumerism in Lima or London, poverty in Dallas or Delhi, the meaning of St. Paul's letter to the Romans in Baltimore or Brasilia—we must always keep in mind the limits of our own language and viewpoints. In 1 Corinthians 13:12 Paul says, "We see through a glass dimly." "But we do see Jesus," states the author of Hebrews (Heb 2:9). "We see through a glass dimly"—this is learning humility and knowing that we do not

---

[1] Jürgen Moltmann, *The Trinity and the Kingdom: The Doctrine of God* (London: SCM Press, 1981), 1.

have God's view of things, that we do not have all the answers or the plans or necessarily the best interpretations of Scripture. Whether we are from the north or south, east or west, the Scriptures' constant reminder, made succinct in the creed's affirmation that Jesus is Lord, is that we are not lords, not little gods who seek to control with knowledge or power. Power and knowledge are only seen in the triune God and the ways in which this God has been revealed to all of creation in Jesus and through the Spirit at work in the church.

When trying to learn about the Holy Trinity and how to live as Christians, it is fundamental for us to remember that the love between the Father, Son, and Spirit offers us a framework for how to think about our own lives and our participation in the divine life. Another word for this type of living is *discipleship*—living into God's calling of God's people, both as individuals and collectively as church. This implies also exercising the prophetic voice within our contexts. That is, the prophetic voice is intimately tied to what it means to live as God's people in the world, enabled by the Spirit to be witnesses for Jesus Christ.

BIBLICAL INTERPRETATION IN LATIN AMERICA

As in any other continent or community, there is no one single way the Bible is read and interpreted in Latin America. Rather, scriptural readings look more like the colors of a kaleidoscope, changing and shifting according to the many contexts and situations in which the Bible is read. Despite this variety, a couple of general

themes have emerged over the past four decades that shed light on the theologies of the doctrine of the Trinity in this vast continent.

First, it is important to note the distinction between the theology of liberation and the Latin American Bible movement.[2] The latter refers to the changes in Bible reading at the popular level, in base ecclesial communities and among the poorest of the poor. The former is the academic, second-order reflection on some of the practices of the base communities and in conversation with key conciliar documents and Western theologies. Precisely because it is more academic, liberation theology is more well known in the West in both Catholic and Protestant circles. What is unique about the Bible movement is that it did not simply offer alternate theological formulations on old themes or different reflections on key dogmas of the church. Rather, it changed the way the Bible was read by placing the reality, that is, the social and economic problems and the oppression of the poor, in the very center. This brought the world of the Bible into the present—a "fluid transition between past and present" that illuminated "the present by considering the manifestations of God in the past."[3] In a similar way, Baptist theologian James McClendon argued that this way of reading the Bible has characterized particular communities throughout Christian history, from Peter's sermon in Acts 3 to African American spirituals of the nineteenth and twentieth centuries. It is what McClendon called the Baptist vision, "this is that, then is now"—a way of appropriating the biblical texts such that not only do they become

---

[2]Paulo Nogueira, "Exodus in Latin America," in *The Oxford Handbook of the Reception History of the Bible*, ed. Michael Lieb et al. (Oxford: Oxford University Press, 2011), 447-52.
[3]Nogueira, "Exodus in Latin America," 448.

a reality for the readers, but they also exercise their prophetic voice on those who read them.[4]

Second, the theologies of Latin America reflect both the political and the ecclesial divisions in the continent. For most of the second half of the twentieth century, Latin American countries were governed by military dictatorships. At the same time, communism and the Cold War played into the psyches of Christians, especially Protestants, who were greatly influenced by conservative missionaries from North America and Western Europe, with the result that too often nothing was done to oppose the dictators and the many abuses of the political system. One could argue that during those decades the prophetic voice of the church was largely silenced, and that theology and biblical interpretation emphasized spiritual transformation and the desire to get to heaven, thus paying little or no attention to what was going on in society. Of course, there were exceptions—individuals and communities that opposed such spiritualizing of the texts—but these were not the dominant voices within Christian circles. The doctrine of the Trinity was an academic discipline, ignored in practice, if not in speech, by most congregations.

Even if not always acknowledged, it was the changes in the Roman Catholic Church after Vatican II—voices and scriptural readings coming from the margins of society—that challenged the status quo and led to what today is known as holistic or integral mission movements in Latin America. This theology, aided by voices such as John Stott, Samuel Escobar, and Orlando Costas, sought to bring together the evangelical

passion for evangelism with social justice practices. While this movement has been largely Christocentric, there have been some theologians and pastors articulating a more robust doctrine of the Trinity. Among such voices, Leonardo Boff is probably the most famous.

Boff, a Brazilian Catholic theologian, reminds us that when speaking of the Trinity we need to recover the proper language, the grammar of our faith—language that is specific to theological discourse and that has been battled over, debated, and fine-tuned over the centuries. At the same time, we must recognize the limitations of our language and affirm the ongoing work of the Trinity in our daily lives. As Boff puts it, if we divorce the Trinity from life, we have given up on justice, peace, love, and salvation.

> The Trinity has to do with the lives of each of us, our daily experiences, our struggles to follow our conscience, our love and joy, our bearing the sufferings of the world and the tragedies of human existence; it also has to do with the struggle against social injustice, with efforts at building a more humane form of society, with the sacrifices and martyrdoms that these endeavors often bring. If we fail to include the Trinity in our personal and social odyssey, we have failed to show the saving mystery, failed in evangelization.[5]

Boff argues that the revelation of God as Trinity happened in the life of Jesus and the work of the Spirit in the community. This does not mean there was no previous communication of the Trinity, "because any true revelation of God's self must be Trinitarian."[6] What is new and unique in Christian theology and in our language of the

[4]"So the vision can be expressed as a hermeneutical motto, which is shared awareness of *the present Christian community as the primitive community and the eschatological community*. In other words, the church now is the primitive church and the church on the day of judgment is the church now; the obedience and the liberty of the followers of Jesus of Nazareth is *our* liberty, *our* obedience." James William McClendon Jr., *Systematic Theology*, vol. 1, *Ethics* (Nashville: Abingdon, 1986), 31.
[5]Leonardo Boff, *Trinity and Society* (Maryknoll, NY: Orbis, 1988), 157.
[6]Boff, *Trinity and Society*, 10.

Trinity is that now God has not just revealed himself to us but has communicated in person. Through Jesus of Nazareth and the Spirit at Pentecost, God takes on human history as God's own and dwells among us in our dwelling place. Yet this emphasis on history as it relates to the doctrine of the Trinity has rarely emphasized the prophetic role and the Spirit's work in the church.

BIBLE, NARRATIVES, AND PROPHETS

Biblical theology in Latin America has often been done in reaction to emphases or major themes coming from the North. In evangelical circles it was done either in reaction to the Roman Catholic majority or in the context of huge numerical growth but little spiritual depth, or both. There is certainly something to be learned from the West, but the danger is that it has led to a neglect of the biblical narratives, allowing the academy to set the tone of doctrinal discussions rather than letting readings of the texts shape and transform lives. The academy is not a place for prophets. Their voices are dampened or dismissed as yet one more interesting idea. It is the reminder of the connection between the Trinity and social justice, and between the Trinity and the politics of God's reign, that is perhaps the greatest inheritance of Latin American trinitarian theology. And if Boff is correct about the implications of the Trinity for daily life, then we must learn to listen to the prophetic voices.

Perhaps Jeremiah and Jonah are unlikely candidates for a discussion about the Trinity. While one cannot cite passages in these books where the triune God is made evident, the narratives themselves and the stories of these men illustrate Boff's point about the ways the Trinity interacts with our understanding of God's call on each of us to work toward justice and salvation in ways that very well might lead to suffering and martyrdom. Furthermore, Jeremiah and Jonah illustrate a kind of obedience (even if they do so begrudgingly) that God demands of God's people and the implied politics of being a faithful community. Being faithful to God's call results in participation in the divine plan for the redemption of all of creation—participation in the life of the Trinity that is being in communion and that challenges the structures of power and politics of this world.

As the story of God's activities with creation and with a particular people within that creation, the Scriptures often contain conflicting substories. There are narratives that suggest competing ways in which God's people listen to and understand the divine calling. One such example of rival narratives is the book of Jeremiah, which recounts the final days of Israel-Judah under Assyrian domination and the bloody transition to domination under Nebuchadnezzar of Babylon. The expanse of the Babylonian Empire led to the destruction of Jerusalem, with its temple and the king's palace burned to the ground in 587 BC, and most of the city's prominent citizens taken into exile. As Old Testament scholar R. E. Clements describes the state of affairs in Judah,

> At one stroke the year 587 witnessed the removal of the two institutions—the temple and the Davidic kingship—which had stood as symbolic assurances of God's election of Israel. Their loss was far greater than the loss of national prestige and left the entire understanding of Israel's special relationship to Yahweh its God in question. What happened demanded total reappraisal and rethinking of Israel's self-understanding as the People of God.[7]

---

[7]R. E. Clements, *Jeremiah*, Interpretation: A Bible Commentary for Teaching and Preaching (Atlanta: John Knox, 1988), 6.

Christopher Seitz suggests that Jeremiah reflects "to a greater degree than other prophetic books a situation of conflict." The conflicts in Jeremiah are numerous—they are within the community in Judah and within also the communities that were exiled to Babylon, and there are still conflicts in Judah after 597 and 587 BC. Moreover, it is precisely the situation of exile that is the focus of the conflicts. These are the very conflicts that gave rise to the distinct tradition in the canon of what is known as the "exilic or Golah tradition."[8] Where is the revelation of God in the exile? What is unique about Jeremiah that enabled him to hear the voice of God's Spirit and to proclaim, even to his own harm, the type of obedience God demanded of God's people?

By the time of Ezra, at the end of the exilic period, the people had learned confession and repentance for the sins of idolatry and syncretism that had characterized most of Israel's life since the giving of the Torah at Sinai and the beginning of exile in Babylon. In Jeremiah we have accounts of the competing narratives of the people's response to the crisis. The remnant in Jerusalem were not able to hear God's voice through Jeremiah—the revelation of God was hidden from them as their end shows. They disappear in Egypt, in idolatry, and Jeremiah is forced to die with them.

In *Reading in Communion*, Stephen Fowl and Greg Jones use Jeremiah's story to show how the moral life must be embodied in particular practices that are shaped by such virtues as patience, hope, and faith.[9] They explain that the situation in Judah was such that it demanded an immediate response—something had to be done. On one hand there was Hananiah, the false prophet, calling the people to join Egypt in a revolt against Babylon and arguing that in doing so the Lord would bring Israel through the war and restore peace to Jerusalem. On the other hand there was Jeremiah, telling the people that subjection under Babylon would last a long time and that they needed to learn to live with it, to be faithful to God in spite of their desperate situation. He instructs them to plant gardens, build houses, marry, and so on. However, as Fowl and Jones point out, the people were not trained to hear the words of God as spoken through Jeremiah—they had not been part of faithful practices that would shape them into faithful people who would be willing to understand and obey Jeremiah's call.

Jeremiah's story does not end in 587 BC. After the siege of Jerusalem, Judah's king Zedekiah is blinded and taken into exile. Nebuchadnezzar leaves a remnant in Judah, including Jeremiah, and Gedaliah is made governor over the province. For a short period, it looked as though the people would finally heed Jeremiah's call. Gedaliah attempted to implement some of the policies suggested by Jeremiah and to follow the prophet's words: "Fear not to serve the Chaldeans: dwell in the land, and serve the king of Babylon, and it shall be well with you" (Jer 40:9-10 KJV). But this brief turn to obedience was short-lived. Led by Ishmael, a descendant of David, the people react against Gedaliah and assassinate him and others who had sought the welfare of the city on Jeremiah's terms. Following Gedaliah's death, Ishmael and his cohorts rebel against Babylon, but they are overthrown by Nebuchadnezzar with equal violence. Then, in fear of further reprisals from Babylon, the rest of the people

---

[8]Christopher R. Seitz, *Theology in Conflict: Reactions to the Exile in the Book of Jeremiah* (Berlin: de Gruyter, 1989), 2, 4-5.
[9]Stephan E. Fowl and L. Gregory Jones, *Reading in Communion: Scripture and Ethics in Christian Life* (Grand Rapids, MI: Eerdmans, 1991), 91.

decide to immigrate to Egypt (Jer 41:16-18). Once again they ask Jeremiah for a word from God, but again he tells them words they are not prepared to hear. He tells them not to go to Egypt but to remain in the land, where they will prosper. For his pronouncements against Israel's unfaithfulness and against Israel's kings and its warfare, Jeremiah is mocked, imprisoned, and suspected of treason. The people reject his word and turn toward Egypt. And, as Karl Barth so poignantly puts it, "[So Israel] returned to the place from which Yahweh has once called and led their fathers by the word of Moses. The difference is that this time the prophet does not lead. . . . And so they disappear and Jeremiah with them. They for their part are given the lie by events. And he is silenced by them as he had been all his life."[10] Jeremiah had the eyes of the Spirit of God to see and to know the type of obedience God demanded of his people and the particular ways God invited the people to participate in God's liberation of them. But the political implications of Jeremiah's prophetic vision included the loss of power, submission to foreign domination, and work toward justice at the local, community level. This was not the kind of God the people wanted to obey.

The story of Jonah highlights the politics of Trinity, though again, one would have to do some serious exegetical acrobatics to come up with Father, Son, and Holy Spirit in the four short chapters of the book of Jonah. That is not the point. Rather, the narrative tells us that the word of the Lord came to Jonah and told him to go to Nineveh, the seat of power of a cruel and ruthless force in the region, and to tell them to repent or face destruction. Nineveh was the capital of the

Assyrian Empire, which was already past its peak when this story was told. It was failing and was plagued by internal corruption and mismanagement. Assur was its god—a violent, cruel, and dominating god, a god who stands in stark contrast to the loving, liberating, covenantal God of Israel. What person in their right mind would want to face Assur?

Jonah is the liberation theologian of his time. He comes from the margins, he is oppressed, his people are suffering, and he is trying to listen to God, to reveal God to his people. So when God says, go to Nineveh, it is like saying, "Don't bother with the margins right now—I want you to go to those in power so that I might redeem them." It is easier to be Nahum and to predict the fall of empire than to preach its salvation. Jonah has his own prejudices and is a grumpy character. But despite his unwillingness, he does not lose the vision of what God demands of him. He also does not lose his courage and finally submits to participating in God's work, even if it means forfeiting his own life at the hands of the enemy.

Victorio Araya argues that faith "in the liberator God of the poor is the profession that God *alone* is liberator in the authentic sense of the word." But how is God liberator? Araya asks, and he answers by suggesting that human beings participate in God's redemptive activities in creation "*from beneath* . . . the God of the Bible is a God with a commitment to human history, a God who assumes the risks of the option for the poor, who remains faithful to the task of re-creating life, and who thus invites us to enter into alliance, a covenant to transform the world by humanizing life."[11]

Jonah and Jeremiah have the eyes to see what God is doing and the link between God's

[10]Karl Barth, *Church Dogmatics*, ed. Geoffrey W. Bromiley and T. F. Torrance, trans. Geoffrey W. Bromiley (Edinburgh: T&T Clark, 1958), IV/1, 474.
[11]Victorio Araya, *God of the Poor: The Mystery of God in Latin American Liberation Theology* (Maryknoll, NY: Orbis, 1987), 149, 150.

revelation to them—which Boff would say is trinitarian, even if the prophets did not articulate it as such—and their participation in God's mission in creation. Being obedient entails participating in the liberating work of God as God is revealed in history.

The danger in many articulations of the doctrine of the Trinity is that they too quickly skip over the biblical stories, making the narratives only secondary to the real agenda. The lesson from liberation theology and the Bible movement in Latin America is precisely this return to the texts, to the stories of Jeremiah and Jonah and so many others, and in making these texts part of our story today. It means learning that the same Spirit who inspired the prophets is at work in the church today and enables the church to have that prophetic voice in whatever context she finds herself.

HAVING THE EYES TO SEE THE TRINITY

Again with Boff, God as Trinity is revealed fully in Jesus and at Pentecost. But in our classrooms and sermons, what Jesus are we teaching? In Latin America there are many faces, many types of Jesus—from the revolutionary Che Guevara to the cute, white, plump little baby in Mother Mary's arms. The doctrine of the Trinity demands that we learn to see Jesus with the eyes of the Spirit so that our own prejudices and politics do not blind us to the obedience to which the Father calls all his people.

How do we discern Jesus, the first-century manual laborer from Palestine, when we see through a glass dimly? The church at Corinth suffered from the same self-absorption and prejudices as did Jeremiah or Jonah. The manifestations of the Spirit in that congregation—dramatic by comparison to most Sunday services—did

not automatically make them more holy or wise. And yet, despite the limitations and sin of the Corinthians, the triune God was made real within that community. How? Why? Part of the answer lies in the fact that God is a missionary God and that the Spirit enables God's prophets to bear messages that relate directly to the people's witness, whatever their context. As Chris Wright observes,

> God sent his prophets to expose the wickedness of his people and to warn them of its dire consequences. . . . The major features of the message of those earlier prophets, sent by God's Spirit, were the fundamental requirements of God's law: to do justice, to show mercy and compassion, and to reject the exploitation of the needy. . . . The prophetic Spirit of *truth* is also the Spirit of *justice*.[12]

These themes of justice and truth are the ones Paul takes on when writing to Corinth. Though the particularity of the issues of that Gentile congregation might be different from those of the people living at the time of Jeremiah or Jonah, the call to be God's faithful people remains the same. This call has everything to do with our participation in the triune life of God.

Father, Son, and Holy Spirit exist in perpetual relationship. John Baxter-Brown notes,

> It is an energetic and dynamic relationship that inevitably is centrifugal in that it is outward looking. The metaphor is not exact, but it suffices here in that the very act of creation displays a fundamental aspect of God's nature: God is missionary. The creative urge, also given to all life, is to create something new whether it be a baby or a piece of art. So it must be with God's people in community: the creative urge is the basis for mission and evangelism, to see God re-create humanity one story at a time.[13]

---

[12]Christopher J. H. Wright. *Knowing the Holy Spirit Through the Old Testament* (Downers Grove, IL: IVP Academic, 2006), 82-83.
[13]John Baxter-Brown, "Evangelism Through the Eyes of Jesus: Reflections on the Trinity" (unpublished notes, Salisbury, UK, 2013).

The metaphor of new birth is very apt, for God is both Creator and Re-creator. If the church is to see Jesus with the eyes of the Spirit and embody the prophetic call to justice and truth, then in such living we reflect something of God's creative nature, and we too will be missionary oriented. It is our calling to be caught up in the Trinity's work of redemption and new creation.

But we need equipping for this task: the Father calls, the Son commissions and shows the way, and the Spirit empowers and comforts. Baxter-Brown captures the reality well: "This can be seen in the rather muddled and messy Corinthian church as Paul highlights the missionary nature of God, embodies the prophetic role in his own ministry, and teaches about the essential nature of the Son's work, especially the central importance of his death and resurrection and the need the Corinthians had (and we have today) of God's Spirit."[14]

Paul's correspondence with the Corinthians displays the urgency of their calling—they must sort out their common life, from sexual ethics to how they share their food—so that their witness in that pagan context is one of truth and justice. Learning to see the way of Jesus with the eyes of the Spirit means learning to live as a particular community that embodies the love of the persons of the Trinity and displays this love to neighbor, whether friend or enemy.

Drawing on Martin Buber's *I and Thou*, Timothy Gorringe argues,

> Responding to the Thou in my neighbour is living within God, within the pattern of correspondences and relations which he calls forth and which constitute created reality. As we relate, we are in the image of God, for the image is the echoing of the relationship God is. As, and only as, we relate we live in the Spirit.

That human beings exist only in community is the most obvious starting point for any anthropology, given the fact that they are formed by language, which is by definition social. . . . There have been philosophies . . . which have sought essential humanness in solitude. . . . Nevertheless, both Judaism and Christianity have in general repudiated this option, affirming community as central to human being. . . . Christianity not only affirms humanity as fellow humanity, but understands fellow humanity as the sacrament of our encounter with God. . . . Through my neighbour I know God . . . the Spirit works and is known in this encounter. . . . The one who is ultimately Other, who stubbornly resists all attempts to fit him in to a ready-made category, is Jesus of Nazareth.[15]

Gorringe is not making a particular point about the Trinity but shows clearly that understanding our place in community is fundamental to being made part of God's life and receiving God's revelation. In his debates with the Corinthians Paul is making the same point—they must understand that how they live as a community has huge implications, in fact, life-and-death implications, for how they exist as God's people. Having the eyes of the Spirit means they see Jesus of Nazareth and live according to that revelation. If their encounters with one another are less than adequate, they not only fail to see Jesus but also fail to show Jesus to those around them—in Boff's words, they run the risk of failing at evangelization.

At the beginning of 1 Corinthians 3 Paul shows the Corinthians that their jealousy, quarreling, and many divisions are directly tied to how they live in the Spirit. Indeed, those who are not spiritual will not receive the gifts of the Spirit (1 Cor 2:14), though Paul has already affirmed in

---

[14]Baxter-Brown, "Evangelism."
[15]Timothy J. Gorringe. *Discerning the Spirit: A Theology of Revelation* (London: SCM Press, 1990), 74-75.

1 Corinthians 1:7 that they are not lacking in any spiritual gift—and how does he know this? He knows because their testimony of Christ has been strengthened in speech and knowledge (1 Cor 1:5-6). It is a dangerous game they are playing, and the apostle is trying his hardest to persuade them again to live lives worthy of Christ.

Like the church in Latin America (and all around the world), there are issues of power and greed that threaten to break apart the community in Corinth. Paul plays on popular conceptions of wisdom and honor to show that the ways the world conceives of such power are very different from the ways of God's Spirit, and it is with the eyes of the Spirit that they must relearn to orient their individual and their collective lives. In the history of God's dealings with creation, God has called the most unlikely people to be his voice and his instruments in a broken world. It is no different with Corinth—some might be wise, but not all; some might be powerful, but not all (1 Cor 12:26-31). God's Spirit rests on very unlikely and often unwilling prophets, asking them to show the world what it means to follow Jesus. For Paul, the Corinthian church is in this great line of people called to challenge wisdom, strength, and might so that the world might know God's justice and be drawn into God's wisdom.

The dynamics of the narrative of 1–2 Corinthians and the reports of Paul's ministry in the book of Acts show both how the apostle is called to be a prophet—calling the people back to justice and truth, to living as the missionary people they are meant to be—and how those who listen to the prophet become prophets themselves. The people of God are called to be a missionary people because in so doing they participate in God's life. Such participation requires and is enabled by the Spirit, who guides and teaches so that the life of Jesus is made real in whatever context the community finds itself. In the Bible movement mentioned earlier, Jesus is not a remote rabbi from the first century but is present in and with the sufferings of the people in poor villages in Peru or an overcrowded prison in megacities such as São Paulo. Being part of the life of the triune God means witnessing to Jesus in words, deeds, and character wherever we are.

Latin American theologians, from the Catholic Boff to the Methodist Miguéz Bonino, have gifted the church with an emphasis of God as Trinity at work in the community. Furthermore, they remind us that this community has been called to be a prophetic voice, a voice for justice and peace, and that such justice cannot be divorced from the life and teachings of Jesus. Insofar as we listen to the Spirit, we are able to see Jesus even in the least of these and to embody in our relationships the obedience to the Father who has called us to himself through the Son and the Spirit.

FURTHER READING

Araya, Victorio. *God of the Poor*. Maryknoll, NY: Orbis, 1987.

Boff, Leonardo. *Holy Trinity, Perfect Community*. Maryknoll, NY: Orbis, 2000.

———. *Trinity and Society*. Maryknoll, NY: Orbis, 1998.

Bonino, José Miguéz. *Faces of Latin American Protestantism*. Grand Rapids, MI: Eerdmans, 1997.

Costas, Orlando E. *Liberating News: A Theology of Contextual Evangelization*. Eugene, OR: Wipf & Stock, 2002.

Gorringe, Timothy J. *Discerning the Spirit: A Theology of Revelation*. London: SCM Press, 1990.

Kärkkäinen, Veli-Matti. *The Trinity: Global Perspectives*. Louisville: Westminster John Knox, 2007.

ASIAN REFORMULATIONS OF THE TRINITY

AN EVALUATION

Natee Tanchanpongs

THIS ESSAY LOOKS to advance the way evangelicals do theology in context by examining proposals by four Asian theologians (Raimundo Panikkar—Indian, Jung Young Lee—Korean, Brahmabandhab Upadhyaya—Indian, and Nozomu Miyahira—Japanese) in their usage of indigenous resources to help reformulate the doctrine of the Trinity. After presenting overviews of these proposals, they are evaluated for biblical authenticity in light of an evangelical framework. The measuring stick used for assessing these proposals is the context-to-text model, which puts forward that a commitment to the primacy of the Bible and an affirmation of the turns to the interpreter's context can coexist only if there is a movement or transformation from context to the text. This model requires elements in the interpreter's context to be dynamic, nonnormative, and modifiable. Out of this context-to-text paradigm, two evaluative criteria will be suggested.

INTRODUCTION

In the article "One Rule to Rule Them All?," Kevin Vanhoozer assesses the modern approach to biblical interpretation. Modernity had searched for the one objective method to rule over the subjectivity of interpreters. With this failed attempt, postmodernity has taken three turns to the interpreter's context. The first is the turn to social location, where the horizons of the interpreters are accounted for more seriously. Moreover, the reality of human situatedness shows that there can never be absolute objectivity from a human standpoint. The second is a turn to social situation, which focuses on the aim of doing theology. On this view, a social context is not only the setting for doing theology but also becomes the objective for doing theology. As such, the goal of theology is to transform society by addressing its ills.[1] Thus social context raises questions, the answers of which lead to praxis for the transformation of the social context. The third is a turn to cultural identity, where cultural contexts provide indigenous resources for doing theology. Thus a theology is contextual if it answers the questions posed by the context, and if it also uses indigenous resources and vernacular categories.

[1] Kevin Vanhoozer, "One Rule to Rule Them All? Theological Method in an Era of World Christianity," in *Globalizing Theology: Belief and Practice in an Era of World Christianity*, ed. Craig Ott and Herold Netland (Grand Rapids, MI: Baker Academic, 2006), 92-99.

Evangelicals are making good progress with the first two hermeneutical turns to context. In the past decade or so, we have been much more aware of the interpretive turn to social location. In 2008, the Theological Commission of the World Evangelical Alliance commissioned a study unit on contextualization. What perhaps distinguishes this group from past efforts made by evangelicals is that the study unit approached contextualization "aware of but not intimidated by postmodern and global challenges."[2] Likewise, mobilization by groups such as the Micah Network has shown a relatively recent push for integral mission among evangelicals in the global context. This is a definitive turn to social situation. We now pay more attention to the injustices in Latin America, the poverty of Africa, and the human trafficking in Asia, and we may look to the Scripture's prophetic voice to speak into these problems of our social situations.

However, it is the third hermeneutical turn, to the interpreter's context, that evangelicals tend to overlook. This turn to cultural identity, if done well, would unlock the full potential of contextualization and aid our understanding of Scripture. But the success of taking such a turn must be measured by how well we use these resources without being held captive by them.[3] As a way forward, I propose that we look at attempts by four Asian theologians in their use of indigenous resources for the reformulations of the doctrine of the Trinity: Raimundo Panikkar's cosmotheandrism, Jung Young Lee's yin-yang, Brahmabandhab Upadhyaya's *saccidananda*, and

Nozomu Miyahira's betweenness-concord. I will point out specific elements in these proposals that substantiate their hermeneutical methods and will then evaluate the legitimacy of these proposals in light of an evangelical framework.[4]

SOME REFORMULATIONS OF THE TRINITY IN ASIA

Raimundo Panikkar (India). Raimundo Panikkar has a Spanish Roman Catholic mother and a Hindu father. He became a Catholic priest and a renowned theologian. Panikkar is a self-proclaimed pluralist who dialogued with the likes of John Hick. He desires to see peaceful coexistence and dialogue between major world religions, an intention and effort that should be commended in an age when religious violence permeates much of our world, and especially in the multireligious Asia.

In the larger picture, Panikkar looks to the doctrine of the Trinity to advance his pluralistic agenda, seeing the mystery of the Trinity as "the ultimate foundation for pluralism."[5] Vanhoozer explains this connection by distinguishing Panikkar's pluralism from "unitive" ones. He appraises Panikkar's work, saying,

> Panikkar wishes to make a suprarational "cosmic confidence in reality," rather than a universal theory of religions, the basis for interreligious conversation and cooperation. Each concrete religion offers only a perspective, a window to the whole. . . . The very incommensurability of the religions is the condition for a kind of trinitarian perichoresis in which each religion is a dimension

---

[2]Cited from Kevin Vanhoozer's recommendation on the back cover of *Local Theology for the Global Church: Principles for an Evangelical Approach of Contextualization*, ed. Matthew Cook, Rob Haskell, Ruth Julian, and Natee Tanchanpongs (Pasadena, CA: William Carey, 2010).

[3]Natee Tanchanpongs, "Developing a Palate for Authentic Theology," in Cook, Haskell, Julian, and Tanchanpongs, *Local Theology for the Global Church*, 109-23.

[4]This framework will be referred to as the context-to-text model, which I will elaborate below.

[5]Raimundo Panikkar, "The Jordan, the Tiber and the Ganges," in *The Myth of Christian Uniqueness: Toward a Pluralistic Theology of Religions*, ed. John Hick and Paul F. Knitter (Maryknoll, NY: Orbis, 1987), 110. Elsewhere Panikkar makes this even more explicit. See Panikkar, *The Trinity and World Religions: Icon-Person-Mystery* (Madras: Christian Literature Society, 1970), 42.

of the other, since each represents the whole of the human experience in a concrete way.[6]

This view of a "suprarational cosmic reality" is Panikkar's trinitarian reformulation, which he calls cosmotheandrism.

While at first glance it may appear that Panikkar draws on the Christian doctrine of the Trinity to help structure religious dialogues and a theology of religions, a closer study shows the contrary. Rather than applying Christian beliefs about the Trinity to a multireligious context, Panikkar uses his multireligious context to reshape traditional understandings of the Trinity. He begins building his trinitarian proposal on *advaitic* (nondualistic) Hinduism, saying that the Father and the Son are neither separate nor one in the same.[7] This neither-nor logic opens up the possibility of moving into a region of the "excluded middle," where the law of noncontradiction does not apply.

Cosmotheandrism involves the confluence of the *cosmos*, *theos*, and *andros*, which forms "the three irreducible dimensions which constitute the real."[8] There is a kind of perichoresis, "indwelling within one another," of these three dimensions of reality.[9] As a result, he sees cosmotheandrism as a trinitarian metaphysics and "the acme of a truth that permeates all realms of being and consciousness."[10] For Christians, this truth is the Trinity. Yet there also exists a generic trinitarian substructure in all other religions. Panikkar is convinced that this substructure is the foundational *oikoumenē* of the world faiths.

Cosmotheandrism functions as a metaphysics that enables Panikkar to realize his pluralistic vision of reality. But as he moves toward his pluralism, Panikkar must radically alter the traditional understanding of the Trinity. In the end, Panikkar's Trinity is neither three nor one—because his "trinity" is really just the Son, and because it constitutes three independent (though interpenetrating) entities: *cosmos*, *theos*, and *andros*.

Jung Young Lee (Korea). Jung Young Lee, a first-generation Korean American, asks, How can God be both one and three at the same time? The problem, according to Lee, is found in the Western tendency to think solely in either-or terms. As such, Lee suggests that we utilize the rich indigenous resources of Asia, specifically the yin-yang framework, to help explicate the doctrine of the Trinity.

There are four main characteristics of Lee's yin-yang logic. First, yin-yang is symbolic thinking. Like Panikkar, Lee suggests that God is unknowable. While Panikkar equates the Father with silence, Lee borrows from the *Tao Te Ching*, which says that "those who know about God do not speak and those who speak about God do not really know him." With this, Lee makes a clear Kantian move to introduce his symbolic thinking: "We must recognize . . . that everything we say or attempt to say about God is not about God himself but about our perception of God through the symbols or images that are meaningful within the limits of our own

---

[6]Kevin Vanhoozer, "Does the Trinity Belong in a Theology of Religions?," in *The Trinity in a Pluralistic Age: Theological Essays on Culture and Religion*, ed. Kevin Vanhoozer (Grand Rapids, MI: Eerdmans, 1997), 58.

[7]Panikkar, *Trinity and World Religions*, 61.

[8]Raimundo Panikkar, *The Cosmotheandric Experience: Emerging Religious Consciousness* (Maryknoll, NY: Orbis, 1993), ix. For further discussion on this, see Jyri Komulainen, *An Emerging Cosmotheandric Religion? Raimon Panikkar's Pluralistic Theology of Religions*, Studies in Christian Mission 30 (Boston: Brill, 2005), 188.

[9]Raimundo Panikkar, "The Myth of Pluralism: The Tower of Babel—A Meditation on Non-violence," *Cross Current* 29, no. 2 (1979): 214.

[10]Raimundo Panikkar, *The Trinity and the Religious Experience of Man* (Maryknoll, NY: Orbis, 1973), xi.

existence in time and space."[11] Lee admits that the Trinity is a symbol that points to God, but prefers to describe the Godhead through the East Asian framework of yin-yang.

Second, yin-yang is based on a both/and logic. Lee maintains that he is not trying to replace either/or reasoning but proposes that we use both/and as a background framework that includes both both/and and either/or structures, thus making yin-yang a more holistic and inclusive approach to the knowledge of God.[12]

According to Lee, relationality is the third characteristic of yin-yang. He posits that "relationship is *a priori* to an entity," in that a given relationship determines what is yin and what is yang. As such, neither yin nor yang is fixed, because something or someone could be yin in one relationship and yang in another. Relativity is thus inevitable.[13]

Finally, change is the ultimate reality in yin-yang. In the end, yin-yang is not a symbol of the beings interacting as yin and yang, but a symbol of the change in their interactions. In other words, what is fundamental to yin-yang relationship is not the being but change. Lee borrows from the *I Ching* in referring to change as "the Great Ultimate," so that being is simply the manifestation of change. Hence, when Lee states that yin and yang are opposites but are united in the Great Ultimate, he is saying that the process of change can integrate elements that seem conflicting or even contradictory.[14]

What looks like a union of two entities in yin-yang construction, Lee insists, is really three.

The symbol of yin-yang should probably be understood as "yin in yang" and "yang in yin." Hence, Lee maintains,

> When two (or yin and yang) include and are included in each other, they create the trinitarian relationship. . . . This inclusiveness can be simply symbolized by the proposition [sic] "in," the inner connecting principle of yin and yang. . . . The Father and the Son are one in their "inness," but at the same time, they are three because "in" represents the Spirit, the inner connecting principle which cannot exist by itself.

He justifies creating threeness from duality through the *Tao Te Ching*, in which it is written, "The Tao gives birth to one. One gives birth to two. Two gives birth to three. Three gives birth to all things."[15]

With this East Asian metaphysical move, Lee claims that everything can be described in terms of yin-yang symbolism, and hence everything can be regarded as a trinitarian act. Furthermore, Lee correlates the biblical concept of the Trinity with what he calls the East Asian trinitarian notion, comprising heaven as Father, earth as Mother, and humanity as their children.[16]

Brahmabandhab Upadhyaya (India). Brahmabandhab Upadhyaya was a nineteenth-century Hindu convert to Christianity (1861–1907). As a Roman Catholic theologian who was fully committed to Thomism, Upadhyaya believed in the Christian gospel message while simultaneously subscribing to a form of natural theology that allowed him to find fragments of

---

[11]Jung Young Lee, *The Trinity in Asian Perspective* (Nashville: Abingdon, 1996), 50, 54.
[12]Lee, *Trinity in Asian Perspective*, 34-35.
[13]Lee, *Trinity in Asian Perspective*, 52-53.
[14]Lee, *Trinity in Asian Perspective*, 27. Lee's theology of change and process theology are similar, with two main differences. First, Lee's theology of change is cyclical, while process theology operates with a linear view. Second, process theology presupposes creativity, whereas Lee's does not (see Veli-Matti Kärkkäinen, *The Trinity: Global Perspectives* [Louisville: Westminster John Knox, 2007], 318).
[15]Lee, *Trinity in Asian Perspective*, 58, 62.
[16]Lee, *Trinity in Asian Perspective*, 52, 63.

divine truth in other religions.[17] These fragments of truth served as a *preparatio evangelica*, on which "the supernatural truths of scripture, which cannot be apprehended through reason, but received as revelation from God, should be grown."[18]

However, Upadhyaya was frustrated with the inability of Christianity to make headway in India, in part because many Western theological expressions were often incomprehensible to Indians. Hence, he spent his whole life looking to give Christianity local Indian understanding using the language and thought form of Hindu philosophies. Timothy Tennent praises Upadhyaya because he "earnestly sought to use the language of advaitic Hinduism as an interpretive bridge or hermeneutic whereby he might be able to better communicate Christianity to enquiring Hindus."[19] Upadhyaya believed he was simply doing with Hindu beliefs what Aquinas had done with Aristotelian philosophy.[20] When Christianity first met Hinduism, the Christians simply dismissed the *advaita* (nondual) Vedanta school of Hindu philosophy as a form of pantheism. On the contrary, Upadhyaya commended it as the highest point that human reason has attained in India, fit to be the starting point for his trinitarian reformulation.

Upadhyaya interacted with Sankara (788–820), the founder of the *advaita* Vedanta school, who posited that *Brahman* is the Ultimate Reality and therefore must be *asanga* ("Absolute") and *nirguna* ("Unrelated"). If this is so, Sankara reasoned, then the world cannot be real because there is no reality outside the Absolute (monistic nondualism). To safeguard the doctrine of aseity, Upadhyaya agreed with Sankara but resolved the monistic problem by making two distinctions: first, between what is necessary and what is contingent in the *Brahman*; and second, between the unchanging essence and the free action of *Brahman*'s attributes. As such, creation is not an intrinsic attribute of the divine nature, and it is not necessary to his nature to create because the *Brahman* is self-sufficiently related *within*.[21] Upadhyaya sums up, saying, "Thus God has an eternal, necessary relationship within himself; but all relationships outside of himself are not necessary, but contingent (*vyavaharika*)."[22] To make this statement, Upadhyaya identified the Trinity with the upanishadic doctrine of *Brahman* as *saccidananda* (*Sat-Cit-Ananda*).

Tennent states that in the later Upanishads, the *Brahman* is often described as *Sat* ("being" or "reality"), *Cit* ("intelligence" or "consciousness"), and *Ananda* ("bliss").[23] For Upadhyaya, strictly speaking only God can be called *Sat*. Only he has absolute, eternal, immutable, and infinite self-existence. All else has contingent existence, is limited in time and space, and is always bounded by change.[24] Consequently, God's *Sat* must imply *Cit*, or "knowledge." As true being, God must know himself, and his

---

[17] Timothy C. Tennent, *Building Christianity on Indian Foundations: The Legacy of Brahmabandhav Upadhyay* (Delhi: ISPCK, 2000), 12.

[18] Orville De Silva, "Upadhyaya, Brahmabandhab," in *Indian Christian Thinkers*, ed. Anand Amaladass (Chennai: Satya Nilayam, 2005), 262.

[19] Timothy C. Tennent, "Trinity and Saccidananda in the Writings of Brahmabandhav Upadhyaya," in *The Gospel Among Religions: Christian Ministry, Theology, and Spirituality in a Multifaith World*, ed. David Brockman and Ruben L. F. Habito (Maryknoll, NY: Orbis, 2010), 183.

[20] *Sophia Monthly* 4, no. 7 (July 1897): 8-9. (*Sophia* was a monthly Catholic journal between January 1894 and March 1899 and became a weekly publication between June 16 and December 8, 1900.)

[21] Tennent, *Building Christianity on Indian Foundations*, 123, 145, 219, 223. Upadhyaya believes the Vedantic philosophers realized that God cannot go outside himself to satisfy his infinite knowledge and bliss. But rather than seeing the intratrinitarian relationship, they either deny reality external to God or see reality as a part of God.

[22] *Sophia Monthly* 4, no. 8 (August 1897): 9.

[23] Many agree that *saccidananda* is the most complete description of the Brahman.

[24] Tennent, "Trinity and Saccidananda," 186, 188.

self-knowledge is expressed in an inward word or image. While our knowledge of ourselves is "accidental and transitory," God's self-knowledge is perfect. This perfect relationship is such that

> His eternal self-comprehension or word is to be conceived as identical with the divine nature and still as distinct from the Supreme Being in as far as he by comprehending himself generates His word. God, knowing himself by producing or generating His own image and word, is called Father; and God as known by himself by this inward generation of the word is called the Word or the Son.[25]

Finally, Upadhyaya identifies God the Spirit as *Ananda*, or bliss. According to him, this term implies that God, who self-exists, is "self-sufficient, self-satisfied and not dependent upon any relation which is not co-terminus with his substance," because that which is "obliged to form alliance with something other than its own self cannot be essentially happy."[26]

Nozomu Miyahira (Japan). Nozomu Miyahira wants the Scripture's understanding of the Trinity to be better understood by the Japanese. He sees the need to rearticulate the traditional Western "three persons in one substance" formulation in a vernacular category. Hence Miyahira suggests building a new formulation on the Japanese idea of "concord" and "betweenness," derived from the ancient rice-growing culture. According to him, the culture of the rice-growing community of Japan produced a way of life that centers on the concepts of *ningen* ("humanity") and *wa* ("concord"). Rice-growing agriculture at that time was labor intensive, requiring a high degree of cooperation. This setting, therefore, produced an ethos of solidarity and concord, which has become definitive in the Japanese understanding of humanity and community. In the historico-etymological study of the word *ningen*, Miyahira refers to Watsuji Tetsuro, who claims that in Japanese context, humans are viewed not just as individual beings but also as beings living "between" others. Thus "*ningen* can mean a human or humans in the community and these two aspects are united in the dialectic relation."[27]

Miyahira explains this further by citing Kimura Bin, who points out that "a self becomes aware of itself when it meets what is not itself." This reality shows up in the Japanese language. While Western languages tend to have only one first-person pronoun, Japanese has more than ten. According to him, this is because "in Japan the self is determined by its relationship with others and is sometimes absorbed into that relationship." Along the same line, according to Hamaguchi Eshun, in Japan "people are highly conscious of their situation or context, and within which they maintain an outside-in perspective."[28]

With this Japanese cultural background, Miyahira begins his reformulation of the Trinity as "three betweennesses and one concord." "Betweenness," as Miyahira presents it, is a specific kind of relationality. A typical theological discussion on relationality today tends to either talk about a general kind of relationality in the Trinity (e.g., "three persons in relation") or focus on relations between a given pair of the trinitarian members (e.g., Father-Son). Betweenness, however, always involves all three persons of the

[25]Tennent, "Trinity and Saccidananda," 186. According to Tennent, this is a summary of Upadhyaya's thought written by A. Heglin, SJ.
[26]*Sophia Weekly* n.s. 1 (September 1900); *Sophia Monthly* 5, no. 8 (August 1898): 119.
[27]Nozomu Miyahira. *Towards a Theology of the Concord of God: A Japanese Perspective on the Trinity* (Carlisle, UK: Paternoster, 2000), 112-15.
[28]Miyahira, *Towards a Theology*, 115, 117, 124.

Trinity. He gives an example of the betweenness that involves the Spirit between the Father and the Son. He writes, "[The] distinctiveness of the Holy Spirit—expressed in the notion of 'procession'—is contrasted with the relationship between the Father and the Son characterised by begetting."[29]

Therefore there are three betweennesses in the Trinity. The first is the Father having the differentiating function of sending the Son and the Holy Spirit, albeit in different ways. Here the Father is between the begotten and the processed. The second is the Son having the differentiating function of sending the Holy Spirit from the Father (Jn 15:26). Here the Son is between the processor and the processed. The third is the Holy Spirit having the differentiating function of life-giver (Lk 1:35; Jn 6:63). Here the Holy Spirit is between the begetter and the begotten.

ON EVALUATIVE CRITERIA FOR BIBLICAL AUTHENTICITY

We must now define criteria to assess these proposals for biblical authenticity. Elsewhere I have critiqued essentialist and structuralist approaches to identify syncretism.[30] Essentialist views focus on preserving the "essentials" of the gospel from being contaminated by cultural or religious contexts. Structuralist approaches define syncretism as a mixing of two or more systems, resulting in inappropriate adaptations, replacements of elements in one system by elements of another. I will not repeat my arguments in full here but will note that if we were to use the essentialist criterion, all four reformulations would be deemed syncretistic, because they have

altered, to some degree, an essential teaching of Christianity. And if we were to use the structuralist criterion, we could not tell which proposals were syncretistic, because the rules for "inappropriateness" are not spelled out.

Given these limitations, I want to propose what I have called above a context-to-text approach to guide our evaluation for biblical authenticity. A commitment to the primacy of the Bible and an affirmation of the turns to the interpreter's context can coexist only if there is a movement or transformation from context to the text. This model requires elements in the interpreter's context to be dynamic, nonnormative, and modifiable.

Furthermore, the context-to-text model parallels the reality of sanctification. In both cases, we always begin from "who we are." In sanctification, we progress in our holiness from who we are as sinners saved by grace. Likewise, our knowledge of Scripture is always mediated through who we are and the things that are already a part of us.[31] This "who we are" includes our indigenous cultural elements. We utilize cultural, religious, and other vernacular concepts embedded in the language as instruments for interacting with and discovering God's Word. In both cases, who we are is affected by sin and is in need of transformation. It is true that we *cannot be* who we are not, but because of sin we must also *become* who we are not. Thus who we are requires a transformation through the work of dual agency. On the one hand, only the Holy Spirit can sovereignly sanctify us toward holy living as marked out by Scripture, and only he can illuminate and

---

[29]Miyahira, *Towards a Theology*, 148.

[30]Tanchanpongs, "Developing a Palate."

[31]This is Michael Polanyi's theory of tacit knowledge. According to him, knowledge is tacit in that there is no direct link to reality through abstract contemplation, but knowledge is always mediated through the body and the things that are already a part of us. Polanyi was a Hungarian Jew who became a Roman Catholic. He had a PhD in physical chemistry but became interested in epistemology and the critique of science's modern positivism and objectivism.

transform our minds toward Scripture. On the other hand, we have a responsibility to appropriately direct our lives (Phil 2:12-13) and our theological works toward that holy living and holy message of Scripture respectively.

The context-to-text model for contextual theology and its connection with sanctification helps us set new criteria for assessing products of contextualization with regard to their biblical authenticity. In both we must ask similar evaluative questions. How do we know whether our life or our theological product displays biblical authenticity? Which directions do they traverse? Are they moving toward Scripture? In Romans 12:1-2, Paul urges Christians to be driven by God's mercy to holy living, and to do so by *moving away from* conformity to the pattern of this world and by *moving toward* God's good, pleasing, and perfect will. Thus, by linking the theological enterprise to sanctification, I propose two criteria for evaluating biblical authenticity.

First, the biblical authenticity of a Christian whose life remains unchanged and unaffected by the transforming power of the gospel must be questioned. A sanctified life is one that is not held captive by one's "who we are" but moves away from it. Therefore, there is no sanctification and no biblical faith if lives remain unchanged and unaffected by the gospel.[32] In the same way, syncretism occurs when a product of contextualization remains captive to a conceptual scheme. As such, there is no movement away from one's contextual framework. We must ask whether the Bible is transforming one's "who we are." A telltale sign of religious syncretism is when a Christian is identical with the society around them. Believers in Jesus Christ must always be reforming away from their sin-

afflicted contexts. Similarly, if contextual elements used in a theological formulation remain unchanged, we might suspect some religious syncretism has occurred.

Second, if the life of a Christian does not change *toward Scripture*, there is also no biblical authenticity. The presence of change in a believer alone does not guarantee biblical authenticity, for one could change toward something other than the Bible. Thus, a sanctifying life is one that continues to embody and move *toward Scripture*. Likewise, syncretism takes place when a theological process does not direct its product toward a proper end of Scripture. Thus, if the first criterion inspects the movement away from the context of the reader, the second checks whether the movement is toward the text of Scripture.

EVALUATION OF THE TRINITARIAN REFORMULATIONS

Panikkar's cosmotheandrism. Panikkar's cosmotheandrism is a clear case of syncretism. There is no significant context-to-text movement of which to speak. In the end, Panikkar is caught in a vicious cycle. His theological effort traverses from his pluralist assumptions to a pluralist metaphysics, which comes back to justify his pluralist agenda. His initial objective is a pluralistic vision, which aims to create a theology of religion valid for more than one religious tradition. In a sense, cosmotheandrism is only his proof text to bring about coexistence and dialogue between the major religions. There is no movement out of his pluralistic "who he is."

In order to maintain his pluralism, Panikkar's interaction with Scripture is only notional and idiosyncratic. His pluralistic assumption dictates the meaning of Scripture by weakening the

---

[32]This is precisely James's argument concerning authentic faith and works in James 2.

tie between Logos and the Spirit in order to "free" the Spirit to be present in other religions and to allow the experience of the reader to "have epistemological priority in the act of reading." As such, Panikkar dehistoricizes the Bible and advances a hermeneutic that gets beyond the texts in their historical contexts to the universal realm in order to relate to diverse particularities.[33] This process makes it more convenient to read the Bible through the lens of other religions.

Lee's yin-yang. Lee's work clearly shows his delight in being Asian, something to be commended in an age where many of us prefer imported products, imported fashions, and imported theologies. But as I read his work, there is a sense that Lee is more concerned about showcasing his culture than talking about the Trinity from a biblical perspective. Veli-Matti Kärkkäinen warns that Lee's proposal threatens to subsume the Trinity into an Asian framework by failing to be critical of his own context. Lee literally tries to force the three of the Trinity into the two of yin-yang. Kärkkäinen calls attention to the fact that "the symbolism of yin-yang—at least at the outset—represents a binitarian rather than Trinitarian structure."[34]

There are many instances where traditional Christian doctrines are being reenvisioned, reinterpreted, and restated. For example, Lee affirms unflinchingly the historical heresy of patripassianism. Lee explains, "Death and resurrection are trinitarian acts because Christ was not only the Son but also the trinitarian God. The death of Jesus on the cross was the death of the Father, who was united with the Son in the Spirit. If the death of the Son was also the death of the trinitarian God, it was also the death of the Spirit as well."[35]

Kärkkäinen continues to point out more unorthodox elements in Lee's proposal. For Lee, the Spirit is both personal and impersonal. Lee justifies this conclusion from a word study of *ruach*, as "wind" (the impersonal aspect) and "breath" (the personal aspect).[36] As such, Lee identifies the Spirit with *ch'i*, which is the vital, creative energy, "mother earth," and the essence of life and all existence.[37] At this point Lee exposes his pantheistic stance, saying, "Because of the Spirit as ch'i, everything that exists is creative and alive. It is, therefore, impossible to separate spirit from matter. In other words, spirit is inseparable from matter, for they are essentially one but have two modes of existence. Because they are inseparable, thinking of matter alone without spirit or spirit alone without matter is illusory." There are many more examples of Lee's subsuming elements of trinitarian doctrine under the East Asian concept of yin-yang, such as the puzzling idea that Jesus is both male and female, the contradictory notion that God is both personal and impersonal, and the process-theological idea that the incarnation is the perfect expression of change.[38] At root is Lee's handling of Scripture. He reinterprets many biblical passages through allegories and various symbol, word, and number games.

---

[33]Vinoth Ramachandra, *The Recovery of Mission: Beyond the Pluralist Paradigm* (Grand Rapids, MI: Eerdmans, 1996), 99.

[34]Kärkkäinen, *Trinity*, 331-32.

[35]Lee, *Trinity in Asian Perspective*, 82, 91-94. Kärkkäinen sums up Lee's heterodox teaching by saying, "The mutuality and interdependency of [yin-yang] symbolism excludes the idea of the immunity of one member of the Trinity (Father) to the experiences of the other (Son). Therefore, Lee is not critical of patripassianism, the idea of God suffering, which was deemed heretical." Kärkkäinen, *Trinity*, 325.

[36]Lee, *Trinity in Asian Perspective*, 96-97.

[37]Kärkkäinen, *Trinity*, 326.

[38]Lee, *Trinity in Asian Perspective*, 71, 78-82, 98; Kärkkäinen, *Trinity*, 319.

For example, concerning the Holy Spirit in the birth narrative of Luke 1, Lee suggests that the conception of Jesus involves two powers—the Holy Spirit and the Most High—and goes on to say that "the familial symbols of the Trinity are definitely established in this story: the Most High as the father, the Holy Spirit as the mother, and Jesus to be born as the son."[39]

Lee resorts to an allegorical reading of the manger as he tries to find support for his cosmo-anthropological view of yin-yang. Lee imagines on, saying, "Jesus in the manger does not belong to human society alone: He also belongs to the animal world of the cosmic order. . . . Thus, Jesus empties himself to fill the manger, and become the lowest form in order to unite both the human and animal worlds." For Lee, death is no longer the ultimate enemy, as Scripture strongly affirms, but it is an integral part of the dialectic of yin-yang.[40]

On the whole, Lee is less concerned about using yin-yang to help clarify and safeguard the integrity of the Bible than he is to use the Bible to proof text and preserve the meaning of yin-yang. Lee's trinitarian reformulation may be less radical than that of Panikkar, but they share similar traits. In their encounter with Scripture, they never move out of their context. For Panikkar, it is his pluralistic assumption that dictates his hermeneutics. For Lee, it is his East Asian yin-yang philosophy. Both theologians see their interpretive contexts as more fundamental, more vital, and they thus become the agendas that drive their reformulations of the doctrine. Both proposals have weak biblical foundations

and are radical revisions of theological tradition, with strong pluralistic orientation.[41]

***Upadhyaya's* saccidananda.** Panikkar's and Lee's proposals fail the epistemic dependency criterion, and their reformulations of the Trinity remain captive to their respective conceptual schemes. Upadhyaya also uses indigenous resources, yet he allows the "text" to transform them where necessary. Upadhyaya is selective about the concepts he employs. For instance, concerning the view of ultimate reality, there are two main schools of thought in Hinduism. *Advaita* Vedantism, a monistic nondualism, advances the view that the world is not real, because there is no reality outside the Brahman. Visistadvaita Vedantism, a form of pantheism, believes that the world is a part of the Brahman. Upadhyaya has to choose between these philosophical stances, neither of which meets the standard of Christian orthodoxy. All things considered, Upadhyaya sees pantheism as a more immediate threat.[42] In contrast, advaitism offers a view of God as the Absolute, something that resembles the doctrine of divine aseity in Thomism. As such, Upadhyaya opts for the *advaita* school as the starting point for his trinitarian reformulation.

Nevertheless, Upadhyaya must contend with the monistic nondualism. As we have seen earlier, Upadhyaya resolves this problem by first making distinctions in the Brahman between necessary and contingent and between unchanging essences and free attributes before he goes on to explicate the Brahman as *sat, cit,* and

[39]Lee, *Trinity in Asian Perspective*, 74.

[40]To this end, Lee writes, "From the cosmo-anthropological perspective, death is inseparable from life, just as life cannot exist independently from death. Life and death are neither enemies to each other nor independent, separable events." Lee, *Trinity in Asian Perspective*, 83.

[41]Robert Letham and Veli-Matti Kärkkäinen, "Trinity, Triune God," in *Global Dictionary of Theology*, ed. William A. Dyrness and Veli-Matti Kärkkäinen (Downers Grove, IL: IVP Academic, 2008), 911.

[42]Tennent, *Building Christianity on Indian Foundations*, 220-21.

ananda. In effect, Upadhyaya has masterfully used the power of discourse to transform the meaning of the Brahman, hence making a context-to-text movement.

Even with this masterpiece, there are two caveats. First, the Hindu philosophy Upadhyaya has chosen as a starting point does not represent the interpretive context of most Indians. He has engaged with intellectual Hindus to win them over to the Catholic faith using "rationalist theism" and has been sharply criticized for being "incomprehensible even to the most learned of Indians" and developing a theology "based on a misguided intellectualism."[43]

Beyond the choice of interpretive context, there is also a second problem: his immediate theological destination is also less than ideal. Upadhyaya, as an ardent Roman Catholic, is concerned about upholding the teachings of his church. Therefore in the best case, biblical integrity can be achieved inasmuch as Thomistic doctrines are biblical. Space does not allow us to elaborate further on this point. Suffice to say that this is a caution against primarily contextualizing a theological tradition as opposed to the Scripture itself.

Miyahira's betweenness and concord. Among the four reformulations, Miyahira's proposal is most promising in light of our context-to-text criteria. He effectively affirms this scheme when he says, "Culture informs us of the framework in which theology can be formed, but culture needs more than that, to be transformed by the exegesis of Scripture." For him, the adaptation of the gospel to a particular culture must be done in such a way as not to weaken the very same gospel.[44] Like Upadhyaya, Miyahira begins with his own cultural context and at once uses the linguistic power of discourse to transform and traverse the cultural elements toward the text.[45] But unlike Upadhyaya, his cultural elements are more colloquial, taken from the everyday experience of common people. And unlike Upadhyaya, Miyahira's immediate "text" is Scripture. In his reformulation of the doctrine, Miyahira directs his attention to the Gospel of John.

Miyahira juxtaposes the Japanese concept of betweenness with the book of John, observing a trinitarian relationship based on the divine internal testimony, that the Son stands in distinct betweenness of the two witness bearers, the Father and the Spirit. Similarly, he sees the concept of concord in John as the unifying relationship of the triune God, a relationship based on knowing, entrusting, and glorifying. First, the Son knows the Father because there is unity between them. No one is fit to be the eyewitness to the Father except the Son, who has close fellowship with the Father. Furthermore, the Father also knows the Son because there is mutual indwelling between the Father and the Son.[46]

Second, the knowing in the Trinity leads to mutual entrusting. In this, the Son does all the redemptive work that the Father entrusts to him. The Father also entrusts all things to the Son, such as authority over all people, authority to execute judgment, and authority to give eternal life, so that the Son may complete the Father's work.[47]

---

[43]Orville De Silva, "Upadhyaya, Brahmabandhab," in *Indian Christian Thinkers*, ed. Anand Amaladass (Chennai: Satya Nilayam, 2005), 262; Madhusudhan Rao, "Lessons from India: Brahmabandhab Upadhyaya and the Failure of Hindu Christianity," *International Journal of Frontier Mission* 18, no. 1 (Spring 2001): 197.
[44]Miyahira, *Towards a Theology*, 4, 177.
[45]An example critique of his own culture is found in Miyahira, *Towards a Theology*, 201.
[46]Miyahira, *Towards a Theology*, 177-79.
[47]Miyahira, *Towards a Theology*, 179-80.

Third, the entrusting relationship leads to glorification by mutual manifesting and honoring. Jesus glorifies the Father by manifesting the Father in his earthly work by fulfilling it, and Jesus honors the Father by doing this work "in absolute obedience to the Father's will." This mutual glorification on earth is rooted in the eternal mutual glorification of the Trinity.[48]

Miyahira explains that this three-pronged unifying concord is motivated by divine eternal love, saying, "The 'concord' as found in the active knowing, entrusting and glorifying is inseparably intertwined with the mutual love between the Father and the Son."[49]

What about the Holy Spirit? Miyahira admits that the Holy Spirit does not appear in John as much as the Father and the Son. Yet he points out that the Holy Spirit is called "another advocate," which connects him with the Son as an advocate. Specifically, Miyahira writes, "After the Son departs, the Holy Spirit as the witness to the Son will guide the disciples into all the truth by not speaking on his own, as the Son does nothing on his own, but speaking whatever he hears."[50] In this trinitarian mutuality, Miyahira argues, the Holy Spirit is also found in the knowing, entrusting, and glorifying relationship with the Father and the Son.

CONCLUSION

In this essay, I have tried to address both material and formal aspects of contextual theology. Materially, I have surveyed four Asian theologians' reformulations of the doctrine of the Trinity and evaluated them for biblical authenticity. On the one hand, Panikkar's cosmotheandrism and Lee's yin-yang have been found wanting. They are undeniably syncretistic because they encounter the problem of epistemic dependency; that is, the message of the Scripture has not been allowed to speak its prophetic voice into the cultures. On the other hand, Upadhyaya's *saccidananda* and Miyahira's betweenness-concord show more potential. They take cultural contexts seriously but at the same time only assign ministerial importance to interpretive contexts. While we cannot dismiss Upadhyaya for not having a high view of Scripture, his theological reformulation is immediately more concerned with preserving and communicating Thomistic doctrine. Miyahira, in contrast, is much more conscientious about engaging directly with the Scripture. In the end, both Upadhyaya and Miyahira can help guide us to increasingly use indigenous resources and vernacular categories in our theological enterprise.

Second, I have used the material aspects of this essay to suggest a way of doing theology in context. Evangelical contextual theology must consist of a movement from one's interpretive context toward the canonically anchored text. But how do we know that we are traversing rightly toward Scripture? In the end, biblical authenticity can be verified only in ongoing catholic dialogue. J. Nelson Jennings is right to say, "Even though there are trustworthy signposts, the path down which such ongoing contextualization processes should go is not a straightforward, given matter. Nor is there any guarantee that syncretism, or contextualization gone awry, will not occur."[51] As such, doing theology in context must be done with great care, which is the impetus for our need of each other in the catholic fellowship of the Word.

---

[48]Miyahira, *Towards a Theology*, 181.
[49]Miyahira, *Towards a Theology*, 182.
[50]Miyahira, *Towards a Theology*, 184.
[51]J. Nelson Jennings, "Suburban Evangelical Individualism: Syncretism or Contextualization?," in *Contextualization and Syncretism: Navigating Cultural Currents*, ed. Gailyn Van Rheenen (Pasadena, CA: William Carey Library, 2006), 175.

Further Reading

Kärkkäinen, Veli-Matti. *The Trinity: Global Perspectives*. Louisville: Westminster John Knox, 2007.

Lee, Jung Young. *The Trinity in Asian Perspective*. Nashville: Abingdon, 1996.

Miyahira, Nozomu. *Towards a Theology of the Concord of God: A Japanese Perspective on the Trinity*. Carlisle, UK: Paternoster, 2000.

Panikkar, Raimundo. *The Trinity and World Religions: Icon-Person-Mystery*. Madras: Christian Literature Society, 1970.

Tanchanpongs, Natee. "Developing a Palate for Authentic Theology." Pages 109-23 in *Local Theology for the Global Church: Principles for an Evangelical Approach of Contextualization*, edited by Matthew Cook, Rob Haskell, Ruth Julian, and Natee Tanchanpongs. Pasadena, CA: William Carey Library, 2010.

Tennent, Timothy C. *Building Christianity on Indian Foundations: The Legacy of Brahmabandhav Upadhyay*. Delhi: ISPCK, 2000.

MOTHERLINESS OF GOD

A SEARCH FOR MATERNAL ASPECTS IN PAUL'S THEOLOGY

Atsuhiro Asano

Not at all. What the Japanese of that time believed in was not our God. It was their own gods.

SHUSAKU ENDO, *SILENCE*

THE CREEDAL CONFESSIONS begin with "We believe in God the Father." The emphasis of the metaphor of *father* in negligence of *mother* sometimes delivers the wrong message that Christianity is patriarchal. Missionary work with such a message has hindered the furtherance of the gospel, especially in so-called maternal societies. Such societies expect the members to relate to others including gods in the way a mother relates to her children. Therefore, a god with paternal dealings is not enthusiastically welcome. Yet the hindrance is a chance to read the Bible with an ear more attentive to motherly voices in it. This author, who is located in a maternal society, reads the epistle to the Galatians, written by one often criticized as a chauvinist, to see whether the God of Christian Scripture is exclusively patriarchal. I contend that Paul reflects the motherliness of God in his vision for nurturing the community.

MATERNAL CULTURE AND A VIEW OF GOD

Silence and motherliness of God. In his historical novel *Silence*, Japanese Catholic author Shusaku Endo depicts the life of a Jesuit missionary, Sebastian Rodrigues, in the heat of the nationwide persecution against Christianity in the Edo era (1603–1867) of Japan. After some years of missionary work, Rodrigues is caught and imprisoned with his flock of believers. Ferreira, an ex-Catholic missionary now apostate, is brought in by the local officials to persuade Rodrigues to renounce his faith in order to save the lives of the Japanese believers who are being tortured in prison. Rodrigues claims that he cannot abandon his God, whose merciful hand is evident on the lives of the native believers. To this Ferreira replies that the people never once believed in the Christian God but sought in God someone else. Later, Rodrigues hears this someone else's voice in prison, revealing himself as Christ, who forgives and lives alongside even those who yield to pressure to deny him. Rodrigues finally announces his apostasy but with his fellow apostate believers secretly seeks after the newly found Christ, who reflects in himself someone other than "Father God."[1]

Endo elsewhere explains that this someone is "Mother God." He further elaborates that, under 250 years of strict prohibition of Christianity during the Edo era, those secret believers, called Sempuku—because after denying Christ they still went underground (*sempuku*) to preserve their faith and lives—were healed of the memory of their betrayal and nourished not by Father God, who is ready to condemn sins, but by Mother God, who is eager to embrace sinners with all their weaknesses. During this era, the victors of faith all died a martyr's death for their courageous confessions, while the apostates survived to preserve the Christian faith. But that faith sees in God a mother's unconditional acceptance of their failures.[2]

When Endo narrates Christian origins in other novels, he focuses on the humanity of Jesus to the exclusion of his divinity in order to focus the reader's attention on the impact of his human suffering on earth. In a similar literary strategy, Endo in *Silence* describes motherliness and fatherliness as almost antithetical to each other—either the paternal religion of Ferreira and of the rest of Western Christianity, or the maternal religion of Rodrigues and of the rest of the apostate believers—in order for the reader to be shocked by the absence of maternal aspects in current Christian theology. By his rhetorical skill of exaggeration, Endo is, so to speak, suggesting that theologians, including New Testament theologians, should examine closely whether Scripture reveals something motherly about the Christian God.[3]

Maternal longing and the discussion of God. Where did the longing for motherliness derive from? It is not simply a theological mutation among the community of the "losers" of faith. The longing is not unique to that historical group; it is the cultural ethos of maternal societies in general to desire motherly relatedness with others, including gods.[4] While in a patriarchal society the father has the authority and power (superego, to use the Freudian language) to regulate the conduct of the child (id) with clear rules and punishment (fear of castration), in a maternal society it is the mother's love of the erring child that brings about a reconciliation. In the latter, violence or confrontation is avoided, and peace and harmony are optimistically (or naively) expected within a society. Such a society, however, does not necessarily emphasize the importance of establishing one's individual selfhood. Thus, "my children are all good children" in the maternal society, while "only

---

[1]The ending of *Silence*, thus the aftermath of Rodrigues's apostasy, is sometimes mistaken. I agree with Kasai's interpretation in Akio Kasai, *Endo Shusaku Ron* [On Shusaku Endo] (Tokyo: Sobunsha, 1987), 153-55.

[2]Shusaku Endo, "Kami No Chinmoku To Ningen No Shogen" [God's silence and human testimony], *Fukuin To Sekai* [Gospel and the world] (September 1966); Endo, *Haha Naru Mono* [Motherliness] (Tokyo: Shincho, 1975), 55. For the history and the theology of the *Sempuku*, or underground communities, see Ann H. Harrington, *Japan's Hidden Christians* (Chicago: Loyola University Press, 1993); Endo et al., *Bosei To Seisei* [Motherliness and holiness] (Tokyo: Kyobunkwan, 1973), 170.

[3]Shusaku Endo, *A Life of Jesus*, trans. Richard A. Schuchert (New York: Paulist, 1978); Endo, *Kirisuto No Tanjo* [The birth of Christ] (Tokyo: Shincho, 1982); Endo, "Ihojin No Kuno" [Agony of Gentiles], in *Endo Shusaku Bungaku Zenshu* [All works of Shusaku Endo] (Tokyo: Shincho, 2000), vol. 13. Endo confesses in this essay that by writing *Silence* (with its emphasis on the motherly aspects of the Christian God) he felt that the gap between Christianity and himself was somewhat filled.

[4]For Japan as a maternal society, see Tomiko Yoda, "The Rise and Fall of Maternal Society: Gender, Labor, and Capital in Contemporary Japan," *South Atlantic Quarterly* 99, no. 4 (Fall 2000): 860-902.

good children are my children" in the patriarchal society.[5] Longing for such relatedness is reflected, for example, in the genesis mythology of the Japanese imperial history in Kojiki (Record of Ancient Things, compiled in AD 712), in which the female sun god, Amaterasu, is peacefully enthroned as the supreme god and relates with other deities as a mother in a sort of indulging way, unlike a typical kingdom myth in which a male god becomes a supreme being by winning the final victory after fierce battles.[6]

Is the maternal longing for God, then, to be regarded as a form of syncretism, as Ferreira of *Silence* condemns the Japanese faith in Christ as "not our God"? Such a judgment seems to depend too much on a patriarchal worldview. With only this view at hand, one may not be able to appreciate fully the riches of who God is. Though the longing for motherliness might be somewhat inflated in the maternal society, that excessive sensitivity may help to point out possible neglected aspects of God in the traditional theological discussion.[7] Indeed, a review of theological textbooks reveals that the parental image of God's relatedness to humans is focused solely on the designation of God as Father.[8] It seems, then, appropriate to be attentive to the evaluation of feminist exegetes in Western societies that motherly aspects are largely neglected in the traditional discussion of God.[9] Indeed, renowned feminist author Ursula Le Guin proposes that the language that embodies motherly relatedness ("mother tongue") be given rightful place alongside "father tongue" in order to attain the sound human communicative experience ("native tongue").[10] The present cultural reading overlaps greatly with the feminist reading, while the latter is primarily concerned with gender, and the former with relatedness.

It is not the intention of this chapter to merely add some presumably positive feminine features to the masculine deity in order to make "him" appear a tenderer and warmer father. Elizabeth Johnson, a prominent feminist theologian,

---

[5]Hayao Kawai and Osamu Fujita, *Do Kangaeru Ka—Haha Naru Mono* [How do we think of motherliness?] (Tokyo: Nigensha, 1977), 164-68. K. Tsuruta, a literary critic, says that while Western novels generally depict the growth of the main character, such a bildungsroman is rare in Japanese novels. Rather, a Japanese hero or heroine often goes on a journey to regress or return to the mother's womb on the way. Kinya Tsuruta, *Haha Naru Mono To Sei Naru Mono* [Motherliness and holiness] (Tokyo: Meiji Shoin, 1986), 3-4.

[6]For example, Zeus against Cronus and Titan in the Greek mythology, and Marduk against Tiamat in the Babylonian mythology. On Amaterasu, see O-no-Yasumaro, *Kojiki* [Record of ancient things], trans. Donald L. Philippi (Tokyo: University of Tokyo Press, 1968).

[7]Takeo Doi explains that the Japanese way of relatedness with others may reflect the pathological overdependence on their parents, in this case especially on their mothers. Doi, *The Anatomy of Dependence*, trans. John Bester (Tokyo: Kodansha, 1973).

[8]Ladd focuses solely on the fatherly relatedness of God in the discussion of theology proper in the Synoptic Gospels. George E. Ladd, *A Theology of the New Testament*, rev. ed. (Grand Rapids, MI: Eerdmans, 1993), 82-85. Erickson refers to the parental metaphor of father in his discussion of the trinitarian confession. Millard J. Erickson, *Christian Theology* (Grand Rapids, MI: Baker, 1983). The one-sided description of the parental metaphor for God is never questioned but rather assumed. Leon Morris, *New Testament Theology* (Grand Rapids, MI: Zondervan, 1986), 248-55. Gaventa points out that the traditional systematic theological discussion largely neglects the implication in Paul's gospel for the lives of women. She takes the example of James D. G. Dunn's New Testament theology. Beverly R. Gaventa, "Is Galatians Just a 'Guy Thing'? A Theological Reflection," *Interpretation* 54 (2000): 267-78, here 269. See James D. G. Dunn, *The Theology of Paul the Apostle* (Grand Rapids, MI: Eerdmans, 1998). While the yearning of motherliness may be more evident in maternal societies, it is to some degree universally felt. It has been suggested by such prominent psychoanalysts as Sigmund Freud and Carl Jung that humans develop their self-understanding and relatedness to others at least partly in the relation to their mothers. Sigmund Freud, *On Sexuality: Three Essays on the Theory of Sexuality and Other Works*, trans. James Strachey (London: Penguin, 1991); Carl G. Jung, *Four Archetypes: Mother, Rebirth, Spirit, Trickster* (London: Ark, 1972). Kawai, a Jungian psychoanalyst, explains that the presence of Great Mother is so strong in maternal societies that it is almost impossible for a child to confront the swallowing mother, let alone to kill her. H. Kawai, *Muishiki No Kozo* [Structure of unconsciousness] (Tokyo: Chuko Shinsho, 1977), 90-91.

[9]Phyllis Trible, "Feminist Hermeneutics and Biblical Studies," *Christian Century* (1982): 116.

[10]Ursula Le Guin, *Dancing at the Edge of the World: Thoughts on Words, Women, Places* (New York: Grove, 1989), 147-60. The power of mother tongue in comparison with father tongue, according to Le Guin, "is not in dividing but in binding, not in distancing but in uniting" (149). Eastman uses Le Guin's concept to interpret Paul in Galatians. Suzan Eastman, *Recovering Paul's Mother Tongue* (Grand Rapids, MI: Eerdmans, 2007).

criticizes some gender-sensitive readings of Scripture that attempt to discover feminine traits of God in the biblical texts but only result in affirming traditional androcentric theology.[11] The present search for motherliness is rather to show that the biblical writers are aware that both paternal metaphors and maternal metaphors (including the very designations of father and mother) are requisite in directing the reader into the mystery of God. One should be aware that the biblical metaphors are significant but only partial and finite tools for describing and explaining the divine reality.[12] Therefore, God is like a father, but never equal to my biological father. One should note that the church decided to employ metaphors to compose the creedal confession, "We believe in God the Father . . ."[13] When Johnson suggests the feminist Trinity of Spirit-Sophia, Jesus-Sophia, and Mother-Sophia, she uses terms that are also metaphors. Each metaphor is partial and finite, never perfect and full. Only when proper metaphors are employed together may we come closer to experiencing the divine mystery.[14]

This essay may be able to contribute to our discussion of God by focusing on how God relates to humans in Scripture. *Motherliness* (as well as fatherliness), being an emotionally loaded word, is rather difficult to define. Some characteristic relational features of maternity are suggested in relation to those of paternity by psychoanalysts and comparative mythologists; for example, inclusion in relation to exclusion, embrace to separation, nourishment to discipline, sympathy to condemnation, and forgiveness to punishment.[15] These antitheses will be kept in mind as the analysis of the text is conducted in the following section. Incidentally, such binary descriptions in the feminist discussion—usually focusing on the character differences between femininity and masculinity—are sometimes considered to reflect a homosocial value judgment.[16] Sarah Coakley's point, therefore, seems appropriate when she surveys a variety of Enlightenment thinkers and criticizes their dualistic view of "domestic and irrational female vs. social and rational male," which affirms a traditional patriarchal social construct in which women, playing a submissive role under the authority of men, are deprived of equal human rights.[17]

Two points should be briefly noted. First, one wonders whether such ideas as inclusion, embrace, nourishment, sympathy, and forgiveness must necessarily be associated with domesticity, irrationality, and therefore submission. The former ideas may be liberated from such politically intentional languages as the latter, when one takes into consideration the aforementioned Amaterasu, the supreme goddess in Kojiki, who

---

[11] Elizabeth A. Johnson, *She Who Is: The Mystery of God in Feminist Theological Discourse* (New York: Crossroad, 1992), 48-49. She comments on such an attempt, saying, "Men gain their feminine side, but women do not gain their masculine side. The feminine is there for the enhancement of the male, but not vice-versa: there is no mutual gain."

[12] Paul Tillich, *Dynamics of Faith* (New York: Harper & Row, 1957), 41-48. See Paul Ricoeur, *The Rule of Metaphor: The Creation of Meaning in Language*, trans. R. Czerny, K. McLaughlin, and J. Costello (London: Routledge, 2003).

[13] See Sallie McFague, *Metaphorical Theology: Models of God in Religious Language* (Philadelphia: Fortress, 1982), 103-44. She comments, "Credal language is both deceptive and powerful; hence, the temptations to idolatry are strong. It is deceptive because it looks like literal language" (115). See also McFague, *Speaking in Parables: A Study in Metaphor and Theology* (Philadelphia: Fortress, 1975), 43-65.

[14] McFague, *Metaphorical Theology*, 115, 177.

[15] Kawai, *Muishiki no Kozo*; Atsuhiko Yoshida, *Nihon Shinwa No Shinso Shinri* [Depth psychology of Japanese mythology] (Tokyo: Yamato Shobo, 2012).

[16] Rosemary R. Ruether, *Sexism and God-Talk: Towards A Feminist Theology* (London: SCM Press, 1983), 111.

[17] Sarah Coakley, *Powers and Submissions: Spirituality, Philosophy and Gender*, Challenges in Contemporary Theology (Oxford: Blackwell, 2002), 89-97.

reigns over all gods and humans, yet as a mother is ready to include, embrace, nourish, sympathize, and forgive.[18] Second, when one exegetes a text, one should be aware that its meanings are conveyed through culturally and historically conditioned words. One's task is primarily not to make an ethical judgment of the culture in history, though it could well be done later. When the Scripture uses the metaphor of father and birthing to describe God, one must first of all ask what picture of God is conveyed with the paternal and maternal metaphors in the historical culture. Then the discussion as to whether those metaphors are appropriate for postmodern sensibilities can be meaningfully begun and maintained.[19] The present chapter is located well within the former process, but not in negligence of the latter discussion.

The present analysis focuses on Paul's letter to the Galatians. The reason for focusing on this text is that it is one of the earliest writings of the church and therefore naturally reflects its earliest understanding of God. Another reason is that Paul is popularly criticized as a chauvinist theologian who may consequently be expected to encourage a paternal understanding of God.[20] If, then, maternal aspects are found even in Paul's theology, maternal theology may be found not altogether foreign to the earliest thinkers and writers of the church.

MOTHERLINESS OF GOD IN GALATIANS

"Male and female" as the image of God (Galatians 3:28). The structure of Galatians 3–4 and the significance of the baptismal triple couplets. It is generally understood that Galatians 3–4 forms the theoretical core of the entire letter.[21] In this section of the letter, Paul repeatedly asks who the true heirs of Abraham are. In the traditional Jewish perspective, Paul's opponents contend that the true Abrahamic heirs are those circumcised under the law. The masculine initiatory rite of circumcision affirms the hierarchical institution based on the paternal genealogy—fathers begetting sons—in which people are ranked and excluded on account of various material differences. In refuting this patriarchal relatedness, Paul emphasizes faith in Christ as the one and only determining factor for inclusion in the Abrahamic family. If paternal relatedness is thus regulated in Galatians 3, it is understandable that the maternal language suddenly becomes conspicuous in Galatians 4 in order for Paul to keep the balance in his theological discussion.[22] Therefore, one encounters in the fourth chapter Jesus' mother (Gal 4:4), the

---

[18]Ruether's criticism of liberal feminism is therefore appreciated. However, her argument for women's rather than men's capacity for greater integration as a human seems to be somewhat doubtful and above all unnecessary in the nature and course of the discussion. Ruether, *Sexism and God-Talk*, 109-15.

[19]Should we replace parental metaphors altogether with the metaphor of friendship? See the discussion in McFague, *Metaphorical Theology*, 184-92. Parental metaphors have much to do with the family metaphor for the Christian community. Questioning the former metaphors may reduce the value of the latter metaphor. Should the value of the traditional institution of marriage be reevaluated?

[20]See J. R. Daniel Kirk, *Jesus Have I Loved, but Paul? A Narrative Approach to the Problem of Pauline Christianity* (Grand Rapids, MI: Baker Academic, 2011), 5. See also Gaventa, who attempts to read something more in Paul's letter to the Galatians, which seems to be a "guy thing." She shares her experience that "for many seminarians, pastors, and laypeople with whom I have talked, it is simply assumed that women will read Paul with suspicion, even with hostility." See Gaventa, "Is Pauline Theology Just a 'Guy Thing'?" chap. 5 in *Our Mother Saint Paul* (Louisville: Westminster John Knox, 2007), 63-75, here 65.

[21]Hans D. Betz, *Galatians*, Hermeneia (Philadelphia: Fortress, 1979), 128; F. F. Bruce, *The Epistle to the Galatians*, New International Greek Testament Commentary (Grand Rapids, MI: Eerdmans, 1982), 214; James D. G. Dunn, *The Epistle to the Galatians*, Black's New Testament Commentaries (Peabody, MA: Hendrickson, 1993), 243.

[22]Brigitte Kahl, "No Longer Male: Masculinity Struggles Behind Galatians 3:28?," *Journal for the Study of the New Testament* 79 (2000): 41-43. In Kahl's expressions, Gal 3 is "decentering the male" and Gal 4 is "recentering the female." It may be that in the expression "male and female" in Gal 3:28 Paul is envisioning some sort of convergence of paternity and maternity.

story of Sarah and Hagar as mothers (Gal 4:21-31), and Paul as a mother in birth pain (Gal 4:19).[23] Thus paternal relatedness of differentiation and exclusion is counterbalanced by maternal relatedness of unification and inclusion.[24]

In the climax of Paul's presentation of antiphallocratic salvation history stands the emancipatory announcement: "There is no longer Jew or Greek, there is no longer slave or free, there is no longer male and female" (Gal 3:28).[25] With the background of the ethnic identity issue in Galatians 2—whether one needs to be a Jew to belong to the church—the first ethnic couplet of "Jew or Greek" is usually considered to be Paul's primary concern among the three couplets.[26] However, if Paul's salvation history is viewed as a critique of the excessive emphasis on the paternal relatedness that privileges Jewish male masters over against others, then the erasure of difference in all of the three couplets should be regarded as significant: Paul realizes the fullness of humanity and riches of relatedness among such humans in the community in Christ. Therefore, in this triple-couplet baptismal formula Paul is envisioning the communal experience of original humanity—"in Christ you are all children of God through faith" (Gal 3:26)—especially for the marginalized members of the community.[27] While the eradication of all three levels of difference is equally important in the community, Paul may have seen the couplet of "male and female" as outstanding because it directly points to the original state of humanity.

"Male and female" and the understanding of God. The third couplet, "male and female," clearly declares the eradication of gender difference. In Christ, there is no difference between male members and female members of the community, "for all of you are one [person] in Christ Jesus" (Gal 3:28). Behind such a relatedness lies a view of God reflected in the creation story.

Exegetes have suggested that Paul had in mind the creation narrative of Genesis as he penned the third couplet.[28] While the other couplets use the connective *nor*, the third couplet uses "and": "male *and* female [*arsen kai thēly*]," not "male *nor* female." It has been argued that Paul uses the irregular *and* as in "male and female" because he draws the expression directly from LXX Genesis 1:27, which says, "and God created humankind [*ton anthrōpon*], according to the image of God he created him, *male and female* [*arsen kai thēly*] he created them." In the Second Temple and rabbinic periods, the fact that Genesis has two accounts of the creation of humankind invited the speculation that original humanity ("heavenly man" in Gen 1) is androgynous, "male and female" at the same time (Philo, *On the Embassy to Gaius* 1.31-32; Megilla 9a; Genesis Rabbah 8:1, 17:6). Probably influenced by the androgynous union in the passage rite of the Greco-Oriental religions, Philo

---

[23]Kahl calls Gal 4 the "mother-chapter" of Paul. Kahl, "No Longer Male," 43.

[24]In the language of liminal theology, the former relatedness is "anti-liminal (= institutional and hierarchical)" while the latter relatedness is "liminal (= anti-institutional and egalitarian)." See Victor Turner, *The Ritual Process: Structure and Anti-structure* (New York: Cornell University Press, 1969); Christian Strecker, *Die liminale Theologie des Paulus: Zugänge zu paulinischen Theologie aus kulturanthropologischen Perspektive*, Forschungen zur Religion und Literatur des Alten und Neuen Testaments 185 (Göttingen: Vandenhoeck & Ruprecht, 1999).

[25]Unless otherwise noted, Scripture quotations in this chapter follow the NRSV.

[26]See Richard N. Longenecker, *Galatians*, Word Biblical Commentary 41 (Dallas: Word, 1990), 156-57.

[27]Atsuhiro Asano, *Community-Identity Construction in Galatians: Exegetical, Social-Anthropological and Socio-Historical Studies*, Journal for the Study of the New Testament Supplement Series 285 (London: T&T Clark, 2005), 187-206.

[28]There is a possibility that Paul is quoting a baptismal saying formed before him among the early believers. Elisabeth Schüssler Fiorenza, *In Memory of Her: A Feminist Theological Reconstruction of Christian Origins* (London: SCM Press, 1983), 209. However, it is possible that it was formulated by Paul and taught among the believers in his first visit to Galatia.

thought that the "earthly man" (Gen 2) will be transformed and return to the androgynous image of God (*Questions and Answers in Genesis* 1.25; see *On the Contemplative Life* 63).[29] Even though Paul himself may not have taught that the image of God was androgynous, his audience was most probably aware of such a worldview in their Greco-Oriental background.[30] Then, "male and female" as the original humanity in the image of God may have been a quite helpful locution to express the vision of the perfect union and equality among the Pauline churches.

The book of Genesis, after narrating the actual creation of the universe, discloses the divine identity as early as in Genesis 1:27. In the Hebrew Bible more than in the LXX, the chiasmic construction emphasizes that the divine image is revealed in the creation of humankind. It is significant that at the very beginning of Scripture the image of God is revealed in terms of male and female. In the phrase "God created humankind in his image," the object of creation is "the Adam [*h'dm*]" (*ton anthrōpon*). The articular noun—Adam with a definite article—suggests that it is not an individual Adam but humankind in general.[31] God's creation of humankind in its wholeness of male and female reflects the image of the Creator. In other words, both the masculine imagery and the feminine imagery need to be employed in the expression of God in order for humans to begin embracing a sound view of God. Since God is the creative source of humankind, as well as the rest of creation, metaphors of both father and mother can be properly

applied to the deity. A lack of awareness of the maternal imagery along with excessive emphasis on the paternal imagery fails to present the fuller picture of who he is. In establishing his community and presenting the new salvation history, for example in Paul's ecclesiology and soteriology, a more holistic view of God is reflected.

Motherliness in the God of Israel. The theology behind Paul's vision of a full and rich union of believers in his community prompts him to describe God with maternal imagery found in the Hebrew Bible. Therefore, "womb [*rḥm*]" is often the physical locus in which God's will is revealed (Sarah in Gen 20:1-18; Leah in Gen 29:31-35; Hannah in 1 Sam 1:1-20). The same Hebrew radical (*rḥm*) in plural form denotes "mercy" or "compassion." Rachel's mourning over the lost fruit of her womb (Ephraim) is met by God's mercy through the child in the divine womb (Jer 31:15-23).[32] "Therefore, my inner parts / womb [*m'h*] trembles for him, I will truly show motherly compassion [*rḥm*] upon him" (Jer 31:20). God's merciful dealing and saving grace is very closely related to the image of a mother giving birth to a child and breastfeeding the child (Ps 22:9-10; Is 46:3-4). Divine mercy is expressed in motherly terms. God indeed says, "I will cry out like a woman in labor, I will gasp and pant" (Is 42:14). When Trible claims that "relinquishing life for the sake of life is the last act of the uterus," the quintessential maternal act almost forecasts the act of Christ on the cross to embrace the sinful children and to writhe for them by bearing upon himself their sins.[33] Then

[29]See Wayne A. Meeks, "The Image of the Androgyne: Some Uses of a Symbol in Earliest Christianity," *History of Religions* 13 (1973–1974): 165-208.
[30]Dennis R. MacDonald, *There Is No Male and Female: The Fate of a Dominical Saying in Paul and Gnosticism* (Philadelphia: Fortress, 1987), 63. Schüssler Fiorenza understands that "male and female" implies the patriarchal marriage system and that Paul is saying that such a system is no longer constitutive in the new community. *In Memory of Her*, 211.
[31]Gordon J. Wenham, *Genesis 1–15*, Word Biblical Commentary 1 (Dallas: Word, 1987), 32-33.
[32]Phyllis Trible, *God and the Rhetoric of Sexuality*, Overtures to Biblical Theology (Philadelphia: Fortress, 1979), 45.
[33]Trible, *God and the Rhetoric of Sexuality*, 37.

what one finds on the face of Christ is not, or at least not only, the paternity of God that defines and concretizes sin on the cross for condemnation, but the maternal body of God that internalizes the sin of humanity and groans with it.[34] Indeed, in 2 Corinthians 5:21, where Paul says, "he made him to be sin who knew no sin," attention tends to be directed to the paternity defining sin, yet in the act of imbuement of sin the maternity embracing sin may well be implied.[35] Probably the most direct and impressive connection of God and mother is found in Deuteronomy 32:18, "You were unmindful of the Rock that begot you, and you forgot the God who writhed in childbirth." Paul may have had this image in mind when he reminded the Galatians how he was relating to them.

Imitation of the writhing God (Galatians 4:19). Paul's motherly labor. At the conclusion of probably the most emotional section of the letter (Gal 4:12-20) comes a surprising expression of Paul's relatedness to the Galatians: "My little children, for whom I am writhing again in childbirth [*ōdinō*] until Christ is formed in you" (Gal 4:19). The appearance of the maternal expression is startling in two ways. First, the imagery concerning children and maturity in the early part of the chapter (Gal 4:1-3) is now chronologically upset by the imagery of the pain of childbirth that naturally foregoes maturity.[36] Second and more importantly, Paul elsewhere explicitly describes his role in relation to his community members as a father, in the sense of spiritually begetting believers in Christ in his mission and developing them. Therefore, "in Christ Jesus I became your father through the gospel" (1 Cor 4:15), and "we deal with each one of you like a father with his children" (1 Thess 2:11; see also Philem 10). We should note, however, that in 1 Thessalonians Paul balances his role as a father with that of a mother, so in the immediately preceding section he says, "We were gentle among you, like a [nursing] mother [*trophos*] tenderly caring for her own children" (1 Thess 2:7).[37]

A maternal self-designation by Paul is not, therefore, absent in the rest of the Pauline letters. However, his use of the word *ōdinō*, and the vivid image of motherhood it implies, is impressive. Paul elsewhere uses the word only twice for the cosmic turbulence in the eschatological context (Rom 8:22; 1 Thess 5:3). The extraordinary word choice—reflecting something physically impossible for Paul—is highly intentional and possibly conditions the reader to read the whole pericope as if it were written by their mother. Though the pericope is often thought of as an interruption in the flow of argument in Galatians 3–4, it could be

---

[34]Keigo Okonogi, *Nihon-Jin no Ajase Konpurekusu* [Japanese Ajase Complex] (Tokyo: Chuo Koron, 1982), 30; Endo, "Kami No Chinmoku To Ningen No Shogen."

[35]Paul, in this verse, may primarily have had the picture of a scapegoat taking on the sin (curse) of the people of Israel in the expulsion rite (Lev 16:20-22; see Gal 3:13). The passive acceptance of the scapegoat (or *pharmakos* in the corresponding Hellenistic rites) may be a helpful metaphor to remind us of the maternity of God.

[36]Dunn, *Galatians*, 240. Commentators generally find the expression to be surprising in the letter as well as in the rest of Paul's letters. Ernest De Witt Burton, *The Epistle to the Galatians*, ICC (Edinburgh: T&T Clark, 1921), 248; J. Louis Martyn, *Galatians*, ABC 33A (New York: Doubleday, 1997), 424.

[37]The word *trophos* is elsewhere translated as "nurse" (see NRSV or Abraham J. Malherbe, *The Letters to the Thessalonians*, Anchor Bible Commentary 32B [New York: Doubleday, 2000], 146), or "wet nurse," in Gene L. Green, *The Letters to the Thessalonians*, Pillar New Testament Commentary (Grand Rapids, MI: Eerdmans, 2002). However, it could well be "nursing mother" or even "mother." Charles A. Wanamaker, *The Epistles to the Thessalonians*, New International Greek Testament Commentary (Grand Rapids, MI: Eerdmans, 1990), 100. See also Walter Bauer et al., *A Greek-English Lexicon of the New Testament and Other Early Christian Literature*, 2nd ed. (Chicago: University of Chicago Press, 1979), 827-28.

explained as Paul's creative rhetoric to appeal to the pathos of the readers.[38]

Ōdinō means "to experience pain and anguish through childbirth," and the noun form ōdin means "birth pang" (Is 23:4; 26:17-18; 45:10; 51:2; 54:1; 66:7-8; Jer 4:31; 30:6; Mic 4:10). "Behold, she suffered birth pain [ōdinēsen] for unrighteousness, she seized pain and gave birth [eteken] to lawlessness" (Ps 7:14). Here, the psalmist uses two verbs (ōdinō and tiktō) to describe childbirth, but the former especially focuses on the suffering of a mother in the action of childbirth. Therefore, the suffering of the day of the Lord before the messianic age is described by the metaphor of ōdinō/ōdin (1 Enoch 62.4; 4 Esdras 4.42). In the Gospels, as well as the Pauline texts referred to above, the term is used in the context of apocalyptic suffering before the new heaven and earth are given birth. "There will be earthquakes in various places; there will be famines. These are the beginning of the birth pangs [ōdinōn]" (Mk 13:8; see Mt 24:8). The end-time suffering, intensified by the metaphor of birth pain, enhances by comparison the salvific jubilance that follows.[39] Therefore, Beverly Gaventa understands Paul's use of ōdinō in Galatians 4:19 in the apocalyptic sense, that is, Paul's missionary "labor" among the Galatians points to the suffering of this age awaiting the fulfillment of salvation in Christ.[40] Considering that Galatians is probably the most apocalyptic of Paul's letters (given the revelation of God's Son in Paul [Gal 1:15-16] and among the Gala-

tians [Gal 3:1-5]), the present pericope and especially Galatians 4:19 could well be considered to reflect Paul's eschatology. If Paul's mimesis of the suffering Christ—Paul suffers as Christ suffers for salvation—is expressed in the apocalyptic language of ōdinō, the relationship of his Christology and his eschatology—Christ suffers as the earth suffers before the joy of salvation—may be glimpsed in this verse. Furthermore, behind these thoughts may lie the view of a God who suffers for his people.[41]

Isaiah 45:10 describes God as a mother suffering pain in giving birth to his people Israel: "The one saying to the father 'what will you give birth to?' or to the mother 'what will you suffer birth pain [ōdinēseis] for?'" Here, the creation of Israel is in focus, as there were people who doubted their divine origin. Louis Martyn finds this verse in Isaiah to be behind Paul's expression in Galatians 4:19.[42] However, probably closer to the context of Paul's missionary suffering is the Song of Moses in Deuteronomy 32:1-43, in which God is described as writhing in birth pain (Deut 32:18) for wayward Israel. Curiously, the LXX translates this verse rather freely, though retaining the maternal features of God. "You forsook God giving birth to you, and forgot God feeding [trephontos] you." Yet the Masoretic Text has it as "You were unmindful of the Rock that begot you [yld], and you forgot the God who writhed in childbirth [ḥûl]." Ḥûl means "to writhe," especially in the pain of childbirth (Is 26:17; 45:10); therefore, the Greek term ōdinō is

[38]Eastman sees the larger pericope of Gal 4:12–5:1 as written in the "mother tongue" to make the bridge between the preceding theoretical section and the following paraenetic section. Eastman, Recovering Paul's Mother Tongue. On this pericope being an interruption, see Burton, Galatians, 236; Franz Mußner, Der Galaterbrief, Herders theologischer Kommentar zum Neuen Testament 9 (Freiburg: Herder, 1981), 304.
[39]Georg Bertram, "ōdin/ōdinō," in Theological Dictionary of the New Testament, ed. Gerhard Kittel and Gerhard Friedrich, trans. Geoffrey W. Bromiley (Grand Rapids, MI: Eerdmans, 1974), 9:672-74.
[40]Gaventa, Our Mother, 32-34.
[41]Both Martyn and Eastman find in ōdinō of Gal 4:19 the pain of God. Martyn, Galatians, 428-29; Eastman, Mother Tongue, 120-21.
[42]Martyn, Galatians, 429.

the natural translation of the Hebrew word as in Isaiah 45:10.[43] In the Song of Moses, which gives the history of a wayward Israel, God's tender care is sadly not met by the faithful response of his children. Through the grief-laden experience of child-rearing, Israel is reminded of their father creating them (Deut 32:6) and of their mother birthing them (Deut 32:18). They should not ignore the authority of fatherly creation nor disregard the pain of motherly procreation.[44] Therefore, Paul's bewilderment and perplexity over the waywardness of the Galatians with respect to the messages of Paul and of his opponents in the pericope (Gal 4:12-20) seem to mirror the motherly anguish of God in drawing unfaithful Israel ever nearer to his/her bosom. God as a mother suffers birth pain for Israel; therefore, Paul imitates God in suffering birth pain for the Galatians as their mother. Thus Paul's missionary relatedness as seen in this pericope reflects his view of a God who relates to his people as a mother does to her children.[45]

Motherly motivation of the salvific pattern. At the beginning of the pericope (Gal 4:12), Paul entreats the Galatians by presenting a curious pattern of unity. "Become as I am, for I also have become as you are." Considering the exigency of the letter, Paul is most probably urging the Galatians to be like Paul, who stands outside the law for the truth of the gospel, as Paul became like the Galatian Gentiles without the law for the truth of the gospel.[46] Paul elsewhere says, "To

those outside the law I became as one outside the law" (1 Cor 9:21). Such a stance to the law probably invited some form of persecution by law-observant Jews, which is a cause for Paul's missionary suffering (2 Cor 11:16-33). In the unity of Paul and the Galatians, salvation is to be reached. In the salvific pattern, Paul suffers, and the suffering brings the Galatians closer to Paul. Paul describes the goal of this salvation process as "Christ is formed in you" (Gal 4:19). Therefore, the reader is naturally reminded of the christological motivation of Paul's missionary suffering.[47] Indeed, the immediately preceding pericope presents the salvific pattern in the history of God's Son. The Son of God was "born of a woman, born under the law . . . so that we might receive adoption as children" (Gal 4:4-5). In other words, the Son of God became like us, so we become the children of God. In a more developed form of salvific pattern, "[God] made him to be sin who knew no sin, so that in him we might become the righteousness of God" (2 Cor 5:21). In the unity of God's Son and humanity, salvation is to be reached. In the salvific pattern, God's Son suffers the vulnerability of humanity, and that suffering brings humans closer to the Son. Furthermore, Christ's salvific passion reflects how God as a mother suffers for Israel.[48] In the history of Israel, God as a mother embraced the vulnerability of his/her children Israel, thus becoming vulnerable her/himself in the pregnancy, and Israel is nurtured to reflect

---

[43]Francis Brown et al., eds., *The New Brown-Driver-Briggs-Gesenius Hebrew and English Lexicon* (Peabody, MA: Hendrickson, 1979), 296-97; Laird Harris et al., eds., *Theological Wordbook of the Old Testament* (Chicago: Moody, 1980), 1:270-71.

[44]Therefore, *yld* and *ḥûl* represent the act of a mother, instead of *yld* pointing to a father's act and *ḥûl* pointing to a mother's act. For *yld* as denoting the birth of a mother, see Prov 23:22. Trible, *God and the Rhetoric of Sexuality*, 62-63.

[45]Being well aware of the Masoretic presentation of God, Paul's image may be closer to the context of Deut 32:18 than Is 45:10.

[46]Burton, *Galatians*, 236-37; Dunn, *Galatians*, 232-33.

[47]Eastman, *Mother Tongue*, 64-65.

[48]Eastman argues that as prophets embodied God's suffering for his people, Paul in his persecution enacts the suffering of Christ. Eastman, "Paul Among the Prophets," 63-88, in *Mother Tongue*, esp. 72-73. I tend to see that God's suffering is reflected in Christ's suffering, and in turn it is reflected in Paul's suffering.

her image. In the unity of God and Israel, salvation is to be reached. In the salvific pattern, God as a mother suffers the vulnerability of Israel, and the suffering brings Israel closer to God. If such a motherly relatedness and unity is the motivation of Paul's dealing with the Galatians, the deconstructionist criticism that Paul's mimesis command—"become like me"—reveals his patriarchal authoritarianism should indeed be reconsidered.[49]

If God's salvation of humanity is described in terms of motherly relatedness to her children, it is understandable that Paul in Galatians refers to the maternal origin of the salvific acts. Thus, for the revelation of God's Son and the call to the Gentile mission, Paul was divinely ordained in his mother's womb (Gal 1:15-16). In the decisive moment of salvation history, Jesus was born of a woman (Gal 4:4). The gospel of Christ is to bear fruit among the Galatians because of Paul's birth pangs (Gal 4:19). Furthermore, the eschatological community, Jerusalem above, is "our mother," in whom regeneration is experienced (Gal 4:26-27).

EPILOGUE: TOWARD A HOLISTIC VIEW OF GOD

Behind Paul's vision of the perfect union in his community lies a view of God whose image is the perfect union of male and female. It is therefore natural that God is presented metaphorically as both a father and a mother in Scripture. Without appreciating the maternal aspect of God, one may lose sight of the divine intention for God's church. When Paul related to the Galatians as a missionary-pastor, he imitated

a God who, as a mother in agony, internalized the vulnerability of Israel. Paul may well have been aware that the maternal relatedness and unity of God was a chief motivation energizing the salvific activities of humanity. Without appreciating the maternal inspiration of the God of the salvific mission, one may misunderstand the divine intention as to how humanity is to be touched by God. Therefore, the theology that fully recognizes the motherliness of God, which painfully embraces vulnerable others, may nurture followers of Christ to reach the richness of Christian being. Yet in the history of the church, commentators and translators have at times been quite conditioned by the paternal worldview. John Chrysostom, for example, comments on the birth pain of Paul in Galatians 4:19; "Did you see his *paternal* care [*splanchna patrika*]? Did you see the anxiety of the apostle's worth? Did you see how he sent out cries much more fierce than of those in labor?"[50] And more recently, the Jerusalem Bible translates Deuteronomy 32:18 as "unmindful now of the God who *fathered* you."

In the early church some attempts were made to preserve a maternal sensitivity toward God, though efforts to secure "orthodoxy" tended to sacrifice this sensitivity. For example, among second-century Syriac churches, God was portrayed as having two breasts full of milk and giving milk to the world out of his (her) breasts, with the Holy Spirit milking him (Odes of Solomon 19.1-4). Probably this maternal expression of God influenced the Syriac translation of John 1:18; whereas in Greek "the only Son . . . is close to the Father's bosom [*kolpon*]," in Syriac

---

[49]Elizabeth A. Castelli, *Imitating Paul: A Discourse of Power* (Louisville: Westminster John Knox, 1991), 86-87; Elisabeth Schüssler Fiorenza, *Rhetoric and Ethic: Politics of Biblical Studies* (Minneapolis: Fortress, 1999), 164-65; Kahl, "No Longer Male," 45-46; Eastman, *Mother Tongue,* 86.

[50]John Chrysostom, *"Hypomnēma eis tēn pros Galatas epistolēn,"* in *Patrologiae Cursus Completus, Series Graeca,* ed. Jacques Paul Migne (Paris: Gaume Fratres, 1857–1866), 61.2:660.

he is close to God's womb (*'ubba*). The interest in the maternal aspects of God among the Syriac churches seemed to be gradually directed toward or limited to the description of the Holy Spirit. Therefore in the Acts of Thomas, the Holy Spirit is a "compassionate mother" (2.27) and "hidden mother" (5.50). This theological tendency is probably preserved in the Gospel of Philip, which points out the error of viewing Mary as conceiving by the Holy Spirit, asking, "When did a woman ever conceive by a woman?" (17). That is, "the power of the Most High [= the word]," rather than the female Spirit, is responsible for Mary's giving birth to Jesus (see Lk 1:35).[51] Aphrahat, "the Persian Sage," who lived during the fourth-century Sassanid dynasty, reflects this old Syrian pneumatology in his expression "Father God and Mother Spirit" (*Demonstrations* 18).[52] Alongside this maternal understanding of the Godhead an androgynous speculation of the Trinity among the Gnostics was developed. The Apocryphon of John seems to assume a trinity of *propatēr* ("original father"), *pronoia* ("foreknowledge"), and *autogenēs* ("one coming to being"). *Pronoia* confesses to be both father and mother (*metropatēr*), and it is also called the spirit (see 2-5). Probably because of the possible association with Gnostic theology, the Syriac churches started in the fifth century to move away from viewing the Holy Spirit as feminine.[53] The Syriac translation for the Greek *pneuma* (the neuter word for "spirit") is *ruḥa*,

and it is feminine, as is the Hebrew *rûaḥ*. Therefore in the Old Syriac version (a translation of the late second to third century), the Holy Spirit is consistently treated as feminine grammatically. Yet in the Peshitta of the fifth century, the Holy Spirit began to be treated as masculine, and in the Harklean version of the early seventh century, it became masculine throughout. The longing for motherliness in the Christian religion is then directed to and contained in the reverence of Mary, the mother of Jesus.[54] Despite the opposition of Nestorius in the christological discussion, Mary was given a title, *theotokos* ("Mother of God"), at the Council of Ephesus in 431. This title was preserved well within the Catholic tradition, and it seems to have enhanced the development of Mariology among the Catholic Church.[55]

Contemporary Protestant churches often resist what they view as excessive reverence for Mary, stimulated partly by the title *theotokos* and partly by the Apostles' Creed, "born of Virgin Mary [*natus ex Maria virgine*]," which is incidentally in the Chalcedonian Definition, "born of Mary the Mother of God."[56] Certainly, the avoidance of her reverence is in part motivated by the fear that such an attitude may cross the line between authentic faith and superstitious beliefs, which by the way is also a concern of *Lumen Gentium* (8.52-69). It may not be proper to think, however, that the motherly involvement in the divine plan of salvation expressed in the Scripture

---

[51]S. P. Brock, "Passover, Annunciation and Epiclesis: Some Remarks on the Term *Aggen* in the Syriac Version of Luke 1:35," *Novum Testamentum* 24 (1984): 227. On the discussion of maternal pneumatology among the Syriac churches, see Fumihiko Takeda, "Josei to shite no Seirei" [The Holy Spirit as feminine in the early Syriac Christian tradition], *Theological Studies in Japan* 47 (2008): 59-86.

[52]On motherliness of the Syriac theology, see Robert Murray, *Symbols of Church and Kingdom: A Study in Early Syriac Tradition* (Cambridge: Cambridge University Press, 1975), 131-58.

[53]Takeda, "Josei to shite no Seirei," 70.

[54]Sasagu Arai, *Shinyaku Seisho No Josei Kan* [New Testament perspectives on women] (Tokyo: Iwanami, 1988), 283-320. See Johnson, *She Who Is*, 50-54.

[55]See articles 53 and 66 of *Lumen Gentium* (*Dogmatic Constitution of the Church*).

[56]Jan Milič Lochman, *Das Glaubensbekenntnis, Grundriß der Dogmatik im Anschluß an das Credo*, 2nd ed. (Gütersloh: Mohn, 1982), 88.

may be readily neglected in the search for "authenticity." The confession of the Marian origin of the Son of God is more than a tool to defend the christological teaching that divinity and humanity are one in the person of Jesus.[57] The motherly involvement in the history of salvation can impress the assertion of the full worth of those who have been largely underestimated in the patriarchal history of humankind.[58] Theology that embraces the fuller expression of who God is helps to enhance an authentic experience among all members of the church and to invite into that experience people of all cultures, even the one that Ferreira in *Silence* declared incapable of accepting or being accepted by "Father God."

A culture with perhaps a pathological longing for maternal dealing still presents a perspective that may be lacking in comparison to the cultures that have long oligopolized the exegesis of Scripture. The cultural reading of the text with the particular perspective may have a place in the attempt to reach toward a yet fuller experience of God. When the author of *Silence* read Luke 22:61, he saw his mother's tears in Jesus' stare at Peter in his denial at the high priest's courtyard.[59] The recognizable gap between the male and the female figures could only be filled by a novelist's instinct, yet the instinct should not be disregarded as a subjective hindrance to the science of exegesis. Exegesis is after all said to be both science and art.[60] One would do well to attend to the rather quiet, if not silent, motherly whisper in the Scripture.

FURTHER READING

Asano, Atsuhiro. *Community-Identity Construction in Galatians.* Journal for the Study of the New Testament Supplement Series 285. London: T&T Clark, 2005.

Doi, Takeo. *The Anatomy of Dependence.* Translated by John Bester. Tokyo: Kodansha, 1973.

Eastman, Suzan. *Recovering Paul's Mother Tongue: Language and Theology in Galatians.* Grand Rapids, MI: Eerdmans, 2007.

Endo, Shusaku. *Silence.* Translated by William Johnston. Rutland, VT: Tuttle, 1969.

Gaventa, Beverly Roberts. *Our Mother Saint Paul.* Louisville: Westminster John Knox, 2007.

Kahl, Brigitte. "No Longer Male: Masculinity Struggles Behind Galatians 3:28?" *Journal for the Study of the New Testament* 79 (2000): 37-49.

McFague, Sallie. *Metaphorical Theology: Models of God in Religious Language.* Philadelphia: Fortress, 1982.

Trible, Phyllis. *God and the Rhetoric of Sexuality.* Overtures to Biblical Theology. Philadelphia: Fortress, 1979.

---

[57]Tyrannius Rufinus, *A Commentary on the Apostles' Creed,* trans. J. N. D. Kelly (Westminster: Newman; London: Longmans, 1955), 42-47.

[58]Lochman, *Das Glaubensbekenntnis,* 97.

[59]Endo, "Gariraya No Haru" [Spring in Galilee], in *Haha Naru Mono* [Motherliness], 167.

[60]Darrell Bock and Buist Fanning, *Interpreting the New Testament: Introduction to the Art and Science of Exegesis* (Wheaton, IL: Crossway, 2006), 17.

HOW TO UNDERSTAND A BIBLICAL GOD IN CHINESE

TOWARD A CROSSCULTURAL BIBLICAL HERMENEUTICS

Zi Wang

THIS CHAPTER SEEKS to study the challenges of translating the term and names of the biblical God in Confucianist (linguistic context) China and to answer this question: What is the relationship between Chinese culture (in particular, Confucianist culture) and the universal claims of Christianity? First, this essay will review the historical debates regarding various translations for the names of God (Shin, Shang-ti) used by Western missionaries (Catholic and Protestant), and subsequently the printed versions of Chinese Bibles. The sociopolitical context of the missionaries will be considered, with a focus on how the gospel was (mis)communicated to the Chinese people.

Indeed, the relationship between Christian faith and Chinese culture is the core issue in the translation of God's name(s). This essay will analyze the conflict between them, explore the process by which the translations were integrated, and propose a crosscultural biblical hermeneutics that focuses on a "fusion of horizons" as a way to avoid miscommunication and misunderstanding. The essay will draw on a

reading of Romans (especially Rom 1:16-17) in dialogue with a Chinese understanding of the biblical God.

How does one accurately express the understanding of the Christian/biblical God in Chinese? Do we use the term Shang-ti or Shin? Or do we use other names? The terminology question became the focus of debate as early as the time of the arrival of Christianity in China. In the subsequent few hundred years, it has been intermittently discussed, and the question is not fully resolved even today. In fact, using Shang-ti to refer to the biblical God has long been a popular practice. When talking about Shang-ti, the vast majority of Chinese people think of the highest Christian Master. However, among Chinese and Western scholars, the issue is complex because behind the term is a conflict between Christianity and Chinese cultures. Therefore, it is directly related to the complex history of the spread of Christianity in China. As the representative of Chinese traditional culture, Confucianism is highly relational (family and society) and particular (heaven, humanity, earth). What is the relationship between this Confucianist culture and the universal claims of Christianity? What kind of impact will this relationship have on the further understanding of the Christian doctrine of God in the Chinese context?

This essay will first briefly survey the doctrine of the Trinity/God in Chinese church history. Second, it will examine the history of "the term question," with special attention to how the interpretation of the Bible has shaped the way people envision the relationship between Chinese traditional culture and the Christian faith. Then the essay will try to respond to the term question from the perspective of a cross-cultural interpretation of the Bible, which is based on the description of the concept of Shang-ti/Heaven in the cultural context of Chinese people encountering the Christian faith. It will also attempt to understand the concept of God in Romans 1:16-17 as an example of the possibilities for dialogue and translation in moving toward a better interaction between Christian faith and Chinese culture.

CHINESE CHRISTIAN UNDERSTANDINGS OF TRINITY/GOD

The effort to understand and proclaim the biblical God in the Chinese context, or to build up Chinese indigenous theology, has been the pursuit of several generations of Chinese scholars and Christians. Notwithstanding, it is still a work in progress, and many church leaders, theologians, and scholars in China have made their own contributions in various ways.

Some preachers from the field of Chinese pragmatic ethics are more concerned with Christians' practical lives rather than the logical analysis of doctrine. Ni Tuo-sheng (Watchman

Nee, 1903–1972), for example, did not pay much attention to Christology or the Trinity in his theology, but devoted himself to the spiritual life and building up the local churches. He stressed the centrality of Christ in the doctrines of Christianity, believing that the aim of God's creation was solely to display Christ's glory, and he believed Christ to be the center of the Godhead, while God revealed himself in Christ and humans become God's sons and daughters in Christ.[1] Accordingly, what Christians should do is to live out the life of Christ.

Zhao Zi-chen (1888–1979), one of the most influential theologians of the twentieth century in China, was the initiator of Chinese contextualizing theology. He devoted himself to interpreting the Christian faith in a Chinese cultural context in an effort to accommodate the tradition to believers' lives. One can hardly find a description of God as omniscient, omnipresent, or omnipotent in his writings. Zhao preferred to introduce a personal God. He thought God was the purest and most perfect standard of personality.[2]

Both Wu Yao-zong (1893–1979), the founder of the Three-Self patriotic movement of Chinese Christianity, and Ding Guang-xun (1915–2012), an outstanding leader of the church in China, are representatives of liberal Christianity (modernist). Wu Yao-zong believed in the Sermon on the Mount and claimed that he was attracted by Christian ethics. All other beliefs derived from the Bible—such as the incarnation, the resurrection, the Trinity, and the parousia—were unbelievable to him. Ding Guang-xun confessed that, at first, he conceived of God as the one with great power who is self-existent and eternal, but eventually he came to argue that the essential characteristic of God is love, which is revealed in

---

[1] See Ni Tuo-sheng, *The Normal Christian Faith* (Taipei: Christian Press, 2001).
[2] Zhao Zi-chen, *Collection of Zhao Zi-chen* (Beijing: Commercial Press, 2004), 1:193.

Christ.[3] However, the representative of Chinese independent churches, Wang Ming-dao (1900–1991), claimed biblical inerrancy. He insisted that only the biblical teachings could guide Christian lives and fiercely criticized the sin of this world and churches including the Three-Self Church.

As a famous scholar in contemporary China, Liu Xiao-feng (1956–) called himself a cultural Christian and committed himself to establishing a foundation of divinity in the reconstruction of Chinese culture. Introducing Karl Barth's theology, he argued on the one hand that God is an absolute "other" and is not a projection of human will, and on the other hand that one's view of God must be closely related to Christology. When people talk about God, they must refer to Christ, since Christ is the Word of God.

As we can see, these Chinese believers paid less attention to the teaching of the Christian God as transcendent than to God as understood through Christ and his love. In other words, what was attractive to these Chinese was how God is involved with human life and shows people a virtue-worthy and civilized way of living.

BACKGROUND: THE TERM QUESTION

Early in the seventeenth century, when Catholic missionaries came to China, the question of whether to use the indigenous name in Chinese culture to translate *Deus* sparked a heated debate among missionaries. Then Jesuit missionary Matteo Ricci initiated the idea that the concept of Shang-ti/Heaven in Confucian classics corresponded to the concept of the Catholic God. It is noteworthy that when Ricci first came to China, he claimed that it was unnecessary to quote and

interpret the Bible when discussing Deus with the Chinese (especially the monks or literati), because the authority of the Bible was meaningless for those who had different beliefs.[4] Ricci thus introduced the concept of Deus, primarily based on Thomistic theology, to the Chinese, demonstrating the existence of Deus through the idea of cosmology and ontology, thus providing the basis for moral philosophy. He also described Deus as without beginning or end, invisible and silent, with great power and wisdom, the supreme good, and knowing everything. Accordingly, Ricci insisted that it is only reasonable that Shang-ti/Heaven in Chinese classics could correspond to the Catholic concept of Deus. However, his successor, Nicholas Longobardi, opposed this view. Even though Longobardi realized that the meaning of Scripture should not be adapted to cater to people with diverse opinions, he acted just as his contemporary missionaries did, namely, paying more attention to systematic theology and neglecting interpretation of the Bible. Therefore, Longobardi also viewed the concept of Shang-ti/Heaven and Deus from a scholastic perspective, arguing that the transcendence of Deus was different from the concept of Shang-ti/Heaven, because Shang-ti/Heaven as a naturalistic concept did not have this characteristic. Then he suggested adopting a transliterated word for Deus. This is part of the well-known rites controversy in Chinese missionary history. The problem of translating the title of the Supreme Ruler in Christianity was called "the term question" (*Sheng-hao-zhi-zheng*) by subsequent missionaries in China. The related debate lasted for more than three centuries.

---

[3]Wu Yao-zong, *No One Has Ever Seen God* (Shanghai: Youth Association, 1947), 96; Ding Guang-xun, "A Chinese Christian's View on God," in *The Collocation of Ding Guang-xun* (Nanjing: Yilin, 1998), 107-12.
[4]Matteo Ricci, SJ, *The True Meaning of the Lord of Heaven* (Taipei: Ricci Institute, 1985), 120, 68.

In 1807, British Protestant missionary Robert Morrison began to translate the first complete Chinese Bible. But this version did not employ a unified Chinese word for the holy name (*sheng-hao*). So, in 1843, fifteen British and American missionaries in China met in Hong Kong with the intention of retranslating the Chinese Bible. In the course of retranslation, these missionaries disagreed on how to translate *elohim* and *theos*. A group dominated by British missionaries insisted on the old translation of Shang-ti, while the American missionaries advocated for the translation of Shin. The two sides persisted in their views on this issue. The debate between William J. Boone of the US Anglican Church and Walter H. Medhurst of the London Missionary Society was very intense. Medhurst insisted that Shang-ti/Heaven was the closest concept to that of the Christian God. He worked from Hebrew and Greek lexicons to research the meaning of *elohim* and *theos*. He noted that *elohim* was derived from the Arabic *Alaha*, which signified "to adore," hence the noun signified the object of adoration, or *numen tremendum*. Likewise, he argued that *theos* in the New Testament meant generally (1) the Creator and Governor of all things that exist; (2) by metonymy, the religion given by God to humanity; (3) any thing that is put in the place of God, such as idols or the devil, when considered as the god of this world; and (4) metaphorically, those who act under the command or authority of God, and are God's vice-regents on earth, such as magistrates and judges. Medhurst thought that this connection was also indicated in the apostle Paul's expression "His eternal power and godhead" (Rom

1:20). Since the meanings of *elohim* and *theos* were understood by both Hebrew and Greek writers to indicate the supreme as well as inferior deities, Medhurst proposed that the Chinese word *Shang-ti/Heaven* expressing the supreme ruler above all could be adapted to translate the name of the biblical God.[5] William Boone, however, rejected this viewpoint, thinking that "among a heathen people no word can be found which will convey, by the meaning which its previous *usus loquendi* has given it, the just ideas of the true God." Therefore, he believed that in translating the Scriptures into the language of a polytheistic nation, it would be better to use a generic name, Shin, for God. He argued that in the Old Testament, the word *elohim* is not a proper name of the true God but is a generic term applied to both heathen deities and to Yahweh. And the Greeks and Romans were polytheists too, so the inspired writers of the New Testament and the apostles chose *theos* rather than Zeus and *Deus* rather than Jupiter to render *elohim* into Greek and Latin. Boone quoted the First Commandment, "I am the LORD your God who brought you out of the land of Egypt, out of the house of bondage. You shall not have other gods before me" (Ex 20:2; Is 44:8; 45:5), to show that the Bible forbids humans to trust, hope in, or rely on any but God and to direct their allegiance to him as the *only* proper object of *religious worship*.[6]

Later, British missionary James Legge and American missionary Elijah Coleman Bridgman also joined the debate. Legge had his famous proclamation: "the *Ti* and *Shang-ti* of the Chinese classics is God—our God—the true

[5]Walter H. Medhurst, "An Inquiry into the Proper Mode of Rendering the Word *God* in Translating the Sacred Scriptures into the Chinese Language," *Chinese Repository* 17 (March 1848): 105-7, 112.
[6]William J. Boone, "An Essay on the Proper Rendering of the Words *Elohim* and *Theos* into the Chinese Language," *Chinese Repository* 17 (January 1848): 17-18, 20.

God." He paid less attention to quoting and interpreting the Bible from his viewpoint. For him, the meaning of the Christian God is axiomatic, that is, he is the Supreme Ruler of humanity. Legge emphasized that all the predicates of Shang-ti are such that we can adopt it in speaking of God "who in the beginning made the heavens and the earth, and who in the fullness of time sent forth His Son, fully to reveal Him to men, and to die, the just for the unjust."[7] Scholars questioning Legge's argument argued that Shang-ti is just another idol of the pagan world. These missionaries reasoned that, according to the Old Testament, all the gods of the nations were idols (Josh 24:2; 1 Kings 20:23; 2 Kings 18:33, 35; Ezra 1:7; Jer 2:11; Ps 14:2-3; 33:12-14; 96:3-5) and that the sin the apostle Paul refers to in worshiping these gods was "idolatry" (Acts 14:16; 17:30; Rom 1:23, 25, 28; Gal 4:8).[8] They believed that, in order to make the Chinese turn away from polytheism and idolatry, they should not use a holy name of the Chinese traditional culture but choose a generic word such as *Shin*. They insisted that their mission was to help people know the true God and turn away from all false gods. The term *Shin* could make the Chinese aware that Yahweh was the true God who made heaven and earth and that the idols they worshiped so far were false gods.[9]

The missionaries who participated in the debate had written numerous articles or booklets published in *Chinese Repository*, *Chinese Recorder*, *China Review*, and other church publications, launching an unprecedented missionary theological debate. However, because the two sides could not reach a consensus, they eventually translated the Chinese Bible into two versions, one of which was published by the British and Foreign Bible Society and called the Shang-ti version, and another published by the American Bible Society and referred to as the Shin version. Both versions are still in use today by churches and scholars.

This debate between British and American missionaries did not come to an end with the two versions of the Chinese Bible. From 1877 to 1878, some missionaries in China and a few Chinese Christians continued to discuss which Chinese term was appropriate for the holy name by publishing a series of argumentative essays in *Church News*. However, some new arguments from the Shang-ti/Heaven camp merit our attention.[10] On one hand, these missionaries thought all the gods of the nations were idols; they believed that God's self-revelation was universal. They quoted Romans 1:19-20, "What may be known about God is plain to them, because God has made it plain to them. Ever since the creation of the world God's invisible qualities—his eternal power and divine nature—have been clearly seen, being understood from what has been made," and argued that, even though the Chinese had not seen the Bible before, they still would have partial knowledge of God. On the other hand, these missionaries tried to prove by interpreting the Bible that *elohim* and *theos* were not generic. They quoted Exodus 20:3, "you shall have no other gods before me," and explained

---

[7]James Legge, *Confucianism in Relation to Christianity, A Paper Read Before the Missionary Conference in Shanghai, on May 11th, 1877* (Shanghai: Kelly & Walsh, 1877), 3.

[8]"Is the Shang-ti of the Chinese Classics the Same Being as Jehovah of the Sacred Scriptures?," *Chinese Recorder* (September–October 1877): 411-26.

[9]"The Meaning of the Word 'Shin,'" *Chinese Recorder* (January–February 1877): 65-93.

[10]Jonathan Lees, "On the Holy Name (*sheng-hao*)," *Church News*, April 13, 1878, in *Sheng Hao Lun Heng* (Shanghai: Shanghai Chinese Classics, 2008), 211-26.

that if there is another *elohim*, then God would not have said, "You shall *have* no other gods," but perhaps only, "You shall not *worship* other gods." Thus, they thought that what God meant here is that people should not use *elohim* to designate anyone besides him (see also Deut 32:17, 39; 2 Sam 22:32; 1 Kings 8:60; 18:21; Ps 96:5).

THE BIBLICAL INTERPRETATION OF THE TERM QUESTION

In the discussion of the term question, there were usually two factions: one advocated the use of *Shang-ti* to translate *God*, while the other advocated the use of *Shin*. However, the problem of translation was in fact more complicated than that because the holy names were not unified in the Bible. There were at least three Hebrew words used to refer to God in the Old Testament.[11] First, *el shaddai* appears in Genesis 17:1; 28:3; 35:11; 49:25 (see also Ex 6:3; Ruth 1:21; Job 5:17; 6:4; 8:3; 13:3). This word was usually used in the time of Abraham to refer to his God. Second, *elohim* is a common word in the Old Testament rendering the supreme Lord, such as in Deuteronomy 4:31 and 1 Kings 18:21. Sometimes it refers to false gods, for instance in Exodus 12:12; Deuteronomy 29:18; 1 Samuel 5:7; and 2 Kings 1:2-3. It can also indicate an angel, as in Psalm 8:5; or it can refer to an earthly ruler, as for example in Psalm 82:1, 6. Third, *YHWH* (Yahweh) is found in Exodus 3:14; 6:3, where God revealed his own name to Moses. This word expresses God's self-existence and appears frequently in the Pentateuch. Later, the Jewish people use the word *adonai* to replace it, as it was too sacred to be pronounced, and it has been translated as *kyrios* in Greek and "Lord"

in English. In the New Testament, *theos* has the same meaning as *elohim*, referring both to the true God and to idols.[12] In other Greek literature, the word *theos* is employed for all objects of worship. And *theos* is usually translated as *Deus* in Latin and "God" in English, representing the Supreme Master. In English, the "Word of God" can be capitalized, or a definite article can be added to refer to the Ruler above all. It can also be used in the plural or with an adjective attached, such as *false*, to qualify a generic concept. But Chinese does not have this kind of grammar, which causes problems in translation. Moreover, the "Word of God" (*elohim*, *theos*) itself has different meanings in different biblical contexts. For example, in Isaiah 42:1, "Here is my servant, whom I uphold, my chosen one in whom I delight," the word *servant* implies God as the Lord. And in Hosea 2:23, "I will say to those called 'Not my people,' 'You are my people'; and they will say, 'You are my God,'" the word *people* shows God as the Ruler. Finally, in Revelation 21:7, "I will be his God, and he will be my son," the word *son* implies God is the Father. Therefore, to respond to the term question is not simply to choose a Chinese word with a fixed meaning but to answer this question: Is what we try to translate the world of the text, the world of translators, or the fusion of two cultural horizons?[13]

Looking back at the discussion of the term question, we can see that, from the perspective of traditional biblical hermeneutics, these Western missionaries did not distinguish between the text and the meaning of the text, which makes the interpretation and use of Scriptures appear arbitrary. They often singled out

---

[11]Lees, "On the Holy Name (*sheng-hao*)," 214-15.
[12]Lees, "On the Holy Name (*sheng-hao*)," 216.
[13]Robert Carroll, "Between Lying and Blasphemy or On Translating a Four-Letter Word in Hebrew Bible: Critical Reflections on Bible Translation," in *Bible Translation on the Threshold of the Twenty-First Century: Authority, Reception, Culture and Religion*, ed. Athalya Brenner and Jan Willem van Henten (Sheffield: Sheffield Academic Press, 2002), 53-64.

fragments of Scripture for their own missionary purposes, not considering either the context of the Scriptures or the context of Chinese readers.

The Western missionaries—whether the Shang-ti or the Shin camp of scholars—imposed their own understandings of God onto the Chinese, that is, they interpreted the Christian God as the supreme transcendental One. They cited the Old Testament (1 Kings 8:60; Ps 20:5; 77:18-19; 83:18; 135:13; Jer 23:6), pointing out that God is characterized by his omnipotence, omnipresence, omniscience, and all-pervading rule and care for all of creation.[14] They believed that Shang-ti of the Chinese cultural tradition, like other nations' idols, might have certain characteristics that belong to God, such as benevolence, clemency, justice, and universal government of God, but still lack God's essential characteristics.[15] First, God is the eternally self-existent one. When Moses asked for God's name in the Exodus text, God replied: "I AM WHO I AM" (Ex 3:14). The text indicates that God is the Supreme Being in whom we live, move, and have our being (see also Ps 90:2; 98:2; Is 40:28; 44:6; 57:15; 63:16; Hab 1:12). Second, God justly and rightfully claims for himself exclusively the homage and worship of all his creatures. In the Ten Commandments, it is said: "I am the LORD your God. . . . You shall have no other gods before me. You shall not make for yourself an idol in the form of anything in heaven above or on the earth beneath or in the waters below. You shall not bow down to them or worship them; for I, the LORD your God, am a jealous God" (Ex 20:2-5). These scholars believed that evidence of a jealous God was found extensively in the Bible, showing that any form of idolatry would incur the wrath of God and bring about punishment (Ex 34:14; Deut 4:23-24; 6:14-15; 7:4; Josh 24:19-20). Finally, God is the Creator of heaven and earth: "I am the LORD, who has made all things, who alone stretched out the heavens, who spread out the earth by myself" (Is 44:24; see also Gen 1:1; Ex 20:11; Neh 9:6; Is 45:12; Jer 10:12; Rev 4:11). God's work of creation demonstrates his excellence and supreme rulership. In their interpretation of the Bible (especially the Old Testament), these missionaries emphasized the transcendence of the biblical God. In the understanding of monotheism, God is absolutely unique to the exclusion of all other gods. In creation, God is the Creator of all things and has the highest authority over all. All in all, this is a transcendent God with great power in the view of these missionaries. This power is described in the Bible through theophanies, as a voice thundering from Sinai, as the mighty influence that fills, fires up, and strengthens the prophets and heroes of Israel for their mission.[16]

Behind the Western missionaries' descriptions of the biblical God as the Most High with great power was a deep-rooted dualism: Creator and creatures, spirit and matter, theology and ethics, and so on. The Christian God as the Creator above all creatures builds up a spiritual relationship with humans, supplying a theological foundation for ethics. The universality of the Christian God is built on his essential characteristic as an eternal objective entity that goes beyond the world and is separated from any concrete cultural identity. Underlying this idea are two basic attitudes toward Western Christianity and the Chinese cultural tradition: (1) either Christianity is irreconcilable with Chinese

---

[14]"Meaning of the Word 'Shin,'" 85.
[15]"Is the *Shang-ti* of the Chinese Classics," 422-25.
[16]J. E. Walker, "Too Straight Is Crooked the Other Way," *Chinese Recorder* (November–December 1877): 519-24.

culture, and Chinese Christians have to choose between the true God and false gods; or (2) Christianity is not incompatible with Chinese culture since there are good parts of Chinese culture that can be fulfilled by the Christian faith. In fact, both of these attitudes reflect a strongly exclusive mindset in the modern missionary movement in China. Western Christianity was treated as the only true religion and absolutely true faith, while the religious beliefs of Chinese culture were either discarded as idolatry or overlooked. In this case, the universality of God became the excuse for missionaries to ignore or reject the possibility of the Christian faith being contextualized in a specific culture.

On one hand, the Christian faith as a religious system is a pursuit and a belief that meets the spiritual and truth-seeking needs of humans, and it does not exclusively belong to any specific nation or location. On the other hand, Christianity also has church communities and social participation in these local settings. That is, the Christian faith has to be related to concrete sociohistorical and cultural traditions. Therefore, Christianity as a religion must incarnate in the Chinese cultural, social, and historical contexts.

A CROSSCULTURAL PERSPECTIVE ON GOD

To understand the biblical God in the context of the Chinese culture, one needs to (1) notice the features of the Chinese term *Shang-ti*/Heaven, which constitutes the preunderstandings of Chinese who come to know the biblical God; and (2) be aware of the context of the Bible, which will fuse with the readers' context in generating meaning. Here we will try to comprehend the biblical God in the context of the Chinese cultural tradition, primarily from Paul's hermeneutics in the book of Romans. There are rich and complex descriptions of God in the Bible. In Paul's letters alone the word *God* appears 548 times, and in Romans it appears 153 times. We will focus on Romans 1:16-17 in order to illustrate an alternative way of understanding the Christian God in the Chinese context.

The contexts of Romans and Shang-ti/ Heaven. Romans 1:16-17 is the *propositio* of the entire epistle's rhetorical structure; that is, it represents the main points of this whole epistle in a brief statement. From a sociohistorical perspective, Paul's aim in writing this letter is to question all claims of cultural superiority and to claim the impartial righteousness of God.[17]

I agree with Robert Jewett's interpretation of Romans 1:16 that "I am not ashamed of . . ." is a strong response to social issues based on the values of honor and shame in the ancient Mediterranean world.[18] In 1 Corinthians 2:2, Paul clarifies that the gospel is "Jesus Christ and him crucified." Obviously, the gospel Paul preached was shameful in the eyes of Roman society. Paul explains this point in detail in 1 Corinthians 1:20-31: "Jews demand miraculous signs and Greeks look for wisdom, but we preach Christ crucified: a stumbling block to Jews and foolishness to Gentiles." There were reasons for Roman society to see the gospel of Christ as shameful. The culture of the first-century world was built on the foundational social values of honor and shame: "Honor was a filter through which the whole world was viewed, a deep structure of the Greco-Roman mind. . . . Every thing, every person, would be valued in terms of

---

[17]Robert Jewett, *Romans: A Commentary*, Hermeneia (Minneapolis: Fortress, 2007), 79.
[18]Jewett, *Romans*, 137.

honor."[19] Status (including social status, cultural status, or even gender status) became a very important standard by which people valued themselves and others in ancient Roman society. In the book of Romans, Paul was seeking support for a mission project in Spain. However, the majority of Spain in the first century was considered a barbaric culture in the eyes of the Romans. Therefore, Paul had to challenge the values of shame and honor and explain God's impartial righteousness. In Paul's view, the values of honor and shame bring about repression and exploitation of people by people, culture by culture, and exploitation is exactly what the gospel committed to change. Therefore, when Paul claimed that he was not ashamed of the gospel, he actually implied a social and ideological revolution inaugurated by the gospel, and suggested that this revolution was countercultural to that of honor and shame.

The reason we can read Romans 1:16 from a sociohistorical perspective is that we share a similar background with Heaven/Ti in the Chinese cultural tradition—a similarity that helps Chinese readers notice and understand the context of Romans.

In the Chinese cultural tradition, people worshiped Heaven/Ti. According to Shang's oracle bones, the most important deity was Ti or Shang-ti (literally, the "god above"), who is in charge of celestial phenomena, natural variations, people's luck, and other gods. In the Chou dynasty, people called this god the "God of Heaven" (*huang-tian-shang-ti*) and started to use the title of "Heaven" (*tian*) more. Duke Chou (ca. 1100 BCE), King Wu's brother, used the argument "the Mandate of Heaven" to defend his new regime. In addition to having all the power

of Ti, Heaven also has the power to establish an earthly reign in realizing the mandate of ruling.[20] Confucius further elucidated the moral principles of Heaven since he reinterpreted Heaven as creator of the moral order.

When Confucius put forward the moral principles of Heaven, he was dealing with the social background of the troubled times of hegemony. Confucius lived during the late stage of the Spring and Autumn period (770–476 BC), when the turbulent civil wars among vassal states caused the decline of the royal family. The prevailing social conditions were characterized by contention for hegemony among the lords, who were continuously fighting for more lands, treasures, and the right of dominion. Confucius described this time by saying that "rites collapsed and music disappeared," which implied moral corruption in his time. In Confucius's view, restoring the rule of virtue in the past (Western Chou dynasty) was the only way to save the immoral, violent world. Because the ruling Chou dynasty embodied the "Mandate of Heaven," Confucius praised the era of the Western Chou Dynasty as the optimal reign: "How splendidly rich it is in all the arts! I prefer the present Chou civilization."[21] Therefore, Confucius understood the Mandate of Heaven as an ethical principle. What he wanted to do was to build up the rule of virtue and moral relations among people by conforming to the Mandate of Heaven, so that the violence could be stopped.

Obviously, both Paul and Confucius are trying to expound a concept of the Christian God and Shang-ti/Heaven, respectively, to overcome suppression and exploitation among humans. The Christian God demands that Roman chauvinism be broken down and that

[19]J. E. Lendon, *Empire of Honor* (New York: Oxford University Press, 2005), 73.
[20]K. K. Yeo, *Confucius and Paul* (Shanghai: East China Normal University Press, 2010), 115.
[21]Confucius, *The Discourses and Sayings of Confucius*, trans. Ku Hung-mi (New York: Kessinger, 2008), 364.

Christ bring salvation to all. And Shang-ti/ Heaven in the Chinese cultural tradition as the moral principle of interpersonal communication requires the eradication of tyrants and restoration of the sage rule. At this point, it is possible to put the Chinese Shang-ti/Heaven and the Christian God into dialogue with each other in a way that is mutually edifying.

The relationship between God/Shang-ti and people. For Paul, God is not only the Creator who is above all creation but also the Creator who participates in human life all along by the cross of Christ. In Romans 1:16-17, the transcendence of God is not only a universality above creatures, like what the Western missionaries pointed to, but also contains his immanence.

In Romans 1:16, Paul says the gospel (of Jesus Christ and him crucified) is the power of God for salvation. The cross of Christ seemed to demean God and overlook the honor and propriety of established religious traditions—whether the Jewish law or the Roman ruler cult. As the cross displayed Christians' most honorable values to the Greco-Roman world in the most shameful way, it revealed the paradox of God's saving power in a compelling way. God the Creator saves this world not as a military leader or a political ruler but as the humblest person crucified on the cross. The cross shows that the power of God is not an absolutely executed strength "over" creatures, but a power "for" salvation of all creatures. And salvation is prepared for everyone (Rom 1:16). The word for "everyone" (*pas*) not only shows the universality of the gospel's range but, more importantly, critiques the phenomenon of different groups or communities devaluing each other. Paul further explains "everyone": first the Jews, then the Greeks (Rom

1:16). Instead of the usual antithesis between Jews and Gentiles, Paul mentions here the "Jews and Greeks [*Hellēnes*]." Abandoning the discriminatory vocabulary of Gentiles, Paul shows that before the salvation of the gospel, there is no special favor or distinction between different groups of people. The Greeks deserve salvation in their own right, not as second-class persons, non-Jews. Meanwhile, Paul's gospel also is different from the salvation proclaimed by Roman imperial propaganda. The Roman ruler cult believed that emperors embodied virtue in a preeminent and salvific manner; emperors were celebrated as savior figures, for they brought the Pax Romana to all Romans. However, the salvation of the gospel of Christ is not only for Romans but also for non-Romans. Therefore, Paul demonstrates that God offers salvation to every group that responds in faith to the gospel of Christ crucified. The evangelical persuasion is thus the means whereby the salvation of the world is now occurring.[22]

Moreover, the gospel revealed the righteousness of God (Rom 1:17, *dikaiosynē theou*). The righteousness of God implies that God's righteousness as the whole saving activity is a divine gift being granted to humanity by God's grace, so that people can be brought back into obedience to God's rulership. In the sense of God acting in accordance with his own nature for the sake of his name, we can say that the gospel reveals what God *is*.[23] God's essential characteristic is revealed by "Jesus Christ and him crucified" (1 Cor 2:2), which means that humans do not need to understand God's saving invitation from a level beyond humanity but to answer God by facing the event of the gospel. This shows God's immanence.

[22]Jewett, *Romans*, 140-41.
[23]Colin G. Kruse, *Paul's Letter to the Romans*, Pillar New Testament Commentary (Grand Rapids, MI: Eerdmans, 2012), 80.

That Chinese readers underline God's immanence in these verses relates to the characteristics of the concept of Shang-ti/Heaven. In Chinese culture, on one hand, the concept of Shang-ti/Heaven does express a theistic belief. In Shijing (Book of Songs), one of the odes reads: "Mighty is God on High [Shang-ti], Ruler of His people below; Swift and terrible is God on High, His charge has many statutes. Heaven gives birth to the multitudes of the people, but its charge cannot be counted upon. To begin well is common; To end well is rare indeed."[24] Shang-ti/Heaven is portrayed as a dignified and powerful Ruler. It creates and dominates the people on earth. There is much evidence to suggest that Shang-ti/Heaven for the ancient people was a Supreme Being, the ultimate benefactor and judge. But on the other hand, Shang-ti/Heaven in Chinese classical texts does not have personhood. In ancient Chinese classics there is no narrative about the interaction between Shang-ti and human beings. This is because there is no sharp distinction between creation and creator in the Chinese cultural tradition. Shang-ti/Heaven is itself creator and also creation.[25] Shang-ti not only creates the world but also is the world itself. Such Chinese pantheistic understanding needs correction from Romans 1, where Paul critiques the collapse of the categories of creature and Creator. Yet the immanent theist understanding of Chinese culture can be a bridge for Chinese Christians to understand the biblical God.

Even though Heaven in Chinese culture does not communicate directly with humans, it conveys its will to humans through oracles and changes in weather or the natural environment.

In other words, by mandate (*ming*, "command") Shang-ti/Heaven responds to the ruling class and instructs rulers about personal virtues. For example, in politics, the authority of rulers is justified by the Mandate of Heaven; ethically, a person lives out the Mandate of Heaven by being attentive to one's moral education. Confucius stressed the unity of people and Heaven from the aspect of moral cultivation. He advocated that the person who truly serves Heaven should pay more attention to his or her own moral cultivation: "A wise and good man is occupied in the search for truth; not in seeking for a mere living. . . . A wise man should be solicitous about truth, not anxious about poverty." And he believed that humans can carry forward the realization of the principles of Heaven by promoting their own morality: "It is the man that can make his religion or the principles he professes great; and not his religion or the principles which he professes, which can make the man great."[26] As we can see, Confucius highlighted that by accepting the Mandate of Heaven and respecting Shang-ti/Heaven, humans are able to educate themselves to achieve a virtuous life.

In the Chinese cultural tradition, there is no direct interaction between Shang-ti/Heaven and humans. The only way humans can respond to the moral principle of Shang-ti/Heaven's self-revelation is via their own enlightenment in the process of moral cultivation. Thus the transcendence of Shang-ti/Heaven in Chinese culture does not lie in relationship with the Supreme One outside the universe, but in the transcendence of the moral force in people's minds. The preunderstanding of the unity of humans and Shang-ti/

[24]Arthur Waley, trans., *The Book of Songs* (New York: Grove, 1996), nos. 255, 261.
[25]Roger T. Ames and Henry Rosemont Jr., *The Analects of Confucius: A Philosophical Translation* (New York: Random House, 1998), 47; Yeo, *Confucius and Paul*, 119.
[26]Confucius, *Discourses and Sayings*, 467-68.

Heaven reminds Chinese readers to note the divine immanence of the biblical God, realizing that the gospel as an event happened in human history and became the way God provided salvation for every creature. Thus a holistic perspective on the Godhead prevents a one-sided understanding of God—such as the Western missionaries had in relation to the term question, stressing the transcendence of God but ignoring his immanence. The Chinese Christian understanding of God hopefully does not swing the pendulum to the end of immanence, but holds to both the transcendence and immanence of God.

The ethical connotations in God's/Shang-ti's self-revelations. Finally, the biblical God and Shang-ti/Heaven in the Chinese cultural tradition demonstrate similar ethical connotations in their self-revelations. For the biblical God, the gospel of Christ equalizes the status of everyone, Jew or Gentile, Greek or barbarian, wise or uneducated, so that in this new interpersonal relationship people will not exploit others and instead will welcome each other. The sage rule under the Chinese Shang-ti/Heaven brings about people's moral enlightenment, as they value each other. In this sense, the Christian God and Chinese Shang-ti/Heaven express a similar aspiration: to welcome others for the sake of building them up. Accordingly, the fusion of the Christian God and the Chinese Shang-ti/Heaven prevents any form of cultural centrism, reminding people that particularity cannot live by itself, and universality cannot turn itself into a mandatory and homogenized rule of law.

In Romans 1:17, Paul indicates that the righteousness of God "is from faith to faith." The phrase "from . . . to . . ." (*ek . . . eis . . .*) can be understood as from (God's) faithfulness to (humanity's) faith.[27] It not only stresses the pervasiveness of the gospel but also reminds us that God's power is not only the abstract strength as expressed in creation but also—decisively—his covenant faithfulness as expressed in the raising of Christ from the dead for the sake of salvation. Paul describes this salvation with the phrase "the righteous will live by faith" (Rom 1:17). Faith is not a cognitive concept but an idea about how humans are to treat each other.[28] Therefore, "from God's faithfulness to humanity's faith" shows that right relationship with God will lead us to a new type of interpersonal relationship. For the goal of divine righteousness is to establish faith communities in which righteous relationships are maintained. God becomes the theological basis of ethics; meanwhile, the salvation of God is related to communities rather than simply to individuals. Therefore, reconciliation and harmonious relations between humans are the result of faith/faithfulness—as in Galatians 5:22, "the fruit of the Spirit." God provided salvation to humanity *through* humanity—so that humanity could answer God's invitation of salvation in humanity itself by being receptive to and living out the whole event of the gospel.

In the Chinese cultural tradition, the highest Master of transcendence is not above the universe, but rather is a moral force that exists in the inner life of a person, guiding people how to live with others.[29] Shang-ti/Heaven as the inner moral force means that in Confucian ethics, moral behavior is offered without expecting something in return but is an expression of ethical acts. In other words, moral behavior is to

---

[27]James D. G. Dunn, *Romans 1–8*, Word Biblical Commentary 38 (Dallas: Word, 1988), 44.

[28]Yeo, *Confucius and Paul*, 379.

[29]Yeo, *Confucius and Paul*, 122.

seek the good by doing good. Therefore, for Confucius, the moral person would know how to choose a lifestyle of goodness. He said, "A man without moral character cannot long put up with adversity, nor can he long enjoy prosperity. . . . It is only men of moral character who know how to love men or to hate men. If you fix your mind upon a moral life, you will be free of evil."[30] Shang-ti/Heaven as the basis of ethics helps humans consciously transform their own lives with others into virtuous living.

We know now that the term question as Western missionaries proposed it ignores the uniqueness of the Chinese cultural tradition, namely: (1) they neglected the Chinese living situation as revealed by the language, and (2) they had a tendency to measure and evaluate the Chinese culture by their Western religious tradition, resulting in miscommunication and misunderstanding. To understand and respect the context of both sides is the beginning of true communication. As we can see, the context of Shang-ti/Heaven would help the Chinese reader to understand the context of the biblical God. More importantly, a preunderstanding about the transcendence of Shang-ti/Heaven as the moral force in the human mind reminds the Chinese reader to pay more attention to the immanence of the biblical God. Eventually, similar ethical requirements become a common space for dialogue between the Christian God and the Chinese concept of Shang-ti/Heaven. From this communication—the fusion of two cultural horizons—the biblical texts can generate new meanings in the Chinese cultural context, thus enriching the Christian faith. Of course, Chinese culture would be enriched through the Christian faith as well, since reading the Bible needs to in-

volve a mutual process between the text and the reader's context.

EPILOGUE: UNIVERSALISM AND CONTEXTUALIZATION

Interpreting Romans 1:16-17 through the pre-understandings of Chinese culture gives us new insight on the biblical God. The crosscultural interpretation of the Bible further provides a way to answer questions about the relationship between the universality of Christianity and the particularity of Chinese culture: to understand the biblical God within the context of Chinese culture is not only possible but also necessary.

The universality of the biblical God is not the same as the universality of God that Western missionaries displayed in the term question. In fact, the universality claimed by Western missionaries, as well as the dualism that informed their view of universality (such as Creator/creatures, materiality/spirituality, naturalism/religion, ethics/theology, etc.), is a distinguishing feature of a modern worldview. This kind of universality is built on a rule of abstract homogenization, which means that only the one who fulfills the unified regulations can be counted as belonging to the category.[31] Therefore, when the missionaries discussed how to translate the holy name, they concentrated solely on the transcendence of God's universality. They neglected the event of gospel as divine immanence, which to the Chinese is the moral essence of being human.

Through a crosscultural biblical hermeneutics we have seen that what Paul criticized was precisely the kind of absolute universality that suppresses everything particular by its own standard. What Paul preached is not a mighty God aloof from all but a mighty God who provides

---

[30]Confucius, *Discourses and Sayings*, 368.
[31]Webb Keane, *Christian Moderns: Freedom and Fetish in the Mission Encounter* (Berkeley: University of California Press, 2007), 9-11.

salvation for humanity through grace and whose power is for every creature. The distinction between Jews and Gentiles in Jewish law, or the discrimination against slaves, women, the uneducated, and those of low status under Roman law, cannot be used to identify Christians: "There is neither Jew nor Greek, slave nor free, male nor female, *for you all one in Christ Jesus*" (Gal 3:28). It means that being Christian does not involve fostering an identity over others: "Glory, honor, and peace for everyone who does good: first the Jew, then for the Gentile. *For God does not show favoritism*" (Rom 2:10-11).

The reason this kind of universalism is possible is that God as the truth is not an abstraction. He was incarnated in the event of gospel. There has been an event, and truth consists in declaring it and then in being faithful to this declaration.[32] That means God as the truth is a universal singularity. He is not a cognitive object but a specific event who enters into human life and asks for humans' responses. God is *the* truth, incarnated in a specific historical social setting. This is why in the Apostles' Creed there is a concrete description about this truth: "conceived by the Holy Spirit, given birth through Virgin Mary, suffered under Pontius Pilate, was crucified, died, and buried; he descended into the death, and the third day was raised again." These details not only show the authenticity of the gospel but also convey that God as an eventful truth bears no privileged relation to any status, community, or culture, but only calls for a response from humans in their living. Hence, the gospel needs to be contextualized. Everyone needs to respond to the Christ event from one's own living conditions.

When we read the Bible from a crosscultural hermeneutical perspective, we will have a holistic view of the Godhead. God is not only transcendent as the Creator but also incarnated in humanity to provide salvation. In the sense of God taking care of all humanity, the Christian faith can be contextualized in the Chinese cultural tradition. To achieve this contextualization, not only does one need to understand the context of Chinese life, but also one needs to respect the specificity of each culture, in order to achieve real communication. As Paul put it, "I have become all things to all people" (1 Cor 9:22). By contextualizing in particular cultures, by encountering and communicating with these cultures, and by "becoming all things," the meaning of the Christian faith is continuously enriched and disseminated.

FURTHER READING

Boone, William J. "An Essay on the Proper Rendering of the Words *Elohim* and *Theos* into the Chinese Language." *Chinese Repository* 17 (January 1848): 17-53.

Jewett, Robert, *Romans: A Commentary*. Hermeneia. Minneapolis: Fortress, 2007.

Kim, Sangkeun. *Strange Names of God: The Missionary Translation of the Divine Name and the Chinese Responses to Matteo Ricci's Shangti in Late Ming China, 1583–1644*. New York: Peter Lang, 2004.

Medhurst, Walter H. "An Inquiry into the Proper Mode of Rendering the Word God in Translating the Sacred Scriptures into the Chinese Language." *Chinese Repository* 17 (March 1848): 105-33.

Ricci, Matteo, SJ. *The True Meaning of the Lord of Heaven*. Taipei: Ricci Institute, 1985.

Yeo, K. K. *Musing with Confucius and Paul: Toward a Chinese Christian Theology*. Eugene, OR: Cascade, 2008.

Zetzsche, Jost Oliver. *The Bible in China: The History of the Union Version or the Culmination of Protestant Missionary Bible Translation in China*. Sankt Augustin, Germany: Monumenta Serica Institute, 1999.

---

[32]Alain Badiou, *Saint Paul: The Foundation of Universalism* (Stanford, CA: Stanford University Press, 2003), 6-13.

JESUS WITHOUT BORDERS

CHRISTOLOGY IN THE MAJORITY WORLD

Part Two

INTRODUCTION TO PART TWO

AN INVITATION TO DISCUSS CHRISTOLOGY WITH THE GLOBAL CHURCH

Stephen T. Pardue

WORLD CHRISTIANITY: SO WHAT?

You may have heard about the tectonic shift in global Christianity that is happening before our eyes. A teacher or a friend may have noted that 80 percent of Christians lived in North America and Europe at the turn of the twentieth century, but currently almost 70 percent live in the Majority World. If you are like many Christians around the world today, you understand that these changes are not just about numbers but also about real people. If you have not experienced church life in a rapidly growing part of the world firsthand, you likely know someone who has, and that means you are connected to the people that this statistical story is all about. The increasing interconnectedness of the world and our awareness of people once invisible to us—a phenomenon often called globalization—ensure that we cannot remain disconnected from what is happening elsewhere.

This massive shift has received significant attention in recent years from missiologists, sociologists, and historians. All of them agree that the trends in global Christianity (decline in Europe and North America, and swift growth on every other continent and Oceania) will con-

tinue more or less unabated for the foreseeable future. Many have pointed out an important reality: the kind of Christianity growing in the Majority World has a number of characteristics that differentiate it from the kind that has historically thrived in the North Atlantic region. Indeed, while the core tenets of the faith may not change from Berlin to Nairobi, its texture and trajectories differ from place to place. What it means, in thought, word, and deed, to make Jesus Lord in Bangkok is quite different from what it means to do the same in Chicago (although there are many commonalities, of course). What's more, in learning what it means for Jesus to be Lord in other places, we often grasp the gospel more fully for ourselves and are more able to see the blind spots of our own locally embodied versions of Christianity. Learning from the church throughout the world, as well as through history, is an essential activity for Christians, since we are a catholic, or universal, church.

This volume exists because it is increasingly evident that Christianity in its current state requires theological resources quite different from those that have been available thus far. The great shift in Christianity's makeup cannot be merely observed as a fascinating phenomenon. If we take the Spirit's work around the world seriously, we are obligated as thoughtful Christians to consider how these shifts should enliven, inform, and challenge the church in its proclamation of and reflection on the gospel of Jesus Christ. The changing world and God's providential use of it for our benefit is what makes the theological task new in every generation and distinct in every place, and so it will not do simply to make the same old theological arguments we always have, as good as they might be. The gospel must be understood in relation to the multiplex cultures where the church proclaims and celebrates Christ's good news. As the church has sought to hear the gospel afresh and anew throughout Christian history, so now the Majority World church is doing the same as it seeks to relevantly apply and faithfully proclaim the gospel where its members live.

But just as it would be a mistake to ignore the best thinking and practice emerging from the Majority World, where the church is currently thriving, it would be equally problematic to do theology only in light of the here and now, ignoring the best aspects of Christian tradition. Theology at its best not only considers the proposals of those present and living but also facilitates the "democracy of the dead," letting our spiritual forebears help us as we sort out our present challenges. The complexity of this interplay of past and present interests should not be underestimated, especially because much of church tradition emerges in the shadow of Western thought, and Christians today are primarily living outside the West.

So we need the strongest theological resources available, from both past and present, both West and East, to do theology in our current context. But theology at its best ultimately takes its cues from somewhere beyond these two streams: God's self-revelation in Scripture. As a theological resource, Scripture does not simply stand alongside traditional and contemporary reflection. Rather, it stands above these two, orienting and judging the theological task from start to finish.

This volume aims to bring all of these resources together, with an eye especially toward discerning how Christians attentive to the global shape of the faith should be interacting with Scripture and tradition. That is, we want to move beyond *mere observation* of world Christianity and into the realm of actually *reading the Bible* and *thinking Christianly* together in light of these realities. In doing so, we want to invite you, the reader, into a lively and rich exchange that is possible today in a way that it never was before. In this conversation, you will meet scholars and pastors from around the globe, and you will see them sort out how Scripture, tradition, and culture fit together to guide the church's theological reflection today. We think you will find this a useful and transforming experience, and we hope that it will inspire further conversation in your community, whether you are in Los Angeles, Madrid, Beijing, Buenos Aires, or Bethlehem.

WHY CHRISTOLOGY?

This second part of *Majority World Theology* deals with the person and work of Jesus of Nazareth. In the original six-volume series, these chapters on Christology made up volume one. We chose this topic to inaugurate the series because it is both easy and hard. It is easy because one of the first things revealed by even a superficial examination of Christianity around the world is that every culture observes Jesus differently, with various culturally relevant nuances.

This is perhaps most notable in Christian art: whatever continent you are on, at least some depictions of Jesus are likely to make him look like the people there.[1] At its worst, there can be a kind of self-idolatry in these depictions—a legitimation of oneself or one's culture by self-projection onto the God-man. But often, something more profound is happening: artists are signifying the contextual nature of the Christian faith and communicating the profound truth that God in Jesus has sympathized with *all* humanity, in all of its bewildering and awe-inspiring diversity.

Jesus is revealed as a person for all people, a singular figure with universal and crosscultural significance. And so when the Gospels are translated into various languages, different things stand out to different people groups, and these diverse emphases lead Christians to latch onto various aspects of Jesus' identity. So, for example, while many Europeans in the nineteenth and twentieth centuries found the image of adoption as sons and daughters to be a guiding metaphor in the New Testament and so highlighted Jesus as brother, they often ignored another image that has been more noticed in other times and places: Jesus as King.[2] These different emphases shape everything from theology to prayer to worship, which is part of what gives Christianity in different places and cultures distinct flavor. And so in the study of Jesus, it is easy to see how people from different times, places, and cultures come to different conclusions about the same biblical data.

But as promising as Christology may be as a starting point for renovating theology in light of global Christianity, it also presents some particular challenges. Students of early church history will recall that Christians spent hundreds of years discussing appropriate and problematic ways of talking about Jesus and his relationship to God. Over the years, the legacy of these debates grew and grew, with the result that creedal treatment of Christology is longer and more specific than creedal treatment of any other doctrine.

And all of this discussion and creed writing occurred in a particular historical and cultural context. That context, generally speaking, has more historical continuity with Western ways of thinking about the world than with the conceptual frameworks that are familiar in the places where Christianity is currently growing. Many languages spoken in the Majority World, for example, lack vocabulary equivalents for common creedal words such as *essence* or *hypostasis*, and this is sometimes (though not always) indicative of a lack of concern for the questions being answered with such terms. In the face of this reality, significant debate has emerged regarding how heavily to favor each of the three sources we mentioned earlier: Scripture, tradition, and culture. And so while Christology is, in some ways, an easy place to begin a renovation of theology in light of contemporary realities, it is not without significant challenges. Yet even in these challenges there lies the potential for tremendous theological profit, as we are forced to stare head-on at the tangle of ancient and contemporary realities that hold together in Jesus Christ.

---

[1]There are, of course, plenty of exceptions, such as images of Jesus that have been exported around the world, in which he is often depicted as a white European or American.

[2]Scot McKnight and N. T. Wright have recently emphasized the shortsightedness of this approach. See Scot McKnight, *The King Jesus Gospel: The Original Good News Revisited* (Grand Rapids, MI: Zondervan, 2011); N. T. Wright, *Jesus and the Victory of God* (Minneapolis: Fortress, 1997).

THE PLAN OF PART TWO

The following chapters take a collaborative approach to the challenge of developing a theological approach to Jesus that makes the most of Christians' best resources, both ancient and contemporary. In concrete terms, we asked eight leading scholars from around the world to discuss what Christology looks like in their region and what they hope it might look like in the future. To help bring focus to the analysis of tradition's contribution to the discussion, we asked each author to investigate the relationship between the Christology of the Chalcedonian Definition and their own contextual christological observations and proposals.[3] This approach to the issue is indebted to Andrew Walls, a scholar who has spent his career calling for recognition of the similarities between what is happening in the Majority World church today and what happened in the first few centuries of Christianity.[4]

Because theological dialogue is best done in person, we helped to bring all the authors together for a few crisp fall days in 2012, during the annual meetings of the Evangelical Theological Society and the Institute for Biblical Research, as part of a consultation called "Scripture and Theology in Global Context." During this time, the authors discussed their papers with each other, as well as with other scholars present at the meetings, and then revised their essays for this book. This approach was designed to foster genuine dialogue between people who would otherwise not get to

see one another, and we are confident that the book is much better because of it.

The eight chapters in part two can be divided into two halves. The first half is written by theologians, reflecting on Christology as an enterprise that unites philosophy, history, and cultural anthropology with reflection on Scripture; the second half is written by biblical scholars, reflecting on Christology through deeper interaction with specific biblical texts freighted with christological significance.

In the opening essay, Kevin J. Vanhoozer reflects on christological developments in the West over the centuries, and considers what kind of continuity is important for contemporary Christians seeking to talk about and worship Jesus in the same way that early Christians did. Next, Victor I. Ezigbo discusses the history of Christology in Africa, considers and critiques contemporary proposals, and then offers his own suggestions for a biblical Christology relevant for Africans. After that, Timoteo D. Gener assesses the available proposals on offer regarding what it means to see Jesus through Asian eyes, and suggests that as members of a minority faith, Christians in Asia are best served by thinking about Christology through a missiological lens. Finally, Jules A. Martínez-Olivieri wraps up the first half of essays by examining christological trends in Latin America, and arguing that the region is an ideal place to bridge the gap between Jesus' heavenly and earthly identities.

In the second half of part two, Yohanna Katanacho reads the Gospel of John as a Palestinian,

[3]The Council of Chalcedon was the fourth ecumenical (worldwide) council convened by the early church, and it was focused especially on how Christians should think about Jesus' divinity and humanity. The substance of the Chalcedonian definition is that Jesus is one person with two natures—divine and human—and that these two natures are neither mixed nor separated. This definition, while rejected by a minority of Christians at the time (and today), has set the tone for much christological debate for more than a millennium. For an accessible introduction to Chalcedon, including primary sources, see Richard A. Norris Jr., trans. and ed., *The Christological Controversy* (Minneapolis: Fortress, 1980).
[4]See Walls's excellent essay, "The Rise of Global Theologies," in *Global Theology in Evangelical Perspective*, ed. Jeffrey P. Greenman and Gene L. Green (Downers Grove, IL: InterVarsity Press, 2012), 19-34.

with a particular interest in its relevance for the Palestinian-Israeli conflict. He argues forcefully that John depicts Jesus as establishing a new world order that precludes approaches to Christology that exclude either Palestinians or Jews. Next, Aída Besançon Spencer takes a closer look at New Testament passages relating to Mary, and then considers and critiques the approach to Mariology and Christology in Latino communities. Andrew M. Mbuvi considers the sacrificial system and its usage in 1 Peter in relation to Christ, offering a close examination of the book from the perspective of an Akamba reader. Finally, K. K. Yeo concludes this collection with an essay that sheds light on the challenge of unity and diversity in New Testament Christologies, and also proposes a Christology that reflects on the image of God from a Chinese perspective.

Given the limited time at the conference and limited space in this book, we cannot claim to represent fully the Christologies emerging from the Majority World. We are aware also that many equally significant voices from other parts of the world are not represented here. We wish to express our thanks to the many individuals and organizations that made this collaborative work possible. We are thankful to the Evangelical Theological Society and the Institute for Biblical Research, each of which graciously hosted our group for its in-person discussions. We are thankful, as well, to the Combs Foundation and First Presbyterian Church of Evanston, which helped make the consultation and this book possible. We owe a debt of gratitude to Jessica Hawthorne for her timely help with the indices, and to Michael Thomson and Jenny Hoffman at Eerdmans for their support for and assistance with the book. Finally, it is with joy that we dedicate this book to our brothers and sisters in the Majority World who are offering us renewed visions of the faith. This collection of essays is from them, for them, and about them.

All three of us who edited this volume are thrilled with the outcome of this collaborative experiment in the renovation of theology. While it should be clear that there are ongoing disagreements regarding what it means to do contextual Christology well, each essay you are about to read is rich with insight that has been gleaned from Christianity around the world and strengthened by interaction with Scripture and tradition. We hope you enjoy the book.

CHRISTOLOGY IN THE WEST

CONVERSATIONS IN EUROPE AND NORTH AMERICA

Kevin J. Vanhoozer

IF THEOLOGY IS the doctrine of "living to God," as seventeenth-century English Puritan William Ames held, then we may define Christology as the doctrine of "living to follow Jesus Christ."[1] This means following his story in the fullest sense of the term *following*: understanding who he is, the significance of what he has done, and how to live to God as Christ's disciples in our present contexts. Christology is faith seeking understanding of its prime confession: "I believe in the Lord Jesus Christ." It is the joyful response of heart, mind, soul, and strength to our Lord's own self-communication. To be a disciple—to perform Christology—means knowing (1) who Jesus Christ is for us "yesterday and today and forever" (Heb 13:8) and (2) how to follow this *same* Jesus today, in *different* contexts. Christology is thus about discerning the same (Christ) in the midst of the different (context).

THE MARRIAGE OF THEOLOGY AND MISSIOLOGY: HOMAGE TO ANDREW WALLS

The history of Christian mission is that of successive translations of the gospel into the languages, thought forms, and practices of other cultures. As Andrew Walls rightly notes, the church, in transmitting the gospel, is simply imitating God's own missionary movement (so to speak), the sending of Son and Spirit: "Christian faith rests on a divine act of translation: 'the Word became flesh, and dwelt among us' (John 1:14)."[2] Theology too is the attempt to translate what we read on the sacred page into sacred doctrine, to restate teaching from God about God in concepts and categories that speak coherently and compellingly to people today. Theology and missiology share a common passion and vocation: to translate the way, truth, and life of Jesus Christ.

The geographic progress of the gospel recorded in the book of Acts ("so the word of the Lord continued to increase," Acts 6:7; 12:24; 19:20) continued after the closing of the canon. This missionary movement and the development of doctrine went hand in hand: "In order to explain in the Greek world who Christ is and what he did and does, a new conceptual vocabulary had to be constructed." Yes, there was conflict and confusion, but in the providence of God, as

---

[1]William Ames, *The Marrow of Theology* (Durham, NC: Labyrinth, 1983), 1.1.
[2]Andrew Walls, *The Missionary Movement in Christian History: Studies in the Transmission of Faith* (Maryknoll, NY: Orbis, 1996), 26.

Walls notes, "the process was hugely enriching; it proved to be a discovery of the Christ. . . . It is as though Christ himself actually grows through the work of mission," and, we might add, theology.[3]

The study of Christianity in the non-Western world affords a glimpse into the future of Christian theology, as well as into the present and perennial fact that all Christian theology is to a greater or lesser extent *contextual*. This is as true of the ecumenical Councils of Nicaea and Chalcedon as it is of North American theology today. The Spirit guides the church into the unity of truth precisely by guiding it into greater diversity: "It is a delightful paradox that the more Christ is translated into the various thought forms and life systems which form our various national identities, the richer all of us will be in our common Christian identity."[4]

Walls divides Christian history into six phases. Watch out for that first postapostolic step; it's a doozy. The gospel's entry into Hellenistic culture has "left its mark on all later Christianity," for better or for worse.[5] Indeed, many today believe that this first step was a serious misstep, not a spring forward but a "Fall back into Hellenistic philosophy."[6] A remnant nevertheless remains who insists that the conciliar formulations of the early church fathers is best seen, by way of contrast, as the evangelization of Hellenism.[7] Whether Western Christology is simply a series of footnotes to this "fall" into Hellenistic philosophy rather than a deepening of the church's understanding of Jesus Christ is the urgent question before us.

PREMODERN ROOTS: THE DEEP-SEATED SHAPE OF WESTERN CHRISTOLOGY

Christology: The question and the project. A newcomer to Western theology might be forgiven for thinking that Western theologians misheard Jesus' question; it is as if he had asked, "*What* do you say that I am?" On the other hand, Dietrich Bonhoeffer thinks that's what Jesus may have been asking in the first place:

> The christological question is fundamentally an ontological question. Its aim is to work out the ontological structure of the "Who?" without plunging on the Scylla of the "How?" or the Charybdis of the question of the "truth" of the revelation. The early Church foundered on the former; modern theology since the Enlightenment and Schleiermacher, on the latter. The New Testament, Paul and Luther sailed through the middle.

Bonhoeffer goes on to distinguish Christology from soteriology, and discusses whether one's work interprets the person or the person the work.[8] Luther believed that if the person is good then his work will be good, even if it does not appear to be so. Still, one cannot conclude that the person is good just because the work is: a work can appear good, but it can still be the work of the devil in the guise of an angel of light. Who a person *is* thus takes precedence over what a person *does*. Christology for Bonhoeffer is first and foremost a matter of "who he is" (the person) rather than "what he does" (the work). Western theology has, with some

[3]Walls, *Missionary Movement*, xvii.
[4]Walls, *Missionary Movement*, 54.
[5]Walls, *Missionary Movement*, 18.
[6]For a description, and rebuttal, of the "theory of theology's Fall into Hellenistic philosophy," see Paul Gavrilyuk, *The Suffering of the Impassible God: The Dialectics of Patristic Thought* (New York: Oxford University Press, 2004), chap. 1.
[7]Robert Wilken speaks of a "Christianization of Hellenism" in *The Spirit of Early Christian Thought* (New Haven, CT: Yale University Press, 2003), xvi.
[8]Dietrich Bonhoeffer, *Christ the Center* (New York: Harper & Row, 1978), 32-33, 37.

prominent exceptions, focused on the project that Bonhoeffer describes.[9]

Background: The Council of Chalcedon. We will not understand Western theology without appreciating its deep roots in the Council of Chalcedon. Philip Jenkins, no stranger to the discussion of global theology, alludes to these roots in the subtitle of his book, *Jesus Wars: How Four Patriarchs, Three Queens, and Two Emperors Decided What Christians Would Believe for the Next 1,500 Years*, though he overstates the role political powers played.[10] It is one thing to explain where a belief came from, or why people came to adopt it, but quite another to assess its truth. His claim that the church's core beliefs "gained the status they did as a result of what appears to be . . . the workings of raw chance" is unconvincing. Readers should read with a critical eye. Fair to say some of the historical sources he relies on are dubious. He quotes Edward Gibbon's *Decline and Fall of the Roman Empire* and its account of the aftermath of Chalcedon, saying, "In the pursuit of a metaphysical quarrel, many thousands were slain."[11]

This so-called metaphysical quarrel was nothing less than an attempt to articulate the central Christian conviction "that God was incarnate in Jesus, that Jesus is God and Man."[12] The early christological councils were attempts to ex-plain the underlying logic and ontology of the biblical teaching and narrative of Jesus Christ with the conceptual tools at hand. This required the deliberations of six councils over a span of 350 years.[13] The most important of these councils for our purposes is Chalcedon (451), and its formulation of the so-called hypostatic union: "two natures in one person . . . without confusion, without change, without division, without separation."

Is this an imposition of Greek metaphysics on the gospel? Must Christians subscribe to a particular theory about "natures" and "persons," to the conceptual scheme of a particular culture? Jacques Derrida deflates whatever totalitarian ambitions metaphysics might have by calling it "a white mythology which assembles and reflects Western culture: the white man takes his own mythology . . . his *logos*—that is, the *mythos* of his idiom, for the universal form of that which it is still his inescapable desire to call Reason."[14] Chalcedon employs the notion of *physis*, or "nature," to refer to those essential characteristics that make an entity one thing rather than another. To say that Jesus Christ is "one person in two natures" is to think of him as having both human-making and God-making properties that coexist alongside each other with no admixture.[15] Does this make Christology a white mythology? Not necessarily. It is possible to read

---

[9]The three most important methodological questions in contemporary Western Christology are (1) should one start "from above" by presupposing the Son's heavenly preexistence, or "from below" with the humanity of the historical Jesus? (2) Which takes priority as to subject matter, Jesus' person or work? (3) What kind of explanation takes priority, ontological or functional (i.e., is Jesus the "Christ" because of what he *is* or what he *does*)? See Myk Habets, *The Anointed Son: A Trinitarian Spirit Christology*, Princeton Theological Monograph 129 (Eugene, OR: Pickwick, 2010), 11.

[10]Philip Jenkins, *Jesus Wars: How Four Patriarchs, Three Queens, and Two Emperors Decided What Christians Would Believe for the Next 1,500 Years* (New York: HarperCollins, 2010).

[11]Philip Jenkins, *Jesus Wars* (New York: HarperOne, 2011), xiv, xii.

[12]D. M. Baillie, *God Was in Christ: An Essay on Incarnation and Atonement* (London: Faber & Faber, 1961), 83.

[13]The relevant councils are Nicaea (325), which proclaimed Jesus *homoousios* with God as opposed to Arius's suggestion that Jesus was a splendid creature; Constantinople I (381), which affirmed the Logos's assumption of a true human soul, contra Apollinaris; Ephesus (431), which upheld the unity of Jesus' person (contra Nestorius) and proclaimed Mary *Theotokos*; Chalcedon (451); Constantinople II (553), which recognized the divine Son as the person that is the subject of both natures (*enhypostatis*); Constantinople III (681), which further clarified Chalcedon, specifying that Jesus had two wills, divine and human.

[14]Jacques Derrida, "White Mythology: Metaphor in the Text of Philosophy," *New Literary History* 6 (1974): 11.

[15]See John McIntyre, *The Shape of Christology: Studies in the Doctrine of the Person of Christ*, 2nd ed. (Edinburgh: T&T Clark, 1998), chap. 4, "The Two-Nature Model," esp. 104-5.

Chalcedon's two-natures-in-one-person formula not as a metaphysical proposition but as a grammatical rule for correct speech about Jesus Christ, a rule that stipulates the kind of thing we *can* say and what we must *not* say. On this reading, Chalcedon exhibits metaphysical restraint: the formula gives us guidance for talking about persons and natures but does not tell us in what each consists.

MODERN REACTIONS TO TWO-NATURE CHRISTOLOGY: FROM METAPHYSICS TO MORALS, HISTORY, AND MYTH (AND BACK AGAIN)

Western theologians have been busy preserving, modifying, or rejecting two-nature Christology. With the advent of modernity, theologians began to react against it, as they did all things metaphysical, largely because of Kant's delimitation of knowledge to things that we can experience in space and time. The two alternatives to the heavenly, metaphysical Christ in the eighteenth century were the Jesus of history and the Jesus of moral value: "The central Christological problem of the present day is not the ontological problem which dominated the patristic period, but the question of the relationship between revelation and history."[16] We begin our survey of modern Western Christology by examining two nineteenth- and three twentieth-century responses to Chalcedon.

From metaphysics to religious-moral function. Enlightenment thinkers such as Kant wanted to be rational and to determine the limits of reason. Kant believed that metaphysics—the attempt to know ultimate reality, things such as God, which transcend space and time—is a futile, speculative ambition that modern thinkers ought to abandon. Theologians can continue talking about God, however, if they are willing to do so in terms not of divine nature but of divine function. "Functional" Christologies focus not on Christ's ontological constitution but on what he does, and on the effects of what he does on others.[17]

Friedrich Schleiermacher (1768–1834) espoused a Christology that was very much a product of its nonmetaphysical times. Jesus says "the kingdom is within you" (Lk 17:21 KJV) because the kingdom—the rule of God in the human will—was first and foremost in him (i.e., his subjectivity). He was uniquely receptive to the divine causality everywhere and always at work in the world. God-consciousness, the feeling of being absolutely dependent on God, "was a real being of God in him."[18] It is precisely as archetype of humanity (the second Adam) that Jesus functions as Redeemer, the ideal example and historical source of God-consciousness, which is to say, divinity itself. Jesus is unlike all other men because of "the constant power of his consciousness of God, which was a genuine being of God in him."[19] For Schleiermacher, the historical Jesus is the Christ of faith because he is the agent of redemption: he is the catalyst who communicates his God-consciousness to the apostles, hence mediating between humanity and God. The apostles in turn communicated this God-consciousness to the church, and it is

---

[16]Alister McGrath, *The Making of Modern German Christology* (Oxford: Basil Blackwell, 1986), 2. On the other hand, McIntyre thinks that the influence of Chalcedon is far from over, not least because even reactions against Chalcedon, such as process theology, "remained deeply under its spell" (*Shape of Christology*, ix).

[17]See Donald Macleod, *The Person of Christ* (Downers Grove, IL: InterVarsity Press, 1998), 245-48.

[18]Friedrich Schleiermacher, *The Christian Faith* (Edinburgh: T&T Clark, 1999), 385.

[19]Cited in John P. Galvin, "Modern Western Christology," in *The Blackwell Companion to Jesus*, ed. Delbert Burkett (Oxford: Wiley-Blackwell, 2010), 359.

through participation in the community that Jesus founded that men and women find redemption, the purging and strengthening of their religious subjectivity.

Albert Ritschl (1822–1889) too began his Christology "from within" the this-worldly historical nexus with Jesus' subjectivity or moral consciousness. Ritschl focuses on Jesus' earthly ministry, in particular his proclamation of the kingdom of God—"the organization of humanity through action inspired by love."[20] Jesus serves as a catalyst for what amounts to an ethical commonwealth, a society that does God's will on earth as it is in heaven. Jesus' "divinity" is a function of his will being perfectly aligned with God's will. When Jesus says, "I and the Father are one" (Jn 10:30), Ritschl hears "one in moral purpose." Jesus' divinity is a function of what he does that is Godlike, namely, giving himself in love for the sake of greater community. In this, Ritschl anticipates twentieth-century Christologies that similarly locate Jesus' significance in terms of what he does to bring about justice, liberation, equality, or anything else that advances the kingdom of God: "Ritschl represented Jesus' continuing influence on the world as that of a powerful moral image that continually energizes the community of the kingdom of God."[21]

Kenosis. So-called kenotic Christology (from *kenōsis*, or "self-emptying," Phil 2:7) attempts to both preserve Chalcedon's two-nature framework and do justice to the realities of Jesus' human psychological development.

How can we reconcile Jesus' divinity with his limited human knowledge and fully human psychology? Instead of saying the eternal Logos assumed or *took on* something (i.e., humanity), Lutheran theologian Gottfried Thomasius (1802–1873) proposed that the second person of the Trinity temporarily *divested* (i.e., emptied) himself of divine attributes incompatible with the normal functioning of the finite human mind. Properties such as omnipotence, omniscience, and omnipresence define God in his relation to the world, but they are not *essential* divine attributes such as truth, holiness, and love. In Thomasius's words: "He [Jesus] exercised no other lordship at all than the ethical one of truth and love."[22]

Subsequent kenotic theologians vacillated between saying that the Son put aside the divine nature and saying that he merely chose not to exercise divine functions such as omniscience while in his incarnate state. What remained constant—the kenotic *cantus firmus*—was the idea that the Son emptied himself of everything not compatible with a genuinely human experience. According to kenotic Christology, Jesus is a divine consciousness within a human nature. According to P. T. Forsyth, "We could not have in the same person both knowledge and ignorance of the same thing."[23] While the overarching framework of kenotic Christology is Chalcedonian, its content is distinctly modern.[24]

The Jesus of history. Twentieth-century European theologians who pursued Christology

---

[20]Albrecht Ritschl, *Justification and Reconciliation* (Edinburgh: T&T Clark, 1900), 3:12.

[21]Stanley J. Grenz and Roger E. Olson, *Twentieth-Century Theology: God and the World in a Transitional Age* (Downers Grove, IL: InterVarsity Press, 1992), 58.

[22]From Thomasius, *Christ's Person and Work*, cited in Claude Welch, ed., *God and Incarnation in Mid-nineteenth-century German Thought* (Oxford: Oxford University Press, 1965), 70.

[23]P. T. Forsyth, *The Person and Place of Jesus Christ*, 2nd ed. (London: Hodder & Stoughton, 1910), 319.

[24]For a recent examination of the viability of the notion of kenosis vis-à-vis Chalcedon, see C. Stephen Evans, ed., *Exploring Kenotic Christology: The Self-Emptying of God* (Oxford: Oxford University Press, 2006).

"from below" did justice to Jesus' humanity another way, proposing to examine the historical evidence for signs that Jesus was (humanly) conscious of his divine identity.[25] Unlike their kenotic counterparts, however, they were unwilling to presuppose a Chalcedonian framework. Belgian Roman Catholic Edward Schillebeeckx (1914–2009) is representative of this approach.[26] Schillebeeckx discovered a Jesus who proclaimed a liberating message (concerning the radical hospitality of God and the liberation of the oppressed from suffering) and practiced what he preached (i.e., by having table fellowship with sinners and healing the sick). Jesus was an eschatological prophet who proclaimed and practiced his powerful "Abba" experience of intimacy with God. Schillebeeckx uses this historical conclusion as a norm for judging all other theological statements about Jesus' identity, including that of Chalcedon. On his view, Jesus' other titles—Lord, Son of God, Christ—reflect the various ways the apostles sought to describe their experience of the significance of the eschatological prophet's work: "This means that all the later titles must be interpreted functionally, not ontologically."[27]

The Christ of myth. The so-called myth-of-God-incarnate theologians represent the most extreme Western rejection of Chalcedon, and of metaphysics more generally. Their "non-incarnational Christology" denies both the pre- and postexistence of Jesus Christ.[28] John Hick, the organizer of the symposium that later became *The Myth of God Incarnate*, argued that Chalcedon was not only inexplicable—how could a mere mortal be God?—but "pernicious" and unjust inasmuch as it limits salvation to the Judeo-Christian tradition alone. It is precisely the exclusivism associated with Chalcedonian Christology—the uniqueness of the God-man—that renders it objectionable to these thinkers. According to Hick, Jesus was "a man approved by God" for a special role, and the incarnation is simply a poetic way or metaphor that the church used to express his significance for us.[29] For a religious pluralist like Hick, viewing Jesus as *one* way rather than *the* way to God "can only be regarded as a gain."[30] However, in the words of one contemporary: "A Savior not quite God is a bridge broken at the farther end."[31]

Revisionist ontologies and metaphysics. Several twentieth-century Christologies revised the tradition in light of newer philosophies. Paul Tillich (1886–1965) was alert to the widespread problem of anxiety and used categories drawn from existentialist philosophy to explain how Christ is the answer to questions implied in human existence. In Tillich's hands, Christology is the answer to the question of how to cope with the anxiety that human existence is not simply finite but threatened by meaninglessness, a form of "non-being." According to Tillich, the story of Jesus' cross and resurrection is a symbolic representation of the power of "new being" to overcome existential estrangement (this is ontology in a new existentialist key). The way Jesus dies shows that it is possible to have victory over anxiety through trust in God—Being itself, the

---

[25]Representative theologians include Wolfhart Pannenberg, Walter Kasper, and Hans Küng.

[26]See Edward Schillebeeckx, *Jesus: An Experiment in Christology* (New York: Seabury, 1979), and *Christ: The Christian Experience in the Modern World* (New York: Seabury, 1980).

[27]Edward T. Oakes, *Infinity Dwindled to Infancy: A Catholic and Evangelical Christology* (Grand Rapids, MI: Eerdmans, 2011), 406.

[28]So Brian Hebblethwaite, *The Incarnation: Collected Essays in Christology* (Cambridge: Cambridge University Press, 1987), 2.

[29]John Hick, ed., *Myth of God Incarnate* (London: SCM, 1977), ix.

[30]Maurice Wiles, "Christianity Without Incarnation?," in Hick, *Myth of God Incarnate*, 9.

[31]Handley Moule, preface to Robert Anderson, *The Lord from Heaven: Chapters on the Deity of Christ* (London: James Nisbet, 1910).

source or ground of one's particular being—whatever the negativities of one's life.[32]

One of the most surprising developments in twentieth-century Christology was the return to metaphysics, though one that employed categories not of being and substance but of becoming and process. Process thinkers follow Alfred North Whitehead in thinking that a focus on events rather than essences allows them to construct a theory of reality that does justice to Einstein's physics. According to process theology, God is not "over" the world, sovereignly decreeing whatever comes to pass, but rather the "soul" of the world who loves and lures the world to actualize its own good. Process theology privileges divine immanence, not transcendence; God acts not on but within the world's natural processes. Hence Christ's incarnation was "not by intrusion from outside but by emergence from within" the world.[33] There is no place for the virgin birth in process theology. Jesus is a man who makes a great leap forward for humanity by perfectly following God's desire for the human creature, the divine lure ("My food is to do the will of the one who sent me," Jn 4:34). In so doing, Jesus acts as catalyst in the becoming of a new kind of human community: the church, a way of being together that transcends the usual divisions of race, gender, and class.[34] Jesus is not the God-man but the human who becomes fully open to the divine influence, the person in whom we best see the divine process of creative transformation.

BACK TO (OR BEYOND) CHALCEDON? CONVERSATIONS IN CONTEMPORARY WESTERN CHRISTOLOGY

We turn now to survey contemporary trends in European and North American Christology. There is a vast amount of material, but little consensus on how to order it. Textbooks disagree about the organizing categories: some treat Jürgen Moltmann (b. 1926) under "The Crucified God," others under "Eschatological Christology," and still others under "Postmodern Christology." The following classification stems in part from an interest in seeing how various approaches (1) attend to the biblical narrative, (2) remain faithful to Chalcedon's ontology, and (3) genuinely contextualize the gospel rather than merely reflect (or impose) the concerns of cultural contexts.

The humanity of Jesus Christ. Though Chalcedon affirms that Jesus Christ is "truly human," contemporary christological discussions make the humanity of Jesus the focal point and assess its significance in new ways. Don Schweitzer concludes his survey of contemporary Christologies with this observation: "The genuine humanity of Jesus is a basic assumption of contemporary Christologies."[35] Whereas Chalcedon asks, "How did God become man?" contemporary theologians ask, "In what does Jesus' humanity really consist, and how can a particular individual who lived in one context be universally relevant, significant to people in every context?"

Faith. Some suggest that Jesus is never more human than when he puts his faith in God. On this view, Jesus is a representative of perfect humanity precisely because, as one who accepts

---

[32]For an evaluation of Tillich's Christology as overly beholden to his mid-twentieth-century context, see Colin J. D. Greene, *Christology in Cultural Perspective: Marking Out the Horizons* (Grand Rapids, MI: Eerdmans, 2003), 128-32.

[33]Norman Pittenger, *The Word Incarnate* (New York: Harper & Row, 1959), 192.

[34]A significant problem with process Christology is that, in principle, other individuals could respond to God's lure too, thus calling Jesus' uniqueness into question.

[35]Don Schweitzer, *Contemporary Christologies* (Minneapolis: Fortress, 2010), 128.

and obeys the word of God (see Heb 11:6), he is the paradigm of covenant faithfulness. T. F. Torrance encourages us to "think of Jesus Christ as believing, trusting, and having faith in God the Father on our behalf and in our place."[36]

Fellow feeling. Many contemporary approaches in the West are sensitive to social context, focusing on "how Jesus empowers those who believe in him to love others, accept themselves, and remain faithful" and viewing Jesus as "the bearer of a universal principle of justice that is not limited by creed or race." Their goal is to apply and expand the patristic axiom, "that which is unassumed is unhealed," so as to include all kinds of human beings. Jesus is the embodiment of the compassion of God, and "the principal evil that Jesus saves people from is a misapprehension of God and a lack of concern for the victims of society."[37]

The awareness of social context has led some to put the accent in Bonhoeffer's question on the person asking it: "Who is Jesus Christ *for us* today?" The "us" in question might be Latinos, African Americans, Asian Americans, or any other marginalized group excluded from the power and influence of the mainstream. Women are a case in point. Elizabeth Johnson observes that the creedal formulation of the incarnation (*homo factus est*) should be translated "was made human," not "was made man."[38] Feminist Christology emphasizes Jesus' full humanity, in particular his loving acceptance and compassion for the outcast, as well as his willingness to subvert unjust social structures, including patri-

archy. It is not his sex but his spirit—his identification with and liberating preference for the poor—that qualifies him as God's representative.

Fallenness. Another conversation that falls under this general rubric is whether Jesus assumed a *fallen* humanity. Those who say yes do so in order to underscore Jesus' identification with sinners. Those who disagree do so to avoid denying Jesus' sinlessness, on the grounds that if Jesus were a sinner he could not be our Savior. This dispute is a good example of how debates about the person of Jesus are inextricably tied to discussions about his saving work.[39]

The (narrative) identity of Jesus Christ. As we have seen, Western theologians typically tended to respond to Jesus' question ("Who do you say that I am?") in one of two ways: (1) by saying *what* he is or (2) by saying what he *does* for us. The 1980s ushered in a new approach that responds by (3) narrating his *identity*, thereby focusing on the *who* question in a new way. Philosopher Paul Ricoeur argues that narrative is not simply a way of packaging information but a cognitive instrument in its own right, capable of providing explanations that elude the grasp of metaphysics. The "turn to narrative" in Christology, often associated with Karl Barth (1886–1968), is thus a high point in twentieth-century Western Christology's attempt to explain how Jesus is the Christ.

Hans Frei (1922–1988) castigated both conservatives and liberals for "eclipsing" biblical narrative. The former read the Gospels as histories, mining them for nuggets of factual information;

---

[36]T. F. Torrance, *The Mediation of Christ*, rev. ed. (Colorado Springs: Helmers & Howard, 1992), 92-93. See further R. Michael Allen, *The Christ's Faith: A Dogmatic Account* (London: T&T Clark, 2009).

[37]Schweitzer, *Contemporary Christologies*, 130, 34.

[38]*She Who Is: The Mystery of God in Feminist Theological Discourse* (New York: Crossroad, 1992), 165.

[39]See further Kelly M. Kapic, "The Son's Assumption of a Human Nature: A Call for Clarity," *International Journal of Systematic Theology* 3 (2011): 154-66, and Oliver Crisp, *Divinity and Humanity* (Cambridge: Cambridge University Press, 2007), chap. 4, "Did Christ Have a *Fallen* Human Nature?," 90-117.

the latter read the Gospels as myth, demythologizing them in search of existential truth. Neither read the Gospels as history-like narratives whose unique purpose is to render personal identity. It is one thing to describe a person by listing that person's objective characteristics, or "properties" (e.g., six feet tall, brown hair, good sense of humor, hardworking). It is quite another to read the Gospels on their own terms, as "realistic" narratives, that identify Jesus as "the-one-who-cannot-be-thought-of-except-as-now-living." In Frei's words: "To know who he is in connection with what took place is to know that he is. This is the climax of the story and its claims. What the accounts are saying, in effect, is that the being and identity of Jesus in the resurrection are such that his non-resurrection becomes inconceivable."[40]

New Testament scholar Richard Bauckham (b. 1946) argues that the unified narrative of Old and New Testaments includes the man Jesus in the unique identity of the God of Israel. "Identity" responds to the *who* question. As God identifies himself to Israel as the one who redeems Israel, rules all things, and alone is deserving of worship, so the New Testament identifies Jesus as one who saves the world, receives worship, and rules all things ("even the wind and the sea obey him," Mk 4:41). Because Jesus does things that only God can do, such as forgive sins, and because God is one (Deut 6:4), Bauckham argues that the biblical narrative drives readers to the inescapable conclusion that Jesus Christ participates in the divine identity. As to *homoousios* ("of the same substance"), far from being a piece of abstract ontological speculation, it instead "functions to ensure that this divine identity is truly the identity of the one and only God."[41]

Focal points in the narrative of Jesus Christ. It is difficult to keep the whole of Jesus' story in mind simultaneously. Many theologians who have made the "turn to narrative" therefore tend to emphasize one moment in Jesus' story and use it as the lens for viewing everything else. Four particular moments stand out as being of particular importance to Western Christology.[42]

Incarnation. For T. F. Torrance, the event that overshadows all others in importance is when God assumed humanity and "became flesh" (Jn 1:14). The incarnation is God's loving "Yes" to every human being. The Son of God enters into a "carnal union" with all humanity. All are objectively "in Christ" and thus (ontologically) related to God, whether they realize it (subjectively) or not. The work of Christ is here identical with his person: Jesus atones for humanity by becoming human and living out a human life (a life that includes death). In Kathryn Tanner's words: "Incarnation becomes the primary mechanism of atonement."[43] Jesus is the one in whom God and humanity coexist in a harmonious relationship. *Homoousios* implies reconciliation.[44]

Crucifixion. No other event better characterizes the story of Jesus than his suffering and death on a cross, which is why Martin Kähler can describe the Gospel of Mark as "a passion narrative with an extended introduction."[45] According to Moltmann, Jesus' crucifixion reminds

[40]Hans Frei, *The Identity of Jesus Christ: The Hermeneutical Bases of Dogmatic Theology* (Philadelphia: Fortress, 1975), 145.

[41]Richard Bauckham, *God Crucified: Monotheism and Christology in the New Testament* (Grand Rapids, MI: Eerdmans, 1998), 71, 78-79.

[42]Other focal points (e.g., the transfiguration; the descent into hell) figure less frequently.

[43]Kathryn Tanner, *Christ the Key* (Cambridge: Cambridge University Press, 2010), 252.

[44]Though I have emphasized the incarnation as a moment, both Torrance and Tanner intend what they say about it to extend to the whole of Jesus' life, and not his birth only. For a critique of Tanner's notion that incarnation is atoning, see Oliver Crisp, *Revisioning Christology: Theology in the Reformed Tradition* (Farnham, UK: Ashgate, 2011), 111-31.

[45]Martin Kähler, *The So-Called Historical Jesus and the Historic, Biblical Christ* (Philadelphia: Fortress, 1964), 80.

us that hope is always for something other than what is present in the world. The cross reveals God's willingness to take on the suffering of the world in order to make all things new. Indeed, Moltmann wrote *The Crucified God* in order to criticize the idea that God sovereignly supports the oppressive status quo: "For me the cross of Christ became the 'foundation and critique of Christian theology.'"[46] Interestingly, nowhere in his book *The Way of Jesus Christ* does Moltmann even mention Chalcedon.[47] He is less interested in speculating on how the cross affects the two natures than in understanding how the death of the Son enables the Father to absorb, and so overcome, all the forces of death and destruction that threaten the world.

Resurrection. Wolfhart Pannenberg (b. 1928) pins his whole Christology on the historical event of Jesus' resurrection. With an eye to biblical (and late Jewish) apocalyptic and eschatology, Pannenberg argues that the meaning of any event of history can only be determined in light of the end of history, for only then will the revelation of God be complete. Pannenberg's signal contribution is to insist that the end of history has broken into the middle of history in the resurrection of Jesus Christ, a harbinger of the general resurrection of the dead that God will bring about at the consummation.[48] Only on the basis of this historical event can we say that Jesus' preaching of the coming kingdom is true. We can also confess that "Jesus is God" (i.e., the future of God's rule and the meaning of universal history), but only *after, and because of,* the resurrection.

Ascension. Some theologians have made the very last incident of Jesus' story—his ascension into heaven (Lk 24:51; see Acts 1:9-11)—rather than the resurrection the climax of Jesus' story, a crucial lens for understanding not only Christology but also the church.[49] The ascension reminds us that the incarnation (i.e., the Son's assumption of human nature-flesh) continues, that Jesus now lives, and that he will return to earth. In ascending, Jesus went up to heaven in our flesh: "I go and prepare a place for you" (Jn 14:2). The ascension reminds us that what is now true of the Son of God—that he has not simply a spiritualized existence but an exalted human, and bodily, existence—will eventually be true for the saints. The ascended Jesus Christ is the hope of the saints' glorification.

Analytic Christology. The relationship of faith and rationality has long been a concern of Western thinkers. Recently, however, a group of theologians has enlisted tools typically used in analytic philosophy and applied them to the project of faith seeking understanding. Analytic theologians prioritize precision, clarity, and logical coherence and seek to clarify basic concepts that play important roles in Christian doctrine.[50] In particular, analytic theologians strive to give as clear a picture as possible of the ultimate constituents of reality, including (as far as is possible) the mystery of the triune God. It follows that analytic theologians are concerned to read the biblical narrative with a view to making (conceptually and ontologically) explicit what is (metaphorically and narratively) implicit.

[46]Jürgen Moltmann, *How I Have Changed: Reflections on Thirty Years of Theology* (London: SCM Press, 1997), 18; see Moltmann, *The Crucified God* (London: SCM Press, 1974).
[47]Jürgen Moltmann, *The Way of Jesus Christ* (Minneapolis: Fortress, 1993).
[48]Wolfhart Pannenberg, *Jesus: God and Man* (Philadelphia: Westminster, 1977).
[49]Gerrit Dawson, *Jesus Ascended: The Meaning of Christ's Continuing Incarnation* (London: T&T Clark, 2004); Douglas Farrow, *Ascension Theology* (London: T&T Clark, 2011).
[50]See Oliver D. Crisp and Michael C. Rea, eds., *Analytic Theology: New Essays in the Philosophy of Theology* (Oxford: Oxford University Press, 2009), esp. the introduction and chap. 1.

Chalcedonian Christology, with its central postulate "two natures in one person," is an apt candidate for analysis, not least because many Westerners charge it with being not only mysterious but also incoherent. Analytic theologians therefore devote considerable energy to refining definitions and clarifying distinctions (e.g., What is "human nature"? Does the God-man have one mind or two?). Thomas V. Morris's *The Logic of God Incarnate* is a good example of analytic Christology.[51] Morris draws a number of helpful distinctions (e.g., Chalcedon's "fully human" does not mean "merely human") in an effort to demonstrate the coherence of the concept of the hypostatic union.

Christology as lens for viewing other doctrines and domains. We turn now from approaches that think *about* Christology to those that think *with* and *through* it. It was Karl Barth who made the famous "turn to Christology," insisting that the history of Jesus Christ—a unified series of personal and agential events—is the sole basis for everything we know about God, true humanity, and their relationship. Barth preserves Chalcedon in a new conceptual key by radically "actualizing" his understanding of both persons and natures, however, insisting that we do not know what "divinity" and "humanity" truly mean apart from Jesus' concrete history.[52] God *is* what he *does* in Jesus Christ: "He acts as God when He acts as a human being, and as a human being when He acts as God."[53] Largely because of Barth's influence, Christology has become not simply one theological locus among others but the key to unlocking every other

doctrine—and not only doctrine! Three examples will have to suffice.

Election. Barth reworks every other doctrine—creation, the divine attributes, anthropology—on the basis of his Christology, thus prompting some to wonder whether Christian theology has perhaps become *too* christological. The doctrine of election is the most stunning example. On Barth's view, God does not choose particular human beings to elect, but rather elects *all* human beings in Christ. There is no electing decree "behind Christ's back." Further, election pertains to God's self-determination not to be God *apart* from his union with humanity in Christ. Election "in Christ" therefore determines both the being of humanity and of God. Hence a "christologically conditioned" doctrine of election is the sum of the gospel: that God essentially is the one who is with us and for us is the totality of the good news.

Metaphysics. Robert Jenson radicalizes Barth's insight, offering a christologically conditioned understanding of God's very being. Specifically, Jenson corrects Greek metaphysics with what he calls a "metaphysics of the gospel" that identifies God's being with the events of Jesus' life. Consistently to follow Barth's "turn to the subject of Jesus Christ" is to substitute Jesus' concrete history for what Western metaphysics traditionally referred to as the Ground of Being. Jesus' *individuality* is constitutive of God's *infinity:* "God is what happens between Jesus and his Father in their Spirit."[54] This is the necessary consequence of turning Christology into first theology, the norm for all speaking and thinking about God.

---

[51]Thomas V. Morris, *The Logic of God Incarnate* (Ithaca, NY: Cornell University Press, 1986).

[52]For a fuller description of Barth's radically actualized Christology, see Paul Dafydd Jones, *The Humanity of Christ: Christology in Karl Barth's Church Dogmatics* (London: T&T Clark, 2008).

[53]Karl Barth, *Church Dogmatics* (Edinburgh: T&T Clark, 1958), IV/2, 115.

[54]Robert Jenson, *Systematic Theology*, vol. 1, *The Triune God* (Oxford: Oxford University Press, 1997), 221. McIntyre wonders whether some theologians ask Christology to perform tasks for which the doctrine was not originally designed.

Ethics. Christology is the attempt to formulate *what is* in Jesus Christ. In Christ there is "the fullness of God" (Col 1:19) and the covenant fellowship (union) between God and humanity. In Christ, as the apostle Paul says, there is "a new creation" (2 Cor 5:17). Christian ethics may be described as the attempt to show how *is* implies *ought* "in Christ." Jesus is not merely a moral example to emulate in our respective contexts; rather, disciples participate in who he is. Jesus Christ is the truth and life of the new creation: he is what God is doing by the Spirit's power to make all things new (Rev 21:5). Viewed through the lens of Christology, ethics is the human response to what Jesus is *now doing* and *now is.*[55] Regardless of their particular context, then, disciples participate in reality rightly only if and when they know who Jesus is and what he is now doing to renew all things. Christology, on this view, is indeed all-encompassing: it directs us how best to become the kind of people that correspond to Jesus' person and work, a person and work that reveals and establishes the really real. Christology says *what is* and *what therefore ought to be.*

CONCLUDING ONTOLOGICAL-CONTEXTUAL POSTSCRIPT: ON THE DEVELOPMENT OF ANY FUTURE GLOBAL CHRISTOLOGY

The question now before us is *how to go on globally* without either letting Western Christology dominate the discussion or dismissing it altogether. If Christology today is "lived in the tension between continuity with the church's doctrinal tradition on the one hand and, on the other, openness to new experiences and understandings of Christ arising out of the particular contexts of suffering and hope," we cannot shirk the question: Whither Chalcedon?[56]

Church history is the story of contextualization as the gospel encountered new frontiers (i.e., a new space) and ethnic groups (i.e., a new people). There are still a few people groups left that have not heard of Jesus Christ; yet global theology poses a distinctly new contextual challenge. It is no longer simply a matter of the gospel entering new contexts, but rather of the *intersection of contexts*, including some that have already received the gospel.

We stand at the threshold of an exciting new stage of church history: "The full-grown humanity of Christ requires all the Christian generations, just as it embodies all the cultural variety that six continents can bring." Andrews Walls acknowledges that all Christians affirm "the ultimate significance" of Jesus of Nazareth but is reluctant to state the coherence of historical Christianity in creedal or propositional form since such formulation "is itself a necessary product of a particular Christian culture."[57] I believe the global church can still and ought to confess that Chalcedon, while not the *whole* truth, is nevertheless "the truth and nothing but the truth," stated in the conceptual terms of the Greco-Roman context.

Is there a global future for Christology without ontology? Must we apologize when using concepts such as *homoousios* for the unbearable *whiteness* of "being"? The ecumenical councils, in invoking ontological terms, showed themselves to be Western, but not necessarily provincial, or metaphysical. Bruce McCormack's verdict is worth pondering: "If Barth has taught

---

[55]So Christopher R. J. Holmes, *Ethics in the Presence of Christ* (London: T&T Clark, 2012).
[56]Daniel L. Migliore, "Christology in Context: The Doctrinal and Contextual Tasks of Christology Today," *Interpretation* 49 (1995): 242.
[57]Walls, *Missionary Movement*, xvii, 23.

us anything, it is that . . . theological ontology can be constructed on the basis of the narrated history of Jesus of Nazareth without the help of metaphysics."[58] I want to make three suggestions about the development of any future global Christology, especially as it concerns the vexed question of Nicaea and Chalcedon's ontology and its normative status. I argue that these creedal statements are essential for thinking rightly about the biblical narratives as stories and histories about Jesus, for maintaining the unity of the church, and for assisting the church to faithfully to improvise new cultural scenes of discipleship in context. In the final analysis, however, we will see that it takes a global village—churches from West, East, and South—fully to say who Jesus Christ is for us today.

1. *What is normative in Chalcedon is not a particular metaphysical scheme but the underlying biblical ontology, not the particular concepts but the underlying judgments that they express.*

Let me explain. To claim that Nicaea and Chalcedon preserve necessary evangelical *judgments* is not to insist that subsequent doctrinal formulations must use Greek, or that Christian cultural practices must be Hellenistic. Everything hinges on the distinction between language and concepts on the one hand, and judgments and wisdom—the ability to draw proper distinctions and make fundamental connections—on the other.[59] Judgments "are intellectual (and therefore moral and spiritual) acts

in which we struggle to order our thinking and speaking in response to reality, and so to think and speak truthfully."[60] To understand the biblical witness theologians must make many kinds of judgments—moral, logical, historical, and yes, ontological: "The Bible conceives life as a drama in which human and divine actions create the dramatic whole. There are ontological presuppositions for this drama, but they are not spelled out."[61] Making "theodramatic" judgments—about the identity of the divine agents in the drama of redemption, about what the drama is about, about what we should do fittingly to participate—is perhaps the quintessential theological skill.

I owe the concept-judgment distinction to David Yeago, who in a seminal essay developed it in connection to Nicaea. He thinks Paul's language in Philippians 2:6, about the Son's *isos theos* ("equality with God"), is saying the same thing as Nicaea's very different concept *homoousios* ("of the same substance"). It is essential "to distinguish between judgments and the conceptual terms in which those judgments are rendered" so that "the same judgment can be rendered in a variety of conceptual terms."[62] The technical concept *homoousios* expresses a nonidentical equivalence with Paul's "equality with God." Chalcedon's "two natures in one person" language is similarly faithful to biblical discourse, not because it repeats the same biblical words or concepts (it does not), but because it

---

[58]Bruce McCormack, "The Person of Christ," in *Mapping Modern Theology: A Thematic and Historical Introduction*, ed. Kelly M. Kapic and Bruce L. McCormack (Grand Rapids, MI: Baker Academic, 2012), 171-72.

[59]Humans typically think, and achieve understanding, by making appropriate connections and distinctions. The mind, most basically, identifies, relates, and distinguishes. Hence the typical form of judgments: "this is an *x*"; "this is not an *x*"; "all *x*'s are *y*'s"; "no *x*'s are *y*'s," etc.

[60]John Webster, *Word and Church: Essays in Christian Dogmatics* (Edinburgh: T&T Clark, 2001), 4.

[61]Reinhold Niebuhr, "Biblical Thought and Ontological Speculation in Tillich's Theology," in *The Theology of Paul Tillich*, ed. Charles W. Kegley and Robert W. Bretall (New York: Macmillan, 1952), 216.

[62]David Yeago, "The New Testament and the Nicene Dogma: A Contribution to the Recovery of Theological Exegesis," in *The Theological Interpretation of Scripture: Classic and Contemporary Readings*, ed. Stephen Fowl (Oxford: Blackwell, 1997), 93.

renders in *different* terms the *same* underlying (ontological) judgments. *It is not the propositional content alone but the biblical judgments of which they are ingredients—that the man Jesus is God; that humanity is not divinity—that are theologically binding.*

This account may be open to what appears to be a serious objection: Why should the rest of the world care about the West's grand ontological obsession? My answer: because the Christian faith necessarily involves certain ontological presuppositions, namely, "the question of being, of what is real and how it is real."[63] Consider, for example, the "ontological difference" between Being and beings. We may not want to use the same expression, but global Christians need to express the same judgment in some way in order rightly to respond to the prime theological imperative (also known as the First Commandment): "You shall have no other gods before me" (Ex 20:3). We can only keep ourselves from idols if we get into the habit of thinking of God in some kind of absolute distinction to all other creatures (i.e., what Western theologians call the "ontological difference").

The church's use of concepts such as nature and person should not be viewed as a betrayal of the faith to philosophical tradition but rather as an attempt, by particular people of faith, to gain a greater understanding of the biblical drama of redemption (i.e., by identifying its protagonist). This is a crucial point. Chalcedon does not define for all time what a person is or what is in a nature; instead, it *provides direction, and a concrete example, for the kinds of things all Christians ought to say about Jesus Christ.* We can speak of Jesus without (cultural) borders but not without some (conceptual) boundaries. For example: "We might say that a 'person' is what there are three of in the Trinity and one in Christ, and 'nature' is what there is one of in the Trinity and two in Christ."[64] What is normative about Chalcedon is the underlying ontological judgment that it preserves, in Greek conceptual form, from Scripture: whatever it means to be human, and whatever it means to be God, Chalcedon stipulates that we must say that the one person Jesus Christ is fully both.

2. *While the Bible alone has magisterial authority, the early catholic consensus has ministerial authority insofar as it displays biblical judgments. It thus provides pedagogical direction and an important opportunity for global theology to display catholic sensibility, which is to say a concern for doing theology in communion with the saints.*

Jesus Christ is "the same yesterday and today and forever" (Heb 13:8). The same cannot be said for Christology. Whereas the previous point dealt with apostolicity (preserving authoritative biblical judgments), the focus here is on the oneness and catholicity of the church and its doctrine. Clearly, the West has not exhausted the riches of the knowledge of Jesus Christ. There is more, much more, to be said on the basis of God's word. However, we should no more despise or relativize the hypostatic union simply because it is culturally situated than we should relativize Newton's Second Law of Motion—$F = ma$ (force = mass × acceleration)—just because he was a seventeenth-century Englishman.

How do we know whether Chalcedon, or our local church, is saying the same thing about Jesus Christ as the apostles? Kevin Hector offers a "postmetaphysical" account of the way one's doctrinal concepts can be judged to be the same.

---

[63]McCormack, "Person of Christ," 150.

[64]Bernard Lonergan, "The Origins of Christian Realism," in *A Second Collection: Papers* (London: Darton, Longman, & Todd, 1974), 259.

Everything depends on *using* concepts in ways that others recognize as attempts to carry on the normative trajectory implicit in a chain of precedent performances recognized as authoritative or, in our case, apostolic.[65] Hector's account relies heavily on our ability to recognize other Christians as "one of us." In the New Testament, this happened dramatically when various groups of people received the Holy Spirit. The illumination of the word-ministering Spirit enables the church eventually to distinguish whether or not a judgment counts as "going on in the same way" as Jesus Christ.

Can we merge Hector's account of the transmission of the faith with that of Walls? In each case it is important to carry on, in the power of the Spirit, the normative trajectory implicit in the church's confession of Jesus as the Christ. Both Hector and Walls acknowledge that the trajectory looks a bit different each time a new use is recognized as going on in the same way. We must not overlook the significance of this point. *The non-Western church can go on in the same way as Nicaea and Chalcedon without having to do so in a slavish, repetitive manner.* Nicaea and Chalcedon are nevertheless important developments that help anchor the trajectory by embodying biblically sound judgments in terms of their respective cultural situations. Subsequent Christologies would do well to continue going on in the same way.

Non-Western Christianity does not need to become Western. Yet non-Western Christianity should strive to stay authentically Christian, and one way to do that is to remain in communion with catholic theological tradition. The way

forward for global theology is so to know both Scripture and tradition well enough to make judgments about whether the church's speech and action today participates rightly in the "same doing"—*homodrao*, one might say—as the biblically attested story of the Christ.

3. *Western Christology is ultimately a matter of regional, perhaps even masterpiece, theater that, while not providing an exhaustive description, nevertheless affords precious insight into the identity of the main protagonist of the drama of redemption.*

No single way of embodying the gospel or identifying Jesus Christ is exhaustive of his way, truth, and life. However, occasional performances—and all attempts to act out theological understanding are "occasional"—can produce permanent gains. I believe the formulas of Nicaea and Chalcedon to be great performances—responses to their own historical contexts that contain lessons for the rest of the church as well.[66]

Like it or not, Western theology is part of the catholic heritage of the church, and hence an intrinsic part of global theology. Whatever the locale, the church's performance of the gospel should be informed by the magisterially authoritative canonical performance of the apostles as well as the ministerially authoritative catholic performance of their successors, Western and non-Western. The goal of global theology is not simply to maintain Chalcedon, of course, but rather to promote what we might call *theodramatic understanding*: a grasp of what God is doing in Christ through the Spirit to renew all things, and a sense of how the

---

[65]Kevin Hector, *Theology Without Metaphysics: God, Language, and the Spirit of Recognition* (Cambridge: Cambridge University Press, 2011), 48.

[66]See further my "'One Rule to Rule Them All?' Theological Method in an Era of World Christianity," in *Doing Theology in a Globalized World*, ed. Craig Ott and Harold Netland (Grand Rapids, MI: Baker, 2006), 85-126.

church in its particular place and time can participate in the action.

If Newton's Second Law holds good for people in twenty-first-century Guatemala and Tibet, how much more ought the global church attend to the Chalcedonian formula, if it correctly identifies Jesus' ontological constitution. To the extent that it makes the ontology presupposed by the biblical drama explicit, doctrinal formulations are true for everyone, everywhere, and at all times. The global church will of course find new things to say about what Jesus Christ means for us today, but I respectfully submit that these new things must go on in the same way—or at least not go *against*—the way indicated by Chalcedon.[67]

What we are after is creative understanding: the ability to go on in the same way, only differently. How can we think this sameness and difference together? I submit that what stays the same is the drama of redemption. The church needs to remain faithful to the apostolic testimony (the inspired transcript), for there is no other gospel, no other drama of redemption. What is different, however, is the scene the local church is now being asked to play. Put differently: the theological judgments about the essential nature of the theodrama must remain the same, but the particular way we perform it—the way we go on—in our present context may differ from previous performances. The task of systematic theology is to form actors with good improvisatory judgment, disciples

who know how to go on in the same way as their Lord in terms of their different cultural contexts. Global theology is a "Pentecostal" plurality of languages and concepts ruled by biblical judgments, especially as these have come to be expressed in the classic formulations of Nicaea and Chalcedon. Creedal Christianity is a precious guide to the global church's confession of Christ, ensuring that it is "according to the Scriptures," grammatically correct no matter what the language or conceptuality.

The task of Christology, says T. F. Torrance, "is to yield the obedience of our mind to what is given, which is God's self-revelation in its objective reality, Jesus Christ."[68] It is only through sustained apprenticeship to Scripture that the church learns how to make judgments about *what is* in Christ and about what it must do to follow Christ today in our myriad present contexts.

Christology requires a plurality of tongues—languages, vocabularies, and concepts. Yet whatever language or conceptual scheme Christians speak and think, let them confess in line with the Chalcedonian (ontological) grammar. Let "every tongue confess *that Jesus Christ is Lord*" (Phil 2:11). That *Jesus is Lord* is the preeminent theological judgment. May the Spirit of Jesus Christ direct the global church, in all its diversity, to go on in the same way—for there is no other way, "no other name under heaven . . . by which we must be saved" (Acts 4:12).

---

[67]See Brazilian composer Heitor Villa-Lobos's comment about the influence of Western counterpoint, paradigmatically expressed in the person and work of Johann Sebastian Bach on his *Bachianas Brasileiras*: "This is a special kind of musical composition, based on an intimate knowledge of the great works of Bach. . . . The composer considered Bach a universal and rich folklore source, deeply rooted in the folk music of every country in the world. Thus Bach is a mediator among all races." I submit that Bach is to Villa-Lobos what Chalcedon is to non-Western Christology.

[68]T. F. Torrance, *Incarnation: The Person and Work of Christ* (Downers Grove, IL: InterVarsity Press, 2008), 1.

FURTHER READING

Dupuis, Jacques. *Who Do You Say I Am? Introduction to Christology.* Maryknoll, NY: Orbis, 1994.

Greene, Colin J. D. *Christology in Cultural Perspective: Marking Out the Horizons.* Grand Rapids, MI: Eerdmans, 2003.

Macleod, Donald. *The Person of Christ.* Downers Grove, IL: InterVarsity Press, 1998.

Macquarrie, John. *Jesus Christ in Modern Thought.* London: SCM Press, 1990.

McCormack, Bruce L. "The Person of Christ." Pages 149-74 in *Mapping Modern Theology: A Thematic and Historical Introduction,* edited by Kelly M. Kapic and Bruce L. McCormack. Grand Rapids, MI: Baker Academic, 2012.

McGrath, Alister. *The Making of Modern German Christology: From the Enlightenment to Pannenberg.* Oxford: Basil Blackwell, 1986.

Migliore, Daniel L. "Christology in Context: The Doctrinal and Contextual Tasks of Christology Today." *Interpretation* 49 (1995): 242-54.

Oakes, Edward T. *Infinity Dwindled to Infancy: A Catholic and Evangelical Christology.* Grand Rapids, MI: Eerdmans, 2011.

O'Collins, Gerald. *Christology: A Biblical, Historical, and Systematic Study of Jesus.* 2nd ed. Oxford: Oxford University Press, 2009.

Schweitzer, Don. *Contemporary Christologies: A Fortress Introduction.* Minneapolis: Fortress, 2010.

10

JESUS AS GOD'S COMMUNICATIVE AND HERMENEUTICAL ACT

AFRICAN CHRISTIANS ON THE PERSON AND SIGNIFICANCE OF JESUS CHRIST

Victor I. Ezigbo

AN AFRICAN CHRISTIAN CHRISTOLOGY should pass both the test of "African-ness" and the test of "Christian-ness."[1] The Christology should demonstrate simultaneously its Christian identity and its relevance to the christological questions of African Christians. The Christology should engage the experience, history, cultures, and religious aspirations of Africans. The Christology should also demonstrate its faithfulness to the understandings of Jesus Christ that are present in the Christian Scripture and the Christologies of the earliest ecumenical Christian councils—in particular, the Councils of Nicaea (325), Constantinople (381), and Chalcedon (451). A Christology that fails to pass these two tests ought not to bear the name "African Christian Christology."

The complexity of these two tests is noteworthy. Christian theologians disagree on what constitutes a faithful or an adequate interpretation of the christological themes in Scripture and the christological statements of the Councils of Nicaea, Constantinople, and Chalcedon. African Christian theologians disagree in their views of the value of Africans' history, experience, cultures, and religious aspiration in constructing Christologies. They also disagree on what constitutes an "appropriate" relationship between Christianity and African indigenous religions. I attempt to deal with the complexity of the two tests by working with the following broad theological framework: an African Christian Christology (1) should use Africans' contexts—experience, cultures, indigenous thoughts, language, and social location—as an indispensable source; (2) should learn from christological statements of the earliest ecumenical councils; and (3) should not be in contradiction with the understandings of Jesus Christ that are expressed in Scripture.

JESUS AS THE PROBLEM OF CHRISTOLOGY: LESSONS FROM THE ECUMENICAL COUNCILS

Many Christian theologians, especially systematicians, are preoccupied with the task of assembling Christian beliefs about Jesus Christ into a

---

[1]The word *Africa* is used in this essay to describe nations in the sub-Saharan African region. This is because the essay focuses only on sub-Saharan African Christianity.

coherent and tidy formula. These theologians have forgotten rather quickly that all Christologies are *human*, and as such, are incapable of encapsulating the full ramifications of God's action in and through Jesus Christ. Theologians, therefore, need the vision of other theologians, particularly those from outside their cultural contexts, church traditions, and religious traditions, in order to successfully imagine, understand, and appreciate the breadth, width, and length of the person and significance of Jesus Christ (Eph 4:12-13). This is because the significance of Jesus Christ will always overflow our theological boundaries. Theologians ought to strive to construct Christologies that identify with the multifarious representations of Jesus Christ in the Bible. Such Christologies also should intentionally engage the religious, cultural, and social issues of the communities for which they are intended.

The earliest Christian communities set the example for this way of doing Christology when the Hebraic Christians expressed Jesus' significance in light of the context of the Jewish notion of God's chosen Messiah. "Everything about Jesus made sense for them in terms of Jewish history and Jewish destiny."[2] Similarly, Hellenistic Greek-speaking theologians such as Justin Martyr (martyred ca. 165) boldly expressed Jesus' significance in the Greco-Roman cultures by presenting him as the divine *logos*—a divine agent through whom God creates and maintains order in the universe.[3] An earlier example of this theological move by the Greek-speaking Christians can be found in the apostle Paul, who

seized the "Hellenistic idea of *pleroma*, the totality of emanations between the transcendent God and the material universe, and identified it with Christ (Col. 1:19)."[4]

In the fourth and fifth centuries, the Councils of Nicaea, Constantinople, and Chalcedon adopted a highly slippery Greek term, *homoousios* ("same substance"), to explain the relationship between Jesus Christ and God (the Father). The Christologies of these councils continue to exert an enormous influence on Christian views of God and Jesus Christ. What lessons can twenty-first-century African Christians learn from the Christologies of these councils? I see two main lessons.

First, there is a *lesson of contextualization*. The attendees of the Council of Nicaea borrowed words and ideas (such as *homoousios*, "similar substance") from their Hellenistic world to articulate Jesus' relationship with God (the Father). That *homoousios* is culturally conditioned is evident in its meaninglessness or limited relevance to the twenty-first-century people who are not schooled in Koine Greek and Hellenistic thought. No Christian community can successfully and meaningfully answer Jesus' question—"Who do you say that I am" (Mk 8:29)—in foreign thoughts and concepts. Our contexts—social locations, cultures, histories, languages, and experiences—supply the cognitive framework we use to interpret and appropriate our encounters with Jesus Christ.

The error of the theologians who do not think contextually is the presumption that their theological questions are universally relevant and, therefore, are not bound by their contexts. For

---

[2]Andrew F. Walls, "Old Athens and New Jerusalem: Some Signposts for Christian Scholarship in the Early History of Mission Studies," *International Bulletin of Missionary Research* 21 (1997): 146.

[3]Justin Martyr, *Apologia* 1.5, in *The Early Christian Fathers: A Selection from the Writings of the Fathers from St. Clement of Rome to St. Athanasius*, ed. and trans. Henry Bettenson (New York: Oxford University Press, 1956), 58-64. See Kwame Bediako, *Theology and Identity: The Impact of Culture upon Christian Thought in the Second Century and Modern Africa* (Oxford: Regnum, 1992).

[4]Walls, "Old Athens and New Jerusalem," 149.

example, a North American evangelical theologian who thinks in this way may be enthusiastic about posing questions relating to open theism and classical theism in an evangelical seminary in Nigeria. It would be surprising, however, if the immediate reaction of most Nigerian students to such questions were not: "Really? Who cares about such questions?" This is because many Nigerian Christians live in cultures where gods are believed to compete for recognition, and that construe omniscience as an essential attribute of any being worthy of the name *God*. Many of these Christians take for granted the omniscience of the Christian God, even though they ground their trust on God's ability to heal, provide, and protect them on God's ability to know God's creation exhaustively. Contextualization reminds us that diversity of culture and thought does not inhibit Christology. On the contrary, diversity of culture and thoughts takes our understandings of Jesus into new realms of thought and meaning.[5]

Second, there is a *lesson of the danger of imperial romance*. The early church's preoccupation with the quest to safeguard the purity of faith and beliefs sometimes led to the physical abuse and deaths of many Christians who propounded the christological positions that lost in the "theological elections" sponsored by the emperors. In the case of the Council of Nicaea (325), Emperor Constantine might not only have influenced the acceptance and insertion of *homoousios* in the creed; he also endorsed and enforced the punishment of the council on those who refused to sign the Nicene Creed. The possibility that Constantine was not interested entirely in the purity of Christian beliefs was demonstrated in his demand for Arius's restoration into the ecclesiastical fellowship and his decision to exile Athanasius, whose theological camp won the debate at the Council of Nicaea. By flirting with the empire, the Council of Nicaea might have unwittingly drawn Jesus Christ into the support of the political agenda of Constantine's empire.[6]

In the sixth century, North African Christianity was tested by the horror of the imperial-ecclesial persecutions when some Copts who opted for the Miaphysite Christology refused to sign the Chalcedonian Definition (451).[7] The persecution of the Copts was so severe that, on hearing the footsteps of the invading Arab Muslims approaching Egypt, they limped for joy and praised God for sending the invaders to rescue them from the hands of the ruthless Melkites, or Chalcedonian Christians. In moments such as this, one wonders whether some Christians have not made Jesus Christ, the embodiment of God's gospel, bad news. Human ambitions, albeit directed toward the preservation of the purity of Christian doctrines, may have denied the gospel its freedom to be God's liberating good news to all people.

AFRICAN CHRISTOLOGY FROM THE 1980s TO THE PRESENT: IMAGINING JESUS CHRIST FROM THE CONTEXTS OF AFRICA

Moving from the sixth century to the sixteenth century through the mid-twentieth century, a careful scholar of African Christianity would notice a similar experience in sub-Saharan Africa. Many Christians who sought to express the Christian message with indigenous religious thoughts were severely hampered by the

---

[5]Walls, "Old Athens and New Jerusalem," 146.
[6]Joerg Rieger, *Christ and Empire: From Paul to Postcolonial Times* (Minneapolis: Fortress, 2007), 69.
[7]Alfred Joshua Butler, *The Arab Conquest of Egypt and the Last Thirty Years of the Roman Dominion* (Oxford: Clarendon, 1978), 158.

traditional Western derogatory attitudes toward African peoples and cultures. The majority of the missionaries who worked in sub-Saharan Africa from the 1400s considered Africans to be irreligious and incapable of conceiving Christian theology adequately without the guiding hands of the West.[8]

In the mid-twentieth century, new opportunities appeared as several Africans, of their own volition, crossed the Atlantic Ocean to study theology and world religions in Europe and North America. Broadly, two kinds of theology emerged: theologies that presented the Christian message as the defeater of indigenous religions of Africa, and theologies that construed the indigenous religions of Africa as *preparatio evangelica*. Some theologians returned to Africa as the protégés of the missionaries who gave them connections to the European and North American funding agencies. Like the missionaries, they aimed to rid Africa of its idolatrous way of life and idolatrous religions.[9] The irony was that the missionaries themselves presented Africans with an idolatrous form of Christianity when they introduced an imperialist and a colonialist Christ whose aim was to civilize the uncivil Africans and to send them on their way to "whiteness."[10] Some theologians, however, began to question the usefulness of foreign theologies for African Christianity. They aimed to construct theologies that took into account the indigenous beliefs and customs of Africa and also to lay theological foundations for the gospel message of Christianity to interact meaningfully with African indigenous religions.[11]

The state of christological discourses in sub-Saharan African Christianity has changed significantly since the 1960s and 1970s. During these periods, because of the pressing theological needs at the time, African theologians focused on broader theological issues of the relationship between African indigenous religions and Christianity. While discussions on the person and significance of Jesus were not entirely absent in the works of theologians, there were no substantive works on Christology. The lack of substantive christological discussions was partly responsible for John Mbiti's comment in 1972 that "African concepts of Christology do not exist."[12] Earlier commentators on the condition of christological discussions in sub-Saharan African Christianity, such as John Taylor and Bolaji Idowu, were highly critical of the ineffectiveness of the "imperialist" Christologies Western missionaries imposed on African Christian communities. In *Primal Vision: Christian Presence amid African Religion*, Taylor wrote: "Christ has been presented as the answer to the questions a white man would ask, the solution to the needs that Western man would feel. . . . If Christ were to appear as the answer to the questions that Africans are asking, what would he look like?"[13] In 1969, Bolaji Idowu beckoned African theologians to seek to discover ways "the

---

[8]For example, see the Annual Report of CMS Committee (May 3, 1921), *Proceedings of the Church Missionary Society for Africa in the East, 1920–1921*.

[9]E. Bolaji Idowu, "The Predicament of the Church in Africa," in *Christianity in Tropical Africa: Studies Presented and Discussed at the Seventh International African Seminar, University of Ghana, April 1965*, ed. C. G. Baeta (Oxford: Oxford University Press, 1968), 426.

[10]Kari Miettinen, *On the Way to Whiteness: Christianization, Conflict and Change in Colonial Ovamboland, 1910–1965* (Helsinki: Suomalasen Kirjallisuuden Seura, 2005).

[11]Idowu, "Predicament of the Church in Africa," 433.

[12]John S. Mbiti, "Some African Concepts of Christology," in *Christ and the Younger Churches: Theological Contributions from Asia, Africa, and Latin America* (London: SPCK, 1972), 51.

[13]John V. Taylor, *The Primal Vision: Christian Presence amid African Religion* (London: SCM Press, 1963), 23.

Christian faith could best be presented, interpreted, and inculcated in Africa so that Africans will hear God in Jesus Christ addressing Himself immediately to them in their own native situation and particular circumstances."[14] Taylor's and Idowu's concerns ignited a new zeal in many African theologians for constructing context-oriented Christologies.

Beginning in the 1980s, some theologians began to do constructive reflections on the person and significance of Jesus.[15] A chronicle of all the Christologies that have appeared in the works of African theologians from the 1980s to the present is beyond the scope of this essay. Instead, I will discuss three christological models that represent the major presuppositions underlying christological discourses in sub-Saharan African Christianity: neo-missionary Christologies, ancestor Christologies, and revealer Christology.

Neo-missionary christologies. *Description and context.* What I call neo-missionary Christologies are the Christologies that retain some Western missionaries' derogatory views of the cultures and indigenous religions of Africa but also seek to contextualize the Christian message in their communities.[16]

These views developed as a result of concerns about the danger universalism posed to African Christianity and simultaneous explorations of the relationship between Jesus Christ and African indigenous religions.

Method and presupposition. Neo-missionary Christologies use a Bible-oriented theological approach that is grounded in a "destructionist presupposition."[17] This presupposition argues that Christianity and Jesus Christ must destroy the core beliefs and practices of the indigenous religions of Africa in order to create true Christian converts. The destructionist presupposition also upholds the position of discontinuity between Christianity and African indigenous religions. These Christologies warn that the assumption of continuity between African indigenous religions and Christianity threatens the uniqueness of Christianity. This assumption is based largely on the belief that African indigenous religions are "human-made" but Christianity is a "divinely instituted" religion.[18]

Assessment. Neo-missionary Christologies have been instrumental in the preservation of the uniqueness of Christianity's theological identity and the primacy of Christian Scripture in the midst of other competing religions in Africa. Byang Kato, a Nigerian evangelical theologian, exemplifies the neo-missionary approach. Although Kato did not write primarily in the field of Christology, christological ideas permeated his theological reflections. Kato warned against African theologians who were critical of missionaries for emphasizing the uniqueness of Christianity. For Kato, "Christianity stands to judge every culture, destroying elements that are incompatible models of expression for its advancement, and bringing new life to its adherents, the qualitative life that

---

[14]E. Bolaji Idowu, "Introduction," in *Biblical Revelation and African Beliefs*, ed. Kwesi A. Dickson and Paul Ellingworth (London: Lutterworth, 1969), 9-16.

[15]Prior to 1980s, the majority of African theologians focused their attention on theology of religions, concentrating on the relationship between Christianity and African indigenous religions. This, of course, does not mean there were no christological works before the 1980s. For example, the All African Conference of Churches in its 1969 official statement insisted that Christology is central to Christian theological discussions.

[16]Victor I. Ezigbo, *Re-imagining African Christologies: Conversing with the Interpretations and Appropriations of Jesus in Contemporary African Christianity* (Eugene, OR: Pickwick, 2010), 55-64.

[17]For extensive discussions on the destructionist presupposition, see Ezigbo, *Re-imagining African Christologies*, 35-42.

[18]Byang H. Kato, *Theological Pitfalls in Africa* (Kisumu, Kenya: Evangel, 1975), 114.

begins at the moment of conversion and culmi- nates eternally with the imminent return of our Lord Jesus Christ."[19] Kato likens the indigenous religions of Africa to cancerous tumors and con- tended that the indigenous religions were un- helpful in expressing the Christian message. "For anyone who has been involved in pagan religion," Kato argues, "the suggestion for 'integral Christi- anity' . . . is like telling an ex-cancer patient that it was a mistake that he received a complete cure. . . . African traditional [or indigenous] religions only locate the problem; the Incarnate risen Christ alone is the answer. Christianity is a radical faith and it must transform sinners radically."[20] Chris- tianity, for Kato, did not merely fulfill the gaps in the indigenous religions (contra the "gap and ful- fillment presupposition").[21] On the contrary, Kato argues that Christianity must destroy the religious aspirations embedded in the indigenous religions of Africa. This view of Christianity is more evident in the work of theologians who follow Kato's theo- logical vision. For example, Tokunboh Adeyemo writes: "Some . . . African theologians have as- serted that Jesus came to fulfill not only the Old Testament but the African traditional expecta- tions. Besides the fact that this is neither biblical nor traditionally true, it is pertinent to ask why the shadow is still embraced (that is, the Tradi- tional Religion) when the perfect reality (Jesus Christ) has come?"[22]

Neo-missionary Christologies are not only interested in discrediting the claims that the in- digenous religions of Africa contain substantive traces of God's revelation and are helpful for ex- pressing the Christian message about God's action in Jesus Christ.[23] These Christologies are also preoccupied with the quest to preserve what Kato called "biblical Christianity" against the threat of universalism. In *Theological Pitfalls in Africa*, Kato attacks theologians he perceives as promoting universalism.[24] For him, the Bible is the inerrant and authoritative word or revelation of God. The Bible, he argues, must be the final authority in judging the truthfulness of any non- Christian religions. And since he judges the in- digenous religions of Africa to be inherently idolatrous, Kato contends that seeing the indig- enous religions as *preparatio evangelica* poses a serious threat to the uniqueness of the Bible, Christianity, and Jesus Christ.

I summarize three major criticisms against neo- missionary Christologies. First, neo-missionary Christologies fail to separate the "Jesus of Christian Scripture" from the "Jesus of Western missionaries." Neo-missionary Christologies are simplistic in their understanding of the complex relations between Jesus and religions, including Christianity. These Christologies, which share some Western missionaries' antagonist attitude toward African indigenous religious beliefs and practices, fail to utilize African indigenous reli- gions as an indispensable source of African Christian Christologies.[25] These theologians have forgotten that many Western missionaries

---

[19]Byang H. Kato, *Biblical Christianity in Africa* (Achimota, Ghana: African Christian Press, 1985), 29.

[20]Kato, *Theological Pitfalls in Africa*, 38.

[21]The gap and fulfillment presupposition states that Christianity fulfills the spiritual aspirations of Africans that the indigenous religions do not satisfy sufficiently. Rather than destroying the indigenous religions, the proponents of this presupposition argue that Christian- ity should build on and utilize the path the indigenous religions have created. For an extensive discussion, see Ezigbo, *Re-imagining African Christologies*, 26-35.

[22]Tokunboh Adeyemo, *Salvation in African Tradition* (Kisumu, Kenya: Evangel, 1978), 29.

[23]E. Bolaji Idowu, *Towards an Indigenous Church* (London: Oxford University Press, 1965).

[24]Kato, *Theological Pitfalls in Africa*, 11-16.

[25]I show later that the indigenous religions of Africa have continued to influence the beliefs, hopes, and practices of many Christians in sub-Saharan Africa.

who worked in Africa from the 1400s to the 1900s asserted themselves as those who embodied the universal ideals of humanity. The missionaries' condemnation of many indigenous cultures and customs of Africa (such as African names) was the product of the dehumanizing views of Africans prevalent in the psychology of Westerners in the eighteenth and nineteenth centuries.[26] Many of the missionaries believed that Africans were savages, intellectually inferior, and morally repugnant people who must be subdued and savaged "by justice, by kindness [and] by [the] talisman of Christian truth."[27]

The missionaries succeeded in creating an impassable chasm between Christianity and the indigenous cultures of Africa, producing Christians who saw the indigenous religious traditions of Africa as anti-Christian, or viewed Christianity as the great defeater of African indigenous cultures. The irony, as many African theologians such as Kwame Bediako and John Mbiti have pointed out, is that most African Christians do not really abandon the indigenous worldviews of Africa in their understanding and practice of Christianity.[28] Many Christians turn to the indigenous religious beliefs and practices when faced with deep religious and spiritual issues.

Neo-missionary Christologies fail to account properly for the dialectics of God's immanence and transcendence in their theologies of religions. For example, polemics preoccupied Byang Kato, a major proponent of neo-missionary Christology, making him a crusader against African indigenous religions rather than a constructive theologian who ought to allow the person and work of Jesus to critique and transform both Christianity and the indigenous religions of Africa.[29] Neo-missionary Christologies' belief that Christianity is judge over other religions is gravely mistaken. We are not to equate Christianity with Jesus Christ or to equate our Christologies with Jesus Christ. Our Christologies cannot be above Jesus' critique. This is because we are prone to distort and misrepresent Jesus, reducing him to *what we want him to be* rather than allowing him to be *who he is* in our Christologies. The apostle Peter was guilty of this christological error when he imagined that Jesus, as Yahweh's Messiah, could not "suffer many things and be rejected by the elders, chief priests and teachers of law, and that he must be killed" (Mk 8:31 NIV). The magnitude of Peter's wrong Christology is revealed in Jesus' stern rebuke: "Get behind me, Satan! You do not have in mind the things of God, but things of men" (Mk 8:33 NIV).

The second criticism against neo-missionary Christologies is their view of conversion, substitution, and replacement. To convert to Christianity, in this sense, is to substitute and replace the core beliefs of African indigenous religion with Christian beliefs and practices, which typically reflect more of Western missionaries' cultures than the teachings of Jesus Christ. This notion of conversion is theologically misleading. This is partly because in the New Testament *conversion* entails "turning toward" or "turning about."[30] A conversion experience implies redirecting and reinterpreting a

---

[26]See Robert Bernasconi and Timothy L. Lott, eds., *The Idea of Race* (Indianapolis: Hackett, 2000).

[27]See Pringle's mission manifesto of 1820. Quoted in Dorothy Hammond and Atla Jablow, *Myth of Africa* (New York: Library of Social Science, 1977), 44.

[28]Kwame Bediako, *Jesus and the Gospel in Africa: History and Experience* (Maryknoll, NY: Orbis, 2004), 21.

[29]Victor I. Ezigbo, "Religion and Divine Presence: Appropriating Christianity from Within African Indigenous Religions' Perspective," in *African Traditions in the Study of Religion in Africa*, ed. Afe Adogame, Ezra Chitando, and Bolaji Bateye (Surrey, UK: Ashgate, 2012), 196.

[30]G. Bertram, *"stréphō," "epistréphō,"* and *"epostrophē,"* in *Theological Dictionary of the New Testament*, abridged vol., ed. Geoffrey W. Bromiley (Grand Rapids, MI: Eerdmans, 1985), 1093-96. See Lk 17:4.

person's previous way of life and beliefs in light of God's action in Jesus Christ. Conversion is an encounter in which a person willingly allows Jesus' understanding of God and humanity to critique and remold the person's previous understandings of God and humanity. This encounter does not require wiping out the person's previous understandings and filling the void with foreign understandings. Rather, the encounter requires redirecting the previous understandings in the direction of Jesus Christ. As Andrew Walls has noted,

> To become a convert . . . is to turn, and turning involves not a change of substance but a change of direction. Conversion, in other words, means to turn what is already there in a new direction. It is not a matter of substituting something new for something old—that is proselytizing, a method that the early church could have adopted but deliberately chose to jettison. . . . Rather, Christian conversion involves redirecting what is already there, turning it in the direction of Christ.[31]

Jesus Christ, a Jew, does not turn Africans into "Jews" before he can truly relate to them. African Christians need not give up their cultural thoughts or adopt Jewish culture before they can meaningfully imagine and appropriate Jesus in their contexts.

The third criticism relates to neo-missionary Christologies' view of "biblical Christianity," which is grounded in the inerrantist view of the Bible. Theologians who advocate neo-missionary Christologies need to reconsider the human elements (cultures, aspirations, and limitations) of the Bible. Neo-missionary Christologies' ideas of "biblical Christianity" do not take seriously the humanness of the Bible. The authors of the Bible, although under the direction or inspiration of the Holy Spirit (2 Tim 3:16-17; 2 Pet 1:20-21), wrote from their contexts—cultures, thoughts, languages, experiences (both personal and communal), and so on. The Holy Spirit's direction of the biblical authors guarantees Scripture's authority in making human beings "wise for salvation through faith in Christ" (2 Tim 3:15). Also, the Holy Spirit's direction of the biblical authors makes Scripture an authoritative text that provides guidance in redirecting our inadequate understandings of God and humanity, and turning them in the direction of Jesus Christ (2 Tim 3:16-17). The humanness of the Bible should remind African theologians that (1) African Christians need not use the Jewish and Greco-Roman christological metaphors in the New Testament in interpreting and expressing their experience of Jesus, and (2) the christological themes in the Bible neither exhaust nor encapsulate the meaning and significance of Jesus Christ. The problem with neo-missionary Christologies' concept of biblical Christianity is that the forms of Christianity that are expressed in the New Testament are clothed in the thoughts, cultures, religious aspirations, religious experiences, and theological questions of the earliest Christian communities. Like Christians everywhere, African Christians have the theological freedom to use African thoughts, concepts, and metaphors to express their understanding of Jesus Christ. Some critics of Kato's theology, such as Kwame Bediako and Mercy Amba Oduyoye, have constructed Christologies that use the indigenous cultures and religions of Africans as a source of theological and christological reflections.[32] The ancestor

---

[31]Walls, "Old Athens and New Jerusalem," 148.
[32]Mercy Amba Oduyoye, *Beads and Strands: Reflections of an African Woman on Christianity in Africa* (Maryknoll, NY: Orbis, 2004); Bediako, *Theology and Identity*, 386-425.

Christology model is one of the products of such reflections, and it is to that model that I now turn.

Ancestor Christologies. *Description and context.* Ancestor Christologies present Jesus Christ as one whose mediatory role between God and humanity fulfills or satisfies the mediatory roles that are ascribed to ancestors in African indigenous religions. Ancestor Christologies seek to bridge the cultural and theological gap between Christianity and the indigenous religions of Africa. Unlike neo-missionary Christologies, ancestor Christologies recognize the value of the indigenous religious beliefs and thoughts of Africans in their expression and appropriation of the person and work of Jesus in Africa.

These approaches developed as a result of explorations of the relationship between Jesus Christ and primal cultures of Africa.

Method and presupposition. Ancestor Christologies are grounded in the claim that Jesus' mediatory role is analogous to the mediatory role ascribed to ancestors in some indigenous religions of Africa.[33] Ancestor Christologies use a culture-oriented theological method that operates with either a gap-and-fulfillment presupposition or a reconstructionist presupposition (or some combination). In the gap-and-fulfillment presupposition, Jesus Christ and Christianity can successfully satisfy the aspirations, hopes, and theological questions of Africans, which the indigenous religions do not satisfy. For the advocates of the reconstructionist presupposition,

Jesus Christ "deconstructs the indigenous religions and reconstructs them in order to create a new religious understanding of the world."[34]

Assessment. Ancestors' actual existence and mediatory functions are central to the beliefs in the indigenous understandings of the ancestor cult. Ancestors are believed to mediate between human beings and gods. They participate in the life of human communities by blessing those who keep the indigenous traditions and customs and by punishing evildoers with misfortune, sickness, or death. They are the guardians and custodians of the moral values of their families and societies.[35] Ancestors are considered "living" because they take spirit or nonphysical forms at death and also because they are alive in the memory of human communities that know and preserve their earthly accomplishments.[36]

Rarely do recent works about African theology or Christology ignore discussions of ancestor Christology models. This is a testimony to the growing influence and acceptance that these approaches enjoy in sub-Saharan African Christianity.[37] Theologians who construct ancestor Christologies see continuity between the cult of ancestors in African traditions and the doctrine of the communion of the saints held by some Christian churches. Some of these theologians devote great efforts to defend the authority of Scripture and the universality of Jesus Christ. Kwame Bediako, for example, has argued that an "understanding of Christ in relation to spirit-power in African context is not necessarily less

---

[33]See Charles Nyamiti, *Christ as Our Ancestor* (Gweru, Zimbabwe: Mabo, 1984), and Uchenna A. Ezeh, *Jesus Christ the Ancestor: African Contextual Christology in the Light of the Major Dogmatic Christological Definitions of the Church from the Council of Nicaea (325) to Chalcedon (451)* (Oxford: Peter Lang, 2003).

[34]Ezigbo, *Re-imagining African Christologies*, 42.

[35]Edward W. Fasholé-Luke, "Ancestor Veneration and the Communion of the Saints," in *New Testament Christianity for Africa and the World: Essays in Honor of Harry Sawyer*, ed. Mark E. Glaswell and Edward W. Fasholé-Luke (London: SPCK, 1974), 213.

[36]John S. Mbiti, *African Religions and Philosophy* (Nairobi: Heinemann, 1969), 25.

[37]For a survey of ancestor Christologies, see Diane B. Stinton, *Jesus of Africa: Voices of Contemporary African Christology* (Maryknoll, NY: Orbis, 2004), 112-42.

accurate than any other perception of Jesus. The question is whether such an understanding faithfully reflects biblical revelation and is rooted in true Christian experience."[38]

For some advocates of ancestor Christologies, Jesus is "proto-ancestor," "ancestor par excellence," or the "greatest ancestor." As the proto-ancestor, Jesus is the "Savior, and the remembrance of his passion, death and resurrection must be retold down the generations, for in him is made visible in a transcendent way that future which the ancestors wish to open up to us."[39] Also, Jesus is the ultimate fulfillment of the mediatory works ascribed to ancestors in the indigenous religions. As Bediako has argued, "Our natural ancestors had no barriers to cross to live among us and share our experience. [Jesus'] incarnation implies that he has achieved a far more profound identification with us in our humanity than the mere ethnic solidarity of lineage ancestors can ever do. Jesus surpasses our natural ancestors also by virtue of who he is in himself."[40]

Criticisms against ancestor Christology usually focus on some Christians who associate the ancestor cult with idol worship or demonic forces. For many of these Christians, especially Protestants, Africa's ancestor cult promotes necromancy, which they judge to be an anti-Christian act or ritual.[41] Christians who grew up with the doctrine of the communion of the saints (such as Roman Catholics), however, are more open to accepting ancestor Christologies. Some theologians have also challenged the usefulness of the ancestor christological model, given the diminishing knowledge of the cult of ancestors in many African communities.[42]

What I consider a more substantial criticism of ancestor Christologies is the unlikelihood that Jesus Christ would have met the requirements for ancestorship if he were an African. Anyone whom the elders and religious leaders found guilty of gross negligence of the traditions and who was executed for such crimes could not become an ancestor. In African indigenous tradition, the forebearers protected their community "against the forces of disintegration by their careful observance of law and custom."[43] Since Jewish religious leaders charged Jesus with the crimes of blasphemy and a gross negligence of some Jewish cultural and religious traditions, it would be very unlikely that Jesus could have qualified as an ancestor in Africa if he was found guilty of the same crimes.

One way of responding to this criticism is to construe the cult of ancestors as a "myth" and proceed from the religious aspiration it creates, not focusing on whether ancestors actually exist. According to Kwame Bediako, the cult of ancestors is the "myth-making imagination of the community that sacralises" it and confers on ancestors "the sacred authority . . . they exercise through those in the community, like kings who also expect to become ancestors." Bediako concludes, "Once the meaning of the cult of ancestors as a myth is granted and its function is understood within the overall religious life of traditional society, it becomes clear how Jesus Christ fulfills our aspirations in relation to ancestral function too." While

---

[38]Bediako, *Jesus and the Gospel in Africa*, 22.

[39]Benezet Bujo, *African Theology in Its Social Context*, trans. John O'Donohue (Eugene, OR: Wipf & Stock, 2006), 82-83.

[40]Bediako, *Jesus and the Gospel in Africa*, 22.

[41]These Christians usually cite Lev 19 as a proof text.

[42]Stinton, *Jesus of Africa*, 123-26, 130-35.

[43]Bujo, *African Theology in Its Social Context*, 22.

Bediako's proposal would be of interest to some Christian theologians, many adherents of indigenous religions may find his proposal offensive because it rejects or dismisses the belief in the actual existence and functions of ancestors.[44] Also, Africans who continue to believe in the existence of ancestors and the relevance of the ancestor cult to African communities may find Bediako's mythological interpretation unhelpful.[45] Herbert Macaulay, the grandson of Bishop Ajayi Crowther, for example, argued that the "African should have been left with his ancestor-worship and that Christianity should not have been allowed to supplant it in certain parts of the continent. Ancestor-worship, it will be readily admitted is Aero-worship, nation-worship, in short patriotism."[46]

I now turn to a revealer Christology model I am proposing as an alternative way to imagine the significance of Jesus' identity and work in sub-Saharan African Christianity.

Revealer Christology. *Description and context.* The word *revealer*, as used here, refers to an individual who embodies a true knowledge of God and humanity and who also communicates such knowledge by redirecting inadequate understandings of God and humanity. The revealer Christology I propose construes Jesus as the revealer of divinity and humanity, through whom African Christians can assess and redirect the knowledge of God and humanity they gained from African indigenous religions and Western forms of Christianity.

This approach arises as a result of an exploration of Jesus' "place" in the interaction of African indigenous religions and Christianity in the practice of Christian beliefs and ethics in sub-Saharan African Christianity.

Method and presupposition. I use a Christocentric approach I prefer to term "communicative and hermeneutical." This presupposition, which is grounded in the traditional Christian belief in Jesus' full divinity and humanity, sees Jesus as God's communicative and hermeneutical act in which African Christians can encounter a true knowledge of God's expectation from God's creatures, in particular human beings.

Revealer Christology: Jesus as God's communicative and hermeneutical act. The ethnographic study I conducted among five different church denominations in Nigeria in 2006 shows that many Nigerian Christians relate to Jesus as only *a* "solution" among many "solutions" to their religious and spiritual needs.[47] To illustrate this christological mindset, I cite two interviewees' responses to the question: "Do Christians in Nigeria go outside of Jesus to seek solutions to their religious and spiritual needs?" Moses Attah, an evangelical Christian from northern Nigeria, said that many Christians in his community consult native doctors and priests of local deities when they sense Jesus' slowness to solve their problems.

> In the north [northern Nigeria], you may have problems with somebody and if you call on Jesus

---

[44]Bediako writes, "The presumption that ancestors actually function for the benefit of the community can be seen as part of the same myth-making imagination that projects departed human beings into the transcendent realm." Bediako, *Jesus and the Gospel in Africa*, 30.

[45]The field research Diane Stinton conducted in Kenya, Uganda, and Ghana shows some African Christians believe that ancestors exist and perform some mediatory roles between humans and gods. See Stinton, *Jesus of Africa*, 123-35.

[46]H. Macaulay, "Religion and Native Customs," *Lagos Daily News* 18, no. 1 (1992), in *A History of Christianity in Asia, Africa, and Latin America, 1450–1990*, ed. Klaus Koschorke, Frieder Ludwig, and Mariano Delgado (Grand Rapids, MI: Eerdmans, 2007), 239.

[47]Ezigbo, *Re-imagining African Christologies*, 136.

the problems may not be solved immediately. Some people will do as we normally say: "Let me put off the shirt of Jesus Christ and put on the cultural shirt." Then they will go to the shrine or any other place to look for help forgetting that Jesus will help them. And sometimes during tribal wars or religious wars between Christians and Muslims some Christians go to the herbalists to collect some charm in order to protect themselves, forgetting that Jesus is there to protect them.[48]

Faith Ukaegbu, a member of a Pentecostal church, shares a similar experience. "Many people go to native doctors to get solutions. Well, the problem is when we [call them] Christians. When we call them Christians we are getting it wrong, because if you are a Christian you cannot go to native doctors no matter the situation. So I don't believe that if you are a Christian you can go to that extent, except you are a backsliding Christian."[49] Ukaegbu's distinction between a "Christian" and a "backsliding Christian" is merely a critique of the practice of deserting Jesus for native doctors and priests of local deities and not a denial of the reality that many Christians relate to Jesus as one among many who provide solutions to their religious and spiritual needs. What drives this practice of deserting Jesus, albeit temporarily, to seek immediate solutions from diviners, native doctors, and priests of local deities? I see three interrelated quests at the heart of these practices: (1) the quest to understand the relationship between the spirit and human worlds; (2) the quest to manipulate, appease, or defeat evil agents in order to attain well-being; and (3) the quest to

identify a reliable agent through whom they can interpret and appropriate their experiences. These quests, which permeate the daily lives of many Christians in Nigeria, are grounded in indigenous religions' teaching about the symbiotic relationship between the spirit and human worlds. In this view of the spirit and human worlds, God, lesser gods, malevolent beings, and ancestors can commune with human beings and interfere in human affairs. Human beings also can manipulate or appease these spirit beings in order to avert their punishments or win their favor.

Many Christian communities in sub-Saharan Africa, as some works written on African Christianity and African indigenous religions have shown, share the same view of the relationship between the spirit and human world.[50] While we should exercise caution in extending the three quests (which are drawn from the religious experience of Nigerian Christians) to other Christians in sub-Saharan Africa, the quests are most likely connected with the emphases on spiritual warfare, prosperity, and the focus on drawing transcendent power from the Holy Spirit to combat demonic forces in the preaching, songs, and lived theologies of many sub-Sahara African Christian communities.[51]

Merely assigning titles such as the "Chief Diviner-Healer" to Jesus Christ does not deal adequately with the root christological issues that are inherent in the three quests.[52] The primary christological issue inherent in the three quests is not the search for a *heuristic* or *pedagogical device* to express a foreign message (about Jesus)

---

[48]Moses Attah, interview by researcher, tape recording, Aba, February 29, 2006, quoted in Ezigbo, *Re-imagining African Christologies*, 136.

[49]Faith Ukaegbu, interview by researcher, tape recording, Aba, May 6, 2006, quoted in Ezigbo, *Re-imagining African Christologies*, 137.

[50]See Vincent Mulago, "Traditional African Religion and Christianity," in *African Traditional Religion in Contemporary Society*, ed. Jacob K. Olupona (St. Paul, MN: Paragon, 1991), 119-34.

[51]J. Kwabena Assmoah-Gyadu, "'From Prophetism to Pentecostalism': Religious Innovation in Africa and African Religious Scholarship," in *African Traditions in the Study of Religion in Africa*, ed. Afe Adogame, Ezra Chitando, and Bolaji Bateye (Surrey, UK: Ashgate, 2012), 165-72.

[52]Joseph Healey and Donald Sybertz, *Towards an African Narrative Theology* (Maryknoll, NY: Orbis, 1996), 85-87.

to Africans. Rather, the primary christological issue is the significance of Jesus to the religious and spiritual questions of Africans. What is needed, therefore, is a constructive Christology that allows Jesus to engage these quests by redirecting them to his vision of God's expectations from humanity. The questions the three quests raise for theologians are: How should these quests function as *sources* for interpreting and appropriating Jesus Christ in Africa? And in what ways could Jesus *engage* these quests in order to answer the questions they generate without betraying his vision for humanity or disregarding the experience of African Christians? An extensive answer to these two questions is beyond the scope of this essay. I only summarize how the revealer Christology I am proposing approaches these questions.

I classify the sources of Christian Christology into two tiers. The Bible belongs to the first tier (in its capacity as the inspired sacred writing) and functions as the final authority in assessing our understandings of Jesus Christ. The Christologies that contradict scriptural teaching about Jesus Christ have failed the primary test of Christian identity. The Christologies of the classical ecumenical councils and the contemporary contexts of local Christian communities belong to the second tier. African Christology should learn from the Christologies of the earliest ecumenical councils. Since the days of the Councils of Nicaea (325), Constantinople (381), and Chalcedon (451), Christian theologians have understood the identity of Jesus in two major parallel ways. We can describe them as the Arian way and the Nicene-Chalcedonian way. The Arian way argues that Jesus is God functionally but not ontologically. God created and has continued to sustain the world through Jesus Christ. But ontologically, Jesus was a special creature of God

and therefore was not the true God. On the contrary, the Nicene-Chalcedonian way argues that Jesus was ontologically divine and human. He was truly God and truly human. Both christological ways, or views, can be explained successfully in Africa because of the indigenous religions' teaching about the mutual relationship and interconnectedness of the spirit world and human world.

The three quests that drive many African Christians' act of consulting native doctors and priests of local deities for solutions to their problems are part of the intellectual and religious contexts of sub-Saharan African Christianity. Recognizing these three quests as sources for African Christology will provide a theologian with the intellectual and religious resources needed to express the person and work of Jesus in a manner that engages concretely with the religious experience of African Christians. By allowing the quests and other experiences of African Christians to become an indispensable source of Christology, the theologian will be drawn into actual christological needs of African Christians. The theologian is also able to avoid the error of imposing foreign christological questions on African Christians.

In light of Jesus' teaching as it is represented in the Gospels, his followers are called to commit to his redirection of their previous understandings of God's expectations from humanity and also their understandings of the place of human beings in the world. This redirection neither occurs in a vacuum nor requires an obliteration of the cultures, intellectual histories, or religious beliefs of those who desire to become his followers. Rather, it is a process in which Jesus invites and enables people, especially his followers, to critique, rethink, and reimagine their previous knowledge and beliefs in light of his vision for humanity and teaching about God. Jesus' response to the questions and religious aspirations of a certain woman of Samaria (Jn 4:1-26) exemplifies his identity as a revealer of true divinity and humanity. In his conversation with the woman of Samaria, Jesus critiques the assumptions of two religions: Judaism and a religion of Samaria. For Jesus, Jews and Samaritans were guilty of "inadequate theology for perceiving God in ways that strip God of the ability to simultaneously interact with and distance God's self from human religions." Jesus invited the woman to rethink her views of God and true worship, not from the Jews' and Samaritans' views of an appropriate worship location, but from his view of God. "But the hour is coming, and is now here," Jesus taught her, "when the true worshippers will worship the Father in spirit and truth, for the Father is seeking such people to worship him" (Jn 4:23 ESV). One of Jesus' aims in the conversation was to critique the theologies of both Judaism and the religion of Samaria and also to "inspire a new imagining of God (on the basis of his identity) from within the perspectives of the two religions."[53]

As the revealer of humanity and divinity, a claim that is grounded in the Christian confession of Jesus' divinity and humanity, Jesus Christ is able to resist our attempts to reduce his significance to what we want him to be. He does not merely provide answers to the questions African Christians are asking about the relationship between the spirit and human worlds, or how to manipulate or defeat evil agents in order to attain well-being, or how to identify a reliable agent through whom they can interpret and appropriate their experiences. Jesus also critiques and redirects these questions.

The Christian who temporarily deserts Jesus for diviners in search of a solution to her barrenness, for example, needs to rethink indigenous understandings of barrenness in light of Jesus' understanding of the value of humanity as God's creatures (Mt 6:25-34). In indigenous African cultures, barrenness is associated with incompleteness and divine curse. These beliefs are shaped by the indigenous African notion of the centrality of human beings in the world. Human beings are to be at the center of existence, and "everything else is seen in its relation to the central position" they occupy.[54] Some Christians continue to hold these beliefs. The revealer Christology proposed in this essay invites such Christians to rethink these indigenous beliefs in light of Jesus' teaching about God and humanity. In this way, Jesus does not merely satisfy the religious and spiritual aspirations of such Christians, but he also reorients the aspirations in a manner that allows his vision of humanity to shape and transform African Christians' questions and religious aspirations. Christians need to know that being a follower of Jesus requires committing to his vision of humanity, in which God, and not human achievements or inabilities, determines human significance and worth. African Christians who search for God's purpose for their lives and the causes of their misfortunes, and who sometimes visit the shrines of native doctors to hear from the ancestors or to solve their problems, can find hope in Jesus, who embodies the true knowledge of divinity and humanity.

CONCLUDING REMARKS

An African "Christian" Christology should show its commitment to the scriptural teaching that

---

[53]Ezigbo, "Religion and Divine Presence," 197-98.
[54]Adeyemo, *Salvation in African Tradition*, 56.

God is in Jesus Christ through the power of the Holy Spirit redeeming, reconciling, and re-molding humanity. The Christology should also use Africa's contexts as an indispensable source. Doing so would allow Jesus Christ to meaningfully engage the christological and theological questions that African Christians' contexts generate for Christology. This means that an African theologian should be intentionally contextual when constructing a Christology for an African community. As the Christologies I examined in this essay show, many African theologians see contextualization as one of Christology's universal traits. Our social locations, cultures, histories, and experiences shape and *ought to shape* our understandings of Jesus' identity and significance. Jesus' question "Who do you say I am?" (Mk 8:29) can only be truly meaningful to contemporary African Christians when they engage it from their own contexts. Revealer Christology offers African Christians the opportunity to commit to Jesus' critique and redirection of their views of himself, God, and humanity without disregarding their contexts.

Further Reading

Bediako, Kwame. *Jesus and the Gospel in Africa: History and Experience.* Maryknoll, NY: Orbis, 2004.

Ezigbo, Victor I. *Re-imagining African Christologies: Conversing with the Interpretations and Appropriations of Jesus in Contemporary African Christianity.* Eugene, OR: Pickwick, 2010.

Oduyoye, Mercy Amba. "Jesus Christ." Pages 151-70 in *The Cambridge Companion to Feminist Theology*, edited by Susan Frank Parsons. New York: Cambridge University Press, 2002.

Schreiter, Robert J., ed. *Faces of Jesus in Africa.* Maryknoll, NY: Orbis, 1991.

Stinton, Diane B. *Jesus of Africa: Voices of Contemporary African Christology.* Maryknoll, NY: Orbis, 2004.

11

CHRISTOLOGIES IN ASIA

TRENDS AND REFLECTIONS

Timoteo D. Gener

WHAT FOLLOWS IS AN overview of Christologies in Asia, and my personal reflections as
an evangelical theologian based in the Philippines. Nowadays, the world we live in has become
"smaller" and globalized. But still genuine conversation and listening seems hard to come by
between and among peoples, even in the body of
Christ. The title of William Dyrness's recent article says it all, "I'm Not Hearing You: The
Struggle to Hear from a Global Church."[1]

Intercultural conversation and hermeneutics
remain vital for biblical interpretation, for we are
often unaware of how cultural blinders limit our
interpretations, even of the gospel. Krister Stendahl's seminal article on Paul and the introspective Western conscience alerted us to this half
a century ago.[2] Mainstream evangelical leaders
and scholars who were responsible for the Willowbank Report on Gospel and Culture (1978)
also made us aware of social and cultural noises

affecting our attempt at universal, monologic interpretations of the Bible and the gospel.[3] Part of
the calling of Christ's followers, as reflected in this
report, is to discern true contextualization from
shallow alternatives. In this vein, what is needed
is not just a knowledge of formal (philosophical)
hermeneutics, but an applied intercultural hermeneutic in service of Christ and his church.[4] The
thrust of the Scriptures tells us that Christ is inseparable from Christian community. The words
of Bishop Azariah of India about a hundred years
ago summarize this connection well:

> But what is Christianity? It is often said that
> Christianity is Christ. That is true; but it is also
> a way of life. "The Way" was the name given to
> it in the days of the apostles. Christianity is not
> a doctrine about God; it is not hero-worship of
> Jesus, it is a scheme of life in a society; it is an
> organism, a family, a brotherhood—whose
> centre, radius and circumference is Christ. In

---

[1]William A. Dyrness, "I'm Not Hearing You: The Struggle to Hear from a Global Church," *Theology, News and Notes* 57, no. 2 (2011):
14-18. See also Stephen B. Bevans and Katalina Tahaafe-Williams, eds., *Contextual Theology for the Twenty-First Century* (Eugene, OR:
Pickwick, 2011), 11-16, 38-52.
[2]Krister Stendahl, "The Apostle Paul and the Introspective Conscience of the West," *Harvard Theological Review* 56, no. 3 (1963): 199-215.
[3]Robert T. Coote and John R. W. Stott, *Down to Earth: Studies in Christianity and Culture: The Papers of the Lausanne Consultation on
Gospel and Culture* (Grand Rapids, MI: Eerdmans, 1980). The paper that emerged out of the consultation, known as the Willowbank
Report, is also available online: www.lausanne.org/content/lop/lop-2.
[4]I still find useful as an introductory orientation for such hermeneutic William A. Dyrness's *Learning About Theology from the Third
World* (Grand Rapids, MI: Zondervan, 1990), with its companion reader, *Emerging Voices in Global Christian Theology* (Grand Rapids,
MI: Zondervan, 1994); also Stephen Bevans, *Models of Contextual Theology* (Maryknoll, NY: Orbis, 1992, 2002).

fellowship with all others who are attached to the Lord, bound together by outward rules and rites and throbbing with one inward pulse and purpose, men and women of all ages, races, tongues, colours, and nationalities have accepted this scheme of life, and separated from all others are more and more experiencing in this fellowship the impetus and power from the Spirit who is its indweller and life-giver.[5]

As we will see, the vitality of Christian witness relates integrally to Christology, since the point of biblical Christology is discipleship in context. The first Christians' path to faith in Jesus as the Christ may actually be called discipleship-in-context Christology, or missiological Christology/ies.[6]

WHAT IS THE ASIAN (CHURCH) SETTING?

Asia is a vast continent and home to the major religions of the world.[7] Asia is also a continent where Christians are a minority, the only exception being the Philippines.

The Federation of Asian Bishops' Conference of the Catholic Church as well as key Asian theologians such as Aloysius Pieris and José de Mesa consider the triple realities of poverty, religions, and cultures as defining the Asian situation in general.[8] While there are developed countries in Asia, such as Japan, China, and Singapore, poverty still characterizes the majority of Asian nations. In these poverty-ridden countries, Christians reread and relate Scripture, and Jesus Christ, to their socioeconomic plight. Likewise, the Scriptures and Jesus Christ are read in the context of the plurality of religions and cultural identities in these communities. The region demonstrates a flourishing of theological ferment that rereads Scripture in ablative terms, by means of Asia and for Asians. These readings characteristically take stock of Asian worldviews, experiences, and concerns.[9]

No less than in the rest of the world, globalization is part and parcel of the new reality that Asians now face.[10] The world has become more

---

[5]Quoted in Susan Billington Harper, *In the Shadow of the Mahatma: Bishop V. S. Azariah and the Travails of Christianity in British India* (Grand Rapids, MI: Eerdmans, 2000), 248.

[6]This direction limits the study from a mere descriptive account (a report) of Asian Christologies to a combination of description and prescription. Peter C. Phan offers a succinct report of Asian Christologies consisting of four Asian theologians in particular: Aloysius Pieris, Jung Young Lee, C. S. Song, and Chung Hyun Kyung. Peter C. Phan, "Jesus the Christ with an Asian Face," *Theological Studies* 57 (1996): 399-430. While I am aware of these theologians and have engaged them myself, my account differs from theirs in that, aside from being confessional (evangelical), I wish to situate christologizing communally, that is, through the local-regional Asian church as a base. I see doing theology as for every Christian, and not just for the experts. See my "Every Filipino Christian, a Theologian: A Way of Advancing Local Theology for the 21st Century," and "Epilogue," in *Doing Theology in the Philippines*, ed. John Suk (Mandaluyong, Philippines: OMF Lit, 2005), 3-23, 219-23. The phrase "discipleship-in-context Christology" combines James H. Kroeger's (discipleship Christology) and Minho Song's (discipleship in context) terminologies. The actual methodology, however, is indebted to José de Mesa, *Following the Way of the Disciples: A Guidebook for Doing Christology in Cultural Context* (Quezon City: East Asia Pastoral Institute, 1996). See also James H. Kroeger, ed., *Knowing Christ Jesus: A Christological Sourcebook* (Quezon City: Claretian, 1989), 13, and Minho Song, "Contextualization and Discipleship: Closing the Gap between Theory and Practice," *Evangelical Review of Theology* 30, no. 3 (2006): 249-63.

[7]As Phan sums it up well, it is "the birthplace of all the major religions of the world, not only Hinduism, Buddhism, Jainism, Zoroastrianism (southern Asia), Confucianism, Taoism, Shintoism (eastern Asia), but also Judaism, Christianity, and Islam (western Asia)." Phan, "Jesus the Christ with an Asian Face," 402.

[8]D. D. Gaudencio Rosales and C. G. Arevalo, S.J., eds., *For All the Peoples of Asia: Federation of Asian Bishops' Conferences Documents from 1970-1991* (Quezon City, Philippines: Claretian, 1997), 13-17; Aloysius Pieris, *An Asian Theology of Liberation* (Quezon City, Philippines: Claretian, 1988); de Mesa, "Making Salvation Concrete and Jesus Real," 3-8; see also Phan, "Jesus the Christ with an Asian Face," 400-403.

[9]See Anri Morimoto, "Asian Theology in the Ablative Case," *Studies in World Christianity* 17, no. 3 (2011): 201-15. For summary reports, see de Mesa, "Making Salvation Concrete and Jesus Real," and Phan, "Jesus the Christ with an Asian Face."

[10]B. Nicholls, T. Lua, and J. Belding, eds., *The Church in a Changing World: An Asian Response* (Quezon City, Philippines: ATA, 2010); Schreiter, *New Catholicity*.

interconnected and "smaller" because of the pervasive role of digital media. Transcultural flows of people and capital globe-wide have also contributed to this shrinking world.[11] While these global flows and exchanges heighten a sense of interconnectedness, globalization also intensifies cultural identities as well as ethnification.[12] A renewed awareness of one's own reality in Asia goes alongside a sense of global interconnectedness.[13] More than ever these call for a new vision of a world church, which takes seriously the role of local and regional churches in the body of Christ worldwide.[14]

As Christian awareness of the global church increases, it is important to note the unique contributions Asia brings to Christ's body as a whole. A look at the documents of the Federation of Asian Bishops' Conference reveals that there are important contributions in the areas of spirituality, meditative prayer, helpful approaches to world religions, and a strong family orientation.[15] It is *this* Asia, with its giftings, to which the Christian church offers Jesus Christ as the one who can provide a fuller meaning and value to Asian people's lives.

Is Asia part of what Philip Jenkins calls "the next Christendom"?[16] Asia is indeed a vast continent, and the numbers do show that Christianity is growing remarkably in Asia. But even if this is so, the figures also show that the "Christian Faith in Asia is still a minority in a vast ocean of Hindu, Buddhist, Confucian, Taoist and Islamic religions."[17] Stephen Bevans, summoning figures from the World Christian Database, likewise describes the Asian church as a minority:

> China . . . with 1.2 billion people, has only about one hundred million Christians by a generous count; India's population of one billion contains about fifty-two million Christians, and Indonesia's twenty-seven million Christians make up less than 10 percent of the country's 226 million people—even though these are more Christians than the entire population of Australia.[18]

The close identification of Christianity in Asia with Euro-American colonization and the church's corresponding lack of rootedness in Asian cultures is likely a major factor for the persistence of this minority status.[19] The lack of cultural roots and engagement fuels doubts that merely planting or multiplying churches is the right agenda for mission in Asian churches today. Asian theologians Emmanuel Gerrit Singgih and Samuel Jayakumar suggest that the presence of

---

[11]See my "Theology and Cultural Identity in Global Exchange" and "Case Study: Identity Crisis of Philippine Migrant Workers," in Nicholls, Lua, and Belding, *Church in a Changing World*, 92-108.

[12]See Schreiter, *New Catholicity*, 27; also Francisco F. Claver, SJ, *The Making of a Local Church* (Quezon City, Philippines: Claretian, Jesuit Communications, 2009).

[13]Emmanuel Gerrit Singgih, "Globalization and Contextualization: Toward a New Awareness of One's Own Reality," *Exchange* 29, no. 4 (October 2000): 361-72.

[14]Karl Rahner called attention to this new understanding of a truly world church and local churches in the Roman Catholic Church ("Toward a Fundamental Theological Interpretation of Vatican II," *Theological Studies* 40, no. 4 [1979]: 716-27). Schreiter labels this new ecclesiological vision as "new catholicity." One senses this ecclesiological tension between global and local even in evangelical circles; see Coote and Stott, *Down to Earth*.

[15]Here I follow the points listed down by Francis X. Clark, SJ, *An Introduction to the Catholic Church of Asia* (Quezon City, Philippines: Loyal School of Theology, Ateneo de Manila University, 1987), 26-29.

[16]Philip Jenkins, *The Next Christendom* (Oxford: Oxford University Press, 2007).

[17]Emmanuel Gerrit Singgih, "Any Room for Christ in Asia? Statistics and the Location of the Next Christendom," *Exchange* 38 (2009): 143.

[18]Stephen Bevans, "What Has Contextual Theology to Offer the Church of the Twenty-First Century?," in Bevans and Tahaafe-Williams, *Contextual Theology for the Twenty-First Century*, 5.

[19]As Dionisio Miranda puts it, "A large part of the failure must be traced back to the alienation or lack of authentic appropriation and [cultural] assimilation by the would-be converters themselves, making them appear no more than clones of foreign missionaries" (*Loob: The Filipino Within* [Manila: Divine Word, 1988], 6).

rapid growth and Christian conversions in Asia does not necessarily mean the church is being obedient to God's work of holistic mission.[20] Rather than "expanding 'Christendom,'" Singgih suggests focusing on expanding "'Christ' or 'Christianness'" in the region. This means becoming a servant church, involved in prophetic, healing ministry, as well as Christians being instruments of Christ's peace and reconciliation among diverse peoples and religions.[21]

CHRISTOLOGY IN THE PLURAL?

Christologies in the New Testament. The plural *Christologies* in this essay's title may suggest a counterpoint to the one Jesus. But biblically speaking, it does not and should not do so here. We have four portraits of the one Jesus in the New Testament Gospels. On the one hand, the four Gospels are what they are because they took into account the location of their respective communities; hence, there was a contextualization of the story of Jesus. On the other hand, the reality of four Gospels underscores a "plurality and diversity in our views about Jesus" while at the same time giving parameters to these views.[22]

In fact, the whole of the New Testament embodies the reality of contextualization.[23] Christolog*ies* in particular point us to the reality of contextual theologizing from biblical times to the present. The biblical writings convey God's transforming word as rooted in particular contexts;

that is, the biblical authors engaged thought patterns and behaviors of people in particular historical times and places. These authors expressed the biblical faith in the God of Israel and of Jesus through the interpretive models and available vocabularies of their day. Similarly, the dual commitment to being faithful to God's word and meaningfully expressing that word in context can be discerned in the thought of Christians of different generations as they do the task of expressing Christology for their own particular times and places. This is what the witness of the Gospels themselves do. The "Gospels . . . are simultaneously a model of how to modernize Jesus without losing sight of the history of Jesus."[24]

In the history and theology of Christian churches, diverse typologies of Christology can be encountered. Following Volker Küster, Veli-Matti Kärkkäinen lists five prominent typologies: (1) the incarnational Christology of the early church and Catholicism; (2) the theology of the cross of Protestantism, especially of the Lutheran tradition; (3) liberation Christology, especially from Latin America; (4) the resurrection and ascension Christology of Eastern Orthodoxy; and (5) the empowerment Christology of Pentecostalism and the charismatic movements.[25]

Approaching Asian Christologies. The way I would describe Christologies in Asia undoubtedly entails some presuppositions, especially regarding theologizing and doing Christology in particular. This admission is not simply

[20]Samuel Jayakumar, "God's Work as Holistic Mission: An Asian Perspective," *Evangelical Review of Theology* 35, no. 2 (2011): 227-41.
[21]Singgih, "Any Room for Christ in Asia?," 143-44.
[22]Richard A. Burridge, *Four Gospels, One Jesus?* (Grand Rapids, MI: Eerdmans, 1994), 174-75.
[23]Daniel Von Allmen, "The Birth of Theology: Contextualization as the Dynamic Element in the Formation of New Testament Theology," *International Review of Mission* 64 (1975): 37-55.
[24]Insightful on this point is Michael F. Bird's "The Peril of Modernizing Jesus and the Crisis of Not Contemporizing Christ," *Evangelical Quarterly* 78, no. 4 (2006): 311.
[25]Veli-Matti Kärkkäinen, *Christology: A Global Introduction* (Grand Rapids, MI: Baker Academic, 2003), 15. For other typologies, see Lesslie Newbigin, *The Finality of Christ* (London: SCM Press, 1969), 65-69, also Newbigin, *Gospel in a Pluralist Society*, 171; also Singgih, "Any Room for Christ in Asia?," 137, which summarizes Pieris's categories from *An Asian Theology of Liberation* (New York: Orbis, 1988), 33.

a matter of situating this study within the larger canvas of theological scholarship. Stating one's methodological preunderstandings in Christology is essential as Christians around the globe come to terms with and contextually engage the growth of christological understandings and traditions from New Testament times down to the present. The word engaging the world is integral to the christological process, even in the Scriptures themselves. To put it another way, the practice of reflection on Christology, as with the practice of theology in general, involves an interaction between biblical faith and our experiences for the sake of Christ's reign, while preserving the normativity of Scripture.[26] Within the Bible itself and the early Christian movement, theological process always demonstrated this interaction between the knowledge of God and the experiences (issues, concerns, needs) of God's people.[27]

On the one hand the work of Christology requires that we probe what the Scriptures reveal about Jesus Christ. The Judeo-Christian tradition represents one pole in the task of doing Christology. Historical and literary study of who Jesus is in the Bible remains essential. However, these are not ends in themselves. For the Gospels themselves proffer the claim that to follow Jesus means to be his disciple in one's own context.[28]

The Gospels demonstrate that to tell the story of Jesus means to follow him "on the road."[29] Here we affirm the relative, not absolute, value of the quest for the historical Jesus, or the pursuit of how much can be reliably discovered about Jesus as a historical figure.[30] For instance, the so-called third quest for the Jesus of history helped better root him in his original, Jewish context. Indeed, the various quests for the historical Jesus have alerted us to the differences "between the Christ proclaimed by the Christian tradition and the Jesus of history."[31] Still the historical Jesus is not the real Jesus. The historical Jesus is "the picture of Jesus that emerges from the application of historical tools and by the formation of historical hypotheses."[32] However, for Christian faith the real Jesus is the resurrected Jesus. He "is not simply a figure from the past but very much and above all a figure of the present, a figure, indeed, who defines believers' present by his presence."[33] In light of the resurrection, the pole of the Judeo-Christian tradition in theologizing involves a continuing recognition of the living Christ in history expressed through the agency of God's people, especially Christ's body, the church. This view of the church entails recognition of the authority of the creeds and the ecumenical councils in interpreting Scripture and defining the meaning of Christian faith and life, though such

---

[26]William A. Dyrness and Veli-Matti Kärkkäinen, eds., *Global Dictionary of Theology* (Downers Grove, IL: IVP Academic, 2008), s.v. "Christology" and "Theological Method." See also Donald K. McKim, who defines "doing theology" as "the process of carrying out theological reflection, articulation and action," in *Westminster Dictionary of Theological Terms* (Louisville: Westminster John Knox, 1996), and Neil Darragh, *Doing Theology Ourselves: A Guide to Research and Action* (Auckland: Accent, 1995). See also Gener, "Every Filipino Christian, a Theologian," 7.

[27]Dyrness and Kärkkäinen, *Global Dictionary of Theology*, s.v. "Theological Method." See also Daniel Von Allmen, "The Birth of Theology: Contextualization as the Dynamic Element in the Formation of New Testament Theology," *International Review of Mission* 64, no. 253 (January 1975): 37-52.

[28]Personal interview with the Philippine theologian José de Mesa, 2012.

[29]Michael F. Bird, "The Purpose and Preservation of the Jesus Tradition," *Bulletin for Biblical Research* 15 (2005): 161-85.

[30]For a useful introduction, see Luke Timothy Johnson, *The Real Jesus* (San Francisco: HarperCollins, 1996); also N. T. Wright, *The Challenge of Jesus: Rediscovering Who Jesus Was and Is* (Downers Grove, IL: InterVarsity Press, 1999).

[31]Thomas P. Rausch, SJ, *Who Is Jesus? An Introduction to Christology* (Quezon City, Philippines: Claretian, 2005), 23.

[32]Bird, "Peril of Modernizing Jesus," 306.

[33]Johnson, *Real Jesus*, 142. See also Robert Jenson, *Systematic Theology* (Oxford: Oxford University Press, 1997), 1:171-73.

authority expressed through confessions is still under the higher authority of Scripture.[34]

The other pole of doing the task of Christology is human experience. Theologizing is a process that speaks to but also draws from human experiences and surrounding cultures to transform them. As we've seen, this is evident in the Bible itself and is essential to the very nature of the theological task. If Christology intrinsically dialogues with not just Scripture but also lived experiences of people(s), then the Asian setting becomes a source for articulating the gospel afresh. Culture is not just a target for evangelization but also a source for expressing and reappropriating the gospel anew.

To understand the different Christologies in Asia, it is important to examine how Asian Christians reread Scripture in light of their own local realities and issues. To express Christology in Asian contexts, it is essential to employ cultural terms and local idioms to express Jesus Christ in these particular settings. Asian Christians see their task "as bringing the vision of Jesus to the masses of Asia. . . . The crucial hermeneutical question for them is not what the historical Jesus looked like but what he means for Asia today."[35] This contextual approach to Christology is also the concern of evangelicals from the Majority World, as evidenced by the work in advancing a *missiological* Christology. Therefore, Christology is not simply about resolving the intellectual puzzle and historical problem of the original Jesus in the Scriptures and in history. Missiological Christology is also

very different from advocacy-driven, Marxist-inspired, liberation Christologies. Rather, it attempts to be both biblical and missiological as it seeks to discover "the meaning and content of Christology for the agenda of mission" in different contexts.[36] It is a biblical Christology "with a missiological thrust, searching for a new model to inspire and mold missionary action."[37]

Evangelical theologians from Latin America highlight four themes in missiological Christology that I find relevant for the Asian context: the identity of Jesus of Nazareth, the marks of Jesus' mission, the meaning of the gospel, and evangelization from the marginalized or the periphery. In this missiological paradigm, the approach to the "historical Jesus" is in contrast with the view of liberal theology of the nineteenth century. Here, the Gospels are seen as essentially reliable historical records of Jesus that provide an adequate basis for the life of the church in mission.[38]

In the Asian setting, I view missiological Christology as an approach that seeks a translation of the biblical Christ into the language, thought forms, and idioms of Asian cultures. Translatability allows the Christian faith to find its home in the diverse cultures of the world, while remaining true to biblical faith. Thus, a missiological Christology in Asian settings seeks a rendering of Jesus Christ in ways that will affect Asian peoples. Accordingly, doing Christology is a process of enculturation, the process by which the church weaves itself into a given culture in a transformative way.[39] This involves *critical syntheses* (or critical contextualization) with

---

[34]See Shirley C. Guthrie, *Always Being Reformed* (Louisville: Westminster John Knox, 1996), 16-30. For a laudable example of how a biblical scholar engages the creeds in relation to Christ and the Gospels, see N. T. Wright, *How God Became King* (New York: HarperOne, 2012), 10-20.

[35]R. S. Sugirtharajah, ed., *Asian Faces of Jesus* (Maryknoll, NY: Orbis, 1993), x.

[36]Vinay Samuel and Chris Sugden, eds., *Sharing Jesus in the Two-Thirds World* (Grand Rapids, MI: Eerdmans, 1983), 277.

[37]Samuel Escobar, "Evangelical Theology in Latin America: The Development of a Missiological Christology," *Missiology* 19, no. 3 (1991): 324.

[38]Escobar, "Evangelical Theology in Latin America," 322-28.

[39]Timoteo D. Gener, "Re-imaging Conversion in Lowland Philippine Setting: The Perspective of Gospel Re-rooting," *Journal of Asian Mission* 3, no. 1 (2001): 43-77.

cultures. It also involves careful interaction with local religious systems toward the development of truly local churches and theologies. Even so, the task requires critical alertness to prevent cultural domestications of the gospel (syncretism).[40]

The local churches (as part of a truly world church) doing their own christological reflections are the articulators and agents (embodiments) of missiological Christologies in their unique settings. José de Mesa offers a useful approach toward developing missiological Christologies in different cultural contexts. He combines sociological description in identifying views of Christ (the reality of projection) with a biblical-theological act of regauging or evaluating these images of Christ toward making the gospel translatable in a new context, in an act of reappropriation of the biblical tradition. Thus the religious experiences and habits of various peoples reveal aspects of their theologies, their understanding of God or Christ, which then need to be assessed biblically and theologically for reappropriation by local Christians.[41]

TOWARD MISSIOLOGICAL CHRISTOLOGIES IN ASIA

If we proceed with the above framework, acknowledging that doing Christology is a process of translation and enculturation of the Word (Jesus Christ) now into Asian settings, what then are some of the Christologies in Asia that offer promising missiological engagement?

Jesus fully human. In many Asian religions God is often featured as inaccessible and distant. As such, a fully human Jesus, or Jesus as God in human form, is good news in Asia. Influenced by the supernaturalist mindset of Asia, there is a tendency among Asian Christians to see Jesus as an angel rather than a full-blooded human being.[42] Alternately, he may just be viewed as one among the many gods that populate the heavenlies.[43] Theologians Lode Wostyn and José de Mesa ask probingly: "Does not Jesus' divinity obscure his power to do so on the grounds that he did not fully share our human condition? It is already a struggle to follow the example of a saint. At most, we can only dream of imitating an angel. Is it not simply preposterous for us to dare follow a God-man?"[44]

Asian churches and theologians respond to a misguided, docetic view of Jesus Christ by recovering the Jesus of the Gospels. One Asian theologian calls this "A Third Look at Jesus."[45] The first look was the way Jesus and first-generation Christians perceived his life and work. The second look at Jesus was the way the Greco-Roman and Western eyes came to understand Jesus. It is this second view that Asians along with the rest of the Majority World churches have received for the past two thousand years. This is the theology expressed in their textbooks,

[40]I have elaborated my views on syncretism in "Engaging with Chung Hyun Kyung's Concept of Syncretism: An Intercultural Dialogue on Mission," *Journal of Asian Evangelical Theology* 19 (March 2015): 43-68.
[41]José de Mesa, "Pastoral Agents and 'Doing Christology,'" *East Asian Pastoral Review* 29 (1992): 111-22. This methodology grounds itself in the "way of the disciples," where the pattern of the disciples' identification of Jesus is taken as a norm for doing Christology. De Mesa's article is expanded into a book, *Following the Way of the Disciples: A Guidebook for Doing Christology in Cultural Context* (Quezon City, Philippines: East Asia Pastoral Institute, 1996). On the connection between the translatability of the gospel and the incarnation, see Timothy C. Tennent, *Invitation to World Missions* (Grand Rapids, MI: Kregel, 2010), 323-53.
[42]José de Mesa and Lode Wostyn, *Doing Christology: The Re-appropriation of a Tradition* (Quezon City, Philippines: Claretian, 2005), 2.
[43]This domestication of the gospel was something that Lesslie Newbigin rallied against. See *The Gospel in a Pluralist Society* (Grand Rapids, MI: Eerdmans, 1989), 3.
[44]De Mesa and Wostyn, *Doing Christology*, 2.
[45]Carlos H. Abesamis, *A Third Look at Jesus* (Quezon City, Philippines: Claretian, 1988).

catechisms, and church homilies. The stress has been on the deity of Christ and salvation understood primarily in terms of Christ's atonement for our sins. The third look is a look at the original Jesus by and through the eyes of the poor. For Carlos Abesamis, the poor are not any kind of poor. Rather, these poor are the "awakened, struggling and selfless poor, who want to create a just, humane, and sustainable world. Jesus and the poor stand on the same ground and view life from a similar vantage point." This third look illuminates two essential insights. First, Jesus as a human being was in vibrant communion with God the Father and was filled with divine power; and second, Jesus was totally poured out in the mission of God's reign, which was about total salvation, human and cosmic.[46] Christian life and service informed by this third look would be characterized by personal holiness and social commitment.

Evangelical theologians in Asia resonate with the need to recover the Jesus of the Gospels for contextual ministry. Vinay Samuel and Chris Sugden have noted that past historical-theological Christologies usually neglect Jesus' humanity and servanthood to the poor and the marginalized (including his inclusion of women). This unfortunate neglect has produced a truncated gospel. Recovering Jesus' identification with the poor and proclamation of their restoration would provide a major resource to recapture the holism of the gospel Jesus proclaimed. Citing the messianic manifesto in Luke 4, Vinay Samuel and Chris Sugden insist, "For

Jesus there was no such thing as an understanding of the good news without its relation to the poor. The gospel and the poor were integrally related in the announcement and activity of Jesus. That is why even those who are rich, to whom this good news was announced, had to approximate to the poor to receive it (e.g., the rich young ruler)."[47]

The witness-reception of Jesus Christ amid Asian religions. Asia is characterized by a plurality of religions. Asian Christians have need to work out their christological understanding in plural and diverse religious contexts; Hindu, Buddhist, and Chinese cultural contexts are among these. Hindu conceptions of Jesus are more elaborate and diverse than those of many other non-Christian faith traditions. Christological formulations first articulated by Hindus are quite unprecedented in Asia.[48] Indeed, popular Hindu leaders such as Keshab Sen (1838–1884) and Mohandas Gandhi (1869–1948) even professed love for Jesus Christ and saw Christ's lasting importance for India while not renouncing their Hindu way of life.[49] R. S. Sugirtharajah demonstrated personal admiration and fondness for Jesus and his teachings. He appreciatively used *diverse Hindu images of Jesus*, which include:

- Jesus as Supreme Guide to human happiness (Rajah Ram Mohum Roy)

- Jesus as True Yogi and Divine Humanity (Keshab Chendur Sen)

- Jesus as Jivanmukta (One who has attained liberation while alive) (Vivekananda)

[46]Carlos H. Abesamis, SJ, *Backpack of a Jesus-Seeker: Following the Footsteps of the Original Jesus* (Quezon City, Philippines: Claretian, 2004), 11, 16-24.

[47]Vinay Samuel and Chris Sugden, *Evangelism and the Poor: A Third World Study Guide* (Bangalore: Partnership in Asia, 1983), 20; also Chris Sugden, *Seeking the Asian Face of Jesus* (Oxford: Regnum, 1997).

[48]Sugirtharajah, *Asian Faces of Jesus*, 57.

[49]Sunil Stephens, "The Significance of Jesus Christ in Hindu-Christian Dialogue," in *Naming the Unknown God* (Mandaluyong: OMF Lit and Asian Theological Seminary, 2006), 114-21.

- Jesus as the Son of Man, seeking the last, the least, and the lost (Rabindranath Tagore)

- Jesus as the Supreme Satyagrahi (love and fighter for truth) (Mahatma Gandhi)

- Jesus as Advaitin (one who has realized destiny with Brahman-God) (Swami Akhilananda)

- Mystic Christ (Radhakrishan)[50]

Indian Christians later imitated the Hindu approach with their own sketches of Jesus using their own cultural and philosophical resources. For example, Jesus is described this way:

- Jesus as Prajapati (Lord of creatures) (K. M. Banerjee)

- Jesus as Cit (Consciousness) (Brahmobandhav Upadhyaya)

- Jesus as Avatara (Incarnation) (A. J. Appasamy, V. Chakkarai)

- Jesus as Adi Purusha (the first person) and Shakti (power-strength) (P. Chenchiah)

- Jesus as Eternal Om (logos) (S. Jesudasan)[51]

These Hindu and Indian Christian cultural and philosophical images of Jesus are not immune from criticisms even within India. Present-day Indian Christian *dalits* and tribals view these articulations as favoring the Sanskrit tradition, which was the "very system instrumental to their own oppression and marginalization."[52] Lesslie Newbigin, longtime missionary to India, was quite aware of this, and therefore insisted on returning to the Christ of history as the key toward

a truly salvific Christology in light of the Hindu and Indian religiocultural realities.[53]

Buddhist-sensitive conceptions of Jesus Christ favor the image of *Jesus as a poor monk*, where the monastic model approximates Asian aspirations and ideals. Asia is the "oldest and the largest generator of monasticism, besides being the inheritor of the largest portion of the world's poverty."[54] Hence Aloysius Pieris posits the relevance of the image of Jesus as a poor monk for Buddhist settings in Asia. The recovery of the meditative dimension from the monastic influence is something Asian evangelicals could use to enrich and deepen their traditions. Instead, they remain critical of the reduction of evil and sin to mammon and greed, and the gospel to liberation from oppression. Evangelicals in the Majority World insist on the fullness of the gospel as ultimately deliverance from sin, evil, and death. Though they do not exclude the bodiliness and materiality of salvation, they resist its reduction to socioeconomic liberation.[55]

With reference to Islam, one must distinguish Christology in Islamic contexts from Islamic Christology. Christology in an Islamic context is a Christian Christology that developed in a Muslim setting and was addressed to it, while Islamic Christology is a specifically Muslim or Qur'anic view of Christ. Christology in Islamic contexts often makes the doctrine of the Trinity the focal point of christological reflection. Modalism and Nestorianism are often considered, but the ancient Christian churches from the Islamic East in general continue to uphold

[50]Sugirtharajah, *Asian Faces of Jesus*, 3.

[51]Sugirtharajah, *Asian Faces of Jesus*, 4.

[52]Sugirtharajah, *Asian Faces of Jesus*, 4.

[53]Lesslie Newbigin, *The Gospel in a Pluralist Society* (Grand Rapids, MI: Eerdmans, 1989), 66-79.

[54]Pieris, *Asian Theology of Liberation*, 57.

[55]Simon Chan, "Evangelical Theology in Asian Contexts," in *The Cambridge Companion to Evangelical Theology*, ed. Timothy Larsen and Daniel J. Treier (Cambridge: Cambridge University Press, 2007), 230.

traditional christological doctrine following its Chalcedonian or non-Chalcedonian form. However, Muslims find the generational language about Christ as the only-begotten Son of God to be most offensive to their theology. Sura 112 of the Qur'an makes it clear that "God neither begets nor is begotten." Hence, Michael Nazir Ali proposes the language of procession (the Son "proceeding" from the Father; see Jn 8:42) rather than *generation* as a better point of departure in talking to Muslims about the person of Christ. Qur'anic naming of Jesus also "lends itself more to 'processional' than to 'generational' language." *Jesus as prophet* is the most frequent title ascribed to Jesus in the Qur'an. However, there are other titles for Jesus in the Qur'an that allow an opening for a discussion of Jesus as more than a prophet. *Almasih* (messiah) is applied to Isa in the Qur'an, and was blessed by Allah to be such (19:31, also 3:49). Such messiahship is also supported or confirmed by the Holy Spirit (2:253; 5:110). Jesus is also called Kalimah, or Word (3:45; 4:171), and Abd Allah (servant of Allah, 19:30, also 4:172; 43:57-59).[56]

Christians living side by side with Muslims need to live Christianly and not merely debate or converse with them about Jesus and their religion. Christology is intimately linked with a Christian lifestyle, lived in community. "The compulsion to believe in Jesus being the son from living like Jesus" are closely aligned. If Muslims name Jesus as Almasih, it is "up to them to choose to enquire more of the Jesus of the Gospel if they are attracted by the life of the Christian."[57] Increasingly, living Christianly is far more effective in reaching Muslims, in achieving shalom, than evangelism by words alone.[58] The story of the Peacebuilders Community in the southern Philippines is one great example of this.[59]

Chinese Christologies are linked to China's past history of evangelization, which goes back to Nestorian Christians arriving in China as early as 635, and then the Franciscans, led by John of Montecorvino, who arrived in 1294.[60] A Nestorian Buddhist Christology portrayed the incarnation through "the story of *Avalokitesvara*, a male *bodhisattva* who took on female form and became known to the Chinese as Guan Yin, the goddess of mercy. . . . *Jesus is like a bodhisattva* in his mission to save others." Later, when the Jesuits arrived in China in 1582, Matteo Ricci and his companions explored missionary strategies that presented Christ gradually to the Chinese so as not to favor premature conversions. In a catechism that Ricci published, *The True Meaning of the Lord of Heaven*, Christ was presented as teacher and performer of miracles. Ricci then compared Christ to China's great teacher, Confucius, concluding that Christ was greater than any king or teacher. A fuller account of the Christ event was given by Diego de Pantoja, one of Ricci's close companions. He emphasized the salvific value of the passion of Jesus through his elaboration of the *Doctrina Christiana* as well as *The*

[56]Effendy Aritonang and Triawan Wicaksono Kho, "A Study of Jesus' Offices and Roles in the Qur'an," in *Naming the Unknown God*, ed. E. Acoba et al. (Mandaluyong, Philippines: OMF Lit and Asian Theological Seminary, 2006), 84.

[57]David Emmanuel Singh, "Christian Relations with Muslims: Review of Selected Issues and Approaches," *Transformation* 22, no. 1 (January 2005): 59-60.

[58]For a theology of community that thrives on this approach, see Emo Yango, "Toward a Theology of Communities in the Kingdom of God," *Phronesis* 10, no. 1 (2003): 7-27.

[59]See PeaceBuilders Community, http://peacebuilderscommunity.org/ (accessed April 28, 2020).

[60]In what follows I draw from Ary C. Dy, *Building a Bridge: Catholic Christianity Meets Chinese-Filipino Culture* (Quezon City, Philippines: Jesuit Communications Foundation, 2005), 58.

Recitation of the Passion of the Savior, which Chinese Catholics recited during Holy Week.

After Ricci, other missionaries such as Giulio Aleni labored in China from 1582 to 1610. Aleni in particular pushed for greater Christ-centeredness in the missionary approach, but informed by extensive knowledge of Chinese culture and language. Aleni used the Chinese language to tell the story of Jesus in publications such as *The Life of Jesus in Words and Images* and *The Life of Our Lord Jesus Christ*. He countered Chinese objections to the incarnation in his *Learned Conversations of Fuzhou*. Aleni wrote the first Chinese text fully devoted to Christology, *Introduction to the Incarnation of the Lord of Heaven*.

Moving to the present scene, with Chinese culture today increasingly becoming globalized, the search is no longer for a single Chinese Christology but for Chinese *Christologies*. The Chinese classics remain vital dialogue partners in cultural theologizing and apologetics, as in the writings of K. K. Yeo.[61] Ary Dy proposes, however, that the image of the suffering Jesus will continue to speak to the Chinese masses, where suffering remains a prevailing experience. Another possibility is a Christology that draws on the place of words in Chinese culture. One sees this in the film *Hero*, which contains many scenes where someone gazes long and hard at a word or piece of calligraphy, seeking to understand the character of the writer. Such meditative acts can affect one's character and way of life. Presenting Jesus Christ as the Word, then,

may be a rich and dynamic way of addressing Chinese culture.[62]

Christ and supernaturalism in popular piety. *Jesus as lord of the spirits.* Pentecostal and charismatic experience continues to dominate Asian forms of Christianity. One might even say this is Protestantism's dominant worldwide folk religion. Based on the figures from the *World Christian Encyclopedia*, Asia is second only to Latin America in terms of the number of Pentecostal and charismatic adherents, and it is fast catching up.[63] At least a third of the Asian Christian population is charismatic or Pentecostal, and the number continues to increase. What is most distinctive about the Pentecostal-charismatic movement is the "strong emphasis of the Holy Spirit as understood in the New Testament."[64] Thus Everett Wilson's statement that "Pentecostalism, the faith of apostolic signs and wonders, represents itself as a self-validating expression of primitive Christianity" is authenticated in the Asian arena.[65] Viewed through the lens of this defining characteristic, the Pentecostal-charismatic movement may be seen as a phenomenon that is indigenous to Asian Christianity and not as an imported movement from North America. The Azusa Street revival in twentieth-century America does not define Asian charismatic Christianity. Various pre-Azusa (nineteenth century) and post–Azusa Street Pentecostal and charismatic forms abound in Asian Christianity.[66] Central to the

---

[61]See, in addition to his essay in this volume, K. K. Yeo, *What Has Jerusalem to Do with Beijing? Biblical Interpretation from a Chinese Perspective* (Harrisburg, PA: Trinity Press International, 1998).

[62]Dy, *Building a Bridge*, 65.

[63]Allan Anderson, "The Charismatic Face of Christianity in Asia," in *Asian and Pentecostal*, ed. Allan Anderson and Edmond Tang (Oxford: Regnum, 2005), 2.

[64]Hwa Yung, "Pentecostalism and the Asian Church," in Anderson and Tang, *Asian and Pentecostal*, 41.

[65]Everett A. Wilson, "They Crossed the Red Sea, Didn't They? Critical History and Pentecostal Beginnings," in *The Globalization of Pentecostalism: A Religion Made to Travel*, ed. Murray W. Dempster et al. (Oxford: Regnum, 1999), 110; as quoted in Hwa Yung, "Pentecostalism and the Asian Church," in Anderson and Tang, *Asian and Pentecostal*, 41.

[66]Hwa Yung, "Pentecostalism and the Asian Church," in Anderson and Tang, *Asian and Pentecostal*, 43-48.

Pentecostal movement's christological practice is a strong, Christ-centered orientation to healing and to confronting demonic spirits, invoking especially the image of Christus Victor (the Victorious Christ).[67] The vision of the victorious Jesus (Col 2:15) serves as a central motif in the formulation of the gospel to Asian peoples.[68]

Jesus among folk Catholics.[69] The picture of Asian Christologies would be incomplete if we did not include an example of how folk Catholics view Jesus Christ in the Philippines. The prevalence of poverty and suffering makes the Nazareno (Nazarene) a favorite image of Jesus among the Filipino masses. The image is that of a life-size portrayal of Jesus clad in a maroon robe, crowned with thorns and carrying a large wooden cross in semikneeling position. Tens of thousands line the streets waving white hand towels, chanting "Viva señor," and lighting candles. Hundreds of devotees risk life and limb as they jostle their way up to the platform to touch the image.

What lies behind this popular devotion? Close analysis of this phenomenon reveals one particular motivation. As Jesus suffers, he understands the sufferings of people, and asks them to carry their own cross. He is no stranger to suffering, and this provides a point of identification with the Filipino devotee. Thus, most of the devotees of the Nazareno have made *panatas* (lifelong commitments of service) in exchange for a request for healing, good health, work, or other needs. One observer, Teresita Obusan, who has studied this very closely, called this devotion to the *Señor* a faith of basics.

Such faith, stripped of everything but the essential, is less concerned with a good afterlife than it is in receiving assistance now, while one is alive. Another researcher puts it this way: "This is a God whom they understand as somebody who died for them exclusively. So they love, and must love fervently, somebody who is willing to undertake such a sacrifice for them. To the masses, there is no other way to reciprocate."[70]

The people's understanding of what Jesus brings about in their lives (salvation) is closely related to who Jesus is for them (Christology). This translates into the following projective (local) images of Christ among devotees:

- If Christ is the bringer of *kagalingan* (healing), *himala or milagro* (miracles), then Christ to them is the Wonder-Worker and Healer *(Mapaghimala).*

- If Christ brings God closer to them in their suffering, then Christ to them is their *Kuya or Amang* (Brother or Father), worthy of their *sakripisyo* (sacrifice) and *pagdamay* (solidarity, feeling-with).

- If Christ grants their requests, then Christ for them is *Poon or Panginoon* (Lord), worthy of submission and *panata* (vows).

These local images show the cultural dimensions of Christology as seen from folk religious experiences. There the longing is for the Christ who heals, who is a divine source of power, a provider, yet one who feels with them in their pain—as their friend. It reveals a longing for salvation that

---

[67]Wonsuk Ma, "In Jesus' Name! Power Encounter from an Asian Pentecostal Perspective," in *Principalities and Powers: Reflections in the Asian Context* (Mandaluyong, Philippines: OMF Lit and Asian Theological Seminary, 2007).

[68]See also Melba Maggay, *The Gospel in Filipino Context* (Manila: OMF Lit, 1987), 4.

[69]This section is taken from a group project on doing local theology at the Asian Theological Seminary led by Dr. George Capaque and me, "Poverty, Religion and Culture in the Devotion to the Black Nazarene," in *The Church and Poverty in Asia*, ed. Lee Wanak (Mandaluyong, Philippines: OMF Lit and Asian Theological Seminary, 2008), 108-27.

[70]Karl De Mesa, quoted in *Inside Quiapo* (Manila, n.d.), 18.

involves the material and the bodily, not just dwelling on the spiritual and the afterlife.

This calls for a rereading of the Bible informed by folk yearnings about Christ and salvation. Rereading Scriptures with these cultural understandings of Christ and salvation, we come to more fully appreciate the fullness of who Christ is and what the Bible really means by salvation. In Asian Christology, reference is often made to Christ as Lord of the spirits as a contextual image.[71] However, Christ as Wonder-Worker, Healer, Friend, and Brother—images often neglected in typical presentations of Christology— are equally important to several Asian contexts.[72]

CONCLUDING REFLECTIONS

First, we have emphasized that Christology in light of the Gospels is discipleship-in-context Christology (see Jn 20:30-31). Therefore, the true test of any Christology is in how it assists authentic following of Christ in one's own context. An authentic understanding of Christ's significance draws from the Bible, but is always socially embodied and expressed through a community's engagement with the word in their respective societies and cultures. The practice of articulating Christology is a threefold process of identification of cultural understandings of Christ and salvation, biblical-theological evaluation, and reappropriation in local contexts.

Second, the recovery of the kingdom of God as central to the life and teaching of Jesus Christ continues to revitalize Majority World churches. This is also true in the Asian church, with its challenge to live Christianly and do mission holistically. Asia in particular is a setting that calls for cultural rootedness, holistic mission, and social-public transformation.

Third, doing Christology as a missiological act takes account of the social, cultural, and geographic location of Christian communities, and seeks to transform these locations with the light of Christ. Thus, we see the flourishing of indigenous practical Christologies in Asia engaging issues of Asian religiousness and poverty, and reclaiming human and cultural dignity for the sake of Christ and his church.

Finally, all the above developments witness to the work of the Spirit, as a witness to the reality of Pentecost, where we hear cultures, peoples, tribes, and nations, speaking in their native languages of the great deeds that God has done (Acts 2:8, 11) and continues to do in and through Jesus the Christ.

FURTHER READING

Chan, Simon. "Evangelical Theology in Asian Contexts." In *The Cambridge Companion to Evangelical Theology*, edited by Timothy Larsen and Daniel J. Treier. Cambridge: Cambridge University Press, 2007.

De Mesa, José. *Following the Way of the Disciples: A Guidebook for Doing Christology in a Cultural Context*. Quezon City, Philippines: East Asia Pastoral Institute, 1996.

Gener, Timoteo. "Contextualization." Pages 192-96 in *Global Dictionary of Theology*, edited by William Dyrness, Velli Matti Kärkkäinen, Simon Chan, and Juan Martinez. Downers Grove, IL: InterVarsity Press, 2008.

———. "Re-visioning Local Theology: An Integral Dialogue with Practical Theology, a Filipino Evangelical Perspective." *Journal of Asian Mission* 6, no. 2 (2004): 133-66.

---

[71]Maggay, *Gospel in Filipino Context*, 4.

[72]Even the current quest for the historical Jesus sees this image as crucial to the Gospel portrait. A recent restatement of this comes from Ben Witherington III, *The Jesus Quest* (Downers Grove, IL: InterVarsity Press, 1997), 185-95, 211-12. Chapter 7 is suggestive on Jesus being Brother.

Gener, T. D., L. Bautista, and K. J. Vanhoozer. "Theological Method." Pages 889-98 in *Global Dictionary of Theology*, edited by W. Dyrness, V. M. Kärkkäinen, S. Chan, and J. Martinez. Downers Grove, IL: InterVarsity Press, 2008.

Greenman, Jeffrey P., and Gene L. Green, eds. *Global Theology in Evangelical Perspective.* Downers Grove, IL: InterVarsity Press, 2012.

Schreiter, Robert. *The New Catholicity: Theology Between the Global and the Local.* Maryknoll, NY: Orbis, 1997.

Stephens, Sunil. "The Significance of Jesus Christ in Hindu-Christian Dialogue." Pages 109-26 in *Naming the Unknown God.* Mandaluyong City, Philippines: OMF Literature and Asian Theological Seminary, 2006.

Sugirtharajah, R. S., ed. *Asian Faces of Jesus.* Maryknoll, NY: Orbis, 1993.

Wanak, Lee, ed. *The Church and Poverty in Asia.* Mandaluyong City, Philippines: OMF Literature and Asian Theological Seminary, 2008.

_12_

¿QUIÉN VIVE? ¡CRISTO!

CHRISTOLOGY IN LATIN AMERICAN PERSPECTIVES

Jules A. Martínez-Olivieri

PRESENTING A SUCCINCT summary of the ethos of Christian theology in Latin America, and Christology in particular—contextualized in its plurality as well as its common elements—is a difficult task. This chapter aims to present the common threads that shape Latin American christological reflection. I attend to the major theological movements in the region: Catholic liberation theology and Protestant Christology. The purpose is to survey how each construes Christology as faith seeking *Gloria Dei, vivens homo* (the glory of God is the human fully alive), that is, to engage in theological and historical discourse that strives to articulate the transformation that Jesus, as the Christ of God, brings to human life.[1] In this pursuit, I also highlight the important methodological, hermeneutical, and dogmatic elements that shape the doctrine of Jesus Christ in Latin America.

A PRÉCIS OF LIBERATION THEOLOGY IN LATIN AMERICA

Background. By 1977, liberation theology had begun to make inroads into academic theo-logical circles. A key aspect that drew attention to this movement was its proposal of an innovative way of doing theology. Christian theology is to be a praxis-oriented and politically transformative discourse, a critical reflection on Christian praxis in light of Scripture and the life of the church.[2] The Conference of Latin American Bishops in Medellín, Colombia, is widely seen as the birthplace of liberation theology. Held in 1968, this conference constructively engaged the results of Vatican II, suggesting a hermeneutical criterion to guide theological reflection: the perspective of the poor. Hugo Assmann provided a provocative rationale for the emergence of liberation theology:

> If the historical situation of dependence and domination of two-thirds of humanity, with its thirty million per year dying of hunger and malnutrition, does not become the point of departure of any Christian theology—even in the rich and dominating countries—theology will not be able to situate and realize historically its fundamental themes. . . . This is why [it] is necessary to save theology from its cynicism.[3]

---

[1]This paradigmatic phrase comes from Irenaeus of Lyons.
[2]Gustavo Gutiérrez, "The Task and Content of Liberation Theology," in *Cambridge Companion to Liberation Theology* (New York: Cambridge University Press, 1999), 29.
[3]Hugo Assmann, *Teología desde la praxis de liberación* (Salamanca, Spain: Sígueme, 1973), 40.

The explicit admission and embrace of the locality and environment in which faith is practiced as a *locus theologicus* intends to show the originality of liberation theology in contrast to traditional (classical) theology and modern European theology.[4] Gustavo Gutiérrez lucidly explains a key factor that spurred the emergence of liberation theology in Latin America. The nonbeliever who questions the logic and structure of the Christian worldview does not pose the main challenge to the Christian faith. Instead, the challenge comes from

> the non-human, that is, from whom is not recognized as a human by the ruling social order: the poor, the exploited, the one who is systematically and legally divested of his being human, the one who hardly knows what it means to be human. . . . Therefore, the question will not refer to the mode that must be used to talk about God in an adult world, but more so to the way that [God] has to be announced as a Father in a non-human world, [and] to the consequent implications of the fact of saying to the non-human that [he] is a child of God.[5]

Liberation theology is better grasped as a theological movement than one strict mode of doing theology. Though it is true that such theology first emerged from the Roman Catholic quarters in Latin America, the adjective *liberation* has become a way to refer to a range of explicitly contextual theologies that focus their theological concerns on triangulating the world, church, and Scripture in light of the themes of oppression, violence, and discrimination in their respective contexts.[6] To this end, there is a plurality of liberation theologies today. Some of them concentrate on responding to international economic oppression, while others take on issues such as classism, racism, gender, and sexual violence. This also helps us understand why liberation theology is not the only theology in the Latin American region. For although many Roman Catholic and Protestant theologians share some of the fundamental intuitions of the movement, such as the perspective of the poor, many do not identify with liberation theology. Nevertheless, one must grant that some of the most important general contributions from Latin America to Christian theology are embedded within this movement, particularly as it evolved, refined, and broadened its scope in its systematic development.

Theology and method. The theological method in liberation theology was very early defined around the central political and economic preoccupations that were affecting the social and ecclesial contexts in which the Christian faith is lived. We can identify fundamental intuitions that shape theological methods in liberation theologies, as well as in Protestant theologies that share liberation priorities. First, the fundamental commonality is a soteriological orientation. The Christian concept of salvation includes not only present communion with God and the hope of life after death; salvation also entails liberation from societal manifestations of sin in present historical experience. Hence, while affirming a final eschatological salvation

---

[4]J. Batista Libânio, "Panorama de la teología de América Latina," in *Panorama de la teología Latinoamericana*, ed. Juan J. Tamayo-Acosta (Navarra, Spain: Verbo Divino, 2002), 60.

[5]Gustavo Gutiérrez, "Praxis de Liberación: Teología y anuncio," *Concilium* 96 (1974): 366.

[6]A central concern of Gustavo Gutiérrez's critique is the theory of economic dependence of Latin American countries with the United States as a social evil, not only discrimination. This focus on dependence as a social evil distinguishes Latin American theology from African American theology, which focuses primarily on racism as a discriminatory social and ideological structure embedded in the culture. See Gutiérrez, *Teología de la liberación: Perspectivas*, Verdad e Imagen (Salamanca, Spain: Sígueme, 1990), chap. 1.

for humanity and creation with God, Latin American theology insists on the praxis of faith and the active pursuit of justice for the other. As the Catholic Episcopal Conference in Puebla, Mexico, pronounced in 1979, to think of salvation as integral liberation means to stress both the subjective aspect (liberation from personal sin) and the historical aspect (liberation from the actual economic, sociopolitical, and cultural situation), which qualifies as "social sin."

In this vein, the fundamental contribution and continuing relevance of liberation theology lies in bringing the primacy of praxis and the perspective of the poor to the center of theology.[7] These hermeneutical criteria are the pillars of a reenvisioned theology—a theology that is not naive about the extent of its rootedness in particular contexts and that is explicitly programmatic in its historical and political implications.

Rosino Gibellini considers that liberation theology introduced into theological language a linguistic innovation. For the word *liberation* is infused with a semantic range that surpasses its conventional use.[8] The language of *liberation* refers back to the biblical traditions of the historical dynamism of God's rescue of and restorative justice among his people. Theologically, *liberation* refers to a soteriological category that, when applied to the historical experience of the church, speaks of God's salvation at three levels: (1) the sociopolitical level: liberation of the oppressed from their oppressors ("exploited classes, marginalized races, despised cultures");[9] (2) the anthropological level: liberation that

allows for the attainment of a society of equals; and (3) the theological level: liberation from sin, which is the ultimate source of all evil and injustice, through a life of communion and participation. Hence, for liberation theologians, the word *liberation* does not merely signify a topic in theology. It does not refer to another theology of the genitive but to an orientation and manner of doing theology—what Hugo Assmann called "a theology from the praxis of liberation."[10]

In order to attend to these dimensions of the concept of liberation, a corresponding methodological approach is employed whereby the aforementioned levels are analyzed. Clodovis Boff articulates these three aspects as the socioanalytical dimension, the hermeneutical mediation, and the mediation of praxis.[11] Using this epistemological analysis, Leonardo Boff states that the goal of liberation theology is "to articulate a reading of reality starting from the poor and from the interest of the liberation of the poor; in function of this, [it] utilizes the human and social sciences, reflects theologically and proposes pastoral actions that alleviate the way of the oppressed."[12] The method presupposes a personal stance that precedes the theological task. Theology is always and strictly a second act of faith. The first act is one of commitment to the Lord Jesus Christ and his work, primarily by adopting his preferential approach toward and treatment of the weakest in society. This is a political, ethical, and evangelical option in favor of the poor. It is a political option in that the theologian must always work within a set of social spaces where she must side with those who

[7]Antonio González, *The Gospel of Faith and Justice* (Maryknoll, NY: Orbis, 2005), 2-10.
[8]Rosino Gibellini, *La Teología del siglo XX*, Coleccion Presencia Teológica (Santander, Spain: Sal Terrae, 1998), 378.
[9]Gustavo Gutiérrez, *La fuerza histórica de los probres* (Salamanca, Spain: Sígueme, 1982), 243.
[10]Assmann, *Teología desde la praxis*, 40.
[11]Clodovis Boff, "The Method of Theology of Liberation," in *Systematic Theology: Perspectives from Liberation Theology: Readings from Mysterium Liberationis*, ed. Ignacio Ellacuría (Maryknoll, NY: Orbis, 1996), 17-21.
[12]Gibellini, *Teología del siglo*, 378.

are the victims of systemic oppression. It is an ethical option because it is a moral response to the unacceptable reality of material misery and its detrimental effects on the Majority World. And it is an evangelical option because the commitment is based on the eschatological blessings of the Gospels regarding the fate of the poor (e.g., Mt 25:35-46): "the poor are the eschatological criteria of salvation/perdition."[13] Hence, the impoverished masses are the indispensable theological loci.[14]

A Précis of Protestant Theology in Latin America

Two trajectories. One can trace theological production among Protestants according to two different but complementary trajectories. The first trajectory is the one associated with the historically Protestant churches (Lutheran, Methodist, Presbyterian, and Reformed). The key theologians representing these churches are Rubem Alves, Emilio Castro, Julio de Santa Ana, and José Míguez Bonino. The second trajectory is the one associated with the Fraternidad Teológica Latinoamericana and is represented by evangelicals such as C. René Padilla, Samuel Escobar, and Emilio Antonio Núñez.

Míguez Bonino offers a helpful typology that identifies the "faces of Protestantism": the liberal face, the evangelical face, the Pentecostal face, and the ethnic face. In terms of theological distinctiveness, the two broader categories are the liberal and evangelical faces—categories that, to some extent, overlap sociologically with one another in the context of an ecclesial family. Still, the distinctions are valuable.

The liberal face of Protestantism refers to church communities that resulted from the missionary efforts of historical or mainline denominations in North America. This tradition is amicable to and promotes many aspects of modernity (e.g., liberal democracy, progress, education, human rights, and freedom). Theologically, the Holiness revival movements in the United States, the social view of the gospel, and liberalism influence it. Traditional theological themes (e.g., the doctrine of God, Christology, ecclesiology, and revelation) are not necessary objects of formal dogmatic elaboration, but we can identify key emphases in regard to the practice of theology. There is an insistence on theological reflection based on concrete historical realities—an explicit effort to locate reflection in context, distancing the theologian from what could be considered *in principio* abstract discussions without historical relevance. To this end, biblical themes such as justice and salvation are treated in light of the experience of pastoral ministry and the meaning of being a church in historical development. The goal is the articulation of "a situated theology, strongly critical in relation to theoretical theological construals," with the aim of achieving a satisfactory relationship between the experience of faith (which implies practical and ethical commitments) and its theory.[15] The role of theology is to provide an orientation and accompaniment in the search for a more humane society.

The evangelical face is also tied to the Latin American situation (poverty, violence, and political oppression). The evangelical face identifies

---

[13]Gibellini, *Teología del siglo*, 379.

[14]Leonardo Boff, *Teología de la político: Sus mediaciones* (Salamanca, Spain: Ediciones Sígueme, 1980).

[15]Celina A. Lértora Mendoza, "Teologias latinoamericanistas reformadas y evangélicas," in *Teología en America Latina*, ed. Carmen-Jose Alejos-Grau and Jose-Ignasi Saranyana (Madrid: Iberoamericana, 2002), 445.

those Christians who receive their heritage from the Holiness and revivalist movements in the United States, but, in contrast with the ecumenically oriented churches, it promotes the experience of salvation on more subjective and individual terms. Evangelicals in Latin America are theologically orthodox but are generally politically liberal since they do not share the conservatism of their counterparts in the United States. For evangelicals, to be liberated from sin is to be freed not so much from the sinful oppression of others but from the experience of personal sin. Life is to be lived in holiness, which often entails not only moral purity but also a tension between the people of God and the rest of society. Evangelicals are also heirs of the Protestant Reformation, with a distinctive emphasis on the paradigmatic *solas*—*sola Scriptura, sola fide, solus Christus,* and *sola gratia.* Salvadorian theologian Emilio Antonio Núñez characterizes *evangélicos* as "theocentric, biblicentric, christocentric, and pneumatological."[16] In a similar vein, David Stoll identifies the *evangélicos* as those who "pursue social issues without abandoning evangelism, deal with oppressive structures without endorsing violence, and bring left- and right-wing Protestants back together again."[17]

Salvation and liberation. Soteriology in Protestantism emphasizes the theme of Christian salvation as communion with God through Jesus Christ, maintaining that the God of the Bible is a God who reconciles people and transforms so-

cieties.[18] In order to emphasize that the Christian view of salvation from sin is an affirmation of God's kingdom-establishing activity lived in historical reality (a transcendence experienced in history), Protestants have also used the nomenclature of salvation as *liberation.* The common denominator is that the concept of liberation-salvation is informed via Christology: Jesus Christ paradigmatically fulfills the Old Testament trajectories of the exodus freedom and the prophetic visions of God's actions to free the people of Israel from internal oppression and the oppression exerted by foreign political powers. In Jesus, the messianic vocation is redefined in terms of liberation of the captives—the sinners, the sick, the afflicted, the poor, and the victims. Hence, since salvation entails liberation from sinful captivities, both personal and societal, it is not a metahistorical concept or experience but "a reality indissolubly tied to the history of human beings."[19]

JESUCRISTO EL SALVADOR: THE SHAPE OF CHRISTOLOGY IN LATIN AMERICA

We are now ready to present a concise overview of the emphases of contemporary Christologies in Latin America by providing a summary of Catholic and Protestant approaches. What I am suggesting is that *Christology in Latin America moves from a focus on the history of Jesus and its soteriological significance toward an account of Jesus the Christ, who calls for participation in the kingdom of God.*

---

[16]Emilio A. Núñez, "Towards an Evangelical Latin American Theology," *Evangelical Review of Theology* 7, no. 1 (1983): 125-31.

[17]As cited in Daniel Salinas, *Latin American Evangelical Theology in the 1970's: The Golden Decade,* Religion in the Americas (Leiden: Brill, 2009), 15. David Stoll, *Is Latin America Turning Protestant: The Politics of Evangelical Growth* (Berkeley: University of California Press, 1990), 131.

[18]The formation of the Fraternidad Teológica Latinamericana (Latin American Theological Fellowship) in the 1970s began a new evangelical discourse: one lining up with creedal orthodoxy, in line with the Reformation heritage, emphasizing theology as a contextual missional discourse, taking a more sophisticated view of Scripture, promoting an interdenominational ethos, and having social relevance. See José Míguez Bonino, "Las iglesias protestantes y evangélicas en América Latina y el Caribe: un ensayo interpretativo," *Cuadernos de teología* 14, no. 2 (1995): 31.

[19]José D. Rodriguez, *Introducción a la teología,* 2nd ed. (Mexico: Publicaciones El Faro, 2002), 17.

The most mature treatments of Christology have come from the systematic Christologies of Leonardo Boff and Jon Sobrino. Though a systematic Christology monograph has yet to be produced from within the Protestant tradition, fine introductions are found in Nancy Bedford's *La porfía de la resurrección: Ensayos desde el feminismo teológico latinoamericano*, an exploration of the contributions of feminist theology for Christology; Alberto García's *Cristología: Cristo Jesús: Centro y praxis del pueblo de Dios*, a systematic outline gathering the contributions of both Latino US theologians and Latin American Protestants; Antonio González's *The Gospel of Faith and Justice*, which considers the relationship between Christology, the kingdom of God, and the Trinity on the one hand, and the mission of peace, justice, and reconciliation of the church on the other hand; and, most recently, Samuel Escobar's *En busca de Cristo en América Latina* traces the history and developments of the doctrine of Christ in evangelical thought.[20]

Access to Jesus. Contemporary christological method presents two main trajectories for approaching the meaning of the life and work of Jesus as God's Messiah. The first trajectory can be identified as "from above," or "descending." It refers to the way in which the knowledge of Jesus' identity and praxis begins through an epistemic movement from the trinitarian life to the mediator and herald of the kingdom of God in the power of the *pneuma* (Spirit). Hence, the confession of the Christ, the Son of God, gains its dogmatic priority and intelligibility under the purview of trinitarian doctrine.

The second trajectory is traditionally identified as "from below," or "ascending." Here the humanity of Jesus is established as the material foundation for Christology. Christology begins with the *facta* and *verba* of Jesus' human life, with the aim of moving toward the confession of his divinity. This approach emphasizes Jesus' human aspects that identify him very early in his life as part of an ethnic minority in Galilee, while also focusing on the actions that portray him as being within the milieu of the expectations of the kingdom of God. Emphasis on the singular humanity of Jesus is one of the distinctive methodological contributions of Latin American theology, as the development of Christology in Latin America has centered on paying attention to the historical Jesus.[21] This is the case paradigmatically with liberation theology, but it is also a key aspect of contemporary Protestant Christologies. We begin with an overview of the former.

A liberation Christology. *Leonardo Boff.* In christological work in Latin America, Leonardo Boff's contribution in *Jesus Christ Liberator* is a catalyst for reflection on the life and work of Christ.[22] How does one speak about Jesus and his salvation in a way that is relevant to the struggles of a great majority of people who live in subhuman conditions of impoverishment and oppression? In Boff's proposal, this approach to Christology includes at least five constructive elements that speak to the experience of liberation.

---

[20]Nancy E. Bedford, *La porfía de la resurrección: Ensayos desde el feminismo teológico latinoamericano*, Colección FTL (Buenos Aires: Kairós, 2008); Alberto L. García, *Cristología: Cristo Jesús: Centro y práxis del pueblo de Dios*, Biblioteca Teológica Concordia (St. Louis: Concordia, 2006); Samuel Escobar, *En busca de Cristo en América Latina* (Buenos Aires: Ediciones Kairos, 2012).

[21]For an introductory survey of these methodological options in Christology and their respective goals, see Wolfhart Pannenberg, *Jesus, God and Man* (Philadelphia: Westminster, 1968).

[22]For a succinct summary of the argument, see Leonardo Boff, *Jesus Christ Liberator: A Critical Christology for Our Time* (Maryknoll, NY: Orbis, 1978), 43-48.

First, it must give primacy to the anthropological element over the ecclesiastical, for the central issue facing the church is a humanity that needs to be humanized, not a church that needs institutional presence. Second, it must favor the utopian over the factual. The reign of God entails a historical experience of a changed reality in favor of the creation of a new human being after the likeness of Christ and his praxis. Third, a critical rather than dogmatic perspective must be adopted. More specifically, the issue is how one discerns that which is liberative from that which is not. Mere confession of Christ does not provide the criteria to make such a judgment. Doctrinal confessions about Jesus as the Christ of God that begin with the creeds, though emphasizing the New Testament resurrection motif, do not offer a sufficient foundation to inform the praxis of disciples because theological confessions need the historical context of Jesus—namely, his words, actions, and death—to gain coherence and practical relevance. Fourth, the method must prioritize the social-communitarian dimension over the personal. That is, it must create a space to speak to the collective implications of the message of Jesus. Finally, the method must retain the primacy of orthopraxis over orthodoxy, right acting over right dogma, highlighting the praxeological core of Jesus' message.

These priorities allow for a view of Jesus of Nazareth as the "liberator," a contextually relevant way of presenting Jesus in Latin America. Boff explains that such a christological title highlights the freedom Jesus brings from the conscience of sin and all kinds of alienations, particularly the human condition of broken

relations toward each other and God. The praxis of Jesus is both the historical realization of the concrete kingdom of God and the beginning of the process of liberation. Jesus' confrontation with the world and the oppressors of his time, as well as his violent death, must be understood as the reaction to his liberative action. The resurrection is hence the irruption in history of the anticipated and definitive liberation whereby the utopia of the kingdom becomes *topia* in history.[23] The resulting thesis for a liberative Christology focuses on the nature of the reign of God: "The Kingdom, although it might not be of this world by its origin (its origin is in God), it is present in our midst, manifesting itself in processes of liberation."[24] To follow Jesus is to seek after his cause and plenitude.

Jon Sobrino. The most complete outline of Christology from a liberation perspective is offered by Salvadorian theologian Jon Sobrino, beginning with his *Cristología desde América Latina: Esbozo a partir del seguimiento del Jesús histórico* (Christology from Latin America: An Outline Beginning with the Following of the Historical Jesus).[25]

Sobrino's Christology is characterized by an interest in soteriology as it relates to a specific historical and political context in which the existential questions posed to faith do not come from secularism and atheism but, rather, center on the meaning of the good news of salvation for the impoverished, the violently oppressed, and the excluded of this world. Despite the immense cultural, religious, and ethnic plurality in the continent, it is still true that these groups share common life struggles.

---

[23]Gibellini, *Teología del siglo*, 389.
[24]Leonardo Boff, *La fe en la periferia del mundo: El caminar de la Iglesia con los oprimidos* (Santander, Spain: Sal Terrae, 1981), 44.
[25]Jon Sobrino, *Cristología desde América Latina: Esbozo a partir del seguimiento del Jesús histórico*, 2nd ed., Colección teologia latino-americana (Ciudad Mexico: Editiones CRT, 1977). For the English translation, see *Christology at the Crossroads: A Latin American Approach* (Maryknoll, NY: Orbis, 1978).

In this Christology, Jesus' ultimacy and transcendence is established from three basic premises: (1) the aim of liberation theology is the reality of God's kingdom, (2) the ethos of this theology is a critical reflection on praxis, and (3) the *locus theologicus* is the poor of this world. The goal is to provide not only a reorganization of the christological task but a reformulation of Christology as the basis of liberation, that is, as salvation from all kinds of evils, especially those that manifest themselves in the perpetuation of poverty, oppression, and violence.

In this vein, Christology has an eschatological structure based on the relationship between the Jesus of history (along the lines of the modern new quest for the historical Jesus) and the dual referents of the kingdom of God and the God of the kingdom. Approving of most modern Christologies' insistence that the final reality for Jesus was not himself, nor God *in directo*, but the kingdom of God, Sobrino argues that we can only come to know it in and through Jesus. For Sobrino, these are "indispensable realities for theology, giving it a basis on which better to organize and grade Jesus' multiple external activities, to conjecture his inner being, and, undoubtedly, to explain his historical fate of dying on the cross."[26] The kingdom is the principal category that provides both direction for Christian praxis and hope for life.

The kingdom of God, as a primary metaphor for God's transcendent activity in history, functions as an organizing category from which this liberation theology claims "a totality from which it can deal with all theological subjects."[27] The resurrection event, although embracing all aspects of faith (the ultimate meaning of history, a radical hope, the defeat of death, etc.), is not a clear enough paradigm to inform how we should live and act *now* in history in light of the conditions that negate the very life that the resurrection offers. The kingdom is proposed to have more explanatory power for discipleship.

If the subject matter of Christology is Jesus as the Christ of God, the access to its material content should be "from below," via the close examination of historical accounts in the Gospels. Christology has two fundamental moments: the texts of revelation that speak of the historic presence of Jesus Christ, and the actual reality of Christ's presence today in which true faith in Christ finds its expression.[28] Hence, the formal presupposition is that Jesus of Nazareth is the Christ of God, whereas the methodological presupposition is that an "ascending" Christology is as valid as, or even more fruitful for discipleship than, the dominant "descending" Christologies that begin with the ultimate realities of the faith: the triune God and the incarnation of the Son. More so, there are at least a posteriori considerations that support the emphasis on Jesus of Nazareth: the historical tendency to ignore Jesus' own historical life and priorities, even where there is a confession of faith in Christ, and the terrible consequences of confessing Christ while using him to legitimize the idols of history, political powers, and inhumane and anti-Christian oppression. The reason for focusing on history is not demythologization, but to move toward the "de-pacification" and "humanization" of Jesus in a way that recovers his historicity as integral for faith and praxis today.

The road that leads to the confession of Jesus as the Christ of God is through Jesus of Nazareth, by considering his concrete history in its totality

---

[26]Jon Sobrino, *Jesucristo liberador: Lectura histórico-teológica de Jesus de Nazaret* (Madrid: Trotta, 1991), 67.
[27]Sobrino, *Jesucristo liberador*, 123.
[28]Sobrino, *Jesucristo liberador*, 23.

and recognizing his praxis as central to our understanding of his life and mission. In this sense, liberation Christology attempts to historicize the Christ event and thus follows the path of many modern theologies with their so-called historical turn. The "historical Jesus" represents the point of departure, which is better understood as the practice of viewing the historical Jesus as the history *of* Jesus.[29] Through this history, with faith in his Father, obedience to his mission, in death and resurrection, Jesus is confessed as the Son of God.

Latin American Protestant Christology. The historical consciousness that Christology found in the twentieth century encouraged Protestants to prioritize the historical and political dimensions of theological discourse in order to galvanize Christian discipleship. But it also presents an opportunity to critically bring to the forefront of Christology the role of history, ethics, and ideologies. It is a methodological option that has inspired a renovation of Christian discipleship and grounded the work of theology with a deep concern for the praxis of the faith.

In Protestant Christology in Latin America, the confession that Jesus is the one unbegotten Son, the Logos, surely provides the ontological presupposition on which Christian faith delves into the mystery of God, for which creedal orthodoxy serves as the standard. However, the work of Christology in Latin America among Protestant theologians also advances under the methodological proposal that it is equally legitimate, or even more necessary from the systematic perspective, to approach Jesus as the Christ of God via the historical particularity of Jesus as the man from Nazareth. It is the at-

tention to Jesus' historical life that permits the very possibility of his anthropological identification as fully human. The retrieval of the humanity of Jesus in its historical Jewish expression provides the ground for any attempt at ontological reflection on the significance of Jesus' divinity and helps the faith avoid reductionism. This is a general achievement of contemporary Christology that is adopted in Latin America.

Argentinean Lutheran Guillermo Hansen proposes that to think about Jesus' humanity and divinity is to delve into the notions of transcendence and immanence: the complete otherness of God and the complete presence of God in the dynamism of creative existence. The path toward thinking theologically about Jesus begins with the presupposition that in this human being there is an extraordinary mediation—an irruption of divine transcendence in immanence, which consequently implies that in the person of Jesus we find a projection of immanence into transcendence. This *doble via* (double way) is what allows us to "confess that in Jesus the divine makes itself present, but it is also what allows us to christologize the divine, that is, identify transcendence with Jesus."[30]

Therefore, when Christians assert that Jesus reveals God and vice versa, and that in this human being the criterion to discern the ultimate meaning in history is found, theology is claiming to "comprehend the 'ultimate' from a figure that can be historically located and correlated to key social, political and cultural dimensions," as Guillermo Hansen puts it—thereby emphasizing that in the life events of Jesus one finds the divine reality. That is, in virtue of the only undivided person (e.g., Chalcedon and *the comunicatio*

[29]Jon Sobrino, *Jesús en America Latina: Su significado para la fe y la cristología* (Santander, Spain: Sal Terrae, 1982), 112-13.

[30]Guillermo Hansen, "¿Se conmueven los cimientos de la cristología?: La tercera búsqueda del Jesús histórico y la respuesta 'alquímica' de la teología," *Cuadernos de teología* 25 (2006): 134.

idiomatum) of Jesus, it is possible to attribute to God that which is human. Jesus christologizes divinity itself.[31] Consequently, knowledge of Jesus Christ is both a confession of faith of the highest order—that this man Jesus is truly of God, from God, and very God—and a historical apprehension and affirmation of Jesus as the Nazarene from Galilee. To believe in Jesus Christ is not only a theological confession but also a trust in and will to enter into *secuela Christi* (following of Christ). As Christians, says Nancy E. Bedford, "we believe in God through Jesus by God," and "we recognize in Christ the *deiformity* of Jesus but also the *christoformity* of God."[32] What she means is that in order to understand the person and work of Jesus, we are inevitably referred to God in his life, and when we think about God, we are inevitably drawn to think of God as seen through Jesus. Christian faith results from a historical epistemological access to Jesus, existentially internalized by the Holy Spirit.

Christology in holistic perspective. Proposing that christological discourses must be evaluated not only for their coherence but also their material content in accordance with the whole gospel and how they function in concrete situations, Bedford outlines the contours of a Latin American feminist Christology.[33] The goal is constructive: to represent Jesus of Nazareth as the Christ in whom the triune God acts as God with us and for us, for the sake of justice, righteousness, and transformation. Bedford shares the conviction that Christology must be understood in trinitarian terms. Analyzing the dominant religious and cultural images of Jesus in Latin America—as the suffering victim or the celestial monarch—she emphasizes that theologians need to avoid "toxic christologies": discourses about Jesus that function as tools for maintaining the status quo and domination of the other, particularly women. In Bedford's judgment, a trinitarian approach to Christology provides the "pneumatic space" where the continuation of faithful praxis and explication of the meaning and relevance of the gospel of Jesus are realized in the freedom of God's people. That is, "When the strength of the Spirit of God acts to overcome the limitations and hierarchies of gender, new spaces are created through the trinitarian economy of God so that the church functions as a home full of life."[34] This approach to Christology has the strength of highlighting the pneumatic dimensions of Christology and ecclesiology, as well as the social implications for gender issues and the integral wellbeing of women and children who fall victim to physical and emotional abuse by men: the logic of patriarchal violence.

Christology and the limits of creedal orthodoxy. Latin American theology has an uneasy relation in its reception of the christological dogma embodied in the Nicene and Chalcedonian Creeds. It affirms the binding nature of the dogma but questions its relevancy for the contemporary challenges of the church in Latin America. The concentration on the historical dimension of salvation with its focus on recovering the centrality of Jesus' concrete actions aims to fix what are perceived as inherent limitations of the creeds: the emphasis on transcendence at the expense of the historical, the stress on Jesus as divine at the expense of the importance of his historical

---

[31]Hansen, "¿Se conmueven los cimientos de la cristología?," 134-35.

[32]Nancy E. Bedford and Guillermo Hansen, eds., *Nuestra Fe* (Buenos Aires: Instituto Universitario ISEDET, 2008), 111.

[33]Nancy E. Bedford, "Otra vez la cristología," *Cuadernos de teología* 27 (2008): 39n9.

[34]Bedford, "Otra vez la cristología," 49.

humanity, and the lack of attention to the ethical dimension of Christology. It is charged that the Christian tradition disassociated the mediation of God's presence in history (Jesus) from the mediation of God's will.

Therefore, although the significance of the creeds is affirmed, the interpretation of the councils—of Chalcedon in particular—reveals a distinction made between the biblical testimony concerning Jesus' identity, and the metaphysical and philosophical mediations that conditioned the theological language of the milieu. Arguably the major difference between classical Christology and the Christologies arising in Latin America is found in the language used to elucidate the mystery of the identity and work of Jesus of Nazareth. It is often argued that creedal Christology in its treatment of the identity and work of Jesus operates with the philosophical terminology of "nature, persons, substance, accident, essence, subsistence, hypostatic union, *communicatio idiomatum*, vicarious satisfaction, etc."[35] This kind of conceptual language did not necessarily diminish the spirituality of the early church fathers and Christian communities, but the language became "more technical and abstract, less narrative and experiential," over time, contributing to the eventual bifurcation between the being of Jesus and his salvific work.[36]

Hence, the authority of the creeds is relative to the necessities of their originating context. The contention is that while "the Nicene Creed and the Chalcedonian definition systematized in metaphysical language the biblical data concerning Christ as fully God and fully man and as the indivisible one . . . they lost sight of Jesus's concrete actions in history," obscuring in the process Jesus' life and humanity, as well as his identification with and concern for the poor and the marginalized of his time.[37]

The main limitation of creedal Christology is its tendency toward abstraction consequent on its use of philosophical conceptuality—making the doctrine of Christ susceptible to historical indifference. The recovery of the history of Jesus in person, practice, options, and destiny is what grants theology the material content to appropriate the work of Jesus of Nazareth as the work of God for the sake of humanity and creation. The creeds need the fundamental corrective of the focus on the good news as an announcement primarily directed toward the victims of institutionalized exclusion and violence, as well as to all who are subject to all kinds of captivities. This critique is of particular importance in evangelical Christianity in Latin America, which despite its acknowledgment of the full humanity of Christ is nevertheless affected by docetism. This influence makes it difficult to establish relationships between doctrine and social ethics because such minimizing of the full humanity of Jesus as compared to his divine identification functionally rejects the materiality of the incarnation.[38]

Catholic and Protestant Christologies locate in the history of Jesus the arrival of the *eschatón*. At the center of the Christian confession of Jesus is his mission, his preaching, his relationship with his *Abba*, and the Spirit revolving around the proclamation of the arrival of the kingdom of God. The death and resurrection of Jesus are

---

[35]Juan-José Tamayo-Acosta, ed., *Diez palabras claves sobre Jesús de Nazaret* (Estella, Spain: Verbo Divino, 1999), 12.

[36]Bedford and Hansen, *Nuestra Fe*, 122.

[37]C. René Padilla, "Toward a Contextual Christology from Latin America," in *Conflict and Context: Hermeneutics in the Americas* (Grand Rapids, MI: Eerdmans, 1986), 81.

[38]Padilla, "Towards a Contextual Christology," 83. Docetism refers to a Christology in which Jesus' humanity is conceived as an apparent quality of his personhood. That is, Jesus only appears to be fully human.

understood not only in the context of the grand biblical narrative of God's redemptive work and in the paradigm of his divine and human identity, but in light of the actions of Jesus of Nazareth, the history of Israel, and God's identification with those actions. The liberation of the masses subjected to sin in its personal, collective, and structural manifestations depends on the cross and resurrection of Jesus, as he is the representative of both the true human and the victims who long for God's ultimate justice.

In the royal announcement of the fulfillment of this reign, Jesus Christ is analytically indispensable to comprehension of it because to announce the kingdom is to announce Jesus Christ, and to announce Jesus Christ is to announce the kingdom. The theological inseparability of Jesus and the kingdom is due to the Gospels' datum that "the function of Jesus after paschal consists in introducing and exercising God's reign in history: 'God was in Christ reconciling the world to himself.'"[39] Antonio González summarizes the relationship between Christology and the kingdom as follows: "The reign of that king is none other than the reign of God. Precisely for that reason, the separation of the proclamation of the Christ, that is, of the Messiah or the anointed one, from the proclamation of the reign of God makes no sense at all. There is not, nor can there be, a Christ without a reign."[40] In emphasizing Jesus' integral historical personhood and the presupposition of the presence of transcendence (i.e., God was in Christ), theology in Latin America hopes to discern a pattern and content for theological ethics. As C. René Padilla argues: "If the Christ of faith is the Jesus of history, then it is possible to speak of social ethics for Christian disciples who seek to fashion their lives on God's purpose of love and justice concretely revealed."[41] The ethical dimensions of christological discourse give rise to an exercise in faithful creativity where contemporary Christians seek to prolong the logic of Jesus' praxis in their different cultural and political settings.

Christology and the cross. Theologians in Latin America approach the soteriological question of Jesus' death on the cross with both historical and theological emphases. Theologically, the death of Jesus is central to the intelligibility and power of the gospel. Jesus redeems from sin, is a substitution for sinners, conquers death, defeats Satan, brings reconciliation and forgiveness, justifies and makes people just, and provides hope for the victims of sin by shining the light of love and justice for the liberation of humanity.

In terms of the reality of history, the death of Jesus is seen as the historical outcome of his confrontation with political and religious authorities: suffering for the sake of justice and calling his disciples to follow his example of sacrifice. Liberation theology places strong emphases on the historical causes of the crucifixion. The death of Jesus was a political murder, a fate sealed by the conflictive religious and political nature of his message and the kind of life he lived and expected others to live. The life of Jesus cannot be relativized, and the question "Why was he killed?" needs to be anchored in a material reality. The danger of decontextualizing and relativizing the life of Jesus is that the political conditions of the cross event are lost, and the main addressees of his message—the humble, the poor, women,

---

[39]Antonio González, *El evangelio de la paz y el reinado de Dios*, Colección FTL (Buenos Aires: Ediciones Kairos, 2008), 51-52. See also chaps. 2-3. The English translation of chaps. 2-5 can be found in González, *Gospel of Faith and Justice*, chaps. 2-4, 7. Other cited passages include Mk 1:14-15; Acts 28:31; Rom 1:4; 14:17; 1 Cor 4:20; Phil 2:9-11; Col 4:11.
[40]González, *Gospel of Faith and Justice*, 72.
[41]Padilla, "Towards a Contextual Christology," 89.

and other marginalized groups—therefore become invisible both in the testimony in Scripture and in our societies.[42]

Bedford shares this concern and believes that in the historical conditions of the cross we can "find, therefore, the truth about the system in which we live"—with its systemic violence against those made weak in society, particularly women—and "the way in which the triune God proceeds, whose fidelity to his creation we confess and in whose mercy we are immersed in following Jesus."[43] In the historical and theological density of the cross, there is healing for victims and transformation for victimizers. To avoid an abstract conception of salvation and to protect the integrity of Christology, theology needs to affirm that the death of Jesus was the consequence of his announcement that the kingdom of God had arrived.

CONCLUSION

Amid the legacy of violent colonialism, political Christendom, dictatorships, civil wars, discrimination, exclusion, and poverty, the person of Jesus Christ becomes in his historicity and humanity the Lord and Son who ushers in the kingdom of God and calls on all men and women to follow him. The one who calls is the Jesus who reaches the poor, who calls for universal repentance, and who heals victims and transforms victimizers. His gospel is the announcement of the arrival of the reign of his Father present in his words, actions, and choices. His ethos is shaped by a life filled and moved by the power of the Spirit to bring life. The cross is the result of Jesus' mission, confronting a world of violence, idolatry, and evil. It is also the way in which God's self-giving stands as an event for us who

believe, but also against the antikingdom of corruption and injustice. Salvation is in history but is not limited to history. Christology from a Latin American perspective is an ascending Christology elaborated on the historical self-abasement of the Christ of God and the hope of his salvific global will.

The aforementioned proposals are in a continual process of development, as theologians are working on a series of challenges. An explanation is needed regarding how to define the nature of history with a concomitant account of divine action. If God's action in history is understood—as Míguez Bonino, Bedford, and González argue—as the action of the trinitarian God, accounts of Jesus as the trinitarian Son and of his salvific mission in relation to the revelation of the Father and the activity of the Spirit are needed. Moreover, we still need to better elucidate the impact of a recovery of the Jesus of history on our understanding of the presently reigning eschatological Jesus, a reigning that finds its elaboration through pneumatology. Also needed is a theological elaboration of the nature and use of Scripture as an authoritative source for epistemic access to the carpenter from Nazareth and the *norma normans* for orthopraxis.

It is notable that the common aim of Latin American Christologies is to articulate a transformative Christology that avoids the practical and discursive dualisms between a heavenly savior and an earthly liberator. The unity of Jesus Christ—avoiding the dichotomy of the Jesus of history and the Christ of faith—and of exegesis and dogmatics is a challenge too. This unity is sought between ethics and ontology, between a social and an individual vision of salvation. The task is to relocate the history of Jesus Christ at

---

[42]Padilla, "Christology and Mission," 28.
[43]Bedford, *La porfía*, 142.

the beginning of Christology. The burden is to provide an account of how the history of Jesus offers people a vital and indispensable foundation for love, life, and hope.

FURTHER READING

Escobar, Samuel. *En busca de Cristo en América Latina.* Buenos Aires: Ediciones Kairos, 2012.

González, Antonio. *The Gospel of Faith and Justice.* Maryknoll, NY: Orbis, 2005.

Lois, Julio. "Christology in the Theology of Liberation." Pages 169-94 in *Mysterium Liberationis,* edited by Ignacio Ellacuría and Jon Sobrino. Maryknoll, NY: Orbis, 1993.

Míguez Bonino, José. "Latin America." Pages 16-43 in *Introduction to Third World Theologies,* edited by John Parratt. Cambridge: Cambridge University Press, 2004.

Padilla, C. René. *Mission Between the Times: Essays on the Kingdom.* Rev. ed. Carlisle, UK: Langham Monographs, 2010.

Sobrino, Jon. *Christ the Liberator: A View from the Victims.* Maryknoll, NY: Orbis, 2001.

READING THE GOSPEL OF JOHN
THROUGH PALESTINIAN EYES

Yohanna Katanacho

THERE IS NO DOUBT in my mind that all of us read the Gospel of John from a particular perspective.[1] We are all shaped by our social, political, cultural, and religious assumptions. This is very true in Israel-Palestine. For example, some Messianic Jews in Israel-Palestine believe that Jesus is the Jew par excellence who lived in a Jewish culture.[2] They read the Gospel of John from this point of view.[3] Other Jews are troubled by the Jesus presented in the Gospel of John, since he describes some Jews as "unbelieving descendants of the devil (8:44), blind, sinful, and incapable of understanding their own scriptures."[4] Further, some Israeli Jews are not interested in Jesus Christ at all. They call him "Yshu," which is a Hebrew acronym that means "may his name and memory be obliterated!"[5] Others in Israel-Palestine emphasize that there is a continuum between the native people of the land throughout the centuries. Consequently, Jesus and contemporary Palestinians share the same geopolitical location.[6] The geographical and sociopolitical continuity makes Jesus not only a Palestinian but also a Palestinian identification figure. The identity and actions of Jesus embody the hopes of Palestinians and represent them, more so than other nations. Many Palestinian Muslims see him as a Palestinian prophet,

[1] For a survey of approaches to the Gospel of John, see Frank Pack, "The Gospel of John in the Twentieth Century," *Restoration Quarterly* 7 (1963): 173-85; Harold Songer, "The Gospel of John in Recent Research," *Review and Expositor* 62 (1965): 417-28; Robert Kysar, "The Gospel of John in Current Research," *Religious Studies Review* 9 (1983): 314-23; Mark Stibbe, *The Gospel of John as Literature: An Anthology of Twentieth-Century Perspectives* (Leiden: Brill, 1993).

[2] It is important to keep in mind that first-century Judaism is neither equivalent to the Old Testament nor identical with twenty-first-century Judaism. The Jewishness of the first-century Jesus is not like the Jewishness of contemporary Jews. Sadly, the Jewishness of Jesus seems to be highlighted in Israel in a way that alienates him from Palestinians and alienates Messianic Jews from the global church. It becomes a barrier instead of being a channel in which the blessings of God are brought forth. In addition, it is important to note that the Gospel of John uses the label *Jew* in a context of hostility. We need to keep in mind that John himself is a Jew and that the word *Jew* in the Gospel of John does not represent the position of all the Jews in the first century, let alone the Jews throughout history.

[3] Messianic Jews have a spectrum of views concerning Jesus Christ. Some accept the traditional Christian views, while most of them refuse the language of the Nicene Creed and prefer to express the identity of Jesus in Jewish categories. Few refuse the theology of the Nicene Creed. For a detailed discussion on Messianic Jewish Christology, see Richard Harvey, *Mapping Messianic Jewish Theology* (Milton Keynes, UK: Paternoster, 2009), 96-139.

[4] Adele Reinhartz, "A Nice Jewish Girl Reads the Gospel of John," *Semeia* 77 (1997): 179. See also Adele Reinhartz, *Befriending the Beloved Disciple: A Jewish Reading of the Gospel of John* (New York: Continuum, 2001).

[5] See, for example, the Jesus Boat Museum on the Sea of Galilee; the English explanation about the first-century boat uses the label *Jesus*, but the Hebrew text uses *Yshu*. I complained to the administration of the museum, but they insisted on using what is common in Israel.

[6] Mitri Raheb, "Toward a Hermeneutics of Liberation: A Palestinian Christian Perspective," in *The Biblical Text in the Context of Occupation: Towards a New Hermeneutics of Liberation*, ed. Mitri Raheb (Bethlehem: Diyar, 2012), 11-27.

and some of them believe that the Gospel of John predicted the coming of Muhammad, the prophet of Islam.[7] On the other hand, many Palestinian Christians see Christ as the Son of God who was born in the Palestinian town of Bethlehem. Several Palestinian liberation theologians affirm that the Palestinian Jesus is again facing Herod, but this time it is an Israeli Herod.[8]

It seems that many who pay attention to Jesus are far from the Chalcedonian Christ who is an inclusive figure that embodies all of humanity.[9] Instead, a particular Christ is conceived who is exclusive by definition. Consequently, the ontological Chalcedonian reality that Christ is fully human is lost in the mix. While the Chalcedonian Definition makes an indispensable ontological contribution to our Christology, it does so while sidestepping any functional dimension.[10] Another problem is that the connection between Christ's full humanity and his particular ethnicity is not addressed. The notion that Christ is the Jewish peacemaker, not only between humanity and God but also between the Jews and the nations, is not developed. It does not define the Jewishness of Jesus at all. In short, the need for studying Jesus Christ beyond Chalcedonian expressions is clear.[11] The Scriptures no doubt are able to enrich our understanding of Chalcedonian Christology; they can help us focus on

concerns that have not been addressed before. Consequently, I propose reading the scriptural story of Jesus of Nazareth combining the human and divine spatiotemporal realities from a functional point of view. How can the Jewish Jesus who is born in Palestine and is fully human be a peacemaker or a liberator? How can he represent both Palestinians and Jews as the humble and suffering servant as well as be the resurrected Christ? How can the Gospel of John help us unpack the concept of the full humanity of Jesus in the context of the Palestinian-Israeli conflict? The Gospel of John is a fruitful place to contemplate the inclusive reality that Christ brings forth.

The exclusive particularism that is rooted in national and ethnic visions of the identity of the Christ is in tension with the depiction of Christ in the Gospel of John. John is advocating a Christocentric worldview in which important particulars of Pharisaic Judaism are deconstructed, making way for an inclusive vision of Christ and his kingdom. As John deconstructs major elements of Pharisaic Judaism, his new world order reorganizes the world in relation to Christ. In the following paragraphs I discuss the "new beginning" in the Gospel of John, holy space, holy time, holy experience, holy community, and holy land. These components not only are important in the Gospel of John but are also foundational

---

[7]Some Muslims believe that the Paraclete in the Gospel of John points to Muhammad the prophet of Islam. For further details, see the following Arabic resources: Ahmed Hijazi Al-Saqa, *Paraclete: It Is the Name of the Prophet of Islam in the Gospel of Jesus* (Cairo: Al-Muty'y, 1972), 4, 29. See also the Arabic book of Faruq Abed Al-salam, *Muhammed, Peace Be upon Him, in the Gospel of John* (Cairo: Markaz Al-salam lltjhyz Al-fani, 2006).

[8]Some examples of Palestinian liberation theology are Naim Ateek, *Justice and Only Justice: A Palestinian Theology of Liberation* (Maryknoll, NY: Orbis, 1989); Naim Ateek, *A Palestinian Christian Cry for Reconciliation* (Maryknoll, NY: Orbis, 2008); Mitri Raheb, *I Am a Palestinian Christian* (Minneapolis: Fortress, 1995). For further details about mapping Palestinian theology, see Yohanna Katanacho, "Palestinian Protestant Theological Responses to a World Marked by Violence," *Missiology: An International Review* 36 (2008): 289-305.

[9]For understanding Chalcedonian Christology in the context of nineteenth- and early twentieth-century discussions, see Mark Nestlehutt, "Chalcedonian Christology: Modern Criticism and Contemporary Ecumenism," *Journal of Ecumenical Studies* 35 (1998): 175-96. See also James Moulder, "Is a Chalcedonian Christology Coherent?," *Modern Theology* 2 (1986): 285-307. For understanding the context and theology of the Chalcedonian Creed, see Frances Young, "The Council of Chalcedon 1550 Years Later," *Touchstone* 19 (2001): 5-14.

[10]William Baker, "The Chalcedonian Definition, Pauline Christology, and the Postmodern Challenge of 'From Below' Christology," *Stone-Campbell Journal* 9 (2006): 81-82.

[11]In suggesting the need to move "beyond Chalcedon" in this way, I do not suggest contradicting Chalcedonian Christology or denigrating its contribution.

for Pharisaic Judaism.[12] They shape the new world order presented in John. Limits of space prevent me from going into great detail, but my analysis of the dominant conceptual structures in the Gospel of John has implications for the Palestinian-Israeli conflict—one marked by strong theo-political patterns—that I draw out.[13] I also reflect, from a Palestinian point of view, on the Chalcedonian Christology that avers that Jesus is "fully human."

A New Beginning

Scholars agree that the beginning of the Gospel of John echoes the beginning of the book of Genesis.[14] It starts with the phrase "in the beginning"; there are references to life and light as well as creation in both passages. Some would even see seven days recast in John 1–2.[15] In the Gospel of John a new stage is clearly initiated in which Christ is all in all. Christ, the God-man person, is not only the transcendent reality but is also the immanent eschatological reality. Through his presence the divine reality is revealed, touched, heard, and seen. The heavens open and the Spirit of God appears (Jn 1:32-34). The invisible God becomes visible (Jn 1:14, 18). The full union between God and humanity becomes a reality that bursts forth with grace and truth (Jn 1:14, 17). The God-man not only is with God but is also with humanity. He is not only in

heaven but he is also humble enough to be found in Nazareth, a small backwater town.[16]

The incarnation is a central theme in John 1, but alone is not sufficient to mark this new beginning. After the Son entered the world and the Spirit appeared, pilgrims were able to see heaven open while the angels of God were ascending and descending over Jesus Christ (Jn 1:51). This angelic scene, along with the phrase "a true Israelite without deceit" (Jn 1:47), echoes the story of Jacob when he received the promises of God and when he had the vision of the gate to heaven (Gen 28:17). Genesis tells us that through Jacob's descendants all the nations will be blessed and he and his descendants will inherit the land (Gen 28:13-14). Jesus applies these verses to himself, in his own first-century context. Jesus is making the assertion here that the King of Israel has been revealed and he will establish the kingdom of God on earth. The words "from now" (Jn 1:51) bring to a close the chapter that starts with the phrase "in the beginning" (Jn 1:1). It paves the way for anticipating a new world and world order in which heaven and earth are connected. Heaven is open through Jesus, and the secrets of the Father are revealed through him. As John 1:18 sums it up, Jesus is the only perfect exegete of the Father and of the divine realities. The Greek word *exēgēsato* that is used in John 1:18 means "make

---

[12]I am simply reading John in its final canonical form from a literary point of view. I agree with Craig Blomberg that "recent scholarship has adequately demonstrated that the canonical form of John is replete with thematic unity, literary artistry and intentional characterization." Craig Blomberg, "The Globalization of Biblical Interpretation: A Test Case—John 3–4," *Bulletin of Biblical Research* 5 (1995): 3. See also E. Ruckstuhl, *Die literarische Einheit des Johannesevangeliums* (Göttingen: Vandenhoeck & Ruprecht, 1987); R. Alan Culpepper, *Anatomy of the Fourth Gospel* (Philadelphia: Fortress, 1983).

[13]For an introduction to the Palestinian-Israeli conflict, see Alex Awad, *Palestinian Memoirs: The Story of a Palestinian Mother and Her People* (Bethlehem: Bethlehem Bible College, 2012). See also Salim Munayer and Lisa Loden, eds., *The Land Cries Out* (Eugene, OR: Wipf & Stock, 2012). The former resource is clearer and more specific in presenting the Palestinian side of the story, but the latter resource presents both Palestinian and Jewish points of view.

[14]See, for example, George Beasley-Murray, *John* (Dallas: Word, 2002), 10.

[15]D. A. Carson, *The Gospel According to John* (Grand Rapids, MI: Eerdmans, 1991), 168. See also Stephen Kim, "The Relationship of John 1:19-51 to the Book of Signs in John 2–12," *Bibliotheca Sacra* 165 (2008): 323-37.

[16]James Strange informs us in the *Anchor Bible Dictionary* that Nazareth was a small agricultural village with only 480 residents (Strange, "Nazareth," in *Anchor Bible Dictionary*, ed. David Noel Freedman [New York: Doubleday, 1992], 4:1050).

fully known" or "give a description or a detailed report." John uses the medium of signs that point to Jesus Christ to give content to this description.

The first sign (Jn 2:11) illustrates the new beginning mentioned in the previous paragraph. It is important to notice that John is speaking about signs, not miracles or wonders.[17] Signs are supposed to lead us to something else. John informs us that the signs should lead us to believe that Jesus is the Messiah and the means to life (Jn 20:31). The wedding at Cana is the beginning of a series of signs. It is the first sign. God started his work in the first Testament with a couple, and now he starts a new work with another couple in a wedding. Weddings in first-century Jewish culture symbolized God's relationship with Israel. It is worth taking time to notice a couple of things about this story.

First, water is important in the Gospel of John. In John 1, we see the waters of baptism. In John 2 we encounter water being transformed into wine. In John 3 Nicodemus had to be born from the water and the spirit-Spirit. In John 4 Christ gives the Samaritan woman water that springs with eternal life. In John 5 another sign is connected to water. In John 6 we see Jesus walking on the water. In John 7 Jesus talks about the living water (i.e., the Holy Spirit). In John 9 Jesus asks the blind man to wash in Siloam, another water scene. In John 11:55 we are reminded of the importance of water to cleansing. However, in John 13 Jesus states that water does not guarantee cleansing. Last, in John 19:34 water is mentioned yet again. To say the least, it seems that John is really interested in using water as a motif. The water in John 2 was needed for cleansing.[18]

Religious people had to ritually cleanse themselves in order to keep the requirements of first-century Judaism. The text implies that all the water jars are filled with water. In other words, Jesus resolves the problem of not having wine and creates a new problem. There is no longer water at the wedding. People no longer have any ritual means to cleanse themselves.

This leads me to my second observation. What is the means of cleansing if there is no water? The Gospel of John is like a tapestry; certain themes or words run through it. One of these important words is *hour*. Jesus tells his mother that his hour has not yet come. At the same time he performs the sign. Jesus is pointing out that the basis of the coming messianic age that is full of joy is not miracles but is the hour. He clarifies that the hour has not come. The "'hour' becomes a theological leitmotif that encapsulates Jesus' passion, his glorification, and human redemption."[19] John uses the label *hour* in John 7:30; 12:23, 27; 13:1; 17:1. Taken together, these texts clarify that John uses the word *hour* to refer to the cross and glorification of Jesus Christ. Put differently, the hour becomes the indispensable foundation for the new world order, or the messianic age. It is associated with all the elements of the new world order and it is the means by which the elements of Pharisaic Judaism are transformed and integrated into a Christocentric reality. The cleansing water of Judaism cannot be transformed into the messianic wine without the hour and all the meaning it carries. The Christ event centered on the hour becomes the starting point for reading the main elements of Judaism, that is, holy space, holy time, holy experience, holy community, and

---

[17]The term *Book of Signs*, now widely accepted by most Johannine scholars in reference to John 1:19–12:50, is usually associated with C. H. Dodd. See Dodd, *The Interpretation of the Fourth Gospel* (Cambridge: Cambridge University Press, 1953), x.

[18]For further details, see Wai-Yee Ng, *Water Symbolism in John: An Eschatological Interpretation* (New York: Peter Lang, 2001).

[19]Craig Morrison, "The 'Hour of Distress' in Targum Neofiti and the 'Hour' in the Gospel of John," *Catholic Biblical Quarterly* 67 (2005): 590.

holy land. The hour becomes the lens in which we see the incarnation.[20] This eschatological reality is the hermeneutical lens for interpreting not only the signs of Christ but also his identity. We cannot understand the humanity of Christ only from the perspective of his birth or the incarnation. We also need to understand his humanity from the perspective of the cross. Not only is Jesus a Jew, but he is also the Savior of the nations. While his Jewishness makes it possible for him to embody the hopes of biblical Israel and fulfill its destiny, his identity as the Savior of the world highlights a reality that transcends exclusive attitudes toward the nations. Both Jews and Gentiles are equally the objects of God's salvation. His humanity is the means of full redemption and reconciliation with God, humanity, and the cosmos. His humanity is the space in which we can touch God and be in fellowship with him. It is an inclusive humanity, not a form of exclusive Jewishness. It is appropriate now to move to my second concern, that is, Christ as the true temple (Jn 2:19-21).

HOLY SPACE

Holy space plays a central role in Second Temple Judaism, as the temple was the center of religious life in first-century Judaism. Interestingly,

the Gospel of John places the cleansing of the temple right after the wedding at Cana, continuing to develop the Johannine theme of a new world order. John tells us that Jesus refers to himself as the temple (Jn 2:21). This is significant in light of the new realities centered on Jesus Christ, but also significant in light of the fact that John places the cleansing of the temple with Jesus entering Jerusalem. Unlike the Synoptic Gospels, which put the cleansing of the temple at the end of the ministry of Jesus, John presents it between the wedding at Cana and meeting Nicodemus in order to highlight the new world order in which Christ replaces the temple.[21]

The section from John 2:1 that ends with John 4:54 has several clues about how John treats "space" as we compare the stories of Nicodemus and the Samaritan woman. John 3 showcases a man, a Jewish religious leader, while John 4 narrates a conversation between Jesus and a despised Samaritan woman, someone who would have been seen as a second-class citizen in first-century Israel.[22] The Jewish leader comes at night (usually a negative in the Gospel of John), while the woman comes during the day.[23] The leader perceives Christ in a limited and distorted way, while the woman is able to confess not only that Jesus is

---

[20]This approach is clear in the works of medieval Arab theologians. See, for example, the Arabic texts of chaps. 6, 7, and 8 of *Summa Theologiae Arabica* as found in Joshua Blau, *A Handbook of Early Middle Arabic* (Jerusalem: Hebrew University Press, 2002), 73-82.

[21]The issue of replacement theology has been polarized and politicized to the extent that people are usually misunderstood whenever they use the word *replace* in my context. Many have associated replacement theology with anti-Semitism, and consequently it is very difficult to address the pertinent theological issues without encountering ad hominem arguments. I simply reject the view that the church replaces the Jews because they are condemned by God (punitive replacement theology). In using the word here, I am simply stating that Jesus Christ embodies the hopes of biblical Israel and fulfills them. All the nations, including the Jews, are called to join the community of Jesus Christ, who is the only Savior of the world. The society of Christ does not replace the society of Israel, but Christ transforms the latter society into the church. Further, the church, or the society of Christ, existed in the society of Israel but became visible and able to fulfill its calling through Jesus Christ.

[22]On Jn 3, see, for example, Blomberg, "Globalization of Biblical Interpretation," 4. Carson says, "John may intend a contrast between the woman of this narrative and Nicodemus of chapter 3. He was learned, powerful, respected, orthodox, theologically trained; she was unschooled, without influence, despised, capable only of folk religion. He was a man, a Jew, a ruler; she was a woman, a Samaritan, a moral outcast. And both needed Jesus." Carson, *Gospel According to John*, 216. See also Mary Pazdan, "Nicodemus and the Samaritan Woman: Contrasting Models of Discipleship," *Biblical Theology Bulletin* 17 (1987): 145-48.

[23]John does not want us to forget that Nicodemus came at night. See Jn 3:2; 19:39. Several important manuscripts add that Nicodemus came at night in Jn 7:50. For further details, see Nestle-Aland, *Novum Testamentum Graece* (Stuttgart: Deutsche Bibelgesellschaft, 1994), 273.

the Christ but also that he is the Savior of the world. Clearly the author of the Gospel of John prompts a comparison of these two figures. The comparison will not be complete if we ignore the idea of holy space, which is central in John 4:20-25. In John 3 Jesus tells Nicodemus that the presence of the Spirit of God is not limited to a specific place (Jn 3:8). The work of the Spirit of God might be everywhere, and those who are born of the Spirit might be everywhere.

This idea is expanded in Jesus' conversation with the Samaritan woman. Here Jesus says that the temple of Jerusalem is no longer needed for worshiping the Father. Jesus denies the monopoly as to the true place of worship to the Pharisaic Judaism of his day because true worshipers do not emphasize the place of worship but the nature of worship. Worshipers cannot please God more when they pray on the temple mount. True worship is defined by the nature of God as revealed in Jesus Christ, not by the place of worship. Indeed, John has already pointed out this divine reality in John 1:14. This verse states that Jesus became a tabernacle in our midst.[24] The concept of connecting Jesus to the house of God is further seen in John 1:51, where we are reminded of the ladder of Jacob and the house of God, Beit El (Bethel). Jesus is the true house of God and the true temple.[25] This assertion is a challenge both to Judaism and to Islam. Any perception that the temple mount, with or without the temple, is the place in which God is found or will be found in the future is undermined by what Jesus says in John. In short, the humanity of Jesus is the space in which all humanity meets God. It is a space of reconciliation between God and human beings.

Divinity and humanity are fully reconciled in Jesus Christ. Humanity cannot be fully reconciled with itself without Jesus Christ. The house of God is a human being. God, through Christ the temple, is accessible to every human being who believes in Jesus Christ. There is thus no room for ethnic pride or exclusiveness.

HOLY TIME

As with holy space, a concept the Gospel of John deconstructs only to reconstruct it in his Gospel christologically, John similarly deals with another central element in Judaism, holy time. Israel's worship has always been centered on one specific religious calendar. The most prominent element of Israel's calendar is the Sabbath day. As Adele Reinhartz reminds us, the Sabbath is a foretaste of the world to come.[26] John mentions two signs that happened on a Sabbath: healing of the crippled person in John 5 and healing of the blind man in John 9. He informs us that Jesus healed a crippled man on a Sabbath (Jn 5:9) and asked him to carry his mattress. Consequently, the Jews were upset because they were not allowed to carry anything on a Sabbath (Neh 13:15-23; Jer 17:21-22). They were angry with Jesus because he healed a man on a Sabbath (Jn 7:23) and because he made mud to heal a blind person on a Sabbath (Jn 9:14). In fact, John informs us that the Jews wanted to kill Jesus because he broke the Sabbath (Jn 5:16). Jesus responds with an interesting explanation. He claims that God works on the Sabbath (Jn 5:17). The signs that Jesus performs are actually the work of God himself, since the Son cannot do anything apart from the Father and can do everything the Father

---

[24]We can translate the first part of Jn 1:14 in the following way: "and the Word became human and dwelt among us." The verb *dwelt* is related to the concept of pitching a tent or a tabernacle, and one of its compound forms is used in the Septuagint to refer to the tabernacle. This verb might be perceived as a figure of speech connected to God's abiding and gracious presence.

[25]For further details, see Paul Hoskins, *Jesus as the Fulfillment of the Temple in the Gospel of John* (Milton Keynes, UK: Paternoster, 2007).

[26]Reinhartz, *Befriending the Beloved Disciple*, 117.

does. Furthermore, if the Jews accept circumcision on Saturday, why would they not accept salvific healing on the same day? Jesus thus challenges the Jews not to be satisfied with superficial interpretations of their Jewish faith (Jn 7:22-24). The Sabbath is associated with the work of God in his creation. It is associated with the rest of God in the unspoiled world of Genesis 1, and it is associated with eschatological rest. In a fallen world, the Sabbath becomes an eschatological reality. On the Sabbath human beings rest from their works and hope for the full restoration (see Heb 4:9). The eschatological Sabbath cannot be found apart from the work of Christ, who is fully God and fully human. Christ himself embodies our Sabbath, being the first signpost and the first fruit of the coming age.

HOLY EXPERIENCE

Jesus not only deconstructs the rituals in the wedding at Cana, replaces the temple in John 2, and fulfills the Sabbath in John 5; he also recapitulates one of the most important traditions in Judaism: the exodus and the wilderness traditions. In John, Jesus is the new Moses. Jacob Enz explains that both Jesus and Moses were unrecognized deliverers (Ex 2:11; Jn 1:11), and both are connected to the sign of the serpent (Ex 4:4; Jn 3:14). Both the Gospel of John and the book of Exodus are built around a series of signs, both mention hardening of hearts (Ex 14:8; Jn 12:37-40), and both have prayers of intercession (Ex 32–33; Jn 17). Enz demonstrates that many other similarities between Moses and Jesus can be found. For example, both Moses and Jesus are connected to manna (Ex 16:4, 15; Jn 6:35) and to light (Ex 13:21-22; 14:20; Jn 8:12).[27] Though Enz may overstate his case, he is right about seeing a connection between Moses and Jesus, between the Gospel of John and the book of Exodus (see especially Jn 6–8). Jesus is the bread in John 6, the water in John 7, and the light in John 8. He is thus not only the center of Passover but also the center of the wilderness experience.

There is no doubt that Israel's Passover is important in the Fourth Gospel. Israel's Passover is a reminder of at least four things: (1) God rescued Israel from death (Ex 12:12-13), and the angel of death passed over the homes of the children of Israel. (2) God is holy and hates evil; so Israel is not to have any yeast (which symbolizes evil). (3) The Passover is the beginning of a new calendar in which God brings forth life. (4) The Passover is the feast of liberty. John connects the Passover (Jn 6:4) to the wilderness experience (Jn 6:31). He declares that Jesus is the sacrifice of the Passover (Jn 6:53-58) and is the true manna or bread that comes down from heaven. John is again reconstructing Israel's experience in a Christocentric way. John also describes Jesus as the source of living water. This descriptor alludes to Israel's experience in the wilderness, when God gave them water out of the rock. This reconstruction of the exodus runs even deeper. John names Jesus as the light. As Israel went out of Egypt, received the manna, drank the water from the rock, and was led by a pillar of fire, so Jesus is the manna, the water, and the light. These are all visible images that hark back to Exodus. However, in each case, John expands the target audience beyond the limits of Israel. The bread is for the world (Jn 6:33), the water is for anyone who is thirsty (Jn 7:37), and the light is for the whole world (Jn 8:12). In John, Jesus is the source of life, whether the life of liberation from Egypt or the

---

[27]Jacob Enz, "The Book of Exodus as a Literary Type for the Gospel of John," *Journal of Biblical Literature* 76 (1957): 208-15.

life that is associated with maintaining Israel in the wilderness. Jesus is also the source of guidance, since in John's presentation, Israel's experiences are meaningless without Christ. This radical reconstruction leads to a dangerous tension, as Jesus questions the absoluteness of the identity markers of the children of Abraham in John 8.

HOLY PEOPLE

The identity of ancient Israel is rooted in father Abraham as well as in their liberation from Egypt.[28] Their liberation is the consequence of their unique identity and connection to Abraham, who is chosen by God. When God elected Abraham, he also elected his seed to rule the Abrahamic kingdom and endowed them with a unique status. They are considered God's firstborn son (Ex 4:22-23). Rabbi Akiva said, "Even the poorest in Israel are considered as freemen who had lost their estates, for they are the sons of Abraham, Isaac, and Jacob."[29] Jesus deconstructs both the concept of liberation as understood by his audience and their connection to Abraham and the God of Abraham. First, he claims that true Abrahamic sonship-daughtership is intimately related to the works of Abraham. It is not defined by descent but by faith commitments that are revealed in works. To be part of the "seed" of Abraham does not make one a child of Abraham.[30] The work of Jesus' Jewish opponents, however, reveals a satanic dimension, for they are seeking to kill Jesus

Christ, who is greater than Abraham. In fact, Abraham believed in Jesus (Jn 8:56), for he is the Great I AM! John is claiming that one cannot accept Abraham and refuse Jesus. One cannot benefit from Abraham's blessing without Jesus Christ. Christ has to be at the center of the identity of Abraham's true children. In John's perspective, Abraham's seed cannot see the kingdom of God if they do not accept Jesus Christ and live as his disciples. When Jesus reached out to the Samaritan woman, he was enlarging the scope of the Abrahamic blessings. Stated differently, no one can claim Abrahamic benefits without acting like Abraham. If John's Jesus preached today, he would claim that no Israeli Jews can be children of Abraham until they act like Abraham and stand with oppressed Palestinian refugees. Similarly, John's Jesus would challenge that no Palestinians can be true followers of Jesus unless they identify and empathize with the survivors and victims of the Holocaust.[31] God's design includes both Palestinians and Israeli Jews. The Jesus of John makes this a reality we dare not ignore.

Second, the followers of Jesus Christ are the community of the free ones. Establishing the community of Christ is a clear concern in the Gospel of John. The children of God are those who accept Jesus Christ (Jn 1:12) and are born of the Spirit (Jn 3:6). They are not necessarily members of the synagogue (Jn 9:34). John argues that the path to freedom is the liberation that comes from Jesus Christ. In John 12, John

---

[28]It is interesting that Egypt is often called the house of the slaves (Ex 13:3, 14; 20:2; Deut 5:6; 6:12; 7:8; 8:14; 13:6; Josh 24:17; Judg 6:8; Jer 34:13; Mic 6:4). Paul Hoskins argues that in John's typology sin corresponds to the Egyptians, who are holding the children of Israel in bondage. Paul Hoskins, "Freedom from Slavery to Sin and the Devil: John 8:31-47 and the Passover Theme of the Gospel of John," *Trinity Journal* 31 (2010): 47-63, here 56.

[29]Cited in Stephen Motyer, *Your Father the Devil?: A New Approach to John and the "Jews"* (Carlisle, UK: Paternoster, 1997), 173.

[30]Elsewhere I have argued that DNA cannot be the identity marker of biblical Israel. See Yohanna Katanacho, *The Land of Christ: A Palestinian Cry* (Bethlehem: Bethlehem Bible College, 2012).

[31]I have been influenced by the statement of Frederick Herzog, "No man can see the kingdom of God unless he becomes black," which is quoted in Blomberg, "Globalization of Biblical Interpretation," 11.

elaborates the theme of freedom. This chapter discusses the entry into Jerusalem. Unlike the Synoptic Gospels, John explicitly mentions the palm branches, which were the symbol of freedom since the Maccabean revolt.[32] He presents the entry into Jerusalem in the midst of a big demonstration. Members of Jewish religious communities were laying out the palm branches and even chanting provocatively. Their cries were quoting Psalm 118:26, with a twist, since they were adding to it the phrase "king of Israel." They were ready to overturn Rome if Jesus were willing to be their leader. In contrast, John describes Jesus riding into Jerusalem on a colt, a symbol of peace. John then quotes Zechariah, also with a minor twist. John uses the words "fear not" instead of "rejoice." Then he adds "behold your King." The first step toward freedom is looking at Christ without fear. John pairs Jesus' entry into Jerusalem with the desire of the Greeks to see Jesus. When Judah the Maccabean cleansed the temple in 167 BC, he kicked the Gentiles out of the temple. The Synoptic Gospels show Jesus cleansing the temple, but not from Gentiles. Rather, the cleansing is from some Jews who abused the temple. John, on the other hand, openly discusses including Gentiles in the community of God. Stated differently, for John, the path to freedom is not lined with palm branches or heard in the militant ethnocentric approach. Rather, freedom occurs when the seed of wheat will die, and the plant is the new community where the enemy becomes a brother. The community of Jesus Christ is not any parochial ethnocentric community. The community of Jesus Christ is composed of those who, like the

seed of wheat, die and are reborn into the community of peace and brotherhood. This is the way of freedom and the way to create a new community. It is the path of the Jewish Jesus—the Savior of the whole world.

In short, this community appears in its embryonic form in the part of the Gospel some scholars refer to as the "Book of Glory" (Jn 13–20:31).[33] In this book, Christ calls his disciples "my children" (Jn 13:33) as a sign of creating his community. It is a Jewish community but with a Christocentric understanding of Jewishness. The children of Christ (Jn 13:33) are the children of God (Jn 1:12). Christ informs his children that he will not abandon them or leave them as orphans. The new community of God envelops the ones who abide in the vine (Jn 15:1-5) and are led by the Spirit (Jn 16:13).

Holy Land

After (1) restructuring the concept of the cleansing water in the wedding at Cana, (2) replacing the temple with Jesus in John 2, (3) pointing out that Jesus is the Sabbath in John 5, (4) rebuilding our perception of the exodus and wilderness traditions in a Christocentric way, and (5) reshaping the major markers of being the children of Abraham and consequently the children of God, John then leads us to reconsider the concept of the holy land from a Christocentric point of view.[34]

In John 10, Jesus declares that he is the good shepherd and the door. The good shepherd is described as leading the going in and out of the sheep and finding pasture. It's plausible that the image of the good pasture refers to the Promised

---

[32]It is interesting to note that the current ten-shekel coin in Israel has a palm tree.

[33]For further details about the Book of Glory, see Raymond Brown and Francis Moloney, *An Introduction to the Gospel of John* (New York: Doubleday, 2003), 307-15.

[34]In response to Christian Zionism, I have argued elsewhere that Christ, not Israel, is the owner of the land. See Yohanna Katanacho, "Christ Is the Owner of Haaretz," *Christian Scholar's Review* 34 (2005): 425-41.

Land. This claim gains strength in light of the way John develops his theology of the new world order. John's treatment of the temple, the Sabbath, prominent experiences in the wilderness, and the sonship-daughtership of Abraham all contribute to understanding the tension between the synagogue and the followers of Christ in John 9. This undergirds how we understand what John is saying about the holy land in John 10. A new exodus is happening, and a more fulfilling holy land is given. The connection of John 10 to the Promised Land can also be seen in the similar expressions found describing the Promised Land in the book of Numbers. The book of Numbers discusses the topic of entering into the Promised Land and asserts that ancient Israel needed a shepherd. Moses prays, saying, "May the LORD, the God who gives breath to all living things, appoint someone over this community to go out and come in before them, one who will lead them out and bring them in, so the LORD's people will not be like sheep without a shepherd" (Num 27:16-17 NIV). The thematic and linguistic similarities suggest reading these texts together in a canonical context. Further, it is interesting that both leaders, Jesus and Joshua, have the same name in Hebrew. Jesus is the New Testament Joshua who will not kill the local inhabitants of Palestine but will destroy the wolf by offering himself as a sacrifice. These declarations are discussed in the context of the Feast of Dedication (Jn 10:22), which highlights liberty; the Maccabean revolution discussed earlier also lends background and credence to this reading. Jesus not only is interested in the land but is also interested in the people of the land. Instead of killing the inhabitants of the land, he is willing

to die in order to save them. His identity as the Savior of the world shapes his behavior toward the inhabitants of the land.

Second, the concept of the holy land in John 10 is also related to the concept of a good shepherd in the Old Testament. The Old Testament is full of places where God is described as the good shepherd. One passage that contains several similarities with John 10 is Ezekiel 34. I have discussed elsewhere the centrality of this text as it relates to the Arab-Israeli conflict.[35] I focus here on the biblical connection between the two texts. The flow of the text in Ezekiel is extremely important. The literary unit, which starts in Ezekiel 33:21 and ends in Ezekiel 37:28, opens with a clear discussion of Abraham and inheriting the Promised Land (Ezek 33:24). Then Ezekiel talks about the bad shepherds of Israel, pointing out that God will bring a new David, who will be the good shepherd (Ezek 34:23-24). The theme of the new David is also found at the end of the literary unit, where we also encounter the themes of one people and one shepherd. There will no longer be any division. David will be the one shepherd who will lead the people into the Promised Land (Ezek 34:24-25). This time there will not be another exile. Obviously, the book of Ezekiel is not talking about the historical David who died hundreds of years before the times of Ezekiel. Ezekiel is talking about a Davidic figure. This David will be the good shepherd who will unify the people of God, lead them into the Promised Land, and fulfill the Abrahamic promises. Simply put, Jesus claims that he is this good shepherd. John is rethinking the theme of the Promised Land in a Christocentric way. No one can truly enter this land without Christ as the door. Christ is not only the door; he is also the way (Jn 14:6). Unless he

---

[35]Katanacho, *Land of Christ*, 58-65.

washes our feet, we cannot be on the way to life and we cannot find the door that leads to life. This leads me to my final point in the Christocentric world order, that is, new creation.

A NEW CREATION

Many scholars have pointed out the similarities between John 1 and Genesis 1–2. Jeannine Brown, however, adds important insights related to the theme of new creation in the Gospel of John.[36] Jesus blew the Spirit on his disciples in John 20:22. This is reminiscent of Genesis 2:7, when God blew his breath into Adam and Eve.[37] Both scenes are set in a garden (see Jn 18:1, 26; 19:41; 20:15). In the first garden Adam fell; the curse as well as death entered our world. In the second garden the second Adam was able to overcome any temptations. He transformed the graveyard into a spring of life. This life will change the whole world. John includes the need to accept Jesus (Jn 1:12) and accept the Spirit (Jn 20:22). This is the path that brings life. This is the path of the new world order and John's way of restructuring Pharisaic Judaism. It is not an approach that replaces the Jewish people or claims that they are cursed because of the crucifixion of Christ. It does not seek to exclude any ethnicity but to highlight the centrality of Jesus Christ, the Savior of the world. Christ does not reject Israel but embodies its deepest hopes and is the climax of its restoration.

CONCLUDING REMARKS

John presents a new world order in which he deconstructs major elements in Pharisaic Judaism and reconstructs them in relation to Christ.

There are several implications of this insight that relate to the Palestinian-Israeli conflict. First, Jews and Palestinians need to resist the temptation of exclusive contextualization. Christ is fully human, and he can represent both Palestinians and Jews. Christ's humanity cannot be defined in an exclusive way. This is the way of the Chalcedonian Definition and is our way. It is indeed important to understand the kind of Christ we follow. He is not the Christ who refuses Palestinians or Jews or anyone else. He is not the Christ who excludes others from dialogue.[38] All people are equally loved by God, created in his image, and so we value all human beings without exception. Every human being is a gift from God. In addition, the value of humanity is not only related to being created in the image of God but is also related to the incarnation, in which God became human, elevating the value of humanity and transforming the fallen creation into a glorified one. The Christ event is the means of transforming us into the children of God. Jesus indeed was born in a Jewish culture, but his human identity redefines Jewishness in inclusive ways. Put differently, in Jesus Christ historical Jewishness cannot be separated from eschatological Jewishness. Not only is Jesus a historical Jew, but he is also the eschatological Jew par excellence, who redefines Jewishness in inclusive ways and embodies its deepest hopes. He is indeed fully human and can represent all human beings.

Second, our perception of holy space and the promises of land should not be divorced from a Christocentric worldview. Any credible

---

[36]Jeannine Brown, "Creation's Renewal in the Gospel of John," *Catholic Biblical Quarterly* 72 (2010): 275-90.

[37]Most commentators connect Jn 20:22 with Gen 2:7. See, for example, Beasley-Murray, *John*, 380-81; Thomas Brodie, *The Gospel According to John: A Literary and Theological Commentary* (Oxford: Oxford University Press, 1993), 569; Carson, *Gospel According to John*, 651; Andreas Köstenberger, *John* (Grand Rapids, MI: Baker, 2004), 575; Andrew Lincoln, *The Gospel According to Saint John* (Peabody, MA: Hendrickson, 2005), 499.

[38]Based on studying John 1, Rafiq Khoury, a Palestinian theologian, affirms that the Christ in whom we believe is a servant and is the Christ of dialogue. See *For the Sake of Open Borders Between Eternity and Time: Towards an Incarnational Theology on the Soil of Our Country* (Bethlehem: Al-Liqa' Center, 2012), 145. The book is in Arabic.

interpretation of the Old Testament must take into consideration the New Testament *relecture* (rereading) of Pharisaic Judaism and its major components as they are represented in the Gospel of John. Our perception of the temple, the Sabbath, the exodus and wilderness traditions, the sonship-daughtership of Abraham, and holy land needs to be influenced and perhaps redefined by a Christocentric worldview. John's *relecture* is possibly the best way forward. The Chalcedonian Christ must be restored to the hermeneutical center. Jesus is fully human. Both Palestinians and Jews can see him as their hero and Savior.

FURTHER READING

Abed Al-salam, Faruq. *Muhammed, Peace Be upon Him, in the Gospel of John.* Cairo: Markaz Al-salam lltjhyz Al-fani, 2006.

Ateek, Naim. *Justice and Only Justice: A Palestinian Theology of Liberation.* Maryknoll, NY: Orbis, 1989.

———. *A Palestinian Christian Cry for Reconciliation.* Maryknoll, NY: Orbis, 2008.

Awad, Alex. *Palestinian Memoirs: The Story of a Palestinian Mother and Her People.* Bethlehem: Bethlehem Bible College, 2012.

Beasley-Murray, George R. *John.* Nashville: Thomas Nelson, 1999.

Blau, Joshua. *A Handbook of Early Middle Arabic.* Jerusalem: Hebrew University Press, 2002.

Brown, Raymond, and Francis Moloney. *An Introduction to the Gospel of John.* New York: Doubleday, 2003.

Carson, D. A. *The Gospel According to John.* Grand Rapids, MI: Eerdmans, 1991.

Culpepper, R. Alan. *Anatomy of the Fourth Gospel.* Philadelphia: Fortress, 1983.

Dodd, C. H. *The Interpretation of the Fourth Gospel.* Cambridge: Cambridge University Press, 1953.

Enz, Jacob. "The Book of Exodus as a Literary Type for the Gospel of John." *Journal of Biblical Literature* 76 (1957): 208-15.

Harvey, Richard. *Mapping Messianic Jewish Theology.* Milton Keynes, UK: Paternoster, 2009.

Hijazi, Ahmed. *Paraclete: It Is the Name of the Prophet of Islam in the Gospel of Jesus.* Cairo: Al-Muty'y, 1972.

Katanacho, Yohanna. "Christ Is the Owner of Haaretz." *Christian Scholar's Review* 34 (2005): 425-41.

———. *The Land of Christ: A Palestinian Cry.* Bethlehem: Bethlehem Bible College, 2012.

———. "Palestinian Protestant Theological Responses to a World Marked by Violence." *Missiology: An International Review* 36 (2008): 289-305.

Khoury, Rafiq. *For the Sake of Open Borders Between Eternity and Time: Towards an Incarnational Theology on the Soil of Our Country.* Bethlehem: Al-Liqa' Center, 2012.

Köstenberger, Andreas. *John.* Grand Rapids, MI: Baker Academic, 2004.

Kysar, Robert. "The Gospel of John in Current Research." *Religious Studies Review* 9 (1983): 314-23.

Lincoln, Andrew. *The Gospel According to Saint John.* Peabody, MA: Hendrickson, 2005.

Motyer, Stephen. *Your Father the Devil? A New Approach to John and the "Jews."* Carlisle, UK: Paternoster, 1997.

Moulder, James. "Is a Chalcedonian Christology Coherent?" *Modern Theology* 2 (1986): 285-307.

Munayer, Salim, and Lisa Loden, eds. *The Land Cries Out.* Eugene, OR: Wipf & Stock, 2012.

Ng, Wai-Yee. *Water Symbolism in John: An Eschatological Interpretation.* New York: Peter Lang, 2001.

Pack, Frank. "The Gospel of John in the Twentieth Century." *Restoration Quarterly* 7 (1963): 173-85.

Pazdan, Mary. "Nicodemus and the Samaritan Woman: Contrasting Models of Discipleship." *Biblical Theology Bulletin* 17 (1987): 145-48.

Raheb, Mitri. *I Am a Palestinian Christian.* Minneapolis: Fortress, 1995.

———. "Toward a Hermeneutics of Liberation: A Palestinian Christian Perspective." Page 7 in *The Biblical Text in the Context of Occupation: Towards a New Hermeneutics of Liberation*, edited by Mitri Raheb. Bethlehem: Diyar, 2012.

Reinhartz, Adele. *Befriending the Beloved Disciple: A Jewish Reading of the Gospel of John*. New York: Continuum, 2001.

———. "A Nice Jewish Girl Reads the Gospel of John." *Semeia* 77 (1997): 177-93.

Songer, Harold. "The Gospel of John in Recent Research." *Review and Expositor* 62 (1965): 417-28.

Stibbe, Mark. *The Gospel of John as Literature: An Anthology of Twentieth-Century Perspectives*. Leiden: Brill, 1993.

FROM ARTEMIS TO MARY

MISPLACED VENERATION VERSUS TRUE WORSHIP OF JESUS IN THE LATINO/A CONTEXT

Aída Besançon Spencer

THE CHALCEDONIAN DEFINITION amplified the Nicene Creed, in response to such persons as Nestorius, who (probably) argued that God cannot have a mother. The definition added that Jesus Christ had two natures without confusion: "because of our salvation begotten from the Virgin Mary, the *Theotokos*, as regards His manhood."[1] Evangelical Hispanics agree that Mary was *Theotokos*, mother of God, literally, "God-bearing," implying that Jesus was God even in the incarnation.[2] According to Justo González, Nestorianism is not a temptation for Hispanic Christians because Hispanics, who themselves suffer, "feel the need to assert that the broken, oppressed, and crucified Jesus is God" and, yet, Jesus must be divine, "for otherwise his suffering has no power to redeem."[3] Veneration of Mary was not a major concern during the early church years. Ironically, though, as time developed, what was intended to affirm Jesus' deity and humanity and Jesus' ability to promote human salvation instead came to affirm Mary as almost a semigod, one without sin,

who had the power of special mediation. This, then, lessened Jesus' humanity and ability to mediate directly on behalf of humans.

This chapter seeks to approach the topic of Christology from a Latina feminist evangelical perspective and, therefore, focuses on the relationship of Mary and Jesus and intercession. The challenge is to esteem Mary but not deprecate Jesus.

Some biblical themes are highlighted in Latin American Christian culture, such as the priority of the (Christian) family and the importance of one's mother. Four main topics are covered in this chapter. (1) Originally, devotion to Mary appeared to replace devotion to mother goddesses, especially Artemis of Ephesus. (2) Veneration of Mary is not necessary because Jesus is the sympathetic and unique intercessor, as explained especially in 1 Timothy 2:5-7. God can appeal to males and females. In contrast, focusing on Mary's feminine attributes and Jesus' masculine attributes is more akin to pagan worship of female and male deities. Jesus can represent all

---

[1]J. N. D. Kelly, *Early Christian Doctrines*, 2nd ed. (New York: Harper & Row, 1960), 311-12, 318, 339-40.

[2]*Latinos* is used to represent Spanish- and Portuguese-speaking men and women in the Americas. *Hispanic* is used when primarily Spanish-speaking people in the Americas are indicated.

[3]Justo L. González, *Mañana: Christian Theology from a Hispanic Perspective* (Nashville: Abingdon, 1990), 148-49.

humans effectively. (3) Mary is an example of a humble disciple with limitations. (4) Authority is key in this discussion. Nevertheless, aside from intercession, different aspects of Mary's character have been highlighted through the years in Latino/a cultures. These bring out different aspects found in her Magnificat (Lk 1:46-55): the conquering Mary, the suffering Mary, and the liberating Mary.

VENERATION IN THE LATINO/A CONTEXT

> Meanwhile, standing near the cross of Jesus were his mother, and his mother's sister, Mary the wife of Clopas, and Mary Magdalene. When Jesus saw his mother and the disciple whom he loved standing beside her, he said to his mother, "Woman, here is your son." Then he said to the disciple, "Here is your mother." And from that hour the disciple took her into his own home. (Jn 19:25-27 NRSV)

With this event, Jesus began what would become one of the blessings in the Latino/a culture and, for some, a snare. Normally, a widow would live with the former husband's family, if we agree with the tradition that Mary was now a widow.[4] His family legally had the obligation to maintain the husband's former wife (Mishnah Ketubbot 4:12; 12:3). Mary could also have lived with one of her other sons, such as James, Judas, Joseph, or Simon (Mt 13:55-56). Instead, with this event, Jesus established the priority of the Christian family over the blood family. Jesus had already prepared the disciples in many ways, for example, when he responded to the woman in the crowd who said to him, "Blessed is the womb that bore you and the breasts that nursed you" with "Blessed rather are those who hear the word of God and obey it!" (Lk 11:27-28 NRSV), or when his mother and siblings are identified as whoever does the will of God (Mk 3:31-35). When they stood watching Jesus' crucifixion, John tells us that from that hour "the disciple took [Mary] as his own into his own home" (Jn 19:27). John must first have brought her back to Galilee. Eventually, John brought Mary to Ephesus in Asia Minor.[5] And, in this region, the misunderstandings about Mary began to occur. Part of the over-the-line veneration may have arisen from the very area where John and Mary lived, Ephesus in Anatolia of Asia Minor.

The Latino/a culture emphasizes the family. Christians not related by blood can become welcomed into a blood family. Latinos also emphasize devotion to one's mother. Even when I worked at the maximum-security state prison of New Jersey (Trenton State Prison), the male Latino inmates included in their own publication poems dedicated to their mothers, for example:

> Cuando digo que lloramos por la mujer,
> yo me refiero a mi viejecita Santa,
> la mujer que me dio el ser, que soy,
> yo lloro por esa mujer,
> por mi madre, compañeros.
> ("When I say that we should weep
>   for womankind,
> I refer to my dear elderly Saint,
> the woman who gave me being, I am,
> I weep for that woman,
> for my mother, my companions.")[6]

---

[4]Joseph is active in the early years of Jesus' life and ministry, but there is no mention of him later (Mt 1:18-25; 2:13-15, 19-23; 13:55; Lk 2:4, 16, 33, 43; 4:22; Jn 1:45; 6:42).

[5]The early church had firm traditions of John's movement to Ephesus. The Council of Ephesus (431) affirmed that Mary was in Asia with John (Eusebius, *Church History* 3.20, 23, 31; 4.14; 5.8, 24; F. W. Farrar, *The Early Days of Christianity* [New York: Funk & Wagnalls, 1883], 379, 393).

[6]Raul Acosta Jr., "La celda #34," *El Mensaje: Trenton State Prison News* 1, no. 1 (February–March 1974): 25.

But Latinos also emphasize devotion to Mary, which is sometimes helpful and sometimes harmful. For instance, in a lovely song dedicated to the Virgin of Rocío, Isabel Pantoja in her album *Desde Andalucía* (RCA, 1988) sings of the miraculous virgin as "la más bonita, la más guapa, la más bella" (the most beautiful) in the world, who came from heaven to stay in Isabel's own country, Spain, "madre mía del cielo" (my heavenly Mother). She lives in Andalucía, "Viva la madre de Dios!" Such passionate devotion to Mary, celebrating her beauty and thus her feminine qualities, combines with nationalistic pride and an appealing melody to make the Vírgen del Rocío attractive to many.

In popular Roman Catholicism of today, especially in Spanish-speaking countries and in churches and homes across the world, sometimes adherents feel more comfortable praying in intercession to Mary than to Jesus.[7] (1) What are some of the reasons for venerating Mary? (2) Why should it not happen? (3) How does Mary's own example encourage us to honor Mary but venerate and employ the intercession of Jesus? (4) After addressing these questions I will summarize the various Latino/a views on Mary.

Why venerate Mary? The renowned Williston Walker in his standard *A History of the Christian Church* explains, "There seems little doubt that the cult of the Virgin originally attracted and replaced the devotion that had been offered to the 'mother goddesses' of Egypt, Syria, and Asia Minor; at the same time, however, it was her role as the chosen vehicle of the Incarnation which set her, in Christian eyes, above martyr or apostle as the noblest and holiest of human persons."[8] The veneration of Mary in Asia Minor may be seen in such evangelists as Gregory Thaumaturgus (born ca. 213), who claimed that the apostles and the Virgin appeared to him and guided his work.[9] In particular, Ephesus in Asia Minor became a crucial place for exaltation of Mary. A basilica was dedicated to the Mother of God when the ecumenical council of 431 met there.[10] A sanctuary dedicated to Artemis in Ephesus was rededicated to Mary.[11] This church is said to be the first of its kind dedicated to the Virgin. The original building was built circa 117–138. There are remains of the building that can be seen even now.[12] The veneration of Mary appears to have developed first in Asia Minor and Palestine and then spread to the West after the close of the sixth century, with a wave of Christian refugees fleeing from the Islamic invasions.[13] In a time of "obscurantism, superstition, and credulity,"

---

[7]Sixto J. García agrees: Mary has played a "traditionally seminal role . . . through the centuries in Hispanic prayer and liturgy." García, "A Hispanic Approach to Trinitarian Theology: The Dynamics of Celebration, Reflection, and Praxis," in *We Are a People! Initiatives in Hispanic American Theology*, ed. Roberto S. Goizueta (Minneapolis: Fortress, 1992), 121.

[8]Williston Walker, Richard A. Norris, David W. Lotz, and Robert T. Handy, *A History of the Christian Church*, 4th ed. (New York: Charles Scribner's Sons, 1985), 192. John McGuckin mentions the context of Isis, a great Mother, combined with Artemis. McGuckin, "The Early Cult of Mary and Inter-religious Contexts in the Fifth-Century Church," in *Origins of the Cult of the Virgin Mary*, ed. Chris Maunder (New York: Burns & Oates, 2008), 10-11.

[9]Justo L. González, *The Story of Christianity I* (San Francisco: Harper & Row, 1984), 99; Henri Daniel-Rops, *The Book of Mary*, trans. Alastair Guinan (New York: Hawthorn, 1960), 92.

[10]Walker et al., *History of the Christian Church*, 192.

[11]Leonardo Boff adds, "When the pagan devotees of the goddesses and virgins were converted, they simply substituted Mary for the goddess known by such and such a title, often retaining the corresponding ritual forms and even the statue of the goddess or virgin in question, with just a change of name." Boff, *The Maternal Face of God: The Feminine and Its Religious Expressions*, trans. Robert R. Barr and John W. Diercksmeier (San Francisco: Harper & Row, 1987), 218.

[12]Fatih Cimok, *A Guide to the Seven Churches* (Istanbul: A Turizm Yayinlari, 1998), 43.

[13]Walker et al., *History of the Christian Church*, 192. For example, a basilica was built at Gethsemane at the possible place of Mary's burial to commemorate the "falling asleep" and later assumption of the Virgin. A church in Jerusalem marked the nativity of Mary. See also Farrar, *Early Days of Christianity*, 379.

Pope Gregory the Great of Rome (540–604), in contrast to earlier Christian teachers who had sought to preserve Christian faith free of popular superstition, "readily accepted the stories circulating at this time as if they were simple and direct confirmation of Christian faith."[14] When Pope Gregory observed the Feast of the Assumption (August 15), he informally recognized Mary's resurrection.[15] Popular Christianity became institutionalized. But not until the 1800s and 1900s did some of these popular teachings become dogma. In 1854, Pope Pius IX's bull *Ineffabilis Deus* officially declared that the Virgin Mary, "in the first instant of her conception," was "preserved untouched by any taint of original guilt."[16] In 1950, Pope Pius XII concluded that

> the majestic Mother of God, from all eternity united in a mysterious way with Jesus Christ . . . , immaculate in her conception, in her divine motherhood a most unspotted virgin, the noble ally of the Divine Redeemer . . . should be carried up, in body and soul, to the celestial glory of Heaven, to reign there as Queen at the right hand of her Son, the immortal King of the ages. . . . Therefore we . . . declare . . . as dogma revealed by God, that the Immaculate Mother of God, ever-Virgin Mary, on the completion of the course of her earthly life, has been taken up, in body and soul, to the glory of heaven.[17]

From humble believer, Mary had now become the queen of heaven, able to intercede with a believer's petition to the more remote Jesus and the most remote Father.

How might this dogma about Mary have been related to the original context of Ephesus, where Mary had lived with John? There were four groups of pagan cults in ancient Anatolia: Zeus, the Mother goddesses, Mēn, and the champions of divine justice and vengeance.[18] The most widely worshiped god in Central Asia was Zeus. According to Stephen Mitchell, "The gods of pagan Anatolia were not abstract and remote. At Lystra they could walk among their people and make themselves seen or heard. After centuries of Christian or Christianizing thought, entangled in attempts to articulate the ineffable, the problems of understanding paganism do not lie in penetrating its mysteries but in perceiving the obvious, the gods made manifest." The pagan gods were plain for all to see. The organization called the Xenoi Tekmoreioi worshiped Artemis in particular. There were many shrines to the mother of the gods. Zeus and his mother were worshiped. Zeus was remote, although awesome, and to be reached through the agency of divine intermediaries. The Phrygians in general were orgiastic worshipers of the mother of the gods. Syncretization was common. The heresy of Montanism began in Anatolia in 170. Celibate asceticism had great appeal. By the end of the third century, Christians outnumbered the rest of the population. Belief in a remote and rarified Zeus transferred to belief in a remote highest God of the Jews and Christians. How better to reach Zeus than through his mother, and then how better to reach God than through his mother, Mary?[19]

Why should veneration of Mary not happen? An important key for transformation may be to refocus from Mary to Jesus, as the sympathetic intercessor, the only mediator, a

[14]González, *Story of Christianity I*, 247.

[15]Daniel-Rops, *Book of Mary*, 110.

[16]Walker et al., *History of the Christian Church*, 351.

[17]Henry Bettenson, *Documents of the Christian Church*, 2nd ed. (New York: Oxford University Press, 1963), 281.

[18]Stephen Mitchell, *Anatolia: Land, Men, and Gods in Asia Minor* (Oxford: Clarendon, 1993), 19, 28.

[19]Mitchell, *Anatolia*, 11, 12, 16, 18-20, 22, 28, 30, 37-44, 48-51, 57, 63, 114.

human for humans. Vatican II repeated that Christ is the one Mediator.[20] This is the same message that Paul emphasized when writing to Timothy, who was serving at Ephesus in the first century: "For God (is) one, one (is) also a mediator between God and humans, human Christ Jesus, the One having given himself (as) a ransom in behalf of all, the witness to (his) own times, for which I myself was appointed a preacher and apostle (I speak truth, I do not lie), a teacher of Gentiles in faith and truth" (1 Tim 2:5-7).[21] The first two clauses (1 Tim 2:5) have two key theological ideas. A Jew would heartily affirm the first clause, as Moses summarizes: "Hear Israel, (the) Lord our God (*elohim*), (the) Lord (is) one" (Deut 6:4). According to Deuteronomy, believers are to love the Lord with their whole being (Deut 6:5-6). Jews were renowned in ancient times for their belief in one God, symbolized, for example, by Judith's proclamation to the Gentile magistrates: we "acknowledge no god but the Lord" (Judith 8:20 REB). Roman historian Tacitus describes the Jews as despising the gods, having "a purely spiritual monotheism . . . for them, the Most High and Eternal cannot be portrayed by human hands and will never pass away" (*History* 5.5). Judaism had been prominent in Asia Minor. God-fearers who were attracted to Judaism's monotheism were ready to accept Christianity.[22] Why did Paul include the clause "God is one" in 1 Timothy 2? He appears to imply that God is unique in that God genuinely wants people to be saved (1 Tim 2:4). God also is the only being capable of saving people

and the only deity before whom a human needs approval. God is also able to accomplish salvation completely within the Godhead. The one who requires purity from humans and the one who can accomplish that purity are the same. Later in 1 Timothy, monogamous marriage or a *one*-flesh union will reflect humans being created in the image of *one* God.[23]

The pagan Gentiles might find several offensive aspects in Paul's statement. First, many would believe in a variety of gods for a variety of purposes and peoples. As Artemidorus explained, "What the gods signify for men, goddesses signify for women. Gods are more auspicious for men than goddesses; goddesses are more auspicious for women than gods" (*Onirocritica* 4.75). Similarly, some today find the female Mary more approachable than a male Jesus. Andrew M. Greeley, for instance, explains, "Mary reveals the tender, gentle, comforting, reassuring, 'feminine' dimension of God." He describes her also as "the only mother goddess currently available."[24] For example, one man mentions that he used to pray to Mary instead of God when he was really desperate: "I felt that as a woman she would be more compassionate than God the Father. Now that my image of God has both male and female attributes, I find God more approachable."[25] At Ephesus, many would place the gods in a hierarchy with Artemis at the top. Pausanias summarizes the ancient sentiment:

All cities worship Artemis of Ephesus, and individuals hold her in honour above all the gods. The reason, in my view, is the renown of the

---

[20]Walker et al., *History of the Christian Church*, 699; Vatican II, Dogmatic Constitution on the Church, no. 62.

[21]Unmarked translations are by the author when necessary to reflect the literal Greek or Hebrew of the original Bible.

[22]Mitchell, *Anatolia*, 32-33, 35-36, 43.

[23]For example, 1 Tim 3:2, 12; 5:9. See also Aída Besançon Spencer et al., *Marriage at the Crossroads: Couples in Conversation About Discipleship, Gender Roles, Decision Making and Intimacy* (Downers Grove, IL: InterVarsity Press, 2009), 28-30.

[24]Andrew M. Greeley, *The Mary Myth: On the Femininity of God* (New York: Seabury, 1977), 17, 123.

[25]Aída Besançon Spencer et al., *The Goddess Revival: A Biblical Response to God(dess) Spirituality* (Eugene, OR: Wipf & Stock, 1995), 127.

Amazons, who traditionally dedicated the image, also the extreme antiquity of this sanctuary. Three other points as well have contributed to her renown, the size of the temple, surpassing all buildings among men, the eminence of the city of the Ephesians and the renown of the goddess who dwells there.[26]

The temple was one of the seven wonders of the ancient world. When Antipater saw the temple "that mounted to the clouds," the other wonders lost their brilliancy for, "Lo, apart from Olympus, the Sun never looked on aught so grand!"[27]

Artemis was often pictured with bow and arrow and stag. The priestesses and priests of the Ephesian Artemis would model a celibate religious lifestyle in honor of the virgin goddess.[28] The temple of Artemis at Ephesus was also renowned as an asylum for the innocent, yet simultaneously Artemis could be a slaughterer (see Acts 19:27).[29] She could use her arrows to protect but also to attack. One etymology for her name was "slaughterer, butcher."[30] Artemis could protect mothers and kill them. Many considered her the "mediator," capable of saving "all" (see 1 Tim 2:4-5). In addition, Ephesus had shrines sacred to Zeus, Cybele, Demeter (mother of the gods), Apollo (Artemis's brother), Asclepius (god of healing), Aphrodite, Dionysus,

Hygeia, Pan, Isis, Hecate, Marnas (river god), Leto (Artemis's mother), Athena, Serapis, Eros, and deified emperors such as Augustus.[31] The Bible, in contrast, asserts that there is only one God who can serve all needs, including salvation, for all people.[32]

The pivotal teaching in Deuteronomy 6:4 also contains an allusion to plurality within the one God. *One* can refer, for example, to two people united in marriage (Gen 2:24) or to all humans when they have one language (Gen 11:1, 6). *Elohim* is an abstract plural word for "God," but it uses a singular verb when referring to the unique living God (e.g., Gen 1:26-28). The Lord has *one* "name," but three persons ("the Father and the Son and the Holy Spirit"; see Mt 28:19).[33] Thus, after God's revelation to Paul (Acts 9:4-5; Gal 1:11-12, 16-17; 1 Thess 2:13) and his own reflection, Paul can assert that God is one but yet that one God has three persons (see also, e.g., 2 Cor 13:13).

Christ Jesus is the only mediator between God and humans. Paul places in juxtaposition the terms *humans* and *human* in 1 Timothy 2:5. Even though Jesus was born a male, Jesus only uses the generic self-description "human" (*anthrōpos*, not *anēr*), because if Jesus is to represent humans (male and female) he himself

---

[26]Pausanias, *Description of Greece*, trans. W. H. S. Jones, Loeb Classical Library (Cambridge, MA: Harvard University Press, 1926), 4.31.8.

[27]*Greek Anthology*, trans. W. R. Paton, Loeb Classical Library (Cambridge, MA: Harvard University Press, 1918), 9.58; Epigrams of Saint Gregory 8.177.

[28]"Virgin" may simply refer to being unmarried, and at the temple sex was prohibited between husband and wife (W. M. Ramsay, *The Cities and Bishoprics of Phrygia* 1 [Oxford: Clarendon, 1895], 95, 136).

[29]Jerome Murphy-O'Connor, *St. Paul's Ephesus: Texts and Archaeology* (Collegeville, MN: Liturgical, 2008), 26, 44, 123-24, 135-36, 150-51. See further Aída Besançon Spencer, "Setting. Temple of Artemis," in *The Pastoral Letters*, New Covenant Commentary (Eugene, OR: Cascade, 2013).

[30]N. G. L. Hammond and H. H. Scullard, eds., *Oxford Classical Dictionary*, 2nd ed. (Oxford: Clarendon, 1970), 126; H. G. Liddell and R. Scott, *A Greek-English Lexicon*, rev. H. S. Jones and R. McKenzie (Oxford: Clarendon, 1968), 248; Martin P. Nilsson, *1 and 2 Timothy and Titus*, African Bible Commentary Series (Grand Rapids, MI: Zondervan, 1971), 509; Euripides, *Iphigenia in Tauris* 35, 40, 381-84, 1458-61. Another etymology is "safe and sound" (Artemidorus Daldianus, *Onirocriticon* 2.35; Strabo, *Geography* 14.1.6).

[31]Peter Scherrer, ed., *Ephesus: The New Guide*, trans. Lionel Bier and George Luxon (Selçuk, Turkey: Graphis, 2000), 58-61, 70, 80, 86-87, 92-94, 134-35, 151, 170-71, 188, 198-201, 209-13.

[32]E.g., Spencer et al., *Goddess Revival*, 81-85.

[33]See Spencer et al., *Marriage at the Crossroads*, 28-29.

must be "human" first of all.[34] He is the counterpart to "the *Adam*," "humanity" (made of male and female; Gen 1:26-28). A "mediator" (*mesitēs*) is in a middle (*mesos*) position between several parties (Gal 3:20), in this case two: God and humans.[35] Job cried out to God the dilemma: "If I wash myself with soap and cleanse my hands with lye, yet you will plunge me into filth, and my own clothes will abhor me. For [God] is not a mortal, as I am, that I might answer him, that we should come to trial together. There is no *umpire* [or mediator, *mesitēs*] between us, who might lay his hand on us both" (Job 9:30-33 NRSV). But Jesus is this unique umpire or mediator (God *and* human). As Paul also explains to the Corinthians, God is "the one reconciling [humans] to himself through Christ" (2 Cor 5:18). Humans did not obey God's first covenant. Jesus set them free from the sins committed under the first covenant so that they could become heirs under a new covenant (Heb 8:6–9:15; 12:24).

What kind of mediator is Jesus? He is "the One having given himself (as) a ransom [*antilytron*] in behalf of all, the witness to (his) own times" (1 Tim 2:6). *Antilytron* harks back to Jesus' words to his disciples: "the Son of Humanity did not come to be served but to serve and to give his life a ransom for many" (Mt 20:28 [*lytron anti*]; see also Mk 10:45). In that context, Jesus uses his own example as a model for servant as opposed to tyrant leadership (Mt 20:25-27). In 1 Timothy 2, Paul uses the concept as an explanation of the means by which God saves all people. Salvation

has already been done willingly by Jesus. Jesus has given his life in exchange for and on behalf of all people to save them.[36] His function as a ransom was displayed in Jesus' lifetime, the "lamb" who was sacrificed (e.g., 1 Cor 5:7). Thus, in the syncretistic culture and times of Asia Minor that eventually affected even the church, Paul has reiterated monotheism, the uniqueness of God who alone is able to save and cleanse men as well as women. Today, however, some Spanish and English translations of 1 Timothy 2:5 mute Jesus' humanity:

> un solo mediador entre Dios y los hombres: Jesucristo hombre (Reina-Valera 1995, La Biblia de las Américas, Nueva Versión Internacional)

> one mediator between God and men (man), the man (Man) Christ Jesus (KJV, NKJV, RSV, NEB, REB, TEV 1966, NIV 1984, ESV)

In 1 Timothy 2:5, *anthrōpoi* is in the plural to refer to all humans, while Jesus is described as *anthrōpos* (singular). Even though Jesus may have been a male, Paul here describes him as a "human," even placing the two instances of *anthrōpos* next to each other ("mediator between God and humans, human Christ Jesus") to highlight the humanity of Jesus. If Paul had emphasized Jesus' *maleness*, then women might wonder whether Jesus was an apt representative or mediator for women. But, for their salvation, Jesus must be representative of women *and* men, as inclusively human (see also Jn 10:33; 11:50; 1 Cor 15:21; Phil 2:8). As a matter of fact, in the New Testament Jesus never once uses *anēr* ("man") as a self-description.[37] Thus, translations such as

---

[34]Not *anēr*, "male." Spencer et al., *Goddess Revival*, 99-101. See also Mark Strauss, "Linguistic and Hermeneutic Fallacies in the Guidelines Established at the 'Conference on Gender-Related Language in Scripture,'" *Journal of the Evangelical Theological Society* 41 (1998): 246-47.

[35]Joseph Henry Thayer, *Thayer's Greek-English Lexicon of the New Testament* (Marshallton, DE: National Foundation for Christian Education, 1889), 401.

[36]Thayer, *Lexicon*, 50.

[37]Spencer et al., *Goddess Revival*, 99, 253n13.

the following render best the generic meaning and language of the original Greek:

> "God and humankind, Christ Jesus, himself human" (NRSV) or

> "God and humanity, the human Christ" (CEB).[38]

Rendering the original generic Greek should also serve as a basis to satisfy those who seek a female, racial, or cultural deity figure. Jesus as "human" is representative of women and men and is over all cultures.

The author of Hebrews also writes of Jesus' ability to be the perfect mediator between God and humans. While Jesus is the heir of all things and very God, creator, superior to angels, priest forever, and high priest in heaven (Heb 1:2-14; 3:1; 7:17, 21, 24; 8:1; 10:21-22), he offered his own blood for eternal redemption, which results in outer and inner cleansing and an eternal inheritance for humans set free from sins (Heb 9:12-18). He is the one perfect sacrifice (Heb 9:27; 10:14). However, Hebrews also explains the full identification of Jesus with humans. The one who sanctifies and those who are sanctified have one Father. They are brothers and sisters. Both have flesh and blood. Because Jesus and humanity are like siblings in every respect, Jesus becomes a merciful and faithful high priest, a sacrifice for atonement for sins. Jesus was tempted so he can help humans who are tempted. Jesus is both forerunner and high priest. Jesus is able to save completely those who come to God through him because he always lives to intercede

for them. Therefore, humans can draw near to God, without any additional intercessor (Heb 2:11-18; 7:25; 10:21-22).[39]

Mary may have been an empathetic human, but she does not have the power of God to succeed fully in her intercession. If God is not remote, God, the Trinity, can serve as God's own intercessor. Elizabeth Johnson summarizes that the growth of Mary's mediation stemmed partially from "a deficient Christology." The divinity of Jesus Christ was stressed "to the point where his real humanity slipped from view or seemed unreal. In this situation the simply human Mary seemed more approachable. In addition, the gracious mercy of God in Christ had been partially eclipsed by emphasis on God's just judgment."[40]

How does Mary's example encourage us to honor Mary but venerate and employ the intercession of Jesus? Mary as a thinking (Lk 1:29, 34; 2:51) and faithful believer should be honored. Her humility is laudable. Even though she could not fully comprehend what would be happening to her, and despite the stigma and her possible execution, she agreed with the angel: "Behold the Lord's slave, let it be with me according to your word" (Lk 1:38). She believed the angel's word to her would be fulfilled (Lk 1:45). She comprehended and welcomed the fact that God, the Mighty One, was doing great things for her (Lk 1:48-49). At Cana, she was willing to let Jesus handle the problem in his own way, even if she had not understood that his time had not yet come (Jn 2:1-4). She was present with others at

---

[38]See also NIV Inclusive Language ed., CEV, NCV. See Aída Besançon Spencer, "Exclusive Language—Is It Accurate?," *Review and Expositor* 95 (1998): 383-95. In Spanish, Jesus could be described as "un ser humano," as in "los seres humanos: el ser humano Jesucristo," or "la humanidad: humano Cristo Jesús." See *Palabra de Dios para Todos* and *Biblia la Palabra Hispanoamericana.*

[39]Antonio González reiterates the importance of Jesus as the only mediator between God and humans in order to promote "an egalitarian community" free of all domination, where "no messianic figure" with "theocratic authoritarianism" can govern in God's place and where no priest other than Christ is necessary. González, *The Gospel of Faith and Justice* (Maryknoll, NY: Orbis, 2005), 84-85.

[40]The post-Reformation growth of Mary's mediation might be attributed to "a deficient pneumatology." Action universally attributed to the Holy Spirit was attributed to Mary. Elizabeth A. Johnson, "Mary as Mediatrix," in *The One Mediator, the Saints, and Mary: Lutherans and Catholics in Dialogue VIII*, ed. H. George Anderson, J. Francis Stafford, and Joseph A. Burgess (Minneapolis: Augsburg, 1992), 324.

the crucifixion of her own son, even though by facing this horror "a sword would pierce" her own soul (Lk 2:35; Jn 19:25). She, along with her family, were devoted to prayer, waiting in Jerusalem with the other disciples for the coming of the Holy Spirit (Acts 1:14). Her praise to God is also exemplary. Her song of praise in Luke 1:46-55 has been studied by many for its emphasis on the liberation of the oppressed, God as Savior, the favorable position of the humble (especially the slave and hungry and poor), and the irony of life, with God reversing positions so the result is joy. Her appropriation of God's message in the Old Testament affected Jesus, James, and eventually Paul.[41]

Nevertheless, because of her humility, I think she would be horrified to discover the undue attention she has received from some replacing veneration due to her son, Jesus, Son of the Most High, Emmanuel, God with us, the Lord (Mt 1:23; Lk 1:31-32, 35; 2:11). She was blessed among women, but blessed because of "the fruit of her womb."[42] She was not blessed in herself. The role of Mary is a difficult problem for ministry in Latin America. Do we emphasize her so much that she becomes an intercessor replacing even popular devotion to Jesus, or do we ignore her so as not to confuse anyone? God's action toward her and her response remind us of our great loss if we ignore her. Mary reminds us to pay attention to those who look least significant. They may very well be God's channel of work, and the cornerstones of God's work and models for all of us. However, the lowly are human too. The lowly

are sinners also. Even Mary probably had doubts about Jesus when the family went to restrain him, for they were saying, "He has gone out of his mind" (Mk 3:20-22, 31-35).[43] She also did not understand how he could stay behind in Jerusalem at age twelve: "Did you not know that I must be in my Father's house?" But Mary and Joseph "did not understand what he said to them" (Lk 2:49-50). Jesus himself, although concerned for care of his mother, saw that priority toward the Christian community and obedience to him superseded the importance of his own family: "'Who is my mother and who are my brothers and sisters?' And, after having looked around at the crowd sitting around him, he says, 'Behold my mother and my brothers and sisters, for whoever may do God's will, that person is my brother and sister and mother'" (Mk 3:33-35; see also Mt 12:46-50; Mk 8:19-21).[44]

SUMMARY AND SURVEY OF LATINO/A VIEWS OF MARY

One might not consider that the treatment of Mary would affect one's understanding of Jesus. However, in predominantly Roman Catholic countries of Latin heritage, such as those where Spanish, Portuguese, and Italian are spoken, emphasis on Mary is highly stressed, sometimes to the detriment of attention toward Jesus himself as God and the perfect intermediary between God and humans. According to Diego Irarrazabal, even many Catholic "pastoral theologians claim that (Marian devotion) takes the place of prayer to God."[45] Overexaltation of

---

[41]See also Aída Besançon Spencer, "Position Reversal and Hope for the Oppressed," in *Latino/a Biblical Hermeneutics: Problematic, Objectives, Strategies*, Semeia Studies (Atlanta: Society of Biblical Literature, 2013).

[42]Luke 1:42: the second clause ("blessed [is] the fruit of your womb") explains the first clause ("blessed [are] you among women").

[43]Possibly because Jesus was not eating and was accused of being demon possessed, his family was concerned for him.

[44]See also Eric D. Svendsen, *Who Is My Mother? The Role and Status of the Mother of Jesus in the New Testament and Roman Catholicism* (Amityville, NY: Calvary, 2001).

[45]Diego Irarrazabal, "Mary in Latin American Christianity," in *The Many Faces of Mary*, ed. Diego Irarrazabal, Susan Ross, and Marie-Theres Wacker (London: SCM Press, 2008), 102.

Mary can approach or become a kind of goddess worship.[46] Latin Americans adhere to Mary as "the Life-Mother," the maternal face of God. In some other contexts, in reaction, Mary can become completely ignored.[47]

In early Christian worship up to the fourth century, the place accorded to Mary was minimal. No Marian liturgy has been found up to that point, although some apocryphal writings, such as the Gospel of James, exhibit an independent interest in Mary.[48] When the fifth-century church strived to explain Christ's nature, to combat Nestorius the Council of Ephesus highlighted that "the Holy Virgin is the Mother of God" (*Theotokos*, or "God-bearer"), the "mother of him who is Emmanuel," not "the mother of God the Word" nor the "Mother of Christ" (*Christotokos*).[49] After the Council of Ephesus succeeded in its proclamation of Mary as the "Mother of God," Christians sang about the triumph of the "God-bearer."[50] Henri Daniel-Rops concludes that the later dogmas about Mary are not based on any New Testament text but are implied by it. By the sixth or seventh century these dogmas of Mariology were held by many Christians and eventually recognized by many Roman Catholic theologians and religious

leaders. Dogma developed to follow practice. Divine revelation was not seen as confined to Scriptures, but it "extends itself and shows itself through the Church."[51] Authority for dogma is a key difference between believers: Is the locus of authority Scripture only or Scripture plus?

All believers point to similar scriptural passages to understand Mary. However, different aspects of the same larger passage (Lk 1:46-55) may be emphasized in different times and by different readers. Possibly, Luke 1:51-52 and Revelation 12:1 and Mary as queen of heaven might be emphasized by nations who want to use Mary as their patron: God "hath shewed strength with his arm; he hath scattered the proud in the imagination of their hearts. He hath put down the mighty from their seats" (KJV) ("Quitó de los tronos a los poderosos" [Reina-Valera 1995]). Even though the woman probably represents Israel giving birth to the new Israel in Revelation 12, some equate the woman with "a crown of twelve stars" (Rev 12:1) with Mary, who was assumed into heaven.[52] This is the triumphant Mary, the patron of Catholic Christendom, the general of the conquering army fighting infidels. Mary has become "Our Lady of Liberation." In Constantinople, according to Clodovis Boff, the

---

[46]Spencer et al., *Goddess Revival*, 34-35.

[47]Jeannette Rodriguez, "Tonanzin Guadalupe: From Passion, Death, to Resurrection," in Irarrazabal, Ross, and Wacker, *Many Faces*, 108, 113; Irarrazabal, "Mary in Latin American Christianity," in Irarrazabal, Ross, and Wacker, *Many Faces*, 104; Nora O. Lozano-Díaz, "Ignored Virgin or Unaware Women: A Mexican-American Protestant Reflection on the Virgin of Guadalupe," in *Blessed One: Protestant Perspectives on Mary*, ed. Beverly Roberts Gaventa and Cynthia L. Rigby (Louisville: Westminster John Knox, 2002), 86, 89.

[48]Daniel-Rops, *Book of Mary*, 82-83; Raymond E. Brown, Karl P. Donfried, Joseph A. Fitzmyer, and John Reumann, eds., *Mary in the New Testament: A Collaborative Assessment by Protestant and Roman Catholic Scholars* (Philadelphia: Fortress, 1978), 248, 293. Beverly Roberts Gaventa, *Mary: Glimpses of the Mother of Jesus* (Minneapolis: Fortress, 1995), 133-45, has the Protevangelium of James.

[49]Philip Schaff and Henry Wace, eds., *Nicene and Post-Nicene Fathers*, Second Series (Peabody, MA: Hendrickson, 1900), 14:206-10.

[50]Among others, Richard M. Price notes that Marian piety "received a powerful spur from the defeat of Nestorius and the definition at the Council of Ephesus that Mary is rightly styled *Theotokos*." Price, "The *Theotokos* and the Council of Ephesus," in *Origins of the Cult of the Virgin Mary*, 99.

[51]Daniel-Rops, *Book of Mary*, 113, 93-94, 98, 100, 102, 109-10.

[52]For example, Bonaventura Rinaldi, *Mary of Nazareth: Myth or History?* (Westminster, MD: Newman, 1966), 153-56. The seed of the woman refers to believers in Jesus (Rev 12:10, 17; 14:12). Thus, the woman appears to represent Israel birthing the new Israel, where her twelve stars represent the twelve tribes. Zion, the old Jerusalem, births the church, the new Jerusalem, who appears in its glory in Rev 21:2. The vision of Rev 12 alludes to numerous Old Testament imagery: Israel as a woman in travail who hides to escape anger and is pursued by a dragon (Is 26:17–27:1); Zion or Jerusalem has travailed (Is 66:7-13); the Sinai wilderness as a place Israel was brought by God to escape Egypt (Ex 19:1-6); wrath as a river (Is 59:19); believers as ruling with a rod of iron (Ps 2:9; Rev 2:26-28; 19:15).

Mother of God became the patron of the imperial capital, replacing the old goddesses Rea and Fortuna. In the liberation of Mexico, La Morenita (an Indian version of Mary) was the symbol of the liberating army.[53]

Other readers might emphasize Luke 1:48: "For (God my Saviour) hath regarded the low estate of his handmaiden: for, behold, from henceforth all generations shall call me blessed" (KJV). Mary is "the slave" (*la sierva*) of God. This view might highlight Mary as a model of submissive, obedient, passive, self-sacrificing motherhood. Such thinking produced a parallel culture of *marianismo* that gave space for androcentrism with expectations for women such as: (1) do not forget a woman's place; (2) do not forsake tradition; (3) do not be single, self-supporting, or independent-minded; (4) do not put your own needs first; (5) do not wish for more in life than being a housewife; (6) do not forget that sex is for making babies—not for pleasure; (7) do not be unhappy with your man or criticize him for infidelity, gambling, verbal and physical abuse, alcohol or drug abuse; (8) do not ask for help; (9) do not discuss personal problems outside the home; and (10) do not change those things that make you unhappy that you can realistically change.[54] *La Madre Dolorosa*, the suffering Mary as a mother with seven swords piercing her heart, is symbolic of this view of Mary.[55]

Since Vatican II, the Magnificat has become instead the emblem of a social Mariology, "Our Lady of Liberation," a Mary who is prophetic and liberating but usually nonviolent.[56] For example, María PilarAquino says, "In the base communities [of Latin America] Mary is seen in terms of commitment to the restoration of justice and the affirmation of hope. She gives new meaning to the existence of the people of God, because in her own person she ratifies God's compassion and power to turn the suffering of the poor and oppressed into joy and abundance." Some Latin Americans observe that there is a gap between popular devotion and the New Testament sources. A new figure of Mary is emerging, "one that is prophetic and liberating, committed to the struggle for justice, faithful to her God and her people."[57] The reversal of positions in Luke 1:52-53 might be emphasized: God put down the mighty but also "exalted them of low degree. He hath filled the hungry with good things; and the rich he hath sent empty away" (KJV). Mary has always been a symbol of public charity, but now she is a proponent of social change as well, especially of improvement of the poor, and, if necessary, restriction of the rich.[58]

Mary is loved and ever-present in the lives of women in Latin America. Every Catholic schoolgirl is exposed to at least one of the many Marian images or apparitions. Even Protestants recognize Guadalupe (the Mexican Mary) as a cultural symbol. Mary is a symbol especially for women and mothers in their daily life in Latin

---

[53]Clodovis Boff, "Toward a Social Mariology," in Irarrazabal, Ross, and Wacker, *Many Faces*, 44-46, 48; Irarrazabal, "Mary in Latin American Christianity," 99.

[54]Lozano-Díaz, *Blessed One*, 90-91; Irarrazabal, "Mary in Latin American Christianity," 97-98, 100; Rosa Maria Gil and Carmen Inoa Vazquez, *The Maria Paradox: How Latinas Can Merge Old World Traditions with New World Self-Esteem* (New York: Putnam's, 1996), 8.

[55]Rodriguez, "Tonanzin Guadalupe," 106.

[56]Boff, "Toward a Social Mariology," 44, 48, 50-51.

[57]María Pilar Aquino, *Our Cry for Life: Feminist Theology from Latin America*, trans. Dinah Livingstone (Maryknoll, NY: Orbis, 1993), 172, 175.

[58]Boff, "Toward a Social Mariology," 45-46; Irarrazabal, "Mary in Latin American Christianity," 100; Rodriguez, "Tonanzin Guadalupe," 113; C. Hugo Zorrilla, "The Magnificat: Song of Justice," in *Conflict and Context: Hermeneutics in the Americas*, ed. Mark Lau Branson and C. René Padilla (Grand Rapids, MI: Eerdmans, 1986), 220-37.

America.[59] An interpreter's emphasis affects their differences in understanding Christ. Mary may be construed as the liberator, as was her Son; the suffering servant, as was her Son; the conqueror, as was her Son; but *not* as the intercessor, as is her Son.

FURTHER READING

García, Alberto Lázaro. *Cristología. Cristo Jesús: Centro y Praxis del Pueblo de Dios.* St. Louis: Editorial Concordia, 2006.

Gaventa, Beverly Roberts, and Cynthia L. Rigby, eds. *Blessed One: Protestant Perspectives on Mary.* Louisville: Westminster John Knox, 2002.

Geisler, Norman, and Ralph E. MacKenzie. "Mariology." Pages 299-330 in *Roman Catholics and Evangelicals: Agreements and Differences.* Grand Rapids, MI: Baker, 1995.

González, Antonio. *The Gospel of Faith and Justice.* Maryknoll, NY: Orbis, 2005.

González, Justo L. *Mañana: Christian Theology from a Hispanic Perspective.* Nashville: Abingdon, 1990.

Irarrazabal, Diego, Susan Ross, and Marie-Theres Wacker, eds. *The Many Faces of Mary.* Concilium 2008/4. London: SCM Press, 2008.

Johnson, Elizabeth A. "Mary as Mediatrix." Pages 311-26 in *The One Mediator, the Saints, and Mary: Lutherans and Catholics in Dialogue VIII,* edited by H. George Anderson, J. Francis Stafford, and Joseph A. Burgess. Minneapolis: Augsburg, 1992.

Some New Testament passages on contemporary Christology significant for Latin American scholars:
    Jesus Christ as mediator: 1 Timothy 2:5-6
    Jesus Christ as liberator of the oppressed and promoter of God's reign: Luke 4:18-19; 5:29-32, 36-39; 6:20-26; 7:36–8:1

---

[59]Carmiña Navia Velasco, "Mary of Nazareth Revisited," in Irarrazabal, Ross, and Wacker, *Many Faces*, 19; Rodriguez, "Tonanzin Guadalupe," 106; Irarrazabal, "Mary in Latin American Christianity," 97-98.

15

CHRISTOLOGY AND *CULTUS* IN 1 PETER

AN AFRICAN (KENYAN) APPRAISAL

Andrew M. Mbuvi

SEVERAL CULTIC IMAGES are used in 1 Peter—sacrifice, temple, priesthood—to present the person and work of Jesus in relationship to the Petrine community.[1] Indeed, 1 Peter begins with a sacrificial expression of defining the believers as having been "sprinkled" with the blood of Jesus Christ (1 Pet 1:2). One question that could be asked is how the Petrine community would have understood the person and the work of Jesus given the letter's rather strong use of cultic imagery and language. Related to this would also be how this Petrine perspective would fit with Chalcedon's formulations of the person and work of Jesus Christ.

This language of blood and sacrifice, and its related aspects of purity, is sprinkled throughout the letter of 1 Peter and practically begs to be read in tandem with cultures where the notion of animal (and in some instances human) sacrifice played (and continues to play) a significant

role in religious rites.[2] Many African communities practiced (and some continue to practice today) animal sacrifices for various religious purposes, including prayer, cleansing and purification rites, thanksgiving, protection from malevolent spirits, and birth rites. With these elements in mind, one wonders whether beginning the presentation of the gospel message, as most Western missionaries did in sub-Saharan Africa, with the assumptions of the Chalcedonian Creed created a biased perspective about how to understand the person and work of Jesus Christ.[3]

When foreign missionaries failed to understand African religious cosmology (much less to regard it positively), and to incorporate African idioms that could communicate the gospel message of Jesus Christ in ways relevant to the African mindset, they imposed culturally Western idioms that never fully embraced the totality of African religious reality.[4] This was

---

[1]By cultic I mean the sacrificial system of animals that used to take place in the temple in Jerusalem. Without the temple, which was destroyed by the Romans in AD 70, there were no more sacrifices, but the language that had been used about it was transformed to talk about spiritual sacrifices (e.g., 1 Pet 1:2; 2:8-12).

[2]Gerhard Lindblom, *The Akamba of British East Africa: An Ethnological Monograph*, 2nd ed. (New York: Negro Universities Press, 1969).

[3]Robert Schreiter, *Constructing Local Theologies* (Maryknoll, NY: Orbis, 1985), ix. With emergence of non-Western theologies, "Western theologians came to the realization that their own theology has just as much sociocultural bias as any other."

[4]This is a point that has been made in virtually all studies of the role of missionaries in sub-Saharan Africa.

perhaps motivated in part by a European sense of superiority based on the racist evolutionary science of the day, but also by a certain interpretation of such a texts as 1 Peter 1:18-22: "For you know that it was not with perishable things such as silver or gold that you were redeemed from *the empty way of life handed down to you from your forefathers/ancestors*" (NIV).[5] Yet African converts to Christianity, especially those with no formal Western education, automatically interpreted their new religion through the lens of their African cosmological reality and not the Neo-Platonic thought embedded in Western Christian creeds.[6]

Perhaps a more fruitful endeavor would be using such cultic connections already established and intricately developed in such works as 1 Peter, which find strong parallels in some African communities. I am careful not to simply point an accusatory finger at the missionaries because, in spite of what one may consider their shortcomings, the vibrancy of African Christianity today owes a lot to those men and women who left family, friends, and homes, and sometimes sacrificed their lives to be buried in African soil, in order to bring the gospel message

to the African continent.[7] Nevertheless, one cannot overlook the fact that an overarching condemnation of *religio Africana* as heathenish and devilish, and therefore subject to obliteration and replacement with culturally Western Christian notions, was a byproduct of Western missionary hubris that was part and parcel of the European colonialism enterprise in Africa.[8]

Kwame Bediako points to two aspects of African missionary encounter that created a theological quandary for the African convert to Christianity: (1) European ethnocentrism that denigrated the African religion, worldview, and culture; and (2) the resultant eradication of religious tradition, memory, and identity. To find their identity, African Christians would have to reconnect with their past.[9] And in order to have a relevant African theology and Christology, they would have to construct them within an African idiom and religious reality.[10] The result has been a concerted cry for the redemption of the African religious reality, by African scholars, as a legitimate storehouse of spirituality that *complements* rather than *contradicts* the biblical worldview.[11]

---

[5]A simplistic equation of the African religions with the Greco-Roman religion that most likely formed the background of this passage would be misleading and shortsighted, as it would fail to appreciate that other perspectives on the backgrounds of converts are also present in the New Testament (e.g., Acts 17).

[6]J. N. K. Mugambi, *Christianity and African Culture* (Nairobi: Acton, 1989), 50.

[7]See Lamin Sanneh, *Translating the Message: The Missionary Impact on Culture* (Maryknoll, NY: Orbis, 1989), who shows that Christianity in Africa only thrived after the Bible had been translated into African languages and was then fully embraced by those communities as an expression of their own religion in their own idiom.

[8]Albert Schweitzer, the eminent German scholar, doctor, and missionary to Lambaréné Gabon, Central West Africa, in the early part of the twentieth century, probably typifies the European missionary attitudes to Africa and Africans. In spite of his sacrificial humanitarian and medical services in Lambaréné, Schweitzer's attitude toward the African people he came to serve was pejorative and racist ("The African is my brother—but he is my younger brother by several centuries," *The Observer* [1955]: 10-23). While Schweitzer is known to have assailed colonialism for its mistreatment of the colonized on the basis of difference (cultural or skin color) before leaving Germany for Lambaréné as a medical missionary, these remarks about Africans as "younger brothers" were made only after he had spent considerable time with the Africans in close proximity. He is also said to have repudiated these remarks later.

[9]Mercy A. Oduyoye, *Hearing and Knowing: Theological Reflections on Christianity in Africa* (Maryknoll, NY: Orbis, 1986), 10, agrees when she states, "Any theology that hopes to be relevant [in Africa] will have to take into account the theological presuppositions that underlie the African worldview and social organization." For this to happen, "the people's primal religion has to be related to and grounded in the community's daily life" (23-24).

[10]Sanneh, *Translating the Message*, 172-90.

[11]Mugambi, *Christianity and African Culture*, 33-34.

COLONIAL AND POSTCOLONIAL AFRICAN RESPONSE TO THE WESTERN MISSIONARY ENTERPRISE

I can delineate in a continuum at least three primary reactions to missions in Africa. First, initial African converts to Christianity, in their zeal to please their Western "masters," totally rejected their African religion and culture. But since the religious aspect of life in African spirituality cannot be conveniently demarcated from other aspects of life, permeating virtually every aspect of life, this initial radical rejection of their past hounded the African converts, many of whom in times of crisis found themselves reverting to African religious rituals and practices.[12]

Second was the formation of African Initiated Churches in reaction to perceived significant contradictions between their interpretation of the Bible, when they read it for themselves, and how the Western missionaries interpreted it.[13] The biggest concern for such groups was that they observed within the biblical narratives and teachings aspects and elements that were fairly closely aligned to their African worldview but which either the missionaries interpreted differently or failed to mention at all (e.g., polygamy).[14]

The third line of response was the largely postcolonial scholarly rejoinder by African Christian theologians. They have sought to counter the missionary caricature of African religious reality by publishing their own research, which has argued that the African religious past not only was compatible with biblical teachings and worldviews, but may even have been complex enough to serve as a sufficient platform in preparation for the gospel message that would eventually be brought by Western missionaries.[15] They have also sought to expose the missionaries' complacency, duplicity, and collusion with racially and economically motivated European colonizing of Africa.

More recently, the African theological scenario can be characterized as pluriform and dynamic, guided by a desire to respond to the politico-socio-economic-cultural concerns of the African community. There is, for example, a growing body of theological reflection championed by Musa Dube that has focused on providing an African biblical premise for doing theology in the midst of the AIDS epidemic in Africa.[16] Other studies have explored the theological implication of African Initiated Churches, the growth of Pentecostal churches, the emergence of the prosperity gospel, and the

---

[12]African novels are an excellent resource for stories that depict this transition and subsequent struggles. See especially the Heinemann's African Writers series, published in London with such works as Chinua Achebe's *Things Fall Apart* (1958), *No Longer at Ease* (1960), and *Arrow of God* (1964); Ngugi wa Thiongo's *The River Between* (1965), *Weep Not Child* (1964), and *A Grain of Wheat* (1967); and Mongo Beti's *Le Pauvre Christ de Bomba* (1956) (English translation: *The Poor Christ of Bomba*).

[13]Perhaps this instance would clearly explain the conflicting perception of Western missionaries. The Africans who ended up forming the independent churches were able to read the Bible in their languages because the missionaries had labored to do the translations and to teach them how to read. They could only criticize and disagree with the missionaries' perspectives because they had benefited from the missionary education and translation projects. The same is true for African novelists and theologians.

[14]While polygamy did become a hot-button subject between Western missionaries and African Christianity, the practice of polygamy was hardly as widespread as the attention it garnered. It was probably the easiest way to show the clear contrast of a Western worldview that was so radically monogamist emerging out of Victorian conservatism and an African culture that seemed to reflect the polar opposite.

[15]John S. Mbiti's "Preparatio Evangelica" concept. See also E. Bolaji Idowu, *Olodumare: God in Yoruba Belief* (London: Longmans, 1962); Mbiti, *African Traditional Religion: A Definition* (London: SCM Press, 1973); Mbiti, *African Philosophy and Religion* (London: Heinemann, 1969).

[16]Musa W. Dube, *The HIV and AIDS Bible: Selected Essays* (Scranton, PA: University of Scranton Press, 2008); Dube, *Theology in the HIV and AIDS Era Series* (Geneva: World Council of Churches, 2007).

phenomenon of megachurches in Africa.[17] Emmanuel Katongole's African Theology Today series and Dube, A. M. Mbuvi, and D. Muwayesango's *Postcolonial Perspectives in African Biblical Interpretations* showcase this growing diversity.[18]

How Does Christology Figure in This African Scenario?

A quick survey of African theological scholarship reflects that Christology has undoubtedly been the central subject of the modern African theological discourse of the past quarter-century or so.[19] However, it bears reminding that African connections with Christianity go all the way back to the New Testament itself (Acts 8:26-40), and claims can be made to such historical figures as Origen, Clement of Alexandria, Tertullian, Cyprian of Carthage, and Augustine of Hippo as African theologians.[20] However, their theological trajectory contributed to much of what is today Western theology and not necessarily to recent sub-Saharan African theological development.[21] One may distinguish at least three trends that

have characterized christological conversation in African beginning with writings from the 1960s (the period of independence from colonialism for most African nations) to the present.

The initial phase, starting in the 1960s, was largely characterized by theology proper, where the concern was to redeem the African conception of God that had essentially been demonized and tarnished in the wake of the Western missionary enterprise in sub-Saharan Africa.[22] Works of such luminaries of African theology as John Mbiti of Kenya, Bolaji Idowu of Nigeria, J. B. Danquah of Ghana, Harry Sawyerr of Sierra Leone, Mulago gwa Cikala of the Democratic Republic of Congo, G. M. Setiloane of South Africa, and Kwame Bediako of Ghana, just to name a few, played key roles in legitimizing conceptions of deity by African Christian scholars, making them, at once, African and Christian.[23] Even though his major works are from the 1980s and 1990s, I place Bediako here since he explains that his perception of African theology in the postmissionary era "is as much a response to missionary underestimation of the value of African pre-Christian tradition, as it is

---

[17]Introduction to *A Study of African Independent Churches* (Gweru, Zimbabwe: Mambo, 1987); John S. Pobee and Gabriel Ositelu II, *African Initiatives in Christianity* (Geneva: World Council of Churches, 1998).

[18]Emmanuel Katongole, ed., *African Theology Today*, vol. 1 (Scranton, PA: University of Scranton Press, 2002), especially chap. 1, by Chris Ukachukwu Manus, "Methodological Approaches in Contemporary African Biblical Scholarship: The Case of West Africa," 1-22.

[19]C. U. Manus, "African Christologies: The Centrepiece of African Christian Theology," *Zeitschrift für Missionswissenschaft und Religionswissenschaft* 82 (1998): 3-23; Charles Sarpong Aye-Addo, "Akan Christology: An Analysis of the Christologies of John S. Pobee and Kwame Bediako in Conversation with the Theology of Karl Barth" (PhD diss., Drew University, 2011).

[20]C. F. Hallencreutz, "From Julius Africanus to Augustine the African: A Forgotten Link in Early African Theology," *Zambezia* 15 (1988): 1-25.

[21]Thomas C. Oden, *How Africa Shaped the Christian Mind: Rediscovering the African Seedbed of Western Christianity* (Downers Grove, IL: InterVarsity Press, 2007). Coptic and Ethiopic traditions are African and originated in the same region, and may have influenced some of these early theologians.

[22]This is not a naive and blanket statement of blame on missionaries, as it is clear to any observant person that the diverse characteristics of Western missionaries and their sending organizations produced different results in different African communities. Indeed, one of the major writings that on the whole defends a positive assessment of African religious worldview—no matter its shortcomings of trying to place African (Bantu) religions within a Western philosophical framework—is the work of Belgian missionary to Congo Placid Tempels's *La Philosophie Bantoue* (Paris: Présence Africaine, 1949). See also John Mbiti's assessment of the impact of Western missionaries in Africa, both positive and negative: *African Religions and Philosophy* (London: Heinemann, 1969), 236.

[23]John S. Mbiti, *Concepts of God in Africa* (London: SPCK, 1970); Idowu, *Olodumare*; Harry Sawyerr, *Creative Evangelism: Towards a New Christian Encounter with Africa* (London: Lutterworth, 1968); J. B. Danquah, *The Akan Concept of God* (London: Frank Cass, 1968); Mulago gwa Cikala, *Un Visage Africain du Christianisme, l'Union Vitale Bantu Face À l'Unité Vitale Ecclésiale* (Paris: Présence-Africaine, 1965); G. M. Setiloane, *The Image of God Among the Sotho-Tswana* (Rotterdam: A. A. Balkema, 1976).

an *African* theological response to the specific and more enduring issues of how the Christian Gospel relates to African culture."[24]

The second stream was Christology proper. Following John Mbiti's lament four decades ago that there was a lack of distinctly African Christology, the following three decades saw an explosion of christological studies that sought to give a uniquely African image of Jesus.[25] The focus was largely on the study of African Initiated Churches, which prompted analysis of their distinct appropriations of the words and works of Jesus.[26] Kofi Appiah-Kubi of Ghana identifies what he sees as the three central christological functions in these communities: Jesus as mediator between humans and God, much in the same way African ancestors and spirits were; Jesus as liberator from oppression; and Jesus as healer of sicknesses.[27] Robert Schreiter, in *Faces of Jesus in*

Africa, has gathered together, under the broad topics of enculturation and liberation, christological perspectives that include Master of Initiation, Elder Brother, Great Ancestor, Great Chief, Ideal Elder, Liberator, Mediator, King, and Healer.[28] Thus, the struggle had commenced to make the person of Jesus relevant to the everyday realities of Africans. Diane Stinton, who adds the categories of Jesus as Life-Giver and Jesus as Leader (chieftaincy) to the list, concludes in her study that the notions of health, mediation, and liberation stand as the central elements in African Christology.[29] It follows that Jesus has been understood in light of societal roles that would make him more relevant to the worldviews of the various African communities.

A third and more conservative African response has been driven by Western evangelicalism's strong influence on church leadership, as

---

[24]Kwame Bediako, *Theology and Identity: The Impact of Culture upon Christian Thought in the Second Century and Modern Africa* (Oxford: Regnum, 1992), xvii.

[25]John S. Mbiti, *Bible and Theology in African Christianity* (Nairobi: Oxford University Press, 1986), 176-227.

[26]See Pobee and Ositelu II, *African Initiatives in Christianity*.

[27]Kofi Appiah-Kubi, "Jesus Christ: Some Christological Aspects from African Perspectives," in *African and Asian Contributions to Contemporary Theology*, ed. John S. Mbiti (Geneva: World Council of Churches, 1976), 51-65.

[28]Robert Schreiter, ed., *Faces of Jesus in Africa* (Maryknoll, NY: Orbis, 1991).

On Jesus as Master of Initiation, see A. Sanon, "Jésus, Maître d'initiation," in *Chemins de la Christologie Africaine*, ed. F. Kabasélé, J. Doré, and R. Luneau (Paris: Desclée, 1986), 143-66; Sanon, *Enraciner L'évangile: Initiations Africaines et Pédagogie de la Foi* (Paris: Cerf, 1982).

On Jesus as Elder Brother, see François Kabasélé, "Christ as Ancestor and Elder Brother," in Schreiter, *Faces of Jesus in Africa*, 116-27.

On Jesus as Great Ancestor, see Charles Nyamiti, *Christ as Our Ancestor: Christology from an African Perspective* (Gweru, Zimbabwe: Mambo, 1984). Bénézet Bujo, *African Theology in Its Social Context* (Maryknoll, NY: Orbis, 1992), uses the term *Proto-Ancestor* since, for him, there should not be assumption of any equality of Jesus with ancestors, but Jesus is the ancestor par excellence. Rodney Reed and Gift Mtukwa, "Christ Our Ancestor: African Christology and the Danger of Contextualization," *Wesleyan Theological Journal* 45, no. 1 (2010): 144-64, point out concerns about this christological category: (1) there is a danger that conceiving of Christ as an Ancestor may actually encourage people to think of their ancestors as intermediaries, while the Scriptures clearly teach that we have just one mediator between God and humanity—Jesus Christ; (2) Africans may be encouraged to actually worship the ancestors and place them in a position that only God should hold by offering to them sacrifices and oblations; (3) it seems to make Jesus just another human being rather than God incarnate; and (4) the Scriptures clearly condemn necromancy (consulting the dead), and that is precisely what happens in much focus on the ancestors. To all these challenges, Oduyoye, *Hearing and Knowing*, 9, poses this question: "Why is the relationship of the African with the 'living-dead' any more idolatrous than the observances of All Souls Day and All Saints Day?"

On Jesus as Great Chief, see J. S. Pobee, *Toward an African Theology* (Nashville: Abingdon, 1979), 94-98. Bujo, *African Theology in Its Social Context*, uses the term *Proto-Ancestor* to dispel any possibility that the ancestors and Jesus could be equals. Jesus as the proto ancestor not only *precedes* but also *supersedes* the "ancestors."

On Jesus as Ideal Elder, see P. N. Wachege, *Jesus Christ Our Muthamaki (Ideal Elder): An African Christological Study Based on the Agikuyu Understanding of Elder* (Nairobi: Phoenix, 1992).

On Jesus as King, see Chris U. Manus, *Christ, the African King: New Testament Christology* (Frankfurt am Main: Peter Lang, 1993).

On Jesus as Healer, see Cécé Kolié, "Jesus the Healer?," in Schreiter, *Faces of Jesus*, 128-50.

[29]Diane Stinton, *Jesus of Africa: Voices of Contemporary African Christology* (Maryknoll, NY: Orbis, 2004). See also Clifton R. Clarke, *African Christology: Jesus in Post-missionary African Christianity* (Eugene, OR: Pickwick, 2010).

reflected in Byang Kato's work, and reprised but better grounded in Kombo's trinitarian reflection. However, this response has been heavily criticized, especially by Bediako.[30]

This essay makes initial forays into the topic of Christology with the hope of enriching our understanding of 1 Peter's use of cultic language through comparison with select African cultic practices. This involves analysis of how 1 Peter uses the Jewish *cultus* within a first-century Christian context to relate it to the religious life of the Gentile believers to whom the letter is addressed.[31] So where cultic language is used, these passages will be read in light of some pre-Christian cultic religious practices of the Akamba of Kenya, the community to which I belong. The cultic traditions make a comparative and analytical study between the cultic language in 1 Peter and that of the Akamba on practice of sacrifices, a tantalizing prospect. As Mercy Amba Oduyoye and others have pointed out, there is a need to relate the Christian message to the traditions and indigenous religions of recipient African communities.[32]

CHRISTOLOGY AND *CULTUS* IN 1 PETER

I have argued elsewhere that 1 Peter's prevalent vocabulary of holiness (*hagiasmos*—1 Pet 1:2, 15-16; 2:5, 9; 3:5-7), with its close link to the *cultus*, calls for every facet of life to be subject to holiness, since the premise of holiness is God, who calls *all*

to holiness in *all* aspects of life. "It is a holiness that is grounded in their involvement in this world which must find its outworking in the midst of all the challenges of pilgrim life."[33] This all-encompassing understanding fits well with the African religious perspective, which assumes that everything that happens in life has a spiritual cause.[34] Indeed, Mbiti's famous maxim that "Africans are notoriously religious" would then be a welcome perspective for reading 1 Peter's injunctions to holiness, since it seems to have similar expectations of its readers.[35]

Second, Western individualistic understanding of salvation "in the heart" contrasts with the African notion of salvation in the community by overcoming the spirit world.[36] As Edward Fasholé-Luke points out, sacrifice in Africa, as a means of atonement, necessitates communal allegiance that is inseparable from the cultic exercise.

> The object of ritual and cultic acts is to sustain the social and the cosmic order—the two can hardly be separated. So the means of fellowship are not meant to provide for the communion with the gods but to enlist these powers in support of the community. Rituals are primarily of two kinds: sacrifices and magic. Sacrifices and libations are meant to appeal to the goodwill of the gods or spirits; magic (both white and black) seeks to manipulate in more mechanical ways forces that cannot be dealt with by appeal.[37]

[30]Byang Kato, *Theological Pitfall in Africa* (Nairobi: Evangel, 1975). See also trinitarian studies by Mika Vähäkangas in Katongole, *African Theology Today*, 69-84; James H. Kombo, *The Doctrine of God in African Christian Thought: The Holy Trinity, Theological Hermeneutics, and the African Intellectual Culture* (Leiden: Brill, 2007); Bediako, *Theology and Identity*, 387-425.
[31]In line with most of the recent scholarship on 1 Peter, I hold the position that the original audience is Gentile but probably made up largely of initial converts to Judaism who elsewhere in the New Testament are referred to as "god-fearers" (Acts 10:2, 22; 13:36; 17:4, 17). See Andrew Mbuvi, *Temple, Exile and Identity in 1 Peter* (London: T&T Clark, 2007), 6.
[32]Oduyoye, *Hearing and Knowing*, 23.
[33]Mbuvi, *Temple, Exile, and Identity*, 80-83.
[34]Bolaji Idowu, *African Traditional Religion: A Definition* (London: SCM Press, 1973).
[35]Mbiti, *African Religions and Philosophy*, 1.
[36]William A. Dyrness, *Learning About Theology from the Third World* (Grand Rapids, MI: Zondervan, 1990), 165.
[37]Dyrness, *Learning About Theology*, 51.

For this reason, the book of Hebrews has attracted significant attention from African theologians because it provides ready-made cultural and religious categories that align fairly well with those found in African communities: high priest-priests, angels-spirits, ancestors, sacrifices, and the like.[38] However, a book such as 1 Peter, which also shares some elements with Hebrews, has hardly been explored for its distinct elements that could serve as grounds for developing a theological framework that is consistent with African religiosity. First Peter itself cannot be said to have a Christology that can be easily labeled, but it does develop cultic images that foreground the work of Jesus and that can allow for a formulation of a Petrine Christology.[39]

As Paul Achtemeier points out, "The Christology in 1 Peter is better conceived of as a series of images than a coherent disquisition on the nature of Christ," and therefore it is important to look at all the passages that paint a picture of Jesus in cultic terms to get a more complete sense of Petrine Christology.[40] The different first-century contexts of recipient communities in the New Testament evoked different images of Jesus. In the Gospels, for example, Jesus is the Good Shepherd, Son of God, Son of Man, and the Vine, just to name a few. All these metaphors try to contextualize for the audiences what might be otherwise too complex or foreign to grasp.[41]

In 1 Peter, one can delineate some images of Jesus as the "perfect sacrifice" (1 Pet 1:2-3; 2:18-22), the "chief cornerstone-capstone" (1 Pet 2:4-10), "the divine warrior" or "triumphant victor" (1 Pet 3:18-19), and the "shepherd and overseer of souls" (1 Pet 2:25; 5:4). We will look at some of these passages more closely.

1 Peter 1:2. The metaphor of blood sprinkling in 1 Peter 1:2 evokes Old Testament sacrificial practices where animal blood was sprinkled for diverse reasons, including protection from calamities such as blood on doorposts to stop the angel of death (Ex 12), establishing a covenant with God (Ex 24), purification of the people (Num 19), or as part of an annual tradition at Yom Kippur (Day of Atonement) in which blood was sprinkled on the mercy seat or atonement cover of the ark of the covenant (Lev 16:11-19).[42] While libations of beer, water, and other drinks were common in most African communities, blood sprinkling was generally rare and usually preserved for more serious situations afflicting the community, including droughts, floods, and plagues.[43]

In such cases, the community elders or spiritual leaders would sprinkle a domestic sacrificial animal's blood at the deity's shrine or a designated location. In addition, blood sprinkling was sometimes done by priests, medicine men, or medicine women during

---

[38]Peter Nyende, "Hebrews' Christology and Its Contemporary Apprehension in Africa," *Neotestamentica* 41 (2007): 361-81. See also a distillation of his dissertation from University of Edinburgh: Nyende, "Why Bother with Hebrews? An African Perspective," *Heythrop Journal* 46 (2005): 512-24. See also David Ekem, "The Author of Hebrews: A Great Dialogue Partner and Interpreter of the Gospel," *AICMAR Bulletin* 3 (2004): 1-25; Kwame Bediako, "Jesus in African Culture: A Ghanaian Perspective," in *Emerging Voices in Global Theology*, ed. William A. Dyrness (Grand Rapids, MI: Zondervan, 1994), 93-126.

[39]Paul Achtemeier, "Christology in 1 Peter: Some Reflections," in *Who Do You Say That I Am? Essays on Christology*, ed. Mark Allan Powell, Jack Dean Kingsbury, and David R. Bauer (Nashville: Westminster John Knox, 1999), 141.

[40]Achtemeier, "Christology in 1 Peter," in Powell, Kingsbury, and Bauer, *Who Do You Say That I Am?*, 140. See Leonhard Goppelt, *A Commentary on 1 Peter*, trans. J. E. Alsup (Grand Rapids, MI: Eerdmans, 1993), 247. Goppelt identifies at least four passages in 1 Peter that are clearly christological in nature (1 Pet 1:18-21; 2:22-25; 3:18-22, 4:6). I would like to add 1 Pet 1:2, 3; 2:4-10 to this list.

[41]Dyrness, *Learning About Theology*, 164-65.

[42]Joseph Gutmann, "The Strange History of the *Kapporet* Ritual," *Zeitschrift für die Alttestamentliche Wissenschaft* 112 (2000): 624-26.

[43]Lindblom, *Akamba*, 224-25: "Krapf tells how the Akamba said that on account of his arrival [a strange pale-colored individual], the rains would not come, for which reason they killed a sheep and sprinkled the path with its blood."

healing sessions.[44] Since the notion of sin in African religious thought is primarily from the vantage point of relational and moral offense to others or to the deity rather than it is legal, the necessity of Jesus' human sacrifice would communicate the gravity of the offense against God that needed to be appeased.[45]

Similarities are doubtless present in Israelite and African understandings of sacrifice.[46] For example, both used animal blood offerings, plant or grain offerings, and even human sacrifice. The idea that sacrifices are a means of interceding with the divine when the community is facing a catastrophe is true for both communities and would be fertile ground to explain the need for the sacrificial death of Jesus in cultic terms that would be familiar to the African religious outlook.[47] Perhaps more jarring for a Western individual in the nineteenth century would have been encountering the existence of human sacrifice during extreme calamities in some African communities such as the Akamba.

However, the Akedah (Abraham's "sacrifice" [binding] of Isaac) in Genesis 22, or even such commands about "passing over to YHWH the first born" as found in Exodus 13:12, perhaps capture remnants of the practice of human sacrifice in early Israelite cult.[48] In fact, a recent study concludes that "human sacrifice in the Israelite cult . . . functioned . . . as a means of capital punishment through which the land and nation were cleansed."[49]

Such an understanding would have facilitated drawing on these existing connections to articulate in familiar terminology the once-and-for-all human sacrifice of Jesus. In a passage such as this it would have helped the community to come to an understanding of the need to forgo the practice while maintaining the efficacy of the event by substituting Jesus.[50] Jesus is the "perfect sacrifice," requiring no further sacrifices![51] What makes him perfect? First Peter 2:20-22 explains that he was sinless, without defect, and so a perfect gift.[52]

---

[44]I remember witnessing a special ceremony for my grandfather to bless his children, grandchildren, and great-grandchildren. He drank water and sprayed (sprinkled) it from his mouth to eagerly waiting kin, who, owing to the number, scrambled to get the drops of water.

[45]J. Omosade Awolalu, "Sin and Its Removal in African Traditional Religion," *Journal of the American Academy of Religion* 44 (1976): 275-87.

[46]Christopher Simon Mngadi, *The Significance of Blood in the Old Testament Sacrifices and Its Relevance for the Church in Africa* (Pretoria: University of South Africa Press, 1981); Knut Holter, "The First Generation of African Old Testament Scholars: African Concerns and Western influences," in *African Identities and World Christianity in the Twentieth Century*, ed. Klaus Koschorke and Jens Holger Schjørring (Gottingen: Ottoharassowitz GmbH, 2005), 149-65.

[47]Justin S. Ukpong, "The Problem of God and Sacrifice in African Traditional Religion," *Journal of Religion in Africa* 14 (1983): 187-203; Ukpong, *Sacrifice: African and Biblical; A Comparative Study of Ibibio and Levitical Sacrifices* (Rome: Urbaniana University Press, 1987).

[48]Jason Tatlock, "The Place of Human Sacrifice in the Israelite Cult," in *Ritual and Metaphor: Sacrifice in the Bible*, ed. Christian Eberhart (Atlanta: Society of Biblical Literature, 2011), 33-48. In 1 Pet 3:21 Noah's flood prefigures the resurrection of Jesus Christ, but it is peculiar that after using all the sacrifice language, 1 Peter does not turn to the Akedah as a sure connection for the interpretation of Jesus' sacrificial death.

[49]Tatlock, "Place of Human Sacrifice," in Eberhart, *Ritual and Metaphor*, 47-48.

[50]Jon Levenson, *The Death and Resurrection of the Beloved Son: The Transformation of Child Sacrifice in Judaism and Christianity* (New Haven, CT: Yale University Press, 1993), x: "In point of fact, those roles [sage and prophet], even if real, have historically been vastly less important in Christian tradition than Jesus' identity as sacrificial victim, the son handed over to death by his loving father or the lamb who takes away the sins of the world."

[51]Dyrness, *Learning About Theology*, 165, laments, "My students in North America have always had a hard time understanding why God had to send his Son to die as blood sacrifice for sins, but they are drawn to images that portray Jesus as healing our estrangement from God. Students in Africa, by contrast, have no trouble with the idea of sacrifice, and they readily see Christ's death as placing him in the position of power with reference to God—death being commonly understood this way in Africa."

[52]This was probably the reason that a child was the one sacrificed among the Akamba, since not only was a child still connected to the spirit world, but she or he had not lived long enough to have failed in any responsibilities and so was perfect.

When connected to his role in the afterlife (1 Pet 3:18-20), the stakes are raised, since now Jesus, in his postdeath state, has entered the realm of the spirits and ancestors. Talking of Bantu communities, of which the Akamba are a part, François Kabasélé argues, "Christ is the Elder Brother *par excellence*: it is to him alone that offering must be made. Or again: once we know Christ, all of the offerings must henceforth be made through him. It is the eldest brother who makes an offering to the Ancestors and to the Supreme Being on behalf of the rest."[53] The shortcoming of this analysis is that it fails to incorporate the cultic elements well-developed in 1 Peter—that of Jesus himself as the perfect sacrifice. He is not simply the conduit through whom sacrifices are made. Instead, he is the perfect sacrifice that nullifies all others.[54]

1 Peter 1:18. Comparison with the lamb may more closely align this text with Exodus 12 and the Passover, which could find parallels in African animal sacrifice that were (and are) a common part of African religious practice. Certain specifications, just like the spotlessness of the Passover lamb, also accompany these sacrifices. However, reference to Jesus' precious blood would conjure thoughts of human sacrifice that was formerly practiced only in times of severe visitations, when it was necessary to propitiate the creator deity, to whom all life belongs, in an exceptional manner. Among the Akamba, the child required for the purpose was kidnapped, usually from the neighboring Kikuyu country. In the region around Machakos, Kenya, a child was taken from the rain clan (*mbaa-mbua*), and the mother received goats in compensation for her loss. The child was smeared with fat and buried alive with a goat at the *ithembo* (altar). Atoning sacrifice was already present in the Akamba worldview—the death of one person for the sake of the many![55] Jesus' sacrifice has to be understood within this framework in order to gain full appreciation within the Akamba cosmology.

This understanding then makes perfect sense of referring to Jesus in sacrificial terms in 1 Peter 1:2, 18. The sacrifices made to appease or seek favor from the spirits would be here replaced by Jesus, the "human" sacrifice that appeases the spiritual world and inoculates the threat that it poses to those in the world of the living. It is true that the parallels here between the Akamba sacrificial system and the biblical text are not without exception. For example, Jesus' sacrifice does more than appease the spirit world; it triumphs over it (1 Pet 3:18-22), and Jesus is a willing participant, which is not the case in the Akamba sacrifice. Jesus' sacrifice, however, can be understood as a certain restoration of harmony between the spiritual and the physical worlds that installs Jesus as the ultimate authority and the perfect conduit between the realms. As such, the difference is that while the sacrifices offered had temporary effect, Jesus'

---

[53]François Kabasélé in Schreiter, *Faces of Jesus*, 122.

[54]Resurrection from the dead (1 Pet 1:3) has no African parallel. Death is transition to the spirit world, with both advantages and disadvantages. Death may be salvation for the individual but not the society. Going on to the land of the dead, especially as an old person, was a good thing. Not so for a young person, which prompted reincarnations or haunting by the dead person's spirit. Names such as Musyoka and Kasyoka ("one who returns") still persist even though many people identify with Christianity today; the notion of reincarnation still undergirds the naming. In some communities, naming after a dead relative, usually one who was beloved, anticipates that his or her spirit will be present in the newly born child. Whether the new baby counts as the same exact person who had died is unclear. Also, among the Akamba, a child is referred to a *keimu* ("little spirit") for at least about six months after birth because children originate from the spirit world and may choose to return to that world (probably a view prompted by the high mortality rate of infants).

[55]Lindblom, *Akamba*, 224, 120.

personal sacrifice—a once-and-for-all act—
holds until the time will come to give account
before God (1 Pet 4:5).

First Peter 3:18-22; 4:6. Karen Jobes notes
that this passage is considered one of the most
challenging to interpret in the whole of 1 Peter
and possibly in the New Testament. Even Reformer Martin Luther seems to have thrown his
arms up in despair, noting that "I still do not
know for sure what the apostle meant." Ancient
reference to the passage as *descensus ad inferos*
("harrowing of hell") by Clement and Origen
and attributed to the Apostles' Creed has no historical basis, since the phrase first appeared in
Rufus (400), replacing the original "and was
buried."[56] This may suggest a later Greco-
Roman interpretation of the understanding of
the passage that has subsequently remained enshrined in today's version of the creed.

William Dalton's groundbreaking study of this
passage undermined the *descensus* interpretation
and other ancient interpretations of the passage
that had maintained that a "pre-incarnate Christ,"
through Noah (e.g., Augustine), had preached
the "good news" to the people who died during
Noah's flood. Dalton instead argued for the
christological understanding of this passage that
portrays Jesus as Christus Victor (Victorious
Christ), who conquers the disobedient spirits (in
upper heavens) and proclaims victory and their
subjection in his ascension to the right hand of
God in heaven. Using Jewish literary background, especially 1 Enoch, Dalton equates the

disobedient spirits with the fallen angels in
Genesis 6 and not with human spirits.[57]

Nevertheless, the phrase "dead in the flesh,
alive in spirit" has remained a *crux interpretum*
for the majority of Western commentators of 1
Peter. There seems to be a lot of exegetical gym-
nastics to align the part of being "alive in the
spirit" with Jesus' *bodily* resurrected form or
divine nature, which is itself a problem since the
phrase says "alive in the spirit" (*zōiopoieō tō
pneuma*) and not "alive in the body" (*zōiopoieō
tō soma*), and as such has influenced how the
whole section is interpreted.[58] However, in contrast to J. S. Feinberg, who understands the
phrase to mean Christ's bodily resurrection, an
Akamba reading would understand the reference to mean simply that, even after going
through death, Jesus was still alive in the "spirit
world," where he made proclamation.[59] In the
Akamba cosmology the physical and the spirit
worlds interact seamlessly, and this makes such
a reading quite sensible.[60]

Such a reading, however, remains in contrast with that of most Western scholars, for
whom the passage, according to Jobes, refers
"either to the two spheres of Christ's existence
(the earthly sphere versus the eschatological)
or to two modes of his personal existence (in
human form before his death and in glorified
form after his resurrection)."[61] Western perspectives seem to generally perceive death as a
negative state that has to be countered by a
positive state of being alive in the flesh, and so

---

[56]Karen Jobes, *1 Peter* (Grand Rapids, MI: Baker, 2005), 236, 241.

[57]William J. Dalton, *Christ's Proclamation to the Spirits* (Rome: Pontifical Biblical Institute, 1965), 18, 118.

[58]Dalton, *Christ's Proclamation*, 19-20; John H. Elliott, *1 Peter: A New Translation with Introduction and Commentary*, Anchor Bible 37B (New York: Doubleday, 2000), 647.

[59]J. S. Feinberg, "1 Peter 3:18-20: Ancient Mythology, and the Intermediate State," *Westminster Theological Journal* 48 (1986): 315.

[60]This perspective is also distinct from the early church's notion of *triduum mortis* (separation of soul and body), as the whole person can exist in the spiritual state.

[61]Jobes, *1 Peter*, 242. See also Elliott, *1 Peter*, 650-51.

they posit the resurrection or glorification as the interpretation of the phrase.[62]

In contrast, among the Akamba, vocabulary for death includes such euphemisms as *kwitwa* ("to be summoned or called," presumably by the deity or the ancestors and spirits) and *kuthumuwa* ("to rest" from earthly labors). Parallels in the Hebrew Bible include, for example, the euphemism "resting with the fathers" (e.g., 1 Kings 2:10; 11:43; 2 Chron 32:33). In essence, then, death is not a disappearance into nothingness but a transition into a different state of being. It is a transformation from the physical (not in the Platonic sense) to a spiritual state that is in a spiritual world, very much a reflection of the physical world we live in but invisible to the human eye. These worlds are connected not vertically but horizontally, and the boundary is porous where the ancestors and spirits (themselves really also human spirits whose identities have long been forgotten) can traverse between the two worlds.[63]

Therefore, in light of how 1 Peter 3:18-19 is laid out, it makes complete sense if understood in light of the African worldview that perceives death as a *transition* to a new state of being that is neither negative nor positive, but simply different: a "spiritual" existence that can still incor-

porate the physical.[64] As 1 Peter 3:19 announces, it is in this state (spiritual state) that Jesus preached to the spirits that were in prison, following his death in the body. It was not in his resurrected state but in his "spiritual state" that he went (not descended) into the spiritual world of spirits and ancestors to preach.[65] Appeals to the Jewish notion of seven heavens in order to resolve the issue are still focused on where Jesus went and not on what the spiritual state is.[66]

From an African perspective, it is Jesus "who has gone into heaven and is at God's right hand—with *angels*, *authorities*, and *powers* in submission to him" (1 Pet 3:22). He goes into this sphere with God's power; he is able to overcome triumphantly all the threats of this world of spirits and to establish his reign even in this realm.[67] A realm that is recognized by the African worldview as source for both fortune and misfortune has been accessed by Jesus, who is able to bring his message to it.[68] It is a world of "living-dead" ancestors and spirits whose intrusion into the world of the living is an accepted reality of a porous divide that was managed by sacrifice as a means to appease any perceived infringements or to seek favors. Jesus establishes authority over all spheres of life, the physical and the spiritual, making proclamation of his gospel

---

[62]Achtemeier, "Christology in 1 Peter," in Powell, Kingsbury, and Bauer, *Who Do You Say That I Am?*, 141; Elliott, *1 Peter*, 686.

[63]Mbiti, *African Religions*, 26; Mugambi, *African Culture*, 51.

[64]Mugambi, *African Culture*, 51.

[65]Elliott, *1 Peter*, 650-51. Diane Stinton also points out that a christological category such as "Christ the Ancestor" may be more popular in academic circles than it actually is on the local church level.

[66]See Dalton, *Christ's Proclamation*; Elliott, *1 Peter*, 658-60. This is not to ignore the connection of the Noah story in the passage but maintains that the spirits there referenced are not simply angels, as most scholars argue, but include the spirits of people who rebelled too. (So Wayne Grudem, *The First Epistle of Peter* [Grand Rapids, MI: Eerdmans, 1998], 215-17.)

[67]Thus, Bediako, "Jesus in African Culture," in Dyrness, *Emerging Voices*, 103: "But if Jesus has gone to the realm of the 'spirits and the gods,' so to speak, he has gone there as Lord over them in much the same way that he is Lord over us. He is therefore the Lord over the living and the dead, and over the 'living-dead,' as the ancestors are also described. He is supreme over all the 'gods' and authorities in the realm of the spirits. So he sums up in himself all their powers and cancels any terrorizing influence they might be assumed to have upon us."

[68]Daniel Kasomo, "An Investigation of Sin and Evil in African Cosmology," *International Journal of Sociology and Anthropology* 1 (2009): 145-55: "In nearly all African societies, it is thought that the spirits are either the origin of evil or agents of evil. When human spirits become detached from human contact, people experience or fear them as 'evil' or 'harmful.' . . . Mystical power is neither good nor evil in itself: but when used maliciously by some individuals it is experienced as evil" (147).

and authority, and sits on the "male hand" side of God, a place of power![69] So, in this passage alone, 1 Peter has combined the images of Jesus as liberator and Christus Victor.

Such a reading then makes sense of the reference to "spirits in prison" (1 Pet 3:19) if understood in light of 1 Peter 4:5-6: "But they will have to give account to him who is ready to judge *the living and the dead*. For this is the reason the *gospel was preached even to those who are now dead*, so that they might be judged according to men in regard to the body, but live according to God in regard to the spirit." This would be a reference to the human spirits of ancestors, in which case the proclamation is for those who died before having a chance to hear the gospel message preached (the "living-dead" ancestors), and thus giving them an opportunity to accept the message.[70] This was a vexing concern for most early African converts to Christianity. This passage provides the possibility of comfort in knowing that the ancestors, who died before the advent of the modern missionary endeavor in Africa, still have the chance to hear the gospel of Jesus Christ.[71]

The one critique that such a reading raises for those who want to interpret Jesus in the model of ancestor is that Jesus goes into this spirit world not to dwell but to "preach" and then come back to life and into heaven. By not remaining in the spirit realm, he cannot be classified as ancestor in the same respect that an African ancestor is.[72] While the ancestor can return to the physical realm only in spirit form and in dreams, Jesus' return is in body and spirit, and in full subjugation of all spirits, angels, ancestors, and powers.

Christological images are quite variegated in 1 Peter. Nevertheless, this brief survey has shown that those images, when interpreted from an African perspective, can be fruitfully understood while being appropriated differently from the common Western readings.

CHALCEDONIAN DEFINITION REVISITED: WHERE DO THE CREEDS FIT IN ALL THIS?

Creeds mostly seem to function simply as part of the recitation in worship among the Western missionary–planted churches in Africa, but do not seem to hold much sway beyond that.[73] By giving prominence to the Bible itself (the *Word* of God), the creeds have been generally relegated to a noninfluential category with the exception of perhaps the Roman Catholic Church. Treating the creeds as sealed documents has meant there has not been any push to develop other elements of Christology.[74] Seen from the

---

[69]Bediako, "Jesus in African Culture," in Dyrness, *Emerging Voices*, 103. For the Akamba and most Bantu communities, the right hand is the male hand, while the left hand is the female hand. The Akamba traditionally buried the men lying on the right side and the women on their left. Lindblom, *Akamba*, 224.

[70]So Goppelt, *1 Peter*, 289: "Proclamation of the gospel is encountered by the dead when they are dead and that their death here, as in v. 5, is *literal*" (emphasis added). Contra Elliott, *1 Peter*, 650, who argues the spirits are "angels."

[71]Interestingly, a parallel perspective could be said to have been maintained by the early church, including Cyril of Alexandria, Origen, Clement of Alexandria, Athanasius, and Gregory of Nazianzus.

[72]Fergus J. King, "Angels and Ancestors: A Basis for Christology?," *Mission Studies* 11 (1994): 10-26.

[73]John H. Leith, *Creeds of the Churches: A Reader in Christian Doctrine from the Bible to the Present*, 3rd ed. (Nashville: Westminster John Knox, 1982), 555.

[74]Clarke, *African Christology*, 1-2: "The approach to theology taken in the council of Nicea, AD 325, which declared that Jesus was *homoousios* (one in being or one in substance) with the Father, and the council of Chalcedon 451 statement that the two natures of Christ (the divine and the human) are without division or separation, is not an African approach to theology." The effort of those on the side of "orthodoxy" to castigate any challenges to the creeds with pronouncement of "heterodoxy" or even "heresy" has meant that these culturally limited creeds have often assumed a universal authority in Christian communities, yet may not have found much relevance in how different local communities do theology or Christology. This rigidity and resistance to interrogation or change may be more grounded in the Platonic philosophy of sense perception that is encrusted in Western education and culture.

list of African christological concerns outlined in this essay, it is clear that issues central to the Chalcedonian Council (the relationship of the divinity and humanity of Jesus) hardly ever show up.

For the most part, christological writing in Africa seems to be intent on finding and creating christological categories and issues that are pertinent to African religious concerns. Even in a passage such as 1 Peter 3:18-22, which may invite such a conversation, the African focus instead turned to the movement of Jesus between the spiritual and the divine spheres. While it is true that the Chalcedonian Definition builds on the Nicene Creed, which does highlight the cultic aspect of Jesus being "crucified under Pontius Pilate," even there it does not explicitly connect Jesus' crucifixion to any other cultic imagery. As Clifton Clarke points out,

> The ecumenical councils, such as the ones held at Nicea AD 325 and Chalcedon AD 451, had on this basis of preserving Christian orthodoxy sought to establish a single faith throughout the empire. This, they thought, represented revealed truth and therefore did not recognize how their own cultural, social, and political influence would determine the shape of their Christological construction.[75]

What Clarke does not also mention is that in the fourth century (306–337), Christianity had been transformed from a minority religion in the Roman Empire to *the* imperial religion, following the conversion of Emperor Constantine. So, while prior to 313 Christianity could be characterized as having been a voice of justice and dissent against empire, afterward it had been co-opted as the state religion and partner in power, unfortunately with the very devastating results of persecuting "pagans" and heretics.[76]

Yet, creeds themselves were prompted by the encounter of Christianity with Greco-Roman culture and religion. So, if Christologies were from the very beginning the products of the encounter of the gospel message with different cultures, then one wonders whether there is need to revisit the creeds themselves, given the more recent Christian encounters within African, Asian, and Latin American cultures.

FURTHER READING

Achtemeier, Paul. "Christology in 1 Peter: Some Reflections." Pages 140-53 in *Who Do You Say That I Am? Essays on Christology*, edited by Mark Allan Powell, Jack Dean Kingsbury, and David R. Bauer. Nashville: Westminster John Knox, 1999.

Bediako, Kwame. *Theology and Identity: The Impact of Culture upon Christian Thought in the Second Century and Modern Africa*. Oxford: Regnum, 1992.

Elliott, John H. *1 Peter: A New Translation with Introduction and Commentary*. Anchor Bible 37B. New York: Doubleday, 2000.

Katongole, Emmanuel, ed. *African Theology Today*. Vol. 1. Scranton, PA: University of Scranton Press, 2002.

Mbiti, John S. *African Religions and Philosophy*. London: Heinemann, 1969.

Mugambi, J. N. K. *Christianity and African Culture*. Nairobi: Acton, 1989.

Schreiter, Robert, ed. *Faces of Jesus in Africa*. Maryknoll, NY: Orbis, 1991.

---

[75]Clarke, *African Christology*, 6.

[76]Samuel Lieu and Dominic Montserrat, eds., *From Constantine to Julian: A Source History* (London: Routledge, 1996), 213-14.

16

BIBLICAL CHRISTOLOGIES
OF THE GLOBAL CHURCH

BEYOND CHALCEDON? TOWARD A FULLY
CHRISTIAN AND FULLY CULTURAL THEOLOGY

K. K. Yeo

UNDERSTANDING WHO Jesus Christ was in Scripture has been a vexing problem ever since Jesus asked of his disciples: "Who do you say that I am?" (Mt 16:15; Mk 8:29; Lk 9:20). The world has changed, but the theological challenge remains the same: understanding who Jesus was and who Christ is to readers in AD 50–100 (New Testament times), 325 (Council of Nicaea: the unity of nature between Christ and God), 451 (Council of Chalcedon: two natures in one person of Christ), and 2014 (these essays from the Western and Majority Worlds). With the rise of historical methods, new hermeneutics, and voices from the Majority World, it is evident from the assortment of Christologies in the biblical witnesses that while Jesus is singular, Christology is plural, as the essays in this section also reveal.[1]

All contributors to this section face two issues: first, the unity and diversity of biblical Christologies—that is, the question of the center (organizing principle) and the unity (underlying aspect in the diversity) of the Bible; and second, the meaning and task of theology—that is, the method and content of Christology as well as Scripture reading. I begin with a hermeneutical question regarding the unity-diversity issue of (i.e., the differences and similarities between) biblical Christologies and that of Chalcedon. Next, I proceed with a theological discussion of the ontology of Christology (implied from the ontology of Christ): what it *means* to be "fully God and fully human," as the global church partners among ourselves in the *logos-dao* Christology, and as contextual Christologies from the Majority World move forward to a global Christology. Finally, I attempt to begin an ecumenical discourse through a distinctly Chinese Christology of *renren* (a person who loves) that helps us to understand Christ(ians) as the image(s) of God. It will be clear that my

---

[1]All Christologies (understandings of Christ) have soteriological biases regarding how Christ will fulfill various human needs or predicaments. Philipp Melanchthon says, "To know Christ is to know his benefits" (cited in Wilhelm Pauck, ed., *Melanchthon and Bucer*, Library of Christian Classics 19 [Philadelphia: Westminster, 1969], 21). It is important, however, that we know the person of Christ through his work in our lives (i.e., christological anthropology), not through our experience (i.e., anthropological Christology).

attempt here is to write and embody, as much as possible, a fully Christian-biblical and fully Chinese-cultural Christology.

CHINESE CHRISTIAN CHRISTOLOGIES

When we survey the landscape of biblical Chinese Christologies, it is apparent how adolescent Chinese Christian scholars are in becoming "fully biblical and fully Chinese." The majority of Chinese biblical scholarship still betrays the assumption that biblical interpretation can be a-cultural (naively or deliberately), and some of these readings have become tacitly Western to the point of replacing whatever is Chinese.[2] Among those Chinese writings that attempt to be aware of their dual-nature-in-one person identity, it is noteworthy that particular biblical texts and topics are favored in christological studies. The Chinese christological palate favors John's Gospel over the Synoptics, particularly the philosophical word *logos* and *dao*.[3] If Synoptic Christologies are discussed, they are linked to the kingdom-of-God discourse pertaining to the socialist sociopolitical reality of modern China.[4] Paul's writings to Gentile readers are preferred over Jewish documents (Hebrews, James) in the New Testament, as Chinese scholars are preoccupied with Pauline Christology that speaks to a moral self or Confucian morality.[5] A more in-depth investigation may reveal that the books of Hebrews and James

are actually rich resources for Christian Chinese Christologies since they reflect themes pertinent to the Chinese such as the revelation of God in historical past (tradition) and fulfillment of Christ (for Jewish and Chinese cultures); Sabbath rest, christological-redemptive rest, and *tai-ji* (Great Ultimate) as well as Confucian musical delight (*yue*) and ecstasy-elevation (*xing*); Christ in space and time and the cyclical and linear worldviews in Hebrews and China (*yin-yang* space and time); the wisdom Christ in James and the Daoist sages in Chinese cultures; and wisdom Christology and metaphoric language of Chinese.[6] Christological texts in the Apocalypse are used often in a dualistic sense to address the Chinese cyclical worldview and the moral vacuum of present-day China. A more engaging crosscultural reading awaits future Chinese scholars as the Apocalypse and Chinese texts are read through lenses such as the sacramental Lamb of God and various Chinese rituals of cosmological anthropology; poetic justice in worship in the Apocalypse and aesthetic transformation of selfhood and nationhood in Chinese culture; and the process and goal of history and a Chinese worldview.[7]

There is fresh air around the table when Chinese scholars continue to read their cultures biblically and read the biblical texts in their own languages. Taking seriously the composite contexts of Scripture and the complex horizons of

---

[2]On historical survey of Christian Chinese theologies and biblical interpretation, see my article "Chinese Interpretation," in *The Oxford Encyclopedia of Biblical Interpretation*, ed. Steven L. McKenzie (Oxford: Oxford University Press, 2013), 1:103-12; also my "Paul's Ethic of Holiness and Chinese Morality of *Renren*," in Charles H. Cosgrove, Herold Weiss, and K. K. Yeo, *Cross-Cultural Paul: Journeys to Others, Journeys to Ourselves* (Grand Rapids, MI: Eerdmans, 2005), 104-40.

[3]See multiple essays addressing this hermeneutic in He Guanghu and Daniel H. N. Yeung, eds., *Sino-Christian Theology Reader*, 2 vols. (Hong Kong: Institute of Sino-Christian Studies, 2009). See also the works of Liu Xiaofeng (in China), and *The Biblical Library* series (K. K. Yeo and Liang Hui, eds. [Shanghai: Shanghai VI Horae]).

[4]See the works of Wu Leichuan, T. C. Chao, Y. T. Wu, Jia Yuming, and Bishop Ting Guang-hsun.

[5]See the works of scholars in the previous footnote, and also Watchman Nee and Wan Szekar.

[6]On wisdom Christology, see K. K. Yeo, *Zhuangzi and James* (Shanghai: Huadong Shifan Daxue VI Horae, 2012). On Christ in space in time, see Yeo, "The Meaning and Usage of 'REST' (*katapausis* and *sabbatismos*) in Hebrews 3:7–4:13," *Asia Journal of Theology* 5 (1991): 2-33.

[7]K. K. Yeo, "Hope for the Persecuted, Cooperation with the State, and Meaning for the Dissatisfied: Three Readings of *Revelation* from a Chinese Context," in *The Book of Revelation in Intercultural Perspective*, ed. David Rhoads (Minneapolis: Fortress, 2005), 200-221.

the Chinese world (whether in China or overseas), with its multiple nationalities, regional groups and dialects, diverse cultures, pluralistic religions, and sociopolitical realities, Chinese Christologies such as those in the *Sino-Christian Theology Reader* have begun to address the following topics: (1) the reinterpretation of the biblical understanding of revelation (Chia Yuming) and reason (Chow Lien-hwa) and the incarnation of Christ (Chao Tzuchen) in the present cultures of China; (2) Christian ethics of resurrection hope in the Bible (You Xilin) in light of the consanguineous Marxist ideology of the new China; (3) faith in Christ and the interaction with other faiths (Chow Lien-hwa); (4) Christ and Chinese Marxism (Zhang Xian) and secular humanism (Wang Xiaochao); and (5) Chinese feminist theology (Gao Shining, Kwok Pui-lan, and K. K. Yeo).

BIBLICAL CHRISTOLOGIES AND CHALCEDON: DIVERSITY (CONTEXTS) AND UNITY (ONTOLOGY)

Like the pluralistic milieus of the New Testament and the Chalcedonian Council, the authors of the essays in this section gather in our diversity two millennia later still naming Christologies (plural) from our particular contexts (United States and Europe, Palestine, sub-Saharan Africa, Kenya, Latin America, Mexico, the Philippines, and China) and yet befriend one another as we seek the unity and fullness of Christ. Neither biblical writings nor Chalcedon's creedal formulations represent an abstract (see Martínez-Olivieri's caution that abstraction that "leads to historical apathy") and comprehensive (possibly leading to

an authoritarian voice) theology of Christ. Rather, they are historical documents, embedded in particular space and specific time, though their impact has endured beyond their contexts.

The Proclaimer (Jesus) became the Proclaimed (Christ); that is, only Jesus is normative, and no Christology is absolute. For example, Chalcedon was correcting the error of the Nestorian division of Christ's two natures and the Eutychean error that Christ had only one nature. Based on biblical witnesses and employing Greco-Roman philosophical acumen, the creed defines christological orthodoxy by holding to the full deity of Christ, the full humanity of Christ, the distinction of the two natures of Christ, and the unity of Christ's person.[8] Following what Andrew Mbuvi calls a "culturally constructed" creed, many Western Christologies hold to the two natures of Jesus as neither a mixing, nor a union, nor a compound of divine-human substance, but the personal and functional unity with God (although Christ has an independent will). This view does not contradict New Testament Christologies. In the New Testament, Jesus' divinity and humanity are non-conflicting, as revealed in Jesus' relationship of self-surrender and self-dedication (humanity) to the personal community of the triune God (divinity) in order to exhibit God's reign.

The subtitle of my essay, "Beyond Chalcedon?," does not bring into doubt the validity of the creed to address the controversies at that time. Rather, the question is a hermeneutical one: Is orthodoxy as formulated in the creed comprehensive enough, given its contextual response to the Nestorian and Eutychean heresies? It is

---

[8]The creed holds "the two natures existed before the union but became one at the Incarnation, . . . Christ is declared to be one Person in two Natures, the Divine of the same substance as the Father, the human of the same substance as us, which are united unconfusedly, unchangeably, indivisibly, inseparably" (cited in F. L. Cross and E. A. Livingstone, eds., *The Oxford Dictionary of the Christian Church*, 3rd rev. ed. [Oxford: Oxford University Press, 2005], 318).

notable that it was not accepted by the Oriental (Armenian, Coptic, Ethiopian, and Syrian) Orthodox churches.[9] The question "Beyond Chalcedon?" can best be answered if we compare and contrast Chalcedonian Christology with that of the New Testament and note the limited *catholicity* of its explicitly stated Christology and the subsequent problem of violence against the Copts (as highlighted by Victor Ezigbo).

Kevin Vanhoozer writes in his essay, "What is normative in Chalcedon is not the particular concepts but the underlying judgments, not a particular metaphysical scheme but the underlying biblical ontology." I agree with Vanhoozer that "a particular metaphysical scheme" is not normative, but Vanhoozer's proposal needs further discussion. For whatever these "underlying judgments" and the "underlying biblical ontology" are, they are still related to the "particular concepts" about the ontology of Christ (fully God and fully human). After all, Christ's reality (two natures in one person) is the reality out of which the triune God has created the world. I would argue that it is this ontology of Christ that Western Christology struggles with when discussing "high Christology" or "low Christology," Christology "from above" or Christology "from below." It is the same christological issue that liberation theology affirms by holding to "both heavenly savior and earthly liberator" (Jules Martínez-Olivieri), and the same issue raised when African Christology believes in indigenous spirituality and Christian faith. My reservation is not with the concepts but the *scope* of the concepts, with the single lens of Chalcedon. That is why I still prefer using the compound lenses of the biblical Christologies.

Indeed, the biblical ontology of Chalcedon is *selective*. The "beyond" I refer to in the subtitle

of the essay is not intended to invalidate Chalcedon. My proposal to the global church is to return to the richness and variety, thus the *true catholicity*, of New Testament Christologies, and the expansive nature of biblical hermeneutics evident in the fourfold Gospels and the Pauline Christologies. That we are given four Christologies of the Gospels based on the Evangelists' variegated and nuanced portrayals of the historical Jesus reveals the crosscultural hermeneutical task of theology in the lived experience of the first readers:

1. Responding to a Jewish Christian community in the midst of a Gentile world, the Gospel of Matthew constructs a Christology of Jesus as the new Israel, new presence of God (Emmanuel), new Moses and new law, new David and new kingdom, new covenant and new faithfulness. Matthew's *biblios geneseos* (book of genesis-genealogy, Mt 1:1) is a new scriptural reading of the Old Testament in light of Jesus Christ, thus fulfilling rather than abolishing the Old Testament.

2. Aiming to encourage the persecuted Roman Christians in the 60s, the Christology of the Gospel of Mark is about the crucified Messiah (Mk 8:29; 12:35; 13:21; 14:61; 15:32), who is the Son of God (i.e., the fully human one; Mk 1:1, 11, 24; 3:11; 5:7; 9:7; 15:39). This good news (Mk 1:1) of Mark is about a Christology of the cross and service.

3. Luke's ordered narrative has a Christology of the universal Savior (Lk 1:47, 69; 2:11), as he defends the legitimacy and goodness of Christian faith to the Roman Empire, and as he narrates the reign of God expanding in the empire.

---

[9]E. Fahlbusch and G. W. Bromiley, eds., *The Encyclopedia of Christianity* (Grand Rapids, MI: Eerdmans, 1999-2003), 1:464.

4. Addressing issues in Pharisaic Judaism, John's Gospel writes the Book of Signs (Jn 1:19–12:50) about a Christology of the transcendent Wisdom-Jesus tabernacled in human history, the Great "I AM" who created and worked miraculously in the chaotic world.

It was not the purpose of the Chalcedon Council to read the Christologies of the fourfold canonical Gospels in light of their historical meaning. We can see how the council was reading the New Testament faithfully, but contextually, with a crosscultural hermeneutic that addressed their philosophical and contextual issues, those being the challenges of the Nestorians and the Eutycheans. The focus on the two natures of Christ and the discussion regarding the technical usage of Greek and Latin (at times using slippery terms such as *homoousios* [same substance] in Ezigbo; "white mythology" in Vanhoozer) certainly is true to the spirit of New Testament Christologies *selectively*; thus it was not their intention to embody the richness of the Gospels' and Paul's Christologies. Chalcedonian Christology, being a contextual Christology, does not attempt to provide a comprehensive Christology of the global (catholic) church.

Global Christologies seek creative dialogues toward (1) a *catholic* faith based on biblical Christologies that honor multiple and interacting worldviews, (2) a global theology that respects crosscultural and shifting contexts in which faithful communities embody real-life issues, (3) a translatability of the Scripture that upholds various dynamic vernaculars and hermeneutics, and (4) a roundtable symposium of proclaiming and worshiping a biblical Christ portrayed in varied Christologies.

One of the best examples of diversity in unity regarding Christologies can be found in the biblical witnesses in the epistles of Paul. Gadamerian hermeneutics of preunderstanding and horizon fusing is evident in Paul's understandings of Christ.[10] To the Thessalonian Christians, he speaks of Christ the Coming One who is the Judge and their hope. To the Galatians, he speaks of Christ the Crucified One, lifting the curse of the law, thus bringing in the nations (Gentiles) as the people of God (together with the Jews) to be the new creation in Christ. To the Roman Christians, he speaks of Christ as God's Righteousness to judge, save, and welcome all regardless of race (Jews or Gentiles) and culture (Greeks or barbarians) so that they may become God's beloved community. In speaking to the Corinthian Christians, Paul seeks to bring them to a higher spiritual awareness via the "crucified Christ" (1 Cor 1:23; 2:2), in order to deconstruct the civilization ideals of power (Romans), religion (Jews), and wisdom-philosophy (Greeks). Through such self-deconstruction, they are then able to reconstruct a holistic life found only in the "weakness" of God, a "miracle-less" faith, and "foolish" understanding. To the Corinthian Christians in 2 Corinthians, when contesting the theology of the superapostles (2 Cor 11:5; 12:11), Paul speaks of Christ as the Reconciler of humanity to God (2 Cor 5:11-21), of the congregation with its church leader (Paul; 2 Cor 2), as well as of the Macedonian believers with the Jerusalem church (2 Cor 8–9). For Paul, the unity of his Christologies in all his epistles is Christ, "who has died, is risen, and will come again," yet we see in individual epistles that his Christologies translate dynamically into different foci, shed light on various themes, and always speak

---

[10]For more, see K. K. Yeo, *Rhetorical Interaction in 1 Corinthians 8 and 10: A Formal Analysis with Implications for a Cross-Cultural, Chinese Hermeneutic* (Leiden: Brill, 1995), 15-43.

forth in a prophetic and priestly way to the needs of the congregations. The compound lenses of Paul's Christologies are certainly much more powerful and expansive than those of Chalcedon. In keeping with previous chapters in this volume, the following section is my Christian Chinese attempt to listen to the voices around the table. It is also an opportunity for me to project my voice, so that together we can embrace global Christologies and go "beyond" the scope of Chalcedon, reaching back to the fountainhead of Christologies, the Bible.

GLOBAL CHRISTOLOGIES AND (BEYOND) CHALCEDON: BIBLICAL MANDATE AND ESCHATOLOGICAL TRUTH

Our task is not to construct only *one* abiding and unifying principle from the four corners of the earth in order to arrive at a coherent, systematic Christology of the Bible. Rather, we wish to encourage faithful interpretations of biblical witnesses in their polyphonic, yet harmonized, proclamation and theologizing of Jesus Christ from diverse cultures. There are two ways we can do this: (1) discern and celebrate (a mutual learning process) the commonalities and the differences of biblical Christologies of the global church; or (2) covenant with each other to work together toward a Christian ritual of confession and loving Christian friendship when contentious points of our biblical Christologies emerge.

The way the global church is diversified in unity demonstrates its priestly and prophetic calling in the world, thus transforming it (Timoteo Gener calls this missiological Chris-

tology). The church will live out the biblical mandate of preaching, translating, and exegeting Jesus Christ as it acknowledges the eschatological nature of Truth.[11] The ontology of Christ is ultimately not simply significant in and of itself, but rather in the ontology of christological theology. That is, Christ's ontology enables "every tribe and language and people and nation" (Rev 5:9; 7:9; 13:7; 14:6; see Acts 2:1-13) to be fully Christian and fully Chinese-Palestinian in their *theologizing*, which constitutes part of Christian worship. Jesus Christ is the Reality that makes all realities, cultures, and meaning systems true, beautiful, and good. Because Jesus Christ does not speak heavenly tongues in his revelation of God, Christianity does not have a sacred language. The gospel of the church is neither culture specific nor language specific.[12] Jesus is the Eternal Word enfleshed (Jn 1:14), as the gospel of Christ and Christian doctrines are always proclaimed and understood "incarnationally" within their own cultures "in-linguistically."

All the essays in this section are akin to eight sides of a prism that allow us to view Jesus Christ from, and in interaction with, their various vantage points. An individual on their own is limited in the ability to reflect Christ's glory and meaning. But all facets, when held together and in tension, reflect Christ's fuller glory in eschatological openness and richness of meaning. As a Christian Chinese, I find a lot of overlapping concerns and conclusions in our biblical interpretations, and my views on many theological and interpretive issues are greatly clarified and expanded by these. Many essays contribute to the discussion of the symbiotic relationship

---

[11]K. K. Yeo, "Response: Multicultural Readings: A Biblical Warrant and an Eschatological Vision," in *Global Voices: Reading the Bible in the Majority World*, ed. Craig Keener and M. Daniel Carroll R. (Peabody, MA: Hendrickson, 2013), 27-37.

[12]As Lamin Sanneh writes, Christianity from its beginning until now has been "a translated religion without a revealed language" (Lamin Sanneh, *Whose Religion Is Christianity?* [Grand Rapids, MI: Eerdmans, 2003], 69).

between the spirit and human worlds (Ezigbo, Mbuvi, Spencer, Gener) and the fluidity between past and present worlds (Katanacho, Yeo). All essays see the hermeneutic act of theology as something salvific, whether to the individual, the community of women (Latin American feminist discussion in Martínez-Olivieri) or the poor (Gener), the system of oppression (Katanacho and Martínez-Olivieri), or even the culture (Gener and Yeo).

All eight essays follow the path of the biblical paradigm that warrants us to take local language, context, and culture seriously for a good cause. When theology is translated into local tongues, and the Bible is used to address contextual issues, the culture is transformed (or fulfilled or converted and turned to Christ, rather than substituted; see Ezigbo), and the Scripture demonstrates its sacredness. It is sacred in the sense that the Bible has the power to speak life across space and time. Moreover, these essays highlight another aspect of global theology, that is, how global Christologies are understood and lived out in their contexts around the roundtable, for the purpose of edifying others. Let me use the example of the Chinese translation of John's Gospel and show how it has helped me to appreciate a Chinese Christology of *dao* that enabled me to see Christ more fully than simply reading the word *Word* in the English version or *logos* in the Greek Bible.

***A Chinese Christology of* dao.** The Greek word *logos* is translated as *dao*, a Chinese word having three meanings: (1) the cosmic or creative principle, (2) the personal truth or embodied wisdom, and (3) the verbal word (speech) or communal dialogue.

1. Jesus is portrayed in John's Gospel as the Creator of the cosmos, evident in the parallel motif of the first chapters of John and Genesis. God-Jesus is the Creator of order from chaos, light from darkness, and meaning from void.

The word *logos* in Stoicism and the word *dao* in Chinese thought have similar ideas: the foundation of truth and the principle that holds all things together. John probably used the word *logos* because it held a crosscultural meaning for both Jewish and Gentile readers that the universe has coherent structures sustaining itself. The notion of *dao* speaks of wholeness and integrity in the Chinese understanding of the universe. Indeed, Jesus, as the creative *dao*, takes human form and keeps on working and performing miracles. These works and miracles are called "works" (*erga* in Greek) and "signs" (*semeia* in Greek) in John's Gospel and reflect the glory of the Father.[13]

2. The *logos* Christology speaks of Jesus as personified wisdom, as the word *dao* would be understood by Chinese readers. *Dao* means wisdom, truth, and knowledge that has the character and vitality of life. In the same light, Jesus as wisdom-*logos*-*dao* comes to us through the Hebrew tradition of wisdom (*hokmah* in Hebrew) as we have known it in Proverbs 8—the personal wisdom and the personal Creator, presented in female imagery. Understood in a patriarchal setting, the use of female imagery is certainly a creative and crosscultural endeavor (see also Martínez-Olivieri's and Spencer's discussions on Christ and women in different cultural contexts). The wisdom-*dao* Christ has personhood; he is not just an abstract principle. Thus, Jesus Christ the personal *dao* has to be an

---

[13]For example, the so-called first miracle Jesus performed at Cana, turning water into wine, is for the sake of "revealing God's glory" (Jn 2:11). The resurrection of Lazarus from the dead is also for the sake of "God's glory" (Jn 11:40). The greatest sign is, of course, the cross (Jn 12:23), where Jesus reveals the glory of God.

incarnated logos. The personal *dao* takes the form of flesh and blood, wear and tear. "In the *dao* was *life,* and the *life* was the light of humanity" (Jn 1:4). Two favorite words John uses in the Gospel are *ginoskō* (know) and *alētheia* (truth). Truth is equivalent to wisdom in John's Gospel, personified wisdom with which one can interrelate. To know is to embrace and be embraced by the embodied truth as one enters into that I-thou relationship. So the *dao* was "full of grace and truth" (Jn 1:14); "grace and truth came through Jesus Christ" (Jn 1:17).

3. If the creative-*dao* Christ speaks of theological creativity, the wisdom-*dao* speaks of incarnated personhood, then the rhetorical-*dao* speaks of communal dialogue, since the universe is a communicative life-world, not an isolated island. Jesus is the rhetorical *dao*, as the Chinese Catholic Bible translates: "In the beginning was the speech [Protestant Bible in Chinese uses *dao*]." The creation is more than *ex nihilo* (out of nothing); it is also a creation of meaning from meaninglessness via God's saying, "Let there be . . ." God created the orderly universe (cosmos) by means of word-speech.

Jesus is the Word of God that makes sense of human language. Jesus is the rhetoric of God that allows the Holy One and human beings to communicate with him. Jesus manifests God by means of what he says. The direct speech of Jesus in John's Gospel is imperative because the reve-

lation of this *dao*-Christology of God is happening on Jesus' own lips. So the self-claim of Jesus ("I am the . . .") is unique to the Johannine Gospel.[14]

John is aware that while words have their creativity, they also have limitations. When the limitation of words is evidenced, silence is used in John (e.g., Jn 8:24: "If you [pl.] do not believe 'I am,' you will die in sin"). The question is: "I am" what? The Greek text is silent.[15] Words cannot really express and reveal who "I AM" is.[16] That words cannot really express who God is does not mean that speech is useless. It is all the more necessary to use words. John, the master of language, uses irony, metaphor, and dialogue as ways to transcend the limitations of language. That richness of *dao*-speech is reflected in *Daode Jing* (the scripture of Daoism by Laozi).[17]

Although language has its limitations, it still is the best medium by which to express the mystery of the unknown and to be in constant conversation with truth within a community. The Johannine Jesus is in constant conversation with God and people: Jesus' conversation with Nicodemus on being "born again," with the unnamed Samaritan woman concerning the living water, and with the Jews concerning the "Wonder Bread." Jesus talks to God the Father in John 17, which is truly the Lord's Prayer. The rhetorical *dao* reveals the truth by telling, praying, and listening to truth. He is the truth (Jn 14:6), but few

---

[14]I am the bread of life (Jn 6:35-40); I am the light of the world (Jn 8:12; 9:15); I am the good shepherd (Jn 10:11); I am the gate (Jn 10:7); I am the resurrection (Jn 11:20-27); I am the way, the truth, and the life (Jn 14:6); I am the true vine (Jn 15:1).

[15]Erroneously, some of the English and Chinese translations say, "If you do not believe I am the Christ" or "If you do not believe I am he"; that addition of "the Christ" or "he" is unwarranted. Silence is a better expression here.

[16]Also, the twofold ending of John, Jn 20:30 and Jn 21:25, hints at the same meaning. John 20:30, "Jesus did many signs . . . that are written in this book," and Jn 21:25, "so many other things that Jesus did if recorded in the books, the world could not contain them," are not stating the obvious; they are the acknowledgment that Jesus the Word of God cannot fully be expressed by our words. Thus, Jesus is the Great "I AM" mentioned in Ex 3:14 ("I am who I am").

[17]"The *dao* that can be told of is not the eternal *dao;*
    The name that can be named is not the eternal Name.
    The Nameless is the origin of Heaven and Earth;
    The Named is the mother of all things" (*Daode Jing,* chap. 1).

seem to know the truth.[18] When the Spirit of truth (Jn 14:17; 15:26) comes, "he will guide us into all the truth" (Jn 16:14).

The *logos-dao* Christology of John 1:1-5 reminds us of the passion and boldness of John to communicate the gospel of Jesus Christ cross-culturally. He dares to work with the biblical text (Hebrew Scripture) together with the Greek philosophical tradition of his time. And those who follow in John's footsteps, as the ones who translate the Bible into other local languages, will discover unique Christologies in the vernaculars of people all over the world.

CHINESE CHRISTOLOGY (*RENREN*) AND CONTEXTUAL-GLOBAL *IMAGO DEI* CHRISTOLOGIES: CHRIST(OLOGIES) AS THE IMAGE(S) OF GOD

The most challenging issue in christological discussion across cultures is the contesting soteriologies (work of Christ), and thus the competing Christologies, especially in the heated milieus of religious claims.[19] Many essays in this volume wrestle with this aspect of Christology (Ezigbo's discussion on African theology; Mbuvi's discussion on the missionary denigration of African religion; Gener on Asian plurality of religions), differing only in degree.

We believe that Jesus comes not to abolish the old but to fulfill and to renew it. This is true of the Jewish law and of cultural ideals as well. My task is to offer a Christian Chinese Christology (and

soteriology) that explains Jesus as the fulfillment of the Confucian ideal of "being human" (*ren*).[20]

Confucius's "soteriological concern" is that people do not know how to coexist together, and that the government-politic has used force to alienate citizens, that rituals (*li*) make us fallen, and music (*yue*) that beautifies our souls is corrupted. According to Confucius, the greatest cultural danger is that people thought they could love God without loving people. So Confucius teaches people to actualize the mandate of heaven (*Tianming*) by committing themselves to love (*ren* = human-relatedness), for what makes human beings (*ren*) is love (*ren*; see *Analects* 12:22), thus the term *renren* (who love). The similar biblical concept is love (*agapē*). *Ren* (love) is not simply a psychological term related to the ontological aspect of human beings; rather, it is inclusive of virtue or spiritual condition.[21] *Ren* (love) connotes all the moral qualities that govern relationships among people, thus human-relatedness has love as the cardinal principle.[22] In other words, to be a *renren* is to express and to participate in the holy as a dimension of all truly human existence. "Virtue does not exist in isolation; there must be neighbors," says Confucius (*Analects* 4:25). "In order to establish oneself, one helps others to establish themselves; in order to enlarge oneself, one helps others to enlarge themselves" (*Analects* 6:28). Therefore, the lostness of humanity is primarily brokenness, isolation, and dehumanization. Thus (here I am

---

[18] As Pilate asks, "What is truth?" (Jn 18:38). Truth is to be located in theological discourse. Jesus tells Pilate that the rhetorical *dao* came into the world "to bear witness to the truth" and that "every one who is of the truth" hears his voice (Jn 18:37). Jesus prays that the Father may sanctify his followers in the truth, for his "word is truth" (Jn 17:17, 19).

[19] For various views on the relationship between Christianity and other religions, see John Hick and Brian Hebblethwaite, eds., *Christianity and Other Religions, Selected Readings* (Philadelphia: Fortress, 1981).

[20] See K. K. Yeo, "Christian Chinese Theology: Theological Ethics of Becoming Human and Holy," in *Global Theology in Evangelical Perspective: Exploring the Contextual Nature of Theology and Mission*, ed. Jeffrey P. Greenman and Gene L. Green (Downers Grove, IL: IVP Academic, 2012), 102-15.

[21] Herbert Fingarette, *Confucius: The Secular as Sacred* (New York: Harper & Row, 1972), 37-38. Mencius says, "Human-heartedness [*ren*] is the mind of human beings; righteousness is the path of human conducts" (6a, 11).

[22] Fung Yulan, *A Short History of Chinese Philosophy*, ed. and trans. Derk Bodde (New York: Macmillan, 1948), 69-73.

going beyond the Confucian anthropology and soteriology toward that of a Christian, or better still, a Christian Chinese anthropology), the salvation Jesus offers and epitomizes is that of wholeness and worthiness of humanity—human beings are created *as* the image of God (1 Cor 11:7; Jas 3:9). Humans represent God in managing the earth and reflecting God's glory in the world (they are the light of the world).[23] Jesus has revealed for us what it means to be fully human, in his being both with God and with people. Jesus' openness and empathy toward sinners, outcasts, the separated, the disowned, and the rejected reveal the extent of his full divinity encountering his full humanity. Christ is fully human, and together in one person he *is* also the *imago Dei* (Col 1:15; Heb 1:3) who lives and gives his life totally for others and for God, not himself. In doing so, he has not lost but has fully encountered himself and the triune God.[24]

New Testament Christology has no problem understanding Jesus *as* the *imago Dei*, but speaking of human beings, the Hebrew preposition *bet* in the Old Testament texts (Gen 1:26-27; 5:1-3; 9:6) is often translated as "in" (God has an image and we are created *in* his image, or *has* his image) rather than as "as" or "in the capacity of" (God has no image of his own other than we, being created *as* his image).[25] I take David Cline's view (*as* rather than *in*), but I explain the content of image as relationship with God (thus dwelling in God's Spirit-presence) and among people (thus communion-friendship with others in order to be fully human). The function of such relationships is to represent God.[26] The first dimension of *imago Dei* is reflected in humanity's corporeal-animated creatureliness that encounters God, his word, and his presence. It is that gifted ability to enter into relationship with God (with all we are—mind, heart, soul, will, body) that allows humans creatures *to be* God's image in the world.[27] Second, the image of God as seen in the creation account, with the clause "male and female he created them," not only emphasizes that both male and female are created "as our image" and "as our likeness," but also explains "image" and "likeness" as the social self (or *co*humanity of male and female in the first *pair* of humanity) relating and encountering each other toward psychosomatic wholeness, intimacy-fulfillment, and glory-dignity.[28]

The human predicament is that one tends to live apart from God's presence (not for God's glory) and subsequently lives a narcissistic life that leads to losing one's self (Mt 10:39; Lk 9:24; Jn 12:25). The alienation between I and self, between self and other, between other and the world, between humanity and God is called the distortion or corruption of the *imago Dei*. That constitutes sin, falling short of the glory of God (Rom 3:23). Jesus is the Christ precisely because in his incarnation, life, death, and resurrection,

[23]The image (Hebrew *tselem*, Greek *eikōn*, Latin *imago*) and likeness (Hebrew *demuth*, Greek *homoiosis*, Latin *similitudo*) of God is the ideal-fully human mentioned in the Bible (Gen 1:26; 5:2; 9:6) having similar denotations of royal lordship (Ps 8:5; see Heb 2:6-8), esteem (rather than as slaves to gods, as some ancient Near Eastern creation myths propose), and physico-spiritual uniqueness (immanence representative of the transcendent Creator God on earth) as that of Confucian understanding of ideal man (*junzi*). On the Genesis text, see Claus Westermann, *Genesis 1–11: A Commentary*, trans. John J. Scullion (London: SPCK, 1984), 146; on human beings as "God's vice-regent on earth," see Gordon J. Wenham, *Genesis 1–15* (Waco, TX: Word, 1987), 31.
[24]"In Christ there is no male or female" (Gal 3:28). This does not speak of unisexuality in Christ but of the equality of male and female. See also Martínez-Olivieri's and Spencer's essays in this part of the volume.
[25]The latter view is that of David Cline; see his "The Image of God in Man," *Tyndale Bulletin* 19 (1968): 53-103.
[26]See also Karl Barth, *Church Dogmatics* (Edinburgh: T&T Clark, 1958), III/1, 197-98.
[27]See Claus Westermann, *Genesis 1–11: A Commentary*, trans. John J. Scullion (Minneapolis: Augsburg, 1984), 156.
[28]See Hans Walter Wolff, *Anthropology of the Old Testament*, trans. Margaret Kohl (London: SCM Press, 1974), 159. As Cline writes, "It is the *homo* [*human*], not the *animus* or the *anima*, that is the *imago Dei*" (Cline, "Image of God," 86).

he lives fully *as* the *imago Dei* (2 Cor 4:4; Col 1:15) and thus reconciles and restores the broken *imago Dei* to be the new humanity-creation (Rom 8:29; Eph 2:15; 4:22-24; Col 3:9-11) for us. Human beings as created as the *imago Dei* does not mean that they are divine beings. Rather, humans are always *creatures* of God because the inbreathing of God's breath-Spirit, thus making the human "a living *nephesh*," does not make the human a divine being. For humans do not possess a divine part (spirit); Cline writes: "Breath is not a 'part' of man, but the principle of vitality itself, which remains in God's possession and may be withdrawn by Him as He pleases."[29] But Christians living as the new humanity are being changed into the likeness of Christ from one degree of glory to another (2 Cor 3:18). Ezigbo is correct when he says, "Theologians need the vision of other theologians . . . to successfully imagine, understand, and appreciate the breadth, width, and length of the person and significance of Jesus Christ (Eph 4:12-13)."

The "fully human" language in both Confucian ethics and biblical Christology emphasizes complete love for others (Rom 13:8). Jesus can complete salvation because he is fully God *and* fully human. Only the fully divine, who is infinitely righteous and glorious, can forgive infinite sin against God and cover the infinite shame and curse against human beings themselves: namely, that we have fallen short of God's glory. Through the power of righteousness, justice, and glory, only the fully human Jesus can restore and save "less than human" humanity from the power of sin. Thus the unity of Jesus' divinity and humanity is God's work of reconciliation based on Jesus' faithfulness and love. The divine can enter the sphere of humanity and

become "fully human," *yet* Jesus is *still fully divine*, and eschatologically, the "all in all" (1 Cor 15:28; Gal 3:28; Eph 1:23; Col 3:10). No human being can be fully divine and "all in all," but the unity-communion we (the fully human) can have with God (the fully divine) is a divine gift and invitation to us all.

Christ manifests the I-Thou relationship with God and with people most perfectly. This line of thought is close to Confucius's understanding of the transcendence of heaven, best known in its representation of immanence in ethical life. It is the virtue of human beings that reveals the beauty, order, and sacredness of heaven. The mandate of heaven has endowed us and is calling us to be moral-spiritual selves, to thankfully receive God's indwelling Spirit in us. As God's image, we are summoned "to live as God's representative within creation, that is, to be that image through whom God's presence and self-manifestation in creation may be found."[30]

CONCLUSION

As God's image, we are called to be free expressions and diverse representations of our oneness with God, with one another, and harmony with God's world, just as the global church should be. Indeed, as God's image, we the new humanity in Christ are moving to the eschatological reality of the glorified church by virtue of the Lamb of God, the Alpha and the Omega. Christ makes sense of all our theologies, including our Christologies. The God of the Bible is Christlike; creation has Christ as the firstborn, and humanity created as God's image is re-created as *imago Christi*. God's world, after all, is not anthropocentric but Christocentric—in creation, redemption, and consummation.

---

[29]Cline, "Image of God," 89.

[30]Stanley J. Grenz, "Jesus as the *Imago Dei*: Image-of-God Christology and the Non-linear Linearity of Theology," *Journal of the Evangelical Theological Society* 47 (2004): 623.

FURTHER READING

Brown, Raymond E. *An Introduction to New Testament Christology*. Mahwah, NJ: Paulist, 1994.

Cosgrove, Charles, Herold Weiss, and K. K. Yeo. *Cross-Cultural Paul: Journeys to Others, Journeys to Ourselves*. Grand Rapids, MI: Eerdmans, 2005.

England, John C., and Archie C. C. Lee, eds. *Doing Theology with Asian Resources, Ten Years in the Formation of Living Theology in Asia*. The Programme for Theology and Culture in Asia 1983–1993. Auckland, New Zealand: Pace, 1993.

Guanghu, He, and Daniel H. N. Yeung, eds. *Sino-Christian Theology Reader*. 2 vols. Hong Kong: Institute of Sino-Christian Studies, 2009.

Kärkkäinen, Veli-Matti. *Christology: A Global Introduction*. Grand Rapids, MI: Baker Academic, 2003.

Patte, Daniel, et al., eds. *Global Biblical Commentary*. Nashville: Abingdon, 2004.

Pelikan, Jaroslav. *Jesus Through the Centuries: His Place in the History of Culture*. New Haven, CT: Yale University Press, 1999.

Yeo, K. K. *Musing with Confucius and Paul: Toward a Chinese Christian Theology*. Eugene, OR: Cascade Books, 2008.

THE SPIRIT OVER THE EARTH

Part Three

PNEUMATOLOGY IN THE MAJORITY WORLD

INTRODUCTION TO PART THREE

PNEUMATOLOGY IN THE MAJORITY WORLD

Gene L. Green

THE HOLY SPIRIT IN SCRIPTURE AND CHRISTIAN THEOLOGY THROUGH HISTORY

"In the beginning God created the heavens and the earth. Now the earth was formless and empty, darkness was over the surface of the deep, and the Spirit of God was hovering over the waters" (Gen 1:1 NIV). The biblical story begins with God. He is the Creator of all things, and the divine Spirit is his active agent to bring order to chaos.[1] Throughout Scripture the biblical authors have also viewed the Holy Spirit as God's agent to empower human beings for work, especially as they become his prophets who express his will (Heb 3:7-11; 1 Pet 1:10-12; 2 Pet 1:20-21). We learn from these authors that the Spirit empowered Jesus for his ministry in fulfillment of Isaiah's messianic prophecy (Lk 4:16-21; see Is 61:1-2). Upon his ascension, Jesus gave the church the Holy Spirit so that his people could carry out the work he ordained (Acts 1:6-8; 2:32-36). Scripture ascribes these and other roles to the Holy Spirit, and the church through the centuries has reflected on its teaching regarding the person and work of the Spirit of God.

After the New Testament era, discussion about the Spirit continued in earnest as the church sought to articulate the nature of God and the relationship between the Father, Son, and Holy Spirit. The Cappadocian fathers—Basil of Caesarea, Gregory of Nyssa, and Gregory of Nazianzus—vigorously defended the Spirit's divinity as they recognized and described the trinitarian foundation of Christian theology. The Nicene Creed (325) affirmed the church's belief in the Holy Spirit as the third member of the Trinity. The Council of Constantinople (381) reiterated Nicaea's affirmation of the Spirit's divinity and then elaborated on the nature and role of the Holy Spirit in this way:

> We believe in the Holy Spirit, the Lord, the
> Giver of Life,
> who proceeds from the Father and the Son.
> With the Father and the Son
> he is worshiped and glorified.
> He has spoken through the Prophets.

Although the Eastern and Western churches have debated the question of whether the Spirit proceeds from both the Father and the Son, they

---

[1]Not all biblical commentators would identify the "Spirit of God" as the "Holy Spirit." While a context-sensitive exegesis of the passage may lead to the conclusion that the author of Genesis is speaking about the wind (*ruach*) of God, later Christian interpreters have read the passage within the context of the canon and Christian theology and so identify God's *ruach* (which may also be translated "Spirit") as the third person of the Trinity.

are in entire agreement that the Holy Spirit is divine and personal. While the Western church's belief in the procession of the Spirit from both the Father and the Son may seem to imply the subordination of the Spirit to the other members of the Trinity, the church affirmed that the Spirit's divinity was on a par with that of the Son and the Father. The Holy Spirit and the Son are not "derived Deities" despite the begetting of the Son and the procession of the Spirit.[2] Another way to articulate this is to say that the Father, Son, and Holy Spirit are consubstantial, that is, of the same and not similar substance.

At the same time, Athanasius carefully distinguished the Spirit from creation. In his *Letter to Serapion*, Athanasius celebrates the full divinity of the Spirit, saying, "For as the Son, who is in the Father and the Father in him, is not a creature but pertains to the essence of the Father . . . so also it is not lawful to rank with the creatures the Spirit who is in the Son, and the Son in him, nor to divide him from the Word and reduce the Triad to imperfection" (1.21). The Holy Spirit is not a creature but a full member of the divine Triad.

While the fathers were carefully working out the question of the being of the Spirit in relationship to the other members of the Trinity and creation, they also reflected on the Spirit's agency. Nicea states that he is the sovereign "Lord" and that all life has its source in him, "the Giver of Life." Moreover, "He has spoken through the Prophets." The Spirit has a particular role in revelation, which, in the creed, is tied tightly to the prophets. Additionally, the creed points in the direction of the church, since following the "third article" it confesses: "We believe in one holy catholic and apostolic church." Ecclesiology and pneumatology cannot be drawn asunder since it is through the Spirit's agency that Christ establishes his church.

With each succeeding generation the church's understanding of the person and work of the Holy Spirit has deepened and widened, becoming a great and powerful river at the end of the twentieth and the beginning of the twenty-first century.[3] Although the creed makes critical affirmations regarding the person and work of the Holy Spirit, it hardly reflects the whole of the biblical witness and does not answer many questions that have arisen in the church's long march up to this day. During the medieval period attention was drawn to the experience of the Holy Spirit. The mystics held the day, but for them this experience was the privilege of those set apart for the religious life. We find, for example, Bernard of Clairvaux (1090–1153) in the monastery, where he wrote *Sermons on the Song of Songs*, which promotes the devotional life, regarded as "a gift of the Holy Spirit." Thomas Aquinas (1225–1274) entered a Benedictine monastery and later became a member of the Dominican Order of Friars. In a life given over to theology and devotion he affirmed that the Holy Spirit is love, proceeds in love, and distributes his gifts accordingly. With the dawn of the Reformation, however, Luther's understanding of the "priesthood of all believers" opened the door to understanding how the Spirit works for sanctification in every Christian, not just those devoted to the medieval conception of the spiritual life. The Reformers emphasized the Spirit's role in relation to the Word and sacraments, whereas

---

[2]Thomas F. Torrance, *The Trinitarian Faith: The Evangelical Theology of the Ancient Catholic Church* (Edinburgh: T&T Clark, 1988), 112.
[3]For the history of the doctrine of the Holy Spirit, see Anthony C. Thiselton, *The Holy Spirit—in Biblical Teaching, Through the Centuries, and Today* (Grand Rapids, MI: Eerdmans, 2013); Veli-Matti Kärkkäinen, *The Holy Spirit: A Guide to Christian Theology* (Louisville: Westminster John Knox, 2012).

some Radical Reformers turned to the Holy Spirit as the one who leads the believer, thereby decoupling the Spirit from Word and sacrament.

CONTEMPORARY WESTERN AND MAJORITY WORLD DEVELOPMENTS IN PNEUMATOLOGY

Until recently, Western theology has focused more on Christology and less on the person and work of the Holy Spirit. A turning point came with the rise of Pentecostalism at the start of the twentieth century and Vatican II (1962–1965). The renewed emphasis among Roman Catholics falls on the Spirit's work within the church. *Lumen gentium* begins its ecclesiological reflection by stating, "Christ is the Light of nations. Because this is so, this Sacred Synod gathered together in the Holy Spirit eagerly desires, by proclaiming the Gospel to every creature, to bring the light of Christ to all men, a light brightly visible on the countenance of the Church." On the Protestant side, the rise of Pentecostalism in North America and globally has brought with it laser-focused attention on the empowerment that comes through the Spirit of God, which enables the church to fulfill its role as witness in the world (Acts 1:8). Out of this movement arose a number of notable North Atlantic Pentecostal scholars, including Gordon Fee, Russell Spittler, and Frank Macchia, who emphasize God's presence and power through the Spirit. Non-Pentecostal theologians, such as George-Yves Congar, Jürgen Moltmann, and Wolfhart Pannenberg, have also been deeply concerned with the Holy Spirit and ecclesiology, renewal, and especially life in all its forms.[4]

Unsurprisingly, the church in the Majority Word has begun renewed reflections on the role of the Holy Spirit in the church and in the world. The church in the Majority World is "self-theologizing." That is, it recognizes its responsibility as part of "one holy catholic and apostolic church" to make its own contribution to the universal or Catholic discussion about theology that has unfolded through the ages within the Western and Eastern churches. From within Africa, Christian theologians have embraced a theology of the Spirit that underscores the way he confronts other spiritual powers in the world. The Holy Spirit is part of a power encounter that finds few parallels in the West, where the church has, at times, forgotten Paul's statement that "our struggle is not against flesh and blood, but against the rulers, against the authorities, against the powers of this dark world and against the spiritual forces of evil in the heavenly realms" (Eph 6:12).

Within Asian theologies, the Holy Spirit is not separated from the material world, as is common in Western theology, but is the primary essence of reality. Instead of opposing dichotomies, the Spirit is not outside the world but is "the complementary pair of *yin* and *yang*" that organizes all things.[5] Questions about the role of the Holy Spirit within the complex of religions in Asia is another concern that occupies Asian theologians. In Latin American theology, the place of the Spirit in the community and the social implications of his presence are topics of concern. Although the role of the Spirit in personal transformation and empowerment for ministry receives prime attention within Latin American Pentecostalism, the social dimension of the Spirit's work receives attention among theologians who face the socioeconomic injustices of the region. The church in the Majority World is self-theologizing, and this is abundantly evident in the development of contemporary pneumatology.

---

[4]Thiselton, *Holy Spirit*, 373–419.
[5]Veli-Matti Kärkkäinen, ed., *Holy Spirit and Salvation: The Sources of Christian Theology* (Louisville: Westminster John Knox, 2010), 420.

BIBLICAL AND THEOLOGICAL REFLECTIONS IN THIS SECTION

The authors of this section share a commitment to Scripture as God's Word and recognize that their reading is always from and to a particular place, time, and cultural matrix. Contextualization is inherent in the affirmation that Scripture is truly God's Word that is spoken in human words. The biblical scholars who speak in these pages—Zakali Shohe, Hua Wei, Samuel Ngewa, and René Padilla—all reflect on the biblical text in concert with their particular *Sitz im Leben* (situation in life), which gives rise to fresh questions and insights regarding the Spirit's work as witnessed in the Word. The theologians from the Majority World—Ivan Satyavrata, David Ngong, and Oscar García-Johnson—as well Asian American scholar Amos Yong, who is the author of the opening chapter, all attend to the theological heritage from the West but recognize that the emphases and formulations developed there are not fully adequate to address the theological necessities of their communities. In other words, both the biblical scholars and theologians in this section are connected deeply with Scripture and the tradition, but they also dialogue extensively with their context and their cultures. All theology, and all biblical studies, is contextual. We may embrace this fact without severing ourselves from Scripture or tradition. Indeed, the insights the authors present benefit the whole church since they are vital contributions to a genuinely catholic theology. Theology through the centuries has always been contextual. While we may read the ABCs of theology—Augustine, Barth, and Calvin—we always need to recognize that the theological alphabet ends with WYZ—Wei, Yong, and Zakali. And so it must be this side of the es-

chaton, since now we know in part, awaiting that day when we will know even as we are fully known. Dimly reflected revelation will give way to face-to-face clarity (1 Cor 13:9-12). Until that time we need one another, the voices of brothers and sisters through the centuries, and those who come to all of us from around the globe. We always get by with a little help from our friends. A few notes about each of the authors and chapters may help as you read along the grain of their concerns and questions that are related to the context of their reading and reflection.

Amos Yong is a familiar voice to anyone reading in the area of contemporary pneumatology. In his chapter he briefly surveys both the Western and Eastern Orthodox traditions regarding the Spirit before providing an overview of some Majority World pneumatology. The brilliance of Yong's chapter is that he ties the traditions together with global developments while, at the same time, reflecting on their connection with the Nicene Creed. Of particular interest is his emphasis on life through the Spirit and its implications for our understanding of God's agency in creation. He stands, along with Majority World theologians, in opposition to Enlightenment-inspired dualism that would want to preserve a sharp divide between spirit and matter. His concern is to show "the immanence of the divine breath within the fabric of created materiality." In this he speaks as an Asian American theologian.

Ivan Satyavrata brings us into the heart of pneumatological reflection from India. In a world where the influence of *advaitic* Hinduism is pervasive, he takes pains to underscore that the Holy Spirit should not be "confused with the human spirit," or be viewed as "an impersonal, immanent force." He closely links the Holy Spirit with Christ—he is the Spirit *of Christ*. The themes here are familiar to anyone reading the Fathers, but the turn comes in his dialogue between the biblical witness and the "personalist *bhakti* strand within Hinduism," which he sees as offering "much more promise for Christian contextual engagement in India." In other words, he finds resonances between the early Christian emphasis on the personality of the Spirit and a devotional strain within Hinduism. As he says, "the Holy Spirit is a means by which God makes his personal presence felt among his people, the church, the community of the Spirit." He ties his argument up with Christology in stating, "the ultimate purpose of the Spirit's floodlight ministry is to mediate the presence of the risen Christ, and to create and deepen an awareness of the reality of Jesus in human experience." His emphasis on personal relation and Christology melds historic theological orthodoxy with contextual insights. The seriousness with which he takes cultural influences derived from Hinduism in his theological reflection is characteristic of much Majority World theology. Cultural perspectives can be both critiqued and affirmed in this dance with Scripture and tradition.

Zakali Shohe writes from the Indian context as well, with special attention to Nagaland in northeast India. She examines the role of the Spirit in Romans 8:14-17 from a relational perspective and draws out the significance of this passage for both Christians and society in India. The Spirit allows the believer to use the filial address "Abba Father," thus identifying all believers as coheirs with Christ. For her, life in the Spirit is not about power but relationship. This Spirit-inspired relationship is a manifestation of the eschatological unity of God's people. Relationship and unity inspired by the Spirit lead to acceptance of the other. But Shohe is not content to stop at the doors of the church. While under-

standing that the church has not lived up to its full reality in the Spirit, she boldly states that, as unified community, "the church as an institution needs to be a model of openness by taking initiative in bridge building and creating platforms for meeting points." In other words, the church is an eschatological sign to the wider community, and this relationality is part of Christian witness and social renewal. Shohe sees a much broader role for the Spirit than personal piety and powerful evangelistic campaigns. Social hopes are tied to the Spirit's work.

Wei Hua writes from a Chinese perspective on one of the enduring problems of Christianity in his country. How should Christians respond to the rites of ancestors and Confucius? After detailing the history of the controversy, Hua explains the meaning of these rites, understanding that they "have many dimensions, and these dimensions are clearly intertwined." He vigorously denies that due reverence is the same as idolatry, which both Confucius and he reject. The surprise in his chapter comes as he examines 1 Corinthians 8–10, where Paul reflects on the practice of eating meat offered to idols. May one participate in these rites? Hua proposes that the answer Paul gives is not a simple *yes* or *no*, as even a casual reading of 1 Corinthians reveals. This biblical reflection undergirds his discussion of the rites issue. Hua does not simply present a facile comparison between China and Corinth. He understands within Christian practice, both then and now, a fulfillment and renewal of culture. Thus, he concludes, "Just as the Jewish law had been fulfilled in the power of the Spirit by Gentile Christians, and the Roman customs had been renewed in Paul's time, so also the Chinese commemorating rights can be renewed and obeyed by Chinese Christians as 'humanizing' etiquette (*li*) in the power of the Holy Spirit, who moves and works through all believers." Hua, as other Majority World biblical scholars and theologians, is struggling and thinking deeply about how Christianity and culture can critically coexist so that the gospel becomes truly contextualized and is not seen as a foreign entity but as the fulfillment of hopes. His desire in the end is expressed in the final prayer: "May the Spirit of God help the global church in China not to be Christianity *in China*, but to be *Chinese* Christianity." He is able to get to this point because he understands that Christian identity is wrapped around the reception of the Holy Spirit. Christian *koinonia* is possible within a diverse community, one that includes Jews, Gentiles, and Chinese, without the dissolution of their cultures.

Samuel M. Ngewa brings his biblical expertise to bear on the work of the Holy Spirit in Acts 2; 8; 10; 19. Like Shohe, he focuses on inclusion as he discusses the Spirit's work among Samaritans, Gentiles, and those who reside in the ends of the earth. "What God seems to be doing in the book of Acts" is "bringing people of all races and nations under the same umbrella." In Acts that inclusion is not tied with ethnicity—Jews, Samaritans, and Gentiles all gather together due to the work of the Spirit. While he celebrates the way that the Spirit brings together those of different ethnicities, Ngewa asks why it was that the location of the East African Revival, Rwanda, succumbed to genocide. "The unfortunate thing," he says, "is that even persons who claimed to be Christians were involved in such killings. These serve as examples of many such conflicts all over the continent of Africa and beyond. Even within the church itself, there have been deep conflicts, with some of them centering on such matters as speaking in tongues and other such dramatic gifts of the Holy Spirit." Ngewa's essay is a realistic plea for the church to

model and live the realities of its faith: one God for all the races of the world, one Savior, the same Spirit, and one family of God. And so he concludes, "All divisions on the basis of race, tribe, or the like have no place in the church of Christ." He understands that perceptions must be changed by God. The Spirit's presence should break down prejudice wherever it occurs.

David Tonghou Ngong traces the development of a Christian theology of the Spirit in Africa, beginning with the North African theologians. He, along with other African Christians, wants the global church to remember that the most significant trinitarian reflection came out of North Africa. He urges that the African church move beyond simply emphasizing the function of the Holy Spirit to examining the place of the Spirit in the Trinity, as did the early North African theologians. Ngong reflects on the Pentecostalization of African Christianity with its concomitant emphasis on pneumatology. He wants to draw together Nicea and contemporary African theology while at the same time rejecting Western Enlightenment rationalism. As part of this concern, Ngong notes that African cosmology is not otherworldly but deeply connected with life as it is lived here and now. For him, theology is worked out on the road of life, but this does not divorce him from the Nicene Creed. In his discussion of African spirituality, he focuses on experience through the power of the Spirit and the transformative function of the Spirit. He emphasizes the belief in the existence of spirits and notes that it is not a superstition but rather a reality that can only be confronted via the power of the Spirit through Jesus Christ. Moreover, spirituality is not simply a question of the believer's individual life but for the community and, indeed, the whole of society. Human flourishing that comes through the

Spirit is communal and is connected to threats to its survival. His chapter ends with a question about religious pluralism in Africa, a theme taken up by García-Johnson as well.

Oscar García-Johnson pens what will be, for many readers of this volume, one of the most challenging chapters. Western theology commonly reflects on general and special revelation, with its overriding emphasis being on God's revelation through Christ and Scripture. But the affirmation of general revelation brings with it entailments not often discussed in the West. Within African Christianity the question often arises: "Did God bring the missionaries to Africa, or did the missionaries bring God?" If we respond that God brought the missionaries to Africa, the question becomes: "Where, then, was God before the missionaries came?" García-Johnson presses the question within the frame of colonial theology. Was there a presence of the Spirit in the Americas before the colonial era? In answering the question, he moves toward seeing the Spirit outside the gate and, in doing so, wishes to uncover an indigenous theology of the Spirit. He reminds us of Melchizedek, Abraham, Balaam, and Paul's quotation of a Greek poet at the Athenian Areopagus (Acts 17) as he tries to trace out the "pneumatological continuity" between the preconquest and postconquest communities of the Americas.

García-Johnson takes a journey into ancestral folk traditions in the Americas. While he does not examine theological trends within contemporary indigenous communities in Central and South America, this could well be a further stage of reflection. While objecting to the West being the *locus theologicus* par excellence, he affirms the Nicene Creed since "early Christian teachers emphasize the Spirit as a Revealer and Giver of Life." The concern expressed here is one every reader needs to take with the utmost seriousness. Does the gospel come into culture as an alien entity, or has God prepared the way, given perspectives, and raised expectations, which are then fulfilled in the gospel? The colonial mentality is one that see the gospel as a conquering and pulverizing force over indigenous peoples and beliefs. The consequence of this perspective has been the devastation of indigenous communities across the Americas, which lost life, land, and culture due to misconceived notions of Christian mission. García-Johnson, as a Central American, pushes back against that heritage and attempts to re-envisage the wideness of God's agency while not losing hold of Christ and his centrality.

The final chapter of this anthology comes from one of the senior statesmen of Majority World theology, C. René Padilla. Since the first Lausanne Conference in 1974, Padilla has been a leader in the development of Latin American evangelical theology. That theology, which developed parallel to and is not derivative from liberation theology, places special emphasis on *misión integral* (integral mission). The gospel of Christ is the in-breaking of the kingdom, or the rule of God through both word and deed. As such, the gospel is transformative not only for the life of the individual or the gathered community of believers, but also for society as a whole. In his chapter, Padilla emphasizes the work of the Spirit "as the source of power for life and hope, especially among the poor." The experience of the Spirit in Latin America, mostly among Pentecostals, occurs in the midst of deep poverty and social oppression. "The mission of the Messiah in the power of the Spirit," Padilla states, "is oriented toward the most vulnerable persons in society: the poor, the prisoners, the blind, the oppressed." So radical was Jesus' ministry among these people that the socioeconomic changes were big enough to be regarded as signs of "the coming of a new era of justice and peace—'the year of the Lord's favor,' the Jubilee year (see Lev 25)—a metaphor of the messianic era initiated in history by Jesus Christ." Those who are swept up by the wind of the Spirit become part of an "empowered, transnational, multilinguistic, intercultural movement for justice." The Spirit empowers the church and allows it "to experience the kingdom of God as a present reality." The values of the kingdom are here present in history in anticipation of that final day when all will be complete.

The authors of these chapters take us on the journey of the Spirit, whose workings are wider than the individual heart. Issues of community and relationality are paramount, often stemming from the relational dimension of the Trinity. The community where the Spirit works is not only the church but also the wider society, both before and after the coming of the gospel. The Holy Spirit is not antithetical to culture, as he both critiques and affirms. Each of these authors deeply appreciates the heritage of Nicaea but understands that the Spirit is restless. There is work to be done in the world, healing and redemptive work, that began in the first moments of creation and continues in the present out to the eschaton. The Spirit was, and is, and will be over all the earth.

■ ■ ■

This section, along with the other sections in this volume, is the product of a strong community effort to facilitate the discussion about emerging Majority World perspectives in biblical studies and theology. We want to thank the authors for their literary contribution and for their willingness to gather in San Diego in November 2014 for the annual meetings of the Evangelical Theological Society and the Institute for Biblical Research (unfortunately, Ngewa and Satyavrata were unable to attend). We are all indebted to the Rivendell Steward's Trust, ScholarLeaders International, and the SEED Research Institute for their financial support and tremendous encouragement. Many of the scholars could not have attended these gatherings without the gracious help these agencies offered. Thanks also goes out to the leadership of the Evangelical Theological Society and the Institute for Biblical Research for creating space for this important discussion about pneumatology. Michael Thomson of Eerdmans has been an indefatigable supporter and counselor all along the way, and, once again, we tip our hats to him. Thanks are also due to Langham Partnership International and Langham Literature for supporting the global publication and distribution of the volumes that originally made up this book. Pieter Kwant of Langham Literature has been an energetic ally, and we offer him our thanks. Jessica Hawthorne, teaching assistant extraordinaire, prepared the indexes. We are all indebted to her. And, as always, we are grateful to God for his answers to prayers so that this global project could move forward. *Soli Deo gloria!*

17

I BELIEVE IN THE HOLY SPIRIT

FROM THE ENDS OF THE EARTH
TO THE ENDS OF TIME

Amos Yong

THE FIRST SECTION of this chapter provides an overview of the broad spectrum of the Christian tradition and highlights the diversity of its pneumatological thinking, especially in the Eastern Orthodox tradition, Majority World theologies of the past century, and modern pentecostal-charismatic movements. Building on such foundations, the second section of the chapter revisits the third article of the Nicene Creed and suggests how such global perspectives can enrich contemporary pneumatological resourcement even as the latter might be disciplined in light of historic Christian commitments.

The doctrine of the Holy Spirit—pneumatology—is experiencing a contemporary renaissance that promises to correct its relative neglect by the classical tradition.[1] Yet the claim that the Spirit historically has been the "shy" or "hidden" member of the Trinity tells us only half the story when assessed in a world Christian context.[2] This chapter revisits the broad spectrum of the Christian tradition and highlights the diversity of its pneumatological thinking, especially in the past century. Such pneumatological pluralism reflects both the many ways in which the divine breath encounters people across space and time and the various modalities through which understanding of such occurs.[3] Contemporary "third article theology"—which refers to the theology of the Spirit (pneumatology) and theology informed by a Spirit-oriented approach (pneumatological theology)—retrieves and elaborates on the third article of the creed both by being anchored in the revelation of God in Christ and by being open to wherever and however the wind of God blows.[4]

This chapter begins descriptively with an overview of pneumatology in a global historical context, and then shifts toward a constructive theology of the Spirit that is simultaneously a theology inspired by the Spirit (pneumatological theology). As a pentecostal theologian,

[1]See Veli-Matti Kärkkäinen, *Pneumatology: The Holy Spirit in Ecumenical, International, and Contextual Perspective* (Grand Rapids, MI: Baker Academic, 2002), 9.

[2]Frederick Dale Bruner and William Hordern, *Holy Spirit: Shy Member of the Trinity* (Minneapolis: Augsburg, 1984).

[3]Nomenclature for the Spirit based on the Hebrew *ruach*—literally "wind" or "breath"—preferred and introduced by Donald L. Gelpi, *The Divine Mother: A Trinitarian Theology of the Holy Spirit* (Lanham, MD: University Press of America, 1984).

[4]See Myk Habets, ed., *The Spirit of Truth: Reading Scripture and Constructing Theology with the Holy Spirit* (Eugene, OR: Pickwick, 2010).

I find inspiration from the New Testament book of Acts, especially in a number of phrases in the early chapters.[5] The narration of Luke, the author, about Peter's day of Pentecost sermon—quoting from the prophet Joel: "God declares, . . . I will pour out my Spirit upon all flesh" (Acts 2:17)—invites consideration of the global character of Christian pneumatological reflection, especially non-Western voices and perspectives.[6] Even before this, Luke records Jesus telling the disciples that they will receive the empowerment of the Spirit to be his witnesses "to the ends of the earth" (Acts 1:8). The Greek in this case, *eschatou tēs gēs*, refers not only to the spatial breadth of the earth but more technically to its temporal ends as well, the ends of the times of the earth, in fact.[7] Both aspects of the Spirit's outpouring—the spatial and the temporal—are reiterated at the end of Peter's day of Pentecost homily, where the gift of the Spirit is promised "for you, for your children, and for all who are far away, everyone whom the Lord our God calls to him" (Acts 2:39).[8] So if the first part of this chapter attempts to document the breadth of pneumatological reflection "upon all flesh," the second section seeks to think creatively with the historical and dynamic deposit of faith, particularly with the Nicene confession about the Spirit, in ways appropriate to the third-millennium global context and beyond.

POURED OUT ON ALL FLESH: PNEUMATOLOGY IN GLOBAL HISTORICAL PERSPECTIVE

This initial mapping proceeds along three lines. I begin with Eastern Christian understandings of the Spirit in order to ensure that this important historic stream is not neglected in any constructive pneumatology for the present time, move on to more recent Majority World perspectives, and conclude with developments in pentecostal-charismatic and renewal theology. Throughout I highlight minority reports on theology of the Spirit in order to gain traction and momentum vis-à-vis the dominant Western pneumatological tradition for when we turn to the second part of this chapter.

Eastern Christian pneumatology. There is no doubt that the achievement of a fully trinitarian orthodoxy, one that speaks not just to the Son's relationship with the Father but also includes the Spirit, would not have been secured apart from the efforts of theologians in the Eastern, or Greek-speaking, church in the fourth century. The Cappadocian fathers—Basil of Caesarea, Gregory of Nyssa, and Gregory of Nazianzus—each played crucial roles in arguing against those who did not believe the Spirit to be divine as the Son and the Father.[9] Against these so-called Spirit-fighters (Greek *pneumatomachians*) from the region of Macedonia, these champions of trinitarian faith followed out the theological logic of the church's

---

[5]Especially relevant for the following is Amos Yong, *The Spirit Poured Out on All Flesh: Pentecostalism and the Possibility of Global Theology* (Grand Rapids, MI: Baker Academic, 2005), among a number of other works that will be cited in due course.

[6]Unless otherwise noted, all Scripture quotations will be from the NRSV. Although perhaps controversial, I believe that the "all flesh" reference includes not only all classes regardless of gender, age, or social status (Acts 2:17-18) but also, potentially and eschatologically, all cultural-linguistic groups (following Acts 2:8-11). For discussion, see my commentary, with Anh Vince Le, "Acts 2," in *Global Bible Commentary Online* (2013), ed. Michael J. McClymond, www.globalbiblecommentary.org/index.html?book=Acts&chapter=2.

[7]See Vitor Westhelle, *Eschatology and Space: The Lost Dimension in Theology Past and Present* (New York: Palgrave Macmillan, 2012), 132.

[8]This line of pneumatological thinking is further exemplified in another of my books: *Who Is the Holy Spirit? A Walk with the Apostles* (Brewster, MA: Paraclete, 2011).

[9]For example, Basil the Great, *On the Holy Spirit*, trans. David Anderson (Crestwood, NY: St. Vladimir's Seminary Press, 1980), and Gregory of Nyssa, "On the Holy Spirit," §§19-26, in *Gregory of Nyssa*, ed. Anthony Meredith (London: Routledge, 1999), 35-45.

hallowed practices of baptism into the triune name and of prayer and worship offered to the Spirit, and insisted that such liturgical commitments sustained over centuries would be invalid apart from the implicit recognition of the Spirit's divine essence and character.[10] Their efforts not only secured creedal elaboration on the deity of the Spirit (at the Council of Constantinople in 381) but also have profoundly affected the main lines of Christian pneumatological reflection even in the Western tradition.

For our purposes, however, it would be a mistake to overlook the distinctive features of early Syriac pneumatology given their shaping of Cappadocian thinking about the Spirit. Second- and third-century Syriac sources clearly delineate the role of the Spirit in the process of Christian initiation.[11] The Spirit is invoked in the prebaptismal anointing of new catechumens, is present to generate faith and active in healing, cleansing, and purifying them through their new birth of baptism in water, and enables their reception of the Messiah in their first Eucharist, thus accompanying their initiation from death to eternal life. While numerous biblical symbols for the Spirit are prevalent in these sources (e.g., the Spirit as fire, dove, or oil), it is the regenerative work of the Spirit that is prominent: to indwell believers, to catalyze new birth and sonship, to sanctify and bring about union with God. For these early Syriac pastors and leaders, then, this life-giving

Spirit stimulated symbolic reflection about a divine motherhood that nurtured, refreshed, and purified human creatures in order that they might participate in the divine nature.[12]

The Eastern emphasis on salvation as union with God and deification has given rise to a distinctive spiritual tradition across the Orthodox world. In this framework the life-giving work of the Spirit includes first and foremost the sanctifying formation of saints, and Pentecost becomes a symbol, then, of a community devoted to the spiritual path of disciplined ascent to the divine presence from the mundane and fallen world of creaturely passions.[13] Yet this tradition of contemplative praxis has also, when explicated with certain intellectual resources informed by philosophical idealism and even gnosticism, opened up to controversial theological developments. The pneumatology of Russian Orthodox thinker Sergei Bulgakov (1871–1944), for instance, set against the backdrop of his Christian divine-humanity and Neo-Platonic sophiology (philosophy of divine wisdom), led to charges of heresy that, although eventually formally absolved, marked his views as at least disconcerting, if not flawed and aberrant.[14] Yet some of Bulgakov's central notions, such as the *kenōsis* of Spirit in creation and the Spirit's gift of love being made available as a continuing Pentecost, resonate with important pneumatological themes both East and West,

---

[10]For a brief overview of the pneumatomachian position, see Stuart George Hall, *Doctrine and Practice in the Early Church* (Grand Rapids, MI: Eerdmans, 1992), 153-54.

[11]See especially the insightful studies of Joseph Chalassery, *The Holy Spirit and Christian Initiation in the East Syrian Tradition* (Rome: Mar Thomas Yogam and St. Thomas Christian Fellowship, 1995); Emmanuel Kaniyamparampil, *The Spirit of Life: A Study of the Holy Spirit in the Early Syriac Tradition* (Kerala, India: Oriental Institute of Religious Studies, 2003); and Sebastian P. Brock, *The Holy Spirit in the Syrian Baptismal Tradition*, 3rd ed., Gorgias Liturgical Studies 4 (Piscataway, NJ: Gorgias, 2008).

[12]Brock, *Holy Spirit*, 176, notes that "in the earliest literature up to about AD 400 the Holy Spirit is always treated grammatically as feminine," and that this applies also to liturgical prayers (i.e., a Trinity of Father, Mother, and Son); this begins to change so that after about the sixth century, *ruah* as masculine predominates except in liturgical and poetic texts.

[13]A Russian Orthodox account is that of I. M. Kontzevitch, *The Acquisition of the Holy Spirit in Ancient Russia*, trans. Olga Koshansky, ed. Abbot Herman (Platina, CA: St. Herman of Alaska Brotherhood, 1988).

[14]Sergius Bulgakov, *The Comforter*, trans. Boris Jakim (Grand Rapids, MI: Eerdmans, 2004).

even as they are both consistent with and arguably intrinsic to Orthodox sensibilities and spiritual life. If Orthodox theologians have by and large prided themselves on retrieving the patristic tradition rather than reconstructing what has been received and handed down from the ecumenical church of the first millennium, Bulgakov is exemplary of those within this Eastern Christian milieu who have attempted to creatively reappropriate inherited resources according to the pneumatological dynamic of a continuing Pentecost.

Nevertheless, Orthodox pneumatology remains largely scriptural in foundation, liturgical in orientation, and poetic in expression. Contemporary Orthodox pneumatologies generally draw from the patristic heritage and attempt biblical articulation in ecumenically relevant categories.[15] Over time, then, the main lines of Orthodox thinking about the Spirit have permeated Latin traditions and contemporary Western theologies so much so that it almost goes without saying that efforts to formulate a pneumatology relevant for the twenty-first-century global context will be deeply shaped by Eastern thought in essential respects.[16] Yet it is important not to take for granted these Orthodox resources that remind us about the feminine dimension of pneumatology as well as the intimate and irrevocable connection between theological ideas and spiritual praxis.

Contemporary trends in the Majority World. If Orthodoxy has contributed distinctively to the texture of pneumatological reflection throughout the Christian tradition, then the emergence of Christianity as a world religion in the twentieth century has extended reflection on the Holy Spirit to the Majority World. The following in no way exhaustively summarizes the state of the discussion—the many gaps of which the rest of this section fills in—but rather highlights a few developments relevant to the constructive task ahead of us. What we will see is that Asian, African, and Latin American developments have the capacity to enrich if not complicate pneumatological thinking for the present time.[17]

The Asian context of course defies summarization, even when it comes to developments in pneumatology. It is not just that there is a diversity of thinking about the Holy Spirit across the Asian continent but also a reconsideration of what vehicles—for example, storytelling, dance, music, drama—best mediate and communicate the Spirit's presence and activity.[18] Nevertheless, the scope of form and content is commensurate: different modalities of experiencing the Spirit lead to a range of pneumatological reflection. Limiting our focus to the Indian subcontinent at this juncture, we can see a spectrum of thinking about the Spirit, from a more traditionalist approach on the one side to more distinctively Indian versions on the other.

[15]Two examples from diverse Orthodox communions include Fr. Tadros Y. Malaty, *The Gift of the Holy Spirit*, The Coptic Orthodox Church and the Dogmas 7 (Cairo: Anba Reuiss; Alexandria: St. Mark and Pope Peter Church, 1991), and John Oliver, *Giver of Life: The Holy Spirit in Orthodox Tradition* (Brewster, MA: Paraclete, 2011).

[16]See, for example, the work of Stanley M. Burgess, whose material in his earlier *The Holy Spirit: Eastern Christian Traditions* (Peabody, MA: Hendrickson, 1989) is incorporated within and effortlessly interwoven into his later *Christian Peoples of the Spirit: A Documentary History of Pentecostal Spirituality from the Early Church to the Present* (New York: New York University Press, 2011).

[17]Note that the following is not intended to be reductionistic in its treatment of Majority World contributions; the selectivity of what follows cannot be justified apart from the anticipated project in the second part of this chapter. For other equally selective but no less helpful overviews of Global South pneumatological developments, see Kärkkäinen, *Pneumatology*, chap. 6, and Veli-Matti Kärkkäinen, ed., *Holy Spirit and Salvation: The Sources of Christian Theology* (Louisville: Westminster John Knox, 2010), chaps. 15-17.

[18]See John C. England and Alan J. Torrance, eds., *Doing Theology with the Spirit's Movement in Asia*, ATESEA Occasional Papers 11 (Singapore: ATESEA, 1991).

On the one hand, more evangelical approaches tend to parallel Western pneumatologies, both in the use of primary biblical and doctrinal categories and in concerns about overemphasis on indigenous sources believed to tend toward syncretism.[19] On the other hand, the search has been underway for more than a century for an authentic Indian theological paradigm, and this has included thinking about matters pneumatological as well. At the forefront of at least this latter trajectory have been Indian theologians such as Aiyadurai Jesudasen Appasamy (1891–1975), Pandipeddi Chenchiah (1886–1959), and Vengal Chakkarai Chettiar (1880–1958), each of whom has attempted to articulate pneumatological realities according to categories derived from Indian cultural, philosophical, and even religious traditions.[20] If the *bhakti* spirituality lends itself to understanding the Holy Spirit in terms of *antaryamin*, referring to the immanent and indwelling divine presence, especially in the soul (Appasamy), then yogic praxis is suggestive of the Spirit as the spiritual power, "supra-mind," and cosmic energy of the new creation (Chenchiah), and the Vedic tradition emphasizes the relationship between the human spirit and the Holy Spirit using *Brahman* notions of *paramatman-atman* (Chakkarai). The latter runs parallel to the efforts of Indian feminist theologians to think about the Spirit in terms of power and of the Vedic *sakti*, the material dimension of *Brahman*, symbolized in *Devi*.[21] The challenge in the Indian context is the monistic underpinnings of Hindu philosophical and contemplative traditions that blur the distinction not only between divine and creaturely spiritual realities but also between the Spirit of the historical Jesus of Nazareth and the more ambiguous spirit of the cosmic (dis- or preincarnate) Christ. So while there is ongoing debate about whether Christian theology in India ought to be Hinduized, the open question persists about the need for specifically Indianized features to be articulated.[22]

The way forward has to be a dialectical conversation between the received historic tradition of orthodox Christianity and Indian thought forms.[23] Approached carefully, *atman*, *antaryamin*, and *sakti* can be understood as "analogous to the Spirit," and in the long run, these notions can potentially "throw light on our understanding of the Holy Spirit and evoke certain hidden aspects of Christ and the Spirit."[24] The discussion has to proceed deliberately and be engaged patiently, however. Theological advances are usually not made overnight.[25]

The call for a more dialogical approach applies not only along the East-West axis, but also

---

[19]See Indian pentecostal theologian Ivan Satyavrata, *The Holy Spirit: Lord and Life-Giver* (Downers Grove, IL: IVP Academic, 2009), including his guarded reaction (in chap. 4) to the by-now-infamous invocation of Korean spirits of *han* by Chung Hyun Kyung at the opening ceremony of the World Council of Churches General Assembly in 1991. For the text of Chung's speech, see her "Come Holy Spirit, Renew the Whole Creation," in *The Ecumenical Movement: An Anthology of Key Texts and Voices*, ed. Michael Kinnamon and Brian E. Cope (Grand Rapids, MI: Eerdmans, 1996), 231-37.

[20]P. V. Joseph, *Indian Interpretation of the Holy Spirit: An Appraisal of the Pneumatology of Appasamy, Chenchiah, and Chakkarai* (Delhi: New Theological College–ISPCK, 2007).

[21]T. Mercy Rani, *Assailants of the Spirit and Upholders of "Sakti": An Indian Feminist Assessment of the Holy Spirit* (Bangalore, India: South Asia Theological Research Institute, 2003).

[22]Joseph, *Indian Interpretation of the Holy Spirit*, 130; see Kirsteen Kim, *Mission in the Spirit: The Holy Spirit in Indian Christian Theologies* (Delhi: ISPCK, 2003).

[23]An example is Christina Manohar, *Spirit Christology: An Indian Christian Perspective* (Delhi: ISPCK, 2009), who interacts with both Western and Indian voices.

[24]Manohar, *Spirit Christology*, 295.

[25]For further discussion of the state of pneumatology in the Indian context, see Ivan Satyavrata's essay in this section.

along the North-South axis. One difference when thinking about African theology in general and pneumatology in particular is that the legacies of Tertullian of Carthage and Augustine of Hippo inform both traditions.[26] The former's time with the charismatic Montanist movement may be of new relevance in the contemporary African context, since what is most pressing on this front is the combination of indigenous spirit-type churches over the past century alongside, amid, and against pentecostal-charismatic movements.[27] Across the continent, then, the kind of Christianity that is most vibrant is pneumatic in sensibility, orientation, and praxis, with manifestations of miracles, exorcism and deliverance, signs and wonders, healings, and other Spirit-related phenomena. Alongside concomitant emphases on being "born again" prevalent in especially pentecostal and charismatic churches, however, there are also extensive concerns about witchcraft, the practice of which is sustained by the African cosmology and worldview. Anxieties about witchcraft hence persist across the spectrum of African Christianity, wherever a pneumatic spirituality is prominent.[28]

If evil spirits remain to haunt the living because of tragic or untimely deaths, the Holy Spirit has been suggested as the "grant ancestor"—alongside the Father as the "proto-ancestor" and the Son as the "great ancestor"—that is, as the "source of a new life, and the fountainhead of Christian living . . . [who] sustains the entire line of humanity by embracing the beginning as well as the end of human spiritual destiny."[29] This is "a kind of pneumatology from below" wherein the divine Spirit retains consanguinity with the living and mediates communication between the human and celestial domains through prayers, rituals, and periodic visitations (i.e., dreams, visions), but yet remains distinct from other ancestor spirits in being eternal in nature (rather than subject to death), in residing within, not just existing external to, human beings, and in sanctifying and enabling the fruit of everlasting life in the image of the "great" and "proto" ancestors.[30] Nevertheless if Western thought spiritualizes, soteriologizes, and eschatologizes the work of the Holy Spirit, African thought focuses on the material, physical, and socioeconomic work of the Spirit as an extension of the blessings of Christ in the present life.

Parallels between African and Latin American pneumatologies derive at least in part from the slave trade. African spirituality arrived in the New World through forced migration, and slave religion merged with indigenous traditions over the next few centuries. Against the backdrop of Roman Catholic saints, a range of ancestor spirits appeared, some more distant from but others more accessible to and engaged with the living.[31] But if African pneumatology

---

[26]Tertullian is a major resource for A. Okechukwu Ogbonnaya, *On Communitarian Divinity: An African Interpretation of the Trinity* (St. Paul, MN: Paragon, 1998).

[27]Both types are delineated and discussed in Allan H. Anderson, *African Reformation: African Initiated Christianity in the Twentieth Century* (Trenton, NJ: Africa World, 2001); see Cecil M. Robeck Jr., *Prophecy at Carthage: Perpetua, Tertullian, and Cyprian* (Cleveland, OH: Pilgrim, 1992).

[28]This includes within the charismatic renewal in African Roman Catholicism; see the discussion of witchcraft, for instance, in Clement Chinkambako Abenguni Majawa, *The Holy Spirit and Charismatic Renewal in Africa and Beyond* (Nairobi: Catholic University of Eastern Africa, 2007), chap. 19.

[29]Caleb Oluremi Oladipo, *The Development of the Doctrine of the Holy Spirit in the Yoruba (African) Indigenous Christian Movement*, American University Studies VII, Theology and Religion 185 (New York: Peter Lang, 1996), 107.

[30]Oladipo, *Development of the Doctrine of the Holy Spirit*, 108.

[31]See Joseph M. Murphy, *Working the Spirit: Ceremonies of the African Diaspora* (Boston: Beacon, 1996); Claude F. Jacobs and Andrew Jonathan Kaslow, *The Spiritual Churches of New Orleans: Origins, Beliefs, and Rituals of an African-American Religion*

has remained this-worldly in the material and existential sense, Latin American thinking about the Spirit has been this-worldly in the sociopolitical sense, especially in the hands of liberation theologians. The latter's spirituality of the poor is, of course, also concerned with the materiality of salvation, but its liberative praxis seeks to change the world and its social, political, and economic structures in cooperation with the divine Spirit, "the start of creation's road back to the Father."[32]

Pneumatology across the global renewal movement. We must also briefly survey pneumatological thinking inspired by the emergence of the global pentecostal and charismatic renewal movement in the twentieth century. If the classical pentecostal theology insisted on a sharp dualism between the good Holy Spirit and demonic local or indigenous spiritual entities, contemporary pentecostal and charismatic thought is more nuanced.[33] Led by the recognized dean of pentecostal studies Walter J. Hollenweger, there is much greater awareness that the effectiveness of pentecostalism as a religion of the Majority World derives at least in part from a spirituality that is contextualizable among indigenous cultures, cosmologies, and worldviews.[34]

If there is a distinct gulf between the Holy Spirit and other spirits in pentecostal theology, the lines are much more blurred in practice, as the "principalities and powers" are never unambiguously good or bad so that healings, miracles, signs and wonders, glossolalia, or manifestations of other so-called spiritual gifts have to be discerned on a case-by-case basis.[35]

Two distinct trajectories of pentecostal pneumatology are noteworthy for our purposes: those crafted by Hispanic theologians and those in search of a global pneumatological theology. The former have engaged, not surprisingly, with liberation-theological themes, urging attentiveness to how pentecostal spirituality and perspective is conducive not only for otherworldly foci but also for this-worldly soteriological concerns.[36] In each case, substantive attention is placed on socioeconomic realities, albeit the approach is informed by a deeply pentecostal and Latino(a)-Hispanic spirituality, one that is affectively shaped and that motivates a distinctive pentecostal orthopathy and orthopraxy. The goal here is not only to theorize or theologize about the Spirit, but also to nurture a pentecostal "social spirituality" through which the divine breath can transform the world.[37]

(Knoxville: University of Tennessee Press, 1991); Samuel Cruz, *Masked Africanisms: Puerto Rican Pentecostalism* (Dubuque, IA: Kendall Hunt, 2005).

[32]José Comblin, *The Holy Spirit and Liberation*, trans. Paul Burns (Maryknoll, NY: Orbis, 1989), 186.

[33]This dualism is arguably of one cloth with "colonial pneumatology," a view of the spirit-world shaped by Enlightenment and Western presuppositions about Majority World cultures; see, for example, J. W. Westgarth, *The Holy Spirit and the Primitive Mind: A Remarkable Account of a Spiritual Awakening in Darkest Africa* (London: Victory, 1946).

[34]Walter J. Hollenweger, *The Pentecostals: The Charismatic Movement in the Churches* (Minneapolis: Augsburg, 1972) and *Pentecostalism: Origins and Developments Worldwide* (Peabody, MA: Hendrickson, 1997); see Harvey G. Cox, *Fire from Heaven: The Rise of Pentecostal Spirituality and the Reshaping of Religion in the 21st Century* (Reading, MA: Addison-Wesley, 1995). On Hollenweger's stature in pentecostal studies, see Lynne Price, *Theology Out of Place: A Theological Autobiography of Walter J. Hollenweger* (London: Sheffield Academic, 2002).

[35]See Allan Anderson, *Moya: The Holy Spirit in an African Context* (Pretoria: University of South Africa Press, 1991); Wilma Davies, *The Embattled but Empowered Community: Comparing Understandings of Spiritual Power in Argentine Popular and Pentecostal Cosmologies* (Leiden: Brill, 2010); and Opoku Onyinah, *Pentecostal Exorcism: Witchcraft and Demonology in Ghana* (Blandford Forum, UK: Deo, 2011). On the importance of spiritual discernment, see Kirsteen Kim, *The Holy Spirit in the World: A Global Conversation* (Maryknoll, NY: Orbis, 2007), chap. 7.

[36]Leading the way are Eldin Villafañe, *The Liberating Spirit: Toward an Hispanic American Pentecostal Social Ethic* (Grand Rapids, MI: Eerdmans, 1993), and Samuel Solivan, *Spirit, Pathos and Liberation: Toward an Hispanic Pentecostal Theology* (London: Bloomsbury T&T Clark, 1998).

[37]On social spirituality, see Villafañe, *Liberating Spirit*, chap. 4.

Asian and African pentecostal pneumatologies are still on the horizon. However, the quest for a global pentecostal theology is well underway, and the major developments along this line are robustly pneumatological in orientation.[38] The emphases here are not only on formulating or extending discussion on the Christian doctrine of the Holy Spirit, but on rethinking Christian theology itself, as well as its constitutive doctrines, from a pneumatological perspective. Hence pneumatological themes are woven into other theological loci, resulting oftentimes in new insight on established doctrines and formulations.[39] The intuition driving these explorations is that the pentecostal and charismatic encounter with the Spirit inspires not only theologies of the Spirit (pneumatology) but also has the capacity to expand thinking toward a more vigorously articulated trinitarian theology.

TO THE ENDS (OF THE TIMES) OF THE EARTH: TOWARD A THIRD-ARTICLE THEOLOGY

This section seeks to press forward in part by looking backward. The goal is to contribute toward a global theology that both builds on the

preceding and thinks pneumatologically with the early church, in particular the third article of the Nicene Creed:[40] "We believe in the Holy Spirit, the Lord and Giver of life, who proceeds from the Father, who with the Father and the Son together is worshiped and glorified, who spoke by the prophets."[41] Each clause of this affirmation will serve as a springboard for engagement with non-Western and Majority World resources in order to sketch the contours of a historically rooted pneumatological theology that is nevertheless relevant for the twenty-first-century world context.

The Lord, the giver of life. That the divine wind is the Spirit of life is clear from the scriptural witness to its bringing forth and sustaining animal and human creaturely breath (Gen 1:30; 2:7; Job 34:14-15; Ps 104:29-30).[42] Yet these ancient Hebraic reflections on the breath of YHWH remain pertinent for Majority World theologians. Amid rapid social change, poverty, injustice, and environmental degradation, the communal-forming, health-giving, interpersonally harmonizing, and ecologically nurturing work of the Spirit is potent, if not actually salvific.[43] Even if some forms of pentecostal and

---

[38]For example, Yong, *Spirit Poured Out on All Flesh*; see also volumes in the Pentecostal Manifestos series published by Eerdmans: Frank D. Macchia, *Justified in the Spirit: Creation, Redemption and the Triune God* (2010); Wolfgang Vondey, *Beyond Pentecostalism: The Crisis of Global Christianity and the Renewal of the Theological Agenda* (2010); and Nimi Wariboko, *The Pentecostal Principle: Ethical Methodology in New Spirit* (2011).

[39]Leading the way in North America has been charismatic Baptist theologian Clark H. Pinnock, *Flame of Love: A Theology of the Holy Spirit* (Downers Grove, IL: InterVarsity Press, 1996); and charting a similar path in the eastern hemisphere is mainline Korean Methodist theologian Jong Chun Park, *Crawl with God, Dance in the Spirit: A Creative Formation of Korean Theology of the Spirit* (Nashville: Abingdon, 1998).

[40]In this respect, the theological methodology at work here resonates with that of Oscar García-Johnson's transoccidentalist approach (see his chapter in this section of the volume), which seeks to bring non-Western voices into the wider theological conversation so far dominated by Western perspectives, but in a way that neither merely displaces the latter nor gives only lip service to the former. As should be clear in what follows, my own proposal involves retrieval of the Western canon within a global context even as I seek to engage with global (non-Western) perspectives from outside the Western theological tradition. The key is to respect the alterity of each even while forging not a third way (which would inappropriately synthesize or syncretize both) but a more enriched harmony of diverse, disparate, and sometimes not altogether coherent accounts.

[41]An exemplary model in this regard is Joel C. Elowsky, ed., *Ancient Christian Doctrine*, vol. 4, *We Believe in the Holy Spirit* (Downers Grove, IL: IVP Academic, 2009).

[42]See also David H. Jensen, ed., *Lord and Giver of Life: Perspectives on Constructive Pneumatology* (Louisville: Westminster John Knox, 2008); Jürgen Moltmann, *The Spirit of Life: A Universal Affirmation*, trans. Margaret Kohl (Minneapolis: Fortress, 1992).

[43]Paul Murray, Diego Irarrázaval, and Maria Clara Bingemer, eds., *Lord and Life-Giver: Spirit Today* (London: SCM Press, 2011).

charismatic emphasis on prosperity theology are unbalanced and the expectation that the Spirit will bring about maximal material health and wealth is unsound, the cries and prayers of the faithful for divine blessing and favor in the present life are both instinctive and in accord with the biblical testimony.[44] The point is that the work of the life-giving Spirit has been understood perennially as having implications for human material well-being and flourishing.

Two theological points are worth noting in this regard. First, the divine Spirit bestows not only new (everlasting, eternal) life but also historical (material, fleshly) life. The life-giving Spirit thereby imbues both spiritual and creaturely vivacity. In contradistinction to the dualism between spirit and matter bequeathed by modern Enlightenment assumptions, Anglican theologian Eugene Rogers has in recent times accentuated just this material dimension of the Spirit's character and work, in conversation with Eastern Christian theological resources.[45] The strength of Rogers's thesis is to highlight the working and resting of the Spirit on bodies, including the materiality of the Spirit's primary modus operandi in the life of Christ: his annunciation, conception, baptism, transfiguration, resurrection, and ascension. Rogers's material pneumatology is thus not materialistic but christological: the identity of the Spirit in the light of Christ is not ethereal but palpable, tangible, and historical. Such a pneumatological construct—

informed not only by the biblical witness but also by the early Syriac emphases on the feminine features of the Spirit—undermines the modernist binary of spirit as opposed to matter and illuminates the immanence of the divine breath within the fabric of created materiality.[46]

The second point to be noted is that the prominence of the Spirit as material and creaturely life-giver begs reconsideration of the relationship between the Spirit of creation and the Spirit of Pentecost. Classical Reformed pneumatology presumes a sharper distinction between the Spirit that gives life and the Spirit who births new life—through justification and especially sanctification—in Christ. This is consistent with the Protestant scholastic *ordo salutis* (order of salvation) that also separates common grace from saving grace, or general revelation from special revelation. Yet even if the regenerative work of the Spirit is not denied, identification of the Spirit as life-giver undermines notions of creaturely life as being bereft of the divine breath.[47] Again, the goal is not to equate the Spirit of creation and of re-creation or Pentecost, but to acknowledge that any hard-and-fast bifurcation between the two goes beyond the scriptural witness.[48] Acknowledgment of the continuity, rather than discontinuity, between the Hebraic wind of YHWH and the apostolic Spirit of Jesus reopens old questions and raises new ones about the relationship between the older and newer covenants, Testaments, and peoples of God.

---

[44]See Katherine Attanasi and Amos Yong, eds., *Pentecostalism and Prosperity: The Socioeconomics of the Global Charismatic Movement*, Christianities of the World 1 (New York: Palgrave Macmillan, 2012).

[45]Eugene F. Rogers Jr., ed., *After the Spirit: A Constructive Pneumatology from Resources Outside the Modern West* (Grand Rapids, MI: Eerdmans, 2005).

[46]The wider scheme of Rogers's agenda includes a theology of sexuality that seeks to move beyond a rigid male-female distinction. One can appreciate the proposed pneumatology without having to agree that male-female is just another type of modernist duality. The way forward is to recognize the biblical normativity of male and female but develop a range of pastoral strategies that are discerning about the challenges attending to the differentiations of human sexuality in the present time.

[47]This is the argument also of John R. Levison, *Filled with the Spirit* (Grand Rapids, MI: Eerdmans, 2009).

[48]As clearly articulated also a generation ago by C. F. D. Moule, *The Holy Spirit* (Grand Rapids, MI: Eerdmans, 1978), 7-12.

Among a number of other tasks, then, a theology of the third article includes a theology of creation. More precisely, what opens up is a pneumatology of creation, even a pneumatology (rather than just theology) of nature itself, since the work of the Spirit not only rests on material bodies but also animates the very dust of the ground if not the stardust of the cosmos.[49] Such a pneumatological and theological vision, however, is not just theoretical but also potentially practical. The liberative, transformative, and salvific work of the life-giving Spirit in this case is not limited to the practice of spiritual disciplines but also includes the deployment of scientific, political, and socioeconomic rationalities in order to effect change and bring about the common good.[50] Hence, when assessed as the Spirit of life, pneumatology opens up to theology's interface with the broad scope of the scientific and anthropological disciplines. Theology of life as an inter- and multidisciplinary undertaking is here fundamentally pneumatological.[51]

Who proceeds from the Father. It is well known that the addition of the *filioque* clause (the Spirit proceeds not only from the Father but also from the Son) by the Roman Church has been a perennial source of dogmatic division between East and West.[52] While there are many implications that follow from retention, or not,

of the *filioque*, for our purposes one important question for pneumatology in the global context relates to how to understand the economies of the Son and the Spirit in relationship to the religious traditions of the world. On one reading, assertion of the *filioque* subordinates the economy of the Spirit to that of the Son and, concomitantly, defines the soteriological work of the triune God ecclesiologically (the church being the body of Christ); in this case, then, any consideration of the religions would either be ecclesiological (subsuming the diversity of religions within the sphere of the church), or without theological warrant altogether. An alternative approach, apart from the *filioque*, insists on the economies of Son and Spirit as related and yet distinct, as the two hands of the Father, to use Irenaeus's metaphor; following this line of thought, if the religions were to be understood in relationship to this pneumatological economy, then their domain would be related to but yet also distinct from that of the church, defined christologically.[53] The need to attend to the world religions on their own terms, not just understand them according to christological or even ecclesiological categories, is what motivates this proposal. Simultaneously, application of the Irenaean metaphor of the two hands of the Father to the theology of religions not only risks

[49]For example, Amos Yong, *The Spirit of Creation: Modern Science and Divine Action in the Pentecostal-Charismatic Imagination*, Pentecostal Manifestos 4 (Grand Rapids, MI: Eerdmans, 2011); see Native North American theologians such as Randy Woodley, *Shalom and the Community of Creation: An Indigenous Vision* (Grand Rapids, MI: Eerdmans, 2012), and Terry LeBlanc, "New Old Perspectives: Theological Observations Reflecting Indigenous Worldviews," in *Global Theology in Evangelical Perspective: Exploring the Contextual Nature of Theology and Mission*, ed. Jeffrey Greenman and Gene L. Green (Downers Grove, IL: IVP Academic, 2012), 165-79.

[50]David Tonghou Ngong, *The Holy Spirit and Salvation in African Christian Theology*, Bible and Theology in Africa 8 (New York: Peter Lang, 2010), makes this argument in the African context, especially vis-à-vis pentecostal churches, urging embrace of spiritual, material, and scientific means to respond to the poverty widespread across the African continent. See also his chapter in this part of the volume for a briefer treatment of pneumatology in an African context.

[51]See Wolfgang Vondey, ed., *The Holy Spirit and the Christian Life: Historical, Interdisciplinary, and Renewal Perspectives*, CHARIS: Christianity and Renewal—Interdisciplinary Perspectives 1 (New York: Palgrave Macmillan, 2014).

[52]The classic defense of the *filioque* is Photios, *The Mystagogy of the Holy Spirit*, trans. Joseph P. Farrell (Brookline, MA: Holy Cross Orthodox Press, 1987).

[53]I have summarized these issues in my *Beyond the Impasse: Toward a Pneumatological Theology of Religions* (Grand Rapids, MI: Baker Academic, 2003), chap. 4.

bifurcation of the economies of the Son and the Spirit but also, from an Orthodox perspective, fails to secure the interconnections between (a pneumatologically rich) trinitarian theology and ecclesiology.[54] The problem, of course, is that to ask about whether the religions are salvific in Christian terms is a nonstarter since the religions invoke neither Christ nor the biblical way of salvation—that is precisely why they are *non-Christian* traditions; yet defining them in relationship to Christ (as needing to be fulfilled by Christ or as lacking Christ's saving power, for instance) misrepresents the religious other in defining them negatively, precisely what Christians hope to avoid in terms of their own representation to people of other faiths.

Any pneumatological and trinitarian theology of religions will need to give both a christological and an ecclesiological account as part of a comprehensive approach. The latter locus, related to the church, will need to resist triumphalism while also empowering appropriate Christian missional praxis. Toward this end, a pentecostal theology of hospitality, based on the outpouring of the Spirit on all flesh, empowers members of the church to be hosts of those in other faiths amid the presence of the welcoming Father even while enabling them to be guests of religious others just as Christ sojourned in a far country and was received by strangers.[55] This involves bearing witness from out of Christian commitment even as it discerningly welcomes the gifts of others as potentially enriching and even transforming Christian self-understanding. Such a pneumatological praxis may also have the capacity to reconcile all people—indeed, "everyone whom the Lord our God calls to him" (Acts 2:39)—to the Father according to the image of the Son even if the trinitarian identity of God is not clearly perceived by those in other faiths not fully or formally initiated into the Christian church.

That the life-giving Spirit also proceeds from the Father thus invites consideration of how the world's religious traditions, insofar as they are life-giving conduits of goodness and holiness, are also related to the primordial source of all living creatures.[56] Pentecostal theologian Koo Yun thus pneumatologically reframes the classical doctrine of general revelation in dialogue with East Asian philosophical and religious sources (particularly the classic *I Ching*).[57] Distinguishing the formal dimension of the Spirit of God as being present and active in all cultures and even religious traditions from the material aspect of the Spirit of Christ (and the church and its missional arm), Yun suggests what he calls a chialogical pneumatology and theology—following the East Asian cultural, philosophical, and religious concept of *chi*, which is at least

---

[54]For an Orthodox response, see Paraskevè (Eve) Tibbs, "A Distinct Economy of the Spirit? Amos Yong, Pentecostalism and Eastern Orthodoxy," in *The Theology of Amos Yong and the New Face of Pentecostal Scholarship*, ed. Wolfgang Vondey and Martin W. Mittelstadt, Global Pentecostal and Charismatic Studies 14 (Leiden: Brill, 2013), 221-38. On the dualism that may be threatening the incarnational and pentecostal missions, see Gerald R. McDermott and Harold A. Netland, *A Trinitarian Theology of Religions: An Evangelical Proposal* (Oxford: Oxford University Press, 2014), chap. 2, esp. 53-57; my response to McDermott and Netland is published as "Toward a Trinitarian Theology of Religions: A Pentecostal-Evangelical and Missiological Elaboration," *International Bulletin of Mission Research* 40, no. 1 (2016): 1-12.

[55]For details regarding such a hospitality praxis vis-à-vis people in other faith traditions, see Amos Yong, *Hospitality and the Other: Pentecost, Christian Practices, and the Neighbor*, Faith Meets Faith (Maryknoll, NY: Orbis, 2008).

[56]On the world's religious traditions being life-giving conduits, I follow the church fathers at Vatican II, who affirmed: "The Catholic Church rejects nothing of what is true and holy in these religions"; see *Nostra aetate* §2 ("Declaration on the Relation of the Church to Non-Christian Religions," in *Vatican II: The Conciliar and Post-Conciliar Documents*, ed. Austin Flannery, OP, new rev. ed. (Boston: St. Paul's Books and Media, 1992), 738-43, here 739.

[57]Koo Dong Yun, *The Holy Spirit and Ch'i (Qi): A Chialogical Approach to Pneumatology* (Eugene, OR: Pickwick, 2012).

semantically parallel to the Hebrew *ruach* or the English *wind* or *breath*—whereby the cosmic Spirit is generally revelatory of the divine even in the world religions. Others have forayed in similar directions, albeit seeking not only theological but also sociopolitical cache in observing how points of contact between Christian pneumatology and East Asian notions of *chi* are suggestive for reconfiguring democratic public spaces that are egalitarian, liberative, and life giving.[58] While these efforts remain distinctive on multiple fronts and precipitate new perspectives, insights, and questions—not to mention precipitate questions that heretofore have not yet garnered answers agreed on across the ecumenical spectrum—each seeks to think theologically in conversation with East Asian religious and philosophical sources via a pneumatological bridge and demonstrates the potential for rethinking the procession of the Spirit from the Father in our late modern and pluralistic global context.[59]

Who with the Father and the Son together is worshiped and glorified. Yet even if the original Nicene-Constantinopolitan Creed did not include the *filioque*, the following clause leaves no doubt that the Spirit is worshiped and glorified together with—neither more nor less than—the Son. Hence there can be no pneumatomonism

(as if focused only on the Spirit) even as there cannot be a Spirit-Father binitarianism that neglects the Spirit or the Spirit's relationship with the Father and the Son. Any theology of the third article as well as pneumatological theology, then, will have to include both a Spirit Christology and a pneumatologically configured trinitarian theology.[60]

Classical Spirit Christologies regularly treated pneumatology as an appendix to the person and work of the Son. But what if christological reflection not only began with but also understood the Spirit as essential to the identity and achievements of the Son?[61] On the one hand, there is no doubt that the Spirit is understood as the Spirit of Jesus and the Spirit of Christ, and that the Pentecost sending of the Spirit was by the Son from the right hand of the Father (Acts 2:33). On the other hand, the Word is incarnate by the Spirit, and Jesus of Nazareth is the anointed Messiah—the Christ—through the empowering Spirit. Further, there is also no recognition of the Son apart from the Spirit (see 1 Cor 12:3), so that authentic acknowledgment of the Son is always and already pneumatically mediated. Last but not least, even any initial confession of the Son awaits both moral and behavioral confirmation, usually related to manifestations of the fruit of the Spirit, and final or eschatological verification

[58]For example, Grace Ji-Sun Kim, *The Holy Spirit, Chi, and the Other: A Model of Global and Intercultural Pneumatology* (New York: Palgrave Macmillan, 2011), and Hyo-Dong Lee, *Spirit, Qi, and the Multitude: A Comparative Theology for the Democracy of Creation* (New York: Fordham University Press, 2014); see Jung Young Lee, *The Trinity in Asian Perspective* (Nashville: Abingdon, 1996), chap. 5, for more on the Holy Spirit and *chi*.
[59]For another foray at this intersection of pneumatology and world religions, but this time on an aesthetic register, see Jonathan A. Anderson and Amos Yong, "Painting Pentecost: The Spirit-Filled Painting of Sawai Chinnawong," *Christian Century*, May 28, 2014, 30-33.
[60]Such a third-article theological project that begins with the work of the Spirit is well underway—for example, Myk Habets, ed., *The Spirit of Truth: Reading Scripture and Constructing Theology with the Holy Spirit* (Eugene, OR: Wipf & Stock, 2010), and Amos Yong, with Jonathan A. Anderson, *Renewing Christian Theology: Systematics for a Global Christianity* (Waco, TX: Baylor University Press, 2014).
[61]Suggestive is Sammy Alfaro, *Divino Compañero: Toward a Hispanic Pentecostal Christology* (Eugene, OR: Wipf & Stock, 2010); see also Roman Catholic theologian Ralph Del Colle, *Christ and the Spirit: Spirit-Christology in Trinitarian Perspective* (Oxford: Oxford University Press, 1994), and Baptist theologian Myk Habets, *The Anointed Son: A Trinitarian Spirit Christology* (Eugene, OR: Wipf & Stock, 2010).

(Mt 7:21-23). For all of these reasons, besides others, any Spirit Christology must proceed at least methodologically as if both hands of the Father were equally definitive. Put alternatively, a Spirit Christology is the flip side of a christological pneumatology, with both approaches mutually and variously informing each other.[62]

Finally, for present purposes, if the Spirit is worshiped and glorified together with the Son and the Father, then the Spirit is not only the culmination of the doctrine of the Trinity but also constitutive of trinitarian confession.[63] If so, then the triune nature of the Christian God is simultaneously patrological, christological, and pneumatological. Anything less than a fully articulated pneumatology—whatever is possible within present horizons—will be deficiently trinitarian. More weightily, if the Spirit is the eschatological horizon through which all creation is reconciled in the Son to the Father, then there is also a fundamental sense in which "now we see in a mirror, dimly" (1 Cor 13:12), not only because of epistemological constraints but because the full glory of the triune God is yet to be revealed, if not achieved. Christian pneumatology thus charts new trajectories for trinitarian theology, and does so, as can be seen through this exploratory essay, by inviting reassessment of Christology, the theology of religions and of interfaith encounter, the theology of creation, and global theology, among other traditional and newly emerging theological loci.[64]

INTERIM CONCLUSION: WHO SPOKE BY THE PROPHETS

The concluding clause to the third article is that the ancient prophets spoke through the Holy Spirit. The question left for consideration is whether the Spirit's speaking through the prophets was merely a thing of the (ancient Hebrew) past. This specific confession is itself drawn from the apostolic witness (2 Pet 1:21), so it must be assumed at least that the Spirit continued to speak through the followers of Jesus the Messiah, beyond the prophets of ancient Israel. If so, then by extension, in a post-apostolic context, does the Spirit speak similarly and perhaps in an ongoing way through the church? Orthodox Christians urge that there is a sense in which the earliest ecumenical councils were vehicles of the Spirit even as the Roman Catholic magisterium suggests there are limited albeit no less real occasions in which the Spirit has spoken and continues to speak through the ecclesial hierarchy. Contemporary pentecostal and charismatic movements insist on *sola Scriptura* (with the Reformers against Catholic and Orthodox emphases on the tradition of the church) and on the ongoing manifestations of the gifts of the Spirit (here in opposition to dispensationalist theologies that argue that such ceased with the apostolic period). For theology, not just pneumatology, in a global context that engages with Majority World voices and perspectives, one senses that this question will continue to be debated, even if part of an affirmative "answer" to it consists in arguments such as those found in this chapter and section of the volume.

[62]I develop these points in my essay "Christological Constants in Shifting Contexts: Jesus Christ, Prophetic Dialogue, and the *Missio Spiritus* in a Pluralistic World," in *Mission on the Road to Emmaus: Constants, Contexts, and Prophetic Dialogue*, ed. Stephen B. Bevans and Cathy Ross (Maryknoll, NY: Orbis, 2015), 19-33; see also Amos Yong, *The Missiological Spirit: Christian Mission Theology for the Third Millennium Global Context* (Eugene, OR: Cascade, 2014), part 4.

[63]Pentecostal theologians are leading the way in this discussion: Steven M. Studebaker, *From Pentecost to the Triune God: A Pentecostal Trinitarian Theology* (Grand Rapids, MI: Eerdmans, 2012), and William P. Atkinson, *Trinity After Pentecost* (Eugene, OR: Wipf & Stock, 2013); see also Aaron T. Smith, *A Theology of the Third Article: Karl Barth and the Spirit of the Word* (Minneapolis: Fortress, 2014).

[64]See my *Spirit of Love: A Trinitarian Theology of Grace* (Waco, TX: Baylor University Press, 2012).

FURTHER READING

Congar, Yves. *I Believe in the Holy Spirit*. Translated by David Smith. 3 vols. in 1. New York: Crossroad, 1997.

Kim, Kirsteen. *Joining in with the Spirit: Connecting World Church and Local Mission*. London: Epworth, 2009.

Macchia, Frank D. *Baptized in the Spirit: A Global Pentecostal Theology*. Grand Rapids, MI: Zondervan, 2006.

Rasmussen, Ane Marie Bak. *Modern African Spirituality: The Independent Holy Spirit Churches in East Africa*. London: I. B. Tauris, 2009.

Rogers, Eugene F., Jr., ed. *The Holy Spirit: Classic and Contemporary Readings*. Chichester, UK: Wiley-Blackwell, 2009.

Thiselton, Anthony C. *The Holy Spirit—in Biblical Teaching, Through the Centuries, and Today*. Grand Rapids, MI: Eerdmans, 2013.

Yong, Amos. *Pneumatology and the Christian-Buddhist Dialogue: Does the Spirit Blow Through the Middle Way?* Studies in Systematic Theology 11. Leiden: Brill, 2012.

18

THE SPIRIT BLOWS
WHERE IT WILLS

THE HOLY SPIRIT'S PERSONHOOD
IN INDIAN CHRISTIAN THOUGHT

Ivan Satyavrata

IN THIS CHAPTER, a critical survey exposes the significant influence of *advaitic* (nondualist) Hinduism on Indian Christian pneumatology. I argue that the Holy Spirit's personhood is consequently undermined and even denied in Indian Christian thought. The personalist *bhakti* Hindu tradition offers more positive prospects for constructive engagement with and meaningful contextualization of the Christian faith in India.

In his discourse on the nature and importance of the new birth in John 3, Jesus uses the metaphor of the wind in illustrating to Nicodemus the mysterious and sovereign nature of the Holy Spirit's workings: "The wind blows where it wills. You hear its sound, but you cannot tell where it comes from or where it is going" (Jn 3:8). These words of Jesus offer real hope and promise to a generation that seeks reality beyond the world of cold logic, deductive reasoning, and academic analysis. All around us we see evidence of a hunger for spiritual experience and an upsurge of interest in spirituality. Daoism, Tibetan and Zen Buddhism, Spiritualism, Kabbalism, yoga, New Age spirituality, and various forms of Eastern

mysticism are all an integral part of Western culture today. People in our world are perhaps more aware and accepting of the realm of the spirits today than ever before in recent history.

But is this openness to the world of religious experience essentially healthy or detrimental to the future of biblical Christian faith? This chapter is an attempt to draw from the Indian experience of the gospel-culture encounter in addressing this question, and to help us see both the pitfalls and possibilities of relating the Christian conception of God as Spirit to notions of spirit (or Spirit) within non-Christian cultural traditions. The Indian experience is helpful in this regard because the subject of the Holy Spirit occupies a place of natural prominence in India due to the ancient tradition of spirituality in the subcontinent. Indians thus naturally tend to think of God as spirit (or Spirit). This positive orientation to spirituality within the dominant religious culture presents the Christian witness in India with potential opportunities and challenges.

My principal concern in this chapter is to clarify the biblical account of the Holy Spirit in the context of myriad prevailing conceptions of "spirit" in India, some of which overlap, while others compete with, the biblical notion. How does the Christian understanding of the Holy Spirit relate to other ideas of spirit, such as *Brahman, atman,* or *sakti* in Hinduism? Must we always view the Holy Spirit in essentially personal terms, or can we look beyond the personalist language and regard the Spirit as an impersonal, abstract force? Can we accommodate the traditional understanding of the Holy Spirit with impersonalist conceptions of spirit (or Spirit) in other faiths in the interest of affirming common ground in interreligious dialogue?

We will see that relating the Christian idea of the Holy Spirit with prevailing notions of spirit in other religious traditions and cultures does have some serious pitfalls. But are there any prospects for positive engagement with Hindu spirituality that could provide stepping stones to dialogue and potential enrichment of traditional Christian understandings of the Spirit? Perhaps an even more pressing existential question, as increasing numbers of people of other faiths move into the neighborhood, into our shrinking global village, is the following: Is the Spirit at work among people of other faiths and cultures? Some Christians find it easy to offer a glib, unqualified no to this question. At the other extreme, we have those who say a simple yes, and have no difficulty accepting that the Spirit is present and at work everywhere in the same way as he is among the believing community.

The Bible does teach that the Spirit is present and active everywhere in creation. But is God's omnipresence and spiritual immanence simply to be equated with the active, dynamic influence of the Holy Spirit poured out on the church on the day of Pentecost? The New Testament describes the Holy Spirit, the Spirit of God, as pre-

eminently the Spirit of Jesus: the one who was promised by Jesus, who was bestowed by Jesus, and who imparts life, based on the redemptive work of Jesus. Our search for points of contact between Christian and other notions of Spirit (or spirit) will thus have to take into account the normativity of Christ as a crucial yardstick. A balanced approach will thus affirm the distinctiveness of the Christ-centered presence and activity of the Spirit within the community of faith, while also exploring Christocentric criteria for identifying and discerning the Spirit's work in the world in the midst of people of other faiths and no faith.

As a prelude to my survey of Indian pneumatological reflections I briefly compare Christian and Hindu notions of spirit (or Spirit). The main body of the chapter is devoted to a critical survey of representative Indian pneumatological contributions. I conclude with a summary evaluation of the extent to which the Holy Spirit's personhood has been adequately affirmed in the Indian Christian tradition, and offer a positive critique indicating prospects for constructive engagement.

THE "SPIRIT" IN INDIA: CHRISTIAN AND HINDU CONCEPTIONS

Christian theology has found it necessary since its inception to express itself in categories relevant to its missional context. The church, which was born and initially nurtured in the cultural environment of Palestinian Judaism, eventually had to adopt the ideas and vocabulary of Greek culture as a result of its encounter with the Greco-Roman world. In a similar vein, since the nineteenth century, Christian thinkers in India have attempted to meaningfully engage the majority Hindu culture by seeking to relate Christian truth to Hindu thought forms and terminology. An approach to pneumatology that is sensitive and critical seems essential for effective contextualization of the gospel in India, given the pronounced "spirit" orientation within Hindu culture.

The importance of pneumatology to the Indian tradition is highlighted in the following observation by one of India's most creative and stimulating Christian thinkers, P. D. Chenchiah: "The future of Christianity will ultimately depend upon the discovery of the Indian Church of the tremendous importance of the Holy Spirit and of its capacity to communicate that spirit to the Hindu."[1] This observation is based on the fact that Indians tend to think of God as spirit. One indication of this is that the Hindu philosophical language, Sanskrit, is rich with "spirit" terminology, such as *atman* (spirit, soul) and its cognates *paramatman* (supreme spirit), *antaratman* (inner spirit), *jivatman* (human spirit), *antaryamin* (inner ruler), *sakti* (power), and *adhyatmikta* (spirituality). Inasmuch as *Brahman* (ultimate reality) is identified with the *paramatman* (supreme spirit), ultimate reality is understood in essentially spiritual terms. Much of Hindu religion focuses on the relation of the *atman* to the *paramatman*. Spirituality pervades all of Hindu philosophy and culture.

This positive orientation to spirituality within Hindu thought has, however, presented the Christian witness in India with some potentially serious pitfalls in its task of contextualization. The danger arises largely due to the fundamental difference between the Christian view of God as a tri-personal being and the veiled agnosticism within the Hindu conception of God. Although

there are primarily two traditions in classical Hindu thought—one that speaks of the Absolute as an impersonal Spirit and the other of a personal God—the latter has tended to be eclipsed by the former.

Neo-Hinduism has tried to bridge the divergent tendencies in one of two ways. Most frequently, the personalist strand is subordinated to the traditional *advaita* (nondualism) view, as an essentially inferior conception, a concession to the popular devotion of the untutored masses. Alternatively, the absolutist and personalist ideas of God are treated as complementary truths, culturally conditioned expressions of the same ultimate mystery, and the personalist conception is subsumed within the dominant *advaitic* view.[2] The Absolute is thus viewed as beyond all conceptions of personality and impersonality. Where personality is ascribed to God, it is treated merely as a symbol, as the highest category to which human beings are able to relate.

The crucial question for Christian theism then is: Does the biblical personalist language about God have an ontological reference? More specifically, is there an adequate biblical basis for the Christian notion of the Holy Spirit's personhood?

The identity and activity of the Holy Spirit in the New Testament is always intrinsically bound up with the person and work of Jesus Christ.[3] The Spirit's bestowal on people is clearly linked to the ministry of Jesus (Mt 3:11; Mk 1:8; Lk 3:16) and, more specifically, to his glorification (Jn 7:37-39). It is, thus, in the ministry of the Spirit, especially in relation to the person and work of

---

[1] D. A. Thangasamy, *The Theology of Chenchiah* (Bangalore, India: Christian Institute for the Study of Religion and Society, 1966), 218.

[2] For the views of two of the most influential modern Hindu philosophers, S. Radhakrishnan and Sri Aurobindo, see M. Braybrooke, *Together to the Truth* (Madras: Christian Literature Society, 1971), 49-52.

[3] The treatment of the New Testament material in the following paragraphs is largely based on Ivan Satyavrata, *The Holy Spirit: Lord and Life-Giver* (Nottingham, UK: Inter-Varsity Press, 2009), 72-74.

Christ, that the personhood of the Spirit is most clearly disclosed in the New Testament.

The strongest evidence for the personhood of the Spirit in the Gospels comes to us in two authentic sayings of Jesus. In the first of these (Mk 3:29; see Mt 12:31; Lk 12:10) Jesus warns his hearers of the serious consequences of blaspheming against the Holy Spirit. In the second instance (Mk 13:11; see Mt 10:20; Lk 12:12) Jesus assures his disciples that the Spirit will help them by speaking through them when they are called to testify during times of persecution. Thus, Jesus clearly regarded the Holy Spirit as a personal being who could be blasphemed against, and on occasion could speak through people.

The book of Acts is filled with references to various personal activities of the Holy Spirit. On several occasions in Acts the Spirit is said to speak (Acts 1:16; 8:29; 10:19; 11:12; 13:2; 28:25). He is also one who forbids (Acts 6:6), thinks about what is good (Acts 15:28), appoints (Acts 20:28), sends (Acts 13:4), bears witness (Acts 5:32; 20:23), snatches (Acts 8:39), and prevents (Acts 16:7), and he can be lied to (Acts 5:3), tempted (Acts 5:9), and resisted (Acts 7:51). The evidence for Paul's belief in the personal character of the Spirit is also convincing. The Spirit, according to Paul, testifies (Rom 8:16), intercedes (Rom 8:26), knows (1 Cor 2:11), teaches (1 Cor 2:13), determines (1 Cor 12:11), gives life (2 Cor 3:6), calls out (Gal 4:6), and can be grieved (Eph 4:30).

The Gospel of John, too, refers to the Spirit in clearly personal terms. The Spirit variously teaches and reminds (Jn 14:26), testifies (Jn 15:26), and guides and speaks (Jn 16:13). When Jesus refers to the Spirit (who has come from the Father) as *allos paraklētos* (another Advocate; NRSV) in John 14:16, he clearly implies that he

himself is the present *paraklētos* (Advocate). The Spirit was thus regarded as a person in the same sense that Jesus was. Similar personal references to the Holy Spirit may be found in other parts of the New Testament as well. The Spirit is described as speaking (1 Tim 4:1), predicting the future (1 Pet 1:11), and addressing God's people in the writings of the Old Testament (Heb 3:7). The book of Revelation records a number of instances when the Spirit is said to speak (Rev 2:7, 11, 17, 29; 3:6, 13, 22; 14:13).

Christians who take the authority of the Bible seriously have thus always insisted that, despite the limitations of human language, in speaking of God the Spirit as personal they are speaking of him as he really is. The language is not merely figurative or anthropomorphic, nor is it meant to reflect some subordinate aspect of God's nature. While one of the central affirmations of Christianity is that God, the ultimate reality, is personal, the highest conception of God in Hinduism is that of the impersonal absolute, *Brahman*. We turn now to a critical survey of the pneumatological reflections of select Indian Christian thinkers and see how they deal with this fundamental theological divergence in their attempts to meaningfully correlate Christian and Hindu notions of "spirit."

A CRITICAL SURVEY OF THE HOLY SPIRIT'S PERSONHOOD IN SELECT INDIAN THINKERS

The first Indians to have reflected seriously on Christian theological themes were, ironically, not Christians, but pioneers of the Hindu Renaissance in India: Ram Mohan Roy, who founded the Brahmo Samaj, and one of his successors in the movement, Keshab Chandra Sen.[4]

---

[4]Ram Mohan Roy is widely regarded as the first Indian to have engaged in serious scholarly interaction with the Christian faith. See Robin Boyd, *An Introduction to Indian Christian Theology* (Delhi: ISPCK, 1991), 19.

Ram Mohan Roy devoted much of his life to a polemic against Hindu polytheism and idolatry. Consequently, he vehemently opposed the Christian doctrine of the Trinity, favoring the Arian view of the person of Christ and rejecting totally any idea of the Holy Spirit's personality. He devotes an entire chapter of one of his writings to "The Impersonality of the Holy Spirit."[5] He regards the Spirit as merely the holy influence and power of God; he is neither self-existent nor a distinct personality. This influence or power was instrumental in the virginal conception of Jesus and is also the means by which men are guided in the path of righteousness.[6]

Keshab Chandra Sen is a crucial figure in the development of Indian Christian thought. As Robin Boyd observes, "Many of the conceptions and categories which have become familiar in the writings of later Indian theologians were first stated by Sen."[7] The highest point of Sen's theological creativity is, perhaps, his exposition of the Trinity in terms of the Vedanta concept of *Saccidananda*. He seems to have been the first to draw on this concept in interpreting the Trinity in the Indian context. The nature and expression of his thought are such as to leave it open to conflicting interpretation, making his teaching the subject of much theological controversy.

In his famous lecture, "That Marvellous Mystery—the Trinity," Sen explains the correspondence between *Saccidananda* and the Trinity:

> The Trinity of Christian theology corresponds strikingly with the Sachchidananda of Hinduism. You have three conditions, three manifestations of Divinity. Yet, there is one God, one substance, amid three phenomena. . . . Whether alone, or manifest in the Son, or quickening humanity as the Holy Spirit, it is the same God, the same identical Deity, whose unity continues indivisible amid multiplicity of manifestations . . . the true Trinity is not three persons, but three functions of the same Person.[8]

There is a tendency toward modalism in Sen's trinitarian thinking. In fact, Sen seems to have regarded the Trinity as only a symbol, with the three members, Father, Son, and Holy Spirit, simply pointing to the reality of God in different ways. In his careful study, Roy Pape notes the importance of the Holy Spirit in Sen's Christology. He compares Sen's approach to a Spirit-Christology, which views Christ as an incarnation of the Holy Spirit. Thus, the Holy Spirit is the presence and activity of God focused in Jesus Christ, the "transforming" activity of God, the "Sanctifier" and "Savior." Pape thus concludes that in Sen's thought "the Holy Spirit is God personally and powerfully at work in Christ the Son and in all who follow Christ."[9]

The problem, however, arises when one considers Sen's fondness for personification and dramatic imagery. One thus detects a certain ambiguity in Sen's thought when he speaks of the Spirit in terms of a "divine enthusiasm" or "a pervading passion," or in language such as the following: "In one favoured spot on earth is the Eternal Sun reflected; thence the concentrated rays of heaven's light are diffused by the inspiration of the Holy Spirit. . . . Already the Holy Ghost has shaken the foundations of our carnal nature, and brought Christ into us as a living

[5]Boyd, *Introduction*, 24.

[6]B. J. Christie Kumar, "An Indian Christian Appreciation of the Doctrine of the Holy Spirit: A Search into the Religious Heritage of the Indian Christian," *Indian Journal of Theology* 30, no. 1 (1981): 29.

[7]Boyd, *Introduction*, 27.

[8]Keshub Chunder Sen, *Lectures in India* (London: Cassell, 1904), 2:16-18.

[9]W. Roy Pape, "Keshub Chunder Sen's Doctrine of Christ and the Trinity: A Rehabilitation," *Religion and Society* 11, no. 3 (1964): 65, 69.

force. The storm-wave of inspiration has touched us, bringing Christ into us all."[10]

Sen leaves us in little doubt as to the basic *advaita* orientation of his conception of God when he declares: "Lo! Within Jesus is concealed the Holy Spirit, and as you go deep into the Holy Spirit you discover at last the Invisible Supreme Essence. . . . In the inmost recesses of every man's soul is the Supreme God."[11]

Nehemiah Goreh has justly been regarded as the most deeply versed in Hindu learning of all Indian Christians. Also one of the most conservative Indian Christian theologians, Goreh affirms the orthodox view of the Spirit's personhood: the Holy Spirit is for him the Spirit of God and the third person of the Trinity. He uses the Gospel of John as his principal source in what is essentially an exegetical defense of the orthodox position. According to Goreh, the language of Scripture clearly shows that the Holy Spirit is God and not merely a creature. John's use of the pronoun *ekeinos* (that) in the masculine gender, as well as the title *ho paraklētos* (the Advocate) in referring to the Spirit, are among the arguments he uses to establish that the Holy Spirit is "a Person, and not a quality or power, in the abstract sense of the word."[12]

Brahmabandhab Upadhyaya is a striking example of a Hindu who found the bridge to an indigenous form of Christianity in the teachings of K. C. Sen. Upadhyaya had a passionate concern for the formulation of a Hindu expression of Christian faith and life in India, and was convinced that the Vedanta philosophy must be made to render the same service to the Catholic faith in

India as to the Greek philosophy in Europe. A fair portion of his theology consists of an exposition of some of Sen's creative insights from a somewhat more orthodox perspective.

A devout Roman Catholic, Upadhyaya sought to combine the Thomist idea of God as pure Being with the Vedanta conception of *Brahman*. His teaching on the Holy Spirit comes in the context of his exposition of the Trinity: "God comprehends Himself by one act of eternal knowledge. The knowing self is the Father, the known self or the self-begotten by His knowledge is the Son; and the Holy Ghost is the Spirit of reciprocal love proceeding from the Father and the Son."[13]

Upadhyaya elaborates Sen's interpretation of the Trinity as *Saccidananda* in a classic Sanskrit hymn of devotion. The Father is described as *Sat* (Being), the Son as *Cit* (Consciousness or Intelligence), and the Spirit, which proceeds out of the union of Sat and Cit, as *Ananda* (Bliss). The verse describing the Holy Spirit says: "Proceeding from the union of Sat and Cit, gracious Spirit, pure Ananda Sanctifier, Inspirer, revealing the Word, our Life-giver!"[14]

At first glance the language of this hymn seems to point toward an orthodox understanding of the Spirit's person. But inasmuch as *Ananda* (Bliss, Joy) is grounded in the impersonalist monism of *advaita*, it merely denotes an abstract attribute—at best an aspect of *Brahman*. As Christie Kumar is careful to note, "Here the very idea of the Christian Trinity as persons is missing."[15]

In fairness to Upadhyaya, it must be observed that he was convinced that the conception of God

---

[10]Sen, *Lectures*, 42-43.

[11]Sen, *Lectures*, 35.

[12]A. M. Balwant Paradkar, *The Theology of Goreh* (Madras: Christian Literature Society, 1969), 82.

[13]Brahmabandhab Upadhyaya, "Hinduism and Christianity as Compared by Mrs. Besant," *Sophia* 4 (February 1897): 8.

[14]Brahmabandhab Upadhyaya, "Our Personality," *Sophia* 5, no. 10 (October 1898): 146-47.

[15]Christie Kumar, "Indian Christian Appreciation," 33.

in *advaita* Vedanta is not impersonal. His own definition of personality as "self-knowledge" would, strictly speaking, only apply to his interpretation of *Cit* (Intelligence) as the second person of the Trinity. He thus still comes short of adequately affirming the personhood of the Spirit.

Aiyadurai Jesudasen Appasamy, in contrast to Upadhyaya, turns to the personalist theistic tradition of *bhakti* as an instrument for formulating an Indian Christian theology. He uses the word *antaryamin* (inner ruler) to denote the Holy Spirit—the immanent God dwelling by nature in all people. There is, however, a certain ambiguity about Appasamy's use of *antaryamin*, for he also occasionally uses the term in referring to the immanence of Christ in the preexistent Logos. Appasamy's interpretation and use of this term does suggest a concern to affirm the Spirit's personhood.

Despite Appasamy's adoption of the *bhakti* philosophical framework and his consequent rejection of the *advaitic* conception of God in his approach to Christian mysticism, he is clearly attracted to it. He thus discerned with positive appreciation both personal and impersonal aspects in the Johannine conception of God. Boyd observes that this accommodation to *advaitic* mysticism may be prompted by "the uncomfortable feeling . . . that for the millions in India the conception of God as *nirguna Brahman* will always rank as higher than that of any kind of personal revelation."[16]

Pandipeddi Chenchiah was one of the most original and radical Indian thinkers. He was convinced that pneumatology would play a decisive role in shaping Christian thought in India, and would, in fact, "become the cornerstone of Indian Christian theology."[17] Chenchiah rejected both the absolute monism of *advaita* and the personal mysticism of *bhakti*, opting instead for Sri Aurobindo's modern but indigenous evolutionary line of thought.

Chenchiah used the Sanskrit terms *mahasakti* (great power) and *sakti* (power) in referring to the Holy Spirit. The word *sakti* in Hinduism is associated with an extraordinary power. Christie Kumar comments: "It [*sakti*] is an energy coming into individuals by means of which people are able to do unique things and utter certain predictions."[18] Furthermore, *sakti* is often personified as the goddess of power in popular Hinduism. Chenchiah believed that the traditional Hindu understanding of *sakti* as personalized divine energy prepares the way for a fresh interpretation of the Holy Spirit that is at the same time both Christian and distinctly Indian. He found the idea of an external power of *sakti* coming in and transforming humanity from within extremely appealing, foreign as it is to the traditional (*advaitic* and *bhakti*) forms of Hindu spirituality. His teaching was that as *mahasakti*, the Holy Spirit introduces new life and power into the lives of believers and is the dynamic means by which the entire cosmos is being transformed and incorporated into Christ as the new creation.[19]

In Chenchiah, we observe again the common tendency in Indian Christian theology to confuse the identities of Christ and the Holy Spirit: "the Holy Spirit is the Universal Jesus," and, "the Holy Spirit is the power that descended vertically in the human stream in Jesus." His description of the Holy Spirit as "the new cosmic energy" and

---

[16]Boyd, *Introduction*, 129-30.
[17]D. M. Devasahayam and A. N. Sudarisanam, eds., *Rethinking Christianity in India* (Madras: Hogarth, 1938), 161.
[18]Christie Kumar, "Indian Christian Appreciation," 29.
[19]Thangasamy, *Theology of Chenchiah*, 217-18.

statements such as "the Holy Spirit is the energy beyond Creation which as Christ has flowed into the world" make us doubt the extent to which he accepted the personhood of the Spirit as an ontological reality.[20]

Vengal Chakkarai, of all Indian Christian thinkers, makes the most extensive use of Hindu terminology, although his theological reflections display no specific philosophical affiliation. The Holy Spirit occupies a vital place in his thought and is, in fact, the starting point of his Christology: "it is from the Holy Spirit our *antaryamin*, the Indweller, that we start our enquiry concerning the nature of the person of Jesus."[21] The relation between Jesus and the Spirit, according to Chakkarai, is simply one of identification: "the Holy Spirit is Jesus Christ in the human personality . . . the Holy Spirit is Jesus Christ himself taking his abode with us . . . the Holy Spirit is Jesus Himself."[22] He identifies the Holy Spirit with the risen, living Christ at work in the world today, and thus sees his work as a continuing part of the incarnation, or *avatara*.

When it comes to the question of the Spirit's personhood, Chakkarai seeks to preserve what he regards as scriptural ambiguity. He perceives a tension within the New Testament between the representation of the Spirit in personalist terms in John's Gospel and Luke's description of the Spirit in Acts as a kind of influence or force. He thus concludes that "the Spirit is evidently in its nature both personal and impersonal."[23] While he does sometimes refer to the Holy Spirit in personal terms, a close perusal of his writings seems to reveal a basic conception of God that is essentially *advaitic* in nature. He totally rejects,

for instance, the idea of personality in God—on the grounds that it is a "Western" concept—supporting instead the common *advaitic* claim that *aham* (ego or personality) is in some way a limitation on universality. Consistent with this line of thinking is his belief that the "Christ of experience" whom we now worship and who lives in our hearts is a "universal spirit" who is outside the realm of mere human personality. It seems evident that for Chakkarai personality is a human and historical constraint that must not be applied to pure divinity.

In the concluding paragraphs of his discussion of the Spirit's functions, Chakkarai distinguishes between our unrestricted worship of the Father and the Son and our somewhat "mysterious" relationship with the Spirit. A deeper understanding of the latter, he believes, "leads us to the heart of religion as we have known it in one of its most powerful manifestations in India." The *advaitic* orientation is unmistakable, especially when in his subsequent concluding explanation we read: "He [the person who has the Spirit] stands in the tumultous [*sic*] ocean as a beholder, alone and without a second, he whose world is the Brahman . . . *in his own self only he beholds the self, he beholds all as self* . . . he becomes a Brahmana, he whose world is the Brahman."[24] Thus, Chakkarai's attempt to formulate a "Christology of the Spirit" without adequate grounding in the New Testament historical account leads him to an *advaitic* view of Christ that negates the Holy Spirit's personhood.

The tradition inaugurated by Brahmabandhab Upadhyaya of seeking a positive relationship between Christianity and *advaita* philosophy has

---

[20]Devasahayam and Sudarisanam, *Rethinking Christianity*, 55.

[21]V. Chakkarai, "Jesus the Avatar," in *Vengal Chakkarai*, ed. P. T. Thomas (Madras: CLS, 1981), 1:123.

[22]Chakkarai, "Jesus the Avatar," 124-25.

[23]Chakkarai, "Jesus the Avatar," 153.

[24]Chakkarai, "Jesus the Avatar," 156-157, emphasis added.

remained very much alive within Roman Catholic theology in India. Its popularity and influence has increased considerably in recent years, in some measure due to the blessing and support extended to the interreligious dialogue movement by Vatican II. We consider briefly the views of three representatives of this school of thought: Jules Monchanin, Swami Abhishiktananda (Henri Le Saux), and Raimundo Panikkar.

Jules Monchanin was a French Benedictine missionary whose work represents, in some ways, the fulfillment of Upadhyaya's highest aspirations. He assumed the Sanskrit name Parama Arubi Anandam, testifying to his special devotion to the Holy Spirit, the Supreme (*Parama*), Formless (*Arubi*), Bliss (*Anandam*). Along with Swami Abhishiktananda, Monchanin founded the Saccidananda Ashram, a monastery devoted to the adoration and contemplation of the Trinity. It was in his understanding of the Trinity as *Saccidananda* that Monchanin carried forward the work of Upadhyaya, perceiving in the Christian doctrine of the Trinity the solution to some of the common antinomies in Hindu thought.

The Spirit occupies an important place in Monchanin's thought. He often insists that it is the third person of the Trinity whom India "awaits" with special eagerness: "the Divine Spirit, the 'uncircumscribed' Person, who appears only under fluid forms, breath, water . . . fire . . . the mysterious immanence of all in every one and of every one in all. He is the very one whom India is awaiting."[25]

Thus, the Spirit, according to Monchanin, is the all-pervasive "Indwelling God"—who is the least circumscribed in his manifestation, the least anthropomorphic, and the most spiritual—at the meeting point of India's quest for the personal God and the impersonal Absolute.[26] Regarding the question of divine personhood, like Upadhyaya, Monchanin seems to begin with the assumption that personality can be attributed to the *nirguna Brahman* of *advaita* philosophy. He then goes on to speak of the Trinity as constituting three "centers of personality": "For us God is neither the impersonal nor the unimpersonal. In his intimate life he is Three persons. . . . He is Sat, he is Cit, he is Ananda, Being, Consciousness, Bliss—in such a manner that he constitutes three centres of personality, each one polarised by the other two."[27]

In spite of this seemingly clear affirmation of trinitarian personalism, however, elsewhere Monchanin seems to be groping for a fresh, "non-anthropomorphic" notion of divine personhood that might more easily be accommodated within the *advaitic* framework: "Perhaps the notion of person also has to be reshaped since the person in God is relationship itself." He thus maintains that "the constitutive element of the divine person is co-esse: each is a Person only by his relation to the other."[28]

In so redefining the concept of divine personality, Monchanin believes that he can fulfill the deepest aspirations of Hinduism for a God who is absolutely simple and absolutely one, and who is not personal (if personal implies even the slender duality of an "I-thou" relationship of a conscious being with an object outside itself).[29]

[25]Jules Monchanin, *Swami Parama Arubi Anandam: [Fr. J Monchanin], 1895–1957: A Memorial* (Tiruchirapalli, India: United Printers, 1959), 103.

[26]Joseph Mattam, "Modern Catholic Attempts at Presenting Christ to India," *Indian Journal of Theology* 23, no. 4 (1974): 209.

[27]Monchanin, *Swami*, 200.

[28]Jules Monchanin, "The Quest of the Absolute," in *Indian Culture and the Fullness of Christ*, ed. Jules Monchanin and Swami Abhishiktananda (Madras: Catholic Centre of Madras, 1957), 50-51.

[29]Monchanin, *Swami*, 186.

Monchanin's solution to the Hindu quest for a personal-impersonal God must be commended for its skillful blending of some elements of Western apophatic mysticism (the belief within some Christian mystical traditions that God can only be described by humans in terms of what cannot be said of him) with the *advaita* philosophy of Sankara. But it hardly does justice to the full-blooded personalism of the New Testament understanding of the Holy Spirit.

Swami Abhishiktananda (Henri Le Saux) develops the basic ideas of Monchanin in a somewhat more radical direction. Abhishiktananda also regards *advaita* as the highest form of Hinduism and is convinced that the deepest and best Hindu (*advaitic*) experience finds its true fulfillment in the Christian mystical experience. How does Abhishiktananda understand *advaita*? According to him, *advaita* simply means "neither God alone, nor the creature alone nor God plus the creature, but an indefinable non-duality which transcends at once all separation and all confusion."[30] All of his theology is thus conditioned by a commitment to this *advaitic* framework. As a result, he is much more deferential in his attitude toward *advaitic* Hinduism than either Upadhyaya or Monchanin.

The importance of the Spirit in Abhishiktananda's thought is determined by the fact that Christianity is primarily a spiritual reality, a living experience in the Spirit. The Christian life must, therefore, be lived at the level of the Spirit: "in the cave of the heart"—the secret and deep place where each individual meets God, the place of ultimate encounter, where the spirit of man becomes one with the Spirit of God.

Like Upadhyaya and Monchanin, Abhishiktananda follows the line of K. C. Sen in his understanding of the Trinity as *Saccidananda*. The Spirit is thus "the supreme revelation of Ananda, the Bliss of Being."[31] It is difficult to see how Abhishiktananda can continue to speak of the Spirit in personal terms within his *advaitic* framework, although he does so on occasion: "the Unspoken and Unbegotten Person who . . . whispers in the sanctuary of the heart the eternal ABBA."[32]

A clue to the solution may lie in Abhishiktananda's reference to the Spirit as a personification of *ekatvam*, the mystery of *advaitic* unity. This may explain why he often speaks of the Spirit in abstract, impersonal terms. He likens the Spirit to the primal energy of *sakti*, "an immeasurable powerful energy," surging up from within man's own inner being, the innermost center of the soul. This is far from the personal language of christological trinitarianism, but Abhishiktananda leaves us in no doubt about his essential *advaitic* orientation in the following assertion: "In reality the *Advaita* lies at the root of the Christian experience. It is simply the mystery that God and the world are not two. It is this mystery of unity, *ekatvam*, that characterizes the Spirit in God, and in the whole work of God."[33]

Raimundo Panikkar, an influential proponent of the interreligious dialogue movement, devoted his theological endeavors to bringing the Hindu religious experience and Christian faith into a common form of expression.[34] In exploring the relationship between Christianity and Hinduism, Panikkar simultaneously attempts to harmonize two prominent schools of thought, *advaita* and *bhakti*, but his

---

[30]Swami Abhishiktananda, *Hindu-Christian Meeting Point: Within the Cave of the Heart* (Delhi: ISPCK, 1976), 107.

[31]Abhishiktananda, *Hindu-Christian Meeting Point*, 88.

[32]Swami Abhishiktananda, *Prayer* (Delhi: ISPCK, 1967), 63.

[33]Abhishiktananda, *Prayer*, 100, 109; see Mattam, "Modern Catholic Attempts," 212.

[34]J. B. Chettimattam, "R. Panikkar's Approach to Christology," *Indian Journal of Theology* 23 (1974): 219.

distinct preference for the former is evident in the basic orientation of his thought.[35] He thus finds it easy to blend the Christian and *advaitic* Hindu conceptions of the Supreme Being: "He [God] is the ultimate Subject, the Substance—the basis of everything—the *Brahman* identical to the *atman*, hence the primary Cause, the unmoved mover, the ultimate Creator, the infinite Goodness, the perfect Idea, the utmost Justice, the Supreme Being."[36] The influence of *advaita* philosophy on his conception of God is evident in his distinct reticence to use personhood as a category for describing the essential nature of God. He thus warns against the "great temptation" of personalism, which he describes as anthropomorphism.[37]

Panikkar has his own distinctive understanding of personhood in relation to the Trinity. According to him the term *persons* cannot be used of the Trinity as a real analogy due to the absence of a viable point of reference for the analogy either within or without the Trinity itself. It is not true that God is three persons, since *persons* in the trinitarian context is an equivocal term, which has a different meaning in each case:

> There is no God except the Father who is his Son through his Spirit—but without three "who's" or "what's" of any sort. . . . There is not a *quaternitas*, a God-divine nature, outside, inside, above or beside the Father, the Son and the Holy Spirit. Only the Son is Person, if we use the word in its eminent sense and analogically to human persons: neither the Father nor the Spirit is a Person.[38]

God the Spirit is, in Panikkar's thought, the "immanent" God, whom he associates with the spirituality of intuitive inwardness, the *jnana* of *advaita* philosophy. Panikkar is deeply enamored of "the way par excellence of *advaita*," which with its emphasis on divine immanence offers the solution to some of the "enormous difficulties" posed by the classical personalist conception of God.[39]

Panikkar turns to the teaching of the *Upanishads* in quest of a solution to the question as to whether one can conceive of an authentic spirituality that is not based on interpersonal dialogue, in which God is not a "thou." The Spirit is thus clearly identified with the *atman* of the *Upanishads*, both signifying the same reality, divine immanence. Panikkar clearly does not conceive of this divine immanence in personal terms: "An immanent God cannot be a God-Person, 'someone' with whom I could have a 'personal' relationship, a God-Other. I cannot speak to an immanent God." For him, the personal conception of God is clearly inadequate: "In short, is the mystery of God exhausted in his unveiling as Person?"[40] The God of the *Upanishads*—the immanent Spirit who is not other, not person, not one with whom we enter into relationship—seems to hold a deeper fascination for him.

The Spirit is, therefore, one whom we realize in the depths of our being—the Ground of Being beyond our outward self. We realize him inwardly through silence and through inwardness. Hence, the realm of the Spirit is the realm of

---

[35]For a more detailed critique, see Vinoth Ramachandra, *The Recovery of Mission: Beyond the Pluralist Paradigm* (Delhi: ISPCK, 1999), 76-108; Ivan Satyavrata, "The Holy Spirit and Advaitic Spirituality," *Dharma Deepika* 1 (1995): 49-60.

[36]Raimundo Panikkar, *Myth, Faith and Hermeneutics* (New York: Paulist, 1979), 356.

[37]Raimundo Panikkar, *The Trinity and the Religious Experience of Man* (Maryknoll, NY: Orbis, 1973), 24.

[38]Panikkar, *Trinity*, 52.

[39]Panikkar, *Trinity*, 27, 39.

[40]Panikkar, *Trinity*, 31, 29.

mysticism and inward realization, not that of devotion or adoration of transcendent majesty: "One cannot have 'Personal relations' with the Spirit. One cannot reach the Transcendent, the Other, when one is directed towards the Spirit. One cannot pray to the Spirit. . . . One can only have a non-relational union with him."[41]

There are echoes here of a view of the Spirit's personhood, which we have earlier seen underlying the thought of Chakkarai, Monchanin, and Abhishiktananda, although in Panikkar the tendency is more explicit. His deference to *advaita* eventually leads him to empty the Trinity of any idea of selfhood and to an explicit denial of the Holy Spirit's personhood. For Panikkar, the spirit or the *atman* of *advaitic* Hinduism is merely an aspect of *Brahman*, the abstract, impersonal Absolute or Ground of Being. Panikkar's description of the Spirit's work amounts to little more than an attempt to clothe *advaitic* spirituality with the language of Christian theology.

WHERE THE HOLY SPIRIT BLOWS IN INDIA: A SUMMARY ASSESSMENT AND PROSPECTS

There is a natural tendency in Indian Christian thought toward "pneumatomonism," in which it is easier to conceive of God as spirit (or Spirit), rather than the Holy Spirit as God. This is largely due to the fact that as a result of the influence of *advatic* Hindu nondualism in India, it is easy for the Holy Spirit to be confused with the human spirit or to be viewed as an impersonal, immanent force. Consequently, the dominance of *advaita* in Hindu thought is reflected in the Christian discussion as well, with the impersonalist conception of the Absolute by and large holding a greater attraction than the idea of a

personal God for both Hindu and Christian thinkers alike.

With the clear exception of Nehemiah Goreh and A. J. Appasamy, the pneumatology of all the Indian thinkers surveyed bears the influence of *advaitic* nondualism. Ram Mohan Roy's strict monotheism, focused on *Brahman*, the Supreme Being of Vedanta, had no place at all for a personal Holy Spirit. His successor Sen's conception of the Trinity as *Saccidananda* set the tone for a whole new approach in enculturation that sought to relate the Christian gospel to Hindu *advaita*. Sen accordingly identified the Christian view of God with the highest conception of God in Hinduism, the *nirguna Brahman* (undifferentiated Being) of *advaita*.

Following this line of thought, Brahmabandhab Upadhyaya attempted somewhat unsuccessfully to affirm divine tri-personhood within the framework of an *advaitic* interpretation of the Trinity. His theological successors, Jules Monchanin and Swami Abhishiktananda, move even further away from a personalist conception of the Spirit in their eagerness to demonstrate ontological continuity between Christian and *advaitic* mystical experience. Raimundo Panikkar's understanding of the Spirit as the "immanent God" of *advaita* represents the ultimate destination in this journey from Christian to *advaitic* spirituality since the idea of personhood in relation to the Spirit is emptied of any meaningful content.

The same tendency toward an impersonalist conception of the Spirit may also be observed in thinkers such as Chenchiah and Chakkarai, who do not otherwise seem to display a conscious preference for *advaita* as a philosophical system. Even someone with strong personalist convictions such as A. J. Appasamy feels the need to make room for an impersonal conception of God within his personalist *bhakti* framework. This mystical fascination with the *advaitic* impersonalist conception of Spirit/spirit among Indian Christian thinkers is not altogether inexplicable given the context in which they theologize. However, Claude Welch's insightful comment in the context of his discussion of the significance of the *filioque* clause helps highlight the crucial point at which Indian pneumatological reflection urgently needs to be more firmly grounded in the New Testament witness:

> When the Christian speaks of the Holy Spirit, he does not refer to just any spirit or spirituality, certainly not to the spirit of man, or merely to a general immanence of God, but to a Holy Spirit consequent upon the event of objective revelation and reconciliation in Jesus Christ the Son. Where in Christian history the Spirit has not been clearly recognized as the Spirit of the Son . . . there has arisen what H.R. Niebuhr calls a "unitarianism of the Spirit."[42]

The neglect of this crucial perspective appears to be the main weakness of Indian Christian pneumatology. The Holy Spirit is not just any spirit and must not be confused with the human spirit, a general divine immanence, or an impersonal monist conception of spirit such as *Brahman-atman*. The Holy Spirit is preeminently the Spirit *of Christ*, and the Christian concept of the Trinity is derived from the historical fact of the incarnation.

There are profound implications of accommodating impersonalist conceptions of Spirit/spirit into Christian theology—a compromise that has a far-reaching impact on the essential nature and perhaps even the survival of the Christian faith. A major consequence of a notion of spirit that is emptied of divine personhood is that it ultimately erodes any basis for robust ethical engagement. The Christian ethic of loving service is grounded in the biblical conception of God as tri-personal: God as loving Father; the Son as divine love incarnate; and the Holy Spirit as the one who pours out God's love into the hearts of Christ-followers. Apart from the Holy Spirit's personhood, the foundation of this ethic is considerably weakened, if not altogether eliminated.

A second, perhaps more serious, consequence relates to the emergence and growing popularity of the modern phenomenon called religious pluralism—the perspective that all religions, more or less, offer equally valid ways of leading people to God. Religious pluralism celebrates diversity of religious experience and expression as good and healthy, and is skeptical of claims that any one religious tradition can be normative for all. This perspective finds strong resonance in an influential strand of philosophical Hinduism that readily subsumes all other religions within its doctrine of the essential unity of all religions with direct realization of the Supreme Being as the ultimate goal of a universal religion of the spirit. Religious pluralists in seeking to ascribe value to non-Christian religious experience thus often tend to stray away from biblical faith when they try to speak of the Spirit or the Trinity apart from the Christ-event in history.

John offers the following words of caution in his first epistle: "This is how you can recognize the Spirit of God: Every spirit that acknowledges that Jesus Christ has come in the flesh is from God, but every spirit that does not acknowledge Jesus is not from God" (Jn 4:2-3). The Holy Spirit is not the only spirit at work in the world—there are other "spirits" in the world. Spiritual discernment, the gift of "discerning of spirits"

---

[42]Claude Welch, "The Holy Spirit and the Trinity," *Theology Today* 8 (April 1951): 29.

(1 Cor 12:10), is thus a critical need if we are to have a biblically informed understanding of the Spirit's true identity in order to distinguish between genuine and counterfeit manifestations of the Holy Spirit's presence.

Jesus promised that the Spirit of truth would guide us into all truth and that he would testify about and bring glory to him (Jn 15:26; 16:13-14). This provides us with a helpful key for identifying where and how the Spirit is at work outside the church: we discern the authentic presence of the Spirit through his Christward witness—the Spirit always points, attracts, and leads to Christ. A commitment to Christ-centeredness as normative in spiritual discernment thus enables us to follow the Spirit in freely pursuing truth, beauty, and goodness wherever they may be found. When we find such elements in the midst of non-Christian religions and cultures, we celebrate their presence, affirm them as pointers to Christ, and use them to deepen and enrich our understanding of the gospel of Christ.

Our survey of Indian Christian pneumatology has illustrated why the *advaitic* tradition within Hinduism, despite its influence, presents seemingly insurmountable obstacles to constructive dialogue. There is, however, a personalist *bhakti* strand within Hinduism that has held a great attraction for Indian Christians such as A. J. Appasamy, Narayan Vaman Tilak, and H. A. Krishna Pillai, among others.[43]

The term *bhakti*, rendered variously as "service," "worship," "loyalty," "homage," and "loving devotion to God," denotes in its widest sense adoration of and loving devotion to the deity.[44] It in-

cludes most of the principal aspects of Indian religion and has had widespread influence in India. While there are different schools of thought within the broader *bhakti* tradition, the essential core of *bhakti* includes the idea of a personal God who can be loved and worshiped, and remains distinct from the *bhakta* (devotee). The object of the *bhakta's* total emotional abandonment and singular devotion is her *ishtadevata*, the deity of her choice, who bestows his grace on and fills her with his *anand*, indescribable peace and bliss. The *bhakta* suffers the agony of separation until through single-minded devotion her soul finds ultimate realization in union with God.[45]

We find a positive Christian approach to *bhakti* spirituality best illustrated in a key Indian Christian figure of the previous century, Sadhu Sundar Singh.[46] A careful analysis of Sundar Singh's thought suggests that his Christian experience was subconsciously shaped by *bhakti* elements imbibed during his pre-Christian formative years, some of which were appropriated later in his Christian theological formation. The influence of *bhakti* on Sundar Singh's approach is pronounced, although his framework represents a synthesis of elements from different strands of the *bhakti* tradition.

The earliest extensive teaching on *bhakti* is to be found in the *Bhagavadgita*, a deeply devotional text, with *bhakti* as the central theme of its message, telling of the soul's immortality and of a caring God's saving and reassuring love for each individual.[47] Among the various Hindu scriptures Sundar Singh was exposed to in his early years, the *Bhagavadgita*, which he had

---

[43]Boyd, *Introduction*, 112-43.

[44]G. M. Bailey and I. Kesarcodi-Watson, eds., *Bhakti Studies* (New Delhi: Sterling, 1992), 1-6.

[45]David Carlyle Scott, ed., *Kabir's Mythology* (Delhi: Bharatiya Vidya Prakashan, 1985), 22-23.

[46]For a more detailed assessment of Sundar Singh's thought, see Ivan Satyavrata, *God Has Not Left Himself Without Witness* (Oxford: Regnum, 2011), 139-96.

[47]J. Miller, "Bhakti and the Rig Veda—Does It Appear There or Not?," in *Love Divine: Studies in Bhakti and Devotional Mysticism*, ed. Karel Werner (Richmond, Surrey, UK: Curzon, 1993), 6, 21-24, 31; J. Lipner, *Hindus: Their Religious Beliefs and Practices* (London: Routledge, 1998), 134-35.

memorized by the age of seven, was a key formative influence.[48] The *bhakti* framework thus seems to have served as a preparation for Sundar Singh's reception of the Christian faith.

Sundar Singh's pre-Christian *bhakti* framework prepared him for his experience of Christ at a number of significant points: the view of God as a loving, personal Creator, distinct from and yet immanent in his creation; the acceptance of the possibility of the incarnation; the understanding of nature as a channel of divine revelation; the recognition of the divine authority of the written Word; the conception of sin as moral evil and salvation as the fulfillment of the soul's quest for union with God resulting in moral perfection of the soul; and the recognition that salvation comes at the gracious initiative of God. His understanding of salvation was strongly conditioned by the *bhakti* mystic quest for union with the divine. His view of the self in its relation to God resonates deeply with *bhakti* spirituality, in which mystical union with the divine is viewed as communion between two free personalities rather than absorption in the absolute: "God is our Creator and we are His creatures; He is our Father, and we are His children. . . . If we want to rejoice in God we must be different from Him; the tongue could taste no sweetness if there were no difference between it and that which it tastes. . . . To be redeemed does not mean to be lost or absorbed into God. We do not lose our personality in God; rather we find it."[49]

Sundar Singh observed the Spirit at work universally, as much in his mother's deep religious devotion as in his own dramatic conversion to faith in Christ. He believed that non-Christians,

while needing "the fullest light" that Christ gives, already have some access to the Holy Spirit and to the light of Christ (the Sun of righteousness):

> Non-Christian thinkers also have received light from the Sun of righteousness. The Hindus have received of the Holy Spirit. There are many beautiful things in Hinduism, but the fullest light is from Christ. Every one is breathing air. So every one, Christian as well as non-Christian, is breathing the Holy Spirit, though they do not call it by that name. The Holy Spirit is not the private property of some special people.[50]

Within Singh's theological framework, people thus have direct intuitive and mystical access to the Logos-Christ and to the Holy Spirit: the essential *bhakti* aspiration for union with God is fulfilled in a mystical encounter with the "living inward Christ" of experience. However, the historical facts concerning the life and ministry of Jesus as recorded in the New Testament are vital, ensuring continuity between the "inner Christ" of experience and the Christ of history. The *bhakti* mystical quest is thus fulfilled in an experience of mystical encounter with the "living inward Christ," in which the seeker's heart is transformed, is set free from sin, and finds true inner peace and bliss.

Sundar Singh's willingness to appropriate aspects of the Hindu tradition is also clearly evident in his adoption of the *sadhu* (holy person) lifestyle, an integral aspect of his expression of Christian discipleship.[51] He thus succeeded in embodying a form of Indian Christian discipleship that penetrated the heart of the gospel, and yet seemed "to have access to the innermost

---

[48]Friedrich Heiler, *The Gospel of Sadhu Sundar Singh*, trans. Olive Wyon (New Delhi: ISPCK, 1989), 37.
[49]Quoted in Heiler, *Gospel of Sadhu Sundar Singh*, 242.
[50]Quoted in B. H. Streeter and A. J. Appasamy, *The Sadhu: A Study in Mysticism and Practical Religion* (Delhi: Mittal, 1987), 232.
[51]Heiler, *Gospel of Sadhu Sundar Singh*, 55-56.

chambers of Indian spirituality."[52] The personalist *bhakti* devotional strand within Hinduism thus holds much more promise for Christian contextual engagement in India, and its influence can be observed in many grassroots Christian movements today. The popular Christian piety in mainline churches, many evangelical churches, and house church movements is commonly characterized by elements of *bhakti* devotional worship, and is especially evident in younger Pentecostal and charismatic church and mission movements.

Spirit-theology in India urgently needs to recapture a profound sense of the Holy Spirit's "holy-ness." The Holy Spirit is not merely an impersonal celestial force (*sakti*), or some abstract link between the Father and the Son (*ananda*). Nor must he be equated with any preexistent presence or influence already within humanity (*antaryamin*). He must not be confused with a general spiritual immanence, an impersonal divine influence, the human spirit, or some sort of supernatural spiritual being. He is the transcendent *Holy* Spirit, distinct and separate from his creation. He is the Spirit *of God* and *of Christ*, the personal presence of God himself: the dynamic personal, holy, *sakti* of Christ—the *Khrista-sakti*.

The Holy Spirit is the means by which God makes his personal presence felt among his people, the church, the community of the Spirit. The ultimate purpose of the Spirit's floodlight ministry is to mediate the presence of the risen Christ, and to create and deepen an awareness of the reality of Jesus in human experience.[53]

> On the last and greatest day of the Feast, Jesus stood and said in a loud voice, "If anyone is thirsty, let him come to me and drink. Whoever believes in me, as the Scripture has said, streams of living water will flow from within him." By this he meant the Spirit, whom those who believed in him were later to receive. Up to that time the Spirit had not been given, since Jesus had not yet been glorified. (Jn 7:37-39)

FURTHER READING

Boyd, Robin. *An Introduction to Indian Christian Theology*. Delhi: ISPCK, 1991.

Christie Kumar, B. J. "An Indian Christian Appreciation of the Doctrine of the Holy Spirit: A Search into the Religious Heritage of the Indian Christian." *Indian Journal of Theology* 30, no. 1 (1981): 29-35.

Kim, Kirsteen. "The Holy Spirit in Mission in India: Indian Contribution to Contemporary Mission Pneumatology." *UBS Journal* 1 (2003): 57-66.

Lipner, Julius. *Hindus: Their Religious Beliefs and Practices*. London: Routledge, 1998.

Richard, H. L. "A Survey of Protestant Evangelistic Efforts Among High Caste Hindus in the Twentieth Century." *Missiology: An International Review* 25 (1997): 419-45.

Stephen, M. *A Christian Theology in the Indian Context*. Delhi: ISPCK, 2001.

---

[52]Eric J. Sharpe, "The Legacy of Sadhu Sundar Singh," *International Bulletin of Missionary Research* 14 (1991): 161; see Heiler, *Gospel of Sadhu Sundar Singh*, 231.

[53]Satyavrata, *Holy Spirit*, 80; see J. I. Packer, *Keep in Step with the Spirit* (Grand Rapids, MI: Baker, 2005), 49-50, 56-58. *Floodlight* is Packer's expression in *Keep in Step*, 57.

19

REDEFINING RELATIONSHIPS

THE ROLE OF THE SPIRIT IN ROMANS AND ITS SIGNIFICANCE IN THE MULTIETHNIC CONTEXT OF INDIA

Zakali Shohe

THE RELATIONAL ASPECT of the Spirit in the Pauline epistles is important to consider in understanding the place of the Spirit in Paul's thought. Furthermore, it is also significant in a multiethnic context. To this end the chapter investigates the role of the Spirit in Romans 8:14-17 and highlights its significance in the multiethnic context of India.

The context of India is one of diverse ethnic groups and races that are interdependent. This interdependence can be economic, political, or social. Yet despite this interdependence, there is also the tendency to protect one's own ethnic group, and this can result in conflict and division. Hence, it is important to redefine boundaries, not abandoning distinct ethnic identities, religions, and denominations, while at the same time being open and accepting of differences in a multiethnic context. With this in mind, this chapter examines the role of the Spirit in Romans 8:14-17 from a relational perspective and draws out its significance for Christians in India.

Studies on the Spirit and the ethical life have predominantly focused on the material *pneuma* (Spirit) as a means that provides an ontological transforming effect.[1] These studies regard Paul's notion of the Spirit as *Stoff* (matter). They focus on the transformation of believers that takes place through the *stofflich* (material) notion of the Spirit. Volker Rabens refers to this model as "static." He proposes instead a relational model of the work of the Spirit based on the actual effects attributed to the Spirit in Judaism and Paul. Rabens describes his model: "It is primarily through deeper knowledge of, and an intimate relationship with, God, Jesus Christ and with the community of faith that people are transformed and empowered by the

---

[1]Ernst Käsemann identifies Christ with *pneuma*, which transforms believers by their partaking in the sacrament of the Lord's Supper. *Pneuma* is seen as a sacramental gift through which the sacrament effects the transformation of people (Käsemann, "The Pauline Doctrine of the Lord's Supper," in *Essays on New Testament Themes*, Studies in Biblical Theology [London: SCM Press, 1964], 108-35, esp. 118-25). F. W. Horn also suggests an ontological transformation by the Spirit. According to him, Paul adopts the material concept of the Spirit, which is transferred sacramentally, especially through baptism (Horn, "Holy Spirit," in *The Anchor Bible Dictionary*, ed. David Noel Freedman [New York: Doubleday, 1992], 3:271-76). Volker Rabens in his monograph discusses this approach in detail. He especially analyzes the stand of Käsemann, Peter Stuhlmacher, and Horn on the "infusion-transformation" approach (*The Holy Spirit and Ethics in Paul: Transformation and Empowering for Religious-Ethical Life* [Tübingen: Mohr Siebeck, 2010], 2-20).

Spirit for religious-ethical life."[2] The approach in this chapter is also relational, but it aims to investigate Romans 8:14-17 in particular within the context of Spirit-guided relationships.

A BRIEF OVERVIEW OF ROMANS 8:14-17

In line with the view that Paul in Romans is addressing a mixed community of Jews and Gentiles, this chapter looks at the Spirit language in such a setting.[3] In taking this stand, I do not intend to argue for Jew-Gentile unification as Paul's sole purpose for writing Romans. In recent years many studies have come up with a variety of reasons why Paul wrote Romans.[4] The epistle itself gives evidence of the many purposes of Paul, but it is beyond the scope of this chapter to go into details. Hence, keeping in mind the Jew-Gentile context of Romans, this chapter takes up the role of the Spirit in redefining relationships. In looking at the pericope, I avoid a detailed discussion of every exegetical issue arising from the text. Instead, I concentrate on how Romans 8:14-17 contributes to the role of the Spirit in redefining relationships. In relation to the Spirit language in Romans 8:14-17, this

chapter highlights two aspects: the leading of the Spirit and the defining role of the Spirit.

The leading of the Spirit. For Paul the criterion for the status of children of God is the leading of the Spirit (Rom 8:14). It is generally accepted that *agontai* (being led) with the dative *pneumati* (by Spirit) suggests the enthusiastic nature of believers and is an active indication of being led by a spiritual force.[5] The overtone of active and ecstatic behavior in the use of the dative *pneumati* is also found in other Pauline epistles (e.g., 1 Cor 12:2; Gal 5:18). Furthermore, the notion of "being carried away" by a compelling force or surrendering to a spiritual force was also dominant in the Greco-Roman world, especially in magical texts, where *agein* (to lead) was used in reference to gods, spirits, or ghosts of the dead. These agents were commanded to lead a person supernaturally.[6]

Romans 8:14 also reflects active indication, which need not necessarily be an audacious ecstatic experience.[7] Instead, it is possible to interpret "being led" by the Spirit in connection with "being led" by the cloud in the exodus narrative.[8] In the exodus narrative, the cloud is

---

[2]Rabens, *Holy Spirit*, 120, 123, 128.

[3]See Karl Paul Donfried, *The Romans Debate*, rev. and exp. ed. (1977; repr., Peabody, MA: Hendrickson, 1991); Andrew Das, *Solving the Romans Debate* (Minneapolis: Fortress, 2007); John Murray, *The Epistle to the Romans*, New International Commentary on the New Testament (Grand Rapids, MI: Eerdmans, 1959, 1965), 2:172-74; Paul J. Achtemeier, *Romans: Interpretation* (Atlanta: John Knox, 1985), 215; W. S. Campbell, "Why Did Paul Write Romans?," *Expository Times* 85, no. 9 (1973–1974): 268; C. E. B. Cranfield, *A Critical and Exegetical Commentary on the Epistle to the Romans*, International Critical Commentary (Edinburgh: T&T Clark, 1975), 1:17-22; 2:694-96; Ernst Käsemann, *Commentary on Romans*, trans. and ed. G. W. Bromiley, 4th ed. (London: SCM Press, 1980), 366. Offering an alternate view that Paul is addressing a Gentile community are A. Andrew Das, "'Praise the Lord, All You Gentiles': The Encoded Audience of Romans 15:7-13," *Journal for the Study of the New Testament* 34, no. 1 (2011): 101-2; Joshua D. Garroway, "The Circumcision of Christ: Romans 15:7-13," *Journal for the Study of the New Testament* 34, no. 4 (2012): 306.

[4]See L. Ann Jervis, *The Purpose of Romans: A Comparative Letter Structure Investigation* (Sheffield: JSOT Press, 1991); A. J. M. Wedderburn, *The Reasons for Romans* (Edinburgh: T&T Clark, 1988); Lo Lung-Kwong, *Paul's Purpose in Writing Romans: The Upbuilding of a Jewish and Gentile Christian Community in Rome* (Hong Kong: Alliance Biblical Seminary, 1998); Robert Jewett, *Romans: A Commentary* (Minneapolis: Fortress, 2007), 80-91.

[5]Ernst Käsemann defines this experience: "Paul was not so timid as his expositors. He could appropriate the terms of the enthusiast because he took 'Christ in us' seriously." *Commentary on Romans*, 226. James D. G. Dunn and Robert Jewett follow Käsemann in reading *agesthai* with the dative as indicating an enthusiastic and active force. Dunn embraces the NEB's rendering "moved by the Spirit." Dunn, *Romans 1–8*, 450; Jewett, *Romans*, 496.

[6]For references to texts, see Jewett, *Romans*, 496 (esp. n231).

[7]Also, Jewett, *Romans*, 496. But not necessarily as in the Corinthian and the Thessalonian contexts (1 Cor 12–14; 1 Thess 5:19-22).

[8]For this reading of *agō* I am indebted to Francis Watson, who introduced me to it in the course of our discussion at Trinity Theological College, Singapore, September 30, 2014.

identified as the presence of God that leads the Israelites (Ex 14). There is no direct reference to the Spirit in the text from Exodus, but Paul alludes to this event in 1 Corinthians 10:1-5 and links the Spirit with the exodus. In considering the Corinthians passage, it is possible to understand being led by the Spirit in Romans 8 as parallel to being led by the cloud. The cloud is the presence of God with the Israelites, and the Spirit in Romans 8:14 can also be seen as the presence of God in the lives of believers.

Elabete (you received, Rom 8:15) probably points to the initial experience of life in the Spirit, while *agontai* (being led, Rom 8:14) refers to the ongoing leading of the Spirit. For the relationship does not stop with the initial experience, but the Spirit continues to guide believers by connecting them to God as well as to other believers. Paul's emphasis is on the ongoing Spirit-guided relationship in the experience of heirship, where all believers share Christ's heirship in the family of God (Rom 8:15-17). For the Spirit is active in guiding believers to a new status as children of God, and this status redefines their relationship within the family of God. It is the Spirit who defines the place of believers in the family of God.[9] This is further elaborated in Romans 8:15-17 with the use of familial images.

The defining role of the Spirit. Having established the criteria for being called "children of God" (Rom 8:14, 16), Paul goes on to highlight the defining role of the Spirit with the use of familial images (Rom 8:15-17). He draws on powerful relationship language from the ancient Mediterranean world that binds its members together in kinship. The family was a basic social institution, and references to it were used in people's everyday language in relation to one another.[10] The familial images in Romans 8:14-17 also point to a relationship that, according to James Dunn, is a status by "divine choice."[11] Paul aims to redefine what it means to be adopted as children of God through receiving the Spirit of God.[12]

Four characteristics define the role of the Spirit of God. First, in Romans 8:14-15 the Spirit is described as the "Spirit of adoption." In these verses the status of the children of God is defined in relation to the Spirit. This relationship is made possible through "adoption," which for Dunn is either through "the Spirit which effects adoption, or the Spirit which expresses adoption."[13]

The metaphor of adoption occurs throughout the Pauline epistles, especially in Romans (Rom 8:15, 23; 9:4; Gal 4:5; Eph 1:1). It is possible that Paul uses the metaphor in his exhortation to the Roman believers because the notion of adoption was common in Greco-Roman law and custom.[14] This practice was not prevalent in its legal form among the Jews, but the notion of adoption, especially divine adoption, is also found in Jewish sources.[15] Ernst Käsemann rejects the original

---

[9]See Dunn, *Romans 1–8*, 451.

[10]Philip Esler, *Conflict and Identity in Romans: The Social Setting of Paul's Letter* (Minneapolis: Fortress, 2003), 247.

[11]James D. G. Dunn, "Spirit Speech: Reflections on Romans 8:12-27," in *Romans and the People of God: Essays in Honor of Gordon D. Fee on the Occasion of His 65th Birthday*, ed. Sven K. Soderlund and N. T. Wright (Grand Rapids, MI: Eerdmans, 1999), 83. See also Dunn, *Romans 1–8*, 526.

[12]See Dunn, *Romans 1–8*, 451; Jewett, *Romans*, 497 (following Dunn's position).

[13]Dunn, "Spirit Speech," 83.

[14]It is beyond the scope of this chapter to discuss the Greco-Roman institution of adoption. See James M. Scott, *Adoption as Sons: An Exegetical Investigation into the Background of ΥΙΟΘΕΣΙΑ in the Pauline Corpus*, Wissenschaftliche Untersuchungen zum Neuen Testament 48 (Tübingen: Mohr Siebeck, 1992), 3-13.

[15]God as the father and Israel as the son (Ex 4:22; Is 43:6; Sirach 51:10; Tobit 13:5). Scott presents a detailed study in *Adoption as Sons*, 61-117. See also Cranfield, *Romans*, 1:397-98.

sense of adoption in the Greek term *huiothesia* (Rom 8:15).[16] However, such rejection overlooks the overall intention of Paul, especially in terms of the role of the Spirit as redefining boundaries. Dunn rightly comments that Käsemann's rejection "is both unfounded and misses the point." Dunn goes on to affirm that Paul draws *huiothesia* from the Greco-Roman world, and his use of the term indicates that a believer is transformed not only from a slave to a freed man but also from a freed man to an adopted child of God.[17] It is thus possible to refer to the notion of adoption as redefining a person's relationship with God. This new status of believers is experienced through the guidance of the Spirit.

Second, the new status of believers gives them the privilege to cry "Abba Father" (Rom 8:15). *Krazomen* (we cry) is taken as referring to *pneuma* (Spirit), "in whom we cry." It can be either an intense and loud cry or an "urgent and sincere crying to God," regardless of whether loud or soft, formal or informal, public or private.[18] However, we cannot conclude with certainty whether *krazomen* stands for a loud, soft, spoken, or silent cry, but it is possible to regard it as an expression of connecting to God where believers can freely express themselves. Such connection with God is realized through the leading of the Spirit.

The filial address "Abba" in Paul's exhortation should not be interpreted merely on the basis of its semantics, but, more importantly, in the context of the divine-human relationship. Emphasizing the experiential side, M. M. Thompson hypothesizes that the "Abba"-cry (Rom 8:15) and

the Spirit's bearing witness with our spirit (8:16) have been misinterpreted as an intimate relationship with God. Thompson states that *krazein* (to cry) cannot be an expression of an emotional state of believers, for it occurs in a prophetic context in Romans 9:27. It refers to the "Spirit-inspired nature of Isaiah's speech." She concludes that *krazein* in 8:15 emphasizes the "ultimate source," which points to the power of the Spirit at work.[19] The problem with Thompson's conclusion is her overemphasis on the experiential aspect of the Spirit over against the relational aspect. It is also a relationship since believers are adopted as children of God, pointing to a different level of relationship from slavery and fear. This relationship receives expression through the Spirit-inspired cry to God. In the words of Dunn, "It is a relationship he is describing, not just an experience. But Paul's language does not permit us to forget that the relationship in view is one which for Paul was expressed in intensity of feeling as well as intimacy of expression."[20] Supporting the view that the "Abba"-cry is not just an experience but also connotes relationship, Rabens says: "The 'Abba'-cry does not designate isolated experiences but a continuous loving relationship which, like every active relationship, has an experiential side."[21]

Third, Paul is emphasizing joint witness. Romans 8:16 further affirms the role of the Spirit in redefining the place of believers: "The Spirit bears witness with our Spirit that we are children of God." The Greek *syn-* compounds (*syn*: with, together with) in relation to the Spirit appear often in Romans 8: the Spirit

[16]Käsemann, *Romans*, 227, following Theodor Zahn, *Der Brief des Paulus an die Römer* (Leipzig: Deichert, 1925).
[17]Dunn, *Romans 1–8*, 452.
[18]Dunn, *Romans 1–8*, 453; see also Cranfield, *Romans*, 1:399.
[19]Marianne Meye Thompson, *The Promise of the Father: Jesus and God in the New Testament* (Louisville: Westminster John Knox, 2000), 126.
[20]Dunn, "Spirit Speech," 85.
[21]Rabens, *Holy Spirit*, 226-27.

bears witness together with us (Rom 8:16); the Spirit leads believers to a relationship with Christ, with whom they become "joint heirs," and also "suffers together with" in order that they might be "glorified together with" (Rom 8:17); the Spirit comes along to offer aid in our weakness (Rom 8:26); and the Spirit works all things together for good (Rom 8:28). These *syn*-compounds emphasize a close "relationship between two people or matters."[22]

The prefix *syn-* (with) in the compound verb *symmartyreō* (bear witness together with) carries the meaning of accompaniment ("bear witness with"), but it can also refer to an intensive force ("bear witness to"; see Rom 2:25; 9:1).[23] Some scholars prefer the latter meaning, while others argue that the dual witness affirms the believer's new relationship to God.[24] The requirement of two or more witnesses is also found in Deuteronomy 17:6; 19:5, in 2 Corinthians 13:1, and in the practice of adoption in the ancient Greco-Roman world.[25] In Romans 8:16, it probably refers to a joint witness in order to affirm the adoption by adding more than one witness. The Spirit confirms the new status of believers in God's family. It is a change from slaves to children. Accordingly, Robert Jewett writes, "Since the Spirit impels believers to utter their prayers directly to their 'Abba,' this is a powerful experiential confirmation of their status as children of God. Since the Spirit con-

firms that they belong to God, there is no longer any basis for anxiety about their status."[26]

Thompson offers a different view, noting that in Romans 8:16 Paul is explicitly referring to the work of the Spirit in enabling the Gentiles to acknowledge God as their source of life and not the believer's "sense of sonship."[27] I agree with Thompson that the Spirit enables the Gentiles, but focusing only on this aspect in Romans 8:16 misses the filial relationship in Romans 8:14-15, especially the work of the Spirit in witnessing with our spirit and in confirming the filial relationship that believers share with God.[28] For in their status as children of God, believers become heirs of God (Rom 8:17).

Fourth, believers share status with Christ as "coheirs" (*synklēronomoi*; Rom 8:17; see Gal 4:7). Christ is not directly addressed as the heir, but believers are called to share as coheirs with Christ. In this regard Christ as heir suggests the concept of the "son of God" (Mk 12:7; Heb 1:2). The Spirit leads believers to a new status as children of God through adoption, and they share with Christ as coheirs. This points to the relationship between God, Christ, and the Spirit. In the Pauline epistles (and the New Testament as a whole) there is no explicitly articulated doctrine of God as in the classical documents of the church, such as the Nicene Creed. However, as David Yeago argues, the New Testament contains implicit and explicit

---

[22]See Gordon D. Fee, *God's Empowering Presence: The Holy Spirit in the Letters of Paul* (Peabody, MA: Hendrickson, 1994), 562.

[23]See Walter Bauer, William F. Arndt, F. Wilbur Gingrich, and Frederick W. Danker, *Greek English Lexicon of the New Testament and Other Early Christian Literature*, 3rd ed. (Chicago: University of Chicago Press, 2000), 617-19, on *martyreō* and its related roots.

[24]For the latter meaning ("bear witness to"), see Geoffrey W. Bromiley, ed., *Theological Dictionary of the New Testament* (Grand Rapids, MI: Eerdmans, 1967), 4:508-9; Cranfield, *Romans*, 1:402. For the former meaning ("bear witness with"), see Rabens, *Holy Spirit*, 216.

[25]Rabens, *Holy Spirit*, 216-17, follows James D. G. Dunn, *The Epistle to the Galatians* (Peabody, MA: Hendrickson, 1993), 219; Trevor J. Burke, *Adopted into God's Family: Exploring a Pauline Metaphor*, New Studies in Biblical Theology 22 (Downers Grove, IL: InterVarsity Press, 2006), 150-51. See also Douglas J. Moo, *Romans* (Grand Rapids, MI: Zondervan, 2000), 504.

[26]Jewett, *Romans*, 500.

[27]Thompson, *Promise of the Father*, 128.

[28]So also Rabens, *Holy Spirit*, 227-28.

judgments concerning the crucified and resur-rected Jesus of Nazareth.[29]

In Romans 8, the relationship of God and Jesus is that of Father and Son. Jesus is identified as an heir in God's family. As heir of God, Jesus has been identified with God, and as such shares God's unique privileges as the firstborn of all (Col 1:15). The Spirit also acts on behalf of God as "the Spirit of God" (Rom 8:14) by leading be-lievers in relating to the Father in their identity as coheirs with Christ. Romans 8 also reflects a community building and strengthening one an-other in the Spirit. Furthermore, Jesus is iden-tified as Christ in Romans 8:17, signifying his exaltation, and in his exaltation Jesus has been identified with God.[30] In looking at the text from the relational perspective it is possible to see the connection between God, Christ, and the Spirit. Christ and the Spirit cannot be separated from God, for God is identified in the person of Jesus as the "Son of God" and heir, and the Spirit in this text is the presence of God, signifying the triune God.

Believers are coheirs not through physical de-scent but through divine call and appointment. As Jesus addresses God as "Abba Father," so also believers address God as "Abba Father" and attest themselves as children of God and coheirs with Christ. The Spirit establishes this rela-tionship and links believers to Jesus. This then defines a person as a believer.[31] Sonship and in-heritance are grounded in a new creation. The idea of inheritance is important in Paul, for the promise given to Abraham is now mediated through Christ (see Gal 3:16, 29; 4:1, 7), and be-lievers, both Jews and Gentiles, are coheirs of the promise (Rom 8:17; Eph 3:18).[32]

Thus far, this chapter has analyzed the Spirit language in Romans 8:14-17 and highlighted two aspects. The first is the criterion for the believer's status as a child of God, that is, the leading of the Spirit. The second is the defining role of the Spirit with the use of familial images. Having analyzed the role of the Spirit in the text, the next step is to redefine relationship in the context of the Spirit.

REDEFINING RELATIONSHIP IN THE CONTEXT OF THE SPIRIT

Spirit and language of intimacy. The word *rela-tional* is not found in the Pauline epistles. In fact, Paul does not even use the words *relationship* and *relational* in the context of the Spirit lan-guage. However, the concept of relationships plays an important role in his ministry and the-ology.[33] This observation is also made by Dunn, who says, "Paul's theology is relational."[34] There are terms and phrases pointing to the idea of relationship, as is also found in Paul's approach to the Spirit. For example, the prepositions *syn* (with, together with) and *en* (in) point to rela-tionship, particularly the notion of being in Christ or with Christ. Familial images such as *huiou theou* (son of God), *huiothesias* (adoption), *abba ho patēr* (Abba Father), *tekna theou*

---

[29]David S. Yeago, "The New Testament and the Nicene Dogma: A Contribution to the Recovery of Theological Exegesis," *Pro Ecclesia* 3, no. 2 (Spring 1994): 153.

[30]Yeago makes a similar argument in his discussion of the message of early Christians on Jesus' exaltation, though not in relation to Romans ("New Testament and the Nicene Dogma," 154).

[31]See Dunn, "Spirit Speech," 84.

[32]J. H. Friedrich, "*klēronomos, ou, ho*," in *Exegetical Dictionary of the New Testament*, ed. Horst Balz and Gerherd Schneider (Grand Rapids, MI: Eerdmans, 1991), 2:298-99.

[33]This is also my hypothesis in "Paul's Use of 'Familial Images' and Their Significance for the Understanding of His Ministry" (MTh thesis, United Theological College, 2003). See Rabens for a list from the Pauline epistles (*Holy Spirit*, 135-37).

[34]James D. G. Dunn, *The Theology of Paul* (Grand Rapids, MI: Eerdmans, 1998), 53.

(children of God), *klēronomoi* (heirs), and *synklēronomoi* (coheirs) highlight family relations (Rom 8:14-17).

The relational approach is also discussed in detail by Rabens, with exegetical evidence from the epistles of Paul.[35] Yet, unlike Rabens, the main question this chapter takes up is how the Spirit enables the redefinition of boundaries. My reading of Romans 8:14-17 indicates that the role of the Spirit in the redefinition of boundaries occurs in the Spirit-guided relationship. This relationship is made more significant with the use of familial language.

Spirit-guided relationship: A redefined boundary. Paul states that "in the Spirit" the Roman communities share a new identity, which is built on Israel's self-understanding of being people chosen by God. The new identity is emphasized with the use of diverse terms such as *huiou* (son; Rom 8:14, 19), *huiothesia* (adoption; Rom 8:15, 23), and *tekna theou* (children of God; Rom 8:16, 21).[36] In the context of the new relationship as children of God, K. K. Yeo makes an insightful remark from the perspective of honor and shame: "Believers made righteous by the act of God in Christ have been given the honor of being sons of God."[37] In the light of the Spirit language in Romans 8, it is thus possible to look at the Spirit of God as the agent of honor. It guides believers to God through adoption and thus leads them to experience the honor of this new identity. It is the Spirit that guides believers and connects them to God through adoption. Their adoption into the family of God gives them the privilege of calling God "Abba Father."

The link between the Spirit and divine heirship broadens beyond people groups by defining believers at Rome as adopted into the family of God. Their status in the family of God is affirmed through a joint witness where "the Spirit" and "our spirit" witness together. This joint witness points to the importance of a community in relation building that redefines boundaries. Furthermore, the Spirit-guided relationship narrows the gap between Jewish and Gentile believers through their acceptance of one another. This relationship is given shape and made significant through the use of familial images. Thus, it is the Spirit who empowers and connects believers at the personal and the corporate levels of relationship.

Spirit-guided relationships: A basis for hope. The divine acceptance of believers as children of God allows them to enter into a new relationship. The entrance into a new relationship is not an end in itself, but the Spirit-guided status that believers share, as coheirs with Christ and with one another as a faith community, provides an eschatological hope for the "unseen" (see Rom 8:24-25; 15:13). Heirship is also grounded in future hope (Rom 8:23), for the inheritance of believers is also an object of hope.[38] Believers look forward to the promise of glorification (Rom 8:17).

---

[35]Rabens, *Holy Spirit*, 121-24.

[36]See J. Ross Wagner, "'Not from the Jews Only, But Also from the Gentiles': Mercy to the Nations in Romans 9–11," in *Between Gospel and Election*, ed. Florian Wilk and J. Ross Wagner, Wissenschaftliche Untersuchungen zum Neuen Testament 257 (Tübingen: Mohr Siebeck, 2010), 418.

[37]K. K. Yeo, "From Rome to Beijing: One World One Dream," in *From Rome to Beijing: Symposia on Robert Jewett's Commentary on Romans*, ed. K. K. Yeo (Lincoln, NE: Kairos Studies, 2013), 16. The monograph *From Rome to Beijing* is important for its crosscultural reading of Romans.

[38]The word group *klēronomos* in its eschatological sense also occurs in the context of judgment (Mt 25:34; 1 Cor 6:10; Gal 5:21). The phrase "inherit eternal life" also occurs within the eschatological frame (Mt 19:29; Mk 10:17; Lk 18:18; 10:25; Col 3:24). See W. Foerster, "The Word Group *klēronomos* in the LXX," in *Theological Dictionary of the New Testament*, ed. Gerhard Kittel, trans. Geoffrey W. Bromiley (1965; repr., Grand Rapids, MI: Eerdmans, 1984), 3:782-84; Friedrich, "*klēronomos, ou, ho*," 2:298-99.

Paul ends the section (Rom 8:14-17) on the believer's existence in the Spirit with a condition (Rom 8:17). He demands that as fellow heirs with Christ, believers "suffer with him so that we may also be glorified with him." The notion of present suffering and future glorification is further developed in Romans 8:18-30. Believers look forward to the future glorification as fellow heirs with Christ, a hope that is unseen but for which they patiently wait (Rom 8:24-25). Believers remain part of the present world, in which suffering and difficulties are inevitable (Rom 5:3-5). In their coming together as a worshiping community, believers strengthen one another and abound in hope as they look forward to final glorification (see Rom 8:17; 15:7-13).[39]

It is thus possible to say that the Spirit-guided relationship provides hope, for it involves a future relationship between individuals, communities, and groups. As Jürgen Moltmann puts it, "Every relationship to another life involves the future of that life, the future of the reciprocal relationship into which one life enters with another." It is a "relational eschatology," for it concerns the ongoing relationship built on the truthfulness and the mercy of God (see Rom 9–11; 15:8-9).[40] In accepting one another as fellow believers in the family of God, the members of the community continue to hope in nurturing their relationship in a meaningful direction. The hope of believers is a move toward building a sense of connectedness among Jews and Gentiles and their openness to accepting one another through the guidance of the Spirit. In Romans 15:13, hope is connected with worship. Such a connection also appears in Romans 5:2,

where hope is connected with giving praise to God—a hope that is unseen (Rom 8:24-25) but kept alive through the common worship of Jews and Gentiles.

Summary. Thus far, this chapter has attempted to identify the role of the Spirit in redefining relationships. The concept of relationship is elaborated with the use of familial images. This relationship is redefined through the guidance of the Spirit at both the personal and the corporate levels. From the above analysis of Romans 8:14-17, it can be said that the language used for the Spirit describes relationship, one expressed in openness to accept the "other," one not belonging to the same people group (Rom 15:7). The Spirit redefines or moves people in terms of boundaries; the Spirit not only guides believers in their present life as a faith community, but also gives them hope to look forward to final redemption. The Spirit guides individual believers in relating to God as children in the family of God as well as in their openness to accepting one another, both Jews and Gentiles. This Spirit-guided relationship also provides hope for believers in their coming together as a worshiping community. Having identified the relation-building nature of the Spirit, I now draw insights from my reading in the context of India.

A PNEUMATOLOGICAL RELATIONAL ELEMENT IN THE CONTEXT OF INDIA

Context of India: A brief overview. India is a land of diverse cultures, faith traditions, and ethnic identities. The multiethnic context and rich cultural diversity provide an opportunity to be open to, learn from, and respect one another.

---

[39]While I understand that there are many home churches in Rome, in this chapter I use the singular ("a worshiping community"), which also represents these home churches.

[40]Jürgen Moltmann, *The Church in the Power of the Spirit: A Contribution to Messianic Ecclesiology*, 2nd ed. (London: SCM Press, 1992), 134.

Even people within the same region share rich cultural diversity, administration, and policies. This is true especially for the northeast region of India. Eight different states comprise northeast India: Assam, Arunachal Pradesh, Manipur, Meghalaya, Mizoram, Nagaland, Sikkim, and Tripura. The region is characterized by its rich ethnic, cultural, religious, and linguistic diversity.

However, the danger in the context of diversity lies in being overprotective of one's identity at the expense of the other people groups. When an ethnic identity or a faith tradition is rooted in pride, there is the danger that the dominant group's identity becomes a threat to others. In India, the Brahmanic, or Sanskritic, culture is meant to represent the Indian culture, or what it means to be Indian.[41] The other people groups enter the mainstream by assimilating into the Hindu fold, whereby the tribes are identified in the Hindu polity.[42] This means "entering the caste fold from the lowest level."[43] In such a context the minority communities are involved in conflict in order to preserve their ethnic or faith identity over against the dominant one; they may experience discrimination at the personal level in either workplaces or public places to varying degrees.

Today in India, instead of celebrating diversity, there is a tendency among various groups to be suspicious. Mistrust stops people from being open and accepting of those who do not belong to their race, religion, or people group, and this is true even in an ecclesial setting. In such a context of conflict, differences, and atroc-ities, Christians as individuals and the church as an institution in India are called to redefine relationships in the ecclesial sphere as well as in the social sphere.

Spirit and relationality. Paul's exhortation on the Spirit-guided relationship that moves beyond the traditional boundaries of people groups is relevant for Christians in India. In the pluralistic context of religions and multiethnicity, which continue to remain a challenging issue in the Indian context, S. J. Samartha refers to the Spirit that brings the unity of the Father and the Son and also brings believers in Christ together as the Spirit of oneness.[44] In Samartha's view, the Holy Spirit "not only makes it necessary for us to enter into dialogue, but also to continue in it without fear, with full expectation and openness."[45] Chenchiah describes the Holy Spirit as a great creative power and energy that brings transformation in the political and social structures of the world.[46] Thus, the Spirit transcends the traditional understanding of the people of God and redefines relationships. It is the Spirit who redefines the people of God, for all who are led by the Spirit are children of God, heirs and coheirs with Christ. In his chapter in this section Wei Hua also highlights the role of the Spirit in building new relationships in the life of believers. This notion of the Spirit is important especially in our understanding of Pauline pneumatology because in Paul's writings we see that the Spirit redefines an individual believer's status before God, and that this is also the case in the incorporation of both Jews and

---

[41]G. S. Gurye, *The Scheduled Tribes* (Bombay: Popular Prakashan, 1963), 211. See also G. N. Dash, *Hindus and Tribals* (New Delhi: Decent Books, 1998), 3.

[42]Gouranga Chhattopadhyay, "The Problem of Tribal Integration to Urban Industrial Society: A Theoretical Approach," in *The Tribal Situation in India*, ed. K. Suresh Singh (Simla: Indian Institute of Advanced Study, 1972), 491.

[43]Hukato Shohe, "Developing a Christology from Sumi Naga Context" (PhD diss., Senate of Serampore College [University], 2014), 202.

[44]Stanley J. Samartha, *One Christ—Many Religions: Toward a Revised Christology* (Maryknoll, NY: Orbis, 1991), 83.

[45]Stanley J. Samartha, *Two Cultures: Ecumenical Ministry in a Pluralist World* (Bangalore, India: Asian Trading Cooperation, 1997), 1-14.

[46]P. V. Joseph, *Indian Interpretation of the Holy Spirit* (Delhi: ISPCK, 2007), 72.

Gentiles in the body of Christ. This creates space for openness to accept one another in a faith community.

The Spirit guides believers into community, where their acceptance of one another provides hope (Rom 15:7-13), for it encompasses the future of the relationship that is established. In their acceptance and openness to one another believers abound in hope that strengthens and nurtures their relationship in a constructive and meaningful direction. The relationship does not end with its initial experience, but believers grow together as they look forward to the hope of final redemption.

This understanding of the Spirit as one who guides believers into community and openness by redefining boundaries is significant for Christians and the church in India. The relation building of the Spirit is obvious in the life of the church, in spite of the many limitations imposed on it by human-created structures in thought and attitude. In India, the church is seen as a remnant of the imperialist heritage. Christians are many times looked on as agents of imperialism or traitors of nationalism or indigenous cultures and religions at worst, or as passive or unconscious agents of Western culture at best. In this context, the reaching-out and relation-building nature of the Spirit continues to manifest itself in various ways in the ecclesial sphere. Both the church as an institution and individual believers continue to identify with and engage in diverse ways at the personal and the corporate levels, in creating space for openness and acceptance, for building a community of faith, and for learning from one another through the guidance of the Spirit.

For instance, northeast India has a long history of insurgency. In fact, most of the states

there in recent years have been affected by violence and conflict. In Nagaland, separatist violence started in the 1950s, and the conflict has escalated, especially since the late 1970s.[47] The Nagas have had a long history of conflict with the government of India and have also suffered at the hands of the Naga insurgency, which is fragmented into various factions. The conflict between the government of India and the various people groups, particularly in the northeast region, has led to much hardship and animosity between the people of mainland India and those of the northeast region. There have also been various occasions when the churches or church-related nongovernmental organizations from mainland India and northeast India have come together to share their visions and missions and to create a platform where they can work together to address issues related to the conflict between mainland India and the various people groups.

The relational nature of the Spirit is visible in the witness of the church in Nagaland. Nagaland, a state in northeast India, is a land of ethnic diversities; yet 80 to 90 percent of the people there are Christians. The Naga society is multicultural and multilingual in nature. The different ethnic groups have been intolerant of one another since colonial times. This was mainly to protect their ethnic identity and their territory. In the past, different ethnic groups were seen as a threat to one another. However, the church as the body of believers in Christ has played its part at different levels. Today many Nagas have gone from being suspicious of the other ethnic communities to acceptance and acknowledgment of the contribution of others. The Nagaland Baptist Council of Churches creates platforms where the different

[47]Ajai Sahni, "Survey of Conflicts and Resolution in India's Northeast," www.satp.org/satporgtp/publication/faultlines/volume12/Article3 .htm#2, accessed April 28, 2020.

ethnic groups can come together to share the visions and missions of their churches and work together to address issues related to conflict and social evils. The contributions of the members irrespective of ethnic group are appreciated, and the members continue to learn from one another and grow together as a faith community.

The other platform where the relational nature of the Spirit is manifested at the ecclesial level is the effort of the Council of the Naga Baptist Churches. This platform aims to bring the Nagas from different ethnic groups together at the ecclesial level, although administrative division within India and the international border between India and Myanmar divide them. While it is still at its nascent stage, it is one organization that brings all Nagas together under one umbrella. It may not sound like much to people unaware of the division and fragmentation of the Nagas living in different administrative states in India and Myanmar. For the people who have virtually no means of coming together, the Council of the Naga Baptist Churches is doing yeoman service in reaching out and creating a meeting point for building relationships, which has remained impossible since the schism of the national political parties fighting for independence.[48]

These are just a few instances where we find the relation-building nature of the Spirit manifested in the life of the church and its members. Nonetheless, in spite of the efforts that the church and individual Christians in some contexts are making, in general relationship building continues to remain a challenge in India.

Challenges for the church in India. While the efforts of the church and its members provide glimmers of hope in building rela-

tionship between groups, other elements in this activity hinder the work of the Spirit. First, the long history of ethnocentrism of the various ethnic groups in India, as well as the different tribes in northeast India, has created stereotypes that hinder open and true relationships among the various people groups. Such stereotyped images are also visible in the life of the church among diverse ethnic Christian groups and denominations. Division and mistrust hinder the growth of Christians as a community of faith and a witnessing community. Second, the relation-building nature of the Spirit may be experienced beyond the ecclesiastical walls in a wider social sphere. For this, the church needs to create platforms for interracial-ethnic, interregional, interfaith, and intrafaith efforts and participation to reflect on the social evils, injustices, and conflicts and to build a just community and restore positive rapport.

The Spirit guides the church to redefine relationships by creating space for openness to accept one another. However, on many occasions in a multiracial-multiethnic context, instead of seeing the beauty in diverse groups coming together, people are building walls and forming divisions on the basis of race and ethnicity. There are also instances where the church has remained silent on the atrocities and violent acts committed in the name of freedom movements, nationalism, or integration. For example, India is a country of diversity, with many races, many ethnic people groups, and a plurality of religions, but aims to promote unity in diversity. Yet, the problem of racism continues to exist in many parts of the country. Atrocities against people from northeast India committed by mainland Indians are a common experience for

---

[48]I am indebted to Hukato Shohe for the information about the Council of the Naga Baptist Churches.

many residing or traveling outside their home states. These atrocities prevail at workplaces, in educational institutions, and in public places as well as in the private sphere. Christians at the personal level have shared their concern on different occasions, in their personal interactions as well as in social gatherings, but the church as an institution has remained silent on the atrocities against northeast India. People from mainland India also experience atrocities in northeast India. But the church in the region does not address this issue. Even when it comes to caste atrocities, the church as an institution has remained passive.

No one can fully blame the church in India for being silent on many issues, since for some time it has been seen as an alien religion that entered the native land. However, the church in India as an institution needs to go beyond the ethnic, denominational, ritual, and doctrinal differences and address the atrocities against minority groups. It needs to create awareness among its members on the importance of accepting and respecting people from all ethnic groups. One of the challenges for Christians in India is to acknowledge multiple identities and roles. Believers in Christ cannot be exclusively Christians in their personal relationship with God and ignore the community. Christianity does not draw away individual believers from the faith community of believers, the wider sphere of the society, or their own culture and traditions, but it demands that its members participate in a different way. Our multiple identities and roles continue to persist in life even after we become Christians, but they should be utilized for the service and the glory of God.

Thus, the church as an institution needs to be a model of openness by taking initiative in bridge building and creating platforms for meeting points. The church in India can draw insights from Paul's exhortation on the Spirit-guided relationship. The leading of the Spirit plays an important role in the life of believers. Thus, it is important to listen to the voice of the Spirit, for it is the Spirit who guides believers into community and openness. For at the heart of it is the notion of relationality. Such a relationship recognizes the "other" and is expressed in an openness to accept the other and strengthen one another as a witnessing community.

The Christian faith calls us to bring people together, transcending boundaries and building positive rapport. We need to go beyond our ethnic identities, denominational boundaries, and doctrinal boundaries, and redefine our boundaries as a witnessing community through the guidance of the Spirit. If the church in India can transcend the boundaries of ethnic groups and denominations and come on a common platform to discuss issues, this will be a witness that speaks louder than any proclamation.

The Spirit-guided relationship brings people together and promotes acceptance and harmony rather than divisions and conflict. It brings believers together as a faith community. As members belonging to the world, believers continue to strengthen one another in their trials and sufferings. In their openness to accepting one another, Christians in India through the guidance of the Spirit will be able to grow and build one another up despite their ethnic and denominational differences.

Christians can be witnesses in their coming together and looking forward to the eschaton. Hope for the future glorification in the Spirit-guided life provides strength and confidence for Christians in India as they persevere in their faith amid hardships and sufferings. C. René Padilla emphasizes the notion of the Spirit as one that provides hope in the context of suffering and hardship in his chapter in this section. He looks at the work of the Holy Spirit as a power that provides hope in the context of poverty. Such a notion of the Spirit is important because the Christian hope provides a reason to press on and anticipate transformation and change in the face of hardship, poverty, injustice, and suffering. However, in this chapter I present the notion of the Spirit as one that provides hope within the context of the worshiping community. Being in a community of believers that is open and accepting of one another strengthens the members to abound in hope and gives them confidence to nurture and build their relationship in a meaningful direction as they look forward to the final glorification.

CONCLUSION

Virgilio Elizondo notes that it is not possible for borders to disappear and that differences cannot completely fade away. Nonetheless, differences need not necessarily divide people and keep them apart as me and you, we and they. Instead of becoming fences of separation, differences can serve as marking regional characteristics, which is definitely appealing and humanizing. Elizondo further stresses that each individual needs the other to be fully human; in encountering others, more about us is revealed as well as about others.[49] Elizondo's perspective enriches our redefining of boundaries, for every time a border is crossed and a bridge is built, Christians in India get another opportunity to critique the past and through the guidance of the Spirit move toward creating space for openness and being a witnessing community. Instead of seeing the diverse ethnic groups, denominations, and doctrines as the dividing line between individuals and groups, Christians can view them as a meeting point from which we build bridges and grow together in respect and solidarity. In this way the relation-building nature of the Spirit can be manifested in the life of the church, which itself will be a witness to the wider social sphere.

FURTHER READING

Dunn, James D. G. "Spirit Speech: Reflections on Romans 8:12-27." In *Romans and the People of God: Essays in Honor of Gordon D. Fee on the Occasion of His 65th Birthday*, edited by Sven K. Soderlund and N. T. Wright. Grand Rapids, MI: Eerdmans, 1999.

Fee, Gordon D. *God's Empowering Presence: The Holy Spirit in the Letters of Paul*. Peabody, MA: Hendrickson, 1994.

Jewett, Robert. *Romans: A Commentary*. Hermeneia. Minneapolis: Fortress, 2007.

Joseph, P. V. *Indian Interpretation of the Holy Spirit*. Delhi: ISPCK, 2007.

Rabens, Volker. *The Holy Spirit and Ethics in Paul: Transformation and Empowering for Religious-Ethical Life*. Tübingen: Mohr Siebeck, 2010.

Yeo, K. K., ed. *From Rome to Beijing: Symposia on Robert Jewett's Commentary on Romans*. Lincoln, NE: Kairos Studies, 2013.

---

[49]Virgilio Elizondo, "Transformation of Boundaries: Border Separation or a New Identity?," in *Negotiating Borders: Theological Exploration in the Global Era*, ed. P. Gnanapragasam and E. S. Fiorenza (Delhi: ISPCK, 2008), 28-29.

PAULINE PNEUMATOLOGY AND THE CHINESE RITES

SPIRIT AND CULTURE IN THE HOLY SEE'S MISSIONARY STRATEGY

Wei Hua

AFTER PROVIDING a brief survey of Chinese pneumatology in the field of biblical studies, this chapter describes the evolution of the Chinese rites controversy, which addressed the question of the traditional commemorating rites of ancestors and Confucius. It then draws insights from Pauline pneumatology, focusing on the relationship between custom and law in Chinese culture and the Holy Spirit, since it is only the Holy Spirit who can initiate and maintain the identity of a Christian. The commemorating rites of ancestors and Confucius are Chinese customs that should be acknowledged and absorbed into the Christian faith through the fulfilling and transforming work of the Holy Spirit. Historically, the rites controversy ended with the Roman Catholic Holy See's concession, and, in light of that issue, the chapter raises a theological question regarding the necessity and possibility of a *Chinese* Christianity rather than Christianity *in China*.

As "an apostle to the Gentiles" (Rom 11:13), Paul launched three missionary journeys, primarily to establish churches in Mediterranean cities. Through his letter writing, he showed Jews and Gentiles the path to Christian faith based on the cross of Christ and the work of the Holy Spirit. With the help of a culturally sensitive and transformative missionary strategy and by means of countercultural accommodation, Gentile Christians soon became the majority of the church in the first-century Jesus movement. Christianity spread rapidly in the Roman Empire soon after and eventually "conquered" the empire as it became its state religion.

By comparison, in the third mission of Christianity to China, the Jesuit Matteo Ricci (1552–1610) advocated a missionary strategy of adaptation, which was well received by the Ming and Qing governments and Chinese intellectuals. He was attacked later by missionaries from other Catholic orders. In this so-called Chinese rites controversy, the Holy See banned Chinese Christians from practicing commemorating rites of ancestors and Confucius. Consequently, the Chinese emperor Kangxi (1654–1722) canceled the proclamation right of Christianity in China. This vigorous conflict led to a fatal failure of the Chinese mission over the next several hundred years.

It is widely believed that the Holy See should assume primary responsibility for this failure. However, significant questions remain: Why did the Holy See's judgment of the Chinese rites lead to a dead end? What mistakes did the Holy See make in its missionary strategy with regards to the dynamic of culture and the Spirit? Numerous studies have focused on the historical facts of the controversy, but this chapter deliberates on the theological causes behind it.

This chapter first presents a brief survey of Chinese pneumatology within biblical studies. It then traces the historical development of the Chinese rites controversy, detailing the two opposite views on this issue. Drawing insights from Pauline pneumatology, especially regarding the relationship between the Holy Spirit and Chinese custom and law, the chapter then argues that it is only the Holy Spirit who can initiate and maintain one's identity as a Christian, and that the Holy Spirit must be an agent of transformation in a culture receiving the gospel. In other words, the commemorating rites of ancestors and Confucius are Chinese customs that should be acknowledged and absorbed into the Christian faith through the fulfilling and transforming work of the Holy Spirit. We know that, historically, the rites controversy finally ended with the Roman Catholic Holy See's concession, and perhaps that in itself indicates a hindsight acknowledgment regarding the necessity and possibility of a Chinese Christianity.

CHINESE PNEUMATOLOGY

Many Chinese scholars have written commentaries on the book of Acts or a biblical theology of the Holy Spirit. Yet only a few take seriously the context of Chinese culture, and these scholars focus primarily on the relationship between biblical exegesis and dialogues with Chinese classics. In biblical exegesis, Watchman Nee (Nee Duo-sheng of Shanghai), a famous theologian and church leader, founded churches called "the Little Flock" or "the Local Church" in Mainland China prior to 1949. He believed that in the Old Testament the Holy Spirit came "upon" (*epi*) people, which is an external endowment. But in the New Testament, besides coming "upon" people, the Spirit also comes to dwell "in" (*en*) people, which is internal empowerment. Nee saw two gifts of the Holy Spirit in the New Testament. After the resurrection, Jesus breathed on his disciples, and they received the Easter gift of the Holy Spirit that would give them abundant life (Jn 20:22). Fifty days later, God himself filled the apostles with the Pentecost gift of the Holy Spirit (Acts 2:1-13), which would "grant them the power for Christian ministry."[1] Nee's exegesis of the Holy Spirit influenced deeply the house churches in Mainland China and continues to do so today.

After the founding of the People's Republic of China in 1949, the center of Chinese biblical studies shifted to Hong Kong, Taiwan, and the Chinese diaspora. This new generation of biblical scholars, including Huiyuan Bao, Roland Y. K. Fung, and Zhibang Zhong, closely followed the exegetical methods and even the theological positions of their Western counterparts. Generally, these scholars agreed that the Hebrew term *ruach* corresponds to the Greek word *pneuma*, which can be translated into "wind," "breath," or "Spirit" in Chinese. *Pneuma* can refer to the human spirit or to the Holy Spirit, "the

---

[1]See Watchman Nee, *The Communion of the Holy Spirit* (New York: Christian Fellowship, 1994), 37-43, 49-67, 79-83. See also Archie Hui, "The Pneumatology of Watchman Nee: A New Testament Perspective," *Evangelical Quarterly* 75, no. 4 (2003): 3-29.

mediator and way of salvation for all human beings."[2] Receiving the Holy Spirit is a necessary step in the process of repentance, baptism, and rebirth.

Not contradicting the biblical exegesis on pneumatology of other Chinese scholars, K. K. Yeo has devoted much of his work to going beyond exegesis to promoting a dialogue between the Bible and Chinese classics in an attempt to address contextual issues faced by his Chinese readers. In his earlier work, he investigated the problem of eating idol-meat in 1 Corinthians 8 and 10 and proposed a rhetorical and crosscultural hermeneutics that addresses Chinese ancestor "worship" or reverence.[3] His recently published monograph, *Musing with Confucius and Paul: Toward a Chinese Christian Theology*, critically synthesizes Confucius's ethical teachings in the *Analects* and Paul's theology in Galatians. He sees the work of the Holy Spirit as more effective than Confucius's benevolence (*ren*), thus fulfilling *ren* and overcoming human or cultural differences because "love your neighbors" and "love your enemies" (Mt 5:43-48; Lk 6:27-36) can truly consolidate the five Confucian basic relationships (*wulun*).[4]

THE CHINESE RITES CONTROVERSY

During the final years of the Ming dynasty, the Jesuits introduced Christianity to China.[5] Matteo Ricci arrived in Macau in 1582 and then preached the Christian faith in southern China. In the next several years, he dressed first as a Buddhist monk and later as a Confucian mandarin. He made friends with Chinese intellectuals and officials, and even wrote books in Chinese. Regarding the "term question" (which name should be used for God), he translated "God" into *Shang-ti* (Heaven), a word that appeared frequently in ancient Chinese classics. He did not regard the rites commemorating ancestors and Confucius as idolatry but permitted Chinese Christians to participate in them. This missionary strategy of adaptation, called "the Rules of Ricci," was followed by other Jesuits.

The Jesuits and other missionaries fiercely debated two questions: whether the "God" of Christianity could be translated as *Shang-ti* (Heaven or Lord of Heaven), or could only be transliterated into Chinese; and whether Chinese rites were idolatrous and consequently prohibited among Chinese Christians. In Chinese missionary history, this debate is called the Chinese rites controversy. However, in the earlier period, the term question gave way to the rites question.[6] The Jesuits and other missionaries, the Holy See, and the Chinese emperor Kangxi were all involved in the debate on these Chinese rites.

In 1643, arising out of his opposition to the Jesuits' missionary strategy of adaptation,

[2]See Zhibang Zhong, *Commentary on the Gospel of John* (Shanghai: Shanghai Sanlian, 2008), 1:190-91.
[3]See K. K. Yeo, *Rhetorical Interaction in 1 Corinthians 8 and 10: A Formal Analysis with Preliminary Suggestions for a Chinese, Cross-Cultural Hermeneutic* (Leiden: Brill, 1995), 180-211.
[4]See K. K. Yeo, *Musing with Confucius and Paul: Toward a Chinese Christian Theology* (Eugene, OR: Cascade, 2008), 253-66; K. K. Yeo, "Paul's Way of *Renren* in Romans 13:1-10," in *From Rome to Beijing: Symposia on Robert Jewett's Hermeneia Commentary on Romans*, ed. K. K. Yeo (Lincoln, NE: Kairos Studies, 2013), 469-79.
[5]For the historical details of the Chinese rites controversy, see George Minamiki, *Chinese Rites Controversy: From Its Beginning to Modern Times* (Chicago: Loyola University Press, 1985); Tiangang Li, *Chinese Rites Controversy: Its History, Literature and Significance* (Shanghai: Shanghai Classics, 1998); Liwei Wu, *The Chinese Rites Controversy: The Encounter of Civilizations and Powers* (Shanghai: Shanghai Classics, 2007).
[6]For more details, see Zi Wang, "How to Understand a Biblical God in Chinese: Toward a Cross-Cultural Biblical Hermeneutics," in *The Trinity Among the Nations: The Doctrine of God in the Majority World* (Grand Rapids, MI: Eerdmans, 2015), 140-60.

Dominican Juan Bautista de Morals submitted his seventeen opposing opinions to the Holy See. In 1645, Pope Innocent X issued an encyclical that disapproved of the adaptive Jesuit strategy and banned Chinese rites among Chinese Christians. Martino Martini, a Jesuit working in China, was called back to Rome by the Society of Jesus to make a counterargument, claiming that Chinese rites were essentially secular and political rites that simply honored ancestors or Confucius. In 1656, Pope Alexander VII issued another encyclical permitting the Chinese rites.

Nevertheless, in 1693, as a vicar apostolic managing church affairs in Fujian province, Charles Maigrot imposed a ban in his diocese. He insisted that the encyclical issued in 1656 was based on Martini's misleading report and, as a result, Chinese Christians were not permitted to participate in the rites commemorating ancestors or Confucius. The rites controversy agitated the Chinese emperor Kangxi. In 1704, Pope Clement XI issued an encyclical in favor of Maigrot's decision and sent Carlo Tommaso Maillard de Tournon to publish it in China. Without notifying the Qing government beforehand, the ambassador published this encyclical in Nanjing the following year and ordered the Jesuits to be obedient to the Holy See or face excommunication. Emperor Kangxi was outraged. He ordered the detention of the ambassador and Maigrot and expelled them from China. As for the other missionaries, he reassured them that, as long as they abided by "the Rules of Ricci" and received a permission paper, they would be granted free missionary privileges in China. In addition, on three occasions Emperor Kangxi sent messengers carrying his letters to the Holy See, in hopes of continuing the diplomatic negotiations.

In 1715, Pope Clement XI issued a new encyclical, *Ex illa die*, which reiterated the previous ban against the traditional rites. In the following year, again without notifying the Qing government in advance, the encyclical was published in Beijing. Emperor Kangxi gave the order to arrest the publisher and send all copies back to Rome. Dispatched by the Holy See, Charles Ambrose Mezzabarba arrived in Beijing in 1720. Emperor Kangxi read the Chinese translation of the ban and, in 1721, gave the order to revoke the legal status of the Chinese mission. In 1742, Pope Benedict XIV issued an encyclical, *Ex quo singulari*, which reaffirmed the ban of 1715 and even prohibited missionaries from debating these issues further.

PAUL ON THE HOLY SPIRIT, LAW, AND CUSTOM

The Chinese rites controversy involves numerous significant historical details. However, "the difficulty is not how to restate this controversy, but how to explain it."[7] The challenge is to explain it theologically. The controversy seems to center on the debate about whether the commemorating rites of ancestors and Confucius constitute idolatry. A deeper analysis will show that the controversy erupted because the Holy See did not correctly understand the relationship between the Holy Spirit and Chinese custom and law.

In first-century missionary circumstances, Paul demonstrated the role of the Holy Spirit in initiating, sustaining, and consummating the Christian faith. He dealt with the relationship of the Holy Spirit, the Jewish law, and Gentile custom by focusing on the agency of God's Spirit among cultures.

---

[7]Sun Shangyang, *Chinese Christianity Before 1984* (Beijing: Xueyuan, 2004), 369.

"Having started in the Spirit" (Galatians 3:3). In contrast to John the Baptist's water baptism for repentance, Jesus baptized with the Holy Spirit for rebirth (Mt 3:11; Mk 1:8; Lk 3:22; Jn 1:33; 3:5). Jesus also promised that, after his ascension, the Holy Spirit, the Advocate, would be sent on believers, teaching his disciples everything so that they could preach his gospel to the ends of the earth (Mk 13:11; Jn 7:39; 14:26; 15:26; 16:13; Acts 1:5). The disciples received the Holy Spirit at Pentecost and "began to speak in other languages" (Acts 2:4).[8] Paul asked the Ephesian disciples, "Did you receive the Holy Spirit when you became believers?" (Acts 19:2). After receiving a negative response, he baptized them in the name of Jesus and laid his hands on them as the Spirit baptized them. John 3:8 reads, "The wind blows where it wishes, and you hear its sound, but you do not know where it comes from or where it goes. So it is with everyone who is born of the Spirit" (ESV). Indeed, rebirth in the Holy Spirit should be the starting point of Christian faith for everyone.

New Testament pneumatology suggests that following Jesus before his death or just hearing the gospel does not constitute a fully Christian process. Believers in Christ need to be baptized by the Holy Spirit so that their discipleship and religious identity become completely confirmed.[9] Paul understood that the reception of the Holy Spirit was an identity marker that confirmed the faith of any Christian, whether Jewish or Gentile. James Dunn argues that although "in Christian tradition it has become customary to think of the gift of the Spirit as a deduction to be drawn from a correct confession or properly ad-

ministered sacrament," in Pauline pneumatology, the "definition of a Christian" originated in receiving the Holy Spirit, not in a confession or a sacrament. Paul illuminates this principle when he writes, "For all who are led by the Spirit of God are children of God" (Rom 8:14), and "anyone who does not have the Spirit of Christ does not belong to him" (Rom 8:9).[10] Paul tells the Galatians explicitly that, "having started with the Spirit" (Gal 3:3), they must "also be guided by the Spirit" (Gal 5:25), in order that they may bear good fruits for God and build a close relationship with God.

Having received the Holy Spirit, Jews and Gentiles are called "Christians" (Acts 11:26) because they share the same religious identity and become children of God. This spiritual relationship makes them all heirs of the inheritance of Abraham promised by God. Having the same religious identity does not cancel national, racial, cultural, or gender differences among Christians, nor does it erase economic, legal, or social inequalities. These differences and inequalities are now transformed into a Christian *koinōnia*, which is a new marker of how the Spirit of God is working in a diverse community. What is most significant about this marker is that human differences have been released from the power of sin and, consequently, are accepted by God in the hope of eternal life. As Paul writes, "There is no longer Jew or Greek, there is no longer slave or free, there is no longer male and female; for all of you are one in Christ Jesus" (Gal 3:28).[11] Differences among human beings are not erased, but domination arising

---

[8]Except where otherwise noted, biblical quotations follow the NRSV.

[9]David Coffey, *"Did You Receive the Holy Spirit When You Believed?": Some Basic Questions for Pneumatology* (Milwaukee, WI: Marquette University Press, 2005).

[10]James D. G. Dunn, *The Theology of Paul the Apostle* (Grand Rapids, MI: Eerdmans, 1998), 430-31.

[11]As J. Louis Martyn comments, "Religious, social, and sexual pairs of opposites are not replaced by equality, but rather by a newly created unity." Martyn, *Galatians: A New Translation with Introduction and Commentary* (New Haven, CT: Yale University Press, 1997), 377.

from these differences is eliminated. The work of the Holy Spirit is therefore to foster the uniqueness of individuals and cultures, but also to rid them of the discrimination these differences might bring to any community.

While the role of the Holy Spirit is universally recognized, the early church also faced a difficult and urgent question, that is, whether and how the Jewish law was still abiding for Jewish and Gentile Christians. This is not simply a question of "right theology" but a theological question embedded in a dynamic cultural context. In the first century, some Jewish Christians thought that, besides receiving the Holy Spirit, Gentile Christians also had to abide by the Jewish law, especially circumcision and the law of purification, in order that they might join in the holy covenant between God and Israel. They believed this was "right theology." However, Paul thought of both theology and culture, so he admonished the Galatians that becoming a Christian was not about subscribing to the Jewish works of the law (becoming a Jew) but about God's grace enabling one to receive the Holy Spirit in order to be fully who one is (as created by God, i.e., "a Gentile").

Paul's assertion, "If you are led by the Spirit, you are not subject to the law" (Gal 5:18), may appear to be an exegetical issue. In fact, without the cultural context, this verse does not make a lot of sense. For circumcision and the law of purification are cultural symbols to Jews that may still have religious meaning. To Gentile Christians, however, circumcision of the flesh would mean ceasing to be a Gentile (in the most robust sense and therefore without the tainting of sin) and instead becoming a Jew, although the concern about becoming a believer is there too. To address both ethnic (Gentile) and salvation

(Christian) issues, Paul teaches that circumcision of the flesh has been replaced by circumcision of the heart (Rom 2:29) and a water baptism that does not have racial, gender, or social distinctions. Paul explains that the inheritance was promised to Abraham long before the promulgation of the Mosaic law, and now "in Christ Jesus the blessing of Abraham might come to the Gentiles" (Gal 3:14), making the point that inclusion of Gentiles among God's people is more highly prioritized (in Abraham) than Jewish distinctiveness (in Moses).[12] Therefore, after receiving the Holy Spirit, Gentile Christians by faith become "born according to the Spirit" (Gal 4:29) and are fully qualified to inherit the Abrahamic blessings originally announced to the First Testament people of God.

The Jewish law. For Jews, the law given by God through Moses is holy and irrevocable; circumcision of the flesh even becomes a sign of their cultural and religious identity as the "people of God." In the Gospel narratives, we read that Jesus frequently "violated" the written laws, as he understood the Jewish law self-critically, out of his deep conviction that "until heaven and earth pass away, not one letter, not one stroke of a letter, will pass from the law until all is accomplished" (Mt 5:18). In other words, a self-critical practice of the Jewish law will bring about its fulfillment and greater effectiveness and benefits to more people, but "blind" obedience from others may actually reduce the power of the law for good. When asked the basic tenets of the Jewish law, Jesus explained that all the law could be summarized by two commandments: love God (Deut 6:4-6) and love your neighbor (Lev 19:18). This is the mega principle of the law and also of the work of the Holy Spirit.

---

[12]See Yeo, *Musing with Confucius and Paul*, passim.

For Jesus, the law is sacred. It is a means to allow God's love to touch more people, not to yoke them to the fine print of the law and restrict their behavior.[13] No wonder Jesus proclaims, "The Sabbath was made for humankind, and not humankind for the Sabbath" (Mk 2:27). Paul's teaching in the book of Romans confirms this view of the law.

In his gospel mission to the Gentiles, Paul accurately grasps the two sides of the law. On the one hand, the law promulgated to the Jewish people "is holy, and the commandment is holy and just and good" (Rom 7:12). On the other hand, the purpose of the law is to reveal to the human race the power of sin that entraps them, first with the Jewish people: "through the law comes the knowledge of sin" (Rom 3:20). But the law does not make them stop sinning or become righteous. In other words, in theological terms, the purpose of the law is Jesus Christ, because "Christ is the end of the law" (Rom 10:4).[14] After the advent of Christ, Paul thinks that the Jews are released from the law and justified by God, not by obeying the law but by believing in Christ. That is to say, the law has been fulfilled or accomplished by Christ's faithfulness. However, this faithfulness does not abolish the law. For example, as a Jewish Christian, Paul not only followed his Jewish vow and had his hair cut off in Cenchreae (Acts 18:18), but he also circumcised Timothy and made a sacrifice in the temple (Acts 16:3; 21:23-26). Indeed, Jews are not compelled to be Gentiles upon conversion any more than Gentiles are compelled to be Jews.

Jewish Christians still may observe the law, but as a marker of their religious identity only. The law by itself is insufficient to be a sign of salvation and must be affiliated with the work of Christ.[15] As a Jewish tradition and custom, the Jewish law cannot justify or save Jews, for the Jewish custom and tradition have been fulfilled by the gospel and love of Jesus Christ (Rom 13:10). K. K. Yeo argues that, facing the agitators in Galatia, Paul criticized the cultural and religious imperialism of his Jewish opponents. Paul uses the crucifixion of Christ to deconstruct Jewish ethnocentrism and reconstruct the Jewish law via the Spirit of the law in love. What Christ had accomplished on the cross has been illustrated by the coming of the Holy Spirit because "the Spirit is the one who fulfills the promise of God." In other words, it is the Holy Spirit who has transformed or extended the salvation of God from a Jewish law-centeredness in the old age to the Spirit-led grounding in the new age.[16]

Circumcision and the law of purification can distinguish Jews from Gentiles, but they cannot be used to differentiate Christians from non-Christians because national and ethnic identities will constantly need to be challenged and fulfilled by religious identity. In other words, the Spirit of God constantly engages cultures to overcome ethnocentrism and to transform them into cultures that will reflect God's glory and kingdom values. Gentile Christians joined the holy covenant, not by obeying the law but through faith in Jesus Christ and in the power

---

[13]See Yeo, *Musing with Confucius and Paul*, 258-59, for a discussion of the ritualizing process of the law in accordance with the Confucian understanding of *li* (ritual).

[14]See Robert Jewett, *Romans: A Commentary* (Minneapolis: Fortress, 2007), 634.

[15]Just as Augustine argued later, the Jewish law never was intended to have a divine function in salvation, but because of its long history, it now becomes "an ancient tradition" (*paternarum traditionum*) and "an enduring custom" (*diuturnam consuetudinem*) for the Jewish people. See Augustine, *De mendacio* 5.8; *Contra Faustum Manicheum* 19.17.

[16]Yeo, *Musing with Confucius and Paul*, 83-84, 310.

of the Holy Spirit. Jewish agitators and opponents in Galatia stubbornly insisted that, for Gentiles, obeying the law was a prerequisite for becoming a Christian. Thus they committed the error of "nationalistic presumption and ethnic restrictiveness."[17]

The Gentile custom. As a part of daily life in the Mediterranean world, people usually sacrificed wine and meat to pagan gods during local festivals, which included many non-Christian religious elements. Being invited to join in a banquet in a pagan temple also was a token of friendship. Jewish Christians in the diaspora were sometimes bothered by these activities, and Gentile Christians in Corinth were confused by this invitation. Christian theology viewed sacrifice to pagan gods as idolatrous, and joining in such a banquet as idol worship (1 Cor 8:7-10; 10:19-21). If this was so, could Gentile Christians enter pagan temples, and then drink wine and eat meat with their pagan families, relatives, or friends? If they did these things, were they participating in idol worship? Like the Chinese rites controversy, these questions created a fierce conflict in the early church and still do so in the church today in China.

In the Corinthian church, believers were divided into two groups: the weak-conscience ones, who regarded consuming food offered to idols as idolatry, and "those who possess knowledge," who believed this kind of eating and drinking was not idolatrous. As we can see, the use of such labels highlights the mutual misunderstanding among Corinthian Christians. To ease tensions, Paul postulates two main prin-

ciples. First, no idols really exist because we know that "'an idol is nothing at all in the world' and that 'there is no God but one'" (1 Cor 8:4 NIV). For "those who possess knowledge," participating in such a banquet does not necessarily lead to idolatry. Yet, Paul seriously limits their participation in banquets held within the confines of pagan temples (such as the Asklepion) because a temple banquet is no doubt honoring a pagan god.[18] In essence, as Paul argues, this pagan sacrifice is a sacrifice to devils, for one may not participate in the table of the Lord and the table of devils (1 Cor 10:21). Second, for "the weak" eating meat in temple banquets should be prohibited since the practice cannot heal their weak conscience. Instead, it defiles them. Due to community concerns, knowledge is less important than love of brothers and sisters, for "knowledge puffs up, but love builds up" (1 Cor 8:1). Taking Paul himself as an example, personal freedom or right has to give way to the edification and salvation of others (1 Cor 9:19-22).[19]

Although not all traditional customs are prohibited, there are limits to the practices. These are defined by concerns for the well-being of others in the community. In the new community life in which Christ is the head, brothers and sisters are "all made to drink of one Spirit" (1 Cor 12:13). In the same faith of Christ, the Holy Spirit has granted them the same religious identity; no longer is anyone able to boast of her glory based on her national, cultural, or social status. Every Christian becomes a child of God and equal in faith.[20] In Pauline pneumatology, this same identity will not cancel their differences, but the

---

[17]John M. G. Barclay, "'Neither Jew nor Greek': Multiculturalism and the New Perspective on Paul," in *Ethnicity and the Bible*, ed. Mark G. Brett (Leiden: Brill, 2002), 202.

[18]Joseph A. Fitzmyer, *First Corinthians: A New Translation with Introduction and Commentary* (New Haven, CT: Yale University Press), 331.

[19]Yeo, *Rhetorical Interactions*, passim.

[20]Jewett, *Romans*, 137.

Holy Spirit opens the way for believers to view their cultural differences anew, that is, not in the old way of cultural discrimination but now from a new perspective of appreciating other cultures (especially cultural ideals) in order to overcome cultural blind spots. Being a Christian does not require Jewish Christians to abandon the law or Gentile Christians to obey the letter of the law (to be proselytized into Judaism), but it does require both Jewish and Gentile Christians to observe the spirit of the law (2 Cor 3:6).

As to the role of the Holy Spirit, Paul states the following.

First, the theological function of the holy law has been fulfilled by faith in Christ and in the power of the Holy Spirit. Jewish Christians may still obey the law but with a new sense of spiritual renewal whereby the Spirit of God in the end times is baptizing Gentiles to his kingdom. Jewish Christians cannot impose the Jewish law on Gentile Christians.

Second, the cultural function of pagan customs has been revised and renewed also by faith in Christ and in the power of the Holy Spirit. After a person receives the Holy Spirit, the Jewish law and pagan customs are not obstacles to the Christian faith but can be accomplished and updated in the love of God and neighbors. Any controversial actions should be delimited and guided by this love.

THE COMMEMORATING RITES OF ANCESTORS AND CONFUCIUS: CHINESE CUSTOM OR LAW?

In the Chinese rites controversy, the Jesuits aligned with the Chinese emperor and Chinese intellectuals, and they submitted their statements of defense to the Holy See to argue for the secular, political nature of the commemorating rites of ancestors and Confucius. There are six

kinds of sacrificial rites involved in the controversy: sacrifice in funeral mourning, sacrifice to a town god by local officials, sacrifice to Heaven by the emperor, commemorating rites of ancestors, commemorating rites of Confucius, and rites to living people.

The commemorating rites of ancestors and Confucius are the most controversial ones. In the first rite, participants are descendants of a family or patriarchal clan, and other people are not allowed to enter the family temple. Participants display meat and fruits in front of the ancestors' memorial tablets, and they burn incense and candles, kowtow, and then share food in a family banquet. In the second rite, participants usually are Chinese intellectuals who have a good reputation for knowledge and some social status. Many of them are imperial officials. On the first and fifteenth days of the month, they enter a Confucian temple, kowtow, and burn incense in front of Confucius's memorial tablet. Every spring and autumn, the central and local governments must hold a grand commemorating rite in the Confucian temples. As in the first rite, participants display meat and fruits, and then share them in a friendly banquet.

As we can see, Chinese rites have social, political, cultural, ethical, and religious dimensions, and these dimensions are clearly intertwined. By participating in these rites, Chinese people can consolidate their close relationships among families, clans, and social strata—being filial to parents, loyal to superiors, trustworthy to friends, and reverent to the cosmic Logos. Furthermore, they can show their respect to Confucius and thus loyalty to emperors, for an empire is also regarded as a family, with the emperor as its father.

The challenge comes when we seek to distinguish between culture and religion, secular and sacred. This is not possible. Every religious belief is developed in a certain culture, and every culture also contains a kind of religious belief. For example, in its external form, the commemorating rites of ancestors are similar to worship rites in Chinese folk religions. Even the common people who do not possess knowledge pray to their ancestors for protection. Unsurprisingly, these two rites may be suspect as being idol worship by foreigners, such as Western missionaries in the time of the Qing dynasty.

The task of a theologian is to attempt to delineate culture from religion, or better still, as Yeo advocates, to read ethics theologically and to read cultures christologically, thus finding creative ways to fulfill cultural aspirations. As Yeo explains, we cannot "speak of Confucianism as a religion, because for me and many Chinese it is more a way of life in pursuit of virtue and in the formation of community."[21] Indeed, the essence of the Chinese rites differs from that of Roman pagan rites, first, in that the objects of Chinese commemorating rites are not powerful gods but deceased relatives and loved ones, including fathers, grandfathers, and Confucius, who was regarded as a sage on morality and knowledge. Second, unlike religion or idolatry, the purpose of the Chinese commemorating rites is not to pursue any supernatural power but to express thanksgiving to ancestors and to pay secular respect to Confucius. We can see that neither of these is an idol in the Christian sense. Also, the word *worship* is too strong. Thus, *reverence* may be a better word. Our biblical hermeneutic needs to take on the power of the Spirit in order to access our cultures not in their outward forms

only but, more importantly, contextually through their inward spiritual dynamics.

It is noteworthy that another author in this section, Zakali Shohe, analyzes the role of the Spirit in Romans 8:14-17 from a relational perspective precisely to bring about a similar pneumatological effect in Asian contexts. Shohe convincingly demonstrates that the Spirit redefines the broader identities of people, including ethnic, cultural, economic, political, and religious ones. These identities will guide Christians to a new status as children of God and then bear witness to a new religious identity in Christ.

The commemorating rites of ancestors and Confucius have two functions. For ordinary people, they are Chinese folk customs and become part of their daily lives, like the customs of Gentiles in Paul's day. But for intellectuals, these rites have been practiced for more than two thousand years and have constituted the core of Chinese traditional ritual and law (*lifa*), which constructed a social order and a moral system for China. Similar to Jewish law, Chinese ritual and law shape national and cultural identities for Chinese people.

By using a hermeneutics of pneumatology to respond to the rites controversy, I do not mean to suggest Chinese rites are perfect but that the Spirit of God will continue to renew such rites, leading the Chinese people to their intended purpose. In his early work, Yeo has suggested how Chinese ancestor "worship" can be renewed by Chinese Christian theology today. If practitioners have any fear or bondage at all, the gospel can proclaim a message of hope and freedom to them.[22]

---

[21]Yeo, *Musing with Confucius and Paul*, 80; see also 81-83, 385-86.

[22]Yeo, *Rhetorical Interactions*, 217-20. See also his "The Rhetorical Hermeneutic of 1 Corinthians 8 and Chinese Ancestor Worship," *Biblical Interpretation* 2, no. 3 (1994): 298-311, and his *Ancestor Worship: Rhetorical and Cross-Cultural Hermeneutical Response* (Hong Kong: Chinese Christian Literature Council, 1996) (in Chinese).

As the founder of Confucianism, Confucius criticized sharply the sacrificial rites of the Shang and Zhou dynasties, as he attempted to remove any superstitious elements and retain only their edifying (moral) function. Therefore, Confucius's allowable sacrifices were not part of religion or idol worship. If distortions have crept into sacrificial practice, then of course it is proper to address the issue of distortion and engage it with the gospel of Christ.

Confucius did not believe in the existence of gods or ghosts: "The topic the Master did not speak of was prodigies, force, disorder, and gods" (*Analects* 7.21).[23] He denied the ancient practice of divination. Nevertheless, he supported practice of sacrifice and the commemorating rites of ancestors. He even paid much attention to the rightfulness of sacrificial objects and rites: "Unless I enter into the spirit of a sacrifice, it is as if I did not sacrifice" (*Analects* 3.12). In other words, if Chinese rites are done merely for show, then they lose the power to shape identities of people; the Spirit of God can empower Chinese to practice these rites out of their intended purpose of living a moral life, thus exhibiting the fruits of the Spirit (Gal 5).

Regarding filial behaviors, Confucius insisted that "when your parents are alive, comply with the rites in serving them; when they die, comply with the rites in burying them and in offering sacrifices to them" (*Analects* 2.5). The reason for this seeming paradox is that Confucius highly valued the moral edifying function of these rites. Offering sacrifices to gods can enlighten a person about his natural position in the entire universe and encourage him to imitate the Dao (the Way) of the cosmos. In this ritual of imitation, he will constantly improve his intelligence and moral conscience. Meanwhile, offering sacrifices to ancestors can enlighten him about his position in society, and make him call to mind his parents' and ancestors' virtue and merits. In this reminiscence, "the virtue of the common people will incline toward fullness" (*Analects* 1.9). This Confucian language of morality is compatible with Paul's language of sanctification, but Paul believes that it is the Holy Spirit that enables believers to live a life of holiness, rather than an individual's effort.

As Confucius demanded, each person must be filial to his parents and offer sacrifices to them when they die. After that, his parents also become the object of commemorating rites. In this edifying process, he will retain love and a good moral conscience from his childhood; recognize the social relations between husband and wife, father and son, emperor and subjects; abide by established social regulations and moral principles; and gradually become a virtuous and peace-loving citizen. "It is rare for a man whose character is such that he is good as a son and obedient as a young man to have the inclination to transgress against his superiors; it is unheard of for one who has no such inclination to be inclined to start a rebellion" (*Analects* 1.2). Thus, after these stages of life, he will accomplish good merits like his parents and ancestors. The Holy Spirit can baptize all these teachings to allow Chinese Christians to live out the spirit of the biblical law in Chinese contexts.

From the Han dynasty to the Qing dynasty, Confucius and his teachings were highly praised. He became a brilliant model of knowledge and morality. In such a long history, he was enshrined as "The Holiest Master and Teacher." The Confucian classics were assigned as sole references for

---

[23]For the *Analects*, this essay uses D. C. Lau, trans., *The Analects* (Beijing: Zhonghua, 2008).

imperial examinations, and the commemorating rites of Confucius also became significant political affairs from the court to local places. According to Confucius, these commemorating rites were intended to express respect to him. Yeo points out that often in Chinese history, however, royal cults would distort and use Confucius's ethic for their own concentration of power. It is this abusive power of the government that needs critical engagement with the democratic and salvific work of the Holy Spirit.[24]

Historically, the commemorating rites of ancestors and Confucius constitute a long custom or even a holy law for the Chinese people, although this holiness was not stated explicitly as coming from God. Chinese Christians can nevertheless, based on their biblical understanding, know that much of Confucius's teaching is in line with biblical teaching. This is a significant point regarding how the Spirit of God has revealed, created, worked, moved, and shaped cultures that are not explicitly traced to the Bible. Amos Yong's chapter in this volume is particularly reflective as we discern this issue. As he advocates, a Spirit-oriented approach is "anchored in the revelation of God in Christ and . . . being open to wherever and however the wind of God blows." The Spirit of God has always blown and moved in Chinese cultures, from ancient times until today.

Unlike the Gentiles in Paul's time, participants in Chinese rites do not worship any pagan gods. But as we saw in the case of the Jewish law, participants in Chinese rites are performing the spirit of the biblical commandments. For example, showing filial piety to parents is one of the core teachings of the Ten Commandments (Ex 20:12), and forgoing rebellion is similar to fulfilling Jesus' and Paul's social principle of serving God and Caesar (Mk 12:17; Rom 13:1-7). Moreover, this edifying process is similar to the sanctifying work of the Holy Spirit in the Christian language. Filialness, loyalty, trustworthiness, and reverence all are encompassed in the commandment to love one's neighbors. In Paul's theology, "love (*agape*) is made virtuous by overcoming human differences in the power of the Spirit."[25]

THE MISSIONARY FAILURE AND ITS THEOLOGICAL CAUSES

Liwei Wu notes that in ancient Chinese society "a rite is not merely a cultural symbol, but plays an indispensable role in the social administration. As a part of social regulations, Chinese rites also represent a kind of imperial power."[26] If a Chinese person does not participate in the commemorating rites of ancestors and Confucius, his choice signifies a betrayal of his family and rebellion against the Chinese government. If the Chinese people are banned from these rites, then they are asked not to be Chinese. As a result, they would rather simply reject Christianity. In this context, Matteo Ricci advocated a missionary strategy of adaptation, which gave Chinese Christians freedom of choice, but a freedom in line with how the Spirit of God is creating and blowing in the Chinese land and culture. Ricci even argued for the secular nature of these rites through his industrious study of Chinese classics, which may be seen as cultural fulfillment in the process of the meeting of the Bible and Chinese classics.

---

[24]See Yeo, "Paul's Way of *Renren*," 469-79.
[25]Yeo, *Musing with Confucius and Paul*, 261.
[26]Wu, *Chinese Rites Controversy*, 102.

Dressed as Western Confucians, the Jesuits maintained a close association with Chinese intellectuals and officials. Because of their contributions to the empire, they quickly gained the favor of the emperor. Emperor Kangxi even legitimized their mission in China. As we know, the early church experienced numerous persecutions, which finally ended with the Edict of Milan, issued by Constantine, the emperor of the Roman Empire. Compared to their predecessors, the Jesuits' conversion of the Chinese people to Christianity went well. However, the missionaries of other orders did not understand Chinese language, culture, and customs, looking only at the outward forms rather than at the spirit of the rites. Thus, they concluded that the commemorating rites of ancestors and Confucius were idolatry and banned Chinese Christians from observing them—not knowing that the ban killed the spirit of a culture and almost eliminated the soul of a group of people.

In this controversy, Chinese Christians became the biggest victims. Contrary to the situation in the Corinthian church, almost all Chinese Christians believed that Chinese rites had nothing to do with idolatry but were endowed with a deep spirituality in line with teachings of the Bible. Participation in Chinese rites never disturbed their faithful conscience but allowed them to make peace with the empire and Confucian society in which they lived, while allowing the Spirit of God to work out salvation in changing cultures. Not surprisingly, the ban from the Holy See met with fierce opposition from the Jesuits, the Chinese emperor, and Chinese Christians.

The ban lasted until the 1930s, when the Holy See eventually lifted the ban on the Chinese rites while dealing with the "Sophia University event" in Japan and the official commemorating rites of Confucius in the pseudo-Manchukuo. In 1939, the Propaganda Fide published the encyclical *Plan compertum est*, issued by Pope Pius XII, in which Chinese Christians were allowed to participate in Chinese commemorating rites. Although never acknowledging the former encyclicals' error, the Holy See actually reverted to its 1656 position, which recognized that the Jesuits' judgment on the nature of the Chinese rites was correct, namely, that these rites in essence were not idolatry but a long-term Chinese custom and tradition. In 1941, the Propaganda Fide issued an additional order that reflected the spirit of Pauline pneumatology: "You should absolutely avoid drafting a list of what is prohibited or permitted, in order that these old disagreements would not stir up again a fierce controversy in its new form," but "should let those priests and good laity to make their decision in individual circumstances according to their own conscience."[27] That is to say, with the love of God and brothers and sisters, Chinese Christians have the freedom to participate in Chinese commemorating rites because they have received the Holy Spirit.

In the Chinese rites controversy, there were at least three critical issues, from which we can learn important lessons regarding culture and the Holy Spirit.

First, the Holy See debated with the Jesuits on the relationship between the catholicity of the Christian faith and its contextualization in China. The focus was whether this universalized faith could be localized and indigenous in various contexts. The Pentecost event in Acts,

---

[27]Ray Noll, trans., *100 Roman Documents Concerning the Chinese Rites Controversy (1645–1941)* (San Francisco: Ricci Institute for Chinese-Western Cultural History, 1992), chap. 100.

with multiple tongues in gospel proclamation, confirms that contextual theologies of the gospel are the will of God and involve the movement of God's Spirit. It will take faith in the Spirit to allow the Spirit to work in new lands, cultures, languages, and contexts.

Second, the Holy See debated with the Chinese emperor on the relationship between church and state. The focus was whether the Holy See should respect the political authority of the Chinese Empire and offer criticism only when church and state assumed an uncritical alliance that concentrated power and downplayed kingdom values. The Jesuits asked the Holy See to follow their admonition: "Do not violate the principles of Confucianism, and never try to intrude into the imperial power."[28] Here, Paul's discussion of the responsibility of Christians and government leaders to serve the Roman Empire in Romans 13 suggests a dual citizenship of Christians.[29]

Third, the Holy See debated with Chinese Christians on the relationship among the Holy Spirit, custom, and law, and the focus was whether it was necessary to abandon national customs once the Chinese received the Holy Spirit. This was the core of the controversy. In the seventeenth and eighteenth centuries, the Holy See neither followed the teachings of biblical pneumatology nor kept a more open attitude for an equal and patient dialogue with their Chinese counterparts. The simple and crude ban issued in 1742 did nothing positive for the Chinese mission, but only intensified the Holy See's conflict with the Jesuits, the Chinese government, and Chinese Christians—resulting in a fatal end to its Oriental missionary project.

CONCLUSION

Just as the Jewish law had been fulfilled in the power of the Spirit by Gentile Christians, and the Roman customs had been renewed in Paul's time, so also the Chinese commemorating rites can be renewed and obeyed by Chinese Christians as "humanizing" etiquette (*li*) in the power of the Holy Spirit, who moves and works through all believers.

As a historical event, the Chinese rites controversy has passed. But for China, the problem of a Chinese Christianity is still a heated topic for the church and the government. After the revolution of 1911, China was no longer a dynastic empire but became the People's Republic of China. By that time, the Chinese government recognized and respected freedom of belief and religion, and the question of understanding and living that freedom often hinged on the letter or the spirit of the law. As the Chinese rites controversy demonstrates, the Holy Spirit plays a critical role in initiating and maintaining Christian identity in a changing culture or context. If we wish to find the right way for the Christian faith to spread in China, we must trust the power of the Spirit at work in diverse cultures, acknowledge the spirit of Chinese traditional customs, and absorb the ideals of Chinese civilization into the Christian faith. In this mutual inspiration, promotion, critique, and fulfillment, Christianity will accomplish its localization and indigenization, while also growing and learning from the global church's multiple cultures. May the Spirit of God help the global church in China not to be Christianity *in China*, but to be *Chinese* Christianity.

---

[28]Wu, *Chinese Rites Controversy*, 81.
[29]See Yeo, "Paul's Way of *Renren*," 469-79.

Further Reading

Jewett, Robert. *Romans: A Commentary*. Minneapolis: Fortress, 2007.

Minamiki, George. *Chinese Rites Controversy: From Its Beginning to Modern Times*. Chicago: Loyola University Press, 1985.

Noll, Ray, trans. *100 Roman Documents Concerning the Chinese Rites Controversy (1645–1941)*. San Francisco: Ricci Institute for Chinese-Western Cultural History, 1992.

Wu, Liwei. *The Chinese Rites Controversy: The Encounter of Civilizations and Powers*. Shanghai: Shanghai Classics, 2007.

Yeo, K. K. *Musing with Confucius and Paul: Toward a Chinese Christian Theology*. Eugene, OR: Cascade, 2008.

———. *Rhetorical Interaction in 1 Corinthians 8 and 10: A Formal Analysis with Preliminary Suggestions for a Chinese, Cross-Cultural Hermeneutic*. Leiden: Brill, 1995.

PNEUMATOLOGY

ITS IMPLICATIONS FOR THE AFRICAN CONTEXT

Samuel M. Ngewa

THE VISIBLE ASPECT in relation to the role of the Holy Spirit, in the African context, has been more divisive than unifying. Many of those who have claimed to have been blessed with the gifts of the Holy Spirit, especially the gifts of healing and speaking in tongues, have always assumed spiritual superiority over those who do not have such gifts. Sermons promoting such an understanding have often been drawn from the book of Acts, particularly Acts 2, where we have an account of what happened on the day of Pentecost. The main objective of this chapter is to underline that the Holy Spirit of the book of Acts, and for that matter the New Testament as a whole, is a unifying Spirit and not a divisive one. He brings together not only individuals but also races to think together and serve God as one united family of God. When this unifying role of the Holy Spirit is placed in the forefront, all his gifts, as shown in other parts of the New Testament, fall neatly into place.

Pneumatology comes from two Greek words, *pneuma* and *logos*. *Logos* literally means "word,"
but when it is put together with another word it means "study of."[1] *Pneuma* means "spirit," whether spirit of man or Spirit of God.[2] It is also translated "wind."[3] In this chapter *pneuma* refers to the Spirit of God (Holy Spirit), and so *pneumatology* means "study of the Holy Spirit."

Most works on the Holy Spirit have two main sections, one dealing with the person of the Holy Spirit and the other dealing with the work of the Holy Spirit. The section on his person deals with such matters as his deity and whether he is actually a person or a thing, while the section on his work deals with what he has done (e.g., in the Old Testament, in the life of Jesus, and in the New Testament church) and does (e.g., his ministries of indwelling a believer and giving gifts for ministry to church and society). By its very nature, an examination of his person tends to be philosophical, while a study of his works is usually more descriptive. The descriptive rather than the philosophical is characteristic of the African context.

Jesus in John 3:8 compares the work of the Holy Spirit with wind and says, "You hear its

---

[1]We add *logos* to *theos* (God) to derive "theology" (study of matters related to God), to *kosmos* (world) to derive "cosmology" (study of the universe), and to *astēr* (star) to derive "astrology" (study of stars), for example.

[2]Spirit of man: Acts 7:59 (spirit of Stephen) and Acts 18:25 (spirit of Apollos). Spirit of God: Acts 2:17 (my Spirit) and Acts 16:7 (the Spirit of Jesus).

[3]John 3:8 is a good example.

sound, but you cannot tell where it comes from or where it is going."[4] One implication of this is that the Holy Spirit's work can be evident even without a philosophical analysis of who he is in his essence. There may be little systematic analysis of who the Holy Spirit is in the African context, but there are millions of people in whose lives he has left a tremendous impact. We can learn about him by examining what he has done.

Being one of the three persons of the Trinity, the Spirit is eternal, and therefore his work is eternal.[5] For the purpose of this chapter, however, I limit the discussion to his work in the African context, particularly in the eastern part of Africa, in the twentieth century and into the twenty-first century.

One major and documented story on the Holy Spirit at work in Africa is the East Africa Revival, referred to by Timothy Morgan as "Africa's Azusa Street." Notable at its beginning was a team of a missionary (Joe Church) and an African (a Ugandan, Simeon Nsibambi). All differences set aside, these two saw the need for the African church to live out its theology. It is one thing to say that we believers are the salt and light of the world (Mt 5:13-16), and it is another for our lives to reflect that truth. Morgan says these two men were moved by "the lifelessness of African churches, the ruthlessness of colonialism, society's pervasive corruption, and the moral failure of Christian leaders."[6]

Church (a graduate of Cambridge University working as a missionary in Gahini in Rwanda) had gone to Uganda in 1929 to catch up on some rest. There he providentially met Nsibambi, and as the two studied the Bible and prayed together, their spirits were united in advancing a life of holiness for the church of Christ.[7] As Church worked from his mission station in Rwanda in the following years and Nsibambi devoted himself to the ministry of preaching in Uganda, the fire of revival caught momentum. Its effect was felt not only in Rwanda and Uganda, where it originated, but also in Burundi, Kenya, Tanzania, and Congo. Its effect, to some degree, has lasted to this day. Festo Kivengere (d. 1988), who has been labeled as the Billy Graham of Africa, was the product of this movement.[8] Its chief characteristic was confession of sin and commitment to live a life of holiness. In some extreme cases, some of its members saw themselves as holier than those who were not in the movement. There were also situations where the confession of sin was taken as the central mark of spirituality, making some members confess sins that they actually had not committed. In such cases, the desire to appear spiritual led to the sin of pretense. Such weaknesses did not help in keeping the movement as steady as it should have been, and so what we have today is more of the effect of the revival than continuity with it. Overall, however, it was evident that the Holy Spirit was at work in Africa.

---

[4]Unless otherwise noted, Scripture quotations in this chapter follow the NIV.

[5]The three persons of the Trinity are God the Father, God the Son, and God the Holy Spirit (Mt 28:19; 2 Cor 13:14).

[6]Timothy C. Morgan, "Africa's Azusa Street," March 28, 2006, www.christianitytoday.com/ct/2006/marchweb-only/113-23.0.html. The Azusa Street Revival in Los Angeles under William J. Seymour, April 9, 1906–1915, was marked by unrelenting preaching against sin and some miraculous signs such as speaking in tongues ("Azusa Street Revival," Wikipedia, en.wikipedia.org/wiki/Azusa_Street _Revival, accessed April 28, 2020).

[7]For a detailed history of this relationship, see Richard Gehman, "The East African Revival," East Africa Journal of Evangelical Theology 5, no. 1 (1986): 36-56; Kevin Ward, "'Tukutendereza Yesu': The Balokole Revival in Uganda," Dictionary of African Christian Biography, 1991, https://dacb.org/histories/uganda-tukutendereza-yesu/.

[8]Frederick Quinn, "Festo Kivengere, 1919–1988," Dictionary of African Christian Biography, 2002, https://dacb.org/stories/uganda /kivengere-festo.

Another story testifying to the work of the Holy Spirit in Africa centers on the ministry of Joe Kayo (b. 1936), who in 1970 founded the Pentecostal Deliverance Church of Kenya but also ministered in Uganda and Zambia.[9] It is from Kayo that in 1971 I heard the most convincing message about the need for speaking in tongues. His sermon was taken from Acts 2, and on reflection (I was one of those who did not speak in tongues during the meeting) I wondered whether he was right to use a narrative to promise all of us the gift of speaking in tongues if we were truly saved. There are many today who carry Kayo's message, citing Acts passages as proof texts. This is an issue that is at the center of this chapter and is discussed extensively below. In summary, however, many, like Kayo and their disciples, have given the impression that the power of the Holy Spirit is "a private possession of those who have been baptized in the Spirit."[10] This feeling, just as was the case among some members of the East Africa Revival, resulted in a holier-than-thou attitude. Many looked at believers in the mainline denominations as unsaved just because they did not speak in tongues. Instead of unifying the church, it brought division and factions in some quarters.

While the East Africa Revival as promoted by Church and Nsibambi and the Pentecostal Deliverance Church under Kayo stand out, they do not exhaust the story. Many African independent (at times called "instituted" or "indigenous") churches also "place emphasis on the Holy Spirit,

with accompanying manifestations of joy, tongues and power, on healing and exorcism, on personal testimony."[11] This is not to mention the ministries of Assemblies of God fellowships and the many mainline denominations that recite the Apostles' Creed every Sunday.[12] In this creed is the statement, "I believe in the Holy Spirit."

Experience must be founded on knowledge, just as knowledge without experience is not adequate. The personal experiences among the members of revival and charismatic movements cannot be downplayed. However, they would be richer if founded on good exegesis of the Scriptures. Impatience "with the idea of using the Bible for sustained teaching on theological issues" must be replaced with a careful examination of the passages on which we build our experiences.[13] Since the book of Acts has been used extensively in promoting the claims of these experiences, this chapter sets out to examine some of those key passages exegetically and from them draw some lessons for the church of Christ in Africa today.

THEOLOGICAL AND EXEGETICAL EXAMINATION

Almost all mainline denominations recite the Apostles' Creed every Sunday. What it contains, however, is just an assertion that belief in the Holy Spirit is one of the pillars of the faith. The Nicene Creed (325) says a little more, for it states that the Holy Spirit is "the Lord and Giver of Life; who proceedeth from the Father and the Son;

---

[9]Pew Research Center, "Historical Overview of Pentecostalism in Kenya," August 5, 2010, www.pewforum.org/2010/08/05/historical -overview-of-pentecostalism-in-kenya; Francis Manana, "Kayo, Joseph," *Dictionary of African Christian Biography*, 2000, https://dacb .org/stories/kenya/kayo-joseph.

[10]Albert Nolan, *God in South Africa: The Challenge of the Gospel* (Grand Rapids, MI: Eerdmans, 1988), 115.

[11]Diane Stinton, "Africa, East and West," in *Introduction to Third World Theologies*, ed. John Parratt (Cambridge: Cambridge University Press, 2004), 119.

[12]The Assemblies of God has fellowships in many parts of the continent and emphasizes the work of the Holy Spirit, particularly the gift of speaking in tongues.

[13]Ward, "Tukutendereza Yesu."

who with the Father and the Son together is worshipped and glorified; who spake by the Prophets."[14] The creed states something about his deity (he is worshiped and glorified with the Father and the Son), his being sent by the Father and the Son as taught in John 14:16; 16:17, his role in inspiration (he spoke by the prophets), and his ministry in the life of a believer (he is the Lord and Giver of Life). Thus, though this creed was meant to answer some wrong teachings of the time, it touches on the most essential teachings of the Scriptures concerning the Holy Spirit. He is a person and not a thing (e.g., power or influence of God), he is equal with the Father and the Son, and he has a ministry to do.[15] These facts need to be kept in mind even as we examine his work in the passages from Acts below.

As we do so, it is important to keep in mind that the book of Acts is a narrative, and narrative's primary function is to tell us what happened and not what should happen. This does not take away the fact that the God who did something in the past is the same God today and so can do the same thing again. However, it

serves as a caution not to impose demands on a sovereign God for what he chooses to do, when to do it, and how it will be done.

Four key passages to be considered in this chapter are Acts 2; 8; 10; 19. These four passages are about the outpouring of the Holy Spirit in Jerusalem on the day of Pentecost, in Samaria, in the house of Cornelius, and in Ephesus, respectively.

Acts 2. The focus of Acts 2 is Jews. Jewish believers are the first to receive the Holy Spirit. The story, however, begins earlier than Acts 2, for in Acts 1:8 Jesus had told the apostles (*apostoloi*) that they would be his witnesses (*martyres*) in all of Judea (beginning in Jerusalem), in Samaria, and to the ends of the earth.[16] The time frame for this was given as after the Holy Spirit had come upon them (Acts 1:8).[17] Even more significantly, Jesus said that their new status would be one in which they had "power" (*dynamis*).[18] Once the Holy Spirit had come upon them, they would be equal to the task.

Jesus' promise that the apostles would receive power upon their reception of the Holy Spirit was fulfilled on the day of Pentecost and when

---

[14]This is cited from Wayne Grudem, *Bible Doctrine: Essential Teachings of the Christian Faith* (Leicester, UK: Inter-Varsity, 1999), 474.

[15]In his determination to safeguard the unity of God, Arius (d. 336) identified only the Father as God, labeling the Son as God's first creation while reducing the Spirit to God's power or influence. This wrong teaching is today propagated by the Jehovah's Witnesses, who are zealous in door-to-door visitation. While their Kingdom Halls may not be fully packed, their enthusiasm in evangelism is felt in many parts of Africa. In spite of the Greek noun *pneuma* (Spirit) being neuter, the New Testament uses a personal pronoun (*ekeinos*) whenever referring to the Holy Spirit.

[16]"Apostles" in Acts 1:2 is taken to refer to the Eleven (the Twelve less Judas Iscariot). This is made clearer by the addition of "whom he [Jesus] had chosen." The significance of a witness is that the person qualified to be one is someone who has gone through an experience needed to achieve that status. The eleven were to be witnesses concerning Jesus because they had been with him—seeing what he was doing and hearing what he was teaching.

[17]This is not to be understood as if the Holy Spirit were inactive in the lives of God's people before the day of Pentecost. The Old Testament uses such terms as "coming upon," "filling," and "putting on" to describe his activity in the lives of judges such as Othniel (Judg 3:10), Gideon (Judg 6:34), Jephthah (Judg 11:29), and Samson (Judg 14:6); civil administrators such as Moses (Num 11:17), Saul (1 Sam 10:10), and David (16:13); craftsmen such as Bezalel (Ex 31:4); and prophets such as Ezekiel (Ezek 11:15) and Micah (Mic 3:8). All these, however, were task-oriented fillings. On the day of Pentecost the Holy Spirit came to dwell (Rom 8:11; 1 Cor 2:12; 6:19-20), seal (2 Cor 1:21-22; Gal 1:13; 4:30), and empower (1 Cor 12–14). God the Father was the most involved in the affairs of his people in the Old Testament, God the Son in the Gospels, and God the Holy Spirit after the day of Pentecost. It would be wrong, however, to assume that the other two persons of the Trinity were inactive when in a given period the focus was on one of them.

[18]The idea behind *dynamis* is the needed energy to perform the task. When a car or machine is said to have lost power, it means that something that makes it keep moving has gone wrong. When that is fixed, the power is restored. The apostles needed the person of the Holy Spirit to move the good news they had witnessed Jesus teach and do, in both near and far locations. Their activities were accomplished with *dynamis*, and their gospel was a gospel of *dynamis*, even as Paul says in Rom 1:16.

they were "all" (*pantes*) in one place (Acts 2:1).[19] Whether only the Twelve or the 120 (the more popular view), these were persons who had experiences to share and a message to pass on. Views are divided on whether the "one place" was a private house or a hall within the temple, and there is no good reason for anyone to be dogmatic in support of one against the other.[20] In any case, its location was such that a crowd could gather to hear the message being proclaimed. What is most significant is what happened that day.

The manner in which the Holy Spirit came upon this group of Jews was "as a sound like the blowing of a violent wind" and "what seemed to be tongues of fire" (Acts 2:2-3). The wind symbolism here may be taken to signify real power in action though invisible, while the tongues of fire may signify the presence of the Lord (see Ex 3:2). The incident left no doubt that the promised Holy Spirit had come.

The result of this incident is fourfold: all were filled with the Holy Spirit (Acts 2:4), all began to speak in other tongues (Acts 2:4), Peter preached the main message for the day (Acts 2:14-40), and about three thousand believers were added that day (Acts 2:41).

The act of filling with the Holy Spirit may have as its focus either character or service. When the focus is character, it may be viewed as a permanent endowment. It is a status that controls the manner in which a person responds to life in general (e.g., Acts 6:3; 11:24; 13:52). Paul summarizes this in what he refers to as the fruit of the Spirit in Galatians 5:22-23. When the focus is service, however, the act is accompanied by a task performed (e.g., Mk 1:41). It is service that is the focus of Acts 2:4. Filling in this sense is an enabling that may go with a short-lived assignment or a long-term task. It can be repeated as many times as there are tasks to be performed. We see it repeated in the cases of Peter and Paul, and this was also the sense in which believers of Acts 4:31 were filled with the Holy Spirit.[21] These two foci of the filling of the Holy Spirit must always be kept in mind when we express our theological positions on a given passage. While character-related filling of the Holy Spirit is expected of

---

[19]The group meant by "all" here could be the Twelve (at this point Matthias has been chosen to replace Judas Iscariot; Acts 1:26) or the 120 mentioned in 1:15. Luke uses the term "apostles" (*apostoloi*) for the 12 (1:2) and "brothers" (*adelphoi*) for the 120. The term "brothers" here is used of all who identified with the apostles on the issue of the message from and about Jesus. Acts 1:14 mentions some women as part of this group also. While I take the position that the "all" is the twelve apostles, the reasons are not strong enough to totally dismiss the view that it can be the 120 brothers. The "all," however, needs to refer to a group the crowd can single out (Acts 2:7). The Twelve had some identity as Jesus' apostles. See C. S. C. Williams, *A Commentary on the Acts of the Apostles* (New York: Harper, 1957), 62, and F. W. Beare, "Speaking with Tongues: A Critical Survey of the New Testament Evidence," *Journal of Biblical Literature* 83 (1964): 236. For the view that 120 were meant, see W. G. MacDonald, "Glossolalia in the New Testament," *Bulletin of the Evangelical Theological Society* 7 (Spring 1964): 60; William Neil, *The Acts of the Apostles*, New Century Bible (Greenwood, SC: Attic, 1973), 72; F. F. Bruce, *The Book of Acts: The English Text with Introduction, Exposition and Notes*, New International Commentary on the New Testament (Grand Rapids, MI: Eerdmans, 1981), 68; John Williams, *The Holy Spirit: Lord and Life-Giver* (Neptune, NJ: Loizeaux Brothers, 1980), 190; I. Howard Marshall, *Acts*, Tyndale New Testament Commentaries (Leicester, UK: Inter-Varsity, 1980), 68; John B. Polhill, *Acts: An Exegetical and Theological Exposition of Holy Scripture*, New American Commentary (Nashville: Broadman, 1992), 97; Joseph A. Fitzmyer, SJ, *The Acts of the Apostles*, Anchor Bible (New York: Doubleday, 1998), 238; Craig S. Keener, *Acts: Exegetical Commentary*, vol. 1, *Introduction and 1:1–2:49* (Grand Rapids, MI: Baker Academic, 2012), 795.

Pentecost, also referred to as the Feast of Weeks, was one of the three major feasts for Jews (the other two being the Passover and the Feast of Tabernacles). It was celebrated in June when the weather was generally good, so many people were normally in attendance. It was a fitting time for many to witness the fulfillment of the promise that the Holy Spirit would fill Jesus' followers at Jerusalem.

[20]See Keener, *Acts*, 1:796-99. For the private-house view, see Heinrich A. W. Meyer, *A Critical and Exegetical Handbook to the Acts of the Apostles* (Winona Lake, IN: Alpha, 1883), 83; R. C. H. Lenski, *The Interpretation of the Acts of the Apostles* (Minneapolis: Augsburg, 1934), 58; Polhill, *Acts*, 97; for the hall-within-the-temple view, see Neil, *Acts of the Apostles*, 72; Bruce, *Book of Acts*, 67.

[21]Peter must have been a participant in the filling of Acts 2:4, since he turned out to be the preacher of the day, and Luke reports the same experience for him in Acts 4:8. In Acts 9:17-20, Saul (Paul) was filled with the Holy Spirit and spoke in the synagogue; in Acts 13:9-11, he was filled with the Holy Spirit and announced punishment on Elymas.

all believers (Eph 5:18), task-related filling may be limited to those assigned a specific task. Also, while character-related filling is meant to be a permanent status, service-related filling may be seasonal. God may fill us with the Holy Spirit in a special way for a task in the twenty-first century that was not a necessary task in the twentieth century. In such a case, what makes the difference between us in the twenty-first century and those in the twentieth century is not the level of spirituality but the nature of tasks. The task of establishing the church in Jerusalem called for a filling that was special. We see it in the further results.

The first outcome of the filling of the Holy Spirit was that "all" began to speak in tongues (Acts 2:4). If we limit the "all" to the team of twelve (see discussion above) referred to as apostles, we can say that the apostles spoke in tongues. It is clear that *glōssa*, translated as "tongue" here, has several meanings.[22] What interpreters are divided on is when it needs to be viewed as a language and when it needs to be viewed as some kind of ecstatic utterance. We also need to be careful not to read into Acts what we have in 1 Corinthians, and vice versa, for this may result in misinterpretation of one or the other.[23] Each passage must be read within its own context and literary type.

We observe in Acts 2 two phrases: "in other tongues" (*heterais glōssais*) in Acts 2:4 and "in our tongues" (*hēmeterais glōssais*) in Acts 2:11. Luke's choice of words makes it clear that the *glōssai* here do not point to speech out of this world but speech within the context of the languages spoken by those listening.[24] Luke says about the speech in Acts 2 that some of those who heard it described it as "declaring the wonders [*ta megaleia*] of God" (Acts 2:11). A list of those who heard is given in Acts 2:9-11. These took home not only the miracle of Galileans (Acts 2:7) speaking in languages of many parts of the world but also a message of what God had done. Though not stated specifically, part of the message of the Twelve here must have been that Jesus had risen from the dead. God had raised Jesus up, sealing that Jesus was his Son and not even death could hold him in the grave. This is a message so close to God's heart that we should not be surprised if he gives the same gift to a missionary of the twenty-first century, enabling her to declare the wonders of God in Christ.

The other outcome of the filling in this incident of Acts 2 centers on Peter. In Acts 2:14, Luke says that Peter addressed the crowd.[25] His

---

[22]It can mean the physical tongue (Lk 1:64; 16:24), nation or people (Rev 5:9; 7:9; 10:11; 14:6), or a language or ecstatic utterance. No references are given for the last two, but they are at the center of the discussion above.

[23]Even if there may be other passages (e.g., Gal 5:18-20; Col 3:16; 1 Thess 5:19-20) that some interpreters regard as relevant to the issue of tongues (see I. J. Martin, "Glossolalia in the Apostolic Church," *Journal of Biblical Literature* 63 [1944]: 126), it is the book of Acts and 1 Cor 12–14 that deal with the matter directly. Mark 16:17, of course, mentions it specifically, but the ending of Mark has its own textual difficulties.

[24]The attempts to present what happened in Acts 2 as a miracle of hearing (see George B. Gutten, *Speaking with Tongues: Historically and Psychologically Considered* [New Haven, CT: Yale University Press, 1927]) rather than a miracle of speaking goes against Luke's choice of words. Menzies's position that the incident combined a miracle of speaking unintelligible tongues and a miracle of understanding those tongues (Robert P. Menzies, "The Role of Glossolalia in Luke-Acts," *Asia Journal of Pentecostal Studies* 15, no. 1 [January 2012]: 52) is based more on assumption (to support "tongues" in Acts 2 as glossolalia) than the more plain reading of the narrative.

[25]We are not told what language (*glōssa*) Peter spoke in addressing the mixed crowd, but he probably spoke a language everyone present would be assumed to understand, even if it would be a second language. His primary audience was the Judeans (Jews), who may also have been the ones making the comment of Acts 2:13, for they did not know some of the dialects (Acts 2:6, 8). In any case, Greek, Aramaic, and Hebrew were languages possibly spoken among the disciples and proselytes (R. H. Gundry, "The Language Milieu of First Century Palestine: Its Bearing on the Authenticity of the Gospel Tradition," *Journal of Biblical Literature* 83 [1964]: 404-8), and Aramaic was the lingua franca of commerce for countries listed in Acts 2:9-11 (F. J. Foakes-Jackson, *Acts of the Apostles* [London: Hodder & Stoughton, 1931], 12).

sermon on the Day of Pentecost and as reported by Luke in Acts 2:14-39 begins by showing that what was happening was fulfillment of Scripture (Acts 2:16-21), followed by a summary of the Christian message (Acts 2:22-36) and concluding with the invitation to repent and be baptized.[26] Peter tells his hearers that their obedience to his invitation to repent will be followed by their reception of the Holy Spirit. The literal translation of the Greek, in Acts 2:38, as to what they will receive is "the gift of the Holy Spirit," which can be understood as the gift that comes from (taking "of the Holy Spirit" as genitive of source) or is connected with (qualitative genitive) the Holy Spirit.[27] It is better, however, to read this in view of Acts 1:8. The Holy Spirit who had come upon those gathered together on the Day of Pentecost is a blessing to be enjoyed by all those who repent and believe in the Lord Jesus Christ. The Holy Spirit himself (epexegetical genitive) is that gift.[28] What accompanies the reception of him is secondary. For the Jews on the day of Pentecost, it was accompanied by the gift of speaking in other languages. They were enabled to proclaim the good news to all who had come together for the Feast of Pentecost. Luke reports that three thousand people were saved that day (Acts 2:41). The church was born in response to a message whose central character was Jesus. It was born in response to faith in this risen Jesus, and everyone who believed received

the Holy Spirit. This, however, was a congregation of Jews and proselytes (Acts 2:5). Witnessing in Jerusalem and Judea (Acts 1:8) had taken place.

Acts 8. In New Testament times, the three broad categories of communities were Jews, Samaritans, and Gentiles. Acts 2 focuses on how Jews received the Holy Spirit. The focus of Acts 8 is Samaritans. Jews regarded Samaritans as one degree nearer than Gentiles, but still not full-fledged members of the house of Israel.[29] Different happenings in history had brought the Jewish general attitude toward Samaritans to a level where a Jewish rabbi would instruct his fellow Jews, "Let no man eat bread of Cuthites (the Samaritans) for he who eats their bread is as he who eats swine's flesh," and would also teach Jews to pray "and Lord, do not remember the Samaritans in the resurrection."[30] In Acts 8:17, however, Samaritans received the Holy Spirit—the same person whom Jews had received in Acts 2. The significance of this was that God, the owner of the church, welcomes to his family Samaritans just as he welcomes Jews. There are some key details in the narrative that should be noted:

1. The Samaritans who received the Holy Spirit were persons who had been preached to by Philip but had not received the Holy Spirit at the point of their believing (Acts 8:5, 16).[31]

---

[26]Jesus of Nazareth's death was in the plan of God. He was raised and lives forevermore as Lord. He is God's provided object of faith. Joel had prophesied what was taking place.

[27]It is this particular understanding of this passage that has led to some reading the gift of tongues into it, of course, raising the question why one gift from the Spirit, out of many as listed in 1 Cor 12; 14, would be singled out.

[28]See also Wayne Jackson, "What Is the 'Gift of the Holy Spirit' in Acts 2:38?," www.christiancourier.com/articles/715-what-is-the-gift -of-the-holy-spirit-in-acts-2-38, accessed April 29, 2020.

[29]T. H. Gaster, "Samaritans," in *Interpreter's Dictionary of the Bible*, ed. G. A. Buttrick (Nashville: Abingdon, 1962), 4:191.

[30]R. Kent Hughes, *Acts: The Church Afire* (Wheaton, IL: Crossway, 1996), 111. See a summary of these happenings in Samuel M. Ngewa, *The Gospel of John for Pastors and Teachers* (Nairobi: Evangel, 2003), 473-74.

[31]Luke in Acts 8:5 says that these were the dwellers of "the city of Samaria" ([tēn] polin tēs Samareias). Since "Samaria" was used for the region in New Testament times, identification of the exact city has included Sebaste, which was the capital city of the region (Barclay

Some have argued that the delay needs to be seen within the context of Philip's limitations in clarity of message or authority.[32] Others have maintained that the delay needs to be explained within the context of the Samaritans' faith being deficient.[33] These, however, seem to be conclusions that do not have full support from the narrative.[34] The reason seems to lie elsewhere, as I will mention below.

2. The Samaritans' reception of the Holy Spirit was in the presence of, and under the ministry of, Peter and John. The apostles in Jerusalem had sent Peter and John (Acts 8:14) after they heard that Samaria had received the word of God. We are not told how they had heard, but it is possible that Philip himself was party to the message sent to the apostles. The message could have been that the Samaritans had received the word of God but there was no external evidence that they had received the Holy Spirit. The standard of measuring or for knowing whether the Holy Spirit had come would have been the experience of the Jews in Acts 2. This had not happened to the Samaritans, though they had believed and had been baptized (Acts 8:12), and it would have concerned Philip.

3. The ministry of Peter and John to these Samaritans included "laying hands on them" (Acts 8:17), and the result was that the Samaritans received the Holy Spirit. By implication, there was some external indicator that this had happened. Whether this was speaking in tongues, as we see later in Acts 10:46, or another sign we cannot say for sure. It is, however, reasonable to assume that God did provide an indicator that was visible to all. The laying on of hands was also an external demonstration of fellowship.

The situation, therefore, seems to be one in which the Samaritans believed but did not receive the Holy Spirit, as would have been expected. Philip is not sure why this is the case and so sends a message to the apostles in Jerusalem on the matter. The apostles send Peter and John to evaluate the situation. They pray for and lay hands on the Samaritans, and the Samaritans receive the Holy Spirit. The delay in receiving the Holy Spirit is caused by neither the weakness of Philip's preaching nor the deficiency of the Samaritans' believing. The delay is God's providence that the apostles, and for that matter the representatives of the Jerusalem church, would be part of and witnesses to the Samaritans also receiving the Holy Spirit. This in itself would be God's own stamp on the oneness of the church of Christ, whether Jews or Samaritans. Barriers are broken in Christ, and that is confirmed by the Samaritans being partakers of the same

---

M. Newman and Eugene Nida, *A Translator's Handbook on the Acts of the Apostles* [London: United Bible Societies, 1972], 173; Fitzmyer, *Acts*, 402); Neapolis, which was the religious headquarters (Lenski, *Interpretation of the Acts of the Apostles*, 316); or even Gitta, the birthplace of Simon the Magician, if the Greek article is left out of the text, reading "a city" (Bruce, *Book of Acts*, 183).

[32]Johannes Munck, *The Acts of the Apostles: Introduction, Translation and Notes*, Anchor Bible, rev. William F. Albright and C. S. Mann (Garden City, NY: Doubleday, 1967), 75; G. H. C. Macgregor, "The Acts of the Apostles," in Buttrick, *Interpreter's Bible* (Nashville: Abingdon, 1954), 9:110.

[33]J. D. G. Dunn, *The Baptism of the Holy Spirit* (Naperville: Alec R. Allenson, 1970), 65; A. Hoekema, *Holy Spirit Baptism* (Grand Rapids, MI: Eerdmans, 1972), 32.

[34]For example, the narrative does not tell us that Peter and John preached a clearer message than Philip had preached but simply that they prayed for them (Acts 8:15) and laid hands on them (Acts 8:17). Also the comment of Luke in Acts 8:16 (the Holy Spirit had not fallen on any of them) implies that there was some abnormality to what would be expected under normal circumstances.

Spirit as the Jews in Acts 2.[35] At a secondary level, there is also the vivid picture of one of the seven deacons (Acts 6:3-5) and two of the twelve apostles (Peter and John) cooperating in the mission of God.[36] They show a unity as the leaders and that unity is to be lived by all—whether Jews or Samaritans (and later, in Acts 10, Gentiles also).

Acts 10. The third key passage is Acts 10, with the narrative extending from Acts 10:1–11:18. While Acts 2 centered on Jews and Acts 8 centered on Samaritans, this passage centers on Gentiles (Acts 11:1, 3). From the perspective of Jerusalem, while Jews belonged to the inner circle and Samaritans to the middle circle, Gentiles belonged to the outer circle. The Gentile representative in the narrative is Cornelius, who was a centurion (man of authority) as well as a God-fearer (Acts 10:1-2). The narrative presents to us some notable details, including the following:

1. Divine preparation of Peter for the ministry to and on behalf of Cornelius, his household, and his friends (Acts 10:9-21). Peter had his views about Gentiles, and those views had to be refuted by the Lord's own intervention through a vision.

2. Divine guidance of Cornelius and his messengers (Acts 10:1-8, 21-23). The Lord gave specific instructions to Cornelius as to whom he would send for and where that person would be found.

3. Peter's obedience and the results (Acts 10:24-29, 44). The message to Peter was clear. He was left with the options of obeying and doing what in his view had seemed as impossible or disobeying and knowing that he was acting against the Lord's clear instructions.

4. Shock of those in Jerusalem (Acts 11:1-3) and Peter's explanation of what exactly happened (Acts 11:4-17), followed by those in Jerusalem having no choice but to accept what had happened (Acts 11:18). It all pointed to the providence of God.

Some of the key phrases (or statements) related to the narrative and pointing us to the providence of God in uniting all believers into one body include the following:

1. God is no respecter of persons (*ouk estin prosōpolēmptēs ho theos*; Acts 10:34).[37] Peter says that this is a fact that he has been taught (*katalambanomai*; Acts 10:34) through the vision God used to prepare him.[38] If it had been left up to him, Gentiles would have been meant to stay outside the kingdom of God or come into it by way of passing through the path of Judaism. God, however, says that they also need to have direct access, and Peter has now learned this. The vision was not for Peter's glorification but for his education in the school of God. He learned that "it is God's will that Gentiles become part of God's

---

[35]I. Howard Marshall describes this overcoming of hostility between Jews and Samaritans as "a step towards the greater of bringing Jews and Gentiles together." He then adds, "If this is correct, it may provide the clue to the undoubted problem presented by the fact that the Samaritan believers did not receive the Spirit until the apostles laid hands on them" (*Acts*, 153).

[36]C. K. Barrett, *Acts*, International Critical Commentary (Edinburgh: T&T Clark, 1994), 1:412.

[37]The verb "is" (*estin*) is here to be taken as a gnomic present, that is, God's nature once we come to know who he is for sure. Peter was aware of this truth before, but only on theoretical terms. Now he knows it practically. In God there is no discrimination or class. He accepts all on the basis of faith in his Son Jesus Christ, even as Peter preached in this narrative (Acts 10:36-43).

[38]Literal translation of *katalambanomai* is "I realize, understand, perceive," and in this context it can be translated, "I have come to understand" (perfective present), for it is a status that God's preparation of him has helped him to achieve. God has caused him to look beyond the limitations of his earlier perceptions. In other words, God has prepared him to see people the way God sees them and not the way the ordinary Jew would.

people without the obligation of obeying prescriptions of the Mosaic law."[39]

2. Every person, from any nation, is accepted by God (*dektos autō estin*; Acts 10:35) so long as there is fear of God in him.[40] This is another statement of Peter's newest education in this narrative. He now knows this.

3. Those of the circumcision (Jews) who were believers were astonished (*exestēsan*) because the gift of the Holy Spirit was poured on Gentiles also (Acts 10:45).[41] That Jews and Gentiles stood on equal footing before God was clear, and, as Kent Hughes puts it, "There was no denying that fact now. Seven witnesses had seen it, including an apostle!"[42]

The "pouring" (*enkchutai*; Acts 10:45) of the Holy Spirit captures the same thing as the "falling" (*epepesen*; Acts 10:44) of the Holy Spirit upon all those who heard the word, and the speaking in tongues (Acts 10:46) is not what is described here as the gift of the Holy Spirit (see note 41) but the external demonstration that the Holy Spirit (who himself is the gift) had been received by Cornelius and his relatives and close friends also.[43]

The center of this phenomenon is, therefore, not that Gentiles spoke in tongues but that they received the Holy Spirit, the reception of which was confirmed by the external demonstration of speaking in tongues.[44] They received the same Holy Spirit the Samaritans had received in Acts 8 and the Jews had received in Acts 2. In other words, Jews, Samaritans, and Gentiles were equal guests in God's house, to dine on the same food and enjoy the same blessings. By the same Holy Spirit, God had sealed the unity of all the communities of the first century. Jews, Samaritans, and Gentiles were brought together into one body, and all of them on equal footing. The issues that had led to the separation of and discrimination between Jews and Samaritans, and the fact that Gentiles could only be accepted by partaking of "Jewishness," were all broken down. In Christ all are one family, the family of God.

Acts 19. Acts 19 does not focus on ethnic distance from what would have been expected in view of God's earlier dealing with the Jews as his chosen nation but on distance in terms of location. It represents "a remote part of the earth" (Acts 1:8) when Jerusalem is seen as the beginning point. The narrative tells us about the following:

1. Paul going to Ephesus, on his third missionary journey, and finding twelve disciples who were baptized only in the baptism of John (Acts 19:1, 6)

2. Paul asking them whether they had received the Holy Spirit when they believed and their answering, "No, we have not even heard there is a Holy Spirit" (Acts 19:2)

---

[39]Fitzmyer, *Acts*, 448.

[40]This *estin* is also a gnomic present. It is what God does on the basis of his nature.

[41]The gift of the Holy Spirit (*hē dōrea tou hagiou pneumatos*) here may be taken as the Holy Spirit himself, taking the genitive *tou hagiou pneumatos* as epexegetical. The literal meaning of *existēmi* is "to stand outside oneself, to be out of one's mind," and in this context it has the idea of being surprised, for what was happening was out of the expected. For a Gentile to have equal spiritual experience with a Jew was not normal.

[42]Hughes, *Acts*, 152. Regarding "seven," in Acts 11:12, Peter mentions brothers who had gone with him.

[43]The verb *encheō* (I pour out) focuses on the source. In this case, it is God who pours out. The verb *epipipto* (I fall on) focuses on the recipients. Taking it in relation to *encheō* (see above), the experience of the Gentiles was that they experienced the Holy Spirit falling on them while at the same time the Jews were surprised at the act of God pouring the Holy Spirit on the Gentiles.

[44]It is the reception of the Holy Spirit that Peter also emphasizes (Acts 11:15) when he states his case to the effect that God had received Gentiles just as he had received Jews and when that happened, Peter had no choice but to accept it (Acts 11:17) and allow it to change his perception.

3. Paul, on realizing that they had received only John's baptism, explaining to them the meaning of John's baptism and its relationship to Jesus (Acts 19:3-4)

4. Paul baptizing them, placing his hands on them, and their reception of the Holy Spirit and speaking in tongues (Acts 19:5-7)

The identity and spiritual state of these twelve have been matters of discussion in scholarship. There are some who have advanced the view that the twelve had been disciples of Apollos, who himself knew only about the baptism of John (Acts 18:25) until Priscilla and Aquila "explained to him the way of God more accurately" (Acts 18:26).[45] Others have suggested that they were disciples of John the Baptist.[46] These two positions are not incompatible. They could have been disciples of John the Baptist who also looked up to Apollos as their teacher.

As to their spiritual state, there are some who view them as not saved, while there are others who view them as believers.[47] While it may be difficult to be 100 percent certain, there are some details in the text whose weight cannot be ignored:

1. Luke's use of "disciples" (*mathētai*) without qualifying them to be John the Baptist's,

Apollo's, or someone else's.[48] It is not unreasonable to see Luke's use of the term here to be equivalent to "believers," that is, disciples of Jesus Christ. The argument that these twelve men only had the appearance of being disciples but they were not seems to take away from Luke the more obvious meaning when he simply says, "he (Paul) found some disciples."[49]

2. The use of the aorist participle *pisteusantes* (believed) gives some support to the view that these twelve were believers (no matter how deficient their understanding was) whose reception of the Holy Spirit had not taken place yet.[50]

The key issue for our argument here is that they had not received the Holy Spirit, though they had believed. However, after Paul baptized them in the name of Jesus (Acts 19:5) and laid his hands on them, "the Holy Spirit came on them and they spoke in tongues prophesying" (Acts 19:6). Fitzmyer's statement that Paul laid his hands on these twelve as a representative of the twelve apostles is in agreement with what God seems to be doing in the book of Acts, namely, bringing people of all races and nations under the same umbrella.[51]

---

[45]Examples include Merrill F. Unger, *New Testament Teaching on Tongues* (Grand Rapids, MI: Kregel, 1971), 64; Bruce, *Book of Acts*, 385.

[46]Examples include Marshall, *Acts*, 306; Bastiaan van Elderen, "Glossolalia in the New Testament," *Bulletin of the Evangelical Theological Society* 7, no. 2 (1964): 55.

[47]Examples of those who view them as believers include Ned B. Stonehouse ("Repentance, Baptism and Gift of the Holy Spirit," *Westminster Journal of Theology* 13 [1950–1951]: 12), Lenski (*Interpretation of Acts*, 780), and Bruce (*Book of Acts*, 385). Hoekema (*Holy Spirit Baptism*, 42), William J. Larkin Jr. (*Acts*, IVP New Testament Commentary [Downers Grove, IL: InterVarsity Press, 1995], 272), Marshall (*Acts*, 305), Fitzmyer (*Acts*, 643), and Ajith Fernando (*Acts*, NIV Application Commentary [Grand Rapids, MI: Zondervan, 1998], 506) are examples of those who take the view that these twelve were not saved.

[48]Other places where Luke uses the title "disciples" in Acts are Acts 6:1; 9:10; 11:26, and in these passages the title is interchangeable with the term "Christians."

[49]The Greek is *kai eurein tinas mathetas*, with the aorist verb *eurein* simply reporting what happened. It is a fact of history. Larkin (*Acts*, 272) says that Luke uses "disciples" for the twelve because "at first their outward identification with believers led Paul to take them as such." Marshall (*Acts*, 306) also says, "They appeared to be disciples but they are not. . . . Luke describes them as they appeared to Paul." But then, why would Luke promote the same misunderstanding years later?

[50]The aorist participle is usually used for an action antecedent to the action of the main verb though it can also be simultaneous with the action of the main verb if the main verb is also in the aorist tense. Paul presumes here that the twelve had believed, and it is on that basis that he is asking them whether they had also received the Holy Spirit.

[51]Fitzmyer, *Acts*, 644.

What happened in these four incidents can be summarized as follows:

Table 21.1

Group	Spiritual Status	Historical Timing	Significance
12 or 120 Jews	disciples of Christ	day of Pentecost	The Counselor (Jn 14:26) has come, and a movement of Spirit-indwelt and -empowered believers has begun.
Samaritans	believers	after Philip preached to them and Peter and John laid hands on them	Samaritans are in also.
Gentiles	believers	as Peter was speaking	Gentiles are in also.
12 disciples at Ephesus	believers (disciples)	after Paul laid hands on them	Believers from the uttermost part of the earth are in also.

Looking at Acts 8; 10; 19, one wonders why persons who have believed do not receive the Holy Spirit, as would be expected in view of such passages as Romans 8:9 and Ephesians 1:13.[52] The mystery lies in what God wants to establish in the context of these four outpourings of the Holy Spirit recorded in Acts. Acts 2 marked the fulfillment of the promise of Acts 1:8, and the other three outpourings marked the uniting of other people groups into that body of believers established on the day of Pentecost. Samaritans (Acts 8), Gentiles (Acts 10), and those living at the uttermost parts of the world (Acts 19) were fully welcomed into the same body established in Acts 2. There would no more be classification of persons who joined this movement on the basis of race, whether Jews, Samaritans, or Gentiles, whether near Jerusalem as the beginning point or as far away from there as Ephesus.

IMPLICATIONS FOR THE TWENTY-FIRST-CENTURY CHURCH

When we put together Acts 2; 8; 10; 19, we see a God who is involved in mission to make his own people from Jewish, Samaritan, and Gentile communities. He not only controls the timing of events, but he also provides visible demonstration of the oneness he is creating so that everyone who is genuine cannot question the evidence. This has implications for us today:

1. There is only one God for all the races of the world.[53] It is not every race or tribe with their God or a Supreme Being who should not be disturbed, but one God on a mission for all.[54] He does not need "a whole army of inferior gods and a long line of ancestral spirits" to connect with his people.[55] He himself is at work among his people.

---

[52]In these passages and others, a believer receives the Holy Spirit immediately after exercising faith in Christ. In fact, Rom 8:9 asserts that anyone without the Holy Spirit is not a believer.

[53]The God of Isaac (Yahweh) was also the God of Ishmael (Gen 17:19-27). There is no reason why Muslims and Christians (in Africa) or Jews and Palestinians (in the Middle East) cannot find a basis for unity as they relate to each other. Calling the Creator of heaven and earth by different names should be seen as a matter of the tongue (languages) and not a necessary basis for irreconcilable differences.

[54]Samuel Ngewa, "The Biblical Idea of Substitution Versus the Idea in African Traditional Sacrifices" (PhD diss., Westminster Theological Seminary, 1987), 59.

[55]Charles Salala, "The World of the Spirits: Basukuma Traditional Religion and Biblical Christianity," in *Issues in African Christian Theology*, ed. Samuel Ngewa, Mark Shaw, and Tite Tienou (Nairobi: East African Educational, 1998), 136.

2. There is only one Savior for all races of the world.[56] It is no longer each people group with their set sacrifices, but God's Son has been given as a sacrifice for the salvation of all.

3. There is the same Spirit for all races of the world. It is no longer the ancestral spirits serving as intermediaries, but God's gift (third person of the Trinity) baptizing believers into one body, one family.[57]

4. There is one family of God, no matter the people group.[58] All the tribes are given a common identity, membership in God's family that is found in the church of Christ.

5. All divisions on the basis of race, tribe, or the like have no place in the church of Christ. We do not deny that different races and tribes exist, but in terms of how we relate they should not make any difference.

6. God's true servants allow God to change their perceptions about people even when the inherited perceptions had drawn lines of demarcation on the basis of race or tribe. History cannot be erased. There were colonizers and the colonized, the "them" and the "we," but all these become things of the past as we are united in Christ.

As believers, unity defines our mission and goal in life. God laid the foundation, and we must build on it if we desire to be judged by him as faithful servants. Oneness also increases our level of effectiveness.[59] The principle of "united we stand, divided we fall" has been proven over and over again. It is not only true in political and social arenas but also in our spiritual ministry. Clarence Shuler's statement that "it is hard to change what has been ingrained" is totally accurate, but we must choose to act like our God, who purposely provided a church that is unified, no matter what boundaries had existed before.[60]

Once the unity established on the basis of Acts is guarded, the exercise of the gifts of the Spirit as taught in the Epistles becomes a blessing rather than a curse. We use the gifts for the good of the one family of God. Exercise of gifts should by no means be a source for division. God started a united church, and it is our mission to maintain that unity, even as we use our different gifts among ourselves.

With this as our understanding of the will of God in doing his mission, we may ask, How are we doing in the African context, and beyond, in following his footsteps? How are we doing in accepting all people groups as God accepts them? As a way of challenge, not condemnation, it is ironic that in the very country (Rwanda) where the East Africa Revival started, one of the worst genocides was witnessed in 1994, with division on ethnic lines being in the background.[61] It is also equally surprising that in the very country

---

[56]That God has declared one as Savior of the world is a fact that one who believes the Bible to be God's Word cannot run away from. It is not a creation out of a sense of superiority but acceptance of God's own declaration (Mt 3:17; Mk 9:35; Jn 3:16). This, therefore, should also not be seen as a basis for animosity against each other. It should be viewed as a point of difference of opinion (some accepting God's declaration and others not) but should not be a basis for wars.

[57]Kenneth Little, "The Mende in Sierra Leone," in *African Worlds: Studies in the Cosmological Ideas and Social Values of African People*, ed. Daryll Forde (Oxford: Oxford University Press, 1954), 115.

[58]Paul captures this well in Eph 4:4-6.

[59]There has been, in our times, the unfortunate withdrawal of ministry funds from a kingdom of God–related ministry, not because the needs of the ministry had ceased but simply because the person who had sourced the funds (whether Jew, Samaritan, or Gentile—using these figuratively) had moved. That contradicts the fundamental principle God established as he united the church in the first century. We need to keep dear to us God's deep desire that the church lives and acts as one—no matter the location.

[60]Clarence Shuler, *Winning the Race to Unity: Is Racial Reconciliation Really Working?* (Chicago: Moody, 1998), 59.

[61]It is estimated that between 500,000 and 1,000,000 persons were killed in one hundred days (April 7 to July 15, 1994), with some sources putting the figure at 800,000 ("Rwandan Genocide," Wikipedia, en.wikipedia.org/wiki/Rwandan_Genocide, accessed April 28, 2020;

(Kenya) where Joe Kayo's ministries started, there were clashes in 2007 causing the loss of many lives, with division along tribal lines being evident.[62] The unfortunate thing is that even persons who claimed to be Christians were involved in such killings. These serve as examples of many such conflicts all over the continent of Africa and beyond. Even within the church itself, there have been deep conflicts, with some of them centering on such matters as speaking in tongues and other such dramatic gifts of the Holy Spirit. No wonder George Williams laments, "It is regrettable that in the course of Christian history the great scene constructed by Luke has repeatedly led to divisions and factions among Christians."[63] Who has failed? Is it the Holy Spirit, or is it us? Certainly not the Holy Spirit! His uniting work is with us just as it was in the accounts discussed here from Acts. What, then, is it that we need to relearn again and again about the Holy Spirit as we see his work in the book of Acts?

1. The Holy Spirit removes all barriers—whether racial, tribal, status, or any other. He removed the wall between Jews, Samaritans, and Gentiles and formed one body, his church. When we see divisions in the church, then there is lack of obedience to the will of God. The church must model what it means to live as members of one family, and society will follow suit.

2. The Holy Spirit breaks down all prejudices. Peter was taken through a dramatic experience before he could imagine himself ministering to Cornelius for direct access to the kingdom of God. Prejudices stood in his way, and those had to be broken. We are all familiar with the stereotyping that goes on—most of it along racial or tribal lines. No matter how historically correct some of the observations behind the stereotyping are, they must all be broken down once we are in Christ. We are called to view others the way God does. He treats Jews, Samaritans, and Gentiles the same, on the basis of faith in Christ.

3. The Holy Spirit uses us at the level of our gifts or assignments, calling all of us into a ministry of cooperation. God used the deacon Philip and the apostles Peter and John together to bring the Samaritans in, as full-fledged members of God's household. What matters is not who or what we are (bishop, pastor, professor, lecturer, etc.) but what God wants to use us for. Such an attitude removes all unhealthy competition and envy. We thank God for the gifts he gives us (1 Cor 12–14; Eph 4:11-12) and pray that we will manifest his fruit (Gal 5:22-23) as we serve him in the twenty-first century, each of us in our corner.

As a continent of fifty-four countries and hundreds of people groups, Africa provides a fertile ground for differences and conflict. The story, however, does not have to be as gloomy as it appears at times. Most African countries have a

---

"Rwandan Genocide," History, www.history.com/topics/africa/rwandan-genocide, accessed April 28, 2020). If one works with the 800,000 figure, this comes to 8,000 persons per day.

[62]It is estimated that between eight hundred and twelve hundred lives were lost ("Deadly Clashes in Kenya Fuel Fears of Election Violence," *Guardian*, September 13, 2012, www.theguardian.com/world/2012/sep/13/kenyan-tribal-clashes-116-dead, and "Death Toll Nears 800 as Post-Election Violence Spirals out of Control in Kenya," *Guardian*, January 28, 2008, www.theguardian.com/world/2008/jan/28/kenya.international); the killers were apparently targeting people on the basis of their ethnic background.

[63]George H. Williams and Edith Waldvogel, "A History of Speaking in Tongues and Related Gifts," in *The Charismatic Movement*, ed. Michael P. Hamilton (Grand Rapids, MI: Eerdmans, 1975), 104-5.

high percentage of Christians, and Bible preaching is on almost every corner. God on his part has given to every believer, no matter the race, tribe, or status, the gift of the Holy Spirit, the Spirit of unity. The church in Africa is called on to practically demonstrate what unity is all about. It is not loss of personal identity but a breaking down of all the barriers that hinder us from relating to others as members of one family. After the church has lived this truth out, then it has the authority to preach it to others. Acts 2; 8; 10; 19 provide the basis on which to build as we strive to this end. A continent of conflict and strife can be turned into a continent of harmony and love by obeying what God shows us to be his will from the Acts accounts. Such harmony is a blessing not only within the context of the church but also in society at large, for it addresses the "us" and "them" mentality that is the core cause of tribalism, nepotism, tribal clashes, civil wars, and other such social evils the African continent often suffers from.

FURTHER READING

Bruner, Frederick Dale. *A Theology of the Holy Spirit: The Pentecostal Experience and the New Testament Witness.* Grand Rapids, MI: Eerdmans, 1970.

Gaffin, Richard B., Jr. *Perspectives on Pentecost: New Testament Teaching on the Gifts of the Holy Spirit.* Phillipsburg, NJ: P&R, 1979.

Gehman, Richard. "The East African Revival." *East Africa Journal of Evangelical Theology* 5, no. 1 (1986): 36-56.

Hamilton, Michael P., ed. *The Charismatic Movement.* Grand Rapids, MI: Eerdmans, 1975.

Parratt, John. *Introduction to Third World Theologies.* Cambridge: Cambridge University Press, 2004.

22

WHO IS THE HOLY SPIRIT IN CONTEMPORARY AFRICAN CHRISTIANITY?

David Tonghou Ngong

THIS CHAPTER BRIEFLY tells the story of how the contemporary African theology of the Spirit came to emphasize the function of the Holy Spirit rather than the place of the Spirit in the Trinity, and proposes that the functional understanding of the Holy Spirit ought to be recalibrated. Moreover, the place of the Spirit in trinitarian life needs to be addressed.

In order to better understand who the Holy Spirit is in contemporary African Christianity, one needs to undertake a panoramic survey of the phases of Christianity in Africa.

PHASES OF THE CHRISTIAN THEOLOGY OF THE SPIRIT IN AFRICA

African Christianity can roughly be divided into three phases: (1) early Christianity in Roman North Africa, Egypt, Nubia, and Ethiopia; (2) precolonial African Christianity, which saw the continuation of Christianity in Egypt and Ethiopia, was dominated by Roman Catholicism in sub-Saharan Africa, and was found especially in regions such as present-day Nigeria (Benin and

Warri) and Angola and Democratic Republic of Congo (the Kongo); and (3) colonial and postcolonial Christianity. The first phase is traditionally thought to have begun in first-century Egypt, and what is left of it today is Coptic Christianity in Egypt and Ethiopian Christianity. The second phase mostly began in the late fifteenth century and had almost completely disappeared by the middle of the eighteenth century. The third phase was heralded by the rise of the modern missions movement in the late eighteenth century but gained significant traction from the nineteenth century. The Christianity brought to Africa during this third phase is currently the most vibrant form of Christianity in the continent and is the focus of this chapter.[1]

First phase. There were significant reflections on the person and work of the Holy Spirit during the first phase of Christian presence in Africa, especially as demonstrated in the works of early African theologians such as Tertullian of Carthage, Cyprian of Carthage, Augustine of Hippo, Origen of Alexandria, and Athanasius of

---

[1]For a good introductory work on the history of Christianity in Africa, see Elizabeth Isichei, *A History of Christianity in Africa: From Antiquity to the Present* (Grand Rapids, MI: Eerdmans, 1995).

Alexandria.[2] When debates about the nature of the Christian God were just beginning, it was Tertullian (ca. 160–ca. 220), partly influenced by his membership in the Holy Spirit movement known as Montanism, who argued that God should be understood as three distinct and related *persona* (persons), Father, Son, and Holy Spirit.[3] Even before contemporary African Pentecostals began speaking of the Holy Spirit as transformer of persons, Cyprian (ca. 200–ca. 258), who is mostly known for his doctrine of the centrality of the church in the Christian life, had noted that transformation of human beings is an important function of the Holy Spirit. Cyprian maintained that the Holy Spirit played this transformative role in his own conversion to the Christian faith.[4]

Origen (ca. 185–254), who began the systematic process of reflecting on the Trinity that significantly influenced how the Trinity would be understood in Christian theology, argued that, as a member of the Godhead, it is the Spirit who probes the things of God and makes the knowledge of God available to human beings. In other words, Christian spirituality is dependent on a proper understanding of the place of the Spirit in trinitarian life.[5]

When in the fourth century some Christians questioned whether the Holy Spirit was God, it was Athanasius (ca. 296–373) who argued that the Spirit should be understood as fully God, thus contributing to the theology of the Spirit that was to influence the Nicene-Constantinopolitan Creed, or Nicene Creed, of 381.

Augustine (354–430) is in a league of his own in the pneumatological reflections of this phase because his statement of who the Holy Spirit is came to form the official position of the Western church and contributed to the split between the Western and Eastern churches. Augustine argued that the Holy Spirit proceeds from the Father and the Son (*filioque*), contradicting the Nicene position that the Holy Spirit proceeds from the Father alone. Augustine's idea that the Holy Spirit is a gift from the Father and the Son and the communion, or love, that unites them has also been influential in reflections on Holy Spirit in the Western church.[6]

The above are brief examples of the significant reflections on the person and work of the Holy Spirit in the first phase of the church in Africa. Even though the focus of this chapter is not on the pneumatological reflections of this first phase, contemporary African pneumatology can benefit from appropriating some elements of the pneumatology of this phase.

Second phase. During this phase there was little, if any, pneumatological reflection in Africa. Christianity in North Africa and Nubia had been eliminated, Coptic Christianity in Egypt had declined due to the expansion of Islam, and Ethiopian Christianity continued. Explorers, traders, and missionaries from Europe, especially from Portugal, Spain, and Italy, began to engage sub-Saharan Africa. Beginning in the fifteenth century, Roman Catholic missionaries began to evangelize the people on the coasts of west,

---

[2]Carthage is in present-day Tunisia, Alexandria in present-day Egypt, and Hippo in present-day Algeria. Roman North Africa includes present-day Libya, Algeria, and Morocco.

[3]Tertullian, *Against Praxeas* 1-2. Even though the extent to which Montanism influenced Tertullian's theology is debated, Tertullian seems to suggest in *Against Praxeas* 2 that his understanding of trinitarian theology is based on instruction from the Paraclete, or the Holy Spirit. For this debate, see Jaroslav Pelikan, "Montanism and Its Trinitarian Significance," *Church History* (June 1956): 99-109; Andrew McGowan, "Tertullian and the 'Heretical' Origins of the 'Orthodox' Trinity," *Journal of Early Christian Study* 14, no. 4 (2007): 437-57.

[4]Michael A. G. Haykin, "The Holy Spirit in Cyprian's *To Donatus*," *Evangelical Quarterly* 83, no. 4 (2011): 321-29.

[5]Gregory K. Hillis, "The Holy Spirit and Prayer in Origen's *On Prayer*," *Cistercian Studies Quarterly* 49, no. 1 (2014): 3-26.

[6]Adam Kotsko, "Gift and *Communio*: The Holy Spirit in Augustine's *De Trinitate*," *Scottish Journal of Theology* 64, no. 1 (2011): 1-12.

central, and southeast Africa.[7] While Christianity was fleeting in west and southeast Africa, it took root to some extent in central Africa, especially in the Kongo. Even though this second phase would not last, partly because Christian missionaries became entangled in the slave trade, it contained one of the most important manifestations of popular pneumatology in African Christianity.

This popular pneumatology appeared toward the end of the seventeenth century in the Kongo through the work of a charismatic young woman, Dona Beatrice Kimpa Vita (d. 1706), whose pneumatology could be seen as perhaps the earliest example of enculturation of the Christian faith in sub-Saharan Africa. As we will see below, versions of her pneumatology are still found in Africa today. She was trained as a *nganga*, or spirit medium/healer, but she later became a Christian when she experienced miraculous healing through the spirit of Anthony of Padua (1196–1231), a Portuguese Franciscan saint who was popular in Kongolese Christianity through Portuguese evangelization of the Kongo.[8] Borrowing from the language of spirit possession common in African indigenous religions, Kimpa Vita claimed that she had been possessed by the spirit of Anthony and she went about healing and preaching what would today be called an Afrocentric gospel. She said that Mary, Jesus, and the apostles of Jesus were all Africans and that Jerusalem was in the Kongo. She was declared a heretic and, like Joan of Arc, burned at the stake, in 1706.[9]

Third phase. The focus of this chapter is on the pneumatological reflections of the third phase of African Christianity, which began with the missionization and colonization of Africa in the nineteenth century. Contemporary African pneumatology should be understood as partly a reaction against the Western Christianity that was brought to Africa by Christian missionaries and partly the desire of Africans to make their belief in the Holy Spirit meaningful in their various contexts. Generally speaking, the reaction has been rooted in the call for Christianity in Africa to be led by Africans and expressed in African idioms and life-worlds. This call is made against the background of Western demonization and denigration of things African in favor of things Western, so that becoming Christian in Africa came to be synonymous with becoming Western. The demonization of African life-worlds meant that Africans had to become Western if they were to be "good" Christians. It is this perception of the gospel and Western culture as equivalent that much of contemporary African theology and pneumatology is contesting.

Roughly four reactions against Western, or colonial, Christianity may be outlined in this phase. The first is the emergence, in the nineteenth century, of what is called Ethiopian Christianity, a form of African Christianity that emphasizes African, rather than Western, leadership in African churches. Here Africans broke away from some of the churches that were planted by missionaries and started African-led churches that were similar in most respects except leadership to the churches from which they had broken away. A second reaction, which

---

[7]There was no Protestantism at the time.

[8]This Anthony is not to be confused with the Egyptian hermit, Antony the Great.

[9]See Sigbert Axelson, "Arguments About 'Fetishes' in Europe and Kongo During the Great Awakening of Kimpa Vita (1684–2 July 1706)," *Swedish Missiological Journal* 96, no. 2 (2008): 127-38; John K. Thornton, *The Kongolese St. Anthony: Dona Beatriz Kimpa Vita and the Antonian Movement, 1684–1706* (Cambridge: Cambridge University Press, 1998); Alexander Ives Bortolot, "Donna Beatriz: Kongo Prophet," *The Metropolitan Museum of Art*, October 2003, www.metmuseum.org/toah/hd/pwmn_4/hd_pwmn_4.htm.

may be connected to the first, is the moratorium movement in the mid-twentieth century, where African church leaders demanded that there should be an end to Western missionary leadership in African mainline churches. This vision has been realized because most African churches today are led by Africans.

A third reaction, which began in the early twentieth century, is the development of what has been called African Independent Churches or African Initiated Churches. These are prophetic movements that were led by charismatic leaders, and they include the Harrist, Kimbanguist, Aladura, Roho, and Zionist churches that began with an emphasis on the presence of the Spirit of Jesus Christ in the life of Christians. With the arrival of Western Pentecostalism in Africa in the early twentieth century, there would later emerge a fourth reaction, which is now described as neo-Pentecostal/charismatic.[10] The third and fourth reactions to Western Christianity have been described as Pentecostal-type churches, and contemporary African pneumatology, both popular and academic, has largely been centered on the beliefs and practices of these churches.[11] This chapter also focuses on these churches.

With the Pentecostalization of African Christianity, a phrase that describes the tendency to stress the presence of the Spirit in most African churches today, one may say that a dominant theological theme in contemporary African Christianity is pneumatology.[12] However, most of the popular and academic reflections on the Holy Spirit coming from Africa have been focused on what the Holy Spirit does rather than on the place of the Spirit in the Trinity. At one level, this is understandable given that the person and work of the Spirit, like the person and work of Christ, can hardly be separated. This notwithstanding, Christian theology, as expressed in the Nicene Creed, speaks of the Holy Spirit as the third member of the Trinity, and it is necessary to reflect on what this means.

The remainder of this chapter first discusses some of the current themes of African pneumatology, arguing that this pneumatology has focused on the functions, rather than the person, of the Spirit. It then makes three proposals for future reflections on the Holy Spirit in Africa. The first is that the reactive nature of African Christian discourse in general, and African pneumatology in particular, needs to be questioned in light of the contribution of such discourse in defining African identity in the modern world in which the continent is marginalized. Second, African pneumatology needs to engage the question of religious pluralism in the continent. Third, African pneumatology needs to address the question of the Spirit as the third member of the Trinity.

---

[10]See Ogbu Kalu, ed., *African Christianity: An African Story* (Trenton, NJ: Africa World, 2007); Ogbu Kalu, *African Pentecostalism: An Introduction* (New York: Oxford University Press, 2008); and J. Kwabena Asamoah-Gyadu, *Contemporary Pentecostal Christianity: Interpretations from an African Context* (Eugene, OR: Wipf & Stock, 2013).

[11]For other classifications of this phase of African Christianity, see Birgit Meyer, "Christianity in Africa: From African Independent to Pentecostal-Charismatic Churches," *Annual Review of Anthropology* 33 (October 2004): 444-74; Ogbu U. Kalu, "The Third Response: Pentecostalism and the Reconstruction of Christian Experience in Africa, 1970–1995," *Journal of African Christian Thought* 1, no. 2 (December 1998): 1-21; Allan H. Anderson, *African Reformation: African Initiated Christianity in the 20th Century* (Trenton, NJ: Africa World, 2001).

[12]For examples of pneumatological reflection in non-Pentecostal contexts, see Elochukwu Eugene Uzukwu, *God, Spirit, and Human Wholeness* (Eugene, OR: Pickwick, 2012); Ferdinand Nwaigbo, "*Instrumentum Laboris*: The Holy Spirit and the Signs of the Times for the Second Synod for Africa," *AFER* (December 2010): 598-624; George Bebawi, "With the Desert Fathers of Egypt: Coptic Christianity Today," *Road to Emmaus* 10, no. 3 (Summer 2009): 3-37.

THEMES IN CONTEMPORARY AFRICAN PNEUMATOLOGY

Rejecting Western Enlightenment rationalism has been crucial to current reflections on the Holy Spirit in Africa. Western missionaries and the churches they planted in Africa were influenced by Enlightenment rationalism that denuded the world of the spiritual, making the human mind the arbiter of all truth. Rationalism undermined the spiritual imagination by declaring it to be superstitious, primitive, and a stage in human life that would eventually be overcome by advances in science and technology. This view of things led Western missionaries and the churches they planted not to take seriously the African cosmology that sees the universe as spiritually charged. In this cosmology, causation is not only material but also spiritual, and human beings make sure to carefully negotiate both the physical sphere and the spiritual sphere in order to ensure their well-being. Because missionaries and the churches they planted did not take this life-world seriously, they failed to appeal to the African masses, because most people saw these churches as saying and doing things that did not directly address their concerns. According to this narrative, the critical concerns of most Africans can only be adequately addressed if African cosmology is taken seriously.

The above point may be connected to the African understanding of religion: religion in African cosmology is not concerned with the otherworldly but rather with how life is lived in the here and now. In fact, religion in Africa is focused on ensuring that humans live long and fruitful lives, characterized by having offspring (preferably many) and enjoying overall material well-being. Thus, religions that do not engage the spirit world with the aim of helping people experience this fullness of life will hardly travel far in Africa. By neglecting to address the connection between the spiritual world and the material world in the quest for human flourishing, Western missionaries and the churches they planted are accused of missing a significant opportunity to speak to the concerns of Africans. It is argued that the African Initiated Churches and other pneumatic churches take this life-world seriously and thus appeal to the people, hence resulting in the significant growth of the church in Africa today.

This life-world is taken seriously through acknowledging that belief in the existence of spirits is not irrational, primitive, or superstitious. Rather, it is a legitimate way to perceive the world. Thus, the solution to the concerns that this life-world raises is to be found not in denying its basic assumptions, as Enlightenment rationalism did, but in positing the Spirit of Jesus Christ as the power that can address the concerns of the African universe and ensure human flourishing.[13] However, this pneumatology does not focus on discussing how the Holy Spirit is the Spirit of Jesus Christ but rather on the function of the Spirit in helping Christians deal with the concerns of their life-world. It is understood that one can only experience the power of the Spirit through Jesus Christ. When people accept Jesus Christ as their Lord and Savior, they begin to experience the power of the Spirit through various manifestations of the Spirit, including speaking in tongues, personal transformation, empowerment, protection, prophecy, and healing,

---

[13]It is important to note here that the Holy Spirit is understood to be the Spirit of Jesus Christ. In fact, the Holy Spirit is often conflated with Jesus Christ as the power in the name of Jesus is also the power of the Spirit.

among others.[14] We are going to look at each of these manifestations in turn.

Speaking in tongues (glossolalia) does not carry equal weight for all Christians who emphasize the presence of the Spirit in Christian life. Sometimes, those who speak in tongues tend to see such pneumatic expression as something that all genuine Christians must experience, so that speaking in tongues seems to be what distinguishes genuine from nongenuine Christians.[15] However, there are other Christians who emphasize the presence of the Spirit but do not see glossolalia as a central marker of the presence of the Spirit. In spite of these differences, the debate about the doctrine of subsequence, the idea that, after conversion, a Christian has to experience an additional "infilling" of the Holy Spirit, has not been dominant in African popular and academic pneumatology, as has been the case in the West.[16]

Another important manifestation of the Spirit is personal and communal transformation. We saw above that Cyprian of Carthage was one of the earliest to speak of the transforming function of the Holy Spirit, holding up his own conversion as an example. Such personal transformation could be seen as the process of sanctification because it is expected that once a person accepts Christ as his Lord and Savior, his character has to change. This change in character means that one has become a new creation who lives by the ways of God rather than the ways of the world. This transformation is often described as a "born again" experience. This born-again experience is especially manifested in how one relates to elements of African traditional cultures. One who is being transformed by the Spirit is expected to refrain from participating in elements of African traditional cultures that are thought to be inimical to both the Christian life and one's personal well-being. Thus, one of the evidences of spiritual transformation is to "make a complete break with the past."[17] Refraining from participating in activities such as those that venerate the ancestors and in certain funeral rites are among the means of making this break with the past. The goal of making this break seems to be that the life of a Christian should be different from that of a non-Christian.[18]

The transformative function of the Spirit is, however, not limited to individual lives; it extends to the rest of society. Kimpa Vita of the Kongo was perhaps the first to link the presence of the Spirit with the transformation of society as a whole when, indwelt by the spirit of Anthony of Padua, she preached the vision of a transformed Kongolese society. Some may find the fact that Kimpa Vita was indwelt by the spirit of Anthony to be troubling, given that the spirit of Anthony is not the Holy Spirit. Reading her narrative in this way would, however, not do justice to the context in which she lived and

---

[14]For more on this, see J. Kwabena Asamoah-Gyadu, *African Charismatics: Current Developments Within Independent Indigenous Pentecostalism in Ghana* (Leiden: Brill, 2005).

[15]Francis Muchingura, "The Significance of Glossolalia in the Apostolic Faith Mission, Zimbabwe," *Studies in World Christianity* (April 2011): 12-29.

[16]See James D. G. Dunn, *Baptism in the Holy Spirit* (Philadelphia: Westminster, 1977), 2; Roger Stronstad, "Forty Years On: An Appreciation and Assessment of *Baptism in the Holy Spirit* by James D. G. Dunn," *Journal of Pentecostal Theology* 19 (April 2010): 3-11.

[17]It has been suggested that this call for a complete break with the past has actually not been successful, since much of African Christianity is still conducted against the background of African traditional religious cultures. See Birgit Meyer, "'Make a Complete Break with the Past': Memory and Post-colonial Modernity in Ghanaian Pentecostal Discourse," *Journal of Religion in Africa* 28, no. 3 (1998): 316-49; Matthew Engelke, "Past Pentecostalism: Notes on Rupture, Realignment, and Everyday Life in Pentecostal and African Independent Churches," *Africa* 80, no. 2 (2010): 177-99.

[18]Benson Ohihon Igboin, "Bias and Conversion: An Evaluation of Spiritual Transformation," *Evangelical Review of Theology* 37, no. 2 (April 2013): 166-82.

preached. Hers was a context in which the Spirit was spoken of in the idiom of spirit possession, which is still the case in much of Africa today.

In much of Africa, it is believed that people can be possessed by certain spirits.[19] Even though these spirits may be said to be different from the Holy Spirit, some scholars have seen the idea of spirit possession as significant to the development of Pentecostalism in America. The fact that the Azusa Street Revival, which is seen as the genesis of Pentecostalism in America, was led by a black person, William Seymour, has led some to posit this African spirituality of spirit possession as standing at the roots of Pentecostalism in America. The experience of spirit possession, which often led to trance experiences, was carried over by African slaves who were brought to the Americas, and this informed their practice of the Christian faith in America. The Azusa Street experience of the Spirit is seen as a manifestation of spirit possession, interpreted in light of the Holy Spirit.[20]

Thus, the fact that Kimpa Vita was indwelt by the spirit of Anthony should be placed within a context in which spirit possession and pneumatology go together. The spirit of Anthony could therefore be seen as shorthand for the Holy Spirit, who sometimes works through holy people. Because Anthony was a holy person, his spirit was holy and thus a manifestation of the Holy Spirit. Even though some evangelical thinkers would find this view controversial, speaking of the spirit of a saint should not be unmoored from the broader theological and pneumatological context in which a saint's life is understood, because the spirit of a saint is not just a personal spirit but also a spirit that participates in the divine Spirit. In essence, it is a spirit that has been divinized.

When this spirit inhabited Kimpa Vita, she preached not only a gospel of personal transformation but also one of societal transformation. In fact, she preached a gospel that called for the burning of all fetishes, making no distinction between crosses and rosaries that Europeans carried and the talisman that the Kongolese carried. All were to be burned because carrying them did not demonstrate reliance on the power of God for protection. Growing up in a war-torn society, Kimpa Vita also preached a gospel that called for peace and restoration of society as a whole. This vision of the Spirit as transformer of society continues in the preaching of many African churches and Christians today.[21]

The theme of transformation is often connected to that of empowerment. It is the Holy Spirit who empowers people for personal transformation. It is the Holy Spirit who empowers societies so that they can be transformed. In fact, without such empowerment there can be no transformation. The empowerment of the Holy Spirit enables people to do and be what they would otherwise not be able to do and be. Thus, people develop moral excellence and spiritual insight only through the empowerment of the Holy Spirit. People succeed in business and jobs only through the empowerment of the Holy Spirit. Many Christian

---

[19]See Susan J. Rasmussen, "Spirit Possession in Africa," in *The Blackwell Companion to African Religions*, ed. Elias Kifon Bongmba (Oxford: Wiley-Blackwell, 2012), 184-97.

[20]For more on the African influence on the beginnings of Pentecostalism in America, see Walter J. Hollenweger, *Pentecostalism: Origins and Developments Worldwide* (Peabody, MA: Hendrickson, 1997), 18-24; see also Estrelda Y. Alexander, *Black Fire: One Hundred Years of African American Pentecostalism* (Downers Grove, IL: InterVarsity Press, 2011), 28-60.

[21]See Philomena Njeri Mwaura, "Integrity of Mission in the Light of the Gospel: Bearing Witness of the Spirit Among Africa's Gospel Bearers," *Mission Studies* 24 (October 2007): 189-212; Clifton R. Clarke, "Pan-Africanism and Pentecostalism in Africa: Strange Bedfellows or Perfect Partners? A Pentecostal Assist Towards a Pan-African Political Theology," *Black Theology* 11, no. 2 (July 2013): 152-84.

worship services are interspersed with testimonies of specific ways in which the Spirit has empowered people for personal transformation.

Further, Christian missions would not be possible without the empowerment of the Holy Spirit. In a recent reflection on the place of the Spirit in the missions of African Initiated Churches, Ghanaian scholar Thomas Oduro argues that African Initiated Churches do not rely so much on money for missions as they do on the Holy Spirit.[22] He tells the story of how a leader of an African Initiated Church in Nigeria, Agnes Okoh, told her congregants in 1963 that the Spirit had informed her that the first foreign land where the church would do missions would be Ghana. It took thirty-four years for this prophecy to be fulfilled, as the church waited on the movement of the Spirit! The prophecy was fulfilled when someone in Ghana invited the church to do mission work there.

All in the church are empowered for Christian missions through charismatic gifts. As recorded in 1 Corinthians 12, different spiritual gifts are given to members of the church so that they can together work for the building up of the church. With the prominence of Pentecostalism in African Christianity, some have argued that there has been a democratization of charisma, that is, an emphasis is now placed on the fact that all members of the church are (to be) endowed with spiritual gifts. In this case, members of the clergy are not the only ones who are especially endowed with charismatic gifts; every member of the church has an important role to play in the ministry of the church because everyone is given a spiritual gift to be used in the church. Ghanaian scholar of Pentecostalism Asamoah-Gyadu has used the expression "12/70 paradigm shift" to make this point.[23] In this equation, twelve is related to the twelve apostles of Jesus Christ, and seventy is related to the seventy disciples Jesus sent out for mission in Luke 10. The twelve apostles, in this scheme, represent the members of the clergy and a situation where the ministry of the church is left to the members of the clergy. However, the seventy disciples Jesus sent out represent the whole congregation rather than only members of the clergy. Thus, through the Spirit's dispensing of charismatic gifts, all members of the church have a role to play in the church's ministry.

This democratization of charisma notwithstanding, not all gifts of the Spirit are created equal. One of the spiritual gifts that is playing a significant role in contemporary African Christianity is the gift of prophecy.[24] Prophecy in this case does not so much have to do with the speaking of truth to power, as many prophets in the Hebrew Bible did, but rather with the ability to peer into spiritual things, to see spiritually what is past and what may happen in the future, the ability to unveil future hidden things, as found in the book of Revelation. Prophecy here is not so much directed toward society as a whole, as many Old Testament prophecies were, but rather toward particular individuals or a particular congregation. These prophets are akin to African traditional seers or medicine men and women who perform diagnostic and healing roles, discerning the causes of particular maladies and

---

[22]Thomas A. Oduro, "'Arise, Walk Through the Breadth and Length of the Land': Missionary Concepts and Strategies of African Independent Churches," *International Bulletin of Missionary Research* 38, no. 2 (April 2014): 86-89.

[23]J. Kwabena Asamoah-Gyadu, *Contemporary Pentecostal Christianity: Interpretations from an African Context*, Regnum Studies in Global Christianity (Eugene, OR: Wipf & Stock, 2013), 59-78.

[24]Cephas N. Omenyo and Wonderful Adjei Athur, "The Bible Says! Neo-Prophetic Hermeneutics in Africa," *Studies in World Christianity* (April 2013): 50-70.

then prescribing solutions. For example, if someone fails in a venture, she may visit a seer to find out why she did not succeed.

Through divination, the seer may say, for example, that the failure is due to the fact that one has not paid due recognition of a particular ancestor and it is the anger of this ancestor that is orchestrating the failure. The seer will then prescribe what needs to be done in order to appease the wronged ancestor and so earn his benevolence. Sometimes, Christian prophets may stipulate that in order for one to succeed, one would need to sever all ties to traditional religions, which may include family ties. Traditional religions, in this context, are often seen as avenues for demonic blockages, and they need to be set aside for blockages to be unclogged. This is part of the context in which Christians are urged to make a complete break with the past. The past (connection to elements of African indigenous religions, such as ancestor veneration) may still be affecting the present in a negative way, and in order for this negative influence to be arrested, ties with the past need to be severed. The prophet, like the seer in indigenous religions, helps Christians to navigate the various intricacies of the spiritual realm in order to sever such ties and so enhance their well-being. The prophet, like the seer, is also seen as a healer because she not only diagnoses but also makes prescriptions for a cure. Some have argued that the charismatic gift of prophecy sometimes overshadows the Holy Spirit because the prophet, rather than the Spirit, is seen as the source of the healing power.

The healing ministry of the prophet brings us to the theme of the Holy Spirit as healer.[25] This is another important pneumatological theme in African Christianity. Here the Spirit is seen as healer of all kinds of illnesses, from cancer to HIV and AIDS to barrenness. The power of prayer for miraculous healing is important, but healing is also mediated through holy people (such as prophets), holy places, and holy things. While prayer can be conducted anywhere, some places have been especially established as places of spiritual power, such as Moria for the Zion Christian Church in South Africa.[26] Holy objects that may be used for healing are holy water and anointed oil. Again, the connection between these holy people, holy places, and holy things and the Holy Spirit still needs to be given clearer theological articulation in African Pentecostal pneumatology. That is, theological arguments for why the Spirit works through these things rather than other objects or why the Spirit works through these objects rather than no object at all needs clearer articulation if Christians are to be spared from being tethered to these things rather than the immaterial Spirit.[27] One way of thinking about this is that acknowledging that some objects have special healing power is to acknowledge the distinction between the sacred and the profane. Thinking in terms of sacred and profane may be helpful, but it may fall afoul of the much-needed element of African spirituality that stresses that everything is sacred.[28] Serious work needs to be done in this area.

---

[25]See Cephas N. Omenyo, "New Wine in an Old Wine Bottle? Charismatic Healing in the Mainline Churches in Ghana," in *Global Pentecostal and Charismatic Healing*, ed. Candy Gunther Brown (New York: Oxford University Press, 2011), 231-50; Paul Gifford, "Healing in African Pentecostalism: The 'Victorious Living' of David Odeyopo," in Brown, *Global Pentecostal and Charismatic Healing*, 251-66.
[26]Anderson, *African Reformation*, 100-101; Asamoah-Gyadu, *Contemporary Pentecostal Christianity*, 51-52.
[27]Recent to the time of this writing some Christians in Ghana died in a stampede when they went to obtain holy water from a holy man from Nigeria. See "Ghana Stampede Kills Four at TB Joshua's Church," *BBC News*, May 20, 2013, www.bbc.com/news/world-africa-22595573.
[28]Laurenti Magesa, *What Is Not Sacred? African Spirituality* (Maryknoll, NY: Orbis, 2013).

Finally, the Spirit is seen as protector against all malevolent spirits. Special focus is directed at malevolent spirits because these are spirits that affect human life in negative ways, thus diminishing human flourishing. Of particular concern to most African Christians is the belief in witchcraft. Witchcraft, roughly stated, is the belief that some human beings possess the ability to appropriate spiritual powers in selfish ways that benefit them but harm others. As was the case in the Middle Ages in Europe, many African Christians hold witchcraft responsible for various human misfortunes such as certain illnesses, poor harvest, deaths, and accidents. Because life has become increasingly harder for many Africans in a world that is modernizing, elements of this hardship are often interpreted in terms of witchcraft.[29] In pre-Christian Africa, people often shielded themselves from the effects of witchcraft through the help of medicine men or women who provided medicines that acted as vaccines against witchcraft activities. For many Christians, however, protection against witchcraft is the work of the Spirit of Jesus Christ. Thus, it is widely believed that those who are Christians, especially Christians who belong to Pentecostal churches, become immune to the activities of witches because they are protected by the Spirit. However, in cases where one is already affected by witchcraft or other negative spiritual powers, deliverance or exorcism is often performed.[30]

From the pneumatological themes discussed above, it can be seen that the focus is on how the Holy Spirit functions in the Christian life to enable human flourishing. This emphasis on human flourishing is understandable given that most Africans face daunting threats to their survival. The recent spread of the Ebola virus in some West African countries highlighted the urgency of some of these threats. These are threats that need to be overcome through the power of the Spirit. The emphasis on human flourishing has, however, led to the dominance of what is called the gospel of health and wealth, or the prosperity gospel, especially in popular pneumatology. This prosperity gospel has received significant critique by those who see it as an inadequate understanding of the gospel.[31] While there is some truth to these critiques, there are three directions that pneumatological reflections in African Christianity may fruitfully pursue.

First, African pneumatology should reconsider the relationship between the supposedly Western rationalistic worldview and the supposedly African spiritualistic worldview. Second, African pneumatology has to engage the question of religious pluralism, especially in an Africa that seems to be increasingly experiencing conflicts that have religious dimensions. Third, African pneumatology must place more focus on the place of the Spirit in the Trinity, reading the third person of the Trinity as divine gift and love who unites divine life, on the one hand, and who unites human and divine life toward eschatological consummation, on the other.

CONCLUDING PROPOSALS

With the rise of the discipline of world Christianity, it has become important to demonstrate

---

[29]See Jean Comaroff and John Comaroff, eds., *Modernity and Its Malcontents: Ritual and Power in Postcolonial Africa* (Chicago: University of Chicago Press, 1993).

[30]See Opoku Onyinah, "Deliverance as a Way of Confronting Witchcraft in Modern Africa: Ghana as a Case History," *Asian Journal of Pentecostal Studies* 5, no. 1 (January 2002): 107-34.

[31]Paul Gifford, "The Prosperity Gospel in Africa: Expecting Miracles," *The Christian Century*, July 10, 2007, 20-24; Lovemore Togarasei, "The Pentecostal Gospel of Prosperity in African Contexts of Poverty: An Appraisal," *Exchange* 40 (October 2011): 336-50.

how Christians around the world practice the faith differently.[32] Situated in the context of post-colonialism, voices that were stymied by colonial discourses are now being raised in the postcolonial era. Also, the tendency toward homogenization that seems to be engendered by globalization is being resisted through appropriation of the local. In these contexts, it makes sense for African Christian theologians to stress the African difference in pneumatological reflections by pitting the African against the Western. However, pitting a supposedly African spiritualistic worldview against a supposedly Western rationalistic worldview does not sufficiently take into account the complex nature of African and Western worldviews, thus leading to a slanted pneumatology. What is taken to be the African spiritualized life-world is only a part of the African life-world. While it should be admitted that the life-world of most Africans is highly spiritual in nature, it should not be forgotten that it is also highly rationalistic and even instrumental. One African theologian has even suggested that the African life-world is so highly pragmatic that it may discourage belief in God.[33] This is so because many Africans often seek what works in life so that their reliance on God is based on their understanding that God will improve their lives. Gods that are seen as indifferent to human well-being are sooner abandoned.[34]

It is also the case that what is depicted as a Western rationalistic worldview is only part of the Western imagination. In the West, we find highly spiritualistic worldviews, which explains why Pentecostalism is flourishing not only in Africa and among adherents of indigenous religions but also in Western countries such as the United States. Even more, what is depicted as the African life-world today has historically been a significant element of the Western imagination.[35] Life-worlds everywhere historically have both spiritualistic and rationalistic elements so that the separation of the two is only a recent phenomenon. Separating the two has often led to an emphasis on rationality, as was the case during the Enlightenment, or on ecstatic spirituality, as is the case in contemporary African pneumatological reflections. An adequate pneumatology is one that sees the Spirit as active in both the ecstatic and the rationalistic, the imaginative and the technical, the spiritual and the scientific.[36] Seeing the Spirit as manifested in both the ecstatic and the rationalistic is especially important because many of the problems Africa faces today are to be addressed not only miraculously but also technically or scientifically.

Take the Ebola outbreak in 2014 as an example. The spread of the virus was made worse not only by the fact that Ebola is an inherently deadly virus but also by the fact that the medical infrastructure was shamefully lacking. A recent study has demonstrated how measures by the International Monetary Fund contributed to the weakening of medical infrastructures in the West African

---

[32]Lamin Sanneh, *Whose Religion Is Christianity? The Gospel Beyond the West* (Grand Rapids, MI: Eerdmans, 2003).

[33]See Eloi Messi Metogo, *Dieu peut-il mourir en Afrique? Essai sur l'indifférence religieuse et l'incroyance en Afrique noire* (Paris: Karthala, 1997).

[34]Toyin Falola, *Culture and Customs of Nigeria* (Westport, CT: Greenwood, 2001), 35.

[35]See Richard Fletcher, *The Barbarian Conversion: From Paganism to Christianity* (New York: Holt, 1997).

[36]For more on the importance of bringing together the ecstatic and the scientific in contemporary African pneumatology, see David T. Ngong, "Stifling the Imagination: A Critique of Anthropological and Religious Normalization of Witchcraft in Africa," *African and Asian Studies* 11 (2012): 144-81. For more on the Spirit as entailing both the ecstatic and the rational, see John R. (Jack) Levison, "Recommendations for the Future of Pneumatology," *Pneuma* 33 (2011): 79-93.

countries that have been significantly affected by the virus.[37] The imagination that seeks scientific causes of human failure and success should not be seen as bereft of the Spirit, but rather as part of the movement of the Spirit to enable human flourishing. In fact, during the Ebola outbreak, one of the leading Pentecostal healers in Africa, the Nigerian T. B. Joshua, cautioned those infected to stay in their countries rather than come to him for healing. While he is believed to be able to heal some illnesses miraculously, he demonstrated his limits during this outbreak.[38]

Another important area that needs to be investigated in African Christian pneumatology is the multireligious context of the continent. As Nigerian scholar of religion Jacob Olupona has recently observed, "Interreligious relations in Africa today have achieved a nearly unprecedented fever pitch of intolerance, thanks in large part to the rapidly growing popularity of radical forms of Evangelical Christianity and Islam."[39] I have described this intolerance elsewhere as simply toxic.[40] This intolerance is found not only between Christians and non-Christians but especially among Christians. In fact, churches that emphasize the presence of the Spirit describe those churches that do not appear to do so as "dead churches," sometimes creating tension among Christians. How can pneumatological reflections speak to this situation? I cannot go into any depth in dealing with this matter here. However, as Pentecostal theologian Amos Yong has shown, one of the most fruitful

theological loci for dealing with questions of interreligious conflicts is pneumatology, because the Holy Spirit resists domestication in the Christian faith and forces Christians to see that the Spirit blows where it pleases, including contexts of Christian and non-Christian religions.[41] From this perspective, it makes sense to take seriously the idea, found in the Hebrew Bible, that it is the Spirit of God infused in all human beings that animates us all (Gen 2:7). If the Spirit of God (*ruach adonai*) is present in all human beings, how is this related to the gift of the Spirit of Jesus Christ to Christians? C. René Padilla's contribution in this part of the volume touches on this question, but it needs to be fleshed out from an interreligious perspective.

The question of how the *ruach adonai* in the Hebrew Bible relates to the Spirit of Jesus Christ in the New Testament leads us to the need to reflect on the person of the Holy Spirit in trinitarian life. Since the Holy Spirit is understood to be the Spirit of Jesus Christ, how is the Spirit distinct from Jesus Christ? In the history of the development of Christian doctrine, it was strenuously argued, especially in the fourth century, that the members of the Trinity—Father, Son, and Holy Spirit—should be regarded as one but three, as united but distinct. The question of how the Spirit is the same as but distinct from the Father and the Son is not irrelevant because what we say about the place of the Spirit in the Trinity has important implications for the Christian life.

[37]Alexander Kentikelenis et al., "The International Monetary Fund and the Ebola Outbreak," *The Lancet*, December 21, 2014, www .thelancet.com/journals/langlo/article/PIIS2214-109X(14)70377-8/fulltext.

[38]Ben Ezeamalu, "Nigeria: T. B. Joshua Asks Ebola Victims to Stay in Their Countries," Allafrica.com (August 4, 2014), http://allafrica .com/stories/201408050164.html.

[39]Jacob K. Olupona, *African Religions: A Very Short Introduction* (Oxford: Oxford University Press, 2014), 33.

[40]David Ngong, "African Pentecostalism and Religious Pluralism," in *Pentecostal Theology in Africa*, ed. Clifton Clarke (Eugene, OR: Wipf & Stock, 2014), 193.

[41]Besides Yong's chapter in this part of the volume, see also "The Spirit of Hospitality: Pentecostal Perspectives Toward a Performative Theology of Interreligious Encounter," *Missiology* 35, no. 1 (January 2007): 55-73.

Perhaps it is at this point that African Christians may borrow from one of the significant ancestors of the faith, Augustine of Hippo, who put considerable thought into this matter and came up with the idea that the Spirit could be understood as a gift from the Father and the Son and as the love that unites them.[42] According to Augustine, the Holy Spirit is the eternal, nonidentical, self-giving of the Father and the Son. This self-giving is eternal and nonidentical because the Father, as source of the Son, has always begotten the Son so that the way the Son gives himself back to the Father is as Son. Here the eternal reciprocity of nonidentical (similar but different ways of) self-giving is understood as the Spirit. However, the Spirit is not only what the Father and the Son give to each other; the Spirit is also what the Father and the Son give to Christians so that the spiritual gifts are understood not just as single gifts, such as the gift of tongues or the gift of prophecy, but rather as the gift of the Spirit itself. It is this gift of the Spirit that enables Christians to participate in divine life.

Further, Augustine sees the Spirit as the love that unites the Father and the Son so that the greatest gift of God is not a particular gift but the gift of the Spirit of love, which graces Christians and the world with divine life and enables them to participate in God. By integrating Christians and the world into divine life, it is the Spirit who guarantees eschatological consummation, thus enabling Christians not to focus only on the Spirit's role in enabling human flourishing in the present. Also, because the gift of the Spirit is beyond anything that Christians can give back to God, the idea of the Spirit as gift interrupts the narrative of prosperity theology that sometimes depicts Christians as having a transactional relationship with God.[43] Finally, because the Spirit of God is the love that unites Father and Son, the Spirit ought to be seen as a source of unity rather than disunity, as often seems to be the case where claims to charismatic gifts are made. Addressing the question of the person of the Spirit in the life of the Trinity enables Christians to speak a little more clearly about the importance of ensuring present human flourishing and our ultimate participation in divine life.

FURTHER READING

Anderson, Allan H. *African Reformation: African Initiated Christianity in the 20th Century.* Trenton: Africa World, 2001.

Asamoah-Gyadu, J. Kwabena. *African Charismatics: Current Development Within Independent Indigenous Pentecostalism in Ghana.* Leiden: Brill, 2005.

———. *Contemporary Pentecostal Christianity: Interpretations from an African Context.* Regnum Studies in Global Christianity. Eugene, OR: Wipf & Stock, 2013.

Clarke, Clifton, ed. *Pentecostal Theology in Africa.* Eugene, OR: Pickwick, 2014.

Kalu, Ogbu. *African Pentecostalism: An Introduction.* New York: Oxford University Press, 2008.

Ngong, David Tonghou. *The Holy Spirit and Salvation in African Christian Theology: Imagining a More Hopeful Future for Africa.* New York: Peter Lang, 2010.

Uzukwu, Elochukwu Eugene. *God, Spirit, and Human Wholeness: Appropriating Faith and Culture in West African Style.* Eugene, OR: Pickwick, 2012.

[42]Augustine, *The Trinity: A Translation for the 21st Century*, trans. Edmund Hill, OP (Brooklyn: New City, 1991), 15.5.

[43]For the Holy Spirit as disrupting gender and capitalistic economic discourses, see Sarah Coakley, "Why Gift? Gift, Gender and Trinitarian Relations in Milbank and Tanner," *Scottish Journal of Theology* 61, no. 2 (May 2008): 224-35; Kotsko, "Gift and *Communio*," 1-12.

23

IN SEARCH OF INDIGENOUS PNEUMATOLOGIES IN THE AMERICAS

Oscar García-Johnson

THIS CHAPTER SEEKS to uncover and recover important elements in ancestral traditions of the Americas with an eye on discerning pneumatological continuity between the pre-Columbian and post-Columbian communities. My basic question is, What are we Christians to make of God's occasional encounters with cultures and religions of the Americas before the European conquest and beyond their occidentalized socio-religious representations, given the fact that God's wider revelatory presence has also been present in the Americas? By using an alternative theological approach, I proceed to disarticulate over-Westernized categories to open up a path for a contextual pneumatology from the Americas.

Robert Johnston begins his book *God's Wider Presence* with the following:

> What are we as Christians to make of those occasional encounters with God in our everyday lives that seem more real than everyday reality . . . ? Whether observing a sunset, . . . feeling awe as we have joined others and the Other in communal acts of justice, or being ushered into the divine Presence by a work of art, music, or literature, such experiences are . . . more than mere deductions based on the footprint of God's act of creation.

They are more than mere echoes or traces of his handiwork, though that is sometimes how they are described by Christian theologians.[1]

These lines carry on the centuries-old tension between general and special revelation (and theology and culture) in traditional Western theology's effort to make sense of how God is present and operates in the world. Johnston, however, situates this tension in "the disconnection between the church and the world" and the "irrelevancy of the church in the culture of the West." Hence, "if God has indeed revealed himself through creation, conscience, and culture then we ourselves are impoverishing ourselves in our relationship with and knowledge of God to the degree we are insensitive to that divine Presence in others." How then do we Christians cope with these issues in our postmodern (Western) and postcolonial (non-Western) worlds? Johnston argues that the gifts of new theological questions (Elizabeth Johnson) and the interlacing of various disciplines-approaches (Cecilia Gonzalez-Andrieu) are indispensable tools for a constructive theological task. Furthermore, the Spirit has persistently operated outside the walls of the

---

[1]Robert K. Johnston, *God's Wider Presence: Reconsidering General Revelation* (Grand Rapids, MI: Baker Academic, 2014), xiii.

church, and "Christians are called to witness to the fact that God has been and continues to be active throughout creation and history, . . . active apart from Jesus Christ through the Spirit who remains the Spirit of Christ."[2]

In response to Johnston's challenge to elaborate a constructive theology informed by a wider revelatory presence of God, I confess that my first impulse, as a Latino/a theologian born in Honduras, is to hide behind the Western layer of my existence, to let those ancestral voices be guided by traditional Western questions. My second impulse, on the other hand, tends to resist such Western hegemony and seeks vindication by appealing solely to my indigenous legacy, although I have difficulty recognizing it. Fortunately, living in the Latino/a US diaspora has taught me a third impulse: a way of asking questions about God, community, life, and the world at the border of my existence. This way of interrelating ideas, experiences, theories, and traditions represents an alternative theological approach seeking to avoid gathering and organizing knowledge in either a Western or an anti-Western way. I call this approach transoccidentalism, which means that the interpreter positions herself beyond Westernized descriptions and categories that define one's identity and reality.

Transoccidentalism is a way of sensing, thinking about reality, and relating to God, creation, community, Scripture, and everyday life (*lo cotidiano*) at the exteriority of those ideas, categories, traditions, and institutions that Western culture has deemed essential and primary for modern thinking and Western

Christianity. Transoccidentalism is a way of reaching beyond the shell of Western conceptual dependency toward a new horizon where original thought and independent research are possible by trespassing the totalizing categorizations built by traditional theologies and paradigms that have organized the world into first, second, third, and fourth worlds. So we ask, If God's wider revelatory presence has also been present in the Americas, what are we Christians to make of God's encounters with cultures and religions in the Americas before the European conquest and beyond their Western representations?

This chapter does not offer a theology of religions from the Americas, because my first task is to repair the false Western assumption that the originating cultures of the Americas had no religion of their own, only mythology. In the same breath, the idea of Christianity in the Americas as merely a Western implant needs serious revision.[3] The broad picture shows God's wider revelatory presence also in the religions of the Americas. In particular, I argue that the West and the Americas should be considered two incarnational spaces (without hegemony) where the Sprit of the triune God freely reveals himself at the exteriority (prior to and beyond) the logic of Western coloniality-modernity. Correspondingly, I endeavor to uncover and recover important elements in ancestral traditions of the Americas in order to discern a pneumatological continuity between the preconquest and the postconquest communities.

The reader should be aware that my transoccidental approach does not follow the normative

---

[2]Johnston, *God's Wider Presence*, xvi-xvii, 214.

[3]See José Rabasa, "Thinking Europe in Indian Categories, or, Tell Me the Story of How I Conquered You," in *Coloniality at Large: Latin America and the Postcolonial Debate*, ed. Mabel Moraña, Enrique D. Dussel, and Carlos A. Jáuregui (Durham, NC: Duke University Press, 2008), 48.

historical- or systematic-theological methodology or present a comprehensive view of all that the Western category of pneumatology implies in all the main religious expressions of the Americas. It will keep an eye on potential activities of the Spirit at the exteriority of coloniality-modernity—in those places, symbols, and peoples previously neglected and negated by Western methodologies. Hence, this chapter begins with the invention of the colonial project of the Americas and its Christian tradition on the encounter of Europe and the New World inhabited by its originating cultures. The first section takes apart the hegemonic Western frameworks that justify the covering of indigenous knowledge at the expense of potential pneumatological contributions. The second part articulates a constructive theological-cultural framework where we can see an indigenous pneumatology.

GEOPOLITICS OF CHRISTIAN KNOWLEDGE

The place where theology is formed matters.[4] Place matters because language, culture, and traditions are never neutral carriers of ideas; they always shape what they convey. Theology develops in a particular place out of the interaction, not between Scripture and culture, but between some version of the Christian tradition and the indigenous traditions of that place—both cultural and religious. We then must understand theological differences at the fundamental level of how we come to know about God, or in our case, the Spirit of God and his work in and with creation. In this new theological process, we

must face the geopolitics of knowledge—the way race, geography, ethnicity, politics, economics, gender, and so forth play into the construction and transmission of knowledge in the form of ideas, categories, and narratives. This critical aspect becomes especially important when a wealth of disciplines claim epistemic hegemony over others. Then we must uncover the epistemic dominance hidden under the assumption that such a wealth of knowledge—situated in a particular culture, history, race, and ethnicity—is fundamental, universal, and inescapable. This has been the case with Western theology in respect to non-Western–minority theologies.

According to Paul Borthwick, a missionary and educator in contact with Africa, Western Christianity in the majority world faces the challenge of pluralism, globalization, and territorialism, which a Zimbabwean brother sums up like this: "What you in the West call 'globalization' we call 'Americanization.'"[5] In the same vein, William Dyrness notes how the Western tradition is a special mix of influences: Greek philosophy, European paganism, medieval scholasticism, the Reformation, and the Enlightenment.[6] This tradition currently comes under the charge of Orientalism (Edward Said) and Occidentalism (Walter Mignolo) in its ethnocentric self-representation in relation to the Majority World, instrumentalized through Christianity, colonial-neocolonial projects, philanthropy, education, science, technology, and the like.

Occidentalism in theological studies. In an article titled "Retheologizing the Americas," I present two theological orientations correlated

---

[4]We argued this in William Dyrness and Oscar García-Johnson, *Theology Without Borders: Introduction to Global Conversations* (Grand Rapids, MI: Baker Academic, 2015), chap. 3.

[5]Paul Borthwick, *Western Christians in Global Mission: What's the Role of the North American Church?* (Downers Grove, IL: InterVarsity Press, 2012), 69-76.

[6]Dyrness and García-Johnson, *Theology Without Borders*, chap. 3.

with Occidentalism that have dominated theological thinking in Latin America and its diaspora for five centuries.[7] The first I label the pro-occidentalist orientation. In this orientation, scholars and practitioners tend to limit themselves to mimicking Western methodologies and transplanting Western ideas, models, and ambitions into Latin America or its global diaspora. Obviously, the identifier *Western* is invisibilized or disguised under universal categorizations. The theological canon here revolves around "master" figures of the West—Augustine, Aquinas, Luther, Calvin, John Wesley, Edwards, and so on.[8] This orientation assumes that European theology and history are the *locus theologicus*, the universal norm, the seat of orthodox faith. Orthodoxy and original scholarship, in the Majority World, are presented as finished products of the Western Christian tradition. As a result, all that is left for Latino/a scholars and ministers to do is to contextualize, which is misunderstood as making Western ideas and practices work for the Americas.

The second orientation I call counteroccidentalist, which raises questions rooted in particular local contexts that are generally antagonistic to hegemonic Western ideas, structures, and patterns of action that perpetuate injustice and dependency. Orthodoxy is dethroned by orthopraxis, and Western-rooted scholarship is bypassed in attempts to do original contextual research. Represented here are theories and traditions from the progressive liberal schools of the West as well as their Latin American counterparts, liberationist movements, and critical

evangelical factions (e.g., the Latin American Theological Fellowship).

Both orientations have informed reflection and practice in the Americas and have played into the logic of coloniality-modernity—one promoting Occidentalism and the other opposing it. The result is a deficit in autonomous Christian thinking and independent research. The point of gravity for autonomous thinking, Walter Mignolo and the decolonial school argue, is Western epistemologies. Until one disengages or delinks from the epistemic dialectic vested in Western coloniality-modernity, one cannot offer a truly autonomous and liberating option.[9] I illustrate next how both orientations have been present in predominant theological traditions since the birth of Latin America, in both Roman Catholicism and Protestantism.

The idea of Christian tradition in the Americas. A number of significant Latin American–Latino/a intellectuals have come to the consensus that the idea of Latin America cannot be understood without the idea of coloniality, as well as the history of the expansion of Western Christianity across the Americas, as a key element in the Euro-American self-understanding as a civilizing force. Mignolo's manifesto, *The Idea of Latin America*, points this out:

> From the sixteenth-century Spanish missionary Bartolomé De Las Casas to . . . the twentieth-century British historian A. J. Toynbee, all we can read (or see in maps) about the place of the Americas in the world order is historically located from an European perspective that passes as universal. . . . History is a privilege of European

---

[7]Oscar García-Johnson, "Retheologizing las Américas: A Transoccidental Approach," *Journal of Hispanic/Latino Theology* 10, no. 2 (2014): 9-24.

[8]For a review of significant Western theologians and how their theologies contribute to colonizing uses of theology, see Don H. Compier, Kwok Pui-lan, and Joerg Rieger, *Empire and the Christian Tradition: New Readings of Classical Theologians* (Minneapolis: Fortress, 2007).

[9]See this argument articulated in Walter D. Mignolo, *Desobediencia Epistémica: Retórica de la Modernidad, Lógica de la Colonialidad y Gramática de la Descolonización* (Buenos Aires: Ediciones del Signo, 2010).

modernity and in order to have History you have to let yourself be colonized. . . . Perspectives from coloniality, however, emerge out of the conditions of the "colonial wound," the feeling of inferiority imposed on human beings who do not fit the predetermined model in Euro-American narratives.[10]

Western Christianity in the invention of America. At the beginning of the Americas there were two crosses: the historical event of the conquest and the theological meaning of that event in light of the Jesus of Christendom.[11] Whether one stands in the Protestant faction (e.g., liberals, *evangélicos*, Pentecostals) or in the Roman Catholic faction (e.g., official religion, popular religion, liberationist movements), excavating the origins of Christianity in the Americas will take us right to the conquest and back to deal with the historical consequences in our time.[12]

The cross and the sword arrived in the New World as inseparable pieces of a shock-and-awe Spanish campaign intending to appropriate the natural resources of the newly discovered land in order to fund the Crusades in the Holy Land. The acquisition of the West Indies marked the land with a cross. In a letter to the Spanish royalty, Columbus writes: "And in every land where your Highness' ships arrive, and in every cape, I send out the order to place a high cross."[13] With this distinctive practice, comments Puerto Rican theologian Luis Rivera-Pagán, "Columbus placed crosses in strategic spaces as a symbol of [his] taking of possession."[14]

Violence, invasion, and Christian faith are historically united under the symbol of the cross, explains Rivera-Pagán, marking the Americas as a possession of the Church and the Spanish kings. "Behind the evangelizing cross," he concludes, "hides the not-so-veiled conquering sword."[15] This account, without denying some of the great contributions of Western culture, sees the process of colonization, evangelization, possession of the land, and history making also as a tragedy marked by invasion and violence. The traditional Western history, however, sees the Americas as having been discovered and civilized by Europeans, something the natives are expected to be thankful for and proud about. *Discovery* and *invention-invasion* are not merely two different terms, argues Mignolo, but refer to two very different paradigms for interpreting Latin American history.[16]

Western tradition against pre-Columbian traditions. A case in point is the scholarship produced by Spanish Jesuit José de Acosta in his *Historia Natural y Moral de las Indias*, published in 1590:

In many ways the light of truth and reason works in them to some small degree; and so most of them acknowledge and confess a supreme Lord and Maker of all, whom the Peruvians called Virachocha, adding a very excellent name such as Pachacamac or Pachayachachic, which means the creator of heaven and earth, and Usapu, which means admirable, and other similar names. They worship him, and he was the chief

---

[10]Walter Mignolo, *The Idea of Latin America*, Blackwell Manifestos (Malden, MA: Blackwell, 2005), xii.

[11]A reworking of Jürgen Moltmann's famous quote: "At the beginning of Christianity there are two crosses"; see "The Cross as Military Symbol for Sacrifice," in *Cross Examinations: Readings on the Meaning of the Cross Today*, ed. Marit A. Trelstad (Minneapolis: Fortress, 2006), 259.

[12]See the four descriptions, or faces, according to José Míguez Bonino, in Bonino, *Faces of Latin American Protestantism: 1993 Carnahan Lectures* (Grand Rapids, MI: Eerdmans, 1997).

[13]Christopher Columbus and Consuelo Varela, *Los Cuatro Viajes: Testamento*, El Libro de Bolsillo (Madrid: Alianza Editorial, 1986), 245.

[14]Luis Rivera-Pagán, *Evangelización y Violencia: La Conquista de América* (San Juan: Editorial Cemi, 1991), 15, my translation.

[15]Rivera-Pagán, *Evangelización y Violencia*, 15, my translation.

[16]See Mignolo, *Idea of Latin America*.

god that they venerated, gazing heavenward. And the same belief exists, after their fashion, in the Mexicans. . . . Yet it has greatly astonished me that even though they do have the knowledge that I mention, *they have no word of their own with which to name God. . . .* So those who preach or write for the Indians use our Spanish *Dios. . . . This shows what a weak and incomplete knowledge they have of God, for they do not even know how to name him except by using our word.*[17]

Acosta was, by all contemporary standards, one of the finest Christian scholars to set foot in the Americas at the beginning of the colonial era. Yet this great scholarship that brought together an appetite for objective truth, the classical disciplines of Greece and Rome, and the willingness to rigorously investigate the New World was plagued with Eurocentrism, historiographic neglect, and epistemic misrepresentation. On the one hand, Acosta's scholarship sought to give visibility and stature to the natives of the New World by conceptualizing them under a more universal history—the European. On the other hand, "its feebleness lies in its assumption that Amerindian knowledge did not count in the same way that the Greco-Latin tradition did."[18] While Acosta's account affirms certain Amerindian elements, it does so within a preconceived and neglecting historiography. This is, indeed, a Western hermeneutical pattern that has marked scholarship, church mission, and ministry since the beginning of the Americas.

Assuming that history is the horizon of epistemology, it follows that a neglecting historiography is the horizon of a demeaning episte-

mology. Certainly, Acosta acknowledged in Amerindian theology the categories that resembled his own tradition: "the light of truth and reason," "a supreme God," "the creator of heavens and earth." This resemblance is what made natives worthy of evangelism and Christianization. But the "recorded information in the form of pictographic images on paper, stone, and pottery, hieroglyphics, temples and pyramids used to pass down oral histories of their beliefs" was ignored, neglected, or in many cases vigorously destroyed.[19]

In short, Acosta can be identified as a proto-occidentalist theologian, perhaps the first in the Americas. Acosta's self-understanding of the Christian tradition worked against an understanding of the indigenous-local traditions. Scholarship and Christian mission that negated the indigenous-local traditions hindered the possibility of discerning how the Spirit of God was present and active in ways that were different from in the West and yet not inferior. This negation played into how deeply Christianity penetrated the Amerindian religious imagination (evangelism, discipleship, and mission). Indeed, to see indigenous religious practices as demonic activities has been a common assumption among Western missionaries and their disciples.

Enrique Dussel concludes that Christianity did not go deep enough into the religious imagination of the originating cultures. In his classic work, *A History of the Church in Latin America*, one of Dussel's conclusions is that a significant portion of the native population of the Americas still "longs for complete evangelization," and

---

[17]José de Acosta, *Natural and Moral History of the Indies*, trans. Frances López-Morillas (Durham, NC: Duke University Press, 2002), 256-57, emphasis added.

[18]Walter Mignolo, "Introduction," to Acosta, *Natural and Moral History of the Indies*, xviii. See also Mignolo, "Introduction," to Acosta and Ivonne del Valle, "José de Acosta: Colonial Regimes for a Globalized Christian World," in *Coloniality, Religion and the Law in the Early Iberian World*, ed. Santa Arias and Raúl Marrero Fente (Nashville: Vanderbilt University Press, 2014).

[19]See Lee M. Penyak and Walter J. Petry, *Religion in Latin America: A Documentary History* (Maryknoll, NY: Orbis, 2006), 1-2.

hence supplements the official religion with folk Catholicism. This form of Catholicism has always been present and nowadays is the majority in the Americas.[20]

Protestantism against traditioned Catholicism in Latin America. Would these preconceived hegemonic frameworks change with the incursion of Protestantism? The short answer is not much, for at least two main reasons. First, Western Christianity never developed a functional theology of religions able to consider a wider revelatory presence of God outside Western culture:[21] (1) the apologists during early Christianity borrowed from Hellenistic sources, yet paganism was judged or ignored; (2) Augustine used Plato, but subjected every epistemology to the knowledge of Christ as the standard epistemic system; (3) Aquinas learned Aristotle through the Arabs, yet had little patience with nonbelievers and "infidels"; (4) Luther focused on purifying and reforming the church, and his anti-Semitic impulses are well documented in the last period of his life; (5) Calvin showed no desire to dialogue with or learn from other faiths; (6) John Wesley came the closest to a theology of religions by focusing on the "inward voice" (initial revelation) and "spiritual senses" but ended up subjecting general revelation to special revelation (Christ).

Second, the incursion of Protestantism and the political independence of the Latin American nations in the nineteenth century delayed the progress of autonomous theological thinking by bringing new imperial powers into its intellectual landscape. The political independence weakened significantly the influence of Iberian Catholicism over Latin American civic and political life, while Western Protestantism was used to build the layers of knowledge and power that yoked Latin America to a new superpower, the United States of America. After all, Latin America was ready for a different theological tone and emphasis, one able to offer progress as an exit from three centuries of colonialism, which historically had imposed tragedy, poverty, and spiritual emptiness. Consequently, a glorious theology with a triumphalist Christ—one we can find in selected biblical narratives, some aspects of creedal formulations, and Pentecostal hymnology—was passionately embraced and conceptualized as the living Christ of the *evangélicos* in diametrical opposition to the "other Christs" of the Americas, particularly the Spanish-Catholic crucified Christ. Christ has reached Latin America! (Protestants did shout).

The epistemological and ecclesiastical shift that had characterized the Protestant Reformation in Europe three centuries earlier had now set foot in the Americas—along with the excesses accumulated by the post-Reformer thinkers: to be Protestant was to be anti-Catholic and fight against all forms of popular piety that attempted to give meaning to the Roman Catholic faith by means of "idolatrous" rituals. A new epistemic element was added as well: that Christ was mediated through the Holy Spirit in the personal experience of *el culto Pentecostal* (the Pentecostal worship service). Interestingly,

---

[20]Dussel combats here the reductionistic concept of "mixed religions," or syncretism, by arguing that not all the layers of understanding of the indigenous people surrendered to Christian knowledge as presented by the Christendom preaching of that epoch. See Enrique D. Dussel, *A History of the Church in Latin America: Colonialism to Liberation (1492–1979)* (Grand Rapids, MI: Eerdmans, 1981), 62-71. Adding to this, Orlando O. Espín argues that popular Catholicism is the "least invaded cultural creation of our people and the locus for the most authentic self-disclosure" ("Grace and Humanness: A Latino/a Perspective," in *We Are a People! Initiatives in Hispanic American Theology*, ed. Roberto S. Goizueta [Minneapolis: Fortress, 1992], 148).

[21]Johnston, *God's Wider Presence*, 201-5.

although there is evidence of indigenous Pente-costal revivals in South America before and at the same time as the so-called Azusa Street Revival of 1906–1910, such happenings have been neglected in the normative historical accounts of Western Pentecostal Christianity.

THE SPIRIT OUTSIDE THE GATE: UNCOVERING AN INDIGENOUS THEOLOGY OF THE SPIRIT

A shared assumption among US Latino/a theologians holds that culture is an elemental locus of human and divine action in the theological process. What needs discernment, however, is how culture should be perceived and used as a category able to embrace both the transcendence of God's Spirit and the complexity and diversity of people's identities. Thus, we must avoid as much as possible the assumption that our modern anthropological and theological tools can objectively interpret culture or cultural practices as reflecting God's activity and character, or even human essence and purpose without conditions. We find this oversight in most modern Western theological processes—and in non-Western theologies depending on Western methods.

Ungating the Spirit from the Western canonical imagination. The colonial-imperial legacy orienting modern theology begs for an understanding of tradition that is able to see the Spirit's activity prior to and beyond the Western hegemonic theological categorizations. Scripture accounts for a wider revelatory presence of God in other cultures and religions. Key biblical scenes containing non-Israelite religious sources shape the Judeo-Christian biblical imagination of the people of God: the high priest of Salem,

Melchizedek, commissioning Abraham (Gen 14); the Transjordan diviner Balaam blessing Israel (Num 22); Paul speaking at Mars Hill about one of the Athenians' altars referring to "an unknown god" and alluding to the words of the Greek poet Epimenides (Acts 17).[22]

Later on, early Christian believers struggled to discern the signs of the Spirit of God in the created realm. Creedal formulations attest to this discerning process, recorded, for example, in the Nicene Creed, with phrases such as *Spiritum Sanctum, Dominum et vivificatium* (the Holy Spirit, the Lord, the Giver of Life). Early Christian teachers emphasized the Spirit as a Revealer and Giver of Life. They learned and communicated this insight with fear and trembling. This insight, in itself, challenges any attempt to gate the Spirit within specific formulas, conceptualizations, or practices. Yet the threats of Gnosticism, Eunomianism, the Pneumatomachi, and other traditions declared "heretical" by the religious-political establishment of the time led to a gating of the Spirit of God within confessional statements, such as the Nicene-Constantinopolitan Creed, and these statements were deemed untouchable.

However, while creedal formulations were being constructed in the main cities of the empire, thousands of Christians in the deserts of Egypt and Palestine and missionary movements elsewhere were testifying to the revealing and powerful presence of the Holy Spirit, the Revealer and Giver of Life. In addition, very early in Christian history the Syriac tradition associated the Holy Spirit with the femininity of God, due in part to the Hebrew word *ruach*. This traditioning of the Spirit as "she" was subsequently replaced (or subsumed) by devotion to Mary.[23]

---

[22]I follow here Johnston's basic listing (*God's Wider Presence*, 203).

[23]Joel C. Elowsky, *We Believe in the Holy Spirit*, Ancient Christian Doctrine (Downers Grove, IL: IVP Academic, 2009), xxi.

This is to say that while creeds and conceptualizations registered important aspects of the interaction of the Spirit of God with local cultures, other traces of the Spirit were challenging the epistemic gates being constructed in the centers of imperial and ecclesial power. Thus, it is inappropriate to regard creeds and canonical artifacts as gated revelations whose keys were given only to a handful of clergy, politicians, and theologians of the Western church. It goes without saying that the so-called *filioque* clause controversy left an unhealed wound in the body of Christ precisely because of an imperial gating decision of the Latin church. Global Christianity requires a different paradigm of dealing with the Spirit of the triune God's interaction with creation.[24]

Retraditioning the Spirit outside the gate of coloniality-modernity. The Spirit of God has a history, comments Joel Elowsky, that can be traced in church confession with categories such as "the Inspirer and Revealer, the Lord and Giver of Life, and the Spirit's relation to the Father and the Son."[25] How dominant factions of the Western church came to use the categories of canon, creeds, and tradition with regard to the Spirit, however, says more about the gating-imperial tendencies of the Constantinian church than about the revelation of the Spirit of God itself.

When I speak in Latin America, the Caribbean, and the United States on the subject of global Christianity, it is not uncommon for me to face some resistance on the basis that we are in danger of losing the legacy of the Christian tradition. More specifically, I perceive fear that the so-called shift of the center of Christianity from the Global North to the Global South might have adverse consequences after all, leading to a suspicion that global Christianity is not attending to orthodox ways of reflection and practice. Simultaneously, I also face a warm-hearted welcome by many who are beginning to celebrate the recovering of an early Christian spirit when doing reflection and mission in different local cultural contexts. The truth is that the shift in the center of Christianity will sooner or later end the hegemony of the Western legacy, and the logic of coloniality-modernity, but not necessarily result in losing the traces of the Spirit, the Revealer and Giver of Life, and the Christian legacy itself.

The Christian tradition has been and will continue to be territorialized and deterritorialized by the Spirit of the triune God in history, which implies understanding *tradition* as a "common Christian identity narratively construed." This understanding of Christian tradition is well articulated by Dale Coulter, who argues that since the beginning,

> [Tradition] became embodied in the rule of faith articulated by such second-century figures as Irenaeus of Lyons, Clement of Alexandria, and Tertullian of Carthage. It did not remove the need to negotiate between local forms of inculturated Christianity, but it implicitly called for such forms to dialogue with the whole by calling parts of the common identity into question without fundamentally altering the basic contours of the narrative that God was in Christ reconciling the world.[26]

I concur with Coulter and contend that the key to the continuity of the Christian tradition does not rest on an archival-historiographic logic

---

[24]This is eloquently argued by Amos Yong in his contribution to this part of the volume. See also his *Beyond the Impasse: Toward a Pneumatological Theology of Religions* (Grand Rapids, MI: Baker Academic, 2003).

[25]Elowsky, *We Believe in the Holy Spirit*, xv. See also Jürgen Moltmann, *The Spirit of Life: A Universal Affirmation* (Minneapolis: Fortress, 1992).

[26]Dale M. Coulter, "On Tradition, Local Traditions, and Discernment," *Pneuma* 36 (2014): 2-3.

rooted in Western culture, but on the incarnational power of the Spirit of the triune God, who reveals truth and gives life to every culture and generation everywhere. In turn, local cultures will do well to negotiate a common Christian identity that does not negate the gift vested in their peoples' own particularities as creatures of God bearing the *imago Dei*. According to Coulter, it was through just such negotiating that the canon and the Christian tradition emerged and reemerged in the early stages of Christian history and in the history of renewal movements.

In short, what legitimates the Christian tradition must not be understood as a gate in the form of a creed, canon, hierarchy, sacrosanct succession, or enlightened culture that sees itself as the civilizing center of the world. To understand the West as the *locus theologicus* par excellence—a particular context entrusted with the treasures of the Christian faith universal—is the result of a logic of coloniality-modernity and not of divine revelation. It is the decolonial Spirit of God in and with creation, "conscience and culture"—with traces in the West in the form of Lord, Revealer, and Giver of Life—that ultimately validates any human form of Christian tradition.[27]

TRACES OF THE SPIRIT IN THE AMERICAS

In this chapter I have maintained that theology develops in a particular place out of the interaction not between the Scripture and culture, but between some version of the Christian tradition and the indigenous traditions of that place—both cultural and religious. We then must understand theological differences at the fundamental level of how we come to know about God, or in our case, the decolonial Spirit of God and his work in and with creation (and conscience and culture). How could we apply this argument in the particular context of the Americas? I can envision three ways.

The pacifying Spirit in originating cultures. Since the beginning, a neglecting historiography and a demeaning epistemology have informed Western scholarship, church mission, and ministry in the Americas, as the case of José de Acosta illustrates. Acosta saw features of Amerindian religiosity that resembled his own tradition (e.g., the light of truth and reason, a supreme God, the Creator of heavens and earth), which made natives worthy of Christianization. Yet the indigenous records and oral traditions were generally ignored or destroyed. Peter and Roberta Markman observe that, throughout the development of Mesoamerican religion, "the primary meaning" of reality "is consistently expressed through the central metaphor of the mask. As Octavio Paz realized, art 'serves to open doors to the other side of reality,' and the mask through its dynamic linking of external reality to that other side of reality, the inner world of the numinous, consistently 'opened the door' from the literal to the spiritual for the peoples of Mesoamerica."[28] The logic of coloniality-modernity requires a concrete and manageable category able to define, manipulate, and represent the other in literature and research in ways that facilitate the production of knowledge, history, and the exercise of power. But a mask,

---

[27]Johnston, *God's Wider Presence*, 190-99.
[28]Peter T. Markman and Roberta H. Markman, *Masks of the Spirit: Image and Metaphor in Mesoamerica* (Berkeley: University of California Press, 1994), xx.

Paz rightly observes, functions only as a door (not a gate) "to the other side of reality."[29]

In Mesoamerica, for instance, in the Náhuatl language, this God was called Quetzalcóatl ("Feathered Serpent"). Latin American theologian Elsa Tamez has reflected on this indigenous faith in the light of God's revelation in Scripture. Quetzalcóatl, she notes, was worshiped in all the stages of Mexican history and is the supreme source of all the other, lesser powers and spirits. Especially interesting is the consistent characterization of this God as acting always on behalf of humanity, creating them, providing them corn to grow, and giving them wisdom to build homes, invent the calendar, and create art. Most surprising is the way Quetzalcóatl is shown struggling against the lord of death, even injuring himself in order to give humanity life.[30]

According to this narrative, the blood from this injury is mixed with human bones and rescues humans from the world of death. Those who have told this story across the generations confess that their continued life is due to this self-sacrifice of Quetzalcóatl. (In one version of the story other gods realize they have to model the self-sacrifice of Quetzalcóatl so that life in the universe can continue.) Tamez concludes: "These are the revelations of the God of life, the God who understands, a compassionate being who gives life to God's creatures."[31] It may well be that the Spirit of God, Giver of Life, was masked in local expressions of Quetzalcóatl for the natives of this context. Jojo Fung makes a similar case for a comparative pneumatology by focusing on the parallels between the *ruach-elohim* conception of the Christian tradition and those of the Creator Spirit–Grand Spirit found in ancestral spiritualities of Latin America, the United States, Australia, New Zealand, and Canada.[32]

Theological attention to these masks might be the key to understanding how certain indigenous cultures in the preconquest period were able to assimilate important elements of Western Christianity after the European conquest and give them local meanings that fit their epistemic universe. If I can support this claim, then I can establish my case for a pneumatological continuity, rather than rupture, where we can discern the traces of the Spirit in the Americas outside the gate of coloniality-modernity. A notable case in favor of this argument comes from the colonial history of the Tira de Tepechpan, a minor *altepetl* (city-state) in central Mexico.

This pictographic artifact is the result of two hundred years of artistic interpretation of history, whose main goal was to "establish the antiquity, autonomy, prestige" of the political, religious, and intellectual traditions of the patron city.[33] Lori Boornazian Diel, working through the interpretation of the Tira de Tepechpan, describes the historical, political, and religious implications of Painter A's work:

> The entrance of the Spaniards into Tepechpan is depicted with a symbolic representation revealing the new entanglement of indigenous and European art forms. Above the year 1 Reed (1519), Painter A drew a cross and dove floating towards the time line. . . . As European conventions for

---

[29]See Octavio Paz, *El Laberinto de la Soledad y Otras Obras* (New York: Penguin, 1997), chap. 2.

[30]See Elsa Tamez, "Reliving Our Histories: Racial and Cultural Revelations of God," in *New Visions for the Americas: Religious Engagement and Social Transformation*, ed. David B. Batstone (Minneapolis: Fortress, 1993), 33-56.

[31]Tamez, "Reliving Our Histories," 39.

[32]See Jojo M. Fung, "A Post Colonial-Mission-Territorial Hermeneutics for a Liberation Shamanic Pneumatology," *Voices* 36 (April–September 2013): 123-47.

[33]See Lori Boornazian Diel, *The Tira de Tepechpan: Negotiating Place Under Aztec and Spanish Rule* (Austin: University of Texas Press, 2008), 1.

Christianity, the cross and dove easily transferred to Aztec pictorial writings as a hieroglyphic construction signifying Catholicism and the Holy Spirit.... The message is that Christianity arrived quickly and peacefully in Tepechpan. Meanwhile, a brutal military conquest was unfolding in Tenochtitlan and would last much longer.[34]

Let us avoid unnecessary technicalities here and pay attention to how history and meaning are produced by indigenous intellectuals in preconquest and colonial times. To begin, the preconceived Western idea that originating cultures lacked aesthetic capacities, intellectual traditions, and critical thinking is immediately challenged.

That Christian traditional symbols, such as the dove and the cross, are incorporated into local narratives, not innocently but exercising a degree of historical manipulation in order to provide an account of what happened in Tepechpan in contrast to Tenochtitlan, is of theological interest. Obviously, the history of Tepechpan takes precedence over that of Tenochtitlan in this representation. Second, a peaceful encounter between this indigenous community and the Spaniards is suggested, while Tenochtitlan is portrayed as a place of chaos and destruction.

Independently of the accuracy of this historical interpretation, just as in early Christian contexts, we can see how indigenous intellectuals are negotiating epistemic meanings with a particular version of Christian tradition (Iberian Roman Catholicism), hence facilitating a new version of indigenous Christianity. The dove symbolizes peace in European Christian history, and Painter A knows it and incorporates it into the new historical narrative of the *Mexica* community immediately after the conquest. The dove represents the Spirit of God, Revealer and Giver of Life, who territorializes as the Pacifier Spirit.

Traditional Christian rationalities in the West reduced the understanding of the Spirit to the invocation of the Spirit (epiclesis) in the Eucharist (Roman Catholicism) and illumination in biblical interpretation and proclamation (Protestantism). This resulted in an epistemic and pneumatological rupture or discontinuity with regard to the religious imaginations of the originating cultures, which included alternative rationalities for understanding spirits and rituals.[35] Consequently, a different paradigm is discerned in Amerindian cultures and hybrid communities. Once we take this "outside the gate" approach, the Spirit of God, the Revealer and Giver of Life, can be recognized through the masks of local spiritual powers such as Quetzalcóatl. This might be the door to understanding other masks and discerning a pneumatological correlation among different traditions within and outside the Americas.

The decolonial Spirit in popular religiosity: Folk Catholicism. We have always known in the Americas that there are two churches: the official and the popular. While the official version of Roman Catholicism has promoted epistemic rupture with indigenous traditions, the popular (folk) version of Latin American Catholicism has sought continuity. This is true not just of Roman Catholicism but of Western Protestantism as well. I address Pentecostalism next. For now, let us remember Enrique Dussel's conclusion that a significant portion of the native population of the Americas still "longs for complete evangelization," hence supplementing the

---

[34]Diel, *Tira de Tepechpan*, 73.
[35]I elaborate more on these Western rationalities in my article "Eucaristía de Comunión: Sacramento de la Iglesia Glocal," *Vida y Pensamiento* 33, no. 1 (2013): 125-59.

official religion with folk Catholicism that has always been present. Popular Catholicism maintained a degree of continuity with indigenous traditions through devotion to Mary, in many local forms. The most significant is Our Lady of Guadalupe, "la Emperatriz de las Américas" (the Empress of the Americas).

Virgilio Elizondo, considered the father of US Catholic Latino/a theology, interprets the significance of Our Lady of Guadalupe in the Americas. Our Lady of Guadalupe arguably appeared in 1531 on a rural hillside in Tepeyac (Mexico) to a native by the name of Juan Diego, and asked him to be her messenger to the Holy Church. In the words of Elizondo: "The apparition marked a spiritual beginning in America. Out of the chaos of the moment, a new people would emerge through the process of *mestizaje*, the mixing of people, biologically, culturally and religiously. In the midst of chaos, darkness and suffering, the Word became our flesh and dwelt among us through the appearance of the *Mestiza* Virgin of Guadalupe." It is lamentable that for almost two centuries Protestants in Latin America and the US diaspora have not been able to figure out what to do with Our Lady of Guadalupe—apart from demonizing her devotion. Elizondo, a popular speaker in US Protestant settings, usually corrects some of the Protestant misunderstandings by pointing out that Our Lady of Guadalupe is not a soteriological artifact to substitute for Jesus Christ, but "a precious gift of the infinite love of our heavenly Father."[36] We notice here a pneumatological resonance with the Pentecost event (Acts 2), where the decolonial Spirit is the gift of love from the heavenly Father through which the church, a new creation in Christ, is born.

The healing Spirit in popular religiosity: Pentecostalism. We also find traces of the Spirit in the continuities between the originating cultures and Pentecostalism. For instance, we find the gift of prophecy to be a central component of ancient Mayan religion. Munro Edmonson tells us that Mayan religious symbolism was readily accessible to all Mayans. Yet within this mystical religion Mayans needed "faith in the specialists who are trained to interpret its complexities," and the Mayan peoples "shared a genuine prophetic tradition."[37] This prophetic tradition had a deep impact on how society functioned. Prophecies could be used to confirm old traditions or establish new ones. Marcelino Tapia reports that among the Guaranies and Tainos a chief could maintain his status as long as he continued to serve the community. Part of his service included prophesying, interpreting dreams, and singing.[38] Edmonson makes clear that the Mayans did not practice some sort of blind faith, for "beyond the priests lies the final test of their knowledge: the test of time."[39] Like the Guarani, the Mayans would not hesitate to replace priests and prophets found to be a sham.

When referring to Pentecostalism per se, Samuel Solivan makes an important observation: one of the sources of Pentecostal theology is the "discerning witness of the community of faith." In addition, when an individual

[36]Virgilio Elizondo, "Our Lady of Guadalupe, Gift of a Loving God," Duke University, December 5, 2011, https://faithandleadership.com/virgilio-elizondo-our-lady-guadalupe-gift-loving-god.
[37]Munro S. Edmonson, "The Mayan Faith," in *South and Meso-American Native Spirituality*, ed. Gary H. Gossen (New York: Crossroad, 1993), 73-74.
[38]Marcelino Tapia R., "La Antropología, la Espiritualidad Indígena y los Desafíos para la Misión de la Iglesia en el Siglo 21," in *Espiritualidades Indígenas, Interculturalidad y Misión Integral*, ed. Lourdes Cordero and Marcelo Vargas (Buenos Aires: Kairos, 2010), 47.
[39]Tapia R., "La Antropología," 73.

acts unethically or claims to have received revelation from the Spirit, observes Solivan, the community immediately acts to protect its integrity by quickly correcting "the individual in light of the Word and the tradition of that community."[40] It appears that Mayas, Guaranies, Tainos, and Pentecostals all hold to the scriptural instruction to test the spirits (1 Jn 4:1).

A form of the gift of divine healing was also present in preconquest communities. Ancient Andean religions practiced divine healing rituals using native herbs, part of an understanding of *Pachamama* (mother earth), who provided sustenance and health, as long as natives remained grateful to and in harmony with nature.[41] Mayan faith included a strong belief in the healing powers of the priest, although it was always tested. There were Mayans who helped cure ailments with herbs, and midwives attended to pregnant women, but the priest was the one with the power to heal serious illnesses. The ability to cure the ill gave evidence of the priest's personal power, a power given by the gods.[42] The same approach to the health and well-being of the tribe is seen in the Amazon, where normal ailments such as the common cold and coughs could be treated with herbs and home remedies; serious or abnormal illnesses could only be tackled by the *pajé*—an Amazonian healer.[43] The correlation between ancestral healers and Pentecostal healers is hard to miss here.

The shamans in the Mapuche religion had similar healing rituals and understood illness as attacks from evil spirits. In order to achieve healing the Mapuche shaman often had to perform special rituals that required singing, trances, and divination. While the Mapuche shaman underwent rigorous training under a respected shaman, power was only given by the supernatural world, and it was confirmed through dreams, visions, or omens.[44] Again we see parallels between the Mapuche shamanic traditions of Chile and the prophetic Pentecostal movement.

Latino Pentecostal theologian Eldin Villafañe, in his *Introducción al Pentecostalismo: Manda Fuego, Señor*, describes Pentecostalism in the Americas as a complex, multifaceted religious movement with multiracial, multicultural, and multiethnic dimensions.[45] In addition to its Western emphasis on the Fourfold Gospel (Christ saves, baptizes, heals, and is coming soon), Pentecostalism implicitly considers the worship service as the *locus theologicus* (the worship service is the theology, and the theology is the worship service). This socioreligious configuration, among other things, has enabled Pentecostalism to offer indigenous-local communities in the Americas a degree of continuity in their experience of the Spirit as Creator Spirit–Grand Spirit and the Spirit of the Christian God, the Revealer and Giver of Life—worshiped in community. We also see clear correlations between significant religious institutions: healers and shamans (Amerindians) and apostles and prophets (Pentecostalism).

[40]Samuel Solivan, *The Spirit, Pathos and Liberation* (Sheffield, UK: Sheffield Academic Press, 1998), 106.
[41]Darío López, "Interculturalidad y Misión Integral," in Cordero and Vargas, *Espiritualidades Indígenas, Interculturalidad y Misión Integral*, 73.
[42]Edmonson, "Mayan Faith," 79.
[43]R. Andrew Chesnut, "Exorcising the Demons of Deprivation: Divine Healing and Conversion in Brazilian Pentecostalism," in *Global Pentecostal and Charismatic Healing*, ed. Candy Gunther Brown (New York: Oxford University Press, 2011), 179.
[44]Louis C. Faron, "The Mapuche of Chile: Their Religious Beliefs and Rituals," in Gossen, *South and Meso-American Native Spirituality*, 361-62.
[45]See Eldin Villafañe, *Introducción al Pentecostalismo: Manda Fuego, Señor* (Nashville: Abingdon, 2012).

Further Reading

Batstone, David B. *New Visions for the Americas: Religious Engagement and Social Transformation*. Minneapolis: Fortress, 1993.

Cordero, Lourdes, and Marcelo Vargas, eds. *Espiritualidades Indígenas: Interculturalidad Y Misión Integral*. Consulta Teológica 2008. La Paz: Ediciones Kairos, 2010.

Dussel, Enrique D. *A History of the Church in Latin America: Colonialism to Liberation (1492–1979)*. Grand Rapids, MI: Eerdmans, 1981.

Dyrness, William C., and Oscar García-Johnson. *Theology Without Borders: Introduction to Global Conversations*. Grand Rapids, MI: Baker Academic, 2015.

Gossen, Gary H., and Miguel León Portilla. *South and Meso-American Native Spirituality: From the Cult of the Feathered Serpent to the Theology of Liberation*. World Spirituality. New York: Crossroad, 1993.

Johnston, Robert K. *God's Wider Presence: Reconsidering General Revelation*. Grand Rapids, MI: Baker Academic, 2014.

Mignolo, Walter. *The Idea of Latin America*. Blackwell Manifestos. Malden, MA: Blackwell, 2005.

Penyak, Lee M., and Walter J. Petry. *Religion in Latin America: A Documentary History*. Maryknoll, NY: Orbis, 2006.

24

THE HOLY SPIRIT

POWER FOR LIFE AND HOPE

C. René Padilla

UNTIL FAIRLY RECENTLY, theological reflection on the person and work of the Holy Spirit was never given much attention on the part of evangelical theologians. There was, of course, a sort of implicit theology present especially in the Pentecostal movement, strongly influenced by North American fundamentalism. This chapter attempts to show that this situation has significantly changed in the past few decades with the emergence of new voices (mainly but not exclusively Pentecostal) that are exploring the subject in depth. The basic focus in Latin American pneumatology is on the Holy Spirit as the source of power for practical life (including the mission of the church) and of hope, especially in the context of poverty and oppression.

At the second global conference of the International Fellowship of Mission Theologians, held in Tlayacapan, Mexico, from May 28 to June 1, 1984, thirty-seven theologians from the Majority World dealt with a subject that they regarded as central to the life and mission of the church all over the world: life in the Spirit.[1] The words with which Orlando Costas introduced one of the plenary papers read at that conference are as relevant today as they were at that time:

> In the Two-thirds World—that part of contemporary life representing a religious and cultural mosaic of very poor, very weak and very oppressed people—the most significant trait of Christian experience is life in the Spirit. Wherever one goes in the Two-thirds World, one finds signs of the Spirit: a growing number of Christians and of new churches . . . joy in the midst of suffering, and a challenging hope in a context of death.[2]

Power for life and hope are made possible by the presence of the Holy Spirit in the Christian experience of people living in a world deeply affected by powerlessness and hopelessness. Costas's statement synthesizes the basic thrust of the official Tlayacapan Declaration that emerged from that International Fellowship of Mission Theologians conference and especially underlines the Spirit's ministry among people living in "contexts of massive poverty, feudal

---

[1] International Fellowship of Mission Theologians is an international network of evangelical mission theologians representing the Latin American Theological Fellowship, the African Theological Fellowship, and Partnership in Mission Asia. The first conference was held in Bangkok, Thailand, on March 22-25, 1982. The proceedings, edited by Vinay Samuel and Chris Sugden, were published under the title *Sharing Jesus in the Two-Thirds World* (Grand Rapids, MI: Eerdmans, 1985).

[2] Orlando E. Costas, "La vida en el Espíritu," *Boletín Teológico* 18, nos. 21-22 (June 1986): 7, my translation.

oppression, bureaucratic corruption, and ethnic and class discrimination."[3]

Like the Tlayacapan Declaration, I acknowledge that the work of the Spirit is present and visible in the new life that he imparts to every person living under the lordship of Jesus Christ regardless of socioeconomic status. For two reasons, however, I have chosen to deal in this chapter with the work of the Spirit as the source of power for life and hope, especially among the poor. The first reason is that, although there is plenty of material on this subject, this perspective is oftentimes neglected in favor of other perspectives that are commonly regarded as more closely related to the work of the Spirit, such as his work of sanctification and charismatic gifts.[4]

The second reason is that, at least in Latin America, the large majority of people who vividly experience the presence of the Spirit (most of them Pentecostal) as the source of power for life and hope in the midst of dire poverty and oppression are not the sort of people who reflect and write on this subject. As José Míguez Bonino has put it, "The Latin American evangelical tradition is strongly pneumatic. As expressed in the 'revivals' or the 'holiness movement' in the nineteenth century and in

Pentecostalism in the twentieth century, the adscription to 'the work of the Spirit' has been very basic. And yet, none of these movements has developed a true theology of the Spirit."[5]

As we move into the proposed subject, we need to take into account that the work of the Spirit is inseparable from the work of God the Father and the work of God the Son. In the God that was revealed in Jesus Christ, unity and diversity are combined in such a way that in all that the Spirit does there is a perfect correlation and interpenetration derived from the *perichoretic* communion that characterizes the trinitarian unity of Father, Son, and Holy Spirit.[6] This does not deny the distinctive action of the Holy Spirit, but it points to the fact that such action is properly understood when seen as action of the triune God. Taking this into account, we focus first on the work of the Spirit of God in creation and history, then on his role in Jesus' mission, and finally on his work in the life and mission of the church.

THE SPIRIT OF GOD IN CREATION AND HISTORY

The first reference to God's *ruach* is in Genesis 1:2, which the NIV renders: "Now the earth was formless and empty, darkness was over the

---

[3]Tlayacapan Declaration, *Boletín Teológico* 18, nos. 21-22 (June 1986) 110, my translation.

[4]For other work on this subject, see, for instance, the full treatment by Gordon D. Fee, *God's Empowering Presence: The Holy Spirit in the Letters of Paul* (Peabody, MA: Hendrickson, 1994), esp. 864-95; Clark H. Pinnock, *Flame of Love: A Theology of the Holy Spirit* (Downers Grove, IL: InterVarsity Press, 1996), esp. 185-214. For a Roman Catholic perspective, see Carlos I. González, *El Espíritu del Señor que da la vida: Teología del Espíritu Santo* (México City: Conferencia del Episcopado Mexicano, 1998), and José Comblin, *O Espíritu no mundo* (Petrópolis, Brazil: Voces, 1978).

[5]José Míguez Bonino, *Rostros del Protestantismo latinoamericano* (Buenos Aires: Nueva Creación, 1995), 121, my translation. This book was translated into English and published under the title *Faces of Latin American Protestantism* (Grand Rapids, MI: Eerdmans, 1997). It must be added, however, that since that book was published, a few Latin American Pentecostal theologians have at least in part filled the gap with commendable theological works on the Spirit. See, for instance, Bernardo Campos, *De la Reforma protestante a la pentecostalidad de la Iglesia: Debate sobre el Pentecostalismo en América Latina* (Quito: Ediciones CLAI, 1997); Leopoldo Sánchez, *Pneumatología: El Espíritu Santo y la espiritualidad de la Iglesia* (St. Louis: Editorial Concordia, 2005); Darío López R., *La fiesta del Espíritu: Espiritualidad y celebración Pentecostal* (Lima: Ediciones Puma, 2006); López R., *Pentecostalismo y misión integral: Teología del Espíritu, teología de la vida* (Lima: Ediciones Puma, 2008); Daniel Chiquete and Luis Orellana, eds., *Voces del Pentecostalismo Latinoamericano III: Identidad, teología, historia* (Concepción, Chile: Red Latinoamericana de Estudios Pentecostales, 2009).

[6]*Perichoretic* is an adjective is derived from *perichorēsis*, a Greek term coined in theology in the sixth century to refer to the union of the Father with the Son and the Spirit.

surface of the deep, and the Spirit of God was hovering over the waters." Both the translation of *ruach* by "Spirit" and the use of a capital *S* at the beginning of the term suggest that the translators opted for a reading of the text in which the word *ruach* refers to the Spirit of God, the third person of the Trinity. This interpretation may be rejected as an anachronism because it attributes to the author of the text a trinitarian concept of God without taking into account that the concept of God as the triune God did not take shape before the coming of Jesus Christ. The least that can be said in response to that objection is that the reality of the Trinity precedes the human experience of it, concerning which the New Testament bears witness. This experience broadens the horizon for the interpretation of *ruach* in the Old Testament and thus contributes to the construction of the basis for the Christian doctrine of God as the triune God, a doctrine whose essential ingredients are found in the New Testament (see Mt 28:19; 1 Cor 12:4-6; 2 Cor 13:14; 2 Thess 2:13-14; Titus 3:4-6; 1 Pet 1:2; Heb 6:4; Jude 20-21; Rev 1:4-5).

If the NIV interpretation of *ruach* in Genesis 1:2 as referring to the Spirit of God is accepted, this is the first reference in Scripture to the Spirit's role in relation to creation. The verb that the NIV translates as "hovering" connotes the idea of flying round about—the action that, according to Deuteronomy 32:11, God performs in order to protect his people in the desert "like an eagle that stirs up its nest and hovers over its young." The image points to the Spirit of God spreading his wings over the surface of the water and escorting the whole process of creation, through which the chaos is transformed into the cosmos (order) and out of the darkness emerge the multiple forms of existence that constitute the universe. Thus, right from the first chapter of

the Bible it becomes clear that the Spirit's action is not limited to the "spiritual" sphere but includes material reality, the stage for human history. The whole of creation, both material and immaterial, is the result of God's action, in the power of the Holy Spirit, through his Word—the same Word that later on will become flesh and make his dwelling among us in the person of Jesus Christ (Jn 1:14). There is no basis here for a Manichean dualism that places spiritual reality over against material reality and relates the former with good—Light—and the latter with evil—Darkness. According to Scripture, when God's creative work was finished "God saw that all that he had made [including material reality], and it was very good" (Gen 1:31).

All of created reality has the purpose of reflecting God's glory, and the work of the Spirit is oriented toward the fulfillment of that purpose. In both the original as well as in the new creation—the topic of the history of salvation—everything proceeds from the Father through the Son in the power of the Spirit, and everything returns to the Father in glory through the Son in the power of the Spirit. The Spirit who was "hovering over the waters" during the first creation was the same Spirit of holiness through whom Jesus Christ our Lord was "declared with power to be the Son of God by his resurrection from the dead" (Rom 1:4) and will also be the Spirit through whom, in the final stage of creation, God will give life to the mortal bodies of those in whom he lives (Rom 8:11). As in the case of Jesus Christ's ministry, the Spirit's ministry has cosmic dimensions.

This biblical perspective on the work of the Spirit in connection with creation raises a number of questions with regard to Christian involvement in society in relation to issues that the majority of Christian believers everywhere generally regard as merely "secular." If the work of the Spirit of God is limited to the sphere of redemption and the church, those "worldly" issues have no place in the Christian agenda. If, on the contrary, the intermediary God is present in creation and history, all issues that affect human beings, regardless of race, sex, or socioeconomic status in the present world, become a matter of Christian concern. The Tlayacapan Declaration on this subject is quite relevant:

> The Spirit's creative work can be seen in all the spheres of life—social, political, economic, cultural, ecological, biological, and religious. It can be seen in anything that awakens sensitivity to the needs of people—a sensitivity that builds more just and peaceful communities and societies and that makes possible for people to live with more freedom to make responsible choices for the sake of a more abundant life. It can be seen in anything that leads people to sacrifice on behalf of the common good and for the ecological wellbeing of the Earth; to opt for the poor, the ostracized, and the oppressed, by living in solidarity with them for the sake of their uplift and liberation; and to build love relationships and institutions that reflect the values of the Kingdom of God. These are "life sacraments" that glorify God and are made possible only by the power of the Holy Spirit.[7]

An outstanding value of this statement is that, at a time when ecological topics were almost completely ignored by evangelical Christians, it included ecology and "the ecological wellbeing of the Earth" among the spheres of life in which "the Spirit's creative work can be seen." Since the Tlayacapan Declaration was issued, what Bob Goudzwaard called "ecological vulnerability"

has increased to such a degree that the very survival of planet Earth is under threat.[8] The damaging effects that corporate capitalism has produced on a global scale can hardly be exaggerated. Among these effects are the depletion of the ozone layer, acid rain, loss of biological diversity, toxic chemical wastes, deterioration of agriculture, destruction of human health, deforestation, the problem of energy supply, and the one effect that perhaps more than any other places a big question mark regarding the future of life on planet Earth: global climate change.

Space does not allow a detailed discussion of the huge impact that climate change is having on the poor. Suffice it to say that, beyond doubt, the sector of the population most deeply affected by the present ecological collapse consists of the people at the bottom of the social scale, commonly regarded as nonpersons. As Pope Francis in his encyclical *Laudate si: On Care for Our Common Home* has rightly stated, "Today . . . we have to realize that a true ecological approach *always* becomes a social debate on the environment, so as to hear both *the cry of the earth and the cry of the poor.*"[9] In light of this dreadful double cry, one of the greatest challenges that we Christians face today is a rediscovery of the ecological dimension of God's mission in which we are called to participate on the basis of the recognition that the Spirit of God is active in creation and history. As John Taylor has put it, "The Spirit of God is ever at work in nature, in history and in human living, and wherever there is a flagging or corruption or self-destruction of God's handiwork, he is present to renew and energize and create again. Whenever

[7]Tlayacapan Declaration, 106, my translation. See John Taylor, *The Go-Between God: The Holy Spirit and the Christian Mission* (London: SCM Press, 1972), 16-17.
[8]Bob Goudzwaard, *Capitalism and Progress: Diagnosis of Western Society* (Toronto: Wedge, 1979), 136.
[9]*Laudate Si: On Care for Our Common Home*, chap. 5, sec. 49. On this subject, see my chapter titled "Globalization, Ecology and Poverty," in *Creation in Crisis: Christian Perspectives on Sustainability*, ed. Robert S. White (London: SPCK, 2009).

faith in the Holy Spirit is strong, creation and redemption are seen as one continuous process."[10]

THE SPIRIT OF GOD IN JESUS' MISSION

From the perspective of the Synoptic Gospels, Jesus is the archetype of the man who has been anointed by the Spirit of God in order to fulfill the mission that God has committed to him. Several New Testament passages explicitly refer to the close relation between the Spirit's action and the events through which Jesus accomplished redemption: his incarnation (Mt 1:18; Lk 1:35), his earthly ministry (Lk 4:18), his crucifixion (Heb 9:14), his resurrection (Rom 1:4), and his ascension (Eph 1:19-23).

Before the initiation of his earthly ministry, when Jesus was baptized by John the Baptist, the Spirit descended on him "in bodily form like a dove. And a voice came from heaven: 'You are my Son, whom I love; with you I am well pleased'" (Lk 3:22; see Mt 3:17; Mk 1:11). This narrative is followed by the description of the temptation in the desert. The Synoptic Gospels mention that "Jesus was led into the desert to be tempted by the devil" (Mt 4:1; Mk 1:12; Lk 4:1). Both the baptism and the temptation are part of Jesus' preparation for his earthly ministry. Both events are explicitly related to the Spirit's action, and the Gospel of Luke mentions the Spirit again with reference to the initiation of that ministry: "Jesus returned to Galilee in the power of the Spirit, and news about him spread through the whole countryside" (Lk 4:14). Note the connection that this text establishes between the Holy Spirit and Jesus' Galilean option—the option for the marginalized sector of the population living in Palestine at the time.[11] Jesus, who has been anointed as the Son of God and a prophet, goes from town to town throughout Galilee, "teaching in their synagogues, preaching the good news of the kingdom, and healing every disease and sickness among the people" (Mt 4:23; see Mt 9:35). Clearly, in Jesus' case the anointing of the Spirit is not a subjective or ecstatic experience, but an experience of the Spirit of power for life and hope related to his public ministry, much of which is dedicated to the most vulnerable sector of the population. This observation is ratified by Jesus' manifesto at the synagogue of Nazareth, at the beginning of his ministry, according to Luke 4:18-19:

> The Spirit of the Lord is on me,
>   because he has anointed me
>   to preach good news to the poor.
> He has sent me to proclaim freedom for the
>   prisoners
>   and recovery of sight for the blind,
> to release the oppressed,
>   to proclaim the year of the Lord's favor.

Space does not allow a full analysis of this passage, but the following observations are relevant here. In the first place, the opening reference to the Spirit must be viewed in light of the definition of Jesus' mission: the purpose of the anointing of the Spirit is the fulfillment of Jesus' messianic mission. An important antecedent of New Testament pneumatology is the relation of God's *ruach* with two Old Testament figures: the Messiah and the suffering Servant of the Lord. The prophet Isaiah foresees the coming of David's descendant, "from the stump of Jesse," on whom

[10]Taylor, *Go-Between God*, 27.
[11]See Orlando Costas, "The Evangelistic Legacy of Jesus: A Perspective from the Galilean Periphery," in *Liberating News: A Theology of Contextual Evangelization* (Grand Rapids, MI: Eerdmans, 1989), 49-70. According to Costas, "Galilee is the place where Jesus established his messianic credentials, built the base of the messianic community, and began to experience his messianic sufferings for the world" (55).

the *ruach* of the Lord—"the Spirit of wisdom and of understanding, the Spirit of counsel and of power, the Spirit of knowledge and of the fear of the Lord"—will rest (Is 11:1-2). In line with this prophetic vision of the suffering Servant of the Lord, Jesus is anointed by the Spirit in order to fulfill his messianic role. For him, the Spirit's anointing and the mission are inseparable.

In the second place, the mission of the Messiah in the power of the Spirit is oriented toward the most vulnerable persons in society: the poor, the prisoners, the blind, the oppressed. The passage read at the synagogue in Nazareth is Isaiah 61:1-2, in which the prophet addresses a group of disappointed Jews shortly after the exile. The quotation, however, includes an additional phrase taken from Isaiah 58:6, "to release the oppressed," which in its original context has definite social connotations. Israel's oppressed are those who, feeling totally unable to cover their basic needs, have sold themselves as slaves. The only hope for them, as for all who are in positions of disadvantage in society, is the cancelation of their debts and their liberation from oppression. As Walter Brueggemann has pointed out in relation to this passage, "the verbs of deliverance refuse to accept as a given any circumstance of oppression."[12]

In the third place, Jesus was convinced that his ministry was to promote radical socioeconomic changes big enough to be regarded as signs of the coming of a new era of justice and peace—"the year of the Lord's favor," the Jubilee year (see Lev 25)—a metaphor of the messianic era initiated in history by Jesus Christ, in other words, the kingdom of God.[13] Both the reference to Isaiah 61:1-2—one of the songs of the

Servant of the Lord in Isaiah—and the arrival of the year of the Lord's favor give to Jesus' ministry an eschatological note. In fact, Jesus' claim is that in his own person and work the Old Testament messianic promises are being fulfilled. What Jesus is announcing is nothing less than the arrival of a new age in human history. Anointed by the Spirit of God, the Messiah is the agent of eschatology in the process of fulfillment. According to Judaism at that time, the Spirit of God had departed from this world, and his return would bring in the fulfillment of messianic expectations. Jesus' announcement, therefore, must be understood as the affirmation of the beginning of a new age of justice by the power of the Spirit manifested in his own person and work.

Jesus' own ministry, synthetically described throughout the Gospels, provides elements for understanding his programmatic Nazareth manifesto: he focuses his ministry on the needy not only from a physical and economic perspective but also from a social and spiritual dimension, according to the will of God. It is evident that his mission includes the restoration of harmony of people with God, with each other, and with creation. It is, in one word, a shalom mission. His presence, his actions, and his words are signs of the kingdom of God, concrete manifestations of the work of the Holy Spirit in the age of fulfillment. His words in Matthew 12:28 point in that direction: "[If] I drive out demons by the Spirit of God, then the kingdom of God has come upon you."[14] The Spirit is God's eschatological gift that makes "the year of the Lord's favor" a present reality through the person and work of Jesus Christ—the embodiment of the

---

[12]Walter Brueggemann, *Theology of the Old Testament: Testimony, Dispute, Advocacy* (Minneapolis: Fortress, 1997), 208.
[13]See Robert B. Sloan Jr., *The Favorite Year of the Lord: A Study of Jubilee Theology in the Gospel of Luke* (Atlanta: Scholars Press, 1977).
[14]Note that in the parallel passage in Mk 11:20 "the Spirit of God" is replaced by "the finger of God."

prophetic hope not just for his disciples, but for the multitudes who are attracted by his ministry.

In fact, although much of Jesus' ministry is dedicated to his disciples, especially to the twelve he chose to train as his apostles, it is by no means restricted to them.[15] At times he is so pressed by the crowds who gather around him that "he and his disciples were not even able to eat" (Mk 3:20). The Gospel of Matthew provides the key to understanding Jesus' unwanted popularity: "When he saw the crowds, *he had compassion on them*, because they were harassed and helpless, like sheep without a shepherd" (Mt 9:36). Already in Old Testament times God had revealed himself as a God full of compassion for the poor and the oppressed, "a parent of the orphan, the widows' champion . . . [who] gives the friendless a home and brings the prisoner safe and sound" (Ps 68:5-6). The God who reveals himself through Jesus as God's Messiah is this God-man of boundless compassion who was anointed by the Spirit to be the source of power for life and hope, especially among the poor. As Gustavo Gutiérrez puts it, "The works on behalf of the poor and the needy identify Jesus as the Messiah."[16]

THE SPIRIT OF GOD IN THE MISSION OF THE CHURCH

The promise of the Holy Spirit. The Holy Spirit who is active in Jesus' mission is also active in the life and mission of the church. Already in the Old Testament there are traces of God's promise that at the end of times the Holy Spirit's ministry will not be limited to a select group (i.e., Israel) but will be extended to the whole people of God regardless of ethnic background. Ezekiel

36:26-27 and Joel 2:18-32 deserve special mention as two passages that are in the background of New Testament teaching on this subject. The prophet Ezekiel foresees a new era in which Israel will receive a heart inclined to obey God's commandments, that is, "a new heart," "a heart of flesh" in place of their "heart of stone," a heart that will open the way for the enactment of a "new covenant" and God's promise: "you will be my people, and I will be your God" (Ezek 36:26-29). The fulfillment of this promise, reiterated by Jeremiah (Jer 31–33), will be mediated by God's *ruach*. According to the prophet Joel, the messianic outpouring of God's *ruach* will not be limited to Israel. God's promise is embracing: "And afterward, I will pour out my Spirit on all people. Your sons and daughters will prophesy, your old men will dream dreams, your young men will see visions. Even on my servants, both men and women, I will pour out my Spirit in those days" (Joel 2:28-29). The sphere of action of God's *ruach* includes men and women, young and old. No one is excluded. This promise is the climax of a whole series of elements that, beginning with Joel 2:18, are combined in order to give a vision of the salvation that God will bring into effect for his people. Joel brings together all the basic elements of the spirituality that result from the Spirit's action in human life and can be synthesized in love for God and love for one's neighbor. This is the spirituality that Jesus Christ confirms in his ministry and his teaching as well as in his lifestyle. It is also the spirituality that the church needs for its life and mission.

This promise becomes clearer in the preaching of John the Baptist, the forerunner of the Messiah,

---

[15]A classical work on the Twelve is one that was originally published in 1871 but has endured the test of time, as is the case of few theological works in the history of the church: A. B. Bruce, *The Training of the Twelve* (Grand Rapids, MI: Kregel, 1971).

[16]Gustavo Gutiérrez, *Beber en su propio pozo* (Salamanca, Spain: Ediciones Sígueme, 1984), 60, my translation.

who defines the difference between his own ministry and that of Jesus in the following terms: "I baptize you with water. But one more powerful than I will come, the thongs of whose sandals I am not worthy to untie. He will baptize you with the Holy Spirit and with fire" (Lk 3:16; see Mt 3:11; Mk 1:8). In the final chapter of his Gospel, Luke returns to John the Baptist's announcement by quoting Jesus' words to his disciples right before his ascension: "I am going to send you what my Father has promised; but stay in the city until you have been clothed with power from on high" (Lk 24:49). The reference to the Spirit is not explicit, but it seems clear that the content of the Father's promise to which these words refer is the outpouring of the Spirit, with which the disciples will be "clothed with power from on high." The same promise made by Jesus to his followers appears again at the beginning of the book of Acts, this time with an explicit reference to the Holy Spirit: "Do not leave Jerusalem, but wait for the gift my Father promised, which you have heard me speak about. For John baptized with water, but in a few days you will be baptized with the Holy Spirit" (Acts 1:4-5). God's promises are many, but this one is the Father's promise par excellence.

As we will see further on, Pentecost marks the fulfillment of this promise of Jesus to his disciples. On the basis of the two passages that have been quoted, however, it is clear that this promise has implications for God's mission: it is closely related to the extension of the gospel to all nations. This is made evident by several expressions that are repeated in the context of the two passages and suggest a missiology that takes as its starting point the outpouring of the Spirit: "witnesses" (Lk 24:48; Acts 1:8), "power" (Lk 24:49; Acts 1:8), and "to all nations" and "to the ends of the earth" (Lk 24:47; Acts 1:8).

Jesus' words in Acts 1:8 are of special importance with regard to the role of the Spirit in relation to God's mission through the church: "But you will receive power when the Holy Spirit comes on you; and you will be my witnesses in Jerusalem, and in all Judea and Samaria, and to the ends of the earth." This is Jesus' response to a question that his disciples have asked him: "Lord, are you at this time going to restore the kingdom to Israel?" (Acts 1:6)—a question that shows that the disciples have not given up the nationalistic messianic aspirations that apparently encouraged them to follow Jesus from the beginning. Jesus' project, however, is not the reestablishment of Israel's kingdom but the formation of a new humanity in which God's purpose for human life and for all of creation will be fulfilled. His disciples will participate in that project as "witnesses" who, beginning in Jerusalem, will spread the good news of the kingdom "to the ends of the earth." And for that purpose they will receive the power of the Holy Spirit.

Therefore, what we have in Acts 1:8 is not a missionary mandate but the ratification of the risen Lord's promise to send his Holy Spirit to his disciples (see Lk 24:49; Jn 20:21) in order to empower them for the fulfillment of God's mission "to the ends of the earth." The Lord's premise is that this mission cannot be carried out merely on the basis of human effort, but in the power of the Spirit. When that premise has been forgotten, the cost that throughout history the church has had to pay in terms of failures and frustrations has been exceedingly high. "The Lord of the harvest" has so designed the crop that the gleaning of it does not depend on sophisticated techniques, or on human strategies, or on financial resources, but on the Resource that he himself provides for that purpose.

Pentecost and the church. From a Christian perspective, Pentecost and the church of Jesus Christ are inseparable realities, and both of them jointly point to the presence and action of the Holy Spirit. In order to understand them, however, they need to be approached in light of Jesus' purpose in sending his Spirit. To speak of Pentecost is to speak of the power of the Holy Spirit that, in fulfillment of Jesus' promise, God gives to his people for the spread of the good news of the kingdom in all nations. The church that emerges out of Pentecost is by nature a missionary community.

At the same time, to speak of Pentecost is to speak of the church as a pneumatic community—the community of the Spirit. At the beginning of the first volume of his two-volume work, Luke relates the Holy Spirit with Jesus' baptism (Lk 3:21-22) and with his messianic ministry (Lk 4:18). At the beginning of the second volume of his work, he relates the Holy Spirit with the church. Pentecost is the baptism of the church, through which God enables it to continue Jesus' mission to the very end of time.

We now turn our attention to what may be regarded as the key passage for understanding the Holy Spirit's role in the life and mission of the church in Acts 2, which may be divided into three parts: the Pentecost event (Acts 2:1-13), the meaning of Pentecost (Acts 2:14-39), and the results of Pentecost (Acts 2:40-47).

The Pentecost event (Acts 2:1-13). The Feast of Pentecost was one of the three annual festivals with which the Jewish people used to celebrate the harvest, and it was held for fifty days (hence the reference to *pentēkostē*, meaning "fifty" in Greek) after the Passover—the beginning of the harvest. Luke simply mentions that the outpouring of the Holy Spirit took place "when the day of Pentecost came" (Acts 2:1), without drawing any conclu-

sions from this fact. The important issue is what follows: the Spirit of God descended on the 120 disciples of Jesus Christ gathered in Jerusalem. As we have already stated, this is the baptism of the church, an event concerning which three observations are relevant here.

First, it was both a personal and a social experience. The author seems to make an effort to communicate this idea when he states, on the one hand, that the disciples "saw what seemed to be tongues of fire that separated and came to rest *on each of them*" (Acts 2:3) and, on the other hand, that "they were *all together* in one place" (Acts 2:1) and that "*all of them* were filled with the Holy Spirit" (Acts 2:4). The experience of the Spirit is not a private experience but an experience in which the personal and the social dimensions are brought together.

Second, it was an experience in which the Holy Spirit manifested his presence through apparently "natural" phenomena, namely, "a sound like the blowing of a violent wind" (Acts 2:2) and "what seemed to be tongues of fire" (Acts 2:3). They are elements probably taken from the theophanies, or visible manifestations of God, in the Old Testament: wind, a symbol of power; fire, a symbol of purification. The reference to them is clearly related to John the Baptist's announcement: "He [Jesus] will baptize you with the Holy Spirit [*pneuma* = wind] and with fire" (Lk 3:16).

Third, it was an experience that made possible the proclamation of the gospel to "all nations," an anticipation of the evangelization that, beginning in Jerusalem, was to reach "the ends of the earth" (Acts 1:8). Luke leaves no room for doubts about the international character of the multitude that was present in Jerusalem for the celebration of Pentecost. He states that the city of Jerusalem was full of God-fearing Jews who had come from the diaspora, "from every nation under heaven" (Acts 2:2:5). Then he includes a long list of the nationalities represented (Acts 2:9-11a), a list that puzzles New Testament scholars because of its apparent lack of coherence. What Luke seems to want to bring into relief, however, is that on the day of Pentecost, by the Spirit of God's action, "the wonders of God" (Acts 2:11) were proclaimed to people from many nations, a symbol of the whole inhabited world (the *oikoumenē*).

The purpose of glossolalia (speaking in tongues, Acts 2:4) on the day of Pentecost can only be understood in light of God's intention that the gospel be proclaimed to all nations of the world. It was not an ecstatic or mystical experience but a resource for mission. This conclusion is supported by the statement that each of the people present "heard them speaking in his own language" (Acts 2:6), and by the comments made by the listeners: "Then how is it that each of us hears them in his own native language?" (Acts 2:8), "we hear them declaring the wonders of God in our own tongues!" (Acts 2:11). On the day of Pentecost God gives the church the power it needs to communicate his Word to all the nations. By the action of the Spirit all nations are recognized as part of the one human race and placed within the context where the gospel is announced in order to give shape to a new humanity with members "from every nation, tribe, people, and language" (Rev 7:9). As Peter Goodwin Heltzel puts it, "Pentecost provides a template for the Christian movement as a Spirit-empowered, transnational, multilinguistic, intercultural movement for justice."[17]

A piece of information that should not be overlooked is that the first messengers of the gospel were Galileans (Acts 2:7), that is, people whom the inhabitants of Jerusalem generally regarded as inferior. Is this not a sign of how oftentimes throughout the history of the church the Spirit of God manifests his power and humility?

The meaning of Pentecost (Acts 2:14-39). Despite the diversity of the languages represented at Pentecost, all the people can hear the proclamation of the gospel in their own language, and that provokes great amazement (Acts 2:12). There are, however, "others," a minority, who do not understand what is going on and make fun of those speaking in tongues, saying that the messengers are drunk (Acts 2:13). That induces Peter to present an interpretation of the meaning of Pentecost, on which we can make the following observations.

First, Peter explains the Pentecost experience in light of Scripture. The quotation of Joel 2:28-32 is an open window that enables us to see the use of the Old Testament in the New Testament. I cannot analyze this subject in detail, but I can point out that the quotation resembles what in the Dead Sea Scrolls is called a *pesher*, that is, an interpretation of the Old Testament in light of a contemporary event that is understood as the fulfillment of an eschatological prophecy. From this perspective, with the coming of Jesus, the Messiah, the new age has arrived and God is fulfilling his promises and carrying out his purpose in history. From this eschatological perspective, what has just happened is what the prophet Joel predicted—"the day of the Lord" has arrived, and God has poured out his Spirit on all people, including sons and daughters, young and old, men servants and women servants, without making distinctions. Pentecost means the creation of a new humanity in which God "democratizes" the

---

[17]Peter Goodwin Heltzel, "The Holy Spirit of Justice," in *The Justice Project*, ed. Brian McLaren, Elisa Padilla, and Ashley Bunting Seeber (Grand Rapids, MI: Baker, 2009), 48.

experience of the Spirit and consequently makes it possible that all the members of the church prophesy. All of them participate in the proclamation of the good news of salvation in Jesus Christ. Beyond doubt, this is the key to understanding the evangelization process that has taken place since the earliest history of the Christian church. They become active "amateur" missionaries anxious to spontaneously share the gospel with others. As Orlando Costas puts it: "The early church interpreted the ministry of evangelization as a communal mission. The traditions of the New Testament, which interpret both Jesus' evangelizing ministry and the various apostolic missions of the early church, affirm categorically that evangelization is not the private property of gifted individuals but rather the responsibility of the whole people of God."[18]

Second, Peter explains the Pentecost experience from a christological perspective. According to him, the sender of the Spirit is Jesus of Nazareth, "a man accredited by God" by miracles, wonders, and signs that God did through him (Acts 2:22), who was crucified (Acts 2:23), raised from the dead (Acts 2:24-32), and "exalted to the right hand of God" as Lord and King (Acts 2:33-36). From that position of universal authority to which he has been exalted by the Father, he has sent the Spirit and invested the church with power to be his witness "to the ends of the earth." As is made clear by Matthew 28:16-20, this universal lordship of Jesus Christ is the basis for the mission of the church to all nations.

Third, Peter links the Pentecost experience with the call to repent and to be baptized "in the name of Jesus Christ" as well as with the promise of forgiveness of sins and the gift of the Holy Spirit (Acts 2:37-39). Any person who responds to the call receives the promise. The gifts of the Spirit have the same outreach as his call. Therefore, the church is open to receive any person willing to change his attitude, to place his life under the lordship of Jesus Christ, and to share with others the good news of salvation in Jesus Christ.

The results of Pentecost (Acts 2:40-47). The results of the Pentecost experience are amazing. In a sense, they point to what the church can expect throughout the centuries as a result of the work of the Holy Spirit in it and through it. These results may be synthesized as follows.

First, there is *evangelization.* The small community of disciples is unexpectedly transformed into a church that even today would be considered large. Note that this growth is the direct result of the preaching of the gospel in the power of the Spirit: "Those who accepted his [Peter's] message were baptized, and about three thousand were added to them that day" (Acts 2:41). Further on, however, another important datum, closely related to this growth, is added: "And the Lord added to their number daily those who were being saved" (Acts 2:47). There is no doubt with regard to the subject of the action, but it is also clear that the Lord uses several means to accomplish his purpose: the proclamation of the gospel (Acts 2:41), "many wonders and miraculous signs . . . done by the apostles" (Acts 2:43), love expressed in terms of mutual sharing and communion among the believers (Acts 2:44-46), a worship spirit (Acts 2:47), and "the favor of all the people" (Acts 2:17). Today there is plenty of evidence to show the dangers of a unilateral emphasis on "church growth" defined in terms of numeral growth accomplished

---

[18]Costas, "Evangelistic Legacy of Jesus," 134. See Michael Green, *Evangelism in the Early Church* (London: Hodder & Stoughton, 1984).

mainly, and sometimes even exclusively, through the oral communication of the gospel.

Second, there is *apostolic teaching*.[19] The presence of the Spirit is made evident through a theological awakening in all the community: "They devoted themselves to the apostles' teaching" (Acts 2:42). It is not a sterile intellectualism but a genuine search for a deep understanding of God's truth revealed in Jesus Christ and mediated through the apostles, so as "to call people . . . to the obedience of faith" (Rom 1:6; see Rom 16:26). The apostolic teaching (the *didachē*) is at the center of every church that is open to the work of the Spirit.

Third, there is *fellowship*. The Spirit creates new relationships in the body of Christ. In the case of the church in Jerusalem, because of his presence the believers "devoted themselves . . . to the fellowship" (Acts 2:42). The extent of this fellowship is clarified in the following verses, which refer to the believers' mutual sharing of material things (Acts 2:44-45; see Acts 4:32-37). The same Spirit who sends "what seemed to be tongues of fire" (Acts 2:3) motivates the believers to sell their possessions and goods and to give "to anyone as he [or she] had need" (Acts 2:45).[20] Although this passage is descriptive rather than prescriptive, it clearly illustrates how the Christian community created by the Spirit affects personal relationships to such an extent that it includes radical change in the economic field—a field in which, perhaps more than in any other, the authenticity of both our trust in God as the only true sustainer of our lives and our concern for our neighbors, especially the poor and needy, is tested.

Fourth, there is *celebration*. Luke points to this ingredient of the communion created by the Spirit as he affirms that the believers in the church of Jerusalem "devoted themselves . . . to the breaking of bread and to prayer" (Acts 2:42). This is apparently a reference to the celebration of the Lord's Supper (probably as part of a community meal) and to joint prayer at community meetings. Other data that are added further on enrich the picture: "Every day they continued to meet together in the temple courts. They broke bread in their homes and ate together with glad and sincere hearts, praising God and enjoying the favor of all the people" (Acts 2:46-47). Clearly, the community that results from Pentecost is a concrete manifestation of the power of the Spirit and a hopeful sign of the fulfillment of God's purpose for humankind.

The picture would not be complete, however, without the words with which the passage closes: "And the Lord added to their number daily those who were being saved" (Acts 2:47). The preaching of the gospel and the community life that the believers experience as a result of Pentecost are the means that the Spirit of God uses to accomplish a purpose that transcends the Jerusalem church: the creation of a new humanity that confesses Jesus as Lord of history and lives in light of that confession. As in Jesus' case—the purpose of whose anointing he himself defined in the synagogue of Nazareth— the experience of the church in Jerusalem resulted in a mission oriented toward the transformation of every aspect of human life including, as we have seen, its material basis.

---

[19]For a valuable essay on the apostolic teaching, see Oscar Cullmann, "The Tradition," in *The Early Church*, ed. A. J. B. Higgins (London: SCM Press, 1956), 55-99.

[20]These words echo Deut 15:4: "There should be no poor among you." "Both the gift of the Spirit and the gift of sharing in community are essential and belong together. Spiritual life cannot be genuine without solidarity with all God's people, particularly those in need." Ross Kinsler and Gloria Kinsler, *The Biblical Jubilee and the Struggle for Life* (Maryknoll, NY: Orbis, 2000), 143.

Conclusion

A brief analysis of the book of Acts throws into relief the spread of the gospel in Jerusalem, Judea, and Samaria, and to "the ends of the earth." As we move from Acts to the Epistles, however, we are surprised that the emphasis shifts from the Spirit's action in relation to the mission of the church to the Spirit's power in other areas of the Christian life such as the gifts that he provides for the building up of the church (1 Cor 12), love (Rom 5:5), the Christian character (Gal 5:19-26), holiness (1 Pet 1:2), Christian unity (Eph 4:3), and so on. It becomes evident that the same Spirit who empowers the church for mission is also the Spirit who empowers the church to confess Jesus Christ as the Lord of the totality of life and to experience the kingdom of God as a present reality. This is, in fact, God's call to the church between the times of Christ: to live by the power of the Holy Spirit according to the values of the kingdom of God inserted into history in the person and work of Jesus Christ, in the hope that he who began a good work in the church will in the end carry it on to completion to the glory and praise of God.

Further Reading

Corrie, John, and Cathy Ross, eds. *Mission in Context: Explorations Inspired by J. Andrew Kirk*. Burlington, VT: Ashgate, 2012.

Darko, Daniel K., and Beth Snodderly, eds. *First the Kingdom of God: Global Voices on Global Mission*. Pasadena, CA: William Carey International University, 2014.

Padilla, C. René. "Globalization and Christian Mission," "Globalization and Greed," and "The Globalization of Solidarity." *Journal of Latin American Theology: Christian Reflections from the Latino South* 9, no. 2 (2014): 17-90.

———. *Mission Between the Times: Essays on the Kingdom*. Rev. ed. Carlisle, UK: Langham Monographs, 2010.

SO GREAT A SALVATION

SOTERIOLOGY IN THE MAJORITY WORLD

Part Four

INTRODUCTION TO PART FOUR

SOTERIOLOGY IN THE MAJORITY WORLD

K. K. Yeo

As a young Chinese born and raised in Malaysia, I encountered the living Christ through reading the Bible for salvation in the middle of the flux and vicissitudes of life. In the nihilistic and secular worldview of my youth, I yearned for meaning in life amid despair and dissonance. I hoped for racial reconciliation and peaceful coexistence among all people in a multireligious and racial country. I lamented that my relatives went through the Cultural Revolution (1966–1976) and prayed often for the national salvation of China.[1] Although I knew the *need* of salvation for all, I was not clear about the meaning of salvation and how the biblical God had anything to do with actualizing salvation in our world. I was puzzled by sermons I heard that declared salvation was mainly about "saving one's soul from the eternal torment of hell."

THE TRADITIONAL LANDSCAPE AND BIBLICAL REPERTOIRE

Traditional theories of salvation. What is salvation? Is salvation the same as redemption, liberation, enlightenment, awakening, for-giveness, attaining nirvana, or going to heaven? Theories of salvation abound in world religions and Christian theologies. Traditionally, and primarily in the North Atlantic West, soteriology (the doctrine of salvation) is construed as the following:

1. mystical theory, the orthodox understanding of salvation as divinization of the human being via communicability of the divine-human nature and, later in Christian history, Friedrich Schleiermacher's understanding of God-consciousness

2. ransom theory (Athanasius, Origen, Irenaeus, Martin Luther, and Karl Barth), which views salvation based on the vicarious atonement of Jesus (Is 53:10, "an offering for sin"; Rom 3:22-25; Heb 10:12, 14; Mk 10:45) and thus understands Jesus as the Victor (Johann Christoph Blumhardt; as in Gustaf Aulén's Christus Victor) over enemies such as chaos, darkness, the devil, or sin and death

3. satisfaction theory, or the juridical view (Cyprian, Gregory the Great, Ambrose,

[1]See K. K. Yeo, "Hope for the Persecuted, Cooperation with the State, and Meaning for the Dissatisfied: Three Readings of *Revelation* from a Chinese Context," in *From Every People and Nation: The Book of Revelation in Intercultural Perspective*, ed. David Rhoads (Minneapolis: Fortress, 2005), 200-221.

Augustine; then Anselm of Canterbury, *Cur Deus Homo?* [*Why the God Man?*]), which argues that the salvation of humanity can be attained only by Jesus Christ the God-human, who alone can make satisfactory reparation for the wounded honor of God (against the previous view that the debt is paid to the devil)

4. penal substitutionary theory of the Reformers (John Calvin, J. I. Packer, Donald G. Bloesch), which interprets salvation as Christ's bearing human sins in their place, thus taking the punishment on the behalf of sinners because sinners violated the demands of God's law, which requires God's holiness and justice from humanity (against the view of satisfying God's honor)[2]

5. moral example theory (Peter Abelard, Friedrich Schleiermacher, Horace Bushnell), which holds that salvation is the work of Jesus Christ, whose death on the cross sets an example for people to imitate Christ morally, so that they will become fully human

6. participatory soteriology (James F. McGrath, Mark M. Mattison, Marcus J. Borg, and John Dominic Crossan), which sees the ones "in Christ" as those who participate in Christ's atonement work as they follow the path of dying and rising so that they themselves may be internally transformed.[3]

Daniel Treier, in his lead chapter in this section, has given us a more detailed exposition of the Western understandings of salvation, from the Orthodox, Catholic, Lutheran, Calvinist, Anabaptist, Arminian, Wesleyan, to the Pentecostal. I agree with Treier, who observes that the chief lacunae in traditional dogmatic soteriology are the sociopolitical and cosmic dimensions of salvation. However, I attribute the cause of such lacunae to the Western tendency to read Scripture and construct theology without paying much attention to Scripture's contexts and that of readers. Thus, by reading abstractly and turning inward on themselves, Western soteriologies, according to Treier, focus too exclusively on the personal blessings of participation in the new covenant.

The biblical semantic of "God saves" ("Jesus" in Hebrew). The Bible offers us a rich semantic and expansive repertoire about salvation, all pointing to God as the Creator (Is 40:12-31) and Savior (Is 43:14-44:6). Genesis 1 affirms that God created by means of redeeming, so that God made or created (*bārā'*, appearing forty-seven times in the Old Testament to describe God's action) as God called or named (speech-act) creation into being by delivering or redeeming them from the primordial chaos.[4] The Old Testament calls God the Savior (Is 45:15, 21) who brings salvation (Is 49:6) and who raises up saviors to deliver Israel (Judg 3:9, 15; 6:36).

Consistent with the Colossians passage that names Jesus as the divine agent of creating and redeeming all things (Col 1:15-20), the Nicene-Constantinopolitan Creed (AD 381) refers to the Son's creating ("through whom all things were made") and saving (what Jesus did "for us and for our salvation") functions. The verb "save" (*sōzō*) in the Septuagint and New Testament (Jn 3:17) and the noun "salvation (*sōtēria*) describe

---

[2]Donald G. Bloesch, *Essentials of Evangelical Theology: Life, Ministry, and Hope*, vol. 1, *God, Authority, and Salvation* (San Francisco: Harper & Row, 1978), 148-222.
[3]Marcus J. Borg and John Dominic Crossan, *The First Paul: Reclaiming the Radical Visionary Behind the Church's Conservative Icon* (New York: HarperCollins, 2009), 137. See also Jarvis Williams, "Violent Atonement in Romans: The Foundation of Paul's Soteriology," *Journal of the Evangelical Theological Society* 53 (2010): 579-99.
[4]Gerald O'Collins, *Jesus Our Redeemer: A Christian Approach to Salvation* (Oxford: Oxford University Press, 2007), 23.

the Lord or God in terms of "my Savior" (Lk 1:47) or the one who gives "salvation from our enemies" (Lk 1:71). The word "Lord" in some biblical texts can refer to either God or Jesus, such as Jude 5, which speaks of "Jesus [a textual variant: the Lord] who once for all saved a people out of the land of Egypt."[5] The Lord's Prayer uses a synonym, *ryomai* (deliver, rescue), of *sōzō*: "deliver us from the evil one" (Mt 6:13). In Matthew 27:42-43, the two words are used in the same sentence, serving as a pleonasm to emphasize the meaning of salvation: "He saved [*sōsai*] others; he cannot save himself. . . . He trusted in God; let God now deliver [*rhysasthō*] him." Likewise, in Romans 11:26 the use of a synonym is not redundant but highlights the thought: "All Israel will be saved [*sōthēsetai*], as is written, 'out of Zion will come the Deliverer [*rhyomenos*].'" Pointing beyond personal salvation, the sociopolitical contexts of these texts are prominent, as is the wide array of cognate words below. Treier's chapter seeks to critique the overly personal emphasis of salvation in Western Christianity, and using biblical theology he works hard to retrieve robustly the new-creation aspects of salvation, such as its sociopolitical and cosmic dimensions.

"Liberation" (*eleutheria*) is a cognate of "salvation." Liberation *from what* is often the debate. Three New Testament verses seem to indicate liberation is on the personal, sociopolitical, and even cosmic levels: "If the Son has liberated you, you will be liberated indeed" (Jn 8:36); "the law of the Spirit of life in Christ Jesus has set you free from the law of sin and death" (Rom 8:2); "creation itself will be liberated from the bondage of decay and will enter upon the glorious liberty of the children of God" (Rom 8:21). Both Latin American scholars in this section, Jules Martínez-Olivieri and Milton Acosta, as well as First Nations Canadian scholar Ray Aldred, work with this aspect of salvation in their chapters. But their perspectives on the "materiality of salvation" have particular nuances because their contexts are not the same.

A similar question could be asked about the next cognate, "redemption" (*apolytrōsis*; Rom 3:24): Redemption *from what*? Romans 3:24 is silent, but it does mention redemption as God's gift. Other scriptural verses mention redemption from the wrath of God (Rom 5:9); the power of sin (Eph 1:7, 14; Rom 5) and the power of death (Rom 6:23); the curse of the law (Gal 3:13); and the devil (Heb 2:14; 1 Jn 3:8). It is interesting that in the Old Testament God is called the *gōʾēl* (Redeemer; Ps 19:14), but never in the New Testament is God or Jesus called Redeemer (*lytrōtēs*). The redemption metaphor comes from the context of the slave market (such as Ex 21:8, Egyptian slavery; Is 51:11; 59:20, Babylonian captivity; Rom 6:13-14, first-century Roman society). But the point is always about the new status of freedom. Thus the Bible speaks of the redeemed people as God's own possession (Ex 15:16; 1 Pet 2:9), ransomed with a price (Is 35:10; 51:11; 62:12; 1 Cor 6:20; 7:23; 1 Tim 2:6). Elaine Goh's chapter seems to use this category well as she examines how Ecclesiastes can be used to speak to the redemption needed for Chinese who possess the mentality of fearing death, overconfidence, and workaholic tendencies.

Another favorite biblical word for salvation is "reconciliation" (*katallagē*; Rom 5:10-11; 2 Cor 5:18-20), translated by William Tyndale as "atonement"

---

[5]The Nestle-Aland Greek New Testament 27th edition renders Jude 5 as "the Lord once for all saved a people out of the land of Egypt," but the 28th edition renders it as "Jesus once for all saved." See Institute for New Testament Textual Research, *Novum Testamentum Graece: Nestle-Aland* (Peabody, MA: Hendrickson, 2013 [28th ed.]; Stuttgart: Deutsche Bibelgesellschaft, 2004 [27th ed.]).

and thus focusing on overcoming the enmity between God and humanity (at-one-ment) rather than the broken relationships among people. Paul here is probably not using the Old Testament or Hebraic idea of atonement sacrifice (Lev 16) but the Greco-Roman background of transforming hostility into friendship or love. Such a relational and interpersonal connotation appeals to Majority World Christians, such as Sung Wook Chung, who examines the painful tension between North Korea and South Korea.

The last two terms are controversial, depending on the interpretive frame one uses to understand the concepts. "Being set right" (*dikaioumenoi*; Rom 3:24) is often used to mean "vindicating" in the context of justice where God stands with the weak or the oppressed, thus justifying them (Ps 82:1-3). But the second meaning is also used in the Bible: reversing the lowly from shame to honor (Ps 31:1-2); thus the shameful cross in the New Testament *sets right* the distorted value system of glory (aesthetic) and obscenity (shame).[6] Unfortunately, the second meaning has often been ignored, especially in legal Western societies, and is picked up by Elaine Goh, Ray Aldred, and Emily Choge Kerama in the Asian, Native North American, and African chapters, respectively, in this section.

The most controversial cognate word for salvation is *hilastērion,* translated as either "propitiation" or "expiation." "Propitiation" refers to the salvific work of Christ in placating divine justice or appeasing the wrath of God (Rom 3:25; Heb 9:5; see *hilasmos,* 1 Jn 2:2; 4:10).[7] My preferred translation, "expiation," traces its theological roots to the Hebrew word *kappōret,* that is, "mercy seat" on the ark of covenant in the Holy of Holies, thus indicating that "God loved us and sent his Son to be the expiation [*hilasmos*] of our sins" (1 Jn 4:10).[8] Jesus Christ is "the expiation [*hilasmos*] not only for our sins but also for the sins of the whole world" (1 Jn 2:2). Gerald O'Collins writes of *hilastērion* in this regard as "wiping away":

> The LXX never introduces this verb or related words (e.g. *exilaskomai*) to speak of sinners appeasing or rendering favorable an offended God [propitiation]. It is rather God who expiates, purifies, and deals with sin (e.g., Ezek 16:13). Likewise in the NT it is God who is the agent or subject of expiator activity, lovingly providing the "*hilastērion,*" his only Son, who is the means and the place for wiping away the stain of sin.[9]

Soteriology is not simply about atoning sacrifice but also about offering love. Salvation is not simply "saved from," but also "saved to"; not simply delivery from sin and death, but also restoration to fullness of life; not simply suffering servant but also reigning king; not simply death and crucifixion, but also resurrection and consummation; not simply forgiveness, but also regeneration; not simply wrong and sin overcome, but also love and life abundant.[10] In short, salvation in the biblical understanding means God's creative deliverance of people in their situation of need from that which threatens wholeness of life, impedes the order of creation, and disrupts God's redemption in the world.

---

[6]Robert Jewett, *Romans: A Commentary*, Hermeneia (Minneapolis: Fortress, 2006), 281.

[7]C. E. B. Cranfield, *A Critical and Exegetical Commentary on the Epistle to the Romans* (Edinburgh: T&T Clark, 1975), 1:217.

[8]J. D. G. Dunn, *The Theology of Paul the Apostle* (Grand Rapids, MI: Eerdmans, 1998), 213; J. A. Fitzmyer, *Paul and His Theology: A Brief Sketch* (Englewood Cliffs, NJ: Prentice Hall, 1989), 64.

[9]O'Collins, *Jesus Our Redeemer*, 17.

[10]See K. K. Yeo, *The Spirit Intercedes: New Testament in Prayers and Images*, trans. (into Chinese) Joseph Wang and May Lin (Taipei: Campus Evangelical Fellowship, 2011), 236-51.

God so loves the Majority World. God's expansive love is expressed indigenously in global contexts through the back roads and alleys of African villages, the new trails of Latin American valleys, and the highways of Asian cities. From the perspective of "saved from" to "saved to," here the language of the contributors to this section varies, reflecting the myriad soteriological expressions in the New Testament: from sin to God (Acts 3:19), from death to life (1 Jn 3:14), from bondage to freedom (Philemon), from brokenness to wholeness (2 Cor 12:9), from enmity to reconciliation (Eph 2:16), from evil to goodness (Rom 12:21), from despair to hope (1 Thessalonians). Just as these metaphors are multiple throughout Scripture, then, so also are the interpretations of soteriology in church history and even today: from guilt to judicial justification (John Calvin), from chaos to order (Gregory of Nazianzus), and from obscenity to beauty (Hans Urs von Balthasar).

Sin and Salvation: Toward a Soteriology of Truth, Goodness, and Beauty

Soteriology presupposes hamartiology (the doctrine of sin), but "sin" (or the "*power* of sin") is understood as all that impedes God's creation of superabundant life.[11] Yet salvation is not simply sin being broken, evil overcome, wrong forgiven. Salvation is also the broken image of God restored, God's presence and love and justice fully realized, and paradise regained—encompassing the past and present to the end of time (eschaton). The problems of humanity and the world we live in are real: the morbid condition of the brokenness in human beings and in their well-being with their Creator and creation, the

prevalence of sin that binds and curses life in the cosmos, and the sting of death that obliterates the shalom of earthly flourishing.

There are three hermeneutical frames of sin and salvation, which should be understood as complementing rather than competing with one another since the semantic domain of all three categories is found in the Bible. The first perspective is that of goodness and evil in a moral sense. This view holds that a moral universe of goodness is in essence the psychological health of human beings or the well-being of humanity. The perversion of the order of the moral universe means a departure from its norm; thus, sin is sickness of the soul (Ps 32:3-5). Salvation then involves finding a cure, a therapy, often resorting to "medications" for healing. Examples are the ritual laws (Lev 13–15) on what is clean and what is unclean, and illnesses such as leprosy (Mt 8:2-4) and blindness (Jn 9), which are regarded as sins.

The second frame assumes a truthful and legal universe, for God is the Lawgiver, and the laws are divine imperatives for human beings to maintain the principles of all things. Sin is missing the mark (*hamartia*), doing wrong (*ḥāṭā'* or *'āwâ*), or rebelling (*pāša'*) against the rules. Sin is law-breaking (1 Jn 3:4), the result of which is guilt (Ps 32), and thus salvation is "forensic" justification. The Reformers especially favored this juridical understanding of sin (penal) and judicial atonement.

The third view assumes a holy and beautiful universe, one that is covered with its Creator's presence and glory. God as the beautiful wisdom (Prov 8) is the true nature of creation's web of relationship and its worthiness. Sin means one has "fallen short of the glory of God" (Rom 3:23), and salvation is to have God's image restored in

---

[11]For more, see J. Richard Middleton and Michael J. Gorman, "Salvation," in *The New Interpreter's Dictionary of the Bible*, vol. 5, S–Z, ed. Katharine Doob Sakenfeld et al. (Nashville: Abingdon, 2009), 45-61.

humanity (2 Cor 3:18) and being clothed in glory (Rom 13:14; Gal 3:27).

In sum, salvation is that which is good, true, and beautiful. As Paul writes, "Do not be conformed to this age [*aiōn*], but be transformed [a major aspect of salvation] by the renewing of your minds [*noos*], so that you may discern what is the will of God—what is good [virtuous/morality] and acceptable [delightful/beauty] and perfect [whole/truth]" (Rom 12:2). The interplay of goodness, truth, and beauty can suggest an understanding of salvation as a process in which the aesthetic brings truth and good to our authentic selves and that of the cosmos. Jesus is the image of God (see Col 1:15; Heb 1:3), and he offers and epitomizes the wholeness and worthiness of humanity as their salvation. Indeed, "the grace of God has appeared bringing salvation to *all* human beings" (Titus 2:11).

SOTERIOLOGY OF THE GLOBAL CHURCH IN THE MAJORITY WORLD

How should we understand soteriology in our pluralistic world, especially in the Majority World in which pre- or extrabiblical knowledge of God abounds in the context of religious diversity? I find it interesting that not even one contributor to part four addresses this crucial issue. For if Christ is sui generis, would Cyprian's dictum— *extra ecclesiam nulla salus* (outside the church there is no salvation)—still hold true today?[12]

Traditionally, three views have emerged from the debate over this question:

1. All religions lead to God and to the salvation of all people (universalism, pluralism, e.g.,

Origen, Irenaeus, Ernst Troeltsch, John Hick; or annihilationism, the belief all nonbelievers will be destroyed after death).

2. Salvation is universally available through Christ, who is predestined to do so (inclusivism, e.g., Justin Martyr's "Logos among Greeks and Socrates," Clement of Alexandria's "philosophy brought salvation to the Greeks as the Laws did to the Hebrews," Thomas Aquinas's "baptism of desire," Karl Barth's "election of Christ").

3. Salvation is available only in Christ (exclusivism, restrictivism, or particularism: R. Douglas Geivett, W. Gary Phillips).[13]

From the discussion above, we know that the traditional debate regarding Acts 4:12 ("there is no salvation through any else except Jesus; for there is no other name under heaven given among human beings by which we must be saved"), especially in the Majority World, remains challenging. Among the qualified inclusivistic views is that of Lesslie Newbigin and Alister McGrath, who argue for the assurance of salvation in Christ but acknowledge that they themselves are agnostic regarding those who have not heard of the gospel. Thus, they believe in the prevenient grace of God at work through the Spirit. McGrath writes: "I have stressed that there is a specifically Christian understanding of salvation, which is grounded uniquely in the life, death, and resurrection of Jesus Christ. To affirm that there is a distinctively Christian understanding of salvation is not to deny that other faiths offer salvation in their own terms."[14]

---

[12]The context in Cyprian's dictum is not about religious diversity but about his emphasis on belonging to the church of Christ, against the schism within the church. See Olli-Pekka Vainio, "Salvation and Religious Diversity: Christian Perspectives," *Religion Compass* 10, no. 2 (2016): 28.

[13]Dennis L. Okholm and Timothy R. Phillips, eds., *Four Views on Salvation in a Pluralistic World* (Grand Rapids, MI: Zondervan, 1996); Vainio, "Salvation and Religious Diversity," 27-34.

[14]Okholm and Phillips, *Four Views on Salvation*, 176.

Maybe Majority World scholars are not shying away from the "whether there is salvation outside the church" question but responding by living out the breadth of biblical salvation (see "The Biblical Semantic of 'God Saves' ['Jesus' in Hebrew]" above), being both true and critical of their *Sitz im Leben* (life situation). Thus, besides the intellectual rigors of the presenters at the Evangelical Theological Society (November 19, 2015) and the Institute of Biblical Research (November 20, 2015) "Scripture and Theology in Global Context" sessions, I am most touched by their personal stories. Ray Aldred shared how the European settlers conquered his land and destroyed his identity, and thus how "God as liberator" to the European settlers was "God the conqueror" for Native Americans. Elaine Goh recounts what a burden it is for Asian Chinese to fear being losers, and thus what a gospel of salvific hope the book of Ecclesiastes has become to them. Emily Choge Kerama tells the story of being born with a congenital defect in a Kenyan family and how her Christian parents witnessed to the power of God despite all odds.

While Western scholarship is often either prejudiced by cultural blind spots or prideful in its assumption of its own "normative" culture-less theology, many Majority World scholars educated in the West are tempted to mimic their mentors and make a contextual-global hermeneutic an afterthought, or worse, to resist the project this series promotes. The chapters in this section are by no means perfect, but the contributors are seeking to live out their faith dynamically, faithful to the Scriptures and critical of their cultural assumptions. Similar to the rich young ruler in Luke 18, who thought practicing the law meant keeping the commandments (Lk 18:20-21), our presenters aim to complement one another on

that "still one thing lacking" (Lk 18:22) in each of our lives. "Still one thing lacking" has something to do with us "entering the kingdom of God" (Lk 18:17) or "inheriting eternal life" (Lk 18:18) by living out *the spirit* of the law. Contextually, it is selling his possessions and helping the poor for the rich ruler; it may suggest other requirements depending on context—such as embracing one's cultural identity (for the First Nations of Canada) or continuing to yearn for reconciliation between North and South (for the South Korean)—the strengthening of one's character as one participates in the suffering of Christ.

Thus, soteriology is a self-theologizing and existential act that is well served by the deep imbrication of theology, Scripture, and readers' contexts. The indicative and imperative moods of salvation must be held in tension. This tension calls believers into not simply abstract imputed righteousness. This tension calls all to real participation in, and a sharing in the merit of, Christ's righteousness (Mt 5:20; Rom 2:5-13; Phil 2:12-13), thus affirming the primacy of grace and the necessity of works, similar to "faith without works is dead" in James (Jas 2:17) and "obedience of faith" in Romans (Rom 1:5; 16:26).

CONCLUSION

The doctrine of salvation in the Majority World is not a theological construct or abstract idea but a matter of life or death. Christians in the Majority World find the Philippian jailer's question, "What must I do to be saved?" (Acts 16:30), a significant and timely reflection in the twenty-first century. However, in most developed countries, especially in Europe and North America, faith in science and material prosperity, as well as a preference in cosmopolitan culture for therapies, often condition people to reduce or even brush aside their problems of plight, sin, and "lostness" and, subsequently, their need of salvation.[15]

Many who live in the Latino/a contexts of conflict, oppression, and violence are desperate to find liberation, peace, and hope.[16] African Christians address their world, which is plagued with HIV/AIDS, poverty, and war, by looking for a soteriology of emancipation from such ills and evils.[17] Asian multireligious, scriptural, linguistic, and racial social realities inevitably cry out for a soteriology that addresses natural disasters, epidemics, child labor, human trafficking, and dissymmetry of wealth. Christians of indigenous groups in the United States, Borneo, and Australia wrestle with a soteriology that will save their land and bring them an identity of nationhood, political freedom, and self-determination. Understanding soteriology in one's context is nothing new. In *Salvation in the New Testament*, Jan G. van der Watt is adamant that "the documents of the New Testament [cannot] be classed as abstract theological treatises. They should rather be seen as reflecting [in the ancient world] the integration of the message into particular situations of the people involved in the first and original communication process."[18]

The hope of the volume editors is that you will read this section in conjunction with other sections in this volume. For soteriology is the megatheme of Scripture, "the integrating center of Scripture [and] the coordinating center of

theology."[19] The salvation motif is prevalent in the Bible and Christian theology because of the "many dimensions" of soteriology by which "most key theological issues . . . converge."[20] Soteriology is symbiotically related to the nature and work of God the Savior (theology; the author of salvation), the person and deeds of Christ (Christology; the agent of salvation), the work of the Spirit (pneumatology; the agency of salvation), the need and being of humanity (anthropology; together with the creation, the recipient of salvation), the identity and function of the church (ecclesiology; the channel of salvation to the world), the process and goal of history (eschatology; salvation consummated).

I believe that soteriology is about God's pneumatology of universality (God's working out his plan of salvation in the whole creation) that has a christological inclusivity (of all who are saved). Therefore, the church lives out that eschatological hope proleptically (Søren Kierkegaard's "life can only be understood backwards; but it must be lived forwards") and prophetically (mercy and justice) to the ends of the earth.[21] Majority World scholars in this section come to us from among the nations, and they offer us the courage and the grace to care for the world redemptively without borders.

■ ■ ■

The volume editors wish to give thanks to many of our friends who partner with us in this project, witnessing to the global church in action

---

[15]Lee E. Snook, *The Anonymous Christ: Jesus as Savior in Modern Theology* (Minneapolis: Augsburg, 1986).

[16]For an extensive bibliography by Majority World scholars apropos the use of the Bible to address their situation of life that calls for salvation, see K. K. Yeo, "The Bible in the Majority World," in *Oxford History of Dissenting Protestant Traditions*, vol. 5, *The Twentieth Century: Themes in a Global Context*, ed. Mark Hutchinson (Oxford: Oxford University Press, 2018).

[17]Charles Nyamiti, "Contemporary African Christologies: Assessment and Practical Suggestions," in *Paths of African Theology*, ed. Rosino Gibellini (Maryknoll, NY: Orbis, 1994), 66.

[18]Jan G. van der Watt, ed., *Salvation in the New Testament: Perspective on Soteriology* (Leiden: Brill, 2005), 505.

[19]Joel Green, *Salvation* (Atlanta: Chalice, 2003), 2.

[20]David Ford, *Theology: A Very Short Introduction* (Oxford: Oxford University Press, 2014), 103.

[21]Howard V. Hong and Edna H. Hong, eds., *The Essential Kierkegaard* (Princeton, NJ: Princeton University Press, 2000), 20.

regarding soteriology in the global context of Scripture and theology. We are grateful to the authors in this section for providing numerous drafts of their presentations at the 2015 Atlanta conference of Evangelical Theological Society and Institute for Biblical Research. We are indebted to ScholarLeaders International (especially Evan Hunter), the Rivendell Steward's Trust, and the SEED Research Institute (John Shen, Moses Cui) for their generous financial and prayer support. The leadership of the Evangelical Theological Society, Institute for Biblical Research, and Society of Biblical Literature has provided hotel space and efficient logistical support for our conferences. Michael Thomson of Eerdmans continues to believe in our work and guide us to navigate smoothly through publishing waters. Chris Wright, Pieter Kwant, and Mark Hunt of Langham Partnership International encourage us and partner with us in publishing our work, but also in caring for the future scholars of the Majority World.

I praise God for the global church living out the mission of God sacramentally (salvation in and through the body of Christ), every time we meet, "breaking bread" at academic conferences or online/iCloud. Oh, "so great a salvation!" (Heb 2:3). I echo Paul's words as a prayer: "For we are the aroma of Christ to God among those who are being saved and among those who are perishing; to the one a fragrance from death to death, to the other a fragrance from life to life" (2 Cor 2:15-16).

25

THE NEW COVENANT AND NEW CREATION

WESTERN SOTERIOLOGIES AND THE FULLNESS OF THE GOSPEL

Daniel J. Treier

THE FOCUS OF THIS opening chapter is to provide an overview of Western soteriologies. This overview begins by complicating the term *Western* before sketching eight soteriological traditions: Orthodox, Catholic, Lutheran, Calvinist, Anabaptist, Arminian, Wesleyan/Holiness, and Pentecostal. Next the overview concludes with recent trends affecting Christ's accomplishment of atonement and justification as well as the Spirit's application of salvation in believers' sanctification and glorification. After this overview comes possible critique, both internal and external, regarding Western soteriological tendencies.

From liberationist and Majority World perspectives, the sociopolitical and cosmic dimensions of salvation are the chief lacunae in traditional dogmatic attempts to represent the gospel's fullness. Such incomplete soteriologies focus too exclusively on the personal blessings of participation in the new covenant. Hence I conclude by suggesting that "new creation," with which the Old Testament prophets surround the new covenant, might fill up what is lacking in the soteriologies surveyed here—without divorcing sociopolitical and cosmic concerns from the new covenant's personal elements.

My primary goal is to provide an overview of "Western" soteriologies (assuming the quotation marks around this label "Western" throughout). This overview indicates that sociopolitical and cosmic dimensions are the chief aspects of salvation neglected by traditional dogmatics. Such incomplete soteriologies focus too exclusively on the personal blessings of participation in the new covenant, which the end of this chapter addresses particularly in terms of Jeremiah 31. I conclude by suggesting that "new creation," a theme of God's saving action with which the Old Testament prophets surround the new covenant, might fill up what is lacking in the soteriologies surveyed here—without divorcing sociopolitical and cosmic concerns from the new covenant's personal elements.

"WESTERN" TENDENCIES

Western soteriological tendencies reflect both major historical traditions and influential recent trends. Of course, such an assignment requires a gargantuan level of generalization, beyond the usual oversimplification that all education requires.

Such generalization begins with the very label *Western*: in one sense it really means Northern, as opposed to Majority World theologies located largely in the Global South. In another sense, soteriologically, *Western* references the Augustinian tradition, which has generated Catholic and Protestant socially embodied arguments over many centuries. Yet the contrast implied in the present context, concerning Majority World theologies, probably includes the Orthodox tradition as well, since its heritage of *theosis* (deification) overlaps considerably with the Catholic tradition and even some Protestant accounts. Finally, for all the differences between Augustinian and Eastern tendencies, together they present another complexity: Augustine and other classic figures were African or Middle Eastern, not European—however Latin or Greek their language and however Roman their context. Hence *Western* functions quite imprecisely, as an omnibus contrast term.

Likewise, the boundaries of *soteriology* are fuzzy—overlapping with Christology, especially for atonement; pneumatology, especially for sanctification; and eschatology, especially for glorification. Systematic theology as modernity knows it, seeking an *ordo salutis* (order of salvation) that logically arranges the Spirit's application of Christ's saving benefits, is a comparatively recent invention. Its meandering development exacerbates the challenge of accurately characterizing Western soteriologies. Should Orthodox soteriology focus on creedal consensus, later theologians' tendencies, or priestly and popular beliefs?

Should Catholic soteriology focus on official dogma, catechetical material, historical eras, or geographical regions, let alone variety among priests, theologians, and the laity? For Protestant soteriologies, similarly, if their welter of systematic theologies reduces formal, printed variety to a somewhat manageable set of traditions and tendencies, then various denominations and popular trends quickly make such moments of apparent consensus less manageable. The following overview attempts to address both the gospel that is formally proclaimed and on occasion, however complex, what is apparently implied or actually practiced.

Traditions. The preceding qualifications notwithstanding, this overview of Western soteriologies begins with the major traditions they encompass. For all their variety, each somehow prioritizes salvation from sin and its consequences. Plus all of them ultimately focus on salvation's personal dimensions.[1] Yet each helpfully contributes an animating principle from which to learn.

Orthodox: Theosis *beyond mortal corruption.* The Orthodox tradition has its focus and limits tied to early creedal consensus. Neither the informal rule of faith nor its later creedal formulations canonized a particular atonement theory or soteriology.[2] The first article of the Nicene Creed ("one God . . . maker of heaven and earth") implies that salvation involves the Creator's establishing full and final lordship over the entire cosmos. Its second article ("one Lord . . . who for us and for our salvation") focuses on the Son's incarnation for us and our salvation, rehearsing his divine identity and earthly pilgrimage. The

---

[1] At least their orthodox or traditional or conservative versions do so. Modernist or liberal versions, arising since the Enlightenment(s), share common tendencies that transcend the distinctiveness of the traditions profiled here. Thus these profiles sketch the originating, conservative and distinctive, tendencies—leaving aside older liberal emphases on human freedom and a moral kingdom of God. Liberationist influence on contemporary progressive theologies surfaces here when highlighting traditional blind spots.

[2] Very emphatically, John McIntyre, *The Shape of Soteriology: Studies in the Doctrine of the Death of Christ* (Edinburgh: T&T Clark, 1992), 2.

"descent into hell" from the Apostles' Creed only adds soteriological implications depending on debated interpretations. The second article's closing reminder of divine judgment ("he will come again to judge the quick and the dead") and an eternal kingdom highlights the respective ends that soteriology puts at stake. The third article, on the Holy Spirit, then, insists on baptism as the key soteriological entry point ("one baptism for the remission of sins") and implies a set of key endpoints: forgiveness of sins, the resurrection of the dead, and the life of the world to come.

Orthodox theologies emphasize this soteriological entry point of baptism, consistent with liturgical tradition. They emphasize the end point of *theosis*, consistent with the focus on resurrection: such deification, or divinization, does not make a human into God himself, but it does involve the saved human "participating in the divine nature" in a creaturely way. Broadly speaking, this soteriology centrally addresses mortal corruption. Each human imitates Adam's sin after having inherited his fallen mortality, with fleshly desires misdirected and disproportionate due to fear of scarcity. Christians experience God's forgiveness through the sacrament of the Lord's Supper. Salvation remakes humanity in union with the resurrected Christ by the Holy Spirit. Ultimately people transcend mortal corruption and become full (albeit still human) "partakers of the divine nature" (2 Pet 1:4) in resurrected bodies. In the meantime, the church's liturgy mediates union with the incarnate Christ so that once again humans can grow in virtue. Ascetic figures and groups underscore Orthodoxy's emphasis on efforts to undergo such transformation of mortal desire.

Catholic: Sacramental renewal unto the beatific vision. The Catholic tradition shares the creedal outline of salvation reclaiming God's creation through the Son's incarnation and atonement, with the Holy Spirit mediating union with Christ through the church. People enter into new life (regeneration) at baptism, appropriate renewing grace through the sacraments (especially the Eucharist), and will enjoy its completion in a form of *theosis*.

Although Orthodoxy rejects the Pelagian idea that humans can grow toward righteousness apart from redeeming grace, the Augustinian concept of original sin is different from the Eastern one. Classically, Catholic theology has Adam's sin being not just necessarily imitated by humans (through corrupted desire stemming from cursed mortality) but imputed to them through real biological connection or another form of representation. Medieval Catholicism also made humanity's soteriological end somewhat more specific, construing *theosis* in terms of the beatific vision ("Blessed are the pure in heart, for they will see God" [Mt 5:8]).[3] While transcending cognition, this beatific vision involves the mind's eye, as it were. In between original sin and the beatific vision, medieval Catholicism applied an intricate legal and ontological construal of soteriological merit, along with a sacramental system for receiving grace.

Medieval Catholic soteriology's more technical terms resulted in less communal and cosmic focus than earlier creedal consensus might have supported (and Orthodox liturgies might claim). Modern Catholic soteriology is more amenable to those broader soteriological aspects, consistent with the doctrines of creation and churchly catholicity. Meanwhile, both

---

[3]Unless otherwise noted, Scripture quotations in this chapter follow the NIV.

Catholicism and Orthodoxy emphasize human dignity and freedom to pursue renewal in the divine likeness, reflecting more positive anthropologies than many Protestant soteriologies.

Lutheran: Justification by faith alone. Protestant soteriologies initially were and often remain critical of perceived errors of Catholic belief and practice. Yet Martin Luther, remaining as Catholic as possible, retained baptismal regeneration, the real sacramental presence of Christ, and Augustinian tendencies regarding original sin and divine predestination. Reemphasizing gracious divine initiative and the bondage of the human will, Luther believed that justification by faith alone was a biblically necessary break with the Roman Church—the article by which the church stands or falls.[4] Justification is preeminently an initial declaration of God's forgiveness and the believer's imputed righteousness in Christ, not an ongoing process of infusing Christ's righteousness into the believer—who must always cling to Christ, rather than cooperate with sacramental grace, for assurance. A cluster of changes followed this one, including "affirmation of ordinary life" as spiritually equal to the monasticism that Luther eventually rejected.[5]

Accordingly, the Lutheran account of sanctification champions freedom and gratitude. Freed from concern over personal righteousness, believers gratefully love God and serve their neighbors as they truly need. Works of love emerge from faith but are never the basis for justification or Christian assurance. Law and gospel do not really contrast the Old and New Testaments; instead, they are contrasting aspects involved in encountering any biblical Word. A first use of the law preserves earthly society by restraining human wickedness in the temporal kingdom; a second use confronts sinners with their need for God's grace in Christ. The gospel focuses on making this offer of forgiveness, inviting people to enter God's eternal kingdom.

Calvinist: Election unto union with Christ. While John Calvin shared Luther's commitment to justification by faith alone, he was more inclined to think centrally from union with Christ. Luther certainly depended on that union: justification by faith alone is not a "legal fiction," as often alleged, because believers in covenantal union with Christ enjoy a glorious exchange—his benefits for their sin—as with joint marital property. Some recent scholarship also suggests that Luther's soteriology was more ontological than previously thought.[6] Yet Calvin, less inclined to start with Catholic commitments altered only when necessary, instead sought a wholesale, ordered biblical theology for catechesis. His soteriology placed union with Christ in the overarching position, within which justification and sanctification became double graces.

As Luther's and Calvin's successors battled Catholics, Radical Reformers, and each other, they developed confessions, catechisms, and elaborate scholastic systems. Such Calvinism became known for predestinarian and covenantal or federal emphases: eternally the triune God predestined the salvation of the elect—the Father willing to send the Son, the Son agreeing to become incarnate and atone for their sin, and the Spirit agreeing to unite the elect with Christ. According to the five points of Calvinism under the

---

[4]For example, "The Smalcald Articles," in *The Book of Concord: The Confessions of the Evangelical Lutheran Church*, ed. Robert Kolb and Timothy J. Wengert (Minneapolis: Fortress, 2000), 301.

[5]Charles Taylor, *Sources of the Self: The Making of the Modern Identity* (Cambridge, MA: Harvard University Press, 1992), 211-85.

[6]For example, Tuomo Mannermaa, *Christ Present in Faith: Luther's View of Justification* (Minneapolis: Fortress, 2005).

acronym TULIP, all humans after the fall become (1) *totally* depraved (not absolutely depraved, but sinful in every aspect), which is addressed by (2) *unconditional* divine election (God does not merely foresee but rather determines who will be saved), (3) *limited* atonement (Christ dies specifically for the elect), (4) *irresistible* grace (the Spirit regenerates the elect, effectually calling them to faith), and (5) *perseverance* of the saints (regeneration preserves the elect in faith throughout their pilgrimage). Salvation's blessings are for those elected to have Christ (rather than Adam, due to imputation of original sin) as their federal head—representing them before God.

Calvinism emphasizes God's redemptive rule over the entire cosmos more than other Protestant traditions.[7] Correspondingly, Calvinists often pursue more cultural transformation. Such implications of redemption, however, do not displace personal salvation from its classical centrality. Calvinism adds a third use of the law to direct believers' pursuit of sanctification. But God's present work of cultural transformation outside the church remains common, not specifically redemptive, grace.

Anabaptist: Radical, communal discipleship. The third Reformation-era Protestant tradition involves the more radical and Anabaptist Reformers. Because they rejected infant baptism and believed that only confessing believers' baptism was biblical, they were labeled "rebaptizers"—for requiring that believers once baptized as infants be baptized again to become church members.

Radical Reformers were less wedded to justification by faith alone than magisterial Protestants;

in some cases they opposed it. Like Lutheran Pietists soon after the Reformation, Puritans later, and others since, they placed justification in a larger context with different emphases. They emphasized pursuit of personal discipleship in small Christian communities. These communities would be alternative societies, typically modeling the nonviolent practice of Jesus while waiting eagerly for God's kingdom to come in fullness. Radical soteriologies were more biblicist, less formal, and correspondingly less consistent. Yet, separatistic tendencies and periodic aberrations aside, their core commitments have become widely influential in recent decades.[8]

Arminian: Freedom for faith. Within Reformed circles, seventeenth-century Dutch thinkers such as Jacobus Arminius retained broadly Protestant soteriology while rejecting Augustinian/Lutheran accounts of the will's bondage and Calvinist accounts of divine sovereignty. Classic Calvinism became formally defined by the Synod of Dort and its rejection of the Arminian alternative. Arminianism then appeared within various traditions, offering no sharply defined and comprehensive system. In general, Arminian soteriologies emphasize human freedom (often labeled "libertarian") to accept or reject the gospel, with divine election being conditional (God foreseeing who will fulfill the condition of believing) or corporate (God deciding to form a servant community in the world rather than deciding the eternal destiny of particular persons). In some Arminian accounts human freedom seems to be a natural function of creation, but in others it is a universal redemptive blessing of prevenient

---

[7]Famously, Abraham Kuyper: "No single piece of our mental world is to be hermetically sealed off from the rest, and there is not a square inch in the whole domain of our human existence over which Christ, who is Sovereign over all, does not cry: 'Mine!'" (*Abraham Kuyper: A Centennial Reader*, ed. James D. Bratt [Grand Rapids, MI: Eerdmans, 1998], 488).

[8]Particularly through John Howard Yoder regarding the politics of Jesus, and Stanley Hauerwas regarding communal ethics of Christian virtue.

grace—grace that comes before the possibility of human faith, as a result of Christ's work on the cross or the Spirit's convicting work in the heart.

Wesleyan/Holiness: The second blessing unto perfect love. A distinctive Arminian family is the Wesleyan/Holiness tradition, in which the possibility of human freedom for faith clearly stems from prevenient grace. If Lutherans and Calvinists are stereotypically monergistic, emphasizing that salvation is due to God's grace alone, then Wesleyans are synergistic, emphasizing that salvation involves human cooperation in a sense—exploring how divine grace works.[9]

John Wesley embraced justification by faith alone; indeed his "conversion" involved the strange warming of his heart when hearing Luther's treatment of Romans.[10] But Wesley did not want this objective aspect of Christian assurance to prevent believers from vigorously pursuing perfect holiness or subjectively receiving assurance in light of their growth in grace. He insisted that biblical commands regarding holiness, even perfection, implied the possibility of graced obedience, enjoying this end of salvation here and now. Wesley's focus was the heart, so perfection would not involve loss of finite weakness or error, or legally blameless lack of inadvertent sin, but complete love of God and neighbor. If Calvinists and Lutherans championed Romans, with the latter marginalizing James, then Wesleyans renewed interest in 1 John.

Realizing Christian perfection would involve ongoing growth in grace, putting sin to death and putting on Christ. But sanctification would involve more than slow, sometimes steady, progress. Christian perfection would involve seeking a special work of grace after conversion,

generally labeled a second blessing. Such holiness meant a primarily personal focus concerning salvation, yet Holiness groups were frequent pioneers in nineteenth-century evangelical social reform: they were more typically involved in abolitionist, temperance, and women's suffrage causes than others. Meanwhile, populist commitments enabled Wesleyans to transform the Anglo-American landscape of church life. Such alternative movements as the Keswick Convention reflect broad Holiness outlines despite altered details: pursuit of a higher plane of sanctification through repeated crises of postconversion filling with the Holy Spirit that punctuate ordinary life. Such approaches have had widespread evangelical influence.

Pentecostal: The baptism and gifts of the Holy Spirit. Emerging from the Holiness tradition is the family of Pentecostal movements originating near the turn of the twentieth century. Just as an Arminian stance cuts across church traditions—with Baptists, for example, being either Arminian, Calvinist, or an amalgam—so Pentecostal beliefs and practices, or openness to them anyway, cuts across other ecclesiastical and soteriological traditions.

Classic Pentecostalism emphasized not merely holiness but empowerment for bold ministry and joyful living. The second, or postconversion, blessing was baptism with the Holy Spirit, with its initial evidence being glossolalia, or speaking in tongues. Most classic Pentecostals did not say that a person is unsaved without such an experience, but such an experience was to be normatively sought. Various Pentecostal denominations promoted this experience and the distinctively supernatural gifts of the Spirit.

---

[9]Thomas A. Langford, *Practical Divinity: Theology in the Wesleyan Tradition*, vol. 1, rev. ed. (Nashville: Abingdon, 1998), especially 249-51.

[10]John Wesley, "The Aldersgate Experience," in *John Wesley*, ed. Albert C. Outler (New York: Oxford University Press, 1964), 51-69.

The charismatic movement arose in the middle of the twentieth century across a range of churches, celebrating charismata and promoting Spirit baptism, albeit with less emphasis on the "initial evidence" of tongues. The Vineyard movement arose in the late twentieth century to continue celebrating charismatic and missional empowerment, often adopting a more Reformed account of progressive (less episodic or crisis-oriented) sanctification. Today *Pentecostal* is a broad adjective globally, having lost theological specificity concerning the classic Spirit baptism evidenced by tongues-speaking. Pentecostal soteriologies generally see themselves remedying more classical—not just Protestant but also Catholic and even Orthodox—deficiencies, bringing the Holy Spirit's work out from under the shadow of excessive Christ-centeredness.

Trends. Accordingly, one of the significant soteriological trends across various traditions is greater emphasis on the Holy Spirit's work. Western Christians and churches are increasingly aware of God's empowering presence within Global South Christianity. Simultaneously, traditional atonement-oriented accounts of salvation, tending toward anthropological pessimism and soteriological exclusivism, are increasingly unpopular in the West. Yet these do not exhaust recent soteriological trends, the rest of which loosely correspond to a traditional dogmatic outline.

Christ's accomplishment: Atonement and justification. Christ's work of atonement has frequently been reinterpreted in nonviolent or victorious terms, while justification by faith has been subject to both ecumenical dialogue and extensive debate in Pauline scholarship.

Justification is not a significant feature of Orthodox soteriologies. Catholic soteriology adopted a broadly Augustinian account involving transformative righteousness, in which justification itself is not primary except in debate with Protestants. Catholic soteriology does not teach justification by meritorious works but justification by faith as fulfilled in love. This love relates transformative righteousness to ontological renewal through infusion of sacramental grace. Believers do not merit salvation as an achievement but as a fitting divine response to human appropriation of grace. By contrast, Protestants typically define justification not as a process of infusion but as the initial imputation of Christ's righteousness—at minimum a declaration of forgiveness based on Christ bearing believers' sins.

Until recently atonement theology operated with a distinction between the person and the work of Christ. The former comprised the focus of Christology; the latter fell into an ambiguous space, partly christological and partly soteriological. Magisterial Protestants developed complex accounts of the *ordo salutis* in which justification became a primary benefit, the initial application of Christ's atoning work.

Ever since the Socinians of the early Protestant era, penal substitutionary atonement—according to which Christ suffered the punishment deserved by human sinners—has had opponents. Early in the twentieth century Gustaf Aulén, a Swedish Lutheran, proposed a threefold typology of atonement theologies.[11] Aulén's widely used typology suggested that (1) objective views, orienting atonement around change on God's side, arose in the Middle Ages when Anselm treated atonement in terms of

---

[11]Gustaf Aulén, *Christus Victor: An Historical Study of the Three Main Types of the Idea of Atonement*, trans. A. G. Herbert (repr., Eugene, OR: Wipf & Stock, 2003).

God's offended honor. Such objective views bear hallmarks of feudal or legal or other realities in their originating contexts. (2) Subjective views, orienting atonement around change on the sinner's side, also arose in the Middle Ages, thanks to Peter Abelard. Yet subjective views focus on Christ's moral example or influence to the exclusion of other scriptural concepts, so they became widespread only in the modern era and are viewed as liberal, captivated by contemporary concerns. Aulén suggested that this binary opposition between objective and subjective views was not original to the Christian tradition, which had previously been characterized by (3) classical views orienting atonement around Christus Victor—Christ triumphing over all hostile powers, including sin, death, and the devil.

Aulén's work appealed to many who recognized that no single atonement theory had been canonized in the early creeds, who reveled in patristic or subsequent diversity, and who rejected the penal substitution model. Modern thought finds blood sacrifice and pessimistic anthropologies distasteful. Aulén's work opened a door through which feminist and other critiques of penal substitution walked all the more forcefully. To some, penal atonement theories entail "divine child abuse," fostering male violence along with female victimization—glorifying Jesus' suffering at the hands of an angry divine Father. Catholic René Girard is representative of other recent antiviolence theories, reinterpreting Christ's sacrifice sociologically as an exposure of societies' scapegoating mechanisms.[12]

Alternatives to penal substitution have arisen periodically among more conservative Protestants. For instance, some Wesleyans find penal substitution to be extrinsic to their tradition and appeal to governmental models, in which Christ's sacrifice reflects God's justice in overcoming sin without addressing divine wrath for specific sinners. Alternatives have also arisen among biblical scholars: some argue that Scripture does not contain the penal substitution model, while others argue more modestly that Scripture does not require it.[13] In such accounts, Scripture provides multiple metaphors from which theologians are free to choose as contextually appropriate. Unifying these objections to penal substitution is the general charge that it is Lutheran and Reformed, not broadly evangelical, reflecting an outdated and excessively Pauline theology to the exclusion of other biblical priorities.

Traditional Protestants have responded by defending the presence of penal substitution in Paul's letters and its coherence with the rest of Scripture: substitution is not merely one metaphor among others but the reality underlying them, and the cross is integral to establishing God's kingdom as the fulfillment of Israel's story.[14] The historical contexts of penal substitution are receiving their due.[15] Implications of

---

[12]René Girard, *Violence and the Sacred* (Baltimore: Johns Hopkins University Press, 1979).

[13]For example, Joel B. Green and Mark D. Baker, *Recovering the Scandal of the Cross: Atonement in New Testament and Contemporary Contexts* (Downers Grove, IL: InterVarsity Press, 2000), which generally claims the latter but sometimes seems to imply the former.

[14]Simon Gathercole, *Defending Substitution: An Essay on Atonement in Paul*, Acadia Studies in Bible and Theology (Grand Rapids, MI: Baker Academic, 2015); John R. W. Stott, *The Cross of Christ* (Downers Grove, IL: InterVarsity Press, 1986); Jeremy R. Treat, *The Crucified King: Atonement and Kingdom in Biblical and Systematic Theology* (Grand Rapids, MI: Zondervan, 2014). Further defending penal substitution are several essays by Henri Blocher, including "*Agnus Victor*: The Atonement as Victory and Vicarious Punishment," in *What Does It Mean to Be Saved? Broadening Evangelical Horizons of Salvation*, ed. John G. Stackhouse Jr. (Grand Rapids, MI: Baker Academic, 2002), 67-91.

[15]For example, Adonis Vidu, *Atonement, Law, and Justice: The Cross in Historical and Cultural Contexts* (Grand Rapids, MI: Baker Academic, 2014).

divine child abuse and allegations of promoting violence or victimization are eliciting more intentionally trinitarian accounts: the Father, Son, and Spirit together lovingly accomplish our salvation; the Son lays down his life of his own accord, and the Father does not punish a mere human but mysteriously pours out judgment on the Son in the bond of the Spirit's love.[16] This trinitarian emphasis has also elicited attempts to recover the patristic fullness on the subject, which includes victory alongside considerable mention of sacrifice—more than Aulén's followers have acknowledged. These trinitarian accounts include efforts to integrate Christ's incarnation more fully with his atoning work: his identification with fallen humanity already begins its healing.[17]

Justification as the declaration of forgiveness tightly correlates with penal substitutionary atonement. Though earlier modern alternatives to penal substitution may have been moralistic in their visions of the divine kingdom and human transformation, current alternatives are typically more optimistic or even universalistic regarding human salvation.[18] Forgiveness seems to involve sheer divine fiat or radically incarnational divine identification with our plight, not a divine work of gracious justice involving the cross.

The most substantial contemporary development concerning justification is the so-called new perspective on Paul. In brief compass, this perspective rejects the Lutheran parallel between Paul's "Judaizing" opponents and medieval Catholicism. Such a parallel suggested that just as Paul's opponents based sanctification or assurance on law-keeping in response to covenantal grace, so later Catholic belief errantly based justification on transformative righteousness through sacramental grace. Rejecting this parallel, newer perspectives on Paul characterize Second Temple Judaism in terms of covenantal nomism, not legalism or works-righteousness: works of the law simply demarcated God's (Jewish) covenant people (from Gentile pagans), with circumcision expressing initial commitment to the covenantal obligation of keeping Torah.

In that case Paul's critique of his opponents chiefly opposed ethnocentric failure to recognize prophetic fulfillment of Gentile inclusion in Christ, not soteriological failure to champion the "faith alone" anthropology of true grace. Key Pauline texts, accordingly, may have in view the faith(fulness) of Christ rather than faith in Christ as what decisively accomplishes our salvation.[19] Apocalyptic readings proceed on this basis to suggest that Paul's gospel is more radically gracious than the Protestant Reformation suggested: not even human faith functions as any kind of condition for participating in the new reality of union with Christ, which has invaded and upended our earthly history.[20]

However, neither apocalyptic nor any of the various new-perspective readings have vanquished more traditional accounts. Certainly the

[16]For example, Hans Boersma, *Violence, Hospitality, and the Cross: Reappropriating the Atonement Tradition* (Grand Rapids, MI: Baker Academic, 2004).

[17]This enduring emphasis of T. F. Torrance (and family) now finds advocates under the heading "evangelical Calvinism."

[18]See, for example, Robin A. Parry and Christopher H. Partridge, eds., *Universal Salvation: The Current Debate* (Grand Rapids, MI: Eerdmans, 2003).

[19]One way of getting up to date on such issues in Pauline scholarship is to examine the most important recent contribution: John M. G. Barclay, *Paul and the Gift* (Grand Rapids, MI: Eerdmans, 2015). Barclay appropriates aspects of the "new perspective," especially its thicker treatment of first-century Judaism, while retaining theological aspects of the earlier Protestant tradition.

[20]Douglas A. Campbell, *The Deliverance of God: An Apocalyptic Rereading of Justification in Paul* (Grand Rapids, MI: Eerdmans, 2009).

newer scholarship has led to more careful portrayals of first-century Judaism, with corresponding debates about how its nomism relates to Pauline arguments. But if "works" must be addressed more chastely, still the traditional Protestant approach has contemporary exegetical and theological defenses—including the identification of misunderstandings and excessively narrow presentations from which it too suffers.[21]

The Spirit's application: Sanctification and glorification. Trends concerning sanctification involve regeneration, spirituality, and glorification, or *theosis*. For some, regeneration is the initial event of being made new by the Spirit, either logically preceding faith (as for most Calvinists and those affirming baptismal regeneration) or proceeding from it (as for most Arminians). For others, *regeneration* is a virtual synonym of *sanctification*, denoting a process of renewal rather than initial reception of a new nature. Apart from interest in conversion as more process- and less event-oriented, few current trends affect regeneration as such.[22] In some circles, though, the positional aspect of sanctification—associated with justification as an initial event—is gaining renewed emphasis. Sanctification terminology in the Bible usually addresses being set apart positionally as God's people, a status that contains a continual calling toward holiness—yet not itself a process involving human initiative. When (instead) that process of sanctification (in more systematic-theological

terms) is in view, the biblical-theological terminology focuses on being renewed, being transformed, growing in grace. From this perspective sanctification needs more emphasis on divine initiative than many views of the Christian life provide.[23]

Spirituality has certainly received contemporary theological attention. Classic theologians' spiritual priorities are being recovered, with particular attention to Christian virtues and practices.[24] Interest in spirituality without religion has elicited theological pursuit of authentic Christian responses to that cultural trend. Protestant openness to *theosis*, with attention to the contemplative end of our earthly pilgrimage, stems partly from trends in Pauline studies and connections with other New Testament corpora.[25] Perhaps it also stems from neglected aspects of Christ's work—broadening atonement beyond the cross to consider implications of his incarnation, earthly ministry, burial, resurrection, and ascension. Even on traditional Pauline terms, Western soteriologies need better accounts of Romans 4:25 ("He was delivered over to death for our sins and was raised to life for our justification"), especially in light of the encompassing trinitarian vision of Romans 8.

Speaking of *theosis*, and/or glorification, completes our overview of the *ordo salutis*. Orthodox and Catholic accounts of salvation's final end have remained relatively stable, with the Orthodox rarely pursuing a technical *ordo* and

---

[21]Theologically, R. Michael Allen, *Justification and the Gospel: Understanding the Contexts and Controversies* (Grand Rapids, MI: Baker Academic, 2013); more historically, D. A. Carson et al., eds., *Justification and Variegated Nomism*, 2 vols. (Grand Rapids, MI: Baker Academic, 2001–2004).

[22]For example, Richard V. Peace, *Conversion in the New Testament: Paul and the Twelve* (Grand Rapids, MI: Eerdmans, 1999).

[23]David Peterson, *Possessed by God: A New Testament Theology of Sanctification and Holiness*, New Studies in Biblical Theology (Grand Rapids, MI: Eerdmans, 1995).

[24]For example, Ellen Charry's recovery of patristic and other premodern figures (*By the Renewing of Your Minds: The Pastoral Function of Christian Doctrine* [New York: Oxford University Press, 1997]); pastoral interest in Jonathan Edwards; Hauerwas's aforementioned influence; Simon Chan, *Spiritual Theology: A Systematic Study of the Christian Life* (Downers Grove, IL: InterVarsity Press, 1998).

[25]For example, Michael J. Gorman, *Inhabiting the Cruciform God: Kenosis, Justification, and Theosis in Paul's Narrative Soteriology* (Grand Rapids, MI: Eerdmans, 2009).

the Catholic one being largely sacramental in nature. Yet their classic underpinnings challenge contemporary Protestants who have become more aware of patristic Christology. If early arguments for the Son's full divinity tie salvation tightly to the incarnation—God taking on humanity in Christ so that believers might take on the divine nature in him—then salvation cannot solely consist in an atoning transaction accomplished by a human sacrifice (however flawless) on the cross. Such transactional myopia is actually not the classic Protestant view, but popular aberrations need correction: if Christ's full divinity is soteriologically essential, then evangelical theologies must more fully integrate incarnation and atonement, correspondingly relating salvation's end to the fullness of bearing the divine image.

As *theosis* rises in Protestant prominence, however, the communal embrace of humanity in the incarnation and the cosmic reach of its implications have elicited critique of limited notions of glorification. Sometimes it seems as if spiritual life and divine likeness do not involve the social, earthly dimensions of created humanity but instead transcend those tempting obstacles. Few theologies say as much, but many in Western traditions live as such. Again, popular aberrations need correction: *theosis*, the beatific vision, or glorification—by whatever name—is not individualistic, disembodied, passive, eternal gazing on the divine essence after the present universe has been annihilated. Against

such assumptions, based on texts such as 2 Peter 3, there has been increasing biblical-theological emphasis on new creation and historical-theological emphasis on resurrection. In light of Christ's incarnation and his resurrection as the firstfruits of ours, true Christian teaching resists an unhealthy dualism between the material and the spiritual.[26] Rather than escaping from the body, community, and the cosmos, Christians wait in hope for God to make all things new. Yet such an emphasis introduces further critique of Western soteriological blind spots.

INTERNAL AND EXTERNAL CRITIQUE

For all their variety, Western accounts of salvation strive for some comprehensiveness by encompassing past, present, and future. Regarding the past, forgiveness of sin initiates new life; regarding the present, transforming grace works that new identity into patterns of living; regarding the future, the fullness of eternal life involves bodily resurrection and complete personal renewal in the joyful immediacy of God's presence. These soteriologies encompass the full history of human lives in this way, but particular persons are their focus. What therefore do they neglect?

The answer of some classically liberal and nearly all liberationist theologies, whether in the West or abroad—as well as other indigenous theologies from the Majority World—involves the gospel's sociopolitical and cosmic dimensions.[27] To mention a very concrete example, conservative Western soteriologies speak of "justification" and

---

[26]Illustrating this emphasis are J. Richard Middleton and N. T. Wright, among others in biblical studies; historical works such as Carolyn Walker Bynum, *The Resurrection of the Body in Western Christianity, 200–1336* (New York: Columbia University Press, 1995); widespread Reformed worldview thinking in Christian higher education; and the account of the resurrection's ethical implications in Oliver O'Donovan, *Resurrection and Moral Order: An Outline for Evangelical Ethics*, 2nd ed. (Grand Rapids, MI: Eerdmans, 1994).

[27]In conference dialogue, Jules Martínez-Olivieri plausibly suggested that liberationist theology is a sufficiently established tradition, even in the West, to be included in the first section of this chapter—with its theme running along the lines of "salvation as historical experience." The reason for keeping the present arrangement is that each of the Western traditions sketched above has one or more church denominations distinctly named in association with its originating soteriology. By contrast, liberationist theologies suffuse various churches but have not claimed any particular, major denomination as their own.

"righteousness" rather than "justice." What a difference such connotations make![28] Accordingly, traditional accounts narrowly construe salvation's future, overemphasizing personal destiny in disembodied, individualistic, and unearthly ways. Additionally, they ignore their own contextual character, applying adjectives only to other soteriologies—as if other indigenous accounts are syncretistic or at least situated whereas the West's are just fundamentally scriptural.

Traditional reactions to such critiques can be grudging or dismissive. Although evangelical Protestant theologians have begun to address the gospel's corollary matters of systemic evil and structural sin, those efforts have been sufficiently late and modest that the issues remain barely acknowledged at the popular level.[29] Corresponding soteriologies remain personally focused. Similarly, though professional or episcopal Orthodox theologies may have a slightly more cosmic focus, national and popular features of church life complicate any claim regarding soteriological holism. Catholic soteriology, meanwhile, made liberation theology possible but also necessary.

The Catholic response to liberation theology has been complex. On occasion the Vatican has disciplined figures within that movement officially, while more often resisting aspects of its perspective. Yet the Vatican clearly adopted much liberationist critique of late modern global capitalism along with increased emphasis on God's embrace of the poor, while most liberationist figures remain in good churchly standing.

Much liberation theology appealed to the Bible for its broader account of sin and salvation, with the exodus as a starting point plus the prophets and Gospels as additional support.

Conservative critique addressed liberation theology's biblical priorities and proportions, often regarding what is not said more than what is. Official Vatican critique addressed Marxist theory and revolutionary practice as much as anything else. Still other critique came from seemingly more sympathetic quarters. Native Americans, among other indigenous or First Nations groups, faulted the exodus paradigm for failing to address its corollary, the conquest. This worry is not just conceptual but historical: the conquest of Canaan became a paradigm for European colonizers in America.[30] More broadly, postcolonial theorists critique liberation theologies for redeeming aspects of Scripture as if they were authoritative; the very notion of biblical authority is allegedly oppressive, if not most or all biblical content. By their own acknowledgment, though, such postcolonial thinkers frequently are not pursuing Christian theology but another enterprise that, despite its importance, must be seen in external rather than internal terms.[31]

Liberationist critique of traditional Western soteriologies originated among Majority World oppressed peoples, at priestly and popular levels. Soon liberationist models arose among marginalized groups within the West, as black theologies illustrate. Feminist theologies, with their womanist (emerging from black women) and

---

[28]An example mentioned by C. René Padilla in personal conversation.

[29]For example, Michael O. Emerson and Christian Smith, *Divided by Faith: Evangelical Religion and the Problem of Race in America* (New York: Oxford University Press, 2001), profiling the "cultural toolkit" with which evangelicals contribute to racialization.

[30]As detailed, for example, in Sacvan Bercovitch, "The Typology of America's Mission," *American Quarterly* 30, no. 2 (1978): 135-55.

[31]See especially the work of R. S. Sugirtharajah, surveyed by Daniel J. Treier, *Introducing Theological Interpretation of Scripture: Recovering a Christian Practice* (Grand Rapids, MI: Baker Academic, 2008), chap. 6. But note the evangelical contribution of Kay Higuera Smith et al., eds., *Evangelical Postcolonial Conversations: Global Awakenings in Theology and Praxis* (Downers Grove, IL: IVP Academic, 2014).

mujerista (emerging from Latin American women) descendants, further illustrate the complexity of marginalization and oppression: they appropriate earlier liberationist elements while pursuing further liberation from aspects of those very movements. Various liberationist concerns now vie for influence in mainline Protestant and progressive Catholic circles. The complexity is illustrated in the interface with inter-religious dialogue: Should contextual theology in southern Asia appropriate mainstream Hindu notions for the sake of dialogue, or side with Dalit persons for the sake of liberation?

Naming such complexities must not distract us from the central critique at issue. Traditionalist Western soteriologies apparently focus so much on the gospel's personal benefits, in particular concerning an individual's eternal destiny, that they neglect its communal and cosmic, perhaps even bodily, dimensions. Traditionalists find this personal focus emerging naturally from biblical texts. Hence we face this question: Are there lines of biblical teaching that widen soteriology's focus, while fitting alongside the personal aspects in the rest of the picture? Or do those other lines of biblical teaching generate a competing soteriological picture that minimizes or even lacks personal salvation?

BIBLICAL REFORM?

Such questions about traditional soteriologies and alternative possibilities probably inform the apocalyptic readings of Paul mentioned previously, and almost certainly elicit the aforementioned interest in biblical corpora beyond

Pauline theology: Jesus in the Gospels bearing the healing kingdom of God in person; catholic epistles calling for moral transformation and addressing its cosmic context (which, incidentally, Paul addresses too!); the exodus and other Old Testament paradigms such as the Jubilee fostering hope for liberation and justice; and the prophets denouncing the injustice, individualism, and idolatry of the covenant people's soteriological status quo. These biblical resources—and theological resources stemming from existing Majority World interest in such scriptural teaching—are deep and wide.

The remainder of this soteriological overview can only hint at one modest suggestion concerning the new covenant and its context of the new creation. The basis of this suggestion lies in the significance of the new covenant for the traditional focus on personal salvation. Jeremiah 31:31-34, not least in its use by Hebrews (Heb 8:7-13), presents a twofold focus: forgiveness of sins and transforming knowledge of God—loosely but dogmatically put, justification and sanctification. Even contemporary readings of Paul, with their communal focus, recognize the importance of these concepts for creating God's covenant people as a new humanity in Christ.

Simultaneously, given extensive recent concern over supersessionism, the new covenant is important for keeping Christian soteriology anchored in the hopes of Israel's Scriptures—resisting appeals to Jesus Christ that would replace Old Testament faith with a merely human revolutionary program or a misguided churchly one.[32] Far too often, Jews have needed liberation

---

[32]As defined by R. Kendall Soulen, "According to this teaching [supersessionism], God chose the Jewish people after the fall of Adam in order to prepare the world for the coming of Jesus Christ, the Savior. After Christ came, however, the special role of the Jewish people came to an end and its place was taken by the church, the new Israel" (*The God of Israel and Christian Theology* [Minneapolis: Fortress, 1996], 1-2). Racially anti-Semitic, and religiously anti-Judaic, forms of supersessionism leave Christians much to regret and repent for. New Testament claims about covenantal change are more complex, though, attempting to appeal in an internal sense to Israel's Old Testament hope.

from oppressive Christianity's theological roots. So, however we construe the creation of a new humanity in Christ, Christians dare not lose the biblical and loving particularity of God's covenant history with Israel.

The new covenant is biblically important, moreover, for theologically integrating divine initiative and human transformation. Atonement—initially and vitally involving forgiveness of sin—depends on what God alone does in self-giving love. The resulting sanctification of God's people has both initial and ultimate dimensions that are divinely accomplished, plus an ongoing dimension that is divinely enabled. Yet that ongoing dimension, despite only being realized in the ultimate fullness of divine presence, is our very human calling: becoming holy as God is. These are not the only dimensions of new-covenant saving hope, but they anchor such hope in loving divine initiative rather than human self-help— whether individual or communal or revolutionary or systemic. At the same time, the Old Testament prophets refuse to allow forgiven persons to wallow in idolatrous brokenness, as if continually calling on God with blood-stained hands. Judgment begins with the household of God, whose new covenant members must call on the Lord out of genuinely contrite hearts—not complacent appeals to a supposedly privileged position.

Admittedly, a comprehensive account of new-covenant saving hope is impossible in this space. Yet, if the soteriological importance of that hope has been established, then we may turn briefly to its content. For that content the Isaianic new-creation and new-exodus passages, which shaped Jesus' self-understanding and prominent

New Testament themes, would surely deserve substantial attention. They indicate that Jesus' presentation of the divine reign inaugurates the fulfillment of Jewish hopes regarding bodily healing, communal restoration, and creational shalom. The New Testament is replete with newness: Jesus called for new wineskins to hold the new covenant's new teaching, new commandment, new name, new song, and so forth.[33]

In suggesting the Old Testament prophetic context of new creation for scriptural reform of the new covenant's overly personal application, the remaining task is to highlight broader soteriological elements in Jeremiah 31. Jeremiah 31:1 immediately sets the end of this saving hope in a communal context: God living with a restored, unified covenant people. As ensuing verses such as Jeremiah 31:5 indicate, restoration will delight this people in the fruit of the land. In Jeremiah 31:6 they go to worship as a people, not just individuals. Jeremiah 31:8 includes marginal persons in this joy: the blind, the lame, and pregnant women. No outdated social markers or ritual boundaries of cleanliness need keep anyone from joining in worship. In Jeremiah 31:9 the water of repentant tears gives way to physical streams and smooth paths. Radiant joy over creation's good things embraces not just the land's abundance but also animals in Jeremiah 31:12. The cosmic blessings of new-covenant hope appear in the freedom with which the text uses physical imagery to convey holistic, even spiritual, flourishing. The restored joy in Jeremiah 31:13 and abundant provision in Jeremiah 31:14 affect every possible group in the community.

Jeremiah 31:15-22 indicates that repentance is vital to the promised restoration and the new reality it brings. Colin Gunton helps to

---

[33]Carl B. Hoch Jr., *All Things New: The Significance of Newness for Biblical Theology* (Grand Rapids, MI: Baker, 1996).

explain what is at stake: God's saving renewal of creation—as full-orbed as it will be—must begin by addressing sinful humanity because our misdirected and aggregated wills are the crux of the problem.[34] We are those who turn God's good creation into a source of idols, whose idolatry warps human cultures into systemic bearers of injustice and manifestations of broken relationships, and whose fearful and rapacious self-interest harms all that God lovingly made.

Back to Jeremiah 31, God shows particular interest in the disadvantaged according to Jeremiah 31:25-26, where weary laborers are promised refreshment. The fecundity and flourishing of people and animals in Jeremiah 31:27-28 are not inimical to the personal accountability in Jeremiah 31:29-30. For the new covenant in Jeremiah 31:31-34 makes people right with God and new on the inside, inaugurating the covenant community and creation's full healing. God appeals to creation in Jeremiah 31:35-37 as the reassuring basis of promised restoration: as surely as God lovingly made and sustains all things, so God promises to make the people new. Whatever the debated ecclesiological and eschatological implications, hope of new-covenant restoration for the covenant people takes physical form in a remade, ever sacred city of Jerusalem.

CONCLUSION

Even this brief overview of Jeremiah 31 underscores that the new-covenant context of new creation should be more prominent than Western soteriologies suggest. Many recent biblical debates and traditional dogmatic concerns over personal justification and sanctification still have a significant place in that framework. But then

we can distinguish their initially prominent, even somewhat central, dogmatic place from their becoming so central that they exclude other soteriological concerns as rivals. The communal and cosmic dimensions of God's new-covenant promises integrate Pauline theology and the rest of the New Testament more holistically. Attention to the new covenant further means reckoning with the Old Testament Scriptures, and thus Israel's identity and hope, more adequately.

One way of engaging the Majority World perspectives reflected elsewhere in this volume goes beyond framing them merely in terms of alternative concepts, differing contexts, and critique of or even opposition to dominant Western patterns. All of those elements may be prominent. Yet Majority World accounts often provide examples of the narrative theology for which Western intellectuals have been calling—but with rather modest results of their own. By contrast, other chapters in the present volume frequently provide narrative density to problematic Western readings of the Bible—both those that have been directly colonizing and others that have myopically produced unintended consequences. At minimum, Majority World theologies put problematic aspects of dominant traditions under a narrative searchlight that can also highlight alternative ways of engaging biblical soteriology. At maximum, Majority World theologies raise challenging questions about the very conceptual forms dominating Western traditions, given their systematic aspirations. And Majority World theologies help us to imagine more concretely what the fullness of salvation might look like in particular human lives, communities, and local contexts.[35]

---

[34]Colin E. Gunton, *The Triune Creator: A Historical and Systematic Study*, Edinburgh Studies in Constructive Theology (Grand Rapids, MI: Eerdmans, 1998), especially 168.

[35]For a noteworthy North American example, see David H. Kelsey, *Imagining Redemption* (Louisville: Westminster John Knox, 2005).

The communal and cosmic dimensions of the biblical hope for a new creation underscore not only the context for salvation's personal dimensions and their complementary divine promises, but ultimately the fullness of Christian hope. They force us to reckon with the plight of so many people and other creatures in God's world—neither indulging in self-justifying escapism, nor despairing of change, nor arrogating to ourselves another gospel of human making.

God has promised a new creation starting with a new humanity—and that renewal begins with my own heart. But it does not end there: God renews my heart not only to receive forgiveness, return loving worship, and bear grateful witness. This renewal also frees me from bondage—to my idolatrous self and other powers—so that I may learn to love all my neighbors and thereby participate in the healing of all creation.

FURTHER READING

Catechism of the Catholic Church. Washington, DC: U.S. Catholic Conference, 1997.

Demarest, Bruce. *The Cross and Salvation.* Foundations of Evangelical Theology. Wheaton, IL: Crossway, 1997.

Hill, Charles E., and Frank A. James III, eds. *The Glory of the Atonement: Biblical, Theological, and Practical Perspectives.* Downers Grove, IL: InterVarsity Press, 2004.

Luther, Martin. *The Bondage of the Will.* Translated by J. I. Packer and O. R. Johnston. Old Tappan, NJ: Revell, 1957.

McCormack, Bruce L., ed. *Justification in Perspective: Historical Developments and Contemporary Challenges.* Grand Rapids, MI: Baker Academic, 2006.

McKnight, Scot. *The King Jesus Gospel: The Original Good News Revisited.* Grand Rapids, MI: Zondervan, 2011.

Oden, Thomas C., ed. *The Justification Reader.* Grand Rapids, MI: Eerdmans, 2002.

Stackhouse, John G., Jr., ed. *What Does It Mean to Be Saved? Broadening Evangelical Horizons of Salvation.* Grand Rapids, MI: Baker Academic, 2002.

Stott, John R. W. *The Cross of Christ.* Downers Grove, IL: InterVarsity Press, 1986.

Tidball, Derek, David Hilborn, and Justin Thacker, eds. *The Atonement Debate: Papers from the London Symposium on the Theology of Atonement.* Grand Rapids, MI: Zondervan, 2008.

26

TELLING OUR STORIES

SALVATION IN THE AFRICAN CONTEXT

Emily J. Choge Kerama

AFRICA IS RAVAGED by many ills—Ebola, HIV/AIDs, malaria, hunger, and extreme conditions of poverty—yet it is in Africa that the shift of gravity in the spread of the gospel has moved. This raises questions: What is the understanding of salvation in the African context? Why is there such a widespread response to the gospel? Is salvation seen to deal with these existential situations, or does it provide an escape from misfortune? What are the stories behind these two contrasting pictures of Africa? What are the stories behind the success, and what are those to the contrary? Are we able to imagine a future for salvation in the African context as it encounters powers and principalities? What type of salvation will grapple with these powers? This chapter seeks to bring out a holistic understanding of salvation in the African context. What does it mean to be saved in an African context?

I was born into an African Christian home. My father was a first-generation African Christian, and my mother was a second-generation African Christian. The first missionaries had come to the coast of present-day Kenya in 1844. Dr. John Ludwig Krapf and Dr. John Rebmann landed at the Kenyan coast in 1844,

and they did some work among the coastal people without much success. My maternal grandfather found himself at the Kenyan coast and was converted to Christianity by Church Missionary Society missionaries in the early 1920s. When he went back to his homeland, he invited the Church Missionary Society missionaries to come to his home area in Nandi in the western part of Kenya. My father was among the first to join the Christian school and church started in the 1940s through the influence of my grandfather. He did not go to school much since he was twenty years old at the time, but he became an evangelist and a teacher of the gospel from that time. He married my mother in the early 1950s, and I was born in November 1959, the third child of my parents.

I was a special child. I was born with a congenital defect that resulted in my left leg ending about six inches above the ground. I did have a right foot, though it was somewhat constricted. This was a challenge to my parents. I remember hearing my father exclaim, "What will become of this child?" In a traditional African setting, a child with disabilities was considered a misfortune, and her birth was interpreted as a curse or a punishment from God. However, because of his faith in Jesus Christ, my father believed in a good God, and he had the assurance that God would one day perform a miracle in my life. I remember he took me to some prayer rallies but nothing happened to my leg. Then he made the decision to take me to a school for girls that had been started by my grandfather. I was six years old at the time. The difficulty was that the boarding school started with standard five (grade five), and I needed to start from standard one. However, through the intervention of African hospitality, the matron and caretaker of the girls' boarding school offered to take me into her home and allowed me to attend the nearby mixed primary school until I could join the boarding school. I lived in her house for four years, and she treated me as one of her children until I was able to go to the boarding school. This changed my life because I was given the opportunity to go to school and also to hear the gospel.

When I was in high school (another school started by missionaries), doctors from the mission hospital in Kijabe came to my school. They examined my leg and recommended that the only way they could correct the problem was to do an amputation. I was fourteen years old. The surgery was performed in December 1974, and I went back to school and walked with crutches for about six months. This did not interrupt my studies. Then I was fitted with a crude artificial leg—no foot, and just plain wood. I think I saw a character in *Pirates of the Caribbean* with one similar to it. It was not nice, but I was able to walk. Needless to say, I have had so many legs since then that I could display them in a museum to show the technological advancement of orthopedic work in Kenya.

The beauty of it all is that the helpless child who could not walk long distances was provided with basic education, and her father, who had had the courage to defy the African beliefs about curse and misfortune, was able to attend his daughter's graduation in 2004 in Pasadena, California, when he was eighty-four years old. He traveled all the way from Kenya, not knowing much English, so that he could witness the miracle of his daughter. He witnessed not only my graduation but also my running and completing a half marathon with a prosthetic leg. This, I think, is the power of salvation, the power of the gospel to transform the lives of people who are in dire situations like my own and bring them to be seated with princes. This is just amazing for me. I would like to see and hear stories that demonstrate the power of salvation to transform and confront the powers of physical deformity, mental malaise, and all other restrictions that have kept people enslaved in the continent of Africa and the world at large. So what is the existential situation for most people in Kenya? What are the powers and principalities from which they need deliverance and salvation?

SALVATION IN THE AFRICAN CONTEXT

In the area of systematic theology in Africa there has not been much reflection on the experience of salvation from an African perspective. Catholic theologian Agbonkhianmeghe Orobator has written *Theology Brewed in an African Pot*, a work that uses most of the original sources in the African context such as stories, proverbs, myths, and prayers. Orobator writes: "To the African religious worldview, stories and narratives are important elements of this worldview. Without pictures or paintings, narrative accounts were created and transmitted from one generation to the next, telling of the lives, times, and deeds of our forefathers and foremothers."[1] The book is easy to read, and since Orobator gives theology a narrative base it is also very interesting. The only drawback is that he does not include a chapter on salvation per se, but I look at what he says about Christology.[2] There is also a collection of essays, *Issues in African Christian Theology*, that covers a range of subjects in systematic theology, including salvation. This collection is, like African Christian theology itself, a work in progress since, as the editors confess, "Christianity is being translated at high speed into modern African culture in almost every area except theology."[3] In the area of salvation, I would commend a classic from within the African context by Tokunboh Adeyemo, *Salvation in African Tradition*.[4] But there are not many recent works in the area of salvation. Nevertheless, with regard to deliverance and salvation from spirits and powers in the African context there is much lively activity.[5] I engage with these works with regard to salvation from the powers because this was an area that was neglected by European missionaries when they brought the gospel to Africa, as confessed by a recent missionary:

> The issue of traditional African beliefs in the invisible world has been neglected in the past as if the gospel had nothing to say about it. . . . This was a serious failure in the effective discipling of

new believers. Too often it left them with the impression that the gospel had nothing to say about the invisible world and the menace it represented—apart from the prohibition of all contact with it.[6]

An African theologian confirms the same:

> Unfortunately, many Western missionaries who came to Africa were unaware of the African worldview. Influenced by the philosophies of the age of Enlightenment these missionaries readily dismissed the spirit world as being nothing more than a figment of the imagination. This left most African converts with no biblical teaching in relation to the spirit world, thereby leaving a huge gap in the faith of the African Christian.[7]

Another area where we see lively activity among scholars in Africa is Christology.[8] This shows that in the African context they take seriously the person who is the deliverer or the bearer of salvation. Most African authors show that Africans knew God but they did not know Jesus Christ. Orobator acknowledges, "*Jesu Kristi* has gained popularity on the lips of African Christians. . . . Songs have been written, liturgies composed, and humorous stories told about Jesus in local languages." But he also notes, "Africans' quest for 'who Jesus is for us' cannot be satiated by simple formulas and models developed in foreign cultural contexts." Therefore, there are many names, titles, models, and proposals for

---

[1]Agbonkhianmeghe E. Orobator, SJ, *Theology Brewed in an African Pot: An Introduction to Christian Doctrine from an African Perspective* (Nairobi: Paulines, 2008), 106.

[2]The chapter bears the interesting and appropriate title: "I Said 'God Had a Son,' But I Did Not Say 'He Had a Wife!'"

[3]Samuel Ngewa, Mark Shaw, and Tite Tiénou, eds., *Issues in African Christian Theology* (Nairobi: EAPH, 1998), vii.

[4]Tokunboh Adeyemo, *Salvation in African Tradition* (Nairobi: Evangel, 1979).

[5]See Opoku Onyinah, *Pentecostal Exorcism: Witchcraft and Demonology in Ghana* (Dorchester, UK: Deo, 2012); Kwabena Donkor, ed., *The Church, Culture and Spirits: Adventism in Africa* (Silver Springs, MD: Biblical Research Institute, 2011).

[6]Keith Ferdinando, *The Battle Is God's: Reflecting on Spiritual Warfare for African Christians* (Bukuru, Plateau State, Nigeria: ACTS, 2012), 6.

[7]Charles Salala, "The World of the Spirits: Basukuma Traditional Religion and Biblical Christianity," in Ngewa, Shaw, and Tiénou, *Issues in African Christian Theology*, 137.

[8]Many books have been written on Christology in Africa, including the following: Kwame Bediako, *Jesus in Africa: The Christian Gospel in African History and Experience* (Akropong, Ghana: Regnum, 2000); J. N. K. Mugambi and Laurenti Magesa, eds., *Jesus in African Christianity: Experimentation and Diversity in African Christology* (Nairobi: Acton, 1998); Charles Nyamiti, *Christ Our Ancestor* (Harare, Zimbabwe: Mambo, 1986).

Jesus in the African context, "the ancestor, the diviner, the traditional healer, the chief, the guest, the life giver, family, friend, loved one, member, initiator, mediator . . . liberator, black messiah." One of the most interesting titles recorded by Orobator is one coined by a prison inmate: "Jesus the bulldozer."[9] And now we look at an attempt to formulate a creed from the African context.

THE NICENE CREED

There has not been much engagement with the Nicene Creed from an African perspective on a scholarly theological basis. I found one essay on the Apostles' Creed, and it shows that Africans appropriate the creeds as part of their worship.[10] Since my father was an Anglican priest and I grew up most of my life in that church, I was exposed to the Nicene Creed in my mother tongue. The things I remember most in that prayer book were the prayer of Chrysostom and the Nicene Creed. When I read them in my mother tongue, I had no idea that I was connecting with the historic faith of the church. Later, when I studied for my master's of divinity at a seminary in Nairobi, I realized that these were important people in the church and that the creed was historic, though there had been many challenges and controversies about the selection of its words.

What I can say about this creed and salvation is that it shows that we as the people of God are one people through the ages, and we should not be divided by schisms that have rocked the church across the years. The early church fathers formulated this creed so that they could be united in their profession of faith, and we can share in their struggles regarding what it meant

to confess Christ as Savior in that Greek and Latin context. With regard to the Nicene Creed in the African context I have found one theological reflection. It is called the Maasai Creed, and the first two articles are as follows:

> We believe in the one High God, who out of love created the beautiful world and everything good in it. He created man and wanted man to be happy in the world. God loves the world and every nation and tribe on the earth. We have known this High God in darkness, and now we know him in the light. God promised in the book of his word, the Bible, that he would save the world and all the nations and tribes.
>
> We believe that God made good his promise by sending his Son, Jesus Christ, a man in the flesh, a Jew by tribe, born poor in a little village, who left his home and was always on safari doing good, curing people by the power of God, teaching about God and man, showing the meaning of religion is love. He was rejected by his people, tortured and nailed hands and feet to a cross, and died. He lay buried in the grave, but the hyenas did not touch him, and on the third day, he rose from the grave. He ascended to the skies. He is the Lord.[11]

This is the Jesu Kristi whom people have experienced as the Lord. And they turn to him in their troubles and in turn give him names such as "Jesus the bulldozer."

THE SAD STORIES OF AFRICA'S EXISTENTIAL SITUATION

In order to give Jesus the opportunity to bulldoze the problems of Africa, we need to examine some of the worrying trends in the continent. While there are stories of success such as mine, it is important to hear other stories so that we

[9]Orobator, *Theology Brewed in an African Pot*, 72-73, 76-77.
[10]Eshetu Abate, "Confessing Christ in the Apostles' Creed," in Ngewa, Shaw, and Tiénou, *Issues in African Christian Theology*, 175-85.
[11]Vincent Donovan, *Christianity Rediscovered* (Maryknoll, NY: Orbis, 2003), 158.

can draft a story of salvation that will be able to speak to the true picture of the African situation.

Children with disabilities. I was inspired to share my story in this chapter because on October 24, 2015, I went to visit a group of mothers whose children have spina bifida and hydrocephalus. October 25 is International Spina Bifida and Hydrocephalus Day, so these parents had come to spend the night together to encourage and support one another. I am chair of the advisory board of Bethany Kids, an organization that helps provide surgical interventions to children with these conditions in Africa, working mainly in Kenya. That day I needed to talk to these parents and children. Seeing them reminded me of my condition, and I could imagine where many of them lived: places with no running water, no paved roads, and very dire conditions of poverty. I shared my story with them. You could have heard a pin drop! They were so attentive and took in every word. At the end, they registered their appreciation for me sharing my life story with them. They were touched by the story and wondered how we could get a school for them so that their children could learn without stigma and discrimination. One of the challenges their children face is urinary and bowel incontinence.

I did not have an answer for them, but I told them that our organization had been trying to get money to expand the children's hospital in Kijabe so that it could take in more children and perform more surgeries. We had not even thought of schools for them. In Kenya, there are two such schools that have been started by the Salvation Army, in Thika and Kisumu. Bethany Kids has been improving the restroom facilities in Thika. From this request, it is evident that there is a need

for schools like this all over the country. How can the church preach the gospel of salvation to these parents and children with disabilities without addressing such pressing needs?

Growing individualism. Conditions of children with disabilities are made worse by the growing individualism in the African culture. Africa in the past was known for its communal culture and worldview. One famous quote from a Kenyan philosopher, John Mbiti, sums it up this way: "I am because we are, and because we are therefore I am."[12] This strength of community is seen when people are in dire need and there is no cushioning from a social welfare system or social security system. Neighbors, friends, and relatives usually pay for funerals, doctor bills, and weddings. However, this system is slowly being strained, and we can see in urban areas a growing sense of individualism and a narrative of isolationism. We have these high walls that separate one house from another, and people do not seem to know their neighbors anymore. In fact, there are cases where neighbors have been attacked and the closest neighbor does not even know it happened. Thieves and criminals have found this isolation easy to exploit. They come and confront homeowners at the gates of their yards and ask them to drive in. A passerby will not even notice what is happening, thinking that these are visitors accompanying the owner of the house. Now, the government is trying to introduce what is known as the Nyumba Kumi Initiative—that you have to know at least ten of your neighbors. Does the gospel of our salvation have something to say about this story of growing individualism? What should be done to change this narrative of despair?

---

[12]John S. Mbiti, *African Religions and Philosophy* (London: Heinemann, 1969), 108.

Rampant poverty. While there is growing individualism and violence in urban areas, rural areas have not been spared. Many move from rural areas into urban areas, and since they do not get jobs, they swell the population of informal settlements and slum areas. Nairobi is the home of one of the largest slum areas in the world. However, the population continues to grow in certain rural parts of the country (Kisii and Maragoli), and the land continues to dwindle. The land that supported a few people is forced to hold many more people, and the area where food crops used to grow is dwindling. Because of this pressure for land, we are hearing news stories about things that never used to happen in the country. Young people on the coast of Kenya are accusing their parents of witchcraft and hounding them out of their homes so that they can get the land from them. These elderly parents are forced to run to houses of refuge to escape from their children. In parts of the country where the pressure for land is acute, we have also heard of many accusations of witchcraft and gruesome executions without government intervention because the community does not know how to deal with these issues. Does the gospel have something to say to the poor and those who suffer because of false accusations? How does it help us understand the beliefs that misfortunes and deaths are caused by people?

The double-edged sword of young people. Africa is a young continent. Most of the population is under the age of forty-nine, and this has great potential for the development and success of the country. Evangelists have said that the best time to introduce people to the gospel is when they are young. If you enter most of the churches in Kenya, the percentage of young people is really high. What can be done to reach and then keep these young people in the church? What is the gospel that will really get them to commit their lives to God so that they can avoid the ravages of HIV/AIDs, other sexually transmitted diseases, drugs, alcoholism, and crime due to unemployment? One-quarter of those who enter primary school manage to get into high school. The government has tried to introduce free primary education, but the retention is not very effective, and at the end of primary school many are not able to enter high school. So the question is, Where do these young people go? The Kenyan media has exposed some ugly incidences of young people who have been found engaging in irresponsible sex, drugs, and alcohol abuse, which illustrates the temptations young people face. What is the gospel that will resonate with these young people? Is an African understanding of salvation able to confront the narratives of sexual immorality, drug abuse, and alcoholism?

The prosperity gospel. What is being preached in our churches? The health, wealth, and prosperity gospel continues to be taught. The leaders of the church demand that the parishioners "plant a seed" and say they will reap abundantly from God. What we see is the contrast of the wealth of the leaders of such churches and the poverty of the members, who give everything they own to support these leaders. The leaders are very wealthy, and they display all the trappings of such wealth: the latest model cars, expensive homes, and all sorts of luxury items. Most recently a renowned evangelist in Kenya came to my town. Traffic came to a standstill because of adherents who came from far and wide to give allegiance to this "Mighty Prophet of God." The cars that were part of the entourage were the latest and most expensive models, and the display of wealth of this evangelist was absolutely immoral.

Political leaders are not exempt from this type of lifestyle. Once the population has elected them, they use their offices not to serve the electorate who put them there, but to accumulate wealth for themselves. The prophetic edge that religious leaders once provided to political leaders has been dulled because they are doing the same things, so the sheep are without a shepherd in the literal sense. How can the gospel of our salvation confront the challenges of wealth and prosperity?

The threat of international terrorism. In Kenya we not only face internal demons and powers; we also have to contend with the international terrorism that has wreaked havoc within our country. We have faced this since 1998, when the US embassy was bombed, causing suffering and heartache in many lives. In 2013, one of the most gruesome attacks was the hostage-taking at the West Gate Mall in Nairobi, where several people died. The most recent attack was the taking of Garissa University, where we saw innocent young university students being butchered. Kenya is a country of religious pluralism, although the Christian population is the large majority. Christians and Muslims have lived in harmonious relationships in the past, but these attacks have brought suspicion and frustration as people of different faiths have attempted to relate to one another. What is the gospel of our salvation that will facilitate dialogue and not fuel violence in our country? How will we relate to people of other faiths, especially when they are hostile to us?

REVERSING THE STORIES OF SADNESS: FACTORS AFFECTING AFRICA'S RECEPTIVITY TO THE GOSPEL

Having listened to some of the sad stories and conditions within the African continent, we can turn now to the story behind Africa's receptivity to the gospel.

Dependence on God. Africans are notoriously religious. This is evident from the number of churches spread throughout Africa's villages and cities. Even in the primal religions of Africa, every community had a name for God, and when the Bible was translated into these languages the name for God was retained. African theologian Kwame Bediako used to say that the missionaries did not bring God to Africa, but God brought the missionaries to Africa. Orobator notes,

> Anyone coming to Africa for the first time cannot but notice the strong and profound sense of the divine that pervades the ordinary lives of many Africans. Often it has been misrepresented as superstition and fatalism. The awareness of the divine is so strong that you can see, hear, feel, and touch it in the way people talk, behave, even worship, sing and dance.[13]

No wonder there was a response to the gospel that has really been so overwhelming that Christianity has become a non-Western religion. Some of the beliefs and the practices in the Old Testament resonate with those of the African culture. For example, when there was misfortune or they needed to appear before God, the people of the Old Testament offered sacrifices of animals without blemish. Wilbur O'Donovan mentions four or five categories of sacrifice in traditional practice, including propitiatory, substitutionary,

---

[13]Orobator, *Theology Brewed in an African Pot*, 128.

mediatory, communion, and gift sacrifice.[14] There was opportunity for individual and also communal repentance when there had been a misfortune. This resonates in an African context. Sin and salvation are not just personal; they have a communal element. When we break relations with one another, we need to mend those relationships. This means that the corporate aspect of sin and salvation touching the individual is well understood in the African context.

Dependence on each other: The church as the extended family of God. The communal nature of African culture is also one that attracts Africans to the gospel. Salvation is not just individual; it also means bringing one into the community of faith that is known as the church. This relational aspect of the gospel means that people are not alone; they belong, as it were, to an extended family. This is one of the strongest aspects of Christianity that has propelled the spread of the gospel in Africa. Now that the family system has broken up due to modernization and urbanization, the place that most people find a sense of belonging is the church. Whenever there are functions such as funerals, weddings, and other social gatherings, what brings people together is the family of the church. Nowhere is this more strongly expressed than in the churches of the diaspora. Africans faced with the prospect of alienation and disorientation in a new culture that is strange and alien in every way find solace and comfort in the newly established churches among indigenous populations in various parts of the world. Even if members were not strong churchgoers in their home countries, they will go to these church gatherings in order to find support. There they find connection with their roots and culture, and

with this, they are not only able to meet the needs of those who have come to the new country, but also to extend a hand to those back at home.

When my husband and I came for my sabbatical to Atlanta and my mother-in-law passed away in Kenya, we went to the Kenya American Community Church in Marietta and shared our situation. I know and I applaud the African sense of community, but even so the response amazed me. At the end of the service, the pastor called us to the front of the church and told the congregation about our situation—that we had lost our mother and we needed to go back home to bury her. As always, this was unexpected, and we did not have the finances, so he told them to come forward and greet us. As the church members came forward, they gave something small to help us return home to Kenya. Within about twenty minutes, the people of God had raised $1,300 for us, and this was enough in addition to what we already had to take us back home. We were so grateful for this family of God who supported us during this time of need. A strong sense of community is carried over into the new places where Africans go and settle.

Celebration and music. Another conduit that brought African people to listen to the gospel is music and celebration within Christian worship. Africans celebrate with music and dance in all kinds of activities: birth, initiation, marriage, and death. One has to be sent home in style. That the newfound faith had music in its worship enhanced this element of African culture. The traditional hymnbook and the songs in it cannot be recognized when they are sung in indigenous languages. The words have been translated into the languages, but they now

---

[14]Wilbur O'Donovan, *Biblical Christianity in African Perspective* (Carlisle, UK: Paternoster, 1996), 104.

have four or five tunes, depending on the community in which they are sung. One of the songs that I know, "My Hope Is Built on Nothing Less," has five or more tunes. In Kiswahili it has been translated as "Cha Kutumaini Sina." This shows that Kenyans have received these songs and made them their very own. Songs bring out emotions and feelings that cannot be expressed in any other way. In traditional African gatherings, some songs require a call-and-response so that all the people participate in the service. The African Mass within the Catholic Church that incorporates singing and dancing is really an occasion to witness. One theologian notes:

> In Africa, worship is never complete without singing and dancing, otherwise that worship would be considered cold and dead. Every aspect of the liturgical celebration is accompanied by joyful, vocal, and bodily expressions.... A shared belief of many Africans is that anything that is good must necessarily overflow. As one African proverb says, a good pot of okra sauce cannot be confined to the cooking pot with a lid. It must bubble up and overflow.[15]

The translation of the Scriptures into African languages. One thing that has allowed the gospel to make inroads into the African continent is the translation of the Scriptures into African languages. It has preserved the languages and the cultures of the people for whom it has been translated. These translations have been a resource for young people who have gone away to school and therefore would not have been able to know their languages. Thus, the work of Bible Societies in translating the Bible into African languages is invaluable.[16] Students in the universities can study these African lan-

guages, and usually the literature that is most available for study is the Bible. One of the first translations was the Nandi Bible (1938). After twenty years another translation, the Kalenjin Bible, incorporated about ten dialects. A recent translation is the new Nandi Bible. Older people had complained that the combined translation did not quite capture the essence of the language as the original one had.

Provision of a holistic salvation. When missionaries came to Africa they did not divide the temporal and the sacred. They did not just emphasize preaching the gospel and saving souls. At the time the debate about whether the focus should be on the social justice or evangelism was yet to emerge. Evangelism came at the same time as the establishment of mission schools, hospitals, and farming stations. If that had been maintained, the scenario would have been different in Africa. Missionaries knew that they had to minister to the whole person, but today that holistic aspect is not seen. In fact, those who are supposed to minister to people who come to church exploit them instead. However, holistic ministry is something that originally helped Africans be receptive to the gospel.

LESS EMPHASIZED STORIES OF SALVATION

I use the pilgrim motif that runs throughout the Scriptures, particularly in the book of Hebrews, as the metaphor that brings together the neglected aspects of salvation with the stories of success in the African context.

The pilgrim motif in Scripture. The people of God are enjoined to live as pilgrims and exiles in a foreign land. One who exemplifies this life is the father of faith, Abraham. Even in the

---

[15]O'Donovan, *Biblical Christianity*, 135.
[16]See also Bediako, "Understanding African Theology," 65.

Promised Land, he still lived in tents because he was looking for a "city with foundations" whose maker and founder was God (Heb 11:10). The people of Israel were told to embody this attitude even as they showed hospitality to those who were aliens in their land. They needed to remember that they had been aliens and strangers in the land of Egypt and so they were to be kind to strangers. The stories and wise sayings of Africa have much to say about traveling and being a stranger, which exposes one to danger but at the same time opens one to the hospitality and generosity of hosts. One such saying is *safari ni taabu* (travel and you will encounter many challenges), but another one counters this: *safari uone mengi* (travel and you will see much). One proverb from Ghana notes: "One who has not traveled thinks that the mother's cooking is the best." All these sayings and proverbs give guidance, so that we know that we are not self-sufficient in our journey of salvation. Rather, we need God, we need one another, and we need courage so that we can overcome the challenges that we meet on the way.

So, as we look at aspects of salvation that we should pay attention to in the African context, the pilgrim motif helps to tie all these things together. The first aspect of this is that we need to emphasize the identity of Christ as the pilgrim par excellence, who for the joy that was set before him endured the cross (Heb 12:2-3). Therefore, the church in Africa needs to proclaim the lordship of Jesus Christ over powers and principalities.

This Christ who is proclaimed in the book of Hebrews is higher than the angels, than Moses, and than the sacrificial system of the Old Testament. This means that Jesus Christ can deal with the world of powers and principalities that have been predominant in the African worldview. One author notes:

> The issue of traditional African beliefs in the world has been neglected in the past as if the gospel had nothing to say about it. Part of the reason for this is that in the nineteenth and twentieth centuries the good news of Jesus Christ was brought to Africa largely by western missionaries. In many cases their worldview no longer had much place for the notion of sorcerers and very little place for spirits either, despite abundant biblical testimony to their existence. Consequently, they had given little—if any—thought to these matters even though they are of central importance in the African conceptions of reality. They had no biblical responses to the pressing questions of their new converts, because they never had to face those questions in their own experience. . . . Failure to address the issue of witches and spirits from a solidly Christian perspective left a whole area of life unredeemed—excluded from the saving power of the gospel, so that new believers felt obliged to use the remedies they had trusted in before they knew Christ.[17]

The need for the proclamation of Christ over these powers is very evident in that recently there have been accusations of witchcraft against women, children, and older people. With the rapid social and economic changes and the breakdown of the family structure, it has been notable that even children have accused their parents of witchcraft so that they can inherit their lands. As I mentioned previously, this has been seen in the coastal part of Kenya. This aspect of the lordship of Christ cannot be overemphasized, as these practices are designed mainly to alleviate the sufferings of human beings harassed by spirits. Though Africans believe in a supreme being, they also have myths to

---

[17]Ferdinando, *Battle Is God's*, 6-7.

show that God has withdrawn from human affairs, so that people are constantly harassed by and threatened by all sorts of enemies, including spirits and sorcerers. Keith Ferdinando writes,

> They must defend themselves, or seek to appease or destroy their attackers. But the Biblical worldview while recognizing the existence of spirits and sorcerers as well as the harm they do to human beings, understands them in the context of a cosmos ruled by a sovereign God who is intimately involved in his creation and who is good and constantly accessible to his own people.[18]

But the proclamation of Christ over the powers should not be restricted to mystical powers or unseen powers; it also needs to confront political power that allows rampant corruption, nepotism, and various forms of social injustice. In the past the church has played a role in being the voice of the voiceless even as the powers of politics suppressed their voices. This was the case from the 1970s to the early 1990s in Kenya. There were leaders of great repute in the church such as Bishop Henry Okullu, Bishop Alexander Muge, and Bishop David Gitari. In South Africa, the church played a role in bringing liberation from the apartheid system. It is not clear where these voices have gone or whether there are new leaders who can take the place of these fearless leaders and their prophetic proclamation.

The church that transcends ethnic and national barriers. Another aspect that needs to be emphasized in the proclamation of the gospel of salvation in the African context is that the people of God transcend all national and ethnic barriers. This is also a strand that comes from the pilgrim motif. There are many "one another" exhortations in the book of Hebrews that show that Christians are not indi-

vidualistic, lone-ranger people. The communal element is well emphasized, and it finds resonance within the African setting. However, what has worked against this is that when the gospel was brought into the African environment, various denominational bodies came to different parts of the country. For example, in Kenya, the Methodist Church is predominant in the eastern part of the country, the Presbyterian Church is foremost in central Kenya, and the Anglican Church is in parts of western Kenya. This means that the church is divided according to various tribal and ethnic communities. It has meant that sometimes the church has been tied to political interests rather than being loyal to brothers and sisters of another community and Jesus Christ. In 2007 and 2008, there were tribal clashes in Kenya, and one church building was burned. This should have caused outrage, but instead one could see that loyalties to ethnic communities were stronger than loyalty to the body of Jesus Christ. Focusing on interdependence will counteract the negative narratives of individualism, the neglect of vulnerable children and youth, and even care for the stranger in the face of terrorist activities.

Hospitality as a mark of pilgrims. One of the strong aspects of African culture that needs to be incorporated into the church is hospitality. This was built into the African system from time immemorial. Africa supported the family of Jacob in Egypt, and they were hosted there until Israel became a great nation (Gen 46:3; 47:13; Ex 1:5-7). Jesus in his early years was hosted in Africa when his parents had to escape the wrath of the evil King Herod (Mt 2:13-15). The word *mgeni* for "stranger" and "guest" in Africa is the

---

[18]Ferdinando, *Battle Is God's*, 45-46.

same word. Thus, strangers are to be welcomed as guests. But in recent years some people have noted that such hospitality has become a museum relic. There have been incidences of xenophobic attacks in various parts of the continent, such as those recently in South Africa. One wonders how the practice of hospitality can be recovered. Since this is a central virtue in Scripture right from the beginning, we have to restore this as a key component in the African church. There are many resources within the African setting that give us guidance on how we can practice hospitality in the midst of modern challenges. One such saying is "mgeni siku ya kwanza, siku ya pili mpe Jembe" (a guest is only a guest for two days; on the third day give him a hoe). The wisdom in this saying is that the efforts of the stranger and the host are combined to make provision for the community. It is not just one-sided. All work together for the good of the community. It means that even as Christians live in their communities, they will make a difference like the early Christians made. A second-century Christian writer comments on the effectiveness of such a stance: "They lived in their homeland as a foreign land and in their foreign land as their homeland" (Epistle to Diognetus 5.5).

CONCRETE STORIES OF HOLISTIC SALVATION THAT AFRICA NEEDS

The ministry of Bethany Kids. I began this chapter with my story of the power of the gospel and how it transformed my father to transcend the prejudices and the fear of misfortune and curses until I experienced that power and became an agent of transformation. I have also shared the story of children with disabilities who are helped by Bethany Kids. This is a ministry that started in a mission hospital. A missionary doctor, Dr. Richard Bransford, was inspired to start this ministry because his daughter Bethany was born with spina bifida. The hospital treating these children at Kijabe was very small. Dr. Bransford started training surgeons from all over Africa so that they could also help such children. The work has now expanded to Sierra Leone, Uganda, and Madagascar. Mobile clinics doing follow-up work go to various parts of Kenya visiting children and giving them help. In these places, they are able to identify new cases and refer them to Kijabe. It is indeed a ministry that is giving hope to Africa's children. This is part of the healing ministry that Jesus gave his disciples to do, and this aspect of salvation is vital for the church in Africa.

The ministry of the Africa Christian Initiation Program. The Africa Christian Initiation Program is a ministry that some professors from Moi University started in 2004 to respond to the needs of young people in the community. I mentioned earlier the rich resource of youth in Africa. In traditional Africa, rites of passage were very important in the transition from one stage of life to another. With the coming of the gospel, however, most of these rites, especially female circumcision, were considered barbaric and condemned. No effort was made to learn what roles and functions these practices played in the community. One thing such rituals did was transmit values and teachings. Because of the rapid changes to which the community has been subjected, it was found that many young people were not prepared to face life's challenges. They were turning to drugs and alcohol, and many were at risk of being infected with HIV/AIDS. Adolescence is a crucial stage in the development of a person, and Africans had recognized this, which is why they had rites of passage.

A group of women came together and put together a program. They decided they would invite young people and their parents. The boys would be offered circumcision, and they would be operated on by a doctor. They rented a boarding school facility because this was done when students were on school holidays. The boys healed for a week while being taught the lessons of what it means to be a man as well as being mentored by model young and older people. The following week the girls were invited, and they joined the boys in class. They were taught important things such as health, how to take care of their bodies, appreciation for their physical bodies, how to avoid peer pressure related to drugs and alcohol, time management, and other important information for this stage of their life. The training manual that came out of this is titled *My Life Starting Now: Knowledge and Skills for Young Adolescents*, by Lucy Y. Steinitz and Eunice Karanja Kamaara. We have been doing this for the past ten years, and we are soon going to launch a study to evaluate how effective this program has been in transforming the lives of young people. This is part of the holistic salvation that Africa needs. It recognizes the values of the practices and traditions of African people and incorporates them into the modern system for the good of the people of God.

CONCLUSION

The gospel has the power to transform lives; as Paul notes in Romans 1:16, "it is the power of God for the salvation of everyone who believes; first for the Jew, then for the Gentile." I have highlighted such examples, and I believe there are many more instances in the whole of the continent. However, there are powers in the African continent that, if not confronted and tamed for the good of the gospel, will be harmful and detrimental to the social, physical, spiritual, and economic welfare of the people of God. Among such powers are the traditions and practices that exclude those with disabilities, women, and children. There are great stories in this continent of how these powers and principalities have been overcome, and these stories need to be heard and celebrated. Armed with the resources of the pilgrim motif from the Bible and enriched by the practices of hospitality, we will be able to hear stories such as those of Bethany Kids, who have transcended the odds for those with disabilities. There are stories of how practices have been transformed into avenues of blessing rather than a curse for Africa's children. Such is the story of the Africa Christian Initiation Program, which is transforming and giving hope, salvation, and life in abundance to Africa's children.

FURTHER READING

Donkor, Kwabena, ed. *The Church Culture and Spirits: Adventism in Africa.* Silver Spring, MD: Institute of Biblical Research, 2011.

Elolia, Samuel K. *Religion, Conflict and Democracy in Modern Africa: The Role of Civil Society in Political Engagement.* Eugene, OR: Wipf & Stock, 2012.

Ferdinando, Keith. *The Battle Is God's: Reflecting on Spiritual Warfare for African Believers.* Bukuru, Plateau State, Nigeria: ACTS, 2012.

Katongole, Emmanuel M. *A Future for Africa: Critical Essays in Christian Social Imagination*. Scranton, PA: University of Scranton Press, 2005.

Ngewa, Samuel, Mark Shaw, and Tite Tiénou, eds. *Issues in African Christian Theology*. Nairobi: East Africa Educational Publishers, 1998.

O'Donovan, Wilbur. *Biblical Christianity in African Perspective*. Carlisle, UK: Paternoster, 1996.

Onyinah, Opoku. *Pentecostal Exorcism: Witchcraft and Demonology in Ghana*. Dorset, UK: Deo, 2012.

Orobator, Agbonkhianmeghe E. *Theology Brewed in an African Pot: An Introduction to Christian Doctrine from an African Perspective*. Nairobi: Paulines, 2008.

27

LUKE 4:18-19 AND SALVATION

MARGINALIZATION OF WOMEN IN THE PENTECOSTAL CHURCH IN BOTSWANA

Rosinah Mmannana Gabaitse

LUKE 4:18-19 HAS ALWAYS been interpreted as Jesus' roadmap. In the Pentecostal context in Botswana, the text is taken seriously, as it announces Jesus' mission, which was later to become the program of the church through the Holy Spirit. The interpretation of this text, however, has always been highly spiritualized, emphasizing spiritual blindness, spiritual poverty, and spiritual oppression and release, with little or no focus on sociopolitical and physical blindness, poverty, and oppression. Spiritualizing texts is one of the characteristics of Pentecostal biblical interpretation. To a large extent this influences the way Pentecostals deal with the marginalization of women in its various manifestations. Oftentimes, the marginalization of women is minimized, ignored, or highly spiritualized. While the marginalization of women is ignored, women in Botswana and Africa in general experience dual patriarchies from indigenous cultures and the Pentecostal church. Since patriarchy is oppressive, women are denied the

right to experience the joy of holistic salvation on earth. In this chapter I seek to demonstrate that in Luke 4:18-19 Jesus was not only offering to release people from spiritual blindness, poverty, and oppression. He also offered people physical and social release from any system of oppression such as patriarchy. This chapter begins by offering a brief overview of Luke 4:18-19 in order to establish that salvation is holistic. I move on to discuss how patriarchy within Pentecostal hermeneutics and theology together with the patriarchy from indigenous cultures denies Pentecostal women the experience of holistic salvation.[1] I will further demonstrate that Luke 4:18-19 affirms that complete salvation is available and possible in the social world.

As a matter of interpretation and agenda, some interpreters of Luke 4:18-19 spiritualize the poor, the blind, and the oppressed and ignore the social aspect of the text, while others give the text both spiritual and social dimensions. A Pentecostal reading emphasizes spiritual aspects of

---

[1] Setswana (the culture of Botswana) is highly patriarchal, and therefore Setswana attitudes about women are reinscribed within Pentecostal hermeneutics. Further, Botswana in general is highly patriarchal. Patriarchy is found everywhere, in state policies, in laws, and in the seating arrangements for men and women during weddings and funerals.

salvation much more than the physical and the social.[2] This kind of interpretation emphasizes that salvation is eschatological and mainly concerned with the soul in preparation for the afterlife. It ignores and minimizes the experiences of social, economic, political, and cultural suffering in patriarchal societies such as Botswana where the marginalization of women is very real.[3] Spiritualizing texts is problematic because the equality of men and women, which was inaugurated by Pentecost in Acts 2 and is alluded to in texts such as Galatians 3:28, is oftentimes spiritualized as well. When Marea Mpuse and I carried out research in 2011–2012 among Pentecostal churches in Botswana on how they interpret Luke–Acts in general, some respondents stated,

> Pentecost makes men and women equal on a spiritual level, women can preach both in the church and crusades, they can lead praise and worship, they preach on Sunday. But the Holy Spirit does not make men equal to women on a day to day basis. This means that in terms of authority, men have the authority over women at home and even in the church.[4]

Although writing within the Western context, Amos Yong argues that Pentecost, an event inaugurated by the Holy Spirit, should effect the empowerment of human beings in "concrete and political ways." That effect has not been translated into equalizing the status between men and women in Pentecostal churches. Yong argues that Pentecost should effect equality in male-female relations in home, church, and society. However, through the selectiveness of the Pentecostal hermeneutic, the Holy Spirit seems to give women recognition only in "things spiritual and ecclesial" while they are still located "in spheres under male domination."[5]

The Pentecostal church in Botswana and surrounding countries such as Zimbabwe and South Africa teaches and enforces male supremacy with legislative force.[6] Spiritualizing

---

[2]When it comes to the marginalization of women, gender relations, gender inequality, and the position of women in the home, Pentecostals gravitate toward the spiritual. But when it comes to material things such as the acquisition of wealth and prosperity theology, Pentecostals emphasize that these must be enjoyed in the social world and in the present. This demonstrates that Pentecostals apply their hermeneutic selectively.

[3]In this chapter, marginalization of women refers to any action, practice, teaching, or belief that disadvantages women and places them in an inferior status as compared to men. This may include but is not limited to stigmatizing women's leadership, using language of domination during biblical interpretation, pushing the ministry of women to the margins, committing violence against women, subordinating women to the authority of men through language and hermeneutic, and making women invisible in roles they play in church by minimizing their status as the weaker vessel. The worst form of marginalizing women is violence against women in any shape or form, be it physical, financial, or emotional.

[4]The analysis of this research can be found in Rosinah Mmannana Gabaitse, "Towards an African Pentecostal Feminist Biblical Hermeneutic of Liberation: A Case Study of Interpreting Luke-Acts with Botswana Women" (PhD thesis, University of KwaZulu-Natal, Pietermaritzburg, 2013).

[5]Amos Yong, *The Spirit Poured Out on All Flesh: Pentecostalism and the Possibility of Global Theology* (Grand Rapids, MI: Baker Academic, 2005), 45, 40.

[6]It must be noted here that although African cultures and Pentecostal churches are patriarchal, not all women in Africa are abused and helpless, and not all Pentecostal men in Africa are abusers just because the culture privileges the male over the female. That the Pentecostal churches preach the supremacy of a male and that all men reap the patriarchal dividends and benefits cannot be disputed. The literature cited below demonstrates that texts such as Eph 5 are interpreted literally to support male prestige and to call women to submission. In some churches, although the male is given a privileged position supported by the above texts, husbands are encouraged to also love their wives into submission, that is, husbands are encouraged to love their wives so that the wives will not have a problem submitting to their authority, thus demonstrating a softer, gentler side of patriarchy. Further, even though Pentecostal churches are patriarchal, they emphasize the belief that when a person is born again, his old being is transformed and he becomes "a new creation and a new man." The expectation from the Pentecostal church is that the person will stop drinking alcohol, using bad language, and having multiple sex partners. Stopping these can make a Pentecostal husband treat his wife better than husbands who are not "born again." However, the darker and harder side of patriarchy is that some men are more forceful with their wives, as I demonstrate below, because of the language of domination that characterizes the Pentecostal hermeneutic. Further, patriarchy becomes destructive when

texts and social problems has resulted in Pentecostal women experiencing marginalization that ranges from bad financial decisions by husbands that affect wives to different kinds of violence.[7] Yet, if Luke 4:18-19 can be read and interpreted to emphasize and elevate not only spiritual salvation but physical, sociopolitical, and economic salvation, the marginalization, exclusion, and subjugation of women could be critiqued easily. Using Luke 4:18-19 to critique the marginalization of women should not be a challenge to Pentecostals because Luke–Acts is prescriptive and normative for the development of most Pentecostal theologies. Furthermore, Luke–Acts in general emphasizes multidimensional salvation, justice, and egalitarian existence.[8] Therefore, Luke–Acts as a whole and Luke 4:18-19 in particular can provide the Pentecostal church with frameworks that denounce the marginalization of women in its various manifestations. Because of its emphasis on the work of the Holy Spirit in directing Pentecostals' existence, the Pentecostal church should be inherently egalitarian. But it is not, as I demonstrate in the sections that follow.[9]

SALVATION IN LUKE–ACTS

Lukan scholars agree that the message of salvation is central to Luke–Acts.[10] Although Luke 4:18-19 does not use the usual "salvation" terminology, such as *sōtēr* (savior), *sōtēria* and *sōtērion* (salvation), and *sōzō* (to save), what it describes and what Jesus sets out to do are acts that demonstrate salvation. David Bosch describes Luke's understanding of salvation as the "total transformation of human life, forgiveness of sin, healing infirmities and release from any kind of bondage." Further, salvation is the reversal of the consequences of sin committed against God and human beings.[11] Similarly, Mark Powell views salvation in Luke–Acts as "participation in the reign of God." He further argues that salvation has both present and future dimensions so that it means "living life, even now as God intends it to be lived." However, he argues that Luke puts more emphasis on salvation as a possibility in the present through his repeated use of the term *today*. Further, according to Powell, Luke does not differentiate between what we might classify as "physical,

---

women are told by the people in authority (clergy) to stay in life-denying situations through the use of a few texts that seem to advance male supremacy. Interpretation has consequences. When both men and women are taught daily that a man is superior, that teaching can translate into how men and women live their lives in the home and church.

[7]It is ironic that the Pentecostal church, which claims to follow the experience of Pentecost as outlined in Acts 2, fails to live up to its name in terms of the gender injustice that it propagates. Elsewhere I have argued that Pentecostals "not only have a dependence on the Holy Spirit and trace this dependence back to the original Pentecost experience as recorded in Luke-Acts, they place the role of the Holy Spirit at the center of their hermeneutic. . . . The liberating power of the Holy Spirit is not just on issues of theology but the Holy Spirit is also experienced by men and women as a power that liberates. This goes to say that once the Holy Spirit is placed at the center of Pentecostal hermeneutic, the hermeneutic must necessarily be liberatory because the Holy Spirit is inherently liberatory. However, in spite of this, the liberatory role of the Holy Spirit is not necessarily emphasized and recognized, especially when it comes to elevating the status of women. This is the reality of Pentecostal frames of reading that need to be engaged." Gabaitse, "Towards an African Pentecostal Feminist Biblical Hermeneutic of Liberation," 6-7.

[8]Ben Witherington III, *Women and the Genesis of Christianity* (Cambridge: Cambridge University Press, 1990); L. Swindler, *Biblical Affirmations of Women* (Philadelphia: Westminster, 1979).

[9]The Holy Spirit should be able to subvert cultures of domination, including frames of reading and interpreting the Bible that subordinate women. But it is not happening in the Pentecostal church in Botswana, because of the belief that the authority of the man is ordained by God, and therefore there is nothing wrong with using the Bible to support the subordination of women to men. However, I strongly argue that the subordination of women is inconsistent with the work of the Holy Spirit, who levels inequalities between people, as demonstrated throughout Luke–Acts. For example, it was through the Holy Spirit that Gentile-Jewish tensions were resolved. Acts 15:28 is especially profound, where Peter says, "It has seemed good to the Holy Spirit and to us not to burden you with anything beyond the following requirements" (NIV). It was through the Holy Spirit that Mary, a woman, became a vessel for God's salvation in Lk 2.

[10]J. B. Green, *The Gospel of Luke*, New International Commentary on the New Testament (Grand Rapids, MI: Eerdmans, 1997).

[11]D. Bosch, *Transforming Mission: Paradigm Shifts in Theology of Mission* (Maryknoll, NY: Orbis, 1991), 107, 117.

spiritual and social aspects of salvation. . . . God is concerned with all aspects of human life and relationships, and so, salvation may involve the putting right of any aspect that is not as it should be."[12] In this chapter, I adopt Powell's and Bosch's definitions of salvation as "participation in the reign of God" and "total transformation of human life and living life as God had intended." The poverty, blindness, and oppression mentioned in Luke 4:18-19 refer not just to spiritual aspects of being human. They involve all aspects of being human, including the social, political, and economic. John Nolland cautions that the poor in Luke 4:18-19 should not be spiritualized because Jesus was "deeply concerned with the literal, physical needs of men," as much as he was with their spiritual needs.[13] This kind of interpretation is helpful, as it can serve as a yardstick for communities of faith to engage with the actual experiences of the marginalization of women in practical ways.

LUKE 4:18-19: JESUS SETS THE CAPTIVES FREE

Luke 4:18-19 presents Jesus reading and quoting from Isaiah 61:1-2. Jesus proclaims,

> The Spirit of the Lord is on me,
>> because he has anointed me
>>> to proclaim good news to the poor.
> He has sent me to proclaim freedom for the
>> prisoners
>>> and recovery of sight for the blind,
> to set the oppressed free,
>> to proclaim the year of the Lord's favor.
>> (NIV)

Jesus uttered these words on the Sabbath, in a synagogue in Nazareth, his hometown. Therefore,

he was aware of the challenges his listeners faced. Jesus came to perform five tasks: to proclaim good news to the poor, to proclaim freedom for the prisoners, to proclaim recovery of sight for the blind, to release the oppressed, and to proclaim the year of the Lord.

Throughout the Gospel of Luke, Jesus' claims in Luke 4:18-19 are accompanied by tangible acts of healing the blind and the sick, feeding the poor by multiplying loaves and fish, and forgiving sins. Jesus heals those who are spiritually blind (Lk 2:30; 7:39; 18:10) and physically blind (Lk 7:21; 18:35-43). Jesus provides for the economically poor (Lk 11:41; 12:33; 14:13; 18:22). People are healed from debilitating illness that has held them captive (Lk 6:9; 8:48), the lame walk (Lk 7:22), and the lepers are cleansed (Lk 17:19). Jesus delivers people who are possessed or held captive by demons (Lk 4:35). All these demonstrate salvation in tangible ways. Throughout his mission, setting the captives and the oppressed free was at the center of his ministry. He tells people, "Go and tell John what you have seen and heard: the blind receive their sight, the lame walk, lepers are cleansed and the deaf hear, the dead are raised up, the poor have good news preached to them" (Lk 7:22 ESV).

Perhaps the oppression in Luke 4:19 refers to sociopolitical captivity. Jesus' listeners appreciated these words, considering that the Jews were under Roman rule at the time. Although the Jews exercised some freedom, it was limited because of the system of governance. Jesus did not fully explain the oppression he was referring to, but we can infer that Jesus was aware that there were systems and circumstances that oppressed people and denied them life in abundance. He was aware that there were cultures

---

[12]M. A. Powell, "Salvation in Luke-Acts," *Word and World* 12, no. 1 (1992): 5, 6, 8.
[13]J. Nolland, *Luke 1–9:20*, Word Biblical Commentary (Waco, TX: Word, 1989), 197.

and economic and sociopolitical systems that held people captive. After stating his intentions, he executed his tasks by delivering people who were possessed by demons (Lk 4:31) and debilitated by sickness (Lk 4:39). Blindness, poverty, and oppression undeniably make human life and human existence uncomfortable and undesirable. Whichever way one interprets this text, it is clear that there are conditions and systems that bind people and keep them under oppression. These are conditions in which people find themselves that require salvation. Jesus was, therefore, intentional in dismantling these systems of oppression through providing tangible solutions to people inhabiting those systems. He was intentional about challenging oppression in its various manifestations, be it illness or poverty or evil spirits.

Further, Jesus stated that he had come to proclaim the year of the Lord's favor. He made reference to the Jubilee year mentioned in Leviticus 25, which was celebrated every fiftieth year. The Jubilee year required agricultural work to stop for the land to rest. The Israelites knew that the "the land shall not be sold in perpetuity, for the land is mine; with me you are but aliens and tenants" (Lev 25:23 NRSV). According to this text, the land belonged to God and it had to be distributed, perhaps equally to all Israelites so as to alleviate poverty and to give dignity to those who were landless. In the Jubilee year, debts were canceled, and slaves and servants were released and set free. To the first-century Palestinian, Jesus' words that he was under anointing to proclaim the year of the Lord were very profound given that the majority of the people were in debt and under a heavy tax burden imposed by the Romans.[14] They would immediately think of the economic relief the Jubilee year brought because of debt cancelation. They would experience an uplift in social status and dignity because of land redistribution, and slaves would celebrate real freedom because they were released. The year of Jubilee, therefore, was the year of justice and jubilation, the year that reminded the Israelites about equality, dignity, and care of those less privileged. It was a year that eliminated economic and social inequities among the Israelites, when all people owned land and all were free.

Finally, in Luke 4:21 Jesus stresses that the salvation that he has described in Luke 4:18-19 will be experienced *today*. His use of the adverb *today* indicates that salvation has a present dimension as much as it has a future dimension.[15] Further, Luke's Jesus demonstrates that salvation is meant for all people; it is physical, present, eschatological, spiritual, and social as well. Luke's Jesus is interested in the welfare of women. He empowers them; hence some women subsidize his ministry (Lk 8:1-3). Luke's Jesus is also interested in Gentiles and those who occupy a lower status and were underprivileged during the first century.[16]

PATRIARCHY IN THE PENTECOSTAL CHURCH AND AFRICAN CULTURES

That Pentecostalism provides greater freedom for women cannot be denied.[17] Cheryl Johns

---

[14]R. Horsley, *A People's History of Christianity-Christian Origins* (Minneapolis: Fortress, 2010).

[15]F. P. Viljoen, "Luke, the Gospel of the Saviour of the World," *Nederduits Gereformeerde Teologiese Tydskrif* 44, nos. 1-2 (2003): 199-209.

[16]Witherington, *Women and the Genesis of Christianity*.

[17]P. Mwaura, "Gendered Appropriation of Mass Media in Kenyan Christianities: A Comparison of Two Women-Led African Instituted Churches in Kenya," in *Interpreting Contemporary Christianity: Global Processes and Local Identities*, ed. O. U. Kalu and A. Low (Grand Rapids, MI: Eerdmans, 2008); K. Asamoah-Gyadu, "'Fireballs in Our Midst': West Africa Burgeoning Charismatic Churches and the Pastoral Role of Women," *Mission Studies* 15-16, no. 296 (1998): 21; A. M. Boadi, "Engaging Patriarchy: Pentecostal Gender Ideology and Practices in Nigeria," in *Religion, History, and Politics in Nigeria: Essays in Honour of Ogbu U. Kalu*, ed. Chima J. Korieh and Ugo G. Nwokeji (New York: University Press of America, 2005), 182.

writes, "In many ways Pentecostalism is not a culture that overtly suppresses women's abilities and gifts. From the early days of the movement women have been affirmed along with men as recipients of the same Spirit who distributes gifts and callings."[18] Pentecostalism has been hailed as gender friendly, opening up spaces for women and providing greater freedom for women.[19] Pentecostal churches are perceived as spaces where men and women "relate to each other on the basis of equality."[20] Further, Pentecostalism is a space where the Holy Spirit is experienced by men and women as a power that liberates.[21]

However, the Pentecostal space is ambivalent toward women. Scholars note that Pentecostalism is full of tensions, contradictions, and ambiguities as women are still expected to preserve traditional expectations of male prestige while they are empowered by the Holy Spirit to preach, speak in tongues, and prophesy. Johns points out that in regards to women, "Pentecostalism is a culture of both exclusion and embrace," and it is a place where "biblical roles of men and women restrict the ministry of women."[22] It is a place where women's leadership is sometimes "stigmatised and demonized."[23] Sarojini Nadar, Isabel Phiri, and Masenya Madipoane writing in the South Af-

rican context; Sidney Berman writing in Botswana; and Rekopantswe Mate writing in the Zimbabwean context all argue that Pentecostal biblical interpretation can be life denying to women and, further, that women are oftentimes pushed to the periphery.[24] Similarly, Nigerian scholar Ogbu Kalu argues that in Pentecostal churches "men tend to use the Bible to justify women's exclusion or relegation to the periphery."[25] What is discernible from the above scholars is that as much as Pentecostalism is a space of embrace, it is also a space of exclusion. This exclusion and embrace cloaks women in invisibility even when they are supposed to be visible especially through the unction of the Holy Spirit, who works among men and women equally and is no respecter of persons.[26] Further, the scholars cited above show that the marginalization of women is a reality within Pentecostal movements, and this marginalization is structurally supported by biblical interpretation. Pentecostal biblical interpretation and theology are full of the gendered language of domination and subordination.

Men are given enormous power over women in home, in church, and in public and women still experience hierarchical exclusion due to patriarchal norms that are maintained through the

---

[18]C. Johns, "Spirited Vestments or Why the Anointing Is Not Enough," in *Philip's Daughters: Women in Pentecostal-Charismatic Leadership*, ed. E. Alexander and A. Yong (Eugene, OR: Pickwick, 2009), 170.

[19]Mwaura, "Gendered Appropriation of Mass Media," 279; Kalu, *African Pentecostalism*, 149.

[20]Boadi, "Engaging Patriarchy," 182.

[21]Gabaitse, "Towards an African Pentecostal Feminist Biblical Hermeneutic of Liberation," 6.

[22]Johns, "Spirited Vestments," 170, 174.

[23]Mwaura, "Gendered Appropriation of Mass Media," 279.

[24]S. Nadar, "Journeying in Faith: The Stories of Two Ordained Indian Women in the Anglican and Full Gospel Churches in South Africa," in *Herstories: Hidden Histories of Women of Faith in Africa*, ed. I. Phiri, B. Govinden, and S. Nadar (Pietermaritzburg: Cluster, 2002), 144-58; M. Masenya, *How Worthy Is the Woman of Worth: Rereading Proverbs 31:10-31 in African-South Africa* (New York: Peter Lang, 2004); S. Berman, "Of God Image, Violence Against Women and Feminist Reflections," *Studia Historiae Ecclesiasticae* 41, no. 1 (2015): 122-37; I. Phiri, "Why Does God Allow Our Husbands to Hurt Us? Overcoming Violence Against Women," *Journal of Theology for Southern Africa* 114 (2002): 19-30; I. Phiri, "Domestic Violence in Christian Homes: A Durban Case Study," *Journal of Constructive Theology* 6, no. 2 (2000): 85-110; R. Mate, "Wombs as God's Laboratories: Pentecostal Discourses on Femininity in Zimbabwe," *Africa, Journal of the International African Institute* 72, no. 4 (2002): 566.

[25]Kalu, *African Pentecostalism*, 150.

[26]The Pentecostal church must be a space of equality, not just in the spiritual realm but in tangible physical, social, and political ways.

use of the Bible.[27] This poses a challenge especially since most African theologians have consistently argued that indigenous cultures in
Africa and the church are patriarchal. African
theologians such as Mercy Oduyoye, Brigalia
Bam, Masenya Madipoane, Sarojini Nadar, and
Musa Dube have demonstrated that the patriarchal African culture and church mutually reinforce each other in marginalizing women. African attitudes about women are reinscribed
within the church's theology so that the two mutually reinforce each other in allocating women
to a marginal status.[28] Oduyoye rightly captures this mutuality: "We see the visible manifestation of patriarchal structures and hierarchies
. . . in the church or in African cultures wherever
we encounter the subordination of women's services or a refusal to listen to women's voices."[29]
In Botswana, the dual patriarchies of Setswana
and Pentecostal contexts are not static and isolated from the

> wider impacts of globalization and the hybrid cul-
> tural forms which global encounters produce. Eu-
> ropean and American cultural forms are highly
> influential within Botswana. This further compli-
> cates the position of a Motswana Pentecostal
> woman who must contend not only with the dual
> patriarchies of the Pentecostal church and
> Setswana culture but also with the import of as-
> pects of wider global forms. This importation does

not happen monolithically but selection frequently
reflects pre-existent patterns of power and patriarchy, rendering new forms of oppression.[30]

Therefore, women within the Pentecostal church
are not only doubly marginalized. They have to
contend with marginalization due to the impor-
tation of global cultures as well.

While female submission is reinforced
through language and some cultural practices in
the Setswana culture, Pentecostals advance hermeneutical approaches to the Bible that enslave
and deny women an experience of salvation as
described in Luke 4:18-19. A negative gender discourse lurks within Pentecostal hermeneutics,
theology, and practice because a few texts are
used to propagate gender inequality by reinforcing the idea of male supremacy. This is done
through promoting male leadership, male power,
and male control, and through advocating hierarchical relationships. Scholars of Pentecostalism
have begun to pay attention to the oppressive
nature of biblical interpretation toward women.[31]

For example, Mate condemns Pentecostal
movements for advancing teachings found in
most African cultures that perpetuate and
maintain patriarchal ideologies such as female
submission to the point of calling women to
blind obedience, that is, women must submit to
their husbands even to the point of death.[32] African women theologians have consistently

[27]Nadar, "Journeying in Faith"; Berman, "Of God Image, Violence Against Women and Feminist Reflections"; Phiri, "Why Does God Allow Our Husbands to Hurt Us?"; Phiri, "Domestic Violence in Christian Homes"; Mate, "Wombs as God's Laboratories."

[28]M. A. Oduyoye, *Introducing African Women's Theology* (Maryknoll, NY: Orbis, 2001), 12, 28; B. Bam, "Women and the Church in (South) Africa: Women Are the Church in South Africa," in *On Being Church: African Women's Voices and Visions*, ed. Isabel A. Phiri and Sa-rojini Nadar (Geneva: World Council of Churches, 2005), 13; Masenya, *How Worthy Is the Woman of Worth*; D. Ramodibe, "Women and Men Building Together the Church in Africa," in *With Passion and Compassion: Third World Women Doing Theology*, ed. V. M. M. Fabella and M. A. Oduyoye (Maryknoll, NY: Orbis, 1996); M. W. Dube, *Postcolonial Feminist Interpretations of the Bible* (St. Louis: Chalice, 2000), 95, 108.

[29]M. A. Oduyoye, *Beads and Strands: Reflections of an African Woman on Christianity in Africa* (Accra, Ghana: Regnum Africa, 2002), 97.

[30]Gabaitse, "Towards an African Pentecostal Feminist Biblical Hermeneutic of Liberation," 56.

[31]S. Nadar, "The Bible Says! Feminism, Hermeneutics and Neo-Pentecostal Challenges," *Journal of Theology for Southern Africa* 134 (July 2009): 153; Mate, "Wombs as God's Laboratories," 566; R. M. Gabaitse, "Pentecostal Hermeneutics and the Marginalisation of Women," *Scriptura* 114, no. 1 (2015): 1-12.

[32]Mate, "Wombs as God's Laboratories," 566.

pointed out that violence against women in Africa is endemic and very serious. They have further maintained that patriarchy provides a breeding ground for all marginalization of women, especially forms of violence.[33] Isabel Phiri conducted research on violence against women among Pentecostal Indian women in Durban, and her data reveal chilling details of the violence that happens within Christian homes perpetuated by born-again husbands using a few texts from the Bible that seemingly support the marginalization of women. As a follow-up to this research, she published another essay in which she argues that Christian women are not immune to experiences of violence in their homes.[34]

Tinyiko Maluleke and Sarojini Nadar, also writing in a South African context, describe horrifying incidents of domestic violence in Christian Pentecostal homes. They tell the story of Khensani, a black South African Pentecostal woman who for years was subjected to severe beating and other kinds of violence by her husband. Numerous counseling sessions had taken place, and many times Khensani ran away from her marital home, after which her senior aunts and uncles would return her home. Maluleke and Nadar write,

> In the last few years of their marriage they had both become born again Christians belonging to a Pentecostal church. Yet this reality did not change the situation of domestic violence to which Khensani was subjected to time and again. If anything, their new found faith and its theology appeared to reinforce the idea of male supremacy in marriage. Often Khensani appealed

to the pastor for intervention, but he would only show her scripture verses that "proved" that she was wrong to complain and to question her husband's "right to violate her."[35]

What is discernible from Maluleke and Nadar's narration of the story of Khensani and Phiri's research on violence is that, first, pastors are not actively denouncing the marginalization of women. Second, Pentecostal pastors are agents of patriarchy, and they endorse a hermeneutic that fundamentally disagrees with Luke 4:18-19 because it oppresses women. Third, the accounts demonstrate how pastors use Scripture verses to maintain a hierarchical order between men and women. Biblical interpretation is used to keep women in life-denying situations, something Phiri classifies as spiritual violence:

> When a woman's faith is used to keep her from finding help and leaving an abusive situation, by telling her she must endure, submit, return . . . she is led to believe that the abuse is her fault, and that if she seeks to leave, she is un-Christian and will be condemned by God. The Bible is quoted to her literally and out of context, particularly passages that serve to "put her in her place," condemn divorce or glorify suffering.[36]

This is a demonstration of how patriarchy is not threatened or destabilized in the Pentecostal church. Failure to overtly and intentionally destabilize patriarchy denies many African women such as Khensani an opportunity to experience release from oppression while suffering is made normative through the selective use of the Bible.

One of the other aspects of Pentecostal theology that denies women an experience of salvation is the dualistic understanding of the

---

[33]N. Njoroge, "The Missing Voice: African Women Doing Theology," *Journal of Theology for Southern Africa* 99 (1997): 81.

[34]Phiri, "Domestic Violence in Christian Homes," 93, 95, 99.

[35]T. Maluleke and S. Nadar, "Breaking the Covenant of Violence Against Women," *Journal of Theology for Southern Africa* 114 (November 2002): 11.

[36]Phiri, "Domestic Violence in Christian Homes," 95.

world. The world is divided into the spiritual world and the physical/social world, and the spiritual world is more important. When Christian women such as Khensani and the women in Phiri's research experience violence, their experiences are "hyperspiritualized" and rationalized. They are told to "fast more," "seek God more," submit to their husbands more, or hold on to the hope that "God will not allow you to go through things, which you cannot manage to handle."[37] Stories of women being told to ignore actual experiences of pain and trauma are many. To these women, salvation is abstract, as it does not translate into the social, political, and economic world that Khensani and the women in Phiri's research inhabit. Because of Pentecostals' tendency to spiritualize, they fail to overtly challenge and deconstruct the marginalization of women with a clear, loud, and unambiguous voice. While spiritual experience and prayer are essential to Pentecostal living, both men and women must be taught that violence committed against women is not normal. In addition, they should be taught that the marginalization of women in any form and shape is not acceptable because it denies women an experience of salvation in the social world.

There is danger in emphasizing spiritual experience while downplaying social experience because political, social, and religious systems that support the oppression of women are not challenged. Further, when people suffer in the social world, they may despair and lose the joy of the salvation that, according to Pentecostal teaching, is the right of those who have accepted Jesus as their personal Savior and have accepted the full gospel. Johns argues, "Pentecostals have

failed to clearly enunciate the ontological and soteriological implications of the liberating power of the full gospel. As a result, they have created an environment characterized by ambiguity and confusion."[38]

A thorough analysis of salvation in Luke–Acts and an analysis of Luke 4:18-19 in particular demonstrates that there is no need for spiritual and social salvation to exist in antagonism. Allan Anderson captures this: "The power of the Holy Spirit has more than just spiritual significance. It also has to do with dignity, authority and power over all types of oppression. God loves and desires the welfare of the whole person: and so needs his Spirit to bestow that divine, liberating ability and strength."[39]

Luke 4:18-19: A Critique of the Marginalization of Women and Violence Against Women

What does proclaiming good news to the poor and setting the captives free look like in the contemporary world? What does Jesus' declaration mean for Pentecostal women who are faced with masculine interpretations of the Bible that do not take their experiences of suffering seriously? The existence of the unfavorable conditions described in Luke 4:18-19 is real, and these conditions prevent human beings, both men and women, from experiencing complete salvation. The oppression described in Luke 4:18-19 can be imposed on people by political, sociocultural, and economic systems. For example, suffering caused by violence against women is imposed on women through a patriarchal system of governance that thrives when certain groups of people are enslaved. Some women continue to be materially poor because

---

[37]Phiri, "Domestic Violence in Christian Homes," 105.
[38]Johns, "Spirited Vestments," 174.
[39]A. Anderson, *Moya: The Holy Spirit in an African Context* (Pretoria: University of South Africa Press, 1991), 63.

patriarchy creates economic inequalities between men and women. Jesus was aware that as much as salvation was a present reality and could be experienced and enjoyed by people regardless of ethnicity and gender, there were systems that prevented people from experiencing it (Lk 11:52). It was necessary for those systems to be dismantled. Therefore, Luke 4:18-19 is a relevant text because it points to the existence of systems that deny people an experience of salvation. Contemporary Pentecostals could use this passage as the basis on which to intercept and deconstruct patriarchal practices that prevent women from experiencing complete salvation. There is no reason for any woman who has given her life to Jesus and believes in Pentecost to be kept captive and oppressed by any system, theology, or frames of reading and interpreting the Bible.

An encounter with Jesus should be life giving because the gospel in general and Luke 4:18-19 in particular liberates. Luke 4:18-19 is subversive as it exposes the oppressive lies of patriarchy that women experience violence because they fail to "submit enough" or "pray more" or they are untamed. The text demonstrates that people suffer because they are denied salvation in the social world through systems of domination. Luke 4:18-19 should unsettle and judge the church not only for failing to make it possible for women to experience fullness of life because they inhabit patriarchal oppressive spaces, but also for using the Bible to advance and support patriarchal norms that oppress women, thus colluding with the Setswana culture in oppressing women. Therefore, the Pentecostal church has to reflect on the heart of the mission of Jesus, which was to set people free.

In fact, the Pentecostal church sins against women through enforcing an oppressive system that maintains male domination and female subordination. The sin of the Pentecostal church translates into individual men's sins such as those of Khensani's husband, who violated his wife as a way of demonstrating power and control based on a false interpretation of the Bible. It is ironic that the language of subordination that results in the marginalization of women is found in a community that is led by the Holy Spirit and believes in the Pentecost narrative of Acts 2. The Holy Spirit, who directs Pentecostal living, is transformative and radical; hence the Spirit is often referred to as an "equal opportunity employer."[40] Elsewhere I have argued that "Pentecost is a rejection of exclusion and marginalization. The Pentecost narrative was communal, *all* are praying, *all* are assembled (2:1), *all* are filled with the Spirit (2:4), the Spirit is for *all* flesh (2:17), the Holy Spirit is given to 'each of you' (2:37)."[41] Through the Holy Spirit, Pentecost gives us a glimpse of an egalitarian, transformed community of faith where discrimination on the basis of gender does not exist. It is in the construction and maintenance of gender inequalities through biblical interpretation that the marginalization of women is made normative. The existence of gender inequalities takes away from the Pentecostal church the opportunity to be the real church of Pentecost, the church led by the Holy Spirit where exclusions were ignored for a while.[42]

---

[40]E. S. Spencer, *The Gospel of Luke and Acts of the Apostles* (Nashville: Abingdon, 2008), 67.

[41]Gabaitse, "Towards an African Pentecostal Feminist Biblical Hermeneutic of Liberation," 178.

[42]As much as Pentecost was egalitarian, I am aware that as the story of the church progressed male leadership was sometimes preferred (Acts 6). However, the story of Acts is a story of how the Holy Spirit moves the church toward egalitarian existence. It is a story in which God will pour God's Spirit on the young men, the old men, and the young women, the free and the slaves. So that even if the church in Acts may gravitate toward male leadership, God has made a promise through the Holy Spirit for the equality

Conclusion

In this chapter I have demonstrated the darker side of Pentecostal hermeneutics and theology much more than the positive side. The positive side of Pentecostal hermeneutics and theology includes but is not limited to women prophesying under the influence of the Holy Spirit and women not bound by traditional rules of dress and Levitical taboos. I point out the darker side of Pentecostalism because there is potential to make the Pentecostal space truly egalitarian, embracing men and women equally, if texts such as Luke 4:18-19 are read to advance multidimensional salvation. Luke 4:18-19 is a powerful resource that the Pentecostal church can use to transform social lives of women who are experiencing patriarchal oppression from indigenous and global cultures.

A saved Pentecostal community should advance hermeneutics and theology that affirm salvation for all people regardless of gender, ethnicity, or race. A Spirit-led and saved community continuously seeks ways of transforming unequal gender relations and affirming the lives of its members so that men and women experience jubilee and social salvation. For this to happen, the Pentecostal church needs to acknowledge that its frames of reading and interpreting the Bible contradict the work of the Holy Spirit, who through Jesus declared that "I have come to set the captives free." This can also happen if the church can take the experiences of women's marginalization seriously by acknowledging that it has caused women pain through its hermeneutics. In addition, the Pentecostal church has to ac-

knowledge that cultures of oppression need to be challenged because they cause women real problems such as trauma from violence inflicted on them. Therefore, Luke 4:18-19 could be a resource for the Pentecostal church to acknowledge that patriarchal practices of subordinating women rob them of experiencing salvation and that Jesus came to set human beings free from oppression.

Biblical texts are living and have the potential to transform lives if they are allowed through the Holy Spirit to do so. Luke 4:18-19 is transformative enough to explode and challenge the patriarchal framework of Pentecostal theology and hermeneutics. Pentecostals could use this text to challenge the unjust and unfair cultural practices that rob women of an experience of social salvation. It is a text that could critique laws and practices that repress women and children, as much as they critique cultures that allow violence to happen and ways of uncritically reading texts such as Ephesians 5 to support the authority of the husband over the wife. Laws, practices, and cultures that oppress and uncritically read the Bible are not consistent with salvation described in Luke 4:18-19. Jesus' proclamation of holistic salvation must be the message adopted by the Pentecostal movements and the church in general because the church is the representative of Christ on earth. The kind of salvation Luke–Acts presents "knows no distinction between the physical, spiritual and social."[43] Salvation takes different forms and shapes, depending on circumstances and contexts. However, the end results of salvation are the same for all humanity, and God desires a healed, whole humanity.

---

of all people, and that promise subverts even the culture of Luke–Acts. See Gabaitse, "Pentecostal Hermeneutics and the Marginalisation of Women," 11.

[43] J. B. Green, "Salvation to the End of the Earth: God as the Saviour in the Acts of the Apostles," in *Witness to the Gospel: The Theology of Acts*, ed. I. H. Marshall and D. Petersen (Grand Rapids, MI: Eerdmans, 1998), 89.

Human beings are saved when their souls are saved and when their circumstances allow for sociopolitical, physical, and economic salvation as well.

FURTHER READING

Seim, T. K. *The Double Message: Patterns of Gender in Luke-Acts.* Edinburgh: T&T Clark, 1994.

Shillington, G. *An Introduction to the Study of Luke-Acts.* New York: T&T Clark, 2006.

Thomas, C. "Women Pentecostals and the Bible." *Journal of Pentecostal Theology* 5 (1994): 41-56.

West, G. "Reading the Bible Differently: Giving Shape to Discourses of the Dominated." *Semeia* 73 (1996): 21-38.

Williams, D. K. "'Upon All Flesh': Acts 2, African Americans and Intersectional Realities." Pages 289-310 in *They Were All Together in One Place: Toward Minority Biblical Criticism*, edited by B. Randal, Ben Tat-Siong, and F. Segovia. Atlanta: Society of Biblical Literature, 2009.

28

CON LAS VENAS ABIERTAS

THE HOPE OF LIFE AND SALVATION IN LATIN AMERICAN THEOLOGIES

Jules A. Martínez-Olivieri

IN THIS CHAPTER the doctrine of salvation in Latin America is construed as a divinely enacted experience that begins in historical reality with the transformation of people freed from both personal and collective expressions of sin for life in communion with God and neighbor. The contextual realities of Latin American theologians in the late twentieth century provided a historical occasion to elaborate on the concept of sin and liberation, which amounted to new emphases. Explorations of sin and salvation among Roman Catholics and Protestants share some overlap, but diverge in a few important ways. This chapter seeks to assess the differences, articulating their hermeneutical intuitions and the subsequent conclusions that were produced by their doctrinal formulations.

In 1971, Edwardo Galeano published a book titled *Con las venas abiertas de America Latina*.[1] It was one of the most visceral accounts of the consequences of the power relations between Europe and the United States over Latin America, which resulted in economic exploitation. Armed with powerful, critical rhetoric, Galeano brought

to the center of political discussion how international political policies had affected the people in Latin America, particularly the forgotten masses of the impoverished and those ravaged by violence. In hindsight, the economic and political conditions were even more complex, and Galeano underestimated how corrupt local governments were equally responsible for the systemic evils that plagued many countries in the region. Still, the suffering of the masses in Latin America, and in many postcolonial regions of the world, is an undeniable and grotesque fact.

Christian theology in Latin America was born from this unacceptable reality of a multitude of peoples suffering in the absence of social justice, economic well-being, and the possibility of a livable life. The rise of Roman Catholic liberation theology and Protestant theology is in part the result of Christians thinking critically about the relevance of Christian salvation, the life of the church among the most vulnerable, and the witness required to proclaim that Jesus is the Lord of life and liberator of humanity.

---

[1] See Eduardo Galeano, *Open Veins of Latin America: Five Centuries of the Pillage of a Continent*, 25th anniversary ed. (New York: Monthly Review, 1997).

My task in this chapter is to offer an exposition of the doctrine of salvation in Latin American theologies. As such, it is necessarily a selective exercise that can suffer for its brevity, but one that can nevertheless provide a map of the theological terrain. I do not pretend to speak for all of the voices but simply aim to zero in on a few frameworks to see how their intuitions illustrate the broader trends in Latin America. And even so, within a single tradition there can be variety. For our purposes, this chapter broadly traces the soteriology of liberation theology in its Roman Catholic and Protestant depictions.

THE HOPE OF LIFE AND SALVATION

Christian theology in Latin America presents itself as an attempt to take on the question of how to discern God's presence in a situation of destitution and human turmoil.[2] The challenge is connected to the political nature of christological and soteriological discourse. The primary challenge is not tethered to philosophical naturalism or materialism of a secular Western society, but rather what is communicated by the actions and attributes of God, who is already assumed in Jesus Christ. This gospel emphasis takes a notable interest in speaking against and deconstructing the political and religious ideologies that diminish human life. This God is the God of life and liberation.[3]

According to the Christian faith, salvation is the central need of humanity. It is the experience of being saved by God from sin and its effects. Sal-

vation is a gracious divine act whereby human beings are brought into right communion with God and neighbor, and as such are saved from alienation from God and neighbor (personal sin), as well as sin in its communal expressions in political, economic, and social systems that perpetuate inhuman conditions (structural sin). This restored communion with God and neighbor activates an alternative human praxis that confronts these structural evils. Salvation, hence, is understood in part as a future eschatological reality free of evil that breaks into present human history. Salvation is in history; that is, it has a definitive historical referent but is not limited to history. Consequently, the Christian experience of salvation can be seen in three dimensions: (1) as redemption, deliverance from sin; (2) as flourishing in grace toward wholeness (sanctification); and (3) as satisfaction of the deepest human longings for transcendence (eternal life). The concept of salvation is manifested in all three senses.[4]

Theological reflection in Latin America exemplifies this consciousness of the contextuality of human theologizing. Theology, as human discourse done in faith, takes the concerns of the historical moment that shaped the life experiences, cultures, and linguistic mediations of its producers. Theological proposals do not enjoy a de facto transcultural relevance.[5] In Latin American theology, doctrine finds validation in the public orthopraxis of the church. That is, the church community is a visible sign of the truth of Christian theology. Theology serves the

---

[2]*Latin America* is a geopolitical term used to refer to the territories comprising Mexico, Central America, the Caribbean, and South America. See Alan Barnard and Jonathan Spencer, *Encyclopedia of Social and Cultural Anthropology* (London: New York, 1996).

[3]Rolando Muñoz avers: "The problem is more so the 'idolatry' of the privileged groups and the 'cults,' those who more or less consciously use 'God' to legitimize their accumulated wealth, their excluding knowledge, their power of domination; is the 'atheism' of the dominant groups that believe that God 'does not see' the exploitation of the poor and the assassination of the innocent, that He 'does not hear' the clamor of the oppressed." Muñoz, *Dios de los cristianos* (Santiago: Ediciones Paulinas, 1986), 29.

[4]See Olegario González de Cardedal, *Fundamentos de cristología: meta y misterio* (Madrid: BAC, 2006), 2:lx-lxii.

[5]Gerardo A. Alfaro, "¿Cómo hacer teología evangelica? Preliminares de un método teológico evangélico," in *Teología evangélica para el contexto latinoamericano: Ensayos en honor al Dr. Emilio A. Nuñez*, ed. Oscar A. Campos (Buenos Aires: Kairos, 2004), 58-59.

people of God by plotting possibilities for expressing the faith and judgments that correspond to the gospel and the testimony of God's communication in Jesus Christ.

Two Soteriological Traditions: Catholic Liberationist and Protestant

Approaches to soteriology can generally be divided between Roman Catholic liberation theology and Protestant theologies, although there are shared methodological, thematic, and practical convergences between them. For Protestantism, I make use of José Míguez Bonino's typology of the "faces" of Protestantism in Latin America.[6]

Liberation theology on salvation. Some scholars have labeled theologies of liberation as a type of retrieval theology. However, liberation theologians are quick to clarify that liberation theology is not another theology of the genitive. Or, stated differently, it is not merely another theology with a new adjectival clarifier in the list of many others. It is not a mere attempt to retrieve one aspect of dogmatic reflection that was ignored or undervalued. Neither is it a theological application of a dogmatic locus to politics and sociology, although it is analytically interested in both. Instead, the adjective modifying *theology* is intended to categorically reconfigure Christian theology as a theology predicated on the confession that God in Christ is the liberator of humanity. Hence, as Ignacio Ellacuría argues, liberation theology should not be understood as a form of political theology, but as a theology of the reign of God focusing on how all dogmatic

areas of theology should be framed in their liberating dimension.[7] Methodologically, the primary object is not politics in itself, but the church, as Christ's broker of embodied salvation. The church has a decided preference for theologizing in light of those who suffer, and on the centrality of Christian praxis as a verification of gospel commitment.

The concept of liberation in liberation theology has a biblical referent that points to the scriptural testimony of God rescuing and establishing justice among his people.[8] Liberation is a soteriological concept that attempts to capture the historical experience of divine redemptive acts. Gustavo Gutiérrez explained three fundamental soteriological levels: (1) the sociopolitical level: the liberation of those "exploited classes, marginalized races, despised cultures"; (2) the anthropological level: liberation for the attainment of a society of equals; (3) the theological level: liberation from sin, which is the origin of all evil and injustice, for a life of communion and participation.[9]

Therefore, history is the realm of divine action in which human transformation is experienced. The cognitive content of salvation has a narrative shape. It begins with the acts of Jesus in his ministry. Jesus' own praxis is liberating; he is the messianic liberator. Leonardo Boff argues that Jesus is the "liberator of the conscience oppressed by sin and by all kinds of alienations; liberator of the sad human condition in its relationships towards the world, each other and towards God."[10]

---

[6]Míguez Bonino suggests several "faces" of Protestantism in Latin America: the ethnic, liberal, evangelical, and Pentecostal. See José Míguez Bonino, *Faces of Latin American Protestantism* (Grand Rapids, MI: Eerdmans, 1997).

[7]Ellacuría, *Historicidad de la salvación*, 325.

[8]Rosino Gibellini, *La Teología del siglo XX*, Coleccion Presencia Teológica (Santander, Spain: Sal Terrae, 1998), 378.

[9]Gustavo Gutiérrez, *La fuerza histórica de los probres* (Salamanca, Spain: Sígueme, 1982), 243.

[10]Leonardo Boff, *Jesucristo Liberador* (Santander, Spain: Sal Terrae, 1980), 253.

Jesus' designation as liberator enjoys more theological capital than Jesus as represented in the language of the ecumenical creeds. The status of creedal Christology (e.g., Councils of Nicaea, Chalcedon, Ephesus) in contemporary theology in Latin America is somewhat ambivalent. The creeds are considered a valuable (though not normative) dogmatic and hermeneutical framework in Latin American theologies among both Roman Catholics and Protestants. The confessional language provides grammatical rules (fitting concepts) that safeguard the identity of the agent of salvation in the gospel, in its own time and across generations. However, even as the identity of the Savior is ontologically specified, the work of the Savior in saving humanity and the shape of the praxis of his followers is not a concern reflected in the creeds. Hence, the creeds do not offer a sufficient foundation for the mission of the church. The creeds are not formulated in a way to give doctrinal preference to Jesus' example—namely, his message and actions. In a narrative conception of salvation, the praxis of Jesus is identified as the historical realization of the kingdom of God and the basis of the process of liberation. The ecumenical creeds, given their attention to metaphysical and theological issues regarding Jesus' divinity and trinitarian ontology, do not assess the material content of the historical expression of salvation based on his praxis. The creeds, therefore, do not pay attention to the content of God's kingdom, which should be fundamental to soteriology. However, when the historical actions of Jesus genuinely shape a broader vision of salvation, then the expectations of God's reign described by the creeds become more meaningful.

Liberation Christology privileges Jesus' proclamation of the kingdom and its advancement. The Gospels skillfully highlight Jesus' actions on behalf of the impoverished. His actions on behalf of victims who suffered a plurality of maladies constitute the establishment of the rule of God in history. Jesus is depicted as the definitive mediator of the kingdom, summoning people to live under God's rule.[11]

Fundamental to the Christian view of salvation is the notion that God's acts in human history are open to human apprehension. Divine action not only sustains the faith of the church but also shapes the embodiment of Christian praxis. In Latin American theologies there is a methodological, pastoral, and missional interest in the historicity of salvation as a public experience of the faith. Praxis, specifically Christian praxis, refers to actions characterized by the intent to transform situations that negate the kind of life that the gospel offers. It promotes holistic well-being for all human beings.

For liberation theologians, Christian praxis has a potential salvific role to play to the extent that it is the consistent testimony of Christians involved in the shaping of a just world—a praxis of salvation. That is, Christian social and political involvement should seek "maximal coincidence between what God wants from human beings and what human beings do." Ellacuría goes further, proposing that human praxis has a soteriological capacity, a "formally salvific power" that shapes, even saves history, not apart from, but in collaboration with God.[12]

Both Roman Catholic and Protestant theologians agree that the modern theological scheme of two histories, a sacred history and a profane

---

[11]Jon Sobrino, *Jesus the Liberator: A Historical-Theological Reading of Jesus of Nazareth*, trans. Paul Burns and Francis McDonagh (London: Burns & Oates, 1994), 108-9.

[12]Ellacuría, *Historicidad de la salvación*, 327, 341.

history, is not sustainable for theology given the Scriptures' rendering of human history as the single space of divine action and human participation. God's actions and human praxis are not logically dichotomous but complementary. God's activity is always related to human beings' activity. In fact, God's activity is so intimately connected to human activity that it can be said that human actions bear the presence of God. The agency of God is principally human activity. "There is an omnipresence of God in history," Ellacuría says, that is not reducible to the natural or supernatural.[13]

The divine presence in history leads liberation theology to deal with the idea of transcendence. Transcendence is framed as the divine reality that sustains history in time and space, while extending beyond it, not against it or in contraposition to it. Transcendence is not over history or beyond it but through history. The referents for this view of transcendence in history are the exodus event and the incarnation. In the exodus event, the paradigmatic salvific event of the Old Testament, the salvific gift of freedom from slavery comes as covenantal freedom for a people, so that they might worship the Lord and in doing so become an alternative society. Worship is dependent on the sociopolitical experience of liberation. In the incarnation, the eternal and transcendent God communicates himself in the Son's humiliation. This is where the eternal and contingent come together in unity but without confusion. Hence, human history is the "privileged field to show the irruption of the transcendent God as the unseen novelty that opens human contingency to divine hope."[14] For this reason, the

nature of salvation is inextricably linked first to how God relates to history.

In terms of the Gospel narratives, liberation is what Jesus defined as integral to his reign. Jesus' messianic mission is displayed by his healings, exorcisms, and confrontations with those who religiously and politically oppressed the masses. It is acutely portrayed by his giving of food to the multitudes, and the formation of a new community of sacrificial service to neighbor. These are the signs of the kingdom. These are the historical conditions that both confirm Jesus' identity and provide the content of his liberating work. Salvation and liberation are, primordially, a material, sociopolitical, and verifiable experience. Salvation is not fully lived unless it reaches the temporalities of human existence.[15] In light of the scriptural testimony of a God who intervenes to save, salvation refers to God's ultimate activity of bringing shalom (the Hebrew conception of wholeness and right relationship between Creator and creation) to humanity. Liberation refers to those conditions in history, personal and collective, that point to the presence of God's liberating actions.

One of the main contributions of liberation theology to Christian dogmatic theology is the conceptual expansion of sin as an alienating condition of relational brokenness. The expansion includes societal structures that threaten human flourishing and the very possibility of human life. To be saved is to experience God in Christ liberating people from personal sin and the "objectification of sin" in social and political life: the impoverishment of the masses; the marginalization of those on the periphery; the oppression and killing of women, children,

---

[13]Ellacuría, *Historicidad de la salvación*, 327-28.
[14]Ellacuría, *Historicidad de la salvación*, 332.
[15]Ellacuría, *Historicidad de la salvación*, 340.

and indigenous groups; and the sex trafficking of millions under the logic of supply and demand. Groups who are doubly oppressed by patriarchy, political subjugation, and racism are victims of what Xavier Zubiri calls "historical sin."[16] These conditions are structures that work against essential aspects of the God who offers abundant life in Christ. God is a God of life, justice, and love. The salvation enacted by God in Christ includes the hope of liberation from these maladies by creating a messianic people that through the inhabitation of the Spirit confront the oppressions of the world, whose sociopolitical praxis is a testimony to the God who calls human beings to just lives. God, in Christ, enacts redemption in them, so contradicting the historical structures of sin with the emergence of new historical "structures of grace."[17] Structures of grace are established in the cross and the resurrection, as these events are interpreted in light of the arrival of God's kingdom. Those who have been impoverished and oppressed by sinful religious, secular, and political systems now are understood as privileged recipients of the reign of God.[18]

How do people and ecclesial communities maintain preference toward the impoverished and oppressed? Jesus' example and his own resistance to oppression prevent the Christian faith from the temptation to decontextualize (and overspiritualize) his mission—which is also their mission. Where the social, political, and religious aspects of the cross are neglected, the most

vulnerable and preferential beneficiaries of the gospel become obscure.[19] Significantly, the death of Jesus is the consequence of this proclamation. It is the death of a human being whose life is identified with the transcendent God.[20]

Consider briefly feminist liberation theologies as one particular expression. Feminist theology in Latin America is critical reflection on the experience of God by women. Women not only suffer oppression like men, but are doubly oppressed for their gender by the prevailing logic of patriarchalism and its patterns of domination. Feminist theology seeks "to transform the causes that produce the impoverishment and violence against women as a social group, with the goal of advancing towards new social relations based on justice and the integrity of life for women and all organisms of the Earth." For some feminist theologians, ignoring the historical causes of the cross is dangerous, as it makes the meaning of salvation susceptible to ideological uses. Sadly, in some religious communities the idea of atonement has been used to perpetuate the suffering of women, proposing that suffering is inherent to a life that emulates Jesus' own suffering.[21]

Nevertheless, Roman Catholic feminist theologians and liberation theologians are hesitant to elaborate on the metaphysical effectiveness of the atonement. They feel more comfortable viewing the death of Jesus primarily in light of its theological symbolic power. For Jon Sobrino, the effectiveness of the cross lies in the capacity

---

[16]X. Zubiri, *Naturaleza, historia, Dios* (Madrid: Alianza Editorial, 1963), 394.

[17]Ellacuría avers: "The first question is to see what is there of grace and what is there of sin in men and in history, but a grace and sin not seen primarily from a moral point of view, and even less from the point of view of fulfilling laws and obligations, but seen primarily from that which makes the life of God present in the midst of men" (*Historicidad de la salvación*, 356-57).

[18]Sobrino, *Jesus the Liberator*, 67.

[19]Nancy E. Bedford, *La porfía de la resurrección: ensayos desde el feminismo teológico latinoamericano*, Colección FTL (Buenos Aires: Kairós, 2008).

[20]Sobrino, *Jesus the Liberator*, 220.

[21]Maria Pilar-Aquino and Elsa Tamez, *Teología feminista latinoamericana*, Pluriminor (Quito: Ediciones Abya-Yala, 1998), 16, 158.

to evoke a pattern of life in light of the kingdom of God. The power of the cross lies "in the form of an exemplary cause more than of an efficient cause."[22] However, to be saved is to come to new subjective and objective realities. Subjectively, the experience of liberation is constituted by faith and love for God and neighbor. Objectively, to be saved is to be liberated for the production of a new praxis and an alternative social order. Humans are both saved and made free through the Spirit of Jesus, who brings freedom and makes Christians coparticipants in God's redemptive history.

Protestants on salvation: Evangelical, Pentecostal, and ecumenical. Soteriology in the Protestant tradition has historically been a central concern for both theology and the mission of the church. Protestants emphasize the theme of Christian salvation and liberation from sin for a life of communion with God and love of neighbor. This God saves people and transforms societies beset by personal and structural evil.[23] As I have argued elsewhere:

> Protestants have also used the nomenclature of salvation as liberation. . . . The concept of liberation/salvation is informed via Christology: Jesus Christ paradigmatically fulfills the OT trajectories of the exodus freedom and the prophetic visions of God's actions to free the people of Israel from internal oppression and the oppression exerted by foreign political powers. In Jesus the messianic vocation is redefined in terms of liberation of the captives—the sinners,

the sick, the maltreated, the afflicted, the poor, and the victims. Hence, since salvation entails liberations from sinful captivities, personal and societal, it is not a meta-historical concept or experience but "a reality indissolubly tied to the history of human beings."[24]

For Protestants, the kingdom also serves as an interpretative lens for soteriology.[25] Jesus' salvific praxis is understood in light of God's kingdom-establishing actions. The consequence of people being saved from fundamental sin (and the praxis of sin) is the formation of an alternative society, a people under the lordship of Christ. The community of the liberated is constituted by God's grace extended to the most vulnerable: women, children, the impoverished, and victims who dream for justice.[26] These are the primary recipients of the kingdom. Samuel Escobar argues: "'To preach the gospel to the poor, To heal the broken hearted, To preach deliverance to the captives and recovery of sight to the blind, To set at liberty them that are bruised.' These are words that cannot be spiritualized in a world like ours, where there are millions of persons who are poor, brokenhearted, captive, blind and bruised."[27] Through his death, Jesus redeems from personal and collective slavery. He is the one true innocent who brings redemption. He is the liberator of humanity, the mediator of the life of God beyond any human or state mediation.[28] Orlando Costas says:

---

[22]Sobrino, *Jesus the Liberator*, 230.

[23]José Míguez Bonino, "Las iglesias protestantes y evangélicas en América Latina y el Caribe: Un ensayo interpretativo," *Cuadernos de teología* 14, no. 2 (1995): 31.

[24]See my "*¿Quién Vive? ¡Cristo!* Christology in Latin American Perspectives," chapter 12 in this volume.

[25]José D. Rodriguez, *Introducción a la teología*, 2nd ed. (Mexico: Publicaciones El Faro, 2002), 17.

[26]See Justo L. González, *Jesucristo es el Señor*, 2nd ed. (Lima: Ediciones Puma, 2011).

[27]As cited by Sharon E. Heaney, *Contextual Theology for Latin America: Liberation Themes in Evangelical Perspective*, Paternoster Theological Monographs (Colorado Springs: Paternoster, 2008), 142.

[28]C. René Padilla, "Christology and Mission in the Two Thirds World," in *Sharing Jesus in the Two Thirds World: Evangelical Christologies from Contexts of Poverty, Powerlessness and Religious Pluralism*, ed. Vinay Samuel and Chris Sugnen (Grand Rapids, MI: Eerdmans, 1983), 28.

Jesus unequivocally shifted the whole concept of salvation—from benefit and privilege to commitment and service. To be saved by faith in Christ is thus to come to Jesus where he died for the world and gave his life for its salvation; it is to commit oneself to those for whom he suffered. Salvation lies outside the gates of the cultural, ideological, political, and socio-economic walls that surround our religious compound and shape the structures of Christendom. It is not a ticket to a privileged spot in God's universe but, rather, freedom for service.[29]

That salvation lies outside the "structures of Christendom"—that is, the shared moral vocabulary, sociopolitical organization, and ecclesial practices associated with cultures under the influence of Christianity—is a de facto intuition in the Pentecostal face of Protestantism. Pentecostalism is the fastest-growing tradition of Christianity in Latin America and in the Majority World.[30] Pentecostals share theological commitments with *evangélicos*, particularly with the paradigmatic Reformation *solas*, a pietistic ethos of personal devotion, and emphasis on evangelistic mission. At the same time, great emphasis is placed on conversion as a moment of crisis when the old life, subjected to the slavery of sin, is liberated to a new, holy life (morally and liturgically) dedicated to serving God through the empowerment of the Holy Spirit.[31] In Pentecostal theology, to be saved from sin is not only to be freed from fundamental sin but also to be liberated from the

"infra-human conditions"—not metaphorically, but concretely—that keep human beings in spiritual chains to the enemy of souls, Satan.[32] The cross of Christ has an intensely personal effect on those who come to faith in Jesus and are united to him by the Spirit: it makes them fully human. The Holy Spirit's fullness in individual lives has the power to change those impoverished and marginalized so that they become proclaimers of a new and just life.[33] The victims of personal and collective sin are given the resources necessary to be considered actors in the work of love and justice, and by the empowerment of the Spirit, the church becomes a center of social liberation.[34] Samuel Solivan argues, "Orthodoxy, narrowly defined as propositional truth, dehumanizes revelation and elevates the cognitive. . . . We are not saved by what we know but by whom we know, and how God informs and transforms our lives and our neighbors' lives."[35] For Pentecostals, the application or experience of salvation extends beyond the intellectual apprehension of the gospel or the knowledge of doctrinal truths. Salvation stems from a personal encounter with the Lord of life, Jesus. Christians are people who respond not to propositions but to a divine narrative of cosmic rescue. The individual's encounter with the Spirit that testifies to Christ is verified in the new habits of individual piety in the church, which validates the reality that Christ is a Savior.

---

[29]Orlando E. Costas, *Christ Outside the Gate: Mission Beyond Christendom* (Maryknoll, NY: Orbis, 1982), 191.

[30]See Ondina E. González and Justo L. González, *Christianity in Latin America: A History* (New York: Cambridge University Press, 2008), 270-96.

[31]José Míguez Bonino, *Rostros del protestantismo latinoamericano* (Grand Rapids, MI: Eerdmans, 1995), 64.

[32]Dario Lopez R., *Pentecostalismo y misión integral: Teologia del Espíritu, teología de la vida* (Lima: Ediciones Puma, 2008), 103.

[33]See Eldin Villafañe, *El Espíritu liberador: hacia una ética social pentecostal hispanoamericana* (Grand Rapids, MI: Eerdmans, 1996).

[34]Lopez, *Pentecostalismo y misión integral*, 103-4.

[35]Samuel Solivan, *The Spirit, Pathos and Liberation: Toward an Hispanic Pentecostal Theology*, Journal of Pentecostal Theology Supplement (Sheffield, UK: Sheffield Academic Press, 1998), 62-63.

Pentecostals articulate a view of salvation as liberation for a full and blessed life that enjoys divine acts of liberation. To this extent, there is a parallel interest in the materiality of salvation that is a feature of liberation theologies.[36] At the same time, there is a strong apocalyptic impulse that views salvation in terms of the ultimate eradication of evil in the world by Jesus in the *parousia*. This is a conviction that finds little elaboration in liberation theology.

Recently there have been attempts at renewing soteriology in a way that accommodates the liberal face of Protestantism and its concern for social transformation. Some theologians have found theological capital in a move toward a panentheistic view of salvation.[37] Panentheism construes God's relation to the world as ontologically necessary. It suggests that the world is part of God's being and that the divinity of God is part of the world, although the divine being transcends the world.[38] Jorge Pixley adopts process theology to make such a case.[39] He argues that this is the most fitting theological framework for the biblical testimony regarding God's liberating actions in the history of Israel, in the person of Jesus, and the demand for human participation. Pixley argues, "If human beings, like God, are creators at any moment of history, this means that God cannot, or does not desire, to impose his will against the will of the creators. The creative action of God is manifested in his will for all and each of the creatures. But that will does not impose itself,

but through *persuasion*. . . . Therefore the future is always open."[40]

Even though the cross and the resurrection are the center of the drama of redemption, Jesus' proclamation of the arrival of the kingdom to his generation was simply wrong. Even God, Pixley argues, is subject to his relations. God cannot simply circumvent the creative actions of creatures who resist his rule. For Pixley, the metaphysics of process theology help explain why the kingdom of God did not immediately arrive. The arrival of a new reality to the world is a collaborative, even codependent effort of divine and human will. Nothing in human reality objectively changes in the atonement of Jesus. For process theologians, divine agency and action are inextricably and necessarily entangled in temporal processes. God's relations with the world are internal to the divine being; hence, they effect and compel divine action. God's will to save, then, can be interpreted as God's will to call humans to experience the Spirit who operates in Christ so that they might in turn imitate the praxis of Jesus, even in his suffering. This proposal is consistent with the basic intuition in liberation theology that God is a God of salvation in history.

LIBERATION: IS THERE LIFE BEFORE DEATH?

Human beings, due to their fallen nature, create cultures of violence, impoverishment, and dehumanization. Xavier Zubiri calls this social

---

[36]See Miroslav Volf, "Materiality of Salvation: An Investigation in the Soteriologies of Liberation and Pentecostal Theologies," *Journal of Ecumenical Studies* 26, no. 3 (1989): 447-67.

[37]Roman Catholic theologians such as Ivone Gebara and Leonardo Boff began to move to a process view of God in the 1990s. But their attention was primarily directed to the doctrine of God, not to soteriology per se. See Ivone Gebara, *Longing for Running Water: Ecofeminism and Liberation* (Minneapolis: Augsburg Fortress, 1999); Leonardo Boff, *Ecología: Grito de la tierra, grito de los probres* (Madrid: Trotta, 1996).

[38]See John W. Cooper, *Panentheism: The Other God of the Philosophers—From Plato to the Present* (Grand Rapids, MI: Baker Academic, 2006).

[39]In process theology, the God-world relationship not only is construed as metaphysically interdependent, but also God is seen as sharing in the metaphysical categories of process, such as temporality, relatedness, and change.

[40]Jorge V. Pixley, *La Biblia, teología de la liberación y filosofía procesual: El Dios liberador en la Biblia*, Tiempo Axial (Quito: Abya-Yala/UPS, 2009), 56.

consolidation of sin *pecado de los tiempos* (sin of the times), or *pecado histórico* (historical sin).[41] The gospel's liberating announcement confronts this antikingdom reality, for it posits that salvation is accomplished through the life, death, and resurrection of Jesus Christ. "God was reconciling the world to himself in Christ, not counting people's sins against them" (2 Cor 5:19).

Certain formulations of salvation, or liberation, come across as reductionistic. For instance, when the theologian conceives and describes the significance of Jesus' death only in terms of a superb exemplary action, its transcendent consequences will be left undervalued. The cross is treated as an epic event. For example, the death of Jesus is sometimes described as the result of the political and religious persecution of a messianic leader and his group of revolutionaries who were crushed under the weight of history. Jesus identified with people in the margins of society and died in solidarity with them. The execution of Jesus reveals that God identifies with the victims. Solidarity and work in favor of those who need it most is a Christian calling, obligation, and virtue.

But this rendering of salvation, though affirming the historical acts and the character of God, tends to minimize the metaphysical aspects of Christ's actions. First, God is in solidarity with the victims of sin as the one who liberates them for a future of cosmic reconciliation and justice. This liberation is overwhelmingly portrayed in Scripture as God's irruption in history in speech and acts, especially in the person of Jesus, the crucified Messiah for the sins of the world. Divine action is primarily effectual, not merely exemplary. God's liberating actions are experienced both historically (al-

ready) and eschatologically (not yet) for those in union with Christ. Second, salvation entails the shaping of an embodied existence according to the telos of God in Christ through faith. It is the experience of the restoration project of creation. God in Christ through the Spirit is the one who reigns, and human beings are called to participate in this reigning activity.

Therefore, a more fully realized (and even embodied) definition of salvation promotes disciples who participate in the exaltation of the crucified, resurrected Son, who is the true human being. To the extent that the experience of salvation is in the "already" of temporal existence, it is conceived as liberation. Salvation points to the union with and participation in the reign of the Lord Jesus through the Spirit for the creation of a world of perpetual shalom.

The *ekklēsia* is commissioned to embody this renovation of human life, particularly in the face of suffering. It does so by rehearsing a drama of another possible world in a social space (i.e., local church); it taps into the collective imagination of another possible humanity. Life *before* death is an imminent concern. Latin American theology has influenced contemporary literature with the exploration of this new human praxis that longs for a different future. Isabel Allende in her novel *Eva Luna* draws a vivid portrait of such a person, Huberto Naranjo, as he changes/transforms into a new human:

> Outwardly, [he] was made of stone, but as the months passed by, something primal softened and broke on the inside, and from within, a new fruit came forth. The first symptom was compassion, unknown to him, since he had never received it from anybody nor had he ever had the occasion to practice it. Something warm was

[41] Antonio González, *Trinidad y liberación: La teología trinitaria considerada desde la perspectiva de la teología de la liberación*, Colección Teología latinomericana (San Salvador: UCA, 1994), 77.

growing behind his hardness and silence, something like an unlimited affection for others, something that surprised them more than any of the other changes he had suffered thus far. He started to love his comrades, wanting to give his life for them; he felt a powerful desire to hug them and tell them: I love you, brother. Then that feeling extended itself until it encompassed the entire anonymous multitude of the town, and he understood that the rage had turned around.[42]

Beginning with the most vulnerable of humanity, men and women are not only united to Jesus the liberator but are empowered to live as a gathering of a new people, becoming both witnesses to and actors in the reign of the triune God.

FURTHER READING

González, Antonio. *The Gospel of Faith and Justice*. Maryknoll, NY: Orbis, 2005.

Gonzalez, Justo, and Ondina E. Gonzalez. *Christianity in Latin America: A History*. New York: Cambridge University Press, 2008.

Martínez-Olivieri, Jules A. *A Visible Witness: Christology, Liberation and Participation*. Emerging Scholars. Minneapolis: Fortress, 2016.

Sobrino, Jon. *Christ the Liberator: A View from the Victims*. Maryknoll, NY: Orbis, 2001.

---

[42]Isabel Allende, *Eva Luna* (Mexico: Edivisión, 1989), 170.

29

FROM WHAT DO
WE NEED TO BE SAVED?

REFLECTIONS ON GOD'S JUSTICE
AND MATERIAL SALVATION

Milton Acosta

THIS CHAPTER EXPLORES the general understanding of salvation in some prayers in the book of Psalms, in the New Testament, and in Latin American theologies (liberation theology and the Latin American Theological Fellowship) in order to highlight the materiality of salvation as an expression of God's justice. The continuity of the materiality of salvation from the Old to the New Testament is more evident than it seems at first, perhaps because the apostle Paul's theology of salvation and suffering has been so dominant. Latin American theologies are in many ways a return to the importance of the continuity between the Old Testament and the New Testament on the importance of God's justice and the materiality of salvation.

A significant portion of the Psalms is prayers of individuals who see themselves as poor and oppressed, and ask God to deliver them from these social evils (Ps 35:10). This understanding of soteriology occupies a prominent place in Latin American theologies. By Latin American theol-

ogies I mean documents produced by both liberation theologians and by theologians affiliated with the Latin American Theological Fellowship (Fraternidad Teológica Latinoamericana). Given the multiplicity of voices, emphases, and theological methods, it is not possible to speak of "one" theology. For liberation theologians salvation has been articulated as liberation, and for the Latin American Theological Fellowship as integral redemption. Perhaps the two main questions that drive these theologies are, "What do human beings need to be saved from?" and "How are they going to be saved?" For the most part Latin American theologians coincide in stating that the people of Latin America need to be saved from poverty and oppression. Contrary to popular belief, most theologians have envisioned a salvation from these evils through peaceful means, while only a few have endorsed violent ones.

A large portion of the Latin American soteriological discourse has to do with material salvation.[1] On this, these theologies are in

---

[1]This is what Miroslav Volf called the "materiality of salvation," which is present in two movements that have been particularly strong in what is known today as the Global South. Miroslav Volf, "Materiality of Salvation: An Investigation in the Soteriologies of Liberation and Pentecostal Theologies," *Journal of Ecumenical Studies* 26, no. 3 (1989): 447-67.

agreement with the Old Testament, where God is committed to save humanity and particularly his people from any form of threat to their well-being. Thus, when believers of the Old Testament ask God to save them, they are usually referring to an enemy of flesh and blood or to a situation of social injustice, and not so much to sin.

In Latin American evangelical piety, however, salvation has been understood mainly as salvation from sin and eternal damnation. That is, God saves us from condemnation in order to give us eternal life. This may be the reason why in the face of social injustice evangelicals in Latin America have a tendency to favor a response along the lines of Christian maturity, sanctification, and sharing in Christ's passion. More recently, a significant number of churches have added the message of the prosperity gospel as the focus of their prayers and the goal of faith.[2]

My question is, "What do we need to be saved from?" First, I summarize how that question is answered in the book of Psalms, which represents well the Old Testament on this issue. Second, I look at a few New Testament examples that highlight the materiality of salvation. Third, I present a brief summary of how the question of salvation has been answered by both liberation theologians and Latin American Theological Fellowship theologians.

I propose that our first response to social evils and social enemies should not be a prayer for the salvation of the victimizers and another for the eternal life of the victims but a rejection of these evils in the form of a prayer for salvation. Action might be required at some point, but our focus here is on prayers that result from a biblical understanding of salvation, not on the specifics of how these evils should be dealt with.[3]

THE OLD TESTAMENT

The biblical idea of salvation has to do largely with three things: forgiveness of sin, deliverance from danger, and the afterlife. In the Old Testament salvation alludes mostly to deliverance from individuals or situations that pose a threat to life and well-being, be it individual or collective.[4] The main issue is perhaps some form of injustice such as corruption, monopoly, or oppression, among others. Forgiveness of sins may be part of salvation (e.g., Ezek 37:23; Ps 79:9) but is not nearly as common as deliverance from real physical enemies. Eternal life is a theology still undeveloped in the Old Testament.

One obvious place in the Old Testament to see a theology of salvation at work is the book of Psalms. Prayers to God for deliverance from earthly enemies exist because of the simple yet fundamental conviction that God saves. This appears to be the case even in prayers that sound more like a complaint to a God described in some cases as absent or indifferent. This suggests that in order to be interpreted and understood, psalms have to be prayed and felt.[5]

Prayer for salvation in the Old Testament. Regardless of the condition of the victim in the psalms, prayers asking for salvation emanate

---

[2]There will of course be exceptions, and the gap may not be as wide nowadays, but this brief description shows that in Latin America, as in many other contexts, the theology produced by academics travels on one road, while the church runs on another one. Even though this document is not in itself a proposal to bring theology closer to the church, and vice versa, it is worth asking why theology has not influenced the church as much as it could and what can be done to remedy the situation beyond the old mutual blaming game.

[3]See the works by C. René Padilla on integral mission: *Global Poverty and Integral Mission* (Oxford: Church Mission Society, 2009), and *Mission Between the Times* (Carlisle, UK: Langham Monographs, 2010).

[4]Church of England Doctrine Commission, *Contemporary Doctrine Classics: The Combined Reports* (Norwich, UK: Church House, 2005), 344.

[5]Luis Alonso Schökel and Cecilia Carniti, *Salmos I y II* (Estella, Spain: Verbo Divino, 1992). See also Hilario M. Raguer Suñer, *Para comprender y vivir los salmos* (Estella, Spain: Verbo Divino, 2010), 67.

from the idea of God and his role in situations of human injustice and violence. Some prayers show more clearly the conviction that God will save or has saved the penitent from a specific danger. Clearly, material deliverance is understood as a form of salvation.

Psalms is the Old Testament book where the idea of salvation and prayer comes together more than in any other. These prayers have at least three underlying premises: (1) God gets involved in human affairs for the sake of justice, (2) God intervenes in favor of those who believe in him, and (3) prayers of gratitude occur when the former two are true, and prayers for deliverance are poured forth when God appears apathetic or unable to intervene.

God gets involved in human affairs for the sake of justice. The idea here is not that God gets involved in human affairs on demand. It is simply that a good number of prayers in the book of Psalms presuppose that the kingdom of God rests on justice and righteousness. Referring to Psalms 28–30, Christoph Schroeder holds that "the practice of justice and righteousness is a crucial factor for the activation of YHWH's power in favor of the petitioner. The practice of evil . . . is a perversion and a damage to creation; it will lead YHWH to respond by reverting the evil against its doers."[6]

Starting with the first two psalms, the idea of divine participation in human affairs is very clear. In Psalm 1, evil people will perish, while the righteous will stand. In Psalm 2, an apparent psalm of enthronement, the enemies of God's people are threatened if they rebel against God's anointed king. We know that Israel and Judah

were never a real threat to the great empires of the ancient Near East. Hymns such as Psalm 2, however, were perfectly normal, just like national anthems say things that are not literally true but are culturally appropriate for the occasion.[7] Most psalms confirm that one fundamental premise for prayer is the belief that God is interested in human affairs for the sake of justice and righteousness.

There are many psalms that ask God to establish justice. In Psalm 94, for example, God is asked to shine because justice has been perverted. Social enemies are described as oppressors who abuse the poor, the orphan, and the widow, the people whose voices are not heard or do not have the resources to stand up for their rights.[8] God seems to be very attentive to the situation of these people and their prayers (Ps 18:5-7, 17). The conviction expressed in these prayers is that God will destroy individuals who use their power to subjugate and abuse others. According to Psalm 146, God executes justice for the oppressed, gives food to the hungry, sets the prisoners free, opens the eyes of the blind, lifts up those who are bowed down, loves the righteous, watches over the sojourners, upholds the widow and the fatherless, and brings to ruin the way of the wicked (Ps 146:7-9).

Psalms describe the enemies of justice as people who trust in their wealth and boast about it. Violence is also a common trait of these individuals (Ps 86), whose lack of understanding makes them comparable to beasts (Ps 49). These are social enemies who have no fear of God or civil laws, and are not likely to be persuaded by reasonable arguments. Some psalms address

---

[6]Christoph O. Schroeder, *History, Justice, and the Agency of God: A Hermeneutical and Exegetical Investigation on Isaiah and Psalms* (Leiden: Brill, 2001), 221.
[7]The Colombian national anthem says that all our evils are over and that the whole world understands the words of Christ.
[8]Even animals are saved by God! (See Ps 36:6; 147:9.)

them just to say that God will destroy them. The predominant language is "deliver me" (*haṣṣîlēnî*), but in some cases God's actions and the victims' actions to eliminate victimizers are one and the same thing (e.g., Ps 18:37-43; 41:10). This is the foundation of prayers that ask for justice and salvation for those who trust in the steadfast love of God (Ps 52:8). Thus, God's justice and righteousness are objects of meditation, prayer, and discourse (Ps 71).

We may partially conclude that (1) justice is a common concern in the psalms, (2) victims of injustice expect God to act in their favor, and (3) justice is done when social enemies are removed.

What do we need to be saved from? People who are victims of social enemies for prolonged periods of time face the danger of despair, the sense of having been abandoned by God. Therefore, salvation from enemies is also salvation from hopelessness and unbelief: "By this I know that you delight in me: my enemy will not shout in triumph over me" (Ps 41:11; see Ps 6:4).[9] Perhaps as an encouragement in these situations, there are psalms that proclaim that God is a guardian who does not fall asleep (Ps 121:3-7; 59:5).

Justice should be promoted by legislation, upheld by all citizens, and defended by judges. Since these three seem to fail rather frequently, affecting especially the weaker population, salvation from all forms of injustice becomes a permanent cry to God in the psalms. There are prayers against favoritism in the courts and a command to the contrary: "Rescue the weak and the needy; deliver them from the hand of the wicked" (Ps 82:4). God, the "judge of the earth"

(Ps 82:8), is called on because earthly judges do not do what they are supposed to. The establishment of justice on earth is also understood as part of God's sovereignty.[10]

Along with injustice, people need salvation from physical danger. The main concerns in these prayers were not traffic or climate change, which are very important. Rather, they talk about the snare of the fowler, pestilence, the terror of the night, arrows that fly, destruction (Ps 91), all sorts of evils such as violent men, venomous tongues, wicked hands, and arrogant people (Ps 140). Salvation in these cases is understood as having a long life well lived.

The petitioner in the psalms also needs to be saved from false hopes, like warriors and their weapons. There is a consistent warning in the Old Testament against trusting in military intelligence and power; faithfulness to God is more important (Ps 146:3; 147:10-11).[11] This, however, does not imply the elimination of armed forces (Ps 35).

Gratitude and complaint. The world of the psalms appears quite dangerous. People are mistreated, abused, threatened, and persecuted. At times life feels like sleeping around lions (Ps 57:4). This is why the cry "keep me," "hide me," and other petitions to the same effect are so common in these prayers. These are enemies of flesh and blood who pose a mortal threat to the person who prays (Ps 17:8).

Perhaps the absence of justice on earth created the urgency in the people of God to think and produce so much literature about this issue. One common irony in prayers for justice is the need to be saved from judges, precisely the

---

[9]In ancient times this did not lead to atheism but to polytheism. Several gods could be better than one if the one you have appears unable to save you. Unless otherwise noted, Scripture translations in this chapter follow the ESV.

[10]J. Clinton McCann, "Righteousness, Justice, and Peace: A Contemporary Theology of the Psalms," *Horizons in Biblical Theology* 23 (2001): 115.

[11]For a complete study of the theme of not trusting in military power, see José Luis Sicre, *Los dioses olvidados: Poder y riqueza en los profetas preexílicos* (Madrid: Cristiandad, 1979).

people responsible for imparting justice (Ps 58; 60; 109:30-31). Those who are meant to be protectors are the ones who "eat up my people as they eat bread" (Ps 53:4). The identity of the enemies is not always clearly stated, but these are people who also pray to God for help but there is no response for them (Ps 18:41).

There seem to be other grounds besides justice on which prayers for salvation are addressed to God. Some psalms state that people in vulnerable situations are saved because of God's mercy (Ps 31:16), because "he delighted in me" (Ps 18:19), or because "I am your servant" (Ps 143:12). In some cases there is a clear affirmation of justice as a retribution for the believer's righteousness and cleanness. In fact, "in the Psalms it is almost always *the righteous* who are suffering, and they are generally suffering not because they have been bad, but rather because they have been faithful."[12] The reasoning of these prayers seems to be that God shows mercy to the merciful, "and with the crooked you make yourself seem tortuous" (Ps 18:26).

God's favorable response to a prayer for deliverance provokes, quite naturally, celebration and words of exaltation. It is one important way by which God becomes real. In some cases the issue is described using court language where evil people are judged, sentenced, and condemned to perpetual ruin. Witnessing the end to injustice is understood to be one of the ways by which God "avenges blood" and remembers those who seek him, that is, the poor.

That about two-thirds of the psalms are lamentations or contain lament implies that it was not uncommon for people in ancient Israel and Judah to have their very existence threatened and, as a result, their faith challenged permanently. Can God save? Prayer, then, is often simultaneously a declaration of belief and unbelief, celebration and lament.

One expression that sums up the idea of salvation in the Psalms is that God restores fortunes. The return of the exiles and the exodus are perhaps the ultimate instances of salvation in the Old Testament. In the case of the exiles who returned to Judea, salvation brought laughter, shouts of joy, and even praise to God from other nations (Ps 126:1-4).

It is possible to speak of God in the abstract, but theology makes little sense unless there is some connection to the world as we, as human beings who live on this earth, know it. Although this sounds very obvious, perhaps it helps us understand that knowledge of God as Savior in the psalms has to do with actual acts of salvation from enemies who can cause physical harm. It is the experience of salvation that produces descriptions of God as rest for the soul, rock, refuge, loving, powerful (Ps 62), and many others that are used to worship God.

As indicated above, the psalms also show that salvation does not always occur in the time or in the way that it is expected, and on occasion not at all. This is also part of the picture in the prayers about salvation. The psalms that express this uncertainty about God's salvation or that complain to God for not being aware of what happens to his people are called psalms of lament. In some cases God is accused of being deaf, mute, asleep, hidden, or indifferent to the suffering of the righteous (Ps 12; 28; 54; 83). In some psalms there is the puzzling combination of uncertainty and assurance. Social evils are denounced, and the certainty of God's salvation is also affirmed.

---

[12]McCann, "Righteousness, Justice, and Peace," 122, emphasis original.

Complaints and laments to God are expressions of faith. It is precisely because of that that the psalmists make these affirmations and questions about God's ability to save (Ps 80). Two common questions are, "How long, O God?" and "Where are you, God?" (Ps 89). These questions presuppose that God is absent when and where he should be present and performing some salvific act.

One of the major theological challenges expressed in the Psalms is simultaneity of the prosperity of evil people and the disgrace of the righteous. In such circumstances, the righteous are tempted to follow the path of the wicked. God seems unable to save and indifferent to sin, which goes against God's expected behavior. The petitioners in these prayers need to be saved in order to believe and to avoid taking the path of corruption and injustice (Ps 18:39-49). In at least one case (Ps 55), in the face of unresolved violence, crime, injustice, cruelty, and deceit, the only alternative seems to be to escape.

Some psalms are perhaps comparable to videos that show a person of authority committing some kind of abuse. They are shown to stir up some sentiments of outrage and indignation in viewers. Psalm 74 talks about the destruction of the temple, the absence of prophets, and God's indifference. Even worse, God seems to be acting against everything he believes (Ps 79)! What could be more tragic than that? But this is done to remind God of who he is. And the reason for doing all this is that God simply cannot disappoint those who trust in him, that is, the poor and the oppressed.

Psalm 80 seems to be a national cry for salvation. God is described as pastor, Lord of hosts, and farmer who should save his people. But the pastor is asleep, the Lord of hosts is somewhere up there wrapped in clouds, and the farmer has completely abandoned his vineyard. From the perspective of this psalm, having faith means asking difficult questions to God and about God when God does not save (Ps 102). Why is God punishing us? Shouldn't he be dealing with the pagans instead? Why are we being punished because of sins committed by our ancestors (Ps 79)? The "how long?" and the "why?" in the Old Testament generally suggest that faith has reached a dangerous limit. These observations show that the theology of salvation in the Psalms is complex. In some instances there is an acknowledgment that the people of Israel have been disobedient and their judgment is well deserved (e.g., Ps 78). But that's not always the case. The psalms of lament seem to express an unbearable incongruity between theology and facts, between faith and experience. We might very well ask whether this incongruity is caused by God's revelation itself or by expectations that all human beings would come up with given a chance to present all our petitions to an almighty God whom we believe is on our side.[13]

To summarize, this brief survey of salvation in the Psalms shows:

1. Life was hard for many people.
2. God's presence and power were not always evident.
3. People protested to God and prayed to God for deliverance.
4. Salvation is a central issue in the book of Psalms.
5. Prayer makes sense because God saves.

[13]For a more detailed study of this issue, see Craig C. Broyles, *The Conflict of Faith and Experience in the Psalms: A Form-Critical and Theological Study* (Sheffield: JSOT Press, 1989); Carleen Mandolfo, *God in the Dock: Dialogic Tension in the Psalms of Lament* (London: Sheffield Academic Press, 2002).

THE NEW TESTAMENT

Many general and specific works are available on salvation in the New Testament, some of them quite detailed.[14] Perhaps it might be safe to say that most works published on soteriology represent the perspective of the New Testament. This happens because of the Christ event. Since we do not have in the New Testament anything comparable to the book of Psalms, I have selected some texts and themes in order to observe what seems to be the dominant response to injustice when it is based on the New Testament.

God's interest in human affairs is present throughout the New Testament. In fact, the incarnation is considered the climactic event in salvation history. The life, death, and resurrection of Jesus together constitute God's ultimate salvific act in favor of humanity. We must ask two questions, however: Is the presentation of salvation in the New Testament developed exponentially regarding the atonement and the afterlife, and underdeveloped in matters of life this side of the grave? Or is our reading of the New Testament regarding these issues inadequate?

What do we need to be saved from? According to Luke's Gospel (Lk 4:17-21), Jesus read the section in the scroll of Isaiah that talks about the liberation of the poor, the oppressed, and the marginalized and concluded that this was a description of his person and ministry. Rosinah Gabaitse has clearly shown in her chapter in this section that this is the road map for Jesus' ministry, but that in the context of Botswana where she lives there is a tendency to remove the mate-

riality of this description of salvation and to turn to spiritual poverty, oppression, and marginalization. The very fact that a chapter has to be written to warn against spiritualizing these words shows that Christians in many parts of the world do not see in the New Testament what some see in the Old Testament, that God is in the business of material salvation as well.

When Zacchaeus acknowledged that he had robbed his fellow citizens in the business of collecting taxes, he decided to give half of his wealth to the poor and to restore fourfold the money he had stolen. Jesus said in response to his decision, "Salvation has come to this house" (Lk 19:8-10). In this case salvation has to do with doing justice, stopping corruption, and restoring social order. This is clearly in line with the Psalms and with Luke 4 quoting Isaiah, which clearly shows the continuity between the Old Testament and the teaching of Jesus on the material aspects of salvation, such as the practice of justice and care for the poor, which demonstrate what it means to love God.[15] Thus, it would be a distortion of the New Testament to limit soteriology to forgiveness of sin and the afterlife. The idea of salvation in the New Testament is rich and complex.

Suffering and salvation. In Acts 4, Psalm 2:1-2 is applied to Jesus in order to affirm that this anointed king has been killed "according to the definite plan and foreknowledge of God." This is said by people who are being persecuted because of Christ. The disciples' request for protection seems short and mild. They pray that God would "look upon their threats" and grant them boldness to continue preaching and to perform signs and wonders by the power of God.

---

[14]For example: Charles H. Talbert, Jason A. Whitlark, and Andrew E. Arterbury, *Getting "Saved": The Whole Story of Salvation in the New Testament* (Grand Rapids, MI: Eerdmans, 2011); Brenda B. Colijn, *Images of Salvation in the New Testament* (Downers Grove, IL: IVP Academic, 2010); J. G. Van der Watt, ed., *Salvation in the New Testament: Perspectives on Soteriology* (Leiden: Brill, 2005); Gary W. Burnett, *Paul and the Salvation of the Individual* (Leiden: Brill, 2001).

[15]Christopher M. Hays, *Renouncing Everything: Money and Discipleship in Luke* (New York: Paulist, 2017).

The way Psalm 2 is used provides a scriptural explanation for Jesus' death, but it seems to suggest that the rulers of the earth who revolt against the Lord and his anointed have succeeded. The verses quoted seem to change the tone of the psalm as a whole. The issue of God's sovereignty might be present in both texts (the whole psalm and what is quoted in Acts 4), but in its New Testament context does not seem to offer any hope of divine protection from social crimes, such as the injustice of killing an innocent. We could say that this is precisely the paradox of salvation, but the point is that the issue of justice is overridden and that those who want to follow this king should be prepared to be the objects of similar injustice. This text seems to set a foundation and a pattern for other stories and future reflections in the rest of the New Testament about suffering for the sake of Jesus, especially in the writings of Paul on this issue.

We must not overlook, however, that Christians are trying to survive in an antagonistic environment. Yet the political discourse of resistance is shot throughout, with Revelation being the climax of this thread that we see in Luke 4. In short, there is more oppositional discourse in the New Testament than we realize. Jesus' cross and resurrection is the center point here, given the use of the cross as a tool of political repression and domination.

The result of the prayer in Acts 4 is that the disciples got what they asked for: fear was gone, the gospel was preached, and miracles occurred. And even more, they were filled with the Holy Spirit. Justice does not seem to be a concern here, but there is resistance on the part of the apostles to the political pressure of the priests and Sanhedrin. They were jailed, but God delivered them; clearly, the powers are challenged, the authorities are dishonored, and the apostles are honored. The church does not have an army to jailbreak, but God sends his angel instead!

In his teaching about prayer, Jesus tells the story of a widow who is the victim of a corrupt justice system (Lk 18:1-8). A judge does not do his job, and nobody cares. However, the apparently helpless widow has a powerful weapon—nagging—and she knows how to use it. The conclusion is that this widow will be given justice by the unjust judge because of her persistence; he gets exasperated, and she will not go away. The story seems to be in line with some prayers about justice in the psalms. For this reason some versions of the Bible reference some psalms next to it (Ps 9:8; 58:11; 94:2).

It seems to be that on the issue of suffering, Paul and other New Testament authors are not following the theology and experiences of the Psalms, but other texts, perhaps Job and Habakkuk. Paul finds strength in weakness, and sees distress, personal crises, and unanswered prayers as opportunities to trust God and his grace in those situations where justice on this earth is not done. Death is victory because it is a way to participate in the sufferings of Jesus, who died but conquered death by being resurrected. This eschatological hope means that both the faithful and the wicked will receive their recompense, a prominent theme in the Gospel of Luke.[16] So there will be justice.

This short selection of texts shows that salvation in the New Testament has to do with believing in Jesus for the forgiveness of sin and the assurance of eternal life. Salvation is also linked to protection from death in the form of healings and an unhealthy religious system.[17] And it also has to do with salvation from social evils.

---

[16]Hays, *Renouncing Everything.*

[17]These seem to be the main two foci of salvation in the New Testament observed by various authors. See Van der Watt, *Salvation in the New Testament.*

LATIN AMERICAN THEOLOGIES

Justice is a prominent issue in Latin American theologies, particularly because of its links to the theology of the kingdom of God and its relevance to the Latin American context. There are multiple forms of violence suffered by the poor and society as a whole. Therefore, it is only natural that Latin American theologies since their early days invite people to seek justice and to promote the values of the kingdom of God throughout the continent. Traditionally, Latin American theologies have seen government and big corporations as the main cause of poverty and oppression. Today the sources of violence have diversified, and we see that the agents of violence have multiplied, in part due to the absence and weakness of the state.

What follows is not meant to be a summary of the main ideas in Latin American theologies. It is simply a small selection of how some theologians in the continent have answered the question, "What do we need to be saved from?"

Liberation theologies. In typical liberationist terms, Brazilian theologian Leonardo Boff warns against the danger of an "antithetical dualism" where theology has to choose between "human liberation and salvation in Jesus Christ." The way out of this problem lies in the proposal of an *"integral liberation* that embraces all the dimensions of human life: corporal-spiritual, personal-collective, historical-transcendent." This is evident in the Lord's Prayer: *"the essence of Jesus's message—*the Lord's Prayer—*has been formulated in a prayer, not as a dogma."*[18]

One key insight in liberation theologies is that "in order for God to liberate his creation . . . *it is necessary for human beings to participate* lest they are reduced to mere spectators; otherwise, the kingdom of God would be inhuman and an imposition. As it is, this world is not the kingdom; but with God's intervention and man's conversion acting on this world, it is transformed into the place of God's kingdom."[19] Boff adds,

> The coming of this kingdom is not mechanical, it does not preclude human collaboration. The kingdom is *God's* kingdom, but it has to become *man's* kingdom. God does not save the world and humanity all by himself, for he has made humans partners in the messianic task until one person becomes sacrament of salvation to another. And this partnership is so decisive that its outcome impinges upon the eternal salvation of man.[20]

In brief, humans do the liberating, but this is from God because "it is God who moves and penetrates human action in such a way that liberation can be considered as God's work."[21]

Jesus' disciples' request that he teach them how to pray was like asking him for a summary of his message. Seen in this light, "prayer functioned as a type of *creed* that granted unity and identity to the group."[22] This is how Boff integrates ecclesiology, liberation, and prayer. Prayer becomes the incarnation of the kingdom of God in the church without being limited to it.

The reason why salvation has to be material is that "no matter how high the Spirit soars, no matter how deep our mystical probings, or how metaphysical our abstract thinking, the human being will always be dependent on a piece of

---

[18]Leonardo Boff, *El padrenuestro: La oración de la liberación integral* (Madrid: Ediciones Paulinas, 1982), 12, 14, emphasis original.
[19]Boff, *El padrenuestro*, 25.
[20]Boff, *El padrenuestro*, 91.
[21]Leonardo Boff, *Gracia y liberación del hombre: experiencia y doctrina de la gracia* (Madrid: Ediciones Cristiandad, 1980), 208.
[22]Boff, *El padrenuestro*, 30.

bread, a cup of water—in short, on a handful of matter. The material infrastructure is so important that ultimately we find it the root and ground of everything we think about or plan or do." The kingdom of God, which is central in the Lord's Prayer, breaks through and sprouts whenever there is reconciliation and the establishment of just structures in society. For Boff the kingdom of God is present when friendships are restored and whenever a person recovers her dignity.[23]

The centrality of liberation in liberation theology presupposes that the Christian response to injustice will not be a theology of suffering, but a theological formulation centered on both divine and human actions against suffering caused directly by human hands or in the form of institutions. Therefore, prayer becomes action.

In his book on Christology, Boff points out that the Latin American context is more interested in anthropology than in ecclesiology, for one simple reason: it is the human being who needs help. The materiality of salvation is not in the visible institutions of the church, but in the needs of people. Theology reflects "on reality right where it bleeds." The goal is not a permanent confrontation but a more human and fraternal world. For that theology has to identify as a fundamental problem the marginalization caused by established social structures. Without this, social reconciliation is impossible. In this context Boff includes loving both friends and enemies. Reconciliation can happen if there are a liberation of the human condition, a conversion of the person, and a reshaping of the world of the person. In the end "what saves is love, disinterestedly accepting

the other and being completely open towards God. Here there is no more friend or enemy, neighbor or not neighbor. There are only brothers and sisters." No violence is needed to accomplish this.[24]

According to Boff, Jesus was not interested in understanding and explaining evil but in "assuming it and defeating it with love." It is at this point perhaps where Boff reconciles salvation and suffering:

> Jesus's behavior opened a new possibility for human existence, more precisely, an existence of faith in an absolute sense, even in the face of absurdity, such as the death caused by hatred towards the one who only just loved and sought to do good among men. For this reason Bonhoeffer says that Christians today are called to live that weakness of Christ in the world.[25]

Where Christians have to be careful for Boff is in the timing of liberation. This is not expected to occur immediately because it could make the situation of the oppressed even worse: "For a [liberating] action to be effective, knowing how to wait is crucial. Thus, faith has to be elaborated and live a mystical dimension of liberation to the point of a general regime of oppression." So for Boff liberation becomes a permanent spiral because new captivities appear constantly.[26]

In brief, liberation theology "reflects radically about the salvific mystery in its historical dimension. It is a protest against all forms of fatalism, against all paralyzing sacralization and against any theological speculation disembodied of the world." It has helped theologians all over the world to think of the material

---

[23]Leonardo Boff, *The Lord's Prayer: The Prayer of Integral Liberation* (Melbourne: Dove Communications, 1983), 75, 82.
[24]Leonardo Boff, *Jesucristo el liberador: Ensayo de Cristología crítica para nuestro tiempo* (Santander, Spain: Sal Terrae, 1983), 63-64, 73, 81, 91, 94, 123, 125.
[25]Boff, *Jesucristo el liberador*, 130.
[26]Boff, *Gracia y liberación*, 117, 203.

implications of salvation, or "the liberating power of the Gospel."[27]

La Fraternidad Teológica Latinoamericana. This section is mostly based on a book that C. René Padilla has described as a "mature fruit" of the theological thinking elaborated by various theologians affiliated with the Latin American Theological Fellowship: *To Be, to Do and to Say: Biblical Foundations of Integral Mission.*[28] This is not a book specifically about prayer, but through its contents we can glean some ideas about how Christians facing oppression and injustice would pray and act.

In the first essay, Old Testament scholar Edesio Sánchez states that in the book of Deuteronomy faithfulness to God has to be understood as the practice of social justice and "the pursuit of a society rooted in justice, peace and love." In other words, "the mission of God's people is founded on two inseparable components: absolute faithfulness to YHWH and social justice."[29]

In this light, biblical monotheism is not just a matter of rejecting other gods, "but also the inescapable responsibility to work hard so that both in oneself and in others the image of God may be reserved without distortions or disguise [*disfraz*]." The best example of this is obviously the book of Exodus, where a community of slaves is liberated from oppression in the form of slavery. "This is the heart of God's mission, and will also be the *locus* and *ethos* of the mission of the church."[30] This liberation is God's answer to the cries of the Israelites in Egypt (Ex 3).

In an essay on the prophets, Esteban Voth holds that the prophets of Israel had a message against unjust structures and the objectification of human beings and for the "construction of theological realities that sought the complete well-being [*bien integral*] of the person." This is so because God's justice "cannot be divorced from God's holiness." In biblical prophetic discourse justice is "always a theological term. The concept of justice is rooted in God's very being, who is just and also requires and demands justice from all human beings." Voth also stresses that in the perspective of the prophets, not doing justice is one of the ways human beings profane God's name (Ezek 36:20). Often when God intervenes powerfully to demand or to establish justice, this is not a pretty picture.[31]

In his application of the prophetic message to the Latin American context, Voth states,

> An integral mission practiced today must take the example of Isaiah seriously. The Latin American context is plagued with situations where the foreigner, the widow, the orphan and the weakest of the population are scorned. These situations are legitimated by legislation or the interpretation of the law. The church, as a community, has the challenge not only to denounce but to transform these cruel realities.

According to Voth, the church should follow the example of the prophets insofar as they saw social injustice as situations that must be confronted directly and unambiguously.[32]

Sánchez and Voth, two Latin American Old Testament scholars, do not see social injustice primarily as an opportunity for spiritual growth

---

[27]Johannes Feiner and Magnus Löhrer, eds., *Mysterium Salutis: Manual de teología como historia de salvación* (Madrid: Cristiandad, n.d.), 5:261, 264.

[28]C. René Padilla and Harold Segura, eds., *Ser, hacer y decir: Bases bíblicas de la misión integral* (Buenos Aires: Ediciones Kairos, 2006).

[29]Edesio Sánchez Cetina, "Misión integral en el Pentateuco," in Padilla and Segura, *Ser, hacer y decir*, 10-11.

[30]Sánchez Cetina, "Misión integral," 14, 35.

[31]Esteban Voth, "Los profetas y la misión integral," in Padilla and Segura, *Ser, hacer y decir*, 156, 169-70.

[32]Voth, "Los profetas y la misión integral," 175.

but as a form of evil that God does not tolerate and Christians should not either. Nevertheless, Voth acknowledges that since the prophets spoke out against the choking forces of the establishment, there are real dangers involved in prophetic preaching. Referring to the case of Ezekiel, Voth states, "The prophet has such passion for life that he is willing to risk his own life."[33] This means that, as for some liberation theologians, liberation and integral mission do not imply the solution to all social problems once and for all. It is a matter of faithfulness to God and to his revelation in Scripture.

A third author whom we consider from this book on the biblical foundations of integral mission is Juan Carlos Cevallos, who wrote an essay on the Synoptic Gospels. As with Sánchez and Voth, Cevallos sees in the life and words of Jesus a call to seek justice on earth. Since the state is not divine or the ultimate reality, Christians can never relinquish their role as critics of all acts of institutional injustice.[34]

According to Cevallos, the ideas of justice and compassion are so important in the message of Jesus about the kingdom of God that they "cannot be understood apart from a decision to serve God." In other words, since God cares especially for the victims of injustice and oppression, that is, the weak and the marginalized, indifference to their plight becomes a serious sin because it has to do with God's very being and his kingdom: "Jesus was never passive when he saw the injustice of the powerful and the privileged people. Nor was he ever a promoter of the *status quo*."[35] Cevallos then sees a continuity

between the teaching and preaching of the Torah, the prophets, and the Psalms and the teaching and preaching of Jesus regarding justice and the kingdom of God, a continuity in the materiality of salvation. The prophetic role of the church means "unmasking the oppressors" within and outside the church.[36]

The emphatic call of the followers of Jesus to seek justice and to stand up for the rights of the weaker members of society implies that for La Fraternidad Teológica Latinoamericana theologians, salvation has a clear and important material component. We could even say that the materiality of salvation is central to the biblical message.

Another repeated issue in dealing with the issues of injustice is the price paid by those who speak out. The goal is not to make new enemies but reconciliation. Therefore, Cevallos insists that Christians should also follow Jesus in his commitment to the practice of nonviolence and forgiveness.[37]

The final author we consider from this book is Justo González, who focuses more on salvation in his essay on integral mission in the book of Acts. González acknowledges that "the preaching of the Gospel and the salvation of souls are both part of the church's mission, integral mission . . . [which] has to do with human history, the nations, the freedom that people should have to 'dwell in the land.'"[38]

Acts is the New Testament book where we expect to see the practice of what the other authors have said about justice and salvation from the Old Testament and the Gospels. And we do find it, but in the form of samples, not as a

---

[33]Voth, "Los profetas y la misión integral," 179.
[34]Juan Carlos Cevallos, "La misión en los evangelios sinópticos," in Padilla and Segura, *Ser, hacer y decir*, 183, 187.
[35]These ideas are based on Matthew's use of Is 32:1-20.
[36]Cevallos, "La misión en los evangelios sinópticos," 211, 217, 220-21.
[37]Cevallos, "La misión en los evangelios sinópticos," 249.
[38]Justo González, "La misión en Hechos," in Padilla and Segura, *Ser, hacer y decir*, 301.

church-wide program for the undoing of poverty, oppression, and marginalization and the establishment of justice.

Thus, González also says that "true salvation not only has to do with eternal life but with victory over all the evils that hurt the body and the whole of life." Jesus is the only source of salvation, but his field of action is not limited to the church: "Wherever there is health, wellbeing, happiness, victory over the powers of evil, there is Jesus, who is the only source of all salvation. . . . The mission of Jesus is so big, so encompassing, that it reaches much further than our preaching and what it may accomplish." One example of salvation in the early church is the sharing of goods. The testimony here is of "salvation from greed, economic injustice, dehumanizing poverty." Wherever a person is freed from any of these evils, there is salvation.[39]

CONCLUSION

According to Miroslav Volf, "Classical (and to a large extent modern) Protestant theology since Luther has retained his radical distinction between salvation and well-being and denied that salvation can be partly experienced in the realm of bodily existence in the world."[40] Even if this thinking cannot be traced back to Luther in every work on soteriology, the truth is that the distinction does exist. This perhaps explains why in some Christian traditions salvation is mainly or merely a matter of forgiveness of sins and eternal life.

As we have seen, material salvation is a central theme in the Old Testament. Salvation is also understood in material terms in Latin American theologies under the general idea that salvation has to do with the whole person. As far as the New Testament is concerned, we see that salvation also includes the body and what happens to it on the earth. Human suffering caused by social evils does play a spiritual role in both the Old and the New Testaments, but it is not an acceptance of it.

Christians who suffer from social evils will certainly have to deal with this situation, both personally and in their communities. But the Bible does not stop there. A victim may forgive a criminal, but, according to the Bible, criminals have to be held accountable for their crimes, no matter who they are. This would sound quite obvious to many people. The reason for bringing it up is that there are Christians who live in places where criminals are the law, rights are not respected, and people live in constant fear. If God does not save them, no one is going to save them. Praying psalms of deliverance from their enemies becomes normal, and their elimination a reason to praise God fervently.[41]

Volf has shown that it makes a lot of sense that theologies with a stronger emphasis on the materiality of salvation, such as liberation theology and Pentecostalism (and more recently the so-called prosperity gospel), would flourish in places where socioeconomic needs are greater. As is always the case, context drives theology.

Material salvation becomes important whenever and wherever there is a need for material salvation. John Coffey describes the role of material salvation as freedom from slavery in various Western movements: Protestants from the Roman pope, Puritans who experienced an

---

[39]González, "La misión en Hechos," 309-12.

[40]When soteriology deals with issues related to social evils, disease, and the economy, it is said that such theology is interested in the "materiality of salvation." Volf, "Materiality of Salvation," 453.

[41]This is what a group of Christians coming from a very violent area of Colombia told me in an interview in 2012. It does not always mean their death but the inability to carry on any criminal activity.

exodus and year of Jubilee, and Oliver Cromwell, who was seen as the English Moses. These and other movements had to do with liberation from religious and civil slavery. Colonists in what is today the United States interpreted their emancipation from the British similarly.[42]

This confirms what has been said in various ways: "Religion as a social phenomenon can function only in the context of culture, and any abstraction of a religion from the cultural context in which it is manifested will distort its essential features." The other side of this is that the biblical message is appropriated through a hermeneutic that the readers of the Bible can understand in terms of both its method and the degree to which it responds to their needs.[43]

Perhaps a confirmation of Volf's affirmation about material salvation in Luther can be found in John Coffey's words: "While oppression and liberation are indispensable biblical categories, they are penultimate ones. In Christianity, love is a more fundamental concept than freedom, and liberation must be crowned by reconciliation, a truth powerfully modeled by Martin Luther King and Desmond Tutu."[44]

My concern here is not that God has to eliminate all suffering and make all Christians rich. That would be nice for many, but that is a view that cannot be defended from the whole testimony of the Bible. As D. L. Baker has said, "Even in the New Testament there are unrealized hopes for the establishment of justice and the end of salvation history."[45] The point is that soteriology has a direct bearing on Christian attitudes toward social evils, as the Psalms clearly show. A more complete biblical view of salvation could affect the prayers of Christians and in favor of Christians who are victims of serious social enemies, such as injustice, corruption, and violence.

FURTHER READING

Baker, D. L. *Two Testaments, One Bible: A Study of Some Modern Solutions to the Theological Problem of the Relationship Between the Old and New Testaments*. Downers Grove, IL: InterVarsity Press, 1976.

Boff, Leonardo. *The Lord's Prayer: The Prayer of Integral Liberation*. Melbourne: Dove Communications, 1983.

Broyles, Craig C. *The Conflict of Faith and Experience in the Psalms: A Form-Critical and Theological Study*. Sheffield, UK: JSOT Press, 1989.

Burnett, Gary W. *Paul and the Salvation of the Individual*. Leiden: Brill, 2001.

Church of England Doctrine Commission. *Contemporary Doctrine Classics: The Combined Reports*. London: Church House, 2005.

Coffey, John. "'To Release the Oppressed': Reclaiming a Biblical Theology of Liberation." *Cambridge Papers* 18, no. 4 (December 2009): 1-4.

Colijn, Brenda B. *Images of Salvation in the New Testament*. Downers Grove, IL: IVP Academic, 2010.

Mandolfo, Carleen. *God in the Dock: Dialogic Tension in the Psalms of Lament*. London: Sheffield, 2002.

McCann, J. Clinton. "Righteousness, Justice, and Peace: A Contemporary Theology of the Psalms." *Horizons in Biblical Theology* 23, no. 2 (2001): 111-31.

---

[42]"Yet even as they praised God for political deliverance, white Americans held hundreds of thousands of Africans in chattel slavery, and the English had become the world's greatest slave traders." John Coffey, "'To Release the Oppressed': Reclaiming a Biblical Theology of Liberation," *Cambridge Papers* 18, no. 4 (December 2009): 1.

[43]Jesse Mugambi, "Africa and the Old Testament," in *Interpreting the Old Testament in Africa: Papers from the International Symposium on Africa and the Old Testament in Nairobi, October 1999*, ed. Mary N. Getui, Knut Holter, and Victor Zinkuratire (New York: P. Lang, 2001), 10, 16.

[44]Coffey, "'To Release the Oppressed,'" 3.

[45]Baker, *Two Testaments, One Bible*, 137.

Mugambi, Jesse. "Africa and the Old Testament." Pages 7-26 in *Interpreting the Old Testament in Africa: Papers from the International Symposium on Africa and the Old Testament in Nairobi, October 1999*, edited by Mary N. Getui, Knut Holter, and Victor Zinkuratire. New York: P. Lang, 2001.

Padilla, C. René. *Global Poverty and Integral Mission*. Oxford: Church Mission Society, 2009.

———. *Mission Between the Times*. Carlisle, UK: Langham Creative Projects, 2010.

Padilla, C. René, and Harold Segura, eds. *Ser, hacer y decir: Bases bíblicas de la misión integral*. Buenos Aires: Ediciones Kairos, 2006.

Schroeder, Christoph O. *History, Justice, and the Agency of God: A Hermeneutical and Exegetical Investigation on Isaiah and Psalms*. Leiden: Brill, 2001.

Sicre, José Luis. *Los dioses olvidados: Poder y riqueza en los profetas preexílicos*. Madrid: Cristiandad, 1979.

Talbert, Charles H., Jason A. Whitlark, and Andrew E. Arterbury. *Getting "Saved": The Whole Story of Salvation in the New Testament*. Grand Rapids, MI: Eerdmans, 2011.

Van der Watt, J. G., ed. *Salvation in the New Testament: Perspectives on Soteriology*. Leiden: Brill, 2005.

Volf, Miroslav. "Materiality of Salvation: An Investigation in the Soteriologies of Liberation and Pentecostal Theologies." *Journal of Ecumenical Studies* 26, no. 3 (1989): 447-67.

30

AN INDIGENOUS REINTERPRETATION OF REPENTANCE

A STEP ON THE JOURNEY TO RECONCILIATION

Ray Aldred

UNDER THE CANADIAN colonial enterprise, salvation for indigenous people was defined as becoming Western and civilized. Conversion for indigenous people meant repenting of indigenous identity, putting it off, and becoming Western, or enfranchised into Canadian society. Conversely, contextual Cree theology reinterprets conversion and repentance as an embracing of the Creator's fulfillment of all that our traditional spirituality longed for. Repentance is turning to Christ by embracing a God-given indigenous identity as a true human being. This reinterpretation of repentance is also sufficient for nonindigenous North Americans as they embrace their own responsibility through repentance moving toward reconciliation.

The idea for this chapter flows out of the attempt to try to hold two identities—Christian and Nehiyaw (Cree, Indian) or Nehiyawiwin (Cree identity)—together within one person.[1] Indigenous people take seriously their indigenous and Christian heritage. They value the spiritual legacy of their ancestors and their own

indigenous experiences.[2] However, room was not always made for the indigenous experience and spirituality within North American Christian identity. This chapter is an attempt to work through some of these difficulties in hopes of promoting the possibility of a "peace treaty" between the two.

Under the Canadian colonial enterprise, salvation for indigenous people was defined as becoming Western and civilized. Conversion meant repenting of indigenous identity and becoming Western, or enfranchised into Canadian society. Conversely, contextual Cree theology would reinterpret conversion and repentance as an embracing of the Creator's fulfillment of all that our traditional spirituality longed for. Repentance is turning to Christ by embracing a God-given indigenous identity as a true human being. This reinterpretation of repentance is also sufficient for nonindigenous North Americans as they embrace their own responsibility through repentance moving toward reconciliation that could be described

---

[1] Arok Wolvengrey and Freda Ahenakew, *Nēhiyawēwin: Itwēwina* (Regina: Canadian Plains Research Center, University of Regina, 2001).
[2] James Treat, *Native and Christian: Indigenous Voices on Religious Identity in the United States and Canada* (New York: Routledge, 1996), 2-8.

using the principles of restorative justice: telling the truth, or complete disclosure; listening with the heart and not just the intellect; and engaging in a shared plan built on a return to the ongoing historical indigenous treaty process.

COLONIZED CONVERSION AND REPENTANCE

The problem of reconciling indigenous and Christian identity in Canada is not just a result of the enforcement of assimilationist policies by some denominations through residential schools. These policies were made possible because in Canada there was a general consensus among Euro-Canadians that indigenous people were a problem to be solved. For example, Mohawk lawyer Patricia Monture-Angus, in her book *Journeying Forward: Dreaming First Nations Independence*, observes that as recently as 1991 Judge Allan McEachern of the British Columbia court, ruling on an aboriginal land claim, described aboriginal people as a "disadvantaged" part of a "national problem."[3] The judge's words could be construed as paternalistic at best, which describes the past 150 years and encapsulates our current state of affairs in indigenous-Canadian relations.

The problem with the Western church was not necessarily its definition of salvation but its interpretation and application of salvation, repentance, and sin. Theologians such as Stanley Grenz point out, "God's activity encompasses all creation, but humankind is his focus. The Spirit applies Christ's work to humans, effecting our union with the Lord and with each other in Christ's community."[4] This definition of salvation is suitable for the purposes of the chapter. Part of the problem was the Western church's presumption that it "owned" salvation to the extent that it defined for indigenous people what salvation would look like.[5] Jesus Christ of the Nicene Creed brought salvation, but the Western church's interpretation of what that meant resulted in indigenous people being looked down on and seen as wild people who were part of a wild land. As John West, Church of England missionary to the Indians, stated, his goal was "to cultivate the heath and convert the heathen."[6]

What was necessary for indigenous people was to repent of their wild way of life and turn to the Christian way of living. Repentance was a contrite turning from sin, but for Canada, developing as a modern nation-state, aboriginal people were immoral by virtue of being indigenous. In colonial Canada, like much of the civilized world, it was necessary for all things wild to become settled. "Settlement, with its attendant emphasis on property and possession, is the bridge that links socioeconomics of colonial civilization with the Christian ideology of moral cultivation."[7] Aboriginal people had a problem fitting into Canadian society because they were immoral. The wild land needed to be cultivated, and wild indigenous people needed to be converted and civilized.

This was a popular view of colonized indigenous people, as postcolonial scholar Laura Donaldson points out. Thomas Jefferson, like most

---

[3]Patricia A. Monture-Angus, *Journeying Forward: Dreaming First Nations' Independence* (Halifax, NS: Fernwood, 1999), 50-53.

[4]Stanley J. Grenz, *Theology for the Community of God* (Grand Rapids, MI: Eerdmans, 2000), 405.

[5]Paul Ricoeur, *Figuring the Sacred: Religion, Narrative, and Imagination*, trans. David Pellauer, ed. Mark I. Wallace (Minneapolis: Fortress, 1995), 148.

[6]James S. Scott, "Cultivating Christians in Colonial Canadian Missions," in *Canadian Missionaries, Indigenous Peoples: Representing Religion at Home and Abroad*, ed. Alvyn Austin and James S. Scott (Toronto: University of Toronto Press, 2005), 22.

[7]Scott, "Cultivating Christians," 29.

Euro-Americans of his time, considered aboriginal men and women as not following proper decorum.[8] A generation later, on the Canadian side of the border, John MacDonald continued this colonial way of thinking, believing the problem with Indians was a moral problem.[9] The solution then was to have proper moral training, which could be achieved through residential schools.[10] This was the view of indigenous people in Canada. As a memorandum from Catholic principles makes plain, "Cardinal among these virtues was moral training . . . 'all true civilization must be based on moral law.' Christianity has to supplant children's Aboriginal spirituality, which was nothing more than 'pagan superstition'; that 'would not suffice'; to make them 'practise the virtues of our civilianization and avoid the attendant vices.'"[11] Thus, the Western conception of Christianity was aimed at making "Indians" better behaved by giving them a civilized European identity. Thus, conversion to Christianity becomes synonymous with becoming "White" civilized "Natives" while at the same time conquering and taming the wilderness to become something that could be bought and sold.[12]

Residential schools. The goal of the residential school system was to resocialize indigenous children.

The residential school system was an attempt by successive governments to determine the fate of aboriginal people in Canada by appropriating and reshaping their future in the form of thousands of children who were removed from their homes and communities and placed in the care of strangers. Those strangers, the teachers and staff, were, according to Hayter Reed, a senior member of the department in the 1890s, to employ "every effort . . . against anything calculated to keep fresh in the memories of the children habits and associations which it is one of the main objects of industrial education to obliterate." Marching out from the schools, the children, effectively resocialized, imbued with the values of European culture, would be the vanguard of a magnificent metamorphosis: the "savage" was to be made "civilized," made fit to take up the privileges and responsibilities of citizenship.[13]

Residential schools and assimilation policies were to "obliterate" every relationship indigenous children had with their traditional way of life so that they could become civilized Christians.

Children were removed from their homes so that the relationship with the land would be severed. Terry LeBlanc, Mikmaq scholar, notes that the residential school system failed to understand the deep connectedness indigenous people had with the land.[14] The land would no longer be the mother of indigenous children; the residential school would be their "mother" and "would fit them for a life in a modernizing Canada."[15]

---

[8]Laura Donaldson, "The Sign of Orpah: Reading Ruth Through Native Eyes," in *The Post-colonial Biblical Reader*, ed. R. S. Sugirtharajah (Malden, MA: Blackwell, 2006), 162.

[9]J. R. Miller, "The State, the Church, and Residential Schools in Canada," in *Religion and Public Life: Historical and Comparative Themes* (Toronto: University of Toronto Press, 2001), 110.

[10]The Davin Report entrenched residential schools, modeled after American industrial schools, as the way to resocialize indigenous children. See Flood Davin, "Report on Industrial Schools for Indians and Half-Breeds, 1879," in *Reconciling Canada: Critical Perspectives on the Culture of Redress*, ed. Jennifer Henderson and Pauline Wakeham (Toronto: University of Toronto Press, 1879).

[11]"Report of the Royal Commission on Aboriginal People: Looking Forward, Looking Back," ed. Government of Canada (Ottawa: Minister of Supply and Services Canada, 1996), 339.

[12]Scott, "Cultivating Christians," 22-23.

[13]"Report of the Royal Commission on Aboriginal People," 335.

[14]Terry LeBlanc, "Mission and Power—Case Studies and Theological Reflection: #1 Residential School: Policy, Power and Mission," in *Edinburgh 2010 Conference* (Edinburgh: n.p., 2010), 6.

[15]"Report of the Royal Commission on Aboriginal People," 335.

Not only were the residential schools to break the relationship between land and indigenous children, but they were also to destroy the children's relationship with their family. The justification for this process included co-opting aboriginal leaders' permission to remove children from homes and place them in schools.[16] Even if parents resisted sending their children to residential schools, the policy was enforced because government and church officials believed that if the children were to be "saved" they needed to be taken from the negative influence of their parents who were stuck in their "wigwam ways."[17]

Another key relationship that was targeted for "obliteration" was the relationship between indigenous children and their traditional culture or spirituality.[18] Therefore, traditional spirituality was to be replaced with European Christian values and morals. "A wedge had to be driven not only physically between parent and child but also culturally and spiritually."[19]

Christianity was reduced to a European Christian conception. Indigenous spirituality was seen as another religion or possibly a kind of heresy. Ephraim Radner notes that the church's slow expansion of the concept of heresy justified violence in other settings and for the church; thus indigenous spirituality had to be eradicated.[20] The church justified violence toward indigenous people by vilifying indigenous spirituality and thus making it necessary to eradicate deviant indigenous faith.

Indigenous children were subjected to institutional pressure that severely damaged all of the primary relationships of their human existence: their relationship with the land, their relationship with their parents and community, and their relationship with the Creator through their spirituality. If the effects of the cursing of creation and humanity, as seen in Genesis 3, are a warping of the relationships between humanity and creation, between man and woman or family, and between God as Creator and human beings, then residential schools entrenched the curse and followed the same pattern of cursing in its impact on indigenous peoples' lives. Salvation, or conversion, then was seen as needing to repent or turn from the sinful indigenous life and put on the "white robes" of Western Christianity.[21]

Relocation of the Sayisi Dene. Residential schools were not the only assimilationist policy of the past 150 years that "obliterated" aboriginal relationships. The relocation policies of the 1950s also took their toll on aboriginal identity. The forced relocation of the Sayisi Dene to Churchill, Manitoba, serves as an example and shows the impact of relocation on the same primary relationships of indigenous people affected by residential schools.

The Sayisi Dene were nomadic hunters long before the coming of the Europeans. Europeans came to Canada and wanted land. The missionaries helped pave the way by learning the language of the people and converting people to Christianity. It was a former Methodist missionary who was the treaty commissioner in 1910, getting the reluctant Sayisi Dene to sign Treaty 5. Even though they would not be forcibly

---

[16]Austin and Scott, *Canadian Missionaries, Indigenous Peoples*, 24.

[17]"Report of the Royal Commission on Aboriginal People," 338.

[18]James William McClendon and Curtis W. Freeman, *Systematic Theology*, rev. ed. (Waco, TX: Baylor University Press, 2012), 1:66-74.

[19]"Report of the Royal Commission on Aboriginal People," 340.

[20]Ephraim Radner, *A Brutal Unity: The Spiritual Politics of the Christian Church* (Waco, TX: Baylor University Press, 2012), 76-109.

[21]William Apess, *On Our Own Ground: The Complete Writings of William Apess, a Pequot, Native Americans of the Northeast*, ed. Barry O'Connell (Amherst: University of Massachusetts Press, 1992), lxvi-lxvii.

moved until 1956, this was the beginning of the move. Western people became convinced that every fur-bearing animal was endangered. To keep the caribou safe, the Dene were moved to Churchill because they were seen a threat. There more than one-third of the people died from various causes. The people were taken from the land. They were given little time to pack their things. Living in Churchill without proper shelter, the ability to hunt, or a means to earn a living, they were reduced to living on "welfare vouchers and macaroni rations."[22]

Again, Western society did not take into account the relationship that indigenous people had with land. Survivor of the move Charlie Ki-thithee said: "The land and the people were one. That was the secret of our life. . . . This is how the creator looked after us. He put animals onto our land so that we could provide for our people."[23]

As a result of the separation from the land, there was a cascading effect on the other primary relationships. Relocated to Churchill, many of the people developed drinking problems. The relationships between family members eroded. "In 1968, community development worker Phil Dickman wrote: 'There is practically nothing today that binds the children to their parents and prepares them to carry adult responsibilities.'"

The relationship with land was broken, which led to a breakdown in family relationships, which resulted in such spiritual and social destruction that Ila Bussidor tells of the shame she felt over her own identity: "We lived in a slum in total darkness. As a child, I learned what it felt like to be inferior to another race, to be less than

the next person because I was Dene. Because of the racism we faced every day, I was ashamed to be Dene. I wished I belonged to another race of people."[24] It is not surprising then that some indigenous people have become ambivalent about their own indigenous identity. Many have seen all of their relationships damaged through generational trauma. Therefore, repentance for Indian people has been cast as a negative thing. Just like conversion, repentance meant giving up one's identity, to turn from being First Nations and embrace the new Christian identity, an identity that just happened to look like Western European identity.[25] To be converted to Christ meant you gave up being Native. You developed hatred and regret for being made this way, and you longed to be "whiter than snow."

This is the narrative of many aboriginal people in Canada. As a result of the degradation that has come about as a result of the assimilation policies such as relocation, residential schools, and underlying racism, many indigenous people are left feeling conflicted about their own identity. The gospel was used to try to annihilate aboriginal identity. Catholic and Protestant alike did this. It was systematic and pervasive. Conversion and repentance became synonymous with giving up aboriginal identity.

Repentance is seen as embracing one's own depravity and turning to God, but this translated into self-hatred by aboriginal people. I am the third generation of my family growing up not wanting to be Indian. My mother told everyone we were mostly French and Scottish. At my grandmother's funeral my brother, in true Cree

---

[22]Ila Bussidor and Üstün Bilgen-Reinart, *Night Spirits: The Story of the Relocation of the Sayisi Dene*, Manitoba Studies in Native History (Winnipeg: University of Manitoba Press, 1997), 50-55, 4.
[23]Bussidor and Bilgen-Reinart, *Night Spirits*, 37.
[24]Bussidor and Bilgen-Reinart, *Night Spirits*, 4.
[25]Marie Therese Archambault, "Native Americans and Evangelization," in *Native and Christian: Indigenous Voices on Religious Identity in the United States and Canada*, ed. James Treat (New York: Routledge, 1996), 139.

fashion, made a joke to ease the pain. As all the indigenous people were arriving for the funeral, he leaned over and said, "I wonder when all the French and Scottish relatives are going to get here." I also grew up hating that I was aboriginal, wanting so much to just fit in, because in fitting in, I would escape the pain, or so I thought.

Some indigenous people suggest communal identity as nations of indigenous people is not redeemable by God. A book published by the Christian and Missionary Alliance in the United States expressed this message; it offered the theological opinion that people were redeemable, but not culture.[26] This could be construed as saying that in order to be Christian we must give up our indigenous culture or spirituality, which amounts to our humanity.[27] This kind of statement is a continuation of the teaching of residential schools that reduced aboriginal identity to something less than human.

As Ila Bussidor expressed shame over her own identity, many indigenous people become self-conscious about their "otherness" and feel shame. In a sense, they feel estranged from themselves. They feel shame for their own identity. They want to be something else, and to solve this pain in their soul they resolve to stop being "Indian." Sadly, many have taken it further and thought that the only solution to pain is to stop feeling. They then go to any length to accomplish that, even if it means taking their own life. "Self-contempt" or "other-contempt," all flowing out of illegitimate shame, is the legacy of the assimilation policy of the Canadian government and the churches.

Thankfully we have turned a page or changed our minds, in keeping with the idea of repentance. Aboriginal people continue to struggle against institutionalized assimilationist pressures. However, a shift in the understanding of indigenous peoples' identity is occurring. An embracing of indigenous identity by aboriginal people could be described as a repenting from self-hatred to embracing a God-given indigenous identity. An identity that gives hope despite continued attempts by Western hegemony to suppress or assimilate indigenous identity. A hope that could flow out of Christianity, that does not seek to replace indigenous identity but could be seen as trying to heal or fulfill indigenous identity.

REPENTANCE AS A DECISION TO LIVE

There are two aspects of repentance that could fit within an indigenous world that would allow repentance to be reconfigured as a decision to turn and embrace the life the Creator has provided. *Michiyuwasewin* in Cree captures the idea of feeling sorry or repenting. This is an older word used in some of the teaching material of the early Methodist missions.[28] In a modern Cree dictionary the word for repentance, *kweskatisiw*, has the idea of changing one's way of life.[29] Both of these definitions would fit within a theological definition of repentance, but they must be reinterpreted within a changing context.

---

[26]Craig S. Smith, *Boundary Lines: The Issue of Christ, Indigenous Worship, and Native American Culture* (Glendale, AZ: Native American Association of the Christian and Missionary Alliance, 2000).

[27]Among Saskatchewan First Nations the terms *spirituality* and *culture* are used interchangably. See Jacqueline Ottmann, "First Nations Leadership and Spirituality Within the Royal Commission on Aboriginal Peoples: A Saskatchewan Perspective" (MEd thesis, University of Saskatchewan, 2002).

[28]John Semmens, William Isbister, and John McDougall, *The Hand-Book to Scripture Truths, or, the Way of Salvation: Words of Admonition, Counsel and Comfort* (Toronto: Methodist Mission Rooms, 1893), 3; E. A. Watkins, "Repentance," in *A Dictionary of the Cree Langage*, ed. Ven. R. Faries (Toronto: Church of England in Canada, 1938).

[29]Wolvengrey, "Repent," in *Nēhiýawēwin: Itwēwina*.

Repentance is a contrite turning from sin. Sin in a First Nations context refers to a "falling out of balance" into self-consciousness, which causes shame.[30] Indigenous people, whose relationships have been under attack and severely damaged, have been pushed "out of balance," resulting in illegitimate shame that can be construed as sin. Calling this illegitimate shame "sin" is not another attempt to heap guilt on abused people by telling them they are to blame for their problems. Rather, it is conceiving of sin as something that traps people, unable to effect change without grace from the Creator. This is a grace that is available if one embraces one's own situation and identity that the Creator has provided. Repentance then involves sorrow for a lost identity. It is turning to embrace a Creator-given indigenous identity, and taking responsibility begins to work toward healing all relationships.

This latter version of repentance could be understood as taking responsibility. Responsibility is not primarily about guilt but about an opportunity to live in another way. As such, repentance could become an act of dreaming about what it would be like to put relationships back together, healed or made whole. The idea of taking responsibility could fit within modern indigenous thought. Monture-Angus believes taking responsibility is what is at the heart of indigenous freedom, or self-determination, as she calls it: "I have realized that self-determination is both a personal issue and a collective yearning. As I have come to understand it, self-determination begins with looking at yourself

and your family and deciding if and when you are living responsibly. Self-determination is principally, that is first and foremost, about our relationships."[31] Thus the gospel of Jesus Christ could bring hope to aboriginal people for a better day in the future. I am struck by the hope that the wounded Christ brings to aboriginal people that we will not die. Somehow, even in the midst of great pain and intensity of rage, there is one who understands. It is the abused Christ who identifies with our own abuse. It is from this place that one can then turn to this Christ and embrace life. Repentance has then ceased to be a decision to hate one's own earthly identity and has become a decision to embrace our broken identity and to live. Repentance is to change my mind about my own despised identity as something having value.

Hope is found in taking responsibility and turning to heal the relationships that have been damaged. For the Sayisi Dene it meant returning to their former territory. They are attempting to restore their relationship with the land. Returning has enabled some to begin to work on healing their wounds. The Dene understood that if we do not heal our wounds they will be passed on to our children.[32] The land is the place where this healing can occur. Again, responsibility for relationship with the land must be understood as a primary human relationship.[33] For example, Naomi Adelson writes, "A sense of health is ultimately rooted in what it means to 'be Cree,' and being Cree has everything to do with connections to the land and to a rich and

---

[30]Joseph E. Couture, Virginia Margaret McGowan, and Ruth Couture, *A Metaphoric Mind: Selected Writings of Joseph Couture* (Edmonton: Athabasca University Press, 2013), 15-16.

[31]Monture-Angus, *Journeying Forward*, 8.

[32]Bussidor and Bilgen-Reinart, *Night Spirits*, 142.

[33]Sophie McCall, *First Person Plural: Aboriginal Storytelling and the Ethics of Collaborative Authorship* (Vancouver: University of British Columbia Press, 2012), 120.

complex past."[34] Repentance as turning to embrace indigenous identity then could mean to reject the teaching of residential schools that land is a commodity and to remember it as part of family, as our mother.[35]

Colin Gunton reminds Christians that we share a continuity with all that is nonhuman by virtue of our being created.[36] Therefore, one of our primary relationships is with creation or land. Indigenous elder and Anglican priest Andrew Wesley teaches that at the heart of indigenous spirituality is understanding your creation story, a story that tells you of your connection to the land.[37] When this connection is made, you can stand on the land and feel it welcome you home.[38]

We are part of creation, and as such we are responsible for living in relationship with the Creator and the created order. Karl Barth affirms that our identity as created individuals means we are responsible to God, the Creator. He maintains that in Acts 2:38, every individual is confronted with the need to repent, to give up a life apart from God, to embrace the only life possible, life with God. Repentance can be seen as a return or a responding to God and entering again into this responsibility.[39] This does not mean that we are responsible for our own salvation—this is entirely the work of God—but we enter again the relationship with the Creator that brings our life into its proper frame of reference. That is, we are to live out our obedience to the Creator as a response to his grace. This idea of repentance as a return to responsibility is in keeping with the understanding of repentance as a turn to embrace indigenous identity.

When repentance is primarily characterized as the feeling of remorse over wrong, it becomes a matter of negative emotions, to which we apply forgiveness to take them away. This does nothing to address the need to actually change one's conduct or way of living. Repentance is more than just a feeling of guilt that can be assuaged by talk of forgiveness. Instead of thinking in terms of repentance as primarily negative, by conceiving of repentance as a turning away from sin toward life, repentance could be interpreted as taking responsibility for one's life and working toward repairing the primary relationships of life. This includes the relationship with God the Creator, relationships with other human beings, relationships with the rest of creation, and relationship with ourselves.

Since God has created human beings and elected to be gracious to them, a natural response to the Creator is thankfulness.[40] Barth describes this as the returning of grace back to God. It is interesting that this circle of thanksgiving defines Cree spirituality. In the fall you pray for good hunting and in the fall you give thanks for good hunting.[41] Thanksgiving is part of indigenous spirituality in response to living in a good land.[42] Barth would affirm that thankfulness is important, but it must be thankfulness

---

[34]Naomi Adelson, *"Being Alive Well": Health and the Politics of Cree Well-Being* (Toronto: University of Toronto Press, 2000), 15.

[35]LeBlanc, "Mission and Power," 93; Couture, McGowan, and Couture, *Metaphoric Mind*, 4; Monture-Angus, *Journeying Forward*, 60.

[36]Colin E. Gunton, *The One, the Three, and the Many: God, Creation, and the Culture of Modernity* (New York: Cambridge University Press, 1993), 3, 13.

[37]Andrew Wesley, "Traditional Aboriginal Spirituality" (paper presented at the Consultation on First Nations Theological Education, Thornloe University, Sudbury, Ontario, May 21, 2009).

[38]Neal McLeod, *Cree Narrative Memory: From Treaties to Contemporary Times* (Saskatoon, SK: Purich, 2007), 61-70.

[39]Karl Barth, *Church Dogmatics*, trans. G. W. Bromiley (Edinburgh: T&T Clark, 1957), II/2, 670; III/2, 192.

[40]Barth, *Church Dogmatics*, III/2, 174.

[41]Arthur Noskey made this observation in a personal conversation in 2009.

[42]Clara Sue Kidwell, Homer Noley, and George E. Tinker, *A Native American Theology* (Maryknoll, NY: Orbis, 2001), 33.

directed to the Creator, not merely the characteristic of thankfulness. Thus, knowledge of the Creator is integral to fulfilling this responsibility to live in thankfulness to the Creator. Human life is to be lived in response to the word of God. God's word summons humanity into existence. This word or summons continues to call human beings to a responsible relationship with God that is new every day. As Barth defines this responsibility: "We have stated that the being of man as responsibility is response, being in the act of response to the Word of God. But if it is as it responds, then it is a being which knows, accepts and affirms the Word of God and therefore God Himself. . . . To be responsible before God is to know God."[43]

Repentance as turning to embrace indigenous identity also includes taking responsibility for healing the wounds of abuse that have separated family members and communities. Again, Barth is helpful in that he points out that repentance is more than just feelings of remorse; there is a need to come to grips with our actual situation and respond to the grace of God.[44] This might aid in healing from colonialism, though the trauma from residential schools is more complicated than just removing colonial or neocolonial policy. Monture-Angus makes this point:

> If colonialism brought our nations to this point, then undoing colonialism must be the answer . . . [but] it is not just colonial relations that must be undone but all of the consequences (addictions, loss of language, loss of parenting skills, loss of self-respect, abuse and violence and so on). Colo-

nialism is no longer linear, vertical relationships—colonizer does to colonized—it is horizontal and entangled relationships (like a spider web).[45]

Monture-Angus is not speaking from a purely Christian perspective, but her words can still be informative for a reinterpretation of repentance for Christians. Repentance can involve trying to work through the wounding by revisiting "dark stories," which can serve as tools for healing.[46] It is reimagining the individual story by embracing the good things from our past history but also remembering the difficulties. The act of embracing one's story and continuing to share it recasts pain and difficulty as a source of hope by showing that indigenous identity remains despite facing traumatic events. Telling and listening to our stories ensures we do not forget our relatives who have passed on. It also ensures that we are not romanticizing some lost ideal, trying to engage in a kind of primitivism as a form of escapism to some premodern period.[47] Rather, it is trying to embrace identity, as it exists, by attempting to build on roots of strength that are within indigenous culture. This is accomplished by retelling difficult stories in a way that advances healing.[48]

It is not only relationships between individuals in one's own family or group that need to be healed, but there is also a responsibility to attempt to return to or heal treaty relationships between indigenous people and newcomers. This idea is part of what it means to be indigenous or connected with land. Right relationship requires a location; it must be grounded on the

---

[43]Barth, *Church Dogmatics*, III/2, 176.

[44]Barth, *Church Dogmatics*, II/2, 768.

[45]Monture-Angus, *Journeying Forward*, 11.

[46]Bussidor and Bilgen-Reinart, *Night Spirits*, xix.

[47]Robert J. Schreiter, *The New Catholicity: Theology Between the Global and the Local*, Faith and Cultures Series (Maryknoll, NY: Orbis, 1997), 25.

[48]McCall, *First Person Plural*, 120.

earth.[49] As covenant, the treaty has a spiritual and locative dimension. The relationship with the "other" is captured in the shared narrative of the treaty, particularly as the practice of treaty making in Canada developed. J. R. Miller points out that treaties evolved in Canada from "friendship compacts" eventually to covenants between newcomers, indigenous people, and the Creator.[50] The braid of sweetgrass illustrates this idea. One strand represents newcomers, another strand the First Nations, and the third the Creator. For the Lakota the smoke from the sweetgrass fills the whole universe, and in doing the ceremony we make peace as we become like relatives.[51] Newcomers, including church officials, engaged in the indigenous ceremonies that made us like relatives or family.[52] Thus, in the healing of relationships, treaty relationships must be healed. The treaty also serves as a source of healing. As a shared narrative, it legitimates or creates shared space. The treaty holds the individuals and groups they represent together because, as covenant, the relationship is more important than the exact particulars.[53]

The healing of all relationships is premised on returning to an indigenous identity that affirms the goodness of the created world. The starting point for indigenous spirituality is the appreciation of a beautiful world. Doug Cuthand writes: "Our people believe that the earth and all the creatures that live on it are a gift from the Creator. This beautiful land of lakes, forests, rivers, plains, and mountains is a gift from the Almighty and it must be respected and treated properly."[54] In indigenous spirituality this appreciation for a beautiful world is thanksgiving. In the circle of harmony, if you receive something, you give something back; in this way we live in harmony with all things.[55] Repentance is seeking to live in right relationships or in balance with Creator and creation. This is the vision and ideal that indigenous spirituality is seeking. However, it will take time to heal. Ila reminds us, "Healing doesn't happen just once. We have to be healed again and again."[56] In seeking the healing of significant relationships with creation, family, clan, community, and all others, indigenous people return or reinvigorate their relationship with *kise-manitow* (Creator).

A reinterpreted understanding of repentance as a turning to embrace an identity given by the Creator is therefore in keeping with traditional understandings of what it means to be indigenous in Canada. Interestingly, the basic meaning of repentance as a contrite sorrow for sin and a turning to a new way of living has not needed to be altered. The context has meant repentance has to be reconfigured as hope through taking responsibility. If Christian repentance and salvation is a large enough concept to conceive of turning to Christ as being a return or embracing of a Creator-given indigenous

---

[49]Monture-Angus, *Journeying Forward*, 36, 60.

[50]J. R. Miller, "Compact, Contract, Covenant: The Evolution of Indian Treaty-Making," in *New Histories for Old: Changing Perspectives on Canada's Native Pasts*, ed. Theodore Binnema and Susan Neylan (Vancouver: University of British Columbia Press, 2007), 84.

[51]Black Elk, Joseph Epes Brown, and Michael F. Steltenkamp, *The Sacred Pipe: Black Elk's Account of the Seven Rites of the Oglala Sioux* (New York: MJF Books, 1996), 103; Leo J. Omani, "Perspectives of Saskatchewan Dakota/Lakota Elders on the Treaty Process Within Canada" (PhD diss., University of Saskatchewan, 2010), 2, 159.

[52]Jennifer S. H. Brown, "Rupert's Land, Nituskeenan, Our Land," in *New Histories for Old: Changing Perspectives on Canada's Native Pasts*, ed. Theodore Binnema and Susan Neylan (Vancouver: University of British Columbia Press, 2007), 34-35.

[53]Miller, "Compact, Contract, Covenant," 83.

[54]Doug Cuthand, *Askiwina: A Cree World* (Regina: Coteau Books, 2007), 1.

[55]Kidwell, Noley, and Tinker, *Native American Theology*, 33.

[56]Bussidor and Bilgen-Reinart, *Night Spirits*, 132.

identity, it is possible to conceive of conversion or salvation in Christ as fulfillment instead of being a replacement for indigenous spirituality.[57]

REPENTANCE FOR CANADA

Turning to nonindigenous or newcomers to Turtle Island (what some indigenous groups call North America), what does repentance look like for a Canada that has violated the treaty relationship and is complicit in the abuse of indigenous peoples? Would repentance as turning to embrace a God-given identity as a human being be sufficient to begin to work through the difficulties from the nonindigenous side of the relationship? The answer is positive, particularly if the treaty relationship is seen as shared narrative. It is a large enough concept to include a narrative of troubled relationships but also one of a coming back together or healing. Some of the principles from restorative justice will be put to use in this description.[58] Restorative justice is an attempt to heal the damage. In this process the affected parties must tell the truth; they must listen; they must come up with a shared plan to repair the damage. All of these steps come together as an attempt at reconciliation between indigenous peoples and the newcomers. These steps presuppose that indigenous and newcomers will both, through repentance, embrace their indigenous identity as created human beings.

Oliver O'Donovan points out that a national repentance that is rooted in Scripture must embrace a community or nation's collective history and return to its social covenant.[59] He was thinking about the atrocities committed in India by Britain. He states that repentance for the British people involves owning those things on a personal, individual level. In this way history functions as a moral mirror. He writes:

> Until we learn to root that sense of "us" in the history of a living community, it is an empty, powerless thing to speak of what "we" shall do now, what "our" good intentions are. There is an immense pathos in a community's good intentions—a point to recall at a moment when a modern democracy is heady with excitement of making new beginnings, setting its hand to do things which it is conscious of having failed to do.

By remembering past actions and owning them on an individual level, a nation may keep from making the same mistakes again. New national "blanket" policies that are applied to indigenous people would just be a continuation of colonialism. Healing will come when we base our relationships on "caring, sharing truth and strength."[60]

Canada could heed O'Donovan's observations of remembering and returning in working through its own repentance. Remembering could follow the principles of restorative justice of telling the truth and listening. Returning could embrace the historical treaties as a way forward to heal and affirm relationships in Canada. Canada needs to remember the past and confess its shortcomings—not in an apology as a one-way speech act, but in

---

[57]In proposing fulfillment I am not precluding the possibility that the relationship between indigenous spirituality and Christianity could be complementary. Fulfillment might be viewed by some as placing indigenous spirituality in a lower or lesser role. It is beyond the scope of this chapter to address this question, but it is worth noting. George Lindbeck offers a brief taxonomy of possible interfaith relationships. See George A. Lindbeck, *The Nature of Doctrine: Religion and Theology in a Post-liberal Age* (Philadelphia: Westminster, 1984), 52-53.

[58]Pierre Allard, "Restorative Justice: Lost Treasure" (lecture, Canadian Theological Seminary, March 11, 1999).

[59]Oliver O'Donovan, "Community Repentance?," *Transformation: An International Journal of Holistic Mission Studies*, no. 14 (1997): 13.

[60]Monture-Angus, *Journeying Forward*, 12.

a dialogue.[61] In so doing Canada could embrace the stories of past abuse as gifts to help be a mirror for repentance.

The Canadian government has engaged in at least two national attempts to effect reconciliation with aboriginal people: the Royal Commission on Aboriginal People and the apology to the survivors of residential schools. Sophie McCall offers the opinion that Royal Commission on Aboriginal People, commissioned in 1991, missed an opportunity for reconciliation because it did not lead to dialogue but reduced the response flowing out of the stories of people's trauma at the hands of the Canadian government and churches to recommendations.[62] Recommendations do not allow the reader to enter the Royal Commission on Aboriginal People as the second-person *you*. Recommendations sterilize the past and render it incapable of providing the emotive energy to dream of what repentance looks like. The Royal Commission on Aboriginal People was limited in its ability to help individuals enter into the shared Canadian narrative to reconfigure history. Instead, the Royal Commission on Aboriginal People tended to see reconciliation as a way to forget the past.

McCall notes, "In order for reconciliation to be more than a case of amnesia, it must prioritize a politics of difference and a testimony. However, the tendency of RCAP's report is to subsume the testimony within a dominant narrative of progress—from assimilation to self-government, from loss to recovery, from mutual mistrust to reconciliation." She explains that the Canadian state's conception of reconciliation saw indigenous people needing to reconcile themselves to being under the Canadian state.[63] This was not a return to the treaty relationship and a reconciliation of equals. Thus, the Royal Commission on Aboriginal People was ineffective in allowing Canada as the offender to enter into the shared narrative of the treaty. It was limited in its ability to help individual Canadians think through what repentance looks like.

Another opportunity for reconciliation occurred with the 2008 apology by the government of Canada for residential schools. Making the apology was better than not making the apology. Indigenous people have used the prime minister's apology to embrace their wounded identity. Eva Mackey, however, points out that the apology also seems to have been used by the Canadian government not to enter into a dialogue but, as in the Royal Commission on Aboriginal People, to forget about the past and impose new national strategies for fixing aboriginal people.[64] Mackey suggests that an apology that is not a dialogue is only a one-sided speech-act that fails to bring about a change. It fails as an act of repentance because it does not lead to a new way of living for the abuser. A real sign of repentance would be a return to the treaty relationship and a reconceiving of repentance from institutionalized abuse. Justice Murray Sinclair, since the completion of the public Truth and Reconciliation Commission, has said that the apology and the public testimony do not amount to reconciliation. There is a need to stop racism toward aboriginal people and others, to work toward healing the relationship.[65] The Canadian people

---

[61]Eva Mackey, "The Apologizers' Apology," in *Reconciling Canada: Critical Perspectives on the Culture of Redress*, ed. Jennifer Henderson and Pauline Wakeham (Toronto: University of Toronto Press, 2013), 48.

[62]McCall, *First Person Plural*, 110.

[63]McCall, *First Person Plural*, 111-14.

[64]Mackey, "Apologizers' Apology," 50-51.

[65]Justice Murray Sinclair, "Reconciliation Not Opportunity to 'Get over It': Justice Murray Sinclair," CBC, April 18, 2014, www.cbc.ca/news/aboriginal/reconciliation-not-opportunity-to-get-over-it-justice-murray-sinclair-1.2614352.

must embrace the past as their own failures. In a turn of repentance to their identity as human beings in a treaty relationship, Canadians could build on the historic treaty process, moving toward reconciliation with indigenous people.

An ideal apology must lead to dialogue, which involves listening. The Truth and Reconciliation Commission was set up as a response to the apology so that people damaged by residential schools could share their stories and perhaps heal.[66] The public testimonies given at the commission meetings were a gift. They are received as a gift if one enters into a reciprocal relationship with the speaker. If we enter into the story and embrace the pain that we have caused and use the emotional energy to help to begin to change, then we are embracing our own identity as true human beings. This is the kind of listening necessary to continue to move toward reconciliation. McCall would call it entering the story "in the second person." This is not easy, and the stories of the trauma cause some to disassociate. This can be mitigated if the speaker and the listeners understand the goal is healing and restored relationship.[67] Healing and restored relationship is a legitimate goal for all who call the land of Canada home.

Finally, repentance as turning to a new way of life for newcomers could mean a return for all to the treaty relationship where they are also treaty people. As treaty people, Canadians themselves are healed from being strangers in the land. The idea of treaty is the idea of making relations. Through the treaty newcomers and indigenous people were to live like family. This secures a place for the First Nations, and it secures a place for newcomers. The following quote from the office of the treaty commissioner in Saskatchewan emphasizes this point:

> Treaties are beneficial to all people in Saskatchewan. They are considered mutually beneficial arrangements that guarantee a co-existence between the treaty parties. Newcomers and their descendants benefit from the wealth generated from the land and the foundational rights provided in the treaties. They built their society in this new land where some were looking for political and religious freedoms. Today, there are misconceptions that only First Nations peoples are part of the treaties, but in reality, both parties are part of the treaty. All people in Saskatchewan are treaty people.[68]

Repentance for Canada could mean turning and owning the mistakes of the past and embracing identity as human beings under covenant, which for those in Canada includes the treaty.

Repentance, then, as defined in the first section of this chapter as a contrite turning from sin and a turning to embrace an indigenous identity, is large enough to include newcomers. By entering into the shared narrative of a treaty as equals, the possibility exists for a shared identity that does not necessitate the eradication of identity. Instead, it is an opportunity to embrace the past and be open to a future of walking together in the Creator's land in a good way. Functioning as a shared narrative, a treaty allows for a reenvisioning history and becomes a tool for healing.

CONCLUSION

Repenting of self-hatred means indigenous people embracing their own broken identity so

---

[66]Truth and Reconciliation Commission of Canada, "Our Mandate," https://umanitoba.ca/centres/nctr/mandate.html, accessed April 28, 2020.
[67]McCall, *First Person Plural*, 111, 120-21.
[68]Office of the Treaty Commissioner, www.otc.ca.

that they can begin to live again. The decision to repent and live is a decision to begin to put back together the relationships that have suffered so much over the years. Though these relationships have been damaged, they remain in the stories and memories of First Nations people. This repentance is not primarily about guilt but is also about taking responsibility and seeking to rebuild what was broken. It is a decision to embrace the hope that there is another way of life possible, one that exceeds merely surviving. The knowledge that each person and each people who share this space are also in relationship is why aboriginal people continue to advocate for a return to nation-to-nation relationships. This provides hope and resources as we continue to develop as a multicultural society.

This reinterpretation of repentance is large enough to include nonindigenous people who make up the nation of Canada. They can repent by entering the shared narrative of the treaty and embracing the stories of trauma from residential schools and relocation in an effort to own the pain and move toward healing. By becoming "second person" in the story, the listener is able to work through the pain of the past without merely wishing it away. This repentance is a turning to embrace the shared narrative of the treaty process in Canada and goes further than a one-way approach that cuts off dialogue. It is possible to see this returning to the treaty relationship as fitting within the rubric of restorative justice as telling the truth, listening with the heart, and creating a shared plan. This is an attempt at reconciliation by healing the treaty relationship or returning to the treaty relationship for healing. Repentance, as seen as a contrite sorrow for sin and a turning to a new way of life, is understandable in a Canadian context by both indigenous and Christian people. It is then possible to see Christian repentance and salvation as a fulfillment of the harmony hoped for by indigenous spirituality.

FURTHER READING

Apess, William. *On Our Own Ground: The Complete Writings of William Apess, a Pequot.* Edited by Barry O'Connell. Amherst: University of Massachusetts Press, 1992.

Black Elk, Joseph Epes Brown, and Michael F. Steltenkamp. *The Sacred Pipe: Black Elk's Account of the Seven Rites of the Oglala Sioux.* New York: MJF Books, 1996.

Bussidor, Ila, and Üstün Bilgen-Reinart. *Night Spirits: The Story of the Relocation of the Sayisi Dene.* Manitoba Studies in Native History. Winnipeg: University of Manitoba Press, 1997.

Cuthand, Doug. *Askiwina: A Cree World.* Regina: Coteau Books, 2007.

Mackey, Eva. "The Apologizers' Apology." Pages 47-62 in *Reconciling Canada: Critical Perspectives on the Culture of Redress,* edited by Jennifer Henderson and Pauline Wakeham. Toronto: University of Toronto Press, 2013.

Miller, J. R. "Compact, Contract, Covenant: The Evolution of Indian Treaty-Making." Pages 66-91 in *New Histories for Old: Changing Perspectives on Canada's Native Pasts,* edited by Theodore Binnema and Susan Neylan. Vancouver: University of British Columbia Press, 2007.

"Report of the Royal Commission on Aboriginal People: Looking Forward, Looking Back." Edited by Government of Canada. Ottawa: Minister of Supply and Services Canada, 1996.

SALVATION AS RECONCILIATION

TOWARD A THEOLOGY OF RECONCILIATION IN THE DIVISION OF THE KOREAN PENINSULA

Sung Wook Chung

SALVATION HAS TO DO not only with vertical reconciliation between God and humanity but also with horizontal reconciliation between human beings. On the basis of this initial insight, this chapter explores the theme of reconciliation as the main thread that runs through the doctrine of salvation, especially in the context of the division of the Korean peninsula between South Korea and North Korea. In so doing, this chapter attempts to shed soteriological light on the current situation of the division between the two Koreas. In addition, this chapter examines the significance of a trinitarian theology of reconciliation for mutual forgiveness, embrace, and love between the two nations.

Soteriology has been one of the major loci of Christian systematic theology or dogmatic theology in the Western tradition. Among the themes that Western Christian soteriology has traditionally discussed are conversion (faith and repentance), regeneration, redemption, forgiveness of sins, justification, adoption, union with Christ, sanctification, and perseverance of the saints. However, the idea of reconciliation in

the context of soteriology did not attract much interest from Protestant Reformation theology in the sixteenth and seventeenth centuries, including its Lutheran and Reformed versions. Instead, the notion of redemption took a more central place than the idea of reconciliation in Reformed and Lutheran dogmatics.

It was Albrecht Ritschl, a German liberal theologian, who restored the theme of reconciliation as a major soteriological issue in his magnum opus, *The Christian Doctrine of Justification and Reconciliation* (*Die christliche Lehre von der Rechtfertigung und Versöhnung*) in the late nineteenth century.[1] Although Karl Barth attempted to distance himself from the presuppositions and sensibilities of German liberal theology, one of whose leading representatives was Ritschl, he titled the second major theme of his *Church Dogmatics* "reconciliation," not "redemption."[2] He employed the word *redemption* for the title of the third main theme of the *Church Dogmatics*. Thus, for Barth, reconciliation was the notion equivalent to salvation, while redemption was equivalent to the consummation

---

[1] Albrecht Ritschl, *Die christliche Lehre von der Rechtfertigung und Versöhnung*, 3 vols. (Bonn: Adolf Marcus, 1870–1874).
[2] See Karl Barth, *Church Dogmatics*, trans. G. W. Bromiley (London: Continuum, 2004), IV/1, 57-58.

or culmination of the work of salvation. This implies that Barth believed that the central dimension of salvation was reconciliation.

Nevertheless, it is still conventional and customary for many mainline evangelical theologians to use the fourfold scheme of the drama of divine engagement with human beings—creation, fall, redemption, and consummation—to delineate the progress of divine revelation and human history. In evangelical systematic theology, therefore, the theme of salvation is typically discussed under the overarching category of redemption.

Many Korean theologians have worked on soteriology in relation to reconciliation as well. We can identify three major directions and trends in Korean soteriology. First, Korean evangelical theologians have primarily focused on personal and vertical reconciliation between God and sinners. This trend is in line with the dominant tendency within the camp of Western evangelical soteriological reflection. Second, Korean *Minjung* theologians have emphasized the sociopolitical significance of liberation of the oppressed from the tyrannical rule of Korean military power, although *Minjung* theology has been criticized for not paying sufficient attention to the dimension of horizontal reconciliation between the oppressors and the oppressed.[3] Third, some revisionist theologians have attempted to reinterpret the idea of salvation by incorporating Korean cultural and religious ethos, utilizing such notions as *han*, honor, and shame.[4] It is regrettable, though, that Korean theologians

have not paid sufficient attention to the idea of group reconciliation or sociopolitical reconciliation in the context of the division of the Korean peninsula.

One cannot overemphasize the significance of the idea of reconciliation in relation to the Christian doctrine of salvation. The fundamental meaning of the idea of salvation in Christian theology is removing enmity and hostility between God and human sinners, which is the result of human rebellion against God. Furthermore, the central aspect of salvation consists in the idea of the restoration of a friendly and harmonious relationship, because the basic character of enmity between God and human sinners is construed to be mutual: God detests the state and actions of human sinners, and human sinners hate the holy and righteous God.

Salvation involves not only vertical reconciliation between God and humanity but also horizontal reconciliation between human beings. As Genesis 3 demonstrates, the break of the vertical relationship between God and humanity had a serious impact on the horizontal relationship between the man and the woman, who otherwise had been enjoying a friendly relationship. They began to blame and accuse each other, and a wall of hostility was erected between them. To be sure, horizontal reconciliation is a natural and necessary consequence of vertical reconciliation, and as the apostle Paul proclaims in Ephesians 2, horizontal reconciliation always involves a mediator and the demolition of the wall of enmity, mutual forgiveness, mutual embrace, and mutual love.[5]

---

[3]In a sense, *Minjung* theology can be viewed as a Korean version of liberation theology. See Paul S. Chung, Veli-Matti Kärkkäinen, and Kim Kyoung-Jae, eds., *Asian Contextual Theology for the Third Millennium: Theology of Minjung in Fourth-Eye Formation* (Eugene, OR: Wipf & Stock, 2007).

[4]See Andrew Sung Park, *The Wounded Heart of God: The Asian Concept of Han and the Christian Doctrine of Sin* (Nashville: Abingdon, 1993).

[5]For an excellent discussion about the themes of reconciliation and embrace, see Miroslav Volf, *Exclusion and Embrace: A Theological Exploration of Identity, Otherness, and Reconciliation* (Nashville: Abingdon, 1996).

On the basis of these initial insights, this chapter explores the theme of reconciliation as the main thread that runs through the doctrine of salvation, especially in the context of the division of the Korean peninsula between South Korea and North Korea. In so doing, this chapter attempts to shed soteriological light on the current division between the two Koreas. In addition, this chapter examines the significance of a trinitarian theology of reconciliation for mutual forgiveness, embrace, and love between the two nations.

SALVATION AS RECONCILIATION: A SOTERIOLOGICAL SKETCH

When Scripture addresses the idea of salvation in its various passages, it typically highlights the theme of reconciliation. In other words, Scripture features reconciliation as the core dimension of salvation given in and through the Lord Jesus Christ. In addition, the notion of reconciliation in the Bible is construed to have three crucial aspects: Jesus the Reconciler, vertical reconciliation, and horizontal reconciliation.

Jesus Christ as the Reconciler. In the discussion of the offices of Jesus Christ in christological discourse, the concept of mediator has played a central role.[6] In addition, the christological concept of mediator implies that reconciliation is one of the major works that the mediator should perform as the representative of both the divine and the human. The mediator becomes absolutely necessary to bridge the gap between the holy God and sinful humanity. As the bridge builder, the mediator should remove the enmity and hostility between the King of the universe and his traitors. In this sense, Jesus Christ the mediator is ultimately the peacemaker and reconciler, as christological tradition has unanimously affirmed.

The New Testament is not silent but explicit about the office of reconciliation that Jesus Christ voluntarily took for us. For example, the apostle Paul proclaims that believers can enjoy peace with God through the blood of Jesus Christ in Romans 5:1, 9-11:

> Therefore, since we have been justified through faith, we have peace with God through our Lord Jesus Christ. . . . Since we have now been justified by his blood, how much more shall we be saved from God's wrath through him. For if, while we were God's enemies, we were reconciled to him through the death of his Son, how much more, having been reconciled, shall we be saved through his life! Not only is this so, but we also boast in God through our Lord Jesus Christ, through whom we have now received reconciliation.[7]

Here Paul describes reconciliation as a result of justification of sinners through faith by grace in Jesus Christ. As justified and forgiven sinners, believers are now completely reconciled to God, the King of the universe. And God is pleased with those sinners forgiven, justified, and reconciled.

Furthermore, Paul stresses the reconciling work of Jesus Christ as follows:

> All this is from God, who reconciled us to himself through Christ and gave us the ministry of reconciliation: That God was reconciling the world to himself in Christ, not counting people's sins against them. And he has committed to us the message of reconciliation. We are therefore Christ's ambassadors, as though God were

---

[6]See John Calvin, *The Institutes of the Christian Religion*, trans. Ford Lewis Battles (Philadelphia: Westminster, 1960); Barth, *Church Dogmatics*, IV/1, 122-28.
[7]Unless otherwise noted, Scripture quotations in this chapter follow the NIV.

making his appeal through us. We implore you on Christ's behalf: Be reconciled to God. God made him who had no sin to be sin for us, so that in him we might become the righteousness of God. (2 Cor 5:18-21)

Paul presents God as the subject who reconciles his rebels to himself in and through his Son Jesus Christ.[8] God committed the work of reconciliation to Jesus Christ, the eternal mediator who is fully divine and fully human.

Vertical reconciliation between God and sinners. In order to restore the broken relationship between God and human sinners by reconciling them to God, Jesus Christ, the eternal Son of God and the second person of the Trinity, voluntarily emptied himself (*kenōsis*), took on human nature, and became a human being through the hypostatic union. So it is appropriate to observe that Christ's incarnation was geared toward reconciliation.[9] Furthermore, Christ was accused as a traitor against Caesar of the Roman Empire and a blasphemer against the God of the Jews, which means he, a sinless person, became a sinner so that he could atone for the human sin of treason and blasphemy against the God of the universe. Jesus Christ voluntarily sacrificed himself (*agapē*) for peacemaking. Paul confirms this truth by saying, "God made him who had no sin to be sin for us, so that in him we might become the righteousness of God" (2 Cor 5:21).

Vertical reconciliation between the holy God and human sinners requires the forgiveness of sins. God forgives human sinners by "not counting people's sins against them" (2 Cor 5:19). On the basis of Christ's atoning work on the cross and in response to sinners' faith in Christ,

God forgives sinners unconditionally once and for all. God's forgiveness is complete in that it covers the sins of the past, the present, and the future. In the context of the new covenant established and endorsed by the blood of Jesus Christ, the mediator of the new covenant, God will never remember our sins. As the writer of Hebrews attests, "But when this priest had offered for all time one sacrifice for sins, he sat down at the right hand of God, and since that time he waits for his enemies to be made his footstool. For by one sacrifice he has made perfect forever those who are being made holy" (Heb 10:12-14).

Horizontal reconciliation between human sinners. The second major dimension of Christ's work of reconciliation is horizontal reconciliation between sinners. Paul affirms this truth by saying, "And he has committed to us the message of reconciliation. We are therefore Christ's ambassadors, as though God were making his appeal through us" (2 Cor 5:19-20). As justified and righteous people reconciled to God in and through Jesus Christ, we are called and appointed to be Christ's messengers of the good news of reconciliation. Just as Jesus Christ the mediator was a peacemaker, we should be like him. In the Beatitudes Jesus proclaims, "Blessed are the peacemakers, for they will be called children of God" (Mt 5:9).

There are two distinct aspects of horizontal reconciliation. The first is the individual aspect, and the second is the communal aspect. On the one hand, the individual aspect is involved with a more private reconciliation between two individuals estranged and alienated from each other. For instance, the biblical story of reconciliation between Esau and Jacob (Gen 33) is an excellent example of the individual dimension of horizontal

---

[8]See Barth's *Church Dogmatics*, IV/1, §57, "The Work of God the Reconciler."
[9]Both Calvin and Barth are correct on this point.

reconciliation. On the other hand, the communal aspect is related to a more public reconciliation between two communities. The biblical witness to the reconciliation between Jews and Gentiles (Eph 2) is a great example of the communal aspect of horizontal reconciliation.[10]

The relationship between vertical and horizontal reconciliation. What is the relationship between vertical and horizontal reconciliation? At the outset, we can affirm that salvation mediated through the gospel of reconciliation embraces both dimensions. In other words, the biblical and theological concept of salvation is comprehensive and holistic enough to include both vertical reconciliation between God and sinners, and horizontal reconciliation between sinners.

However, there is a specific relationship between vertical and horizontal reconciliation: the vertical always precedes the horizontal. Vertical reconciliation gives birth to horizontal reconciliation; horizontal reconciliation is a natural and necessary fruit and evidence of vertical reconciliation.[11] In other words, the vertical is pregnant with the horizontal, and the goal of vertical reconciliation is horizontal reconciliation. Ephesians 2 demonstrates this point perfectly. In the first half of the chapter Paul addresses the vertical dimension of reconciliation, discussing the predicament of human depravity and salvation by grace through faith in Jesus Christ alone. Then, in the second half of the chapter, he deals with the reconciliation between Jews and Gentiles, which Christ's work of salvation makes possible. As Paul declares, "For he himself is our peace, who has made the two groups one and has destroyed the barrier, the dividing wall of hostility, by setting aside in his flesh, the law with its commands and regulations. His purpose was to create in himself one new humanity out of the two, thus making peace" (Eph 2:14-15).

On the basis of our discussion so far, we can conclude that the gospel of reconciliation brings us two main benefits: vertical reconciliation with God and horizontal reconciliation with others. And horizontal reconciliation is not only a natural product originating from vertical reconciliation but also our proper response to it, that is, it is both a gift (*die Gabe*) and a task (*die Aufgabe*). Furthermore, horizontal reconciliation has both individual and communal dimensions.

RECONCILIATION AND SANCTIFICATION FROM A TRINITARIAN PERSPECTIVE

Reconciliation and sanctification. Ever since the entrance of sin into the human world, sinners' reconciliation with God has been a prerequisite for their renewed and restored life. In spite of God's forgiveness of our sins and his declaration of our justification through faith in Jesus Christ, sinful nature (*sarx*) still remains in us. Right after being pronounced right with God by grace alone, we start a lifelong struggle with indwelling sin, which we call the process of sanctification. In this progressive movement toward perfect godliness, the Christian experiences the repetition of the event of reconciliation in its vertical and horizontal aspects.

The Christian is justified once and for all through faith in Jesus Christ. At the same time, she is definitely set apart for God's possession

---

[10]See Jarvis Williams, *One New Man: The Cross and Racial Reconciliation in Pauline Theology* (Nashville: B&H Academic, 2010).
[11]See Christoph Schwöbel, "Reconciliation: From Biblical Observations to Dogmatic Reconstruction," in *The Theology of Reconciliation*, ed. Colin E. Gunton (London: T&T Clark, 2003), 13-38.

(positional and definitive sanctification). Still, she has to go through the challenging process of practical and progressive sanctification. Sometimes she enjoys victories in the uphill struggle for the glory of God. Nevertheless, it is not always so. The Christian often fails to live up to God's expectations, and this makes her estranged from intimate fellowship with God. At this point, God wants her to be reconciled to him again through confessing her sins and acknowledging the assurance of God's forgiving heart. The vertical reconciliation that the Christian has experienced once and for all becomes a repetitive event that she undergoes again and again on a daily basis. This means that her experience of reconciliation once and for all becomes the paradigm for her future experiences of reconciliation in the process of sanctification in the power of the Holy Spirit.

In addition, we tend to fail to love others as ourselves, including our neighbors and enemies. We often get involved in conflicts with others by doing harm to them or being hurt by them. We tend to exclude others rather than embrace them. This creates a "dividing wall of hostility" (Eph 2:14) between us and others. In the context of continuous ups and downs in the Christian life, we have to go through the repetition of the event of horizontal reconciliation as well on a daily basis. Sometimes we should forgive those who hurt us, and oftentimes we should ask forgiveness of those whom we hurt. "Forgive us our debts as we forgive our debtors" (Mt 6:12). We have to repeat the Lord's Prayer and practice it continuously. Throughout the process of sanctification, we experience God's grace and others' mercy in forgiving our sins and transgressions. Furthermore, we practice God's grace and mercy in reconciling to us those who do harm to us. In this sense, we can say that the process of sanctification is the continuous journey of experiencing events of reconciliation, vertically with God and horizontally with others.

Reconciliation: Insights from trinitarian theology. Trinitarian theology can shed significant and further light on the doctrine of reconciliation. When the Christian is equipped with the insights of trinitarian theology, he can lead a life of reconciliation on a deeper level with the power of the Holy Spirit.

Renaissance of trinitarian theology in the twentieth century. Christian theology experienced a renaissance and revival of the doctrine of the Trinity on a global scale in the twentieth century.[12] Karl Barth from the Reformed tradition and John Zizioulas from the Greek Orthodox tradition were two of the most important theologians who made indelible contributions to this revival of trinitarian theology.[13] Roman Catholicism also witnessed a renaissance of the doctrine of the Trinity, primarily through the contribution of major feminist theologians, including Elizabeth Johnson and Catherine Mowry LaCugna.[14]

---

[12]For excellent introductions to this renaissance, see Stanley J. Grenz, *Rediscovering the Triune God: The Trinity in Contemporary Theology* (Minneapolis: Augsburg Fortress, 2004), and Grenz, *The Social God and the Relational Self: A Trinitarian Theology of the Imago Dei* (Louisville: Westminster John Knox, 2001). See also Veli-Matti Kärkkäinen, *The Trinity: Global Perspectives* (Louisville: Westminster John Knox, 2007), and Robert Letham, *The Holy Trinity: In Scripture, History, Theology, and Worship* (Phillipsburg, NJ: P&R, 2004).

[13]John D. Zizioulas, *Being as Communion: Studies in Personhood and the Church* (Crestwood, NY: St. Vladimir's Seminary Press, 1997), and Zizioulas, *Communion and Otherness: Further Studies in Personhood and the Church* (London: T&T Clark, 2006). Among the contributors from the Reformed tradition are Thomas F. Torrance, Colin E. Gunton, and Jürgen Moltmann. Among Lutheran contributors are Robert W. Jenson, Carl Braaten, and Wolfhart Pannenberg.

[14]Elizabeth Johnson, *She Who Is: The Mystery of God in Feminist Theological Discourse* (New York: Crossroad, 2002); Catherine Mowry LaCugna, *God for Us: The Trinity and Christian Life* (New York: HarperCollins, 1991).

Major theological insights from revived trinitarian theology. We can glean four major theological insights from the revival of the doctrine of the Trinity in the twentieth and early twenty-first centuries. First, God is a community or, more technically speaking, a communion of three divine persons who embodies unity in diversity and diversity in unity.[15] So diversity is not contradictory to unity, and unity is not contradictory to diversity. Unity and diversity can coexist in perfect harmony. They are not mutually exclusive. In a sense, the doctrine of the Trinity is a resolution of the perennial philosophical problem of "the one and the many." The triune God embodies both unity and plurality in absolute balance.

Second, since we are called to imitate God (Eph 5:1), we should strive to celebrate and respect diversity and difference rather than dismissing and suppressing them. In the context of the celebration of diversity, we should pursue unity. In the context of endeavoring to materialize unity, we should respect diversity and difference.

Third, the three divine persons exist together in a perichoretic manner. The word *perichorēsis* means mutual indwelling, mutual incoherence, and circumincession: the Father dwells in the Son and the Holy Spirit; the Son dwells in the Father and the Holy Spirit; the Holy Spirit dwells in the Father and the Son. Divine *perichorēsis* entails further that the three divine persons penetrate into, participate in, and depend on one another. Mutual penetration, participation, and interdependence characterize the life of the triune God.

Human beings should pursue a perichoretic relationship with others characterized by mutual openness, penetration, participation, and interdependence. Therefore, extreme individualism that dismisses outright the communal dimension of human life squarely contradicts the way of being of the triune God. Furthermore, extreme collectivism that suffocates celebration of diversity and individuality is opposed to the perichoretic manner of God's existence. Rejecting both uncontrolled individualism and oppressive collectivism, we should strive to embody a communal *perichorēsis*.

Fourth, the triune God is a communion who enjoys the *koinōnia* of mutual love (*agapē*), glorification, welcoming, embrace, respect, hospitality, service (*diakonia*), and submission (*hypotassō*). The Trinity is not an egalitarian community of entities that seek to grasp equal rights but rather a communion of submission (*hypotassō*) to one another, in which individuals set aside their rights to equality (*kenōsis*) and serve one another with self-sacrificing love (*agapē*).

We should strive to embody communions like the triune communion in every area of human life, including the family, workplace, school, society, politics, nations, and international relations. The kingdom of the triune God has already come. It has already begun to affect individual human beings and their communities. Churches are communities that are called to realize a communion like the triune communion. Of course, before the eschaton, we will not be able to accomplish our task completely; but still, churches can be the signposts of the coming kingdom of the triune God, who is a perfect communion.[16]

---

[15]This theological concern began to be described specifically as a focus on the *social Trinity*. But I personally prefer the term *communal Trinity*, since I believe that the triune communion is not merely a society or community.

[16]For an excellent discussion of the life application points of trinitarian theology, see Fred Sanders, *The Deep Things of God: How the Trinity Changes Everything* (Wheaton, IL: Crossway, 2010).

Trinitarian theological insights and reconciliation. First, trinitarian theological insights will prevent human conflicts. When we realize genuinely the truth that diversity and difference should be celebrated, respected, and welcomed, not dismissed and suffocated, many unnecessary conflicts will be prevented between human beings. For example, if we truly grasp the trinitarian truth that racial and ethnic diversity is something to celebrate, rather than to suppress, then racial and ethnic conflicts will decrease significantly. In this context, one may ask, "Why does the Trinity then not legitimize all kinds of diversity and pluralism, including the religious sort?" This question is a legitimate and valid one. It is not difficult, however, to provide an appropriate theological response to the question. Racial, ethnic, gender, and professional differences are indifferent matters to salvation, whereas religious commitments are intrinsically connected to the issue of salvation.[17] If you fall into the trap of religious pluralism, you will ultimately end up denying the absolute uniqueness and finality of Jesus Christ.

Second, trinitarian theological insights will promote reconciliation. When we truly understand the trinitarian truth that we are created and called to pursue and embody communions like the trinitarian communion, promotion of reconciliation through practicing unconditional forgiveness will be a natural step to take after conflicts have occurred.[18] Enmity and vengeance against other people and communities will be condemned as totally contradictory to the calling of the Christian individual and community. In this context, one may raise two questions: (1) Isn't it difficult to see how the triune community can serve as the basis for an ethic of forgiveness and reconciliation inasmuch as the triune persons are never in need of forgiveness and reconciliation with one another? (2) Is it really true that the example of the Trinity requires full and equal fellowship among all human beings? While it may be true that human community mirrors God's own internally relational life, don't human limitations require that community be extended to only a certain few (family, friends, clan, culture, or nation), to the exclusion of others?

In relation to the first question, I would argue that the triune communion can serve as the basis for an ethic of forgiveness and reconciliation even though the triune persons are never in need of forgiveness and reconciliation with one another. This is because both protologically (beginning) and eschatologically (ending) the triune communion should be the model of all communities. In other words, the triune communion was the model for a marriage communion between Adam and Eve in Eden before the fall, and it will be the model for the community of glorified and resurrected people of God in the new heavens and new earth. In order for communities broken by enmity and hostility to be restored to the original model of the triune communion, they should practice forgiveness and reconciliation since the processes of forgiveness and reconciliation are the means through which human beings can reach the goal of embodying the triune communion in their own context.

---

[17]Several theologians (Mark Heim, Amos Yong, Jacques Dupuis, and Raimundo Panikkar) have recently explored theologies of religions with reference to the renaissance of the doctrine of the Trinity, most of which are sympathetic to the pluralist ideology. Keith E. Johnson has refuted those proposals successfully in his *Rethinking the Trinity and Religious Pluralism: An Augustinian Assessment* (Downers Grove, IL: IVP Academic, 2011).

[18]For a Latin American discussion of the inclusion of trinitarian perichoresis as a factor in horizontal reconciliation, see Leonardo Boff, *Trinity and Society* (Eugene, OR: Wipf & Stock, 2005).

In terms of the second question, I would argue that in principle the example of the Trinity requires full and equal fellowship between all human beings. However, in reality, human limitations and sinfulness require that the trinitarian communion be embodied in only a certain few communities, including marriage, family, friends, clan, culture, and nation within history. The triune communion, however, will be embodied completely and universally among all human beings who will be redeemed in Jesus Christ, the Lamb of God, at the eschaton. The glorified and resurrected people of God will be able to transcend the limitations of time and space and their sinful inclinations.

APPLICATIONS TO THE
CONTEXT OF THE DIVISION OF
THE KOREAN PENINSULA

This section focuses on how to apply the soteriological and trinitarian theological insights discussed above to the situation of the division of the Korean peninsula.

Analysis of the situation of the division of the Korean peninsula. Korea was under Japanese colonial rule from 1910 to 1945. During this period the Korean people experienced violent atrocities committed by the Japanese colonial government and were eagerly yearning for their liberation. With the end of the World War II and the defeat of Japan, Korea was politically emancipated but divided into two areas against its will, the northern part occupied and governed by the Soviet Union and the southern part occupied and governed by the United States. In the northern area, north of the thirty-eighth parallel, Korean socialists and communists coop-

erated with the Soviet Union to establish their own government; in the southern area, south of the thirty-eighth parallel, Korean nationalists and democratic republicans collaborated with the United States to found their own government. With the backing of the United Nations and the United States, the Republic of Korea was officially formed in the southern area in 1948, which is today called South Korea. In 1948, the General Assembly of the United Nations confirmed officially that South Korea was the only legitimate nation in the Korean peninsula. Regardless of this UN decision, Korean socialists and communists established the Democratic People's Republic of Korea in the northern area with the support of the Soviet Union and China.

National—even global, depending on one's perspective—tragedy began when the communist North Korea invaded South Korea on June 25, 1950. The Korean War continued for three years.[19] In support of South Korea, sixteen UN allied forces led by the United States participated in the war. China supported North Korea militarily. The Soviet Union helped North Korea economically without sending troops. As a result of this war, about 40,000 US troops, 217,000 South Korean troops, 406,000 North Korean troops, and 600,000 Chinese troops were killed. In addition, about 1 million South Korean civilians and 600,000 North Korean civilians were killed or missing. On July 27, 1953, the war ended with a ceasefire. No official truce was established between the two Koreas, which means, in fact, the two countries are still at war.

What, then, was the main cause of the war? Scholars and historians have presented various theories and analyses about the causes of the

---

[19]Among the best sources for the history of the Korean War are Max Hastings, *The Korean War* (New York: Simon & Schuster, 1988); Bruce Cummings, *The Korean War: A History* (New York: Modern Library, 2011); and David Halberstam, *The Coldest Winter: America and the Korean War* (New York: Hyperion, 2008). A great online source is www.history.com/topics/korean-war.

Korean War. But in a nutshell, it seems appropriate to observe that the Korean War marked the starting point of the Cold War between the communist countries, led by the Soviet Union and China, and the free countries, led by the United States. This means that the Korean War was the tragic theater of global ideological conflict between communism and free-market democracy.

It has already been more than sixty years since the end of the Korean War. But the communist North Korea has never given up its desire to communize South Korea, and it has frequently attacked the capitalistic South Korea, although South Korea has never made a preemptive attack on North Korea. Enmity and hostility between the two Koreas has not dwindled but rather increased in spite of South Korea's numerous efforts to provide humanitarian aid for the hungry and sick in North Korea. North Korea has responded to South Korea's conciliatory gestures and endeavors with violence, cyber invasions, military attacks, and the development of nuclear bombs.[20] As a result, hostile tension between the two Koreas is still increasing on a daily basis, and prospects for reconciliation seem gloomy.

Recognition of the absolute necessity and urgency of reconciliation between the two Koreas. Many factors are causing the division of the Korean peninsula to be prolonged indefinitely: international power struggles between China, Japan, Russia, and the United States; outdated ideological conflict between communism and free-market democracy; the aggressive and belligerent attitude of North Korea; and general disinterest in reconciliation among South Koreans. Whatever the causes may be, we need to recognize that reconciliation between the two Koreas is absolutely necessary and urgent.

The two Koreas share a common language, ethnicity, and historical legacy. Nevertheless, the two Koreas are getting further and further apart from each other in terms of values, worldviews, and lifestyles. Enmity and hostility between the two Koreas has been rapidly increasing because military conflicts continue sporadically, resulting in the deaths and injuries of many soldiers and civilians and further alienation from each other. From the perspective of South Korea, the North Korean government has been committing horrendous atrocities against the North Korean people, including serious abuse of human rights, suppressing and forfeiting the basic freedom of religion and press, and over-controlling citizens' daily lives.[21]

Reconciliation through mutual forgiveness. In this context, reconciliation between the two Koreas should be pursued through the process of mutual forgiveness. It is against human nature for the victims of violence to forgive the perpetrators. For this very reason, we need the gospel and the message of reconciliation that empowers us to forgive our enemies. God reconciled his enemies to himself by sacrificing his Son Jesus Christ. The core message of the gospel of reconciliation is that unconditional forgiveness opens the door to restoration of friendly and harmonious relationship. The two Koreas need to practice unconditional forgiveness toward each other. Without mutual and unconditional forgiveness, the two Koreas will remain divided permanently. This would be the most tragic scenario for the future of the two Koreas.

---

[20]For an excellent discussion of the character of North Korea as a state, see Victor Cha, *The Impossible State: North Korea, Past and Future* (New York: HarperCollins, 2012).

[21]For discussions about human-rights conditions in North Korea, see Barbara Demick, *Nothing to Envy: Ordinary Lives in North Korea* (New York: Spiegel & Grau, 2010), and Jiyoung Song, *Human Rights Discourse in North Korea* (New York: Routledge, 2014).

In order for mutual forgiveness between the two Koreas to occur, the issues of truth telling and acknowledgment of guilt should be dealt with in a genuinely gracious and just manner. Both South Korea and North Korea should tell the truth about their attempts to destroy and harm each other and acknowledge their guilt to each other. And they should ask for forgiveness from each other. This is the first step toward mutual forgiveness. Without truth telling and acknowledgment of sins and guilt, authentic forgiveness can never happen.

We have an excellent example of mutual forgiveness in a sociopolitical context in the case of South Africa. There, many theologians and Christian leaders discussed the issue of reconciliation between the white and the black communities, seeking to remove the mutual enmity and hostility brought about by the policy of apartheid. Desmond Tutu, for example, consistently promoted unconditional and mutual forgiveness between the two communities during apartheid and even after its abolition.[22] Furthermore, 152 theologians and religious leaders signed the Kairos Document, which challenged the policies of apartheid and declared that the oppressors' repentance was required for genuine forgiveness to occur.[23]

Of course, we cannot forgive others on our own. We need supernatural help and empowerment from the Holy Spirit. Natural human beings tend not to forgive but to avenge. We cannot deny that. So we need to pray for the Holy Spirit to work even in unbelieving Koreans for them to open their hearts and forgive their enemies. In fact, we should pray for a miracle!

The South Korean government's responsibility. In the context of the division of the Korean peninsula, the South Korean government should take responsibility for reconciling the North Korean government to itself by practicing unconditional forgiveness and embrace. In spite of the irresponsibility, irresponsiveness, and unchanging hostility of the North Korean government, the South Korean government should act in a different manner. Of course, it would be too idealistic to expect a secular government to act like a religious organization or a church. However, if the South Korean government continues to act like other secular governments in the world, the division of the Korean peninsula will continue endlessly without any hope for reconciliation or reunification.

From 1998 to 2007, when the left-wing political party was in power in South Korea, the government did a good job of embracing North Korea through the so-called sunshine policy, which was focused on supporting both the North Korean government and its people through unconditional economic aid.[24] Many scholars and politicians criticized the South Korean government's sunshine policy because the North Korean government abused and misused its unconditional financial support for developing a nuclear program that threatened the security of South Korea and its neighboring countries, including Japan and the United States, rather than feeding the hungry and healing the sick in North Korea.

It is undeniable that the possibility of the North Korean government's misuse of the South Korean government's economic aid is always

---

[22]See Desmond Tutu, *No Future Without Forgiveness* (New York: Image, 2000).

[23]Harvey J. Sindima, *The Gospel According to the Marginalized* (New York: Peter Lang, 2005), 75.

[24]For an excellent discussion of the sunshine policy by one of its advocates, see Chung-In Moon, *The Sunshine Policy: In Defense of Engagement as a Path to Peace in Korea* (Seoul: Yonsei University Press, 2012). Another good reference is Key-young Son, *South Korean Engagement Policies and North Korea: Identities, Norms and the Sunshine Policy* (New York: Routledge, 2006).

there. Despite that, the South Korean government should not stop providing the North Korean government and people with economic support. To be sure, the South Korean government needs wisdom and discernment here. It must request transparency from the North Korean government to make sure economic aid is being distributed and delivered to the North Korean people according to the desires of the South Korean government and other donors.

Ever since the right-wing political party took power in South Korea in 2008, the sunshine policy has been officially terminated. But we should remember that apart from sacrificial giving and unconditional love and forgiveness, no flower of reconciliation can blossom. We should sow the seed of reconciliation in tears, and eventually we will get a full harvest—both reconciliation and reunification between the two Koreas.

The South Korean church's communal responsibility. As Murray Rae has argued, the church is the sign of reconciliation because it is the community of those forgiven by and reconciled to God.[25] As the communion of forgiveness, the South Korean church should strive to embody the spirit of reconciliation within itself (members loving and forgiving one another) and extend it to the larger society and urge the people of the two Koreas to respond to the message of reconciliation. This is how the South Korean church can fulfill its God-given mission and calling in the context of the division of the Korean peninsula.

From a trinitarian theological perspective, the South Korean church should learn how to celebrate diversity within itself and pursue unity in the context of radical diversity in terms of theological convictions, spiritual experiences, church polities,

and historical legacies. The South Korean church is a totality of extremely diversified organizations, denominations, and traditions. So it is very easy to fall into excessive individualism, suppressive collectivism, or irresponsible pluralism. In the past, the South Korean church failed to live up to the trinitarian ideals of the celebration of diversity, the pursuit of unity, and the embodiment of perichoretic *koinōnia* of *agapē*, *diakonia*, and *hypotassō*. The South Korean church should repent of its past failures and endeavor to become an alternative communion that can give the people of the two Koreas a new hope for the future.[26] Furthermore, it should become a paradigmatic communion that the people of the two Koreas become eager to follow and imitate in an effort to resolve their problems of mutual enmity and hostility.

The South Korean Christian's individual responsibility. Individual Christians in the South Korean church have responsibilities as well. First, they should recognize that God has sent them to the Korean peninsula as messengers of reconciliation. Empowered by the Holy Spirit, they should lead a life of reconciliation in their personal life, families, and churches, and in larger society. In so doing, they should sow the seeds of reconciliation in every area of human life in South Korea with the hope and prayer that their holy endeavor will eventually bear the fruit of reconciliation between the two Koreas. Second, individual Christians in the South Korean church should make every effort to embody trinitarian spirituality, which is characterized by the celebration of diversity; the pursuit of unity in diversity; and the perichoretic life of communion of mutual love, service, and submission. Their prayer should be that their effort will have

---

[25]Murray Rae, "The Remnant People: Ecclesia as Sign of Reconciliation," in *The Theology of Reconciliation*, ed. Colin E. Gunton (London: T&T Clark, 2003), 93-108.

[26]For an excellent discussion of the church as alternative community, see Stanley Hauerwas and William H. Willimon, *Resident Aliens: Life in the Christian Colony*, 25th anniversary ed. (Nashville: Abingdon, 2014).

ripple effects for reconciliation among South Korean people and between the two Koreas.

Getting down to praxis. When it gets down to praxis, how do we lead North Korea to the table? What acts of grace would promote dialogue? These are legitimate questions that require appropriate responses. Considering North Korea's belligerent and warmongering attitude, it will not be easy to draw the North Korean government to the table of dialogue for reconciliation. However, given the complexities of this situation, we need to delve into how a theology of reconciliation can inform the process of reconciling with a cruel and corrupt regime rather than simply trying to conquer it. Again, my suggestion would be that the South Korean government attempt to convince the North Korean government that the South Korean government does not want to conquer it militarily or swallow it up, but rather wants to have a genuine and authentic relationship that is mutually beneficial and that will ultimately result in mutual reconciliation. In addition, the South Korean government can prepare some incentives for North Korean participation in reconciliation dialogues.

Many scholars and professional analysts of the Korean peninsula have become deeply suspicious about the possibility of reconciliation between the two Koreas, especially after North Korea's fifth nuclear detonation (since 2006), conducted on September 9, 2016. The South Korean people have recently claimed that they have been sacrificing and patient enough. Nevertheless, the South Korean government should not stop knocking on the door of North Korea, asking to open the door for a meal of dialogue together (Rev 3:20). We should become like Jesus Christ toward North Korea, asking to return to the normal way of life and promising complete forgiveness. May God bless South Korean efforts to accomplish reconciliation with North Korea!

CONCLUSION

Salvation is reconciliation, and vice versa. South Korean Christians and churches have already experienced salvation as reconciliation. As a result, they are enjoying peace, friendship, and harmony with the triune God and other people. They should recognize that they are called to be the messengers and ambassadors of the gospel of reconciliation revealed in and through Jesus Christ. They should take this responsibility with full seriousness. Through the fulfillment of their God-given mission and calling in the power of the Holy Spirit, they will be able to make a great contribution to the reconciliation between the two Koreas. The reconciliation of the two Koreas is not only our task but also God's gift. For this reason, we keep on praying for the miracle of reconciliation of the two Koreas, planting the seeds of peace in tears. "There is neither Jew nor Gentile, neither slave nor free, nor is there male and female, for you are all one in Christ Jesus" (Gal 3:28).

FURTHER READING

Ateek, Naim Stifan. *A Palestinian Christian Cry for Reconciliation*. Maryknoll, NY: Orbis, 2008.

Doxtader, Erik. *With Faith in the Works of Words: The Beginning of Reconciliation in South Africa, 1985–1995*. East Lansing: Michigan State University Press, 2009.

Gilbreath, Edward. *Reconciliation Blues: A Black Evangelical's Inside View of White Christianity*. Downers Grove, IL: InterVarsity Press, 2008.

Lee, Jung Young. *Marginality: The Key to Multicultural Theology*. Minneapolis: Augsburg Fortress, 1995.

Yung, Hwa. *Mangoes or Bananas? The Quest for an Authentic Asian Christian Theology*. Maryknoll, NY: Orbis, 2014.

32

QOHELET'S GOSPEL IN ECCLESIASTES

ECCLESIASTES 3:1-15; 7:15-22; 11:1-6

Elaine W. F. Goh

ECCLESIASTES IS A BOOK that communicates hope. In Ecclesiastes 3:1-15, Qohelet conveys a realistic depiction of the concept of time. In Ecclesiastes 7:15-22, Qohelet acknowledges that a mortal, striving to be righteous, is nevertheless hampered by human limitations. In Ecclesiastes 11:1-6, Qohelet asserts that human ignorance should not deter one from carpe diem action. These passages suggest life-giving aspects to contend with the mentality of fearing death, overconfidence, and workaholic tendencies among the Chinese. Asian Chinese in general are instructed, through generations of Confucian teachings, to be pragmatic, morally guided, and diligent. Qohelet points out to Asian Chinese the reality confronting these teachings. Qohelet teaches one to live here and now, in line with Asian Chinese pragmatism. This chapter argues that the message of Ecclesiastes offers salvific hope, in line with the gospel and salvation as offered in the Christian faith.

This chapter upholds the theme of salvation history as an Old Testament theology, which accentuates the role of biblical Wisdom literature to convey salvation. With this perception, I survey and evaluate the biblical passages frequently used by some Asian Chinese scholars to construct the Chinese Christian understanding of salvation. In this chapter I suggest that Ecclesiastes offers salvific hope as well. I use three passages taken from Ecclesiastes to illustrate the point. In Ecclesiastes 3:1-15, Qohelet conveys a realistic depiction of the concept of time that reduces the general fear of death. In Ecclesiastes 7:15-22, Qohelet acknowledges that humankind, striving to be righteous, nevertheless has to accept human limitations. This acceptance will guide people to be realistic and reasonable in daily living. In Ecclesiastes 11:1-6, Qohelet asserts that human ignorance should not deter one from taking action. Thus, one can be ready to act without being seen to be a workaholic. The three passages suggest life-giving aspects to contend with the mentality of fearing death, overconfidence, and workaholic tendencies among Asian Chinese. Through generations of Confucian teachings, Asian Chinese have learned to be pragmatic, morally guided, and diligent. Qohelet shows Asian Chinese the need to widen the horizons of these teachings. Nevertheless, Qohelet teaches one to live here and now in line with Asian Chinese pragmatism. As such, this chapter argues that the message of Ecclesiastes offers hope and is consistent with the gospel and salvation proffered in Christian belief.

THEOLOGICAL CONSTRUCTION ON THE THEME OF SALVATION: SOME ASIAN CHINESE PERSPECTIVES

Constructing a Chinese Christian theology is a task taken on by some Asian scholars in recent decades. To summarize, the basic Asian Chinese Christian understanding of salvation, or soteriology, is primarily Christ-centered.[1] Understandably, their theological construction relies heavily on the New Testament. They regard the Christ event as the continuation of salvation history from the Old Testament, which also becomes the defining understanding of the law "before" and "after" Jesus' coming, as mentioned in Galatians 3:23-25.[2] Passages related to the Christ event are generally quoted to articulate the theological understanding of salvation, especially the historical death of Jesus (Heb 2:14-15), the imagery of the cross (Eph 2:16; 1 Pet 2:24), and the blood of Christ (Acts 20:28; Rom 3:25; Heb 9:12).[3] These New Testament passages, as anticipated, have built on the idea of sacrifice in the Old Testament.

Salvation is needed because of the presence of sin. The word *sin* is a somewhat alien concept in Chinese vocabulary. Though it is commonly found in the Bible, it is often understood in light of, or is related to, the idea of shame among Asian Chinese. The Old Testament and the New Testament address the idea of shame in relation to sin as well because of the cultural milieu of the Israelites. In Asian Chinese culture, if a person commits murder, he has to face the law and also bear the shame of giving the family a bad name. Nevertheless, the Asian Chinese way to redeem one's shame is often through one's good works. The idea of salvation in this sense means bringing honor to annul shame.

In the Old Testament, a sacrifice is necessary to eliminate sin. On this founding idea, the New Testament avers that sin, regardless of its form, makes humankind fall short of God's glory (Rom 3:23) and become alienated from God (Eph 4:18). The death of Jesus Christ on the cross represents the sacrifice that is required to deal with sin. Redemption, therefore, takes place through the grace of God. Hence, when articulating salvation in the Bible, grace (*hesed* in the Old Testament, *charis* in the New Testament) is an important idea that Asian Chinese scholars deliberate. As a result of this grace of God, fallen humankind can be made "right," or "justified" (Eph 1:4-6; Rom 3:21-26).[4] This idea of justification is in relation to one's faith and is tied closely to the interpretation of salvation based on Paul's epistle to the Romans.[5] Therefore, understandably, in the theological construction of the Christian doctrine of soteriology, the declaration of one being saved "by grace" and "through faith" (Eph 2:8) is often purposely asserted.[6]

---

[1] These Asian scholars and theologians are mainly from Malaysia, Hong Kong, and Taiwan, as the references suggest.
[2] Kok Hon Seng, *Jialataishu Daolun* [Introduction to the Book of Galatians] (Hong Kong: Logos, 2003), 110.
[3] See, for example, Dao-zong Wu, *Shenzhi Suoxin: Jidujiao Jiyao Zhenli* [Knowing What We Believe: The Fundamental Truth for Christians] (Taipei: China Evangelical Seminary, 2010), 293-96.
[4] On how this "rightness," or "justification," takes place, various Asian biblical scholars differ in their interpretations depending on their perspectives on the Pauline Epistles. See, for example, one that derives from the new perspective on Paul by Lo Lung-Kwong, *Baoluo Xinguan: Luomashu de Zhuti yu Mudi* [New Perspectives on Paul: The Theme and Purpose of the Book to the Romans] (Taipei: University of Donghai Press, 2007).
[5] See a title by Sam Tsang, *Luomashu Jiedu: Jidu Fuyin de Zhanxin Shiye* [An Imperial-Missiological Rereading of Romans] (Taipei: Campus Evangelical Fellowship, 2009).
[6] See, for example, Kok Hon Seng, *Heavenly Vision for Witness on Earth: A Commentary on Ephesians* (Kuala Lumpur: Bridge Communication, 2010), especially 180-88.

In a commentary on the Nicene Creed, a group of Chinese scholars in Southeast Asia further elaborate on the creed. The conviction of the salvation through Christ is partly reflected in the phrase "For us and for our salvation, He came down from heaven."[7] Citing biblical events such as that of God's deliverance through Noah's ark (Gen 6–8), the exodus (Ex 1–14), and the deliverance from sin (Mt 1:21), God's salvation is again affirmed. Their theological construction on salvation also relates Christian faith to the life of the church in Asia. The way of faith, according to Asian Chinese theologians, also relies on passages such as Colossians 1:15-19, which declares that Christ is the head of the church, through him all things have been created, and in him all things hold together.[8]

A dual theme of creation and redemption has also shaped the Asian Chinese theological understanding of salvation.[9] The notion of creation is closely tied in with the creation account in the book of Genesis. This dual theme is reflected in the work of Yee-cheung Wong in his *Old Testament Theology: From Creation to New Creation*, which uses the terms *creation* and *restoration* to narrate the message of the Old Testament.[10] The concept of new creation in his work also builds on the Genesis creation account. In this dual theme, redemption refers to the restoration of the order of things that includes the

human condition, lifestyle, relationships, and the cosmos.

In Chinese understanding, theology is relational. The second paragraph of the Nicene Creed spells out the relationship of the Father and the Son: Jesus Christ is the only Son of God, eternally begotten of the Father, and of one Being with the Father. This declaration is made before affirming in the creed that Jesus Christ is salvation. Salvation, therefore, is based on a relationship, and this relationship is extended "for us" in the creed, making possible reconciliation between God and humankind (Rom 5:10; Col 1:20-22; Eph 2:12-13).[11] The grace of reconciliation is given freely through the death and resurrection of the Lord Jesus Christ (Rom 3:24; 5:11).[12] Based on this theological understanding of reconciliation, the identity of the Asian church is, in some way, defined by reconciling people to God. As an example in practice, such reconciliation through Christ's redemption should have an effect on human living conditions, including solving the problems of poverty in Asia.[13] Salvation, in the sense of the breaking down of oppressive and destructive cycles in that society, will then be truly experienced by all.

The understanding of relationship can be expanded into a constant dialogue between faith and context.[14] Thus, some have advocated for the task of constructing Christian theology from

[7]Yip Ching Wah and Lo Lung Kwong, *We Believe: A Commentary on the Nicene Creed*, ed. Association of Theological Schools in South East Asia (Hong Kong: Chinese Christian Literature Council, 2014), 109-17.
[8]Andres S. K. Tang, ed., *Zai Xinyang Zhisi de Tuzhong* [On the Way of Faith Thinking] (Hong Kong: Logos, 2000), 47.
[9]Watson Hua-zhong Soong, *Shengjing Shenxue* [Biblical Theology] (Taipei: Campus, 1997), 301.
[10]Wong Yee-cheung, *Jiuyue Shenxue: Cong Chuangzao Dao Xinchuangzao* [Old Testament Theology: From Creation to New Creation] (Hong Kong: Tien Dao, 2003).
[11]Zhang-lin Wang, *Shengjing Sibian Shenxue* [Speculative Theology of the Bible] (Taipei: Daosheng, 2008), 119.
[12]See also Tan Kim Sai, *Fuyinlun: Fuyin de Neirong yu Benzhi* [Gospelogy: The Content and Nature of the Gospel] (Selangor, Malaysia: MBS, 2006), 30-48.
[13]Kung Lap Yan, *Quanren Yushen Hehao: Jiaohui de Shenfen* [Ministry of Reconciliation: The Identity of the Church] (Hong Kong: Hong Kong Christian Institute, 2002), 127-40, points out the relatedness between Jesus Christ's redemption and the fate of the poor.
[14]Benedict Hung-biu Kwok, *Chaoxiang Zhengquan Shenxue Sikao* [Toward Complete Theological Thinking] (Hong Kong: Tien Dao, 2004), 27, 33. The notion of theology being relational is inevitably informed by Karl Barth's and Dietrich Bonhoeffer's interpretation of humankind being created "in God's image." See also Tang, *Zai Xinyang Zhisi de Tuzhong*, 133.

Chinese cultural contexts by means of native resources and terminologies. Exploring cultural connections between the Bible and Chinese literature is not new. Archie Lee, for example, has written substantially on cross-textual hermeneutics.[15] Furthermore, the in-depth research by K. K. Yeo to pursue a Chinese Christian theology is notable.[16] Yeo asserts a Chinese Christian theology based on a study on Confucian *xin* (trustworthiness) and Pauline *pistis* (faith). He also compares Confucius to Paul in their pursuit of ethics and virtues as professed in the *Analects* and the book of Galatians. By being creatively faithful to the two living texts, Yeo illustrates effectively both the ethical task and the theological task of Chinese Christians.[17]

Biblical and theological research conducted by Asian Chinese will inevitably face constant pressure. On the one hand, we are informed and nurtured by education from the West; on the other hand, we try to come to terms with the biblical and theological meanings in various Asian Chinese contexts. As Terence Fretheim correctly observes, Christians typically relate salvation to "forgiveness" granted to those who believe in Jesus Christ (Rom 5:8-10).[18] This understanding is shared among Asian Chinese. Furthermore, Chinese Christians in Asia also largely understand the idea of salvation based on the New Testament. Nevertheless, the Christ event and its often-quoted New Testament passages do not exhaust the experience of salvation in the Bible. The Old Testament often speaks of

God as the Lord who saves God's people, for example, through acts of giving, deliverance, and guidance. The idea of God in the Old Testament is depicted through images of king, warrior, and shepherd, among many other metaphors. In the book of Isaiah, for instance, one finds a diversity of metaphors describing God—the Holy One of Israel—as a soldier at war (Is 42:13) and a woman in childbirth (Is 42:14). The two metaphors are rendered in both masculine and feminine understandings, and are related to God's acts of salvation in the Old Testament. In short, the Old Testament's use of salvation language differs from that of the New Testament. The Old Testament articulates different dimensions in understanding salvation or soteriology.

SALVATION HISTORY, WISDOM, AND OLD TESTAMENT THEOLOGY

In this section, I propose an Asian Chinese perspective on constructing an Old Testament theology with a dual emphasis: the theme of salvation history and the role of wisdom. The Old Testament encompasses mixed writings and is highly diverse in terms of its compositions, contents, and themes. Due to this diversity, one is compelled to choose between constructing a coherent Old Testament theology or a combination of Old Testament theologies. The former endeavor strives to find a theological center and usually leads to a marginalization of wisdom's theological perspective.[19] The latter approach attempts to assess theological perspectives

---

[15]See his major works recently collected and published in Archie Lee, *Kuawenben Yuedu: Xibolai Shengjing Quanshi* [Cross-Textual Reading of the Hebrew Bible] (Shanghai: Shanghai Sanlian Books, 2015).

[16]K. K. Yeo, *Musing with Confucius and Paul: Toward a Chinese Christian Theology* (Eugene, OR: Wipf & Stock, 2008). The Chinese version of this title is available; see Yang Keqin, *Kongzi yu Baoluo: Tiandao yu Shengyan de Xiangyu* [Confucius and Paul: An Encounter Between the Heaven Path and the Holy Word] (Huadong: Normal University Press, 2009).

[17]See, for example, Yeo, *Musing with Confucius and Paul*, 403.

[18]Terence E. Fretheim, *What Kind of God? Collected Essays of Terence E. Fretheim*, ed. Michael J. Chan and Brent A. Strawn, Siphrut: Literature and Theology of the Hebrew Bible 14 (Winona Lake, IN: Eisenbrauns, 2015), 363.

[19]Despite many attempts to find the theological center, or *Mitte*, of the Old Testament, none satisfyingly express an Old Testament

alongside Pentateuchal, historical, prophetic, and Wisdom writings. Walther Eichrodt's theme of the covenant belongs to the former endeavor.[20] Gerhard von Rad's salvation history, on the other hand, represents the latter.[21] Both works have generated important contributions but have inevitably marginalized the aspect of wisdom.[22] Brevard Childs considers theology a descriptive discipline of analyzing the Old Testament text in a canonical context and views the final form of the Old Testament by seriously considering its various components as they stand in the canon.[23] In delivering the total message of the Old Testament, von Rad's salvation history is the most telling in my opinion. Childs's canonical approach, on the other hand, has the advantage of maintaining the diversity within the Old Testament. Therefore, despite striving to maintain an Asian Chinese voice, this chapter is also informed by von Rad and Childs.

Within the Wisdom corpus itself, there is theological diversity. Anyone who attempts to construct wisdom's theological perspective should consider the complexity within Proverbs, Job, and Ecclesiastes. Job and Qohelet depart in form and content from Proverbs. On the other hand, all three books share a common wisdom unifying theme. In essence, wisdom is "the ability to cope," "the art of steering," and "the quest for self-understanding and for mastery of the world."[24] Therefore Job's and Qohelet's "voices of protest" should be viewed as an integral and genuine expression of faith, rather than as a rejection of traditional wisdom thought.[25]

CANONICAL WITNESSES TO SALVATION HISTORY

Salvation history in the Torah. Salvation history begins with God creating the world.[26] The biblical creation narrative supplements the Chinese understanding of creation of the world in some ways. For instance, God appears in a human form (Gen 6:1-4).[27] In the biblical account, due to humans' wrongful choices, God

---

theology, and none have succeeded in commanding a consensus. See Roland E. Murphy, *The Tree of Life: An Exploration of Biblical Wisdom Literature* (Grand Rapids, MI: Eerdmans, 2002), 112.

[20]Walther Eichrodt, *Theology of the Old Testament*, 2 vols. (London: SCM Press, 1961, 1967).

[21]Gerhard von Rad, *Old Testament Theology*, 2 vols. (New York: Harper & Row, 1962, 1965).

[22]Gerhard von Rad's later work, *Wisdom in Israel* (Nashville: Abingdon, 1972), which focuses solely on the aspect of wisdom, is regarded by some as his third volume on Old Testament theology as a corrective measure to his earlier endeavor (which neglected Wisdom literature). Most people have a problem locating Wisdom in constructing Old Testament theology. The reason is largely due to the absence of familiar themes, such as election of Israelites, exodus, revelation at Sinai, and covenant. Even more unusual is the lack of well-known figures such as Abraham, Moses, David, and the prophets. The absence of these common Old Testament focuses in Wisdom literature, some claim, presents a universal concern and secular outlook in the Wisdom corpus, hence justifying its marginality. This viewpoint demonstrates a narrow conception of Old Testament theology. The place of Wisdom literature in the present form of the Old Testament can be taken more seriously.

[23]Brevard S. Childs, *Old Testament Theology in a Canonical Context* (London: SCM Press, 1985); Childs, *Introduction to the Old Testament as Scripture* (Philadelphia: Fortress, 1979). Childs's theological reading of the final form of the Old Testament involves a process of integrating larger canonical units of Torah, Prophets, and Writings. This theological mode of study enables a Christian interpreter to apply biblical texts without marginalizing any component that comprises the Old Testament.

[24]James L. Crenshaw, *Old Testament Wisdom: An Introduction* (Louisville: Westminster John Knox, 1998), 9.

[25]Richard Schultz, "Unity or Diversity in Wisdom Theology? A Canonical and Covenantal Perspective," *Tyndale Bulletin* 48, no. 2 (1997): 271-306, here 279, 290.

[26]In this section, "Canonical Witnesses to Salvation History," I focus mainly on Ecclesiastes, a book of wisdom. I wish I could elaborate more on other sections of the Bible (Torah, historical and prophetic books). Alongside many others who identify a theological theme that runs through the Old Testament, I suggest "salvation history."

[27]See a theological reading of the Chinese creation stories of Pan Gu and Nu Wa by Archie C. C. Lee, "Theological Reading of Chinese Creation Stories of P'an Ku and Nu Kua," in *Doing Theology with Asian Resources: Ten Years in the Formation of Living Theology in Asia*, ed. John C. England and Archie C. C. Lee (Auckland: Pace, 1993), 230-36. Lee points out how the Chinese reading of the creation of heaven and earth, and the creation of human beings, identifies with that of the Bible. Lee's work therefore has opened the door to a theological dialogue about creation narratives.

took steps to save his people from the consequences of divine-human alienation. This divine initiative is also notable in Chinese understanding, wherein humans usually aspire to seek God by establishing certain connections with the heavens or by attempting to attain immortality. In the biblical account, it was God who made the connection. In seeking the return of his own people, God chose Abraham and his descendants. He established a covenantal relationship that bound his people with certain expectations and responsibilities. His people embarked on a journey of faith henceforth with notable victories and many pitfalls. Yet God delivered them from the oppressions of their enemies and from the consequences of their choices. The idea of salvation history is reflected through divine faithfulness in the midst of the struggles and rebellions of God's people. This idea of the divine *ḥesed* (faithfulness) is largely reassuring, especially for the Chinese, who as a nation endured a long history of struggles and failures.

Salvation history in the historical and prophetic books. The struggles between divine-human continuums continue in the formation of a nation and then in its fall. Leaders and kings were elected partly in the hope of carrying out the salvific task of shepherding and protecting God's people. However, God's people, including their political leaders, failed to respond according to God's salvific plan. Along with those struggles, God's message of rebuke and restoration was communicated eloquently through various prophets who were called to speak to God's people. Their message varied depending on the dispositions of the prophets and their sociopolitical contexts. Salvation history continues

to mark the journey of God's people in Israel's history nonetheless.

Salvation history in the Wisdom and poetic books. Theology is the *logos* of *theos*. It narrates about God and the faith of God's people. In living out faith, one may either trust human ability for survival or rely totally on God's mercy. There is a tension between human confidence and human limitations within a believer. This tension is also reflected in wisdom writing, and it is often perceived as conflicts of perspectives or wisdom's self-correction. There is a theological reason underlying such a tension. It signifies a journey of faith by a believer alongside salvation history.

Proverbs: A good disciple. A disciple of God embarks on a journey of faith by learning proverbial sayings and admonitions (Prov 1–9). To fear God ensures deliverance from the evil path. A good disciple, therefore, may subscribe to absolute and formulaic certainty (e.g., in Prov 10–22; 25–29). As a new beginner in faith, one exercises discernment, hoping to steer her life safely into harbor and avoid hazards that bring catastrophe to fools.[28] Misconduct such as adultery brings shame to oneself and entails abandonment by the family and the community (Prov 5:7-14; 6:32-35). Every bad consequence, such as suffering, presumes a prior sin or wrongful behavior, and it needs divine redemption. Therefore, one holds fast to God's commandment and lives ethically in order to obtain the goodness of life, while at the same time avoiding calamity and punishment.

Job: A questioning devotee. The faith of a believer in God is tested in the realities of life, prompting tremendous struggles (Job 1–2). Along the journey of such struggles, the absence

---

[28]James L. Crenshaw, "The Concept of God in Old Testament Wisdom," in *In Search of Wisdom: Essays in Memory of John G. Gammie*, ed. Leo G. Perdue, Bernard Brandon Scott, and William Johnston Wiseman (Louisville: Westminster John Knox, 1993), 1-18, here 6.

of God becomes offensive (Job 3–31). The subsequent response from God also appears confrontational rather than therapeutic (Job 38–41). Job's questioning signifies a quest to know God as a faithful follower. This quest is compounded by challenges from Job's three friends. The struggles, however, do not conceal one's hope that God will eventually come to one's assistance. In a momentous theophany, the faithful follower is confronted by God's presence. One realizes that God does not owe an answer to the human quest even though God is the one in charge of running the world (Job 42:2-3). The faith of a questioning devotee is saved through this encounter, by journeying in faith, from "hearing about God" to "seeing God" (Job 42:5).

Qohelet: A skeptical believer. Qohelet appears to have tested the confident assertions about the way the world works and found that they are not always valid. For instance, Qohelet questions the value of wisdom (Eccles 2:12-17) and diligence (Eccles 2:18-23) that are upheld in Proverbs. A faithful follower here faces a threatening skepticism. Ecclesiastes is Job without the theophany.[29] The rhetorical questions in Ecclesiastes 1:3; 2:15; 3:9; 4:8; 6:8, for example, express Qohelet's observations that the truth one once learned is now in question. The realities of life become unpredictable and incomprehensible. A believer has to settle for a less structured attitude without compromising trust in God (Eccles 3:14; 5:7; 7:18; 8:12-13; 12:13). A faith journey arriving at this stage has inevitably embraced a hesitant yet mature aptitude. Salvation history continues, as the tested believer does not cease to believe in God. Qohelet even challenges younger ones to be mindful of the harsh realities in life while at the same time asserting the need

to fear God (Eccles 12:13). This grown believer forgoes hasty judgment and refuses to absolutize any conclusion in life. Such a disciple is both a skeptic and a believer.

The fear of God in wisdom elaborated above reflects both human obedience and doubt in salvation history. Tracing wisdom from Proverbs through Job and eventually to Ecclesiastes, a believer in God embraces Torah obedience while growing in faith. Such obedience demands serious engagement with the harsh issues of life (such as the suffering of the righteous, toil, and death) and with the ultimate presence or absence of God. In this journey of faith, the God-human relationship is retrospective and two-dimensional. The whole process is salvific nonetheless: a believer in God grows from a simple faith to a faith in crisis and then to a renewed faith.

The poetic books. The poetic books in the Old Testament represent the voices of God's people along their journey in salvation history. In the biblical poetic books, human confidence is exemplified through love songs, hymns of praise, and psalms of trust. In the psalms of lament, however, the troubled psalmists reflect on human-God relationships, grieving for unresolved questions and pains. Outcries are heard at both individual and community levels. The psalms of lament (e.g., Ps 13; 69; 83; 88) resemble the Chinese poetic corpus *Shijing* (the Book of Poems), reflecting a common human experience. The psalms of lament as well as the Chinese *Shijing* commonly reflect a quest for divine intervention in times of desperation. God in the Bible, explicitly depicted as an all-powerful deliverer, is, at the same time the psalmists' enemy (e.g., Ps 6:1-5; 17:3-12; 22:1-2). The deity in *Shijing*,

[29]John Goldingay, *Theological Diversity and the Authority of the Old Testament* (Grand Rapids, MI: Eerdmans, 1987), 209.

Tian, is also perceived to be an adversary and is often questioned in human suffering. While some psalmists stress moral conduct as being an agent of change (from the reading of *Shijing*), others find comfort in piety to trust God nonetheless (from the reading of, for instance, Ps 6:8-10; 17:13-15; 22:3-5).[30] Both of these elements of lament speak of how people in Asia would cry over poverty and injustice.

There are various perspectives on salvation history in the Old Testament. A person of faith takes on an attitude shaped by various Old Testament writings. The Bible as a whole is therefore a book of faith. It narrates the salvation that God has provided for people of faith, and the struggles and promises that come along with that faith. We now focus on the book of Ecclesiastes, which also offers hope for faithful people.

Ecclesiastes: A book that offers salvific hope. Qohelet seems to challenge the view that wisdom in the past had given enormous confidence in human intellect.[31] The literary genre of Ecclesiastes is "a vehicle of critical reflection upon traditional values and beliefs."[32] Qohelet recog-nizes wisdom's advantage and that folly is never better.[33] Nevertheless, wisdom has its limits and is subject to failures too.[34] At the point where such limits and failure are experienced in life, there is still hope to cope with them.

In Ecclesiastes, Qohelet launches a search for meaning amid limits and failures. The search is expressed through a compound use of verbs for seeking, finding out, and scrutinizing: *dāraš, tûr* (to seek; Eccles 1:13), *māṣā'* (to find; Eccles 7:24), *bāqāš* (to seek; Eccles 7:25), *ḥēqer* (to search; Eccles 12:9), and *'āzen* (to weigh, in *piel* form; Eccles 12:9).[35] In such pursuits, Qohelet is aware of the challenges in the world where humanity has to live. Qohelet avers that humankind cannot find out what God has done (Eccles 3:11). Qohelet says that even the wise cannot find out what is happening under the sun (Eccles 8:1-17). In short, Qohelet not only draws on the wisdom tradition, but he also brings the tradition to bear on human experiences.[36] Qohelet concludes that wisdom provides no advantage in the grasping of one's destiny—when it does not provide sufficient knowledge, when it is determined by

---

[30]Archie C. C. Lee, "Kuayue Bianjie: Xibolai Shipian yu Zhongguo Shijing dui Renxing de Xiangxiang" [Crossing Boundaries: A Study on Human Nature from the Readings of Hebrew *Psalms* and Chinese *Shijing*], in *YeRu Duihua Xinlicheng* [A New Turn in Confucianism-Christianity Dialogue], ed. Pin-Chao Lai and Jing-Xiong Lee (Hong Kong: Chung Chi College of Chinese University of Hong Kong, 2001), 197-221.

[31]The perceived tension within wisdom thought in Ecclesiastes garners various opinions. Walther Zimmerli, for instance, suggests that Qohelet is engaged in a dialogue with the sages and their traditional wisdom, confronting wisdom's boast to solve every human problem. See Walther Zimmerli, *Sprüche, Prediger Altes Testament Deutsch* 16/1 (Göttingen: Vandenhoeck & Ruprecht, 1963), quoted in Richard J. Clifford, *The Wisdom Literature* (Nashville: Abingdon, 1998), 111. K. Galling, on the other hand, has in mind that with Qohelet, wisdom has entered a crisis situation. See K. Galling, *Die Krise der Aufklärung in Israel* (Mainz: Mainzer Universitätsreden, 1952); quoted in Murphy, *Tree of Life*, 55. Elsewhere, Michael Fox maintains that Qohelet does not attack wisdom or the wise but instead favors wisdom; he nevertheless examines the contradictions observed in human life rather than explain them away. See Michael V. Fox, *Qohelet and His Contradictions*, Journal for the Study of the Old Testament Supplement Series 71, ed. David J. A. Clines and Philip R. Davies (Sheffield, UK: Almond, 1989), 10-12.

[32]Karel van der Toorn, "The Ancient Near Eastern Literary Dialogue as a Vehicle of Critical Reflection," in *Dispute Poems and Dialogues in the Ancient and Mediaeval Near East*, ed. G. J. Reinlink and H. L. J. Vanstiphout (Leuven: Peeters, 1991), 59-75, here 59. The ancient Near Eastern parallels of Job, rather than related to issues of theodicy, have been suggested by van der Toorn to be "literary dialogue" as a vehicle of critical reflection on traditional values and beliefs.

[33]Qohelet appears to be challenging the traditional wisdom, yet this does not mean that Qohelet dismisses wisdom. Wisdom is always better than folly in the book of Ecclesiastes.

[34]Choon-Leong Seow, *Ecclesiastes*, Anchor Bible (New York: Doubleday, 1997), 68.

[35]The rare verb *tûr* connotes an extraordinary measure of firm resolve, more appropriate to spying. The verb is used in Job 39:8 to refer to an animal's search for food, and in Prov 12:26 to imply examining one's friend closely. See Crenshaw, *Old Testament Wisdom*, 116, 134.

[36]Seow, *Ecclesiastes*, 69.

chance, and when it is restrained by death.[37] Recognizing such human limitations is not depressing, but liberating.[38] For in Ecclesiastes, the scope of wisdom has extended to discern the ways to survive meaningfully regardless of circumstances. To Qohelet, life is momentary, and therefore one has to seize the moment by working diligently while at the same time observing the fear of God.

Ecclesiastes exhorts one to live pragmatically in a disorderly world. The motif of the book is often claimed to be one with a negative tone because of the recurrent *hebel* in the book, occurring thirty-eight times altogether. Yet the underlying theme of the book is constructive, and one can view Qohelet's commendation to enjoyment positively. The interplay between the commendation of enjoyment and the injunction to fear God in Ecclesiastes suggests they are positively correlated. Enjoyment of life lies at the heart of Qohelet's vision of piety, which can be said to be an ethic of joy and social responsibility.[39]

There is a positive undertone in Ecclesiastes. First, the recurrent *'ĕlōhîm* (God) in Qohelet's articulation is remarkable. The verbs that have been associated with *'ĕlōhîm* in Ecclesiastes illustrate "a very active God."[40] God is the subject of two frequent verbs: *nātan* (give; Eccles 1:13;

2:26; 3:10, 11; 5:18-19; 6:2; 8:15; 9:9; 12:7) and *'āśâ* (do or make; Eccles 3:11, 14; 7:14, 29; 8:17; 11:5). God is also the one who judges (Eccles 3:17), is angry (Eccles 5:6), and brings all human things into judgment (Eccles 11:9). Therefore, Qohelet affirms divine actions and sovereignty.

Second, *'et-hāʾĕlōhîm yĕrāʾ* (to fear God) is the motive behind Qohelet's quest for meaning. This phrase appears throughout the book (Eccles 3:14; 5:7; 7:18; 8:12-13; 12:13). This fear of God is consistent in the wisdom tradition with aiming to promote godly behavior.[41] In Ecclesiastes 5:1-7, for example, Qohelet makes lengthy remarks about religion. He solicits reverence and one's faithful implementation of the covenant with God. People are advised to fear *'ĕlōhîm* in all that they do.

Finally and most significantly, Qohelet looks at human life through the lens of exception. Traditional teachings distinguish clearly between rights and wrongs, but Qohelet points out their exceptions. Such a perspective is critical and realistic, but not necessarily pessimistic.[42] The exceptions are used as contradictions, raising questions of integrity and authorship. Some have attempted to harmonize Qohelet's view of exceptions, yet have also missed his intended rhetoric.[43] The exceptions raise the possibility of the intended dialectical rhetoric of Qohelet.

[37]Michael V. Fox, "Wisdom in Qohelet," in *In Search of Wisdom*, ed. Leo G. Perdue, Bernard Brandon Scott, and William Johnson Wiseman (Louisville: Westminster John Knox, 1993), 115-31, here 123-26.
[38]Von Rad, *Wisdom in Israel*, 101, states that recognizing human limitations puts a stop to the false security in human wisdom and enables one to be open to the activity of God.
[39]Eunny P. Lee, *The Vitality of Enjoyment in Qohelet's Theological Rhetoric* (Berlin: Walter de Gruyter, 2005), 32-82, 129-34.
[40]Roland E. Murphy, *Ecclesiastes*, Word Biblical Commentary 23A, ed. David A. Hubbard, Glenn W. Barker, and John D. W. Watts (Dallas: Word, 1992), lxviii.
[41]Otto Kaiser, "Qohelet," in *Wisdom in Ancient Israel*, ed. John Day, Robert P. Gordon, and H. G. Williamson (Cambridge: Cambridge University Press, 1995), 83-93, here 90-91. Kaiser distinguishes two epilogists, who engage two levels of "fear of God"; the second epilogist (in Eccles 12:13-14) appears to be more legalistic to Kaiser, with a call for obedience to God's commandment.
[42]For example, like the other sages, Qohelet affirms *'ĕlōhîm* as one who is powerful in Eccles 3:14-15. But there is an exception: at times God keeps humans in ignorance (Eccles 3:10-11). Similarly, God controls the details of human life, but Qohelet professes also that God is distant in human affairs (Eccles 6:1-2, 11-12). In Qohelet's articulation, wisdom is asserted like the traditional teaching (Eccles 2:13; 7:11-12, 19), yet the exception is that wisdom is belittled at other times (Eccles 1:18; 2:15-16; 8:16-17).
[43]Besides harmonizing the "contradictory views," scholars also have tried to identify one of the opinions as an unmarked quotation, or to suggest a dialectic between Qohelet with an opponent. See, for example, T. A. Perry, *Dialogues with Kohelet: The Book of Ecclesiastes: Translation and Commentary* (University Park: Pennsylvania State University Press, 1993).

Leland Ryken calls this rhetoric a "dialectical structure of contrasts."[44] Craig Bartholomew opines that the exceptions are "part of the very fabric of *Ecclesiastes*."[45] Qohelet simply keeps in view two scenarios that are in tension. Through this lens of exception, Qohelet points out life's transitory nature and advocates against life's absolute certainty. Therefore, Qohelet presents a quest for meaningful survival.[46] This quest results in Qohelet's recommendations to embrace a certain attitude, which is a "reconstruction and recovering of meanings," according to Michael Fox.[47]

In short, a realistic attitude toward life is hopeful for God's people in salvation history. Ecclesiastes conveys honest reflections of people who search for hope and meaning in living.[48] After all, wisdom is about a way of directing life, and Ecclesiastes conveys such wisdom for living out salvific hope. As such, the book speaks powerfully to God's people who yearn for hope and meaning. It serves as a pointer to anyone who wrestles with challenges and tensions.

In the context of the marginalization of women within the church in Botswana, highlighted in the chapter by Rosinah Gabaitse in this section, the message of Ecclesiastes offers salvific hope. The tension between the hope of salvation and the challenge of injustice against women is the very fabric of life realities. Similarly, the aspects of the "materiality of salvation" discussed by Milton Acosta in this section convey tensions in the lives of God's people due

to the presence of danger, violence, calamity, and enemies. Qohelet, too, surveys the physical (toil and death), economic (labor and gain), and sociopolitical (injustice and supreme power of the rulers) realms as well. The world does not operate according to our ideal expectations, whether in fairness and justice in the experiences of men in relation to that of women or the realities of suffering from the threats of enemies. These are the exceptions that occur in the life of God's people, who are saved by God's grace yet are marked by fallen human nature. One of the similarities among the struggles of God's people in the Majority World is that we wrestle with the experiential realities of the doctrine of salvation. For God's people, issues of injustice, violence, and social enemies are real. One is nevertheless instructed to seize the opportunity to live right and to be diligently working for better days. Also, embracing certain attitudes in life, such as fearing God amid injustice, unfairness, and danger, can guide one to reconstruct meaning toward authentic witnessing to the gospel. Specifically, what constitutes certain attitudes in life, and how one reconstructs meaning to authentic witnessing, are largely interpretive and are bound by contextual considerations.

READINGS IN THE ASIAN CHINESE CONTEXT

Qohelet's concept of time in Ecclesiastes 3:1-15.
The catalogue of seasons and times in Ecclesiastes 3:1-8 is the most illustrative of Qohelet's

---

[44]Leland Ryken, "Ecclesiastes," in *A Complete Literary Guide to the Bible*, ed. Leland Ryken and Tremper Longman III (Grand Rapids, MI: Zondervan, 1993), 268-80, here 271.

[45]Craig G. Bartholomew, *Ecclesiastes*, Baker Commentary on the Old Testament Wisdom and Psalms, ed. Tremper Longman III (Grand Rapids, MI: Baker Academic, 2009), 81. Bartholomew uses the idea of "gaps," which are opened up in the reading of the book when two contradictory, juxtaposed perspectives are in view.

[46]He communicates this quest through the recurring word *yôtēr* (Eccles 6:8) and *yitrôn*, both meaning "surplus, advantage, or profit."

[47]Michael V. Fox, "The Innerstructure of Qoheleth's Thought," in *Qoheleth in the Context of Wisdom*, ed. A. Schoors (Leuven: Leuven University Press, 1998), 225.

[48]See another similar view by Costa Rican scholar Elsa Tamez, *When the Horizons Close: Reading Ecclesiastes* (Eugene, OR: Wipf & Stock, 2006), especially 1-10.

insistence that God makes everything "beautiful in its time" (Eccles 3:11).[49] In upholding God's "making" (*'āśâ*) in Ecclesiastes 3:11, the list of human events is then depicted in fourteen sets of antithetical parallelisms. The antithetical pairs point out a certain tension. The tension reflects favorable actions (e.g., to live, to laugh, or to dance) or unfavorable ones (e.g., to die, to cry, or to grieve). It does not show any order or pattern but represents life occurrences in a spontaneous manner. Qohelet asserts that there is a time for these human circumstances, but he rules out human determination for the outcome of these circumstances.

Even if humankind does not determine life occurrences, people can still respond to them and discern the appropriate moment for any human activity. Life occurrences are not just out of human control; they are also beyond human comprehension (Eccles 3:11). Yet in the same verse, Qohelet affirms clearly that for God, the scenario is otherwise: God is the one who determines life occurrences for humans. The concept of *'ôlām* (eternity) can be understood as the time-transcending nature of God's activity, which is not bound by time.[50] God puts "eternity" in human hearts, so that people can cope with various situations, one at a time. Therefore, for a human, one can still do well in one's lifetime (Eccles 3:12), as well as eat, drink, and see *ṭôb* (good) in one's toil (Eccles 3:13). The idea of *'ôlām* returns in Ecclesiastes 3:14, describing what God has done, with an added concept of fearing God as one's purpose. This concept of fearing God first appears here and elsewhere in Ecclesiates 5:7 (Hebrew 5:6); 7:18; 8:12-13; 12:13. It is a theological

marker for Qohelet's articulation of life elusiveness. In light of Ecclesiastes 3:15, it is also an affirmation of God's activity in the human realm (Eccles 3:10, 11, 13-14).

On fearing death: Time is in God's hand. Among the taboos in Chinese thought, the idea of death generates a sense of fear. People are fearful of losing everything that has been accumulated in their lifetime. Ecclesiastes 3:1-15 affirms that there is a time for everything in life, including living and dying. The Chinese in general work hard to make life better, more so in Asia, where living is competitive due to rapid social and economic developments. Losing everything at the point of one's death can be frightening because all the hard work that one has done would become void. Nevertheless, Ecclesiastes 3:1-15 avers that even death is beautiful in its time because God is in the picture. The passage, too, is a reminder of the differences between God's actions and human activities. Knowing these differences, one is reminded of the affirmation of eternity, when human works are done in full awareness of God's presence. Furthermore, reading Ecclesiastes 3:1-15 prompts one to fear God yet at the same time endeavoring to live meaningfully in the present. One can still see the good in life and live it out abundantly while one is able to. Death, in this sense, does not cancel out one's possessions, accomplishments, and wealth. For these things have their meaning under God's time-transcending activities. Death also testifies that one has eventually lived to the depth and height of life. At one's death, therefore, one's total achievement in life is being witnessed and celebrated. Death can be called "beautiful" when it comes.

---

[49]Ecclesiastes 3:1-15 is a logical unit by itself, though the thought on timing can be detected again in Eccles 3:17: God "has appointed a time for every matter and for every work." This thought echoes what Qohelet has declared in Eccles 3:1, that for everything there is a season, and for every matter a time. Still, Eccles 3:16 suggests a new turn with the phrase "and again I saw" and new subjects (justice and righteousness).

[50]Seow, *Ecclesiastes*, 171, 174.

Qohelet's view of righteousness in Ecclesiastes 7:15-22. Qohelet's articulations on the topic of righteousness occur in Ecclesiastes 7 three times (Eccles 7:15-16, 20), and in Ecclesiastes 3:17; 8:14; 9:1-2. Most of these articulations appear to question the common pursuit of righteousness. In Ecclesiastes 7:15-22, Qohelet questions the absolute value of being righteous. Ecclesiastes 7:15 states that righteous people do perish in their righteousness, and wicked people have their lives prolonged despite their evildoings. Once again looking through Qohelet's "lens of exceptions," righteous people do not necessarily have better lives, as the wise had commonly thought.

Though this view on exceptions does have canonical witnesses from other parts of the Bible (for instance, the psalms of lament and the prophetic books), Qohelet goes further, advising people, "Do not be overly righteous," and suggesting that "to be overly righteous could be destructive" (Eccles 7:16). Ecclesiastes 7:17-18 are even more perplexing because wickedness and folly "should not be let go." One assumes here that Qohelet does not engage righteousness as affirmatively as the sages do but appears to commend half-hearted righteousness. This leaves him open to the allegation of negotiating immorality. Schooled by Confucian teachings, the Chinese in general believe that righteousness is needed to alleviate social injustice. Therefore, scholars of Chinese descent may find it disturbing and uncomfortable to accept Qohelet's idea of half-hearted righteousness here. Some may even choose to interpret the passage from the lens of the Confucian golden mean to secure

the idea of morality, so that *yi* (righteousness) is still necessary. This reflects Confucian confidence in upholding righteousness to reorder individual and communal life. Righteousness is seen as an initiative to guide human behavior, unlike Qohelet, who stresses human limitation in living out righteousness.

In addition, the passage is understood by some as a warning against self-righteousness, as the adverb *harbēh*, from the word *rābâ*, means "much, many, great" or "numerous" but not "too" or "over."[51] In light of this, it is not an aspect of moral agency that is absent in Ecclesiastes. There is yet another view suggesting that Qohelet's dissent is aimed at overconfidence in righteousness.[52] This warning is directed against the person who lays claim to righteousness as absolutely attainable. This view is consistent with Qohelet's thought against the certainty of wisdom (Eccles 7:23-29; 9:13-16) and of advantage (Eccles 1:3; 3:9; 6:8) elsewhere in the book. In this light, the passage does not advocate unrighteousness. Rather, Qohelet perceives an actual human limitation in trying to live out righteousness. Therefore, "the one who fears God" (Eccles 7:18) finds a balance between being righteous and acknowledging human limitation. The idea of this limitation continues in Ecclesiastes 7:19-22, including the idea of wisdom as well. It is no surprise that Qohelet's address in Ecclesiastes 7:15-22 regarding righteousness appears to be half-hearted. Qohelet is less convinced of the human success in living out righteousness. Regardless of striving to be righteous and wise, one cannot just deny the realities of wickedness and folly in life.

---

[51]For example, R. N. Whybray, "Qoheleth the Immoralist? (Qoh 7:16-17)," in *Israelite Wisdom: Theological and Literary Essays in Honor of Samuel Terrien*, ed. John G. Gammie et al. (New York: Union Theological Seminary, 1978), 191-204, here 191. The adverb *harbēh*, according to Whybray, does not express any value judgment such as "too righteous" in Eccles 7:16, but an ironical sense, that is, a "self-styled *ṣaddîq*"; see 195-96.

[52]Seow, *Ecclesiastes*, 267.

Be confident but not overconfident. Hardworking and diligent, the Chinese are generally confident of what can be done and achieved. Such confidence may mistakenly sneak into our understanding of faith experience, that as long as one attends church worship, tithes, and serves well, one attains the "righteousness" required by the Bible. Being righteous becomes attainable as long as one obeys what the Bible tells us. Righteousness has also become something that can be attained and worked for, such as having a good reputation, holding an important position in Christian ministry, serving many years in Christian ministry, and so forth. One therefore becomes overconfident about living "right," as if that were easy and natural. As a result, some may not be able to cope when fellow Christians fail in witnessing and are involved in scandals and lawsuits. Qohelet advises us to be cautious about such certainty. Overconfidence can be destructive, as Ecclesiastes 7:15-22 suggests. There is an actual human limitation on practicing righteousness in life, and we must simply acknowledge our humanness. A righteous and wise person does not necessarily rule out the chances of being wicked and foolish.

Qohelet's idea of human ignorance in Ecclesiastes 11:1-6. There is an observable double theme of "what a human does not know" and "what a human does know" in Ecclesiastes 11:1-6.[53] In this passage, although human knowledge is limited, the author advises readers "to embark upon life." The idea of action frames the theme of human ignorance. This means that one can be doing something without knowing exactly why or how, yet at the same time be preparing for multiple contingencies. Thus Ecclesiastes 11:1, 6 present the chances for spontaneous actions despite uncertain outcomes.

In Ecclesiastes 11:1-2, Qohelet quotes a popular proverb in the ancient Near East to commend liberality and its proliferation.[54] Some interpret these verses as an investment, whereby *leḥem* (bread) is a metaphor for merchandise. According to this interpretation, one can avoid losing everything in a business venture by dividing one's risks in the investment. However, the idea of *leḥem* as "goods" is unattested elsewhere in the Bible. Besides, one should *māṣā'* (find) more than what is invested from any venture. Yet the idea of profit is not found in Ecclesiastes 1:2 but rather the "getting back" of what is originally sent.[55] Qohelet argues that the

---

[53]Graham S. Ogden and Lynell Zogbo, *A Handbook on Ecclesiastes* (New York: United Bible Societies, 1997), 391. See also T. Francis Glasson, "'You Never Know': The Message of Ecclesiastes 11:1-6," *Evangelical Quarterly* 55 (1983): 43-48, who singles out "you do not know" as the theme in Eccles 11:1-6.

Ecclesiastes 11:1-6 is an independent unit for several reasons. First, the change in subject matter is discernable from the political rhetoric in Eccles 10:16-20 to the economical concern in Eccles 11:1-6. Second, the verbs in Eccles 11:1, 2, 6 are found in the imperative mood, unlike the ones from the preceding chapter, and the one after in Eccles 11:7-8. Third, the passage is framed by a purpose clause that is introduced with *kî* (twice in Eccles 11:1-2, once in Eccles 11:6). Fourth, there is a fourfold expression of "you do not know" in Eccles 11:2, 5 (twice), and Eccles 11:6, which comprise its theme.

[54]The proverb resembles the Egyptian *Ancksheshonq*, which says, "Do a good deed and throw it in the water; when it dries up you will find it." See Miriam Lichtheim, ed., *Ancient Egyptian Literature* (Berkeley: University of California Press, 1980), 3:174. The interpretation of liberality is evident in Prov 19:17, and in the Targum and Midrash, and in the understandings of Rashi, Ibn Ezra, and Rashbam; see Michael V. Fox, *Ecclesiastes*, JPS Bible Commentary (Philadelphia: Jewish Publication Society, 2004), 72, and Thomas Krüger, *Qoheleth: A Commentary*, Hermeneia, trans. O. C. Dean Jr., ed. Klaus Baltzer (Minneapolis: Fortress, 2004), 192.

[55]Seow, *Ecclesiastes*, 335. There is yet another interpretation taking in the sense of beer production; see Michael M. Homan, "Beer Production by Throwing Bread into Water: A New Interpretation of Qoh. XI 1-2," *Vetus Testamentum* 52 (2002): 275-78. According to this interpretation, Qohelet recommends beer production and consumption in risky times, similar to the advice in Eccles 9:7. Isaiah 22:13 is quoted, "Eat and drink for tomorrow we die," to support his thesis. However, Homan might be informed by a pessimistic understanding of Ecclesiastes. Qohelet is recommending a proactive attitude of seizing opportunity amid life's uncertainty, rather than the

unknown future may bring forth desirable results or undesirable misfortunes, yet one can *know* that charitable giving at present is the recommended thing to do. The appropriate action is thus doing something useful, and it is better than doing nothing at all.

In Ecclesiastes 11:3-5, knowing the uncertainties of life, some people refuse to take certain risks to act and consequently end up being unproductive.[56] The double theme of "one does know" and "one does not know" persists. In human ignorance, some people resort to obsessive weather watching, thus halting agricultural efforts and missing the proper time for action.[57] There is an opportunity for sowing and reaping despite not knowing the right time. The danger remains that one who is always watching for the perfect moment will never act.[58] While one cannot ascertain the result, it does not mean one should do nothing at all. The motif "one does not know" reappears twice in Ecclesiastes 11:5, conveying that no one knows how new life begins in a mother's womb, much less the work of God. In short, the action of God is beyond human calculation.

Therefore, in Ecclesiastes 11:6, one should act according to what one knows, without being bothered by what is unknown.[59] There is an imperative followed by a motive clause here. This idea recalls Ecclesiastes 11:1-2, and hence is an *inclusio* of Qohelet's rhetoric. Qohelet advises

that one should live and work according to what one has been taught. Being diligent by sowing seeds in the morning and keeping active in the evening may secure some relative advantages. Taken as a whole, Qohelet is realistic about how much a human does not know, yet how much one can do based on understandable facts. Qohelet's thesis, namely, the twin themes of what humans can and cannot know, is specified clearly in Ecclesiastes 11:1-2, the illustrative materials for these themes are set forth in Ecclesiastes 11:3-5, and concluding advice is offered in Ecclesiastes 11:6.[60]

***Carpe diem but not workaholic and* kiasu.[61]**
The Chinese are generally hardworking. Having vast opportunities for social and economic growth in Asia, many pragmatic Chinese toil diligently to acquire more opportunities and greater advantages. Yet, people at the same time are fearful of failing to secure these opportunities and advantages, especially when they are confronted by factors beyond their comprehension and control. People do not know when it is the best time to act or when a financial crisis will occur. The calculations of uncertainties in life may paralyze some observant and careful people. This is true in business ventures, career planning, and investments. Yet, there is always a place for human efforts. One cannot remain inactive under the pretext of waiting for the best time. Ecclesiastes 11:1-6 conveys that instead of

---

escapism of drinking, being merry, and dying. His interpretation needs to establish links to the previous and subsequent passages concerning beer production. It appears unlikely too that Qohelet would contradict the warning given in Eccles 10:16, and his criticism rendered in Eccles 10:19, by suggesting beer production and consumption here. Ecclesiastes 11:6 appropriately closes the passage in a proactive outlook that advocates human's endeavor. In sum, Eccles 11:1-2 most likely refers to good deeds given freely and plentifully.

[56]Qohelet uses the aphorism of a farmer who awaits perfect conditions to sow and harvest, criticizing the idling state of people who should have done something constructive. There is some predictability from nature; for example, one knows that strong wind and a storm will uproot a tree, but one does not know in which direction it will fall.

[57]William P. Brown, *Ecclesiastes*, Interpretation, ed. James Luther Mays and Patrick D. Miller (Louisville: John Knox, 2000), 103.

[58]Murphy, *Ecclesiastes*, 109.

[59]Crenshaw, *Ecclesiastes*, 181; see also Ogden, "Qohelet 11:1-6," 223.

[60]Ogden, "Qohelet 11:1-6," 227.

[61]*Kiasu* is taken from the Hokkien language, which is a division among Chinese languages, and means an "afraid to lose" mentality.

pondering life's obscurities, one should act promptly based on what one is able to comprehend in order to seize the opportunity. So, on the one hand, this passage informs Asian Chinese of the importance of timely hard work. It is carpe diem advice, directing people to seize the day despite life's uncertainties. It is about human effort, not about blind chance.

Yet, on the other hand, some people may have worked too hard to secure maximum results. Many Asian Chinese have become too busy and are workaholics. To them, profiting the most during their youth will make life comfortable later. Under such circumstances, one may also resort to a *kiasu* mentality. It is a mentality that generally reflects the way some Asian Chinese think: they aspire to have something greater, bigger, or more valuable as compared to others. Yet, there are exceptions to one's experiences in life, and one cannot be sure of everything. There is always the chance that one may face limitations amid many possibilities. It often happens that one may gain this time but lose the next. Again, as Ecclesiastes 11:1-6 suggests, one does not know the certainty of the outcome of one's overdiligence. Therefore, one should just work sensibly and be productive, without compromising the good things in life. Asian Chinese in general, through generations of Confucian teachings, are pragmatic and diligent. Qohelet attunes us to the realistic sides of being so.

Conclusion

Qohelet teaches one to live here and now in line with Chinese pragmatism. This chapter argues for the message of Ecclesiastes that offers hope, in line with the message of salvation as outlined in Christian belief. Wisdom represents one of the three ways in which God's salvation history is being communicated: through the priestly laws, the sages' worldviews, and the prophetic utterances. Within the Wisdom corpus, Proverbs, Job, and Ecclesiastes demonstrate the progress of salvific faith grounded in the fear of God. The book of Ecclesiastes conveys hope between the two extremes of human potential and limitation, its ideal and its realities. The emphasis on human potential harmonizes with the emphasis on covenantal revelation. The two different points of departure should prompt biblical interpreters to defend wisdom heritage in the proclamation of salvation. It is enriching to know that human limitation is acknowledged, not judged, and that human potential is affirmed, not dismissed. The affinity between Wisdom literature and other canonical witnesses is important as we articulate salvation history in biblical theology.

Further Reading

Fox, Michael V. *A Time to Tear Down and a Time to Build Up: A Rereading of Ecclesiastes*. Grand Rapids, MI: Eerdmans, 1999.

Kok, Hon Seng. *Heavenly Vision for Witness on Earth: A Commentary on Ephesians*. Kuala Lumpur: Bridge Communication, 2010.

Lee, Archie C. C. "Cross-Textural Hermeneutics and Identity in Multi-Scriptural Asia." Pages 179-204 in *Christian Theology in Asia*, edited by Sebastian C. H. Kim. New York: Cambridge University Press, 2008.

Lo, Lung-Kwong. *Baoluo Xinguan: Luomashu de Zhuti yu Mudi* [New Perspectives on Paul: The Theme and Purpose of the Book to the Romans]. Taipei: University of Donghai Press, 2007.

Longman, Tremper, III. *The Book of Ecclesiastes*. New International Commentary on the Old Testament. Grand Rapids, MI: Eerdmans, 1998.

Seow, Choon-Leong. *Ecclesiastes*. Anchor Bible. New York: Doubleday, 1997.

Wong, Yee-cheung. *Jiuyue Shenxue: Cong Chuangzao Dao Xinchuangzao* [Old Testament Theology: From Creation to New Creation]. Hong Kong: Tien Dao, 2003.

Yeo, K. K. *Musing with Confucius and Paul: Toward a Chinese Christian Theology*. Cambridge: James Clarke, 2008.

Yip, Ching Wah, and Lo Lung Kwong. *We Believe: A Commentary on the Nicene Creed*. Edited by the Association of Theological Schools in South East Asia. Hong Kong: Chinese Christian Literature Council, 2014.

THE CHURCH FROM EVERY TRIBE AND TONGUE

Part Five

ECCLESIOLOGY IN THE MAJORITY WORLD

INTRODUCTION TO PART FIVE

GOD'S COMMUNITY IN MAJORITY WORLD THEOLOGY

Gene L. Green

AT THE 2016 ANNUAL MEETINGS of the Evangelical Theological Society and the Institute for Biblical Research, a group of seven international scholars gathered to present papers and discuss the nature of the church. One additional presenter from China submitted her paper but was not able to attend the gathering. Four of the group are specialists in biblical studies, and the others are experts in theology. A few participants flew in from their residences in the United States, although their natal homes were Finland, Columbia, and Korea. Others journeyed from Kenya, Uganda, Costa Rica, and Palestine.

All eight of these authors are engaged in developing contextualized biblical studies and theology, and represent the crescendo of voices from the global church who are thinking afresh about the Bible's message and doing theology both from and to their own contexts. All are members of Christ's "one holy, catholic, and apostolic church," as states the Nicene-Constantinopolitan Creed (or the Symbolum Nicaenum of AD 381). While they have each reflected on Scripture and theology in relation to the realities and their experiences within their homelands, they present their findings as an offering to Christ's whole church. Throughout the history of the church around the globe, all biblical reflection and theologizing have been carried out with reference to the immediate contexts of the interpreters. As the Peruvian theologian Dr. Samuel Escobar once said to me, "Toda la teología es contextual."[1] But that does not mean that these theologies and biblical reflections are simply for a particular time, place, and people. Each contributes to a truly catholic or universal theology just as much as the reflections received from early Christian authors in the first centuries or the Reformers of the sixteenth century. From the beginning the church has sought to understand God and his way of salvation in concert with the daily realities believers faced within their communities and societies. They are not only local expressions of the faith but faithful catholic biblical studies and theology, full stop.

---

[1] "All theology is contextual."

ECCLESIOLOGY IN THE MAJORITY WORLD: THE AUTHORS AND THEIR ESSAYS

The design of this volume responds to the repeated questions we have received from colleagues and students who wanted to know what Majority World scholars were saying on a particular topic. While none of the sections presents a comprehensive survey of all the biblical reflection and theological developments within Africa, Asia, and Latin America, they are representative of current thinking among a wide sampling of conservative scholars. Some of the names that appear in this and the other parts are well known in the West and elsewhere. Others are younger scholars in the early stages of their own teaching and writing careers. They are all faithful followers of Christ who hold the Bible as God's authoritative Word. Their essays are fresh winds of God's work throughout the world. Reviews of scholarly tomes such as this one are always varied and useful, but students' responses ring loudest in our ears. They tell about the delight and deepened faith they have discovered through reading along the grain with Christians elsewhere in the world. They come to understand new dimensions of the faith not previously imagined yet wonderfully relevant.

This section on the doctrine of the church, or ecclesiology, vividly demonstrates how reading with a different set of questions and seeing from a non-Western context can broaden our understanding of the gospel. Most trained in the Western academy could not imagine how ecclesiology and a Palestinian Christian theology of the land might intersect, for example. Recently I had the honor of leading a course for the North American Institute for Indigenous Theological

Studies (www.naiits.com) on "Community in the New Testament." Native authors and students pushed out our understanding of God's community to include all creation, as Keetoowah Cherokee scholar Randy Woodley points out in his book *Shalom and the Community of Creation: An Indigenous Vision*.[2] These contextual readings are not a vain syncretism that allows local or traditional values and perspectives to dominate over the gospel. Rather, they seek to be both biblically faithful and culturally relevant, understanding that Scripture is God's Word for all times and cultures. From the beginning God's message has come clothed in culture.

This collection on ecclesiology launches with Veli-Matti Kärkkäinen's essay "Ecclesiology and the Church in Christian Tradition and Western Theology." Anyone reading about developments in Majority World theology will know Kärkkäinen's interest and publications in this field, especially his five-volume systematic theology, titled *A Constructive Christian Theology for the Pluralistic World*. The last volume in this series, *Hope and Community*, builds on his previous work on the church, *An Introduction to Ecclesiology: Ecumenical, Historical and Global Perspectives*. Kärkkäinen baptizes us into New Testament teaching on the church, focusing on its key symbols as the people of God, the body of Christ, and the temple of the Spirit. He moves forward into the creeds, which identify the church's unity, holiness, catholicity, and apostolicity. He recalls, however, that the church's existence is instrumental in God's mission. As he states, "God's community on earth (the church) is graciously drawn into the coming of God's kingdom, his righteous reign over all creation. That makes the church missionary by its very

---

[2]Randy S. Woodley, *Shalom and the Community of Creation: An Indigenous Vision*, Prophetic Christianity (Grand Rapids, MI: Eerdmans, 2012).

nature. The church exists as mission." That the mission has been effective is marked by the church's growth from approximately 10,000 members at the turn of the first century to 2.4 billion members in the first decades of the twenty-first. Moreover, the church has migrated from its center in Europe and North America to the Global South and East. Some readers may not yet realize that Christians living in the North Atlantic region now find themselves on the geographical margins of the church and not at its center. But, Kärkkäinen concludes, the church around the globe faces two great challenges at present: secularism and religious pluralism. "The rise of both secularism and religious pluralism means that the ecclesiologies of the third millennium have to pay attention not only to what is inside the church and within the Christian tradition, but also to the teaching of other religious traditions and the mindset of the secular public." With this observation Kärkkäinen hands off to the other authors in this section, all of whom are keenly aware of the contextual realities that surround them as they develop this third-millennium ecclesiology.

Ruth Padilla DeBorst is a Latina theologian who resides in Costa Rica, where she works with the Comunidad de Estudios Teológicos Interdisciplinarios. Past President of the Latin American Theological Fellowship, Padilla DeBorst has for years been an active participant in the development of Latina/o theological reflection. She possesses the rare ability to present theology lyrically (we could say that she "sings" theology), as readers of her essay will hear. Like many theologians within her context, whether committed to *misión integral* (integral mission) or *las teologías de la liberación* (liberation theologies), Padilla DeBorst traces the relationship between the church and the powers of the day. What does it

mean to live as church under the imperial power of colonial Christendom or under foreign commercial or educational powers? She notes that the Latin American church sometimes has succumbed to triumphalist metaphors alien to the gospel, but she draws hope from developments within the *misión integral* movement, which "seeks to engage followers of Jesus in linking the whole gospel to the whole of life under the lordship of Christ in the power of the Holy Spirit so that the reign of God and God's justice may be made visible in particular historical contexts." Padilla DeBorst traces the ecclesial movement "from below" within the base ecclesial communities and surging Pentecostalism in Latin America. But she understands the church as "a school for citizenship," a people drawn together by the Community-of-Love and called to follow Jesus into the world. They are to then go out to the rest of society together. She quotes the late Orlando Costas, who said the church is called to "move into the neighborhood." This, she notes, "entails sacrificial incarnation in the messiness of socioeconomic, political, and ecological realities." For Padilla DeBorst, the church is not a community separate and aloof, but a community engaged in all of life's hard realities.

Wonsuk Ma, a Korean theologian who for some time directed the Oxford Centre for Mission Studies and now serves as Distinguished Professor of Global Christianity at Oral Roberts University, is fluent in theological developments in Asia and around the globe. Ma reminds us from the start that "the church was born in Asia," yet today in many parts of Asia it seems like a "foreign religion." K. K. Yeo once said that many in China, for example, believe that one must choose whether to be Christian or Chinese since Christianity is regarded as a Western faith. Despite this, however, Ma recognizes distinct ecclesiological developments within the Asian context. Since the region is so vast, however, he opts for presenting two case studies: the post–Cultural Revolution house church called the Word of Life Church and South Korea's well-known Yoido Full Gospel Church. Both these newer churches actively engage with their contexts and shape the received theological traditions around those realties. In other words, newer churches engage in what Justo González called "self-theologizing" in an attempt to bring the gospel into deep dialogue with their cultural contexts. Ma recognizes the central role of these churches' founders in shaping their theological vision.

Among the theological tenets of the Word of Life Church, developed by its founder Peter Yongze Xu, are "(1) salvation through the cross, (2) the way of the cross, and (3) discerning the adulteress," which they identify as the government-registered Three-Self Patriotic Movement. Given their rejection of the state-sanctioned church, Word of Life members believe that suffering that results from "refusing to submit to atheistic government policies" is a mark of the true church. These realities shape the life of their church since, as Ma observes, "there was no identifiable Western 'mother' church to dictate the shape of the church." Added to these realities is the commitment to personal piety, dependence on the Holy Spirit for miracles and guidance, and a deep commitment to mission. On the other hand, the Yoido Full Gospel Church, the world's largest church, headed by David Yonggi Cho, finds guidance in its founder's theology of a "good God" who is able to heal and do the miraculous. Out of this tenet arises the Fivefold Gospel of Jesus as Savior, Baptizer, Healer, Blesser, and Coming King, and

the Threefold Salvation, which embraces "spiritual, physical, and circumstantial (which includes material) salvation." Ma reflects elsewhere on the relationship between Cho's emphasis on blessing and shamanism.[3] The Yoido Full Gospel Church places great emphasis on prayer and presents Jesus as "the answer to all human suffering." In mission the church proclaims "the good God, blessing, healing, and God's intervention on his people's behalf." Both Xu and Cho's churches are born from deep contextualization of the gospel into their respective social contexts without much reflection on the historic traditions of Christian ecclesiology.

Stephanie Lowery was raised in Kenya, where she currently serves as lecturer in systematic theology at Scott Theological College. In 2017 Lowery published a text on African ecclesiology and so is well suited to pen an essay titled "Ecclesiology in Africa: Apprentices on a Mission."[4] Before embarking on constructive work of her own, Lowery outlines prominent themes emerging within contemporary African ecclesiologies. Is the paradigm for the African church the family, with its extended networks that even reach back to the ancestors who are highly venerated? In a simple observation she captures a compelling reason for embracing this model: "If, then, the idea of family points the church back to the doctrine of the Trinity and humans' inherently relational nature, then we ought to give this model more thought, as so many theologians in Africa . . . have done." She notes the caution, however, raised by Georges Titre Ande, who prefers the model of church as a "community of life," life being a key concept within African Christology as well. Lowery also touches on developments

---

[3] Wonsuk Ma, "David Yonggi Cho's Theology of Blessing: Basis, Legitimacy and Limitations," *Evangelical Review of Theology* 35 (2011): 140-41.
[4] Stephanie A. Lowery, *Identity and Ecclesiology: Their Relationship Among Select African Theologians* (Eugene, OR: Pickwick, 2017).

within the African Initiated/Independent/Instituted Churches, which emphasize biblicism, Africanism, and *philadelphia*, or the church as a community of love marked by *koinōnia*. Biblical models that resonate with cultural values are picked up in the African Initiated/Independent/Instituted Churches, such as the church as a priesthood and leaders as prophets. As Lowery says, "While cultural and Old Testament models abound, other ecclesiologies arise from a mélange of cultural, Old Testament, and New Testament references." She adds that some have taken up corporate models from the business world to outline their understanding of the church. In the midst of the diverse richness of African ecclesiologies, however, Lowery is concerned that some churches are reluctant to see themselves as part of the larger "one, holy, catholic, and apostolic" church, given the painful relationship with colonial Christianity. At the end of her essay, Lowery takes a bold step by suggesting, "Those enabled by the Spirit are, I propose, intended to be apprentices." The church is a community of learners who live out God's Word, and, as disciples (that's what an apprentice is, she reminds us), they follow their Master and always learn more from him. She notes that apprentices are also involved in praxis, carrying out the *missio Dei* but doing so in the recognition that they are "aliens and sojourners," people "who are in some sense outsiders in their contexts: they seek to be contextual, without losing their holiness and their divinely granted identity."

The first four essays were written by theologians representing the West, Latin America, Asia, and Africa. However, we designed this section to include biblical scholars alongside them. These participants are well versed in biblical exegesis but also recognize that biblical studies cannot be carried out without reference to one's context. We always read from and to a place, an insight common among Majority World biblical scholars. Their approach to Scripture is not to read it from the balcony, to use the language of John MacKay, but from the road, that place where "life is lived tensely, where thought has its birth in conflict and concern, where choices are made and decisions are carried out."[5] While we expect theologians to ask how the gospel plays out within cultures, some readers may think that biblical interpretation should be done objectively, using prescribed methods and the proper tools. But Majority World biblical scholars read in ways akin to what Hans-Georg Gadamer describes in his seminal text *Truth and Method*. He states, "In our analysis of the hermeneutical process we say that to acquire a horizon of interpretation requires a fusion of horizons," that is, between the biblical author and the biblical reader. He continues, "Every interpretation has to adapt itself to the hermeneutical situation to which it belongs."[6] Insights abound when these scholars read Scripture while acknowledging their place, knowing that they read from and to that place. Their readings honor the authority of Scripture, the apostolic voice, and the fact that the Bible is truly the Word of God for us.

Carlos Sosa Siliezar is a New Testament scholar from Guatemala. His essay, titled "Ecclesiology in Latin America: A Biblical Perspective,"

---

[5]John MacKay, *A Preface to Christian Theology* (New York: Macmillan, 1941), 27.
[6]Hans-Georg Gadamer, *Truth and Method* (New York: Continuum, 2000), 397. See also Gene L. Green, "The Challenge of Global Hermeneutics," in *Global Theology in Evangelical Perspective*, ed. Jeffrey P. Greenman and Gene L. Green (Downers Grove, IL: IVP Academic, 2012), 9-15.

first reads Scripture along the grain of Leonardo Boff's ecclesiogenesis and René Padilla's holistic ecclesiology. Boff, a Brazilian scholar, rejected Roman Catholic hierarchies in the church and favored small base communities that live and read Scripture together. Padilla, an Ecuadorian trained as an exegete, proposed an ecclesiology that supported holistic mission, or *misión integral*. Sosa assesses both their positions. He raises cautions regarding Boff's separation of the ecclesiology of Jesus—if indeed there was one— and that of the early church. Boff believed that "the church was not part of Jesus' intentions," since Jesus taught about the coming of the kingdom of God. The failure to establish God's kingdom resulted in the church becoming "the substitute for the unfulfilled kingdom." Sosa critiques this bifurcation between Jesus and the early church while, at the same time, celebrating Boff's affirmation that laypeople can gather around the Word of God without the intervention of the church. On both counts Sosa's evangelical commitments are evident. On the other hand, Sosa celebrates Padilla's link between integral mission and ecclesiology. Padilla was one of the founders of the Latin American Theological Fellowship, which roots its theology in the concept of holistic mission, so it is no surprise that he links in ecclesiology here. Sosa is clearly more comfortable with Padilla's view, which coalesces Jesus' teaching with what the Gospel writers wrote.

Sosa's own position builds on Padilla, however, by appeal to the Gospel of John. Sosa identifies John 13:34-35 as a pointer to Jesus' idea of a new community of disciples, but he also sees in the text concerns germane to the Latin American context. He remarks that "churches should see themselves as (1) local communities with global awareness, (2) suffering communities that love

the world, and (3) communities where diversity is reconciled." The surprise for many readers outside, and perhaps even inside, the Latin American context is that Sosa views these traits as significant not only for the church in and of itself but also for the wider society. For example, Sosa charges, "Laws that regulate economic agreements between Guatemala and the United States and the European Union are not based on the Johannine idea of love." He draws the Johannine emphasis on love into realms such as business and international law. Sosa stands with a multitude of Majority World scholars who fully embrace a socially engaged faith.

Xiaxia Xue from China was not able to gather with the other scholars in 2016 but provided a provocative paper titled "The Community as Union with Christ in the Midst of Conflict: An Ecclesiology of the Pauline Letters from a Chinese Perspective." Xue reflects on the nature of the church from a Chinese perspective and brings her observations into dialogue with Pauline ecclesiology. She reflects deeply on the various ecclesial bodies in China and Hong Kong, including the Three-Self Patriotic Movement, the house churches, local assemblies, registered churches, and the True Church of Jesus Christ. She points out that the Three-Self Church is connected deeply with the Chinese social and political environment, while, on the other hand, house churches are a resistant group that "refused to compromise with the communist government." The local churches started under the leadership of Watchman Nee introduced the concept of one church in one locality, a theological trend that has influenced the thinking of many North American Christians. Churches in China hold varied understandings of their relationship to God, his kingdom, and their sociopolitical context. Later in her essay she points out the further differences between the churches in China and the Chinese congregations in Hong Kong. In all this she highlights the tensions that exist between the churches. For example, she notes the conflict between the Hong Kong and Mainland churches, which "on the one hand, has its roots in divergent political opinions and, on the other hand, is caused by their different value systems."

When considering the divisions she returns to the creed's confession of one holy, catholic, and apostolic church, but mainly focuses on the varied places within the Pauline letters that address the issue of divisions. In exploring the Paulines, she notes that divisions were part of the life of the church from the very beginning, and so "tension within the church is not an accidental or alien factor." She points out the tremendous diversity within the early churches, including ethnic diversity, and the attendant problems this caused, as evidenced in Galatians. First Corinthians points out the divisions in the church based on varied understandings of leadership that found their roots in the surrounding society's values and the church's economic disparity. While not celebrating division, Xue embraces the idea that division is a natural part of the life of the church, whether in Corinth or in Hong Kong and Mainland China. Indeed, she goes so far as to argue that the very essence of the church is found here: "The Community as Union with Christ in the Midst of Conflict." Paul dealt with the conflicts in the province of Galatia and the city of Corinth, but conflict is natural and, indeed, inevitable in the church. She appeals to Paul, however, in prescribing the solution, based on the sacrificial love of Christ demonstrated on the cross and the recognition

that we are one body. The ancient text is brought into dialogue with Chinese realities and addresses them directly.

Peter Nyende is from Kenya but currently teaches New Testament at Uganda Christian University. He appeals to the book of Hebrews in his essay "The Church as an Assembly on Mount Zion: An Ecclesiology from Hebrews for African Christians." Nyende stands in the midst of other African biblical scholars and theologians who recognize, as did the late Kwame Bediako from Ghana, that "Hebrews is our epistle."[7] Nyende begins by outlining various strains of African ecclesiologies: identity ecclesiologies, focused on the interests and perspectives of a particular denomination; ecumenical ecclesiologies, which attempt to transcend denominational boundaries; and those emanating from the African Initiated Churches, those founded by Africans and oriented to African realities. Nyende points out the necessity of ecclesial studies in Africa, since by 2025 "Africa will have the highest population of Christians on any continent, standing at more than seven hundred million." As he works with the biblical text, Nyende focuses on the notion of God's dwelling, starting in the Garden of Eden and going up through the heavenly Mount Zion (Heb 12:22). Starting with Eden, God's dwelling is accessible to humans. Indeed, the Genesis account shows that "God intended the world to be the place of his dwelling with human beings." Nyende continues the discussion by focusing on the period after the fall, when via the tabernacle and temple God restored "his dwelling among humans and his kingdom in the world." The temple is associated with its location on Mount Zion. The prophets Isaiah and Micah predicted that the temple

---

[7]Kwame Bediako, *Jesus and the Gospel in Africa: History and Experience* (Maryknoll, NY: Orbis, 2004), 27.

would be restored on the highest mountain, "symbolic of Mount Zion's superiority over other houses of divinities because YHWH, its resident, is superior to all other gods." Turning to the New Testament, Nyende draws the line between God's dwelling in the Old Testament and the way the ecclesiology in Hebrews conceptualizes the church as God's dwelling, where Christ is the high priest and where the community worships him. "In some real sense, then," Nyende concludes, "in Christ this community is in God's heavenly house offering prayers and immaterial sacrifices as they are asked to do in Hebrews 13:15." He understands the relevance of this reality for the African church, which, unlike many churches in the West, is keenly aware that the spiritual word interacts with the material world. African ecclesiology lives within the interaction between the material and the spiritual planes. Like all other authors in this section and the rest of this volume, Nyende delves deeply into the biblical text without ever letting go of the cultural, and in this case the spiritual, context in which he and other African Christians find themselves.

Munther Isaac is a Palestinian Christian who currently serves as the academic dean of Bethlehem Bible College. His essay, "Ecclesiology and the Theology of the Land: A Palestinian Christian Perspective," brings together two topics commonly held apart in most Western ecclesiologies. Both Isaac and his colleague Yohanna Katanacho, another author in this volume, have written a biblical theology of the land from a Palestinian perspective.[8] More than one reader will register surprise at Isaac's opening line: "The Palestinian church takes its identity and theology from its

natural and unbroken relationship with the biblical land." He goes on to quote Mitri Raheb, who states, "My self-understanding as a Christian Palestinian has a *territorial dimension*." Those lands are the home of their ancestors, and the interplay between the church and the land shapes their understanding of ecclesiology. Like Katanacho, Isaac points out that the land, known as the Promised Land, belongs to God. As God declares in Leviticus 25:23, "For the land is mine." Isaac deconstructs some contemporary notions of the Promised Land, first showing that the boundaries of God's land in the Old Testament were fluid and that Genesis 15:18-21 emphasizes God's universal dominion. As in the Great Commission (Mt 28:18 NRSV), Christ's dominion is universal: "All authority in heaven *and on earth* has been given to me." The earth is Christ's possession (Ps 2:8). But the church is then tasked to establish new "holy places" in new lands—that is, they "recreate the story of Israel in new lands." In this mission, Jerusalem "no longer has to play a central role in relation to the other new locations, because Jesus is now the cornerstone—the center of the new Christian movement." Isaac wants to show that Christian experience is always rooted in time and space, and, for Palestinian Christians, that place is what many call the Holy Land. Land always matters because it is the place where Christ interacts with the world and his church. As Isaac states, "God is the God of nations and lands, and not just the God of individuals." So for Isaac as a Palestinian Christian, there must be a place for what he terms a "territorial ecclesiology." The church is always rooted in the world and its place is God's place.

---

[8]Munther Isaac, *From Land to Lands, from Eden to the Renewed Earth* (Carlisle, UK: Langham Monographs, 2015); Yohanna Katanacho, *The Land of Christ: A Palestinian Cry* (Eugene, OR: Pickwick, 2013); and Katanacho, "Reading the Gospel of John Through Palestinian Eyes," in this volume.

The land, then, becomes for Isaac a "Fifth Gospel," a place that acts as a witness to God's presence and work in history. Palestinian Christians, then, continue to bear witness to Christ in the very place where the biblical history began. The land tells the story not just of the past but of the presence of God's Palestinian people who reside in that very land. The church then becomes the "Sixth Gospel," the community of faith where God dwells and from which the witness of Christ goes forth. The land for Isaac and for others from his place is, in Sabbah's words, "a dwelling place for God with humanity, and a homeland for all the children of God."[9] With these words, Isaac opens the door to a deeper understanding of the presence of the church in the world, in any land where Christ is named.

Threads in the Ecclesial Tapestry

In discussing ecclesiology, all of these biblical scholars and theologians affirm that they cannot develop a doctrine of the church without reference to the context in which the church lives out its faith in service to Christ. The opening essay by Kärkkäinen, who is not a Majority World theologian but knows the conversation, says that ecclesiologies must take into account both secularism and pluralism in society. In contrast, Nyende names African awareness of the spiritual world as an important contextual consideration. Ma, Padilla, Sosa, Xue, and Isaac all point to the political context of the church as a factor in the development of ecclesiology. Lowery names the cultural values of the family and community as key contextual considerations, while Xue struggles with ecclesial division rather than unity as a prominent consid-

eration in ecclesiology. If indeed all theology is contextual, each biblical scholar and theologian must be a deep and thoughtful reader of the biblical text, the church's theological traditions, and the cultural contexts in which the church defines its being and mission.

Stemming from these contexts, their reflections on ecclesiology bring us theological insights that are not commonplace in discussions about the nature of the church. Padilla sees the church engaged in a holistic mission, playing its role in society under God's reign. The church, then, becomes a school for citizenship. Others likewise emphasize faithful Christian social praxis as a central piece of their ecclesiology. Lowery talks about the church as a body of apprentices in society engaged in praxis, while Sosa sees the church's role in social reconciliation. Isaac's ecclesiology summons us to think about land and place as essential for the church's identity and calling. But both Ma and Sosa remind us that the church is a suffering community and must find its self-understanding in relation to the hostility it experiences within society. The church lives along the way of the cross, and Ma reminds us that this includes the deep life of prayer. Xue walks a similar road by working out an ecclesiology that embraces church division as well as unity. These and other living streams bring us all fresh understanding of what it means to be Christ's church in the world. We are all richer and refreshed by their insights.

Conclusion

Read and savor these essays. Each comes from living on the road in faith. Every author in this volume refuses to rest content with constructing

---

[9]M. Sabbah, *Sawtun Sarikhun Fil Barriya* (*A Voice Crying Out in the Wilderness*) (Jerusalem: Latin Seminary, 2008), 28.

theological abstractions. They all long to understand how life and theology intersect. Readers looking for a neatly outlined systematic theology will not find it here. The categories are set within the interplay between the church's context, its Lord, and his Word. The hermeneutical circle runs between context and Scripture in the development of relevant and theological understanding. All the authors offer their reflections as vital air, water, and food for their communities and also as gifts for Christ's church throughout the world. Read and savor, and learn.

This section, like the rest of the volume, was made possible through the generous work of the authors and the faithful support of their respective institutions. We owe them all hearty thanks for their commitment. Bringing together scholars from around the globe is an enormous logistical and financial undertaking, which would not have been possible without the underwriting of ScholarLeaders International and John Shen from Beijing. The unwavering commitment of Larry Smith and Evan Hunter, president and vice president, respectively, and of Lynn Simmons, who oversees finances, has meant that this dream could become reality. We cannot adequately express our joy for your partnership. We are also indebted to Langham Publishing for publishing this and all the other volumes in the series. Our gratitude to Pieter Kwant, director of Langham Literature, is deep. We also want to thank Suzanne Mitchell for her fine editorial work and Jixun Hu for preparing the indexes for part five. Their labor has made this a highly accessible collection.

We stand in awe at what God is doing through his church around the world and, as always, give him the honor and the glory.

33

ECCLESIOLOGY AND THE CHURCH IN CHRISTIAN TRADITION AND WESTERN THEOLOGY

Veli–Matti Kärkkäinen

THIS CHAPTER SEEKS to provide a concise description of the theology of the church, the Christian community, based on biblical teachings and early Christian intuitions and creedal statements. The missionary nature of the one, holy, catholic, and apostolic church, in the service of the kingdom of God, will be highlighted as well as the church's continual striving for unity in the midst of rampant divisions and splits. The chapter ends with a look at urgent ecclesiological challenges in the religiously pluralistic and secularized global world.[1]

THE EVOLUTION AND RISE OF ECCLESIOLOGY

Senior Catholic ecclesiologist Hans Küng opens his now-classic *The Church* by observing that "though there is much talk nowadays about the Church in the secular world, there is not a corresponding awareness of what the Church is."[2] Whether outside the church or inside, I fear this lack of awareness is even deeper at the beginning of the third millennium!

As important a role as ecclesiology is playing in contemporary theology, we should recall that as a fully developed separate locus, the doctrine of the church did not emerge until the time of the Reformation.[3] This is of course not to ignore the many church-related themes already discussed in the patristic and later doctrinal manuals, particularly sacramentology. It is rather to remind us of the polemical setting of the Reformation theology out of which a full-orbed ecclesiology, an understanding of the "true" church, emerged.[4] Not surprisingly, the construal of first full-scale ecclesiologies at the

---

[1]I have kept the documentation to a minimum because this essay is based on materials (with full documentation) in "Part II: Church," of my *A Constructive Christian Theology for the Pluralistic World*, vol. 5, *Hope and Community* (Grand Rapids, MI: Eerdmans, 2017). I also glean directly from both my *An Introduction to Ecclesiology: Ecumenical, Historical, and Contextual Perspectives* (Downers Grove, IL: IVP Academic, 2002) and my "Ecclesiology," in *Mapping Modern Theology*, ed. Kelly Kapic and Bruce McCormack (Grand Rapids, MI: Baker Academic, 2012), 345-76.

[2]Hans Küng, *The Church* (Garden City, NY: Doubleday, 1976), 11.

[3]Happily enough, we are currently served by a most detailed and reliable history of ecclesiology by senior Catholic theologian Roger Haight, SJ: *Christian Community in History*, vol. 1, *Historical Ecclesiology* (New York: Continuum, 2004); vol. 2, *Comparative Ecclesiology* (2005); vol. 3, *Ecclesial Existence* (2008).

[4]A brief detailed outline of the emergence and history of ecclesiology can be found in Wolfhart Pannenberg, *Systematic Theology*, trans. Geoffrey W. Bromiley (Grand Rapids, MI: Eerdmans, 1998), 3:21-27.

time advanced slowly and had a somewhat haphazard tone due to circumstances.

In the aftermath of the Protestant Reformation, the church's institutional unity was replaced by an ever-intensifying plurality and
multiformity of churches and Christian communities. A couple of centuries later, this diver-
sification was further intensified as the result of
the modern missionary movement, which in
turn forced the Christian communities to construct viable ecclesiologies. Beginning from the
end of the eighteenth century, Christianity
rapidly became a world religion with a presence
and outposts all over the newly developing inhabited world. Noted late historian of doctrine
Jaroslav Pelikan aptly locates the place of the
doctrine of the church at the eve of the last
century of the second millennium:

> As the twentieth century began, each of the major
> churches of a divided Christendom was obliged,
> for reasons of its own, to address anew the doc-
> trine of the church—its place in the mind of Christ,
> its essential message, its nature and identity, its
> marks of continuity, its authority and structure, its
> response to its twofold mission of keeping itself
> "unspotted from the world" and yet of being "the
> salt of the earth," and above all its authentic unity
> despite and beyond its historic divisions.[5]

Alongside the doctrine of the Trinity and pneumatology, ecclesiology has risen to the center of
constructive and ecumenical theological work.
As a result, anyone writing on the doctrine of the
church at the beginning of the third millennium
is fortunate in being able to tap into unprecedented resources and proposals, some of which
will be registered below.

In this essay, the following formative themes
and topics will be briefly presented. We will
begin with a look at the three determinative biblical symbols and metaphors (people, body, and
temple) and the four "marks" of the church as
described in the creed (unity, holiness, catholicity, and apostolicity). All Christian churches
affirm these. That is followed by a discussion on
the lack of unity of the church and the unwillingness of Christian communities to acknowledge each other as true churches. Thereafter, the essay will address the place and role of
the church in God's economy—that is, the
mission and missionary nature of the Christian
community in the trinitarian movement of
God's kingdom. The last major topic to be dealt
with takes a look at the future of ecclesiology and
the new challenges posed by globalization, migration, new forms of ecclesial existence, secularism, and religious pluralism.

A number of essential ecclesiological themes
and topics cannot be discussed at all within the
constraints of this essay. They include liturgy
and worship, sacraments, ministry and ordination, and polity issues.

PEOPLE, BODY, AND TEMPLE: DETERMINATIVE BIBLICAL SYMBOLS AND METAPHORS

Among numerous metaphors and symbols for the
church in the New Testament, the following three
have gained particular importance in Christian
parlance: namely, "people of God" (1 Pet 2:9-10),
"body of Christ" (Eph 1:22-23; 1 Cor 12:27; Col 1:18),
and "temple of the Spirit" (Eph 2:19-22; 1 Pet 2:5).[6]
These metaphors obviously reflect the triunity of
God, whose community on earth the church is.

---

[5]Jaroslav Pelikan, *The Christian Tradition: A History of the Development of Doctrine*, vol. 5, *Christian Doctrine and Modern Culture (Since 1700)* (Chicago: University of Chicago Press, 1989), 282.

[6]A massive study of biblical materials is Everett Ferguson, *The Church of Christ: A Biblical Ecclesiology for Today* (Grand Rapids, MI: Eerdmans, 1996). Famously, almost a hundred images are discerned in Paul Minear, *The Images of the Church in the New Testament* (London: Lutterworth, 1960).

Ecumenically it is of utmost importance that virtually all Christian churches are currently in agreement about the trinitarian basis and nature of the church as well as the anchoring of communion (*koinōnia*) in the shared divine life itself. A brief consideration of each of these, beginning with the last one, helps elucidate the ancient self-understanding of the Christian community derived from the Scriptures.

The Spirit's work in the New Testament is not only present in the individual believer's life; it is also community forming and communally directed. As late Lutheran Wolfhart Pannenberg puts it: "The gift of the Spirit is not just for individual believers but aims at the building up of the fellowship of believers, at the founding and constant giving of new life to the church."[7] This was of course evident on the day of Pentecost, when a *koinōnia* of believers was brought into existence, as beautifully described in Acts 2:42-47.[8] The same Spirit also makes the church charismatic as its members are endowed with various spiritual gifts and capacities for witness and service (Acts 1:8; 1 Cor 12; 14).

As the temple of the Spirit, the church is also the body of the risen Christ, who poured out the Pentecostal Spirit. This is to say that there is a dual foundation for the church, christological and pneumatological. Apostolic father Ignatius taught that "wherever Jesus Christ is, there is the Catholic Church," and another early teacher, Irenaeus, made reference to the Spirit's presence: "For where the Church is, there is the Spirit of God; and where the Spirit of God is, there is the Church, and every kind of grace."[9] The balance between the christological and pneumatological basis of the church honors the deep and wide "Spirit Christology" of the New Testament. In the Gospels and beyond, this "Spirit Christology" comes to the forefront in that, from the beginning of the history of Jesus Christ to his glorious resurrection, there are references to the work of the Spirit, and, conversely, the Spirit's work is everywhere associated with that of the Son.[10] Appropriately, the leading communion-theologian of contemporary times, the Eastern Orthodox John Zizioulas, speaks of the church as *instituted* by Christ and constituted by the Holy Spirit.[11]

The New Testament contains very few references to the church's status as the body of Christ, but body terminology abounds, particularly in the form of "one body" or "one body in Christ." Whereas in 1 Corinthians and Romans the individual community is depicted as a body, in Ephesians and Colossians it is the whole church. In Pauline teaching the main point of employing the body metaphor with regard to individual communities has to do with interrelated virtues and the qualities of love, unity, and working for the common good; just study 1 Corinthians 12–14 to that effect.[12] In the context of the whole church as the body, to the fore is a cosmological Christology and the cosmic work of the triune God working out his eternal purposes toward the reconciliation of all peoples and all of creation.

---

[7]Pannenberg, *Systematic Theology*, 3:12-13.

[8]A massive recent study of all aspects of *koinōnia* is Lorelei F. Fuchs, SA, *Koinonia and the Quest for an Ecumenical Ecclesiology: From Foundations Through Dialogue to Symbolic Competence for Communionality* (Grand Rapids, MI: Eerdmans, 2008).

[9]Ignatius, *To the Smyrnaeans* 8; Irenaeus, *Against Heresies* 3.24.1, respectively.

[10]See my *A Constructive Christian Theology for the Pluralistic World*, vol. 1, *Christ and Reconciliation* (Grand Rapids, MI: Eerdmans, 2013), chap. 8, for the Spirit's role in Christology; and vol. 4, *Spirit and Salvation* (Grand Rapids, MI: Eerdmans, 2016), chap. 2, for Christ's role in pneumatology.

[11]John D. Zizioulas, *Being as Communion: Studies in Personhood and the Church*, trans. John Meyendorff (Crestwood, NY: St. Vladimir's Seminary Press, 1997), 22.

[12]See also Küng, *Church*, 186-89.

The widest and most comprehensive biblical image of the church is the people of God. In the Bible, peoplehood is based on divine election, as first presented with regard to Yahweh's choosing of Israel as his people. That election, however, should not lead to separation (as happened at times with Israel); rather, membership in the community is toward the goal of the gathering of the people of God in the new Jerusalem, as the programmatic vision of the seer of Revelation testifies to (Rev 21:3-4). The people metaphor is also critical in its link with Israel, the "first" people of God. While affirmed by all Christian communities from the beginning, over the centuries there have been immeasurable difficulties in trying to hold together the distinction of the two peoples, "old" and "new," without a harmful separation. Paul's most extensive exposition in Romans 9–11, understandably, has been the focus of millennia-long debates.

These three guiding metaphors of the church, as mentioned, have also been rightly linked with the foundational Christian confession of one God as triune. Hence, already in patristic theology the church was envisioned as an image of the Trinity. Just as each person is made according to the image of the Trinity, so the church as a whole is an icon of the Trinity. This teaching has been particularly pronounced in the Eastern Orthodox tradition.

This trinitarian vision of the church based on the eternal Trinity has also helped the church to foster a robust vision of communion, that is, a communion ecclesiology. The triune God is the eternal communion of Father, Son, and Spirit. Consequently, the church as the communion of human persons may be said to echo that communal, relational existence.

ONE, HOLY, CATHOLIC, AND APOSTOLIC: THE MARKS OF THE CHURCH

In the Nicene-Constantinopolitan Creed (381), confessed by (virtually) all Christian traditions throughout history, the church is believed to be one, holy, catholic, and apostolic. It is to be noted that in the creed, unlike often in later tradition, these four classical marks (also called "notes" or "signs") were not used in any apologetic sense. Furthermore, it is worth noting that rather than carefully formulated, fixed definitions, the marks were most probably added to the creed somewhat haphazardly.

It is important to realize that rather than abstract definitions of the church, the marks are first and foremost an object of faith. Whereas in the creeds we believe in the triune God as Father, Son, and Spirit, when it comes to the third article, an accurate rendering of the original text states that we believe the church. As a result, the marks are as much also statements of hope. Eventually, the four marks become statements of action, because they urge us to realize what is believed and hoped for.[13] It is usual and useful to consider the marks as gifts and tasks. On the one hand, they are gifts from God. We do not make the church one, holy, apostolic, and catholic; only God can. On the other hand, we see too clearly that any church in the world, including our own, is far from those markers. Hence, each description is also a matter of hope, which leads to action for attaining its realization more closely.

Although the oneness or unity of the church has been a spiritual and theological conviction from the beginning of history, we notice that

---

[13]Jürgen Moltmann, *The Church in the Power of the Spirit: A Contribution to Messianic Ecclesiology*, trans. Margaret Kohl (London: SCM Press, 1977), 339-40.

already in the biblical era the church began to encounter splits and has been divided since.[14] Not for nothing are there a number of biblical exhortations to restore and help retain the oneness and unity as the one body of Christ under one head. Repentance is needed as a condition for seeking lost unity (Jn 10:16; 17:20-26; Acts 2:42; Rom 12:3-8; 1 Cor 1:10-30; 12:12-27; Gal 3:27-28; Eph 4:1-6).[15] This same desire to restore unity was also present in early patristic theology, as is evident in ecumenical tracts such as the early third-century *On the Unity of the Church* by Cyprian.[16]

In keeping with the nonapologetic employment of the marks of the church in early Christianity, the meaning of the term *catholic*—literally in Greek, "directed towards the whole"—in Ignatius of Antioch, in whom we find it for the very first time, simply meant the "whole" church in distinction from local communities.[17] There is no indication yet of the later meaning attached to catholicity of "fullness" and "perfection," that is, not lacking in anything; nor is that meaning present in secular Greek. The linking of *catholic* with the *plerōma* ("fullness") of Ephesians 1:23 came later, beginning from the third century, due to polemics and apologetics. Then the term's meaning first came to match materially with *orthodox* and by derivation to mean something like "valid." This came to its zenith with the establishment of Christianity as the only legitimate state religion in Christendom. Quite naturally, the further layers of the term also took on geo-graphical and numerical connotations as the church extended to new territories and grew in membership. By the fifth century, Vincent of Lérins's celebrated formula speaks of "that faith which has been believed everywhere, always, by all."[18] The contemporary understanding needs to remember the original New Testament meaning of the term *catholic* (notwithstanding the lack of the term therein): it simply means the whole church as that which consists of all local churches, which in themselves are full churches insofar as they are in communion with other similar communities. "While the individual local Church is *an* entire Church, it is not *the* entire Church." By derivation, each such local church is truly catholic. In other words, the plurality of local churches does not make either them or the whole church uncatholic; what strips the church(es) off from catholicity is only separation from others, self-sufficiency, and isolation.[19] Furthermore, we have to say that, although spatial extension, numerical quantity, and temporal continuity are not irrelevant to catholicity, they do not alone—or even primarily—constitute it.

The celebrated ecumenical document *The Nature and Mission of the Church* reminds us of the obvious dilemma facing each and every church: "the essential holiness of the Church stands in contrast to sin, individual as well as communal" (#54).[20] Not surprisingly, various tactics have been tried in order to ensure the

---

[14]For examples concerning the unity of the church, see J. N. D. Kelly, *Early Christian Doctrines*, rev. ed. (New York: Harper & Row, 1978), 200-201.

[15]For details, see Küng, *Church*, 352-53.

[16]See Kelly, *Early Christian Doctrines*, 204-7.

[17]Ignatius, *To the Smyrnaeans* 8.

[18]Vincent of Lérins, *A Commonitory* 2.6. For details of this development, see Küng, *Church*, 385-86.

[19]Küng, *Church*, 387-88.

[20]World Council of Churches, *The Nature and Mission of the Church: A Stage on the Way to a Common Statement*, Faith and Order Paper no. 198, 15 December 2005, www.oikoumene.org/en/resources/documents/commissions/faith-and-order/i-unity-the-church -and-its-mission/the-nature-and-mission-of-the-church-a-stage-on-the-way-to-a-common-statement.

church's holiness. An early dispute between the followers of Augustine and the Donatists illustrates this. The latter party sought to ensure holiness by not receiving back into membership the leaders and members who had lapsed under persecution. The Donatists, rather, wanted to cultivate the idea of a "pure church," a principle later followed by free churches throughout their existence. On the other hand, for Augustine and the mainline party, the principle of love and unity of the body was the determining principle, and he advocated for the idea of a "mixed body," the rule adopted later by Protestant, Anglican, and Roman Catholic communities. Therein, the holiness of the church is located in its head, Jesus Christ, rather than in the members (even if the pursuit of holiness in the Christian walk is not unimportant in itself either). Be that as it may, all churches have to live in the dynamic tension between belief in holiness and acknowledgment of the presence of sin and sinful members.

An elusive and pluriform concept both in the New Testament and in later ecclesiastical usage, beginning from the early fathers, *apostolicity* became a commonplace in Christian usage, whether in relation to the church, a bishop, or Christ. Although the adjective *apostolic* never occurs in the Bible (and hardly in other contemporaneous sources), as a noun, the term is of course frequent in the New Testament, most often in Luke and Paul, where its meaning resembles that of "ambassador" (for Christ). The term is not limited to the Twelve, as is often popularly assumed. It can also refer to various persons and groups; Paul himself is of course often its object, and he also mentions "false apostles."

Despite complex debates in later history, it is undisputed that the original meaning of the term *apostolic* simply had to do with the linkage to apostles. Apostolicity, then, essentially involves the continuity of life and faith of the apostles and the apostolic church of the New Testament. That much all ecclesiastical traditions affirm. Differences coming to the surface have to do with the way the linkage with the church of the apostles should be determined. Broadly speaking, two main approaches have been tried without a final consensus having yet been reached. For Orthodox and Catholic traditions, episcopal succession (somewhat differently conceived in each church) serves as the needed evidence. With the laying on of hands, each new generation of bishops is guaranteed to be standing in the line of the apostles. Although Protestant Reformers did not totally do away with the office of bishop, theirs was the claim to the primacy of the apostolic Word, the Scriptures. Where Scripture is preached and followed (alongside the right celebration of sacraments), apostolicity can be assumed. While among the free churches no defined opinion of apostolicity is to be found, recently some Pentecostal theologians have proposed that the presence of the Spirit's charismatic vitality and obedience to Christ's command to evangelize and serve all people should qualify as an indication of apostolicity. The reason for that claim is simple: according to the New Testament testimonies, that is what seemed to be happening everywhere among the communities established and led by the apostles.

As mentioned, the one church of Christ on earth is deeply and painfully divided. The continuing divisions, splits, and conflicts between the churches and their unwillingness to acknowledge each other's ecclesiality is the most critical issue facing the church of the past and tomorrow.

THE UNITY OF THE DIVIDED CHURCH: THE ECUMENICAL CHALLENGE

The question of ecclesiality: What makes the church **church.** The ecumenical challenge, namely, the issue of restoring the unity of the church, has to do with two major challenges. First of all, there is the lack of willingness among various church traditions to acknowledge and embrace the full "churchliness" (ecclesiality) of other Christian communities. Let us name that the question of ecclesiality. The second, related issue has to do with the pursuit of restoring unity among communities that are separated. That is the wider ecumenical challenge. Let us begin with the first one.

Notwithstanding the general consensus about the trinitarian basis of the church based on biblical testimonies and the universally confessed nature of that community as one, holy, apostolic, and catholic, there is a lack of willingness among churches to fully acknowledge other communities' full ecclesiality. The term *ecclesiality* simply refers to what makes the church *church*. In other words, some churches do not consider others as churches but as something less or defective. This wound is particularly deep between the "older" (Roman Catholic and Orthodox) and "younger" churches (free churches and various types of independents), but it also relates to Protestant and Anglican communities, which in this respect stand somewhere in the middle of the debate.

The key debate has to do with the role of sacraments, episcopacy, and personal confession of faith in relation to what makes the church *church*. There are three main positions. First, for Or-

thodox and Catholic ecclesiology, not only does the church carry out the sacraments, but the sacraments first and foremost make the church. This means that only where there is the celebration of the sacrament of the Eucharist (whose attendance requires water baptism), there is the Christian church. And for that celebration to be ecclesiologically valid, there needs to be a bishop whose standing is considered to be linked with the first apostles, as noted above. In sum, this is the "sacramental" and "episcopal" definition of the ecclesiality of the church.[21]

Second, for the youngest Christian family, the free churches, decisive is the presence of a personal confession of faith of the men and women who then gather together as the church. That faith is mediated directly, as it were, and does not necessarily require mediation by the sacraments or office. The celebration of the sacraments of water baptism and the Lord's Supper is an important part of the church's life, but these are not considered ecclesiologically constitutive and, in the case where personal faith is missing, might even be taken as something formal and useless. Furthermore, while among those free churches some have an ecclesiastical office by the name of "bishop," this does not have any ecclesiologically determinative function.[22]

Third, there is the Protestant mainline definition of the church's "foundation" in terms of the administration of the sacraments (baptism and the Eucharist) and the preaching of the gospel, as famously defined in the Lutheran Augsburg Confession (#7). Although for Anglicans and many Protestants (all Lutherans and some Reformed) the theology (of salvation) is sacramental in the

---

[21]Hence, in the following the word *episcopal* (as distinct from the proper name *Episcopal*, i.e. Anglican, Church) is used in that technical theological sense.

[22]This is common among most African-American churches in the United States, as well as in a large number of Pentecostal and other free churches all over the world, particularly in Africa but also in the former Soviet Union, and so forth.

sense that one becomes and is sustained as Christian by the sacraments (when integrally linked with the Word), neither sacraments nor ministerial patterns are considered ecclesiologically constitutive after the manner of Orthodox and Catholic theology. As a result, even if they have a bishop (as a large number of Lutherans do), that office is not constitutive for the being of the church and can also be otherwise.[23]

Now, the ecumenical and ecclesiastical implications are simply these: for Orthodox and Catholics, neither Protestants and Anglicans, regardless of their sacramentality, nor free churches qualify as churches because they lack episcopal and sacramental validity for the reasons explained above. Even the Anglican and Protestant celebration of the sacraments (particularly the Eucharist) is invalid because of the episcopal deficit. On the other hand, for free churches, particularly in the early years of the movements, no amount of appeal to episcopacy or sacraments had any church-constitutive meaning; indeed, putting them at the forefront often elicited a response against mere formal religion! Mainline Protestants (and Anglicans, I suppose) come closest to not having binding reasons for nonrecognition of either free churches (as long as they also honor the sacraments, and they do appreciate the preaching of the Word, after all) or Orthodox and Catholic churches (without endorsing their exclusive appeal to episcopal succession). It is here that the complex and demanding work of the ecumenical movement begins.

The ecumenical movement: The striving for the unity of the church. Nearly everybody would agree that "ecumenicity was the great new fact in the history of the church."[24] A number of initiatives and developments prepared for the coming into existence of the contemporary ecumenical movement, including important ecclesiastical unions and agreements in Europe, North America, India, and elsewhere, with the establishment of the World Council of Churches in 1948 as the most visible sign. A significant early twentieth-century push toward concerted efforts for unity came from the Edinburgh Missionary Conference, whose centennial was celebrated in 2010 in Edinburgh. Ecumenical platforms to deal with social issues (Life and Work) and doctrine (Faith and Order) further helped bring the World Council of Churches into existence.

The Roman Catholic Church and most evangelicals are not officially members of the World Council of Churches. It is not a church but rather a "fellowship of churches," currently about 350 churches from all continents. Its self-understanding was established in the 1961 New Delhi basis statement: "a fellowship of churches which confess the Lord Jesus Christ as God and Saviour according to the scriptures, and therefore seek to fulfill together their common calling to the glory of the one God, Father, Son and Holy Spirit."[25] Its purpose is

> not to build a global "super-church," nor to standardize styles of worship, but rather to deepen the fellowship of Christian churches and communities so they may see in one another authentic

---

[23]A materially similar presentation (limited to Orthodox or Catholic and free churches) can be found in Miroslav Volf, *After Our Likeness: The Church as the Image of the Trinity* (Grand Rapids, MI: Eerdmans, 1997), 130-35.

[24]Pelikan, *Christian Doctrine and Modern Culture*, 282. The most comprehensive and accessible resource on various facets of ecumenism and the ecumenical movement, including the World Council of Churches, is the *Dictionary of the Ecumenical Movement*, ed. Nicholas Lossky et al. (Geneva: WCC, 1991). For key texts, see Michael Kinnamon and Brian E. Cope, eds., *The Ecumenical Movement: An Anthology of Key Texts and Voices* (Grand Rapids, MI: Eerdmans, 1997).

[25]"The Basis of the WCC," World Council of Churches, www.oikoumene.org/en/about-us/self-understanding-vision/basis, accessed April 28, 2020.

expressions of the "one holy, catholic and apostolic church." This becomes the basis for joining in a common confession of the apostolic faith, cooperating in mission and human service endeavours and, where possible, sharing in the sacraments. All these acts of fellowship bear testimony to the foundational declaration of the WCC that the Lord Jesus Christ is "God and Saviour according to the Scriptures."[26]

An important part of the ecumenical work happens constantly in the form of bilateral and multilateral dialogue between Christian churches. In most countries there is a national council of churches (such as the National Council of Churches, USA), which works in close cooperation with Faith and Order, facilitating ecumenical conversations, events, and projects at national, regional, and local levels. There are also a number of informal ecumenical contacts between leaders as well as laypeople at various levels, making a significant contribution to the search for unity. In other words, the term *ecumenical* has to be understood most inclusively and should in no way be limited to what might be called the "official" or "formal" ecumenism (that is, the work done by the World Council of Churches and other such agencies). Recall that the two biggest players in the Majority World, namely, Roman Catholics and Pentecostal-charismatics (as well as the majority of evangelicals), are not affiliated with the World Council of Churches (although Catholics collaborate in many projects).

While there is no agreement about the form and shape of visible unity, the ecumenical movement at large has adopted that as the main goal. There are also a number of dividing issues with regard to ministry, sacraments, and, say, the issues of evangelism and proselytism, which call for patient, long-term consideration and mutual understanding.

"Church as Mission"

The church as the sign of the kingdom of God. The one, holy, catholic, and apostolic church does not exist for itself, but, rather, as the image of the triune God—the people of God, the body of Christ, and the temple of the Spirit—it participates in the wider salvific purposes of God. This forges an integral link between God's community (church) and God's kingdom. This is to say that God's community on earth (the church) is graciously drawn into the coming of God's kingdom, his righteous reign over all creation. That makes the church missionary by its very nature. The church exists as mission.

At the heart of Jesus' proclamation was the announcement of the dawning reign of God that he came to usher in. A shorthand for the divine rule was the term *kingdom of God*. Not only as individuals responding to Jesus' message, but as a community—people, body, and temple—Christians are graciously invited to participate in the coming of this righteous rule. This means that the church serves as the sign of the kingdom of God.

The church in itself is not to be equated with God's rule, as has happened at times during Christian history, particularly at the height of Christendom—to which development the sad history of colonialism in South America tragically testifies, as discussed in Ruth Padilla DeBorst's essay. God's reign, his kingdom, is much wider and more comprehensive than the church or even human society. What the church is is a preceding sign pointing to the coming righteous

---

[26]"The WCC and the Ecumenical Movement," World Council of Churches, http://archived.oikoumene.org/en/who-are-we/background
.html, accessed April 28, 2020.

rule of God in the eschaton, an anticipation of the coming consummation and gathering of all God's people under one God (Rev 21:3-4). The distinction between the sign and the thing to be signified sets the church and its function in relation to God's rule in their proper place, as Wolfhart Pannenberg puts it succinctly:

> A sign points beyond itself to the thing signified. It is thus essential to the function of the sign that we should distinguish them. We must not equate the thing with the sign in its weakness. Only by this distinction can the thing signified be, in a certain sense, present by way of the sign. . . . If the church fails to make this distinction clearly, then it arrogates to itself the finality and glory of the kingdom, but by the poverty and all too human character of its own life it also makes the Christian hope incredible.[27]

Acknowledging the anticipatory and preparatory nature of the church's existence helps avoid uncritical alignment with any political or ideological order. So what is important to note is that as far as the church faithfully functions as the sign, it "has its end not in itself but in the future of a humanity that is reconciled to God and united by common praise of God in his kingdom."[28] Exactly as an imperfect, often-failing sign and instrument, the church shows to the world that it points to something more perfect and permanent.

The missionary nature of the church. This integral relation of the church to the movement of the kingdom of the triune God is aptly described in the Roman Catholic Vatican II's (1862–1865) ecclesiological document, *Lumen Gentium*: "The pilgrim Church is missionary by her very nature" (#2). Importantly, several streams of missiological thinking coalesced in this new acknowledgment of the church's missionary nature. Highly influential was the untiring call from late United Reformed Bishop Lesslie Newbigin, a long-term missionary to India, for considering the West (Europe and the United States) as a "mission field" and thus the need for all churches everywhere to adopt a missional approach and existence.[29] One of the offshoots from that call was the establishment of an ecumenical network and research initiative by the name of "Gospel and Culture"; soon it was followed by similar networks in the United States and beyond.[30] In the American context, a 1998 book titled *Missional Church: A Vision for the Sending of the Church in North America*, a collection of essays by representatives of the Gospel and Our Culture Network, made an effort to bring World Council of Churches discussions of *missio Dei* (the mission of God) and Lesslie Newbigin's missionary insights to bear on North America.[31] The book urges the church to move away from a Christendom model that focuses on maintenance to a missional way of life based on outreach and expansion.

American Presbyterian theologian Darrell Guder reminds us that embracing the missional understanding of the church helps conceive of ecclesiality and the marks of the church in the same dynamic manner: "By 'apostolicity,' we do not merely mean 'the church descended from the apostles,' as important as that is. We mean 'apostolicity' in the active sense of the New Testament verb, meaning 'to be sent out,' and the noun 'apostle' as the 'sent-out' one. The community

---

[27]Pannenberg, *Systematic Theology*, 3:32.
[28]Pannenberg, 45-46.
[29]The best resource to get into basic ideas is Lesslie Newbigin, *The Gospel in a Pluralist Society* (Grand Rapids, MI: Eerdmans, 1989).
[30]See, e.g., the Gospel and Our Culture Network at www.gocn.org.
[31]Darrell Guder, ed., *Missional Church: A Vision for the Sending of the Church in North America* (Grand Rapids, MI: Eerdmans, 1998).

formed by the Holy Spirit through the initial apostolic witness is called to be sent." The second mark, catholicity, would remind the church of "the message . . . to be made known to the ends of the earth, . . . [to be] translatable into the life and experience of every ethnicity, as concretely demonstrated at the first Pentecost."[32]

Typically in Christian tradition, the tasks of the missionary church in the world include worship, liturgy, and sacramental celebration, proclamation of the gospel, cultivating mutual fellowship (*koinōnia*), and engaging in *diakonia* (meeting the various needs of men and women). When placed in the wider context of God's universal purposes over creation, it is appropriate to add to these important tasks and dimensions of ministry the following: working toward equality and justice, whether with regard to gender, economy, or sociopolitical issues; participating in efforts to restore peace and reconciliation at various levels of human communities, from the local to regional to global levels; and helping care for nature and the environment.

IN LIEU OF CONCLUSIONS: NEW CHALLENGES AND NEW OPPORTUNITIES IN THE THIRD MILLENNIUM

The Christian church goes global. From what is estimated to have been fewer than 10,000 Christians in AD 100, Christianity has grown to be the largest religion, with over 2.4 billion adherents.[33] Not only that, but the rapid growth of the church in the Global South (Africa, Asia, and Latin America) has helped shift the center of the church away from the Global North (Europe, North America). The Majority World now houses more than two-thirds of all Christians. By 2050, only about one-fifth of the world's three billion Christians will be non-Hispanic whites.

At the same time, the composition of the church worldwide is changing dramatically. As of now, one-half of all Christians are Roman Catholics, another quarter is composed of Pentecostals and charismatics, and the rest are Eastern Orthodox Christians (by far the largest segment in this section), as well as Anglicans, mainline Protestants, and free churches.[34] This means that Roman Catholics, Pentecostals, and charismatics together constitute three-fourths of the global membership. As a result, conservative and traditional mindsets will be strengthened even as theological liberalism and pluralism reign in Western academia. The "Pentecostalization" of the Christian church in terms of Pentecostal and charismatic spirituality and worship patterns infiltrating all churches is yet another implication of the transformation.

Particularly significant to the future of the Christian church is the rapid and steady growth of Christianity in Africa—which also has become an important exporter of migrant and diaspora Christianity to the Global North.[35] Indeed, as part of the globalization process underway, migration and diaspora have caught the attention of some ecclesiologists and missiologists. According to 2013 Pew Research Center data, of over two hundred million migrants (which constitutes

---

[32]Darrell Guder, "The Nicene Marks in a Post-Christendom Church," Presbyterian Church USA, www.pcusa.org/site_media/media/uploads/reformingministry/pdfs/nicene_marks.pdf, 9-10, accessed April 28, 2020.

[33]Rodney Stark, *The Rise of Christianity* (San Francisco: HarperCollins, 1997), 57-61.

[34]The basic statistical sources are David B. Barrett, George T. Kurian, and Todd M. Johnson, eds., *World Christian Encyclopedia*, 2 vols., 2nd ed. (New York: Oxford University Press, 2001; pages 12-15 contain a useful global summary); and the more recent Todd M. Johnson and Brian J. Grim, *The World's Religions in Figures* (Oxford: Wiley-Blackwell, 2013).

[35]For the currents in African ecclesiology, see the two informative essays in this part of the volume by Stephanie Lowery and Peter Nyende. Among a number of reports and studies on the influence of diaspora Christianity in the West, informative are, for example,

3 percent of the world's population), about one-half are Christians; the United States houses most of them. The next largest number are Muslims (about one-fourth), followed by smaller groupings of other religious affiliations.

New forms of ecclesial existence. An important aspect of the re-formation of the global church has to do with the rise of new forms of ecclesial existence. Regrettably, theologians are still slow to discern and acknowledge the significance of these changes. By and large, doctrines of the church—similarly to ecumenical documents—are still written as if a Christendom model were in place and mainline churches were the only players on the field. Similarly, denominational markers stay intact for theologians and ecumenists, although they have become fluid and at times almost nonexistent among a growing number of church members. Yet in many cases, traditional churches are rapidly losing their former status in both society and Christian imagination—even if the Roman Catholic Church, differently from all counterparts, continues to constitute a majority in many locations. At the same time, new forms of the Christian church are mushrooming and flourishing. Wonsuk Ma's essay on two emerging free church–type ecclesiologies wonderfully illustrates this trend.

Many specialists hold the opinion that the free church congregational model might well be the major paradigm in the third millennium alongside the Catholic one. Owing to the heritage of the Radical Reformation, Christian communities such as the Anabaptists and (later) Mennonites, Baptists, Congregationalists, Quakers, Pentecostals, and some Methodist and Holiness movements, as well as a growing number of independent movements, are usually included under the somewhat elusive concept of "free churches."

Many younger-generation Christian leaders drawn to and influenced by postmodernity have been engaged in ecclesiological experiments known under elusive names such as ChurchNext (2000) and The Liquid Church (2002).[36] The most widely researched among these new forms of ecclesiality are emerging/emergent churches, as they are called in the United States, and fresh expressions of the church, as they are known in the United Kingdom. Highly active in virtual networks and ways of connecting, their ecclesiologies are fluid. They do not always meet in sanctuaries but may instead rent comedy clubs or pubs. Deeply missional in orientation with the focus on praxis and everyday Christian service, they do not typically bother to delve into theological debates about ecclesiology, although many of their leaders may have solid academic training in religion.[37]

Facing religious plurality and secularism. Alongside globalization and the rise of new forms of ecclesial existence, two other major challenges to the church and ecclesiology have been recently identified. They have to do with the simultaneous rise of secularism and religious pluralism. In contrast to the (in)famous "secularization thesis" revived in the secular 1960s, which built on the foundation laid by the great atheists of the nineteenth century (Feuerbach, Marx, Freud, and others) and predicted the death of religion as a

the following: Frieder Ludwig and J. Kwabena Asamoah-Gyadu, eds., *African Christian Presence in the West: New Immigrant Congregations and Transnational Networks in North America and Europe* (Trenton, NJ: Africa World, 2011); Mark R. Gornik, *Word Made Global: Stories of African Christianity in New York City* (Grand Rapids, MI: Eerdmans, 2011).

[36]Eddie Gibbs, *ChurchNext* (Downers Grove, IL: InterVarsity Press, 2000); Pete Ward, *The Liquid Church* (Peabody, MA: Hendrickson, 2002).

[37]So far the most thorough study—ethnographic as well as theological—on both sides of the Atlantic Ocean suggests that emerging churches (1) identify with the life of Jesus, (2) transform the secular realm, and (3) live highly communal lives. Because of these three activities, they (4) welcome the stranger, (5) serve with generosity, (6) participate as producers, (7) create as created beings, (8) lead as a body, and (9) take part in spiritual activities (Eddie Gibbs and Ryan Bolger, *Emerging Churches: Creating Christian Community in Postmodern Cultures* [Grand Rapids, MI: Baker Academic, 2005]).

result of a scientifically based "enlightened" worldview, the world of the third millennium is even more religious than before. At the global level, religions are not only holding their own but are flourishing and (at least in some cases) growing in numbers. Religious plurality is no longer a matter of certain locations and continents but also a reality over the whole globe, including the Global North.

The rise of both secularism and religious pluralism means that the ecclesiologies of the third millennium have to pay attention not only to what is inside the church and within the Christian tradition, but also to the teaching of other religious traditions and the mindset of the secular public. Just think of a topic such as land, a deeply biblical issue but so far largely ignored by theologians; Munther Isaac's essay, from a Palestinian perspective, makes a significant contribution in this regard. Similarly, questions of power and identity, among others, loom large in the contemporary globalized world.

Regarding religious pluralism, two theological subdisciplines provide wonderful help, namely, Christian theology of religions and comparative theology. Theology of religions seeks to investigate the theological value of religions and Christianity's place and function among other religions.[38] Comparative theology builds on that work, as well as the accumulated results of comparative religion—which, as the name indicates, compares religious beliefs and rites without stated theological-philosophical presuppositions in order to accomplish specific and detailed comparisons among religions.

FURTHER READING

Gaillardetz, Richard R. *Ecclesiology for a Global Church: A People Called and Sent.* Theology in Global Perspectives. Maryknoll, NY: Orbis, 2008.

Gibbs, Eddie, and Ryan Bolger. *Emerging Churches: Creating Christian Community in Postmodern Cultures.* Grand Rapids, MI: Baker Academic, 2005.

Haight, Roger, SJ. *Christian Community in History.* Vol. 1, *Historical Ecclesiology.* Vol. 2, *Comparative Ecclesiology.* Vol. 3, *Ecclesial Existence.* New York: Continuum, 2004, 2005, 2008.

Harper, Brad, and Paul Louis Metzger. *Exploring Ecclesiology: An Evangelical and Ecumenical Introduction.* Grand Rapids, MI: Brazos, 2009.

Kärkkäinen, Veli-Matti. *A Constructive Christian Theology for the Pluralistic World.* Vol. 5, *Hope and Community.* Grand Rapids, MI: Eerdmans, 2017.

———. *An Introduction to Ecclesiology: Ecumenical, Historical, and Contextual Perspectives.* Downers Grove, IL: IVP Academic, 2002.

Küng, Hans. *The Church.* Translated by Ray and Rosaleen Ockenden. London: Burnes & Oates, 1967. Reprint, Garden City, NY: Doubleday, 1976.

Mannion, Gerard. *Ecclesiology and Postmodernity: Questions for the Church in Our Time.* Collegeville, MN: Liturgical, 2007.

Moltmann, Jürgen. *The Church in the Power of the Spirit: A Contribution to Messianic Ecclesiology.* Translated by Margaret Kohl. London: SCM Press, 1977.

Pannenberg, Wolfhart. *Systematic Theology.* Vol. 3. Translated by Geoffrey W. Bromiley. Grand Rapids, MI: Eerdmans, 1998.

---

[38]For details, see Paul F. Knitter, *Introducing Theologies of Religions* (Maryknoll, NY: Orbis, 2002); Veli-Matti Kärkkäinen, *An Introduction to the Theology of Religions: Biblical, Historical and Contemporary Perspectives* (Downers Grove, IL: IVP Academic, 2003).

34

CHURCH, POWER, AND TRANSFORMATION IN LATIN AMERICA

A DIFFERENT CITIZENSHIP IS POSSIBLE

Ruth Padilla DeBorst

THIS CHAPTER INVITES READERS to trek through the centuries, looking through theological and historical lenses at the various expressions of church in Latin America. It pays particular attention to diverging practices and understandings regarding church and power, and to the relationship between the church and the powers of the day. Echoing mainly two ingredients of the ancient creed, it explores the double movement experienced by the people of the triune Community-of-Love as it lives out the reign of God, following Jesus in the power and gifting of the Spirit while, at the same time, never making itself fully at home in the world. It posits that it is precisely the holy and apostolic calling of the church that constitutes it as a school of citizenship.

The country was worn down by hyperinflation and a military dictatorship. People who dared question the government's repressive policies were deemed disloyal citizens and made to "disappear." Even so, excitement rippled through the small congregation that sunny March morning at the beginning of the school year. It was ordination day in the Baptist church on the outskirts of Buenos Aires. Young children were first: they raced to the front and sat on the floor. The ministry team, composed of women and men, laid their hands on them. "To learning, growing, being good friends, and following Jesus at home, school, and neighborhood, we ordain you." A resounding "Amen" issued from the rest of the congregation. Next were the high-schoolers, who, in a colorful circle, received their charge. They were followed by college students, who were ordained to explore their vocation and hone their skills for service. Employees, business-people, stay-at-home parents, manual workers, professionals in diverse fields, people in full-time Christian ministry, all were ordained, group by group, to live as citizens of God's kingdom, following Jesus with the gifts and the power of the Spirit in their particular occupations.

The occasion was celebrated with a classic Argentine lunch, *empanadas* and *asado*, in the back yard of the *templo*.[1] Once the meal was over, the chairs were drawn into a circle, and a community

---

[1] *Asado* is Argentine-style barbecue. The term *templo* is frequently employed to name church buildings in Latin America and allows for a helpful distinction between place (*templo*) and people (*iglesia*).

consultation began. The question of the day was: Should there be wine or grape juice for Communion? Historically, the church had always had wine for the Lord's Supper. However, a recently arrived missionary had explained to the ministry team that he was unable to participate in communion because he did not believe Christians should drink alcohol. A frank conversation ensued: "Why should we change simply because a US-American missionary doesn't like our way of doing things?" resisted several young people. "Yet we must find ways to preserve our unity as a church body; we cannot have people excluded from communion." "Additionally, what about the people who are wrestling with drug addiction and alcoholism?" questioned others. "Would it not favor them to not have alcohol in church?" People, younger and older, women and men, freely expressed their perspectives. The discussion proceeded to include volunteers for the after-school program and recruitment of a social worker to work in the rehabilitation center sponsored by the church. And, from that day forward, half the Communion cups were filled with white grape juice and half with red wine.

This paper does not propose to prescribe the proper content of Communion cups, nor to discuss the benefits and drawbacks of congregational modes of church order. Neither does it intend to present an exhaustive review of ecclesiologies generated within Latin America.[2] Instead, it invites readers to trek through the centuries, looking through theological and historical lenses at the various expressions of church in Latin America and paying particular attention to diverging practices and understandings regarding church, power, and the relationship between the church and the powers of the day. It

then posits the church as a school of citizenship in light of its identity as the people of the triune Community-of-Love and its calling to follow Jesus into the world while never making itself fully at home in it. These theological reflections on church, power, and transformation in Latin America and beyond are born out of the dialogue between Scripture, historical analysis, personal experience as a member of the Iglesia Evangélica Bautista de La Lucila, and involvement in a variety of Christian faith communities since then.

CHURCH AND POWER IN LATIN AMERICA: A HISTORICAL TREK

The question regarding *what*, or rather *who*, is the church has received divergent responses and concrete outworkings throughout the history of Latin America. Each of these conceptual and embodied responses rests on theological understandings regarding the nature of God, of humankind, of the relationship between them, and of the relationship between gospel and power. We will note these as we walk through the centuries, after a few clarifications are made. First, a word on power. No realm of creation or human existence is devoid of it. Crucial questions in the analysis of all relationships include: Who exercises power and who is deprived of it? What is the source and nature of power? How, for what, and for whom is that power employed? Although a comprehensive response to these questions is beyond the scope of this paper, the issues themselves are inextricably woven through the entire account and mark the contrasting faces of the Christian church in the subcontinent.

Second, the story of Christianity in Latin America is as complex and diverse as the people,

---

[2]The resources cited at the end of this essay could prove useful for such a study.

cultures, ethnicities, and traditions of the people that compose this vast region that spans from North America, through Central America, and all the way south till Fire Land. Our walk today, then, is necessarily riddled with generalizations and omissions.[3]

The church under imperial power, and followers of "the other Spanish Christ." On the wall of the cathedral of Quito, Ecuador, two plaques register the names of the city founders. Among them is Juan Padilla, my ancestor. I do not share this with pride, however, because Catholic churches such as this one were built on the ransacked ruins of ancient Inca, Aztec, and Maya temples. Colonial Christendom was erected on the pillage and plunder of the native population, who were also my ancestors. The original inhabitants of Abya Yala received the Christian gospel on the blade of a sword when the Spanish and Portuguese conquistadores "discovered" them at the end of the fifteenth century.[4] In the words of John Mackay, "The sword and the cross entered into partnership. It was this partnership, formed in the name of evangelism, in which the sword opened the way for the cross, and the cross sanctified the work of the sword, that constituted the originality of Spanish Christianity."[5]

The god of imperial power blessed military conquest and thirst for wealth, and brought with him unintelligible languages, intractable ill-nesses, and alien cultural traditions. Says Mackay, "While their religious message was entirely devoid of ethical content and their own lives of Christian attractiveness and consistency, the *conquistadores* had a passion for the external rites of Catholicism."[6] The *conquistadores* could piously attend mass on Sunday morning, beat an indigenous slave to death in the afternoon, and rape several indigenous women at night. Deprived of agency and dignity, with no access to the Bible, and simply deriving their understanding of Christianity from the behavior of the Europeans, the people called into being by this imperial god learned to superimpose foreign ritualistic religious practices onto their traditional ways, intermingling them into forms acceptable to the ruling authorities in varying expressions of religious patriotism. Yet they often lacked a deep-seated passion for God, and the consequent ethical commitment that would make itself visible in day-to-day life, their values, their priorities, and their relationships.

A few notable exceptions did make known the "other Spanish Christ," the Christ of the Gospels. Catholic priests such as Antonio Montesinos, and Bartolomé de Las Casas, advocated for the life and dignity of the original inhabitants of the Americas. Jesuit Pedro Claver served for many years in the Colombian port city of Cartagena as a self-appointed "slave to the slaves." As missionaries like these gave their lives away in

---

[3]See Ondina González and Justo L. González, *Christianity in Latin America: A History* (New York: Cambridge University Press, 2008), for a valuable overview. Also find primary sources in Klaus Koschorke, Frieder Ludwig, and Mariano Delgado, eds., *A History of Christianity in Asia, Africa and Latin America, 1450–1990: A Sourcebook* (Grand Rapids, MI: Eerdmans, 2007), 277-418.

[4]Abya Yala is a compound term coined by the Guna (or Kuna) people who live in present-day Panama and Colombia. It means "land of plenitude and maturity" and has been employed by autochthonous groups to refer to what Europeans named America. The usage of the term is customary now in decolonization circles which affirm the rights of indigenous peoples. It is also increasingly being used more broadly as a more felicitous term than "Latin America" since it focuses on the land shared by peoples from many ethnic backgrounds, a continent that is not merely Latin or European but also indigenous, African, and Asian in makeup. This is the sense in which the term is employed in this chapter, interchangeably with the more traditional one, Latin America.

[5]John Alexander Mackay, *The Other Spanish Christ: A Study in the Spiritual History of Spain and South America* (New York: Macmillan, 1933), 26.

[6]Mackay, *Other Spanish Christ*, 37.

compassionate pastoral work, selfless service, and the defense of the dignity of all people, they made God known as the loving one, who protects the weak, affirms diverse cultural values, and builds a faithful community from the bottom up.

During colonial Christendom, the Roman Catholic Church was not only the hegemonic religious power. It was also the keeper of the keys to citizenship. No person was officially born, married, educated, recognized as dead, or buried unless they were Roman Catholic. Since the only registry was the Roman Catholic Church, Protestants, Jews, and people who claimed no faith had no legal personhood and no recourse in the face of abuse. Church and civil power were inextricably bound.

The church under commercial power, and education and the Bible among the people. As the Latin American colonies fought and gained independence from Spain, toward the beginning of the nineteenth century, they began organizing into national entities and sought to gain a place in the "modern" world of progress, technology, and education. In order for the young nations to open commercial relations with the Protestant European nations, they had to break the hegemony of the Roman Catholic Church; otherwise Protestant Christians would not be welcome. Consequently, in many instances, commercial agreements included clauses on freedom of worship.

Immigrant Protestant churches that were formed during the commercial expansion of the British and Dutch powers were often uncritical of the business interests of their nations in the new world, even when the pursuit of those interests demanded the exploitation of indigenous people or involvement in the slave trade. The double ethic of proper religiosity on the one hand and self-interested business practices on the other marked the people who rallied around the god of commercial prosperity. There are fascinating stories of British pirates who read the Bible and prayed before plundering Spanish ships and paying dues to the newly forming countries.[7]

In contrast, there were women and men who sacrificially lived the good news of the reign of God not only in their private lives but also in the public arena, serving especially the more relegated sectors of society and validating their inclusion as full citizens. Their most significant contribution was making the Bible and education accessible to people who had been deprived of them for centuries. Among them, English missionary Allen Gardiner worked among indigenous populations. Scottish missionary James "Diego" Thompson, with the support of the British Bible Society and the Lancasterian Society, distributed Bibles, began a teachers' training college in Peru, and opened schools in the poorest areas for indigenous and black children. He advocated for the education of women, saying, "Female education in my opinion is the thing most wanted in every country; and when it shall be properly attended to, the renovation of the world will go on rapidly."[8]

Along with Francisco Penzotti, known as the first great Latin American promoter of Protestantism, Thompson introduced the New Testament as a school textbook. He also translated the New Testament into the Quechua language so the indigenous people of the Andes and the jungle could read it. For the translation, he

---

[7]See papers published in *Journal of Latin American Theology* 6, no. 2 (2011), and the work of Mexican historian Lourdes de Ita Rubio.
[8]Tomás Gutierrez, "James Thompson in Perú: Protestant Influence in the Beginning of the Republic," *Journal of Latin American Theology: Christian Reflections from the Latino South* 6, no. 2 (2011): 140.

collaborated with willing Roman Catholic priests, who also helped distribute Bibles. This ecumenical and holistic model of mission not only marked many church communities at the time but also opened a track on which future generations were able to tread.

Moving into the early twentieth century, we encounter Latin American Christian intellectuals and activists such as Erasmo Braga and Baez Camargo, and missionaries such as John Mackay and William Morris, who took on roles in public education and in the shaping of public policy for the common good out of their Christian convictions. Through education and new access to Scriptures, "Oppressed sectors like African slaves, freed slaves, and indigenous people heard in the non-conformist Protestant message a call to faith and hope in their fight for freedom."[9]

The church called into being through access to the Bible and education were women and men who knew their dignity as people made in God's image, and for whom faith was not merely a Sunday matter but one that infused the whole of their lives, attitudes, relationships, priorities, values, and transformative presence in the broader society.

The church under global capitalism, and the power of radical discipleship. As geopolitics shifted toward the end of the nineteenth century, and the United States gained ascendancy, mission and empire took a new turn. Latin America continued to feel the impact of foreign mission work, but the origin of the missionaries and the funding for church life and work shifted significantly from Europe, with its Protestant ethos, to North America, with its more independent, "faith-based" evangelical and Pentecostal denominational paradigms. In a century marked by world wars, the Cold War, military dictatorships, revolutions, and growing exploitation, Latin American nations and all sectors of society were wooed or compelled to follow the suit of their powerful northern neighbor. So-called free-trade agreements drew them into the global market, in which everything and everyone is susceptible to being bought and sold. To this day, while US farmers are paid for dumping their crops, Central American farmers watch their corn rot because prices bottomed out, thanks to the surplus shipped from the United States. While US consumers dispose of clothes outdated by the latest fashion, Central Americans slave away in sweatshops with no labor laws to protect them. While capital is free to travel, invested and divested at will and for the benefit of big business, only wealthy people—with passports or visas of the empire—are truly free to come and go. The other millions are held down, deprived of any right to hope for a way out of poverty, free only to be victimized by gangs, die in the desert, or become rejected nobodies in the wealthy north.

As the self-identified evangelical and Pentecostal population grew in the region, and particularly in Central America, churches were not immune to the shining neon lights of consumerism and the illusion that bigger is always better. With a triumphalist spirit, many entered the race for the largest *templo*, the farthest-reaching radio, the record number of members. Many scrambled to mix in with the governing elites and establish business connections that would favor evangelicals' interests. Contemporary "apostles" began to wear, drive, and exude the symbols of success. Massive growth, alliances with state and financial leaders, and the impact

[9]Jaime Adrián Prieto Valladares, "Historical Antecedents of Protestantism, the Beginnings of the Spread of the Bible in Independent Central America," *Journal of Latin American Theology* 6, no. 2 (2011): 186.

of positive images all crowded out any need for suffering. In the understanding of many, the days of being persecuted or excluded for one's faith were buried in the past, when evangelicals were a minority with no say in the makings of their countries.

In stark contrast to these religious expressions were two movements of radical discipleship that sprouted from the seeds of public education and the Bible in the hands of the people that had been planted in Abya Yala during the nineteenth century. Earlier in the twentieth century, these seeds had matured into small but growing local churches, the members of which were known as the "Bible people" and *evangelistas*, and were often persecuted by the Roman Catholic majority. The two indigenous and transnational movements of the mid-twentieth century that generated alternative Christian communities that engaged with the social realities of the context were the *misión integral* movement among radical *evangélicos* and the Roman Catholic *comunidades de base*. As the last stop in our historical trek we turn briefly to these movements, which have been more thoroughly described in other publications.[10] Mention is also made of the Pentecostal movement, which, as such, cuts across the boundaries of traditional church denominations.

The* misión integral *movement. The seeds of the radical *evangélico* movement were sown by early twentieth-century Protestant-evangelical pioneers such as those already mentioned. The first shoots became visible when several Latin American Christian student movements came together in Cochabamba, Bolivia, in 1958 to form the Comunidad Internacional de Estudiantes Evangélicos. And the plant struck root more broadly with the formation and growth of the Fraternidad Teológica Latinoamericana, from 1970 onwards.[11] At the core of both movements was a group of friends, principally three couples—Lilly and Samuel Escobar, Emma and Pedro Arana, and Caty and René Padilla—who built theologically both on their transnational belonging, as each was formed in part in Europe and in the United States, as well as on their Latin American evangelical matrix.[12] They intentionally situated themselves within the Latin American context, which was marked by revolutionary fervor on the one hand and by a lack of solid biblical teaching in churches on the other. They were committed to responding to the issues of that context and strengthening the capacity of the church to contribute out of the stores of their faith to the transformation of society. Together they developed what has come to be known as *misión integral*, a theological-missiological articulation and practice that seeks to engage followers of Jesus in linking the whole gospel to the whole of life under the lordship of Christ in the power of the Holy Spirit so that the reign of God and God's justice may be made visible in particular historical contexts.

For these friends, the vocation of theology was to nourish the mission of the church, so their academic work was pastorally and missiologically directed. The radical, socially all-encompassing

---

[10]See, for example, Samuel Escobar, "Doing Theology on Christ's Road," in *Global Theology in Evangelical Perspective: Exploring the Contextual Nature of Theology and Mission*, ed. Jeffrey P. Greenman and Gene L. Green (Downers Grove, IL: IVP Academic, 2012), 67-85.

[11]See Daniel Salinas, *Latin American Evangelical Theology in the 1970s: The Golden Decade* (Leiden: Brill, 2009); Carlos Mondragón, "Los movimientos estudiantiles como precursores de movimientos teológicos: el caso de la FTL. Consulta 2014: La FTL: Su Identidad y Misión Hacia el Siglo XXI" (paper presented at FTL Consultation, San José, Costa Rica, September 22, 2014).

[12]See Ruth Padilla DeBorst, "Latin American Communities I: *Comunidad Internacional de Estudiantes Evangélicos* and the *Fraternidad Teológica Latinoamericana*," in "Integral Mission Formation in *Abya Yala* (Latin America): A Study of the Centro de Studios Teológicos Interdisciplinarios (1982–2002) and Radical *Evangélicos*" (PhD diss., Boston University, 2016), 94-142.

perspective earned this movement and its adherents the rejection of more conservative sectors of the Latin American church, who to this day write them off as communists. Meanwhile, their respect for Scripture as the Word of God caused more liberal sectors to judge them as far too conservative. Even so, through speaking, teaching, preaching, publishing, and dialoguing in homes, churches, campuses, seminaries, and conferences across Latin America and beyond, and through their own engagement in the life and ministry of local congregations, they influenced the understanding and practice of church for hundreds of church leaders and lay professionals.

The comunidades de base *movement.* The Vatican II process (1962–1965) catalyzed renewal in the Roman Catholic Church, and suddenly millions of people who had never had access to Scripture were able to purchase Bibles in their language. The Bible Societies began selling Bibles across Abya Yala as never before. While previously the Roman Catholic Mass had always been led in Latin, priests were finally allowed to minister it in Spanish. God's Word reached God's people, and in cities, villages, and rural settings, women and men began gathering in circles of Bible study and prayer. So began the Comunidades Eclesiales de Base, gatherings of believers who explored the Bible in light of their context and their context in light of Scripture. Father Armando Márquez Ochoa, head of the Comunidades Eclesiales de Base (El Salvador), explained: "We gathered as a believing community around God's Word, and so we gained a vision of God's kingdom. Out of that vision grew our commitment to the transformation of our context and service in the community."[13] As was

the case with the *misión integral* movement, undergirding the theological articulations of many liberationists was the living, breathing, suffering, and thriving reality of local communities of believers who sought to live into the already inaugurated reign of God.[14]

The Pentecostal and neo-Pentecostal movement. The Pentecostal movement was born early in the twentieth century at the margins of Christian life, among the lower classes; but it grew exponentially in the second half of the century to occupy center stage. It struck a chord of popular religiosity in ways not achieved by the established Catholic Church or the illumined Protestant circles. Central to Pentecostal teaching is the baptism of the Holy Spirit; a focus on emotion, freedom, and spontaneity in worship; a search for holiness; an apocalyptic eschatology; direct access to biblical revelation; and the empowerment of laypeople, including women, many of whom lead churches and freely exposit Scripture.

Over the last forty years, Pentecostal growth became explosive and has resulted in many new denominations, churches, and church members. It has also had a noticeable impact on all denominations, including the Roman Catholic Church. Although initially many Pentecostal preachers rejected education, including theological education, and some considered the Bible to be merely a legalistic compendium of "dos" and "don'ts," many have more recently begun deepening their theological formation, their appreciation for responsible Bible study, their involvement in social matters, and their crosscultural mission initiatives.[15]

---

[13]Father Armando Márquez, personal conversation with author, San Salvador, August 12, 2005.

[14]See Carlos Sosa Siliezar, "Ecclesiology in Latin America: A Biblical Perspective," in this volume for further details on this process.

[15]For an example, see Ruth Padilla DeBorst, "The Social-Ethical Impact of CETI: Formation Nourishing Transformation," in Padilla DeBorst, "Integral Mission Formation in *Abya Yala*," 313-33.

Contrasting postures regarding power are also present in this movement. Native and imported neo-Pentecostal churches and neo-apostolic churches began to consolidate during the last decades of the twentieth century, many of them with strong elements of prosperity gospel, ostentatious buildings, and weak processes of financial accountability. Plenty of megachurch leaders in Latin America today claim their inheritance as children of the sovereign King and feed off their congregations in order to wrap themselves in the trappings of power and prestige of our consumer society. Some see the rapid growth of Pentecostal and evangelical churches as a sure sign that "our time" has come: after centuries of Catholic hegemony, it is now our turn to assert political ascendency and benefit from the privileges of power. In contrast, other Pentecostal pastors and congregations have sacrificially moved into some of the most violence-ridden neighborhoods, befriended gang members, and opened opportunities for them to find livelihoods. As did the Lord they follow, they are making God's love tangible through their embrace of the rejects of society.[16] As a result of his study of Pentecostalism in El Salvador, researcher Timothy Wadkins attributed much of the credit for the "social consciousness" of the Misión Cristiana Elim and the way its leaders "prophetically apply the gospel to El Salvador's crushing social reality" to "a careful reading of the gospels and the somewhat quiet influence of the . . . Latin American Theological Fraternity," and to the Center for Interdisciplinary Theological Studies, generated in Argentina by radical *evangélicos*: "In their two-year training program they emphasize what they call integral ministry—an emphasis on God's comprehensive, incarnational intention of not leaving any human and any corner of the earth untouched by his love."[17]

As we have trekked through the centuries, while the eyes of faith reveal the work of the triune God calling God's people into full life as citizens of God's reign and promoters of God's love and justice in the world, they also lay bare the glory and dust proper to any human venture. This jumbled and paradoxical portrayal points to the ambiguity of the church, a people riddled by the very same challenges as any other human gathering, yet drawn together by the divine Community-of-Love with the highest of purposes: being the dwelling place of that Community—the palpable, historical expression of reconciling love—and living in the world as citizens of a realm governed by the eternal, life-giving Creator of all. The following two sections probe the identity and calling of the church, with a special focus on its capacity and potential as a school of citizenship that is critical of any power that conspires against God's life-giving agenda in the world and that seeks transformation in light of that agenda.

THE CHURCH: A SCHOOL FOR CITIZENSHIP

The people gathered that March Sunday in La Lucila included the unlikely combination of home-making women, students, recovering drug addicts, long-term Christians, professionals from many fields, young people, manual laborers, newly converted Christians, immigrants, high-powered businesspeople, unemployed people, elderly people, foreigners, and native Argentines. After a long week of work and the shared burden of an oppressive government

---

[16]A powerful example is the life, ministry, and writing of Church of God pastor Darío Lopez in Perú.
[17]Timothy Wadkins, letter to Eliberto Juárez, Canisius College, Buffalo, New York, July 1, 2011.

and the climbing cost of living, worship services constituted an opportunity to rest, to celebrate life with music and fellowship, to take personal and national burdens to God in prayer, to regain hope through reflection on God's Word in community, to grapple with ethical dilemmas, and to muster courage for living faithfully throughout the new week. Yet further, for most of the people gathered, church services and assemblies were the only places where they had a voice, their opinion was welcome, and their perspective was respectfully received. The annual ordination service affirmed the lordship of Christ over every dimension of life, as well as the value of each person and every occupation; none of them was more worthy or more sacred than any other. Everyone was recognized as an active member of the community and a responsible citizen in God's economy. Within the faith community, women and men, young and old, gained a clear sense of their identity as members of God's people, of the gifts granted by the Spirit, and of their calling to follow Jesus in the world without belonging fully to it. Theirs was a lived definition of church, experienced less as a static condition and more as the constant double movement Jesus referred to in his prayers and words to his disciples.[18] They were being called out of the world into one body and granted a distinctive identity, and they were being sent into the world in radical followership of Jesus for the sake of God's life-giving, transformative purposes. Without necessarily articulating it in the very words of the Nicene Creed, this double movement experienced by the members of that local congregation echoed that ancient affirmation: they were holy, called out, separate; they were one in spite of their significant social differences; and

they were *apostolic*, grounded in the ministry of the apostles and sent out, as they had been, into the world as witnesses of the good news.[19]

Called out to be the people of the Community-of-Love. Not a place and not an institutional structure, the Greek *ekklēsia* was an assembly of citizens called out from their homes and gathered in some public place. The testimonies and letters compiled in the New Testament depict the *iglesia* (church) as a body politic composed of women and men who are called out of their particularity to integrate into a distinct community. In contrast to the biddings in the *polis*, however, the call is not issued by some passing political authority, but by their sovereign Creator, who in the past had already called a people together to serve as a living, loving witness of God's good purposes in the world (see Gen 18:18; 22:18; 26:4). In contrast to the unity enforced by Roman armies and deterring crucifixions, the church is drawn together by the love of the incarnate, crucified, risen, and ruling Christ. Rather than being held together by crippling fear and grueling taxation, the church is granted unity by the life-giving Spirit, who extends bridges across linguistic, ethnic, and social differences. In sum, through God's gracious action, Christians become the people of the Community-of-Love and citizens of a new realm (Eph 2:13-22; 1 Pet 2:9-10). Citizenship under the rule of this loving community is not purchased or earned; it is not subject to migratory eligibility or dependent on skin color or ethnicity. Belonging, in God's new humanity, is a condition freely granted to all who admit to their created condition, acknowledge Jesus Christ as Savior and Lord, recognize that their very breath depends on the living Spirit, look

---

[18]See Jesus' prayers and words to his disciples in Jn 17:15-18; 20:21.
[19]See Veli-Matti Kärkkäinen's chapter in this section.

forward to God's complete restoration of the entire creation, and live in light of these confessions in the world.

Citizenship under the rule of the Community-of-Love is not some otherworldly, extra-terrestrial, or imagined condition, but a concrete belonging embodied in the church. That real, existing community is portrayed in the unburnished New Testament accounts of the early church as it grew, spread out, and grappled with cultural differences, human greed, power contestations, and external persecution in light of the ultimate leveling and reconciling work of Jesus. They nourished hopeful perseverance by singing their faith, writing letters, and visiting one another. Notable in spite of their growing pains and expressions of fallen human nature is the extrabiblical historical testimony of their contemporaries, who attest to the integrity of the message taught and lived out by these early Christians.[20] In contrast to many churches today, they did not invest in buildings but met in houses. The money gathered from tithes and offerings was then freed up to support the work of missions, to purchase the freedom of slaves, and to care for widows and orphans. Along the way, the church grew because it lived what it preached as an alternative community in which they were tutored in citizenship for life within the church and in society at large.

In like manner today, popular Protestant-evangelical-Pentecostal churches "have become alternative societies that create a closed world where people are accepted and become actors, not on the basis of what gives them status in the world, but of the values that come from their vision of the kingdom of God."[21] The story of that March day in Buenos Aires illustrates this very point. So do the studies of Timothy Wadkins, who, having researched a variety of Protestant-evangelical churches in Central America, discovered that, although "individualized rituals of community building such as prayer, Bible reading, and personal testimony" could be considered socially alienating, they actually serve as "micro acts of democracy." "Over time . . . what begins in conversion and is sustained in the context of such deeply rooted communities of faith and personal piety, could lead to the kinds of social organization that have the power to rise up against injustice, overturn the submissive, status quo politics of traditional Christianity, and lay the foundation of democratic participation and social change."[22]

Again, membership in the ecclesial gathering serves as a practice run for citizenship in the broader society, and leads to the second movement of the church in relation to the broader world.

Called to follow Jesus into the world. While God's people are called out of the world to become an alternative community, they are simultaneously called to enter the world. Says René Padilla, "To speak of the Kingdom of God is to speak of God's redemptive purpose for the whole creation and of the historical vocation that the church has with regard to that purpose here and now, 'between the times.'"[23]

---

[20]A fascinating example is the Epistle to Diognetus. See also Rodney Stark, *The Rise of Christianity: How the Obscure Marginal Jesus Movement Became the Dominant Religious Force in the Western World in a Few Centuries* (San Francisco: HarperSanFrancisco, 1997).

[21]Samuel Escobar, "A Missiological Approach to Latin American Protestantism," *International Review of Mission* 87, no. 345 (April 1998): 170.

[22]Timothy Wadkins, "Getting Saved in El Salvador: The Preferential Option for the Poor," *International Review of Mission* 97, no. 384/385 (2008): 46. Wadkins's work is representative of what Samuel Escobar denominates "a new generation of social scientists working at the micro level [who] have brought to light the transforming nature of the spiritual experience offered by these churches" (Escobar, "Missiological Approach," 170).

[23]René Padilla, *Mission Between the Times: Essays on the Kingdom* (Carlisle, UK: Langham Monographs, 2010), 186.

Recognition that the whole created order belongs to God compels the people who live under God's rule to engage with all dimensions of human experience. The crucial issue is from where and in what manner this engagement takes place. The pattern of the church's involvement must follow that of the King it represents. The amazingly subversive good news is that God, the Creator and Sustainer of all that is, in Christ squeezed into time-limited, earth-bound, suffering human form. God could have remedied all the world's maladies in one grand swoop of life-giving power. But that's not the God of the gospel. God could have spoken justice into our unequal world. But that is not the God of the gospel. God could have decreed sustenance for all that lives—from above, from outside, without getting God's hands dirty. But that is not the God of the gospel. God could have extended a compassionate hand from a distance. But that is not the God of the gospel. Instead, consistent with the relational nature of the Community-of-Love, God chose to enter the world God so loves and, in this way, to bridge the greatest divide of all, the one that separates a broken, fumbling, wandering humanity from its Source of life, from itself, and from the rest of the creation of which it is a part. Further yet, far from entering through the splendorous gates of a Roman imperial family, with all its trappings of grandeur and dominion, God approached a poor Palestinian woman to become a working-class boy in an occupied territory and was first visited by simple shepherd folk. God became a fearful refugee in a foreign land. God became an anonymous worker, carving stone and wood for wealthy folk. God became an itinerant teacher, with no place to rest his head. God befriended women and despised imperial lackeys. God knelt and washed the dusty feet of bewildered and treacherous fishermen. God became a criminal, executed to demonstrate the fate of anyone who dared disturb the deathly Pax Romana. And it was from there, from the bottom up, from inside, from underneath, that God sovereignly effected the most astounding reversal of all times. By entering the darkest darkness, the abyss of death and alienation and sheer aloneness—"Father, Father, why have you abandoned me?!"—God broke those chains of death and alienation and sheer aloneness. God, the Community-of-Love, worked a true peace into the dough of a fractured society, not one precariously pounded together by iron nails and grueling taxation. In Christ, the Creator continued the work of creation. God began fashioning a new humanity by effecting peace, Pax Christi, weaving together the unlikeliest assortment of women and men—slaves, slaveowners, freed slaves, manual workers, wealthy homeowners, Jews and Greeks—into a new humanity.

For the church today, following Christ's choice to set aside his power and "move into the neighborhood" (Jn 1:14 MSG) entails sacrificial incarnation in the messiness of socioeconomic, political, and ecological realities. Following Christ's life choices entails making similar ones: befriending the people who are marginalized by systems of power and exclusion, recruiting them for active ministry, and reinstating them to their rightful place in society. Following the King who chose the way of the cross and rejected violence entails abandoning "Christendom projects," which confuse the kingdom of God with the institutional church, the gospel with culture, and the power of the cross with the power of the sword.[24] Following the King who rose from the dead and rules sovereignly today entails resisting every form of imperialism, relativizing the authority of all rulers, nations, and powers, pledging ultimate allegiance only to the Kingdom of God, and "bearing witness to God's purpose of love and justice revealed in Jesus Christ, in the power of the Holy Spirit."[25]

CONCLUSION

Necessary questions in light of these reflections are: Is the evangelical church in Latin America, in the United States, and around the world living into its calling as a people called out of the world into another primary belonging as the people of the Community-of-Love? Is its life as a community such that all members participate as active citizens and are ordained to contribute as Christians to the broader society? Is the presence and witness of the church in the world distinctive, not thanks to some religious veneer but by virtue of its ethical embodiment of God's reign? Does the church pay ultimate allegiance to the powers of the day or to the Lord of life, the God of history?

The people gathered in La Lucila that March morning were being schooled in these matters. And as they faced the world in light of the Word, and vice versa, they grew in their capacity to live out a different citizenship as active members under the reign of the Community-of-Love in the world.

FURTHER READING

Arias, Mortimer. *Announcing the Reign of God*. Philadelphia: Fortress, 1984.

Cook, Guillermo. *New Face of the Church in Latin America: Between Tradition and Change*. Maryknoll, NY: Orbis, 1994.

González, Ondina E., and Justo L. González. *Christianity in Latin America: A History*. New York: Cambridge University Press, 2008.

Journal of Latin American Theology Special Issue on 19th-Century Protestantism 6, no. 2 (2011).

Míguez Bonino, José. *Faces of Latin American Protestantism*. Grand Rapids, MI: Eerdmans, 1997.

Mondragón, Carlos. *Like Leaven in the Dough: Protestant Social Thought in Latin America 1920–1950*. Madison: Fairleigh Dickinson, 2011.

Padilla, René. "La Nueva Eclesiología en América Latina." *Boletín Teológico FTL* 18, no. 24 (Diciembre 1986): 201-226.

Yamamori, Tetsunao, and C. René Padilla. *The Local Church, Agent of Transformation: An Ecclesiology for Integral Mission*. Buenos Aires: Ediciones Kairós, 2004.

Yoder, John H., Lilia Solano, and C. René Padilla. *Iglesia, Ética y Poder*. Buenos Aires: Ediciones Kairós, 1998.

---

[24]Orlando E. Costas, *Christ Outside the Gate: Mission Beyond Christendom* (Maryknoll, NY: Orbis, 1992), 181. See also José Míguez Bonino, *Toward a Christian Political Ethics* (Minneapolis: Fortress, 2007), 98; Paul John Davies, "Faith Seeking Effectiveness: The Missionary Theology of José Míguez Bonino" (PhD diss., Utrecht University, 2006).

[25]René Padilla, "The Ebb and Flow of Kingdom Theology and Its Implications for Mission," in *Evangelical and Frontier Mission Perspectives on the Global Progress of the Gospel*, ed. Beth Snodderly and A. Scott Moreau (Oxford: Regnum, 2011), 285.

35

TWO TALES OF
EMERGING ECCLESIOLOGY IN ASIA

AN INQUIRY INTO THEOLOGICAL SHAPING

Wonsuk Ma

ECCLESIOLOGY IN ASIA, especially in evangelical and Pentecostal and charismatic circles, has not been adequately articulated. This study examines the shaping of ecclesiology in two "free churches": the Word of Life group in China and the Yoido Full Gospel Church in Korea. The study illustrates the need for theological construction and articulation in Asia, as the former has no ties with churches outside the country, while the latter has developed its own unique understanding of the church. The study also demonstrates that, in these two particular cases, the founders and the social contexts play a significant role in the theological shaping of each community. Hence, their ecclesiologies have been functional in nature, and their sense of a relationship to the historic tradition of ecclesiology is minimal. The urgency is further felt as these two communities represent a thriving and fast-growing segment of Asian Christianity.

ECCLESIOLOGY IN ASIA

The Christian presence on this continent is ancient. In fact, the church was born in Asia. And yet, today, in many parts of Asia, Christianity remains a foreign religion. This directly affects how Christians as well as society understand the community of followers of Christ that is called the church, especially its nature and function.

The historic churches have shown encouraging efforts in reflecting on the engagement between the Christian gospel and sociocultural contexts. The Roman Catholic Church has done impressive theological work, especially after Vatican II. The Federation of Asian Bishops' Conferences has been shaping a new participatory model of the church for decades, particularly paying close attention to a dialogue between church hierarchy and women.[1] Equally active is the publication program of Christian Conference of Asia, which is the regional arm of the World Council of Churches. Again, it has consciously engaged with

---

[1] An extensive study is found in Thao Nguyen, "A New Way of Being Church for Mission: Asian Catholic Bishops and Asian Catholic Women in Dialogue: A Study of the Documents of the Federation of Asian Bishops' Conference (FABC)" (PhD diss., Graduate Theological Union, Berkeley, 2013). For other Catholic resources, see "Publications," Federation of Asian Bishops' Conferences, www.fabc.org/pub_p8.html, accessed April 28, 2020.

Asian contexts and issues.[2] Mainline Protestant churches also seem to have been paying attention to this theologizing process. With their theological identities relatively well established, the natural next step will be to become relevant in the Asian setting. One Christian Conference of Asia publication, although dated, is devoted specifically to the diverse nature of the church and its life in several Asian countries, primarily in response to the historical, cultural, and social context of each church.[3]

When it comes to the evangelical and free churches, including Pentecostal ones, studies of the nature and function of the church are relatively rare, especially ones that take Asian contexts into account. Only recently have some efforts begun to appear among evangelicals.[4] For indigenous churches with little or no affiliation with Western churches, theological reflection is even more scarce. Of course, these churches will have different theologizing processes from historic ones, which received their theology from the Western mother churches. Free churches, unlike the historic churches, tend to be more autonomous, without a mother church or its accompanying well-developed theology. Moreover, even Asian churches that have Western mother churches may exercise relative autonomy in their ecclesial structure and theology.

Two Case Studies

This study is an initial attempt to address the immense need presently in the new churches in

Asia. The approach is to select two church groups in East Asia and trace the development of their ecclesiologies. The first is a house church network in China called the Word of Life Church in Henan Province, a post–Cultural Revolution era indigenous house church. The second is Yoido Full Gospel Church in Seoul, Korea, a Pentecostal congregation with a network of sister and daughter churches. Both are representative of the "newer" churches in Asia.

These two cases are selected for several reasons. Both are extremely influential churches, and both claim a large membership. The Word of Life Church is estimated to have three million followers throughout China, while Yoido Church and its network form the world's single largest congregation, with more than seven hundred thousand members. The rise and growth of the Word of Life Church provides a model for, and its influence on, house church movements in China. Its recent decline also reveals the structural vulnerability of rural house church networks, which rely heavily on their leader-founders. Yoido Church and its founder, David Yonggi Cho, have established a unique Korean interpretation of Pentecostal theology and spirituality. Its "full gospel" theology has had a far-reaching impact on Korean Christianity and beyond. Most importantly, however, my choice of these two was motivated by their active engagement with their contexts, their own reading of the Scriptures, their adaptation or modification of any "received" theology (especially in

---

[2]"CCA Publications," Christian Conference of Asia, www.cca.org.hk/home/publications, accessed October 10, 2016. Although dated, a ten-year process of developing Asian theology with Asian resources is a fine example: John C. England and Archie C. C. Lee, *Doing Theology with Asian Resources: Ten Years in the Formation of Living Theology in Asia* (Auckland: Programme for Theology and Cultures in Asia, 1993).

[3]Kwok Nai Wang, *The Local Church* (Hong Kong: Christian Conference of Asia, 2005).

[4]In the Philippines, for example, Asian Theological Seminary has held a very successful annual theological conference dealing with theological and missional themes. Its proceedings have been published, serving as valuable resources: see "ATS Theological Forum Books," Asian Theological Seminary, www.ats.ph/ats-theological-forum-books/, accessed April 28, 2020. Its first publication was E. Acoba et al., *Doing Theology in the Philippines* (Quezon City, Philippines: OMF, 2005).

the case of the full gospel theology), and the processes of their own theology shaping. This creativity has resulted in some controversies, and yet their theologizing processes are noteworthy.

Approaching the Subject

My focus is on the shaping of local theologies, preferably those perceived among members of the churches. The focus of observation is on the process through which each community has been shaped, and how it is understood to function and operate. On the one hand, it negotiates and interacts with, and sometimes reacts to, the context. On the other hand, it reads and interprets the Bible and draws from Christian traditions. This theology, often unarticulated, is lived out in church and daily life. As I began observing these two churches, I soon realized that traditional theological categories would not be adequate for analyzing the living process of theologization.

This is primarily due to the fact that the received theology and its categories are shaped and sustained in a Western Christendom setting. In such a religious context, the church existed predominantly to provide pastoral care to the parishioners. The world was perceived to be a fully Christian empire, to some degree. In contrast, the Asian church today exists in constant engagement with the world, which is sometimes even hostile to Christianity. The place and function of the church, therefore, is heavily shaped by this context and experience.

I have been immensely aided by several creative inquiries on contemporary ecclesiology. The first is a work by Veli-Matti Kärkkäinen. Well exposed to Asian realities through his mis-

sionary work, he characterizes each of the six major ecclesiological traditions with their theological foci. His exploration of several new and emerging churches and their ecclesiologies (for example, African Independent Churches) is particularly enlightening. The present study is focused on the category of "free church" in Kärkkäinen's categories.[5] Equally refreshing are the ecclesiological categories which Gerald Bray has proposed through his historical study. In his survey of the New Testament church and subsequent persecuted and imperial churches, he ultimately raises the question of what the fundamental tenets of the church might be, in light of diverse traditions and forms.[6] If this question is posed to believers in the Global South, whose population corresponds to two-thirds of the world's Christians, I suspect the responses will be challengingly different from those one gets from the North.

Because of my interest in the construction of ecclesiologies, Simon Chan's book on grassroots theology in Asia has a strong appeal.[7] It is particularly helpful in the case of the Word of Life Church, due to the scarcity of any "magisterial" theology. As Chan proposes, this study will assess each church with regard to both (1) the stories of its members, often expressed in the church's testimonies, sermons, programs, and leaders, and (2) ancient theological traditions, specifically the Nicene-Constantinopolitan Creed.

There are several foci to which I will pay particular attention: the theological formation of the founding leader of each church, the self-understanding of the nature of the church, and the perception of the mission of the church. Relying

---

[5]Veli-Matti Kärkkäinen, *An Introduction to Ecclesiology: Ecumenical, Historical and Global Perspectives* (Downers Grove, IL: IVP Academic, 2002), 194-201, 59-67.
[6]Gerald Bray, *The Church: A Theological and Historical Account* (Grand Rapids, MI: Baker Academic, 2016), viii.
[7]Simon Chan, *Grassroots Asian Theology: Thinking the Faith from the Ground Up* (Downers Grove, IL: IVP Academic, 2014).

on empirical evidence is pertinent in observing the Word of Life Church, as I have had few encounters with founder Peter Xu. For the Yoido Church, I have maintained a reasonable degree of contact with both the clergy and the laity. More published materials are available for this case, which I intend to utilize.

PETER XU AND THE WORD OF LIFE CHURCH

Peter Yongze Xu (1940-). David Aikman categorizes Xu as one of the three "uncles" who served as the founders of three large house church networks in the post–Cultural Revolution era. They were responsible for the miraculous resurrection of Chinese Christianity after the communist takeover of this vast nation. Xu is also linked to today's Chinese Christianity through the previous or "patriarch" generation. Prayed over by his Christian grandfather, he grew up in a Christian family. It is even recorded that he saw visions at the age of five.[8] His first house arrest took place in 1967, and during the Cultural Revolution he was targeted for his "counterrevolutionary" offenses. In 1978, he emerged as a significant house church leader. His evangelistic teams spread beyond Henan Province to various other parts of China. After his imprisonment in 1982, a state persecution began, and many full-time evangelists were sent out for evangelism and church planting. This resulted in the establishment of more than three thousand churches by 1988.

However, Xu was concerned by the widespread emphasis on healing and miracles among many house church networks. Perhaps in reaction to this, his ministry stressed genuine regeneration and discipleship. With an increasing number of house churches and leaders joining Xu, the Born-Again Movement was born and grew to become perhaps the most controversial house church network in the country. The emphasis on a genuine experience of regeneration has also led this network to develop a heavy focus on evangelism.

Xu spent more than two decades of ministry as a fugitive hiding among the "floating population" during this turbulent time. This was also a time when he actively ministered to them, as he kept discovering hidden believers, both active and inactive. It is not unreasonable to suspect that his theology and ministry practices were affected by this experience and shaped through his reflection. The ever-mobile nature of his life must have been particularly significant in the understanding of the nature and purpose of the church (that is, ecclesiology) within his particular historical and social setting. There are two notable aspects of his ecclesiology: (1) how the nature of the church is understood, and (2) what is perceived to be the mission of the church. They are assumed as their theology is practiced, especially in the absence of any articulate theology.

The nature of the church. First, because they often gathered secretly for worship, Bible study, prayer, and fellowship, the marker of the church was not a visible building or an established organizational structure. The church was, and still is to a certain extent, identified primarily as the community of believers regardless of location. The first three points of the seven-point theology of the church concern the purity of the church through genuine conversion. They are: (1) salvation through the cross, (2) the way of the cross, and (3) discerning the adulteress (i.e., the Three-Self Patriotic

---

[8]David Aikman, *Jesus in Beijing: How Christianity Is Transforming China and Changing the Global Balance of Power* (Washington, DC: Regnery, 2003), 73-74, 87.

Movement).[9] This important characteristic of the Word of Life Church, as with most other unregistered churches, has been shaped by three contextual realities. The first is that there was no identifiable Western "mother" church to dictate the shape of the church. The second is the newness of its existence, without a historical link. The third is the social context, which prohibits any open gathering of people for religious activities unless registered. In addition to these contextual factors, it is notable that a reading of the book of Acts likely encouraged and reinforced this understanding of the church.

Second, its given sociopolitical context has kept this unregistered church illegal. Xu developed his serious ministry-consciousness through his (Christian) reading club in his vocational school years. Then his Christian faith was seriously questioned by the authorities "for a nonstop period of forty days," even "forcing him to remain standing for seventeen hours."[10] Subsequently, during the Cultural Revolution, he was in self-exile to hide from the authorities, and mostly separated from his family. Through his life, he experienced several imprisonments and house arrests. Details of how he was treated are not readily available, but I had a glimpse of such a persecuted life. In light of all this, it is not surprising to find in the seven-point theology of the church a theology of the cross. The second point reads: "Take the way of the cross to persevere in faith during suffering." Xin interprets such a period as a theologically formative process for becoming a missionary.[11]

Two junior women leaders from the Word of Life Church studied theology in the seminary where I served as the academic dean. Upon becoming Christian, they offered themselves to the service of the Lord. They participated in different forms of training and were sent to various parts of Henan Province for evangelism and church planting. Eventually, they were arrested by the authorities and sentenced to prison terms. They openly shared about the harsh treatment they had received during their incarceration, including utter humiliation before male prison guards as part of their punishment. They implied that most of their colleagues and leaders went through similar experiences. It was claimed that among ordinary believers, a popular perception was formed that imprisonment was a mark of one's devotion, thus preferable, if not necessary, for a leadership appointment.

The hostility of the world has kept the identity and mission of Christians and the church clear. Christianity is never viewed as a means to upward social mobility, as observed in some Christian sectors. Indeed, being Christian results in a voluntary downward social mobility. At a seminary chapel session, one of the women leaders shared her prayer after she was physically exposed for humiliation: "Thank you, Lord, for considering me worthy of participating in your suffering." As Gerald Bray has noted, persecution was a critical aspect of the early church, and some of the characteristics of this era are very similar to the experience of the Word of Life Church.[12] The seven-point doctrine of the Word of Life Church includes a statement affirming that the official Three-Self Patriotic Movement "embraces worldly authority."[13] The

---

[9]Yalin Xin, *Inside China's House Church Network: The Word of Life Movement and Its Renewing Dynamic* (Lexington, KY: Emeth, 2009), 80-81.
[10]Aikman, *Jesus in Beijing*, 87.
[11]For the whole seven points, see Xin, *Inside China's House Church Network*, 89-90.
[12]For example, the ascetic tendency and the decisive role of episcopacy (or leadership), the spread of the gospel, and an adverse social context largely resonate with the Word of Life Church. See Bray, *Church*, 61-89.
[13]Xin, *Inside China's House Church Network*, 89.

Three-Self Patriotic Movement "registered" churches have lawful status and are visibly organized but operate under government guidance. A distinct mark of the true church in the minds of most house church members, therefore, is suffering for refusing to submit to atheistic government policies.

The third characteristic of the Word of Life Church is that it understands itself to be a community of regenerated people of God. Following the free church model of ecclesiology, each member is expected to have repented of their sins, been forgiven by God, and become incorporated into the community of faith, and that is the church. Xu and the church have consistently stressed the necessity of discipleship, for which a genuine experience of regeneration is essential. Aikman contends that this was a reaction to the increasing Pentecostal faith among the house church networks. To foster such a lifestyle, the church encouraged its members to participate in spiritual retreats where repentance was emphasized and exhorted. Soon, it became common or even "normative . . . for everyone to weep," often for a prolonged period, as evidence of genuine repentance.[14] In spite of repeated denials by Xu and the leaders, many members, including local-level leaders, believe that weeping has obtained a significant theological meaning. The church soon became known as the Born-Again Movement or simply "the Weepers." By the mid-1990s, the security authorities and the Three-Self Patriotic Movement labeled the church as a cult and Xu as a cultic leader. This controversial issue led various house church networks to come together to work out theological and personality

differences and to set criteria for orthodox Christianity. This was further developed in 1998 to create a unified front against the government's persecution by adopting a common statement called "United Appeal of the Various Branches of the Chinese House Church."[15]

The strong emphasis on regeneration and Christian discipleship attracted many Christian groups, especially in the 1980s. A 1998 issue of *Christianity Today* rejected the claim of heresy and estimated that the church had reached about three million members.[16] Like most house church networks, Xu and his church often pray for healing and God's miraculous intervention. The work of the Holy Spirit in evangelism is particularly stressed. However, they do not encourage other spiritual gifts that are common among Pentecostals, such as speaking in tongues or prophecy. Luke Wesley, a Pentecostal academic working in China, concludes the group is evangelical in nature, but not Pentecostal:

> The Word of Life Church represents an interesting mixture of conservative theology and experiential piety. They expect to see miracles, pray for healing, and look to the Holy Spirit for supernatural guidance and deliverance. At the same time, they are generally quite closed to some manifestations of the gifts of the Spirit, such as prophecy and tongues. . . . I would classify this group as non-charismatic.[17]

The mission of the church. Based on the strong emphasis on genuine regeneration, the church has set evangelism as its foremost and primary mission. Xin points out that Xu had a deep appreciation for Christian leaders of previous eras

[14]Aikman, *Jesus in Beijing*, 88.

[15]For the full text, see Aikman, *Jesus in Beijing*, 293-94.

[16]Timothy C. Morgan, "A Tale of China's Two Churches," *Christianity Today*, July 13, 1998, 30-39. Similarly, Daniel H. Bays, *A New History of Christianity in China* (Malden, MA: Wiley-Blackwell, 2012), 195.

[17]Luke Wesley, *The Church in China: Persecuted, Pentecostal, and Powerful* (Baguio, Philippines: AJPS Books), 2004, 48.

and recalls how Xu drew much inspiration from Charles Finney's books that had been hand-copied during a difficult period. In 1983, the church's most important theological process took place when the church's theological position was articulated in the seven points (or "Seven Principles"). They begin with "salvation through the cross" and end with "frontier evangelism." New life in Christ is the absolute foundation for Christian discipleship and mission. The description of the last point is worth quoting, as this is the only one with a specific action plan prescribed: "This is the Great Commission of Christ to the Church for the fulfillment of God's eternal salvation scheme. As Chinese Christians, we are burdened with the one hundred million souls that need salvation. In order that the gospel be preached to all the people in China, frontier evangelistic teams should be organized and sent to the unreached areas."[18]

In the same year, 1983, with the government crackdown renewed, the church's top seventeen itinerant evangelists, called "Messengers of the Gospel," scattered, hiding themselves. The circumstances effectively pushed them into full-time ministry. The authority's persecution and opposition were instrumental in the creation of the powerful evangelistic program of the church, called the "Gospel Band."[19]

More intentionally, the church evolved to create a massive training program to serve the entire process of Christian discipleship, from conversion to evangelism and church planting. Each congregation implemented various levels of training programs, often mobile in location. The completion and publication of the two-volume training manual in 1987 enhanced the development of the training programs. The "missiological cycle" illustrates the life of an evangelist of the church: from short-term training and theological education (called "Seminary of the Field") to leading a member to join the Gospel Band. Eventually, teams of evangelists are sent out to frontier regions to establish house churches.[20]

Within the given social context, the development of house churches drew a large number of women, and thus young women have had a prominent role in leadership. Wesley describes eight leaders of the Word of Life Church, seven of whom were women, while most, if not all, of the leaders that the Philippines seminary trained were women. Xin, who participated in a number of congregations, estimates that about 70 percent of the church's members are women. He also believes that women make up about the same proportion of the Messengers of the Gospel, the backbone of the church's leadership structure.[21] This is common with other house church networks, reflecting the social circumstances in which they exist. In a number of places, Xin stresses the important leadership role of Xu Yongling, Peter's younger sister, especially when he was imprisoned. She may have served as a good role model for women in leadership within the church. However, the recent drastic decline of the Word of Life Church raises a serious question about the very nature and shape of this church, and particularly about the role of leadership. In the absence of strong leadership, the entire church network is now in danger of disintegration. The next case demonstrates a more stable structure.

---

[18]Xin, *Inside China's House Church Network*, 88-90.
[19]Xin, *Inside China's House Church Network*, 91. See 102-5 for details of the training, activities, and fruits of this program.
[20]Xin, *Inside China's House Church Network*, 99.
[21]Xin, *Inside China's House Church Network*, 105.

DAVID YONGGI CHO AND YOIDO FULL GOSPEL CHURCH

The development of this largest single congregation under Cho's leadership has been studied extensively. A brief overview of its half-century history highlights the development of its ecclesiology. Due to the decisive role of Cho in this process, his own theological formation is integral to the church's "full gospel" ecclesiology.

David Yonggi Cho (1936–) and the "full gospel." The development of this largest single congregation in the world is traced in three geographically oriented stages. David Yonggi Cho grew up through the turbulent changes of Korea: Japanese colonialism (1910–1945), independence (1945), the Korean War (1950–1953), military dictatorship (1970s and 1980s), and economic development (from the 1990s on). His conversion took place in his youth as he was dying of tuberculosis: he was healed at the same time as his spiritual birth. This brought a radical transformation to his life and to his attitude toward daily life in this postwar society.

His first tent church, called Full Gospel Church, was established in 1958 on the outskirts of the war-torn capital city of Seoul. Ministering to the urban poor, at the center of Cho's "full gospel" was the gift of healing and miracles. His church always expected the sick to be present, and the ministry of healing has been an integral part of almost all the gatherings of the church. The tent church was looked down on by the general population and by churches in the vicinity. Many objected to the makeshift state of the church building, and even more so to the internal makeup of the church. At the same time, the power of God attracted those who were marginalized and helpless. True to the Pentecostal tradition, this was a church *of* the poor, not one *for* the poor. In fact, Cho himself *was* sick and poor.

When Cho took his congregation to the downtown Sudaemun area in 1961, the venue had been secured by American missionaries as a Central Revival Hall. Cho had regularly served as their interpreter when the main message was hope and healing. The new congregation, therefore, represented a convergence between Cho's full-gospel message and mainstream Pentecostal theology. The church in this urban setting began a new phenomenon that has characterized Korean Christianity until today: the megachurch movement. His passion for church growth is understandable in a context where Christianity was still around 10 percent of the national population at the beginning of the 1960s. While continuing his message of God's power in healing and miracles, he presented a theological notion of a "good God." The exponential growth of his church began to attract the world's attention.

In 1973, he moved the church to Yoido Island, the newly emerging financial center of the capital. During this era, his congregation reached the unprecedented height of claiming 750,000 members. He also theologized his concept of a good God into a Fivefold Gospel and Threefold Salvation. The Fivefold Gospel was an adaptation of the traditional christological formula of the Assemblies of God: he added "Jesus the Blesser" to "Jesus the Savior, Baptizer, Healer, and the Coming King."[22] Based on 3 John 2, his Threefold Salvation includes spiritual, physical, and circumstantial (which includes material) salvation. His emphasis on God's blessing triggered a theological controversy, with many alleging that his

---

[22]Wonsuk Ma, "David Yonggi Cho's Theology of Blessing: Basis, Legitimacy, and Limitations," *Evangelical Review of Theology* 35, no. 2 (April 2011): 140-41.

ministry had shamanistic tendencies or advocated the prosperity gospel. Cho's ministry has expanded globally, and he has become perhaps the best-known Korean in the world.[23] At the same time, the church has increased its mission program. Before his formal retirement, Cho began to strengthen the church's ministry to the socially marginalized. His successor, Younghoon Lee, has taken the social responsibility of the church even further.[24]

"Full gospel" faith as lived out. Why are people attracted to Yoido Full Gospel Church and its massive Jashil Choi Fasting and Prayer Mountain? Their expectations are a valuable window through which the popular perception of Yoido Full Gospel Church can be deduced.

First, Yoido Church has been a popular haven for those who have nowhere to turn. The unique character of the church was defined from the very beginning, and it has continued. Myung Soo Park's analysis of selected published testimonies in the *Shinang-gye* (*World of Faith*), the monthly magazine of the church, points to this. He lists "the last hope for solving problems of life" as the "starting point of Pentecostal spirituality."[25] Almost every teaching opportunity, from Sunday sermons to cell-group Bible studies, contains the message of God's power to solve life's problems. These often include physical and mental illness, family problems such as in marriage and parent-children relationships, financial difficulties, business issues, addiction to gambling and substance abuse, suicidal tendencies, and many more.

To provide various spaces for people to come and experience God's power, the church has developed many prayer programs in addition to the traditional daily dawn prayer and Wednesday evening prayer. The church began a Friday overnight prayer meeting, which spread to almost all the churches in Korea and extended to all the weekdays in the church. It has instituted a special series of prayers, such as Daniel Prayer (for twenty-one days) and 40-Day Dawn Prayer. Members are encouraged to dedicate a designated time frame to pray for a specific need, and fasting prayer was uniquely promoted and encouraged by Rev. Choi, the long-time ministry partner of Cho. The massive Jashil Choi Fasting Prayer Mountain draws thousands of people from different churches in Korea and far beyond. Praying for healing and life's problems is a regular feature of all services in the church.

Second, accordingly, every gathering of the church is a space and time where God's power and love is expected and experienced. Every part of the service is designed to help worshipers to experience an encounter with God, through the Holy Spirit. The lively and contemporary preworship music and prayer welcome the worshipers who fill the auditorium, which was emptied minutes prior by the worshipers of the previous service. The postsermon session of ministry is rather extended. Normally it begins with a corporate prayer time, when each member is encouraged to put their problems into the Lord's care, based on the sermon just heard. The famous three shouts of "Juyo!" ("Lord!") at the

[23]Myung Soo Park, "Globalization of the Korean Pentecostal Movement: The International Ministry of Dr Yonggi Cho," in *Korean Church, God's Mission, Global Christianity*, ed. Wonsuk Ma and Kyo Seong Ahn (Oxford: Regnum, 2015), 228-41.

[24]See Younghoon Lee, "Yoido Full Gospel Church: A Case Study in Expanding Mission and Fellowship," in *Called to Unity for the Sake of Mission*, ed. John Gibaut and Knud Jorgensen (Oxford: Regnum, 2014), 275-84.

[25]Myung Soo Park, "Korean Pentecostal Spirituality as Manifested in the Testimonies of Believers of the Yoido Full Gospel Church," in *David Yonggi Cho: A Close Look at His Theology and Ministry*, ed. Wonsuk Ma, William W. Menzies, and Hyeon-sung Bae (Baguio, Philippines: APTS, 2004), 47.

beginning of this corporate prayer powerfully transform thousands of individuals into a spiritual community. The auditorium-filling prayers and shouts are followed by a prayer led by the preacher. Each member is asked to lay their hand on the part that is ailing, or on the heart if there is a problem other than physical. The prayer is a mixture of petition to God and a command to the force(s) responsible for the problem. This is the real climax of the service, when shouts of "Amen" and "Hallelujah" continue. This ministry session ends with the eruption of praise and thanksgiving.

This modern scene of Yoido Church's worship has its historical roots in the very beginning of the tent church. Cho repeatedly declared that Jesus is the answer to all human suffering, which overwhelmed his life and the tent church.[26] His church was regularly filled by more sick people than healthy ones. The former often included the pastor himself! His radical conversion experience is well documented. On his deathbed, with no hope of recovery from tuberculosis, he experienced not only spiritual rebirth but also physical restoration. The church, by design, is a sacred space where God's reality is encountered and his gracious power is experienced.

Third, this type of spirituality engenders countless narratives of who God is and what God has done. In a typical Pentecostal worship service in the early years, and still today in many parts of the world, sharing of testimonies is a major part of any worship. Normally the participants are not prearranged: anyone can stand up or come forward to tell their story of an encounter with God. The exchange of such life stories is practiced very regularly. Although the sheer size of Yoido Church prohibits a formal service from providing sufficient space for sharing of testimonies, sermons utilize such experiences as a powerful illustration of God's love and power. Moreover, the most active place where such sharing takes place is the weekly cell-group meetings, often in a member's home.

This is the unique and powerful process of grassroots theologization. True to the Pentecostal theological process, members actively contribute to the construction of theology, by either sharing, appropriating, adjusting, or discerning. Also, by articulating their experiences, they often reflect on the teachings of the Bible and the church. This helps the members to build confidence and contents for evangelism. Theologically, this is an example of the "prophethood of all believers," and practically this theological and spiritual orientation is responsible for the numerical growth of the church.

Mission of the church. Closely related to the above, there are three areas the Yoido Full Gospel Church has taken as its unique mission. The first is the spreading of full-gospel faith. At the core is the message of the good God, blessing, healing, and God's intervention on his people's behalf. This was radically opposite to the prevailing otherworldly orientation of Korean Christianity. Coupled with his healing and exorcism, Cho and his church were looked at suspiciously by the mainstream church in Korea. In fact, he was either included in the watch list of doctrinally "questionable" groups or condemned outright as a heretic. He and the church were cleared from the heresy list not long ago.[27] His belief and

---

[26]For example, in his own words, "Pastoring is preaching the gospel of Jesus Christ, leading them to salvation through faith in Jesus, and helping them to serve the Lord as God's people, and to love their neighbors." David Yonggi Cho, "An Interview: Pastoring with the Holy Spirit" [in Korean], in *Charis and Charisma: Church Growth of Yoido Full Gospel Church*, ed. Sung-hoon Myung and Yong Hong (Seoul: Institute for Church Growth, 2003), 14.

[27]For example, the Presbyterian Church of Korea (known as the Tonghap Group) formally classified Cho as a heretic in its 1983 General Assembly and withdrew this decision in 1994.

practice were also linked to shamanism by two well-known Western scholars. Both Harvey Cox and Walter Hollenweger made this link as a positive and successful attempt at connecting Christian faith with the widespread indigenous religious tradition. In this way, they applauded that Cho had successfully made Christianity relevant to the Korean cultural and contemporary context. Hollenweger regarded him as a "Pentecostal Shaman *par excellence*."[28] Understandably, the church emphatically denied such allegations, and, in fact, the church brought Cox to its pulpit a number of times so that he could have a firsthand experience. However, Cho is still viewed by many as a prosperity-gospel preacher.

These controversies prove that Cho's fullgospel faith and ethos has radically challenged normatively practiced Christian beliefs and practices. In the end, he has succeeded in convincing the Korean church of his full-gospel faith. This can be argued on at least two fronts. First, the worship and songs of his church and various prayer programs were adopted by churches across all denominations. They were particularly popular among pastors, who saw that people were attracted to such worship and messages. Through this powerful influence, Cho's Pentecostal spirituality has become a common feature of the Korean church.[29] Second, the growth of his church served as a sure and visible proof of the validity and impact of his full-gospel faith. At the height of the church-growth movement (for example, at the School of World Mission of Fuller Theological

Seminary), the Yoido Full Gospel Church was a favorite illustration. There was a practical side to this as well. His prayer mountain and overnight prayer sessions drew people regardless of their church's theological standing. "Sheep stealing" was a common charge lodged against Yoido Church and its branch worship centers in various parts of the metropolis.

Second, Cho and his church have served as the best advocates of church growth. It began with his strong desire for his church to grow in numbers and influence. This could have been, at least in the early years, a reaction to his dilapidated tent church, which symbolized the downcast status of his members. In the 1960s, the icon of a decent church was Youngnak Presbyterian Church. In many ways, it served as a symbol of Christian glory. Many founding members of the church were land and business owners in the northwestern part of North Korea who had fled the communist regime before the Korean War.[30] It is well known that in the early days of his tent church, Cho and his partner Mrs Jashil Choi (who later became his mother-inlaw) were returning from a disappointing trip downtown after his lottery ticket did not win. As the bus passed a large cinema, which was close to the location of his future downtown church, he said he heard the Holy Spirit say, "Do you see the cinema? I will give you a church which is larger than that."[31]

In 1976, Cho organized Church Growth International to systematically spread the experience and principles of Yoido Church's growth. Its

---

[28]Walter J. Hollenweger, *Pentecostalism: Origins and Developments Worldwide* (Peabody, MA: Hendrickson, 1977), 100n2; Harvey Cox, *Fire from Heaven: The Rise of Pentecostal Spirituality and the Reshaping of Religion in the Twenty-First Century* (Reading, MA: Addison-Wesley, 1995), 100.

[29]For example, the Pentecostalization of Korean Presbyterianism was pointed out by a concerned theologian: Chang-sup Shin, "Assessing the Impact of Pentecostalism on the Korean Presbyterian Church in Light of Calvin's Theology," *Chongshin Theological Journal* 3, no. 1 (1998): 115-31.

[30]Sebastian C. H. Kim and Kirsteen Kim, *A History of Korean Christianity* (New York: Cambridge University, 2015), 173.

[31]David Yonggi Cho, *Dr. David Yonggi Cho: Ministering Hope for 50 Years* (Alachua, FL: Bridge-Logos, 2008), 51.

board members have been senior pastors of megachurches throughout the world. The annual meetings bring a large number of pastors from around the world to hear the experiences of leaders of large churches and cell-group leaders of the church, and to participate in church life.

Third, the church has been widely known for its active mobilization of the laity for ministry, particularly women. Logically this is a natural development: the church has helped to enable its members to have life-changing encounters with God and provided spaces for them to share their stories with people. At the beginning of the exponential growth of his church, Cho decided to organize the church according to the administrative districts of the capital. When he announced to the church that he would select and train lay women to lead the small groups ("cells" in the church language), resistance was strong, both within and without the church, and from both men and women! Soon, however, this empowered women and laity to undertake ministries.

Christianity in Korea has a long tradition of promoting the welfare and education of women. Early Protestant missionaries began many schools, some of which were exclusively for girls and women. Pentecostalism took this Christian contribution to another level. The Korean Assemblies of God, with which the church is affiliated, was one of a few denominations that ordained women ministers. The first women ministers were ordained in 1979.[32] This is extremely significant given the male-privileged social culture in Korea. Cho's cell-group system took this even further by radically sharing ministerial responsibilities with laity (and mostly women)! This is an important contextual and practical expression of Pentecostal theology, which promotes the democratization of ministry to every believer.

FREE CHURCH ECCLESIOLOGY IN ASIA: A PRELIMINARY PICTURE

A close look at the two churches in East Asia raises more questions than when the study began. These two may not be typical enough to represent the incredible variety of free church types in Asia. For example, in India, a recently published study presents the transformation of "Every Home Crusade," a mission operation, into "Christ Groups" through the adaptation of rural Indian culture.[33] Its ecclesiological shaping is quite different from the two cases above.

Notwithstanding this deficiency, this study indicates a close interplay between the social context, church tradition that was transmitted or lack thereof, and the way the gospel is understood. The nature of the church in both networks is defined by their function within their given contexts, perhaps with little or no consciousness of ancient ecclesiological formulae. Because this study used "ground evidence" to understand the nature and function of the church widely understood in each circle, the present ecclesiological description has the advantage of a close connection to actual ecclesial realities in these communities.

Also noticeable in both cases is the decisive role of the leaders in theological shaping. In a free church setting, where each congregation exercises a sufficient degree of autonomy, the leader's role is substantial in shaping the culture, ethos, life, and theology of the congregation. In the case of Yoido Full Gospel Church, Cho "revised" the fourfold gospel of the (US) Assemblies

---

[32]The church's bylaws were amended to allow women to be ordained in 1972. Publication Committee of the 60-Year History, *With the Holy Spirit: A 60-Year History of the Korean Assemblies of God* [in Korean] (Seoul: Assemblies of God Korea, 2013), 103, 108.

[33]Saheb John Borgall, *The Emergence of Christ Groups in India: The Case of Karnataka State* (Oxford: Regnum, 2016).

of God. His experience of healing had a substantial influence on the construction of full-gospel theology. For him, this is part of the recovery of the apostolic ministry as spiritual gifts are restored. The leader's role is especially prominent in independent churches, as in the Word of Life Church. Xu's encounter with hidden Christians during the Cultural Revolution caused him to prioritize genuine repentance and regeneration as the most foundational aspect of Christian faith. Although the apostolic aspect of the Nicene-Constantinopolitan Creed has been interpreted variously, the strong leadership and authority of Xu and Cho are reminiscent in some ways of the apostolic succession in ancient churches. As in some house church networks, Xu's family still holds the church's leadership in Xu's physical absence. Theological controversies notwithstanding, both have been subject to moral, ethical, and legal charges, and they are certainly disturbing.

The recognition of other Christian communities, of the "one" and "catholic" dimensions of the Nicene-Constantinopolitan Creed, is least manifest. The survival experiences of both communities have affected their attitudes. The Word of Life Church was and still is unlawful and subject to various restrictions. The negative attitude toward registered churches in China among house church networks has been caused by and resulted in a narrow definition of the true church. As a Pentecostal congregation, Yoido Church also experienced marginalization among Korean churches. Only lately, partly due to its massive growth and influence, has the church been able to join the National Council of Churches. Today its ecumenical participation and leadership are significant.

The role of the social context is undoubtedly critical in the formation of church life. It is ex-pected that an average member of the Word of Life Church would not consider the presence of a building, church structure, or clergy to be essential for a gathering to be a church. The church's status of lacking legal sanction or recognition has forced them to develop the notion of a church as the gathering of God's people. On the other hand, Cho's Yoido Full Gospel Church has existed in a social setting where religious activities and entities are legally provided for and protected. Nonetheless, it struggled with allegations of unorthodoxy.

It is not unexpected that both groups were caught in theological controversies. This may be seen as an indication of their theological and spiritual creativity, exploring what the church is and what it does beyond the normal boundaries. Their free church state affords this uninhibited freedom. At the same time, it points to a need for a historic framework of Christian orthodoxy to safeguard doctrinal and practical integrity. This is where the ancient catholic nature of the church can be particularly relevant.

How the church is understood to be, and the process through which it is shaped, have direct implications for its mission. The two churches have remarkably stark contrasts in their missions. Both communities uphold the holy nature of the church, set apart as God's people for his mission in the world. But how they understand and try to fulfill it is radically different. The core of Cho's message is blessing, while Xu's is the cross. Their growth is symbolized by a massive auditorium (Cho) or an extensive network of congregations (Xu). Their mission is spreading the message of blessing and church growth (Cho), or evangelism and church planting (Xu). Both invoke the work of the Holy Spirit, to baptize in the Spirit (Cho), or to bring continual cleansing (Xu).

In Asia, more models of the church are expected to appear both in the historic and the free churches. Many historic churches have remained theologically evangelical, while seeking to integrate cultural elements into church life. Free churches will proliferate as some of these churches are now actively sending their missionaries to many parts of the continent and reproducing themselves. The growing passion of the Chinese house churches for the Back to Jerusalem movement is an example.[34] Varying and rapidly changing social contexts, especially in those areas hostile to Christianity, will play a decisive role in the shaping of the church and its understanding of its nature and mission. The two communities, with their leadership now in the hands of a younger generation, face formidable challenges. The population of Korea and China is aging rapidly, and the rise of urban house churches in China is significantly affecting how churches operate. How the de facto denominational function of the Word of Life will respond to the trend among urban churches toward the formation of denomination-like organizations will decisively affect its ecclesiological orientation.[35] It is therefore essential for churches and mission communities around the world to extend their theological hospitality, to watch each other's back, while encouraging creativity that is a gift of the Holy Spirit. This hospitality, as long as it remains an offer rather than an imposition, will give birth to varying dynamic and creative ecclesiologies that are lived out, reflected, and articulated, from both the newer and the older churches in Asia.

FURTHER READING

Chan, Simon. *Grassroots Asian Theology: Thinking the Faith from the Ground Up*. Downers Grove, IL: IVP Academic, 2014.

Kärkkäinen, Veli-Matti. *An Introduction to Ecclesiology: Ecumenical, Historical, and Global Perspectives*. Downers Grove, IL: IVP Academic, 2002.

Phan, Peter C. *Christianity with an Asian Face: Asian American Theology in the Making*. Maryknoll, NY: Orbis, 2003.

Wang, Kwok Nai. *The Local Church*. Hong Kong: Christian Conference of Asia, 2005.

---

[34]A textbook for this movement was recently published by a prominent urban house church leader: Mingri Jin, *Back to Jerusalem with All Nations: A Biblical Foundation* (Oxford: Regnum, 2016).

[35]For example, Brent Fulton, *China's Urban Christians: A Light That Cannot Be Hidden* (Eugene, OR: Wipf & Stock, 2015).

36

ECCLESIOLOGY IN AFRICA

APPRENTICES ON A MISSION

Stephanie A. Lowery

ECCLESIOLOGIES ON THE African continent take many shapes and forms, often drawing on biblical references. Some pattern themselves after Israel, others after angels, and so forth. Many of these models challenge the church worldwide to immerse itself in and tie itself more closely to the Bible. These ecclesiologies also raise challenges with regard to the Nicene affirmation of the church as one and catholic. Finally, a biblical, contextually appropriate model is proposed that links ecclesiology with the *missio Dei*.

Many images may arise in a person's mind when hearing the term *Africa*. From ancient churches in Ethiopia, to sprawling metropolises such as Nairobi, to the deserts of Namibia and Morocco, Africa teems with life and variety. Given the size and diversity of the continent, I have chosen to offer a brief overview of ecclesiological developments in roughly the last century, discussing how these developments and proposals relate to the Nicene Creed's description of the church as one, holy, catholic, and apostolic, and then proposing a way

forward for ecclesiologies in Africa today. From my perspective, the Nicene Creed is a pointed reminder that those in historic or North Atlantic–founded churches in Africa and those outside Africa need to seriously consider developments on the continent if we want to affirm that the church is one and catholic.[1]

As has been said many times before, Africa is a large continent full of diversity, and such diversity should not be ignored or downplayed. However, I will attempt to offer a general overview with some specific examples, in order to provide a wider perspective on ecclesiologies in Africa.[2]

HISTORICAL ECCLESIOLOGICAL MODELS

For the Roman Catholic churches of Africa, their ecclesiological model is something of a given, though there are modifications within that overall framework. The model of "church as family" has generally been enthusiastically embraced by Catholic theologians across the

---

[1] I am using *Western* and *North Atlantic* interchangeably here to refer to a certain region of the world, as well as the broad cultural traits that persons in that region have in common, such as the Enlightenment heritage.

[2] For a more detailed examination of ecclesiologies from historic/mission-founded churches in Africa, see Stephanie A. Lowery, *Identity and Ecclesiology: Their Relationship Among Select African Theologians* (Eugene, OR: Pickwick, 2017).

continent.[3] Protestant theologians too have relied on this imagery of the church, as do African Initiated Churches (churches begun by and for Africans, and led by Africans, generally speaking; they stand in contrast to historic or mission-founded churches with a North Atlantic bias).[4]

In part, this is because the model finds significant biblical support as well as cultural resonance. This description of the church may seem unremarkable to Western ears, but I would suggest that is only because North Atlantic persons may be overly familiar with the terminology, without actually exploring its ramifications in more detail. For one, in African contexts, describing the church as family raises issues of ancestors: Are non-Christian ancestors included in the church, if church is a form of family? Another concern is just what *family* means. At least in Kenya, *family* carries connotations of bloodlines and ethnicity—and ethnic bonds tend to favor insiders. So family notions can consciously and unconsciously reinforce and borrow from the worst of ethnocentrism, and provide justification for treating those who are different or "other" as lesser.

Family models can also be unclear. Amid a ferment of change, what does family mean for Africans today? Old notions have changed in some ways, and it is not necessarily clear just what family entails. For example, some theologians have proposed that the church is like a "clan" of African cultures.[5] But which ethnicity's model of clan? And given how swiftly Africa is changing, it is valid to ask just how much "clan" means to modern, urbanized Africans who have been affected by the West through globalization, among other means.

At the same time, the idea of church as family is compelling, for equally important reasons. The Bible does use extensive familial imagery to describe God's people, and we would all do well to consider just what responsibilities and implications arise from being part of God's household. Also, as many theologians have pointed out, the ecclesial community should be based on the triune God, and human relationality and the ecclesial community do have the ability to reflect the divine Three-in-One in a limited way. If, then, the idea of family points the church back to the doctrine of the Trinity and humans' inherently relational nature, then we ought to give this model more thought, as so many theologians in Africa—both Catholic and otherwise—have done.

While many African theologians from various church traditions embrace this model, a few have rejected it outright. For example, Congolese Georges Titre Ande, of the Anglican Church, insists that the family model should not be used to describe the church in an African context.[6] He goes so far as to claim that the Bible does not use familial language for the

---

[3]Pope John Paul II endorsed this model in the exhortation "Ecclesia in Africa," September 14, 1995, www.vatican.va/holy_father/john_paul_ii/apost_exhortations/documents/hf_jp-ii_exh_14091995_ecclesia-in-africa_en.html#top. A few examples of works by Catholic theologians that embrace this model include Elochukwu E. Uzukwu, *A Listening Church: Autonomy and Communion in African Churches* (Eugene, OR: Wipf & Stock, 2006); Agbonkhianmeghe E. Orobator, *The Church as Family: African Ecclesiology in Its Social Context*, Hekima College Collection (Nairobi: Paulines Publications Africa, 2000); Augustin Ramazani Bishwende, *Église-famille de Dieu dans la mondialisation: Théologie d'une nouvelle voie africaine d'évangélisation* (Paris: L'Harmattan, 2006).

[4]For instance, Paul Mbandi, *A Theology of the Unity of the Church in a Multi-ethnic Context: Toward a Theological Understanding of the Unity of the Church in Relation to Ethnic Diversity* (Saarbrücken: Verlag Dr. Müller, 2010), explores the biblical imagery of the church as the people of God and the household of God—these images describe family or relatives.

[5]John Mary Waliggo, "The African Clan as the True Model of the African Church," in *The Church in African Christianity: Innovative Essays in Ecclesiology*, ed. J. N. K. Mugambi and Laurenti Magesa, African Challenge (Nairobi: Initiatives, 1990).

[6]Titre Ande, *Leadership and Authority: Bula Matari and Life-Community Ecclesiology in Congo*, Regnum Studies in Mission (Oxford: Regnum, 2010).

church, which contradicts biblical evidence (see, e.g., Gal 6:10; Eph 2:19; 1 Tim 3:15; Heb 3:1-6).[7] Yet the stridency with which he opposes this model, and the specific dangers he mentions, should give us pause.

One of his concerns is that familial models are more often rooted in cultural notions of family than in biblical teachings. His own proposal is to root ecclesiology in Christology and the Trinity, describing a "community of life" unified in Christ, an approach designed to give priority to biblical imagery while still contextualizing, taking care that context does not become the determining factor. While I disagree with some of Ande's claims, his work is valuable on several fronts: he contextualizes without idealizing his cultural past and at the same time engages with issues of globalization and the worldwide, catholic church; he also bases his ecclesiology on biblical study. While Ande is a rare voice for his rejection of familial models, it is worth exploring other ecclesiological developments on the continent.

AFRICAN INITIATED CHURCHES' ECCLESIOLOGICAL MODELS

As is well known, African Initiated Churches have blossomed rapidly, much to the delight of theologians and historians. Omenyo views African Initiated Churches as a promising "paradigm" for African ecclesiology, and cites the late Kwame Bediako as support for this view.

Bediako claims African Initiated Churches are significant because they manifest the general trends in African responses to Christianity.[8] One excellent source on African Initiated Churches is Allan H. Anderson, a South African who offers an insider's analysis of the movement. Indeed, Anderson claims that in these African Initiated Churches, Africa has experienced nothing less than a "reformation" that has "revolutionized" Christianity.[9] Indeed, even in 1968 David B. Barrett observed that participants in the African Initiated Church movement were consciously describing their movement as a "radical mission of renewal and reformation," and noted a "striking number of parallels" between the African scene and the European Reformation. He described three specific areas in which African Initiated Churches seek reform: biblicism, Africanism, and *philadelphia*.[10] On the final theme, *philadelphia*, he locates one contribution of African theology in African Initiated Churches: their theology of church as community. Omenyo too emphasizes the importance of koinonia in African Initiated Churches, and views this as an important contribution of African churches to ecumenism in a world that seems to overemphasize the individual.[11] "In short, the movement as a whole has introduced onto the African scene and forcibly drawn attention to a new quality of corporate Christian life and responsibility, a new *koinōnia* (sharing) of warmth, emotion and mutual caring in the

---

[7]Such familial language can be found in the Gospels, Pauline material, and the Catholic Epistles. Christians are those who "belong" to God (Jn 17:9), who are born by God's Spirit to become God's children and coheirs with Christ, their elder brother (Jn 3:1-6; Rom 8:14-17; Gal 4:1-7; Jas 2:5; 1 Pet 3:7). The Old Testament also is filled with language of Israel as God's child or bride, both terms describing kinship.

[8]Cephas N. Omenyo, "Essential Aspects of African Ecclesiology: The Case of the African Independent Churches," *Pneuma* 20, no. 2 (2000): 234; citing Kwame Bediako, *Christianity in Africa: The Renewal of a Non-Western Religion*, Studies in World Christianity (Edinburgh: Edinburgh University Press, 1995), 66.

[9]Allan H. Anderson, *African Reformation: African Initiated Christianity in the 20th Century* (Trenton, NJ: Africa World, 2001), 4.

[10]David B. Barrett, *Schism and Renewal in Africa: An Analysis of Six Thousand Contemporary Religious Movements* (Nairobi: Oxford University Press, 1968), 161-62, 164-69.

[11]Omenyo, "Essential Aspects of African Ecclesiology," 248.

Christian community, together with a new philanthropy of all."[12] Ecclesial *koinōnia* provides fellowship as well as a sense of belonging.[13] If these scholars are correct, then African Initiated Church ecclesiologies (implicit or explicit) deserve closer study.

African Initiated Churches can be categorized in various ways, but are often divided into three categories: (1) African, Ethiopian, or nationalist churches, which did not claim prophetic roots or special manifestations of the Spirit, and were often secessions from mainline or historic European churches; (2) prophet-healing or spiritual churches, which emphasize the Spirit and his power, often draw on the Pentecostal movement, and tend to embrace many traditional practices and models, such as healers with spiritual powers; and (3) Pentecostal or charismatic African Initiated Churches that emphasize the Spirit but are usually more critical of traditional practices and roles than spiritual churches would be.[14]

African Initiated Churches, since they are not constrained by Western influences in the same way that historic/mainline churches are, have more freedom with regard to inculturation and innovation, but there are nevertheless trends that can be seen in this diverse grouping of churches. Some African Initiated Churches, such as the one founded by Ghanaian Prophet Jemisemiham Jehu-Appiah, pattern the church after cultural communal models. So Jehu-Appiah modeled the church on the traditional Fanti court, making himself the king and setting up a dynastic succession.[15] Peter Ropo Awoniyi's study of African Initiated Churches among the Yoruba people in southwest Nigeria notes that African Initiated Churches in that area give chieftaincy titles "as a mark of honour for distinguished member [sic] of their churches."[16] If ecclesial oneness and catholicity were to require a common model for the church worldwide, these models would be problematic, not least because they are quite contextual and thus less likely to be adopted in other contexts. However, we shall now describe ecclesiological trends on the continent.

Adapting cultural models for Christianity can take many forms. Examining Ghanaian African Initiated Churches, Elom Dovlo describes instances "such as the Twelve Apostles Church, [where] traditional priests such as John Nankabah and Grace Tanie . . . simply crossed over from traditional priesthood into Christian priesthood and their long experience in the former greatly influenced their new Christian role." Priesthood is not the only cultural model that has been adopted by Ghanaian African Initiated Churches: the notion of church leader as a prophet was also embraced, and this paralleled "the model of traditional priesthood known in Akan as the Okomfo." Dovlo proceeds to note

---

[12]Barrett, *Schism and Renewal in Africa*, 169. He continues, "It is precisely at this point that independency is making its strongest appeal—the emphasis on brotherly love, the innate apprehension that salvation is found only in community, the need to belong met by fellowship as well-being in community," and so forth (170).

[13]Omenyo, "Essential Aspects of African Ecclesiology," 237.

[14]Anderson, *African Reformation*, 15-19. Ayegboyin and Ukah divide churches in Africa into the following categories: mainline, Ethiopian, African Initiated Churches, or Pentecostal (Deji Ayegboyin and F. K. Asonzeh Ukah, "Taxonomy of Churches in Africa: The Case of Nigeria," *Ogbomoso Journal of Theology*, 13, no. 1 [2008]: 1-21). John Gichimu prefers to categorize African Initiated Churches as either nationalist/Ethiopian/African, Zionist/Apostolic/Aladura, or African Pentecostal ("Theological Education in African Instituted Churches (AICs)," in *Handbook of Theological Education in World Christianity*, ed. Dietrich Werner et al. [Oxford: Regnum, 2010], 368).

[15]Anderson, *African Reformation*, 78-79.

[16]Peter Ropo Awoniyi, "Yoruba Cultural Peculiarity and the Making of African Indigenous Churches in Southwest Nigeria," *Ogbomoso Journal of Theology* 17, no. 2 (2012): 127.

that not just particular roles but whole structures were adapted, including ecclesiologies. Thus, "the Prophet is in traditional parallel a chief. . . . The MDCC and the Ossah Madih Church offer examples of the traditional authority paradigm. They are organised along the lines of the Akan State (*Oman*) which [*sic*; with] the Prophet as the paramount chief and other leaders of appropriate traditional titles, functions and at times regalia."[17]

Jehu-Appiah is certainly not the only one to adopt a monarchical model. Yet some of these monarchical and theocratic models are clearly designed to mirror biblical examples, and not so much cultural paradigms. Interestingly, these models often draw heavily on the Old Testament. For instance, one of the Aladura (praying) churches that arose in Nigeria, breaking off from the Anglican Church, was founded by Garrick Sokari Braide, who renamed his hometown Bakana-Israel and titled himself Prophet Elijah II.[18]

Such churches often refer to their base as Jerusalem, Zion, or Israel, and the leaders are prophets, prophet-healers, or kings. So in South Africa Zulu Zion leader Daniel Nkonyane established a Zion City, and leaders were like Moses, except that they found the Promised Land, and it is in Africa.[19] Others view themselves as lost Jews who must return to Israel.[20] Afolabi's study of Christ Apostolic Church notes many parallels between African and Israelite religious experiences, such as highly valuing sacred sites and elements. Because of the biblical basis and cultural resonances, Afolabi defends the Christ Apostolic Church model against any charges of syncretism: he insists that this church is appropriately contextual and thoroughly evangelical.[21]

While cultural and Old Testament models abound, other ecclesiologies arise from a mélange of cultural, Old Testament, and New Testament references. So, for instance, the AmaNararetha's leader is a healer, Nazirite rules are followed, and a high place and holy mountain have been established.[22] John Marange, founder of the African Apostolic Church of John Marange (or "Maranke"), claimed to be John the Baptist and required converts to obey Old Testament laws.[23] Yet other churches describe themselves in none of these earthly terms but appeal instead to heavenly realities, such as the Eternal Sacred Order of Cherubim and Seraphim, a result of an Anglican prayer group. This church claims to represent angels on earth.

Some African Initiated Churches frame their leadership and ecclesiology more in New Testament terms, describing their leaders as apostles. One of the better-known African Initiated Churches was founded by Congolese Simon Kimbangu, a Baptist who preached for approximately half a year before being jailed. Despite his brief ministry as a free man, his church now has approximately seventeen million members.[24]

---

[17]Elom Dovlo, "African Culture and Emergent Church Forms in Ghana," *Exchange* 33, no. 1 (2004): 35-37.

[18]Anderson, *African Reformation*, 80.

[19]Anderson, *African Reformation*, 96-97. Ezra Chitando's work on the African Apostolic Church of Zimbabwe provides another example of this: for this church, Zimbabwe becomes Zion ("The Recreation of Africa: A Study of the Ideology of the African Apostolic Church of Zimbabwe," *Exchange* 32, no. 3 [July 2003]: 239-49, here 246).

[20]Anderson, *African Reformation*, 118.

[21]Stephen Olurotimi Adeola Afolabi, "Yoruba Cultural Reflections in the Christ Apostolic Church," *Ogbomoso Journal of Theology* 17, no. 2 (2012): 132, 144-45, 149-50.

[22]Anderson, *African Reformation*, 106-7. Unlike Nyende's proposal in this book, this church has designated a literal, physical mountain as its holy place, which reveals a deficient interpretation of the New Testament, particularly the book of Hebrews.

[23]Anderson, *African Reformation*, 116-17.

[24]Aurélien Mokoko Gampiot, "Kimbanguism: An African Initiated Church," *Scriptura* 113, no. 1 (2014): 1.

Kimbangu is viewed as an instrument of the Holy Spirit who brought a new Pentecost, a prophet, and a miracle worker.[25] Kimbangu's own view of himself was more modest: he denied being a prophet, and instead called himself an "envoy," pointing people to Christ. But to members of his church, he is the "Supreme Authority of the Church and the Guarantor of the unity of the Church and its doctrine."[26] Kimbangu's followers sometimes ascribe divine qualities to him, such as omnipresence, or view him as the personification of the Holy Spirit.[27] Akiele concludes by describing Kimbanguist ecclesiology as a "family," a unity of the faithful whose ecclesial activities "create brotherhood, sisterhood."[28] Given the way in which he emphasizes faith as necessary for inclusion in the church, it would seem that this family model, as least, would not include non-Christian ancestors.[29]

Having mentioned all of these models, there are some churches that seemingly reject any of these paradigms and choose their models from more pragmatic, modern sources. Asonzeh Ukah suggests that more recently established Pentecostal churches have a "firm-like structural organization" and are run like businesses that produce and sell commodities. The leadership too derives from business-world paradigms: the church leader is a combination of a chairman, president, and CEO, with the requisite board of trustees. Such a church is led by a person who is a "bank of grace," a "repository of charismata, and a special bridge between his followers and

God"; moreover, "his word is law. He is an oracular instrument and initiator of doctrines."[30] However, even such business-oriented churches may still be unconsciously drawing on cultural notions of holy places. Ukah describes a

> tendency to reconstruct religious geography through the construction of religious camps. Particularly in Nigeria and Ghana, these churches buy up large expanses of land, sometimes measuring well over ten square kilometres, and construct a range of facilities such as auditoriums, schools, guesthouses, dormitories, presidential villas (for VIP guests such as politicians), banks, gas stations and hospitals. These camps, which often constitute an "alternative city," function to showcase a Pentecostal leader's charismata, authenticate the claim to divine authorisation, and produce his brand of Pentecostalism.[31]

Then there are churches that seem to defy the "historic or African Initiated Church" categorization, such as the Orthodox Church of Africa and the Embassy of God. For the Orthodox Church of Africa, its history in one country—Kenya—is of interest for our purposes in this essay. This church has a large number of members from the Kikuyu ethnic group of Kenya. During the 1950s, British colonialists were struggling to suppress the Mau Mau Uprising; when a state of emergency was declared in 1952, the colonial government banned independent churches and schools as well, assuming they too were hotbeds of rebellion. Though begun as an African Initiated Church,

---

[25]Anderson, *African Reformation*, 125-26.
[26]Basile Akiele, "Attributes of Simon Kimbangu: Founder of the Kimbanguist Church," *The Journal of the I.T.C.* 26, no. 2 (1998/1999): 194, 198.
[27]Gampiot, "Kimbanguism," 4-5. Regarding his embodiment of the Spirit, Kimbanguists appeal to Jn 14:15-17, which records the promise to send another comforter, which Kimbanguists identify with their founder.
[28]Akiele, "Attributes of Simon Kimbangu," 206.
[29]Akiele also points to the Trinity as one of the foundational principles of the Kimbanguist church ("Attributes of Simon Kimbangu," 200).
[30]Asonzeh Ukah, "African Christianities: Features, Promises and Problems," in *Working Papers*, ed. Institut für Ethnologie und Afrikastudien (Mainz: Institut für Ethnologie und Afrikastudien, 2007), 15.
[31]Ukah, "African Christianities," 17.

the Orthodox Church of Africa had been accepted officially by the Greek Orthodox Patriarchate of Alexandria in 1946, but "no support was offered to its African congregations in Kenya" during this time, and there was but one Kenyan priest—who was detained by the government—in the country for over a decade.[32]

This case study is significant for multiple reasons: (1) it demonstrates that some African Initiated Churches are seeking out relationships with the church worldwide, even desiring to demonstrate their oneness and catholicity by joining historic or mainline denominations. However, (2) at least for this African Initiated Church, the path was not easy, and it received little support from its partner organization. It seems that the historic church was not offering meaningful partnership to its newly accepted church in Kenya. Finally, (3) despite being accepted into the Greek Orthodox Church as Africans, "there has been an attempt to impose the sense of a 'Greek-centered' cultural identity that seriously haunts the process of enculturation." For instance, non-African leaders sought to change the church's name to "Greek Orthodox." This indicates that historic churches may not have fully grasped or appreciated the place of contextualization amid catholicity and oneness. Njoroge writes, "Through the transformative energies of the Holy Spirit, the incarnation process brings meaning to the message of the Gospel uniquely to every local context. These energies give balance to the universal meaning of the message and the contextualized interpretation and understanding of the Gospel."[33] But if historic churches do not even respect the necessity

of contextualized congregations within their own denomination, there seems little hope of churches from various denominations being able and willing to demonstrate oneness.

There are signs of hope for unity in diversity. Asamoah-Gyadu examines the Embassy of God in Ukraine. While African Initiated Churches are typically churches led by Africans, based in Africa, and targeting Africans, the Embassy of God, unlike other African Initiated Churches in diaspora, is not predominantly African in membership. Also, the language of *embassy* is noteworthy with regard to ecclesiology. This model understands God's children as citizens of God's kingdom and his representatives on earth. In other words, this ecclesiology includes missiology: it goes beyond family language to include the church's raison d'être; it implicitly ties praxis into theology, so that theology does not remain abstract. And given the multiethnic nature of the church, it is succeeding in creating a diverse community, breaking down dividing walls, and demonstrating unity to those around it.[34] This church, then, understands and is manifesting the oneness and catholicity that the Nicene Creed attributes to the church.

CONTRIBUTIONS OF AFRICAN ECCLESIOLOGIES

What, then, are some of the contributions of African ecclesiologies that churches in other regions need to hear? And what do the African Initiated Churches offer that mainline churches seemingly do not? As to the first question, ecclesiologies in Africa value solidarity in very practical ways, and in that regard challenge

---

[32]John N. Njoroge, "The Orthodox Church in Africa and the Quest for Enculturation: A Challenging Mission Paradigm in Today's Orthodoxy," *St. Vladimir's Theological Quarterly* 55, no. 4 (2011): 409, 419-21, 423-24.

[33]Njoroge, "Orthodox Church in Africa," 428-29, 436; see 437.

[34]J. Kwabena Asamoah-Gyadu, "African Initiated Christianity in Eastern Europe: Church of the 'Embassy of God' in Ukraine," *International Bulletin of Missionary Research* 30, no. 2 (April 2006): 73-74.

ecclesiologies in other regions to consider how and to what degree they are visibly demonstrating their unity in Christ. The debate over familial language surfaces this concern with solidarity in the ecclesial community, and examines how that solidarity differs from cultural understandings of communal solidarity.

Second, many ecclesiological emphases in African contexts rely quite heavily and directly on biblical models. As Philip Jenkins has pointed out, the southward shift of Christianity entails taking the Bible seriously.[35] Have North Atlantic ecclesiologies, for instance, had a tendency to be too swayed by contextual models and strayed from biblical teachings about unity among God's people? African scholars tend to be more concerned with the biblical text's application than its background, as several scholars have noted.[36] This may be termed a highly pastoral approach, similar to Ellen Charry's argument that theology should ultimately serve pastoral ends. In other words, it is a timely reminder that Christian doctrine is intended to change lives.[37] Stephen C. Barton similarly advocates for an approach he terms "readerly," meaning that instead of focusing on reconstructing the world in or behind the text, this approach engages deeply with the historical text itself *"as Spirit-inspired,"* with the goal of producing individual and communal transformation.[38] Barton describes this method as "a form of critical reason which is *theological and ecclesial.*"

Aside from their more ecclesial, application-oriented approach, ecclesiologies in Africa also raise the issue of the radical nature of following Christ. Many of these churches expect that their members will make great sacrifices for their church, that they will sacrificially care for each other and live in countercultural ways. This could be called costly ecclesiology. Members in these churches may be required to dress differently, give generously, and make pilgrimages—or even move—to a special location that has been designated as a holy place. These responsibilities and burdens are counted as worthwhile for many people if in return they find a community of belonging and an identity as God's people.

Furthermore, it is worth asking what African Initiated Churches offer that Africans from various backgrounds find so appealing and what weaknesses in mainline ecclesiology they highlight. First, many provide or are based on divine revelation granted to the founder. These churches value communication from God and have no doubt that God actively communicates to God's people today. Second, these churches offer a holistic salvation, which means the leaders can heal, cast out spirits, or provide deliverance from oppression, and so forth. In other words, they are convinced that salvation in Christ affects every aspect of life, and they have confidence that God has the power and willingness to address any of their problems. Third, these churches provide freedom and dignity—freedom from Western

---

[35]See Philip Jenkins, *The Next Christendom: The Coming of Global Christianity* (New York: Oxford University, 2011).

[36]Ukachukwu Chris Manus, *Intercultural Hermeneutics in Africa: Methods and Approaches*, Biblical Studies in African Scholarship (Nairobi: Acton, 2003), 59; Grant LeMarquand, *An Issue of Relevance: A Comparative Study of the Story of the Bleeding Woman (Mk. 5:25-34; Mt. 9:20-22; Lk. 8:43-48) in North Atlantic and African Contexts*, Bible and Theology in Africa 5 (New York: Peter Lang, 2004), 3, 219-20.

[37]Ellen T. Charry, *By the Renewing of Your Minds: The Pastoral Function of Christian Doctrine* (New York: Oxford University Press, 1999).

[38]Stephen C. Barton, "Christian Community in the Light of the Gospel of John," in *Christology, Controversy and Community: New Testament Essays in Honour of David R. Catchpole*, ed. David G. Horrell and Christopher M. Tuckett, Supplements to Novum Testamentum 99 (Leiden: Brill, 2000), 284-85.

control and dignity as African Christians. Fourth, often in African Initiated Churches there is more equality among men and women, and opportunities to lead are open to women, youth, and others who are so gifted. Fifth, many of these churches rely heavily on the Spirit's power, which may indicate that their ecclesiologies are more closely linked to a robust view of pneumatology and the Trinity than other models.

AFRICAN ECCLESIOLOGIES IN LIGHT OF THE NICENE CREED

As we have already noted, ecclesiologies in Africa, whether historic/mission churches or African Initiated Churches or varieties in between, offer both contributions and challenges with regard to the Nicene Creed's description of the church as "one, holy, catholic, and apostolic." Some African Initiated Churches may not be interested in partnering with churches elsewhere in the world, or at least not with Western churches, given the painful history there. In other instances, African churches may be willing to enter crosscultural partnerships, but Western churches are not interested in such partnership. That African Initiated Churches are often praxis oriented may also make Western churches wary, accustomed as they are to doctrinal statements, creeds, and theological literature as a whole. They may ask themselves how they will be able to determine a particular church's apostolicity without formal belief statements. The issue of holiness is one that may be more of a concern for African churches as they examine Western churches, whose seeming liberalness can be off-putting. On the other hand, many Western churches would likely be highly wary of churches that permit polygamy. Yet on the whole, unity,

catholicity, and apostolicity seem most likely to raise concerns.

A NEW MODEL: A COMMUNITY OF APPRENTICES CONTINUING CHRIST'S MISSION

What is the way forward for African ecclesiologies? It would be well-nigh impossible, and not necessarily desirable, to my mind, to propose an ecclesiological model that would attempt to solve or address all issues of a particular church, or be the best choice in every context. So I propose an approach that builds on existing ecclesiological models and is hopefully broad enough to be adapted to various contexts on the continent.

As has been noted, the idea of family is a popular model for the church across denominations on the continent but equally carries significant dangers in a context of ethnocentrism. Therefore, calling the church a clan is not a wise route.[39] The Bible does use familial imagery to describe God's people, but makes it clear that the household of God is distinct from and functions differently from biological families. Also, familial imagery describes what the church is to some degree but does not sufficiently link ecclesiology with the *missio Dei* (though familial metaphors do frequently link ecclesiology with the triune God). African Initiated Churches have also highlighted that ecclesiology should be more closely related to pneumatology, not just Christology. Thus, I propose that the church be described as *the adoptive children of God, who are a community of Spirit-led apprentices gathered for worship and training to continue Christ's mission in the world.*

The emphasis on adoptive children highlights that being a child of God is not a natural right

---

[39]Thanks to Rev. Kioko Mwangangi for his input on this matter.

but a gracious gift, hopefully curbing prideful attitudes and ethnic-like conceptions of the church. The theme of God's free choice of his people runs through the Old and New Testaments. For instance, in Deuteronomy Moses lays out the basis and guidelines for the freed Hebrews who will constitute the nation of Israel. Deuteronomy 7:6-8 emphasizes that God chose the Israelites, not due to their own merit but because of a promise he had made to their ancestors and because of his gracious love. God's sovereign election of God's people is a source of wonder for the apostle Paul (see Rom 8:15-17; 9:4-26; Gal 4, esp. Gal 4:4-7; Eph 1:3-12; 2). This theme also arises in John's Gospel (Jn 1:12; 15:19) and in 2 Peter (2 Pet 2:4-10).

In addition, the call to God's people to realize they are God's children is not a call to be proud but rather a reminder that God's people are to be marked by humility. Jesus tells his disciples that to enter God's kingdom, one must be like a child: humble and dependent, asking for all that they need (Mt 18:3-4). The disciples did not respect or value children much, or at least saw them as an interference and distraction to Jesus' "true" ministry, and for this they were rebuked. Perhaps this rebuke that the people of God are to be like children before their Father is a reminder Christians need to hear again today. To rely on the Father who chooses and keeps his adopted children safe in God's hand (Jn 10:28-29) is to trust in God to lead us and to bring along those who are called to join his people. It is not for God's children to decide whom the Father should adopt into that family.

The emphasis on being Spirit-led is both a call back to Scripture and a reminder that the Spirit unites and guides the church. It also leaves room for the Spirit's present work in manifesting himself to God's people, as well as the Spirit's role in illuminating their minds and grasp of Scripture. This is the same Spirit who empowered Jesus' mission (Is 61:1-2, quoted by Jesus in Lk 4:18-19) and creates new life in God's people. He is the "Spirit of adoption" (Jn 3:5-8; Rom 8:14). The Spirit, as Peter preached at Pentecost, has been poured out on "all flesh" (Acts 2:17-18), enabling the people of God.

Those enabled by the Spirit are, I propose, intended to be apprentices. The concept of apprentices is one that has echoes of the past but resonance today as well, in both rural and urban contexts. An apprentice describes a person who is a learner and who learns in order to apply her trade. Indeed, if we return to the beginning of Deuteronomy, in Deuteronomy 6 God's people are called to actively remember God's acts on their behalf. They are also called to meditate on God's commands, pass them on to their children, and obey them. Thus, they are called to be a community of persons who seek to learn and live out God's words; they are apprentices or disciples (see Sosa's essay in this section on a holistic church as a community of disciples), following their Master and always needing to learn more of him and from him. Like the seventy-two disciples, after learning from Jesus, Christians are sent out for ministry. Then they return from their work to report to their master and continue learning from him. This cycle should be ongoing until Christ returns.

Luke 10 unites the concept of being God's children, the call to learning and praxis, and the *missio Dei* being passed on to Jesus' apprentices: Jesus notes that the workers are few and urges his disciples to pray that God might raise up more harvesters. He then sends the disciples out, after warning them to expect rejection. When the Seventy-Two return, Jesus warns them not to be delighted about the power they have employed in their ministry; their delight should be in the knowledge that they belong to and are known by Almighty God (Lk 10:17-20). The power they wield on behalf of God and for his mission is not what they should focus on. Jesus continues by referring to his apprentices—or disciples—as "little children," a reminder of their dependency on their heavenly Father. They know God only because he has graciously chosen to reveal God's self to these dependent, humble "children." It is both a gentle encouragement and a sharp reminder that one's position in Christ is more important than the power God bestows on God's children. They are not to be commended for their insight, as if they had achieved or earned this knowledge, but to realize that their knowledge of God is a blessing from God, as undeserved as the rain that God sends on the unjust (Lk 10:22-24).

By employing the apprentice imagery and model, the African Initiated Church emphasis on praxis can be carried into ecclesiology, and the *missio Dei* can once again be given its due in ecclesiology as the driving force and task of the whole church. Presumably, this outward focus could help the church move beyond its regional boundaries and have a worldwide focus. An ecclesiology that does not have any outward focus is a crippled one, for it fails to consider the purpose of God's people: they are not to be inward focused, but to go out and represent him in the world and display his love to a world lost in darkness. As Abraham was reminded, he was blessed in order to be a blessing to the world (Gen 12). The *missio Dei* begins with God at creation, as God reaches out to the newly created world, offering to enter into relationship with the creatures made in God's image who will represent God and rule on God's behalf. This mission, driven by the relentless, pursuing love

of this God who—aptly described by Francis Thompson as the "Hound of Heaven"—hunts for his people, who are lost in darkness but nevertheless avoiding their holy pursuer, is not frustrated by the intractability of God's people. That mission continues when the second person of God enters creation as a human being. Nor does this mission end with Jesus' death. Just as Jesus was sent by the Father into the world, so too the people of God are sent out into the world in the Spirit's power, to be ambassadors of Christ and ministers of reconciliation (Jn 20:21).

This church, as Petrine language reminds us, is aware of the fact that the ecclesial identity sets people apart. Specifically, Peter describes God's people as aliens and sojourners (1 Pet 2:4-10), those who are in some sense outsiders in their contexts: they seek to be contextual, without losing their holiness and their divinely granted identity. Because they stand out, and because they are following their Lord's way of life, Christians expect suffering. In the two case studies he presents, Wonsuk Ma's work in this section raises the issue of what place suffering plays in ecclesiologies, a timely question in a world facing increasing religious extremism as well as government persecution.

The apostle Peter also describes God's people as sojourners. These sojourners in particular are on a journey toward their heavenly home, as Peter Nyende points out with his ecclesiology based on the book of Hebrews. Nyende's use of Hebrews is a contribution for ecclesiologies in general, in that he employs a book little used in ecclesiologies. For African churches in particular, the basis in Hebrews engages themes of holy places, God's dwelling, Christ's mediatorial role, among others—themes that should resonate with African Christians. Nyende notes that the purpose of God's residence in Israel is to restore his dwelling among humanity. He reads

Hebrews as calling God's people to worship, which includes prayer and sacrifices on the one hand, and obedience on the other. However, it is important to expand on just what obedience to God involves, if the church is not to be an insular community focused on itself. Peter describes God's people as a royal priesthood, a holy nation, a people belonging to God. The church is set apart to worship God and to proclaim him in the world, which means they gather for worship and are then sent out into the world as witnesses. An ecclesiology that lacks this "sent out on behalf of the world" aspect is incomplete.

The message of Hebrews—that Christ is best, and that all the Israelite religious aspects foreshadowed him—also links well with Munther Isaac's emphasis that the land is God's. Just as all aspects of religious life were pointing to something else and were used by God, so too the land of Israel and all the earth belongs to God. God's people tend it for God, but they are not intended to possess or control it for themselves. All of life, from the land to the religious life as mandated by God, to the national and ethnic identities people hold—all of life is to be submitted to Christ, with the reminder that it all belongs to God, who uses it as God deems fit, in order to fulfill the *missio Dei*. Christians are called to hold lightly to the things of this world; their concern is to abide, know their identity as those united with Christ, and look forward to the fulfillment of God's plans on the final day.

With regard to the day of judgment, eschatology too shapes this ecclesiological construct and its understanding of the *missio Dei* in which the church is invited to participate: the church is called to know not only the nature and origin of its mission but also its goal, as seen in Revelation. The book of Revelation paints a sobering yet hope-filled picture for God's people. They are called to be faithful witnesses amid persecution from both demonic forces and fellow humans. Christians are called to remember they are part of a heavenly battle, one in which Christ is ultimately the supreme victor. As faithful witnesses, God's people are called to speak truthfully, to declare what they know regardless of the consequences. An ecclesiology in Africa—in all parts of the world—needs to address the reality of the spiritual forces attacking the body and teach Christians that suffering is a necessary part of taking up their cross and following their Lord. At the same time, God redeems the suffering God's people endure and reminds them that regardless of the suffering and evil they face, they can trust and hope in Christ's victory over evil. With these points in mind, it is to be hoped that the church can better negotiate the trials and obstacles it faces, while maintaining its unique identity in Christ, an identity of divine grace that glorifies the triune God. One day, God's people will rejoice with their Lord and enjoy a feast with him (Rev 19:1-9). May that day hasten!

FURTHER READING

Ande, Titre. *Leadership and Authority: Bula Matari and Life-Community Ecclesiology in Congo.* Regnum Studies in Mission. Oxford: Regnum, 2010.

Lowery, Stephanie A. *Identity and Ecclesiology: Their Relationship Among Select African Theologians.* Eugene, OR: Pickwick, 2017.

Magesa, Laurenti. *Anatomy of Inculturation: Transforming the Church in Africa.* Nairobi: Paulines Publications Africa, 2007.

Mugambi, J. N. K., and Laurenti Magesa, eds. *The Church in African Christianity: Innovative Essays in Ecclesiology.* African Challenge. Nairobi: Initiatives, 1990.

Nthamburi, Zablon. *The Pilgrimage of the African Church: Towards the Twenty-First Century.* Nairobi: Uzima, 2000.

Nyamiti, Charles. "The Church as Organ of Christ's Ancestral Mediation: An Essay on African Ecclesiology." *Revue africaine de théologie* 15, no. 30 (October 1991): 195-212.

Orobator, Agbonkhianmeghe E. *From Crisis to Kairos: The Mission of the Church in the Time of HIV/AIDS, Refugees, and Poverty.* Nairobi: Paulines Publications Africa, 2005.

———. *Theology Brewed in an African Pot.* Maryknoll, NY: Orbis, 2008.

Ukwuegbu, Bernard. "'Neither Jew Nor Greek': The Church in Africa and the Quest for Self-Understanding in the Light of the Pauline Vision and Today's Context of Cultural Pluralism." *International Journal for the Study of the Christian Church* 8 (2008): 305-18.

Uzukwu, Elochukwu E. *A Listening Church: Autonomy and Communion in African Churches.* Eugene, OR: Wipf & Stock, 2006.

37

ECCLESIOLOGY IN LATIN AMERICA

A BIBLICAL PERSPECTIVE

Carlos Sosa Siliezar

ALTHOUGH ECCLESIOLOGY is still developing in Latin American theology, there are at least two major proposals written from two distinctive angles that use the canonical Gospels as their point of departure: Leonardo Boff's ecclesiogenesis and René Padilla's holistic ecclesiology. After reviewing both proposals, I conclude that Boff's handling of the evidence is not historically accurate and that Padilla's reading of the New Testament can be enhanced by paying attention to the distinctiveness of each Gospel. I then proceed to explore the potential contribution of Johannine thought about community for the articulation of a Latin American ecclesiology.

Protestant Christianity experienced unprecedented growth in Latin America between 1960 and 1990.[1] New denominations and groups were formed, and some older ones were renovated through the influence of Pentecostalism. Most recently, some Latin American countries have

also seen the rise of newer groups called neo-Pentecostal churches. Today, Christianity in Latin America has a diverse and changing face. Not surprisingly José Míguez Bonino, a prominent Argentinian theologian, analyzed Latin American Protestantism, paying attention to its "many faces."[2] However, theological reflections about the nature and purpose of the church in Latin America have not been as copious as its many churches and denominations.[3]

During the 1970s the Roman Catholic Church was dominant in Latin America. They were the first Christians to arrive in this region in the sixteenth century. Priests in Latin America attempted to follow as closely as possible the form, format, and theology of the Roman Catholic Church in Spain and Portugal.[4] For more than three hundred years, there were no formal reflections on the mission and nature of the church produced by Christians born and active in Latin

[1]Christian Lalive d'Epinay, "The Pentecostal 'Conquista' in Chile," *Ecumenical Review* 20 (1968): 16-32; Walter J. Hollenweger, *Pentecostalism: Origins and Developments Worldwide* (Peabody, MA: Hendrickson, 1997); Martin Lindhardt, ed., *New Ways of Being Pentecostal in Latin America* (London: Lexington Books, 2016).

[2]José Míguez Bonino, *Faces of Latin American Protestantism* (Grand Rapids, MI: Eerdmans, 1997).

[3]Veli-Matti Kärkkäinen's essay in this volume, "Ecclesiology and the Church in Christian Tradition and Western Theology," observes that European ecclesiology advanced slowly and with a somewhat haphazard tone due to circumstances after the Reformation. Similarly, ecclesiology in Latin America is advancing slowly and is being highly influenced by contextual circumstances.

[4]John A. Mackay, *The Other Spanish Christ: A Study in the Spiritual History of Spain and South America* (New York: Macmillan, 1933). See also C. René Padilla, "Evangelical Theology in Latin American Contexts," in *The Cambridge Companion to Evangelical Theology*, ed. Timothy Larsen and Daniel J. Treier (Cambridge: Cambridge University Press, 2007), 259-73, here 259.

America. The situation of the Protestant churches was similar. They came to Latin America from Europe and, mainly, from the United States during the nineteenth century.[5] However, they too sought to mimic the liturgy and doctrine of their sending churches. Formal reflections on the nature and mission of the church (ecclesiology) by native Latin American leaders are unknown during this period.

Formal reflections on the nature and mission of the church in this region came first from liberation theologians. Liberation theology emphasizes the social liberation of the poor from their oppressors. A foundation for ecclesiological thought is found in Brazilian thinker Leonardo Boff's work. He articulated an innovative way of looking at ecclesiology from within the Roman Catholic tradition. He used the New Testament, especially the Synoptic Gospels (Matthew, Mark, and Luke), as a source for his reflections. In doing so, he employed the methodologies and results of redaction criticism, an approach that aids the reader in distinguishing between received traditions and the theological work of the Evangelists in handling such traditions. Boff attempted to provide a theoretical framework to understand base communities, groups of lay Christians living and reading Scripture in community without significant interventions from

the hierarchical institution. Boff regarded his proposal as "ecclesiogenesis," that is, the origins (genesis) of the church (*ekklēsia*). The official Roman Catholic reaction to Boff's proposal was not positive, to say the least. His ideas were rejected by the Church in Rome.[6] However, his proposal is still influential in Latin American theology.

Other voices, past and present, coming from the Roman Catholic Church follow Boff's initial insights.[7] Furthermore, Boff's proposal is unique in that he uses the canonical Gospels (Matthew, Mark, Luke, and John) to articulate ecclesiology. Therefore, we will focus here on his proposal.

The other thinker who has attempted to articulate ecclesiology from a Latin American perspective is Ecuadorian theologian René Padilla. He writes from an evangelical orientation. Padilla uses the canonical Gospels in the form we have them in our New Testament today in order to propose an ecclesiology that can serve a holistic mission. He is well known for proposing that the church's mission should be "integral" or "holistic." That means, in a nutshell, "a mission that maintains the unity between justification by faith and the struggle for justice, between faith and works, between spiritual needs and material and physical needs, and between the personal and the social dimensions of the gospel."[8] His ideas are very influential among Protestant and

---

[5]Sidney Rooy, "Religious Tolerance and the Arrival of Protestantism in Latin America," *Journal of Latin American Theology* 6 (2011): 41-69.

[6]Former Cardinal Joseph Ratzinger expressed his disagreements with Boff's ecclesiology in his "notification" *Dominus Iesus*. Boff's vigorous reply is found in his article, "¿Quién subvierte el Concilio? Respuesta al Cardenal J. Ratzinger a propósito de la *Dominus Iesus*," *Revista Latinoamericana de Teología* 236 (2001): 33-48. When quoting from works published in languages other than English, I provide my own translation. See also Harvey Cox, *The Silencing of Leonardo Boff: The Vatican and the Future of World Christianity* (London: Collins Religious, 1989).

[7]G. Olivieri, *Novas formas de ser Igreja* (Andradina, Brazil: Novas Formas, 1995); F. L. C. Teixeira, *A gênese das CEBs no Brasil: Elementos explicativos* (São Paulo: Paulinas, 1988); J. C. Petrini, *CEBs: Um novo sujeito popular* (Río de Janeiro: Paz e Terra, 1984); A. Quiróz Magaña, *Eclesiología en la teología de la liberación* (Salamanca, Spain: Sígueme, 1983). More recent work on ecclesiology comes from Latin American thinkers associated with the official Roman Catholic Church. They pursue insights found in the latest Conference of Bishops (Aparecida, Brazil, 2007). See, for example, Fernando Berríos, "Una comunidad de discípulos misioneros: Líneas eclesiológicas de Aparecida," *Teología y Vida* 49 (2008): 685-97. A recent assessment of Latin American ecclesiology is found in Rodrigo Polanco, "Eclesiología en Latinoamérica: Exposición y balance crítico," *Teología y Vida* 50 (2009): 131-52.

[8]Padilla, "Evangelical Theology in Latin American Contexts," 269.

evangelical churches in Latin America. Although Padilla has shown sympathy for Boff's ecclesiological proposal, a deeper analysis of both ecclesiologies reveals significant differences in the way they handle the biblical texts.[9] Padilla praises Boff for attempting to renew the Roman Catholic Church by going back to the New Testament in order to articulate his ecclesiogenesis. However, as will be shown shortly, their methodologies for approaching the biblical texts are rather different.

Regrettably, there are not many voices in the Latin American Protestant world that articulate ecclesiology from a biblical perspective. Most of the work has been done as theological articulation or as an "evangelical response" to liberation ecclesiology.[10] Therefore, engaging the foundational work of Padilla seems the best option here.

Since both Boff's and Padilla's proposals are theological articulations, it is difficult to provide a deep engagement with the biblical texts they use for support. In what follows, I will include the biblical citations provided by them, but I will not provide close assessment of their work with the biblical text. Instead, I will assess the methodologies they seem to employ when engaging the New Testament. My overall impression is that general ideas from the canonical Gospels,

rather than specific texts from the New Testament, are used by Boff and Padilla to support their views.[11]

After describing and assessing both proposals, I will attempt to perform an exegetical reading of John 13:34-35 and will try to explore the potential contribution of this passage for the articulation of ecclesiology from a Latin American perspective. By "exegetical reading" I mean paying close attention to a particular text in light of its larger literary context.

ECCLESIOGENESIS AND CHRISTIAN ORIGINS

The rise and development of "base communities" was truly innovative in Latin American ecclesiology. Boff, a former priest within the Roman Catholic tradition, described these communities as "new ecclesiological experiences," "a rebirth of the church," "the emergence of a different way of being church," and "a reinvention of the church."[12] These are base communities because laypeople gather together as a church without significant intervention from the hierarchical institution.

Historically, these communities were a response to institutional crises in the Roman Catholic Church. The first General Conference of Latin American Bishops gathered in 1955 in order to find solutions to the lack of clergy in the region. They described the situation as a

---

[9]C. René Padilla, "Introducción: una eclesiología para la misión integral," in *La iglesia local como agente de transformación: Una eclesiología para la misión integral*, ed. C. René Padilla and Tetsunao Yamamori (Buenos Aires: Kairós, 2003), 39-40.

[10]For an example of theological articulation, see Nicolás Panotto, "The Church We Imagine for Latin America: Faith and Identity in Today's Globalized World," *Journal of Latin American Theology* 9 (2014): 139-57. A pioneer and robust evangelical response to liberation theology (including its ecclesiology) is found in Emilio A. Núñez, *Liberation Theology* (Chicago: Moody, 1985). My own essay, Carlos R. Sosa, "Trayectorias de la Nueva Evangelización católica: Un enfoque evangélico," *Kairós* 39 (2006): 61-91, is also an attempt to respond to recent theological developments in Roman Catholic ecclesiology.

[11]This is more evident in Boff's proposal. I have been unable to find a single Bible reference in his description of base communities in Leonardo Boff, *Church: Charisma and Power: Liberation Theology and Institutional Church*, trans. John W. Diercksmeier (New York: Crossroad, 1985), 125-37, even in those places where he argues that base communities are "Born from the Word of God" (127).

[12]These designations are found several times in Leonardo Boff, *Ecclesiogenesis: The Base Communities Reinvent the Church*, 5th ed. (Maryknoll, NY: Orbis, 1986). See also Antonio Alonso, *Comunidades eclesiales de base: Teología-Sociología-Pastoral* (Salamanca, Spain: Sígueme, 1970); R. Muñoz, *La Iglesia en el pueblo: Hacia una eclesiología latinoamericana* (Lima: Centro de Estudios y Publicaciones, 1983); J. Galea, *Uma Igreja no povo e pelo povo* (Petrópolis, Brazil: Vozes, 1983).

"distressing problem."[13] Behind their preoccupation lay the idea that a representative of the hierarchical institution was necessary in order for a community to have a legitimate church. Structurally, these communities come close to what observers of the Protestant world call "free churches."[14]

To the official leaders, base communities seemed an imperfect solution to the problem. Laypeople gathered to read the Bible and to enjoy fellowship (*communitas fidelium*) without necessarily being under the authority of a priest. This situation engendered a new ecclesiology, that is, new theological reflections about the meaning, mission, and nature of the church. An important resource for these new reflections was the New Testament. One of the main driving questions for these new reflections was, "Did the historical and prepaschal Jesus want a church?"[15]

Posing the question this way ensures a sharp distinction between the "ecclesiology" of Jesus (if any) and the doctrinal developments of the early Christians, and anticipates giving greater authority to Jesus' own ideas than to the theological thoughts of the New Testament writers. This question also accepts almost without reserve the results of redaction criticism.[16] This methodology focuses on "the unique theological emphases" that the New Testament writers "place upon the materials they used, their specific purposes in writing their works" and the context "out of which they wrote."[17]

Boff asserts that "the church was not part of Jesus' intentions." Jesus was a Jew who announced the coming of God's kingdom. He preached only to Jews because he wanted them to accept his message of the imminent coming of the kingdom.[18] Boff understands this kingdom as a new world order in which God is the supreme ruler, and as the overcoming of all evil that oppresses the world. In this perspective, Jesus' last supper was not a sacrament for the church but the joyous anticipation of the imminent kingdom. However, the Jews rejected Jesus' mission, and therefore he failed in his attempt to set up God's kingdom on earth. This failure was partially resolved in the cross. Since Jesus realized that he was unable to convince people with his message and works, he won people by taking on himself the sins of the world. Thus, God's kingdom was not fulfilled in a universal sense. Jesus himself then became God's kingdom. His message, demands, and self were the kingdom of God in the present time.

The church, then, is the substitute for the unfulfilled kingdom. On the one hand, there is discontinuity between Jesus' preaching about the kingdom and the beginning of the church. This discontinuity is marked by the cross. On the other hand, there is continuity between Jesus and the church. His resurrection ensures his presence among his followers. Since the kingdom is present in Jesus, the presence of the risen Jesus among his followers allows for continuity between Jesus and

---

[13]William T. Cavanaugh, "The Ecclesiologies of Medellin and the Lessons of the Base Communities," *Cross Currents* 44 (1994): 67-84.
[14]Interestingly, Kärkkäinen, "Ecclesiology," contrasts the Roman Catholic Church with the free church without seemingly noticing the close structural resemblances between Roman Catholic base communities and Protestant free churches.
[15]Boff, *Ecclesiogenesis*, 77. In the following paragraphs I will attempt to summarize Boff's arguments.
[16]This methodology attempts to distinguish between the putative oral and written traditions about Jesus that the Gospel writers received, and their theologically motivated editorial changes and additions to such traditions.
[17]Robert H. Stein, "Redaction Criticism (NT)," in *The Anchor Bible Dictionary*, ed. David Noel Freedman (New York: Doubleday, 1992), 5:647.
[18]This idea is still current in historical Jesus research. See Samuel Byrskog and Tobias Hägerland, eds., *The Mission of Jesus*, Wissenschaftliche Untersuchungen zum Neuen Testament 2/391 (Tübingen: Mohr Siebeck, 2015). Historical Jesus research presupposes that the real Jesus of history was different from the Christ portrayed in the four canonical Gospels. Scholars engaged in trying to recover the putative "real" Jesus from the Gospels are said to be part of the "quest of the historical Jesus."

the church.[19] Notwithstanding this perspective, the disciples did not establish the church immediately after Jesus' resurrection. They still preached the gospel to their fellow Jews and waited for the imminent arrival of God's kingdom. The delay of the parousia, Jesus' second coming to the world, and the wide acceptance of their message among Gentiles drove them to create the church. This they did under the inspiration and guidance of the Holy Spirit.

The disciples started organizing themselves in order to face all the challenges in the world that their life without Jesus would imply. This organization was also necessary because their message was being welcomed among Gentiles. Although the historical Jesus did not conceive of a church of Jews and Gentiles, the disciples decided to preach among non-Jews. They received light, illumination, and inspiration from the Spirit in order to transpose eschatology (the things to come with Jesus' second coming to the world) into the time of the church and to translate the doctrine of God's kingdom into the doctrine of the church. Thus, the church is a temporal and imperfect realization of God's kingdom.

Two important components of the newly created church were the apostles and the Eucharist. The group of the twelve selected by Jesus in order to symbolize the twelve Israelite tribes were now sent to preach the gospel to Gentiles. This sending made them apostles of the gospel. An apostle, then, is a postpaschal, postresurrection, missionary concept.[20] They innovated and preserved traditions according to their own

contextual needs. They even wrote Gospels in which their theological perspectives coexisted along with the historical Jesus' own message. Similarly, the Lord's Supper acquires new meanings after Jesus' resurrection. For the church, the Eucharist is not related to the imminent coming of the kingdom but is instead nourishment for the church, a symbol of unity and the permanent presence of Jesus' sacrifice.[21]

Base communities are still current in Latin America, and their ecclesiology is still developing.[22] The designation of Argentinian Bishop Jorge Mario Bergoglio as the 266th pope of the Roman Catholic Church has raised expectations regarding the future shape of the Church.[23] Pope Francis's first apostolic exhortation, *Evangelii Gaudium* ("The Joy of the Gospel"), published in 2013, devotes several paragraphs which consider "An ecclesial renewal which cannot be deferred" (§§ 27-33). A remarkable paragraph for our purpose is number 29:

> Other Church institutions, basic communities [i.e., base communities] and small communities, movements, and forms of association are a source of enrichment for the Church, raised up by the Spirit for evangelizing different areas and sectors. Frequently they bring a new evangelizing fervour and a new capacity for dialogue with the world whereby the Church is renewed.[24]

A critical evaluation of Boff's ecclesiology should highlight first its positive elements. The most remarkable is the idea that laypeople can gather around God's Word without significant intervention from the "official church." As Pope

---

[19]Leonardo Boff and Clodovis Boff, *Introducing Liberation Theology* (Maryknoll, NY: Orbis, 1987), 76.

[20]Passages such as Lk 6:13 ("Jesus called his disciples . . . whom he named apostles" [ESV]) are not to be attributed to Jesus but to Luke's redaction, according to Leonardo Boff.

[21]Leonardo Boff, *When Theology Listens to the Poor* (San Francisco: Harper & Row, 1988), 101-15.

[22]Stefan Silber, "Los laicos somos la Iglesia: 'Otro modo de ser Iglesia' ya es una realidad," *Alternativas* 30 (2005): 123-46.

[23]Pablo Richard, "Otra Iglesia es posible: El papa Francisco nos abre nuevos caminos," *Alternativas* 46 (2013): 185-98.

[24]Pope Francis, *The Joy of the Gospel* (*Evangelii Gaudium*) (New York: Image, 2014), 26.

Francis states, base communities bring renewal to the church. Furthermore, the idea that laypeople should take an active role in the mission of the church comes close to the emphasis on the priesthood of all believers in Protestant theology. Even the early church fathers from the second century AD such as Ignatius and Irenaeus highlighted the idea that Jesus' presence through his Spirit legitimizes a community as fully Christian.[25]

Another important positive element is the emphasis on God's kingdom. Since this was a major element in Jesus' preaching according to the Synoptic tradition, any ecclesiology should use this topic as a frame of reference. The kingdom of God is universal and not restricted to a particular faith community or local church. It points, as Boff highlights, to a new world order in which God is the absolute ruler.

However, there are some other elements of Boff's proposal that require further consideration. On the practical side, it is very difficult to imagine that members of base communities in Latin America (many of them with low levels of education and living in rural areas) would make a sharp distinction between the teachings of the historical Jesus and the teaching of the Synoptic Gospels. A plain reading of these texts would certainly point to similarities and differences between them, but it is doubtful that such a reading would lead to the conclusion that Jesus' teachings during his earthly ministry were very different from the disciples' later interpretations of them. It remains possible that someone with knowledge of redaction criticism would lead the discussions of a base community so that its

members could reach such conclusions. But then base communities would require a significant intervention from a new kind of "priest," namely, people with a special knowledge about layers of tradition in the final form of the Synoptic Gospels. This new "academic priesthood" goes against the very nature of base communities, in which all the members explore the New Testament without significant intervention from the official Roman Catholic Church.

Boff's claims can also be assessed historically. There is no doubt that Jesus directed his message primarily to Jews. However, not all the evidence supports the contention that the disciples' latter mission to Gentiles was only a later innovation that coexisted along with Jesus' exclusive preaching to Jews. It makes better historical sense to suggest that the disciples' Gentile mission was somehow shaped by Jesus' enduring impact during his earthly ministry.[26]

Judaism during Jesus' time was divided into several groups. On the one hand, some groups such as the Pharisees regarded themselves as "the righteous." This meant that all those who did not fulfill the law in their terms were regarded as "sinners." Thus, the term *sinners* denoted "Jews who practised their Judaism *differently* from the writer's faction. They were 'sinners' . . . but only from a sectarian viewpoint, and only as judged by the sectarians' interpretation of the law."[27] On the other hand, Jesus was remembered as directing his mission to "sinners" (Mk 2:17) and sharing the table with them. He was seen by his detractors as a "glutton and a drunkard, a friend of tax collectors and sinners" (Mt 11:19; Lk 7:34 NRSV).

---

[25]This is shown in Kärkkäinen, "Ecclesiology." He also notices that European ecclesiologies such as that of Wolfhart Pannenberg regard the Spirit as "community-forming" and "communally-directed."

[26]James D. G. Dunn, *Jesus, Paul, and the Gospels* (Grand Rapids, MI: Eerdmans, 2011), 97-98.

[27]Dunn, *Jesus, Paul, and the Gospels*, 100.

Jesus' association with those regarded as sinners might suggest that he saw God's grace open to even those deemed to be excluded from the covenant. It is plausible, then, that knowledge of Jesus' mission led the apostles to conclude that God's grace is not restricted to those who fulfill the law.[28] In preaching to the Gentiles, the apostles were not actually innovating and departing from Jesus' mission. They were taking the next natural step in continuity with Jesus' earthly ministry.

Furthermore, it remains possible that Jesus actually had contact with non-Jewish people. There is evidence that Gentiles used to visit Jerusalem during Jesus' time. The existence of two warning inscriptions written in Greek to prevent Gentiles from entering the inner precincts of the Jewish temple would indicate that some non-Jews used to visit Jerusalem. During Jesus' time, Jerusalem was a "metropolis of international, worldwide significance, a great 'attraction.'" The Synoptic tradition "presupposes without further ado" that Jesus was capable of having a conversation in Greek. We find him talking to a captain from Capernaum, Pilate, and the Syro-Phoenician woman. Furthermore, Galilee, a place where Jesus carried out most of his earthly ministry, offered many opportunities to have contact with non-Jews.[29] Therefore, the portrayal of Jesus' contact with Gentiles should be taken as historically plausible instead of only as a late theological elaboration by the Gospels' final editors.

HOLISTIC ECCLESIOLOGY AND BIBLICAL THEOLOGY

Although the evangelical church has been present in Latin America for many decades, only recently has its ecclesiology started to develop. René Padilla and Tetsunao Yamamori recognized back in 2003 that "a remarkable deficit in Latin American evangelical theology is that found in the area of ecclesiology." Padilla, in particular, has proposed an ecclesiology that can nurture holistic mission.[30] In order to articulate such an ecclesiology, Padilla uses the Gospels, mainly the Synoptic Gospels, in their final form. The driving question of his reading of the New Testament seems to be: How does the Gospels' ecclesiology support the theological concept of holistic mission?

Padilla argues for a holistic ecclesiology that has, at its center, the fulfillment of holistic mission.[31] Only a church that has a holistic ecclesiology is able to make a positive impact in its community and is capable of transforming society. This holistic ecclesiology has four intertwining characteristics. The first, and fundamental, characteristic is commitment to Jesus Christ as Lord of all. The heart of the New Testament is precisely the confession of Jesus as Lord (1 Cor 8:4-6). This confession is tied to the Greek version of the Old Testament, where Yahweh, the God of the Old Testament, was referred to as "Lord." This confession also was a protest against the first-century Roman imperial cult, with its emphasis on the absolute authority of the Roman emperor. The church, then, that confesses that Jesus is Lord over all will have a mission that concerns all aspects of life: for example, economics, politics, culture, society, art, ecology, and community (1 Cor 1:2; see Acts 9:14, 21; 22:16). Christology, the

---

[28]See Dunn, *Jesus, Paul, and the Gospels*, 101, 104.
[29]Martin Hengel, *The "Hellenization" of Judaea in the First Century After Christ*, trans. John Bowden (Eugene, OR: Wipf & Stock, 2003), 9, 11, 17.
[30]Padilla and Yamamori, *Iglesia local*, 7; Padilla, "Introducción," 13-45.
[31]In what follows, I summarize the arguments found in Padilla, "Introducción," 13-45.

acknowledgment that Jesus is Lord over all the earth, is the basis of ecclesiology.[32]

The second characteristic of a holistic ecclesiology is discipleship. Following Jesus means a process of transformation (Rom 10:12-15). The disciple is one who follows Jesus' example and obeys his teachings (Acts 2:42; Rom 6:17; Gal 1:8-9). Jesus taught and showed how to love God, love our neighbors, serve others, be in solidarity with the poor, and be committed to the truth (Mk 10:43-45; Lk 14:25-33; Jn 10:15). The holistic disciple should live as Jesus lived. However, discipleship is not a lonely business. The disciple is part of a Christian community, where they find God's grace. Therefore, the third characteristic of a holistic ecclesiology is community. The holistic church is actually a new humanity. Its testimony is incarnational—that is, it becomes real in the world just as God's Word became flesh and dwelt among us (Jn 1:14; 20:21). The church embodies God's word and is a witness of God's purpose for the whole of creation. The paradigm of the church's mission is Jesus' life, ministry, death, resurrection, and exaltation (Mt 10:18, 24-25; Acts 2:36; 1 Cor 15:25, 56-57; Eph 1:19-20).

This community of disciples is not, however, an end in itself. The Christian community plays a priestly role as intermediary between God and the world. This is the fourth characteristic of a holistic church. Through gifts and ministries, the Holy Spirit empowers the church to perform transformative acts in society (1 Cor 12:4; Eph 4:11-12). These transformations reflect God's purposes for human life and for his whole creation. Each member of the church should use their gifts to advance the transformation of this world. There should not be a sharp distinction between clergy and laymen and laywomen. Every Christian should be actively involved in the mission of the church. The clergy should be more like laypeople, and laypeople should be involved in the ministry of the church.

If our understanding of Christology is based on the confession that Jesus is Lord over all creation, our ecclesiology can then only be a holistic ecclesiology that inevitably leads to a holistic mission. That is, the whole church and all of its members are committed to the transformation of the whole world, following Jesus' example and living under his death, resurrection, and exaltation.

In evaluating Padilla's proposal we should start with his approach. It is a valuable contribution to look at the Gospels in their final form. This is the way that many lay Christians in Latin America would read the New Testament. He hardly makes a distinction between what Jesus taught and what the Gospel writers wrote. This, however, could play against his proposal. Reading the Gospels in their final form and extracting from them a holistic ecclesiology runs the risk of not paying enough attention to the theological distinctiveness of each Gospel and, indeed, of each book of the New Testament.

There is unity of thought across the New Testament. However, this unity should not be maximized beyond what can be seen from the New Testament itself. There are dimensions, perspectives, and contributions from each New Testament book on the topic of ecclesiology. This diversity does not necessarily oppose a holistic ecclesiology. It might be the case that paying attention to the distinct contribution of each Gospel from an ecclesiological perspective may enhance and enrich what Padilla calls holistic ecclesiology.

---

[32]Ecclesiologies from other contexts, however, operate within a trinitarian framework that, in turn, allows a more ecumenical understanding. See Kärkkäinen, "Ecclesiology."

FROM EXEGESIS TO ECCLESIOLOGY

In what follows, I attempt to undertake constructive contextualized biblical reflection on the Gospel of John. My aim is to make a small contribution to Latin American ecclesiology by highlighting some distinctive features of Johannine ideas about community in John 13:34-35.[33] I have intentionally selected the Gospel of John because this seems a neglected text in classic Latin American liberation theology.[34] When it is used as a source of theology, the favorite passage seems to be the story of the Samaritan woman in John 4.[35] I will suggest three dimensions that should be considered in articulating the nature and mission of the church. I will preface each dimension with a brief description of my own observations and experience as a member of the Guatemalan church and society.

Although there is much debate about the extent and form of ecclesiological thought in the Gospel of John, there are at least three indications in John 13:34-35 that point to the idea of a new community of disciples.[36] The first indication is the separation of Jesus from his disciples, explained in John 13:33. Jesus is leaving for a place where his disciples cannot come. This separation entails a new form of existence for the disciples as a group. The second indication is the reference to a "new commandment" in John 13:34. The adjective *new* already points to a distinctive form of community among the disciples.

The disciples will maintain a relationship with Jesus through obeying a new commandment. The third indication is the use of the ideas found in John 13:34-35 in latter Johannine works. In 1 John 3:23 (ESV) we read, "This is his commandment . . . love one another, just as he has commanded us." Similarly, in 2 John 5 (ESV) we find, "I ask you . . .—not as though I were writing you a new commandment, but the one we have had from the beginning—that we love one another." This would imply that the commandment found in John 13:34 was taken as foundational for Jesus' followers after his departure.[37]

How might the Johannine ideas of community found in John 13:34-35 speak to the Latin American context? From a Latin American perspective, I suggest that churches should see themselves as (1) local communities with global awareness, (2) suffering communities that love the world, and (3) communities where diversity is reconciled.

Local communities with global awareness.
Latin American realities are deeply influenced by the global context. In Guatemala, for example, the US Embassy is often found expressing public opinions about the social and political situation of the country. The Dominican Republic-Central America Free Trade Agreement and the Economic Agreement between the European Union and Central America put Guatemala in an economic relationship with the United States and the most

---

[33]A Latin American "popular reading" of this passage is found in Ernesto Cardenal, *The Gospel in Solentiname* (Maryknoll, NY: Orbis, 2010), 543-49.

[34]A notable exception is José Miranda, *Being and the Messiah* (Maryknoll, NY: Orbis, 1976).

[35]For example, Néstor Míguez, "Reading John 4 in the Interface Between Ordinary and Scholarly Interpretation," in *Through the Eyes of Another: Intercultural Reading of the Bible*, ed. Hans de Wit, Louis Jonker, Marleen Kool, and Daniel Schipani (Elkhart, IN: Institute of Mennonite Studies, 2004), 334-47.

[36]For an example of the debate, see Francis J. Moloney, "John 18:15-27: A Johannine View of the Church," in *The Gospel of John: Text and Context*, Biblical Interpretation Series 72 (Leiden: Brill, 2005), 313-29.

[37]A few scholars suggest that the Johannine letters were written before the Gospel of John. See Udo Schnelle, "Die Reihenfolge der johanneischen Schriften," *New Testament Studies* 57 (2011): 91-113. This view, however, is not dominant among scholars.

powerful countries of Europe. This context might point to specific international applications of the love motif found in John 13:34-35. The following thoughts do not attempt to argue that the love command become a central place in all trade agreements. Instead, I suggest that the Johannine love command should be at the center of reciprocal activities between fellow Christians, including business relations.

According to this Johannine text, the most important characteristic of a community of disciples is love. This idea is repeated three times in these two verses: "that you love one another" (Jn 13:34); "you are to love one another" (Jn 13:34); "have love for one another" (Jn 13:35).[38] In the Gospel of John love is a divine characteristic. The first reference to love in this Gospel is found in John 3:16: "For God so loved the world . . ." (see Jn 17:23). God is portrayed several times as loving the Son (e.g., Jn 3:35; 10:17), and Jesus is likewise portrayed as loving the Father (Jn 14:31). This divine community between Jesus and the Father is maintained by love. The Father loved the Son even before the foundation of the world (Jn 17:24, 26). The way the Father shows his love for the Son is by sharing all things with him. The Father has given all things into his hands (Jn 3:35; 13:3).[39]

This love between Christians should extend to all those followers of Jesus living in different countries (Jn 17:20-21). Laws that regulate economic agreements between Guatemala and the United States and the European Union are not based on the Johannine idea of love. Therefore, Christian businesspeople from those regions that benefit from trade with Guatemala should ask: "What would be the best way to show love to my Guatemalan fellow Christians when doing business with them?" "Is it enough to follow the official international laws?"

The way Christians should show love among themselves is by imitating the love that God has for his Son: sharing all things and placing them in his hands (Jn 3:35; 13:3). The love command should be at the center of any kind of relation between Christians from different countries. Even those Christians in the so-called First World who profit from trade with fellow Christians from countries such as Guatemala should reflect on the place of the love command in their business interactions.

Suffering communities that love the world. Christianity is the majority religion in most Latin American countries. This is taken as a blessing by many internal and external observers. However, it carries a risk: society's values and worldview can negatively influence the mission of the church. Guatemala's elected president and vice president (2012) had to resign in 2015 due to allegations of corruption. The president was the guest of honor at the inauguration of the new church building of one of the largest neo-Pentecostal churches in Guatemala in 2013. He was given the pulpit to address thousands of parishioners, although he had never publicly indicated his adherence to any evangelical church. The elected vice president also donated a very expensive flag to be put in this new church building. Three years later it was discovered that money to finance the flag came from corruption in the government. The church was forced to give the flag back.

---

[38]This idea is repeated again in Jn 15:12 and Jn 15:17 (see Jn 17:26). The love motif is prominent in the Gospel of John. For a classic study of this topic, see A. Feuillet, *Le mystère de l'amour divin dans la théologie johannique* (Paris: Gabalda, 1972). For a more recent treatment of this topic, see Sjef van Tilborg, *Imaginative Love in John*, Biblical Interpretation Series 2 (Leiden: Brill, 1993).

[39]This Johannine idea about divine community shaping ecclesial community is an emphasis found in Eastern Orthodox tradition. A robust vision of divine community should be echoed in an ecclesiology of relational existence (Kärkkäinen, "Ecclesiology").

The Gospel of John indicates clearly that God loves the world (Jn 3:16; 17:23). God loves the world because he created it in the beginning (Jn 1:3, 10; 17:5, 26). Jesus shows his love for the Father by loving sacrificially what the Father loves, namely, the world. Jesus' love for the world has two dimensions. The first dimension is his giving his life in order to take away the sins of the world (Jn 10:17; 13:1; 15:13). Through his suffering on the cross, he showed his sacrificial love for the world. The second dimension is his testifying about the world that its works are evil (Jn 7:7). On the one hand, Jesus speaks the truth because he is the light. On the other hand, the world is attached to falsehood and is enslaved in darkness. This is why the world hates Jesus. Ironically, Jesus' love for the world was the cause of his earthly suffering. Because he spoke against falsehood and darkness in the world, he suffered during his earthly ministry. He faced opposition, accusations, threats of death, and persecution.

Christians living in countries such as Guatemala with complex social problems where politics plays a major role might conclude that a "neutral" position is the best way to show love for the world. However, John 13:34-35 clearly indicates that love for the world implies taking a position in favor of the light and the truth and against darkness and falsehood.

If Christians are called to imitate Jesus, one might conclude that evidence that a church follows Jesus is its speaking the truth in the midst of a world full of lies. As long as the church loves the world, the church will suffer hate from the world. This means that an important component of the church's mission is testifying about the world that its works are evil. The disciples who live in a new covenant with Jesus (Jn 13:34) cannot live in covenant with the world.

The "new command" found in John 13:34 is the Johannine equivalent of the new covenant elsewhere in the New Testament. During his last meal, Jesus instituted the observance of the Lord's Supper (Mt 26:28; Mk 14:24; Lk 22:20; 1 Cor 11:25). This celebration would determine the way the disciples would live as a group.[40] The regular, perhaps weekly, observance of the Lord's Supper should shape their existence as a community. The Johannine passage we are considering (Jn 13:34-35) is also set in the context of Jesus' last supper (Jn 13:1-2). However, John omits any overt reference to the actual supper with bread and wine and instead focuses on a dramatic action, Jesus' washing of his disciples' feet (Jn 13:4-12). The Gospel of John lacks the actual institution of the new covenant and instead focuses on the new command that should characterize not the weekly but the daily life of his disciples. This new command should be fulfilled in the context of sacrificial service, just as Jesus washed his disciples' feet.

Communities where diversity is reconciled. Oppression and injustice have deeply marked the history of Latin America. Complex problems have divided Latin American societies and have even created alienation. Guatemala is regarded as one of the most diverse and multicultural countries in the world. Four groups coexist in this country: Maya, Xinca, Garifuna, and Ladinos.[41] Sixty percent of the population is Maya, but the central government is run by a

---

[40]J. Ramsey Michaels, *The Gospel of John*, New International Commentary on the New Testament (Grand Rapids, MI: Eerdmans, 2010), 758-59.

[41]People with strong ethnic ties with pre-Columbian inhabitants of Mesoamerica are called Mayas. Indigenous people culturally different from Mayas are identified as Xincas. People called Garifunas have strong ethnic links with West and Central African people brought to Latin America by Spanish people in the sixteenth century. *Ladinos* is a general term used to refer to all those contemporary inhabitants of Guatemala who can claim Spanish or Portuguese ancestors.

huge majority of Ladinos. Although Mayan people contribute to the rich cultural diversity of Guatemala, one of the major social problems of the country is racism.[42] In the midst of such intricate realities, the church should be the epicenter of reconciliation, transforming the world through the powerful testimony of God's love among them. The church should demonstrate a reconciled diversity.

The diversity of people attracted to Jesus in the Gospel of John is noteworthy. The Johannine Jesus indicates: "when I am lifted up from the earth, I will draw *all people* to myself" (Jn 12:32 ESV). Indeed, we find significant diversity among the people who approach Jesus in the Gospel of John: for example, disciples of John the Baptist (Jn 1:37), a true Israelite such as Nathanael (Jn 1:47), a ruler of the Jews (Jn 3:1), a woman from Samaria (Jn 4:7), a royal official (Jn 4:46), a former blind man (Jn 9:35), a family from the village of Bethany (Jn 11:1-3), Greek pilgrims in Jerusalem (Jn 12:20), the wealthy Joseph of Arimathea (Jn 19:38), and fishermen from Galilee (Jn 21:1-2). This is not surprising because the Word was actively involved in the creation of everything that exists (Jn 1:3, 10), and Jesus' mission as portrayed in the Gospel of John concerns the whole world (Jn 3:16; 12:44-50).

The church, then, should be taken as the privileged space where creation is reconciled to its Creator and where diversity is redeemed. As Jesus departs from the world, he commands his disciples to love one another, just as he loved them (Jn 13:34).[43] During his earthly ministry, Jesus showed his love for his disciples by re-

vealing the Father to them and teaching them the truth. Jesus loved them just as the Father loved him (Jn 15:9). Jesus also loved the world sacrificially, giving his life for the world (Jn 15:13). Jesus showed his love for the Father through obedience to his commandments (Jn 14:31). The love between the Father and the Son is sustained by Jesus' obedience to him (Jn 15:10). In loving one another, the disciples must reflect the same "divine community" between the Son and the Father. Since God loves his creation, the disciples show their love for the Father when they love what God loves, namely, his Son and his creation.

Leonardo Boff was correct to indicate that Jesus' resurrection ensures his presence among his followers. René Padilla also correctly highlights the importance of the confession of Jesus as Lord among the community of disciples. However, from a Johannine perspective, the risen Jesus is present among those disciples who follow the new command to love one another. Jesus will manifest himself to those who love him (Jn 14:21). Even the Father and the Son will come to abide and make their home with those who love Jesus (Jn 14:23). It is not only the confession of Jesus as Lord that ensures his presence among his followers. Jesus is present among those disciples who love one another.[44]

Love is actually what brings God closer to his world. Although the world loves darkness (Jn 3:19), God approaches his creation by sending his Son into the world (Jn 3:16). Those who love Jesus experience a very close encounter with their Creator, since both the Son and the Father

---

[42]Heather E. Mitchel, "Guatemalan Indigenous Youth: Experiences of Ethnic Discrimination and Its Impact" (PsyD diss., Wheaton Graduate School, 2013).

[43]It is worth noting that while the Synoptic Gospels emphasize love for enemies, the Gospel of John highlights love among disciples. See Hugo Zorrilla and Daniel Chiquete, *Evangelio de Juan*, Comentario para Exegesis y Traducción (Miami: Sociedades Bíblicas Unidas, 2008), 443.

[44]This insight is also found in Cardenal, *Gospel in Solentiname*, 443.

come to them and make their home with them (Jn 14:23; see Jn 8:42).

This love has what we might call a missionary goal. If the community of Jesus' followers love one another, "all people will know" that they are his disciples (Jn 13:35). When the disciples love one another just as Jesus loved them, they become perfect in unity (Jn 17:23). The world will then know that Jesus was sent and loved by the Father (Jn 17:23). A community that fulfills the new command is a powerful testimony to the world of the love between the Father and the Son (Jn 14:31). Since loving God is the way creation can reestablish a proper relationship with its Creator, and since loving Jesus means loving God, a community of disciples in which each loves the other as the Son loves the Father is in itself a testimony to the world of God's love.

This threefold perspective provided by John 13:34-35 has the potential to enrich our understanding of the historical confession of the church as contained in the Nicene-Constantinopolitan Creed (AD 381). For centuries, Christians around the world have confessed that the church is "one, holy, catholic, and apostolic."[45] Since the church is one and universal, the idea of local communities with global awareness is more than an ideal; it should be our commitment.[46] Local Christian communities are churches "insofar as they are in communion with other similar communities."[47] Christians from different contexts and geographies should constantly seek collaboration and communion not only for "ecclesiastically related" issues but also for larger social issues such as those described in this essay. This unity and universality also means that all the wonderful dimensions of God's diversity found in creation (Jn 1:3, 10; 17:5, 24) can and will be reconciled in Jesus through his disciples.

The confession of the church as holy does not make it impossible to have contact with the world, which is in darkness. God loves the world and has sanctified Jesus' disciples (Jn 13:10; 17:11, 17) so that they can keep engaging the world with his Word. The only way the church can honor its title of holy is by continually shining its light in the darkness, by constantly bringing life to the world, and by loving a world that hates God. By keeping the tradition of the apostles, especially as contained in the New Testament texts, the church remains faithful to the truth, is sanctified in the truth, and engages a world dominated by lies in order to transform it.

Latin American churches with their distinctive liturgies, traditions, and confessions are part of the holy, catholic, and apostolic church. However, the church is not going to be recognized by the world as followers of Jesus primarily because of its dogmas, rules, or liturgy.[48] Love among one another is what makes churches part of the universal church.

CONCLUSION

Latin American ecclesiology still needs development. The two proposals evaluated here (Boff's and Padilla's) are helpful, but they can be improved. There is a need for more exegetical

---

[45]The received text of the Greek church and the Latin version of Dionysius Exiguus are found in Philip Schaff, *The Creeds of Christendom with a History and Critical Notes* (New York: Harper, 1877), 2:58. Actually, the characteristic construction of this confession in the Greek reception, "we believe in" (πιστεύω + εἰς), is found several times in the Gospel of John (e.g., Jn 2:11; 3:16; 6:35; 11:48; 16:9).

[46]For Jürgen Moltmann, *The Church in the Power of the Spirit: A Contribution to Messianic Ecclesiology*, trans. Margaret Kohl (London: SCM Press, 1977), 339-40, the creed provides "statements of hope" that should become "statements of action." See Kärkkäinen, "Ecclesiology."

[47]Kärkkäinen, "Ecclesiology."

[48]Zorrilla and Chiquete, *Evangelio de Juan*, 443.

work on the New Testament, paying attention to the individual theological contributions of each text. There is also need for an integrative work that can accommodate the rich diversity found in the New Testament texts and their significance to the contemporary church and society.

A reading of John 13:34-35 with attention to the Latin American context, particularly the Guatemalan context, has shown that the category of love should take a prominent place in any ecclesiological articulation. The meaning of this noun is framed and shaped by the larger Johannine thought in which love is the foundation of the unique relationship between the Father and the Son. This divine community is actually extended to all those who love the Son. Jesus and the Father are present with those who love each other. Furthermore, Jesus' followers should follow his example by loving what the Father loves, namely, the world.

A constructive contextualized reading of John 13:34-35 has the potential to nurture Latin American ecclesiology by highlighting the nature of the church as a local community with global awareness, by emphasizing the being of the church as a suffering community that loves the world, and by underscoring its mission of reconciling the creation with its Creator and redeeming diversity.

FURTHER READING

Azevedo, Marcelo de C. *Basic Ecclesial Communities in Brazil*. Washington, DC: Georgetown University Press, 1987.

Boff, Leonardo. *Church, Charism and Power: Liberation Theology and the Institutional Church*. Translated by John W. Diercksmeier. New York: Crossroad, 1985.

Hewitt, W. E. *Basic Christian Communities and Social Change in Brazil*. Lincoln: University of Nebraska Press, 1991.

Kärkkäinen, Veli-Matti. *Introduction to Ecclesiology: Ecumenical, Historical and Global Perspectives*. Downers Grove, IL: InterVarsity Press, 2002.

Núñez C., Emilio A., and William D. Taylor. *Crisis and Hope in Latin America: An Evangelical Perspective*. Pasadena, CA: William Carey Library, 1996.

Padilla, C. René. *Mission Between the Times: Essays on the Kingdom*. Revised and updated. Carlisle, UK: Langham Monographs, 2010.

Sobrino, Jon, and Ignacio Ellacuría, eds. *Mysterium liberationis: Fundamental Concepts of Liberation Theology*. Maryknoll, NY: Orbis, 1993.

38

THE COMMUNITY AS UNION WITH CHRIST IN THE MIDST OF CONFLICT

AN ECCLESIOLOGY OF THE PAULINE LETTERS FROM A CHINESE PERSPECTIVE

Xiaxia E. Xue

THIS ESSAY EXPLORES from a Chinese perspective the essence of the church as described in the Pauline letters. After a brief survey of the historical forms of Chinese ecclesiology, the essay argues that the essence of the church is the community in union with Christ in the midst of conflict. It examines the Pauline churches in Galatia and Corinth, and also the churches in Hong Kong. The essay considers both the earthly and transcendental dimensions of the church. On the one hand, the church is fully human because Christian communities share the human characteristics of tension and fragility. On the other hand, the church is transcendent because its true identity is the body of Christ and it is created by Christ. The church stands as a dynamic community in the process of growing into its fullness. In its continuous struggle and unceasing efforts to achieve unity, the church grows toward greater maturity.

The church is the assembly of the faithful whose marks the Nicene Creed proclaims as "one, holy, catholic, and apostolic." It is, however, not a pure instrument representing God's presence, since throughout history it becomes manifest in the imperfect nature of its members. Conflict is natural to Christian churches. Starting from the early church in the first century and throughout every following age, people have experienced divisions in the church.[1] One instance is the church in Corinth. It was reported that there were several parties in this church. Some claimed to belong to Paul, some to Apollos, some to Cephas, and some even to Christ. Paul cried out to the Corinthian church, "Is Christ divided? Was Paul crucified for you?" (1 Cor 1:13 ESV).

Tension and conflict, even division, were characteristic of the early church, for the church consists of people who think differently due to each one's experiences and identity. Does such intrachurch struggle and fragmentation contradict the great gospel of reconciliation? Of course not. These conflicts and how the early followers dealt with them demonstrate that the church community is not an otherworldly entity

---

[1]Lukas Vischer et al., *Unity of the Church in the New Testament and Today* (Grand Rapids, MI: Eerdmans, 2010), 1-2.

but a real body of flesh-and-blood humans in the process of growing into maturity.[2] The tensions created by the differences of divergent Christian groups challenge the church to become more mature.[3] Lukas Vischer states, "From the very beginning the community had to struggle for its unity. . . . Unity shatters when this struggle ceases. It is destroyed primarily by the hardening of positions, by exclusivity and self-contented isolation."[4] In other words, dealing with the struggle helps to push forward the growth and maturity of the churches.

These conflicts are also rooted in modern churches, as we see in churches in Hong Kong. In contemporary Hong Kong churches, Christians are divided according to their attitudes toward the Chinese central government. Strongly held attitudes trigger fragmentation within the churches. Some wish to continue to relate to and support the churches in Mainland China, and some do not want to. From this conflict arise divisions among them.

This essay aims to explore through Pauline texts how the first Christians dealt with their fragmenting struggles and then make application to modern Asian churches in Hong Kong to clarify the essence and nature of the church. However, one may question how texts from two thousand years ago can address modern church issues. With great insight, Vischer has provided a good reason to use these texts:

> Reasons that compelled the first generations to struggle for community are still valid today. What was true for the authors of the New Testament is still true for the modern ecumenical movement—that with his reconciling work in

Christ God has laid the foundation for a community in love, and that obedience to God involves giving visible expression to this unity. The call to unity is the same, and it is therefore not surprising that the great texts of the New Testament in which the drive to unity has been formulated are also relevant today.[5]

Therefore, this essay will examine the origins of the church and the Nicene Creed to describe and explain both the reality and the ideal nature of the church. Then it will focus on the conflict in Pauline churches and in today's churches in Hong Kong. Third, the way Paul deals with conflicts within the churches will be examined, from which the essence of the church will be derived. Finally, the essay will apply Paul's principles in dealing with such conflicts to the current conflicts in the churches in Hong Kong. But first I will offer a brief survey of Chinese ecclesiologies as examples of dynamic Christian communities and their contexts.

A Brief Survey of Chinese Ecclesiologies

There are many different types of Chinese churches. These include the Three-Self (self-governance, self-support, self-propagation) Patriotic Church, house churches, local assemblies, registered churches, and the True Jesus Church. The Three-Self Patriotic Church is an institutional, state-approved church that was constituted after the communists established the new Red China in 1949. In order to adapt to the new political environment, Three-Self Church leaders decided to show their loyalty to the state by rejecting the influence of foreigners in the areas of leadership,

---

[2]Vischer et al., *Unity of the Church*, 5.
[3]Luke Timothy Johnson, *The Creed: What Christians Believe and Why It Matters* (New York: Doubleday, 2003), 275.
[4]Vischer et al., *Unity of the Church*, 14.
[5]Vischer et al., *Unity of the Church*, 15.

finance, and mission.[6] According to K. H. Ting, the Three-Self Church needed to be independent from foreign countries and to carry out the Three-Self policy because the revival of China required Christians to be in line with the state. Christians henceforth would be accepted as patriotic citizens, thereby enabling more effective evangelism.[7] Also, Y. T. Wu, the first Three-Self Church leader after the establishment of the People's Republic of China, maintained that the most significant expressions of the church were in social action and moral doctrine. Therefore, it was important for him to respond to social and political issues, and Wu participated actively in political movements.[8] For him, Christian ethics that responded to particular social and political issues were important.[9]

If the Three-Self Church's close connection with the Chinese social and political environment is at one end of the spectrum, at the other end are the house churches and their relationship with their political and cultural environment. Wang Mingdao represents those conservatives who refused to compromise with the communist government.[10] In Wang's view, the church is independent of any worldly structure, since "no particular form of church government was essential for the existence of the church." For such conservatives, the function of the church is

twofold: "One was to be separate from the world, and not be conformed to the world. Everything must be done according to the will of God. The other side was to bear witness to the world. It was because the church did not conform to the world that it could be a witness of God."[11] In sum, most conservatives remain separate from social and political issues and believe the church should exist independent from any worldly structure. They insist on walking the way of nonconformity to the world.

The third type of church is the "local assembly" established by Watchman Nee, whose ecclesiology was influenced by the Brethren. Dissatisfied with the fragmentation of the churches caused by denominational differences, Nee called for the unity of different denominations. He introduced the local assembly model of church—one geographical locality, one church.[12] Nee's understanding of God's kingdom was church-centered, and he did not consider it necessary for Christians to exert moral effort to change society since the church revealed and manifested God's kingdom.[13]

Besides these three types of Chinese churches, other churches are affiliated with the state, with and without being affiliated with the Three-Self official churches. In sum, the forms of the church in China are varied. Each type reflects the

---

[6]丁光訓著，《論三自與教會建設》(上海：中國基督教兩會出版，2000年)，5 (English translation: K. H. Ting, *On Three-Self Policy and the Construction of the Chinese Churches* [Shanghai: National Committee of Three-Self Patriotic Movement and National Christian Council of China, 2000], 5).

[7]丁光訓，《論三自與教會建設》，55-65 (Ting, *On Three-Self Policy*, 55-65); Chee Nan Pin, *The Search for the Identity of the Chinese Christian Church: Ecclesiological Response of the Chinese Church in 1949–1958 to the Political Changes* (Hong Kong: WEC International of HK, 2016), 69.

[8]Chee, *Search for the Identity*, 111; Philip L. Wickeri, *Reconstructing Christianity in China: K. H. Ting and the Chinese Church* (Maryknoll, NY: Orbis, 2007), 97.

[9]Chee, *Search for the Identity*, 111.

[10]Thomas Alan Harvey, *Acquainted with Grief: Wang Mingdao's Stand for the Persecuted Church in China* (Grand Rapids, MI: Brazos, 2002), 93-101; Chee, *Search for the Identity*, 124.

[11]Chee, *Search for the Identity*, 125-26.

[12]Chee, *Search for the Identity*, 128.

[13]Chee, *Search for the Identity*, 128, 132; 倪柝聲，《權柄與順服》，第二版，(台北：台灣福音書房，1979)，52-53 (English translation: Watchman Nee, *Authority and Obedience*, 2nd ed. [Taipei: Taiwan Gospel Book Room, 1979], 52-53).

church's understanding of its nature and its relationship with God, God's kingdom, and its socio-political and cultural context.

The Origin of the Church and the Nicene Creed's Statement About the Church

The origin of the church. The word *ekklēsia* focuses on two points, evoking associations in two ways. First "The assembly of the nation Israel, the assembly of God, is behind the word." Second, it evokes associations with popular assemblies in ancient cities, so a local church could be referred to as an *ekklēsia*.[14] Regarding the origin of the church, scholars argue one of two positions. The first is to view the church as being "instituted immediately and directly by the true and historical Christ himself."[15] The second is to regard the church as a post-Easter creation. The second declaration would lead to the ecclesiological discontinuity between the historical Jesus and the risen Jesus. I agree with Vischer's view that "one can speak only of starting points or roots in Jesus that then after Easter led to the formation of the church."[16] In other words, there is no historical root for the church without Jesus, and without the post-Easter proclamation of Jesus' resurrection, there is no formation of the church. The unity of the church hinges on Jesus, whose coming, death, and resurrection are the core of the proclamation of the church community.

The disagreements within the church arise mainly out of the varied identities of church members and the conflicting viewpoints among them. With Jesus, we find there are two groups: the twelve disciples and the other disciples who followed Jesus. The personal identities of the first group varied sharply; for example, Matthew the tax collector and Simon the Zealot would have represented opposing parties in Israel. The second group is larger than the first and includes unclean people, women, and Samaritans, suggesting the openness of the group.[17] The strains within the church in Jerusalem are reported in Acts 6:1 by Luke, who writes of the tensions between the Greek-speaking Jewish followers of Jesus and the Aramaic-speaking disciples. It can be inferred that there were various disputes among group members from the very beginning of primitive Christianity.[18] Surely, members emphasized different points about Jesus and his mission.

The Nicene Creed: One holy catholic and apostolic church. Although from the beginning of the primitive church conflicts existed among church members, this does not mean that they are the essence of the church. We need to turn to a very early statement of faith to understand the concept of ecclesiology. As the oldest of the three ancient creeds, the Nicene Creed stands closest to the original sources of faith, being issued by over three hundred bishops gathered at Nicea on June 19, 325.[19] Moreover, the creed was an innovation for the church that clearly brought the churches into a position of cooperation with a universal creed that took precedence over local

---

[14]Vischer et al., *Unity of the Church*, 55.

[15]For the Latin text please see Heinrich Denzinger and Adolf Schönmetzer, *Enchiridion Symbolorum*, 36th ed. (Freiburg: Herder, 1976), no. 3540. Also see Vischer, *Unity of the Church*, 34.

[16]Vischer et al., *Unity of the Church*, 34, 36.

[17]Vischer et al., *Unity of the Church*, 38-39.

[18]Johnson, *Creed*, 44-45.

[19]Hans-Georg Link, "Fullness of Faith: The Process of an Ecumenical Explication of the Apostolic Faith," in *One God, One Lord, One Spirit: On the Explication of the Apostolic Faith Today*, ed. Hans-Georg Link, Faith and Order Paper No. 139 (Geneva: WCC, 1988), 5. Also see Johnson, *Creed*, 34.

versions.[20] The creed places the statement of the church under the third article:

> We believe in the Holy Spirit,
> the Lord, the giver of life,
> who proceeds from the Father.
> With the Father and the Son he is worshipped
>   and glorified.
> He has spoken through the prophets.
> *We believe in one holy catholic and apostolic church.*
> We acknowledge one baptism for the
>   forgiveness of sins.
> We look for the resurrection of the dead,
> and the life of the world to come. Amen.[21]

The relevant part for the church is the statement, "We believe in one holy catholic and apostolic church." However, what do these four categories (one, holy, catholic, apostolic) say about the essence of the church? Does it mean that the church has these characteristics? The answer is no. In other words, the four characteristics "are the directions into which the church is growing."[22] First, the church is one. This declaration points to the unity (not the uniformity) of the church through the work of the Holy Spirit. The church as "God's chosen people" who call on the name of the Lord (Rom 10:13) is the body of Christ. This unity requires diversity within the community (Eph 4:3-12; 1 Cor 12:4-11). The second mark is holy. It indicates that the church as a corporate entity is called to be different from the world. The otherness of the church makes it challenge and even transform the world through the Holy Spirit's leading. The third mark is catholic. Catholicity refers to the church's universality and its embrace of ethnic and cultural differences (Gal 3:28). The fourth

mark of the church is apostolic. This characteristic refers to the standard by which the church is measured. Luke Timothy Johnson states, "The church in every age must be measured by the standard of the apostolic age as witnessed not by the later tradition but by direct appeal to the writings of the New Testament." These four marks point to the ideal church that has not been and will not be realized yet, for tension and conflict remain natural to human communities, including the church.[23]

The church in its essence is a community that is united with Christ in the midst of tension. On the one hand, it is the body of Christ, the assembly of the faithful in the Spirit, with the four traits as marks of the ideal church. On the other hand, the church through history has been composed of real people with human frailties and natural passions. It has never been a pure instrument perfectly representing God's presence on earth since tension is natural in Christian communities.[24]

A brief summary. Tension within the church is not an accidental or alien factor. It has its place in the historical churches. It already existed in the early church from its beginning since these Christian communities consisted of people with different experiences who came from various ethnic groups (e.g., the Greek-speaking Jewish Christians, the Aramaic-speaking disciples, the Gentiles among the Greco-Roman citizens, etc.). Nevertheless, the Nicene Creed describes the four classic marks of church that provide an ideal goal for the church to realize. Therefore, tension and conflict share a place with the four classic marks of church. The former have existed

[20]Johnson, *Creed*, 33.
[21]Link, *One God, One Lord, One Spirit*, 1, emphasis added.
[22]David Willis, *Clues to the Nicene Creed: A Brief Outline of the Faith* (Grand Rapids, MI: Eerdmans, 2005), 142.
[23]Johnson, *Creed*, 274-75.
[24]Johnson, *Creed*, 254-62.

since the beginning of the earliest church, and the latter will never be fully realized.

The Tensions in Pauline Churches and in Today's Hong Kong Churches

Many factors cause tensions in the Christian communities. Tension started in Jerusalem between the Greek-speaking Jewish followers of Jesus and the Aramaic-speaking disciples because of an argument over the daily distribution of food (Acts 6:1-2). Moreover, different attitudes toward the Torah caused further divisions between the followers of Jesus.[25] In addition, local religious or ethnic factors brought about conflict (e.g., the table-fellowship disputation between the Jewish and non-Jewish Christians in the Antioch event, Gal 2:11-14). Fourth, sociocultural factors led to tensions, such as the partisan problems in the Corinthian church. The last, but not least, aspect is sociopolitical issues. The conflict between Hong Kongers and Mainlanders in China stems from a political issue. In the following pages, the tensions in Galatian churches, Corinthian churches, and modern Hong Kong churches will be examined.

The conflict in the Galatian church. The Gentile mission soon led to the dispute over whether Gentiles should be circumcised and be obedient to the law.[26] This contention threatened the unity of the church. The conflict in the Galatian church was between the Judaizers and Gentile Christians. Paul describes those Jewish Christians as "troublemakers" or "agitators" (Gal 1:7, 10; 4:17) and views their gospel as another, different gospel (Gal 1:6). Regarding the Antioch crisis, when the Torah-faithful visitors came from Jerusalem to Antioch, Peter, Barnabas and some other Jews separated from the table fellowship with Gentile Christians, for they feared the circumcision faction (Gal 2:12). What Peter did gave the Gentile Christians the impression that they must participate in the Jewish rite of circumcision and other rituals, otherwise they could not continue to eat with the Jewish Christians.[27] Paul reproaches Peter sharply for being a hypocrite since he was not acting consistently with the true gospel (Gal 2:14). At Antioch he resisted the troublemakers from Jerusalem, which was a way of expressing his persuasion of the Galatians to stand firm against the agitators in Galatia.[28] For those agitators, Jewish rituals were valued more highly than the new community of Jewish and Gentile Christians. In Galatians Paul argues sharply against this tendency.

The conflict in the Corinthian church. Scholars have suggested that there were different parties in the Corinthian church that followed different leaders (1 Cor 1:12).[29] The factions were reported to Paul through Chloe's household (1 Cor 1:11). The following will explore the underpinnings of the conflict.

First, the opening four chapters of this letter illustrate the factions, quarrels, and divisions among the Corinthian congregation. This

---

[25]Vischer et al., *Unity of the Church*, 44-45.

[26]Regarding Paul's general concept of church in Romans and Galatians, see Stanley Porter, "The Church in Romans and Galatians," in *The New Testament Church: The Challenge of Developing Ecclesiologies*, ed. John Harrison and James Dvorak (Eugene, OR: Pickwick, 2012), 85-102. However, this essay explores Paul's view of church from the perspective of conflict.

[27]Vischer et al., *Unity of the Church*, 58, 67.

[28]Frank J. Matera, *Galatians* (Collegeville, MN: Liturgical Press, 1992), 88.

[29]Craig S. Keener, *1–2 Corinthians* (Cambridge: Cambridge University, 2005), 8. For a general idea of the Corinthian church, see Eckhard J. Schnabel, "The Community of the Followers of Jesus in 1 Corinthians," in *The New Testament Church: The Challenge of Developing Ecclesiologies*, ed. John Harrison and James Dvorak (Eugene, OR: Pickwick, 2012), 103-29.

tension extends through the entire letter, as Margaret Mitchell suggests.[30] In 1 Corinthians 1:10-12, the opening section of the body of the letter, Paul indicates that there are quarrels (ἔριδες, 1 Cor 1:11) and parties who dispute with each other. They claim to belong to Paul, or to Apollos, or to Cephas, or to Christ (1 Cor 1:12). He reproaches them for being of the flesh because they behave according to their human inclinations, with jealousy and quarreling (1 Cor 3:3). The Corinthians' divisions depict the rivalry among them. As David deSilva says, "In many respects these divisions reflect the age-old problem of 'looking out for number one' rather than looking out for the interests of fellow believers."[31] Paul criticizes the Corinthians for being puffed up for following one leader rather than another (1 Cor 4:6-7, 18-19). Their claim of superiority is based on the teacher they consider most authoritative.[32] Moreover, this rivalry or competitiveness exists in the way they measure spiritual gifts and charismatic endowment (1 Cor 12–14). Even at the celebration of the Lord's Supper they compete for the hierarchy of social status.[33]

Second, the conflict in the Corinthian church results in part from their close interaction with Corinthian society. The issue is that they are so attached to the culture that they are very much influenced by it. In 1 Corinthians 1:18–2:5 we read that they are deeply attracted to the wisdom of the world, which is contrary to the gospel. Co-

rinthian society is very competitive, and so are some believers in the church. In 1 Corinthians 12–14, Paul indicates that these believers regard themselves as spiritually superior to other members. As people of the Spirit, they see themselves as above any responsibility toward weaker members. For them, the church has no claim on their lives outside the worship gatherings. Some may even have participated in temple dinners (1 Cor 10:14-22), for they would meet with socially higher-positioned people there. John Barclay suggests that "from their continued participation in temple-dinners . . . those who are socially well-placed set much more store on the opinions of their non-Christian friends than on the feelings of their 'weaker' Christian brothers."[34]

Third, the divisions within the church are also expressed in the hierarchal gaps between the rich and the poor. Paul, discussing the Lord's Supper in 1 Corinthians 11:17-34, teaches the Corinthians not to abuse the church's common meal; in other words, the shared fellowship of the Lord's Supper has been superseded by a divided meal.[35] The rich members came early and went ahead with their own private meals. The poor or the slaves who had nothing came late with nothing to eat. Paul blames the wealthy: "Do you not have homes to eat and drink in? Or do you show contempt for the church of God and humiliate those who have nothing?" (1 Cor 11:22 NRSV). Barclay comments, "The behavior of the wealthier members at the Lord's Supper and the

---

[30]See Margaret M. Mitchell, *Paul and the Rhetoric of Reconciliation: An Exegetical Investigation of the Language and Composition of 1 Corinthians* (Louisville: Westminster John Knox, 1992), 81-83. Also see John M. G. Barclay, *Pauline Churches and Diaspora Jews* (Tübingen: Mohr Siebeck, 2011), 34-35.

[31]David A. deSilva, *An Introduction to the New Testament: Contexts, Methods and Ministry Formation* (Downers Grove, IL: IVP Academic, 2004), 566.

[32]Barclay, *Pauline Churches and Diaspora Jews*, 41.

[33]DeSilva, *Introduction*, 566. DeSilva indicates, "It [the mindset of competition] led to the replication of the hierarchy of social status at the celebration of the Lord's Supper as the rich provided fine fare for themselves and their guests of equal rank in addition to the bread and wine that was distributed to the 'masses' (1 Cor 11:17-31)."

[34]Barclay, *Pauline Churches and Diaspora Jews*, 191.

[35]Gordon D. Fee, *The First Epistle to the Corinthians* (Grand Rapids, MI: Eerdmans, 1987), 535.

legal disputes between members are eloquent testimony to the lack of close affective ties within the church."[36]

In summary, the tensions and fragmentation in the Corinthian church were caused by several factors, such as the low (the poor) and high status (the elites) of the members, and the personal desire to seek superiority in society as well as in the church through spiritual experiences. In a nutshell, the conflict among the Corinthian congregants resulted from their removing Christ from the center and reducing him to the periphery so that they were principally influenced by their cultural value systems. Those who were to overcome the world were overcome by the world.

The conflict in today's Hong Kong churches. In recent years, the tension between Hong Kong and Mainland China has increased sharply, which in turn has influenced the relations of the churches on the two sides. The conflict, on the one hand, has its roots in divergent political opinions and, on the other hand, is caused by their different cultural value systems.

First, the conflict inside the Hong Kong churches results from the sociopolitical context of Hong Kong society. When speaking of the Christian churches in Hong Kong today, this Hong Kong–Mainland conflict has to be kept in sight. Since the handover of Hong Kong's sovereignty to China in 1997, the tensions between

people from Hong Kong and Mainland China have increased, especially in the late 2000s and early 2010s.[37] Most of all, the Hong Kong–Mainland conflict can be attributed to differences in cultural value systems, those of the former being more international while those of the latter are more traditional Chinese. Also, Hong Kong people and Mainlanders have different spoken languages. Most Hong Kongers cannot understand Mandarin, which makes communication complex. The tension can be illustrated in the derogatory names they give each other; for example, the Mainlanders call Hong Kongers "old dogs" and the latter call the former "locusts."[38] Moreover, the conflict is due to the allocation of resources in different sectors. For example, the number of "anchor babies" of Mainland mothers in Hong Kong has been increasing, which results in increased competition for welfare in the city.[39]

The tension between Hong Kongers and Mainlanders is reflected in the churches. For one thing, the Hong Kong churches' ministries on the Mainland have diminished in recent years, for the Hong Kong sponsors have reduced or even canceled their donations to their ministries on the Mainland. For another thing, mutual distrust leads to the doubts that Mainlanders have about the purpose of the Hong Kong churches' aid. This distrust creates obstacles for gospel ministry toward the Mainlanders. In addition,

---

[36]Barclay, *Pauline Churches and Diaspora Jews*, 190-91.

[37]See Custer Charles, "The Conflict of Hong Kong vs. China: What's All the Fighting About?," Thought Co., updated November 12, 2019, www.thoughtco.com/china-vs-hong-kong-687344.

[38]The label "old dogs" comes from a well-known, outspoken professor at Peking University, who indicated that some Hong Kongers in the former colony were "British running dogs." This insulting label caused some Hong Kongers to take to the streets to protest. Then a Hong Kong newspaper called some Mainlanders "locusts" swarming into Hong Kong to grab the resources. See "Dogs and Locusts," *The Economist*, February 4, 2012, www.economist.com/node/21546051.

[39]<800人捐款五日籌十萬高登下週登報促截'雙非'>，載於蘋果日報 ("Hong Kong–Mainland Contradictions," Apple Daily, January 27, 2012, http://hk.apple.nextmedia.com/news/art/20120127/16018621). "Anchor babies" refers to the babies born in Hong Kong by Mainland mothers. Hong Kong opened its door to Mainland Chinese in 2003. Then some Chinese pregnant women went to Hong Kong to give birth so that their babies could obtain Hong Kong citizenship. By doing this, they could skirt the Mainland's one-child policy and gain access to Hong Kong's social-welfare benefits.

the cultural differences make it difficult for the Mainlanders to integrate into local Hong Kong churches, which creates further misunderstanding or distrust between both sides.

Second, churches are also torn apart due to the divergent political opinions between different generations, especially after the Umbrella Movement. The Umbrella Movement started on 28 September 2014 and is "usually considered the day that the theological landscape in Hong Kong changed."[40] It lasted for seventy-nine days and deeply affected Hong Kong's economy, the people's livelihood, and the churches. Some Hong Kongers affirmed the movement as a kind of liberation theology in Hong Kong; others opposed it because for them it had torn society apart.[41] The conflicts and disagreements among citizens also exist in the family, among friends, and within churches. The archbishop of Hong Kong, Paul Kwong, indicated that these political struggles have made many people lose their mutual trust and respect.[42]

A brief summary. Serious conflict resided in the Pauline assemblies (e.g., in Galatia and in Corinth) and continues to be present in Christian communities in modern society. Where there are people, tension occurs. God's assembly consists of human beings, so the tension is natural to Christian institutions. The conflict created by differences among people (e.g., different ethnic groups, various political viewpoints, differences in social status and goals, or incompatible cultural value systems) results in divisions within the church. However, this does not mean that we do not need to deal with the tension, for the essence of the church is based on Christians' union with Jesus Christ. The reality of the church still points to the unity of all God's assemblies with Christ through the work of the Holy Spirit. We may not have realized our ideal yet, but we are in the process toward that final eschatological reality. We are called to move this process forward.

THE ESSENCE OF CHURCH: THE COMMUNITY AS UNION WITH CHRIST IN THE MIDST OF CONFLICT

In the midst of tension, how did Paul respond to the situation? The way Paul reacted to the tension of the church helps us explore his opinion of ecclesiology, particularly the essence of the church. Paul's handling of the disputes in the Galatian and Corinthian churches will be examined using the four marks found in the Nicene Creed.

Paul's viewpoint of ecclesiology based on Galatians. The mark of catholicity: Dealing with the ethnic conflicts between Jewish and Gentile Christians. One of the characteristics of an ideal church is catholicity, a trait expressed in the church's embrace of differences. The conflict in many churches is caused by church members' exclusivity toward others. Paul urges God's assemblies to embrace the diversity of the community.

The conflict between the Jewish and Gentile Christians is first represented in the Antioch table-fellowship event in Galatians 2. In Antioch, obedience to Jewish ritual was vigorously discussed

---

[40]Justin K. H. Tse, "Introduction: The Umbrella Movement and Liberation Theology," in *Theological Reflections on the Hong Kong Umbrella Movement*, ed. J. K. H. Tse and J. Y. Tan (New York: Palgrave Macmillan, 2016), 1.

[41]Yan Kung, "The Umbrella Movement and Kairos: The Church's Theological Encounter with a Political Movement," in Tse and Tan, *Hong Kong Umbrella Movement*, 107.

[42]Elizabeth Cheung, "Hong Kong's Religious Leaders Call for Reconciliation After Political Conflicts," *South China Morning Post*, December 23, 2014, https://www.scmp.com/news/hong-kong/article/1668043/hong-kongs-religious-leaders-call-reconciliation-after-political.

because some Jews demanded exact obedience to the Jewish rites of circumcision and table fellowship so as to differentiate themselves from the Gentiles. This led to tensions between the Jewish and non-Jewish Jesus-followers.[43] In the Antioch crisis, Paul confronted Peter because he was in fear of the circumcision faction (Gal 2:12). Moreover, these tensions in the Galatian church had been expressed through hostility shown among the believers, as Paul implied in Galatians 5:15: "If, however, you bite and devour one another, take care that you are not consumed by one another" (NRSV). Paul also used an allegorical story of Hagar and Sarah in Galatians 4:21-29 to explain the conflict relationship in the church: "But just as at that time the child who was born according to the flesh persecuted the child who was born according to the Spirit, so it is now also" (Gal 4:29 NRSV).

To address the ethnic-conflict issue, Paul appeals to both Christ and Abraham to redefine who God's heirs are. First, Paul deals with the crucial factors (the Gentiles' circumcision and law observance) that caused the ethnic conflicts. He sets Abraham as a universal ancestor (Gal 3:29), and then dissociates the ancestor from the law of Moses and connects him with faith (Gal 3:10-14, 23-25). Second, Paul identifies the descendants of Abraham by their faith in God. Those who believe are the descendants of Abraham (Gal 3:7; οἱ ἐκ πίστεως, οὗτοι υἱοί εἰσιν Ἀβραάμ).[44] By employing Genesis 15:6, he bases descent from Abraham on faith, not circumcision. The third and most important factor for the redefinition of God's people is the role of Christ. Paul intentionally links the singular form

of the "seed" (σπέρμα) with a single descendant, Jesus Christ (Gal 3:16). In Galatians 3:26-29 he includes both Jew and Gentile in Christ: "If you belong to Christ, then you are Abraham's offspring, heirs according to the promise" (Gal 3:29 NAS 1977). Therefore, Paul argues that the ethnic tension between the Jewish and Gentile Christians should be overcome by their faith in Jesus Christ, for all the believers are united with Christ to become the body of the one church.

The mark of apostolicity: Crucified love on the cross in Galatians. The mark of apostolicity refers to the measure of the real church, which is founded on the apostles and their writings. In the midst of the conflicts, Paul's way of reunification is based on Christ's sacrificial love on the cross, and he himself sets an example as a paradigm of conformity to Christ. In Galatians 5:11 Paul says that he was persecuted for the sake of the cross because he does not preach circumcision. Then he reproaches the Judaizers for compelling circumcision in order to avoid persecution (Gal 6:12). All the believers in Galatia are called to imitate the crucified Christ as Paul did: "Brothers, I entreat you, become as I am" (Gal 4:12 ESV). As Paul says in Galatians 2:20 (NRSV), "It is no longer I who live, but it is Christ who lives in me. And the life I now live in the flesh I live by faith in the Son of God, who loved me and gave himself for me." If we live in conformity to Christ, we have no reason to fight against one another due to our different opinions or ethnic identities. Paul in his letters already expressed that Christ's crucified love binds the diverse members into one unified, but not uniform, community.

---

[43]Vischer et al., *Unity of the Church*, 46.

[44]G. Walter Hansen, *Abraham in Galatians: Epistolary and Rhetorical Contexts*, Journal for the Study of the New Testament Supplement Series 29 (Sheffield, UK: JSOT Press, 1989), 109-16; Karin B. Neutel, "'Neither Jew nor Greek': Abraham as a Universal Ancestor," in *Abraham, the Nations, and the Hagarites: Jewish, Christian, and Islamic Perspectives on Kinship with Abraham*, ed. Martin Goodman et al. (Leiden: Brill, 2010), 292-93.

Paul's viewpoint of ecclesiology based on Corinthians. *The mark of holiness: Dealing with cultural and secular conflict.* Instead of being assimilated into contemporary cultures, the church's holiness requires it to be different from its surrounding social milieu and also to challenge and transform culture.

I have discussed the cultural and secular conflict above. First, the Corinthians tore the church apart by splintering into partisan groups following Paul, or Apollos, or Peter. However, they saw no wrong in the divisions, because division was quite common in the hierarchical society of the ancient Mediterranean world.[45] But Paul considers division to be very serious, regarding it as a division of Christ. He asks in 1 Corinthians 1:13, "Has Christ been divided? Was Paul crucified for you? Or were you baptized in the name of Paul?" (NRSV). For Paul, it is Christ himself, not these apostolic leaders, who created the church community. And it is Christ in whom they should boast, not the apostles (1 Cor 1:31). It is Christ alone who is the source of our life and it is he who became for us wisdom from God, and righteousness and sanctification and redemption. Thus the honor belongs to Christ alone (1 Cor 1:29-31).

Second, the competitive secular culture had an effect on the church. The members competed for alliance with these distinguished apostles, and they even participated in the city's temple feasts to make a connection with higher-status groups in society.[46] Paul instructs them that the full power of God is made perfect in weakness (2 Cor 12:9). Paul himself did not teach with words of wisdom but came in weakness and in fear and in much trembling (1 Cor 2:3-4). In addition, he even regarded himself as the rubbish of the world, the dregs of all things (1 Cor 4:13).

Third, the divided Lord's Supper further widened the gap or divisions among church members. Paul asks for true fellowship among all members without any social disruption. Destroying the church's fellowship is an affront to Christ; as he states, "when you . . . sin against members of your family, and wound their conscience when it is weak, you sin against Christ" (1 Cor 8:12 NRSV). It is Christ who creates the community, and all behaviors that damage the fellowship of the community are sin against Christ.[47]

In summary, the problem of the Corinthians was that they were too closely attached to the society so that cultural values infiltrated their lives. Paul asks the Corinthian church to be holy and to live lives different from the social milieu by living out their union with Christ.

The mark of unity: Union with Christ as one body with many members. That the church is one declares its unity, and this unity requires the diversity of the community (1 Cor 12:4-11). When managing the problem of divisions, Paul keeps returning to our union with Christ. The conflict in the Corinthian church resulted from two sets of disordered relationships. Vertically, the members' relationship with Christ had been viewed through their relations with the apostolic leaders. Horizontally, the relationship among members was disordered, for they saw themselves via the secular value system. They favored one over another based on each other's religious authority or social position (1 Cor 4:6).

---

[45]David deSilva, *Honor, Patronage, Kinship and Purity: Unlocking New Testament Culture* (Downers Grove, IL: InterVarsity Press, 2000), 95-104.

[46]Vischer et al., *Unity of the Church*, 86.

[47]Vischer et al., *Unity of the Church*, 86.

Paul provides some foundational principles to deal with these tensions. First, for Paul, church takes place not only in the physical arena but also in the spiritual arena. All members are united with Christ through one Spirit: "For in the one Spirit we were all baptized into one body—Jews or Greeks, slaves or free—and we were all made to drink of one Spirit" (1 Cor 12:13 NRSV). In other words, the Spirit or Christ is the foundation of the unity of church communities. Christ is the center for the creation of a church community. We are called by God into fellowship with Jesus Christ (1 Cor 1:9) and not with any superior human being. All the members who share in this union with Christ are in fellowship with one another.

Second, the horizontal fellowship with one another is like the relationship that our body parts have with each other.[48] Our body cannot live without the parts. Because each member is reliant on the others, when one suffers, all suffer together, and the weaker part is indispensable for the other members of the body. Moreover, the inferior member should be given greater respect and honor. According to Paul,

> the members of the body that seem to be weaker are indispensable, and those members of the body that we think less honorable we clothe with greater honor, and our less respectable members are treated with greater respect; whereas our more respectable members do not need this. But God has so arranged the body, giving the greater honor to the inferior member, that there may be no dissension within the body, but the members may have the same care for one another. If one member suffers, all suffer together with it; if one member is honored, all rejoice together with it. (1 Cor 12:22-26)

A brief summary. Paul's way of dealing with these tensions in the churches in Galatia and Corinth helps us to understand the essence of God's assemblies. Since the beginning of the church, the struggle for unity has not ceased. In his letters, Paul demonstrates an ideal community of Christ—that is, in the midst of conflict the crucified love of Christ has been given so that all Jesus' followers can be renewed and reunited with the Son of God as one body. Christ's community should be one holy, catholic, apostolic church. Each part of the body is indispensable for every other part, and they all build each other up. The communities' fellowship with Christ empowered them to live differently from their social surroundings. The unity of the church is measured by the apostles and their writings. In short, church is a community united with Christ in the midst of conflict. Its true identity is sanctified, but it lives in earthly bodies (1 Cor 15:40).

HOW PAUL'S VIEW OF ECCLESIOLOGY RELATES TO TODAY'S CHURCHES IN HONG KONG

Are the struggles for unity of the first generations of Christians in church communities still valid today? Is what was true in the apostolic period still applicable to today's churches in Hong Kong? At the start of this essay we quoted the good answer provided by Vischer: "The call to unity is the same, and it is therefore not surprising that the great texts of the New Testament in which the drive to unity has been formulated are also relevant today."[49]

It is necessary to admit that tension and conflict are as natural to Hong Kong churches as to any other communities consisting of human beings. Since the Umbrella Movement

---

[48]Vischer et al., *Unity of the Church*, 88.
[49]Vischer, *Unity of the Church*, 15.

of September 2014, the deteriorating relationships within different groups, communities, and churches have become a thorny social issue. Even parents were set against their children and children against their parents. Friends disputed with each other due to their different attitudes toward the central government and Mainland China. These issues remain a serious concern in some Hong Kong churches. Having accepted that the issue of tension is rooted in the churches, we must now explore how Paul's view of ecclesiology might help produce the desired unity.

If Paul could write a letter to the Hong Kong churches, what would he say?

First, Paul might remind us of the crucified love on the cross as the foundation for our mutual love in a community. No matter what kind of tensions exist between Hong Kongers and Mainlanders, as Christians we embrace the same sacrificial love of Christ. Christ so loved us that he gave his life for us, so how can we level charges against those whom God has chosen? How can we separate from each other over different political viewpoints or cultural value systems? We discover Christ in fellowship with our brothers and sisters, particularly in the midst of conflict.

Second, as we are all united with Christ as one body, each member has an indispensable position in the body. Neither Hong Kong churches nor Mainland Chinese churches can live without the other. On the one hand, Hong Kong churches are more developed and have more resources. In many respects, Mainland people can benefit from the advanced resources in Hong Kong, such as the developed administration in churches, valuable theological resources, and well-disciplined theological educators. On the other hand, following the reunification of Hong Kong with Mainland China, Hong Kong churches need skill and wisdom to deal with the Chinese central government. In this the Mainland churches can share various kinds of lived experiences learned over many long years in which their faith has grown strong. In this sense, both Mainland Chinese Christians and Hong Kong Christians are called to embrace and love each other, since we are all members of this one body, Jesus Christ.

In sum, Paul's view of handling the tensions in the church is still applicable to modern churches in Hong Kong. The types of conflicts may vary, but the foundations for dealing with the struggle for unity remain the same.

CONCLUSION

A church in its essence is a community that is united with Christ in the midst of conflict. It demonstrates two perspectives: one earthly and the other transcendental. It is earthly because Christ's communities share the fully human characteristics of tension and fragility. It is transcendental because the true identity of church is the body of Christ and it is created by Christ. The church stands as a dynamic community in the process of growing into its fullness. The continuous struggle and unceasing efforts to achieve unity will make the church grow into greater maturity.

FURTHER READING

Cao, Nanlai. *Constructing China's Jerusalem: Christians, Power, and Place in Contemporary Wenzhou.* Stanford, CA: Stanford University Press, 2011.

Chee, Nan Pin. *The Search for the Identity of the Chinese Christian Church: Ecclesiological Responses of the Chinese Church in 1949–1958 to the Political Changes.* Hong Kong: WEC International of HK, 2016.

Clapp, Rodney. *A Peculiar People: The Church as Culture in a Post-Christian Society.* Downers Grove, IL: Inter-Varsity Press, 1996.

Harvey, Thomas Alan. *Acquainted with Grief: Wang Mindgao's Stand for the Persecuted Church in China.* Grand Rapids, MI: Brazos, 2002.

Pavey, Stephen C. *Theologies of Power and Crisis: Envisioning/Embodying Christianity in Hong Kong.* Eugene, OR: Pickwick, 2011.

Wickeri, Philip L. *Reconstructing Christianity in China: K. H. Ting and the Chinese Church.* Maryknoll, NY: Orbis, 2007.

丁光訓。《論三自與教會建設》。上海: 中國基督教兩會, 2000 (English Translation: Ting, K. H. *On Three-Self Policy and the Construction of the Chinese Churches.* Shanghai: National Committee of Three-Self Patriotic Movement and National Christian Council of China, 2000.)

林榮洪。《王明道與中國教會》。香港: 中國神學研究院, 1982, 1987 (English translation: Lam, Wing-hung. *Wang Ming-Tao and the Chinese Church.* Hong Kong: China Graduate School of Theology, 1982, 1987.)

彭淑卿。《倪柝聲的末世論教會觀》。台灣: 中原大學宗教研究所及台灣基督教文藝出版社聯合出版, 2011 (English translation: Peng, Shu-Ching. *Watchman Nee's Eschatological Ecclesiology.* Taiwan: Graduate School of Religion of Chung Yuan Christian University and Taiwan Christian Literature, 2011.)

39

THE CHURCH AS AN ASSEMBLY ON MOUNT ZION

AN ECCLESIOLOGY FROM HEBREWS FOR AFRICAN CHRISTIANITY

Peter Nyende

IN THIS CHAPTER I classify ecclesiological studies, against which I briefly survey African ecclesiological scholarship. From this survey I show that, relative to ecclesiological studies elsewhere, there is a paucity of literature on ecclesiology within African scholarship. I argue that this paucity puts African Christianity at a disadvantage in the quest of African Christians to be simultaneously African and biblical, thereby embodying an African biblical Christianity. In an effort, therefore, to contribute to African ecclesiological scholarship, I offer a conceptual ecclesiology drawn from Hebrews in which the church is understood as a community approaching God, in Christ, in his heavenly dwelling (the heavenly Mount Zion) to offer him, through the same Christ, prayers and immaterial sacrifices, and to live in obedience to him en route to partaking in the coming fullness of his presence and kingdom. This fullness will result in the realization of God's purposes for creating the world.

I wish to propose from Hebrews a biblical-theological ecclesiology that is at home in Af-rican Christianity. But since the subject of ecclesiology is vast I will begin my paper by classifying academic discourse on ecclesiology, and within that classification give an overview of ecclesiological studies in Africa. This overview will support the view that, although all types of ecclesiological study are found in Africa, more ecclesiological studies from Africa are needed, especially in the area of conceptual ecclesiologies, if the quest for an authentic but biblical African Christianity is to be achieved.

GLOBAL AND AFRICAN ECCLESIOLOGICAL STUDIES

Ecclesiological studies can be classified into three distinct areas of study, namely, identity ecclesiologies, concrete ecclesiologies, and conceptual ecclesiologies. In identity ecclesiologies the content of ecclesiology is focused on, and/or is from the perspective or in the interests of, a given denomination.[1] Ecumenical ecclesiologies are also included in identity ecclesiological studies, although their intent is to transcend

---

[1]See, for example, Walter Kasper, *The Catholic Church: Nature, Reality, and Mission* (New York: Bloomsbury Academic, 2015); Paul Avis, *The Anglican Understanding of Church* (London: SPCK, 2013).

denominational boundaries.[2] African identity ecclesiological studies are found in historical-studies literature on African Initiated Churches, which are churches in Africa that were founded by Africans, in historical-studies literature on various African churches that were started by missionaries, and, in exceptional cases, in studies of the church in a given African country.[3] These African identity ecclesiologies usually discuss the genesis and spread of African churches, together with their peculiarities.

Also to be found within identity ecclesiological research are studies along the lines of race and ethnicity and, to a lesser extent, gender.[4] They are highly contextual in nature and are usually fueled, for various reasons, by the need for ecclesial emancipation from Eurocentric or Western ecclesiologies. Black ecclesiologies in Africa belong to such studies where, for example, Vuyani Vellem articulates a black ecclesiology based on the narrative of the uprising of liberation spirituality.[5]

Concrete ecclesiological studies are ecclesiological studies that focus on the practical and empirical matters of a church or churches. These practical studies include how to be church or a certain kind of church, church order and church polity, church ministry, how to grow a church, what successful or healthy churches look like, church life and membership, and church architecture (from which *ecclesiology* as a technical term was first used).[6] There is a small amount

---

[2]See, for example, Gillian R. Evans, *The Church and the Churches: Towards an Ecumenical Ecclesiology* (Cambridge: Cambridge University Press, 1994); Gesa Elsbeth Thiessen, *Ecumenical Ecclesiology: Unity, Diversity, and Otherness in a Fragmented World* (London: T&T Clark, 2009).

[3]For historical-studies literature on African Initiated Churches, see, for example, F. B. Welbourne and B. A. Ogot, *A Place to Feel at Home* (London: Oxford University Press, 1966); David B. Barrett, *Schism and Renewal in Africa: An Analysis of Six Thousand Contemporary Religious Movements* (Nairobi: Oxford University Press, 1968); Bengt Sundkler and Christopher Steed, *A History of the Church in Africa* (Cambridge: Cambridge University Press, 2000); H. J. Becken, "A Healing Church in Zululand: 'The New Church Step to Jesus Christ Zion in South Africa,'" *Journal of Religion in Africa* 4 (1972): 213-22; M. C. Kitshoff, ed., *African Independent Churches Today: Kaleidoscope of Afro-Christianity*, African Studies 44 (Lewiston, NY: Edwin Mellen, 1996); Allan H. Anderson, *African Reformation: African Initiated Christianity in the 20th Century* (Asmara, Eritrea: Africa World, 2001). For historical-studies literature on African churches that were started by missionaries, see, for example, Walter L. Yates, "The History of the African Methodist Episcopal Church in West Africa: Liberia, Gold Coast (Ghana) and Nigeria, 1900–1939" (PhD diss., University of Hartford, 1967); Adrian Hasting, *A History of African Christianity 1950–1975*, African Studies 26 (Cambridge: Cambridge University Press, 1979); and Ogbu Kalu, *African Pentecostalism: An Introduction* (Oxford: Oxford University Press, 2008). For studies of the church in a given African country, see Kenneth R. Ross, "Current Ecclesiological Trends in Northern Malawi," *Journal of Religion in Africa* 19 (1999): 465-85; Christine Chaillot, *The Ethiopian Orthodox Tewahedo Church Tradition: A Brief Introduction to Its Life and Spirituality* (Paris: Inter-Orthodox Dialogue, 2002); Frank-Ole Thoresen, *A Reconciled Community of Suffering Disciples: Aspects of a Contextual Somali Ecclesiology* (Frankfurt: Peter Lang, 2014).

[4]See, for example, Letty M. Russell, *Church in the Round: Feminist Interpretation of the Church* (Louisville: Westminster John Knox, 1993); De Woong Park, "Towards an Asian Ecclesiology Based on Asian Liberation Theology and Minjung Theology" (PhD diss., Drew University, 2008); C. René Padilla, "A New Ecclesiology in Latin America," *International Bulletin of Missionary Research* 11 (1987): 156-64.

[5]Vuyani S. Vellem, "Black Ecclesiology: Uprising Faith Praxis for the Blackness of Humanity," *The Ecumenical Review* 67 (2015): 651-63. See also Goba Bongonjalo, "Towards a Black Ecclesiology," *Missionalia* 9 (1981): 47-59.

[6]How to be church or a certain kind of church: see, for example, Michael Moynagh, *Being Church, Doing Life: Creating Gospel Community Where Life Happens* (Oxford: Monarch, 2014); C. René Padilla et al., eds., *The Local Church, Agent of Transformation: An Ecclesiology for Integral Mission* (Buenos Aires: Ediciones Kairós, 2004). Church order and church polity: see, for example, Mark Dever, ed., *Polity: Biblical Arguments on How to Conduct Church Life* (Washington, DC: Center for Church Reform, 2001); Steven B. Cowan, *Who Runs the Church? Four Views on Church Government* (Grand Rapids, MI: Zondervan, 2004). Church ministry: see, for example, Robin Greenwood, *Transforming Church: Liberating Structures for Ministry* (London: SPCK, 2002); Brian D. MacLaren, *The Church on the Other Side: Doing Ministry in the Postmodern Matrix* (Grand Rapids, MI: Zondervan, 2000). How to grow a church: see, for example, Bob Jackson, *Hope for the Church: Contemporary Strategies for Growth* (London: Church Publishing House, 2002); George Barna, *Grow Your Church from the Outside In: Understanding the Unchurched and How to Reach Them* (Ventura, CA: Regal, 2002). What successful or healthy churches look like: see, for example, Mark Dever, *Nine Marks of a Healthy Church*, 2nd ed. (Wheaton, IL: Crossway, 2012); and Eddie Gibbs and Ryan K. Bolger, *Emerging Churches: Creating Christian Community in Postmodern Cultures* (Grand Rapids, MI: Baker Academic, 2005). Church life and membership: see, for example, James P. Wind and James W. Lewis, eds., *American Congregations*, vol. 2 (Chicago: University of Chicago Press, 1994); and Scott Thumma and Dave Travis, *Beyond Megachurch Myths: What We Can Learn from America's Largest Churches* (San Francisco: Jossey-Bass, 2007). Church architecture: see, for example, Mark A. Torgerson,

of African literature on concrete ecclesiologies dealing with how to be an indigenous church, being a local church, types of congregations in Africa, church ministry to youth in Africa, and church architecture in Africa.[7]

Conceptual ecclesiologies address the topic of who or what the church is, or simply the nature of the church.[8] For this reason, they are considered ecclesiologies of the first order, are prescriptive in nature, and provide guideposts for concrete forms of being church, of church practice, and doing mission. Studies on the creedal pronouncement of belief in the one, holy, catholic, and apostolic church are in this group of ecclesiological studies and, as such, have inspired a variety of forms of being church. African literature on conceptual ecclesiologies is dominated by understandings of the church based on sociocultural dynamics of family, such as family itself, clan, ethnic group, and ancestor-

hood.[9] Stephanie Lowery's essay in this section concerned with ecclesiology in Africa from the perspective of its developments also points out the predominance of "church as family" in virtually all church groupings in Africa.[10] This dominance she pins on the metaphor's cultural resonance in Africa and the plentiful biblical support for it. But we also have conceptual ecclesiologies based on some aspect of mission, on understandings of sacrament, and on biblical imagery of pilgrims.[11]

THE NEED FOR AFRICAN ECCLESIOLOGICAL STUDIES

The ecclesiological studies highlighted above from other parts of the world are but a representation of a vast literature on ecclesiology, while those from African ecclesiological studies are virtually all that there is. This state of affairs puts Christianity in Africa at a disadvantage in view

---

An Architecture of Immanence: Architecture for Worship and Ministry Today (Grand Rapids, MI: Eerdmans, 2007); Jeanne Halgren Kilde, *Sacred Power, Sacred Space: An Introduction to Christian Architecture and Worship* (Oxford: Oxford University Press, 2003). On ecclesiology, see Gerard Mannion, "What Is Comparative Ecclesiology and Why Is It Important? Roger Haight's Pioneering Methodological Insights," in *Comparative Ecclesiology: Critical Investigation*, ed. Gerard Mannion (London: T&T Clark, 2008), 13-40.

[7]How to be an indigenous church: E. Bolaji Idowu, *Towards an Indigenous Church* (London: Oxford University Press, 1965). Being a local church: see A. Radoli, ed., *How Local Is the Local Church?* (Eldoret, Kenya: AMECEA Gaba, 1993); John Gichinga, *The Local Church* (Kampala: IFES, 1995). Types of congregations in Africa: H. Jurgens Hendriks, *Studying Congregations in Africa* (Wellington, South Africa: Lux Verbi BM, 2004). Church ministry to youth in Africa: Jesse Jackson Mirega, *The Youth and the Church in the 21st Century: A Handbook for Youth Ministry and Pastors* (South Bend, IN: Sahel, 2010). Church architecture in Africa: Richard Tambwe Mutibula, *Towards an African Ecclesiology in Stones: A Theological Cry of an African Newborn Child* (Saarbrücken: VDM Verlag Dr. Müller, 2011).

[8]See, for example, Avery Dulles, *Models of the Church* (Garden City, NY: Doubleday, 1987); Everett Ferguson, *The Church of Christ: A Biblical Ecclesiology for Today* (Grand Rapids, MI: Eerdmans, 1996); Miroslav Volf, *After Our Likeness: The Church as the Image of the Trinity*, Sacra Doctrina (Grand Rapids, MI: Eerdmans, 1997); and Scott MacDougall, *More than Communion: Imagining as Eschatological Ecclesiology* (London: Bloomsbury T&T Clark, 2015).

[9]See Paul J. Sankey, "The Church As Clan: Critical Reflections on African Ecclesiology," *International Review of Mission* 83, no. 330 (1994): 437-49; John Mary Waliggo, "The African Clan as the True Model of the African Church," in *The Church in African Christianity: Innovative Essays in Ecclesiology*, ed. J. N. K. Mugambi and L. Magesa (Nairobi: Acton, 1998), 111-28; A. E. Orobator, *The Church as Family: African Ecclesiology in Its Social Context* (Nairobi: Hekima College, 2000); Oliver Alozie Onwubiko, *The Church in Mission in the Light of Ecclesia in Africa* (Nairobi: Paulines, 2001); Gerald K. Tanye, *The Church as Family and Ethnocentrism in Sub-Saharan Africa* (London: Transaction, 2010); Charles Nyamiti, *Studies in African Christian Theology*, vol. 4, *Christ's Ancestral Mediation Through the Church Understood as God's Family: An Essay on African Ecclesiology* (Nairobi: Catholic University of Eastern Africa, 2010).

[10]See also Stephanie Lowery, *Identity and Ecclesiology: Their Relationship Among Select African Theologians* (Eugene, OR: Pickwick, 2017).

[11]Based on some aspect of mission: see Solomon Andriatsimialomananarivo, "The Missiological Dimensions of African Ecclesiology" (PhD diss., University of South Africa, 2001); Stan Chu Ilo, Joseph Ogbonnaya, and Alex Ojacor, eds., *The Church as Salt and Light: Path to an African Ecclesiology of Abundant Life*, African Christian Studies (Eugene, OR: Wipf & Stock, 2011). Based on understandings of sacrament: Kambere Kasai Florent, "The Church as a Sacrament of Reconciliation and Healing in the Africa Context," *African Christian Studies* 30 (2014): 26-47. Based on biblical imagery of pilgrims: See P. J. Arowele, "The Pilgrim People of God: An African's Reflection on the Motif of Sojourn in the Epistle to the Hebrews," *African Journal of Theology* 4, no. 2 (1990): 438-55; David Zac Niringiye, *The Church: God's Pilgrim People* (Carlisle, UK: Langham Global Library, 2016), although Niringiye does not focus on any African context.

of African Christians' ongoing need for both in-digenousness and faithfulness to Scripture.

The latest statistics project that by 2025, Africa will have the highest population of Christians on any continent, standing at more than seven hundred million million.[12] Alongside this increase Africa has manifold forms of Christianity due to an unrivaled proliferation of churches and denominations.[13] But this numerical strength must be matched by the Christian faith taking root in African culture and thereby being authentically African. For this rooting to happen, African Christians must be helped to think about their faith in African terms; worship and liturgy must be African in thinking, conduct, and instrumentation; Bible interpretation must be through the lens of, and for, African contexts; and theologies must give priority to, and engage with, African needs and realities.[14] The extent, therefore, to which these requirements are met is the extent to which Christianity in Africa takes on authentic African forms. And given that African ecclesiologies are written for, or based on, African churches, more of them would contribute to shaping authentic African forms of Christianity.

Moreover, authentic African forms of Christianity must be matched by fidelity to the Bible for African Christianity to be biblical Christianity, that is, African biblical Christianity. The quest for authentic African Christianity must then be guided by biblical insight or else it will be left at the mercy of what is African, or what is locally expedient and pragmatic for the survival, sustenance, or growth of churches in African cities, towns, and countryside. Otherwise it will

even be at the mercy of ecclesiastical entrepreneurs who are out simply to make money through churches. For this reason, ecclesiological studies, particularly the conceptual kind that are informed directly by the Bible, are critical since they help engender faithful forms of African Christianity. Such studies can help Christian communities in Africa to understand the nature of the church they are a part of and who they are in Christ, and thereby be guide-posts for faithful forms of biblical Christianity that is also African.

I wish, therefore, to articulate an ecclesiology for African Christianity that not only comes from the book of Hebrews but, at the same time, resonates with Africa's spiritual, enchanted world. But since Hebrews's ecclesiology can only be grasped against the background of the Old Testament's literature on God's dwelling from the Garden of Eden to Mount Zion, my ecclesiology is invariably a biblical-theological ecclesiology.

GOD'S DWELLING FROM THE GARDEN OF EDEN TO MOUNT ZION: A BIBLICAL THEOLOGY

The key to appreciating Hebrews's ecclesiology lies in the second of the Genesis creation accounts. The stories of creation are not a discourse with a lot of literary detail and precision telling us everything we need to know about how God created the world. Rather, they are brief stories imbued with imagery and symbolism whose meanings are foundational for understanding the purposes of God for creation, what jeopardized those purposes, and God's plan for restoring those purposes.

---

[12]Todd M. Johnson, Gina A. Zurlo, Albert W. Hickman, and Peter F. Crossing, "Christianity 2016: Latin America and Projecting Religions 2015," *International Bulletin of Missionary Research* 40 (2016): 1.

[13]Paul Kollman, "Classifying African Christianities: Past, Present, and Future: Part One," *Journal of Religion in Africa* 40 (2010): 4.

[14]The rooting of Christianity in Africa is what is called inculturation (or contextualization), and it has been a defining goal of African theology; see K. Davis, "Third World Theological Priorities," *Scottish Journal of Theology* 40 (1987): 85-105.

In Genesis's second account of creation (Gen 2:4-24), the garden of Eden is depicted as God's own dwelling where human beings are placed to care for and tend it (Gen 2:15). This depiction is first seen in God's full accessibility to human beings within the garden, symbolized in God being with the humans and talking with them face to face. Second, it appears in the words used to explain the duties of the human beings in the garden, that is, "work" (*abad*) and "taking care of" (*shamar*), words used to describe Levitical duties of guarding and ministering in the sanctuary (see Num 1:53; 3:7-8; 4:23-26; 18:4). The use of *abad* and *shamar* to designate the duties of human beings in the garden, therefore, implies that the garden was God's dwelling place. Third, the depiction is seen when human beings sin against God, since the movement of God when he finds out the humans' sin is a movement (*hithallek*) specific to one's residence (Gen 3:8; see Lev 26:11-13; Deut 23:14).[15] It was as God was taking a walk in his garden that he confronted the human beings' disobedience to his express command. Fourth, the depiction is seen in the consequence of sin, when human beings are expelled from the garden as God's abode. The cherubim, who are associated with God's presence and throne, guard the garden from human beings so that they cannot reenter it, lest they enjoy what it has to offer (Gen 3:22-24). Finally it is seen in the reference to the Garden of Eden in biblical literature as God's garden (Gen 13:10; Is 51:3; Ezek 28:13; 31:9), thereby underscoring the view that the garden is indeed God's dwelling.

The depiction of the Garden of Eden as God's dwelling where he is fully accessible to humans and where humans live to serve reveals a funda-mental purpose of God's creation of the world: God intended the world to be the place of his dwelling with human beings. God's residence and kingship are inseparable, as later biblical literature makes clear with the ark, the mercy seat, and the cherubim (Ex 25:19-22) in the temple's inner room (*hekal*) making up God's throne or footstool (see Ps 11:4; 99:1, 5, 9; 132:7; Is 6:1-3; 37:16; 60:13; Ezek 10:1-4; 43:6-7; see Num 10:35-36; 1 Sam 4:3-4; 1 Kings 22:19; Mic 4:7). Therefore it is implicit that, by virtue of God's dwelling with humans, he intended to rule the world from his dwelling. In other words, God intended the world to be his place of residence with humans and a part of his kingdom.

However, these purposes were jeopardized by Adam and Eve sinning, which led to their expulsion from God's dwelling (Gen 3:22-24). In calling Abraham and promising him off-spring, land, kings, and blessing to all nations (Gen 12:1-3, 7; 13:15; 15:18-20; 17:6, 16 [see Gen 35:11]), YHWH sets out to restore his residency and kingdom purposes for creation (i.e., Edenic restoration). YHWH clarified this restoration plan by the person of Abraham when he spoke through Moses about Israel's identity as his people and himself as their God, including their vocation as a holy nation and a royal priesthood for the sake of other nations if they were obedient to him (Ex 19:1-6; see Deut 4:5-8; Jer 4:2). He commanded Moses to have the people of Israel build him a sanctuary ac-cording to his design (Ex 25:9-40) so that he could dwell with them (Ex 25:8). But it was through another prophet, Nathan, whom YHWH clarified his restorative plan, according to his kingship promise made to Abraham. He

---

[15]The verb used for movement (*mithalek*) in Gen 3:8 is, as pointed out by Hamilton, "a type of Hithpael that suggests iterative and ha-bitual aspects." Victor Hamilton, *The Book of Genesis Chapters 1–17*, New International Commentary on the Old Testament (Grand Rapids, MI: Eerdmans, 1990), 192.

chose David and his line for kingship to use to exercise his rule (2 Sam 7:4-17; 1 Chron 17:3-15). So the restoration plan of God's residency and kingdom by means of Abraham entailed God's dwelling with Israel in the land under Davidic kings, and then using them to restore both his kingdom and his dwelling with human beings (the nations) in the world.[16]

In the tabernacle and later the temple we have the beginning of YHWH restoring his dwelling among humans and his kingdom in the world. This conclusion is supported by numerous correspondences between the tabernacle and the temple and YHWH's garden dwelling.[17] Furthermore, this correspondence is seen when human beings are referred to as trees in the temple (Ps 52:8; 92:12-13), and in the reference to a river in Jerusalem where the temple is located (Ps 46:4-5; see Ezek 47:1-12), both of which correspond to the setting in the Garden of Eden. This parallelism is also witnessed in the Chronicler's consistent use of God's compound name (YHWH Elohim) in connection with the temple (see 1 Chron 17:16-17; 28:20; 29:1; 2 Chron 1:9; 6:41-42; 26:18), which corresponds to the use of the same name to refer to God in the garden story.[18]

It is important to note here that the temple as God's dwelling was referred to as Mount Zion.

This reference was due to the association of mountains with divine dwellings in ancient Near Eastern cosmology. Numerous studies show that, because they reached to the clouds, mountains were believed in the ancient Near East to be places where the netherworld, earth, and heaven met (the fulcrum of the world, the *axis mundi*), and were therefore believed to be the dwelling place of divinities.[19] As such, mountains were viewed as the hot spots of encounters and communications between humans and divinities. So the temple, and by extension Jerusalem as YHWH's abode, was referred to as a mountain, namely, Mount Zion (Ps 2:6; 3:3-4; 24:3; 99:9; Is 4:5; 8:18; 11:9; 56:6-7; Mic 4:7; Joel 2:1; 2:32), although it was not a mountain. Indeed, the movement of God to the temple as his permanent dwelling was seen to be the movement of God from Mount Sinai, where his presence was felt by the people of Israel definitively (Ex 24:17), to Mount Zion (Ps 68:15-18).

We have already mentioned that the purpose of God having residence in Israel was to restore his dwelling among humans and his kingdom in the world. This was first to start taking effect with Israel, who approached YHWH in his dwelling through all manner of prayers, such as thanksgiving, praise, and petition, as the prayer of Solomon (1 Kings 8:30-45) and the psalmists'

---

[16]See details of this, albeit with different shades and emphases, in T. Desmond Alexander, *From Eden to the New Jerusalem: An Introduction to Biblical Theology* (Grand Rapids, MI: Kregel Academic, 2009); C. Marvin Pate et al., *The Story of Israel: A Biblical Theology* (Downers Grove, IL: InterVarsity Press, 2004), among others.

[17]For details of correspondences, see, for example, Victor Avigdor Hurowitz, "YHWH's Exalted House: Aspects of the Design and Symbolism of Solomon's Temple," in *Temple and Worship in Biblical Israel*, ed. John Day (London: T&T Clark, 2007), 63-110, here 80-81; Elizabeth Bloch Smith, "'Who Is the King of Glory?' Solomon's Temple and Its Symbolism," in *Scripture and Other Artifacts: Essays in Honor of Philip J. King*, ed. Michael D. Coogan and Philip J. King (Louisville: Westminster John Knox, 1994); Gregory K. Beale, *The Temple and the Church's Mission: A Biblical Theology of the Dwelling Place of God* (Downers Grove, IL: InterVarsity Press, 2004), 66-80; D. Sawyer and P. Morris, eds., *A Walk in the Garden: Biblical, Iconographical and Literary Images of Eden*, Journal for the Study of the Old Testament Supplementary Series 136 (Sheffield, UK: JSOT Press, 1992); Margaret Barker, *The Gate of Heaven: The History and Symbolism of the Temple in Jerusalem* (Sheffield, UK: Sheffield Phoenix, 2008).

[18]I am indebted on this point to Stordalen's comprehensive study. For a fuller discussion, see T. Stordalen, *Echoes of Eden: Genesis 2-3 and Symbolism of the Eden Garden in Biblical Hebrew Literature* (Leuven: Peeters, 2000), 457-58.

[19]See, for example, Mircea Eliade, *Patterns in Comparative Religion* (Cleveland: Meridian, 1958), 367-87; Richard J. Clifford, *The Cosmic Mountain in Canaan and the Old Testament* (Cambridge, MA: Harvard University Press, 1972); Robert L. Cohn, "The Mountains and Mount Zion," *Judaism* 26 (1977): 97-115.

petitions and thanksgiving indicate, and through sacrifices and feasts (Lev 1–7:19; 16; 23) YHWH had prescribed. YHWH would in consequence respond to their approaches (Ps 73:15-20; Is 37:14-34) besides revealing his presence one way or another on account of them being in his house. This explains the psalmists' longings for visits to and residence in the temple (Ps 27:4-5; 42:1-2; 84:1-4; 122:1-2), and even their eschatological-like hopes of living there forever (Ps 23:6; 26:8; 27:4). The people of Israel would then go back to their homes and daily lives to live in obedience to God (Ps 15:5; 24:3-4; 36:7-9; see Ps 65:4), consequently experiencing his blessings of life in the land (Ex 19:5; Lev 26:3-39; Deut 7:12-16; Ps 24:5) and becoming a light to the nations (Ex 19:1-6; Deut 4:5-8). Other nations would in turn flock to Zion to be in God's presence and be exposed to his law and ways (Ps 47; 48:1-2; 50:1-2; 67:1-2; 68:28-34; 84:5-7; 87; 96:3-4; 99:1-3; Is 2:2-4; Mic 4:2) and, as a logical implication, go back to their nations and kingdoms to live in obedience to YHWH, as seems to have been the case with the queen of Sheba (1 Kings 10:1-13). Mount Zion as God's dwelling would become a magnet to Israel and to all nations, who would then, respectively, be and come under God's kingdom. Unfortunately, due to Israel's disobedience to God's commandments, this plan did not come to pass.

The preexilic prophets then proclaimed God's judgment on Israel on account of their sins, which ranged from rebellion (e.g., Hos 1:2; 4:1-2, 6-10), injustice, lies, and deceit (e.g., Mic 2:1-2, 8-10; 3:1-3, 9, 11), to violence and murder (see Jer 5:26-28; 9:4-6). In regard to false worship in the temple, their drawing near to God in the temple was not accompanied by obedience to God in their daily living, and this was tantamount to rejecting him (e.g., Amos 2:8; Is 1:12-17), and to idolatry (see Ezek 8:1-18; 16:1-52). Judgment on Israel included the destruction of Jerusalem and the temple, the decimation of Israel's population but for a remnant (e.g., Is 1:7-9; 3:1-8; Ezek 2:10; 4:9-17), and exile (e.g., Hos 9:3-6; 10:3-6; Jer 1:14-15; 5:8-19).

In the same breath the prophets also proclaimed God's restoration of Israel, which showed his intent to still use Israel, Davidic kings, and Mount Zion to restore his dwelling and kingdom. However, the future restoration the prophets prophesied was in some of their oracles indicative of a transformative restoration and not simply a restoration of what had gone before, since some descriptions of the restored state of Israel, Davidic kingship, covenant, land, Jerusalem, and temple could not be reconciled with their current or past states. This transformative restoration is explicit in covenant restoration, since Jeremiah's description of a new covenant meant a radical transformation of the existing one (Jer 31:31-34).

In regard to the prophecy of temple restoration, the restored temple would not just be a rebuilt temple but would be transformed into the highest mountain (Is 2:2-4; Mic 4:1-3), which was in all probability symbolic of Mount Zion's superiority over other houses of divinities because YHWH, its resident, is superior to all other gods. The restored temple would have life-giving waters flowing from it (Ezek 47:1-12; Zech 14:8), perhaps symbolic of God's dwelling supporting life, as was the case with the rivers in the Garden of Eden. It would also be the eschatological site of a great feast for all peoples and the destruction of death and all things that hurt (Is 25:6-8). However, it was not until the advent of Christ that the nature of this transformative restoration was clarified. This clarity is the case in point when the author of Hebrews admonishes his audience to be aware that in Christ they have come to a heavenly temple and city that are ontologically superior to God's dwelling in the past. Indeed, the clarity Hebrews provides on the nature of the restored Mount Zion, to which the church has come, is central to its ecclesiology. It is this connection of Hebrews's ecclesiology with God's past dwelling that makes the discussion of a biblical theology of God's dwelling necessary, without which Hebrews's ecclesiology would not be comprehensible.

ECCLESIOLOGY IN HEBREWS

We can view Hebrews as a sustained rhetorical discourse on Jesus as mediator par excellence.[20] Jesus' mediatorial functions are articulated in comparison with Old Testament prophets and Moses in particular (Heb 1:1-2; 3:1-6), angels (Heb 1:4–2:18), and, for the most part, Aaronic high priests (Heb 1:3; 2:14-18; 4:14–5:10; 6:16–8:7; 9:1–10:18). Given that Jesus' mediatorial functions are largely spelled out in comparison with those of Aaronic high priests, God's dwelling forms a significant part of the content of Hebrews, since priests and Aaronic high priests served in the tabernacle and then in the temple. In consequence, the author of Hebrews (referred to from here on simply as Hebrews, given the book's unknown authorship) envisions his audience (community of faith from here on) as a worshiping community both in their approach to God in his dwelling and in obedient living. This vision of the church is most prominent in Hebrews's unique revelation to the community of faith that they are approaching God on the heavenly Mount Zion and Jerusalem (Heb 12:22) and, therefore, are also receiving God's unshakable kingdom (Heb 12:28).

The subject of God's dwelling (*skēnē*) is articulated in Hebrews in relationship to Jesus' high-priestly role for the community of faith. For the purposes of discussing Hebrews's ecclesiology, we shall pay attention to God's dwelling in relationship to the community of faith. With regard to Jesus, it suffices for the purposes of this chapter only to note that in contrast to Aaronic high priests, Jesus is said to be a minister in the true tent pitched by the Lord (Heb 8:1-2; 9:11, 24).

In the above study on God's dwelling that was a necessary backdrop to Hebrews's ecclesiology, we pointed out that the people of Israel approached God in his dwelling through prayers and the feasts and sacrifices YHWH had prescribed. YHWH would then respond to their approaches and reveal himself to them. This is one half of what constituted worship. Accordingly, in four instances (Heb 4:16; 10:19; 12:18-29; 13:15-16) Hebrews's audience is called on to worship God in his house in ways similar to the people of Israel's worship in the temple.

In the first call, the recipients of Hebrews are encouraged, in view of Christ's high-priestly sympathetic intercessions (Heb 4:14-15), to approach the throne of grace with confidence to receive mercy and grace to help them in their moments of need (Heb 4:16). This has to do with prayers in the house of God, because the mention of God's throne of grace corresponds to God's mercy seat in the temple. In addition, the verb used for "approach" (*proserchōmetha*), also found elsewhere in Hebrews (Heb 7:25; 10:1, 22; 11:6; 12:18, 22), corresponds directly to its use in the Septuagint to denote prayers in the temple, where God's mercy seat resides.[21]

---

[20]Indeed, the speaker in Hebrews characterizes it as "a word of exhortation" (*logos tēs paraklēseōs*, Heb 13:22), which is usually understood as an oral discourse, that is, a sermon (see Acts 13:15).

[21]For more on this word and its cultic context, see J. M. Scholer, *Proleptic Priests: Priesthood in the Epistle to the Hebrews*, Journal for the Study of the New Testament Supplement Series 49 (Sheffield, UK: JSOT Press, 1991), 91-95.

The second call to Hebrews's community of faith to worship God in his house comes in the exhortation to have confidence to enter God's house ("holy places," *tōn agiōn*—Heb 10:19) and to draw near to him (Heb 10:22) because of the blood of Jesus (Heb 10:19). The entering into God's house and drawing near to him presumes that they will engage in worship of the kind that occurred in the temple—prayers and sacrifices—for that is what was prescribed and done there. This presumption is, again, supported by the word for drawing near (*proserchōmetha*) to God being similar to that used for worship in the temple.

Given the preeminence of the third call to the community of faith to worship God in understanding Hebrews's ecclesiology, we shall look at it last. The fourth call to worship comes in the pastoral admonition to the community of faith to offer to God a continuous sacrifice of praise through Jesus, a sacrifice of good deeds and sharing what they own (Heb 13:15-16). Here sacrifices in the prescribed way are commended to the community of faith, since they too worship in God's house. However, in this case the sacrifices commended are not material, as was the case on Mount Sinai, the tabernacle, and Mount Zion, but immaterial. The immaterial sacrifices are in keeping with the kind of house it is. Before we turn to this house below, it is important to note here that Hebrews makes it clear to the community of faith that their approach to God in his house is enabled by Christ: by his sympathetic priesthood (Heb 4:14-15), by his blood (Heb 10:19), and through him now in God's very presence (Heb 13:15).

The third call to Hebrews's audience to worship God in his house (Heb 12:18-29) is essential for understanding Hebrews's ecclesiology given its content: (1) it clarifies the location and nature of God's dwelling; (2) it points to the nature of God's dwelling in relationship to God's past dwelling among the people of Israel, and in so doing helps us to relate God's dwelling to the prophets' prophecies of temple restoration; (3) it ties God's dwelling to God's kingdom; and (4) it mentions both halves of worship (prayers and sacrifices on the one hand, and obedience on the other) as integral to being in God's dwelling.

None of the three calls to worship in God's house in Hebrews directly specifies to the community which house of God is in view, nor its nature. But the nature of the house is indirectly suggested in Hebrews 10:19-22. This is because the house of God the community is encouraged to enter confidently in drawing near to God is the same one in which Jesus the high priest (Heb 10:21) serves. If this is the case, then the house of God in which the community has been called to worship is metaphysical in nature, since Jesus serves in God's house, which is built by God himself (Heb 8:2). It is not of this creation (Heb 9:11). In other words, Jesus serves in God's house—in heaven itself (Heb 9:24). In Hebrews 12:22 the location and thus the nature of God's house are directly specified.

In the said passage (Heb 12:18-29), the author reveals to the community that they have drawn near (*proselēlythate*) to the heavenly (*epouraniō*) Jerusalem, the city of God where Mount Zion is located, to pray and offer sacrifices. In contrast to earthly life, heaven here is not simply spatial, as in the sky above, which would mean that it is beyond the reach of the community of faith who live on the earth. Rather, it is a dimension of existence or life beyond the realms of ordinary human experience, where God's presence is experienced fully and God's will is done because his reign is experienced absolutely (Mt 5:34; 6:10). For this reason, Mount Sinai as God's past dwelling on earth is inferior to the heavenly

Mount Zion. According to Hebrews, Mount Sinai was earthly, and the people of Israel were accompanied by fire, gloom, darkness, the sound of trumpets, and a voice, all of which brought fear and dread (Ex 19:16, 18; 20:18-19). In contrast, Mount Zion is heavenly, and the community of faith finds itself in the company of a myriad of angels, of just ones made perfect, of Jesus, and of God himself. Such a place and company bring forth joyous praise and gratitude.

The prophets prophesied of a transformative restoration of Mount Zion. In Hebrews this promised restoration has occurred, and Mount Zion has been transformed into the heavenly Mount Zion. Hebrews calls the community of faith to worship at this mountain and not at the temple in earthly Jerusalem. In some real sense, then, in Christ this community is in God's heavenly house offering prayers and immaterial sacrifices as they are asked to do in Hebrews 13:15. However, their worship is part of the journey to being fully in God's presence when he restores his dwelling in the world and thereby realizes his purposes for it. Thus God's intent to live among the people of Israel on Mount Zion in order to dwell fully once again with human beings is now taking place through his presence with his people in Christ on Mount Zion above. The destiny of the heavenly Mount Zion and Jerusalem is the fullness of God's dwelling among human beings, as was to have been the destiny of the earthly Mount Zion (a destiny that would have been realized had it not been for Israel's disobedience).

This destiny of Mount Zion is supported in Hebrews's constellation of revelatory pronouncements that point to a future in the fullness of God's dwelling. These revelatory pronouncements mention the powers of an age to come (Heb 6:5), receiving the promised eternal inheritance (Heb 9:15), Christ appearing a second time

to save those who believe in him (Heb 9:28; 10:35-39), better and abiding possessions beyond the earthly ones that are being plundered (Heb 10:32-39), the day of the Lord (Heb 10:25), and the city to come (Heb 11:10, 16; 13:14). This destiny is also seen in John's vision when he witnesses the heavenly Jerusalem come down and God dwelling fully with the redeemed (Rev 21:1-4).

As mentioned, God's house and reign are inseparable, hence God's throne in the tabernacle and temple. This inseparable relationship is clear in Hebrews. By being in God's heavenly house (Heb 12:18-24), the community of faith is before his throne (see Heb 4:16). There, as priest in God's heavenly dwelling, Christ is seated at the right hand of the throne of God (Heb 1:3; 8:1; 12:2). The community is part of God's kingdom, which cannot be shaken (Heb 12:27), and of whose fullness they will partake in the future. The destiny of the heavenly Mount Zion will simultaneously be the restoration of God's kingdom in the world, which results in the realization of God's purposes for God's creation.

Obedience to God in daily living is necessary. This is the other half of worship. Accordingly, Hebrews' audience is repeatedly warned against disobedience. In Hebrews 12:18-29 the relationship between worship in God's house and worship in daily living is most clear. The call to obedience in Hebrews 12:25 immediately follows the revelation that they have come to worship in God's heavenly house (Heb 12:18-24). God's people, Israel, rejected God, who spoke from Mount Sinai, by disobeying him in the desert, and they were punished for it. Now Hebrews warns the community of faith that they will not escape judgment if they reject God by disobeying him (Heb 12:25). Moreover, the revelation that their worship is in the heavenly court prompts the exhortation to obedience

(Heb 12:12-17). To put it differently, their approach to God in the heavenly Mount Zion should be accompanied by their daily obedience. Such worship (*latreuōmen*) is pleasing (*heuarestōs*) to God (Heb 12:28). Other warnings against disobedience in Hebrews (including Heb 2:1-4; 3:7-16; 4:1-11; 12:1-2) should be viewed from this perspective.[22]

To sum up, Hebrews's ecclesiology is of a community approaching God, in Christ, in his heavenly dwelling, to offer him prayers and immaterial sacrifices. They live in obedience to him on the way to being in the fullness of his presence and kingdom, resulting in the realization of God's purposes for creation, which we discussed earlier.

CONCLUSION: HEBREWS'S ECCLESIOLOGY AND AFRICAN CHRISTIANITY

Some years back I argued that the intersection of Africa's spiritual enchanted world and the Christian faith is what accounts for the character of Christianity in Africa.[23] African Christians believe and understand that the spiritual world is in constant interaction with the material world of humans and largely determines its fortunes. For this reason, African Christians, like the rest of the population, are alert to the spirit world, if not preoccupied with it. Thus, Hebrews's ecclesiology, which has to do with a plane of existence not of the material kind, which those in Christ are now a part of, finds hospitable ground in Africa. In consequence, it would readily appeal to African Christians and help them understand in African terms the nature of the church and provide guidance for their faith practices, thus contributing to the formation of authentic African Christians.

In conclusion, Hebrews's ecclesiology is not limited to informing the faith and practices of African Christians' understanding of the nature of the church. God's revelation in Scripture is offered to all those in Christ, wherever they may be. However, I have offered this ecclesiology in light of the observation that people's contexts and history will make certain biblical texts more meaningful and have a greater relevance to them than they would to others. Therefore, although Hebrews's ecclesiology may be appreciated by Christians outside Africa, I think it is an ecclesiology that African Christians would more readily ponder and appreciate.

FURTHER READING

Chaillot, Christine. *The Ethiopian Orthodox Tewahedo Church Tradition: A Brief Introduction to Its Life and Spirituality.* Paris: Inter-Orthodox Dialogue, 2002.

Hendriks, H. Jurgens. *Studying Congregations in Africa.* Wellington: Lux Verbi BM, 2004.

Kitshoff, M. C., ed. *African Independent Churches Today: Kaleidoscope of Afro-Christianity.* African Studies 44. Lewiston, NY: Edwin Mellen, 1996.

Lowery, Stephanie A. *Identity and Ecclesiology: Their Relationship Among Select African Theologians.* Eugene, OR: Pickwick, 2017.

Mugambi, Jesse N. K., and Laurenti Magesa, eds. *The Church in African Christianity: Innovative Essays in Ecclesiology.* Nairobi: Acton, 1998.

---

[22]Indeed, Son (Kiwoog Son, *Hebrews 12:18-24 as a Hermeneutical Key to the Epistle* [Carlisle, UK: Paternoster, 2005]) has argued that the content of Hebrews should be viewed through Heb 12:18-24.

[23]Peter Nyende, "An Aspect of the Character of Christianity in Africa," *Journal of Theology for Southern Africa* 132 (2008): 38-52.

Nyamiti, Charles. *Studies in African Christian Theology.* Vol. 4, *Christ's Ancestral Mediation Through the Church Understood as God's Family: An Essay on African Ecclesiology.* Nairobi: Catholic University of Eastern Africa, 2010.

Onwubiko, Oliver Alozie. *The Church in Mission in the Light of Ecclesia in Africa.* Nairobi: Paulines, 2001.

Orobator, A. E. *The Church as Family: African Ecclesiology in Its Social Context.* Nairobi: Hekima College, 2000.

Sundkler, Bengt, and Christopher Steed. *A History of the Church in Africa.* Cambridge: Cambridge University Press, 2000.

Tambwe, Richards M. *Towards an African Ecclesiology in Stones: A Theological Cry of An African Newborn Child.* Saarbrücken: VDM Verlag Dr. Müller, 2011.

Tanye, Gerald K. *The Church as Family and Ethnocentrism in Sub-Saharan Africa.* London: Transaction, 2010.

Thoresen, Frank-Ole. *A Reconciled Community of Suffering Disciples: Aspects of a Contextual Somali Ecclesiology.* Frankfurt: Peter Lang, 2014.

40

ECCLESIOLOGY AND THE THEOLOGY OF THE LAND

A PALESTINIAN CHRISTIAN PERSPECTIVE

Munther Isaac

THE THEOLOGY OF THE LAND gives insight into our understanding of the meaning of *ekklēsia* (church). This is because God, land, and community are always connected in the Bible. The church is always defined by a context, and that context is the people in a certain time and space. The particularity of the Palestinian church, being located in the biblical land, shapes the ways the Palestinian church understands itself and its identity.

The Palestinian church takes its identity and theology from its natural and unbroken relationship with the biblical land.[1] This is the land where Jesus was born and where many of the Bible events took place. There is an existential relationship between Palestinian Christians and their land. Mitri Raheb, a Palestinian Christian pastor and theologian, puts it this way:

> My identity was stamped by the fact that I was born in this particular place. I feel I have something like a special relationship to David and to Christ—a relationship developed not only by way of the Bible, not only through faith, but also by way of land. I share my city and my land with David and Jesus. My self-understanding as a Christian Palestinian has a *territorial dimension*.[2]

Even though this statement is made with the first-person singular pronoun, one could easily replace the "I" with "we," as in "we the church in Palestine." In other words, the self-understanding of the Palestinian church has a territorial dimension.

Palestinian Christians have written a lot about the theology of the land. When Palestinian Christians speak of the land, they talk about their *homeland* and the homeland of their ancestors. The theology of the land for us is not simply an abstract academic study but a matter of existence and identity. This paper will focus on the interplay between land and church as it shapes the Palestinian Christian understanding of ecclesiology.

---

[1] I use the term "the Palestinian church" as a representation of all the churches and denominations in Palestine today. There are about 45,000 Christians in the West Bank (including East Jerusalem) and Gaza, and about 120,000 in Israel, the majority of whom are Greek Orthodox and Catholic, with a few Protestants. For more, see Rania al Qass Collings, Rifat Odeh Kassis, and Mitri Raheb, *Palestinian Christians in the West Bank: Facts, Figures and Trends* (Bethlehem: Diyar, 2012); Johnny Mansour, *Arab Christians in Israel: Facts, Figures and Trends* (Bethlehem: Diyar, 2012).

[2] Mitri Raheb, *I Am a Palestinian Christian* (Minneapolis: Fortress, 1995), 3, emphasis added.

The first part will look at the land and ecclesiology from a biblical-theological standpoint and consider the question, How does the theology of the land shape our understanding of ecclesiology?[3] The second part will offer insights that are particular to the experience of the Palestinian church in the land today.

THE THEOLOGY OF THE LAND AND ECCLESIOLOGY

The land belongs to God. Palestinian Christians believe and emphasize that the original Promised Land, like all other "lands" in the world, belonged to the Creator God (Gen 1:1; Ps 24:1). And so, when God promised Israel the land, he made it clear that the land would remain *his land* nevertheless: "For the land is mine" (Lev 25:23 ESV). Former Latin patriarch in Jerusalem Michel Sabbah comments: "Land has a particular status in the Bible. It belongs to God. . . . Israel, therefore, could not become the absolute owner of the land: it was only God's guest. The worst possible thing that could befall Israel would be to forget this truth, to settle this land, and to substitute it for God in its worship and values system."[4] Similarly, Palestinian Orthodox theologian Paul Tarazi argues regarding the allotment of the land: "It is an assigning of the tribes to certain parts of that earth, and not an allocation of land to each of the tribes as though each would become the owner."[5]

The claim "for the land is mine" comes in the context of the Jubilee laws (Lev 25). The importance of these laws in Leviticus 25 is that they are a reminder to Israel that *it does not own the land*, for the land belongs ultimately to God (Lev 25:23). Israel is not free to do with the land whatever it wants or to claim eternal possession of it. These laws are a reminder that "land is not from Israel but is a gift to Israel, and that land is not fully given over to Israel's self-indulgence."[6] Such a way of administrating the land is a challenge to the empire concept, where the king owned and administrated the land and the people were mere servants or slaves (1 Sam 8:10-17).

Why a land? The theology of the land must begin by asking the question, Why a land? Why did God promise Abraham a land to begin with?

Why was a particular geography critical in God's plan for history? The significant role of this local geography is counterintuitive, since the covenantal God of Abraham is the Creator of both heaven and earth who proclaims, "For all the earth is mine."[7]

Giving a land as part of the project of redemption highlights that God is committed to his created order and to the redemption of human society. Redemption in the Bible is not merely about individuals, personal piety, or spiritual, existential experiences. It is about redeeming whole societies and communities on earth, who in turn make the church. It is ultimately about redeeming the whole of humanity.

The biblical story line could have been different. God could have given Abraham moral commandments for himself and his family. He could have instructed him to wander around in the world proclaiming the worship of the one

---

[3]The arguments in this section are based on my work *From Land to Lands, from Eden to the Renewed Earth* (Carlisle, UK: Langham Monographs, 2015).

[4]Michel Sabbah, "Reading the Bible Today in the Land of the Bible," Latin Patriarchate of Jerusalem, November 1993, www.lpj.org/fourth-pastoral-letter-patriarch-sabbahreading-bible-today-land-bible-november-1993/.

[5]P. N. Tarazi, *Land and Covenant* (St. Paul, MN: OCABS, 2009), 130.

[6]Walter Brueggemann, *The Land: Place as Gift, Promise, and Challenge in Biblical Faith* (Minneapolis: Fortress, 2002), 59.

[7]E. B. Korn, "Jewish Reflections on Richard Lux's 'The Land of Israel (*Eretz Yisrael*) in Jewish and Christian Understanding,'" *Studies in Christian-Jewish Relations* 3 (2009): 4.

true God. Instead, he chose to bring Abraham to a place, to engage with humans in a certain history and a certain geography, and to create from Abraham's descendants a unique and distinct society—one that would reflect his image on earth in the midst of the nations: the church.

Finally, this pattern of choosing a nation and a land and dwelling in the midst of people underscores God's desire for fellowship with humanity. The Bible portrays God as a God who seeks to dwell among humanity and thus in the midst of communities. This is evident throughout biblical history, whether in the Garden of Eden, the tabernacle, or the temple. It is in this sense that we could describe the faith of Israel as "incarnational."[8] The people of God always embodied the presence of God in their midst, and this becomes a part of their definition. The presence of God in the land was dependent to a certain degree on the presence of the Israelites in the land, for he dwells not merely in the land, but also in the midst of his people: "For I the LORD dwell in the midst of the people of Israel" (Num 35:34 ESV).

THE LAND UNIVERSALIZED: THE PROMISED EARTH

Palestinian theologians look to the land as more than just "Canaan," or modern-day Palestine and Israel. The descriptions of the boundaries of the land in the Old Testament are "fluid."[9] The outline in Genesis 15:18-21 speaks of universal dominion and not merely of a specific territory in the ancient Near East. This is confirmed by

Paul's language in Romans 4:13 that Abraham was promised the "world."

Furthermore, Palestinian theologian Yohanna Katanacho argues, from the well-known words in Genesis 12:1-3, that the "climax of the speech" comes in the statement that "through you all the families of the earth will find blessing." As such, "it seems that the land of Abraham is not going to have fixed borders. It will continue to expand . . . thus increasing in size both territorially and demographically. The land of Abraham will continue to extend until it is equal to the whole earth."[10]

In the New Testament the domain of this kingdom—its land—is the whole earth. The declaration of Jesus at the conclusion of Matthew's Gospel is perhaps one of the most important statements in the New Testament on the theology of the land: "All authority in heaven *and on earth* has been given to me. Go therefore and make disciples of *all nations*" (Mt 28:18-19 ESV). Jesus here receives *all the lands of the earth* as his inheritance. The "Promised Land" has been eclipsed by the breakthrough of what we may call the "promised earth." The land has been *universalized*. The kingdom of Israel is now a universal kingdom. It is not limited to one land or one people, because the king in this kingdom has authority over heaven and earth. This is indeed a fulfillment of the original vision regarding the kingdom of God in the Old Testament. Psalm 2:8 is now a reality: "You are my Son; today I have begotten you. Ask of me, and I will make the nations

---

[8]See N. T. Wright, "Jerusalem in the New Testament," in *Jerusalem Past and Present in the Purposes of God*, ed. P. W. L. Walker (Carlisle, UK: Paternoster, 1994), 58.

[9]The boundaries of the land in the Old Testament roughly make two maps: (1) the land of Canaan and (2) a wider territory (from the river to the river) that includes most of the ancient Near East. We can speak of "micro borders" (Canaan) and "macro borders" (the Euphrates). In addition, in the different periods, the land had different shapes. The allotted land, for example, is different from the land during David's and then Solomon's reign, and in both cases the boundaries went beyond modern Israel and Palestine.

[10]Yohanna Katanacho, *The Land of Christ* (Bethlehem: Bethlehem Bible College, 2012), 80.

your heritage, and *the ends of the earth your possession.*" The risen Christ can now claim this psalm and make it his: he was appointed the Son of God, the nations are his heritage, and the ends of the earth are his possession.

In short, the theology of the land has a universal thrust. We cannot simply speak about the theology of *the land*, but instead we should speak about the theology of *the earth*. The theology of the land is ultimately the theology of the earth, and this, in turn, will take us back to the creation (Ps 24:1).

This universalization of the land is by no means a negation of the role and importance of the land in Christian theology but instead serves only to emphasize its importance. The universalization of the land takes shape in three ways: through expansion, through reproduction, and finally in the consummation.

Universalization by expansion. The coming of Jesus caused the borders of the land to expand. This is particularly evident in Acts 1:8: "You will be my witnesses in Jerusalem and in all Judea and Samaria, and to the ends of the earth." The image envisioned here is that of progression or expansion. As the gospel of the kingdom moved from Jerusalem into Judea, then Samaria, and to the ends of the earth, the borders of the land also shifted outward to include these new places. In this image, the Promised Land grows until it reaches the ends of the earth. In other words, the "land" grows into the "earth." This has important consequences for our understanding of the church and its universal character.

This aspect of the universalization reminds us of the historical nature of Christianity. That is why the Jesus event had to take place *in the land of promise*, and that is why the first church had to be a *Jerusalemite church*. The land plays an integral role in New Testament biblical theology. The reign and presence of God began expanding to the rest of the world *from the land*.

Because of this, the Palestinian church considers itself the original church. Christianity started from Jerusalem, after all, and for Palestinian Christians this is a source of pride.

Universalization by reproduction. Second, and more directly related to our discussion on ecclesiology, the land is universalized in that the mission of the church establishes new "holy places" in new lands. We can refer to this as *establishing new "land realities" in new lands*. As new communities of believers in new lands embody the presence and reign of God, taking responsibility for their territory, they recreate the story of Israel in new lands. In this process, Jerusalem no longer has to play a central role in relation to the other new locations, because Jesus is now the cornerstone—the center of the new Christian movement. The New Testament thus has a decentralized ecclesiology—but it is still territorial. Any place has the potential to become a holy place. Any land has the potential to become a holy land. Any city has the potential to become a holy city or a city on a hill—as evident by the role of Antioch in the early stages of Christianity (Acts 11:25-30). As Gary Burge explains:

> The New Testament . . . brings an ecclesial alternative to the problem of Holy Land. Christians in other lands, lands deeply valued by God, bring with them the possibility of bearing the reality of Christ to these places. Which explains the fundamental basis of Christian mission. This is a divinely appointed task to bring that which the Temple and the land once held—the presence of God—into the nations of the world.[11]

---

[11]G. M. Burge, *Jesus and the Land: The New Testament Challenge to "Holy Land" Theology* (Grand Rapids, MI: Baker Academic, 2010), 131.

This is not to deny that God is present everywhere and at all times. Nor is it a denial of the possibility of divine presence and encounters apart from the church. Yet it remains true that God is present in a special way in the midst of the church. The presence of God in a particular way in the midst of God's people is a biblical principle. In the Old Testament, the presence of God in the land depends to a certain degree on the presence of the Israelites in the land, for he dwells not merely in the land but also in the midst of his people: "For I the LORD dwell in the midst of the people of Israel" (Num 35:34 ESV). Jan Joosten even argues that God's dwelling in the land is "inseparably connected to the fact that he dwells in the midst of the Israelites."[12]

The church, however, brings more than just the presence of God to new lands. It speaks prophetically for God in new lands. It cares for neighbors and the sojourners in new lands. It promotes and embodies the kingdom ideals of justice and equality in new lands. In this way, it creates new land realities in new lands. *The land is universalized when Israel's model is Christified and replicated in new lands.* In addition, the new "land realities" function as a signpost and point forward to the time of consummation, when all the earth will be fully redeemed.

Universalization in the consummation. Third, the universalization of the land is intended to point toward a time when the whole created order will be renewed in the form of a "new heavens and a new earth." This holistic and universal redemption serves to remind us of the goodness of creation. The land is part of God's good creation. The restoration of the land is an integral part of the restoration of the earth—a moment toward which history is

moving. Until this happens, however, the lands continue to groan.

These three aspects of the universalization of the land together make a complete picture. The land is universalized as it expands beyond Jerusalem into new lands. This expansion includes an element of decentralization, which no longer necessitates the central role of Jerusalem in redemptive history. Rather, new land realities are created in new lands, as Israel's model is replicated in new places. This process culminates in a new heavens and a new earth when God intervenes in time and space—by bringing complete redemption to the universe.

THE CROSS AS THE PARADIGM

It is crucial to underscore that declaring a territory as belonging to God and announcing Jesus as Lord over new lands is not done through military or political means. The church cannot rely on power or the secular authorities to implement the reign of God in new lands. The church in the past has erred in trying to enforce the kingdom of God over people and territory—evident, for example, on occasions in the Byzantine Empire, the Crusades, Calvin's Geneva, the Puritans, and colonial history. The role of the church cannot be confused with that of political rulers or civil authorities.

The church conquers the world not by weapons or force; the kingdom of God expands through preaching and evangelism in both words and deeds. *The nonviolent and sacrificial approach of the Messiah determines the nature of his reign and the method and approach of his followers.* The kingdom, though violently resisted (Acts 14:22), is to expand nonviolently—through sacrificial service and the power of the Spirit (1 Cor 2:3-5).

---

[12]J. Joosten, *People and Land in the Holiness Code: An Exegetical Study of the Ideational Framework of the Law in Leviticus 17–26* (New York: Brill, 1996), 192.

EMBODYING THE PRESENCE AND REIGN OF GOD ON EARTH

The church must take seriously the theology of being made in God's image and of being entrusted with vice-regency. The community of believers, collectively, represent God on earth. The local church represents God in a particular village, or city, or land. The believers should take this responsibility seriously. God and the land demand holiness, and the covenant that God made with his people always demands the fruits of justice and righteousness.

The church in all its community-based activities creates, as it were, a sacred arena where God can be encountered. The church community is thus the natural medium of theophany today. The community, liturgy, and sacraments embody and manifest the presence of God within a particular land. The presence of God is a sanctifying presence: it transforms individuals, communities, societies, and lands. Again, this is not to deny the presence of God or divine activity beyond the realm of the church. General revelation cannot be denied (e.g., Acts 17; Rom 1).

The church should also take its priestly task seriously. The church not only represents God within a certain land but also represents a certain land and the people of that land before the face of God. As such, it must continuously engage in prayers of intercession on behalf of the nation and the land (1 Tim 2:1-2).

A church must also recognize its identity as the light and salt of the land. Corrupted salt or a fading light is a recipe for the corruption and darkness of society and land. The church in a particular land must have a sense of accountability toward that land and the people and society of that land. With election comes responsibility.

LAND, COMMUNITY, AND THE CHURCH

The Christian experience today is always rooted in time and space.[13] To be "in Christ" is to be with him *here* and *now*, and this, at the same time, is a *community experience*. To be "in Christ" is to be in him with the community of believers— and this is directly related to the land of that community. The theology of the land emphasizes the role of the community. It is very important that the Christian life demands responsibilities from and to those within the community. The social dimension of the theology of the land helps reclaim this community element in redemption. Chris Wright further proposes that ancient Israel's mission in the land can become a model for the experience of being "in Christ" today. He calls this a "typological understanding of the significance of Israel's land":

> The typological interpretation of the land, which relates it to the person and work of Jesus the Messiah, does not come to a "dead end" with Jesus himself. Rather, it carries the social and economic thrust of Old Testament ethics onwards into the ethics of practical relationships within New Testament Israel, the Messianic community. Citizenship of the kingdom of God most certainly has a social and economic dimension.[14]

Wright's contribution to the theology of the land is immensely important. He avoids any spiritualization or "heavenization" tendencies by anchoring the thesis "In Christ = In the Land" in the experience of the community of believers on earth and also by linking this to a Christian version of Israel's theology of the land. As such, the theology of the land continues to be an important category of faith in Christian theology— with an important role to play in defining the mission and identity of the church.

---

[13]This section is adapted from my book *From Land to Lands*, 366-67.
[14]C. J. H. Wright, *Old Testament Ethics for the People of God* (Downers Grove, IL: InterVarsity Press, 2004), 193, 196.

Land matters. The biblical narrative is a story about land. Covenant, as Walter Brueggemann stresses, never concerned only people and God, *"but the land is always present to the interaction and is very much a decisive factor."*[15] In many Christian circles, the transition from the Old Testament to the New Testament resulted in two dissimilar versions of redemption: the covenant in the Old Testament between God, people, and land became in the New Testament a covenant between God and *individuals—with no reference to land or community*. However, a serious biblical-theological approach to the Bible as a whole must, however, challenge such an approach—especially in light of the fact that the New Testament authors so clearly present the Jesus event as the continuation and climax of the story of Israel.

In the biblical narrative the role of the community is emphasized alongside that of the individual—perhaps even above it. The biblical context of redemption is the community. In many Christian circles, salvation has become a private matter that is not related to land and community. The focus is on God's encounters with individuals, and God is relevant only as he is involved in personal and private matters. But the theology of the land shows that the covenant has always been between *God*, *communities*, and *land*. As Brueggemann powerfully argues:

> It will not do to make the individual person the unit of decision-making because in both Testaments the land possessed or promised concerns the whole people. Radical decisions in obedience are of course the stuff of biblical faith, but now it cannot be radical obedience in a private world without brothers and sisters, without pasts and futures, without turf to be managed and cher-

ished as a partner in the decisions. The unit of decision-making is the community and that always with reference to the land.[16]

God is the God of nations and lands, and not just the God of individuals. The focal point in biblical theology is the community and not the individual. This is not a denial of the need for individuals to make faith decisions. God is the one who meets individuals where they are. However, once an individual believes in the gospel of the reign of God through Christ, they become a member of a community—a family. They are accountable to the community just as the community is accountable to them. *Meaning, mission, and identity can only be defined in the context of the community.* This is the true definition of ecclesiology.

This is where the New Testament concept of fellowship comes into play. Fellowship is not merely a symbolic spiritual articulation of Christian unity in Christ. Rather, "the experience of *fellowship*—in its full, rich, concrete New Testament sense—fulfils analogous theological and ethical functions for the Christian as the possession of *land* did for Old Testament Israelites."[17] Christian fellowship, therefore, manifests itself in the socioeconomic sphere and is interpreted in socioeconomic actions, such as sharing possessions, meeting the needs of the community, and maintaining a system of equality among the members of the fellowship. The experience of the community is central to what it means to be a Christian.

THE CHURCH IN CONTEXT: TERRITORIAL ECCLESIOLOGY

The church is always a church in a context. For Paul Tarazi, this understanding of territorial

---

[15]Brueggemann, *Land*, 200, emphasis added.
[16]Brueggemann, *Land*, 199.
[17]Wright, *Old Testament Ethics*, 195, emphasis original.

ecclesiology is rooted in the foundational relationship between the church and the world. The church, he argues, "is not a separate entity which stands vis-à-vis the world or even in the world." Rather, the church and world are two "faces of the same reality, which is the creation. The world is the first creation; the church is the new one." However, the church and world are at the same time radically different faces of the same reality. While the world is the sinful and not-yet-redeemed creation, the church is that part of creation that has responded to and willingly accepted salvation by and in Jesus Christ. Tarazi then concludes: "Orthodoxy has consistently taken the New Testament expression 'the church of God in such and such a place' to be a basic truth at the core of sound ecclesiology. There is no such thing as an ethereal church of God at large, but the same church of God taking different shades and colours according to its various dwelling places on this earth."[18]

This understanding of ecclesiology is extremely important. It emphasizes the rootedness of the church in the land. *A church in a particular land exists for the sake of that land and takes its mission agenda from it.* The church, in other words, derives much of its purpose from its locale. This is not simply a matter of contextualizing the Christian gospel and making it more "relevant." This has to do with the self-definition of the church. This requires that each church identifies its territory and claims this territory as the realm of its vice-regency. The mission of the church in the world is, after all, a declaration of the sovereignty of the Son of God over all the lands of the world. The local church needs to apply this global reign of Christ in its own distinctive locality. This declaration of sovereignty

can only be done through sacrificial love and service. It cannot be imposed or forced. The biblical meaning of vice-regency is that of service of the other and selfless love of the neighbor. This is how God reigns!

Churches today are defined more in terms of doctrine and beliefs than territory. Mission is defined in reference to individuals and people groups, not territory. Yet the biblical vision of holistic redemption and the paradigm of Israel together suggest a different way of doing church and mission. *The church in a particular land exists with the view that this land will one day become a new, restored creation. Therefore, the church of a particular land must embody, advocate, and implement God's agenda for that land. God's agenda for a particular land must then unify the churches that exist in a particular land toward fulfilling this agenda. A missional theology of the land thinks territorially.*

THE PARTICULARITY OF THE PALESTINIAN CHURCH

One holy, catholic, apostolic church. Palestinian Christians view themselves, naturally, as part of the "one holy, catholic, apostolic church," as the Nicene-Constantinopolitan Creed declares. In fact, the Jerusalem church was part of the first five original seats, though a small one, besides Alexandria, Antioch, Constantinople, and Rome.

Yet the unity of the one church has been jeopardized by the many divisions and conflicts Christians have had among themselves, but especially in conflicts that have taken place in the Holy Land itself. The Jerusalem seat has been coveted over the years, and everyone has wanted to have a foot in Jerusalem, the place where Jesus

---

[18]Paul Nadim Tarazi, "Covenant, Land and City: Finding God's Will in Palestine," *The Reformed Journal* 29 (1979): 14.

was crucified and rose from the dead. This resulted in the presence of many churches and bishops—even two patriarchs—in Jerusalem.

So what do we make of the fact that the church looks different from one locality to another? And what do we make of the fact that these differences and conflicts have resulted in the presence of many churches in Jerusalem today? Tarazi answers:

> As to the oneness of the church, it is a delusion to think that either a centralized administration or a pseudo-theological justification of actual chaos can realize it. The church is one because the Holy Spirit is one. And it is precisely this colorful Holy Spirit who is responsible for the various shades the church takes in its different earthly dwellings, thus making it a richly vested and beautifully adorned bride to the great joy and glory of the bridegroom, the Lord Jesus Christ.[19]

Interestingly, Palestinian Christians identify more in terms of their geopolitical identity than their denominational one. We are Palestinian Christians first, and then Orthodox, Catholics, or Lutherans. The reason for this is twofold: first, the particularity of Palestine as the biblical land, and second, the historical developments and the sense of pride Palestinians feel in response to the Israeli occupation.

The land as the Fifth Gospel. For Palestinian Christian theologians, the original promised land has lost its strictly *theological* and *salvific* significance. It is no longer a distinct "Holy Land" or even a "Promised Land." The New Testament went beyond land to the whole earth, claiming that

Jesus is the ultimate fulfillment of the Old Testament story and that after his death and resurrection, the land has been universalized. In this sense, the land has lost its theological significance.[20]

However, once this critical point has been granted, we can readily acknowledge that the land continues to act as a witness to God's work in history. Michel Sabbah argues that, according to the teachings of Jesus, the committed believer does not need to worship God in a particular place, be it Jerusalem or the Promised Land. True worship is in spirit and truth anywhere in the world. This, however, does not negate the importance of holy places for Christians as places of faith and prayer and destinations for pilgrimage. Rather, priority is given to faith over the place in which one practices one's faith.[21]

The land will always be the historical backdrop or scenery against which the biblical drama took place in actual time and space: the call of Abraham; the birth, death, and resurrection of Christ; and the place where the church first began. So, in this sense, the land still has a special role that it can play within Christian faith—*as a witness.* This is why many have called the land the Fifth Gospel. Palestinian theologian Naim Ateek comments: "St. Cyril of Jerusalem (c. 304–386) considered the various places of Palestine as bearing a true witness to Christ. Such sites . . . were for him an eloquent witness to Jesus Christ. What was true for St. Cyril, the archbishop of Jerusalem in the fourth century, is still true today in the experience of countless pilgrims. Palestine is a fifth Gospel to them."[22]

---

[19]Tarazi, "Covenant, Land and City," 14.

[20]Some have suggested that the land could possibly be the theater of the final drama in salvation history, namely, the place where Christ will return. See R. L. Wilken, *The Land Called Holy: Palestine in Christian History and Thought* (New Haven, CT: Yale University Press, 1992), 47. However, as we have seen, the focus in the final vision of the New Testament is on the new heavens and the new earth, and the new Jerusalem, not on the land.

[21]Michel Sabbah, *Sawtun Sarikhun Fil Barriya* (*A Voice Crying Out in the Wilderness*) (Jerusalem: Latin Seminary, 2008), 31.

[22]N. Ateek, *Justice and Only Justice: A Palestinian Theology of Liberation* (New York: Orbis, 1989), 114.

Palestinian Christians are proud that their church continues two thousand years of Christians witness in the land where it all started. The Jerusalem church is unique in that respect. Tarazi says:

> In digging further into their own background the [Christian] citizens of Jerusalem discover that the unique contribution of their city and their land lies in the holiness of them: Jerusalem is the Holy City and Palestine is the Holy Land. In fear and trembling we realize the weight of such a responsibility, knowing that holiness is God's attribute; still in humility and obedience we accept the fact that the same Holy God has anointed in a unique way Jerusalem and Palestine. In a way the Palestinian Orthodox have no choice, since even our own flesh and blood are products of that land: its dust, its climate, its air, its food, its water—which centuries ago produced the flesh and blood of our Savior and Lord Jesus Christ.[23]

The land today tells a story! It tells the story of a God who has chosen a people and land and dwelt in their midst—eventually bringing from that people and that land a powerful redemption that can reach to all the families and the lands of the earth. It tells the story of a God who blesses but also demands holiness and justice.

It is in this sense that the land can be considered sacred, as British Anglican bishop John Inge argues: "Sacred places will be those which have been associated with sacred stories, places linked with divine disclosure."[24] The land gives a testimony to thousands of years of salvation history. It can, as such, become a place where God is encountered in a special way—especially by people who find themselves in places with which they are familiar from their reading of Scripture. The land functions as a stimulus for spiritual reflection, prayer, and fresh encounters with God. That is why over the centuries Christian pilgrims have visited this land, seeking a deeper encounter with God.[25]

However, we must warn against idolizing the land—something to which this very same land itself testifies. The land serves as a warning against idolizing the land! As Naim Ateek says,

> History teaches us that whoever concentrates heart and mind on the land will be cursed and vomited out of the land. This is what happened to the crusaders, Christians who fell into this trap. The land can, however, *become* holy to those who put their trust in the God of the whole universe, whose nature does not change—a God of justice for all, who desires goodness and mercy for all people living in this and every land.[26]

The Palestinian church constantly declares that *our connection is with the God of the land, the God whose story the land tells, and not with the land itself.* The Crusades and the Crimean War are two examples of how far Christians are willing to go when the land is absolutized over the God of the land. In addition, and as we have seen, there is no guarantee that a holy place will continue to be holy forever—as Jerusalem itself testifies.

---

[23]Tarazi, "Covenant, Land and City," 14.

[24]J. Inge, "Towards a Theology of Place," *Modern Believing* 40 (1992): 47. Inge argued extensively for what he called an "Incarnational" theology of the land, where a place in which God is experienced in a special way can become sacred. It is important to observe that for Inge, any place or land, like a cathedral, could become sacred, and not just the original land of promise. See also his book, J. Inge, *A Christian Theology of Place* (Burlington, VT: Ashgate, 2003).

[25]See the book by Wilken, *Land Called Holy*. See also P. W. L. Walker, *Holy City, Holy Places? Christian Attitudes to Jerusalem and the Holy Land in the Fourth Century* (Oxford: Oxford University Press, 1990).

[26]Ateek, *Justice and Only Justice*, 111.

The living stones—the church—as the Sixth Gospel. Ateek says:

> The Palestinian Christians of today are the descendants of those early Christians, yet this is no cause for *hubris*. With a humility that befits their Lord, they accept it as a privilege that carries with it a responsibility for service. . . . They and their ancestors have maintained a living witness to Jesus and his Resurrection from the beginning of the Church, and they should see themselves dynamically continuing such a witness in the land.[27]

Christians must remember that the people of the land are as important as the land itself when it comes to narrating the biblical story and the story of the land over the centuries. Christians who visit the land must have a connection not just with old stones of old churches but, more importantly, with the "living stones" of the land—the community of faith where God in reality dwells. The presence of God by his Holy Spirit in the midst of the community of faith in the land is what makes this land, as indeed any other land, holy. The people of the land are an integral part of the witness of the land. The testimony of the land apart from the people of the land is an empty testimony. If the land is the Fifth Gospel, then the people of God in the land are, according to Raheb, the "Sixth Gospel": "The Palestinian people are an important continuum from the biblical times until today of the peoples of the land and their distinct cultures. Their understanding of the context is important to understand the text of the bible. They constitute another important hermeneutical key to the bible."[28]

The land as a model. For Palestinian Christians, the theology of the land has a missional role. The theology of the land of biblical Israel—modified in the Jesus event—is a paradigm for Christian communities living in other lands. Ateek argues:

> The land that God has chosen at one particular time in history for one particular people is now perceived as a paradigm, a model, for God's concern for every people and every land. As God commanded the Israelites to obey God's law in their life in the land, so God demands the same from all peoples in their lands. . . . Every nation can say about its own country . . . "This is the Lord's land, and the Lord demands a life of righteousness and justice in our land."[29]

If this is true for any church in a land, then it is certainly true for the Palestinian church. It actually begins here—in Jerusalem. That is why Palestinian Christians believe that their land has a universal mission. In 2009 Palestinian Christian lay leaders, theologians, pastors, and activists from all church backgrounds issued an important document called the Kairos Palestinian Document. In it they said:

> We believe that our land has a universal mission. In this universality, the meaning of the promises, of the land, of the election, of the people of God open up to include all of humanity, starting from all the peoples of this land. In light of the teachings of the Holy Bible, the promise of the land has never been a political programme, but rather the prelude to complete universal salvation. It was the initiation of the fulfillment of the Kingdom of God on earth.[30]

---

[27]Ateek, *Justice and Only Justice*, 113.

[28]Mitri Raheb, "Shaping Communities in Times of Crisis: Narratives of Land, Peoples and Identities" (unpublished conference paper, International Center of Bethlehem, November 2005). See also M. Raheb, "Towards a New Hermeneutics of Liberation: A Palestinian Christian Perspective," in *The Biblical Text in the Context of Occupation: Towards a New Hermeneutics of Liberation*, ed. M. Raheb (Bethlehem: Diyar, 2012), 11-28.

[29]Ateek, *Justice and Only Justice*, 108-9.

[30]Kairos Palestine Document, section 2.3, www.kairospalestine.ps/index.php/about-kairos/kairos-palestine-document, accessed April 29, 2020.

SHARING THE LAND: THE LAND OF PEACE, JUSTICE, AND RECONCILIATION

Palestinian Christians emphasize that God's ultimate vision for "the land" is that it will be like "the garden of Eden," "a dwelling place for God with humanity, and a homeland for all the children of God."[31] That is why Palestinian Christians reject any exclusive claim to the land. The land belongs to God, and as such it is a land for all.

It is evident that the land is a place of hostility, strife, and division. The reality in the land is one of injustice. In 2017 we commemorate fifty years of the Israeli occupation of Palestinian land.[32] There are oppressors, and there are the oppressed. In the state of Israel, not all the people of the land are equal.[33] There are laws that differentiate between ethnicities and religions—against the biblical vision of equality. The resources of the land are not shared equally. Theology has been used in Palestine to justify the occupation and injustice.[34]

In response, Palestinian Christians call for a theology of a *shared land*, which means that all the dwellers of the land share the land and its resources equally and have the same rights—regardless of their ethnicity or religion.

A shared-land theology emphasizes that there are no second-class citizens in this land. No one is marginalized in God's vision of the land. *A shared land is not simply an option; it is the only way forward.* This is the biblical vision, and so it must be the prophetic vision of the church in Palestine and Israel. The reality on the ground is that of walls, yet what is needed is a vision of bridges. *Palestinians and Israelis must think collectively in terms of a common future in which they cooperate—not a divided future in which they separate.*[35]

CONCLUSION

For Palestinian Christians, land, ecclesiology, and identity are interrelated. Furthermore, Palestinian theology makes a strong connection between territory, ecclesiology, and mission. The church as a community of believers defines its identity and mission from its context.

For Palestinian Christians, the context of conflict and occupation has important consequences for the self-understanding of the church. For them, no one can claim possession or ownership of any land. Human beings are only tenants in the land and as such must share the blessings of the land with their neighbors. The Palestinian church emphasizes that the land is something to share, not to possess. It is given as a gift for the good of the society, and is shared equally among the members of the community. The principle of shared and inclusive land means that an ideal church and an ideal land are places where people of all ethnicities and social backgrounds are treated equally.

Finally, the Palestinian church makes every effort to be a place of peace, fellowship, and

---

[31]Sabbah, *Voice Crying Out*, 28.

[32]For more on the history of the Palestinian-Israeli conflict, see B. White, *Israeli Apartheid: A Beginner's Guide* (London: Pluto, 2009).

[33]For the inequality in the state of Israel, see B. White, *Palestinians in Israel: Segregation, Discrimination and Democracy* (London: Pluto, 2012).

[34]See M. Raheb, *Faith in the Face of Empire: The Bible Through Palestinian Eyes* (New York: Orbis, 2014).

[35]Isaac, *From Land to Lands*, 380. Most of the political discussions today center around the idea of a two-states solution, in which Palestinians and Israelis divide the land. The practicality of this solution is now debated since it is becoming more and more impossible to define the borders of each side's territory as a result of the Israeli settlements. This is why many academics and activists today are calling for a one-state solution, in which there is one country and one law but two governments. I believe that the church must not get involved in suggesting political solutions. Rather, the message should be that regardless of which political solution is adopted and implemented, the vision and ideals of God, of justice and equality in the land—indeed, any land—must be respected.

reconciliation, a place where enemies meet and are reconciled. The principle of recommissioning reminds us that the church should be a community of peacemakers. It must be engaged in active and sacrificial peacemaking in the land.

Further Reading

Isaac, Munther. *From Land to Lands, from Eden to the Renewed Earth.* Carlisle, UK: Langham Monographs, 2015.

Katanacho, Yohanna. *The Land of Christ: A Palestinian Cry.* Eugene, OR: Pickwick, 2013.

Raheb, Mitri. *I Am a Palestinian Christian.* Minneapolis: Fortress, 1995.

Sabbah, Michel. "Reading the Bible Today in the Land of the Bible." November 1993. Latin Patriarchate of Jerusalem. www.lpj.org/fourth-pastoral-letter-patriarch-sabbahreading-bible-today-land-bible-november-1993/.

Tarazi, P. N. "Covenant, Land and City: Finding God's Will in Palestine." *The Reformed Journal* 29 (1979): 10-16.

———. *Land and Covenant.* St. Paul, MN: OCABS, 2009.

ALL THINGS NEW

ESCHATOLOGY IN THE MAJORITY WORLD

INTRODUCTION TO PART SIX

ESCHATOLOGY IN THE MAJORITY WORLD

Stephen T. Pardue

IN TOO MANY arrangements of systematic theology, eschatology functions much like an appendix, awkwardly affixed to the core of Christian teaching like an unnecessary limb. Even if it is unintentional, it is hard not to sense some deprioritizing when this part of Christian theology is called "last things," while matters such as prolegomena and revelation get to be called "first things," and the doctrine of God is called "theology proper." Regardless of titles, moreover, it is often the case that these doctrines bear examination only in the twilight of the theologian's attention, rather than in the bright dawn of God and the gospel.

This is a most unfortunate state of affairs, because there is a strong argument to be made that Jesus' teaching—and, indeed, the entire message of his life, death, and resurrection—cannot be rightly understood apart from eschatological commitments and claims. John the Baptist prepares the way for Jesus by proclaiming that "the kingdom of heaven has come near" (Mt 3:2 NIV) and by taking up Old Testament language clearly associated with the day of the Lord, a moment

when Yahweh would intervene in the course of human events with finality, yielding judgment for those in rebellion against him, and perfect redemption for the people of Israel. Thus, the irony: far from being the subject of minor interest that it is now, eschatology was, in the very first declaration of the good news, a star player, a sine qua non.

In the twentieth century, several movements converged to bring eschatology back to the center of theological attention, each in a slightly different way. One of the most influential theologians of the twentieth century, Karl Barth, famously foregrounded eschatology, demanding that Christian theologians break with an increasingly prevalent habit of reducing Christian teaching to a set of ethical principles or philosophical ideals. Barth decried this tendency as a "de-eschatologization" of Christianity, and famously noted in the introduction to his commentary on Romans that "If Christianity be not altogether thoroughgoing eschatology, there remains in it no relationship whatever to Christ."[1] If theology is to be christological, in other words,

---

[1] Karl Barth, *The Epistle to the Romans*, trans. E. C. Hoskyns (Oxford: Oxford University Press, 1968), 314. See also Daniel L. Migliore, "Karl Barth's First Lectures in Dogmatics: Instruction in the Christian Religion," in Karl Barth, *The Göttingen Dogmatics: Instruction in the Christian Religion*, trans. Geoffrey W. Bromiley (Grand Rapids, MI: Eerdmans, 1991), 1:lviii.

it must also be intentionally eschatological through and through. Barth was hardly alone. As Richard Bauckham (himself a significant figure in twentieth-century eschatology) notes, Jürgen Moltmann brought a similar conviction to the project of modern theology, contending that "from first to last, and not merely in the epilogue, Christianity is eschatology."[2] To be sure, Barth, Moltmann, and other twentieth-century thinkers each had their own way of applying the eschatological turn, but all were convinced that eschatology must serve as the dominant interpretive lens through which Christian teaching must be refracted.

At least one key ingredient in this turn was emerging New Testament scholarship that sought to apply new tools and principles of historical scholarship to understanding the person of Jesus. In a rebuke to previous eras, figures such as Albert Schweitzer and later Ernst Käsemann reminded scholars that their understanding of Jesus must not be disconnected from the cultural and political context in which Jesus emerged.[3] Viewed in this light, they contended, it is clear that Jesus is best understood as an eschatological prophet, and any interpretation of his life and work that misses this reality is ultimately pointing toward some formulated ideal rather than the authentic Jesus of Nazareth. While many aspects of the "quests" for the his-

torical Jesus have been discarded, this insight has only gained surer footing in recent years, with a whole raft of new scholarship exploring the import of apocalyptic thought for understanding Jesus.[4]

But eschatology also received a boost in the twentieth century from a less scholarly and more grassroots movement: the rise of dispensationalism. Rooted in the teachings of John Nelson Darby, dispensationalists pushed eschatology to the center of Christian consciousness through an emphasis on decoding biblical prophecies. Dispensationalist pastors and churchgoers spent much of the twentieth century conscientiously searching for connections between unfolding historical events—the rise of the Third Reich, the formation of the modern state of Israel, the dominance of the Soviet Union, to highlight a few examples—and biblical prophecies. Like Christians of all ages, they affirmed and looked forward to the return of Christ; what was new was the outsized attention given to the biblical teachings about the parousia and the events prophesied to precede it.[5]

Dispensationalist churches gained an unlikely eschatological bedfellow in the latter half of the twentieth century: Pentecostal church movements. While Pentecostals differ markedly from dispensationalists in their assessment of the ongoing validity of particular spiritual gifts,

---

[2]Jürgen Moltmann, *Theology of Hope*, trans. James W. Leitch (London: SCM Press, 1967), 16; quoted in Richard Bauckham, "Eschatology," in *The Oxford Handbook of Systematic Theology*, ed. John Webster, Kathryn Tanner, and Iain Torrance (Oxford: Oxford University Press, 2007), 306.

[3]Bauckham, "Eschatology," 306-7.

[4]For an introduction to this trend, see two compilations of essays in honor of a pioneering voice in this area: J. Louis Martyn: Marion L. Soards, and Joel Marcus, eds., *Apocalyptic and the New Testament: Essays in Honor of J. Louis Martyn*, rev. ed. (London: Bloomsbury, 2015); Joshua B. Davis and Douglas Karel Harink, eds., *Apocalyptic and the Future of Theology: With and Beyond J. Louis Martyn* (Eugene, OR: Cascade, 2012).

[5]Perhaps the best-known sensationalist account from this viewpoint was Hal Lindsey's *The Late Great Planet Earth* (Grand Rapids, MI: Zondervan, 1970). However, readers should also note that many dispensationalist scholars, especially from the 1990s onward, sought an approach to the movement that maintained some of its core distinctives but was more circumspect with regard to its analysis of prophecy and contemporary events. See, e.g., Craig A. Blaising and Darrell L. Bock, *Progressive Dispensationalism* (Grand Rapids, MI: BridgePoint, 1993); Craig L. Blomberg and Sung Wook Chung, eds., *A Case for Historic Premillennialism: An Alternative to "Left Behind" Eschatology* (Grand Rapids, MI: Baker, 2009).

they often share a similar commitment to a fore-grounding of eschatology, affirming the imminent return of Christ, looking for the fulfillment of specific biblical prophecies in current world events, and seeing themselves as living "at the end of the age."[6]

ESCHATOLOGY AND THE EXPANSION OF THE MAJORITY WORLD CHURCH

Coincidentally or not, the twentieth century turn toward all things eschatological occurred at almost exactly the same time as an explosion of growth in the Majority World church. As each of these movements advanced the eschatological agenda in different ways, remarkable church expansion was being activated in Asia, Africa, and Latin America. While the beginning of the twentieth century saw only a small fraction of the world's Christians living outside the West, by the turn of the millennium Christians living outside the West were the clear majority. A specific case can help drive home the significance of this broad claim: consider that in spite of decades of persecution and marginalization, Christians in China now outnumber those in the United Kingdom, which was one of the major centers of the world Christian movement throughout the nineteenth and early twentieth centuries.

In many cases, these Majority World expansions were directly linked to eschatological thinking. In Latin America, for example, theologies that emphasized the establishment of the kingdom and the hope that it offered to the poor

and oppressed were instrumental in revitalizing the church and equipping it for ongoing mission. In other cases, there is strong evidence that mission activity in the Majority World was driven primarily by a sense that the church must redeem the brief time left before the second coming, or even that through the making disciples of all nations, the church may be able to hasten the second coming.[7] To return to the contemporary Chinese church, a prominent example of eschatology's ongoing influence in mission is the Back to Jerusalem movement, a loosely organized campaign that sees churches in China supplying an enormous missionary workforce in the years ahead to penetrate the unevangelized nations between China and the Holy Land. The vision of the movement is rooted in a set of very specific convictions about the eschaton: especially that China has been providentially blessed at this specific moment in time, and "that God has given [us] a solemn responsibility to take the fire from his altar and complete the Great Commission by establishing God's Kingdom in all of the remaining countries and people groups in Asia, the Middle East, and Islamic North Africa."[8] The movement explicitly affirms a premillennial eschatology, and, in many cases, includes an affinity for political Israel.[9]

And so we are confronted in the twentieth century with two coinciding trends: what we might call the reeschatologization of Christian theology, and the shift of the church's primary center of gravity to the Majority World. At first

---

[6]For an excellent introduction to distinctives of Pentecostal eschatologies, see Frank D. Macchia, "Pentecostal and Charismatic Theology," in *The Oxford Handbook of Eschatology*, ed. Jerry L. Walls (Oxford: Oxford University Press, 2007), 280-94; Peter Althouse and Robby Waddell, eds., *Perspectives in Pentecostal Eschatology: World Without End* (Eugene, OR: Wipf & Stock, 2010).

[7]Craig Ott, Stephen J. Strauss, and Timothy C. Tennent, *Encountering Theology of Mission: Biblical Foundations, Historical Developments, and Contemporary Issues*, Encountering Mission (Grand Rapids, MI: Baker, 2010), 186-91.

[8]Quoted from backtojerusalem.com in Tobias Brandner, "Mission, Millennium, and Politics: A Continuation of the History of Salvation—from the East," *Missiology: An International Review* 37, no. 3 (2009): 319.

[9]Brandner, "Mission, Millennium, and Politics," 327-28. See Shirley Ho's essay in this part of the volume for a fascinating examination of how these pro-Israel beliefs have influenced the church in Taiwan.

glance, the two developments seem to be of a piece: at the same time that professional Christian theologians were rediscovering the centrality of eschatology for Christian teaching, Christian practitioners had the same thought. Both parties helped propagate a renewed vision for eschatology in their own way—with professional theologians influencing the academic literature on the one hand, and church practitioners influencing in-the-trenches ministry on the other.

But a closer look reveals a far more complicated picture. For example, it is notable that some of these movements have been quite at odds in terms of how Christian eschatology should influence Christian life. At least in certain forms, dispensationalist and Pentecostal theologies often perceive Christian eschatological teaching to have a primarily extractive force: because the world is not my home, and because we are so near to the end of all things, our limited resources are best focused on evangelism and the building up of the church, not on the transformation of this-worldly realities through civic engagement or ecological care.[10] In contrast, theologians such as N. T. Wright and J. Richard Middleton have spilled much ink arguing precisely the opposite: namely, that biblical eschatology should push Christians to greater engagement with this-worldly realities in light of God's desire to renew all things through the church's ministry of reconciliation.[11]

Another complication in the narrative relates to the influence of eschatology in the thought of

Christians in the Majority World. As the essays in this section make clear, eschatology has significantly shaped the dynamics and self-understanding of Christians in the Majority World. And yet, as William Dyrness and Oscar García-Johnson have recently noted, there are "relatively few works that specifically address eschatology outside the West." Specifically, Dyrness and García-Johnson are concerned by the paucity of contextualized reflections on eschatology in the Majority World, "especially in Africa and Asia," where "Western eschatology had a great, and not always positive, influence."[12] If eschatology gained such centrality in Christian theology at just the time that Majority World churches have been expanding, why the shortage of contextually rooted eschatological theologies?

PLAN OF PART SIX

These are just some of the complications that this section of *Majority World Theology* is uniquely positioned to expose, wrestle with, and begin untangling. D. Stephen Long begins the discussion with an insightful examination of the ongoing value of first-century apocalyptic as a resource for contemporary Christian eschatology. After offering a detailed account of the recovery of apocalyptic thought in recent scholarship, he engages with a series of objections to its influence in Christian eschatology. While it is certainly the case that irresponsible interpretations of apocalyptic literature can veer into dangerous territory, Long contends that ridding

---

[10]Many will no doubt identify with James K. A. Smith's description of the evangelical eschatology with which he was initially brought to faith: "It was very much a rapture-ready, heaven-centric piety that had little, if anything, to say about how or why a Christian might care about urban planning or chemical engineering or securing clean water sources in developing nations. Why worry about justice or flourishing in a world that is going to burn up?" (James K. A. Smith, *Awaiting the King: Reforming Public Theology* [Grand Rapids, MI: Baker, 2017], 85).

[11]N. T. Wright, *Surprised by Hope: Rethinking Heaven, the Resurrection, and the Mission of the Church* (New York: HarperOne, 2014); J. Richard Middleton, *New Heaven and a New Earth: Reclaiming Biblical Eschatology* (Grand Rapids, MI: Baker Academic, 2014).

[12]William A. Dyrness and Oscar García-Johnson, *Theology Without Borders: An Introduction to Global Conversations* (Grand Rapids, MI: Baker Academic, 2015), 140.

Christian eschatology of its apocalyptic under-pinnings is a fool's errand. Rather than less apocalyptic imagination, the global church desperately needs a deeper and richer vision of the apocalyptic: one that unveils not only the culminating judgment that awaits the world but also the vision of God dwelling with his people in a new heaven and new earth.

Long's essay explores well the tension with which many of the section's remaining essays wrestle: namely, that between recognizing the future orientation of the Christian faith and the pressing needs confronting the church in the here and now. This theme is echoed in the two succeeding essays, from James Kombo and John Ekem. Kombo starts by offering a fascinating survey of eschatology in African Christian thought. He notes that African Christians approach eschatology not only in cosmic terms—that is, as a consideration of how all things will be restored or reconciled in Christ—but also in very personal terms. In particular, he draws attention to the discussion of what has been termed "the intermediate state," the time between bodily death and bodily resurrection. While this "in-between" time has often been ignored or minimized in Western eschatologies, the African context, with its emphasis on the ongoing life of the ancestors, requires that we articulate how God provides for and governs this phase of life after death. He argues persuasively that Christian theology has internal resources to respond well to these questions and that, in the process, African theological reflection can help Western eschatology be refined and enriched.

If Kombo creates a framework for such enrichment, Ekem provides a concrete example of it. Like Long, Ekem reminds readers that the strange and sometimes unsettling world of apocalyptic literature is an unavoidable feature

of Christian eschatology—it is the language that Jesus chooses to use when asked about the end of all things, and it is also the genre through which Revelation communicates the most comprehensive Christian vision of the end. Ekem specifically examines Revelation 21's vision of the new heaven and new earth, considering how the original author's vision translates and communicates in the contemporary Ghanaian context. The results of his analysis are fascinating. The Ghanaian context reveals shades of nuance and emphasis in Revelation 21 that are easily lost in contemporary English translations, and the African worldview that Kombo so ably described prompts new and interesting questions about the nature of the text and its impact on Christian thought.

The next two essays once again bring together the insights of a systematic theologian and a biblical scholar, this time exploring the dynamics of Christian eschatology in Latin America. Alberto Roldán offers a broad survey of the landscape of eschatology in Latin American contexts, focusing especially on the contrast between dispensationalist eschatology that dominated in the decades after World War II, and the much broader eschatological visions that gained influence in the later part of the twentieth century. Roldán argues that these eschatological movements, especially those that echo Moltmann's insights in *Theology of Hope*, have much to offer the contemporary evangelical church, as they often strike impressive balances between the promise of future salvation and the Christian commitment to here-and-now transformation. He concludes the essay by showing how this plays out in the real world, noting how Christian hymnody tells a particular eschatological story that rightly shapes the posture and perspective of churchgoers.

Nelson Morales is likewise interested in the real-world implications of eschatological teaching, but examines instead the diverse interpretations in Latin American churches of Jesus' famous announcement recorded in Mark 1:15: "The time has come. . . . The kingdom of God has come near" (NIV). Understanding how various networks within the Latin American church have heard and interpreted this declaration turns out to be a potent heuristic for understanding the implications of various eschatological views. Ultimately, Morales argues that evangelicals in Latin America would be wise to make the most of these insights by recognizing both the future fulfillment and the present unfolding of the kingdom in our present world.

The final two essays in the book, from Aldrin Peñamora and Shirley Ho, offer a glimpse of how the church in Asia—a minority nestled in a continent where the major world religions all find their home—understands and articulates the uniquely Christian vision of the end. Peñamora examines four influential movements in Asia and considers how their unusual—and remarkably effective—ministries each depended on a profoundly eschatological vision. Each case study offers a unique insight into how Asian believers have approached the doctrine of eschatology, even as they experience extreme forms of success and blessing (e.g., in the case of David Yonggi Cho's ministry in Korea) and suffering (e.g., Watchman Nee's experience in China). Peñamora argues that while we should be grateful that Christian theology has the diverse resources to speak to the broad array of experiences present in Asia, the Asian church must be especially attentive to the gospel's clarion call to stand alongside the suffering, marginalized, and downtrodden.

Finally, Shirley Ho's essay assesses the eschatological underpinnings of the Zionist movement in Taiwan. Ho is not only an able tour guide—offering readers a remarkable glimpse into a world in which rams' horns are blown, traditional Jewish clothing is worn, and Jewish festivals are celebrated thousands of miles and worlds away from Israel—but more importantly helps to explain the rationale and worldview underlying these practices. After noting how Taiwanese Christians within this movement read a key text about the restoration of Israel, Ho offers her own reading, which artfully connects the world of the original author and audience with Taiwanese history and culture. Using the concept of harmony (*Ta-tung*), she ably narrates a more robust vision of eschatology that is biblically rooted and also contextually formed.

For theology to be eschatological is to acknowledge that the gospel is first and foremost an announcement of good news about God's redemptive kingdom and plan. That this good news is for every people in every culture and place has classically led Christians to affirm that its unpacking is best accomplished with the whole church, allowing the fullness of truth to shine through our diverse cultural identities. This is what it means for theology to be catholic, and it is the fundamental affirmation underlying this volume. It is a great joy to see these two truths come together in this section—that is, not only to see eschatology recognized as a central aspect of all Christian theology, but also to see it assessed in a context of true catholicity. It is our hope that the section will therefore serve as a unique aid to the church in its journey of seeking to apprehend, submit to, and live out the good eschatological news among every tribe, nation, people, and tongue.

Compiling a collection like this is impossible without a team of remarkable people working together. Of course, first on this list are the authors and their respective institutions, for making the time for this project in the midst of their many and varied commitments. They are our heroes. We are also grateful for the steady help of ScholarLeaders in standing behind and beside us as we have developed this volume, and no less so in the case of this section. Larry Smith, Evan Hunter, and Lynn Simons deserve our thanks for seeing the strategic value of *Majority World Theology* from the start. They provided crucial assistance in securing resources and managing logistics to enable scholars from four continents to gather in Boston in November 2017. Without that gathering, this section would not have been possible. We owe a deep debt to Langham Publishing, and especially to Pieter Kwant, Luke Lewis, and Vivian Doub, for their unwavering commitment and assistance in the publication of this section and the rest of the volume. In addition, we wish to thank Suzanne Mitchell for her editorial assistance, and Jixun Hu for his work on the indexes. Finally, of course, we give thanks for the Lord's faithfulness in bringing this project to fruition. All glory to him who was, and is, and is to come.

41

ESCHATOLOGY, APOCALYPTIC, ETHICS, AND POLITICAL THEOLOGY

D. Stephen Long

THIS CHAPTER FIRST examines the perceived failures of apocalyptic in modernity: it is otherworldly; foments an extreme, violent politics; or produces a political Zionism that destabilizes the international political order. For this reason, some theologians divide eschatology from apocalyptic, but this is an unsustainable division. If there were no apocalyptic literature, there would be no eschatology. The key question is how to interpret apocalyptic literature for eschatology. The conclusion offers a theological interpretation of the Apocalypse.

INTRODUCTION

Eschatology is the doctrine of the end times or ultimate things. Eschatology comes from the Greek word *eschaton*, which means "last." It contains many important themes. Here are six of the most important: (1) the restoration of Israel; (2) the coming of the kingdom or reign of God; (3) the renewal of creation; (4) heaven and earth, God's dwelling place and the creaturely dwelling place, coming together in unity; (5) final judgment; and (6) the completion, fulfillment, or perfection of history.

These themes are present in the Nicene Creed, the most universally used expression of faith

among Christians throughout the world. Many recite it weekly, confessing the following words about Jesus:

> For our sake he was crucified under Pontius Pilate,
> he suffered death and was buried,
> and rose again on the third day
> in accordance with the Scriptures.
> He ascended into heaven
> and is seated at the right hand of the Father.
> He will come again in glory
> to judge the living and the dead
> and his kingdom will have no end.

Here is the basic confession of Christian eschatology. Through his death and resurrection, Jesus has been enthroned as ruler of the world. His reign will be one of divine glory. Every Christian worship service is a repetition of Jesus' enthronement as ruler, but it is also a recognition that, as Hebrews 2:8 states, everything is not yet subject to his reign. For this reason, Christians also regularly confess, "Christ is come. Christ has died. Christ will come again." The expectation of his coming anticipates judgment. Although injustice, inequality, hatred, and violence seem to have the last word, no one can finally escape their wrongdoings. They must be accounted for. But the judgment is not to condemn; it brings life—his reign will have no end, and unlike other reigns it will not be based on deception and violence. The petition from the Lord's Prayer that "thy kingdom come, thy will be done, on earth as it is in heaven" expresses this eschatological hope.

The above brief exposition of eschatology presents a Christian eschatology. However, eschatology does not need to be religious; it can also be secular. Reinhold Niebuhr interpreted that period of Western history known as the Renaissance with its emphasis on progress as one side of the development of Christian eschatology. The other side, the Reformation, developed the pessimistic. The former focused on renewal, the latter on judgment.[1] Many thinkers have suggested that Karl Marx's view of a communist society bears strong similarities to Jewish and Christian eschatology. Some have called it a secularized eschatology. Marx sees a dialectic that runs through history moving us toward that stage when, rather than laboring away at a single vocation, everyone engages in various tasks without those tasks becoming their identity: "hunt in the morning, fish in the afternoon, rear cattle in the evening, criticize after dinner, just as I have a mind, without ever becoming hunter, fisherman, shepherd or critic."[2]

While Marx's thought as a secularized eschatology has been suggested by many, fewer seem to have noticed that Adam Smith's *Wealth of Nations* takes its title from a Jewish and Christian eschatological passage, Isaiah 60:5. Isaiah tells the people of Israel what will happen when they return to Jerusalem after exile:

Lift up your eyes and look around;
    they all gather together, they come to you;

your sons shall come from far away,
    and your daughters shall be carried on their
        nurses' arms.
Then you shall see and be radiant;
    your heart shall thrill and rejoice,
    because the abundance of the sea shall be
        brought to you,
    the wealth of the nations shall come to you.[3]

Another source for secular eschatology is technology, when it is assumed that it can deliver what Christian faith hoped for but never delivered: life without end, a promise set forth in some posthuman evolution in which humans merge with technology to create everlasting life.

The above Jewish, Christian, and secular views of eschatology all assume that something is being restored, which also means that something needs restoration. Everything is not as it should be. To see the world as it is and realize that it should not be is the first step in eschatology. The next step is to see the world as it should be coming into existence—lions lie down with lambs, the hungry are fed, pain and suffering no longer exist, justice is done, and wrongs are righted. Eschatology, then, is a teaching about judgment and restoration. It can have a secular goal that suggests that if we follow these economic or political principles, injustices will be overcome and the wealth of nations will come to all. It can have a religious goal. Eschatology is the renewal and restoration of Israel, the church, or of all creation. Its influence in Western society is pervasive, both in secular and religious forms. Yet Western thinkers, religious and secular, have also been concerned that the influence of Jewish and

---

[1] Reinhold Niebuhr, *The Nature and Destiny of Man* (New York: Charles Scribner's Sons, 1964), 2:156-69.
[2] From Marx's *Economic and Philosophical Manuscripts*, in Eric Fromm, *Marx's Concept of Man*, trans. T. B. Bottomore (New York: Unger, 1986), 206.
[3] Unless otherwise stated, Scripture quotations in chapters 41-47 are from the NRSV.

Christian eschatology has had detrimental political and ethical consequences.

The following essay begins with secular and religious thinkers who express grave reservations about eschatology's influence. It then moves to discuss a pervasive feature of Western eschatology that has had, and continues to have, global political repercussions: Zionism, old and new. As other chapters in this section ably demonstrate, the emphasis on a Christian Zionism has had marked global influence. The essay then examines different readings of eschatology, ethics, and politics among diverse contemporary Western thinkers that do not require Christian Zionism. It concludes by suggesting that the most constructive way forward for Christian eschatology is its cultivation of an apocalyptic imagination that arises from a fullness of worship and that is repeatedly relevant for a theopolitical vision.

Perceived failures of apocalyptic. Because it assumes that the world as it is should not be, eschatology can be dangerous. It looks for something other than what exists and that could motivate persons to wish for the destruction of what is for the sake of what is coming. Several Western thinkers expressed grave concern about eschatology. In the nineteenth century, philosopher Friedrich Nietzsche announced the "twilight of the idols." By "idols" he meant theological ideas such as God, the church, and eschatology. He imagined that by our generation these theological ideas would no longer hold people captive. Contemporary political philosopher Mark Lilla announces and laments that "the twilight of the idols has been postponed." Lilla finds it "incomprehensible" that apocalyptic or eschatological ideas are still with us and continue to inform

politics, much to its detriment. He writes, "We are disturbed and confused. We find it incomprehensible that theological ideas still inflame the minds of men, stirring up messianic passions that leave societies in ruin. We assumed that this was no longer possible, that human beings had learned to separate religious questions from political ones, that fanaticism was dead. We were wrong."[4] Notice that he correlates "messianic passions" with fanaticism. To hope for a Messiah, to think one knows who the Messiah is and how he is coming, suggests Lilla, inflames fanatics, who seek to destroy political societies as they currently exist for the sake of the messianic society that is arriving. Lilla characterizes apocalyptic as focusing on revelation. Apocalyptic denies that knowledge of God moves from humanity to God. In contrast, it emphasizes God's unpredictable inbreaking, relativizing the present and political structures. Apocalyptic is catastrophic. It looks for the destruction of the world.

Lilla is not alone in lamenting the ongoing influence of apocalyptic; there is a long tradition of Western philosophers who rejected eschatology because of its political and ethical consequences. Immanuel Kant (1724–1804) was an influential philosopher who focused on how it is that we can come to know what we know. He was less concerned about what eschatology did to politics than about what it did to philosophy. In 1796, he wrote an essay titled "On a Newly Arisen Superior Tone of Philosophy." The "superior tone" arose from religious enthusiasts who thought that they had a mystical vision that gave them certain knowledge. These enthusiasts, he suggested, reduced philosophy to a "mode whereby secrets are revealed." Apocalyptic, he thought, is the unveiling of secrets, so once philosophy took

---

[4]Mark Lilla, *The Stillborn God: Religion, Politics and the Modern West* (New York: Knopf, 2007), 3.

this apocalyptic tone, it "must necessarily promise a surrogate of cognition, supernatural communication (mystical illumination), which is the death of all philosophy."[5] Anyone who thinks that they have a secure source of knowledge from supernatural communication will no longer engage in critical thinking. They will be led by a misguided vision.

G. W. F. Hegel (1770–1831) wrote after Kant and, like him, emphasized political freedom. He also claimed, "Otherworldly eschatology is the enemy of political and economic freedom."[6] If you found your true home in the eschaton, you would not work for the political and economic freedom available to finite human creatures in the here and now. Karl Marx (1818–1883) agreed and developed Hegel's idea in a more critical political and economic vein. Eschatology promised poor workers that even though they were suffering now and not yet receiving their reward, they would be rewarded when they entered the kingdom of God at the end of life. Eschatology was oppressive because it masked the alienation workers should recognize between their labor and its just reward. Eschatology was used by the powerful to sedate the poor and to provide false comfort to the sufferings of the exploited.

Kant, Hegel, and Marx were not alone. From the eighteenth century until today, influential Western philosophers have expressed grave reservations about apocalyptic thinking due to its perceived detrimental effects. It causes people to flee from the world or even hate it, hoping for its destruction. Few of these critics have been as strident as atheist Christopher Hitchens. He accused religion of being "violent, irrational, intol-erant, allied to racism and tribalism, invested in ignorance and hostile to free inquiry." He added to this the charge that it "looks forward to the destruction of the world."[7] Here, too, apocalyptic is the reason for religious violence because apocalyptic envisions a catastrophic end to the world in which everything is destroyed in a great conflagration. These concerns are not unwarranted. In the sixteenth century, especially in Münster, Germany, Christians known as the radical wing of the Reformation thought that the end of the world was coming, and the result was violence perpetrated by them and against them. In 1978, when an apocalyptic sect known as Jonestown committed mass suicide, 909 people died. In 1993, an apocalyptic sect known as the Branch Davidians thought along similar lines, and the result was violence perpetrated by them and against them. Given these sentiments about the dangers of apocalyptic, and the historical events that seem to corroborate them, many Christians have been wary of embracing the doctrine of eschatology.

Zionism: New and old. The controversies swirling around various types of Zionism accentuate the concerns of many Western philosophers and theologians about eschatology. Jewish Zionism was a movement in the latter part of the nineteenth century to provide a homeland for Jews in Israel, including a state. Christian Zionism differs. It is an eschatologically charged political movement that seeks to create political conditions that would lead to the second coming of Jesus. In its fundamentalist, dispensationalist form, Christian Zionism views eschatology as a decoded map, by which we can discern or even encourage the development of conditions that allow

---

[5]I. Kant, "On a Newly Arisen Superior Tone in Philosophy," in *Raising the Tone of Philosophy: Late Essay by Immanuel Kant, Transformative Critique by Jacques Derrida*, ed. Peter Fenves (Baltimore: Johns Hopkins University Press, 1993), 51, 62.
[6]Cited in Luke Bretherton, *Resurrecting Democracy: Faith, Citizenship, and the Politics of a Common Life* (New York: Cambridge University Press, 2015), 227.
[7]Christopher Hitchens, *God Is Not Great: How Religion Poisons Everything* (New York: Twelve, 2007), 56.

Israel's political development to pave the way for Jesus' second coming. This popular movement has little backing among New Testament scholars and theologians. However, one common theme running through the essays in this section is how pervasive something like Christian Zionism is throughout global Christianity. Shirley Ho traces its importance and influence in Taiwan. Alberto Roldán demonstrates the influence of dispensationalist eschatology in Latin American Protestantism, even as he points to movements in Latin America that are now moving away from dispensationalism. Nelson Morales presents an eschatology that is an alternative to this Christian Zionism. The kingdom of God is not the restoration of the "land of Israel," but "a new order inaugurated by Jesus" that can be established wherever his disciples are faithful. James Kombo presents it in terms of an African ontology.

These diverse accounts of eschatology raise the question: What is being restored? Is it a literal return of Jews to Israel and the rebuilding of the temple? A "new" articulation of Christian Zionism argues that eschatology must include not only the land of but also the state of Israel. Gerald McDermott represents the new Christian Zionism, stating,

> We believe that the return of Jews to the land and their establishment of the state of Israel are partial fulfillments of biblical prophecy and so are part of God's design for what might be a long era of eschatological fulfillment. As Mark Kinzer puts it, today's state of Israel both awaits redemption and is a means to it. It is a proleptic sign of the eschaton, which means that it is a provisional sign of the not-yet-actualized consummation.

McDermott distances the "new" Christian Zionism from that found among fundamentalist dispensationalists, who put "Israel and the church on two different tracks," have an "elaborated schedule of end-time events," and view Christians as raptured while Jews and others are lost.[8] The "new" Christian Zionism does not have these convictions, although it does wed biblical prophecy to a defense of the state of Israel.

Nicholas Brown asks what Jesus has restored in his strange victory and makes a biblical argument that the land of Israel must be included in any eschatological vision. He dissects contemporary eschatologies and suggests that they lose the importance of land through three different strategies: "praxification, ecclesiofication and typofication." The first turns the restoration of the land of Israel into an ethical praxis. Wherever this ethical praxis can be found, eschatological restoration has begun. The second views the church as sufficient for restoration. When Jesus claimed that he would destroy the temple and rebuild it, the biblical writers identified his body as the site for restoration. The land is no longer necessary because we have the church as the continuation of Christ's body. The third views the restoration as a political type that can become the pattern for any nation-state.[9] Although Brown agrees in part with these three views, he argues that each of them loses the importance of the land. The land and Jesus' prophetic proclamation of God's reign must be held together. While the three views noted above lose the connection of the land to the kingdom, the "Christian Zionists . . . tend to detach that connection from Jesus'

[8]Gerald R. McDermott, "Introduction: What Is the New Christian Zionism?," in *The New Christian Zionism*, ed. Gerald R. McDermott (Downers Grove, IL: InterVarsity Press, 2016), 14, 11.
[9]Nicholas Brown identifies Glenn Stassen and David Gushee with the first approach, Stanley Hauerwas and John Howard Yoder with the second, and Oliver O'Donovan with the third. See Nicholas Brown, *For the Nation: Jesus, the Restoration of Israel and Articulating a Christian Ethic of Territorial Governance* (Eugene, OR: Pickwick, 2016), 65-83.

proclamation of the kingdom."[10] They lose his prophetic critique.

What is restored in Christian eschatology? From the above discussion on Zionism new and old, it is at least evident that this restoration has political and ethical consequences. The next section examines a different account of eschatology and its relation to those consequences.

ESCHATOLOGY, APOCALYPTIC, ETHICS, AND POLITICS

If it were not for a genre of Jewish and Christian literature known as apocalyptic, there would be no eschatology. Examples of apocalyptic literature can be found in the book of Daniel in the Old Testament and Revelation in the New Testament. The Greek word for Revelation is *apokalypsis*, from which we get the term *apocalypse*. Christian theology has a doctrine of eschatology because of apocalyptic literature. As I noted in the first section above, apocalyptic literature became controversial in the West after the seventeenth century. For a long time, theologians ignored eschatology and apocalyptic by emphasizing Jesus as an ethical teacher who taught about the kingdom of God, something that could be brought about by human effort. In one sense, the popular Christian Zionism of fundamentalist dispensationalism filled the gap this abandonment of eschatology left in more mainline Christian thought.

German biblical scholar and theologian Albert Schweitzer (1875–1965) challenged any understanding of Jesus that could adopt his ethics and abandon his eschatology. Schweitzer argued that the historical Jesus could not be rightly understood apart from his eschatology. However, Schweitzer thought that no modern person could affirm Jesus' eschatology, so the relevance of Jesus for modern times would have to lie elsewhere than in his historical and eschatological context. Since Schweitzer's work, theologians have recognized the importance of Jesus' eschatology for understanding him, but they have responded to it differently. Some have dismissed that context, replacing it with something else, such as the command to love God, neighbors, and enemies. Others have affirmed it but distinguish eschatology from apocalyptic, treating the former as a more general discipline and the latter as a problem to be overcome because of its perceived specificity. Still others do not divide eschatology and apocalyptic and suggest that Christian ethics cannot be understood without apocalyptic.

Schweitzer's retrieval of apocalyptic. One way to avoid apocalyptic was to disregard any sense that Jesus was an apocalyptic thinker. Western biblical scholars and theologians did this by emphasizing Jesus' proclamation of the "kingdom of God," but they did so in such a way that the reign of God he announces is not something that interrupts the world as it is; it is not an in-breaking, but it gradually emerges over time from his ethical teachings. The ethical teachings that were proposed looked much like the dominant ethics of Western, European society. In this tradition of thought, Jesus does not challenge politics as it is but perpetuates it. He gives us resources to do what is already being done, fostering a civilization of democracy and freedom. The difficulty with this tradition of thought, as Schweitzer pointed out, is that it read itself into the historical Jesus and neglected his radical, apocalyptic thinking. After Schweitzer's work, that tradition could no longer consider itself to

---

[10]Brown, *For the Nation*, 192.

be putting forth the historical Jesus. Once Jesus became an apocalyptic prophet, it was not so easy to remake him into the image of a respectable, democratic, Western man.

Schweitzer challenged the liberal interpretation of Jesus that reduced his work to modern ethics by convincingly demonstrating that Jesus' mission could only be understood in his apocalyptic context. Jesus did not expect human beings to create the kingdom of God; it would come about by an in-breaking from God into creaturely existence that Jesus thought was imminent. For that reason, Schweitzer stated, the Jesus who preached the "ethic of the Kingdom of God never had any existence. He is a figure designed by rationalism, endowed with life by liberalism and clothed by modern theology in an historical garb." Because he thought the kingdom of God was about to arrive, he could "throw himself on the wheel of history," sacrificing everything—family, property, relationships, power. God was bringing something completely new, so everything that existed prior to it could be jettisoned. For Schweitzer, eschatology and ethics were contraries. He writes, "There is for Jesus no ethic of the Kingdom of God, for in the Kingdom of God all natural relationships, even for example the distinction of sex, are abolished." Jesus was an apocalyptic prophet who imagined that the end times were about to interrupt human history, but he was wrong. Jesus did not stop history when he threw himself upon the "wheel of history"; it grinded on, destroying eschatological expectation. Jesus' failure as an apocalyptic prophet meant that no one could take those expectations seriously. Thus, rather than creating the conditions for the eschaton, "he has destroyed them."[11]

Ethics in place of eschatology. Schweitzer's work on Jesus' apocalypticism accomplished two things in Western theology. First, apocalyptic returned as a necessary context in which to understand Jesus. Second, apocalyptic was largely considered indefensible. Jesus' mission was inextricably linked with his eschatology, but, because the latter was unacceptable to modern persons, something must replace eschatology if Jesus was to be conceived as relevant. Often, what replaced eschatology was ethics. Take as an example the influential work of Paul Ramsey in his 1950 *Basic Christian Ethics*. He identifies *agapē* or disinterested love as the heart of Jesus' teaching, and he too connects it with eschatology. When Jesus tells us to do something difficult such as love our enemy, give everything to the poor, or resist calling someone a fool, his "strenuous" sayings depend "on his apocalyptic expectation." Agreeing with the American theologian Walter Rauschenbusch (1861–1918), Ramsey argues that Jesus' apocalyptic context is untenable for moderns. We can neither "translate" his love commands from that apocalyptic context without significant loss, nor can we inhabit it. We are caught in a conundrum. Jesus' ethics arise from apocalyptic expectation, but modern, reasonable people cannot inhabit Jesus' eschatological world. What is to be done? Ramsey argues that Jesus' teaching can still have "validity" without the eschatology. The "genesis" of the love commandment in its apocalyptic context has "nothing to do with validity."[12] What Jesus teaches can be differentiated from how he taught it and still function as a Christian ethics. Ethics can be divided from eschatology.

---

[11] Albert Schweitzer, *The Quest of the Historical Jesus: A Critical Study of Its Progress from Reimarus to Wrede* (Baltimore: Johns Hopkins University Press, 1998), 398, 365, 371.

[12] Paul Ramsey, *Basic Christian Ethics* (Louisville: Westminster John Knox, 1993) 36, 41.

Eschatology as necessary for ethics. This longstanding modern division between ethics and eschatology was unstable. Later in his work, Ramsey qualifies his earlier statements about eschatology and affirms its importance for Christian ethics. In so doing, he was following some mid-twentieth-century theological shifts, largely brought about by Swiss Protestant theologian Karl Barth (1886–1968) and Swiss Roman Catholic theologian Hans Urs von Balthasar (1905–1988). They retrieved eschatology and made it central to their theology.

Barth wrote a famous essay in 1922 in which he states that the supposed certainties of Western ethics have become more of a problem than Christian dogma. Ethics can no longer substitute for Christian doctrine. Rather than ethics substituting for eschatology, ethics is intelligible within eschatology. In his famous *Commentary on the Epistle to the Romans* (1922), he states, "Thus it is that all these human possibilities become ethical only in the shadow of the final eschatological possibility."[13] The human possibilities are generosity, mercy, and cheerfulness, especially as they bring a new conception of authority. To bring about this new conception, the human person must be "disturbed." Eschatology disturbs human nature, interrupting and even contradicting it to bring something new.

Fifteen years after Barth's Romans commentary, Balthasar published a three-volume work titled *Apocalypse of the German Soul*.[14] Apocalyptic had never disappeared from Germany, he suggested, but it was negatively present. It often functioned in German literature as the emptying out of God into humanity. The basic teaching of the incarnation that God became human had become a strict passage from the divine to the human. What had been considered divine had become nothing but human. Barth is the only theologian Balthasar cites in his three-volume work; Barth offers a different understanding of eschatology. There is much to appreciate in Barth, but his early work is too dialectical for Balthasar. By that he means that God is only present to humanity as a negation of what it means to be human. Balthasar also affirms apocalyptic, but he does so analogically. The eschaton does not simply negate what comes before but preserves and perfects what is true, good, and beautiful in creation. Balthasar thinks that Barth's later work moved away from dialectic to analogy and thus provided us with a better understanding of apocalyptic and its relation to creation.

An eschatological ethics: The church and the two ages. After Barth and Balthasar, apocalyptic continued to hold an important place for many Christian theologians and ethicists. Three American theologians—John Howard Yoder, James William McClendon, and Stanley Hauerwas—and one British theologian, Oliver O'Donovan, have argued that Christian ethics makes no sense without eschatology. Yoder, McClendon, and Hauerwas draw on eschatology for a "neo-Anabaptist" ethics of nonviolence that makes the church central. Their approach is better called an "ecclesial approach" because Jesus inaugurates a new era to which the church must bear witness. It primarily does so by refusing to use violence to control history. Rather than emphasizing a return to the specific land of Israel, they look to the condition of exile or diaspora as the way God wills the

[13]Karl Barth, *The Epistle to the Romans*, trans. Edwyn C. Hoskyns (London: Oxford University Press, 1968), 449.
[14]Hans Urs von Balthasar, *Apokalypse der deutschen Seele: Studien zu einer Lehre letzten Haltungen*, 3 vols. (Salzburg and Leipzig: Verlag Anton Pustet, 1937–1939).

restoration of all things. The task of Israel and the church is to accept its condition of exile and follow the prophet Jeremiah's counsel in Jeremiah 29:4-7 (ESV):

> Thus says the Lord of hosts, the God of Israel, to all the exiles whom I have sent into exile from Jerusalem to Babylon: Build houses and live in them; plant gardens and eat their produce. Take wives and have sons and daughters; take wives for your sons, and give your daughters in marriage, that they may bear sons and daughters; multiply there, and do not decrease. But seek the welfare of the city where I have sent you into exile, and pray to the Lord on its behalf, for in its welfare you will find your welfare.

In 1954, the Mennonite theologian Yoder wrote an essay, "Peace Without Eschatology," arguing that Jesus' eschatology makes sense of how we should live and act in the world. Yoder's eschatology draws heavily on Colossians 2:15, where Paul tells us that Jesus disarmed the "powers and principalities" or "rulers and authorities" and made a "spectacle" of them. In so doing, he "disarmed" them. The rulers and authorities are now part of an old age. The former age in which they claimed to be gods has been disarmed; they no longer have that kind of power over us. In crucifying Jesus, who was true God and humanity in one person, they were revealed for what they really are: self-absorbed centers of power who reject the things of God. Jesus calls and equips his church to be a sign of the new age, an age in which God's reign has begun and will be fulfilled in the eschaton. Meanwhile, Christians live in the midst of two eons: the new age of the church and the old age of the world. The rulers and authorities of the old age remain. They are crea-

tures that serve God's purposes, but they have been limited in their role.

Yoder gives the following interpretation of the role for the rulers and authorities after Christ's triumph: "The Reign of Christ means for the state the obligation to serve God by encouraging the good and restraining evil, i.e. to serve peace, to preserve the social cohesion in which the leaven of the Gospel can build the church and also render the old aeon more tolerable."[15] The purpose of the ruling authorities has been limited by Christ's victory in his crucifixion, resurrection, and ascension. The real politics now resides with the church and all who witness to the new age that has been inaugurated and whose completion we await. Yoder states,

> The point apocalyptic makes is not only that people who wear crowns and who claim to foster justice by the sword are not as strong as they think—true as that is. . . . It is that people who bear crosses are working with the grain of the universe. One does not come to that belief by reducing social processes to mechanical and statistical models, nor by winning some of one's battles for the control of one's own corner of the fallen world. One comes to it by sharing the life of those who sing about the Resurrection of the slain Lamb.[16]

The first task of Christians is to act within the new age that Christ has established. They act within it consistent with how Christ acted. It is the slain Lamb who can read from the scroll who discloses the "grain of the universe."

Eschatological ethics: An Augustinian approach. Few Christian ethicists link eschatology and ethics as do Yoder, Hauerwas, and McClendon. Few look to the book of Revelation for a political ethic, but Anglican theologian Oliver O'Donovan

---

[15]John H. Yoder, *Christian Witness to the State*, Institute of Mennonite Studies Series 3 (Newton, KS: Faith and Life, 1964), 5.
[16]John H. Yoder, "Armaments and Eschatology," *Studies in Christian Ethics* (Edinburgh: T&T Clark, 1988), 1/1:58. See also David Toole, *Waiting for Godot in Sarajevo* (Boulder, CO: Westview, 1998), 216; Stanley Hauerwas, *With the Grain of the Universe* (Grand Rapids, MI: Brazos, 2001), title page, 230-41.

is an exception. He too links eschatology, ecclesiology, ethics, and politics. In his *War and the American Difference*, Hauerwas acknowledges the similarities among O'Donovan, himself, and Yoder. He writes, "My (and John Howard Yoder's) understanding of the 'doctrine of the Two' shares more in common with O'Donovan than many might suspect."[17] By "the Two," he means the doctrine of the two ages. While the ecclesial approach references this doctrine to argue that Christians should eschew violence, O'Donovan references it in order to advocate for just-war theory.

Rather than focusing on exile, however, O'Donovan focuses on the monarchy. It provides a political pattern that demonstrates what it means for Jesus to be "the desire of the nations." Every nation, explicitly or implicitly, now comes under his judgment. O'Donovan develops the work of one of the most important eschatological theologians in the Western tradition, St. Augustine, and his doctrine of the two cities. Until the eschaton, the two cities—the city of God and the earthly city—exist side by side, the latter learning how to serve the former. It must still use violence, but for limited, political ends. These two approaches to ethics—the ecclesial and Augustinian—are perhaps the two theological approaches to the Christian life most indebted to the twentieth century's retrieval of eschatology for positive purposes.

For O'Donovan, the political significance of the book of Revelation is that the "authority of truth and justice" is now established, an authority that "political society on earth has consistently failed to achieve." This brings "God's word of judgment pronounced in Christ" as the "foundation for a new order of society."[18] The doctrine of the two, he states, is, "before all else, a doctrine of two ages."[19] O'Donovan also links eschatology and ecclesiology. He writes,

> John's eschatological approach to ecclesiology has this point in view: the root of any true political order, in which human beings can relate to God and to each other lovingly, is the conspicuous judgment of God. The good order of society is founded upon a judgment (*dikaiōma*), a declarative act which establishes a justice (*dikaiosune*). Without God's judgments we cannot comprehend how we may live together.[20]

The church, then, is the "root" of true political community. But O'Donovan emphasizes the positive role of judgment by the rulers and authorities in the times between the times. In Christ's resurrection and ascension, creation is vindicated as good in and of itself. O'Donovan distinguishes creation from providence. Creation was always complete, good in and of itself. It has an order that does not need to develop or change. Providence is the historical ordering by which God heals the wounds humans inflict in history.[21] Eschatology is the purpose toward which providence moves; it is "the vindication and perfection of the created order which was always there but never fully expressed."[22] Because John's Apocalypse unveils this purpose, it vindicates creation and reauthorizes secular authority. The rulers and authorities have been made subject to God's sovereignty in Christ,

---

[17]Stanley Hauerwas, *War and the American Difference: Theological Reflections on Violence and National Identity* (Grand Rapids, MI: Baker Academic, 2011), xii.

[18]Oliver O'Donovan and Joan Lockwood, *Bonds of Imperfection: Christian Politics Past and Present* (Grand Rapids, MI: Eerdmans, 2004), 44.

[19]Oliver O'Donovan, *The Desire of the Nations* (Cambridge: Cambridge University Press, 1996), 211.

[20]O'Donovan and Lockwood, *Bonds of Imperfection*, 43.

[21]See Oliver O'Donovan's earlier work, *Resurrection and Moral Order: An Outline for Evangelical Ethics* (Grand Rapids, MI: Eerdmans, 1986), for his account of the vindication of creation and its relation to eschatology and history, especially 31-76.

[22]O'Donovan, *Resurrection and Moral Order*, 53.

even if they do not know it; secular authority is reauthorized within its newly established limited role, learning in history to become subject. In the time between Christ's first and second comings, the secular authority exercises judgment, and, if necessary, it does so through force, coercion, and violence, but only for limited political ends. The eschatological conditions that reauthorize the secular at the same time limit state-sponsored violence.

Every thinker noted in the above section draws on the book of Revelation, the Apocalypse, to spell out an eschatological and ecclesiological ethic. Rather than teaching us to flee the world as some Western philosophers and theologians feared, it teaches us to engage it. Following Schweitzer, these thinkers interpret Jesus as an apocalyptic thinker. Contra Schweitzer, they do not find him to be a failed apocalyptic prophet. Through his resurrection and ascension, creation has been restored, although it still awaits its consummation. None of them focus on the land of Israel as necessary for that restoration in the time between the times. None of them distinguish eschatology from apocalypse. Several modern theologians, however, found it important to distinguish them in order to salvage eschatology from apocalyptic.

Eschatology without apocalypse? German theologian Karl Rahner (1904–1984) was a Catholic contemporary to Balthasar. For him, eschatology is a necessary Christian doctrine that deals in general with last things and requires a "special hermeneutic" to interpret them, but apocalyptic claims to know too much about the end and should be discarded.[23] Apocalyptic goes awry, he avers, because it is often interpreted as an "anticipatory, eyewitness account of a future which is still outstanding." This false hermeneutic leads to "avoidable" difficulties. They are avoidable with a better interpretation. A proper hermeneutic begins not with prognostications about the future, but in "anticipation of what [the Christian] knows here and now about himself and about his salvific present." Or, put otherwise, Rahner states, "eschatology is man's view from the perspective of his experience of salvation, the experience which he now has in grace and in Christ."[24] Rahner worried about developing too much significance from apocalyptic.

American Protestant theologian Charles Mathewes makes a similar distinction between eschatology and apocalyptic; he does so in part to question theologians such as Hauerwas and Yoder for their apocalypticism. He sees detrimental consequences from apocalyptic thinking not only among theologians but also in much of the modern era, especially in American politics, anti-American jeremiads, and Marxist critiques. All, he argues, fall prey to the temptation to "apocalypticism." He distinguishes the "apocalyptic imagination" from "eschatological faith."[25] Like Rahner, Mathewes believes that apocalyptic goes bad when its defenders claim to know "in detail how things will turn out." This claim to know how things will turn out inhibits careful attention to the world as it is so that we might act

[23]Karl Rahner, "The Hermeneutics of Eschatological Assertions," in *Theological Investigations* (New York: Crossroad, 1982), 4:323-46. For a thorough investigation of the relation between apocalyptic and eschatology and their role in political theology, see Kyle Gingerich Hiebert, *The Architectonics of Hope: Violence, Apocalyptic and the Transformation of Political Theology* (Eugene, OR: Cascade, 2017). He addresses Rahner's distinction and Metz's opposition to it on 30-44.

[24]Karl Rahner, *Foundations of Christian Faith: An Introduction to the Idea of Christianity*, trans. William V. Dych (New York: Crossroad, 1987), 431-33.

[25]Charles T. Mathewes, *The Republic of Grace* (Grand Rapids, MI: Eerdmans, 2010), 220-25.

in it with the confidence that "all will be well" without knowing how.[26]

Mathewes makes an important distinction between the way the world is and the way the world should be. An apocalyptic imagination assumes that it knows how the world should be, and thus it ignores acting in the world as it is. Because it acts in concert with an apocalyptic vision, it neglects careful attention to the way the world is and how we must act within it. Philosopher Jeffrey Stout agrees with Mathewes that living by an apocalyptic imagination can be dangerous to seeing and acting in the world as it is. "Some churches," he writes, "are so enraptured by utopian visions of the lion lying down with the lamb that they are unwittingly assisting actual lions in the destruction of actual lambs."[27] By distinguishing eschatology from apocalyptic, Mathewes attempts to hold on to the importance of Christ's victory—all will be well—without it providing too much concrete guidance in addressing how the world is.

Assessing apocalyptic imaginings. Apocalyptic can go horribly awry, so the distinction between eschatology and apocalyptic is important. It goes awry when apocalyptic is interpreted as catastrophic. Rather than being transfigured into God's reign, material, historical reality must be destroyed in a conflagration for the sake of the new. Apocalyptic as *catastrophic* is both ancient and modern, often resulting from a millenarianism in which a thousand-year reign culminates in the coming of the antichrist (the latter term is not found in the Apocalypse). A diabolical ending to history produces a great tribulation.

Catastrophic apocalyptic thinking is not the best interpretation of apocalyptic. It too has led to significant errors. It was a source for serious political violence and inhuman activity in the sixteenth century, both by the Radical Reformers and against them. Christ's immanent return meant that everything we have—property, politics, relations, friendships, morals—should be held to lightly if at all, for it is coming to an end. But catastrophic apocalyptic was not unique to the sixteenth century; it continues into the modern era. It pervades the modern insofar as it assumes that the "modern," the new and improved, is about to arrive, and nothing we have done up to now has prepared us for its coming; it must all be discarded. Everything must be revised, discarded, rethought, reconstructed, possibly destroyed, for the old is always obsolete because of the new that is on the way. This apocalyptic tone is found in modern capitalism's "creative destruction" as well as in some historical performances of Marxism. The catastrophic apocalyptic represents an in-breaking that has no continuity with what came before. It positions the apocalypse in opposition to creation: creation provides no adequate knowledge for ethics or politics because the apocalyptic interruption does not perfect or complete creation; it destroys it.

The above discussion matters because apocalyptic thinking is not one thing. If it is understood as catastrophic, then Rahner's and Mathewes's distinction between eschatology and apocalyptic serves a useful purpose. If, rather than a catastrophe, apocalyptic is taken to be an unveiling, no such distinction is necessary. Instead, the important question is what kind of unveiling this is. Is it an unveiling that arises out of a fullness, affirming creaturely goods? Or is it

---

[26]Mathewes, *Republic of Grace*, 221. He makes similar claims in *A Theology of Public Life* (Cambridge: Cambridge University Press, 2007), 18, 24, 38-39, 127.

[27]Jeffrey Stout, *Blessed Are the Organized: Grassroots Democracy in America* (Princeton, NJ: Princeton University Press, 2010), 42.

an unveiling that negates, falling back unintentionally into the catastrophic?

Apocalypse from the fullness of worship. Apocalyptic arises from the fullness of a worshipful vision that uses images and symbols to show us a reality that could not otherwise be shown because it is something most of us do not see, and even if we do, we too easily lose sight of it. It shows us that the world as it appears to be is not what it is intended to be, and the world as it is intended to be is arriving in unexpected ways. The apocalyptic imagination does not counsel escapism, indifference, or withdrawal; it gives permission to act consistent with a vision partially unveiled.[28] The unveiling offers new possibilities for acting with the grain of the universe. As Michael Gorman says, the apocalyptic visionary "has seen what others have not; indeed he has seen Truth—invisible and future Truth—about the cosmos as it really is and really will be."[29] He has seen this in worship. Apocalyptic is worship and liturgy generating a theopolitical vision that entails acting in harmony with that vision as best one can in the world as it is.

The apocalyptic imagination should frighten and alarm anyone and everyone who takes it on themselves to hold power over others in order to rule and dominate them. For, according to the Apocalypse, this class of people, politicians and merchants, the people we normally extol and thank for their service, can be seen in a very different light: as a beast with ten heads and seven horns. They risk standing on the side of the old

age against the new age coming into existence, defending the world as it is rather than the world as it should be. The apocalyptic imagination performs what Richard Hays calls the "shock of reversal," because it is the slaughtered Lamb and not the "ferocious lion" who holds the key to unlock the truth of political order.[30] The war of the Lamb is not military conquest. It is a battle continuous with the politics present in the Sermon on the Mount. Its power and persuasive force are present in the means the Lamb uses, symbolized by the double-edged sword present in his mouth: his death and his "spoken word." It should come as no surprise to careful readers of the Apocalypse that it gives us this word of caution: "If you kill with the sword, with the sword you must be killed" (Rev 13:10). Gorman succinctly states the theopolitical vision present in the apocalyptic imagination: "Revelation calls believers to nonretaliation and nonviolence, and not to a literal war of any sort, present or future. By its very nature as resistance, faithful nonconformity is not absolute withdrawal but rather critical engagement on very different terms from those of the status quo."[31] That is what the apocalyptic imagination asks of us.

The apocalyptic imagination can be well understood, as George Beasley-Murray has put it, as political cartoon, depicting those convinced that they should take authority to control the levers of violent power as buffoons who are serving principalities and powers that they are unable to recognize.[32] The apocalyptic imagination is poetic,

---

[28]Johann Metz writes, "Imminent expectation will not let discipleship be postponed. It is not the apocalyptic feeling for life that makes us apathetic, but the evolutionistic!" Johann Metz, *Faith in History and Society: Toward a Practical Fundamental Theology*, trans. J. Matthew Ashley (New York: Herder & Herder, 2007), 163; cited in Gingerich Hiebert, *Architectonics of Hope*, 42.

[29]Michael J. Gorman, *Reading Revelation Responsibly: Uncivil Worship and Witness—Following the Lamb into the New Creation* (Eugene, OR: Cascade, 2011), 21-22.

[30]See Richard Hays's *The Moral Vision of the New Testament: A Contemporary Introduction to New Testament Ethics* (San Francisco: HarperSanFrancisco, 1996), 174; Gorman, *Reading Revelation Responsibly*, 108.

[31]Gorman, *Reading Revelation Responsibly*, 109, 79.

[32]Gorman, *Reading Revelation Responsibly*, 19.

hyperbolic, comedic—and necessary, if our lives are not to be completely defined by the sword. The greatest comedic act of all is to love our enemies in their deadly seriousness, not take them too seriously, and let them know that there are alternative ways of being political than by dominating others.

And yet the apocalyptic imagination cannot primarily be a form of *kenōsis* or resistance. The resistance must emerge as a secondary effect of its primary intention: to be infused with the overabundance of God's presence. It is out of this fullness that a proper humility and a lack of resentment gets generated, for resentment is always a sign that confidence is a sham. It is a sign of insecurity in which what one opposes is more determinative for who one is than what one is for. To be for something, to work from a fullness, does not require one opposing those on the "outside," for it is not weakness that directs us to them but a fullness that dares to risk new forms of political engagement, forms that will find analogies that will be recognizable even in their difference. It works with the grain of the universe. The apocalyptic imagination is only for someone taken up into the ecstasy of worship.[33] "Worthy is the Lamb who was slain to receive power and wealth and wisdom and honor and glory and praise" (Rev 5:12 NIV).

CONCLUSION

Eschatology is the cultivation of an apocalyptic imagination through the fullness of vision present in worship. That vision is an *apocalypsis*—

an unveiling that brings together the restoration of Israel, the coming of the kingdom or reign of God, and the renewal of creation. Much like the temple imagery present in Genesis 1, the unveiling reveals God's dwelling place and the creaturely dwelling place coming together in unity.

> See, the home of God is among mortals.
> He will dwell with them;
> they will be his peoples,
> and God himself will be with them;
> he will wipe every tear from their eyes.
> Death will be no more;
> mourning and crying and pain will be no more,
> for the first things have passed away. (Rev 21:3-4)

This unity cannot occur without final judgment, but the judgment is not for condemnation. It is so that every nation can bring its wealth and contribute to the unity God intends.

> I saw no temple in the city, for its temple is the Lord God the Almighty and the Lamb. And the city has no need of sun or moon to shine on it, for the glory of God is its light, and its lamp is the Lamb. The nations will walk by its light, and the kings of the earth will bring their glory into it. Its gates will never be shut by day—and there will be no night there. People will bring into it the glory and the honor of the nations. But nothing unclean will enter it, nor anyone who practices abomination or falsehood, but only those who are written in the Lamb's book of life. (Rev 21:22-27)

To act from this apocalyptic vision is to will the completion, fulfillment, or perfection of history.

FURTHER READING

Barth, Karl. *The Epistle to the Romans*. Translated by Edwyn C. Hoskyns. London: Oxford University Press, 1968.

Gingerich Hiebert, Kyle. *The Architectonics of Hope: Violence, Apocalyptic and the Transformation of Political Theology*. Eugene, OR: Cascade, 2017.

---

[33]I owe this insight to Michael Gorman, who writes that Revelation's "character as resistance literature is actually secondary to, and derivative of, its more fundamental character as worship literature, as a liturgical text" (Gorman, *Reading Revelation Responsibly*, 25).

Gorman, Michael. *Reading Revelation Responsibly: Uncivil Worship and Witness—Following the Lamb into the New Creation.* Eugene, OR: Cascade, 2011.

Hauerwas, Stanley. *Approaching the End: Eschatological Reflections on Church, Politics, and Life.* Grand Rapids, MI: Eerdmans, 2013.

O'Regan, Cyril. *Theology and the Spaces of Apocalyptic.* Milwaukee: Marquette University Press, 2009.

Rahner, Karl. "The Hermeneutics of Eschatological Assertions." Pages 323-46 in vol. 4 of *Theological Investigations.* New York: Crossroad, 1982.

Toole, David. *Waiting for Godot in Sarajevo: Theological Reflections on Nihilism, Tragedy, and Apocalypse.* Boulder, CO: Westview, 1998.

42

THE PAST, THE PRESENT, AND THE FUTURE OF AFRICAN CHRISTIANITY

AN ESCHATOLOGICAL VISION FOR AFRICAN CHRISTIANITY

James Henry Owino Kombo

ESCHATOLOGY IN THE African context remains a major driver of African Christian thought. Conversation around eschatology in Africa embraces the question of death and how the dead exist thereafter, and what the Christian faith says to these questions. The Hebrews 11 language of a "great cloud of witnesses" and the Nicene Creed's statement that "we look for the resurrection of the dead, and the life of the world to come," among other concepts, help anchor eschatology in the African context. Critical aspects of the African worldview—particularly (1) its approach to death, dying, and living on; (2) the question of the ancestors, spirits, and divinities; and (3) the modes of time, events, and seasons in African cosmology—are not just studies in sociology or anthropology, but collectively and individually are windows through which the idea of Christian eschatology may be brought to the African theological situation.

ESCHATOLOGY: THE AFRICAN WORLDVIEW AS A THEOLOGICAL HERMENEUTIC

This essay attempts to use a non-Western ontology, in this case an African worldview, to do theology for African Christianity. What is eschatology? How do I explain the term to my eighty-year-old father, who, though not a theologian, does not use English, is not a tabula rasa, and has lived by the gospel for the better part of his life? *Eschatology* is a word foreign to African theological culture, though the concept it embodies is a religious principle that the African intellectual culture admits.[1]

The principles we take advantage of in articulating eschatology for African Christianity reside in the African worldview. In the African cultural traditions, we find permanent eschatological fixtures in death, dying, and living on; ancestors, spirits, and divinities; and time, events, and seasons. The way these categories stand in the African worldview

---

[1] J. Page, *The Black Bishop* (London: Simpkin, 1910), 282.

allows us to do three things: (1) to see how pre-Christian Africa responded to these categories, (2) to view these notions and experiences as worthy ideas that are capable of being submitted to theological reflection in any forum, and (3) to bring unique African questions and responses to the global theological conversation.

This is all the more relevant given that eschatology is about physical death and its logical spinoff: What happens to people when they die? Not only does the question of time, events, and seasons in the context of this kind of eschatology allow for the utilization of the African ontology as a prism in relation to time, phenomena, and events, but these categories also help us to see how African Christianity is living out these aspects of the African world—What is time, for instance, in relation to death, ancestors, and the problem of relations? How is time related to the fulfillment of history realized in the corporate outlook of eschatology?

As J. S. Mbiti has argued, the shape of the African worldview is highly anthropocentric:

> The human being is placed at the center of the cosmos, but not in an individualistic way. The individual is to be understood in terms of the kinship system to which he belongs. Our relationship thus comes before our individuality. The human being is thus seen not primarily as an autonomous individual, but as a person belonging to a group. He has specific, ongoing and permanent responsibilities towards the members of that group.[2]

Mbiti outlines the African world as follows:

1. God, as the ultimate explanation of the genesis and sustenance of both humanity and all things;

2. Spirits, made up of superhuman beings and the spirits of human beings who died a long time ago;

3. Humans, both those who are alive and those about to be born;

4. Animals and plants, or the remainder of biological life;

5. Phenomena and objects without biological life.[3]

God occupies the number-one category, since he is the Originator and Sustainer of humanity. The spirits, ancestors, and divinities explain the destiny of humanity: humans, who are ontologically below them, are ever moving inevitably toward them. Humanity's position at the very center of this ontology communicates human responsibility and relationships. The next two categories are animals and plants, and natural phenomena and objects. These categories provide both the means by and the theater in which human beings live. This ontology is experienced as a unified, integrated whole, incapable of being disturbed without destroying the entire ontology, including the Creator.

In a world that is configured in these terms, how do we discern a solid eschatology for the Christian community therein? As we have noted, this ontology has a way of speaking to the categories named, and more specifically to the questions of personal eschatology, ancestors, and time. Although the African cultural traditions appear to have spoken so eloquently to these matters, rather than being theological the conversations have unfortunately remained at the ethnographic, linguistic, and historical levels. And so how we understand death, time,

---

[2]Cited in William P. Russell, "'Time Also Moves Backwards': John Mbiti's Traditional Concept of Time and the Future of World Christianity," *Studies in World Christianity* 9 (2003): 88-102, here 96.

[3]J. S. Mbiti, *African Religions and Philosophy* (London: Heinemann, 1969), 20.

or ancestors—categories that themselves are richly theological—has contributed very little to the nature and shape of theological discourse, and much less to a probable approach for Christian eschatology for the African context. This must change, and theology, it appears, must start to take positive advantage of the constructs of the African intellectual culture.

ESCHATOLOGY IN RELATION TO DEATH, DYING, AND LIVING ON

Africa is often caricatured as a space of death. The recent history of HIV and AIDS, long-term armed conflicts, civil wars, and genocide has led to so many deaths that thinking in these terms has only given this notion more currency. Consequently, as "in Europe after the First World War, mourning is replaced by memorialization, by the creation of museums and national memorial parks."[4] Another significant player in all this is the phenomenon of international migration, which has necessitated new technologies such as refrigeration, embalmment, and use of media, particularly video and newspapers: it is reported that the insurance industry is making huge returns on account of these emerging practices. And so, although the "African way of death" is supposedly going the same way as the "American way of death," there are fundamental underlying differences.[5]

Edward Evans-Pritchard thinks that the African funeral rituals are a reality in the African context because death in these societies provoked fear and revulsion. In the thinking of Evans-Pritchard, the dead could only find their place as ancestors, rather than vengeful ghosts, if their loss had been properly registered by their living relatives and the social groups around them. For Evans-Pritchard, therefore, the ultimate purpose of funeral customs was to allow the living relatives and social groups to get on with living.[6]

John S. Mbiti's understanding of the mourning process in Africa focuses on the need to connect the living to the living-dead ancestors and the spirits in the *sasa* and the *zamani*.[7] For him, in death we see "a separation and not annihilation; the dead person is suddenly cut off from the human society and yet the corporate group clings to him. This is shown through the elaborate funeral rites, the dirges and other ways of keeping in touch with the departed."[8] The dirge used by all African communities is a useful means of expressing the inevitable: the dead are praised, honored, and mourned.[9] In this case, therefore, the goal of life is the ability to begin a relationship with the world around—a sort of guaranteed open line for vibrant communication with both the visible and the invisible world. Thus the dead are granted a befitting funeral in which they are prevailed on not to become wandering ghosts

---

[4]Rebekah Lee, "Death and Dying in the History of Africa since 1800," *Journal of African History* 49 (2008): 342-43.

[5]See Jessica Mitford's criticism of the American funeral industry, *The American Way of Death* (London: Simon & Schuster, 1963; rev. ed., 1998); cited in Gary Lederman, *Rest in Peace: Death and the Funeral Haven in Twentieth Century America* (Oxford: Oxford University Press, 2003).

[6]Edward E. Evans-Pritchard, "Burial and Mortuary Rites of the Nuer," *African Affairs* 48 (1949): 51-63, here 62. See also, on the misrepresentations of African beliefs about death, Louis-Vincent Thomas, *La mort africaine: Idéologie funéraire en Afrique noire* (Paris: Payot, 1982).

[7]What is present is what is called *sasa*: this is the word for the time that covers the "now" period, with a sense of immediacy, newness, and nearness. The *zamani*, on the other hand, is the period of termination, the dimension in which everything finds its halting point. See John S. Mbiti, *New Testament Eschatology in an African Background* (London: Oxford University Press, 1971), 23.

[8]Mbiti, *African Religions and Philosophy*, 46.

[9]African Christianity has traditionally not been happy with this—it has castigated elaborate funeral rituals, honoring the dead, and any form of maintenance of links with the dead either in the past or in the present. This continues to be a gray area, and Christians of independent, charismatic, and Pentecostal extraction appear to have sensed the lethargy of the historical forms of Christianity and are making steady inroads among the second-generation Christians.

who suffer the indignity of not living properly after death.

We see here, therefore, a situation that takes the preeminence of death and its theology seriously. In the African approach to death and life beyond the grave, the culture has not only affirmed the reality of death, but it has also ensured that it has left no room for escaping or denying death and life thereafter.[10] The grounding in the African cosmology provides a framework through which we are able to face mortality for what it really is.

The manner in which African cosmology speaks to death and life beyond the grave makes it well suited to offer a new perspective to the wider church on death and life thereafter. Note that for the African situation, in death, the whole person and not just some part of the person continues to live and gets invested with powers to transact as an ancestor. And neither is death merely a private affair that one must face alone; instead, in death one becomes part of the "cloud of witnesses" (see Heb 11). Thus, we continue with hope to learn that life exists beyond the grave. Christian theology talks of resurrected bodies that (1) have a physical nature and (2) are both immortal and imperishable (1 Cor 15:42-43). Elsewhere in Scripture, the immortal and imperishable body is also called a glorified and heavenly body (Phil 3:21; 1 Jn 3:2). What appears to have distinguished these realities from the preresurrection body is not immateriality but the presence of both immortality and imperishability (1 Cor 15:42).

The doctrine of Christ's descent among the dead, though neglected among many traditions of the Christian faith, also offers a significant opportunity in this context. The central significance of this doctrine is its standing for us as a reminder of Christ's lordship over all and the liberation of the dead. By this doctrine, William Russell explains, Christ "liberates our relationships to our own dead, standing in the midst of them, removing all false fear and assuring us of the triumph of love.... Death thus has no victory and does not reduce our loving relationships to non-existence. Our relationships to our loved ones have not been terminated, but are now transformed in him."[11] This doctrine has tremendous pastoral potential for African Christianity given its traditional concern for dead relatives, and its recovery would also be an opportunity for African Christianity to spur a theological recovery of an equal significance to other parts of the world. Now we know that we do not have to fear our dead; on the contrary, Christ has liberated our relationship to the dead.

ANCESTORS, SPIRITS, AND DIVINITIES: LIVING IN THE AFTERLIFE

The African world perceives interpenetration of the seen and the unseen, the visible and the invisible, the sacred and the secular.[12] Lamin Sanneh has focused the discussion on what he sees as Africa's religion, which falls like a shaft of light across the entire spectrum of life.[13] What this means for eschatology is that in the African

---

[10]I find the analysis of Rebekah Lee ("Death and Dying") cited here in full useful: "In the 1970s Philippe Aries argued that, whilst Europeans in the Middle Ages (like primitive peoples) accepted death as part of life, by the twentieth century they were more likely to attempt to deny it. A combination of industrialization, urbanization and the rise of scientific medicine eventually produced a situation in which death became a private affair, and one drained of meaning. Against this picture of death sanitized, medicalized and uneasily denied, African attitudes to death could be viewed with a degree of nostalgia" (342).

[11]Russell, "Time Also Moves Backwards," 96.

[12]Stephen Ellis and Gerrie ter Haar, *Worlds of Power: Religious Thought and Political Practice in Africa* (New York: Oxford University Press, 2004), 14.

[13]Lamin Sanneh, "New and Old in Africa's Religious Heritage: Islam, Christianity and the African Encounter," in *Exploring New Religious Movements: Essays in Honor of Harold Turner*, ed. Andrew F. Walls and Wilbert R. Shenk (Elkhart, IN: Mission Focus, 1990), 64.

world, we have ancestors, spirits, and divinities living within the same space, environment, and plane. Moreover, we do not have another world that we are to occupy once we start talking of "the eschaton," and neither do we bracket eschatological matters in a far-distant future. Those who have already departed occupy abodes in proximity to their living relatives. The good men and women who die dream, at the very best, of becoming ancestors as soon as they transition so that they can continue to patronize their living relatives and acquaintances. It is thus understood that this is our world, and we continue to live in it whether we live or die.

Yet a fundamental question remains particularly problematic in African theology: Where do we go when we die? Where are our ancestors? This is a matter that generated tremendous heat and division between African evangelicals and other groups sometimes called "African ecumenists" in the mid-1970s to the 1980s. The evangelicals believed that J. S. Mbiti's three books—*African Philosophy and Religion* (1969), *The Concepts of God in Africa* (1970), and *New Testament Eschatology in an African Background: A Study of the Encounter Between New Testament Theology and African Traditional Concepts* (1973)—were all built on the platform of theological universalism. Driven by this belief, there arose two responses spearheaded by Byang H. Kato's *Theological Pitfalls in Africa* (1975) and Tokunboh Adeyemo's *Salvation in African Tradition* (1979). Later, J. S. Mbiti wrote *The Bible and Theology in African Christianity* (1987), in which he did two things: first, he laid out publicly his theology of Scripture;

and, second, he specifically invited his theological interlocutors to a candid conversation. Thirty years later this conversation has still not happened, and the question of where our ancestors are remains unanswered.

In the interim, research appears to be unveiling several things: the ancestors and the spirits are not the nuisances they are sometimes thought to be. They raise an important theological question from a pre-Christian African point of view: What happens after we die? The import of this question must be seen from the position of someone who cares deeply about relations; a person who understands that relationships with our deceased relatives and with the world as it is known to us can be expressed in a myriad of ways; one who appreciates the idea that we are indeed moving very quickly to our ancestors, who themselves are real people, and that the only thing that holds us back from being ancestors is the bridge of death standing between us; someone who appreciates that we and our deceased relatives may be in the *sasa* zone today, but soon we will together be in the graveyard of *zamani*. Thus we are not talking about ghosts (*pepo mbaya*—bad spirits), and neither are we talking of a mere system of ideas.

At the outset, it bears noting that while Africa has often been labeled as animistic, rife with ancestor worship or veneration and existing in diffused monotheism, the meaningful application of all of these terms to the primal African worldview is contested.[14] While we cannot resolve all of these matters here, it is important to note up front that the African relationship with ancestors

---

[14]Bolaji Idowu uses this concept to discuss the relationship between the divinities and Supreme Being in Africa according to which divinities serve as "functionaries in the theocratic government of the universe." Accordingly, therefore, the various divinities are apportioned respective duties to undertake in accordance with the will of the Supreme Being. It is also the case that divinities are ministers with different but complementary assignments in the monarchial government of the Supreme Being. Essentially, then, they are administrative heads of various departments. E. Bolaji Idowu, *African Traditional Religion: A Definition* (London: SCM Press, 1973), 170. The term *animism* was coined by anthropologist E. B. Tylor (1832–1917). By it he meant a theory of religion according to which

is best understood not in the context of worship, at least as the term is biblically understood, but in the context of respect and relationship.

The living who relate to the ancestors may choose to communicate those relationships in active expressions, appropriations, and even experiences of the supernatural. Note that these beings—ancestors and the spirits—were once human beings living in the very same villages and holding positions of influence and honor. They live within easy proximity of their descendants and remain a part of their human family, which they continue to actively influence in either direction depending on the inclination or quality of the relationship.[15] Indeed, ancestors are part of the explanation of the African world, giving meaning to benefits, misfortunes and to strains of life in society. They do this not just for the sake of it but because they have immense interest in the welfare of their living descendants. Indeed Victor Uchendu, in his anthropological study among the Igbo, does not just see the influence, but he also brings in what he calls the "equalitarian principle." He explains, "The reverence which the Igbo accord the ancestors has its definition in the transference of the social status of the elder of a kinship group into the realm of the spiritual where in the abode of the ancestors the former head of a family continues to retain the status and the attendant honour and respect which he enjoyed in his former earthly existence."[16]

Then there is the matter of vigilance—the notion that the ancestors keep watch over their living relatives. They reward, but they can also punish in equal measure. Thus they focus on the requirement for discipline on the part of the living relatives and provision of guidance in matters of family affairs, traditions, and morality, as well as assurance of health and fertility. Thus witches, sorcerers, and bad medicine have no powers over a person whose ancestors are alert. But the ancestors and the spirits are also known to punish members of their family in cases of error and moral vice. To that extent, not are only they considered the ubiquitous part of the clan that links both the world we live in and the spirit world, but they are also understood to possess supernatural powers donated to them by the Supreme Being.[17] Thus, they can independently influence such powerful natural phenomena as rainfall and good harvests, and even the attainment of prosperity. On the other hand, such misfortunes as drought, famine, and destructive calamities may also be attributed to ancestors and the spirits.

In the African perspective, then, the dead are in active contact with their living relatives and acquaintances. This contact is seen in the context of providence, guidance, punishment, and protection. In such an environment, it makes sense for African Christianity to conceive eschatology not as some far-distant phenomenon but as an aspect of the doctrine of the providence of God in the here and now. It should assert that God—not the ancestors, nor the spirits, nor the divinities—is the reason for rainfall, a good harvest, and even the attainment

---

religion is a "belief in spiritual beings" that originated in the early idea of attributing life, soul, or spirit to inanimate objects, "defining the religious systems of the lower races, so as to place them correctly in the history of culture," Tylor observed in 1892. See E. B. Tylor, "The Limits of Savage Religion," *Journal of the Royal Anthropological Institute* 21 (1892): 283-301.

[15]J. I. Omoregbe, *Ethics, a Systematic and Historical Study* (Lagos: Joja Educational Research, 1993), 174-77, on Epicurean ethics.

[16]Victor C. Uchendu, *The Igbo of Southeast Nigeria* (New York: Holt, Rinehart & Winston, 1965), 19. See also F. A. Arinze, *Sacrifice in Igbo Religion* (Ibadan, Nigeria: Ibadan University Press, 1970), 19-20.

[17]K. Amponsah, *Topics on West African Traditional Religion* (Accra: McGraw-Hill FEP, 1974), 1:85. See also J. Omosadu Awolalu and P. Adelumo Dopamu, *West African Traditional Religion* (Ibadan, Nigeria: Onibonje, 1979), 272-73.

of prosperity. At the same time, as Russell notes, it should make space for the affirmation that, in death, "our relationships to our loved ones have not been terminated, but are now transformed in [Christ]." As Christians, then, "we must henceforth see all these relationships as existing in Christ."[18]

Although divinities are generally not directly related to the African eschatological vision, they are of massive influence among many African communities, particularly in West Africa. These entities are known variously as gods, demigods, nature spirits, divinities, and the like.[19] It is understood that they exist in the hundreds. For instance, among the Yoruba, there are as many as 201, 401, 600, or 1,700 divinities.[20] Mbiti notes that among the Edo, there are as many divinities as there are human needs, activities, and experiences.[21] Their eschatological significance lies in that they are perceived to be intermediaries between human beings and the Supreme Being. As such, they function as windows through which sacrifices, prayers, and offerings are both understood and presented to the Supreme Being. Although Idowu notes that they do not necessarily distract from direct worship of God, where they are part of reality, their abode and function is considered a halfway house, a purgatory of sorts, which by design is not supposed to be a permanent resting place for the departed.[22]

INTERPRETING TIME, EVENTS, AND SEASONS: MODALITIES OF SPACE AND TIME

Africa's notion of eschatology is inextricably intertwined with time, events, and seasons. Here time, whether past, present, or future, is understood as concrete and substantive. It is thus defined as "a composition of events which have occurred, those that are taking place now and those which are immediately to occur."[23] Time, it is explained, "is universally present, [however] conceptions and experiences of time themselves are not universal but rather historically and culturally contingent. They are dependent on and change with their respective contexts."[24]

It is now widely accepted that the main difference between African and European ideas of time is a recent development in European culture that has redefined the future and given it absolute dominance in comparison to the past and the present. Indeed, as Ulfried Reichardt argues, the "important elements which were used to distinguish European from African cultures in temporal terms in their strong and emphatic sense only emerged during the late eighteenth century." Mbiti appears to have followed this trend very closely in assigning minimal if any significance to the future as a category of time. Reichardt goes on to note,

Time in traditional African societies is radically contextual. In a small subsistence economy and

---

[18]Russell, "Time Also Moves Backwards," 96.

[19]John S. Mbiti, *Concepts of God in Africa* (London: SPCK, 1975), 117.

[20]Francis O. C. Njoku, *Essays in African Philosophy, Thought and Theology* (Owerri, Nigeria: Claretian Institute of Philosophy & Clacom Communication, 2002), 127.

[21]Mbiti, *African Religions and Philosophy*, 119.

[22]E. Bolaji Idowu, *Oludumare: God in Yoruba Belief* (London: Longmans, 1962).

[23]Mbiti, *New Testament Eschatology*, 17. Also key to this view of time is Dominique Zahan, *Religion, spiritualité et pensée africaines*, 2nd ed. (Paris: Payot, 1970).

[24]Ulfried Reichardt, "Time and the African-American Experience: The Problem of Chronocentrison," *American Studies* 45, no. 4 (2000): 465.

small village or tribal units, the mechanics and logistics of the coordination of people's actions and the community's functioning does not presuppose an abstract time scheme; the network of actions can still be coordinated by word of mouth and face-to-face interaction. Consequently, there is no idea of rational, abstract and mechanical time; rather, time is intimately linked with events, rituals, natural cycles, and the supernatural. Time is not understood as being under the control of human beings, not something to be shaped or filled; it is a dimension of the surrounding world, including the gods.[25]

This characterization that compounds time alongside God, events, activities, and seasons allows for a possibility of conceiving potential time and actual time. But more importantly, this conception of time, Mbiti argues, is "the key to our understanding of the basic religious and philosophical concepts."[26] There are seven philosophical notions involved here, namely, (1) that we are moving backward in time toward the past, and we are slowly but surely becoming part of it—time thus moves backward rather than forward; (2) the past to which we are moving belongs to the ancestors and the spirits; (3) on account of this movement, the living dead are our immediate horizon—they are our future. This conception of time is (4) essentially relational. As such, we retain our relationships even in death; death does not redefine or delete how we relate. These relationships (5) nevertheless are not only multiple, but they are also

accentuated in different ways. The time component, as previously noted, is divided into two: (6) *zamani* and *sasa*. In all this, (7) human beings are at the center because they have permanent responsibilities.

It is on this ground that Mbiti argues that time is measured by events.[27] Thus, time is not conceived in a vacuum; rather we say that it is "time for," "time to," or a "time of." Time in this case is designated and not merely numerical or mathematical. Thus, we do not become slaves of time—we master time. In this scheme of things, therefore, calendars represent phenomena—concrete things that happened. For instance, an "oldman" remembers when he was born or when he married in relation to an event or a phenomenon that happened at around the same time. Time becomes a significant marker of events or phenomena. In the case of our "oldman," what is important is that he was born or that he married, not the mathematical exactitude that characterizes the year or month. That time is meaningful only to the extent that he was born or married then; it is a mere beacon in the theater of events.

This conception of time has significant theological consequences. Russell raises questions that deserve further study: "Is this view of time compatible with the Christian faith, or not? What insight into faith does it help us to grasp better? What error does it contain that the Christian faith corrects?"[28]

---

[25]Reichardt, "Time," 469-70. Note also that modern philosophical considerations of time (Henri Bergson, William James, John Dewey, George Herbert Mead, and Alfred North Whitehead) and contemporary theories of time all offer critiques of mechanical time and point out the contextual character of time. This insight is seen in William Faulkner's novels. Mechanical time is no longer considered objective; as Niklas Luhmann points out, time is now used by systems as a medium of their operations. Thus, there is no objective time. What we have now is system-specific time.

[26]In Joseph K. Adjaye, "Time in Africa and Its Diaspora: An Introduction," *Time in the Black Experience*, ed. Joseph K. Adjaye (Westport, CT: Greenwood, 1994), 5.

[27]Mbiti, *African Religions and Philosophy*, 19-22.

[28]Russell, "Time Also Moves Backwards," 89.

CONTACT POINTS

It is now well demonstrated that Christianity is a worldwide phenomenon. As such, it now operates within the contours of a new theological culture that embraces all Christian traditions while at the same time flourishing in the intellectual constructs of Africa, Asia, Latin America, and Oceania. This has been described as "worldwide theology." According to this scheme of things, Christian thought from the cultural margins like Africa and Asia will increasingly manifest an active engagement with historical voices. Thus, African ideas about death, ancestors, spirits, time, and events "will influence theological thinking beyond Africa and may help to resolve ancient conflicts that have divided Christians in the past." Speaking specifically to Mbiti's conception of time, Russell argues that its adequacy should be judged by "whether or not, and in what ways, it might help us to understand better the Christian revelation. The ethnographic, linguistic and historical questions that have dominated the discussion of the idea so far thus recede into the background."[29] In light of the matters discussed here, I now highlight six areas in which African Christian thought may have a salutary impact on wider Christian theology.

The idea of time. Generally, the idea of time is underresearched. In particular, its relationship to context and culture, particularly the African culture, has been generally ignored, leaving in focus only a relatively recent notion of time made popular in modernity. This was already recognized in the 1980s and the 1990s, and today nothing much has happened to change the state of affairs. Some of the outstanding contributions during this period include J. T. Fraser's authoritative publication *The Voices of Time* (1981), which "included contributions on 'non-Western' societies like China and India but conspicuously omitted Africa."[30] Whereas there is a need to fill the gap and bring Africa into the picture, such studies should not merely be critiques of John Mbiti and Dominique Zahan and what they saw of time in the late 1960s and the early 1970s. Instead, further study should focus on time as a multifaceted and contextual phenomenon that is intimately linked and significantly related to events, rituals, natural cycles, and the supernatural. The relational aspect of time is particularly critical: we stand in relation to our deceased relatives, who are our future, since we are moving toward them; we stand in relation to God; and we stand in relation to the rest of God's creation.

Relationships. The issue here is the reality of the living, the ancestors, and the spirits in African ontology and the fact that the living and the dead in fact stand in a permanent and ongoing relationship. In this case, therefore, relationship as a phenomenon is to be viewed as an epistemic handle. The epistemic and eschatological challenge posed by relationship as entrenched in African ontology is itself a matter that African Christianity and worldwide theology will have to deal with. Is it ancestor worship—is it ancestor veneration?[31] What does Scripture say about the relationship between the living and the dead? What relationships are condemned, and which ones may be permitted? Don't we encounter God as a God of ancestors? Isn't he a God of the living, not of the dead? In

---

[29]Russell, "Time Also Moves Backwards," 89.
[30]Adjaye, "Time in Africa and Its Diaspora," 7-8.
[31]C. S. Bae, "Ancestor Worship and the Challenges It Poses to the Christian Mission and Ministry" (PhD diss., University of Pretoria, 2007), 1.

any case, Israel followed their ancestors in faith; we see a similar thing in the case of the Christians in the New Testament in the manner in which they related to the apostles and in the church communities the apostles founded. These questions and many more in the context of relationships as a hermeneutical key may require a new attitude, even perhaps a totally new effort toward another way of looking at the relationship between the living and the dead.

Universalism. An observation was made above about the supposed rift among theology scholars in Africa on the basis of what was understood as universalism. The question was not a Christian theology question but an African ontology question: Where do we go when we die? Where are our ancestors? Mbiti posed these questions in his books *African Philosophy and Religion* (1969), *The Concepts of God in Africa* (1970), and *New Testament Eschatology in an African Background: A Study of the Encounter Between New Testament Theology and African Traditional Concepts* (1973). He subsequently received swift responses from Byang H. Kato's *Theological Pitfalls in Africa* (1975) and Tokunboh Adeyemo's *Salvation in African Tradition* (1979). Later, as mentioned above, Mbiti attempted a truce through his book *The Bible and Theology in African Christianity* (1987), in which he laid out publicly his theory of Scripture and then proceeded to invite his theological interlocutors to a candid conversation. Thirty years later this conversation has still not happened, and the ontological question of where our ancestors are and in what way we might relate with them is largely unanswered.

It appears to me that there are two parallel questions here: eschatology and soteriology. Whereas Byang Kato and Adeyemo appear to be driving at an evangelical soteriological question, Mbiti is pursuing an eschatological agenda informed by his notion of time and relations.[32]

The doctrine of Christ's descent among the dead. This doctrine, which is part of the church's creedal tradition, has often been abandoned in reflections on eschatology due to numerous historical and exegetical puzzles it presents. Fortunately, due to the historical link between African Christianity and its doctrine that the dead remain alive, the controversy associated with this doctrine is minimized, and the significance of this doctrine for eschatology remains. African Christian faith seems very ready to work toward a strong doctrine of "descent among the dead." Note that what this doctrine does is to explain how Christ's time in the tomb helps locate his atoning work within the doctrine of the last things. The robust conversation about the ancestors and the spirits is, in my opinion, an opportunity to once again attend to the doctrine of Christ's descent among the dead. The doctrine remains significant both for its pastoral potential and for its standing for us as a reminder of Christ's lordship over all, including the dead, and his liberation of the dead.

By adopting this orphaned doctrine, reinterpreting it in light of the African theological culture, and raising it to the global church, African Christianity would be making a contribution that it alone is prepared to make at the moment—namely, to declare that Christ "liberates our relationships to our own dead, standing

---

[32]Note that the Roho Christian denomination spread all over East Africa hardly consider themselves saved, and yet they wear turbans and scarves bearing the conspicuous mark of the cross, and they call each other *japolo* (meaning "people of heaven"). The Tukutendereza, on the other hand, are a product of the Puritan movement and believe in the salvation wrought by Jesus Christ and confession of sins.

in the midst of them, removing all false fear and assuring us of the triumph of love. . . . Death thus has no victory and does not reduce our loving relationships to non-existence. Our relationships to our loved ones have not been terminated, but are now transformed in him."[33] We need to take up this challenge, and we need to demonstrate its relevance to African Christianity both for pastoral reasons and for the benefit of the global church.

Reassessing sixteenth-century eschatological controversies. The church in the sixteenth century provided answers to several eschatological questions, including those raised by the Catholic doctrine of acquisition of merit, the doctrine of indulgences, the idea of the communion of the saints, and the idea of purgatory, as well as the Reformers' response to prayers to and for the dead. These well-considered answers addressed the situation of Europe and the questions raised at that time. They were specific to the issues at hand and are not in any way related to the African notions of death, dying, ancestors, spirits, time, events, and seasons studied here. It is therefore inappropriate to link these concepts articulated in the sixteenth century as answers to specific African questions.

The African eschatological ideas discussed here are independent and have their own unique origin and meaning. As Russell argues, the African concepts raised in the context of our own ontology "ought not to be understood in terms of a dispute that is foreign to it."[34]

What the Catholics and the Reformers intended to achieve by their responses to eschatological controversies at the time was an appropriate understanding of Paul's doctrine of justification; the African agenda as demonstrated in this work is primarily cosmological and only secondarily pastoral.

Christ as an ancestor. Ancestors play an important role in African cosmology. As far as these ontologies are concerned, ancestors are deceased members of a community who live within easy proximity of their living relatives and acquaintances as they provide guardianship and support. Many theologians have borrowed the term *ancestor* from respective cultures of reception and used it as a handle for Christ.

Eschatological and trinitarian thinking informs us differently: Jesus is one with the Father and the Holy Spirit in the Godhead. He is God himself. He is not an elevated ancestor, nor is he a Great Ancestor.[35] In African cosmology, ancestors occupy a category below God but above human beings. Christ stands in the midst of ancestors, not as one of them but as "other," "removing all false fear and assuring us of the triumph of love." Because of the work of this Christ, death even for the ancestors themselves is defeated, and our relationships with deceased relatives are not terminated, nor reduced to non-existence. On the contrary, "our relationships with our deceased loved ones are now transformed in him."[36]

---

[33]Russell, "Time Also Moves Backwards," 96.
[34]Russell, "Time Also Moves Backwards," 91.
[35]Note the three distinct functions of ancestors: "liturgical companions to the living"; mediators between God and human beings; and guardians of family affairs, traditions, ethics, and activities. In view of these functions, divergent views arise on whether Christ can be called an ancestor. John Pobee and Bujo readily state that Jesus could be called an ancestor (see Diane Stinton, *Jesus of Africa: Voices of Contemporary African Christologies* [Nairobi: Paulines Publications Africa, 2004], 140-43); Nürnberger disagrees (see K. Nürnberger, *The Living Dead and the Living God* [Pietermaritzburg: Cluster Publications, 2007], 234); while Stinton is noncommittal (see Stinton, *Jesus of Africa*, 165).
[36]Russell, "Time Also Moves Backwards," 96.

Conclusion

Conversations around eschatology in African Christianity have unfortunately been shrunk to a play whose main plot is time and character. We applaud Mbiti for his illustrious and tireless contributions, spanning many decades, to the development of African Christian thought. But African Christianity must now expand its field of play and consciously include more contributors to the conversation while, at the same time, expanding the agenda of eschatology beyond just time. Already, as we have seen, more in the African Christian culture could be and has been discussed: death, dying, and life beyond the grave; ancestors, spirits, and divinities; time, events, and seasons. These are not just issues of philosophy, religious studies, and social sciences—though they have at times been dragged and confined to these corners. These are conversations in eschatology, and where we have processed them as theological responses we must utilize them for pastoral concerns and allow them to inform the thought of worldwide Christianity.

For Further Reading

Adjaye, Joseph K. "Time in Africa and Its Diaspora: An Introduction." In *Time in the Black Experience*, edited by Joseph K. Adjaye. Westport, CT: Greenwood, 1994.

Bae, C. S. "Ancestor Worship and the Challenges It Poses to the Christian Mission and Ministry." PhD thesis, University of Pretoria, 2007.

Evans-Pritchard, Edward E. "Burial and Mortuary Rites of the Nuer." *African Affairs* 48 (1949): 51-63.

Lee, Rebekah. "Death and Dying in the History of Africa Since 1800." *Journal of African History* 49 (2008): 342-59.

Mbiti, John S. *New Testament Eschatology in an African Background*. London: Oxford University Press, 1971.

Nürnberger, K. *The Living Dead and the Living God*. Pietermaritzburg: Cluster, 2007.

Reichardt, Ulfried, "Time and the African-American Experience: The Problem of Chronocentrism." *American Studies* 45, no. 4 (2000): 465-84.

Russell, William P. "'Time Also Moves Backwards': John Mbiti's Traditional Concept of Time and the Future of World Christianity." *Studies in World Christianity* 9 (2003): 88-102.

Tempels, Placide. *Bantu Philosophy*. Paris: Présence Africaine, 1969.

43

REVELATION 21:1-4 FROM AN AFRICAN PERSPECTIVE

John D. K. Ekem

APOCALYPTIC THEOLOGY constitutes a key component of biblical eschatology. Unfortunately, it is a neglected area or at best an endangered species in African biblical scholarship. This chapter critically examines Revelation 21:1-4, one of the most popular texts that has attracted a variety of interpretations on the Ghanaian Christian terrain. This essay argues that eschatological issues emerging from the text have a strong bearing on current African sociopolitical, economic, and religious realities, including ecological conservation.

INTRODUCTION

The interpretation of apocalyptic literature tends to open Pandora's box for biblical scholarship. Texts emerging from this type of literature, as exemplified in Revelation, have attracted a variety of interpretations at academic and nonacademic levels, depending on whether one subscribes to the amillennial, premillennial, millennial, or postmillennial school of thought or to approaches that may be described as preterist, historicist, futurist, or idealist.[1] In the wake of eschatological speculations about how the world will come to an end and the proliferation of books and movies on the subject, an investigation of the nature and significance of apocalyptic texts assumes special importance.[2]

The study and application of such a literary genre to current realities in church and society has emerged as a delicate hermeneutical exercise. Unfortunately, some forms of reading methods or hermeneutical approaches to apocalyptic passages have generated unwarranted extremism, such as religious fanaticism, or apathy in matters of social and political involvement. Unfamiliarity with critical tools for interpreting such literature has thus turned out to be counterproductive. A proper understanding, analysis, and repackaging of apocalyptic texts for specific audiences will positively affect global efforts at social justice and peaceful coexistence.

As a case study, this chapter examines Revelation 21:1-4, which has often served as a beacon of hope for those in distressing situations, particularly in Africa, where multiple challenges confront people in the social, religious, political, and economic spheres.

---

[1] For a discussion of different hermeneutical approaches to the text of Revelation, see Frederick D. Mazzaferri, *The Genre of the Book of Revelation from a Source-Critical Perspective* (Berlin: Walter de Gruyter, 1989), 33-34; David L. Barr, ed., *Reading the Book of Revelation* (Atlanta: Society of Biblical Literature, 2003), 1-6.

[2] As an example of eschatological speculation, see, for example, Hal Lindsey, *The Late Great Planet Earth* (Grand Rapids, MI: Zondervan, 1970).

The proposed hermeneutical approach for this study can be described as eclectic insofar as methods of reading behind the text, within the text, and in front of the text are brought on board to highlight specific issues. To be precise, we can hardly do justice to the text under consideration without coming to grips with its historical, rhetorical, and current contextual nuances.

LOCATING REVELATION WITHIN THE CONTEXT OF APOCALYPTIC LITERATURE

The Judeo-Christian Scriptures contain a variety of literary genres that have engendered extensive scholarly discussions. We can, for example, make mention of Deuteronomic, prophetic, and Wisdom literature, as well as Gospel, apologetic, and epistolary material. Each of these has its own characteristics, some of which overlap with others, and critical scholarly tools are needed to determine their *Sitz im Leben*.

Significantly, apocalyptic literature contains aspects of the abovementioned literary genres while remaining distinct from them in certain respects. Within the apocalyptic literary genre itself, we can identify two main approaches: those that focus primarily on "reviews of history" (e.g., Daniel, Jubilees, 4 Ezra, and 2 Baruch) and those that highlight "otherworldly journeys" (e.g., the Testament of Abraham, Testament of Levi 2-5, and the Apocalypse of Zephaniah).[3] With the help of symbolic language and several literary devices, apocalyptic writers build their message around the following themes:

1. dualism, whereby a sharp distinction is drawn between good and evil, light and darkness, heaven and earth, "this world" and "the world to come"

2. God's sovereignty over history and the cosmos

3. ultimate vindication of the righteous

4. access to divine revelation through intermediary heavenly beings

5. enduring optimism

6. opening of a new chapter in creation

As a key text in the apocalyptic literary genre and the most popular material for some Christian interpretations of the end times, Revelation appears to combine features of all of the above. Apocalyptic material thrives amid persecution and other forms of traumatic experience on the part of its addressees. Thus, while scholars view the material in Daniel, especially Daniel 7-12, against the backdrop of the Maccabean revolt, Revelation is often interpreted in the context of persecution and martyrdom of Christian communities in the first-century Greco-Roman world. William Hendriksen, for instance, considers the purpose of Revelation to be an attempt to "comfort the militant Church in its struggle against the forces of evil."[4] Apocalyptic theologies as envisioned in Daniel and Revelation raise the question of theodicy, the sovereignty of God vis-à-vis the persistence of evil. But their authors try to resolve this ambiguity by pointing to the transient nature of evil phenomena and the fact that God has the final word. Within the canon, Isaiah 24-27; 56-66; Ezekiel; Joel 2:28-3:21; Zechariah 9-14; Mark 13 (and Mt 24; Lk 21:5-36); 1 Thessalonians 4:13-5:11; 2 Thessalonians 2:1-12; 2 Peter 2-3; and Jude also contain interesting ingredients of apocalyptic material. Carl Holladay sums it up:

---

[3]For a concise but very useful discussion, see Carl R. Holladay, *Introduction to the New Testament* (Waco, TX: Baylor University Press, 2017), 837-41.

[4]William Hendriksen, *More than Conquerors. An Interpretation of the Book of Revelation* (Grand Rapids, MI: Baker, 2015), 13.

Revelation has long been recognized as an apocalyptic writing whose language and outlook resonate with these other biblical and non-biblical apocalyptic writings, which were produced between 200 BCE and 200 CE. . . . As the vast body of Jewish and Christian apocalypses became available in critical editions and translations, scholars were able to gain a better understanding of how apocalyptic literature worked, what symbols and images it tended to use, how it related to biblical prophetic books, and what circumstances produced such writings. Understanding the "rules" of apocalyptic writing and how apocalyptic thinkers construed their world enabled scholars to interpret Revelation within the broader context of the ancient world.[5]

The rhetorical nuances of Revelation, with its use of symbolism to respond to a crisis situation in the first century AD, call for a careful approach to the text.[6]

While recognizing some historical realities such as persecution and martyrdom of Christians during the reign of latter first-century AD Roman emperors, we should guard against biblicist-literalistic and allegorical interpretations that carry the danger of unhealthy speculations. Succumbing to the latter does obvious violence to the author's rhetoric of "divine sovereignty trump card" as antidote to the wider negative forces of darkness, dehumanization, wanton destruction of nature, corruptibility, and death. The text of Revelation can be outlined as follows:[7]

Prologue and Opening Vision of Christ (Rev 1:1–3:22)

Opening Heavenly Vision (Rev 4:1–5:14)

The Lamb Opens the Seven Seals (Rev 6:1–8:5)

The Seven Trumpets (Rev 8:6–11:19)

Miscellaneous Visions (Rev 12:1–14:20)

Seven Angels, Seven Plagues, Seven Bowls of Wrath (Rev 15:1–16:21)

The Fall of Babylon (Rev 17:1–19:10)

Final Visions and Epilogue (Rev 19:11–22:21)

THE TEXT OF REVELATION 21:1-4: SOME CONCISE EXEGETICAL REMARKS
Author's translation.

And I saw a new heaven and a new earth. For the former heaven and the former earth have gone out of existence and the sea was no more. And I saw the holy city, [namely], the new Jerusalem, coming down out of heaven from God, prepared as a bride adorned for her husband. And I heard a great voice from the throne saying, "Behold the tabernacle of God is with humankind, and he shall dwell [pitch his tent] with them, and they shall be his people, and God himself shall be with them [as their God], And he shall wipe away every tear from their eyes, and death shall be no more; neither shall there be weeping nor crying nor pain any more, [because] the former things have passed away.

Concise exegesis. Revelation 21 ushers us into a *Theologie der Hoffnung* (*Theology of Hope*), to borrow Jürgen Moltmann's famous title. Following a gloomy picture of judgment and the destruction of whatever constitutes opposition to God's sovereignty and salvific plan, including death and Hades (Rev 20:14), the apocalyptic writer escorts us to witness an interventionist,

---

[5]Holladay, *Introduction to the New Testament*, 838.
[6]For an interesting discussion, see Steven J. Friesen, *Imperial Cults and the Apocalypse of John: Reading Revelation in the Ruins* (Oxford: Oxford University Press, 2001); Young Jang, "Narrative Function of the Apocalypse," *Scriptura* 80 (2002): 186-96. Another useful reading is George Eldon Ladd, *The Presence of the Future: The Eschatology of Biblical Realism* (London: SPCK, 1981).
[7]Extracted from Holladay, *Introduction to the New Testament*, 850-51.

holistic, salvific act of God. This is described in vivid terms as the sight of a new heaven and a new earth (Rev 21:1). In order to erase any doubts regarding the possible threat of antigodly corruptible phenomena, attention is drawn to the previous heaven and the previous earth passing out of existence (Rev 21:1). The sea that symbolizes a threat to the divine scheme of things is also no more (Rev 21:1). But what exactly is the nature of this new heaven and new earth? This has been interpreted in various ways. One school of thought posits that the new heaven and the new earth will be newly created and, for that matter, radically different from the previous ones that have gone out of existence. John Walvoord describes it as an act of new creation rather than a renovation.[8] Another school of thought holds the view that the new heaven and the new earth will be a renewal or transformation of the previous ones that have been corrupted by sin.[9] According to J. B. Smith, the old heaven and earth will not vanish into nothingness.[10] Leon Morris describes the process as the "complete transformation of all things," and Blount views this as a process of radical continuity characterized by a radically transformed

earth.[11] A third school of thought interprets the phrase "a new heaven and a new earth" (Rev 21:1) in a metaphorical sense as a reference to the moral and spiritual transformation of the world.[12] Without necessarily taking a specific stand, Fee cautions against a literal reading of the text.[13] The expression "and the sea was no more" (Rev 21:1) has also been interpreted literally and metaphorically. The literal reading postulates that the new earth will not have a sea in it.[14] According to Walvoord, the only water body will be the river mentioned in Revelation 22:1.[15] John Philips interprets it as a symbolic reference to the Holy Spirit.[16] One can also interpret it as a Johannine apocalyptic symbol of chaos and evil or anything that is contrary to God's salvific will and opposes God's sovereignty.[17] Michael Wilcock alludes to the fact that in ancient mythologies, the sea was representative of the chaos monster Tiamat.[18] Similar to the *Odyssey* in Greek mythology, the sea personifies evil which must be abolished. Craig Keener has also come up with the intriguing suggestion that the disappearance of the sea in John's apocalyptic vision is a probable reference to the end of all human mercantile trade, since God will supply all the

---

[8]John Walvoord, *The Revelation of Jesus Christ* (Chicago: Moody, 1966), 311-13; see also Ben Witherington III, *Revelation*, New Cambridge Commentary (Cambridge: Cambridge University Press, 2003), 252-53; Margaret Barker, *The Revelation of Jesus Christ* (Edinburgh: T&T Clark, 2000).

[9]John Philips, *Exploring Revelation* (Chicago: Moody, 1974), 263-64; Michael Wilcock, *The Message of Revelation: I Saw Heaven Opened* (Nottingham, UK: Inter-Varsity Press, 1975), 197-99; Robert Mulholland, *Holy Living in an Unholy World: Revelation* (Grand Rapids, MI: Zondervan, 1990), 315; Graeme Goldsworthy, *The Gospel in Revelation: Gospel and Apocalypse* (Carlisle, UK: Paternoster, 1994), 132-38; G. K. Beale, *Revelation: A Shorter Commentary* (Grand Rapids, MI: Eerdmans, 2015), 497.

[10]J. B. Smith, *A Revelation of Jesus Christ: A Commentary on the Book of Revelation* (Scottdale, PA: Herald, 1961), 281.

[11]Leon Morris, *Revelation: An Introduction and Commentary* (Leicester, UK: Inter-Varsity Press, 1976), 243; Brian K. Blount, *Revelation: A Commentary* (Louisville: John Knox, 2009), 376.

[12]Charles R. Erdman, *The Revelation of John* (Philadelphia: Westminster, 1929), 154; J. M. Ford, *Revelation: Introduction, Translation and Commentary* (New York: Doubleday, 1975), 360-62.

[13]Gordon Fee, *Revelation: A New Covenant Commentary* (Cambridge, UK: Lutterworth, 2011), 290-93.

[14]Philips, *Exploring Revelation*, 263-64; Walvoord, *Revelation of Jesus Christ*, 311.

[15]Walvoord, *Revelation of Jesus Christ*, 311.

[16]Philips, *Exploring Revelation*, 272-73.

[17]Wilcock, *Message of Revelation*, 198; Witherington, *Revelation*, 253; Erdman, *Revelation of John*, 155; Ford, *Revelation*, 361; Morris, *Revelation*, 243; Blount, *Revelation*, 377.

[18]Wilcock, *Message of Revelation*, 198.

needs of his people.[19] It should, therefore, come as no surprise to us that in the Johannine apocalyptic scheme of things, it disappears from the new order of creation.[20] It is quite obvious from these varied perspectives that there is no consensus regarding the interpretation of Revelation 21:1, even though an overly literal interpretation fails to capture the message the apocalyptic writer is trying to put across by means of symbolic language.

With reference to Revelation 21:2, which deals with the motif of the new Jerusalem, Philips, Smith, and Walvoord share the view that it is a celestial city inhabited by God's sanctified ones, and that this is in keeping with Christ's promise to prepare a place for all believers.[21] Walvoord opines that it hangs like a satellite that God has already prepared.[22] But there is also the literal messianic view that this New Jerusalem is a qualitative restoration of the earthly Jerusalem which was destroyed.[23] Another school of thought represented by Morris, Fee, Graeme Goldsworthy, and Robert Mulholland interprets "the holy city" introduced in apposition to the "new Jerusalem" as a metaphorical reference to a radically renewed community of human existence that becomes the climax of God's regenerative work among mortals, with the church serving as a paradigm.[24] Contrary to Walvoord's view that it is a prepared "hidden satellite," Brian Blount states categorically that the new Jerusalem is "this-worldly" and not "other-worldly."[25]

Its uniqueness lies in that it is God who takes the initiative to renew his creation. Richard Middleton poses the question as to whether the ushering in of a new cosmos presupposes "an obliteration followed by replacement or a reference to some form of (admittedly radical) transformation." Basing his discussion on the use of the verb *parēlthen* ("has passed away") to qualify *ta archaia* ("the old things") in 2 Corinthians 5:17, he argues that this does not in any way connote obliteration. "By analogy, then, the passing away of the present heaven and earth to make way for the new creation is also transformative and not a matter of destruction followed by replacement."[26] Nevertheless, we cannot overlook the influence of apocalyptically loaded prophetic material from Isaiah and Ezekiel on the "theology of radical renewal" in Revelation. David Mathewson has done a thorough study of passages from Isaiah 25:8; 60:1-22; 61:10; 65:15-20; and Ezekiel 40–48 that have a bearing on issues raised by the apocalyptic author of Revelation. Along with others, he observes:

> By this density of Isaian texts utilized according to thematic patterns throughout Revelation, as well as the anticipatory use of Isaian oracles of renewal and the new Jerusalem, John has once again prepared the reader for and has created an expectation of a reuse of Isaian texts relating to eschatological salvation, renewal and the new Jerusalem in the final chapters of Revelation.[27]

---

[19]Craig S. Keener, *Revelation*, NIV Application Commentary (Grand Rapids, MI: Zondervan, 2000), 406.

[20]Fee, *Revelation*, 292.

[21]Philips, *Exploring Revelation*, 264; Smith, *Revelation of Jesus Christ*, 282; Walvoord, *Revelation of Jesus Christ*, 313.

[22]Walvoord, *Revelation of Jesus Christ*, 313.

[23]R. H. Charles, *A Critical and Exegetical Commentary on the Revelation of St John* (New York: Charles Scribner & Sons, 1920), 2:200-201.

[24]Mulholland, *Holy Living in an Unholy World*, 316; Goldsworthy, *Gospel in Revelation*, 137; Morris, *Revelation*, 244; Fee, *Revelation*, 292.

[25]Blount, *Revelation*, 378.

[26]Richard Middleton, *A New Heaven and a New Earth: Reclaiming Biblical Eschatology* (Grand Rapids, MI: Baker Academic, 2014), 205-6.

[27]David Mathewson, *A New Heaven and a New Earth: The Meaning and Function of the Old Testament in Revelation 21.1–22.5*, Journal for the Study of the New Testament Supplement Series 238 (New York: Sheffield Academic Press, 2003), 31; see also Richard Bauckham, *The Theology of the Book of Revelation* (Cambridge: Cambridge University Press, 1993), 132; David E. Aune, *Revelation 17–22*, Word Biblical Commentary 52C (Grand Rapids, MI: Zondervan, 1998), 443-57.

In Mathewson's opinion, in Revelation 21 the author tries to draw a sharp contrast between two epochs: the present order that characterizes corruptibility, and the coming new order that is a qualitatively superior one, precisely because God himself is its architect and executor.[28] The apocalyptic visionary expresses God's sovereignty and "final say" in this "renewal event" when he draws on the concept of a great voice from the heavenly throne (Rev 21:3) that announces God's dwelling or "tabernacling" among humankind (Rev 21:3), an echo of the Johannine Logos's activity in John 1:14. If our author is drawing on the Jewish Scriptures, then he appears to reinterpret the concept of the tabernacle in Jewish thought that symbolized God's abiding presence among Israel (Ex 25:8). God's glorious presence could be experienced in the tabernacle (Ex 40:30-35) and, as Bauckham graphically puts it with reference to the text in Revelation, "The theo-centricity of Revelation . . . is focused again in the description of the New Jerusalem. God's creation reaches its eschatological fulfilment when it becomes the scene of God's immediate presence. This, in the last resort, is what is 'new' about the new creation. It is the old creation filled with God's presence."[29]

Consequently, the author of Revelation leaves no doubt that inhabitants of the new Jerusalem will be God's own people (Rev 21:3). The author is thereby echoing God's promise to dwell with his people Israel and to be their God (Ezek 37:27-28; Zech 8:8) as well as to welcome other nations into the commonwealth of the redeemed (Is 19:24-25; 56:6-8). Similar to Ezekiel's vision in Ezekiel 48:35, "The new Jerusalem becomes

the perfect place for the gathering of the redeemed, a symbol of the long-awaited union of God and his faithful people. God's presence in the city will banish the things of the former order."[30] That being the case, Revelation 21:4 itemizes the removal of all that constitutes a threat to human existence or throws the ecology out of gear, including death, mourning, cries of distress, and pain. The prospects of a positively and radically transformed universe through God's initiative must have constituted an important eschatological hope for the author and addressees of Revelation.

IMPACT OF REVELATION 21:1-4 ON THE GHANAIAN/AFRICAN TERRAIN

In his groundbreaking work titled *New Testament Eschatology in an African Background*, John Mbiti wrestles with the subject of eschatology and its implications for the African concept of time. He draws on examples from his own Akamba society in Kenya and contends that "For the Akamba, Time is not an academic concern. It is simply a composition of events that have occurred, those which are taking place now and those which will immediately occur. What has not taken place or what is unlikely to occur in the immediate future, has no temporal meaning—it belongs to the reality of 'no-Time.'" Mbiti subsequently argues that within Akamba communities, what really matters is the "Long Past" and the "Dynamic Present," and that the "Future," in a linear sense, is nonexistent. He applies this concept of time to his analysis of Revelation 21:1-4, drawing attention to its relevance for the prevailing sociopolitical, economic, and

---

[28]Mathewson, *New Heaven and a New Earth*, 34.

[29]Bauckham, *Theology of the Book of Revelation*, 140. See also John N. Suggit, *Oecumenicus Commentary on the Apocalypse* (Washington, DC: Catholic University of America Press, 2006), 183.

[30]Ranko Stefanovic, *Revelation of Jesus Christ: Commentary on the Book of Revelation* (Berrien Springs, MI: Andrews University Press, 2009), 577-78.

religious challenges on the African continent.[31] The significance of Mbiti's work lies in the question he raises regarding the tension between the linear concept of time that many Western societies are familiar with, and the cyclical dimension that influences the thought patterns of many non-Western societies, including sub-Saharan Africa. Precisely the question that arises is the extent to which futuristic eschatologies that apocalyptic material, including Revelation, seem to champion can resonate with the African context. With particular reference to our subject of investigation, we should query whether the concept of a new heaven and a new earth that Revelation 21:1-4 portrays should, in the African context, be accommodated within the confines of either a futuristic or a realized eschatology, or both. Admittedly, such a query does not lend itself to a simplistic response, given the multiple influences of Westernization, urbanization, and industrialization on traditional African communities. One can argue, nonetheless, that the persistence of traditional African religious worldviews, with their cyclical orientation to events, particularly in matters of holistic salvation, points to the resilience of realized eschatological inclinations on the African terrain. This can be illustrated with reference to the soteriologies and eschatologies of African Independent Churches. These churches are "protest movements" against the "over-Westernization" of European mission-founded churches in Africa, considering that the latter could hardly satisfy the deep-seated needs of their African audiences. Whether we characterize them as "Zionist" or "faith-healing" churches, these African Independent Churches teach their members to look forward to a better land, sometimes referred to as a "new Jerusalem," where peace, prosperity, and righteousness prevail.[32]

In assessing the reception history and impact of the text on "receptor communities" in Africa, it is apposite to examine some mother-tongue translations that have shaped people's theologies. The key issue of vernacularization as a vehicle for theological creativity in Africa also comes to the fore: the critical role of African mother-tongue Bible translations in shaping the future of African biblical scholarship has attracted much attention.[33] Here I will draw on two case studies from Ghana, with which I am most familiar. My two case studies come from the Asante-Twi and

---

[31]John S. Mbiti, *New Testament Eschatology in an African Background: A Study of the Encounter Between New Testament Theology and African Traditional Concepts* (London: Oxford University Press, 1971), 24, 83-85.

[32]Mbiti, *New Testament Eschatology*, 85. On the worldviews of these African Independent Churches, see also John S. Pobee and Gabriel Ositelu II, *African Initiatives in Christianity: The Growth, Gifts and Diversities of Indigenous African Churches* (Geneva: WCC, 1998); Thomas Oduro, *Christ Holy Church International: The Story of an African Independent Church* (Minneapolis: Lutheran University Press, 2007), 18-42.

[33]John D. K. Ekem, *Early Scriptures of the Gold Coast (Ghana): The Historical, Linguistic and Theological Settings of the Gã, Twi, Mfantse and Ewe Bibles* (Rome: Edizioni di Storia e Letteratura, 2011), 156-57. See also two of Ekem's other publications: *Priesthood in Context: A Study of Priesthood in Some Christian and Primal Communities of Ghana and Its Relevance for Mother-Tongue Biblical Interpretation* (Accra: SonLife, 2009), 188-89; "Interpreting *ton arton hēmōn ton epiousion* in the Context of Ghanaian Mother-Tongue Hermeneutics," in *Postcolonial Perspectives in African Biblical Interpretations*, ed. Musa W. Dube et al. (Atlanta: Society of Biblical Literature, 2012), 317-27. See also Bernhard Y. Quarshie, "Doing Biblical Studies in the African Context: The Challenge of Mother-Tongue Scriptures," *Journal of African Christian Thought* 5 (2002): 4-14. For a good discussion of vernacularization, see Kwame Bediako, *Christianity in Africa: The Renewal of a Non-Western Religion* (Edinburgh: Edinburgh University Press, 1995), 59-74; Birgit Meyer, "Translating the Devil: An African Appropriation of Pietist Protestantism—The Case of the Peki Ewe in Southeastern Ghana, 1847–1992" (PhD thesis, University of Amsterdam, 1995), 94-104; John D. K. Ekem, "Jacobus Capitein's Translation of 'The Lord's Prayer' into Mfantse: An Example of Creative Mother Tongue Hermeneutics," *Ghana Bulletin of Theology* 2 (2007): 66-79; Kwesi A. Dickson, *Theology in Africa* (London: Darton, Longman & Todd, 1984), 96-97; John S. Pobee, *Toward an African Theology* (Nashville: Abingdon, 1979). Edwin M. Yamauchi, *Africa and the Bible* (Grand Rapids, MI: Baker Academic, 2004), 205-13, also touches on the thorny subject of Afrocentric biblical interpretation.

Gã translations that I have had the privilege to supervise as Translation Consultant of the Bible Society of Ghana. The Asante-Twi and Gã communities are two major ethnic groups in Ghana, occupying the middle and part of the coastal belt of Ghana, respectively. Asante-Twi and Gã are both tonal languages and belong to the Kwa subgroup of the wider Niger–Congo cluster of languages. Asante-Twi is the most widely spoken language in Ghana, occupying over 40 percent of the linguistic slot. Linguistically, it can also be classified as the dominant dialect of the wider Akan group of dialects, spoken by over 60 percent of the Ghanaian population. This explains why I am using a translation from this dialect as a case study.

Revised Asante-Twi Bible published in 2012 (translation of Revelation 21:1-4).

Section Heading: *Ɔsoro foforɔ ne asase foforɔ* [A New Heaven and a New Earth]

Na mehunu ɔsoro foforɔ ne asase foforɔ, na kane soro ne kane asase no atwam, na ɛpo nni hɔ bio [And I saw a new heaven and a new earth, for the former heaven and the former earth have passed away, and the sea was no longer in existence]. *Na mehunu kuro kronkron, Yerusalem foforɔ, sɛ ɛfiri soro Nyankopɔn nkyɛn resiane, na wɔasiesie no sɛ ayeforɔ a wɔahyehyɛ no ama ne kunu* [And I saw the holy town, New Jerusalem, that it was descending from the presence of the God of heaven, and that it had been prepared as a bride richly adorned for her husband]. *Na metee nne kɛseɛ bi firi ahennwa no mu a ɛse: Hwɛ, Nyankopɔn ntomadan wɔ nnipa mu, na ɔbɛtena mu wɔ wɔn mu, na wɔayɛ ne man, na Onyankopɔn no ara ne wɔn bɛtena* [And I heard a loud voice from the royal stool saying: Look, God's tent is pitched among human beings, and he will dwell in the tent amongst them, so that they become his people, and God himself will dwell with them]. *Na*

ɔbɛpepa wɔn ani ase nisuo nyinaa. Na owuo nni hɔ bio, na awerɛhoɔ ne osu ne yea biara nni hɔ bio, ɛfiri sɛ kane nnɔɔma no atwam [And he will wipe away every tear from their eyes. And death shall be no more, and there shall be no more sorrow or crying or pain, because the former things have passed away].

New Gã Bible published in 2006 (translation of Revelation 21:1-4).

Ni mina ŋwei hee kɛ shikpɔŋ hee, ejaakɛ tsutsu ŋwei lɛ kɛ tsutsu shikpɔŋ lɛ eho etee, ni Ŋshɔ bɛ dɔŋŋ [And I saw a new heaven and a new earth, because the former heaven and the former earth have passed away, and the sea was no more]. *Ni mina Maŋ Krɔŋkrɔŋ lɛ ni ji Yerusalem hee lɛ jɛ Nyɔŋmɔ ŋɔɔ yɛ ŋwei miikpeleke shi, ni asaa lɛ ato tamɔ ayɛmforo ni awula lɛ ahã ewu* [And I saw the Holy Township, which is the New Jerusalem, coming down from God in heaven and made ready as a bride dressed for her husband]. *Ni minu gbee kpeteŋkple ko maŋtsɛ sɛi lɛ mli kɛɛ, "Naa, Nyɔŋmɔ shishilɛhe lɛ yɛ gbɔmɛi ateŋ, ni eeehi shi yɛ amɛteŋ ni amɛaatsɔ emaŋ, ni Nyɔŋmɔ dieŋtsɛ kɛ amɛ aaahi shi* [And I heard a great voice from the supreme royal paramount chair saying, "See, God's dwelling is among humans, and he will dwell in their midst and they shall be called his people, and God himself will dwell with them]. *Ni Nyɔŋmɔ aaatsumɔ amɛhiɛiaŋ yafonui fɛɛ. Gbele bɛ dɔŋŋ, ni nkɔmɔyeli loo blɔmɔ loo nɔnaa ko hu bɛ dɔŋŋ; ejaakɛ tsutsunii lɛ eho etee* [And God will wipe away every tear from their eyes. Death shall be no more, and deep worry or distress cry or suffering shall also be no more; because the previous things have passed away"].

These two mother-tongue translations from Ghana illustrate the technicalities of transferring thought from one language to another. This exercise becomes particularly challenging when attempts are made to repackage theological concepts for different receptor audiences. With reference to the apocalyptic text of Revelation 21:1-4, one needs to tread cautiously in navigating from a first-century AD crisis situation and its theological response, aided by rhetorically loaded apocalyptic literary device, to twenty-first-century existential realities being experienced by some Ghanaian communities. In a typical sub-Saharan African community, where the forces of destruction via political oppression, economic mismanagement and exploitation, social marginalization, religious extremism, and intimidation that generate a culture of silence prevail, it is easy to connect with the concerns of oppressive structures and the prospects of the ultimate triumph of good over evil with apocalyptic literature.[34] That Revelation 21–22 has emerged as the locus classicus of an awaited new cosmos in which forces of negation are thoroughly done away with explains the high premium Ghanaian Christian circles place on it. Revelation 21:1-4 is often read and sung at funeral services as a beacon of hope and comfort for traumatized families and friends mourning the loss of loved ones. The majority of ministers/pastors view the texts in a literal sense and teach them accordingly to their audiences. Many are unaware of the historical and theological background to Revelation, and some avoid preaching from it simply because they are unsure of what exactly it seeks to convey. A few opine that we should not be so engulfed in sociopolitical matters as to lose sight of our inheritance in the new earth that God will prepare for the righteous and called ones.

Coming back to our Ghanaian mother-tongue translations, it is interesting to observe how the nuances of Revelation 21:1-4 are captured for the Asante-Twi and Gã readerships respectively. First, the prospects of a new heaven and a new earth are viewed in both futuristic and realized eschatological terms, such that what is anticipated in the distant future is also hoped for in the present and foreseeable future. The latter is in tandem with the Asante-Twi and Gã concepts of time that are more cyclical than linear. This can be illustrated with the Odwira festival of the Asante-Twi communities and the Homowo festival of Gã communities. Both festivals are occasions to reconnect with the departed members of the community who have attained ancestor status, reconcile with the living, and pray for the ancestors to be reincarnated in the yet-to-be-born. Such an ontological bond between the departed, the living, and the unborn resonates more with a cyclical view of life than with a linear hope for an "end time" characterized by the nullification of the past and present. This throws some interesting light on the portion of the Nicene Creed that states that "we look for the resurrection of the dead and the life of the world to come," which can be considered as a fulfilled reality in traditional Ghanaian thought. Writing with reference to the Odwira festival, Frank Adams makes the following thought-provoking remarks: "The Odwira festival was seen as an 'uninterrupted story' where the past, present and future were united in the Asante historical and cultural experience. . . . It was celebrated as a purposeful sequence of events, from defilement to purification and to renewal; from disintegration to integration; from past to future."[35]

---

[34]Joseph Quayesi-Amakye, *Christology and Evil in Ghana: Towards a Pentecostal Public Theology* (New York: Rodopi, 2013), 51-86.
[35]Frank Kwasi Adams, *Odwira and the Gospel: A Study of the Asante Odwira Festival and Its Siginificance for Christianity in Ghana* (Oxford: Regnum, 2010), 201.

In any case, since the new Jerusalem (Asante-Twi = *Yerusalem foforo*; Gã = *Yerusalem hee lɛ*) is coming down from God himself in order to assume divinely prepared this-earthly dimensions, it should be a welcome antidote to current imperfections within the constraints of human existence. Significantly, the Gã concept of "newness," translated as *hee lɛ*, connotes "divinely breathed radical renewal" and brings out more powerfully the transformation envisaged in Revelation 21:1-4. The Asante-Twi equivalent of *foforo*, though quite apposite, is semantically limited in this context, unless it is qualified with an intensifier pointing to its high quality. In future revisions, translators may consider adding the qualifier *paa* ("very"/"most") to *foforo* in order to achieve a similar effect. The comparison of this new Jerusalem with a bride adorned for her husband, which experience is highly cherished in Asante-Twi and Gã societies, reinforces the qualitative and innovative nature of such a divine initiative. The concept of throne, translated into Asante-Twi and Gã as *ahennwa* and *maŋtsɛ sɛi lɛ* respectively, brings out the element of divine authority that effects positive changes in society for the common good. The Asante-Twi and Gã equivalents are considered as visible representations or shadows of ultimate divine authority. And that is all the more reason why occupants of royal stools/chairs must be people of integrity whose leadership brings good fortune to their communities. As a matter of fact, "royal stools" in Ghanaian traditional contexts symbolizes societal cohesion. If God is truly coming to dwell among human beings, as the Asante-Twi concept of *ntomadan* ("pitching of tent") strongly connotes, then all the forces that dehumanize us ought to disappear and God himself will take the initiative to alleviate our sufferings. In the African/Ghanaian context, we cannot confine this to otherworldly domains lest it lose its relevance for current concerns about human survival and ecological balance.

TOWARD AN AFRICAN ECOCENTRIC ESCHATOLOGY

As African theological educators, the challenges of material poverty, socioeconomic exploitation and marginalization, and religiocultural bigotry constantly stare us in the face. These propel us to rethink the content of the theological education that we have received and are passing on to others. Our theological seminaries, Bible colleges, and university departments of religion and theology usually operate with syllabi that tend to expose students to theological impulses from the North Atlantic region. While these are not harmful in themselves, they carry the risk of producing theologians who are unresponsive to pertinent issues in Africa or, at best, view them with spectacles that may not necessarily address key African concerns. This is particularly the case with eschatological questions. Unfortunately, candidates who undergo training for ministry in churches and the wider community are ill-prepared to recontextualize the theologies they have been taught in the face of other existential realities within their constituencies of ministry. Amazingly, the average Ghanaian/African student of the Bible and theology tends to think futuristically in matters of eschatology, and there is often a myopic worldview of "a pie-in-the sky" soteriology that ignores present-day concerns.[36] Obviously, approaching the text of Revelation 21:1-4 from this perspective is bound

---

[36]See Collium Banda, "Empowering Hope? Jürgen Moltmann's Eschatological Challenge to Ecclesiological Responses in the Zimbabwean Context of Poverty" (PhD diss., Stellenbosch University, 2016), 47; Onesimus Ngundu, "Revelation," in *Africa Bible Commentary*, ed. Tokunboh Adeyemo (Nairobi: WordAlive, 2010), 1603.

to be otherworldly rather than this-worldly, for which reason extremist gnostic as well as Platonic tendencies will threaten to gain the upper hand. Yet it can be argued from the rhetoric of Revelation that the apocalyptic author is drawing attention to a radical renewal of creation by a sovereign God who is not limited by time and space and whose rescue package embraces the entire ecology, including human beings.

Such a comprehensive, soteriologically oriented eschatology is not alien to the New Testament documents, as can be attested from Romans 8:18-25; Ephesians 1:10; and Colossians 1:15-20.[37] This is a cosmic reconciliation, but unfortunately it is hardly prioritized in New Testament scholarship. The clarion call to think ecologically beyond anthropocentric concerns is gaining increasing popularity in Africa, and theologians who focus on environmental ethics are drawing attention to issues of ecological balance that resonate well with the eschatology presented by the apocalyptic visionary in Revelation 21.[38] Joseph Mante, for instance, offers what he refers to as "Ontological Guidelines for an Eco-Theology," drawing on the philosophical-theological concept of *perichorēsis* ("mutual interpenetration"). He argues very persuasively that for contemporary theology to be viable in Africa, it must move away from "A mechanistic view of nature . . . insist on the relationality of every entity to its environment . . . develop an anthropology with proper ecological perspective . . . incorporate salvation history within an ecological framework and, thereby, develop an ecologically-oriented salvation history."[39]

There is no doubt that our theologies will be positively revolutionized if we offer enough space to biblical interpretation that takes the ecology seriously. African reflections on eschatology should include the implications of apocalyptic theology for a balanced ecology as Revelation 21:1-4 champions. We cannot dispute the fact that the Bible is the most important source for African theologizing endeavors. Working diligently to make God's salvific purposes visibly expressed here on earth entails a holistic approach to soteriology and eschatology that should not be exclusively anthropocentric. Our approach ought to be ecocentric and deeply rooted in the agenda of the sovereign triune God. Of particular significance is the fact that questions of eternity in Johannine literature, which includes Revelation, are treated from a cyclical, rather than linear, perspective, because the sovereign God is the one who holds the past, present, and future, bringing them together in a relationship of mutual interdependence.

CONCLUDING REMARKS

This essay has attempted to explore the relevance of apocalyptic literature as a key component of biblical eschatology for the African context. The case study from Revelation 21:1-4 has highlighted the subject matter of radical renewal of creation, not its annihilation, by the sovereign God, whose redeeming presence with humankind and the rest of creation makes all things new. I have argued that the text serves as a locus classicus for a theology of hope for African communities in search of holistic salvation

---

[37]For a thorough discussion, see John D. K. Ekem, *New Testament Concepts of Atonement in an African Pluralistic Setting* (Accra: SonLife Press, 2005), 71-77.

[38]Joseph O. Y. Mante, *Africa: Theological and Philosophical Roots of Our Ecological Crisis* (Accra: SonLife, 2004); see also Ogbu U. Kalu, *Power, Poverty and Prayer: The Challenges of Poverty and Pluralism in African Christianity, 1960–1996* (Asmara, Eritrea: Africa World, 2006), 75-98; Lloyd Timberlake, *Africa in Crisis: The Causes and Cures of Environmental Bankruptcy* (Philadelphia: New Society, 1986).

[39]Mante, *Africa*, 138-39.

amid the hydra-headed challenges confronting the continent. A key issue is the maintenance of cosmic equilibrium via an ecocentric eschatology that is firmly anchored in the triune God. The current state of affairs is beautifully summarized by Steven Friesen: "John's vision for the kingdom of God and his Christ has not yet been realized. Perhaps he would be surprised to learn that it has taken so long or perhaps not. His text has nevertheless remained viable across millennia."[40] It is hoped that this essay will help stimulate further discussion on biblical eschatology and its accompanying apocalyptic theologies, using relevant tools from African biblical hermeneutics.

For Further Reading

Allen, Garrick K. *The Book of Revelation and Early Jewish Textual Culture.* Cambridge: Cambridge University Press, 2017.

Boesak, Allan A. *Comfort and Protest: The Apocalypse of John from a South African Perspective.* Eugene, OR: Wipf & Stock, 2015.

Collins, John J. *The Oxford Handbook of Apocalyptic Literature.* Oxford: Oxford University Press, 2014.

Fiorenza, Elizabeth Schüssler. *The Book of Revelation: Justice and Judgement.* Minneapolis: Fortress, 1998.

Gallusz, Laszlo. *The Throne Motif in the Book of Revelation.* New York: Bloomsbury T&T Clark, 2013.

Glabach, Wilfried E. *Reclaiming the Book of Revelation: A Suggestion of New Readings in the Local Church.* New York: Peter Lang, 2007.

Herms, Ronald. *An Apocalypse for the Church and for the World: The Narrative Function of Universal Language in the Book of Revelation.* New York: Walter de Gruyter, 2006.

Kiel, Micah D. *Apocalyptic Ecology: The Book of Revelation, the Earth and the Future.* Collegeville, MN: Liturgical, 2017.

Lee, Pilchan. *The New Jerusalem in the Book of Revelation: A Study of Revelation.* Tübingen: Mohr Siebeck, 2001.

Smith, Julie M. *Apocalypse: Reading Revelation 21–22.* Provo, UT: Neal A. Maxwell Institute for Religious Scholarship, 2016.

Stephens, Mark B. *Annihilation or Renewal? The Meaning and Function of New Creation in the Book of Revelation.* Tübingen: Mohr Siebeck, 2011.

Trafton, Joseph L. *Reading Revelation: A Literary and Theological Commentary.* Macon, GA: Smyth & Helwys, 2012.

---

[40]Friesen, *Imperial Cults and the Apocalypse of John*, 210.

FROM DISPENSATIONALISM TO THEOLOGY OF HOPE

LATIN AMERICAN PERSPECTIVES ON ESCHATOLOGY

Alberto F. Roldán

IN THIS CHAPTER the author explains the development of eschatology in Latin American perspectives from the classic dispensationalism to the theology of hope of Jürgen Moltmann. The author analyzes the presence of eschatology in Spanish literature especially in Church and Society in Latin America and in the Latin American Theological Fraternity. He also shows the contrast in eschatological visions between classic hymns and the new songs in evangelical churches.

INTRODUCTION

The importance of eschatology within the corpus of systematic theology is beyond doubt. The author of Hebrews states that "in these last days he has spoken to us by a Son" (Heb 1:1), and the Son of God, Jesus of Nazareth, has inaugurated the eschaton. The Nicene Creed affirms that Jesus Christ "will come again with glory to judge the living and the dead; and his kingdom will have no end." In spite of this, eschatology as a theological theme was almost absent from the consideration of many systematic theologies for many years, before seeing a resurgence of interest at the end of the nineteenth century and beginning of the twentieth through the influence of authors such as Albert Schweitzer, Albrecht Ritschl, Johannes Weiss, and others.[1]

Protestant eschatologies—especially evangelical—have largely developed in relation to the concept of the millennium, dividing into historical premillennialism, dispensational premillennialism, postmillennialism, and amillennialism.[2] Although dispensationalism strongly influenced Latin American evangelical churches in the twentieth century, since the middle of the century a change of perspective has emerged, partly because of the influence of several theological movements, including Church and Society in Latin America, liberation theology, and the Latin American Theological Fraternity.

---

[1] For an analysis of the historical route of eschatology in the nineteenth and twentieth centuries, see Alberto F. Roldán, *Eschatology: An Integral Vision from Latin America* [*Escatología: Una Visión Integral desde América Latina*] (Buenos Aires: Ediciones Kairós, 2002), 19-56; Roldán, *Escatología: ¿Ciencia ficción o Reino de Dios?*, 2nd rev. ed. (Buenos Aires: Ediciones Kairós, 2019).

[2] See Roldán, *Eschatology*, 89-114. For a panoramic view of the various views on the millennium, see Robert G. Clouse, ed., *The Meaning of the Millennium: Four Views* (Downers Grove, IL: InterVarsity Press, 1977).

In this essay, we will first consider the difference between classic and progressive dispensationalism, an important distinction given their prominence in evangelical theology in Latin America. Second, we will survey a range of Spanish literature that engages with various perspectives on eschatology, including the significant influence of Jürgen Moltmann's *Theology of Hope*. Third, we will interpret the presence of eschatology in a sample of evangelical songs that offer an important glimpse of the grassroots perspective on eschatology in Latin America. Finally, we will respond to the question, How are the Nicene Creed's eschatological commitments present in Latin American theologies today?

CLASSIC DISPENSATIONALISM AND PROGRESSIVE DISPENSATIONALISM

For much of the twentieth century, evangelical churches in Latin America were heavily influenced by dispensationalism. According to this theological stream, developed by English theologian John Nelson Darby, one of the founders of the Plymouth Brethren movement, and based on a book written by Jesuit Manuel Lacunza, the Bible must be interpreted in relation to different "dispensations" or "economies," ways in which God deals with human beings. It distinguishes several dispensations or stages and makes a strong separation between the Old Testament and the New Testament. In its classic version, the kingdom that Jesus of Nazareth offered to the Jews was the theocratic-Davidic kingdom, which, when rejected, led to the creation of the church, a reality not foreseen in the Old Testament. While Darby was the systematizer of

dispensationalism, the instrument that popularized it was Scofield's Bible, translated late into Spanish but frequently read by English missionaries and then by pastors and believers who had access to it in that language.

The initial success of dispensationalism was due to the strong influence exercised by American fundamentalism and the fact that it constitutes a very complete scheme of the future of history and its eschatological culmination. From the 1960s, nuances in classic dispensationalism gradually modified some inflexible positions. The influence of theologians such as Dwight Pentecost and Charles Ryrie should be mentioned here.[3] Subsequently, a review of classic dispensationalism was made in the book *Progressive Dispensationalism* by Craig Blaising and Darrell Bock.[4] While highlighting broad commitments shared by all dispensational traditions, they advocated for "progressive dispensationalism," a perspective that "offers a number of modifications to classical and revised dispensationalism which brings dispensationalism to contemporary evangelical biblical interpretation."[5]

For Blaising and Bock, the most important aspects of classic dispensationalism are the following: the central dualism that recognizes two different purposes for Israel and the church; an emphasis on dispensations as different economies of God in his relationship with humanity; the heavenly nature of the church; the biblical covenants with Abraham, with Moses, and with Christ; and the difference between the kingdom of God and the kingdom of heaven. In contrast, progressive dispensationalism emphasizes holistic redemption and a progressive revelation, the nature of the church as a reality

---

[3]J. Dwight Pentecost, *Things to Come: A Study in Biblical Eschatology* (Grand Rapids, MI: Zondervan, 1958); Charles C. Ryrie, *Dispensationalism Today* (Chicago: Moody, 1965).
[4]Craig A. Blaising and Darrell L. Bock, *Progressive Dispensationalism* (Grand Rapids, MI: Baker, 1993).
[5]Blaising and Bock, *Progressive Dispensationalism*, 22.

that exists in this dispensation prior to the second coming of Christ, the consistent and historical interpretation of the Bible, and the identification between the kingdom of God and the kingdom of heaven and the presence of this kingdom in our times.

ESCHATOLOGY IN SPANISH THEOLOGICAL LITERATURE

Dispensationalism has had a significant influence on Spanish theological literature on eschatology. For example, in *Eventos del Porvenir: Estudios de Escatología Bíblica* (*Things to Come: Studies of Biblical Eschatology*), Dwight Pentecost examines the hermeneutics of prophecy, covenants in the Bible, and the scriptural meaning of the millennium from a dispensationalist perspective.[6] Similarly, in *Dispensacionalismo, Hoy*, Charles Ryrie critiques covenant theology and explores the meaning of dispensations, the origin of dispensationalism, the hermeneutic of dispensationalism, salvation, the church, and the eschatology of dispensationalism.[7]

In addition to American authors whose works gained influence in the Latin American context, Latin American theologians have also advocated for the dispensationalist view. For example, Evis Carballosa is a Cuban theologian who represents the classic dispensationalist view. In *Cristo en el Milenio*, Carballosa offers an overview of what Christians should expect with regard to the millennium, and also criticizes the amillennial tendency to transpose millennial prophecies into generic descriptions of the eternal kingdom of God.[8]

The decline of dispensationalism in the mid-twentieth century was due in part to the popular influence of books such as Hal Lindsey's *The Late Great Planet Earth*, which, drafted in the midst of the Cold War, posited the USSR as the great antichrist who had to be defeated. The collapse of real socialism and the disappearance of the Soviet Union quickly made this postulate outdated. Lindsey's work is a model of science-fiction eschatology. From a firm conviction of the "secret rapture" of the church and an interpretation of a series of current events—such as the formation of the European Economic Community and the Soviet Union, which represented a perceived peril—Lindsey identified persons and movements as signs of a near end of the world.

Vendré Otra Vez, by George E. Ladd, represents historic premillennialism.[9] The theologian of Fuller Seminary considers the importance of Christian eschatology for the meaning of history. He discusses the second coming of Christ in contemporary theology, the biblical presuppositions, and the relationship between the second coming and the lordship of Christ. The conclusion of Ladd is that the parousia of Christ represents the final irruption of God in history and the consummation of redemption.

Anthony Hoekema's book *La Biblia y el Futuro* is important for the amillennialist perspective.[10] This is a complete exposition of the different perspectives on eschatology. Hoekema develops many aspects of biblical eschatology. He interprets the millennium from a symbolic perspective.

---

[6]J. Dwight Pentecost, *Eventos del Porvenir: Estudios de Escatología Bíblica*, 2nd ed. (Miami: Editorial Vida, 1989).

[7]Charles C. Ryrie, *Dispensacionalismo, Hoy*, trans. Evis Carballosa Tarrasa (Barcelona: Publicaciones Portavoz Evangélico, 1974).

[8]Evis L. Carballosa, *Cristo en el Milenio: La Gloria del Rey de Reyes* (Grand Rapids, MI: Publicaciones Portavoz Evangélico, 2007).

[9]George Eldon Ladd, *Vendré Otra Vez*, trans. Edwin Sipowicz (Buenos Aires: Ediciones Certeza, 1973; original: *Jesus Christ and History* [Downers Grove, IL: InterVarsity Press, 1963]).

[10]Anthony A. Hoekema, *La Biblia y el futuro*, trans. Norberto E. Wolf (Grand Rapids, MI: Subcomisión Literatura Cristiana, 1984).

THE INFLUENCE OF THE THEOLOGY OF HOPE IN THE ACADEMIC ENVIRONMENT

Church and Society in Latin America. Starting in the 1960s, three movements created important changes in the development of eschatology in Latin America. The first was Church and Society in Latin America (Iglesia y Sociedad en América Latina), which lasted from 1961 to 1971 and was the first Latin American Protestant movement devoted to social and political realities. Theologians such as José Míguez Bonino, Richard Shaull, and Rubem Alves considered eschatology to be an important subject. In an article written in 1964 titled "Theological Foundations of Social Responsibility of the Church," Argentinian Methodist theologian Míguez Bonino exposits the theme by focusing on the kingdom of God and the lordship of Jesus Christ. About this last reality he notes that for both Luther and Calvin, Jesus Christ is Lord, although for the German Reformer there are two kingdoms. He adds: "Divine sovereignty in the totality of human reality, individually and socially, is also Calvin's point of departure."[11] To speak of sovereignty, moreover, is to speak of the kingdom and its relationship to the church. This leads Míguez Bonino to refer to the communal structure of the church as a prefiguration of the kingdom. Míguez Bonino criticizes the inversion of the biblical notion of the kingdom of God in Christianity through history. He posits that the dominant idea of the kingdom of God is an individualistic hope for immortal and celestial life but not for the transformation of the world.[12]

In those early works of Church and Society in Latin America, Brazilian theologian Rubem Alves is the one who most emphasizes eschatology and the kingdom of God. In his chapter titled "The Social Ministry of the Local Church," Alves interprets what the action of God consists of. From Jesus Christ we understand the action of God, whose purpose is to lead human history to its initial purpose: love and harmony. God acts dynamically in history by exterminating the powers that rebel against his love, and alters the historical order with chaos and disorder. What place has the kingdom of God in this approach? Alves argues that the kingdom of God represents God's sovereignty over all spheres of life and has radical projections on social and political structures.[13]

Another influential theologian in Church and Society in Latin America was Richard Shaull. In his book *Encounter of Revolution*, Shaull describes the presence of the kingdom in the world, affirming that "God broke into history in Jesus Christ and established His kingdom among men." Shaull explains: "God was present in his kingdom, offering new possibilities of life to men and nations. Jesus healed the sick, fed the hungry, opened the eyes of the blind, and brought good news to the poor. . . . These acts were signs of a reality already present. The kingdom of God had come."[14]

Moreover, this kingdom looks toward a final fulfillment. The incarnation is the beginning but not the end of this kingdom. "We now live 'between the times,'" Shaull explains, and "between these two events, and in this 'interim' God is at work. In it, history moves forward toward the

---

[11]José Míguez Bonino, "Fundamentos Teológicos de la Responsabilidad Social de la Iglesia," in *Responsabilidad social del cristiano*, ed. Rodolfo Obermüller et al. (Montevideo: ISAL, 1964), 25.

[12]José Míguez Bonino, *Doing Theology in a Revolutionary Situation* (Philadelphia: Fortress, 1975), 133.

[13]Rubem Alves, "El ministerio social de la iglesia local," in Obermüller, *Responsabilidad social del cristiano*, 57.

[14]Richard Shaull, *Encounter of Revolution* (New York: Association, 1955), 50, 60.

goal which he has determined for it."[15] Church and Society in Latin America offered a new approach to eschatology in relation to the political and social situation in Latin America.

Latin American Theological Fraternity. The topic of the second meeting held in Lima, Peru, by the Latin American Theological Fraternity was the kingdom of God. Emilio Antonio Núñez talked about the nature of the kingdom of God. The Central American theologian distinguished two dimensions of the kingdom of God, vertical and horizontal, and he showed the immanent and transcendent character of the kingdom.[16]

Moreover, Núñez said, "The church reflects the tension between the 'now' and 'not yet' of the kingdom of God and out of the church it is not possible to think its existence. The church is the simultaneous affirmation of the kingdom of God as a present reality and as a future reality."[17] In Núñez's comments we can see a stark contrast with the dispensationalist theologies of earlier generations. In a similar vein, Samuel Escobar elucidates the negative consequences for social and political questions that sometimes accompany dispensational eschatologies:

> A *dispensational* and *premillennial* theology assumes the vision of a fallen world whose sinfulness is reflected in its structures and ways of life. The kingdom of God will burst into the future. Therefore no kingdom of this world can be considered the kingdom of God. The consequence of this belief should be a critical attitude towards the kingdoms of this world and its opposition to the kingdom of God.[18]

Escobar's arguments stand in stark contrast to the vision of dispensational eschatology that was especially prevalent in the Pentecostal world. In this regard, Howard Snyder, citing Melvin Hodges, asserts that Pentecostals generally believe that the remedy for many of the evils of the earth is to expect the second coming of Christ. According to Hodges, the return of Christ will solve all the social and political problems in the world. The only emphasis of mission is the transformation of persons through the proclamation of the gospel.[19]

Liberation theology. Alongside dispensationalist, escapist eschatology on the one hand, and the politically and socially engaged eschatology of Church and Society in Latin America and Latin American Theological Fraternity, a third stream of thought came to affect evangelical eschatology in significant ways. Jürgen Moltmann published his theology of hope as a response to Ernst Bloch's *Das Prinzip Hoffnung*. Moltmann reshapes the notion of eschatology from being merely a "doctrine of a future" to a "doctrine of hope." Moltmann shows the tension between futurist eschatology and present eschatology. He says:

> "The end of all things," it is said, must either lie wholly and entirely in the future, or have wholly and entirely already come, and thus be present. According to this viewpoint, future and present lie along the same temporal line. So it is also easy to find a reconciling solution when distinguishing in temporal terms between that which is "now already" present and that which is "not yet" present.[20]

Moltmann thinks that this is an apparent solution.

---

[15]Shaull, *Encounter of Revolution*, 61.

[16]Emilio Antonio Núñez, "La naturaleza del Reino de Dios," in *El Reino de Dios y América Latina*, ed. C. René Padilla et al. (El Paso, TX: Casa Bautista de Publicaciones, 1975), 32.

[17]Núñez, "La naturaleza del Reino de Dios," in *El Reino de Dios y América Latina*, 46.

[18]Samuel Escobar, "El Reino de Dios, la Escatología y la Ética Social y Política en América Latina," in René Padilla, *El Reino de Dios y América latina*, 138, emphasis original.

[19]Melvin Hodges, "A Pentecostal's View of Mission Strategy," 88, cited in Howard Snyder, *La Comunidad del Rey*, 3rd ed. (Buenos Aires: Kairós, 2014), 71.

[20]Jürgen Moltmann, *The Coming of God: Christian Eschatology*, trans. Margaret Kohl (Minneapolis: Fortress, 1996), 6; see also Ernst Bloch, *Das Prinzip Hoffnung* (Frankfurt: Suhrkam Verlag, 1959).

Moltmann's theology was deeply influential but was not without its critics. Rubem Alves, for example, first argues that his theology is essentially idealistic. "The pattern for the historical movement which Moltmann offers," Alves writes, "is . . . basically platonic. It is eros . . . which creates the *cor inquietum*. And more than that: God becomes the *primum movens*, as with Aristotle, pulling history to its future, but without being involved in history."[21]

Second, Alves criticizes Moltmann because he fails to do justice to the present reality of God. He says that the biblical communities "did not know a God whose essential nature was the future, the primum movens ahead of history. The Old and New Testaments speak about the historical present of God. The pure futuricity of God is a new form of Docetism in which God loses the present dimension and therefore becomes ahistorical."[22]

What is the difference between the theology of Moltmann and liberation theology (*teología de la liberación*)? The central difference consists in the necessity to adopt political instruments to transform the world. José Míguez Bonino says that from his perspective, the imperative for today in the world is revolutionary action for the transformation of the structures and conditions of life in the economic, political, and cultural spheres. For this Argentinean theologian, the transformation of Latin American societies will not come solely though the conversions of individuals, but through the adoption of political

norms according to the paradigm of the kingdom of God. Míguez Bonino likewise argues that the Christian hope has its ultimate horizon in the shalom of the kingdom of God with the mediation of Jesus Christ.[23]

In general, American missionaries have adopted dispensational theology, but the theologians of Iglesia y Sociedad en América Latina, *teología de la liberación* (theology of liberation), and Latin American Theological Fraternity have adopted the theology of hope. While the former is primarily futuristic in its eschatology, the theology of hope emphasizes one present eschatology to transform the world.

THE PRESENCE OF ESCHATOLOGY IN EVANGELICAL SONGS

The presence of eschatological issues in Latin American liturgical expressions deserves a detailed analysis that is not possible here.[24] Nevertheless, we will examine several examples of hymns that might be called classics within evangelical hymnology, as their eschatological emphases and perspectives stand in significant contrast to similar expressions in some songs in today's Latin American evangelical worship.

Consider, to begin with, the well-known hymn "When the Roll Is Called Up Yonder," which discusses the arrival of the final day in the presence of God:[25]

1. When the trumpet of the Lord shall sound,
    and time shall be no more,
   And the morning breaks, eternal, bright and fair;

---

[21]Rubem Alves, *Theology of Human Hope* (New York: World, 1969), 59. Cited in Timothy Gorringe, "Eschatology and Political Radicalism: The Example of Karl Barth and Jürgen Moltmann," in *God Will Be All in All: The Eschatology of Jürgen Moltmann*, ed. Richard Bauckham (Minneapolis: Fortress, 2001), 106.

[22]Alves, *Theology of Human Hope*, 94. Cited in Gorringe, "Eschatology and Political Radicalism," 106.

[23]José Míguez Bonino, *Christians and Marxists: The Mutual Challenge to Revolution* (Grand Rapids, MI: Eerdmans, 1976), 7-8, 111.

[24]Some concepts in this section have been adapted from the chapter "La Escatología en la Teología Latinoamericana" (Eschatology in Latin American Theology), in Alberto F. Roldán, *Escatología: Una Visión Integral desde América Latina* (Buenos Aires: Ediciones Kairós, 2002).

[25]Text and music: James M. Black, from *Himnario Bautista* (Buenos Aires: Casa Bautista de Publicaciones, 1978), 602.

When the saved of earth shall gather over on
the other shore,
And the roll is called up yonder, I'll be there.

Refrain
When the roll is called up yonder,
When the roll is called up yonder,
When the roll is called up yonder,
When the roll is called up yonder, I'll be there.

2. On that bright and cloudless morning when
the dead in Christ shall rise,
And the glory of His resurrection share;
When His chosen ones shall gather to their
home beyond the skies,
And the roll is called up yonder, I'll be there.
[*Refrain*]

The emphasis of this hymn lies on the final judgment, and the author's poetry seems to be inspired by Revelation 20:11-15. The hymn says that "time shall be no more" but makes no reference to an intermediate period such as the millennium on earth, before consummation. Although it speaks of "the saved of earth," which might be a reference to a corporate salvation, the whole emphasis is on the individual, as the refrain repeats "I'll be there." The phrase "home beyond the skies" seems to ignore the biblical perspective of a new earth. It does not appear on the horizon. As for the influence of this eschatological perspective on the present of Christians, it is reduced to "Let us labor for the Master"—not in terms of transforming the concrete, social world, but simply in talking about "His wondrous love and care."

We can also highlight the words of a hymn widely distributed in Central and South America, written by Felicia and Mariano Beltran and called "How Glorious Will Be That Great Morning":[26]

1. O how glorious will be that great morning
When Christ Jesus will return to be adored.
When the nations as sisters and as brothers
Join to welcome the coming of the Lord.

Refrain
For the brilliance of that dawn
Will outshine the brightest sun.
All its heat and light give way
To God's never-ending day.
No more weeping will remain,
No more grief and no more pain.
For at last Jesus Christ, the Lamb of heaven
'Throned in mercy, forevermore will reign!

2. How we wait for that great glorious morning
When the God of love descends for us to greet;
When the fragrance of Christ will bathe our senses
In the rose light of dawn so rich and sweet.
[*Refrain*]

Written within the same conceptual framework of the classic hymns already mentioned, this Central American poetry returns to the themes of heaven, the heavenly home, and the overcoming of anguish, crying, and pain in a poetic construction saturated with apocalyptic symbols. It affirms that in that heavenly place "the fragrance of Christ will bathe our senses / In the rose light of dawn so rich and sweet." Although all of that is true, it leaves parishioners with the question of how to solve the problems of the here and now, where everything is not rosy. In other words, how can this future perspective help us to change the present state of things?

---

[26]It appears as no. 549 of the hymnal *Celebremos Su Gloria* (*Let Us Celebrate His Glory*). The music of this hymn is by an unknown author, but with arrangements by Roberto Savage, copyright 1953, updated in 1981. The hymn as quoted above has been edited by professors of the Central American Theological Seminary of Guatemala and is dedicated, among others, to Guatemalan hymnologist Alfredo Colom Maldonado (1904–1971). Data provided by Professor Pablo Sosa of the Instituto Superior Evangelico de Estudios Teologicos. Translated into English by Mary Louise Bringle.

A very brief song, still sung in Pentecostal churches and, with ecclesiastical globalization, in many other renewal and neo-Pentecostal churches, is "I'm Going with Him." It says:

> Christ is coming, signs are there;
> Saved souls, He comes to seek.
> Those who slept will stay;
> Those who veiled, will go with Him.
> I go with Him, [3×]
> I do not stay
> I go with Him.

In simple language, the author emphasizes what we have already seen in the classic eschatological hymns: the imminence of the already, with a striking absence of the not yet, and the fact that the signs have already been fulfilled to know that this is true. Christ comes to seek "saved souls," perhaps reflecting an implicit adoption of Greek dualism and the immortality of the soul, to the detriment of the resurrection of the body. With the expression "those who slept will stay," the song seems to adopt the strange hypothesis of a partial rapture: when Christ returns, only those who are watching will be raptured. The ending emphasizes an individualistic profile: "I do not stay, I go with Him."

Finally, it is opportune to cite a different type of liturgical eschatology, one perhaps less pervasive than these others but nevertheless present, especially in the so-called historical churches. As an illustration, we mention "We Have Hope," a hymn written by Argentine Methodist bishop Federico J. Pagura:[27]

> Because He entered into the world and into history,
> Because He broke the silence and the agony;
> Because He filled the earth with His glory,
> Because He was light in our cold night;

> Because He was born in a dark crib,
> Because He lived sowing love and life;
> Because He broke the hard hearts
> And lifted the despondent souls.

> *Refrain*
> That's why today we have hope;
> That's why today we struggle with striving;
> That's why today we look with confidence.
> The future, in this land of mine.
> That's why today we have hope;
> That's why we strive with obstinacy;
> That's why today we look with confidence,
> To the future.
> Because He attacked ambitious merchants
> And denounced wickedness and hypocrisy;
> Because He exalted the children and the women,
> And rejected those who were proud . . .
> Because a dawn saw His great victory
> Over death, fear, lies,
> Nothing can stop His story,
> Nor the coming of His eternal Kingdom.
> [*Refrain*]

The mere reading of the words gives us the clear feeling that we are in the presence of a Christology and eschatology different from those exposed in the previous cases. The central theme is hope and, more precisely, the *why* of hope. It is a hope that is nourished and invigorated by the one who "entered into the world and into history." It summarizes the life of Jesus of Nazareth, his life of love and justice, his choice for the poor and the "downcast soul," and, as a counterpart, his criticism and denunciation of the "ambitious merchants" for their "wickedness and hypocrisy." Where does hope come from? It comes from both the history of Jesus and the eschatological future evident in the resurrection as a proleptic eschatological event ("a dawn saw

[27]The music is by Uruguayan composer Homero R. Perera and has a tango rhythm. Here the words are taken from *Cancionero Abierto* (*Open Hymnal*) (Buenos Aires: ISEDET, 1986), 66.

His great victory over death") and in the blunt affirmation "Nothing can stop His story, nor the coming of His eternal Kingdom." Perhaps the refrain provides the hermeneutic key to understanding this eschatology: We look forward to "the future, in this land of mine." The future of the triumph of Jesus Christ and the kingdom of God must be translated into "this earth," where we await the final consummation. It is, in short, the proposal of a dynamic hope, one that does not resign itself to failure but leads us to "strive with obstinacy."

Immersed in the world of image and sound, and abstracted by the force of music and participatory and emotional worship in churches—aspects that are not negative themselves—we run the risk of not taking into account what is sung, that is, the theological content of the songs. There are no innocent liturgies, hymnologies, or aseptic songs. All songs respond to theological positions and doctrinal emphases, consciously or unconsciously assumed. The samples above have shown that, except in very honorable exceptions, there is a marked celestial and transcendent tendency in classic hymnology and evangelical songs. There is, in general, an assumption of the theory of the rapture of the church and an absence of hope for the world as a dynamic factor in the present. In summary, the eschatology expressed in Latin American liturgy is, in general, dualistic and spiritualistic, or has been directly replaced by other themes that have been instilled in the churches. It should be noted that this brief analysis of classic hymns and more current songs is not done to the detriment of the spiritual blessing and strength they may have provided in the past or continue to offer in the present. It is only a theological analysis of their content. What, then, would be an alternative

eschatology of both the models of systematic eschatology and those expressed in the Latin American cult? An integral eschatology would offer an alternative in this regard.

Conclusion

The Nicene Creed affirms that God's "kingdom shall have no end," and "we look for the resurrection of the dead, and the life of the world to come." The question is, how are these affirmations present in the different schools of eschatology in Latin America? In classic dispensationalism, the kingdom is suspect because Israel rejected the gospel of the kingdom announced by Jesus Christ. All the dimensions of the kingdom of God are thus translated to the future: the millennium and the eternal kingdom. Progressive dispensationalism affirms the presence of the kingdom in the world now, but it is in the theologies of Church and Society in Latin America, the Latin American Theological Fraternity, and liberation theology that we have the clearest, most systematic and most solid reflection on the kingdom of God. Under the clear influence of the theology of hope, Latin American theologians emphasize that it is necessary to transform the futuristic eschatology to an eschatology engaged with the here and now. The resurrection and the eternal life of the world to come must transform the present situations of injustice, poverty, and marginalization into justice, human dignity, and solidarity. This is basically the perspective that the Nicene Creed offers to Latin American theologies. The affirmation "whose kingdom shall have no end" is present in the words of Federico Pagura: "Nothing can stop His story / Nor the coming of His eternal Kingdom."

FURTHER READING

Hendriksen, William. *La Biblia, el más allá y el fin del mundo*. Grand Rapids, MI: Libros Desafío, 1998.

Ladd, George E. *El Apocalipsis de Juan*. Miami: Caribe, 1978.

Míguez Bonino, José. *Militancia política y ética cristiana*. Buenos Aires: Ediciones La Aurora, 2013.

Padilla, C. René, ed. *De la marginación al compromiso: Los evangélicos y la política en América Latina*. Buenos Aires: FTL, 1991.

Reyes-Mate, José-A. Zamora, ed. *Nuevas teologías políticas: Pablo de Tarso en la construcción de Occidente*. Barcelona: Anthropos, 2006.

Roldán, Alberto F. *Escatología: ¿Ciencia ficción o Reino de Dios?* 2nd ed. Buenos Aires: Kairós, 2019.

———. *Reino, política y misión*. Lima: Ediciones Puma, 2011.

Stam, Juan. *Apocalipsis*. 3 vols. Buenos Aires: Ediciones Kairós, 2003–2009.

45

THE KINGDOM OF GOD

LATIN AMERICAN BIBLICAL REFLECTIONS ON ESCHATOLOGY

Nelson R. Morales Fredes

THIS CHAPTER EXPLORES the eschatological concept of the kingdom of God from a Latin American perspective. The first section analyzes the eschatological perspectives of the Nicene Creed. A second section explores the relationship between God's kingdom and the doctrine of the church according to four important Latin American theological viewpoints (traditional Catholicism, liberation theology, the Latin American Theological Fraternity, and dispensationalism) and the way that each of these systems expresses the relationship between kingdom and church in its use of Mark 1:14-15. The study concludes with a consideration of the author's personal approach to the same passage.

INTRODUCTION

The 1970s and 1980s were tumultuous years in Latin America. In the midst of military dictatorships, Christians also made their presence

known. In the circles where I grew up, there was a perception that Jesus' second coming was just around the corner. Prophecy conferences about the end times were common. We were taught to evangelize our neighborhoods in order to accelerate the coming of the millennial kingdom of Jesus. In other circles, ubiquitous poverty and systemic injustice were the concerns. How could we preach salvation without confronting oppressive systems? The kingdom of God must be established here and now in order to eradicate oppression. Many thought that the Nicaraguan political model of liberation was the example to follow.[1] In Europe and the United States, the topic of the kingdom of God was also under discussion.[2] However, the concerns were totally different. Thus, the answers were different.[3]

Today, these distinct trends are still present in Latin America. After a dialogue with the Nicene-Constantinopolitan Creed regarding the present

---

[1] In 1979, the Sandinist movement managed to defeat the army and take control of the country. Liberation theologians, both Catholic and Protestant, interpreted these events as the establishment of the kingdom of God in Nicaragua. Antonio González, "Reinado de Dios y signos de los tiempos," *Encuentro* (2004): 23-34; Ernesto Cardenal Martínez, *La revolución perdida* (Managua: Anamá, 2013), 390-91.

[2] See Christopher W. Morgan and Robert A. Peterson, eds., *The Kingdom of God* (Wheaton, IL: Crossway, 2012); Wendell Willis, ed., *The Kingdom of God in 20th-Century Interpretation* (Peabody, MA: Hendrickson, 1987).

[3] See a detailed bibliography on the issue in Lesław Daniel Chrupcała, *The Kingdom of God: A Bibliography of 20th Century Research* (Jerusalem: Franciscan, 2007); Lesław Daniel Chrupcała, "The Kingdom of God: A Bibliography of 20th Century Research. Update," www.academia.edu/41346521/The_Kingdom_of_God_A_Bibliography_of_20th_Century_Research._Update.

aspect of the kingdom of God, this chapter describes two external influences on Latin American thinking regarding the kingdom of God: traditional Catholicism and dispensationalism. It also presents two local approaches to the issue of the kingdom of God: liberation theology and that of the Latin American Theological Fraternity. It will be apparent that the way the kingdom of God is conceived affects one's ecclesiology. Mark 1:14-15 is recurrently used in all of these approaches. Consequently, after a brief description of the thoughts of each group, an example of their interpretation of this passage is presented. After describing the main interpretive trends in Latin America, I will briefly develop my own contextual reading of the same passage.

DIALOGUE WITH THE NICENE-CONSTANTINOPOLITAN CREED

Given the importance of the Nicene-Constantinopolitan Creed in church history, it is worthwhile to discuss briefly what it contributes to our topic.[4] As it turns out, the kingdom of God seems to have been a secondary issue in the elaboration of the creed. At least, that is the impression received at the first reading. The eschatological aspects in the Nicene-Constantinopolitan creed are mainly christological:

> I believe in one Lord Jesus Christ . . . who for us men, and for our salvation, came down from heaven, and was incarnate by the Holy Ghost of the Virgin Mary, and was made man; he was crucified for us under Pontius Pilate, and suffered, and was buried, and the third day he rose again, according to the Scriptures, and ascended into heaven, and sitteth on the right hand of the Father; from thence he shall come again, with

> glory, to judge the quick and the dead; whose kingdom shall have no end.[5]

The Nicene-Constantinopolitan Creed focuses more on the "not yet" of the kingdom. In fact, the phrase "whose kingdom shall have no end" is located after mention of the judgment of the living and the dead. God the Father is explicitly presented as Creator of heaven and earth, not as King, although his kingship is implied in the imagery of the throne: "sitteth on the right hand of [God]." Except for this phrase, there is no mention of the current presence of Jesus' kingdom. The Holy Spirit is presented as Lord and Life-Giver who spoke through the prophets. There is no explicit mention of his empowering presence in believers. Finally, there is no explicit relationship between the "holy catholic and apostolic church" and Jesus' kingdom.

On the other hand, the "already" aspect of the kingdom could be derived from the creed. In the fullness of time, Jesus the Messiah came to bring us salvation. Today, he shares God's throne. He is seated at the right hand of the Father. His kingdom will have no end. With his first coming, he inaugurated this kingdom. His ministry of salvation permitted us to enter this kingdom and be his disciples through our faith in him. The Holy Spirit is the Life-Giver of humanity.

THE KINGDOM OF GOD IN LATIN AMERICAN ESCHATOLOGY

With this consideration of the Nicene-Constantinopolitan Creed in the background, we will now consider ways that the relationship between the church and the kingdom of God has been addressed within four interpretive frameworks that have strongly influenced Latin American

---

[4]This creed was formulated the first time in Nicaea in AD 325 and later was expanded in Constantinople in 381.
[5]Nicene Creed, as altered in 381, trans. Phillip Schaff, "English Versions of the Nicene Creed," Wikipedia, https://en.wikipedia.org/wiki/English_versions_of_the_Nicene_Creed, accessed February 13, 2019.

eschatology: traditional Catholicism, liberation theology, the Latin American Theological Fraternity, and dispensationalism. We will pay particular attention to the way that each of these views has interpreted Mark 1:14-15. After that, I will present my own reflection on the same passage.

Traditional Catholicism. Latin American Catholic eschatology develops along two fronts, representing traditional and more progressive theological concerns. The mainline Catholic front comes from Europe, through the direction of the doctrine of the church.[6] The second and more influential front has developed locally, through the writings of liberation theologians. There is some overlap, but there are also strong differences. In both cases, God's kingdom is the central axis. This section presents the traditional view, and the next develops the concepts as presented in liberation theology.

Gabino Uribarri presents a good summary of the notable change in Catholic eschatology in the last century.[7] From the beginning of the twentieth century until the 1950s, Catholic eschatology had "a marked neo-scholastic orientation."[8] There was scarce dialogue with prominent topics in the Protestant discussions such as hope and the kingdom of God reflected in the consequent eschatology of Albert Schweitzer or the realized eschatology of C. H. Dodd. During the years prior to the Second Vatican Council, there was growing consciousness about these themes of Protestant concern, such as the focus on life here and now instead of on the afterlife, the hermeneutic of eschatological statements in the Bible, an eschatology pertinent to the world and its problems, and the historical dimension of the kingdom of God. In particular, Catholic eschatology began to include the role of history and the world and not just the hereafter. Studies in literature written during the Second Temple period, in particular literature that related to the end of times, guided a revision of the Catholic hermeneutics of the *eschata*, the last things.[9] After the Second Vatican Council, the topic of God's kingdom became central for Catholic eschatology. Catholic theologians explored the eschatological tensions in the study of the historical Jesus and the Christ of the faith, "their differences, their relationships, and their place in the life of the faith of the church."[10] There was reflection about hope centered in the kingdom. This hope had a historical aspect, without neglecting the hope in the resurrection. Oscar Cullman's expression became representative of the tension between the "already and the not yet" of the presence and implications of the kingdom. The church is at the service of the kingdom of God, even though the difference between the two is not always crystal clear in Catholic literature.[11]

---

[6]The writings of popes, councils, catechisms, and other official documents constitute the doctrine of the Catholic Church.

[7]Gabino Uríbarri Bilbao, "La escatología cristiana en los albores del siglo XXI," *Estudios eclesiásticos* 79, no. 308 (2004): 3-28.

[8]During the neo-scholastic era of Catholic thought in the second half of the nineteenth century, the eschatological topics, called the "newests" (*novísimos* in Spanish), were death, judgment, hell, and glory. There was no discussion on the Christian hope and its relationship with the kingdom of God. During the first fifty years of the twentieth century, the Catholic discussion on eschatology revolved around these topics instead of around the kingdom of God and the related issues discussed widely in Protestant circles.

[9]Uríbarri Bilbao, "La escatología cristiana en los albores del siglo XXI," 11-15.

[10]Uríbarri Bilbao, "La escatología cristiana en los albores del siglo XXI," 16. In this and the following citations, the translations from Spanish to English are my own. With the quest for the historical Jesus, some scholars made a marked distinction between the man of Galilee behind the Gospels and the one drawn by the faith of the first Christians. That distinction was strong during those years after the Second Vatican Council—for example, in the works of authors associated with the Jesus Seminar. Today, many scholars recognize a closer relationship between the so-called historical Jesus and the Christ of the faith—for example, N. T. Wright, Craig Blomberg, and John P. Meier. The Gospels are a truthful testimony of the real Jesus. The Christ of the faith is the same Jesus of Nazareth.

[11]Uríbarri Bilbao, "La escatología cristiana en los albores del siglo XXI," 15-17. Uríbarri points out that the church serves the kingdom

A passage often mentioned regarding God's kingdom is Mark 1:14-15. In Mark's account of the beginning of Christ's ministry, Jesus announces the nearness of God's kingdom. By using these verses to support the foundation of the church, the Dogmatic Constitution on the Catholic Church, *Lumen Gentium*, seems to equate the kingdom of God with the church. The document asserts that even though this kingdom begins to manifest itself through the words, deeds, and presence of Christ, the church constitutes "the initial budding forth of that Kingdom."[12] Later, in 1979, the documents of the Third Latin American Episcopal Congress made this connection between the kingdom and church. Since then, the work and mission of the church have been interpreted as the mission of the kingdom. The Catholic Church is the sign, the visible aspect, of the kingdom. Its mission is to an-

nounce and establish the kingdom among all people.[13] The Catholic Catechism of 1992 uses the same verses of Mark to explain the foundation of the church.[14] Thus, in Mark 1:14-15, Jesus announces the kingdom of God and the beginning of his church at the same time. The church's mission and ministry is the mission of the kingdom. The church is the visible aspect of this kingdom.

Liberation theology. If the topic of the kingdom of God is important for the eschatology of traditional Catholicism, for liberation theology it is the theological center around which all other doctrines revolve.[15] The concept of the kingdom of God is viewed as a utopia, a path to walk in.[16] Liberation theology emphasizes the presence of this kingdom as an answer for those living in oppression and poverty. In the words of John Fuellenbach,

of God but is not equal to it. He quotes as a reference *Lumen Gentium* §5. But, as the next paragraph shows, the difference between the church and kingdom in that document is not so clear. The same happens with the discussion of the issue in *The Eschatological Character of the Church: Kingdom and Church in Select Themes of Ecclesiology* (1984), published by the Congregation for the Doctrine of the Faith, www.vatican.va/roman_curia/congregations/cfaith/cti_documents/rc_cti_1984_ecclesiologia_sp.html.

[12]Catholic Church, *"Lumen Gentium*: Dogmatic Constitution on the Church," in *Vatican II Documents* (Vatican City: Libreria Editrice Vaticana, 2011), §5.

[13]Conferencia Episcopal Latinoamericana, "La evangelización en el presente y en el futuro de América Latina," in *Documentos de Puebla: III Conferencia General del Episcopado Latinoamericano*, ed. Conferencia Episcopal Latinoamericana (Bogotá: Biblioteca Electronica Cristiana, 2008), §226-31. It will be apparent in the next section that the conclusions of the Third Latin American Episcopal Council were more in line with the thoughts of liberation theology regarding the role of the church as an agent of the kingdom than with the doctrine of the church represented by the thought of John Paul II and Benedict XVI.

[14]Catholic Church, *Catechism of the Catholic Church* (Washington, DC: United States Catholic Conference, 2000), §541. The catechism adds that the church is "the Kingdom of Christ already present in mystery . . . on earth, it constitutes the seed and the beginning of this Kingdom" (§669). Pope John Paul II made the same point in his inaugural discourse at the Latin American Episcopal Conference celebrated in Puebla, Mexico, in 1979, against the more political view of the kingdom by the liberation-theology wing of the Latin American Church. Juan Pablo II, "Discurso Inaugural pronunciado en el Seminario Palafoxiano de Puebla de los Ángeles, México," in *Documentos de Puebla: III Conferencia General del Episcopado Latinoamericano*, ed. Conferencia Episcopal Latinoamericana (Bogotá: Biblioteca Electrónica Cristiana, 2008), §1.8.

[15]Jon Sobrino, "La centralidad del 'Reino de Dios' en la Teología de la Liberación," *Revista Latinoamericana de Teología* 3, no. 9 (1986): 247-81; Sobrino, "La centralidad del reino de Dios anunciado por Jesús," *Revista Latinoamericana de Teología* 23, no. 68 (2006): 135-60. See also Juan José Tamayo-Acosta, *Para comprender la escatología cristiana* (Navarra, Spain: Verbo Divino, 2008), 120-86. These thoughts are also present among Protestant theologians. See, for example, Mortimer Arias, "The Kingdom of God," *Westminster Theological Journal* 23 (1988): 33-45; José Míguez Bonino, "El reino de Dios y la historia: Reflexiones para una discusión del tema," in *El reino de Dios en América Latina*, ed. C. René Padilla (El Paso, TX: Casa Bautista de Publicaciones, 1975), 75-95; Elsa Tamez, "Poverty, the Poor, and the Option for the Poor: A Biblical Perspective," in *Option for the Poor in Christian Theology* (Notre Dame, IN: University of Notre Dame Press, 2007), 41-54. Alberto Roldán focuses on this group of Protestant theologians in his chapter on Latin American eschatology in the present work. He highlights the thought of authors such as José Míguez Bonino, Richard Shaull, and Rubem Alves.

[16]See, for example, Ignacio Ellacuría and Jon Sobrino, *Conceptos fundamentales de la teología de la liberación*, vol. 2 of *Mysterium Liberationis* (San Salvador: UCA Editores, 1991); Sobrino, "La centralidad del 'Reino de Dios' en la Teología de la Liberación," 247-81; Jon Sobrino, *Jesucristo liberador* (San Salvador: UCA, 1991), 121-232; Jules A. Martínez-Olivieri, *A Visible Witness: Christology, Liberation, and Participation*, Emerging Scholars (Minneapolis: Fortress, 2016), 55-62.

"The intention of this theology is to recover the historical dimension of God's message and to move that message away from all abstract universalism so that the biblical message may be more responsive to the world of oppression and its social structures."[17] In this sense, their concept of the kingdom of God is linked to the historical reality.[18] The identification with the poor and oppressed in their time of need is a hallmark of true discipleship. In that vein, theological reflection is, according to Martínez-Olivieri, "a second act that presupposes a social location and the commitment resulting from an encounter with Jesus in the lives of the poor."[19] The kingdom of God is present in history, so the church is an agent of the kingdom that brings and advances the presence of the kingdom by confronting oppression and liberating the poor. The fact is that the poor are the primary recipients of the kingdom. For that reason, the kingdom of God serves as the horizon where the church should focus its identity and mission.[20] As Jon Sobrino emphasizes, "[the kingdom] enjoins that the mission of the Church be, like Jesus' own mission, good news to the poor, evangelism and prophetic denunciation, and the proclamation of the Word and historical fulfillment of Liberation. In this way, the church can be today a 'sacrament of salvation.'"[21]

Gustavo Gutiérrez explains Mark 1:14-15 from the perspective of liberation theology. His explanation illustrates the centrality of the theme of the kingdom of God in the eschatology of liberation theology. Furthermore, this explanation reveals the close connection between liberation theology's concept of the kingdom of God and its ecclesiology. He introduces his analysis by highlighting the following: Mark anticipates that Jesus will face "resistance of the powerful of his time." He anticipates this by introducing Jesus' ministry just after John's incarceration. Gutiérrez connects Galilee with the ministry from the periphery, the borders. In Galilee, Jesus "recruits his closest disciples." "In the history that Jesus makes his own, the proclamation of the Kingdom is heard from the lips of those who are not listened to and who struggle for life and for recognition as human beings: the lips of the poor and the marginalized." The proclamation announces the kairos of God, "a propitious moment, a favorable day, a time when the Lord becomes present and manifests himself." The kingdom of God has come. God reveals himself in a special way in human history; his kingdom "is not something purely interior that occurs in the depths of our souls." This kingdom inaugurated by Jesus "is present today in the person of Jesus the Messiah." It is a dynamic reality, Gutiérrez comments, that gives to history its final meaning. "It implies a present development and has not yet attained to its full form."[22]

Jesus' announcement finishes with an invitation to repent and believe the gospel (Mk 1:15).

---

[17]John Fuellenbach, "The Kingdom of God in Latin American Liberation Theology," *Studia Missionalia* 46 (1997): 268.

[18]Jon Sobrino emphasizes that "the theology reformulates and corrects the interpretation of the eschatological reserve as purely relativizing, and insists in that in history, it should be evident that truly it is God who reigns. And because the Kingdom is liberator, that kingship should be noticeable in all the levels in which slavery is present: physical, spiritual, personal, and social slavery." Sobrino, *Jesucristo liberador*, 223.

[19]Martínez-Olivieri, *Visible Witness*, 61.

[20]Ignacio Ellacuría presents a clear argument for this thesis in *Conversión de la Iglesia al Reino de Dios: Para anunciarlo y realizarlo en la historia*, Presencia Teológica 18 (Santander, Spain: Sal Terrae, 1984).

[21]Sobrino, "La centralidad del 'Reino de Dios' en la Teología de la Liberación," 277.

[22]Gustavo Gutiérrez, "Mark 1:14-15," *Review and Expositor* 88 (1991): 427-31.

This is an invitation to enter the kingdom. It implies demands for certain kinds of behavior. Gutiérrez clarifies,

> The acceptance finds expression both in thanksgiving to God and in deeds done for our brothers and sisters. It is in this dialectic that the meaning of the Kingdom emerges. The Kingdom requires us to change our present reality, reject the abuses of the powerful, and establish relationships that are fraternal and just. When we behave thus, we are accepting the gift of the Lord's presence.[23]

At the same time, accepting the invitation is to reject the unjust world that oppresses the poor. It is to denounce the antikingdom. It is to proclaim liberation to the captives and good news to the poor (Lk 4:18-19). This example clearly illustrates the centrality of the theme of the kingdom of God in liberation theology's eschatology. This kingdom is not an abstract idea; it is a concrete expression of God's sovereignty in the real world, which brings liberation to the oppressed.

Latin American Theological Fraternity. The Latin American Theological Fraternity (Fraternidad Teológica Latinoamericana) sees the kingdom of God as a central and unifying theme for eschatology.[24] Jesus introduces the kingdom with his person and ministry. "He is the Messiah in whom the Kingdom of God becomes a present reality. The church is the community that emerges as a result of his royal power."[25] Today, the kingdom of God continues acting in history through the work of the Holy Spirit. In this way, for the Latin American Theological Fraternity, the triad kingdom of God, Holy Spirit, and church are intimately related. René Padilla points out, "As a community of the Kingdom, the church is called to be, through the power of the Spirit, a new humanity in which love and justice, reconciliation and peace, solidarity and forgiveness, new attitudes and new relations take form. In other words, all of what signals the quality of life of the Kingdom [takes form] in the heart of history."[26] As a community of the kingdom, the church imitates its Lord in a holistic mission to the world.[27] "The historical mediation of the Kingdom is not a program but a community that lives by the power of the Spirit."[28] This community of the kingdom performs its mission nurtured by the hope of the fulfillment of the kingdom when Jesus comes again.[29] In this way, the eschatology of the Latin American Theological Fraternity presents a more holistic view of the kingdom of God, one that takes into

---

[23]Gutiérrez, "Mark 1:14-15," 430.

[24]Juan Stam highlights that "the central theme and unifier of eschatology is the Kingdom of God. This theme dominates the Synoptic Gospels; in the Pauline epistles, it takes the form of the lordship of Christ, and Revelation emphatically reaffirms it with the triumph of 'the King of kings and the Lord of lords.'" Juan Stam, *Escatología bíblica y misión de la iglesia: Hasta el fin del tiempo y los fines de la tierra* (San José: Semilla, 1999), 16. See also Valdir R. Steuernagel, "Forty-Five Years of the FTL and Its Biblical Theology: A Bit of Theology Along the Way . . . and Mary," *Journal of Latin American Theology* 11, no. 2 (2016): 15-34; J. Daniel Salinas, *Taking up the Mantle: Latin American Evangelical Theology in the 20th Century*, Global Perspectives (Carlisle, UK: Langham Global Library, 2017), 97-107.

[25]C. René Padilla, "La misión de la iglesia a la luz del reino de Dios," in *Al servicio del Reino en América Latina: Un compendio sobre la misión integral de la iglesia cristiana en Latinoamérica*, ed. Valdir R. Steuernagel (San José: Visión Mundial, 1991), 21.

[26]C. René Padilla, "El Reino de Dios y la historia en la teología latinoamericana," *Cuadernos deteología* 7 (1985): 11.

[27]The holistic proclamation to all creation was the central topic of the Third Latin American Congress of Evangelization in Quito, 1992. Fraternidad Teológica Latinoamericana, ed., *CLADE III: Tercer congreso latinoamericano de evangelización, Quito 1992; Todo el evangelio para todos los pueblos desde América Latina* (Buenos Aires: Fraternidad Teológica Latinoamericana, 1993).

[28]René Padilla points out that this way of seeing the kingdom and the church avoids regarding both concepts as synonyms, and as a result having an ecclesiocentric vision of the Christian mission. At the same time, it also avoids the error of separating the church and the kingdom, turning the latter into a mere "historical project" without a concrete reality. Padilla, "El Reino de Dios," 12.

[29]See, for example, C. René Padilla, *Mission Between the Times: Essays on the Kingdom*, 2nd ed. (Carlisle, UK: Langham Monographs, 2010).

account the work of both the Spirit and the church. Not forgetting the future aspect of this kingdom, it considers its concrete presence in the world today.

A good example of this eschatology is the work of René Padilla. In his article "El reino de Dios y la historia en la teología latinoamericana" ("The Kingdom of God and History in Latin American Theology"), Padilla deals with Mark 1:14-15. He explains that the kingdom of God is not just information about a future event but also a new order inaugurated by Jesus. God's dynamic power is visible through the signs Jesus does. These signs point to Jesus as the Messiah. This new reality has entered the course of history and affects "the human life not only morally and spiritually but also physically, psychologically, economically, socially, and politically."[30]

In this context, Padilla remarks, Jesus presents his message "the time is fulfilled, and the Kingdom of God is at hand; repent and believe in the gospel" (Mk 1:15, Padilla's translation). Paraphrasing Luke 7:22, Padilla insists that this message is not just a verbal message, separated from the signals that corroborate it; this message is "good news regarding something that can be heard and seen." He derives five implications from Jesus' message: (1) it is about a historical fact that affects human life in all its dimensions; (2) it is of public interest—it has to do with all human history; (3) it is linked to the Old Testament prophecies; the *malkut Yhwh* (the kingdom of God) becomes a present reality; (4) it calls for repentance and faith; and (5) it results in the creation of a new community that recognizes Jesus as the Messiah and follows him.[31] In *Mission Between the Times*, using the same passage, Padilla notes four facts with regard to the gospel: (1) "the gospel proclamation itself marks the kairos, the time assigned by God for the fulfillment of his purpose"; (2) "The content of the gospel is not a new theology or a new teaching about God but an event . . . the coming of the Kingdom"; (3) "The reference to both the Kingdom of God and the gospel points to Isaiah 52:7. . . . Jesus sees himself as the herald of a new age in which Isaiah's message—'Your God reigns'—is fulfilled"; and (4) "the proclamation of the gospel is inseparable from a call to repentance and faith."[32]

At this point, some similarities and differences between liberation theology's and the Latin American Theological Fraternity's eschatology appear. The centrality of the kingdom of God in the eschatology of both currents of thought is clear. Furthermore, both of them share the view of a concrete presence of the kingdom in the real world of the needy. Perhaps the main difference is the role of the Holy Spirit. It is an important component in the Latin American Theological Fraternity's eschatology, but is almost absent in liberation theology's. In the same vein, the Latin American Theological Fraternity's approach is more holistic. It does not limit the current activity of the kingdom of God to just a physical/economical liberation; it includes also the proclamation of the gospel of salvation and the spiritual needs of the people.

Dispensational evangelicalism. An important segment of evangelicalism in Latin America considers itself to be dispensational. Alberto Roldán aptly summarizes the main theological distinctives of this system in his chapter on Latin American eschatology in the present book. Classic

---

[30]Padilla, "El Reino de Dios," 10-11.
[31]Padilla, "El Reino de Dios," 11.
[32]Padilla, *Mission Between the Times*, 87-88.

and revised dispensationalism is present mainly among Pentecostals and some other denominations, such as the Central American Mission and the Southern Baptists.[33] In their perspective, the kingdom of God tends to be circumscribed to a soteriological dimension (in the present) or is equal to the millennial/Davidic kingdom (in the future).[34] The kingdom has a present component, defined as a rule or dominion.[35] However, even though today Jesus is King, he does not rule as a king. Jesus' kingdom is still future; it will begin with his second coming. During his earthly ministry, Jesus offered the kingdom; however, since Israel rejected it, the kingdom was postponed.[36] The church is not the kingdom but is included in it; it is the agent of the present form of the kingdom.[37] In this scenario, the mission of the church is mainly to preach the gospel in order to hasten the coming of the kingdom.[38] Eschatology in these circles tends to focus on future events, on the not-yet of the kingdom. There are some aspects of the present form of the kingdom, but usually they revolve around soteriology, as the following example illustrates.

Samuel Pérez Millos has written several commentaries from the dispensational perspective in the series Comentario Exegético al Texto Griego del Nuevo Testamento. Even though this author is a Spaniard, his works are influential in Latin America. In his discussion on Mark 1:14-15, Pérez Millos points out that "the gospel of God" is the message of salvation as a free gift from God. It proclaims to humankind the plan of salvation established from eternity. He defines "kingdom of God" as "the sphere of God's government where God reigns as sovereign and is voluntarily obeyed." It is a spiritual government of God over regenerated people in the present time. "The righteousness of the Kingdom is not external and ceremonial, but internal, from the heart."[39] Pérez Millos argues that in the phrase "the kingdom of God is near," Jesus is announcing the present aspect of the kingdom of God. In Jesus the Savior, the kingdom of God has come near to humanity.[40] Since this kingdom is eternal, it is present and eschatological at the same time. Those who accept the message of salvation enter the spiritual kingdom. Jesus'

---

[33]Currently, there are almost no influential Latin American theologians writing in these circles. The influence is mainly from North American works translated into Spanish. For a description of dispensational evangelicalism in Latin America, see Óscar A. Campos R., "The Mission of the Church and Kingdom of God in Latin America" (PhD diss., Dallas Theological Seminary, 2000), 95-147.

[34]Church theologians Guy Duffield and Nathaniel Van Cleave comment regarding the present form of the kingdom of God: "The present (soteriological) Kingdom of Christ is spiritual and invisible, for it consists of the kingship, power and authority of Jesus as Savior and Destroyer of Satan." The future form of this kingdom is called "eschatological." Guy P. Duffield and Nathaniel M. Van Cleave, *Fundamentos de Teología Pentecostal* (San Dimas: Foursquare Media, 2006), 482. (Original: Guy P. Duffield and Nathaniel M. Van Cleave, *Foundations of Pentecostal Theology* [Los Angeles: LIFE Bible College, 1983], 445.)

[35]Emilio A. Núñez, "La naturaleza del reino de Dios" (paper presented at the II Consulta de la Fraternidad Teológica Latinoamericana, Lima, Perú, December 11-19, 1972), 1-25.

[36]The words of Charles Ryrie have been very influential: "Because the King was rejected, the messianic, Davidic Kingdom was (from a human viewpoint) postponed. Though He never ceases to be King and, of course, is King today as always, Christ is never designated as King of the church. . . . Though Christ is a King today, He does not rule as King. This awaits His second coming. Then the Davidic Kingdom will be realized (Matt. 25:31; Rev. 19:15; 20). Then the Priest will sit on His throne, bringing to this earth the long-awaited Golden Age (Ps. 110)." Charles Caldwell Ryrie, *Basic Theology: A Popular Systemic Guide to Understanding Biblical Truth* (Chicago: Moody, 1999), 298.

[37]Emilio A. Núñez, *Hacia una misionología evangélica latinoamericana* (Santa Fe: Comibam, 1997), 124.

[38]See, for example, Campos R., "Mission of the Church," 127-44.

[39]Samuel Pérez Millos, *Marcos*, Comentario Exegético al Texto Griego del Nuevo Testamento (Barcelona: Clie, 2014), 128-29, 132-33.

[40]For John D. Grassmick, Jesus' audience understood "the kingdom of God" as the messianic kingdom. What Jesus announced was that "the governance of God is near." The kingdom was present in the sense that Jesus, the agent of God's government, was present among them. John D. Grassmick, "Marcos," in *Mateo, Marcos, Lucas*, El conocimiento bíblico: Un comentario expositivo Nuevo Testamento 1 (Puebla, Mexico: ELA, 1996), 133. This series has been widely used among dispensationalists in Latin America.

ministry opens the door to a time of divine fulfillment and calls people to a personal encounter with God and himself.[41] The future aspect of that kingdom is the millennial kingdom that will end with the eternal kingdom.[42] Thus, as mentioned above, Pérez Millos's discussion illustrates that the present aspect of the kingdom of God is spiritual and focused on the salvation of the soul. The eschatology of dispensational evangelicalism is mainly focused on the future and not so much on the present world.

In evaluating the four views presented here of the kingdom of God and its relationship with the church, the words of Benedict XVI are helpful. He summarizes the different interpretations of the kingdom of God in the history of the church under three main groups.[43] The first group sees the kingdom of God as synonymous with Jesus. As Origen called him, he is the *autobasileia* (the self-government). The dispensational approach appears to see the presence of the kingdom of God in this way, in particular due to the close association between Jesus and the land of Israel in this theological view. When Jesus was here, he was King. Currently, he is a king without a kingdom. He will have a kingdom after his second coming. Benedict XVI calls the second interpretive line "idealist." This way of conceiving the kingdom of God sees the activity of the kingdom inside the human being. The kingdom grows in and acts from there. This view seems to be the way both the traditional Catholic and the dispensational approach understand the present aspect of the kingdom. The third interpretive line sees different degrees of relationship and identification between the church and the kingdom of God. The approach of liberation theology appears to conceive of an indirect relationship between the church and the kingdom. The emphasis on the historical and political aspects of the kingdom and the poor as the main recipients of that kingdom tends to set the church aside as simply an agent of the kingdom. For its part, the Latin American Theological Fraternity's understanding of the kingdom sees a closer relationship between the church and the kingdom. Just as in liberation theology, the Latin American Theological Fraternity's thinkers see the historical importance of the kingdom for today. For that reason, they emphasize the holistic mission of the church. The Holy Spirit is the key factor in that mission. In this way, the Latin American Theological Fraternity's conception of the kingdom of God is more trinitarian.

MARK 1:14-15: A LATIN AMERICAN REFLECTION

Mark begins his narrative with a strong eschatological flavor.[44] In the prologue to the entire Gospel (Mk 1:1-15), the author introduces John the Baptist as the forerunner of the Messiah (Mk 1:1-8). In this way, the book begins with the new

---

[41]Pérez Millos, *Marcos*, 134-35. Grassmick is more explicit in asserting that the phrase "the time has come" "emphasizes the distinctive note of fulfillment in Jesus' proclamation." Grassmick, "Marcos," 132.

[42]Pérez Millos, *Marcos*, 133; Grassmick, "Marcos," 133.

[43]Joseph Ratzinger, *Jesús de Nazaret: Primera parte, desde el Bautismo a la Transfiguración* (New York: Doubleday, 2007), 76-82 (*Jesus of Nazareth: From the Baptism in the Jordan to the Transfiguration* [London: Bloomsbury, 2008]).

[44]I approach this from a literary perspective that accepts the text as it is. The relevant bibliography is considerable. See R. T. France, *The Gospel of Mark: A Commentary on the Greek Text*, New International Greek Testament Commentary (Grand Rapids, MI: Eerdmans, 2002); Robert H. Gundry, *Mark: A Commentary on His Apology for the Cross, Chapters 1-8* (Grand Rapids, MI: Eerdmans, 2004); Joel Marcus, *Mark 1-8: A New Translation with Introduction and Commentary*, Anchor Bible (New York: Doubleday, 2000); Marcus, *Mark 9-16: A New Translation with Introduction and Commentary*, Anchor Bible (New York: Doubleday, 2009); Xabier Pikaza Ibarrondo, *Comentario al evangelio de Marcos* (Barcelona: Vida, 2012); Ben Witherington III, *The Gospel of Mark: A Socio-Rhetorical Commentary* (Grand Rapids, MI: Eerdmans, 2001).

exodus and the messenger of the Lord (Is 40:1-5).[45] This connection between the Gospel and the metanarrative of the new exodus frames the ministry of Jesus in the eschatological time of fulfillment.[46] Jesus is the one who will baptize people with the Holy Spirit (Mk 1:8). After Jesus' baptism, the Spirit who has come on him leads Jesus into the desert and temptation (Mk 1:9-12). Jesus comes out from temptation in victory. The apocalyptic scene after the temptation arguably reinforces this eschatological framework (Mk 1:13).[47]

John the Baptist is reintroduced into the scene before Jesus' ministry (Mk 1:14). Now the Baptist is in prison. The reasons for his imprisonment appear later, in Mark 6:14-29. Here the author uses John's situation to introduce Jesus' ministry of proclamation in a context of opposition, adversity, and evil. The forces of the anti-kingdom are already functioning. Jesus comes to the very region where John is prisoner. Galilee is central in the Gospel. Jesus begins and finishes his earthly ministry in Galilee (Mk 1:9, 14; 16:7).[48] Herod Antipas was the ruler of that region. So Jesus performs his early ministry among the people right at the lion's mouth (Mk 1:16, 21, 28, 39; 3:7). His proclamation is public, addressed to all the people.[49] In the same way, Jesus' dis-

ciples will face adversity and will develop their ministry in the midst of opposition (Mk 13:3-23).

Jesus' message is summarized as "the gospel of God" (Mk 1:14). Mark will show that this gospel from God is about the Messiah, the Son of God (Mk 1:1). In Mark 1:14, Jesus continues the work that the forerunner anticipated. John prepared the way of the Lord by preaching repentance (Mk 1:4). Now Jesus announces the good news from God (Mk 1:14) and calls people to repent (Mk 1:15). His preaching is accompanied by doing miracles and confronting unclean spirits. Both actions bring health and deliverance to those in need (Mk 1:21–6:6). Later, as the Lord did, the Twelve preach the same call to repentance and bring health to the needy (Mk 6:12).

In Mark 1:15, the Evangelist presents the content of the gospel. First, Jesus proclaims that "the time has come." The time of eschatological fulfillment has arrived. In line with the new-exodus motif, Jesus the Messiah has appeared. He is the beloved Isaianic Servant on whom the Spirit of God rests (Is 42:1; Mk 1:11). The Holy Spirit guides and empowers him (Mk 1:12; 3:22-30). His disciples also receive the Holy Spirit.[50] In his power, they perform their ministry of

---

[45]For more details on the use of the Old Testament in this passage, see Rikki E. Watts, "Mark," in *Commentary on the New Testament Use of the Old Testament*, ed. G. K. Beale and D. A. Carson (Grand Rapids, MI: Baker, 2007), 113-20.

[46]Rikki Watts makes an important contribution to this topic. See Rikki E. Watts, *Isaiah's New Exodus and Mark*, Biblical Study Library (Grand Rapids, MI: Baker, 2000).

[47]See the brief and recent discussion about the eschatological imagery in Mk 1:13 in John Paul Heil, "Jesus with the Wild Animals in Mark 1:13," *Catholic Biblical Quarterly* 68 (2006): 63-78; Charles A. Gieschen, "Why Was Jesus with the Wild Beasts (Mark 1:13)?," *Concordia Theological Quarterly* 73 (2009): 77-80.

[48]Fernando Méndez points out that of the twelve times Galilee is mentioned in Mark, five are in Mk 1. In this way, in Mark, Galilee is strongly linked to the beginning of Jesus' ministry. Méndez also highlights the fact that even the last two (of the twelve) mentions of Galilee relate to the beginning of the ministry of the risen Jesus. Fernando Méndez, *Marcos*, Comentario Bíblico Mundo Hispano 15 (El Paso, TX: Mundo Hispano, 2012), 32.

[49]Xabier Pikaza points out that Jesus did not stay in the desert—the place of the trial—nor did he go to Jerusalem, besides the temple; rather, he went to Galilee, to his land and his people. Pikaza Ibarrondo, *Marcos*, part 1.1, "Necesidad humana y mensaje de Reino (1,14–3,6)."

[50]In Mark, the presence of the Spirit leading the disciples in their ministry is implicit. In Mk 1:8, the Baptist announces that one more powerful than he will baptize people with the Holy Spirit. In Mk 3:13-19, Jesus sends the Twelve to preach and cast out demons. Immediately after, in Mk 3:20-30, it is clear that Jesus casts out demons by the power and presence of the Holy Spirit. It could be inferred that his disciples cast out demons by the same Spirit. In Jesus' prophecies in Mk 13:11, he exhorts his disciples to not be anxious when appearing before tribunals, because the Holy Spirit will speak through them. Thus, in one point of the narrative, the disciples are

proclamation (Mk 1:7-8; 13:11). Furthermore, Jesus the Messiah announces that in this time of fulfillment, "the kingdom of God has come near." The Isaianic flavor of these first verses in Mark comes across strongly as Jesus echoes Isaiah 52:7 [LXX]: "Zion, your God will reign." The Servant of God is announcing the kingship of God. This eschatological flavor of Jesus' ministry is also present in his disciples' ministry (Mk 13:3-23). They should proclaim the same message until their Lord comes again (Mk 13:10, 24-27).

Even though, since the beginning, God sustains all his creation, he has burst into human history in the presence and ministry of Jesus the Messiah. Jesus' ministry is intimately related to the ministry of his disciples. In fact, immediately after presenting the summary of Jesus' proclamation in Mark 1:14-15, Mark recounts Jesus' calling of the first group of disciples (Mk 1:16-20).[51] Since then, God's kingdom is present through the ministry of Jesus' disciples. Jesus sent out his twelve disciples with the same message (Mk 3:13-15; 6:12). Later, with the help of the Holy Spirit, they will continue their ministry in the midst of adversity and opposition as their Lord did (Mk 13:9-11). This kingdom also waits for a final fulfillment when the Son of Man comes with glory and power (Mk 13:26-27). The certainty of this coming gives hope to his disciples today.

This good news demands an answer from those who hear it. Jesus says, "Repent and believe in the gospel." This call to repentance implies at least two things: it implies sins from which to repent and people who must repent. Those who repent will follow the path of the

Messiah by believing in the gospel. The rich young man is an example of someone who did not want to repent of his love of money. As a result, he could not enter the kingdom of God (Mk 10:17-31). He is like the seed among thorns (Mk 4:19). Other people accepted Jesus' invitation immediately and followed him (Mk 1:16-20; 2:13-14). They are like the seed in good soil: those who hear the word of the kingdom and embrace it (Mk 4:20). Darío López reminds us, "Due to individual, social, and structural sin, human beings act egotistically, looking to their own interests, without any regard for the well-being of their neighbors."[52] Thus, our proclamation of the gospel should not leave out the call for repentance. It should also include a denunciation of the social and structural sins less perceived by many Christian communities. In this sense, repentance is a key for entering the kingdom, but perseverance is also a signal of true discipleship. A disciple repents of their own sins, but must learn to live in a world under the control of the antikingdom. True disciples repent of sin, enter the kingdom of God, and bring the new reality of the kingdom into their world.

The church is the community of Jesus' disciples. As such, it is called to proclaim the gospel of God. As Padilla says, "The mission of the Church is an extension of Jesus's mission."[53] We are still waiting for the coming of our Lord. In the meantime, with the power of the Spirit, we proclaim the good news of salvation. As Núñez comments, "God wants to bless all human beings and the whole human being."[54] So this good news also implies bringing help to those in

---

baptized with the Holy Spirit. It is Luke who lets us know the moment (Acts 2), but in Mark it is implicit.

[51]Osvaldo Vena rightly points out, "Like John, Jesus will need disciples to do his work. For that reason, his ministry does not begin without first calling his first collaborators." Osvaldo D. Vena, *Evangelio de Marcos*, CET (Miami: Sociedades Bíblicas Unidas, 2008), 29.

[52]Darío López R., *La propuesta política del Reino de Dios* (Lima: Puma, 2009), 88.

[53]Padilla, *Mission Between the Times*, 205.

[54]Núñez, *Hacia una misionología evangélica latinoamericana*, 142.

need. This ministry is a visible expression that the kingdom of God is here. In Jesus' ministry, miracles demonstrate his mercy (Mk 6:34). They are not mere bait for evangelistic purposes. Evangelistic activities combined with donations of food or medical support have been common in Latin America. Often, in order for people to receive food, medical supplies, or attention, they are first required to hear the "gospel" and "accept Jesus." In this way, the help turns into mere bait for evangelistic purposes. Instead, the church's mission of proclamation should be accompanied by deeds of mercy. In this regard, Padilla points out, "[The church] is the manifestation (though not yet complete) of the Kingdom of God, through proclamation as well as through social service and action. The apostolic witness continues to be the Spirit's witness to Jesus Christ as Lord through the church."[55]

Thankfully, in Latin America, the practice of using deeds of mercy in their evangelistic efforts as a way to attract converts has declined over the past decade, but it is still a problem. Catholic works of mercy have set a good example showing that a more balanced ministry is possible. Also, many evangelical churches have developed a more integral work among their neighborhoods and in places of greater need. A very good example is the research Claudia Dary presents in her book. It is a study and compilation of the work of several churches located in extremely violent neighborhoods in Guatemala City. The book shows how pastors and churches, priests and parishes are fully involved in rescuing youth from the arms of gangs, with holistic ministries.[56]

The kingdom came before the first disciples of Jesus entered it. So the kingdom of God is not the community of disciples, but it includes them. The kingdom of God includes at least the redeemed creation, believers in God from Adam to the last one, and the holy angels. The church—just as its Lord was—is the herald of the gospel of God. However, there is an antikingdom force that opposes this ministry. In Mark, Satan and the unclean spirits continually opposed Jesus. Jesus also faced the religious and political establishment. In the same way, as agents of this kingdom, we should be a light that shines in the darkness of the world system that is utterly opposed to his kingdom and its values.

CONCLUSION

The eschatological concept of the kingdom of God has long occupied the agenda of Latin American reflection. The concerns have revolved around the presence of the kingdom today. Even though the concept is almost absent from the Nicene-Constantinopolitan Creed, it has been a focus of wide and deep discussion in Latin America. Different approaches have emphasized different aspects of that presence. Dispensational circles have tended to see an absence of the kingdom. That absence has motivated them in their evangelization. For its part, the traditional Catholic Church has centered its focus on the inner presence of that kingdom: church and kingdom are so closely related that it is hard to differentiate between them. In liberation theology, the emphasis lies on the historical and political presence of the kingdom of God. The poor are the main recipients of that kingdom. In this context, the church is an agent of the kingdom and its mission is to bring the kingdom to the oppressed. The Latin American Theo-

---

[55]Padilla, *Mission Between the Times*, 205.

[56]Claudia Dary, *Cristianos en un país violento: Respuestas de las iglesias frente a la violencia en dos colonias del área metropolitana de Guatemala* (Guatemala City: Universidad de San Carlos de Guatemala, 2016).

logical Fraternity presents a more trinitarian approach to the concept. The church is an agent of the kingdom. Through the empowering presence of the Spirit, and as servants of the Lord Jesus, the church proclaims the gospel of God that brings help to those in need.

The summary of Jesus' proclamation of the gospel of God in Mark 1:14-15 is a good example of these different approaches. Jesus has inaugurated the eschaton with his presence and ministry. The kingdom of God is present and manifest today through the ministry of Jesus' disciples, who are empowered by the presence of the Holy Spirit. That same good news announces the victory of God over the forces that oppose his kingship. This victory will be definitive when Jesus comes in glory and power. Then God will manifest his kingdom in all its splendor, and all peoples will praise him.

FURTHER READING

Martínez-Olivieri, Jules A. *A Visible Witness: Christology, Liberation, and Participation.* Emerging Scholars. Minneapolis: Fortress, 2016.

Padilla, C. René. *Mission Between the Times: Essays on the Kingdom.* 2nd ed. Carlisle, UK: Langham Monographs, 2010.

Roldán, Alberto F. *Reino, política y misión: Sus relaciones en perspectiva latinoamericana.* Lima: Puma, 2011.

Salinas, J. Daniel. *Taking Up the Mantle: Latin American Evangelical Theology in the 20th Century.* Global Perspectives Series. Carlisle, UK: Langham Global Library, 2017.

Stam, Juan. *Escatología bíblica y misión de la iglesia: Hasta el fin del tiempo y los fines de la tierra.* San José: Semilla, 1999.

Tamayo-Acosta, Juan José. *Para comprender la escatología cristiana.* Navarra, Spain: Verbo Divino, 2008.

46

ASIA AND GOD'S CRUCIFORM ESCHATOLOGICAL REIGN

Aldrin Peñamora

ESCHATOLOGY PLAYS A crucial role in the way Christians in Asia engage with issues of public or social-political relevance. While the principle of *sola Scriptura* continues to be one of the bedrocks of Asian Protestant Christianity, historical and cultural factors have powerfully shaped it, as exemplified in Korea and China. Sadly, the eschatology that has resulted with the intertwining of history, culture, and Scripture has often led to little or no involvement of Christians in public spaces. This essay seeks to address this issue for the Christian community in order that it might reflect Jesus' cruciform eschatology, which confronted the oppressions of his day in light of the dawning of God's eschatological reign. A proper resolution of this issue is of vital importance for Christians in Asia, where poverty, exclusion, and oppression have for so long been constant and deadly companions of the people.

INTRODUCTION

"From first to last," according to Jürgen Moltmann, "Christianity is eschatology, is hope, forward looking and forward moving, and therefore also revolutionizing and transforming the present."[1]

In Asia, where multitudes of people groups have long been struggling against poverty and oppression, the Christian message about God's restoration of all creation can provide them with much-needed hope in their specific contexts.

Indeed, like all other Christian doctrines, eschatology is contextual. This essay will look at how eschatology, especially premillennialism, was appropriated contextually by the early Korean Presbyterian Church, David Yonggi Cho and the Yoido Full Gospel Church, China's "Back to Jerusalem" movement, and Watchman Nee and the Little Flock church. By presenting and examining the contours of their eschatological views, this essay aims to advance some critical theological insights that will hopefully be of some relevance toward addressing concretely the situations of the poor in Asia.

THE MANY FACES OF ASIA

The diversity of Asia's ethnic groups, histories, cultures, religious traditions, and political systems reflects the pluriformity of Asia. The notion that Asia is one was from antiquity one of convenience, which was firmly established when

---

[1]Jürgen Moltmann, *Theology of Hope* (New York: Harper & Row, 1965), 16.

the world was divided into several continents during medieval times.[2] After World War II, attempts to conceptualize the oneness of Asia in political terms were not lacking, although the underpinnings and goals of those attempts led to contested visions—imperialist, nationalist, regionalist, and the like—that only strengthened the claim to Asia's many-ness.[3] Similarly, even with the notion of Christianity in Asia, an essentialist view of "Christianity" may refer aptly to a unity of basic Christian beliefs in contrast to other Asian faith traditions, but viewed historically the varied and frenzied ways these beliefs and practices have been socially embodied, expressed, and understood make the plural "Christianities" an equally appropriate designation.[4]

For Asia has always been many, with multiple conceptions that draw on various sources, such as interdependence, economic growth, ideational and religious foundations, and other material factors that in different ways have contributed toward shaping the lives and destinies of peoples and nations.[5] It is this pluriformity that obliges the church in Asia to abandon absolutizing claims regarding a particular form of—or way of doing—theology. To insist on such runs the risk of once again expressing colonial tendencies of "intellectual, cultural, sociological, economic and religious imperialism."[6] Aloysius Pieris makes the important point that in Asia many metacosmic religions, such as Confu-

cianism in China and Shinto worship in Japan, took deep root in societies centuries before Christianity arrived. These cannot easily be dislodged by another metacosmic faith, "except by protracted use of coercion—that is, by an irreligious resort to mass conversion."[7]

Poverty and religious plurality are key features of the Asian soil. According to the sixth Christian Conference of Asia, held back in 1977, the "dominant reality of Asian suffering is that people are wasted: Wasted by hunger, torture, deprivation of rights, . . . by economic exploitation, racial and ethnic discrimination, sexual suppression, non-relation, non-community."[8] Today, even with China—and India poised to soon rise—as a superpower, and the influence of other highly developed economies such as Japan, Singapore, and Taiwan, massive poverty is still prevalent in Asia.

Poverty and oppression in Asia, as Peter Phan remarks, is forced and imposed. Historically, it is one of the unhappy and lasting legacies of past and often multiple iterations of political, economic, social, and religious colonization from the West, going all the way back to the arrival in India of Portuguese explorer Vasco de Gama. But while one may easily think of Asia's domination by Western powers, it is important to note that Asian powers themselves, such as Japan, at one time or another also advanced colonial interests, and that Asian despots

---

[2]Atola Longkumer, "Together Towards Life and Contemporary Asian Theology," in *Ecumenical Missiology: Changing Landscapes and New Concepts of Mission*, ed. Kenneth R. Ross et al. (Oxford: Regnum, 2016), 499.

[3]Amitav Acharya, "Asia Is Not One," *Journal of Asian Studies* 69, no. 4 (November 2010): 1002-3.

[4]Peter C. Phan, ed., *Christianities in Asia* (Chichester, UK: John Wiley & Sons, 2007), 1-2.

[5]Acharya, "Asia Is Not One," 1001.

[6]Engelbert Mveng, quoted in Frank Chikane, "EATWOT and Third World Theologies: An Evaluation of the Past and the Present," in *Third World Theologies: Commonalities and Divergences* (Maryknoll, NY: Orbis, 1990), 150-52.

[7]Aloysius Pieris, *An Asian Theology of Liberation* (Maryknoll, NY: Orbis, 1988), 55. Pieris defines metacosmic faith as postulating the existence of "a transphenomenal Reality immanently operative in the cosmos and soteriologically available within the human person either through *agape* (redeeming love) or through *gnosis* (redeeming knowledge)." Jewish and Christian faiths represent the agapeic, while the monastic faiths of Hinduism, Buddhism, and Taoism represent the gnostic (54).

[8]Quoted in C. S. Song, *Theology from the Womb of Asia* (Maryknoll, NY: Orbis, 1986), 187.

and regimes have perpetuated oppressive measures toward Asian subalterns and minoritized citizens because of class (e.g., the Hindu caste system of India), gender (e.g., women), and religion (e.g., Rohingya Muslims in Buddhist-majority Myanmar).[9]

A second thread that connects Asia is the peoples' deep religiosity. As the cradle of the world's major religious traditions, in Asia religion is intertwined with daily life and with the very identity of the people. This is exemplified by the Moros, or Muslims, of Southern Philippines, who consider religious identity to be of utmost importance as citizens of the nation.[10] This aspiration to be recognized as Muslims is at the core of the longstanding conflict in Mindanao.[11]

Religious identity or affiliation is thus often invoked in armed struggles in Asia.[12] Undeniably, many violent conflicts contain religious elements. However, we would be amiss to view religion and violence as intrinsically intertwined. "The idea that religion causes violence," as William Cavanaugh incisively points out, "is one of the most prevalent myths in Western culture."[13] Many elements usually converge to enable violence and armed insurgencies.[14] Indeed, religious symbols, principles, and doctrines have been utilized for various ends that include radical and violent ones.[15] Nonetheless, Asian religions also play a vital role in bringing peace and protesting abuses in society. The Indian independence movement of Mahatma Gandhi and the Philippine "People Power" that brought down a dictator are fine examples. But as conflicts proliferate in religiously pluralistic Asia, conflicts that are increasingly being defined as clashes of civilizations, Phan is correct to observe that they "cannot be resolved without the harmony of religions."[16]

---

[9]Peter C. Phan, "Jesus Christ with an Asian Face," *Theological Studies* 57 (1997): 401. K. M. Panikkar calls the period of Western colonization of Asia the "de Gama epoch," which started from the Portuguese explorer's arrival in India in 1498 and lasted until the end of World War II in 1945. It is a period that is unified by these four features: (1) the dominance of the maritime power of Asia's landmasses, (2) the imposition of an economic life based not on the usual agricultural economy but on international trade, (3) the domination of Europeans over the affairs of Asia, and (4) attempts by Europeans to Christianize Asia. K. M. Panikkar, *Asia and Western Dominance: A Survey of the Vasco de Gama Epoch of Asian History 1498–1945* (London: George Allen & Unwin, 1959), 13-15.

[10]From the word *Moors*, the term *Moro* was used derogatorily by the Spanish colonizers to refer to the Muslims of Mindanao, Sulu, and Palawan in southern Philippines.

[11]At the present time, representing the Moro people in their struggle for meaningful self-determination is the Moro Islamic Liberation Front. Their demand for genuine self-determination is encapsulated in the "Bangsamoro Organic Law" that was signed into law on July 26, 2018.

[12]Bardwell L. Smith, "Religion, Social Conflict and the Problem of Identity in South Asia: An Interpretive Introduction," in *Religion and Social Conflict in South Asia*, ed. Bardwell L. Smith (Leiden: Brill, 1976), 7.

[13]William T. Cavanaugh, *The Myth of Religious Violence: Secular Ideology and the Roots of Modern Conflict* (Oxford: Oxford University Press, 2009), 15. On pages 181-83, Cavanaugh points out various ways in which the myth of religious violence is a useful construct for the West, particularly in reinforcing power in domestic and foreign politics. Although not without many critics, Edward Said put forth a similar notion, arguing that the concept of "Oriental" was conjured by the West for its own purposes. He writes, "Orientalism can be discussed and analyzed as the corporate institution for dealing with the Orient—dealing with it by making statements about it, authorizing views of it, describing it, by teaching it, settling it, ruling over it: in short, Orientalism as a Western style for dominating, restructuring, and having authority over the Orient" (Said, *Orientalism: Western Conceptions of the Orient* [London: Routledge, 1978], 3).

[14]William Gould, *Religion and Conflict in Modern South Asia* (Cambridge: Cambridge University Press, 2012), 309. Gould further makes the point that south Asia should not be defined mainly in relation to religious traditions. The civil war in Sri Lanka, for instance, between the Sinhalese Buddhists and Tamil Muslims, can be viewed superficially as a clash of religions, but, on closer examination, contributing factors include international, domestic, socioeconomic, and religiocultural matters. He ultimately concludes that it is primarily an "ethnonationalist insurgency wherein various communities defined themselves and their antagonists by ethnicity and faith tradition." Berkeley Center for Religion, Peace and World Affairs, *Civil War Along Ethnoreligious Lines* (Washington, DC: Georgetown University Press, 2003), 1-9.

[15]Smith, "Religion, Social Conflict," 7.

[16]Phan, *Christianities in Asia*, 5. A very interesting study was made by Jonathan Fox on how religion contributes to violent conflicts and also to nonviolent protests. He insightfully observes that violence more readily crosses religious lines than do peaceful protests. See Jonathan Fox, "Is Ethnoreligious Conflict a Contagious Disease?," *Studies in Conflict and Terrorism* 27 (2004): 89-106.

Contextual Eschatology in Asia

With the end of World War II, the de Gama epoch came to an end. Song called this a *kairotic* year, a year that did not just affect drastically the lives of countless peoples in Asia but that enabled history to be intelligible and to have meaning. From the ashes of war arose nations that were at long last free—or at least relatively free.[17] In the following we will see how Christians in Korea and China appropriated the doctrine of eschatology in their specific contexts.

A tale of two Koreas. Eschatology and the "queen of suffering." In protesting the persecution of Christians to Roman authorities, Tertullian wrote in his *Apologeticus*, "The oftener we are mown down by you, the more in number we grow; *the blood of* Christians *is seed.*" More than a century later this statement was again proven true by Christians in Korea. Because of the great suffering they have endured in history, Ham Sok Hon, the "Korean Gandhi," called Korea the queen of suffering, and described his nation's suffering in this vivid manner: "Haven't you all nailed my mother to a cross and exposed her private parts to her shame, Red China holding her one arm and Japan grasping the other, while the polar bear holds down her head and the eagle from Rocky Mountains holds down her legs?"[18] Two interlinked events in the history of the Korean Presbyterian Church demonstrate how the Koreans suffered: first, in relation to the early spread of Protestantism, and second, concerning the issue of the Shinto shrines. In these, eschatology played a vital role in upholding and nourishing the growth of the church.

The Korean church grew rapidly between 1895 and 1907. This was a time of great sociopolitical upheaval as the nation was the focal point of two wars that imperial Japan won: against the Qing Empire in the First Sino-Japanese War (1894–1895) and against the Russian Empire in the Russo-Japanese War (1904–1905). With the Japanese colonization of Korea in 1910, Korean Christians experienced continuous persecution, first because of their nationality and later also because of their faith.[19] The failure of the 1919 nonviolent protest against Japan by the Samil Independence movement, which was led by many Korean Christians, became a crucial turning point as the Japanese retaliated ruthlessly by placing thousands in prison and murdering many Korean believers.[20]

This led the people to despair about their sociopolitical situation and contributed to the appeal of premillennial eschatology. During this period of colonization, some notable Korean Presbyterians, led by Sun Joo Kil, also called the "Father of Korean Christianity," Ik Doo Kim, and Hyung Yong Park, persuasively taught and preached a future-oriented and otherworldly Christianity. Ik Doo Kim's emphasis, for instance,

---

[17]Song, *Theology from the Womb of Asia*, 38-40. From 1945 to 1949, nations that were formerly under colonial rule, such as Indonesia, Korea, Philippines, India, and Burma, won their independence, with China establishing a communist regime after several years under civil war. Imperial Japan, of course, was dismantled and became a democratic nation. However, independence was not absolute in some cases, as exemplified in Korea. While 1945 brought an end to Japanese colonial rule, it also marked the beginning of Korea's division into North and South and of falling under the influence of the Soviet Union and the United States, respectively.

[18]This is also the title of his work. See Ham Sok Hon, *Queen of Suffering: A Spiritual History of Korea*, trans. E. Sang Yu, ed. John Sullivan (London: Friends World Committee for Consultation, 1985), x; quoted in Peter Koslowski, ed., *The Origin and the Overcoming of Evil and Suffering in the World Religions* (Dordrecht: Springer, 2001), 9.

[19]Ung Kyu Pak, *Millennialism in the Korean Protestant Church* (New York: Peter Lang, 2005), 109. A good overview of the history of Roman Catholic and Protestant Christianity in Korea can be found in Ig-Jin Kim's *History and Theology of Korean Pentecostalism: Sunbogeum (Pure Gospel) Pentecostalism* (Zoetermeer, Netherlands: Uitgeverij Boeckencentrum, 2003), 31-52.

[20]Doug Sung Choi, "The Roots of Presbyterian Conflicts in Korea, 1910–1954, and the Predominance of Orthodoxy" (PhD diss., Emory University, 1992), 143-44.

"on the millennial Kingdom and eschatology harmonized well with the hope of a suffering people who lost independence and sovereignty during the annexation."[21] The churches thus fixed their eyes on a future world, for the present world was incapable of being saved, and, that being so, Christian duty was perceived in personal and individualistic terms: to preach deliverance, to witness, baptize, and gather out God's elect in preparation for Christ's second coming.[22]

Premillennialism reached the Korean church through Western missionaries who were deeply influenced by D. L. Moody and Arthur Pierson, two pioneers of the eschatological missionary movement after the American Civil War.[23] Through their leadership, the movement spread among college and seminary students. Pierson's concept of "evangelization of the world in this generation" inspired a flood of volunteers who understood Christ's return to be imminent, so his followers needed to spread the gospel all over the world.[24]

Korea proved to be fertile ground. Timothy Lee incisively points out that when Protestant missionaries reached Korea, the people were also searching for a new moral order that the existing ones such as Buddhism, Confucianism, and the Sirhak (Practical Learning) movement of the Choson dynasty had failed to adequately provide.[25] Unhappily, the Puritanical attitude of many early missionaries and their dualistic view toward the world and society inculcated among many Korean Christians a faith that was hostile to indigenous religion and culture.[26] Nonetheless, this did not lead to a total rejection of traditional or folk beliefs. Hang-Sik Cho argues that Christianity in Korea incorporated many aspects of shamanism, which came about through a "cultural colorization" of Christian experience and spontaneous syncretization by Koreans with shamanistic backgrounds.[27] In other words, "the beliefs of Shamanism have enabled Koreans to comprehend more easily the references in Christianity to the idea of God, to evil in the world, to heaven and hell, and to benevolent and evil spirits."[28] This, as we will see shortly, is a charge that has been leveled against David Yonggi Cho, leader of one of the largest churches in the world, the Yoido Full Gospel Church.

The new Christian faith that the Koreans embraced was put to the test by the Shinto shrine issue. After conquering Manchuria, the Japanese government coerced the Korean people to worship at the Shinto shrine, which included performance of religious rites. For the Korean Presbyterian Church, the issue was not merely about a political act of loyalty to the state, or a matter of nonessentials; it was about the very core of the Christian faith, for it entailed a

---

[21]Kwang Jin Paik, "Korean Presbyterianism and the Kingdom Expectation: The Role of Eschatological Motive in the Expansion of the Korean Presbyterian Church, 1884–1945" (PhD diss., Reformed Theological Seminary, 1996), 155; quoting Yong Kyu Park, "Korean Presbyterianism and Biblical Authority: The Role of Scripture in the Shaping of Korean Presbyterianism, 1918–1953" (PhD diss., Trinity Evangelical Divinity School, 1991), 239.

[22]Paul Hang-Sik Cho, *Eschatology and Ecology: Experiences of the Korean Church* (Oxford: Regnum, 2010), 153.

[23]Jaekeun Lee, "McCormick Missionaries and the Shaping of Korean Evangelical Presbyterianism" (MTh diss., University of Edinburgh, 2010), 38.

[24]Paik, "Korean Presbyterianism," 77-79.

[25]Timothy S. Lee, *Born Again: Evangelicalism in Korea* (Honolulu: University of Hawaii Press, 2010), 3-7.

[26]Keel Hee-Sung, "Can Korean Protestantism Be Reconciled with Culture? Rethinking Theology and Culture in Korea," *Inter-Religio* 24 (Winter 1993): 50.

[27]Hang-Sik Cho, *Eschatology and Ecology*. A good study of shamanism in Korea was carried out by Tongshik Ryu in "Shamanism: the Dominant Folk Religion in Korea," *Inter-Religio* 5 (Spring 1984): 8-15.

[28]Boo Woon Yoo, "Response to Shamanism by the Pentecostal Church," *International Review of Mission* 75 (January 1986): 72-73. Yoo adds that "the above characteristics, developed through belief in shamanism, greatly affected the Korean appropriation and expression of Christianity, through revival and Pentecostal enthusiasm and an other-worldly orientation."

religious act of worshiping other gods.[29] The Korean Presbyterian Church resisted, which led to the imprisonment of more than five thousand Christians and the shuttering of around twelve hundred Presbyterian churches.

An important factor enabling the Presbyterian Church to endure Japanese persecution and resist the oppressive measure was its premillennial outlook. Prominent leaders of the Anti-Shinto or Non-Shrine Worship movement, such as Ki-Sun Lee and Ki-Cheul Ju, were convinced of Christ's impending coming that would bring about the fall of all political nations and the establishment of the millennial kingdom. Hence, they exhorted Korean believers to take courage in opposing the Japanese Empire. As the martyred Ju said, the Korean church must dare to die for Jesus, for others, and for the defense of the Christian faith.[30]

Eschatological blessings: Yonggi Cho and the Yoido Full Gospel Church. The Korean people experienced untold suffering yet again when the nation was devastated by the Korean War. It would have been easy to lose hope in this situation. But believing in the gospel message and in the power of the Holy Spirit to give hope to the hopeless, David Yonggi Cho pioneered a "tent church" just a few years after the war in the slums of Dae-jo dong. It was a foundational experience for Cho, who experienced deeply what it meant to be one with his people in that time of utter despair.[31] Hence, his primary motivation for preaching in those early days was to give a message of hope. Cho recounts:

> I started preaching to people in the cursed land of Korea after the war. It was war-torn, broken, destroyed, and poverty-stricken. I had nothing materially to give to the people, but I was putting spiritual resources into their mind. . . . Spiritual resources are the most powerful kind of resource. Without them you cannot have material victory. . . . Soon they got out of their poverty-stricken situation. Jesus Christ through His crucifixion successfully destroyed the curse.[32]

By 1961, Yoido Full Gospel Central Church had grown to 300 members; 100,000 in 1979; 250,000 in 1983; over half a million in 1987. By 2006, it was listed as having 700,000 members.[33] Certainly, much credit can be attributed to Cho for his multiple skills, but, as Wonsuk Ma points out, the bedrock of his ministry that has fueled the phenomenal growth of Yoido Church is his "theology of blessing."[34] This refers to Cho's teaching on the Fivefold Gospel and Threefold Blessing. The former refers to Jesus' role as Savior, healer, blesser, baptizer, and coming king; while the latter, also called "treble blessings," is based on 3 John 2, which refers to the salvation of the soul, health and healing of the body, and material wealth from God.[35]

---

[29]Harvie M. Conn, "Studies in the Theology of the Korean Presbyterian Church," *Westminster Theological Journal* 29, no. 2 (May 1967): 165-66; Kim, *History and Theology of Korean Pentecostalism*, 74-75.

[30]Pak, *Millennialism in the Korean Protestant Church*, 191-92; Paik, "Korean Presbyterianism," 193.

[31]David Yonggi Cho, *Salvation, Health and Prosperity: Our Threefold Blessings in Christ* (Altamonte Springs, FL: Creation House, 1987), 11.

[32]David Yonggi Cho, *My Church Growth Stories* (Seoul: Seoul Logos, 2006), 157.

[33]Vincent Leoh, "Eschatology and Pneumatic Preaching with a Case of David Yonggi Cho," *Asian Journal of Pentecostal Studies* 10, no. 1 (2007): 111.

[34]Wonsuk Ma, "David Yonggi Cho's Theology of Blessing: Basis, Legitimacy, and Limitations," *Evangelical Review of Theology* 35, no. 2 (2011): 143. Cho, of course, has been criticized from various quarters. Gordon Fee, the General Presbytery of the Assemblies of God, US evangelicals, Robert Schuller, and others have refuted Cho's teachings. See Allan Anderson, "The Contribution of David Yonggi Cho to a Contextual Theology in Korea," *Journal of Pentecostal Theology* 12, no. 1 (2003): 89-90.

[35]Ma, "Cho's Theology of Blessing," 144. Ma makes the good point that the theological language of Cho's fivefold theology is closely aligned with the "Pentecostal Four" of the Assemblies of God, with which Cho is known to be affiliated. See also Kim, *History and Theology of Korean Pentecostalism*, 202-6. As to the origin of Cho's teaching on the treble blessings, Myung Soo Park maintains that Cho derived

The fifth element of the Fivefold Gospel, Jesus as coming king, or the gospel of the second coming, refers to Cho's dispensational premillennialism perspective on eschatology. His view conforms to the classic Pentecostal perspective, but, as Ig-Jin Kim remarks, the real strength of Cho's eschatology is its application in daily life.[36] This is based on Cho's already-but-not-yet view of God's kingdom. Whereas the earlier Korean Presbyterian Church emphasized the future advent of Christ and the establishment of the millennium, for Cho, the here and now are also important. Healing, miracles, and the third aspect of the treble blessings, material wealth, are therefore important manifestations of the presence of the in-breaking kingdom.

Because of Cho's emphasis on material blessings as an aspect of eschatology that others see as excessive, his theology is branded as Gibok Shinang (faith that seeks or prays for blessing).[37] As Cho says, "If we do not receive the 'riches' as stated in scripture, we make the poverty of Jesus of no effect. We have an important responsibility: to receive the prosperous life . . . which He makes possible for us by living in poverty."[38]

This emphasis on material blessings has led many from both within and without to identify it as a local brand of America's prosperity gospel and as a shamanization of Christianity in Korea. Harvey Cox is known to have claimed that, as exemplified by Yoido Church, a crucial reason "for Korean Pentecostalism's extraordinary growth is its unerring ability to absorb huge chunks of indigenous Korean shamanism and demon possession into its worship."[39] However, those who disagree with such assessments point to, among other key factors, the uniqueness of the Korean context. As Hwa Yung suggests, "a proper understanding of Cho on this is to see it as illustrative of his efforts to contextualize the gospel in order to address the felt needs of a people."[40] In his insightful study, Chuong Kwon Cho connects the Korean notion of Han as a "contextual factor" that Cho and Yoido, as "institutional factors," are able to address adequately.[41]

China. *China's end-time calling: The Back to Jerusalem movement.* Eschatology has often played a vital role in Christian missions, especially in relation to the Great Commission. For Christians in China's house churches, it is the central motivation. As one of the leaders of the house churches says, "We believe God has given us a solemn responsibility to take the fire from his altar and complete the Great Commission by establishing his kingdom in all of the remaining countries and people groups in Asia, the Middle East, and Islamic North Africa. When this

---

it from Oral Roberts. Myung Soo Park, "David Yonggi Cho and International Pentecostal/Charismatic Movements," *Journal of Pentecostal Theology* 12, no. 1 (2003): 108.

[36]Kim, *History and Theology of Korean Pentecostalism*, 304. See also Hwa Yung, "The Missional Challenge of David Yonggi Cho's Theology," *Asian Journal of Pentecostal Studies* 7, no. 1 (2004): 71-73.

[37]Ma, "Cho's Theology of Blessing," 147.

[38]Yonggi Cho, *Salvation, Health and Prosperity*, 68.

[39]Harvey Cox, *Fire from Heaven: The Rise of Pentecostal Spirituality and the Reshaping of Religion in the Twenty-First Century* (London: Cassell, Petter, Galpin, 1996), 222. A good overview of criticisms of Cho on this aspect is given by Allan Anderson in "Contribution of David Yonggi Cho," 89-93.

[40]Hwa Yung, "The Missiological Challenge of David Yonggi Cho's Theology," *Asian Journal of Pentecostal Studies* 7, no. 1 (2004): 75-76. See also Ma, "Cho's Theology of Blessing," 145-48; Anderson, "Contribution of David Yonggi Cho," 93-99. Park also asserts that instead of drawing from Korean shamanism, Cho drew from the American Pentecostal/charismatic movements in regard to his teachings on material wealth. Park, "Cho and International Pentecostal/Charismatic Movements," 127.

[41]Chuong Kwon Cho, "*Han* and the Pentecostal Experience: A Study of the Growth of the Yoido Full Gospel Church in Korea" (PhD diss., University of Birmingham, 2010), 48. Chuong points to three aspects of *Han*: (1) Korean despair, (2) the oppressed minds of the Korean Minjung, and (3) the Korean cultural archetype.

happens, we believe that the Scripture says the Lord Jesus will return for his bride."[42]

Napoleon's assessment of China—"There is a sleeping giant. Let her sleep. For when she wakes, she will shake the world"—can be aptly related to the massive growth of Christianity in that nation.[43] Chinese Christians in the last century have certainly awakened, and a particular house church network, the Back to Jerusalem movement, has shaken the Christian world with its vision to bring back the gospel to its roots by preaching and establishing fellowships in all the countries, cities, and towns among all ethnic groups between China and Jerusalem.[44]

While many believe that missionary efforts are rooted in Western imperialism, the Back to Jerusalem movement is an indigenous movement that defies such analysis.[45] The movement, says Timothy Tennent, is not under a single organization but "is more of a vision statement that many Chinese Christians have identified with, and yet which provides no formal connection among its adherents."[46] The Back to Jerusalem movement emerged in Shandong Province in the 1920s from independent Chinese churches. Originally part of the Jesus Family house church network, some members later formed the Northwest Spiritual Movement, which Simon Zhao led in the 1940s. Their vision was to preach

the gospel in Xinjiang and beyond. Another Chinese leader, Mark Ma from Shaanxi Province, confirmed Zhao's vision with a vision he also received, which entailed taking the gospel outside China, through Islamic countries, and all the way back to Jerusalem.[47] Missionary Helen Bailey called this group the "Back to Jerusalem Evangelistic Band."[48] Currently the movement envisions having by the year 2030 some twenty thousand Chinese missionaries who will join the global missions force.[49]

Premillennial eschatology adapted to the Chinese situation figures prominently in the Back to Jerusalem movement. It holds that Chinese Christians have been specially called by God to help usher in the second coming of Christ by fulfilling the Great Commission (Mt 24:14). Tobias Brandner observes that Back to Jerusalem movement's eschatological vision has functional psychological implications for Chinese Christians, who have been asking why Christianity has grown very late in China and what role God has for them in the history of salvation.[50] To such questions the Back to Jerusalem movement gives a narrative of history that depicts a shift toward China in God's covenantal relationship, especially now that America has lost its calling due to its history of political aggression. Other cities and nations in the past have also been

---

[42]Quoted in Paul Hattaway, *Back to Jerusalem: Three Chinese House Church Leaders Share Their Vision to Complete the Great Commission* (Carlisle, UK: Piquant, 2003), 20.

[43]James Sung-Hwan Park, "Chosen to Fulfill the Great Commission? Biblical and Theological Reflections on the Back to Jerusalem Vision of Chinese Churches," *Missiology: An International Review* 43, no. 2 (2015): 163-64.

[44]Hattaway, *Back to Jerusalem*, x.

[45]Tim Stafford, "A Captivating Vision: Why Chinese House Churches May Just End Up Fulfilling the Great Commission," *Christianity Today* 48, no. 4 (April 2004): 1.

[46]Timothy C. Tennent, *Theology in the Context of World Christianity: How the Global Church Is Influencing the Way We Think About and Discuss Theology* (Grand Rapids, MI: Zondervan, 2007), 238.

[47][Name witheld], "Assisting House Churches to Become Great Commission Churches" (PhD diss., Southern Baptist Theological Seminary, 2012), 157-58; Hattaway, *Back to Jerusalem*, 12.

[48]Park, "Chosen to Fulfill the Great Commission?," 165.

[49]Steve Z., "Indigenous Mission Movements in China," *Mission Roundtable: The OMF Journal for Reflective Practitioners* 11, no. 3 (September–December 2016), 27.

[50]Tobias Brandner, "Trying to Make Sense of History: Chinese Christian Traditions of Countercultural Belief and Their Theological and Political Interpretation of Past and Present History," *Studies in World Christianity* 17, no. 3 (2011): 219.

called by God for a special purpose, such as Israel, Wittenberg, Zurich, Geneva, and, more recently, America.[51] But in these end times, with their history of persecution, Chinese Christians are perfectly situated to enter into this unique covenant with God.

It must be recalled that Christians in China experienced persecution at the hands of the communist regime from 1950, when the Communist Party supported the formation of the Three-Self Patriotic Movement, which aimed to unify all Chinese Protestant churches under the Communist Party's leadership. Of those persecuted, the indigenous Protestant movements suffered the most.[52] Thus, Liu Zhenying, more famously known as Brother Yun and a key leader of the Back to Jerusalem movement, said, "There is little that any of the Muslim, Buddhist, or Hindu countries can do to us that we haven't already experienced in China."[53] Their crucial role in these end times thus gives Chinese Christians much assurance as they seek to provide the people with an alternative interpretation of their nation's history, especially amid the nation's current experience of economic success, which the Back to Jerusalem movement also sees as bringing decay to the nation's traditional values.[54]

From an eschatological standpoint, therefore, the Back to Jerusalem movement understands God to have orchestrated cultural, political, and socioeconomic factors to prepare them for their special calling. Their ability to speak different languages, knowledge of various cultures, good relationship with Arabs, ability to enter Arab nations without much suspicion, and aptitude for holding meetings in house churches make them appropriate messengers of the gospel.[55] And as Christians in the Middle East are experiencing severe persecution from violent extremists, Christina Lin writes encouragingly:

> As darkness descends upon the region, a light is kindling in the East and spreading west on the Silk Road towards this heart of darkness. What is not reported in mainstream media is that Christianity in the Mideast is not yet facing extinction, as new Christians from the East are migrating to help in the region—Chinese Christians. China, currently experiencing the largest Christian movement in the world, is marching west.[56]

Watchman Nee. Among Chinese Christian leaders, Watchman Nee (Ni Tuosheng) has the distinction of having immense influence both in China and in the global Christian world. He converted to Christianity as a young man during the 1920s, and by the time the Communists came to power in Mainland China in 1949, the indigenous church movement he founded, "the Little Flock," already had seventy thousand members.[57] As China was undergoing social and political upheaval during the first half of the twentieth

---

[51]Brandner, "Trying to Make Sense of History," 220.

[52]Yihua Xu, "'Patriotic' Protestants: The Making of an Official Church," in *God and Caesar in China: Policy Implications of Church-State Tensions*, ed. Jason Kindopp and Carol Lee Hamrin (Washington, DC: Brookings Institution, 2004), 115, 118. The "three selves" stand for self-governing, self-support, and self-propagation. These principles were meant to assure the government that the member Protestant churches were free from foreign influence and supportive of the new communist regime. Rodney Star and Xiuhua Wang, *A Star in the East: The Rise of Christianity in China* (West Conshohocken, PA: Templeton, 2015), 44-45.

[53]Quoted in Hattaway, *Back to Jerusalem*, 58.

[54]Tobias Bandner, "Premillennial and Countercultural Faith and Its Production and Reception in the Chinese Context," *Asian Journal of Pentecostal Studies* 14, no. 1 (2011): 8-9.

[55]J. Park, "Chosen to Fulfill the Great Commission?," 165-68.

[56]Christina Lin, "China's Back to Jerusalem Movement," *ISPSW Strategy Series* 329 (March 2015): 2.

[57]Archie Hui, "The Pneumatology of Watchman Nee: A New Testament Perspective," *Evangelical Quarterly* 75, no. 4 (2003): 3; Liu Yi, "Globalization of Chinese Christianity: A Study of Watchman Nee and Witness Lee's Ministry," *Asia Journal of Theology* 30, no. 1 (April 2016): 98.

century, Christian leaders such as Nee inevitably addressed the social situation that confronted Chinese Christians. His perspective on eschatology played a vital role in this matter.[58]

Through missionary Margaret Barber, Nee came to embrace Brethren ideas such as the absence of church government beyond the local congregation and the dispensational, premillennialist eschatology of influential Brethren teacher John Nelson Darby.[59] Using the New Testament church as a model, Nee rejected denominationalism and the then-prevailing Western missionary culture that presupposed foreign superiority over local Chinese leaders, who were merely hired as "native assistants" of foreign mission agencies instead of getting called by congregations.[60] When the Three-Self Patriotic Movement was established in 1950, calling for indigenization and ecclesial autonomy, Nee believed that the Little Flock embodied those ideals and hence would be tolerated by the communist state. The party state and the Three-Self Patriotic Movement, however, also intended to control churches for the Maoist state, and thus continued to view Nee and the Little Flock church as a threat. He was arrested in 1952 and in 1956 charged with various crimes against the state. Nee died in prison in 1972.[61]

Following Darby and Cyrus Scofield's eschatology, Nee developed a dualistic and pessimistic perspective of society and human history. The turbulence in China only confirmed his convictions.[62] The world, said Nee, is organized by Satan into a system that is antithetical to God. While acknowledging that the world evinces a certain movement toward progress, the crucial question for Nee was: "To what is this 'progress' tending?" The systems that give the world its appearance of coherence—politics, education, art, commerce, law, music—all move toward the setting up in history of the kingdom of the antichrist.[63] He said,

> There is absolutely no solution to the problems of the present system, governments, and society. The problems will be taken care of. When the new heaven and the new earth are inaugurated, the old order with all of its problems will be borne away. Today we do not take care of those problems. We only save people. Even though society at large will be somewhat affected after individuals are saved, our commission is not to save the world.[64]

Nee emphasized "Jesus never touched the question of politics. . . . He came to save individuals from sins. . . . His purpose is to save man. He has no intention other than this."[65] Bernard Erling is thus correct in his assertion that "there

---

[58]Kevin Xiyi Yao, "Chinese Evangelicals and Social Concerns: A Historical and Comparative Overview," in *After Imperialism: Christian Identity in China and the Global Evangelical Movement*, ed. Richard R. Cook and David W. Pao (Cambridge, UK: Lutterworth, 2012), 52-53.

[59]Joseph Tse-Hei Lee, "Watchman Nee and the Little Flock Movement in Maoist China," *Church History* 74, no. 1 (March 2005): 73-74.

[60]Alexander Chow, *Theosis, Sino-Christian Theology and the Second Chinese Enlightenment: Heaven and Humanity in Unity* (New York: Palgrave Macmillan, 2013), 55-56; Grace Y. May, "Watchman Nee and the Breaking of Bread: The Missiological and Spiritual Forces That Contributed to an Indigenous Chinese Ecclesiology" (ThD diss., Boston University School of Theology, 2000), 252-53.

[61]Tse-Hei Lee, "Watchman Nee," 82-87; Bernard Erling, "The Story of Watchman Nee," *Lutheran Quarterly* 28, no. 2 (May 1976): 146-47. A good account of the trial is in chap. 18 of Nee's biography by Angus I. Kinnear, *Against the Tide: The Story of Watchman Nee* (Fort Washington, MD: Christian Literature Crusade, 1974).

[62]Nee's most profound influences are from the Pietist background of the Brethren founders J. N. Darby and George Müller. The writings of dispensationalists, particularly G. H. Pember, Robert Govett, and D. M. Panton, influenced Nee's eschatology. Ken Ang Lee, "Watchman Nee: A Study of His Major Theological Themes" (PhD diss., Westminster Theological Seminary, 1989), 49-53.

[63]Watchman Nee, *Love Not the World*, ed. Angus I. Kinnear (Fort Washington, MD: Christian Literature Crusade, 1970), 12, 14.

[64]Watchman Nee, *The Normal Christian Faith* (Anaheim, CA: Living Stream Ministry, 1993), 178.

[65]Nee, *Normal Christian Faith*, 178-79.

is no suggestion anywhere in Nee's writings that a part of the Christian's responsibility is to seek to build a better world. . . . The world may be used to advance the evangelistic efforts of the church, but Nee is wholly pessimistic with respect to programs of social reform."[66]

For Nee and other Chinese evangelicals of his time, such as Wang Ming-dao, sin is the ultimate cause of the world's depraved condition, and no amount of participation in the social-political sphere will be able to put the world back to its proper purpose. In line with dispensational premillennialism, Nee urgently called his listeners to a life of personal holiness and evangelism.[67] It is not that Nee was against social action altogether. Rather, as Ken Ang Lee points out, the threat Nee and other evangelical leaders "perceived in the Social Gospel was not its emphasis on social concern per se. It was that it emphasized social concern in an exclusivistic way which seemed to undercut the relevance of the message of the Gospel itself."[68]

While Nee looked to Christ's second coming to usher in God's kingdom, he did not consider the world to be in utter chaos. It is indeed fallen, but God has set up earthly governments, and to them Christians owe limited submission. As Nee pointed out emphatically, "God alone is the object of our absolute obedience."[69]

Cruciform eschatology. The foregoing accounts illustrate how Christians in Korea and China confronted the social and political realities of their time armed with the Christian eschatological vision that was articulated through premillennial eschatology. The responses they gave to those particular realities certainly also sought to answer the question that, while in prison, Dietrich Bonhoeffer asked: "Who is Christ for us today?"[70]

The christological emphasis of the question is central to eschatology, and indeed to the Christian view of history. Jesus Christ, according to K. K. Yeo, "defines the end (purpose, goal and fulfillment) of history. . . . Jesus infuses history with meaning, redeeming and consummating history."[71] Pointing out further the significance of the crucified Christ in the future restoration of all things that takes into account the transitory restoration of the oppressed in history, Moltmann remarks, "With the raising of the crucified Christ from the dead, the future of the new creation of all things has already begun in the midst of this dying and transitory world."[72]

Christian eschatology, as mentioned at the beginning of this essay, can only be understood in the context of God's reign that the Christ event inaugurated. Paul Löffler said it well: "The beginning of the reign of God as an event of history

---

[66]Erling, "Story of Watchman Nee," 154.

[67]Chow, *Theosis*, 59.

[68]Ang Lee, "Watchman Nee," 231.

[69]Watchman Nee, *Take Heed* (New York: Christian Fellowship, 1991), 47-50.

[70]Dietrich Bonhoeffer, *Letters and Papers from Prison*, ed. Eberhard Bethge (New York: Collier, 1972), 279.

[71]K. K. Yeo, "An Eschatological View of History in the New Testament: Messianic and Millennarian Hope," *Asia Journal of Theology* 15, no. 1 (April 2001): 43. See also his *Chairman Mao Meets the Apostle Paul: Christianity, Communism, and the Hope of China* (Grand Rapids, MI: Brazos, 2002), 27-56; *Musing with Confucius and Paul: Toward a Chinese Christian Theology* (Eugene, OR: Cascade, 2008), 126-31; and *What Has Jerusalem to Do with Beijing? Biblical Interpretation from a Chinese Perspective* (Eugene, OR: Pickwick, 2018), 194-241.

[72]Jürgen Moltmann, *The Coming of God: Christian Eschatology* (London: SCM Press, 1996), 136; Brandon Lee Morgan, "Eschatology for the Oppressed: Millenarianism and Liberation in the Eschatology of Jürgen Moltmann," *Perspectives in Religious Studies* 39, no. 4 (Winter 2012): 379, 381. In *The Coming of God*, Moltmann's christological basis for his eschatology is found on 194-96. A more expanded explanation can be found in his work *The Way of Jesus Christ: Christology in Messianic Dimensions* (Minneapolis: Fortress, 1993), 181-96.

... and as a hope to be fully realized in the future is the context of the life and ministry of Jesus as well as the key to his words and deeds."[73] This entails perceiving Jesus' earthly ministry to the poor and his confrontations with oppressive powers that led ultimately to the cross as the very shape of God's advancing eschatological kingdom. In other words, God's eschatological kingdom is cruciform. Again, Löffler is instructive when he says that "the suffering of Christ, understood in the context of the beginning kingdom of God, raises above all the issue of power, of the counterpower of Christ versus the established powers of this world."[74]

As an eschatological community, the church therefore needs to go beyond exclaiming "Conversion alone!" by proclaiming the gospel exclusively to the inner recesses of the human heart so that individuals will be taken to heaven away from the earth.[75] It must be ready to follow Jesus, even to the point of suffering, in disclosing concretely and witnessing to God's character of love, justice, and righteousness in anticipation of the fulfillment of his future reign. Kosuke Koyama is right in saying that because God's nature is to be involved with others in history, the "eschatology of the Bible has this basic orientation toward the others."[76]

THIS WORLD OR THE OTHER?

Yonggi Cho's this-worldly eschatology had its contextual roots in Korea's wartime sufferings. Although trained under classical Pentecostal missionaries, his experiences with the suffering Korean people, coupled with a shift in Pentecostal attention to a this-worldly eschatology in the 1960s, helped shape his theology of blessing.[77] Shirley Ho points to similar contextual factors in the case of Taiwanese Christians who have embraced what she calls "Taiwan Philo-Semitic Theology," or a theological preoccupation with Jews/Israel. According to Ho, Taiwan's "underdog" experience and shamanistic culture contributed to their seeking material blessings, as well as their finding a closer affinity with the Jews who are known for their wealth.[78]

Cho's theology of wealth certainly has some contextual and biblical-theological basis, and it provides answers to the material longings of many of Asia's poor.[79] It is nonetheless also fraught with peril. Korea's Tonghap Presbyterian denomination released a study of Cho's theology of blessing in 1983 and stated, among other things, that it tended toward teaching spiritual salvation as a means of receiving blessings in this earthly life, thus connecting God's salvation with worldliness and success-centeredness.[80] Ma also points out that the theology of blessing

---

[73]Paul Löffler, "The Reign of God Has Come in the Suffering Christ: An Exploration of the Power of the Powerless," *International Review of Mission* 68, no. 270 (April 1979): 110. See also Yeo, "Eschatological View of History," 39.

[74]Löffler, "Reign of God," 111.

[75]Roko Kerovec, "The Resurrection of Christ and the Eschatological Vision of the Kingdom of God as the Platform for Evangelistic Practice: The Challenges and Possibilities of the Evangelistic Commission," *Kairos: Evangelical Journal of Theology* 2, no. 2 (2008): 191-92.

[76]Kosuke Koyama, "The Asian Approach to Christ," *Missiology: An International Review* 12, no. 4 (October 1984): 440. See Denis Edwards, *How God Acts: Creation, Redemption, and Special Divine Action* (Minneapolis: Fortress, 2010), 26-33.

[77]Wonsuk Ma, "Pentecostal Eschatology: What Happened When the Wave Hit the West End of the Ocean," *Asian Journal of Pentecostal Studies* 12, no. 1 (2009): 103.

[78]Shirley S. Ho, "The Philosemitic Theology on the Eschatological Restoration of Israel in Taiwan Christianity" (paper presented at the Annual American Academy of Religion and Society of Biblical Literature, Boston, November 2017), 15-16. Like Taiwan Philo-Semitic Theology, the early Pentecostals embraced philo-Semitism mainly upon their appropriation of dispensational premillennialism. See Eric Nelson Newberg, *The Pentecostal Mission: The Legacy of Pentecostal Zionism* (Eugene, OR: Pickwick, 2012), 209-13.

[79]See Ma, "Cho's Theology of Blessing," 145-58; Yung, "Missiological Challenge," 70-76.

[80]Kim, *Korean Pentecostalism*, 207.

is "by nature self-centered," and if it fails to integrate what authentic Christian discipleship means, then its adherents may simply measure the quality of their lives by the blessings they have, ask God for wealth merely out of selfish interests, and seek blessings through unjust and oppressive means. The theological purpose of the blessings is thus of crucial importance.[81]

In contrast, the early Korean Presbyterian Church, Watchman Nee, and the Back to Jerusalem movement took a mainly otherworldly orientation. The early Pentecostals also looked to Christ's imminent return and similarly became preoccupied with missionary zeal for winning souls. Like the Back to Jerusalem movement and the Korean Presbyterians, Pentecostal missionaries from the West, including Filipino *balikbayans* (returning overseas residents) in the 1940s, were convinced, especially after experiencing Spirit baptism, that the Christian calling is primarily about proclaiming the gospel.[82]

Without denigrating the biblical mandate concerning the missionary enterprise, as well as the sufferings that Nee and the other Christians in Asia have experienced, the consequences of their otherworldly eschatology must not be overlooked. One key concern is related to Christian social responsibility. With a particular focus on the imminent return of Christ and the future realization of God's kingdom, Nee and the others were pessimistic about the affairs of this

world, so they disregarded the eschatological import of the church's responsibility to society. Korea's Hang-Sik Cho puts it this way: "The most devastating eschatological teaching in respect to structural social change is a pessimistic fatalism concerning social conditions . . . as espoused by dispensational premillennialists."[83] Here we see the acute relationship between eschatology and ethics. As Rian Venter says incisively, "Eschatology is fundamentally an ethical project— it has performative effects."[84] Or, in this instance, nonperformative.

Justice in the here and now is thus a casualty of such an otherworldly eschatology. Social reforms, engagement in the public sphere, and care for nature and the environment are generally deemed unimportant, since the world is a sinking ship.[85] This notion actually expresses a dualistic cosmology in which the old heaven and earth are expected to pass away to give way to the new (e.g., 2 Pet 3:7), which are not located in the same historical continuity. But if the eschatological kingdom of God is intertwined with the historical Christ event—his life, death, and resurrection—then not only do the old and the new heaven and earth share the same historical platform, but the kingdom of God must also be seen in the context of time and space.[86] Justice, similarly, must be in time and space. That is, it must be historically, culturally, and socially located. As Bradley Johnson notes, based on the apostle Paul's unveiling of a new

---

[81]Ma, "Cho's Theology of Blessing," 158. See also Juliet Ma, "Eschatology and Mission: Living the 'Last Days' Today," *Transformation* 26, no. 3 (July 2009): 195-96.

[82]Ma, "Pentecostal Eschatology," 99.

[83]Hang-Sik Cho, *Eschatology and Ecology*, 192.

[84]Rian Venter, "Trends in Contemporary Christian Eschatological Reflection," *Missionalia* 43, no. 1 (2015): 115.

[85]Adherents of premillennialism are of course not homogeneous in their doctrine and practice, like the revivalists of the late nineteenth century who held on to a pessimistic outlook on the world but, in contrast with other premillennialists of their time, persisted in their social relief work to prepare the poor in receiving the gospel. Bernie A. Van De Walle, *The Heart of the Gospel: A. B. Simpson, the Fourfold Gospel, and Late Nineteenth-Century Evangelical Theology* (Eugene, OR: Pickwick, 2009), 49-51. In regard to dispensationalism and ecology, see Hang-Sik Cho, *Eschatology and Ecology*, 222-24.

[86]Kerovec, "Resurrection of Christ," 192-93.

creation in line with Romans 2:13-14, justice must be achievable in the present. It is not something that only an apocalypse can bring. "Justice, in short, need not be an appeal to, or a promise of, a change in reality that comes from beyond existing reality. If we are to do justice to justice, we will allow it to become possible—to become transformative now."[87]

CONCLUSION: CRUCIFORM ESCHATOLOGY IN ASIA

"The time is fulfilled, and the kingdom of God has come near; repent, and believe in the gospel" (Mk 1:15). To the multitudes of Asia's poor and oppressed, Jesus' proclamation of the in-breaking of God's eschatological kingdom can only be good news. But, before it can be good news to them, it must first be so to the churches in Asia, especially in those nations where Christianity came through colonization. Many Asians certainly have something in common with the Indians who once sent this message to Pope John Paul II: "We used to praise our God in our language, with our gestures and dances, with instruments made by us, until the day European civilization arrived. It erected the sword, the language, and the cross, and made us crucified nations."[88] While it will never be easy for the church in any nation to extricate itself from its painful past, we do well to remember that it is precisely because of such experiences that God inaugurated his kingdom through the risen Christ, who was crucified.

In the previous section, the discussion centered on the this-worldly and otherworldly aspects of eschatology. If we are right in claiming that God's kingdom has already begun its realization through the Christ event, and that it is both a this-worldly and an otherworldly reality, the question for the church in Asia is not only whether it also embodies this tension as an eschatological community, but also from where it comes.

Koyama insightfully remarks: "Christianity has given humanity a new concept of center . . . seen in the life and death of Jesus Christ. In short, Jesus Christ, the center person, establishes his centrality by going to the periphery . . . by being crucified. . . . Thus, Christianity has made it possible, through its eschatology, to have a view from the periphery."[89]

Indeed, in poverty-stricken Asia, the church needs to claim the periphery, where the broken and downtrodden are, as the locus of God's cruciform eschatological kingdom. Amid the temptation to escape from this world by adapting a dehistoricized eschatology or by rejecting the periphery in light of a this-worldly eschatological gospel of prosperity, Asian churches are called to be broken themselves and stretch out their hands in defense of the poor and vulnerable—the Dalits, the Moros, the Minjung, the Rohingyas, and similarly situated people. This includes the environment or the earth, which also groans because of human exploitation (Rom 8:19-25). It is precisely to remind the church, in Asia and throughout the world, of this important eschatological task that Jesus left to us the practice of the Eucharist. David Power's reminder aptly concludes this essay:

Today, at the Lord's table, we need to be particularly mindful of those who have perished through violence, through the senseless death of hunger and illness, or through deprivation of their cul-

[87]Bradley A. Johnson, "Doing Justice to Justice: Re-assessing Deconstructive Eschatology," *Political Theology* 12, no. 1 (2011): 22-23.
[88]K. Koyama, "New World—New Creation: Mission in Power and Faith," *Mission Studies* 10 (1993): 59-77, here 60.
[89]Koyama, "Asian Approach to Christ," 445-46.

tural heritage that is not only a matter of song, dance, and expression, but also of the space and time in which they provide for existence, heritage, and future. To hope even for those dead in

the knowledge of the love of God shown in Christ is one of the qualities of eschatological hope, a hope that leads also to action for justice.[90]

FURTHER READING

Bergmann, Sigurd, ed. *Eschatology as Imagining the End: Faith Between Hope and Despair.* New York: Routledge, 2018.

Braaten, Carl E. *Essays on the Theology and Ethics of the Kingdom of God.* Eugene, OR: Wipf & Stock, 2016.

Phelan, John E., Jr. *Essential Eschatology: Our Present and Future Hope.* Downers Grove, IL: IVP Academic, 2013.

Westhelle, Vítor. *Eschatology and Space: The Lost Dimension in Theology Past and Present.* New York: Palgrave Macmillan, 2012.

Wilfred, Felix. *Asian Public Theology: Critical Concerns in Challenging Times.* Delhi: Tercentenary Publication, 2010.

[90]David N. Power, "Eucharistic Justice," *Theological Studies* 67 (December 2006): 873. In another essay, I relate eucharistic justice to peacemaking initiatives with the Muslims of the Philippines or the Bangsamoro people. See Aldrin M. Peñamora, "Eucharistic Justice: A Christ-Centered Response to the Bangsamoro Question in the Philippines," *Asian Journal of Pentecostal Studies* 19, no. 1 (February 2016): 31-44.

FROM JUDEOPHILIA TO *TA-TUNG* IN TAIWANESE ESCHATOLOGY

Shirley S. Ho

AFTER A CRITICAL ANALYSIS of the prevailing Judeophilia in Taiwanese contemporary churches and eschatological reflections by some Taiwanese Bible commentators, this essay builds on the prophetic text of Isaiah 2:1-5 together with some pertinent New Testament passages and incorporating Chinese political reformer Kang Yu-Wei's vision of *Ta-Tung* to construct a robust Christian eschatology for Taiwan. This is a timely reflection not only for the context in view but also for the global context, where nationalism is gaining ground in ecclesiastical and national policies.

INTRODUCTION

Over the past few years there has been a resurgence of interest among Chinese Christians in the eschatological restoration of Israel. Interestingly, this renewed interest in Israel's national restoration is evident not only among the Chinese community but also in other cultures.[1] In 2017, when US President Donald Trump recognized Jerusalem as the capital city of Israel and effected the transfer of the US embassy to Jerusalem, the policy received two opposing reactions around the world: resistance and support. Among Taiwanese Christians, there were apparently those who held a neutral position, while others expressed some form of support of the policy, some openly and others clandestinely. However, forceful and outright resistance to the policy was almost absent among Taiwanese Christians. This essay will investigate Taiwanese Christians' views of the eschatological restoration of Israel.

Mindful that the Hebrew Bible contains numerous texts on the subject matter, I have chosen to pay close attention to one: Isaiah 2:1-5. This essay comprises three main sections. I shall first provide a summary of how other Taiwanese Bible commentators read the passage. I shall then highlight a Jewish-centered reading and will discuss the rationale for the adoption of that vision of eschatology. Last, guided by Isaiah 2:1-5, New Testament passages, and the reframing of Kang Yu-Wei's *Ta-Tung* utopian conception, I will propose a Taiwanese Christian eschatology, which is to be preferred over a Jewish-centered eschatology since it corresponds more faithfully to the biblical witness.

---

[1]Don Finto, in *God's Promise and the Future of Israel* (Ventura, CA: Regal, 2006), writes: "Three events are shaping our 21st century: Jewish eyes are opening to the revelation that Yeshua is their Messiah; nations long held in darkness are learning of the God who brings redemption to the world through Israel's famous son; and a centuries-long anti-semitic church is beginning to come alive to the Jewish roots of her faith, to acknowledge her sins and to come together with her Jewish brothers and sisters as one flock in God" (101).

THREE REPRESENTATIVE CHINESE READINGS OF ISAIAH 2:1-5

Isaiah 2:1-5 is one of the primary texts in Old Testament Zion theology. This short yet promising passage includes numerous important utopian themes: the house of the Lord, symbolic of the presence of God in Zion (Is 2:2); the congregation of an international community of both Jews and Gentiles (Is 2:3); and adherence to the Torah of the Lord from Zion (Is 2:3). It envisages the Lord as the judge over the international community to achieve common goals of peace and harmony by military disarmament (Is 2:4). Preoccupation with war and violence will be replaced by agricultural cultivation and development (Is 2:4). Finally, "light" will characterize the life of the international community (Is 2:5).

Zion as localized church. The first representative reading of Isaiah 2:1-5 is that of Lin Yong-Tsi, who reads it as a textbook on local church government and management. Regarding the image of military apparatus turned into agricultural tools, he writes, "The proper way to deal with conflict in the church is not through authoritative force, but through love for one another, fellowship, and support. The church is the ideal spiritual kingdom." On Isaiah 2:4, on God's execution of judgment, he argues that the decisions of the local church's officials who are chosen by God should be upheld. He reads the language of Zion's standing out among all others as a reference to the church as superior over earthly standards. He pays particular attention to the moral and Christian character of believers in pursuing holiness and righteousness. Last, he understands "the establishment of Zion" as the

statement of faith and the doctrinal teaching of the True Church denomination, which stands strong and will not be moved by slander and false teachings.[2]

Zion as social justice and peace. Another representative reading is that of Chen Nan-Chou.[3] For him, the passage is a proof text for any discussion on social justice, peace, and reconciliation. He speaks of the racial disharmony and discrimination in the world, particularly in the United States. In his commentary, he inserts an anecdote about how he was once forbidden to enter the United Nations in New York because he comes from Taiwan, not a member state. He hails Martin Luther King Jr., with his famous "I have a dream" rhetoric, as a social activist who promoted social equality. Chen maintains that Jesus' teaching about God's kingdom and Martin Luther King Jr.'s advocacy are the same. Insofar as there is a lack of peace in many parts of the world, he affirms that one can build on the work done by Martin Luther King Jr. and hope that one day there will be true justice and peace in the world. Chen's theologizing resonates well with secular and cultural justice.

Ideal Zion as new Jerusalem. Jeffrey Lu reads the text in relation to Isaiah 65–66 on the vision of the new Jerusalem. This new Jerusalem is the center of international pilgrimage, revelation, and peace. He maintains that the vision speaks of the "Ideal Zion" and that the Ideal Zion is a symbol that goes beyond the historical eighth-century BC Judah and Jerusalem but is *replaced by* the spiritual Zion. The thrice-repeated references to "Jacob" (Is 2:3, 5, 6) and the mention of "Israel" (Isa 4:2) are seen as markers

[2] 林永基 《活讀以塞亞書》 台中: 腓利門實業股份有限公司 [Lin Yong-Ji, *Live Reading on Isaiah* (2009), 35].
[3] 陳南州 《上主是天上任間的主： 以賽亞書 1~39章》 台南:台灣教會報社 [Chen Nan-Zhou, *The Lord Is the Lord in Heaven: Isaiah 1–38* (2016)].

that the vision goes beyond geographical Zion.[4] This highlights the spiritual people of God in an ideal Zion. Quoting 2 Timothy 2:22, he states that the spiritual people of God will be characterized by waiting on God's sovereignty, seeking after God's instructions, upholding God's justice and peace, and pursuing spiritual communities that pray with a pure heart.[5]

TAIWANESE JUDEOPHILIA ESCHATOLOGY

Aside from the above interpretive traditions, Jewish-centered eschatology is the order of the day. The following elements characterize Taiwanese Judeophilia eschatology.

Literal fulfillment eschatology. Taiwanese Judeophilia eschatology is unapologetic that literal reading is the first interpretive principle unless the text before and after suggests otherwise. It argues for a literal reading by rhetorically asking: "Don't the prophecies about the Messiah have to be literally interpreted and literally fulfilled in Jesus Christ? Why then do we not interpret the prophecies about the restoration of Israel literally as well?"[6] Its hermeneutics build on the prophecies about the Messiah, which were literally interpreted and fulfilled in the person of Jesus Christ.

Greater attention is placed on foretelling than on forthtelling. The fulfillment of the prophecy is the centerpiece. Taiwanese Judeophilia eschatology reads the promises of Isaiah 2:1-5 as first fulfilled in 1948, when Israel gained its independence, led by Jewish leader and Prime Minister David Ben-Gurion. The establishment of the modern state of Israel in Palestine is considered the "watershed in human history."[7] Taiwanese Judeophilia eschatology recognizes that through numerous waves of Aliyah Zionist immigration, Israel will continue to return to their land and await its complete fulfillment.[8] Denny Ma associates Isaiah 2:1-5 with Beit Ya'akov Lekhu Venelkha (House, Jacob, Come, Walk). This is an organization founded in 1882 that seeks to establish the restoration of Israel based on this Isaiah passage.[9]

Taiwanese Judeophilia eschatology argues that God's plan for Israel was to first gather them back to their land and then give them a new, circumcised heart and spirit (Ezek 11:18-20).[10] This responds to critics who question the 1948 event as the fulfillment of the prophecies and the lack of differentiation between political and spiritual Israel. Critics prioritize Jewish spiritual repentance, but, for Taiwanese Judeophilia eschatology, spiritual restoration is not enough. The national restoration of Israel is also necessary.

Proponents of Taiwanese Judeophilia eschatology claim that their interpretation and theology is based on the grace, wisdom, sovereignty, and faithfulness of God. "Israel's historical experience has never been experienced by other people groups and nations in the world. They have been colonized by many great and gentile nations, like Egypt, Assyria, Babylon, Persia, Romans, and Ottoman Empire, etc. but they still

---

[4]Jeffrey Shao Chang Lu, *Isaiah*, Tien Dao Bible Commentary [以賽亞 （一）] (Hong Kong: Tien Dao, 2015), 138.

[5]Lu, *Isaiah*, 139.

[6]「以色列復國是否應驗聖經預言？ （二）」 ["Is Israel's National Restoration a Biblical Fulfilment? (Part II)"], www.fundamental book.com/article193.html.

[7]Timothy Lee, 「世界局勢分水嶺：以色列復國」 ["The Watershed in Human History: Israel's National Restoration"], *TruthLoveShare* (blog), May 2010, www.luke54.org/view/18/726.html.

[8]"Is Israel's National Restoration a Biblical Fulfilment? (Part II)."

[9]Denny Ma, *Glory of Redemption: A Commentary on the Book of Isaiah* (Taipei: Tian-en, 2005).

[10]"Is Israel's National Restoration a Biblical Fulfilment? (Part II)."

survive."[11] Israel's survival is a demonstration that God has a distinct plan for them. Taiwanese Judeophilia eschatology cites biblical texts that include non-Jews and pagan Gentiles, yet the sovereign God fulfills his plan for the Jews (e.g., through King Cyrus).

Instead of debating historical-critical issues, the Taiwanese Judeophilia eschatology hermeneutical lens looks at the unfolding fulfillment of these prophecies in contemporary modern history: the current geopolitical situation in the news on the one hand, and the prophecies in the Old Testament on the other hand.[12] Prophecy as a spiritual gift and phenomenon is a lived reality. The national and social developments of the Jews are seen as God at work rather than simply historical events of political, social, and economic causality. Since the ancient prophecies about Israel are currently being fulfilled, contemporary prophecies spoken by pastor-prophets are also deemed trustworthy. This grants license to practice prophecy in modern times.

Jewish-privileged eschatology. Taiwanese Judeophilia eschatology concurs with the prevailing narrative that God has rejected Israel because of their unbelief in Jesus as the Messiah (Mt 8:11-12; Acts 13:46). But it is quick to say that God has not completely abandoned Israel (Rom 11:1-2, 25-29). The rejection of Israel as God's chosen people in human history is deemed temporary and partial. God's irrevocable intention is to restore the fortunes of Israel. Taiwanese Judeophilia eschatology believes that the Jews

have "sacred possession" of the land of Israel (Gen 17:8). "No other nations or countries, ancient or modern, not even USA or England or China have sacred possession of their respective lands. If there was any nation who has a sacred possession of their land, it would be Israel."[13] Peter Lu opines, "On that day, the place of the Jewish nation and Israelites will be higher than other non-Jewish nations."[14] Taiwanese Judeophilia eschatology argues that replacement theology has misunderstood the New Testament texts on unity (Eph 2:14; Rom 3:22; 10:12). Accordingly, unity in the church does not mean that the Gentiles have replaced the Jews in God's salvation history.

Reverend Nathaniel Chou argues that replacement theology has "suppressed" (*fēngshā*) the Jews from the "whole bowl of salvation," leaving the Jews without any share in this salvation. He preaches, "Thank God, as we are transformed, God has revealed his will to us to pay attention to our 'Jewish big brother.' We have to learn from them, love them and honor them. May God lead not only Taiwan but Chinese churches and non-Chinese churches not to 'suppress the Jews' anymore. In the fullness of time, we will see all Jews saved."[15]

Missional eschatology. While others read Isaiah 2:1-5 in theological abstraction and ethical-moral reflection, Taiwanese Judeophilia eschatology is oriented toward evangelism and world missions. This way of reading calls the Chinese churches to participate in the evangelization of the

---

[11]"Is Israel's National Restoration a Biblical Fulfilment? (Part II)."

[12]For example, the article "Proving Biblical Prophecies: Israel Media," *Kingdom Revival Times*, October 16, 2016, is in consonance with pesher reading of Old Testament texts mindful of the two horizons.

[13]"Is Israel's National Restoration a Biblical Fulfilment? (Part II)."

[14]Peter C. S. Lu, *A Commentary on the Book of Isaiah in the 21st Century* (Vista, CA: Christ-Centered Gospel Mission, 2004), 40.

[15] 李容珍與林鈺庭. 「國家祭壇：回轉到神面前得地為業」 [Nathaniel Chou, "National Prayer Altar: Return to God; Land as Inheritance"], in *Chinese Christian Tribune* 3851 (October 2016): 5, www.ct.org.tw/1295078. Rev. Chou spoke about the theme of suppression (*fēngshā* 封殺): how the church in the past suppressed the Jews, Taiwan aborigines, the Jewish festivals, and the Holy Spirit, exhorting Taiwan churches to repent.

Jews. Chinese Christians are viewed as transformative agents. Hence, long- and short-term missions teams are sent to modern Israel. Jewish missions receives more funding than that for other people groups (e.g., Muslims). Prayer rallies for Jews to believe in the Messiah Jesus Christ are on the rise. Proponents self-designate as "watchmen for Israel" (Hab 2:1). Sharing the gospel with Jews is viewed as their divine calling and a chance "to pay the debt of the gospel." Having been recipients of Western missionary work in the past, they are now self-commissioned to take the gospel back to the Jews— hence the Back to Jerusalem movement as a missionary phenomenon and vision of the churches in China. They see themselves on the front line in taking on the missionary responsibility of taking the gospel west and south of China, including the Middle East. They believe that this missionary work is a precondition for Jesus' return and will hasten it (Mt 24:14).[16]

Analogical eschatology. Judeophilia eschatology perceives Jewish restoration as a precondition to Taiwan's national and spiritual renewal. In the vision statement of Tabernacle of David, the goal is to pursue, first, the revival of national Israel and, second, the revival of the churches of Taiwan.[17]

Moreover, the relationship between Israel and the church is expressed not solely in terms of historical priority but also in essence. Chang explains, "Whenever we talk about the election of God's people, it includes Israel as the sand of the seashore and the church as the stars in the sky; all are Abraham's descendants, natural and spiritual descendants. But the spiritual cannot come first; instead, the natural should come first (I Cor 15:46)." In another sermon, he says, "God has used the restoration of Israel as the sign of God's renewal [of the world]; God will also use the church, his spiritual children, to do the work of renewal."[18] Chou identifies Israel as the "big brother" (*Zhǎngzǐ*) of the church. It is believed that the revival of Taiwan as a nation is connected with the revival of Israel.

The connection is demonstrated by restoring and employing Old Testament language and themes in local churches: blowing rams' horns, the use of the language of "altar" (*iìtán*), hoisting Jewish flags, wearing Jewish clothing, celebrating the Jewish feasts and festivals, adopting the Jewish calendar, pitching tents to celebrate Sukkoth, and learning Jewish education and economics.[19] Taiwanese Judeophilia eschatology rationalizes that if Taiwanese churches find their roots in the Jewish faith, they also will be recipients of God's blessings like Israel.

Contrary to Marcionism, Taiwanese Judeophilia eschatology takes the Old Testament to be the authoritative revelation of God. It regards the election of Israel, their history, and culture as God's revelation to humanity rather than simply a medium of God's revelation of his salvation plan. Accordingly, Israel does not just prefigure the church. The concern for the Israel/Jewish calendar,

---

[16]Paul Hattaway, *Back to Jerusalem: Three Chinese House Church Leaders Share Their Vision to Complete the Great Commission* (Carlisle, UK: Piquant, 2003), 20.

[17]A Christian organization that publishes books, writes and produces music, organizes leadership training, etc. "We believe that before the coming of the Lord, there will be a global revival. . . . Such revival at least covers four areas: (1) the revival of Israel; (2) the revival of the glorious church (spiritual Israel); (3) the revival of every tribe, every people and every nation; (4) the revival of all heaven and earth (Rom. 8:18, 21). In the Bible we see the last wave of revival before the 2nd coming of the Christ; the most important movement of revival is restoring the Tabernacle of David." www.hosanna-tod.com/about_us/?parent_id=30, accessed April 29, 2020.

[18]章啟明 [Chang Tzi-Min] 「從以色列的復興認識先見創意文化」 [Discover the Creative Culture from the Revival of Israel], August 2017, www.hosanna-tod.com/festival/?parent_id=1643. On this website is a table that compares the restoration of Israel on the one hand with the renewal of the church.

[19]The philo-Semitism is selective, as it does not adopt the Jewish dietary system.

customs, and practices does not serve as background for understanding Old Testament texts. Instead, this approach makes the Jewish calendar and culture part of God's revelation itself.

THE RATIONALE FOR TAIWANESE JUDEOPHILIA ESCHATOLOGY

One's social and cultural milieu and experience affect one's interpretive strategies and theology. Despite the linguistic, geographical, cultural, and geopolitical distance between Taiwan and Israel, Taiwanese Christians have a magnetic affinity for Israel. I suggest the following three possible social and cultural realities that serve as hermeneutical contexts behind the theology.

First, geopolitically, the Taiwanese perceive themselves as the underdogs or victims of strong, oppressive powers. Despite possessing a democratic government, flag, and monetary system, Taiwan is hard-pressed as an independent sovereign country. The tense relationship between Taiwan and China goes back to 1949. China has moved the international community, including the United Nations, to withhold Taiwan independence from China.[20] Because of this kind of geopolitical humiliation, in addition to the history of Western colonization and the context of a shame culture, Taiwan identifies with the Jews, whose geopolitical sovereignty is also con-

stantly under threat. The Old Testament language of "possessing the land as heritage," "restoration/renewal of the land," and "freedom from bondage" appeals to Taiwanese Judeophilia eschatology and is part of their corporate prayers.

Second, although the Taiwanese are steeped in shamanism and ancestral worship, Taiwan is increasingly a secular and materialistic society. The Taiwanese are more interested in economics than politics.[21] Neighboring the larger economic market of China, the Taiwanese are looking for new paradigms to achieve economic and financial prosperity.[22] In the eyes of the Taiwanese, the Jews are known to be rich, famous, and successful.[23] The Chinese psyche wants to emulate the best practices and practitioners of economic prosperity. This explains the preponderance of Jewish economic management books in the Taiwanese market.[24] Given the combination of the seduction of the prosperity gospel, the force of materialism, and the economic growth and development of Mainland China, it is not surprising that this kind of Judeophilia strikes a chord with many Taiwanese Christians.[25]

Third, Taiwanese culture is grounded in the teachings of Confucianism and Taoism. As a social and ethical philosophy, Confucianism accounts for the personal, social, and environmental realms of human existence.[26] Insofar as

---

[20]Ng Yuzin Chiautong, 「台灣與中國關係的探索」 [An Excursion into the Relationships Between Taiwan and China], in 臺灣國際研究季刊 8, no. 1 (2012): 1-12; Jeanne Hoffman, "Taiwan Trap: New Stories Needed—Rethinking Taiwan and China Futures," *Journal of Future Studies* 21, no. 4 (2017): 1-17; Sui-Sheng Jao, "Chinese Nationalism and Beijing's Taiwan Policy: A China Threat?," *Issues & Studies* 36, no. 1 (2000): 76-99.

[21]Chun-Chi Chang and Te-Sheng Chen, "Idealism Versus Reality: An Empirical Test of Postmaterialism in China and Taiwan," in *Issues & Studies* 49, no. 2 (2013): 63-102.

[22]Shin-Ta Tung, "Economics and Business of Great China from Taiwan's Perspective," 創新與管理 12, no. 3 (2016): 73-94.

[23]In the 2017 Forbes World's Billionaires list, five Jews were in the top fifteen, and seven in the top twenty-five. Mark Zuckerberg is the world's richest Jew. Wang Jianlin from China ranked eighteen, and Li Ka-Sheng ranked nineteen.

[24]Rabbi Daniel Lapin's *Thou Shall Prosper* was translated into Chinese (猶太人致富金律) in 2009. A book by Zvika Bergman titled *Secrets the Rich Jews Know* was translated into Chinese in 2015.

[25]James Ross and Song Lihong, *The Image of Jews in Contemporary China* (Boston: Academic Studies, 2016). Lihong maintains that in China, the fascination with Jewish/Israeli culture is mainly economic and educational, without the religious aspect, unlike in Taiwan. Lihong Song, "Some Observations on Chinese Jewish Studies," *Contemporary Jewry* 29 (2009): 195-214.

[26]Kwok Pui-Lan, "Chinese Christians and Their Bible," *Biblical Interpretation* 4, no. 1 (1996): 127-29. Confucianism is not a religion, for it has little to say about metaphysical and spiritual realities. Should there be any metaphysical reality, it is more an abstract concept than a person.

the Jewish culture has deep moral and ethical traditions regarding family, education, and lifestyle, Taiwanese Christians have a strong affinity for it.[27] Books on Jewish child education translated into Chinese are available in local bookstores.[28] Taiwanese Bible-reading practices focus on the moral teachings rather than on the doctrinal, historical, or political aspects of the Old Testament.

In sum, the observation of Philip Jenkins that the Global South is characterized by "its veneration for Old Testament, which is considered as authoritative as the New" is now confirmed.[29] Taiwanese culture has more similarities with Jewish than with Western and Greek cultures. Regarding the Jews as the big brother of the church resonates well, since ancestral and family solidarity, and respect for the elderly and one's predecessors, are intrinsic aspects of the culture.

TOWARD A TAIWANESE ESCHATOLOGICAL *TA-TUNG* READING OF ISAIAH 2:1-5

The prophet Isaiah's vision in Isaiah 2:1-5 of communal peace and harmony is attractive to Taiwanese culture. The concept of harmony is composed of two Chinese characters 大同, *Ta-Tung*. *Ta-Tung* is an ideology that has reached the popular level as an everyday motto among Taiwanese. It is used to designate major thoroughfares, businesses, edifices, hotels, and educational institutions; and, most importantly, *Ta-Tung* appears among the lyrics of the Taiwan National Anthem. Sun Yat-Sen wrote this anthem to instill among the citizens the pursuit of *Ta-Tung*, translated here as "world peace":

> Three Principles of the People,
> Our aim shall be:
> To found a free land,
> World peace, be our stand.
> Lead on, comrades,
> Vanguards ye are....
> Be earnest and brave,
> Your country to save,
> One heart, one soul,
> One mind, one goal . . .

Confucius once wrote a poem to describe his *Ta-Tung* commonwealth vision:

> When the Great Principle prevails, the world is a Commonwealth in which rulers are selected according to their wisdom and ability. Mutual confidence is promoted and good neighborliness cultivated. Hence, men do not regard as parents only their own parents, nor do they treat as children only their own children. Provision is secured for the aged till death, employment for the able-bodied, and the means of growing up for the young. Helpless widows and widowers, orphans and the lonely, as well as the sick and the disabled, are well cared for. Men have their respective occupations and women their homes. They do not like to see wealth lying idle, yet they do not keep it for their own gratification. They despise indolence, yet they do not use their energies for their own benefit. In this way, selfish schemings are repressed, and robbers, thieves and other lawless men no longer exist, and there is no need for people to shut their doors. This is called the Great Harmony (*Ta-Tung*). [English translation by James Legge]

---

[27]Der-Heuy Yee, 「台灣本地行事邏輯的探討：尋找尚未接上的環節」 [Social Betterment in the Realm of Practical Ethics in Taiwanese Society: In Search of a Missing Link], 慈濟大學人文社會科學學刊 7 (2008): 25-63.

[28]For example, Wendy Mogel, *The Blessing of a Skinned Knee: Using Jewish Teachings to Raise Self-Reliant Children* [孩子需要9種福分：古猶太教的教養智慧] (Scribner, 2008); Sara Imas, *Jewish Mother Gives Three Keys to Children: Viability, Will Power, Ability to Solve Problems* [猶太媽媽給孩子的3把金鑰：生存力、意志力、解決問題的能力] (2015).

[29]Philip Jenkins, *The New Faces of Christianity: Believing the Bible in the Global South* (Oxford: Oxford University Press, 2006), 4-5.

Kang Yu-Wei (1858–1927) captured this utopian vision and developed it further by setting out concrete methods and procedures to achieve it. As a political thinker and reformer of the late Qing dynasty, he wrote the book *Ta-Tung Shu* (The Book of the Great Harmony).

Kang mulls over an alternative to Buddhism's solution to the problem of human suffering. Buddhism's way to overcome suffering is to make human desire extinct—to suppress desire in any way possible. Kang, however, proposes an alternative narrative, speaking strongly about "The Evils of Having Sovereign States." Sovereign states cause different types of human suffering, such as war, violence, and bloodshed. He writes:

> Coming now to the [matter of] existence of states, then there is quarrelling of the land, quarrelling over cities, and the people are trained to be soldiers. In a single war those who die [will number in] the thousands and ten thousands. [They] may meet with arrows, stones, lances, cannon, poison gas. And then again, [they] may be disemboweled or decapitated, [their] blood splashed on the field, [their] limbs hung in the trees. Sometimes they are thrown into a river, dragging each other under. Sometimes a whole city is burned. Sometimes the corpses are strewn everywhere and dogs fight over them. Sometimes half [of the army] lies wounded, and then hunger and pestilence continue the deaths.[30]

His political strategy to achieve sustainable peace and harmony is twofold: complete military disarmament and the abolition of sovereign boundaries. The way he expresses this is powerful: "The desire to bring about peace among men cannot [be accomplished] without

disarmament; and the desire to bring about disarmament cannot [be accomplished] without abolishing sovereign states."[31]

He proposes the abolition of nine boundaries, which will lead to harmony in the one world:

1. Abolishing National Boundaries and Uniting the World

2. Abolishing Class Boundaries and Equalizing [All] People

3. Abolishing Racial Boundaries and Amalgamating the Races

4. Abolishing Sex Boundaries and Preserving Independence

5. Abolishing Family Boundaries and Becoming "Heaven's People"

6. Abolishing Livelihood Boundaries and Making Occupations Public

7. Abolishing Administrative Boundaries and Governing with Complete Peace-and-Equality

8. Abolishing Boundaries of Kind, and Loving All Living [Things]

9. Abolishing Boundaries of Suffering and Attaining Utmost Happiness

Finally, a student of Confucius's three-age paradigm, he envisages that this one world will be the product of evolution in three stages:[32]

> First Stage: The Age of Disorder at the Time the First Foundations of One World Is Laid
>
> Second Stage: The Age of Increasing Peace-and-Equality When One World Is Gradually Coming into Being
>
> Third Stage: The Age of Complete Peace-and-Equality When One World Has Been Achieved

[30]Kang, Yu-Wei, *Ta t'ung shu: The One-World Philosophy of Kang Yu-Wei*, trans. Laurence G. Thompson (London: George Allen & Unwin, 1958), 81.
[31]Kang, *Ta t'ung shu*, 83.
[32]Kang, *Ta t'ung shu*, 72.

To be sure, Kang's *Ta-Tung* vision cannot be indiscriminately adopted as Christian eschatology. In fact, Kang could be censured as naive, a racist, a polygamist, and an atheist according to modern and Christian sensibilities given his views on humanity, race, and marriage. For instance, there is naiveté in supposing that human beings will naturally and progressively become good in the final stage. His racism is observable when he says: "When the One World is attained, there will remain only the white and yellow race. The black and brown race will probably all be swept away from the earth." He is guilty of promoting polygamy, believing that monogamy goes against human nature and desire.[33] Assuredly, Kang's utopian vision falls short of the Christian vision of eschatology. His *Ta-Tung* lacks Christian theistic foundations. Most importantly, a day of judgment is not in his purview. He writes:

> Christianity takes reverence for God and love for men as a teaching of the Good; it takes repentance of sin and judgment after death as its [means of making people] frightened by [doing] evil. In the Age of Complete Peace-and-Equality, [people] will naturally love others, will naturally be without sin. Comprehending the natural workings of evolution, they will therefore not reverence God. Comprehending the impossibility [literally, "difficulty"] of limitless numbers of souls occupying the space [of Heaven], they therefore will not believe in a Day of Judgement. The religion of Jesus therefore, when we have attained One World, will be extinct.[34]

Kang's *Ta-Tung* vision certainly lacks a Christian orientation, but as a nonbiblical text his idea should not be quickly dismissed. Instead, his views may be conceived as a collaborative witness to crucial aspects of Christian and biblical eschatology. They are instructive for theological reflection and provide a guide map for Christian eschatology. Thus, the following discussion is a reappropriation of Kang's concept of *Ta-Tung* infused with christological and ecclesiological underpinnings.

From national self-determination to one administration under Jesus Christ. Kang's problematization of sovereign states and boundaries is the crux in any serious discussion of world peace and human equality. Insofar as sovereign statehood leads to endless war and violence, Kang is unafraid to call out national sovereignty as the elephant in the room in any peace talks. He writes:

> Even the Good and Upright cannot help but be partial each to his own state. Hence, what their wills are fixed upon, what they know and talk about, is always limited to [their own] state. [They] consider fighting for territory and killing other people to be an important duty; they consider destroying other states and butchering their people to be a great accomplishment.[35]

Kang also rightly observes:

> Nowadays disarmament conferences are being held ever more frequently, and such [conferences] aside, whenever individual states make treaties, these treaties are always based upon the principle of disarmament. Nevertheless, so long as the boundaries of states are not abolished, and the strong and the weak, the large and the small are mixed in together, wishing to plan for disarmament is [like] ordering tigers and wolves to be vegetarians—it must fail.[36]

---

[33]Kang, *Ta t'ung shu*, 63, 274-75.
[34]Kang, *Ta t'ung shu*, 274-75.
[35]Kang, *Ta t'ung shu*, 82.
[36]Kang, *Ta t'ung shu*, 83.

Kang's proposal of disarmament may be provocative in modern society, but it is nevertheless in line with the language of demilitarization in Isaiah 2:4, "They shall beat their swords into plowshares, and their spears into pruning hooks; nation shall not lift up sword against nation, neither shall they learn war any more." He further proposes that in the one world, nationalism will be abolished, and everyone will be under one administration. He writes: "In the Age of One World there will be no national struggles, no secret schemes. In great undertakings it will not be necessary to put power into the hands of political leaders or set up autocratic leaders. The laws and regulations of the ten thousand and some hundred administrative [organs] will all be [determined] through universal public discussion."[37]

The Isaiah passage envisions all nations making pilgrimage to Zion as the dwelling place of God (the temple). Although the vision is prefaced and directed to Judah and Jerusalem (Is 2:1), the objective is internationalism. The picture does not encourage hegemonic power or the superiority of one nation over another. Instead, the Lord rules and arbitrates among these nations. The focus of Taiwanese Judeophilia eschatology unwittingly shifts from awaiting the second coming of Christ to awaiting the eschatological restoration of Israel. While Taiwanese Judeophilia eschatology claims that its vision is Christ-centered, its eschatology does not fully exhaust the role of Jesus Christ and the church as the final and perfect revelation of God. Jesus and the church are the ultimate realities prefigured in the Old Testament Law, Prophets, and Writings (Heb 10:1). N. T. Wright argues that a

christological reading of the restoration of Israel in Old Testament eschatological passages leads one to view God's promises in the Old Testament as all fulfilled in Jesus Christ. In Christ every one of God's promises is a "Yes." For this reason it is through Jesus that we say "Amen," to the glory of God. Jesus' resurrection is the fulfillment of the restoration of the temple. Jesus' redemptive work of the whole world fulfills the promise of restoration of the land. Wright says poignantly:

> The NT is unequivocal in its interpretation of the fall of Jerusalem as being inextricably linked to the vindication of Jesus and his people. Jesus' whole claim is to do and be what the city and the temple were and did. Any attempt to claim that they can (on the basis of a supposed "literal" meaning of the many Old Testament promises of restoration, as yet supposedly unfulfilled) has failed to reckon with the total New Testament reading of those promises.... They all have come true in the Messiah (2 Cor. 1:20). This is no simple spiritualization. Rather, these promises, seen now through the lens of the cross and the resurrection, have been in one sense narrowed down to a point and in another sense widened to include the whole created order.[38]

Kang's proposition regarding public discussion on policies may be strategic—in fact, it is very modern and humanistic. This humanism results in the lack of divine administrator in his vision. The biblical vision introduces Jesus Christ as God—the one ushering in the kingdom of God. He reigns as King and Lord over his people. It is this rule that will abrogate the sovereignty of states and self-determination. It will effect the leveling of all nations and the prioritizing of communal life.

---

[37]Kang, *Ta t'ung shu*, 235.

[38]N. T. Wright, "Jerusalem in the New Testament," in *Jerusalem Past and Present in the Purposes of God*, ed. P. W. L. Walker (Grand Rapids, MI: Baker, 1994), 53-77, here 73.

More importantly, Kang is laudable in singling out selfishness as the moral-ethical thrust of the matter. After all, is not "national interest" the operative word we hear in any geopolitical discussion? He incisively writes that "cultivating the spirit of aggressiveness and selfishness, [men] are led to rationalize and justify their narrow-mindedness and cruelty."[39] Make no mistake, selflessness is antithetical to sovereignty, self-determination, and national interest.

Selflessness is the central message of Jesus Christ in his teaching and also in his work at the cross. After all, he sacrificially gave himself up for human beings to rescue them (Gal 1:4; 1 Tim 2:6). Self-denial and selflessness for the sake of others is required of the church of Christ as the people of God in Philippians 2:3-4 ("Do nothing from selfish ambition or conceit, but in humility regard others as better than yourselves. Let each of you look not to your own interests, but to the interests of others"). The New Testament is replete with texts on the people of God maintaining love and peace (1 Cor 13:13; Eph 2:1-17; 4:2; Col 3:12-14).

From geographical attachment to the whole earth for everyone. Kang seeks to abolish sovereign states based on geography. He maintains that "In One World there will be no need to attach importance to geographical factors . . . there being no states or military strong points." The whole earth will be divided for everyone. "In the One World, transportation, communication and settlement of population will open up the whole earth, so that there will no longer be any isolated or backward areas." He adds, "In the Age of One World, the [peoples] of the whole earth will all be self-governing, and the whole earth will be entirely under one great administration, publicly elected by the people."[40]

Similarly, it is unnecessary to be fixated on the sanctity of geographical Jerusalem. Israel's land, election, institutions, and culture should be understood as instruments of God's revelation. Without them, God's revelation would have had no way to reach human beings. Christopher Wright says aptly:

> When prophets spoke about the future, they could only do so meaningfully by using terms and realities that existed in their past or present experience. The realities associated with being Israel in their day included their specific history and such things as the land, the law, Jerusalem, the temple, sacrifices and priesthood. All of these had substantial significance in Israel's relationship with God, and also in Israel's ultimate role in relation to the nations. . . . Thus, for prophets to speak about God's future dealings with Israel and the nations, they had to speak in terms of these contemporary realities.

Wright maintains that there is a transcendent nature to the prophecies as well, such that they go beyond Israel's historical nationhood. He writes: "Moreover, even in the Old Testament itself, there was an awareness that the fulfillment of prophecies that were made in terms of the concrete realities of Israel's life and faith would actually go beyond them. The familiar dimensions of Israel's national life are transcended in various ways."[41]

God's sacred space, historically located in Jerusalem, is now expanded to cover the world as the knowledge of God fills the whole earth ("But the earth will be filled with the knowledge of the glory of the Lord, as the waters cover the sea,"

---

[39]Kang, *Ta t'ung shu*, 82.
[40]Kang, *Ta t'ung shu*, 231-32.
[41]Christopher Wright, "A Christian Approach to Old Testament Prophecy Concerning Israel," in Walker, *Jerusalem Past and Present*, 3-4.

Hab 2:14). Jerusalem is merely a microcosm of God's dwelling place, which is the whole earth. Taiwanese Christians' impassioned interest in mission work by going to remote places to bear witness to the knowledge and glory of God should be understood as a theological act. The sacred space has been redefined to include all parts of the world where God's glory is manifest. "If there are 'holy places' in the land for Christians to visit, they must be regarded, in some senses, as one might regard the grave of a dearly loved friend, perhaps even an older brother."[42]

Kang's concept of whole-earth *Ta-Tung* finds parallels in the biblical vision of the kingdom of God introduced by Jesus Christ. It does not place a high premium on one geographical region over another. N. T. Wright criticizes Judeophilia eschatology, since it undermines what Jesus has accomplished:

> The attempt to carry over some OT promises about Jerusalem, the land and the temple for fulfilment in our own day has the same theological shape as the attempt in pre-Reformation Catholicism to think of Christ as being re-crucified in every Mass. . . . If Jesus was claiming to be, in effect, the new and true temple, and his death is to be seen as the drawing together into one of the history of Israel in her desolation, dying her death outside the walls of the city, and rising again as the beginning of the real "restoration," the real return from exile, then the attempt to say that there are some parts of the Old Testament (relating to Jerusalem, Land or Temple) which have not yet been "fulfilled" and so need a historical and literal "fulfilment" now, or at some other time, is an explicit attempt to take something away from the achievement of Christ in his death and resurrection, and to preserve it for the

work of human beings in a different time and place. The work of Christ is . . . "incomplete."[43]

From racial/class privileging to equalizing all people. Kang's discussion on the abolition of racial and class boundaries, while ideal, is naive and problematic. Although the intention is to abolish the boundaries, his methodology may be faulted as racism for privileging white and yellow skin color over brown and black:

> The silver-colored race is spread out over the globe, while the gold-colored race is still more numerous. These two kinds—the yellow and the white—have occupied the whole world. The strength of the white race is assuredly superior, while the yellow race is more numerous and also wise. But it is an indestructible principle that when [two kinds] join in union they are smelted.[44]

Kang is cognizant that this boundary is the most difficult one to abolish. His method is problematic (racist and sexist), as he proposes mixed marriage, interracial propagation, the nonwhite race practice of migration, and a change of diet to change skin color. When it comes to social classes, he identifies three inferior classes: the inferior race, slaves, and women. For all three, he provides a master plan to abolish these boundaries. Kang's method of achieving the uniformity of color is ludicrous, but the intention to abolish racial discrimination needs a biblical assessment. This is a necessary corrective to a highly Jewish-centered eschatology.

Taiwanese eschatology would do better to embrace the apostle Paul's message:

> For in Christ Jesus you are all children of God through faith. As many of you as were baptized into Christ have clothed yourselves with Christ.

---

[42]Wright, "Jerusalem in the New Testament," 76.
[43]Wright, "Jerusalem in the New Testament," 73-74.
[44]Kang, *Ta t'ung shu*, 141.

There is no longer Jew or Greek, there is no longer slave or free, there is no longer male and female; for all of you are one in Christ Jesus. And if you belong to Christ, then you are Abraham's offspring, heirs according to the promise. (Gal 3:26-29)

Certainly, this passage is not about nondifferentiation but affirms the peace, unity, and equality between the two people groups. It imagines a world where Jews and Gentiles (Taiwanese Christians) are equal. Discrimination of other races (anti-Semitism) and privileging the Jewish race and culture (philo-Semitism) over others and, even worse, over one's own culture should be denounced. Taiwanese Judeophilia eschatology's Judeophilia is a disservice to Taiwanese Christianity. The recognition by Gentile Christians of Jews aWs "big brothers" should be redefined as simply respecting Jewish status as that of the firstborn and those who have historical priority without ascribing them superiority over other people groups. The relationship could be conceived as that of twin brothers rather than as an older-and-younger brother relationship.

Using a Christ-centered ecclesiological lens when reading the Old Testament prophecies will highlight the equal place of Jews and Gentiles in God's redemptive plan in and through Jesus Christ. Also, an ecclesiological lens will reframe the reading from a Jewish-centered one to a universal one, and affirm the diversity of the church as the people of God. Every race/color is a member of the body and contributes to the universal nature of the church. Abolishing differences of race/color is unbiblical (Rev 7:9-10).

From war and violence to productivity and benevolence. Kang supposes that when all the racial, gender, social, and national boundaries have been removed, placing everyone on the same plane, humanity will finally have reached the third stage of one world. In that one world, the world will not be stagnant. The competition arising from acting in selfishness and national interests present in the first stage will be transformed. The people of one world will compete in (1) the pursuit of excellence, (2) the pursuit of knowledge, and (3) encouraging *jen* (human benevolence). All three are simply different aspects of the same method: to rechannel the competitive drive of humanity into a constructive form of competition. There will be no military, economic, political, or social competition, but people will compete to produce the best material goods, to invent new methods, to expand knowledge, and to manifest their *jen* (human benevolence). Through this cooperative kind of competition, the world will not fear the stagnation of civilization or retrogression into the disorderly stage but will continue to progress.[45]

Kang operates within the context of secular and humanistic benevolence (*jen*), but if this *jen* is redeemed from its secular context and reoriented toward Christ and the church, the pursuit of *jen* becomes the "responsibility of the church in the present to anticipate the age to come in acts of justice, mercy, beauty and truth; we are to live 'now' as it will be 'then.' We can only do this. . . . There is no going back to the old lines that demarcate human beings (race, color, gender, geography)."[46] If in the one world "people will honour virtue and not nobility of [blood]," then in the kingdom of Jesus Christ people will live the life of the Beatitudes as the

---

[45]Kang, *Ta t'ung shu*, 49-50.
[46]Wright, "Jerusalem in the New Testament," 76; see a constructive view of *jen* in K. K. Yeo, *Musing with Confucius and Paul: Toward a Chinese Christian Theology* (Eugene, OR: Cascade, 2008), 253-354.

light and salt of the world (Mt 5:13-16).[47] This pursuit of moral virtue rather than power politics is consistent with Isaiah when he imagines the adherence to the Torah of the Lord coming out of Zion.

CLOSING REMARKS

Similar to many other human-centered visions of utopia, another significant weakness of Kang's *Ta-Tung* narrative is its temporal and earthly scope. His *Ta-Tung* is confined to human earthly life. Recognizing the inevitability of human aging and death, Kang can only outline measures to prevent sickness and death in the Age of Complete Peace and Equality in the one world. He presses for a vegetarian diet, cultivation of a healthy environment, effective medical support, facilities to prolong human life, and also the study of Buddhahood and immortality. On the last point on Buddhahood, he is at his wits' end, saying:

> The One World is the ultimate Law of this world; but the study of immortality, of longevity without

death, is even an extension of the ultimate Law of this world. The study of Buddhahood . . . [implies] not [merely] a setting apart from the world, but [an actual] going out of this world; still more, it is going out of the One World. If we go this far, then we abandon the human sphere and enter the sphere of immortals and Buddhas. . . . The study of immortality is too crude, its subtle words and profound principles are not many, and its [ability] to intoxicate men's minds is limited.[48]

This substantial limitation accentuates the superiority and the distinctiveness of the Christian utopia. In the last lines of the Nicene Creed, those who confess Jesus Christ as Lord will inevitably face death—but they will also receive physical resurrected bodies and life. It is only in and through this resurrected body that the pursuit of wisdom and human benevolence (*jen*) in the world to come can reach its ultimate potential. These bodies will flourish in the enduring administration of Jesus Christ, without war and boundaries, and without end.

FURTHER READING

Blaising, Craig, and Darrell Bock, eds. *Progressive Dispensationalism*. Grand Rapids, MI: Baker, 2000.

Finto, Don. *God's Promise and the Future of Israel*. Ventura, CA: Regal, 2006.

Kang, Yu-Wei. *Ta t'ung shu: The One-World Philosophy of Kang Yu-Wei*. Translation and introduction by Laurence G. Thompson. London: George Allen & Unwin, 1958.

Lu, Jeffrey Shao Chang. *Isaiah (1)*. Tien Dao Bible Commentary. Hong Kong: Tien Dao, 2015.

Ross, James, and Song Lihong. *The Image of Jews in Contemporary China*. Boston: Academic Studies Press, 2016.

Walker, P. W. L. *Jerusalem Past and Present in the Purposes of God*. 2nd ed. Grand Rapids, MI: Baker, 1994.

Walls, Jerry L., ed. *The Oxford Handbook of Eschatology*. Oxford: Oxford University Press, 2008.

---

[47]Kang, *Ta t'ung shu*, 245.
[48]*The One-World Philosophy of Kang Yu-Wei*, 275.

CONTRIBUTORS

Milton Acosta (PhD, Trinity Evangelical Divinity School) is an Old Testament professor at the Seminario Bíblico de Colombia in Medellín. He is the author of *El humor en el Antiguo Testamento* (2009) and Old Testament editor of the *Comentario Bíblico Contemporáneo* (2019). His areas of research include rhetorical patterns in the Hebrew Bible, forced migration, and violence in the Bible. He also leads a small group of pastors and academics in Medellín who explore the issue of worship and liturgy in evangelical churches.

Ray Aldred (ThD, Wycliffe College) is the director of the Indigenous Studies Program at the Vancouver School of Theology. He is a Cree from Northern Alberta, Canada. He has written chapters in *Prophetic Evangelicals* (2012), *Evangelical Postcolonial Conversations* (2014), and *Strangers in This World* (2015). He is also a storyteller and grandfather.

Atsuhiro Asano is professor of New Testament studies at the School of Theology, Kwansei Gakuin University, in Kobe, Japan. Asano received his master of divinity at International School of Theology, his master of theology in New Testament studies at Fuller Theological Seminary, and his doctor of philosophy in New Testament studies at the University of Oxford. His books include *Community-Identity Construction in Galatians*.

Gerald Bray is research professor of divinity at Beeson Divinity School and distinguished professor of historical theology at Knox Theological Seminary. He is also the director of research for the Latimer Trust (London) and editor of the Anglican theological journal *Churchman*.

Emily J. Choge Kerama (PhD, Fuller Theological Seminary) is an associate professor at Moi University, Eldoret, Kenya. She has written many essays, among which are "Social Ethics" in *The Global Dictionary of Theology* and "Hospitality in Africa" in the *Africa Bible Commentary*.

Sung Wook Chung (DPhil, Oxford University) is a professor of Christian theology at Denver Seminary in Littleton, Colorado. He is a native Korean and the author and editor of twenty-five books published in English and Korean. Among them are *Admiration and Challenge: Karl Barth's Theological Relationship with John Calvin* (2002), *Christ the One and Only: A Global Affirmation of the Uniqueness of Jesus Christ* (2003), and *Diverse and Creative Voices: Theological Essays from the Majority World* (2015). His current research focuses on trinitarian theology, eschatology, and Christian systematic theology in conversation with other religions.

John D. K. Ekem (DTheol, magna cum laude, University of Hamburg) is professor of New Testament studies and director, Centre for Mother Tongue Biblical Hermeneutics at Trinity Theological Seminary, Legon, Accra, Ghana. He is also the seminary's vice-president responsible for academic affairs. An ordained minister of the

Methodist Church Ghana, he also occupies the seminary's Kwesi Dickson-Gilbert Ansre Distinguished Chair of Biblical Exegesis and Mother Tongue Hermeneutics, and serves as translation consultant for The Bible Society of Ghana. He has supervised the translation and revision of the Bible into several major Ghanaian languages and continues to do so. A member of Studiorum Novi Testamenti Societas (Society for New Testament Studies), he has authored several books on mother-tongue biblical interpretation, including *New Testament Concepts of Atonement in an African Pluralistic Setting* (2005), *Early Scriptures of the Gold Coast (Ghana)* (2011), and, most recently, *A Simplified Greek-English Commentary on the Epistle to the Colossians* (2017), adapted from original commentaries he wrote in the Asante-Twi and Mfantse dialects of Ghana.

Victor I. Ezigbo (PhD, University of Edinburgh) is assistant professor of systematic and contextual theology at Bethel University in St. Paul, Minnesota. His areas of research are African Christian theologies and Christologies, African indigenous religions, and postcolonial theological discourses. He has written a book and several articles in the areas of African theologies, Christologies, and spirituality. He is also the founder of the Centre for Research in Global Christianity.

Rosinah Mmannana Gabaitse (PhD, University of Kwa-Zulu Natal) is a lecturer in biblical studies at the University of Botswana within the Department of Theology and Religious Studies. She is also a postdoctoral fellow in Germany sponsored by the Humboldt Foundation. She researches and publishes in the field of feminist biblical hermeneutics, Luke–Acts, and Pentecostalism. Her research focuses on establishing a link between teaching and researching in a university and grassroots communities, hence some

of her publications on the spread of HIV and AIDS, gender-based violence, and masculinities.

Oscar García-Johnson (PhD, Fuller Theological Seminary) is associate professor of theology and Latino/a studies and associate dean for the Center for the Study of Hispanic Church and Community at Fuller Seminary in California. Born in Honduras, he is an ordained minister with the American Baptist Churches, planted four churches, and worked as a Regional Minister for the American Baptist Churches of Los Angeles for eleven years prior to coming to Fuller. He is the author of *Jesús, Hazme Como Tú: Cuarenta Maneras de Imitar a Cristo* (2014), *The Mestizo/a Community of the Spirit* (2009), and *Spirit Outside the Gate* (2019) and coauthor of *Theology Without Borders: Introduction to Global Conversations* (2015). His current research focuses on critical ecclesiology, decolonial theology, and intercultural/global religious conversations from the South.

Timoteo D. Gener (PhD, Fuller Theological Seminary) is president of the Asian Theological Seminary, Manila, Philippines. A practitioner of local theology and a distinguished member of the World Evangelical Alliance Task Force on Ecumenical Affairs, he has coedited *The Earth Is the Lord's: Reflections on Stewardship in the Asian Setting* (2011).

Elaine W. F. Goh (ThD, South East Asia Graduate School of Theology) is currently a lecturer in Old Testament studies at Seminari Theoloji Malaysia (Malaysia Theological Seminary). She has published a book on Ecclesiastes titled *Wisdom of Living in a Changing World: Readings from Ecclesiastes* (2013). Her areas of research are in Old Testament studies and biblical Wisdom literature. In her dissertation research, she worked on cross-textual hermeneutics between Ecclesiastes and the *Analects*. Her published essays include one on intertextual reading in *Reading Ruth in Asia* (2015).

Antonio González was born in Oviedo, Spain, in 1961. He has a PhD in philosophy (Madrid) and also in theology (Frankfurt am Main). For several years he lived and worked with the Catholic Church in Latin America, moving afterward to a more evangelical comprehension of the Christian faith. He has taught in Latin America, the United States, and Spain. He currently teaches at the Xavier Zubiri Foundation in Madrid.

Gene L. Green (PhD, University of Aberdeen) is the dean of Trinity International University–Florida and professor emeritus of New Testament at Wheaton College and Graduate School. Previously he served as professor of New Testament, academic dean, and rector of the Seminario ESEPA in San José, Costa Rica. He is the author of *Vox Petri: A Theology of Peter* (2020) and four biblical commentaries written in Spanish and English, coauthor of *The New Testament in Antiquity* (2019), and coeditor of *Global Theology in Evangelical Perspective* (2012). His research focuses on the intersection of the Christian faith and cultures, both ancient and contemporary.

Shirley S. Ho (PhD, Trinity Evangelical Divinity School) is an associate professor of Old Testament at China Evangelical Seminary, Taipei, Taiwan. She is a Filipino-Chinese but has resided in Taiwan for thirteen years. Her areas of interest are Hebrew language, Wisdom literature, Old Testament theology, cultural exegesis, contextual theology, and hermeneutics. She has written a number of articles, and she contributed the "Introduction and Notes on Ecclesiastes" to *NIV God's Justice Bible: The Flourishing of Creation and the Destruction of Evil*. She is a Langham scholar and is currently doing her Langham postdoctoral research on the book of Proverbs.

Wei Hua (PhD, Peking University) is associate professor of philosophy and Christian studies at Huaqiao University, Xiamen, China. He has published several articles on biblical and Augustinian studies, including "A Brief Investigation of *Sarx* and *Sōma* in Romans" (2012), "On the Rise of Augustine's Concept of Voluntas" (2013), and "Galatians 2:11-14 and the Exegetical Controversy Between Augustine and Jerome" (2015).

Munther Isaac (PhD, Oxford Centre for Mission Studies) is a Palestinian Christian pastor and theologian. He now pastors Christmas Lutheran Church in Bethlehem and is at the same time the academic dean of Bethlehem Bible College. He is also the director of the highly acclaimed and influential Christ at the Checkpoint conferences and is a board member of Kairos Palestine. Munther is passionate about issues related to Palestinians and Palestinian Christians. He speaks locally and internationally on issues related to the theology of the land, Palestinian Christians, and Palestinian theology. He is the author of *From Land to Lands, from Eden to the Renewed Earth: A Christ-Centered Biblical Theology of the Promised Land* (2015). He earned a master's in biblical studies from Westminster Theological Seminary and a PhD from the Oxford Centre for Mission Studies. He is married to Rudaina, an architect, and together they have two boys: Karam and Zaid.

Veli-Matti Kärkkäinen (DTheol, Habil, University of Helsinki) is professor of systematic theology at Fuller Theological Seminary and docent of ecumenics at the University of Helsinki. A native of Finland, he has also lived and taught theology in Thailand. An ordained Lutheran minister (Evangelical Lutheran Church in America), he is also an expert in global Pentecostal-charismatic issues. A regular participant in theological, missiological, and ecumenical projects and consultations at a global level, he also participates in interfaith dialogues, most recently with Muslims. He is a prolific author, with over twenty books written and edited; the latest include the five-volume series titled A Constructive Christian Theology for the Pluralistic World (2013–2017), whose last volume, *Hope and Community*, sets forth a new vision for ecclesiology (and eschatology) in the pluralistic global world.

Yohanna Katanacho (PhD, Trinity Evangelical Divinity School) is a Palestinian evangelical who studied at Bethlehem University (BSc), Wheaton College (MA), and Trinity Evangelical Divinity School (MDiv, PhD). He serves as the academic dean for Bethlehem Bible College. He has authored several books in English and Arabic, including *The Land of Christ: A Palestinian Cry*, *A Commentary on Proverbs*, *The Seven "I AM" Sayings in the Gospel of John*, and *The King of Peace and His Young Followers*. He is also one of the authors of the Palestinian Kairos Document.

James Henry Owino Kombo (PhD, Stellenbosch University) is a Kenyan Anglican minister and professor of theological studies at Daystar University, Nairobi, Kenya. His outstanding publications include *The Doctrine of God in African Christian Thought* (2007) and *Theological Models of the Doctrine of the Trinity: The Trinity, Diversity and Theological Hermeneutics* (2016). Though focused on theological studies, Kombo continues to serve in the senior management of Daystar University, having been deputy vice-chancellor (academic affairs) for ten years and acting vice-chancellor since November 2015. He is an active member of the Africa Society of Evangelical Theology and editor of the *Africa Journal of Evangelical Society*.

Samuel Waje Kunhiyop (PhD, Trinity International University) served as academic dean and provost of Jos ECWA Theological Seminary (1994–2007) and later served as the first full-time postgraduate head of the South African Theological Seminary, Rivonia, South Africa (2008–2011). He is also a visitor in ethics at Bingham University, Karu, Abuja, Nigeria. He is the current general secretary of Evangelical Church Winning All and executive general secretary of Evangel Fellowship International. He is the author of *African Christian Ethics*, *African Christian Theology*, and many national and international journal articles.

D. Stephen Long (PhD, Duke University) is Cary M. Maguire University Professor of Ethics at Southern Methodist University, Dallas. He is an ordained United Methodist minister in the Indiana Conference. He works at the intersection between theology and ethics and has published over fifty essays and fifteen books on theology and ethics, including *Divine Economy: Theology and the Market* (2000), *The Goodness of God: Theology, Church and Social Order* (2001), *John Wesley's Moral Theology: The Quest for God and Goodness* (2005), *Calculated Futures* (2007), *Christian Ethics: A Very Short Introduction* (2010), *Saving Karl Barth: Hans Urs von Balthasar's Preoccupation* (2014), *The Perfectly Simple Triune God: Aquinas and His Legacy* (2016), and *Augustinian and Ecclesial Christian Ethics: On Loving Enemies* (2018).

Stephanie A. Lowery (PhD, Wheaton College) is lecturer in systematic theology at Scott Christian University in Machakos, Kenya. She grew up in Kenya and returned to live there after completing her PhD. She has a book on ecclesiologies in Africa, *Identity and Ecclesiology* (2017), as well as a forthcoming coauthored article on theological perspectives on identity and community. Her research interests include African theologies, African ecclesiologies, and the doctrine of the Trinity.

Wonsuk Ma (PhD, Fuller Theological Seminary) is a Korean Pentecostal serving as Distinguished Professor of Global Christianity and PhD program director at Oral Roberts University, Tulsa, Oklahoma. He served as a missionary educator in the Philippines (1979–2006), where he launched *Asian Journal of Pentecostal Studies* and *Journal of Asian Mission*. He also served as executive director of the Oxford Centre for Mission Studies (2007–2016), during which time he led the publication of the thirty-five-volume Regnum Edinburgh Centenary Series. He has also participated in various international mission and ecumenical functions, including the Reformed and Pentecostal (Theological) Dialogue (1997–2005), Edinburgh 2010, Lausanne meetings, and various ecumenical conferences including the World Council of Churches and the Global Christian Forum. He has also participated in networks for theological education, including Global Forum of Theological Educators. His research interests include Old Testament theology, prophets, the Spirit of God in the Old Testament, contextual theology, Asian Pentecostalism, Pentecostal mission, and global Christianity. He has authored and edited thirteen books, in addition to numerous scholarly writings.

Jules A. Martínez-Olivieri (PhD, Trinity Evangelical Divinity School) is associate professor of theology at Trinity International University-Florida, adjunct professor of theology at the Seminario Teológico de Puerto Rico, and adjunct professor of theology and philosophy at Universidad Interamericana de Puerto Rico. He is the author of *A Visible Witness: Christology, Liberation, and Participation*.

Andrew M. Mbuvi (PhD, Westminster Theological Seminary) is associate professor of biblical studies and hermeneutics, Shaw University Divinity School, North Carolina. He has published a book on 1 Peter titled *Temple Exile and Identity in 1 Peter* (2007) and is currently working on a commentary on 2 Peter–Jude in the New Covenant Commentary Series.

Nelson R. Morales Fredes (PhD, Theological Studies/New Testament, Trinity International University) is professor of New Testament and hermeneutics at Seminario Teológico Centroamericano, Guatemala. Originally from Chile, he has lived, studied, and taught in Guatemala since 1993. He has written several articles in the journal *Kairós*, encyclopedia entries, a commentary on 2 Corinthians in *Comentario Bíblico Contemporáneo*, and *Poor and Rich in James: A Relevance Theory Approach to James's Use of the Old Testament* in the Bulletin for Biblical Research Supplement Series (2018). He is also a board member of the Evangelical Society for Socio-Religious Studies in Guatemala.

Samuel M. Ngewa (PhD, Westminster Theological Seminary) is professor of New Testament at Africa International University, Nairobi. He is the author of *The Gospel of John for Pastors and Teachers* (2003) and several commentaries in the Africa Bible Commentary Series, including *1 & 2 Timothy and Titus* (2009). He also serves as a pastor with Africa Inland Church, Kenya.

David Tonghou Ngong (PhD, Baylor University) is associate professor of religion and theology at Stillman College in Tuscaloosa, Alabama. He is originally from Cameroon. In addition to many articles, he is the author of *The Holy Spirit and Salvation in African Christian Theology* (2010) and *Theology as Construction of Piety: An African Perspective* (2013).

Peter Nyende (PhD, University of Edinburgh) is an associate professor of New Testament and the head of biblical studies at the School of Divinity of Uganda Christian University. He is also a priest and a canon in the Anglican

Church and a commissioned evangelist with the Church Army Society of Africa. His area of interest in scholarship is the interpretation of the Bible, with a special emphasis on the book of Hebrews, within various African contexts. To this end, he has published a number of articles in leading biblical journals, with the most recent in *Expository Times* (2016) titled "Tested for Our Sake: The Temptations of Jesus in the Light of Hebrews."

C. René Padilla (PhD, University of Manchester) is executive director of Ediciones Kairos and president emeritus of the Kairos Foundation of Buenos Aires, Argentina. In addition to many articles, he has authored or edited more than twenty books, most of them on the subject of integral mission. His main book, *Mission Between the Times: Essays on the Kingdom* (2nd ed., 2010), has been published in English, Spanish, Portuguese, Korean, German, and Swedish.

Ruth Padilla DeBorst (PhD, Boston University) is a wife of one and mother of many, a theologian, missiologist, educator, and a storyteller. She has been involved in leadership development and theological education for integral mission in her native Latin America for several decades. She works with the Comunidad de Estudios Teológicos Interdisciplinarios, a learning community with master's- and certificate-level programs. She coordinates the Networking Team of the International Fellowship for Mission as Transformation and serves on the board of Arocha. She lives in Costa Rica with her husband, James, and fellow members of the Casa Adobe intentional Christian community. Her education includes a bachelor's in education (Argentina), an MA in interdisciplinary studies (Wheaton College), and a PhD in missiology and social ethics from Boston University.

Stephen T. Pardue (PhD, Wheaton College) is associate professor of theology at the International Graduate School of Leadership and the Asia Graduate School of Theology in Manila, Philippines. He also serves as the associate publications secretary for the Asia Theological Association. He is the author of *The Mind of Christ: Humility and the Intellect in Early Christian Theology* (2013) and coeditor of *Asian Christian Theology* (2019). His areas of research include virtue theory, early Christian thought, and contextual theologies.

Aldrin M. Peñamora (PhD Theology, Christian ethics concentration, Fuller Theological Seminary) is executive director of the Commission on Justice, Peace and Reconciliation of the Philippine Council of Evangelical Churches. He is also executive director of the Center of Research for Christian-Muslim Relations. He has taught theology at the Koinonia Theological Seminary, Davao City, Philippines, and is currently a member of the faculty of the Asian Graduate School of Theology, Philippines, and the Asian Theological Seminary, Quezon City, Philippines. As an advocate of just peacebuilding among different faith traditions, especially between Christians and Muslims in the Philippines and Southeast Asia, he is often involved in initiatives aimed at fostering harmonious Christian-Muslim relations. He has published essays on the subject both locally and internationally. Aldrin is married to Christine Ching Peñamora.

Alberto F. Roldán (DTheol, Instituto Universitario Isedet) is from Argentina. He is postgraduate studies director of Instituto Teológico Fiet, Buenos Aires, Argentina, and visiting professor at Lee University, Semisud, Ecuador; South African Theological Seminary, Bryanston, South Africa; and Universidad Adventista del Plata, Libertador San Martin, Argentina. He is a prolific writer, having authored or edited thirty books, including *¿Para qué sirve la teología?* (2011), *Reino, política y misión* (2011), *Atenas y Jerusalén en diálogo: Filosofía y teología en la mediación hermenéutica* (2015), *Hermenéutica y signos de los tiempos* (2016), and *La teología de la cruz como crítica radical a la teología de la prosperidad*, Aportes Teológicos 3 (2018). He is a member of Fraternidad Teológica Latinoamericana and the Society of Biblical Literature, and was awarded "Theological Personality of 2016" by the Asociación Evangélica de Educación Teológica en América Latina. Roldán is also the director of Teología y Cultura, www.teologos.com.ar.

Ivan Satyavrata (PhD, Oxford Centre for Mission Studies) has spent more than twenty years in Christian leadership training but presently serves as senior pastor of the Assembly of God Church in Kolkata, a multilingual congregation, with a weekly attendance of more than four thousand people and a social outreach that provides education and basic nutrition for several thousand underprivileged children. He has authored two books: *Holy Spirit, Lord and Life Giver* (2009) and *God Has Not Left Himself Without Witness* (2011).

Zakali Shohe (DTh, Trinity Theological College, Singapore) is associate professor of New Testament and academic dean at Trinity Theological College (affiliated with the Senate of Serampore College [University]) in Dimapur, Nagaland, India. She has contributed chapters to several monographs and is the coeditor of *Theology in Context*. Her recently published monograph is *Acceptance Motif in Paul: Revisiting Romans 15:7-13*.

Carlos Sosa Siliezar (PhD, University of Edinburgh) is assistant professor of New Testament at Wheaton College, Illinois. He holds a PhD in New Testament language, literature and theology from the University of Edinburgh, Scotland. He is the author of *Creation Imagery in the Gospel of John* (2015) and *La condición divina de Jesús: Cristología y creación en el Evangelio de Juan* (2016).

Aída Besançon Spencer (PhD, Southern Baptist Theological Seminary) is professor of New Testament at Gordon-Conwell Theological Seminary, South Hamilton, Massachusetts, and Extraordinary Researcher at North-West University, Potchefstroom, South Africa. Born and reared in Santo Domingo, Dominican Republic, she earned her PhD in New Testament at Southern Baptist Theological Seminary and the master's of theology and divinity at Princeton Theological Seminary. She has served as a social worker, college minister, and founding pastor of organization of Pilgrim Church in Beverly, Massachusetts. Listed in *Who's Who in the World*, *Contemporary Authors*, and *Who's Who of American Women*, she has authored numerous books and articles, including *Pastoral Epistles* (New Covenant Commentary), *Beyond the Curse: Women Called to Ministry, Paul's Literary Style, 2 Corinthians* (Daily Bible Commentary), and cowritten or coedited *Reaching for the New Jerusalem: A Biblical and Theological Framework for the City, The Global God, Global Voices on Biblical Equality, The Prayer Life of Jesus, Joy Through the Night: Biblical Resources on Suffering, The Goddess Revival*, and *Marriage at the Crossroads*. She has been a visiting scholar at Harvard Divinity School and El Seminario Evangélico de Puerto Rico.

Natee Tanchanpongs is the academic dean of Bangkok Bible Seminary and a pastor at Grace City Church, Bangkok, Thailand. He received his PhD in theological studies from Trinity Evangelical Divinity School in 2007, where he worked in the area of contextual hermeneutics. Thereafter he served the World Evangelical Alliance Theological Commission, in which he worked in a study unit on contextualization. He is married to Bee. They have two children, Maisie and Meno.

Daniel J. Treier (PhD, Trinity Evangelical Divinity School) is Blanchard Professor of Theology at Wheaton College Graduate School. He is an author of four books and an editor of several others. Among his most recent books are *Theology and the Mirror of Scripture: A Mere Evangelical Account* (2015) and *Introducing Theological Interpretation of Scripture: Recovering a Christian Practice* (2008).

Kevin J. Vanhoozer (PhD, Cambridge University) is currently research professor of systematic theology at Trinity Evangelical Divinity School. Previously he served as Blanchard Professor of Theology at Wheaton College Graduate School (2009–2012) and, before that, as senior lecturer in theology and religious studies at the University of Edinburgh, Scotland (1990–1998). He is the author or editor of sixteen books, including *The Drama of Doctrine: A Canonical-Linguistic Approach to Christian Theology* (2005) and *Remythologizing Theology: Divine Action, Passion, and Authorship* (2010). He is married to Sylvie and has two daughters (and fifteen doctoral students). He is an amateur classical pianist and serious reader, and finds that music and literature help him integrate academic theology and spiritual formation.

C. Rosalee Velloso Ewell (PhD, Duke University) is a Brazilian theologian from São Paulo and currently serves as the executive director of the Theological Commission for the World Evangelical Alliance. She has written and edited various books and articles and is the New Testament editor for the *Latin American Bible Commentary*. Rosalee is married and has three children, four rabbits, and twenty chickens.

Zi Wang, born in Beijing, China, graduated and received a PhD from the Department of Philosophy and Religious Studies at Peking University. She is a postdoctoral researcher at the Institute of World Religions in the Chinese Academy of the Social Sciences. Her major research covers biblical studies and the sociology of religion.

Randy S. Woodley (PhD, Asbury Theological Seminary) is Distinguished Associate Professor of Faith and Culture at George Fox Seminary in Portland, Oregon. His books include *Shalom and the Community of Creation: An Indigenous Vision* and *Living in Color: Embracing God's Passion for Ethnic Diversity*. He has authored numerous book chapters and articles in compilations such as the *Dictionary of Scripture and Ethics* and *The Global Dictionary of Theology*.

Xiaxia E. Xue (PhD, McMaster Divinity College) is assistant professor of New Testament at the China Graduate School of Theology, Hong Kong. She was brought up in Fujian province in China and was involved in the youth ministry of her church in her early and college years. After receiving her master's degree in philosophy at RenMin University in Beijing, she was called to study theology. She earned her PhD in New Testament studies from McMaster Divinity College in Ontario, Canada. Xiaxia's teaching includes courses in New Testament Greek, biblical exegesis, Pauline letters, and classes in early Christian origins. She also participates in church ministry in Hong Kong, preaching sermons and teaching adult Sunday school. Her first book is titled *Paul's Viewpoint on God, Israel, and the Gentiles in Romans 9–11: An Intertextual Thematic Analysis* (2016). She has also published several articles and presented several papers at international conferences, including the Society of Biblical Literature. She is one of the editors of the online journal *Dialogismos*.

K. K. Yeo (PhD, Northwestern University) is Harry R. Kendall Professor of New Testament at Garrett-Evangelical Seminary and affiliate professor at the Department of Asian Languages and Cultures at Northwestern University in Evanston. He is an elected member of the Society of New Testament Studies since 1998 and a Lilly Scholar (1999) and Henry Luce Scholar (2003). In the last fifteen years, he has been a visiting professor to major universities in China. He has written or edited more than forty Chinese- and English-language books on critical engagement between the Bible and cultures, including *Musing with Confucius and Paul* (2008), *What Has Jerusalem to Do with Beijing?* (2018), and *The Oxford Handbook of the Bible in China*.

Amos Yong (PhD, Boston University) is professor of theology and mission and director of the Center for Missiological Research at Fuller Theological Seminary in Pasadena, California. He has authored or edited more than forty books, including, most recently, *Renewing Christian Theology: Systematics for a Global Christianity* (2014).

NAME INDEX

SUBJECT INDEX

SCRIPTURE INDEX

Finding the Textbook You Need

The IVP Academic Textbook Selector
is an online tool for instantly finding the IVP books
suitable for over 250 courses across 24 disciplines.

---

ivpacademic.com